2009 | WORLD DEVELOPMENT INDICATORS

 **THE WORLD BANK**

2009 | WORLD DEVELOPMENT INDICATORS

Photo credit: Front cover, Gavin Hellier/Robert Harding World Imagery/Getty Images.

If you have questions or comments about this product, please contact:

Development Data Group
The World Bank
1818 H Street NW, Room MC2-812, Washington, D.C. 20433 USA
Hotline: 800 590 1906 or 202 473 7824; fax 202 522 1498
Email: data@worldbank.org
Web site: www.worldbank.org or www.worldbank.org/data

ISBN 978-0-8213-7829-8

ECO-AUDIT
Environmental Benefits Statement
The World Bank is committed to preserving endangered forests and natural resources. The Office of the Publisher
has chosen to print *World Development Indicators 2009* on recycled paper with 30 percent post-consumer fiber in
accordance with the recommended standards for paper usage set by the Green Press Initiative, a nonprofit program
supporting publishers in using fiber that is not sourced from endangered forests. For more information, visit www.
greenpressinitiative.org.

Saved:
62 trees
43 million Btu of total energy
5,452 pounds of net greenhouse gases
22,631 gallons of waste water
2,906 pounds of solid waste

PREFACE

World Development Indicators 2009 arrives at a moment of great uncertainty for the global economy. The crisis that began more than a year ago in the U.S. housing market spread to the global financial system and is now taking its toll on real output and incomes. As a consequence, an additional 50 million people will be left in extreme poverty. And if the crisis deepens and widens or is prolonged, other development indicators—school enrollments, women's employment, child mortality—will be affected, jeopardizing progress toward the Millennium Development Goals.

Statistics help us understand the events that triggered the crisis and measure its impact. Along with this year's 91 data tables, each section of the *World Development Indicators 2009* has an introduction that shows statistics in action, describing the history of the current crisis, its effect on developing economies, and the challenges they face.

World view reviews the housing bubble and other asset bubbles that preceded it, the global macroeconomic imbalances that fed the bubbles, and the role of financial innovation. *Economy* looks at the record growth of developing economies preceding the crisis. *Environment* reviews the increasing impact of developing economies on the global environment. *Global links* discusses the transmission of the global crisis through the avenues of global integration: trade, finance, migration, and remittances. *States and markets* reminds us that as information and communication technologies change the way we work, they will be part of the solution to the current crisis. *People* contains most of the statistics for measuring progress toward the Millennium Development Goals. Its introduction, prepared by our partners at the International Labour Organization, examines new measures of decent work and productive employment now included in the Millennium Development Goals.

High quality, timely, and publicly available data will be central to managing the response to the crisis. We need high frequency—quarterly or monthly—data on labor markets to better track the impacts of macroeconomic events on people. We also need to know more about the characteristics of households and their response to economic conditions. While income distribution data are improving, they are weak at both ends of the spectrum, missing the very rich and the very poor. We know little about household assets in most developing economies. There is little information on housing markets, and financial data need to be enriched with more information on nonbank financial institutions (such as insurance companies, pension funds, investment banks, and hedge funds) in many countries.

Official statistical agencies need to take a long range view of their public role—to think broadly about data needs and build strategic partnerships with academia and the private sector. In a time of crisis the careful, systematic accumulation of statistical information may seem a luxury. It is not. We need better data now to guide our responses to the current crisis and to plot our course in the future.

The World Bank stands ready to support countries with their statistical capacity-building efforts. We will also continue to maintain the *World Development Indicators* as a rich source of development information, bringing to you new and critical data areas as availability and quality improve. And as always, we welcome your comments and suggestions for making *World Development Indicators* more useful to you.

Shaida Badiee
Director
Development Data Group

ACKNOWLEDGMENTS

This book and its companion volumes, *The Little Data Book* and *The Little Green Data Book,* are prepared by a team led by Sulekha Patel under the supervision of Eric Swanson and comprising Awatif Abuzeid, Mehdi Akhlaghi, Azita Amjadi, Uranbileg Batjargal, David Cielikowski, Richard Fix, Masako Hiraga, Kiyomi Horiuchi, Nino Kostava, K. Sarwar Lateef, Soong Sup Lee, Ibrahim Levent, Raymond Muhula, M.H. Saeed Ordoubadi, Beatriz Prieto-Oramas, Changqing Sun, and K.M. Vijayalakshmi, working closely with other teams in the Development Economics Vice Presidency's Development Data Group. The CD-ROM development team included Azita Amjadi, Ramgopal Erabelly, Reza Farivari, Buyant Erdene Khaltarkhuu, and William Prince. The work was carried out under the management of Shaida Badiee.

The choice of indicators and the contents of the explanatory text was shaped through close consultation with and substantial contributions from staff in the world Bank's four thematic networks—Sustainable Development, Human Development, Poverty Reduction and Economic Management, and Financial and Private Sector Development—and staff of the International Finance Corporation and the Multilateral Investment Guarantee Agency. Most important, the team received substantial help, guidance, and data from external partners. For individual acknowledgments of contributions to the book's contents, please see *Credits.* For a listing of key partners, see *Partners.*

Communications Development Incorporated provided overall design direction, editing, and layout, led by Meta de Coquereaumont, Bruce Ross-Larson, and Christopher Trott. Elaine Wilson created the graphics and typeset the book. Joseph Caponio and Amye Kenall provided proofreading and production assistance. Communications Development's London partner, Peter Grundy of Peter Grundy Art & Design, provided art direction and design. Staff from External Affairs oversaw printing and dissemination of the book.

TABLE OF CONTENTS

FRONT

1. WORLD VIEW

2. PEOPLE

3. ENVIRONMENT

TABLE OF CONTENTS

 ## 4. ECONOMY

 ## 5. STATES AND MARKETS

6. GLOBAL LINKS

BACK

PARTNERS

Defining, gathering, and disseminating international statistics is a collective effort of many people and organizations. The indicators presented in *World Development Indicators* are the fruit of decades of work at many levels, from the field workers who administer censuses and household surveys to the committees and working parties of the national and international statistical agencies that develop the nomenclature, classifications, and standards fundamental to an international statistical system. Nongovernmental organizations and the private sector have also made important contributions, both in gathering primary data and in organizing and publishing their results. And academic researchers have played a crucial role in developing statistical methods and carrying on a continuing dialogue about the quality and interpretation of statistical indicators. All these contributors have a strong belief that available, accurate data will improve the quality of public and private decisionmaking.

The organizations listed here have made *World Development Indicators* possible by sharing their data and their expertise with us. More important, their collaboration contributes to the World Bank's efforts, and to those of many others, to improve the quality of life of the world's people. We acknowledge our debt and gratitude to all who have helped to build a base of comprehensive, quantitative information about the world and its people.

For easy reference, Web addresses are included for each listed organization. The addresses shown were active on March 1, 2009. Information about the World Bank is also provided.

International and government agencies

Carbon Dioxide Information Analysis Center

The Carbon Dioxide Information Analysis Center (CDIAC) is the primary global climate change data and information analysis center of the U.S. Department of Energy. The CDIAC's scope includes anything that would potentially be of value to those concerned with the greenhouse effect and global climate change, including concentrations of carbon dioxide and other radiatively active gases in the atmosphere; the role of the terrestrial biosphere and the oceans in the biogeochemical cycles of greenhouse gases; emissions of carbon dioxide to the atmosphere; long-term climate trends; the effects of elevated carbon dioxide on vegetation; and the vulnerability of coastal areas to rising sea levels.

For more information, see http://cdiac.esd.ornl.gov/.

Deutsche Gesellschaft für Technische Zusammenarbeit

The Deutsche Gesellschaft für Technische Zusammenarbeit (GTZ) GmbH is a German government-owned corporation for international cooperation with worldwide operations. GTZ's aim is to positively shape political, economic, ecological, and social development in partner countries, thereby improving people's living conditions and prospects.

For more information, see www.gtz.de/.

gtz

Food and Agriculture Organization

The Food and Agriculture Organization, a specialized agency of the United Nations, was founded in October 1945 with a mandate to raise nutrition levels and living standards, to increase agricultural productivity, and to better the condition of rural populations. The organization provides direct development assistance; collects, analyzes, and disseminates information; offers policy and planning advice to governments; and serves as an international forum for debate on food and agricultural issues.

For more information, see www.fao.org/.

International Civil Aviation Organization

The International Civil Aviation Organization (ICAO), a specialized agency of the United Nations, is responsible for establishing international standards and recommended practices and procedures for the technical, economic, and legal aspects of international civil aviation operations. ICAO's strategic objectives include enhancing global aviation safety and security and the efficiency of aviation operations, minimizing the adverse effect of global civil aviation on the environment, maintaining the continuity of aviation operations, and strengthening laws governing international civil aviation.

For more information, see www.icao.int/.

International Labour Organization

The International Labour Organization (ILO), a specialized agency of the United Nations, seeks the promotion of social justice and internationally recognized human and labor rights. ILO helps advance the creation of decent jobs and the kinds of economic and working conditions that give working people and business people a stake in lasting peace, prosperity, and progress. As part of its mandate, the ILO maintains an extensive statistical publication program.

For more information, see www.ilo.org/.

International Monetary Fund

The International Monetary Fund (IMF) is an international organization of 185 member countries established to promote international monetary cooperation, a stable system of exchange rates, and the balanced expansion of international trade and to foster economic growth and high levels of employment. The IMF reviews national, regional, and global economic and financial developments, provides policy advice to member countries and serves as a forum where they can discuss the national, regional, and global consequences of their policies.

The IMF also makes financing temporarily available to member countries to help them address balance of payments problems. Among the IMF's core missions are the collection and dissemination of high-quality macroeconomic and financial statistics as an essential prerequisite for formulating appropriate policies. The IMF provides technical assistance and training to member countries in areas of its core expertise, including the development of economic and financial data in accordance with international standards.

For more information, see www.imf.org.

International Telecommunication Union

The International Telecommunication Union (ITU) is the leading UN agency for information and communication technologies. ITU's mission is to enable the growth and sustained development of telecommunications and information networks and to facilitate universal access so that people everywhere can participate in, and benefit from, the emerging information society and global economy. A key priority lies in bridging the so-called Digital Divide by building information and communication infrastructure, promoting adequate capacity building, and developing confidence in the use of cyberspace through enhanced online security. ITU also concentrates on strengthening emergency communications for disaster prevention and mitigation.

For more information, see www.itu.int/.

PARTNERS

National Science Foundation

The National Science Foundation (NSF) is an independent U.S. government agency whose mission is to promote the progress of science; to advance the national health, prosperity, and welfare; and to secure the national defense. NSF's goals—discovery, learning, research infrastructure, and stewardship—provide an integrated strategy to advance the frontiers of knowledge, cultivate a world-class, broadly inclusive science and engineering workforce, expand the scientific literacy of all citizens, build the nation's research capability through investments in advanced instrumentation and facilities, and support excellence in science and engineering research and education through a capable and responsive organization.

For more information, see www.nsf.gov/.

Organisation for Economic Co-operation and Development

The Organisation for Economic Co-operation and Development (OECD) includes 30 member countries sharing a commitment to democratic government and the market economy to support sustainable economic growth, boost employment, raise living standards, maintain financial stability, assist other countries' economic development, and contribute to growth in world trade. With active relationships with some 100 other countries it has a global reach. It is best known for its publications and statistics, which cover economic and social issues from macroeconomics to trade, education, development, and science and innovation.

The Development Assistance Committee (DAC, www.oecd.org/dac/) is one of the principal bodies through which the OECD deals with issues related to cooperation with developing countries. The DAC is a key forum of major bilateral donors, who work together to increase the effectiveness of their common efforts to support sustainable development. The DAC concentrates on two key areas: the contribution of international development to the capacity of developing countries to participate in the global economy and the capacity of people to overcome poverty and participate fully in their societies.

For more information, see www.oecd.org/.

Stockholm International Peace Research Institute

The Stockholm International Peace Research Institute (SIPRI) conducts research on questions of conflict and cooperation of importance for international peace and security, with the aim of contributing to an understanding of the conditions for peaceful solutions to international conflicts and for a stable peace. SIPRI's main publication, *SIPRI Yearbook,* is an authoritive and independent source on armaments and arms control and other conflict and security issues.

For more information, see www.sipri.org/.

Understanding Children's Work

As part of broader efforts to develop effective and long-term solutions to child labor, the International Labor Organization, the United Nations Children's Fund (UNICEF), and the World Bank initiated the joint interagency research program "Understanding Children's Work and Its Impact" in December 2000. The Understanding Children's Work (UCW) project was located at UNICEF's Innocenti Research Centre in Florence, Italy, until June 2004, when it moved to the Centre for International Studies on Economic Growth in Rome.

The UCW project addresses the crucial need for more and better data on child labor. UCW's online database contains data by country on child labor and the status of children.

For more information, see www.ucw-project.org/.

United Nations

The United Nations currently has 192 member states. The purposes of the United Nations, as set forth in the Charter, are to maintain international peace and security; to develop friendly relations among nations; to cooperate in solving international economic, social, cultural, and humanitarian problems and in promoting respect for human rights and fundamental freedoms; and to be a center for harmonizing the actions of nations in attaining these ends.

For more information, see www.un.org/.

United Nations Centre for Human Settlements, Global Urban Observatory

The Urban Indicators Programme of the United Nations Human Settlements Programme was established to address the urgent global need to improve the urban knowledge base by helping countries and cities design, collect, and apply policy-oriented indicators related to development at the city level.

With the Urban Indicators and Best Practices programs, the Global Urban Observatory is establishing a worldwide information, assessment, and capacity building network to help governments, local authorities, the private sector, and nongovernmental and other civil society organizations.

For more information, see www.unhabitat.org/.

United Nations Children's Fund

The United Nations Children's Fund (UNICEF) works with other UN bodies and with governments and nongovernmental organizations to improve children's lives in more than 190 countries through various programs in education and health. UNICEF focuses primarily on five areas: child survival and development, basic Education and gender equality (including girls' education), child protection, HIV/AIDS, and policy advocacy and partnerships.

For more information, see www.unicef.org/.

United Nations Conference on Trade and Development

The United Nations Conference on Trade and Development (UNCTAD) is the principal organ of the United Nations General Assembly in the field of trade and development. Its mandate is to accelerate economic growth and development, particularly in developing countries. UNCTAD discharges its mandate through policy analysis; intergovernmental deliberations, consensus building, and negotiation; monitoring, implementation, and follow-up; and technical cooperation.

For more information, see www.unctad.org/.

United Nations Educational, Scientific, and Cultural Organization, Institute for Statistics

The United Nations Educational, Scientific, and Cultural Organization (UNESCO) is a specialized agency of the United Nations that promotes international cooperation among member states and associate members

PARTNERS

in education, science, culture and communications. The UNESCO Institute for Statistics is the organization's statistical branch, established in July 1999 to meet the growing needs of UNESCO member states and the international community for a wider range of policy-relevant, timely, and reliable statistics on these topics.

For more information, see www.uis.unesco.org/.

United Nations Environment Programme

The mandate of the United Nations Environment Programme is to provide leadership and encourage partnership in caring for the environment by inspiring, informing, and enabling nations and people to improve their quality of life without compromising that of future generations.

For more information, see www.unep.org/.

United Nations Industrial Development Organization

The United Nations Industrial Development Organization was established to act as the central coordinating body for industrial activities and to promote industrial development and cooperation at the global, regional, national, and sectoral levels. Its mandate is to help develop scientific and technological plans and programs for industrialization in the public, cooperative, and private sectors.

For more information, see www.unido.org/.

The UN Refugee Agency

The UN Refugee Agency (UNHCR) is mandated to lead and coordinate international action to protect refugees and resolve refugee problems worldwide. Its primary purpose is to safeguard the rights and well-being of refugees. UNHCR also collects and disseminates statistics on refugees.

For more information, see www.unhcr.org

World Bank

The World Bank is a vital source of financial and technical assistance for developing countries. The World Bank is made up of two unique development institutions owned by 185 member countries—the International Bank for Reconstruction and Development (IBRD) and the International Development Association (IDA). These institutions play different but collaborative roles to advance the vision of an inclusive and sustainable globalization. The IBRD focuses on middle-income and creditworthy poor countries, while IDA focuses on the poorest countries. Together they provide low-interest loans, interest-free credits, and grants to developing countries for a wide array of purposes, including investments in education, health, public administration, infrastructure, financial and private sector development, agriculture, and environmental and natural resource management. The World Bank's work focuses on achieving the Millennium Development Goals by working with partners to alleviate poverty.

For more information, see www.worldbank.org/data/.

World Health Organization

The objective of the World Health Organization (WHO), a specialized agency of the United Nations, is the attainment by all people of the highest possible level of health. It is responsible for providing leadership on global health matters, shaping the health research agenda, setting norms and standards, articulating evidence-based policy options, providing technical support to countries, and monitoring and assessing health trends.

For more information, see www.who.int/.

World Intellectual Property Organization

The World Intellectual Property Organization (WIPO) is a specialized agency of the United Nations dedicated to developing a balanced and accessible international intellectual property (IP) system, which rewards creativity, stimulates innovation, and contributes to economic development while safeguarding the public interest. WIPO carries out a wide variety of tasks related to the protection of IP rights. These include developing international IP laws and standards, delivering global IP protection services, encouraging the use of IP for economic development, promoting better understanding of IP, and providing a forum for debate.

For more information, see www.wipo.int/.

World Tourism Organization

The World Tourism Organization is an intergovernmental body entrusted by the United Nations with promoting and developing tourism. It serves as a global forum for tourism policy issues and a source of tourism know-how.

For more information, see www.unwto.org/.

World Trade Organization

The World Trade Organization (WTO) is the only international organization dealing with the global rules of trade between nations. Its main function is to ensure that trade flows as smoothly, predictably, and freely as possible. It does this by administering trade agreements, acting as a forum for trade negotiations, settling trade disputes, reviewing national trade policies, assisting developing countries in trade policy issues—through technical assistance and training programs—and cooperating with other international organizations. At the heart of the system—known as the multilateral trading system—are the WTO's agreements, negotiated and signed by a large majority of the world's trading nations and ratified by their parliaments.

For more information, see www.wto.org/.

Private and nongovernmental organizations

Containerisation International

Containerisation International Yearbook is one of the most authoritative reference books on the container industry. The information can be accessed on the Containerisation International Web site, which also provides a comprehensive online daily business news and information service for the container industry.

For more information, see www.ci-online.co.uk/.

PARTNERS

International Institute for Strategic Studies

The International Institute for Strategic Studies (IISS) provides information and analysis on strategic trends and facilitates contacts between government leaders, business people, and analysts that could lead to better public policy in international security and international relations. The IISS is a primary source of accurate, objective information on international strategic issues.

For more information, see www.iiss.org/.

International Road Federation

The International Road Federation (IRF) is a nongovernmental, not-for-profit organization whose mission is to encourage and promote development and maintenance of better, safer, and more sustainable roads and road networks. Working together with its members and associates, the IRF promotes social and economic benefits that flow from well planned and environmentally sound road transport networks. It helps put in place technological solutions and management practices that provide maximum economic and social returns from national road investments. The IRF works in all aspects of road policy and development worldwide with governments and financial institutions, members, and the community of road professionals.

For more information, see www.irfnet.org/.

Netcraft

Netcraft provides Internet security services such as antifraud and antiphishing services, application testing, code reviews, and automated penetration testing. Netcraft also provides research data and analysis on many aspects of the Internet and is a respected authority on the market share of web servers, operating systems, hosting providers, Internet service providers, encrypted transactions, electronic commerce, scripting languages, and content technologies on the Internet.

For more information, see http://news.netcraft.com/.

PricewaterhouseCoopers

PricewaterhouseCoopers provides industry-focused services in the fields of assurance, tax, human resources, transactions, performance improvement, and crisis management services to help address client and stakeholder issues.

For more information, see www.pwc.com/.

Standard & Poor's

Standard & Poor's is the world's foremost provider of independent credit ratings, indexes, risk evaluation, investment research, and data. S&P's *Global Stock Markets Factbook* draw on data from S&P's Emerging Markets Database (EMDB) and other sources covering data on more than 100 markets with comprehensive market profiles for 82 countries. Drawing a sample of stocks in each EMDB market, Standard & Poor's calculates indices to serve as benchmarks that are consistent across national boundaries.

For more information, see www.standardandpoors.com/.

World Conservation Monitoring Centre

The World Conservation Monitoring Centre provides information on the conservation and sustainable use of the world's living resources and helps others to develop information systems of their own. It works in close collaboration with a wide range of people and organizations to increase access to the information needed for wise management of the world's living resources.

For more information, see www.unep-wcmc.org/.

World Information Technology and Services Alliance

The World Information Technology and Services Alliance (WITSA) is a consortium of more than 60 information technology (IT) industry associations from economies around the world. WITSA members represent over 90 percent of the world IT market. As the global voice of the IT industry, WITSA has an active role in international public policy issues affecting the creation of a robust global information infrastructure, including advocating policies that advance the industry's growth and development, facilitating international trade and investment in IT products and services, increasing competition through open markets and regulatory reform, strengthening national industry associations through the sharing of knowledge, protecting intellectual property, encouraging cross-industry and government cooperation to enhance information security, bridging the education and skills gap, and safeguarding the viability and continued growth of the Internet and electronic commerce.

For more information, see www.witsa.org/.

World Resources Institute

The World Resources Institute is an independent center for policy research and technical assistance on global environmental and development issues. The institute provides—and helps other institutions provide—objective information and practical proposals for policy and institutional change that will foster environmentally sound, socially equitable development. The institute's current areas of work include trade, forests, energy, economics, technology, biodiversity, human health, climate change, sustainable agriculture, resource and environmental information, and national strategies for environmental and resource management.

For more information, see www.wri.org/.

USERS GUIDE

Tables

The tables are numbered by section and display the identifying icon of the section. Countries and economies are listed alphabetically (except for Hong Kong, China, which appears after China). Data are shown for 153 economies with populations of more than 1 million, as well as for Taiwan, China, in selected tables. Table 1.6 presents selected indicators for 56 other economies—small economies with populations between 30,000 and 1 million and smaller economies if they are members of the International Bank for Reconstruction and Development (IBRD) or, as it is commonly known, the World Bank. A complete set of indicators for these economies is available on the *World Development Indicators* CD-ROM and in *WDI Online*. The term *country,* used interchangeably with *economy,* does not imply political independence, but refers to any territory for which authorities report separate social or economic statistics. When available, aggregate measures for income and regional groups appear at the end of each table.

Indicators are shown for the most recent year or period for which data are available and, in most tables, for an earlier year or period (usually 1990 or 1995 in this edition). Time-series data for all 209 economies are available on the *World Development Indicators* CD-ROM and in *WDI Online*.

Known deviations from standard definitions or breaks in comparability over time or across countries are either footnoted in the tables or noted in *About the data*. When available data are deemed to be too weak to provide reliable measures of levels and trends or do not adequately adhere to international standards, the data are not shown.

Aggregate measures for income groups

The aggregate measures for income groups include 209 economies (the economies listed in the main tables plus those in table 1.6) whenever data are available. To maintain consistency in the aggregate measures over time and between tables, missing data are imputed where possible. The aggregates are totals (designated by a *t* if the aggregates include gap-filled estimates for missing data and by an *s,* for

simple totals, where they do not), median values (*m*), weighted averages (*w*), or simple (unweighted) averages (*u*). Gap filling of amounts not allocated to countries may result in discrepancies between subgroup aggregates and overall totals. For further discussion of aggregation methods, see *Statistical methods*.

Aggregate measures for regions

The aggregate measures for regions cover only low- and middle-income economies, including economies with populations of less than 1 million listed in table 1.6.

The country composition of regions is based on the World Bank's analytical regions and may differ from common geographic usage. For regional classifications, see the map on the inside back cover and the list on the back cover flap. For further discussion of aggregation methods, see *Statistical methods*.

Statistics

Data are shown for economies as they were constituted in 2007, and historical data are revised to reflect current political arrangements. Exceptions are noted throughout the tables.

Additional information about the data is provided in *Primary data documentation*. That section summarizes national and international efforts to improve basic data collection and gives country-level information on primary sources, census years, fiscal years, statistical methods and concepts used, and other background information. *Statistical methods* provides technical information on some of the general calculations and formulas used throughout the book.

Data consistency, reliability, and comparability

Considerable effort has been made to standardize the data, but full comparability cannot be assured, and care must be taken in interpreting the indicators. Many factors affect data availability, comparability, and reliability: statistical systems in many developing economies are still weak; statistical methods, coverage, practices, and definitions differ widely; and cross-country and intertemporal comparisons involve complex technical and conceptual problems that cannot be resolved unequivocally. Data coverage may

not be complete because of special circumstances affecting the collection and reporting of data, such as problems stemming from conflicts.

For these reasons, although data are drawn from the sources thought to be most authoritative, they should be construed only as indicating trends and characterizing major differences among economies rather than as offering precise quantitative measures of those differences. Discrepancies in data presented in different editions of *World Development Indicators* reflect updates by countries as well as revisions to historical series and changes in methodology. Thus readers are advised not to compare data series between editions of *World Development Indicators* or between different World Bank publications. Consistent time-series data for 1960–2007 are available on the *World Development Indicators* CD-ROM and in *WDI Online*.

Except where otherwise noted, growth rates are in real terms. (See *Statistical methods* for information on the methods used to calculate growth rates.) Data for some economic indicators for some economies are presented in fiscal years rather than calendar years; see *Primary data documentation*. All dollar figures are current U.S. dollars unless otherwise stated. The methods used for converting national currencies are described in *Statistical methods*.

Country notes

- Unless otherwise noted, data for China do not include data for Hong Kong, China; Macao, China; or Taiwan, China.
- Data for Indonesia include Timor-Leste through 1999 unless otherwise noted.
- Montenegro declared independence from Serbia and Montenegro on June 3, 2006. When available, data for each country are shown separately. However, some indicators for Serbia continue to include data for Montenegro through 2005; these data are footnoted in the tables. Moreover, data for most indicators from 1999 onward for Serbia exclude data for Kosovo, which in 1999 became a territory under international administration pursuant to UN Security Council Resolution 1244 (1999); any exceptions are noted.

Classification of economies

For operational and analytical purposes the World Bank's main criterion for classifying economies is gross national income (GNI) per capita (calculated by the *World Bank Atlas* method). Every economy is classified as low income, middle income (subdivided into lower middle and upper middle), or high income. For income classifications see the map on the inside front cover and the list on the front cover flap. Low- and middle-income economies are sometimes referred to as developing economies. The term is used for convenience; it is not intended to imply that all economies in the group are experiencing similar development or that other economies have reached a preferred or final stage of development. Note that classification by income does not necessarily reflect development status. Because GNI per capita changes over time, the country composition of income groups may change from one edition of *World Development Indicators* to the next. Once the classification is fixed for an edition, based on GNI per capita in the most recent year for which data are available (2007 in this edition), all historical data presented are based on the same country grouping.

Low-income economies are those with a GNI per capita of $935 or less in 2007. Middle-income economies are those with a GNI per capita of more than $935 but less than $11,456. Lower middle-income and upper middle-income economies are separated at a GNI per capita of $3,705. High-income economies are those with a GNI per capita of $11,456 or more. The 16 participating member countries of the euro area are presented as a subgroup under high-income economies. Note that the Slovak Republic joined the euro area on January 1, 2009.

Symbols

..

means that data are not available or that aggregates cannot be calculated because of missing data in the years shown.

0 or 0.0

means zero or small enough that the number would round to zero at the displayed number of decimal places.

/

in dates, as in 2003/04, means that the period of time, usually 12 months, straddles two calendar years and refers to a crop year, a survey year, or a fiscal year.

$

means current U.S. dollars unless otherwise noted.

>

means more than.

<

means less than.

Data presentation conventions

- A blank means not applicable or, for an aggregate, not analytically meaningful.
- A billion is 1,000 million.
- A trillion is 1,000 billion.
- Figures in italics refer to years or periods other than those specified or to growth rates calculated for less than the full period specified.
- Data for years that are more than three years from the range shown are footnoted.

The cutoff date for data is February 1, 2009.

WORLD VIEW

The world seems to be entering an economic crisis unlike any seen since the founding of the Bretton Woods institutions. Indeed, simultaneous crises. The bursting of a real estate bubble. The liquidity and solvency problems for major banks. The liquidity trap as consumers and businesses prefer holding cash to spending on consumption or investment. The disruptions in international capital flows. And for some countries a currency crisis.

Plummeting global output and trade in the last quarter of 2008 brought the global economy to a standstill after years of remarkable growth, throwing millions out of work. The United States, as the epicenter, has seen unemployment rising to more than 11 million, an unemployment rate of 7.2 percent. Most forecasts show world GDP growth slowing to near zero or negative values, after a 3.4 percent increase in 2008.

What brought about the crisis? Why is it so severe? How quickly has it spread? In this introduction, and in the introductions to sections four (*Economy*) and six (*Global links*), the data describe the events that have brought us to this point. Could the crisis have been anticipated by looking more closely at the same data? Perhaps. Perhaps not. But there is still much we can learn about how these events unfolded.

The crisis must be seen in the context of dramatic changes in the global economy. First, record export-led economic growth in emerging market economies shifted the balance of global economic power, evidenced by their growing share in world output, trade, and international reserves. High savings rates outstripped their capacity to invest in their own economies while policies to sterilize large inflows and protect against financial shocks led to a large build up in international reserves. So poorer economies were financing the current account deficits of high-income economies. Second, financial integration has accompanied expanding trade, spurred by remarkable developments in information technology and financial innovation. This extended the reach of global markets, lowering costs and increasing their efficiency, but also spreading systemic shocks farther and faster.

The financial crisis had its origins in a U.S. real estate asset bubble fed by a boom in subprime mortgage lending. The availability of cheap credit fed asset bubbles in other developed economies and among major emerging market economies. The rapid and massive growth of long-term, illiquid, and risky assets financed by short-term liabilities contributed to the speed with which the crisis spread across the world economy and to its severity.

Global growth will be negative in 2009, and growth in developing economies will fall sharply from the 6 percent or higher rates of 2008. This reflects both a sharp decline in export demand from high-income economies and a major reduction in access to commercial finance and an increase in its cost. Slower growth will inevitably affect the ability of low-income economies to reach the Millennium Development Goals. How far the global recession extends and how long it lasts will depend on the effectiveness of policies adopted by rich and poor economies alike in the months ahead.

Growth accelerated in the 2000s

The years preceding the 2008 global crisis saw the strongest economic growth in decades (figure 1a). Global economic output grew 4 percent a year from 2000 to 2007, led by record growth in low- and middle-income economies. Developing economies averaged 6.5 percent annual growth of GDP from 2000 to 2007, and growth in every region was the highest in three decades (figure 1b). Europe and Central Asia and South Asia had their best decade in the most recent period (2000–07). East Asia and Pacific almost equaled its previous peak, reached before the 1997 crisis. For others the peak was in 1976—before the oil price shocks of the late 1970s and the debt crisis of the 1980s. But growth rates in high-income economies have been on a downward path since the 1970s.

China and India have emerged in recent years as drivers of global economic growth, accounting for 2.9 percentage points of the 5 percent growth in global output in 2007. Low- and middle-income economies now contribute 43 percent of global output, up from 36 percent in 2000. China and India account for 5 percentage points of that increased share.

Exports led growth

Integration of the global economy was marked by a rapid increase in trade. Growth in low- and middle-income economies was led by exports, which grew at an average annual rate of 12 percent over 2000–07. China and India were among the fastest-growing exporters. Export growth was led by manufactures in China and by services in India. Some smaller economies with exports of oil, gas, metals, minerals, or manufactures were also among the fastest growing. Exports from low- and middle-income economies in 2007 made up 29 percent of the world total, up from 21 percent in 2000. Although trade between low- and middle-income economies has been growing, 70 percent of low- and middle-income economies' exports still went to high-income economies in 2007 (figure 1c).

Fast-growing, export-oriented economies attracted new investment (figure 1d). Some of it came from domestic saving. In low- and middle-income economies savings rose from 25 percent of GDP in 2000 to 32 percent in 2007. But growth also attracted foreign direct investment. The contribution of investment to GDP growth in these economies averaged less than 1 percentage point before 2000 but rose to 2.4 percentage points over 2000–07.

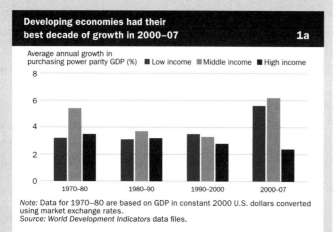

Developing economies had their best decade of growth in 2000–07   **1a**

Average annual growth in purchasing power parity GDP (%)   ■ Low income ■ Middle income ■ High income

Note: Data for 1970–80 are based on GDP in constant 2000 U.S. dollars converted using market exchange rates.
Source: World Development Indicators data files.

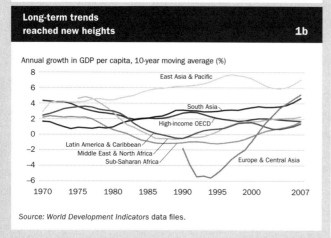

Long-term trends reached new heights   **1b**

Annual growth in GDP per capita, 10-year moving average (%)

East Asia & Pacific
South Asia
High-income OECD
Latin America & Caribbean
Middle East & North Africa
Sub-Saharan Africa
Europe & Central Asia

Source: World Development Indicators data files.

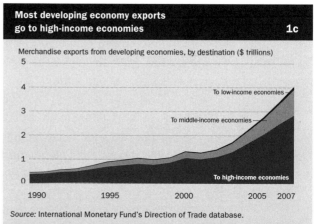

Most developing economy exports go to high-income economies   **1c**

Merchandise exports from developing economies, by destination ($ trillions)

To low-income economies
To middle-income economies
To high-income economies

Source: International Monetary Fund's Direction of Trade database.

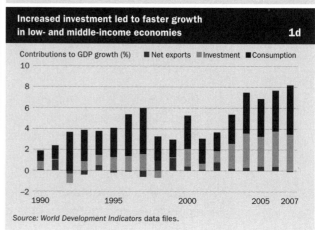

Increased investment led to faster growth in low- and middle-income economies   **1d**

Contributions to GDP growth (%)   ■ Net exports ■ Investment ■ Consumption

Source: World Development Indicators data files.

Structural imbalances emerged

Countries with trade surpluses accumulated capital beyond their capacity to absorb it. Many ran large current account surpluses and accumulated record reserves. Countries with trade deficits financed their current account by increased borrowing abroad. From 2005 to 2007 the five largest surplus economies accounted for 71 percent of total current account surpluses, and the five largest deficit economies, for 79 percent of total current account deficits (table 1e).

China's current account surplus rose from 2 percent of GDP in 2000 to an average of 10 percent during 2005–07 (figure 1f). Oil and gas exporters such as the Russian Federation and Saudi Arabia also saw surpluses balloon. Unlike many high-income economies, Germany went from a deficit of 1.5 percent of GDP in 2000 to a surplus of 6 percent over 2000–07. But some countries with strong export growth had equally strong import growth, with India and Mexico maintaining small current account deficits.

The largest deficits were in high-income economies, with the United States accounting for more than half the world's current account deficits. The U.S. current account deficit increased from 4.3 percent of GDP in 2000 to an average of 6 percent in 2005–07. Spain's rose from 4 percent to 9 percent of GDP.

Countries became more interdependent

As the global imbalance between savings and investment grew, countries with large deficits borrowed from countries with surpluses, while fast-growing exporters depended on expanding markets in deficit countries. China and other surplus economies accumulated record reserves (figure 1g) and sent capital overseas. The United States and other deficit countries consumed more and financed their deficits by issuing more debt and equity (figure 1h).

Savings and investment trends for China, the largest surplus country, and the United States, the largest deficit country, illustrate the growing imbalances. China's savings rate increased, exceeding investment by 11.5 percent of GDP in 2007. In the United States private savings almost disappeared, and investment exceeded savings by 4.6 percent of GDP.

Countries with large reserves invested large portions of their holdings in U.S. Treasury securities, widely regarded as very low risk. At the end of 2008 China was the largest foreign holder of U.S. Treasury securities, at $696 billion, followed by Japan, at $578 billion. Total foreign holdings of U.S. Treasury securities were $3.1 trillion, up from $2.4 trillion in 2007.

Large current account surpluses and deficits were concentrated in a few economies during 2005–07   **1e**

Economy	2005–07 average ($ billions)	Share of all deficit/surplus economies (%)	Percent of GDP
All deficit economies	−1,303		
United States	−749	57	−6
Spain	−113	9	−9
United Kingdom	−74	6	−3
Australia	−47	4	−6
Italy	−43	3	−2
All surplus economies	1,428		
China	372	26	10
Germany	256	18	6
Japan	210	15	4
Saudi Arabia	95	7	27
Russian Federation	76	5	8

Source: International Monetary Fund balance of payments data files and *World Development Indicators* data files.

Current account surpluses and deficits increased   **1f**

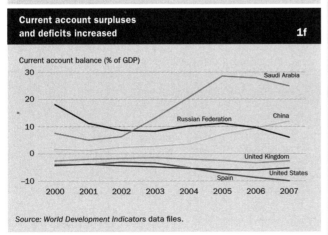

Current account balance (% of GDP)

Source: *World Development Indicators* data files.

Trade surpluses led to large build-ups in reserves   **1g**

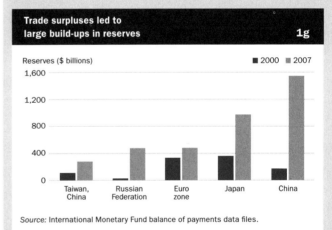

Reserves ($ billions)

Source: International Monetary Fund balance of payments data files.

Trade deficits were financed by foreign investors   **1h**

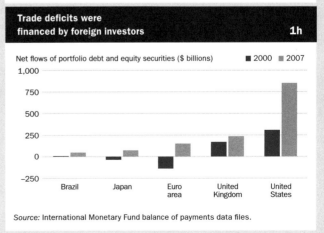

Net flows of portfolio debt and equity securities ($ billions)

Source: International Monetary Fund balance of payments data files.

Foreign investments grew

Private capital flows to low- and middle-income economies more than quadrupled from $200 billion in 2000 to over $900 billion in 2007, reaching 6.6 percent of the economies' collective GDP (figure 1i). Foreign domestic investment accounts for most of those flows, as multinational corporations established footholds in new markets, shifted production sites to take advantage of lower costs, or sought access to supplies of natural resources.

Portfolio investment in bond and equity markets also grew. Foreign investors were drawn to emerging equity markets as the prospects for these economies improved substantially and the returns outpaced those in more developed markets. Net inflows from bonds and commercial bank lending grew from $12 billion in 2000 to $269 billion in 2007 as globalization of the banking industry continued and perceived risk in many low- and middle-income economies dropped to all-time lows (figure 1j).

Brazil, China, India, and the Russian Federation attracted the largest shares of capital flows among developing economies. But foreign domestic investment flows to low-income economies also increased in recent years—some of them coming from developing economies with large current account surpluses—drawn by rising commodity prices into the oil, mineral, and other commodity sectors and into infrastructure projects.

Asset prices rose rapidly as well

Stock market capitalization in low- and middle-income economies increased nearly eightfold, rising from $2 trillion in 2000 to $15 trillion in 2007, or from 35 percent of GDP to 114 percent. Stock markets in Brazil, China, India, and the Russian Federation accounted for $11 trillion. Foreign investors increased their stakes in these markets, which outperformed more developed markets. Foreign holdings of portfolio equity securities increased from $37 billion in 2001 to $364 billion in 2007 in Brazil, from $11 billion in 2000 to $292 billion in 2007 in the Russian Federation and from $17 billion to $103 billion in India, and from $43 billion in 2004 to $125 billion in 2007 in China. Other classes of assets such as housing also appreciated rapidly (figure 1k).

Asset prices rose in part due to more optimistic expectations for future earnings. Price-earnings ratios, a measure of valuation for equities, rose rapidly in low- and middle-income economy stock markets (figure 1l). From 2000 to 2007 ratios rose from 11.5 to 16.6 in Brazil, from 21.6 to 50.5 in China, from 16.8 to 31.6 in India, and from 3.8 to 18.4 in the Russian Federation. And rising housing prices reflected expectations for continuing appreciation.

Private capital flows to developing economies took off in 2002 . . . 1i

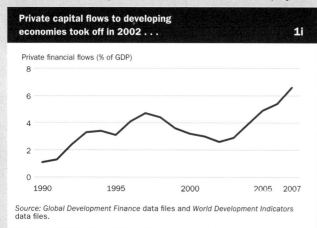

Private financial flows (% of GDP)

Source: Global Development Finance data files and World Development Indicators data files.

. . . And investors perceived less risk 1j

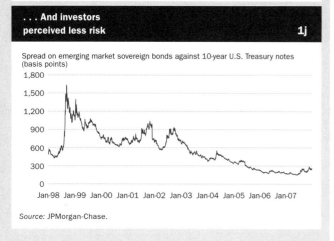

Spread on emerging market sovereign bonds against 10-year U.S. Treasury notes (basis points)

Source: JPMorgan-Chase.

Prices of assets, especially in real estate, were rising rapidly in some countries . . . 1k

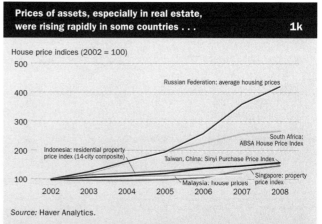

House price indices (2002 = 100)

Source: Haver Analytics.

. . . And so were equity asset valuations 1l

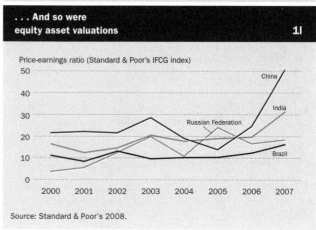

Price-earnings ratio (Standard & Poor's IFCG index)

Source: Standard & Poor's 2008.

External debt declined and changed composition

The Debt Initiative for Heavily Indebted Poor Countries and the Multilateral Debt Relief Initiative have helped some of the poorest and most indebted countries, especially in Sub-Saharan Africa, significantly reduce their outstanding debt. External debt to GNI ratios for Sub-Saharan Africa went from more than 80 percent in the mid-1990s to less than 30 percent today (figure 1m). Elsewhere, especially in Europe and Central Asia, debt increased in recent years. For Croatia, Kazakhstan, Latvia, Romania, and a few small island economies external debt to GNI ratios reached all-time highs in 2007.

As debt ratios fell, many countries gained access to private financing. Private nonguaranteed debt of low- and middle-income economies rose from 24 percent of total debt in 2000 to 37 percent in 2007. In Europe and Central Asia private nonguaranteed debt made up 55 percent of total external debt in 2007. Short-term debt in low- and middle-income economies rose from 13 percent of total debt in 2000 to 24 percent in 2007. In 2007 in East Asia and Pacific short-term debt made up 39 percent of total debt and 55 percent in China. But growing international reserves helped offset the risk of short-term financing in foreign currencies (figure 1n).

Demand for primary commodities increased

Rapid global economic growth drove demand for commodities, boosting prices, especially for oil, metals, and minerals used as inputs to manufacturing. After increasing gradually from 2000 to 2006, prices rose more rapidly in 2007 and into 2008. Food prices also rose, due in part to the production of ethanol from corn and other food crops (figure 1o).

Rising commodity prices benefited exporters, especially in Latin America and the Caribbean and Sub-Saharan Africa. Aside from the terms of trade gains, the higher commodity prices increased government revenues from taxes on commodity exports and attracted foreign domestic investment into commodity exports and supporting infrastructure projects.

But for food and fuel importers the spike in prices has been costly. Current account balances of most oil-importing low- and middle-income economies worsened (figure 1p). Price increases have also pushed up inflation and interest rates, with the impacts especially severe for poor people. In eight countries higher food prices between 2005 and 2007 increased poverty rates by 3 percentage points on average (Ivanic and Martin 2008). Globally, the number of people living on less than $1.25 a day may have risen by more than 100 million before commodity prices began to fall in the latter half of 2008.

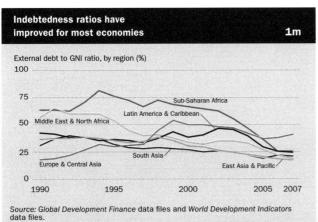

Indebtedness ratios have improved for most economies **1m**

External debt to GNI ratio, by region (%)

Source: Global Development Finance data files and World Development Indicators data files.

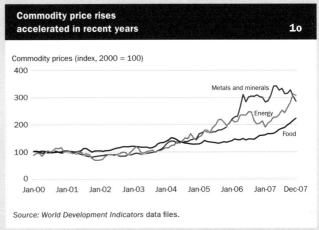

Commodity price rises accelerated in recent years **1o**

Commodity prices (index, 2000 = 100)

Source: World Development Indicators data files.

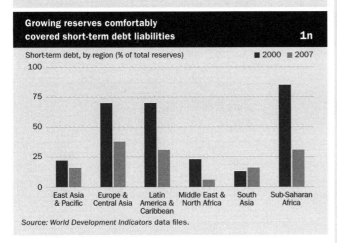

Growing reserves comfortably covered short-term debt liabilities **1n**

Short-term debt, by region (% of total reserves) ■ 2000 ■ 2007

Source: World Development Indicators data files.

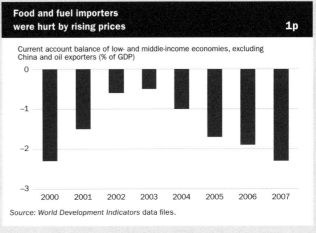

Food and fuel importers were hurt by rising prices **1p**

Current account balance of low- and middle-income economies, excluding China and oil exporters (% of GDP)

Source: World Development Indicators data files.

A perfect storm?

The current global financial and economic crisis is unlike anything the world has seen since the Great Depression nearly eight decades ago. It embraces simultaneous crises in the housing, equity, and financial markets, triggering what could become a global recession. Output and trade declined sharply in the last quarter of 2008 (figure 1q). Projections for 2009 suggest global growth close to zero percent, with strong downside risks. Unemployment is rising sharply in both developed and emerging market economies. The International Labour Organization estimates job losses of up to 50 million in 2009. The United States lost as many as 3.6 million jobs in 2008.

The crisis had its superficial roots in the rise in U.S. household debt (figure 1r), financed largely by home mortgages, many of which did not meet prime underwriting guidelines. When home prices began to fall from their peak in 2006 (figure 1s), mortgage default rates rose sharply and triggered a collapse in mortgage-backed securities. Subprime lending came to an abrupt halt, further driving down the prices of U.S. homes. Investors, their confidence undermined, withdrew funds from other illiquid markets (figure 1t), and investment banks had to liquidate assets or withdraw financing from customers, forcing further deleveraging. Thus, the subprime mortgage crisis became a fully fledged financial crisis (Lin 2009).

The impacts were felt throughout the increasingly integrated global financial markets, attacking stock markets globally and reducing credit availability. Global stock markets lost an estimated $30 trillion in market capitalization in 2008 over their inflated 2007 levels. Rising unemployment and the wealth effects of falling asset prices contributed to a sharp decline in consumer spending. Developing countries suddenly faced a sharp decline in demand for their exports and a drop in commodity prices. As recessionary trends developed, remittances from migrant workers declined, and migrants began returning home.

Three major factors account for the scale of the crisis. Underlying the bubbles in global real estate and stock markets were growing macroeconomic imbalances that fed liquidity into the system, lowering real interest rates and fueling the asset price bubbles. Financial innovations pioneered by major global investment banks turned out to be transmission mechanisms for instability (Lin 2009). And the failure of national financial regulators to effectively regulate global financial markets encouraged investors to take exorbitant risk.

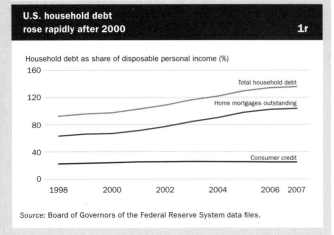

Output in the largest economies slowed or declined in the 4th quarter of 2008　**1q**

GDP (% change from previous year)

■ 2008 Q1　■ 2008 Q2
■ 2008 Q3　■ 2008 Q4

Source: U.S. Department of Commerce, Japan Cabinet Office, Eurostat, China National Bureau of Statistics, Haver Analytics, and World Bank staff calculations.

U.S. household debt rose rapidly after 2000　**1r**

Household debt as share of disposable personal income (%)

Total household debt

Home mortgages outstanding

Consumer credit

Source: Board of Governors of the Federal Reserve System data files.

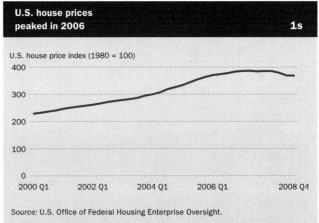

U.S. house prices peaked in 2006　**1s**

U.S. house price index (1980 = 100)

Source: U.S. Office of Federal Housing Enterprise Oversight.

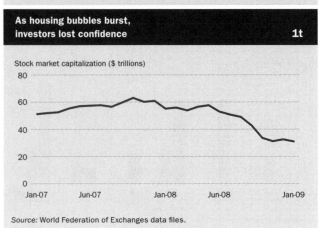

As housing bubbles burst, investors lost confidence　**1t**

Stock market capitalization ($ trillions)

Source: World Federation of Exchanges data files.

Macroeconomic imbalances

Global savings and investment rates have been fairly stable in recent years at 20–22 percent. But these global rates masked a significant shift in the source of savings. In developing economies savings rates rose 7 percentage points of aggregate GDP between 2000 and 2007, exceeding investment rates, while in high-income, Organisation for Economic Co-operation and Development countries, savings rates fell by about 2 percentage points of aggregate GDP.

The growing pool of savings in part of the world reflected the rising new incomes of oil exporters, boosted by record prices, deliberate policies to build up foreign exchange reserves by Asian countries wishing to avoid repeating the experience of the late 1990s, and the excess household and corporate savings in China (figure 1u). Surpluses in Germany, Japan, and some Asian countries were matched by substantial savings deficits, mainly in the United States (figures 1v and 1w). U.S. savings rates fell nearly 4 percentage points between 2000 and 2007, producing a savings-investment imbalance of close to 5 percentage points of GDP.

The rest of the world's savings surpluses left the United States awash in liquidity. U.S.-owned assets abroad doubled between 2000 and 2007 to 128 percent of GDP, reflecting the importance of the United States as a source of both foreign direct investment and portfolio flows (figure 1x). U.S. liabilities rose from 77 percent of GDP to 145 percent over the same period, increasing the negative net liabilities to 17 percent of 2007 GDP. Foreign official assets held in the United States more than tripled, to $3.3 trillion, or 24 percent of GDP, the bulk of it in U.S. government securities, the counterpart to the buildup in reserves in developing and high-income Asia. This kept U.S. interest rates low and stimulated a global "search for yield." It also led investors to underprice risk and shift to risky assets, stimulating a boom in real estate and stock markets globally.

Some see the savings surpluses in developing economies as policy driven, ascribing a passive role to policymakers in industrial economies who benefited from these surpluses. Others see U.S. structural deficits as reflecting profligate spending. Indeed, personal savings in the United States were a mere 1.7 percent of GDP in 2000, falling further to 0.4 percent by 2007 reflecting consumption growth in "substantial excess of income growth" (Summers 2006). But until the crisis rudely interrupted the party, both surplus and deficit countries benefited: the first from high export-led growth; the second from low interest rates and cheap consumer goods, which held inflation down despite large fiscal deficits.

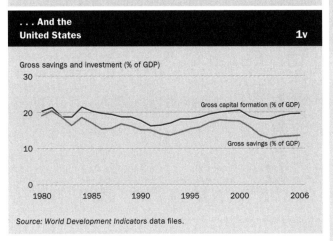

Savings and investment in China . . . **1u**

Gross savings and investment (% of GDP)

Gross savings (% of GDP)

Gross capital formation (% of GDP)

Source: World Development Indicators data files.

. . . And the United States **1v**

Gross savings and investment (% of GDP)

Gross capital formation (% of GDP)

Gross savings (% of GDP)

Source: World Development Indicators data files.

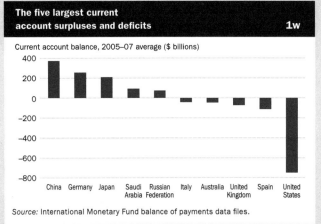

The five largest current account surpluses and deficits **1w**

Current account balance, 2005–07 average ($ billions)

China Germany Japan Saudi Arabia Russian Federation Italy Australia United Kingdom Spain United States

Source: International Monetary Fund balance of payments data files.

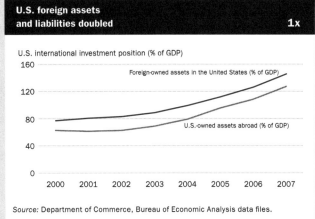

U.S. foreign assets and liabilities doubled **1x**

U.S. international investment position (% of GDP)

Foreign-owned assets in the United States (% of GDP)

U.S.-owned assets abroad (% of GDP)

Source: Department of Commerce, Bureau of Economic Analysis data files.

The role of financial innovation

What distinguishes this crisis from previous crises is the speed and depth of the transmission channels, as a U.S.-based crisis turned global in a matter of months. This reflects the transformation of the financial system during this boom period by the dramatic growth in the share of assets held outside the traditional banking system. The mortgage market, for example, was transformed by an "originate and distribute" model. Mortgage loans, made by loan originators, were resold to financial institutions, which "sliced and diced" pools of mortgages and aggregated them into collateralized debt obligations resold in turn to investors all over the world.

Derivatives, or financial instruments whose value is derived from the value of an underlying asset (commodities, equities, stocks, mortgages, real estate, loans, bonds) or an index (of interest rates, stock prices, or consumer prices), enable those who trade in them to mitigate risk through hedging or to speculate. Derivatives can be bought and sold through over the counter trades between two parties, or they can be exchange traded. Over the counter derivatives had a notional value of some $684 trillion in June 2008 (figure 1y), representing the value of the underlying assets against which the derivatives were issued. But the risk is better measured by the cost of replacing all such contracts at the prevailing market price: their gross global market value rose from $2.5 trillion in June 2000 to a still astronomical $20.4 trillion in June 2008 (figure 1z).

Derivatives were pioneered globally by investment banks, stimulated by high fees. Financial sector profits in the U.S. averaged 29 percent of before-tax profits between 2000 and 2006 (figure 1aa). U.S investment banks quickly grew to rival commercial banks but were not subject to the same regulation. "The scale of long-term risky and illiquid assets financed by very short-term liabilities made many of the vehicles and institutions in this parallel financial system vulnerable to a classic type of run, but without the protections, such as deposit insurance, that the banking system has in place to reduce such risks" (Geithner 2008). Following the collapse of the real estate market and the loss of confidence in mortgage-backed securities, investors began pulling out of these markets, creating liquidity and solvency crises for investment banks.

Underlying these developments lay the failure to properly regulate financial institutions, weaknesses in internal risk management systems, and the failure of credit rating agencies to correctly rate risk. At the end of 2007, there were reportedly 12 triple-A rated companies in the world, but as many as 64,000 structured finance instruments were rated triple-A (Blankfein 2009). Given the size of the market in these new instruments, it is questionable whether any single national authority can regulate cross-border transactions (figure 1bb).

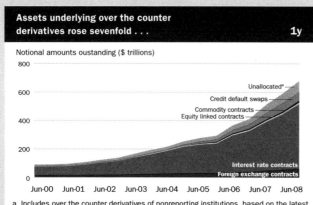

Assets underlying over the counter derivatives rose sevenfold . . . `1y`

Notional amounts oustanding ($ trillions)

a. Includes over the counter derivatives of nonreporting institutions, based on the latest Triennial Central Bank Survey of Foreign Exchange and Derivatives Market Activity in 2007.
Source: Bank for International Settlements data files.

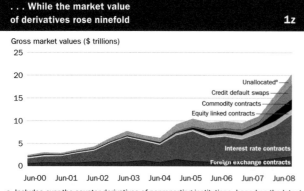

. . . While the market value of derivatives rose ninefold `1z`

Gross market values ($ trillions)

a. Includes over the counter derivatives of nonreporting institutions, based on the latest Triennial Central Bank Survey of Foreign Exchange and Derivatives Market Activity in 2007.
Source: Bank for International Settlements data files.

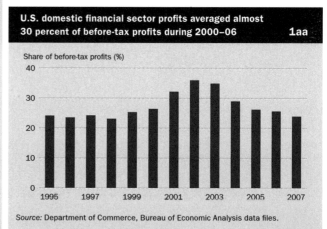

U.S. domestic financial sector profits averaged almost 30 percent of before-tax profits during 2000–06 `1aa`

Share of before-tax profits (%)

Source: Department of Commerce, Bureau of Economic Analysis data files.

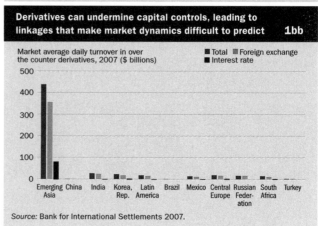

Derivatives can undermine capital controls, leading to linkages that make market dynamics difficult to predict `1bb`

Market average daily turnover in over the counter derivatives, 2007 ($ billions)

■ Total ■ Foreign exchange ■ Interest rate

Source: Bank for International Settlements 2007.

Why financial crises occur so often

Banking systems are inherently prone to crises. Banks borrow short (take in deposits) and lend long. They rely on depositors not to withdraw their deposits all at the same time. But depositor confidence in banks can be shaken by the rising threat of nonperforming loans or by political and economic developments. Even sound banks can be hurt by rumors and a general loss of confidence. When that happens, depositors may demand their deposits, causing a run on banks or a liquidity crisis. If banks sell their assets to maintain their ability to repay depositors, that may reduce the price of their assets and thus their equity base, a solvency crisis.

A recent study notes that banking crises "have long been an equal opportunity menace," (Reinhart and Rogoff 2008, p. 2) affecting developed and developing economies alike. It examines crises beginning with Denmark's financial panic during the Napoleonic war to the current global financial crisis in 66 economies. The Great Depression of the 1930s was the crisis that affected the greatest number of countries in the 109 years ending in 2008. The period immediately after World War II, between the late 1940s and the early 1970s, when financial markets were repressed and capital controls were extensive, was marked by relative calm. Banking crises recurred again after the 1970s following financial and international capital account liberalization (figure 1cc). Major crises in this period included the Latin American debt crisis of the 1980s, the U.S.

savings and loan crisis of 1984, Japan's asset bust in 1992, and the Asian financial crisis of 1997–98 (figure 1dd).

Some key characteristics of banking crises include:
- Periods of high international capital mobility, which have repeatedly produced international banking crises, possibly because they were accompanied by inadequate regulation and supervision (Caprio and Klingebiel 1996).
- Preceding period of sustained surges in capital inflows.
- Preceding boom in real housing prices, followed by a marked decline in the year of the crisis and beyond.
- Preceding expansion in the number of financial institutions.

The cost of bailing out banks following a systemic crisis (the exhaustion of much or all of banking capital) is often high (figure 1ee). A study of 117 systemic banking crises in 93 economies between the late 1970s and 2002 shows that the cost to countries of major crises could amount to as much as 55% of GDP (as with Indonesia in its 1997–2002 crisis; Caprio and Klingebiel 2003). This does not include the cost to depositors and borrowers of wider interest rate spreads from bad loans on balance sheets. The data need to be used with caution, however, because in some cases costs include corporate restructuring while in others they relate to restructuring and capitalization of banks.

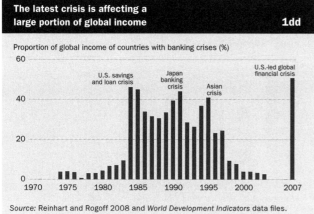

The number of banking crises rose after the 1970s `1cc`

Countries with banking crisis

Source: Reinhart and Rogoff 2008.

The latest crisis is affecting a large portion of global income `1dd`

Proportion of global income of countries with banking crises (%)

U.S. savings and loan crisis · Japan banking crisis · Asian crisis · U.S.-led global financial crisis

Source: Reinhart and Rogoff 2008 and *World Development Indicators* data files.

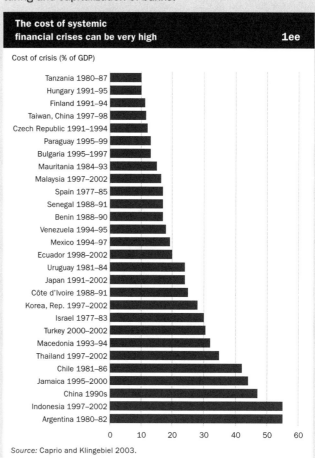

The cost of systemic financial crises can be very high `1ee`

Cost of crisis (% of GDP)

Tanzania 1980–87
Hungary 1991–95
Finland 1991–94
Taiwan, China 1997–98
Czech Republic 1991–1994
Paraguay 1995–99
Bulgaria 1995–1997
Mauritania 1984–93
Malaysia 1997–2002
Spain 1977–85
Senegal 1988–91
Benin 1988–90
Venezuela 1994–95
Mexico 1994–97
Ecuador 1998–2002
Uruguay 1981–84
Japan 1991–2002
Côte d'Ivoire 1988–91
Korea, Rep. 1997–2002
Israel 1977–83
Turkey 2000–2002
Macedonia 1993–94
Thailand 1997–2002
Chile 1981–86
Jamaica 1995–2000
China 1990s
Indonesia 1997–2002
Argentina 1980–82

Source: Caprio and Klingebiel 2003.

The crisis spreads quickly . . .

Past crises show that equity prices typically fall 55 percent over 3.5 years (Reinhart and Rogoff 2008). Housing prices decline an average 35 percent over 6 years. Unemployment rises 7 percentage points over 4 years. Output falls by 9 percent over 2 years. And the real value of government debt rises an average of 86 percent. This pattern is beginning to play out in the major high-income economies. In the fourth quarter of 2008 U.S. gross domestic output contracted by an annualized rate of 6.2 percent, euro area countries by 5.9 percent, and Japan by 12.1 percent.

Many low- and middle-income economies have begun to feel the impact as high-income economy demand for their exports declines. The troubles of the financial sector have increased risk aversion and reduced liquidity, impairing or reversing capital flows to low- and middle-income economy borrowers and equity markets (figures 1ff and 1gg). The subsidiaries of troubled banks are likely to curtail lending, pushing corporations with debt falling due into risk of insolvency. Foreign direct investment flows may also decline as corporations adjust to an increasingly uncertain environment and as plunging commodity prices make some ventures less appealing. Higher unemployment will also reduce workers' remittance flows to low- and middle-income economies.

. . . And developing economies feel the pain

Low-income economies are the most vulnerable to potential losses of official aid, workers' remittances, and foreign direct investment, which often make up a large share of their GDP (table 1hh). But the slowdown in trade could also hurt low-income commodity exporters such as The Gambia, Guinea-Bissau, Nigeria, Mauritania, Mongolia, Papua New Guinea, and Zimbabwe, which are expected to suffer large terms of trade losses as prices fall. Lower commodity prices will reduce both export revenues and fiscal revenues—and discourage foreign direct investment. But food and fuel importers, which have endured soaring prices since January 2007, will get some relief—oil importers such as Kyrgyz Republic and Tajikistan and food importers such as Benin, Eritrea, Ghana, Guinea, Haiti, Madagascar, Niger, Senegal, and Togo may benefit from improved terms of trade.

Remittances have proved surprisingly resilient, rising again in 2008. But they are expected to fall as unemployment rises in high-income economies and some migrants return home. For many low-income economies, remittances are a big part of total capital flows—10 percent of GDP in more than a quarter of them (figure 1ii). And if the pattern of past financial crises is a guide, there is also a risk that official aid will decline. Low-income economies rely heavily on official aid flows, with median official aid at 15 percent of GDP in 2005–07.

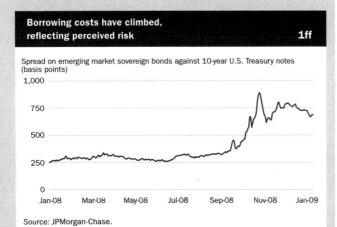

Borrowing costs have climbed, reflecting perceived risk   **1ff**

Spread on emerging market sovereign bonds against 10-year U.S. Treasury notes (basis points)

Source: JPMorgan-Chase.

Equity markets have suffered large losses   **1gg**

MSCI equity price indices (January 2008 = 100)

Group of Seven

Emerging market economies

Source: Morgan-Stanley.

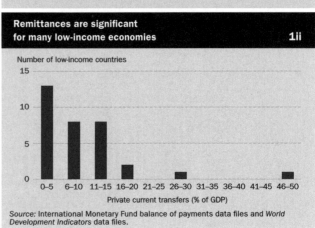

Low-income economies depend the most on official aid, workers' remittances, and foreign direct investment   **1hh**

External financing, 2007 (% of GDP)

Source	Low-income economies	Middle-income economies
Workers' remittances and compensation of employees, receipts	5.7	1.8
Official aid	5.0	0.3
Foreign direct investment, net inflows	4.2	3.7
Portfolio equity investment	1.6	0.9
Bonds	0.2	0.6
Commercial banks and other lending, net flows	−0.1	1.6
Net exports of goods and services	−6.3	2.6

Source: *World Development Indicators* data files.

Remittances are significant for many low-income economies   **1ii**

Number of low-income countries

Private current transfers (% of GDP)

Source: International Monetary Fund balance of payments data files and *World Development Indicators* data files.

Coping with the crisis

In November 2008 China introduced a $585 billion economic stimulus package to counter the global crisis. Other middle-income economies also have stimulus plans. Fiscal responses to the crisis must address short-term risks to macroeconomic stability and long-term fiscal sustainability—while protecting the vulnerable segments of society and the longer term investments that sustain economic growth and human development. About 40 percent of low- and middle-income economies have good fiscal and current account positions, including many larger economies, and may be able to expand fiscal policy without jeopardizing solvency (table 1jj).

In addition to strong fiscal and external positions, a successful fiscal stimulus requires administrative capability to design and implement new programs, or expand existing ones (box 1kk). Getting the timing and size right for a discretionary fiscal stimulus is not easy. Packages often cannot be delivered quickly enough, and expenditures may go to wasteful projects, especially when subject to political pressure. Where administrative capacity is weak, easier to implement options are boosting existing safety net programs, supplementing or replacing faltering foreign financing of infrastructure projects already under way with domestic financing, creating jobs through public works projects, increasing fiscal transfers to subnational governments, and facilitating central bank support of trade financing.

Fiscal positions have generally improved but remain weak for some developing economies · 1jj

Fiscal position (% of GDP; median)

Country group	Public debt 2007	Maximum debt 2002–07	Fiscal balance 2007[a]
Low-income economies[b]	40.5	87.9	−2.4
Large economies	36.7	87.9	−1.9
East Asia and Pacific	40.6	70.1	−2.5
Europe and Central Asia	31.7	77.5	−2.6
Latin America and Caribbean	37.6	55.0	−0.4
Middle East and North Africa	41.2	57.8	−4.8
South Asia	57.1	66.4	−3.4
Sub-Saharan Africa	28.0	93.9	−1.7
Small economies	61.0	87.1	−3.6
Middle-income economies	34.1	51.1	−0.6

a. After official grants.
b. IDA-eligible economies.
Source: IMF 2008b; World Development Indicators data files.

Finding fiscal space in low-income economies · 1kk

Low-income economies can allow fiscal deficits to temporarily increase if they can access financing, but this generally has not been the case in past downturns. Median public debt among low-income economies was 41 percent of GDP in 2007. A quarter of developing economies had public debt of less than 21 percent. Among larger Sub-Saharan African economies median debt was 28 percent.

The ability to borrow depends on the size of the fiscal deficit, the level of government debt, the country's growth prospects, the government's reputation for fiscal management, the structure of debt (maturity, currency), and recent debt history.

Financing a larger fiscal deficit is generally easier if the country's starting external balance and reserve position are strong. A fiscal stimulus package tends to increase the external deficit by bolstering domestic demand. For commodity-exporting countries current account and fiscal deficits tend to rise when commodity prices fall, as at present. Thus a large imbalance or a low level of reserves will tend to limit the size of the fiscal stimulus that is possible.

Protecting the vulnerable

Poor people in developing economies are highly exposed to the global crisis. World Bank estimates for 2009 suggest that lower growth rates will trap 46 million more people below the $1.25 a day poverty line than expected before the crisis. An extra 53 million people will be living on less than $2 a day, and child mortality rates could soar. It is estimated that 200,000–400,000 more children a year, a total of 1.4–2.8 million from 2009 to 2015, may die if the crisis persists.

Poor consumers are the first to be hurt by lower demand for labor and falling remittances. In addition, shrinking fiscal revenues and potential decreases in official aid flows threaten to reduce access to social safety nets and to such social services as health care and education. Households may have to sell productive assets, pull children out of school, and reduce calorie intake, which can lead to acute malnutrition. The long-term consequences can be severe and in some cases irreversible, especially for women and children.

Almost 40 percent of low- and middle-income economies are highly exposed to the poverty effects of the crisis. Yet three-quarters of them cannot raise funds domestically or internationally to finance programs to curb the effects of the downturn.

Recent World Bank Group initiatives · 1ll

Establish a vulnerability fund. The World Bank has proposed a vulnerability fund financed by high-income economies to assist countries that cannot afford to protect the vulnerable. The fund's priorities would be to invest in safety net programs and infrastructure and to finance small and medium-size enterprises and microfinance institutions.

Substantially increase lending by the International Bank for Reconstruction and Development (IBRD). IBRD could make new commitments of up to $100 billion over the next three years.

Fast track funds from the International Development Association (IDA). A facility is now in place to speed $2 billion to help the poorest countries deal with the effects of the crisis.

Respond to the food crisis. Nearly $900 million is approved or in the pipeline to help developing countries cope with the impact of high food prices through a $1.2 billion food facility.

Ensure trade flows. The International Finance Corporation (IFC), a member of the World Bank Group that focuses on the private sector, plans to double its existing Global Trade Finance Program to $3 billion over three years and to mobilize funds from other sources.

Bolster distressed banking systems. IFC is putting in place a global equity fund to recapitalize distressed banks. IFC expects to invest $1 billion over three years, and Japan plans to invest $2 billion.

Keep infrastructure projects on track. IFC expects to invest at least $300 million over three years and mobilize $1.5 billion to provide rollover financing and recapitalize viable infrastructure projects in distress.

Support microfinance. IFC and Germany have launched a $500 million facility to support microfinance institutions facing difficulties as a result of the crisis.

Shift advisory support to help companies weather the crisis. IFC is refocusing advisory services to help clients cope with the crisis. It estimates a financing need of at least $40 million over three years.

Millennium Development Goals

Goals and targets from the Millennium Declaration	Indicators for monitoring progress

Goal 1 — Eradicate extreme poverty and hunger

Target 1.A Halve, between 1990 and 2015, the proportion of people whose income is less than $1 a day	1.1 Proportion of population below $1 purchasing power parity (PPP) a day[1] 1.2 Poverty gap ratio [incidence × depth of poverty] 1.3 Share of poorest quintile in national consumption
Target 1.B Achieve full and productive employment and decent work for all, including women and young people	1.4 Growth rate of GDP per person employed 1.5 Employment to population ratio 1.6 Proportion of employed people living below $1 (PPP) a day 1.7 Proportion of own-account and contributing family workers in total employment
Target 1.C Halve, between 1990 and 2015, the proportion of people who suffer from hunger	1.8 Prevalence of underweight children under five years of age 1.9 Proportion of population below minimum level of dietary energy consumption

Goal 2 — Achieve universal primary education

Target 2.A Ensure that by 2015 children everywhere, boys and girls alike, will be able to complete a full course of primary schooling	2.1 Net enrollment ratio in primary education 2.2 Proportion of pupils starting grade 1 who reach last grade of primary education 2.3 Literacy rate of 15- to 24-year-olds, women and men

Goal 3 — Promote gender equality and empower women

Target 3.A Eliminate gender disparity in primary and secondary education, preferably by 2005, and in all levels of education no later than 2015	3.1 Ratios of girls to boys in primary, secondary, and tertiary education 3.2 Share of women in wage employment in the nonagricultural sector 3.3 Proportion of seats held by women in national parliament

Goal 4 — Reduce child mortality

Target 4.A Reduce by two-thirds, between 1990 and 2015, the under-five mortality rate	4.1 Under-five mortality rate 4.2 Infant mortality rate 4.3 Proportion of one-year-old children immunized against measles

Goal 5 — Improve maternal health

Target 5.A Reduce by three-quarters, between 1990 and 2015, the maternal mortality ratio	5.1 Maternal mortality ratio 5.2 Proportion of births attended by skilled health personnel
Target 5.B Achieve by 2015 universal access to reproductive health	5.3 Contraceptive prevalence rate 5.4 Adolescent birth rate 5.5 Antenatal care coverage (at least one visit and at least four visits) 5.6 Unmet need for family planning

Goal 6 — Combat HIV/AIDS, malaria, and other diseases

Target 6.A Have halted by 2015 and begun to reverse the spread of HIV/AIDS	6.1 HIV prevalence among population ages 15–24 years 6.2 Condom use at last high-risk sex 6.3 Proportion of population ages 15–24 years with comprehensive, correct knowledge of HIV/AIDS 6.4 Ratio of school attendance of orphans to school attendance of nonorphans ages 10–14 years
Target 6.B Achieve by 2010 universal access to treatment for HIV/AIDS for all those who need it	6.5 Proportion of population with advanced HIV infection with access to antiretroviral drugs
Target 6.C Have halted by 2015 and begun to reverse the incidence of malaria and other major diseases	6.6 Incidence and death rates associated with malaria 6.7 Proportion of children under age five sleeping under insecticide-treated bednets 6.8 Proportion of children under age five with fever who are treated with appropriate antimalarial drugs 6.9 Incidence, prevalence, and death rates associated with tuberculosis 6.10 Proportion of tuberculosis cases detected and cured under directly observed treatment short course

The Millennium Development Goals and targets come from the Millennium Declaration, signed by 189 countries, including 147 heads of state and government, in September 2000 (www.un.org/millennium/declaration/ares552e.htm) as updated by the 60th UN General Assembly in September 2005. The revised Millennium Development Goal (MDG) monitoring framework shown here, including new targets and indicators, was presented to the 62nd General Assembly, with new numbering as recommended by the Inter-agency and Expert Group on MDG Indicators at its 12th meeting on 14 November 2007. The goals and targets are interrelated and should be seen as a whole. They represent a partnership between the developed countries and the developing countries "to create an environment—at the national and global levels alike—which is conducive to development and the elimination of poverty." All indicators should be disaggregated by sex and urban-rural location as far as possible.

Goals and targets from the Millennium Declaration | Indicators for monitoring progress

Goal 7	Ensure environmental sustainability

Target 7.A	Integrate the principles of sustainable development into country policies and programs and reverse the loss of environmental resources
Target 7.B	Reduce biodiversity loss, achieving, by 2010, a significant reduction in the rate of loss

7.1 Proportion of land area covered by forest
7.2 Carbon dioxide emissions, total, per capita and per $1 GDP (PPP)
7.3 Consumption of ozone-depleting substances
7.4 Proportion of fish stocks within safe biological limits
7.5 Proportion of total water resources used
7.6 Proportion of terrestrial and marine areas protected
7.7 Proportion of species threatened with extinction

Target 7.C	Halve by 2015 the proportion of people without sustainable access to safe drinking water and basic sanitation

7.8 Proportion of population using an improved drinking water source
7.9 Proportion of population using an improved sanitation facility

Target 7.D	Achieve by 2020 a significant improvement in the lives of at least 100 million slum dwellers

7.10 Proportion of urban population living in slums[2]

Goal 8	Develop a global partnership for development

Target 8.A	Develop further an open, rule-based, predictable, nondiscriminatory trading and financial system (Includes a commitment to good governance, development, and poverty reduction—both nationally and internationally.)

Some of the indicators listed below are monitored separately for the least developed countries (LDCs), Africa, landlocked developing countries, and small island developing states.

Official development assistance (ODA)
8.1 Net ODA, total and to the least developed countries, as percentage of OECD/DAC donors' gross national income
8.2 Proportion of total bilateral, sector-allocable ODA of OECD/DAC donors to basic social services (basic education, primary health care, nutrition, safe water, and sanitation)

Target 8.B	Address the special needs of the least developed countries (Includes tariff and quota-free access for the least developed countries' exports; enhanced program of debt relief for heavily indebted poor countries (HIPC) and cancellation of official bilateral debt; and more generous ODA for countries committed to poverty reduction.)

8.3 Proportion of bilateral official development assistance of OECD/DAC donors that is untied
8.4 ODA received in landlocked developing countries as a proportion of their gross national incomes
8.5 ODA received in small island developing states as a proportion of their gross national incomes

Target 8.C	Address the special needs of landlocked developing countries and small island developing states (through the Programme of Action for the Sustainable Development of Small Island Developing States and the outcome of the 22nd special session of the General Assembly)

Market access
8.6 Proportion of total developed country imports (by value and excluding arms) from developing countries and least developed countries, admitted free of duty
8.7 Average tariffs imposed by developed countries on agricultural products and textiles and clothing from developing countries
8.8 Agricultural support estimate for OECD countries as a percentage of their GDP
8.9 Proportion of ODA provided to help build trade capacity

Target 8.D	Deal comprehensively with the debt problems of developing countries through national and international measures in order to make debt sustainable in the long term

Debt sustainability
8.10 Total number of countries that have reached their HIPC decision points and number that have reached their HIPC completion points (cumulative)
8.11 Debt relief committed under HIPC Initiative and Multilateral Debt Relief Initiative (MDRI)
8.12 Debt service as a percentage of exports of goods and services

Target 8.E	In cooperation with pharmaceutical companies, provide access to affordable essential drugs in developing countries

8.13 Proportion of population with access to affordable essential drugs on a sustainable basis

Target 8.F	In cooperation with the private sector, make available the benefits of new technologies, especially information and communications

8.14 Telephone lines per 100 population
8.15 Cellular subscribers per 100 population
8.16 Internet users per 100 population

---

1. Where available, indicators based on national poverty lines should be used for monitoring country poverty trends.

2. The proportion of people living in slums is measured by a proxy, represented by the urban population living in households with at least one of these characteristics: lack of access to improved water supply, lack of access to improved sanitation, overcrowding (3 or more persons per room), and dwellings made of nondurable material.

	Population	Surface area	Population density	Gross national income		Gross national income per capita		PPP gross national income[a]			Gross domestic product	
	millions	thousand sq. km	people per sq. km	$ billions	Rank	$	Rank	$ billions	Per capita $	Rank	% growth	Per capita % growth
	2007	2007	2007	2007[b]	2007	2007[b]	2007	2007	2007	2007	2006–07	2006–07
Afghanistan	..	652	..	8.1	120	..[c]	..	26[d]	..[d]	..	5.3	..
Albania	3	29	116	10.5	111	3,300	116	23	7,240	107	6.0	5.7
Algeria	34	2,382	14	122.5	48	3,620	108	259[d]	7,640[d]	104	3.1	1.6
Angola	17	1,247	14	43.0	67	2,540	128	72.3	4,270	135	21.1	18.3
Argentina	40	2,780	14	238.7	30	6,040	85	512.4	12,970	78	8.7	7.6
Armenia	3	30	107	7.9	123	2,630	125	17.7	5,870	117	13.8	13.8
Australia	21	7,741	3	751.5	15	35,760	29	702.0	33,400	34	3.3	1.7
Austria	8	84	101	348.9	25	41,960	19	305.6	36,750	21	3.4	2.9
Azerbaijan	9	87	104	22.6	84	2,640	124	56.3	6,570	114	25.0	23.9
Bangladesh	159	144	1,218	74.9	56	470	184	211.4	1,330	177	6.4	4.7
Belarus	10	208	47	40.9	69	4,220	100	104.3	10,750	90	8.2	8.5
Belgium	11	31	351	436.9	20	41,110	21	375.3	35,320	26	2.8	2.0
Benin	9	113	82	5.1	141	570	178	11.8	1,310	180	4.6	1.5
Bolivia	10	1,099	9	12.0	106	1,260	151	39.5	4,150	138	4.6	2.8
Bosnia and Herzegovina	4	51	74	14.3	101	3,790[e]	105	30.3	8,020	102	6.8	7.0
Botswana	2	582	3	11.5	107	6,120	84	24.2	12,880	79	5.3	4.0
Brazil	192	8,515	23	1,122.1	10	5,860	86	1,775.6	9,270	97	5.4	4.2
Bulgaria	8	111	71	35.1	73	4,580	97	85.0	11,100	87	6.2	6.7
Burkina Faso	15	274	54	6.4	130	430	186	16.5	1,120	186	4.0	1.0
Burundi	8	28	331	0.9	188	110	209	2.8	330	206	3.6	−0.3
Cambodia	14	181	82	8.0	122	550	179	24.9	1,720	170	10.2	8.3
Cameroon	19	475	40	19.5	90	1,050	156	39.3	2,120	161	3.5	1.5
Canada	33	9,985	4	1,307.5	9	39,650	22	1,170.7	35,500	25	2.7	1.7
Central African Republic	4	623	7	1.6	174	370	189	3.1	710	201	4.2	2.3
Chad	11	1,284	9	5.8	137	540	180	13.8	1,280	181	0.6	−2.1
Chile	17	757	22	135.8	46	8,190	76	204.7	12,330	82	5.1	4.1
China	1,318	9,598	141	3,126.0	4	2,370	132	7,150.5	5,420	120	13.0	12.4
Hong Kong, China	7	1	6,647	218.6	32	31,560	33	304.3	43,940	13	6.4	5.3
Colombia	44	1,142	40	180.4	37	4,100[e]	103	363.4	8,260	101	7.5	6.2
Congo, Dem. Rep.	62	2,345	28	8.6	121	140	207	17.9	290	207	6.5	3.5
Congo, Rep.	4	342	11	5.8	136	1,540	145	10.4	2,750	152	−1.6	−3.6
Costa Rica	4	51	87	24.7	81	5,520	90	46.9[d]	10,510[d]	92	7.8	6.3
Cote d'Ivoire	19	322	61	17.8	95	920	161	31.1	1,620	175	1.7	−0.2
Croatia	4	57	79	46.4	65	10,460	66	68.9	15,540	68	5.6	5.6
Cuba	11	111	103	..	..	..[f]	..	..	..	..	..	..
Czech Republic	10	79	134	150.7	40	14,580	56	234.5	22,690	53	6.6	5.9
Denmark	5	43	129	302.8	26	55,440	9	201.0	36,800	20	1.8	1.3
Dominican Republic	10	49	201	34.6	74	3,560	109	61.8[d]	6,350[d]	115	8.5	7.3
Ecuador	13	284	48	41.5	68	3,110	120	94.8	7,110	112	2.7	1.6
Egypt, Arab Rep.	75	1,001	76	119.5	49	1,580	144	405.3	5,370	121	7.1	5.2
El Salvador	7	21	331	19.6	89	2,850	121	38.6[d]	5,640[d]	118	4.7	3.3
Eritrea	5	118	48	1.3	178	270	202	3.0[d]	620[d]	204	1.3	−1.8
Estonia	1	45	32	17.2	97	12,830	61	25.3	18,830	62	6.3	6.5
Ethiopia	79	1,104	79	17.6	96	220	205	61.7	780	196	11.1	8.4
Finland	5	338	17	234.3	31	44,300	18	183.9	34,760	28	4.4	4.0
France	62	552	112	2,466.6[g]	6	38,810[g]	25	2,088.8	33,850	32	2.2	1.6
Gabon	1	268	5	9.3	116	7,020	80	17.8	13,410	76	5.6	4.0
Gambia, The	2	11	171	0.5	193	320	195	1.9	1,140	185	6.3	3.6
Georgia	4	70	63	9.3	117	2,120	135	21.0	4,760	129	12.4	13.3
Germany	82	357	236	3,207.3	3	38,990	24	2,857.7	34,740	30	2.5	2.6
Ghana	23	239	103	13.8	104	590	177	31.0	1,320	178	6.3	4.2
Greece	11	132	87	288.1	27	25,740	40	311.5	27,830	43	4.0	3.6
Guatemala	13	109	123	32.8	79	2,450	130	60.3[d]	4,520[d]	131	5.7	3.2
Guinea	9	246	38	3.7	150	400	188	10.5	1,120	186	1.5	−0.6
Guinea-Bissau	2	36	60	0.3	202	200	206	0.8	470	205	2.7	−0.3
Haiti	10	28	349	5.0	143	520	182	10.1[d]	1,050[d]	189	3.2	1.4

	Population	Surface area	Population density	Gross national income		Gross national income per capita		PPP gross national income[a]			Gross domestic product	
	millions	thousand sq. km	people per sq. km	$ billions	Rank	$	Rank	$ billions	Per capita $	Rank	% growth	Per capita % growth
	2007	2007	2007	2007[b]	2007	2007[b]	2007	2007	2007	2007	2006–07	2006–07
Honduras	7	112	63	11.3	109	1,590	143	25.6[d]	3,610[d]	143	6.3	4.3
Hungary	10	93	112	117.5	51	11,680	64	175.6	17,470	64	1.1	1.3
India	1,125	3,287	378	1,071.0	11	950	159	3,082.5	2,740	153	9.1	7.6
Indonesia	226	1,905	125	372.6	23	1,650	141	804.5	3,570	144	6.3	5.1
Iran, Islamic Rep.	71	1,745	44	251.5	29	3,540	110	769.7	10,840	89	7.8	6.4
Iraq	..	438	..	..	..	..[h]	..	..	..	..	..	..
Ireland	4	70	63	207.9	34	47,610	13	164.6	37,700	18	6.0	3.4
Israel	7	22	332	159.2	39	22,170	45	188.9	26,310	45	5.4	3.5
Italy	59	301	202	1,988.2	7	33,490	30	1,792.6	30,190	38	1.5	0.7
Jamaica	3	11	247	8.9	119	3,330[i]	115	14.2[d]	5,300[d]	123	–7.3	–7.7
Japan	128	378	351	4,828.9	2	37,790	26	4,440.2	34,750	29	2.1	2.1
Jordan	6	89	65	16.3	99	2,840	122	29.5	5,150	124	6.0	2.6
Kazakhstan	15	2,725	6	77.7	55	5,020	94	148.7	9,600	95	8.9	7.7
Kenya	38	580	66	24.0	82	640	174	58.1	1,550	176	7.0	4.2
Korea, Dem. Rep.	24	121	198	..	..	..[c]	..	..	..	..	..	..
Korea, Rep.	48	99	491	955.8	14	19,730	48	1,203.6	24,840	50	5.0	4.6
Kuwait	3	18	149	99.9	53	38,420	23	136.7	52,610	4	6.3	3.7
Kyrgyz Republic	5	200	27	3.2	157	610	176	10.4	1,980	165	8.2	7.3
Lao PDR	6	237	25	3.7	151	630	175	12.2	2,080	162	7.9	6.0
Latvia	2	65	37	22.6	85	9,920	69	35.9	15,790	67	10.3	10.9
Lebanon	4	10	400	23.8	83	5,800	87	41.2	10,040	93	2.0	1.0
Lesotho	2	30	66	2.1	171	1,030	157	3.9	1,940	166	4.9	4.3
Liberia	4	111	39	0.5	194	140	207	1.0	280	208	9.4	5.4
Libya	6	1,760	3	55.5	62	9,010	73	90.6[d]	14,710[d]	71	6.8	4.8
Lithuania	3	65	54	33.0	77	9,770	71	56.8	16,830	66	8.8	9.4
Macedonia, FYR	2	26	80	7.1	126	3,470	111	18.4	9,050	100	5.0	4.9
Madagascar	20	587	34	6.4	131	320	195	18.2	930	193	6.2	3.4
Malawi	14	118	148	3.5	153	250	204	10.5	760	198	7.9	5.2
Malaysia	27	330	81	170.5	38	6,420	81	351.2	13,230	77	6.3	4.6
Mali	12	1,240	10	6.1	134	500	183	12.8	1,040	190	2.8	–0.2
Mauritania	3	1,031	3	2.6	166	840	167	6.3	2,000	164	1.9	–0.6
Mauritius	1	2	621	7.0	127	5,580	89	14.4	11,410	86	4.7	4.0
Mexico	105	1,964	54	989.5	13	9,400	72	1,464.4	13,910	74	3.2	2.2
Moldova	4	34	116	4.1	147	1,210[j]	153	10.6	2,800	151	3.0	3.8
Mongolia	3	1,567	2	3.4	156	1,290	149	8.3	3,170	146	10.2	9.2
Morocco	31	447	69	70.7	57	2,290	133	125.1	4,050	139	2.7	1.5
Mozambique	21	799	27	7.1	125	330	194	15.5	730	199	7.3	5.3
Myanmar	49	677	74	..	..	..[c]	..	..	..	..	5.0	4.1
Namibia	2	824	3	7.2	124	3,450	112	10.6	5,100	125	5.9	4.2
Nepal	28	147	197	9.9	115	350	193	29.8	1,060	188	3.2	1.5
Netherlands	16	42	484	747.8	16	45,650	17	646.5	39,470	17	3.5	3.3
New Zealand	4	268	16	114.5	52	27,080	39	107.3	25,380	48	3.0	1.9
Nicaragua	6	130	46	5.5	138	990	158	14.1[d]	2,510[d]	157	3.9	2.6
Niger	14	1,267	11	4.0	148	280	200	9.0	630	203	3.2	–0.1
Nigeria	148	924	162	136.3	45	920	161	260.8	1,760	169	5.9	3.6
Norway	5	324	15	364.3	24	77,370	3	252.6	53,650	5	3.7	2.6
Oman	3	310	8	32.8	75	12,860	59	55.1	21,650	57	7.2	5.6
Pakistan	162	796	211	140.2	43	860	165	412.9	2,540	155	6.0	3.7
Panama	3	76	45	18.4	93	5,500	92	35.5[d]	10,610[d]	91	11.5	9.8
Papua New Guinea	6	463	14	5.4	139	850	166	11.8[d]	1,870[d]	168	6.2	4.2
Paraguay	6	407	15	10.5	112	1,710	139	27.7	4,520	131	6.8	4.9
Peru	28	1,285	22	95.0	54	3,410	113	200.9	7,200	108	8.9	7.6
Philippines	88	300	295	142.1	42	1,620	142	326.4	3,710	142	7.2	5.2
Poland	38	313	124	375.3	21	9,850	70	590.9	15,500	69	6.6	6.7
Portugal	11	92	116	201.1	36	18,950	50	231.1	21,790	59	1.8	1.5
Puerto Rico	4	9	445	..	..	..[k]	..	..	..	..	..	..

1.1 Size of the economy

	Population	Surface area	Population density	Gross national income		Gross national income per capita		PPP gross national income[a]			Gross domestic product	
	millions	thousand sq. km	people per sq. km	$ billions	Rank	$	Rank	$ billions	Per capita $	Rank	% growth	Per capita % growth
	2007	2007	2007	2007[b]	2007	2007[b]	2007	2007	2007	2007	2006–07	2006–07
Romania	22	238	94	137.7	44	6,390	82	266.2	12,350	81	6.0	6.2
Russian Federation	142	17,098	9	1,069.8	12	7,530	79	2,036.5	14,330	73	8.1	8.4
Rwanda	10	26	395	3.1	161	320	195	8.4	860	194	6.0	3.0
Saudi Arabia	24	2,000[l]	12	373.7	22	15,450	54	554.4	22,910	52	3.4	1.2
Senegal	12	197	64	10.3	113	830	168	20.5	1,650	173	4.8	1.9
Serbia	7	78	95	33.5	76	4,540	98	72.6	9,830	94	7.5	8.0
Sierra Leone	6	72	82	1.5	176	260	203	3.9	660	202	6.8	4.9
Singapore	5	1	6,660	148.4	41	32,340	31	220.0	47,950	10	7.7	3.3
Slovak Republic	5	49	112	63.3	59	11,720	63	103.7	19,220	61	10.4	10.3
Slovenia	2	20	100	43.4	66	21,510	46	52.9	26,230	46	6.8	6.2
Somalia	9	638	14	..	..	..[c]	..	..	..	..	..	..
South Africa	48	1,219	39	273.9	28	5,720	88	452.3	9,450	96	5.1	4.1
Spain	45	505	90	1,314.5	8	29,290	36	1,380.0	30,750	37	3.8	2.1
Sri Lanka	20	66	310	30.8	80	1,540	145	84.0	4,200	137	6.8	6.1
Sudan	39	2,506	16	36.7	70	950	159	72.5	1,880	167	10.2	7.7
Swaziland	1	17	67	2.9	164	2,560	126	5.6	4,890	128	3.5	2.8
Sweden	9	450	22	437.9	19	47,870	12	343.0	37,490	19	2.7	2.0
Switzerland	8	41	189	459.2	18	60,820	7	335.3	44,410	12	3.3	2.4
Syrian Arab Republic	20	185	108	35.3	72	1,780	137	88.1	4,430	133	6.6	4.0
Tajikistan	7	143	48	3.1	160	460	185	11.5	1,710	171	7.8	6.2
Tanzania	40	947	46	16.3[m]	98	410[m]	187	48.7	1,200	182	7.1	4.5
Thailand	64	513	125	217.2	33	3,400	114	502.8	7,880	103	4.8	4.1
Timor-Leste	1	15	71	1.6	175	1,510	147	3.3[d]	3,090[d]	147	7.8	4.5
Togo	7	57	121	2.4	168	360	191	5.1	770	197	1.9	−0.7
Trinidad and Tobago	1	5	260	19.3	92	14,480	57	29.9[d]	22,420[d]	56	5.5	5.1
Tunisia	10	164	66	32.8	78	3,210	118	73.0	7,140	110	6.3	5.3
Turkey	74	784	96	593.0	17	8,030	77	946.7	12,810	80	4.6	3.3
Turkmenistan	5	488	11	..	..	..[h]	..	21.0[d]	4,350[d]	130	..	..
Uganda	31	241	157	11.3	108	370	189	32.1	1,040	190	7.9	4.3
Ukraine	47	604	80	118.9	50	2,560	126	316.7	6,810	113	7.6	8.2
United Arab Emirates	4	84	52	..	..	..[k]	..	..	..	..	9.4	5.7
United Kingdom	61	244	252	2,464.3	5	40,660	20	2,063.8	34,050	27	3.0	2.4
United States	302	9,632	33	13,886.4	1	46,040	16	13,827.2	45,840	11	2.0	1.0
Uruguay	3	176	19	21.2	86	6,390	82	36.6	11,020	88	7.4	7.1
Uzbekistan	27	447	63	19.7	87	730	172	65.3[d]	2,430[d]	158	9.5	7.9
Venezuela, RB	27	912	31	207.6	35	7,550	78	337.8	12,290	83	8.4	6.6
Vietnam	85	329	275	65.4	58	770	169	215.4	2,530	156	8.5	7.2
West Bank and Gaza	4	6	616	4.5	142	1,290	148	..	..	..	6.3	2.7
Yemen, Rep.	22	528	42	19.4	91	870	163	49.3	2,200	160	3.6	0.6
Zambia	12	753	16	9.2	118	770	169	14.2	1,190	183	6.0	4.0
Zimbabwe	13	391	35	4.5	145	340	191	..	..	..	−5.3	−6.0
World	**6,610 s**	**133,946 s**	**51 w**	**52,850.4 t**		**7,995 w**		**65,752.3 t**	**9,947 w**		**3.8 w**	**2.6 w**
Low income	1,296	21,846	61	744.3		574		1,929.7	1,489		6.4	4.2
Middle income	4,258	77,006	57	12,393.5		2,910		25,666.2	6,027		8.2	7.2
Lower middle income	3,435	35,510	100	6,542.9		1,905		15,748.8	4,585		10.2	9.1
Upper middle income	824	41,497	20	5,853.9		7,107		9,943.8	12,072		5.8	5.0
Low & middle income	5,554	98,852	58	13,141.1		2,366		27,592.5	4,968		8.1	6.8
East Asia & Pacific	1,912	16,299	121	4,172.8		2,182		9,503.1	4,969		11.4	10.5
Europe & Central Asia	446	23,972	19	2,697.2		6,052		5,018.7	11,262		6.9	6.7
Latin America & Carib.	561	20,421	28	3,252.1		5,801		5,426.0	9,678		5.7	4.4
Middle East & N. Africa	313	8,778	36	883.5		2,820		2,318.7	7,402		5.9	4.1
South Asia	1,522	5,140	318	1,338.7		880		3,853.6	2,532		8.4	6.8
Sub-Saharan Africa	800	24,242	34	761.0		951		1,495.5	1,869		6.2	3.8
High income	1,056	35,094	32	39,685.9		37,570		38,386.0	36,340		2.5	1.8
Euro area	324	2,585	129	11,611.1		35,818		10,554.9	32,560		2.7	2.1

a. PPP is purchasing power parity; see *Definitions*. b. Calculated using the *World Bank Atlas* method. c. Estimated to be low income ($935 or less). d. Based on regression; others are extrapolated from the 2005 International Comparison Program benchmark estimates. e. Included in the aggregates for lower middle-income economies based on earlier data. f. Estimated to be upper middle income ($3,706–$11,455). g. Includes the French overseas departments of French Guiana, Guadeloupe, Martinique, and Réunion. h. Estimated to be lower middle income ($936–$3,705). i. Included in the aggregates for upper middle-income economies based on earlier data. j. Excludes Transnistria. k. Estimated to be high income ($11,456 or more). l. Provisional estimate. m. Covers mainland Tanzania only.

About the data

Population, land area, income, output, and growth in output are basic measures of the size of an economy. They also provide a broad indication of actual and potential resources. Population, land area, income (as measured by gross national income, GNI), and output (as measured by gross domestic product, GDP) are therefore used throughout *World Development Indicators* to normalize other indicators.

Population estimates are generally based on extrapolations from the most recent national census. For further discussion of the measurement of population and population growth, see *About the data* for table 2.1 and *Statistical methods*.

The surface area of an economy includes inland bodies of water and some coastal waterways. Surface area thus differs from land area, which excludes bodies of water, and from gross area, which may include offshore territorial waters. Land area is particularly important for understanding an economy's agricultural capacity and the environmental effects of human activity. (For measures of land area and data on rural population density, land use, and agricultural productivity, see tables 3.1–3.3.) Innovations in satellite mapping and computer databases have resulted in more precise measurements of land and water areas.

GNI measures total domestic and foreign value added claimed by residents. GNI comprises GDP plus net receipts of primary income (compensation of employees and property income) from nonresident sources. The World Bank uses GNI per capita in U.S. dollars to classify countries for analytical purposes and to determine borrowing eligibility. For definitions of the income groups in *World Development Indicators,* see *Users guide.* For discussion of the usefulness of national income and output as measures of productivity or welfare, see *About the data* for tables 4.1 and 4.2.

When calculating GNI in U.S. dollars from GNI reported in national currencies, the World Bank follows the *World Bank Atlas* conversion method, using a three-year average of exchange rates to smooth the effects of transitory fluctuations in exchange rates. (For further discussion of the *World Bank Atlas* method, see *Statistical methods*.) GDP and GDP per capita growth rates are calculated from data in constant prices and national currency units.

Because exchange rates do not always reflect differences in price levels between countries, the table also converts GNI and GNI per capita estimates into international dollars using purchasing power parity (PPP) rates. PPP rates provide a standard measure allowing comparison of real levels of expenditure between countries, just as conventional price indexes allow comparison of real values over time.

PPP rates are calculated by simultaneously comparing the prices of similar goods and services among a large number of countries. In the most recent round of price surveys conducted by the International Comparison Program (ICP), 146 countries and territories participated in the data collection, including China for the first time, India for the first time since 1985, and almost all African countries. The PPP conversion factors presented in the table come from three sources. For 45 high- or upper middle-income countries conversion factors are provided by Eurostat and the Organisation for Economic Co-operation and Development (OECD), with PPP estimates for 34 European countries incorporating new price data collected since 2005. For the remaining 2005 ICP countries the PPP estimates are extrapolated from the 2005 ICP benchmark results, which account for relative price changes between each economy and the United States. For countries that did not participate in the 2005 ICP round, the PPP estimates are imputed using a statistical model.

For more information on the results of the 2005 ICP, see the introduction to *World View*. The final report of the program is available at www.worldbank.org/data/icp.

All 209 economies shown in *World Development Indicators* are ranked by size, including those that appear in table 1.6. The ranks are shown only in table 1.1. No rank is shown for economies for which numerical estimates of GNI per capita are not published. Economies with missing data are included in the ranking at their approximate level, so that the relative order of other economies remains consistent.

Definitions

• **Population** is based on the de facto definition of population, which counts all residents regardless of legal status or citizenship—except for refugees not permanently settled in the country of asylum, who are generally considered part of the population of their country of origin. The values shown are midyear estimates. See also table 2.1. • **Surface area** is a country's total area, including areas under inland bodies of water and some coastal waterways. • **Population density** is midyear population divided by land area in square kilometers. • **Gross national income (GNI)** is the sum of value added by all resident producers plus any product taxes (less subsidies) not included in the valuation of output plus net receipts of primary income (compensation of employees and property income) from abroad. Data are in current U.S. dollars converted using the *World Bank Atlas* method (see *Statistical methods*). • **GNI per capita** is GNI divided by midyear population. GNI per capita in U.S. dollars is converted using the *World Bank Atlas* method. • **Purchasing power parity (PPP) GNI** is GNI converted to international dollars using PPP rates. An international dollar has the same purchasing power over GNI that a U.S. dollar has in the United States. • **Gross domestic product (GDP)** is the sum of value added by all resident producers plus any product taxes (less subsidies) not included in the valuation of output. Growth is calculated from constant price GDP data in local currency. • **GDP per capita** is GDP divided by midyear population.

Data sources

Population estimates are prepared by World Bank staff from a variety of sources (see *Data sources* for table 2.1). Data on surface and land area are from the Food and Agriculture Organization (see *Data sources* for table 3.1). GNI, GNI per capita, GDP growth, and GDP per capita growth are estimated by World Bank staff based on national accounts data collected by World Bank staff during economic missions or reported by national statistical offices to other international organizations such as the OECD. PPP conversion factors are estimates by Eurostat/OECD and by World Bank staff based on data collected by the ICP.

1.2 Millennium Development Goals: eradicating poverty and saving lives

	Eradicate extreme poverty and hunger					Achieve universal primary education		Promote gender equality		Reduce child mortality	
	Share of poorest quintile in national consumption or income %	Vulnerable employment Unpaid family workers and own-account workers % of total employment		Prevalence of malnutrition Underweight % of children under age 5		Primary completion rate %		Ratio of girls to boys enrollments in primary and secondary school %		Under-five mortality rate per 1,000	
	1995–2007[a,b]	1990	2007	1990	2000–07[a]	1991	2007[c]	1991	2007[c]	1990	2007
Afghanistan	..	..	..	..	..	..	..	..	..	..	..
Albania	7.8	..	..	..	17.0	..	96	96	97	46	15
Algeria	6.9	..	35	..	10.2	80	95	83	99	69	37
Angola	2.0	..	..	..	27.5	35	..	..	..	258	158
Argentina	3.4[d]	..	20	..	2.3	..	97	..	104	29	16
Armenia	8.6	..	..	..	4.2	..	98	..	104	56	24
Australia	5.9	10	9	..	..	..	..	101	97	10	6
Austria	8.6	..	9	..	..	..	103	95	97	10	4
Azerbaijan	13.3	..	53	..	14.0	..	..	100	..	98	39
Bangladesh	9.4	..	85	64.3	39.2	..	72	..	103	151	61
Belarus	8.8	..	..	..	1.3	94	92	..	101	24	13
Belgium	8.5	..	10	..	..	79	87	101	98	10	5
Benin	6.9	..	..	..	21.5	21	64	49	73	184	123
Bolivia	1.8	40	..	8.9	5.9	71	101	..	98	125	57
Bosnia and Herzegovina	6.9	..	..	..	1.6	..	..	..	99	22	14
Botswana	3.1	..	..	..	10.7	89	95	109	101	57	40
Brazil	3.0	29	27	..	2.2	90	106	..	103	58	22
Bulgaria	8.7	..	8	..	1.6	90	98	99	97	19	12
Burkina Faso	7.0	..	..	29.6	35.2	20	33	62	82	206	191
Burundi	9.0	..	..	..	38.9	46	39	82	90	189	180
Cambodia	7.1	..	87	..	28.4	..	85	73	90	119	91
Cameroon	5.6	..	..	18.0	15.1	53	55	83	85	139	148
Canada	7.2	..	10	..	..	..	..	99	98	8	6
Central African Republic	5.2	..	..	..	21.8	27	24	60	..	171	172
Chad	6.3	94	..	..	33.9	18	31	42	64	201	209
Chile	4.1	..	25	..	0.6	..	95	100	99	21	9
China	5.7	..	..	..	6.8	105	..	87	100	45	22
Hong Kong, China	5.3	6	7	..	..	102	102	103	98	..	..
Colombia	2.3	28	41	..	5.1	70	107	108	104	35	20
Congo, Dem. Rep.	5.5	..	..	..	33.6	46	51	..	73	200	161
Congo, Rep.	5.0	..	..	..	11.8	54	72	85	90	104	125
Costa Rica	4.2	25	20	..	..	79	91	101	102	18	11
Côte d'Ivoire	5.0	..	..	..	16.7	43	45	65	..	151	127
Croatia	8.7	..	18	..	..	..	96	..	96	13	6
Cuba	..	..	..	..	..	99	93	106	99	13	7
Czech Republic	10.2	7	12	..	2.1	..	94	98	101	13	4
Denmark	8.3	..	..	..	..	98	101	101	101	9	4
Dominican Republic	4.0	39	42	8.4	4.2	62	89	..	104	66	38
Ecuador	3.4	36	34	..	6.2	..	106	..	100	57	22
Egypt, Arab Rep.	9.0	28	25	8.2	5.4	..	98	81	95	93	36
El Salvador	3.3	35	36	11.1	6.1	61	91	102	101	60	24
Eritrea	..	..	..	..	34.5	..	46	..	78	147	70
Estonia	6.8	2	6	..	..	..	100	..	100	18	6
Ethiopia	9.3	..	52	..	34.6	..	46	68	83	204	119
Finland	9.6	..	..	..	..	97	97	109	102	7	4
France	7.2	..	7	..	..	104	..	102	100	9	4
Gabon	6.1	48	..	..	8.8	..	..	..	..	92	91
Gambia, The	4.8[d]	..	..	..	15.8	..	72	66	100	153	109
Georgia	5.4	..	62	..	..	..	92	98	98	47	30
Germany	8.5	..	..	..	..	..	97	99	98	9	4
Ghana	5.2	..	..	24.1	18.8	61	71	79	95	120	115
Greece	6.7	40	28	..	..	..	103	99	98	11	4
Guatemala	3.4	..	..	27.8	17.7	..	77	..	93	82	39
Guinea	5.8	..	..	..	22.5	17	64	45	74	231	150
Guinea-Bissau	7.2	..	..	..	21.9	..	..	..	..	240	198
Haiti	2.5	..	..	..	18.9	27	..	94	..	152	76

Millennium Development Goals: eradicating poverty and saving lives | 1.2

	Eradicate extreme poverty and hunger					Achieve universal primary education		Promote gender equality		Reduce child mortality	
	Share of poorest quintile in national consumption or income % 1995–2007[a,b]	Vulnerable employment Unpaid family workers and own-account workers % of total employment		Prevalence of malnutrition Underweight % of children under age 5		Primary completion rate %		Ratio of girls to boys enrollments in primary and secondary school %		Under-five mortality rate per 1,000	
		1990	2007	1990	2000–07[a]	1991	2007[c]	1991	2007[c]	1990	2007
Honduras	2.5	49	..	..	8.6	64	88	106	106	58	24
Hungary	8.6	7	7	2.3	..	87	96	100	99	17	7
India	8.1	..	..	..	43.5	64	86	70	91	117	72
Indonesia	7.1	..	63	31.0	24.4	91	99	93	98	91	31
Iran, Islamic Rep.	6.4	..	43	..	..	91	105	85	114	72	33
Iraq	..	..	..	..	..	..	..	78	..	53	..
Ireland	7.4	20	11	..	..	..	96	104	103	9	4
Israel	5.7	..	7	..	..	..	101	105	101	12	5
Italy	6.5	16	22	..	..	104	100	100	99	9	4
Jamaica	5.2	42	35	..	3.1	90	82	102	101	33	31
Japan	10.6	19	11	..	..	101	..	101	100	6	4
Jordan	7.2	..	..	4.8	3.6	101	99	101	102	40	24
Kazakhstan	7.4	..	36	..	4.9	..	104[e]	102	99[e]	60	32
Kenya	4.7	..	..	20.1	16.5	..	93	94	96	97	121
Korea, Dem. Rep.	..	..	..	..	17.8	..	..	..	..	55	55
Korea, Rep.	7.9	..	25	..	..	98	101	99	96	9	5
Kuwait	..	..	..	..	..	..	98	97	100	15	11
Kyrgyz Republic	8.1	..	47	..	2.7	..	95	..	100	74	38
Lao PDR	8.5	..	..	..	36.4	45	77	76	86	163	70
Latvia	6.8	..	7	..	..	..	92	101	100	17	9
Lebanon	..	..	..	..	..	..	82	..	103	37	29
Lesotho	3.0	38	..	..	16.6	59	78	123	104	102	84
Liberia	6.4	..	..	..	20.4	..	55[e]	..	..	205	133
Libya	..	..	..	..	..	..	..	..	105	41	18
Lithuania	6.8	..	..	..	..	89	93	..	100	16	8
Macedonia, FYR	6.1	..	22	..	1.8	..	97	..	99	38	17
Madagascar	6.2	84	86	35.5	36.8	33	62	98	96	168	112
Malawi	7.0	..	..	24.4	18.4	29	55	81	100	209	111
Malaysia	6.4	29	22	..	..	91	98	101	104	22	11
Mali	6.5	..	..	29.0	27.9	13	49	57	78	250	196
Mauritania	6.2	..	..	..	30.4	34	59	71	102	130	119
Mauritius	..	12	17	..	..	107	94	102	102	24	15
Mexico	4.6	26	29	13.9	3.4	88	104	97	99	52	35
Moldova	7.3	..	32	..	3.2	..	93	106	102	37	18
Mongolia	7.2	..	..	..	5.3	..	110	109	107	98	43
Morocco	6.5	..	52	8.1	9.9	48	83	70	87	89	34
Mozambique	5.4	..	..	..	21.2	26	46	71	85	201	168
Myanmar	..	..	..	..	29.6	..	..	97	..	130	103
Namibia	1.5	..	21	21.5	17.5	..	77	106	104	87	68
Nepal	6.1	..	..	..	38.8	51	78[e]	59	98[e]	142	55
Netherlands	7.6	..	..	..	..	..	..	97	98	9	5
New Zealand	6.4	13	12	..	..	100	..	100	103	11	6
Nicaragua	3.8	..	45	9.6	7.8	42	73	109	102	68	35
Niger	5.9	..	..	41.0	39.9	18	40	53	71	304	176
Nigeria	5.1	..	..	35.1	27.2	..	72	77	84	230	189
Norway	9.6	..	6	..	..	100	96	102	100	9	4
Oman	..	..	..	..	..	74	88	89	99	32	12
Pakistan	9.1	..	62	39.0	31.3	..	62	..	78	132	90
Panama	2.5	34	28	..	..	..	99	..	101	34	23
Papua New Guinea	4.5	..	..	..	..	46	..	80	..	94	65
Paraguay	3.4	23	47	2.8	..	68	95	98	99	41	29
Peru	3.9	36	40	8.8	5.2	..	101	96	101	78	20
Philippines	5.6	..	45	..	20.7	88	94	100	102	62	28
Poland	7.3	28	19	..	..	96	97	100	99	17	7
Portugal	5.8	19	19	..	..	95	104	103	101	15	4
Puerto Rico	..	..	..	..	..	..	..	..	..	..	..

1.2 Millennium Development Goals: eradicating poverty and saving lives

	Eradicate extreme poverty and hunger					Achieve universal primary education		Promote gender equality		Reduce child mortality	
	Share of poorest quintile in national consumption or income %	Vulnerable employment Unpaid family workers and own-account workers % of total employment		Prevalence of malnutrition Underweight % of children under age 5		Primary completion rate %		Ratio of girls to boys enrollments in primary and secondary school %		Under-five mortality rate per 1,000	
	1995–2007 a,b	1990	2007	1990	2000–07 a	1991	2007 c	1991	2007 c	1990	2007
Romania	8.2	9	32	..	3.5	100	101	99	100	32	15
Russian Federation	6.4	1	6	..	..	..	..	104	99	27	15
Rwanda	5.4	..	..	24.3	18.0	35	35	92	100	195	181
Saudi Arabia	..	..	..	..	..	55	93	84	94	44	25
Senegal	6.2	83	..	21.9	14.5	43	49	69	92	149	114
Serbia	8.3 f	..	23	..	1.8	..	..	..	102	..	8
Sierra Leone	6.1	..	..	..	28.3	..	81	67	86	290	262
Singapore	5.0	8	10	..	3.3	..	..	..	..	8	3
Slovak Republic	8.8	..	10	..	..	..	93	..	100	15	8
Slovenia	8.2	12	13	..	..	..	..	..	100	11	4
Somalia	..	..	..	..	32.8	..	..	..	..	203	142
South Africa	3.1	..	3	..	..	76	92	104	100	64	59
Spain	7.0	22	12	..	..	103	99	104	103	9	4
Sri Lanka	6.8	..	41	29.3	22.8	102	106	102	..	32	21
Sudan	..	..	..	..	38.4	42	50	77	89 e	125	109
Swaziland	4.5	..	..	..	9.1	60	67	98	95	96	91
Sweden	9.1	..	..	..	..	96	..	102	100	7	3
Switzerland	7.6	9	10	..	..	53	88	97	97	9	5
Syrian Arab Republic	..	..	..	..	..	89	114	85	96	37	17
Tajikistan	7.7	..	..	..	14.9	..	95	..	89	117	67
Tanzania	7.3	..	88	25.1	16.7	62	112 e	97	..	157	116
Thailand	6.1	70	53	17.4	7.0	..	101	97	104	31	7
Timor-Leste	6.7	..	..	..	40.6	..	69	..	95	184	97
Togo	7.6	..	..	21.2	..	35	57	59	75	150	100
Trinidad and Tobago	5.5	22	16	4.7	4.4	101	88	101	101	34	35
Tunisia	5.9	..	..	8.5	..	74	120	86	104 c	52	21
Turkey	5.2	..	36	8.7	3.5	90	96	81	90	82	23
Turkmenistan	6.0	..	..	..	..	..	..	..	..	99	50
Uganda	6.1	..	..	19.7	19.0	..	54	82	98	175	130
Ukraine	9.0	..	..	..	4.1	94	101	..	100	25	24
United Arab Emirates	..	..	..	..	..	103	105	104	101	15	8
United Kingdom	6.1	..	..	..	..	..	..	102	102	10	6
United States	5.4	..	..	..	1.3	..	95	100	100	11	8
Uruguay	4.5	..	25	..	6.0	94	99	..	106	25	14
Uzbekistan	7.1	..	..	..	4.4	..	97	94	98	74	41
Venezuela, RB	4.9	..	30	..	..	81	98	105	103	32	19
Vietnam	7.1	..	74	36.9	20.2	..	..	..	..	56	15
West Bank and Gaza	..	..	36	..	..	..	83	..	104	38	27
Yemen, Rep.	7.2	..	..	..	..	..	60	..	66	127	73
Zambia	3.6	65	..	21.2	23.3	..	88	..	96	163	170
Zimbabwe	4.6	..	..	8.0	14.0	97	..	92	97	95	90
World		.. w	.. w	.. w	23.2 w	79 w	86 w c	86 w	96 w	93 w	68 w
Low income		..	..	..	28.0		65		87	164	126
Middle income		..	..	..	22.0	84	93	85	97	75	45
Lower middle income		..	..	..	24.8	83	91	82	95	81	50
Upper middle income		..	22	..	..	90	101	99	103	47	24
Low & middle income		..	..	..	24.1	78	85	83	95	101	74
East Asia & Pacific		..	..	..	12.8	101	98	89	99	56	27
Europe & Central Asia		..	19	..	..	93	98	100	102	49	23
Latin America & Carib.	30	..	31	..	4.4	84	100	98	103	55	26
Middle East & N. Africa		..	37	..	..	78	90	78	96	77	38
South Asia		..	..	..	41.1	62	80	70	89	125	78
Sub-Saharan Africa		..	..	..	26.6	51	60	79	86	183	146
High income		..	..	..	..	..	97	100	104	12	7
Euro area		..	12	..	..	101	..	101	..	10	4

a. Data are for the most recent year available. b. See table 2.9 for survey year and whether share is based on income or consumption expenditure. c. Provisional data. d. Urban data.
e. Data are for 2008. f. Includes Montenegro.

About the data

Tables 1.2–1.4 present indicators for 17 of the 21 targets specified by the Millennium Development Goals. Each of the eight goals includes one or more targets, and each target has several associated indicators for monitoring progress toward the target. Most of the targets are set as a value of a specific indicator to be attained by a certain date. In some cases the target value is set relative to a level in 1990. In others it is set at an absolute level. Some of the targets for goals 7 and 8 have not yet been quantified.

The indicators in this table relate to goals 1–4. Goal 1 has three targets between 1990 and 2015: to halve the proportion of people whose income is less than $1 a day, to achieve full and productive employment and decent work for all, and to halve the proportion of people who suffer from hunger. Estimates of poverty rates are in tables 2.7 and 2.8. The indicator shown here, the share of the poorest quintile in national consumption, is a distributional measure. Countries with more unequal distributions of consumption (or income) have a higher rate of poverty for a given average income. Vulnerable employment measures the portion of the labor force that receives the lowest wages and least security in employment. No single indicator captures the concept of suffering from hunger. Child malnutrition is a symptom of inadequate food supply, lack of essential nutrients, illnesses that deplete these nutrients, and undernourished mothers who give birth to underweight children.

Progress toward universal primary education is measured by the primary completion rate. Because many school systems do not record school completion on a consistent basis, it is estimated from the gross enrollment rate in the final grade of primary school, adjusted for repetition. Official enrollments sometimes differ significantly from attendance, and even school systems with high average enrollment ratios may have poor completion rates.

Eliminating gender disparities in education would help increase the status and capabilities of women. The ratio of female to male enrollments in primary and secondary school provides an imperfect measure of the relative accessibility of schooling for girls.

The targets for reducing under-five mortality rates are among the most challenging. Under-five mortality rates are harmonized estimates produced by a weighted least squares regression model and are available at regular intervals for most countries.

Most of the 60 indicators relating to the Millennium Development Goals can be found in *World Development Indicators*. Table 1.2a shows where to find the indicators for the first four goals. For more information about data collection methods and limitations, see *About the data* for the tables listed there. For information about the indicators for goals 5–8, see *About the data* for tables 1.3 and 1.4.

Definitions

- **Share of poorest quintile in national consumption or income** is the share of the poorest 20 percent of the population in consumption or, in some cases, income. • **Vulnerable employment** is the sum of unpaid family workers and own-account workers as a percentage of total employment. • **Prevalence of malnutrition** is the percentage of children under age five whose weight for age is more than two standard deviations below the median for the international reference population ages 0–59 months. The data are based on the new international child growth standards for infants and young children, called the Child Growth Standards, released in 2006 by the World Health Organization. • **Primary completion rate** is the percentage of students completing the last year of primary school. It is calculated as the total number of students in the last grade of primary school, minus the number of repeaters in that grade, divided by the total number of children of official graduation age. • **Ratio of girls to boys enrollments in primary and secondary school** is the ratio of the female to male gross enrollment rate in primary and secondary school. • **Under-five mortality rate** is the probability that a newborn baby will die before reaching age five, if subject to current age-specific mortality rates. The probability is expressed as a rate per 1,000.

Location of indicators for Millennium Development Goals 1–4 — 1.2a

	Table
Goal 1. Eradicate extreme poverty and hunger	
1.1 Proportion of population below $1.25 a day	2.8
1.2 Poverty gap ratio	2.8
1.3 Share of poorest quintile in national consumption	1.2, 2.9
1.4 Growth rate of GDP per person employed	2.4
1.5 Employment to population ratio	2.4
1.6 Proportion of employed people living below $1 per day	—
1.7 Proportion of own-account and unpaid family workers in total employment	1.2, 2.4
1.8 Prevalence of underweight in children under age five	1.2, 2.19, 2.21
1.9 Proportion of population below minimum level of dietary energy consumption	2.19
Goal 2. Achieve universal primary education	
2.1 Net enrollment ratio in primary education	2.12
2.2 Proportion of pupils starting grade 1 who reach last grade of primary	2.13
2.3 Literacy rate of 15- to 24-year-olds	2.14
Goal 3. Promote gender equality and empower women	
3.1 Ratio of girls to boys in primary, secondary, and tertiary education	1.2, 2.12*
3.2 Share of women in wage employment in the nonagricultural sector	1.5, 2.3*
3.3 Proportion of seats held by women in national parliament	1.5
Goal 4. Reduce child mortality	
4.1 Under-five mortality rate	1.2, 2.21, 2.22
4.2 Infant mortality rate	2.21, 2.22
4.3 Proportion of one-year-old children immunized against measles	2.17, 2.21

— No data are available in the *World Development Indicators* database. * Table shows information on related indicators.

Data sources

The indicators here and throughout this book have been compiled by World Bank staff from primary and secondary sources. Efforts have been made to harmonize the data series used to compile this table with those published on the United Nations Millennium Development Goals Web site (www.un.org/millenniumgoals), but some differences in timing, sources, and definitions remain. For more information see the data sources for the indicators listed in table 1.2a.

1.3 | Millennium Development Goals: protecting our common environment

	Improve maternal health			Combat HIV/AIDS and other diseases		Ensure environmental sustainability					Develop a global partnership for development
	Maternal mortality ratio Modeled estimate per 100,000 live births	Contraceptive prevalence rate % of married women ages 15–49		HIV prevalence % of population ages 15–49	Incidence of tuberculosis per 100,000 people	Carbon dioxide emissions per capita metric tons		Proportion of species threatened with extinction %	Access to improved sanitation facilities % of population		Internet users per 100 people[a]
	2005	**1990**	**2002–07[b]**	**2007**	**2007**	**1990**	**2005**	**2008**	**1990**	**2006**	**2007**
Afghanistan	..	..	..	..	..	..	..	0.7	..	..	..
Albania	92	..	60	..	17	2.2	1.1	1.5	..	97	*14.9*
Algeria	180	*47*	61	0.1	57	3.0	4.2	2.1	88	94	10.3
Angola	1,400	..	..	2.1	287	0.4	0.6	1.4	26	50	2.9
Argentina	77	..	..	0.5	31	3.4	3.9	1.9	81	91	25.9
Armenia	76	..	53	0.1	72	1.2	1.4	0.9	..	91	5.7
Australia	4	..	..	0.2	6	17.2	18.1	4.7	100	100	68.1
Austria	4	..	..	0.2	12	7.5	8.9	1.9	100	100	67.4
Azerbaijan	82	..	51	0.2	77	6.4	4.4	0.8	..	80	10.8
Bangladesh	570	40	56	..	223	0.1	0.3	1.9	26	36	0.3
Belarus	18	..	73	0.2	61	10.6	6.5	0.7	..	93	29.0
Belgium	8	78	..	0.2	12	9.9	9.8	1.3	..	..	65.9
Benin	840	..	17	1.2	91	0.1	0.3	1.5	12	30	1.7
Bolivia	290	30	58	0.2	155	0.8	1.0	0.8	33	43	10.5
Bosnia and Herzegovina	3	..	36	<0.1	51	1.6	6.9	13.1	..	95	28.0
Botswana	380	*33*	..	23.9	731	1.6	2.5	0.5	38	47	5.3
Brazil	110	59	..	0.6	48	1.4	1.7	1.3	71	77	35.2
Bulgaria	11	..	..	..	39	8.6	5.7	1.1	99	99	30.9
Burkina Faso	700	..	17	1.6	226	0.1	0.1	1.0	5	13	*0.6*
Burundi	1,100	..	9	2.0	367	0.0	0.0	1.5	44	41	*0.7*
Cambodia	540	..	40	0.8	495	0.0	0.0	29.8	8	28	0.5
Cameroon	1,000	*16*	29	5.1	192	0.1	0.2	5.4	39	51	*2.0*
Canada	7	..	..	0.4	5	15.4	16.6	1.8	100	100	72.8
Central African Republic	980	..	19	6.3	345	0.1	0.1	0.6	11	31	*0.3*
Chad	1,500	..	3	3.5	299	0.0	0.0	1.0	5	9	*0.6*
Chile	16	56	58	0.3	12	2.7	4.1	2.4	84	94	31.1
China	45	85	85	0.1	98	2.1	4.3	2.4	48	65	16.1
Hong Kong, China	..	86	..	..	62	4.6	5.7	13.2	..	..	57.2
Colombia	130	66	78	0.6	35	1.7	1.4	1.2	68	78	27.5
Congo, Dem. Rep.	1,100	*8*	..	..	392	0.1	0.0	2.5	15	31	0.4
Congo, Rep.	740	..	21	3.5	403	0.5	0.6	1.0	..	20	*1.9*
Costa Rica	30	..	96	0.4	11	0.9	1.7	1.9	94	96	33.6
Côte d'Ivoire	810	..	13	3.9	420	0.4	0.5	3.9	20	24	*1.6*
Croatia	7	..	..	<0.1	40	5.1	5.2	1.8	99	99	44.7
Cuba	45	..	77	0.1	6	3.0	2.2	4.2	98	98	11.6
Czech Republic	4	78	..	..	9	15.6	11.7	1.5	100	99	48.3
Denmark	3	78	..	0.2	8	9.7	8.5	1.6	100	100	80.7
Dominican Republic	150	56	73	1.1	69	1.3	2.0	2.1	68	79	17.2
Ecuador	210	53	73	0.3	101	1.6	2.2	10.4	71	84	13.2
Egypt, Arab Rep.	130	*47*	59	..	21	1.4	2.4	4.1	50	66	14.0
El Salvador	170	*47*	67	0.8	40	0.5	1.0	1.8	73	86	11.1
Eritrea	450	..	8	1.3	95	..	0.2	15.0	3	5	2.5
Estonia	25	..	..	1.3	38	18.1	13.5	0.6	95	95	63.7
Ethiopia	720	4	15	2.1	378	0.1	0.1	1.3	4	11	0.4
Finland	7	77	..	0.1	6	10.1	10.1	1.3	100	100	78.8
France	8	*81*	..	0.4	14	6.4	6.2	2.5	..	..	51.2
Gabon	520	..	..	5.9	406	6.5	1.2	2.1	..	36	6.2
Gambia, The	690	12	..	0.9	258	0.2	0.2	2.2	..	52	5.9
Georgia	66	..	47	0.1	84	3.2	1.1	1.0	94	93	8.2
Germany	4	75	..	0.1	6	12.3	9.5	2.2	100	100	72.3
Ghana	560	*13*	17	1.9	203	0.2	0.3	3.7	6	10	3.8
Greece	3	..	..	0.2	18	7.1	8.6	2.1	97	98	32.9
Guatemala	290	..	43	0.8	63	0.6	0.9	2.4	70	84	*10.1*
Guinea	910	..	9	1.6	287	0.2	0.2	2.2	13	19	*0.5*
Guinea-Bissau	1,100	..	10	1.8	220	0.2	0.2	2.4	..	33	*2.2*
Haiti	670	*10*	32	2.2	306	0.1	0.2	2.3	29	19	10.4

	Improve maternal health			Combat HIV/AIDS and other diseases		Ensure environmental sustainability					Develop a global partnership for development
	Maternal mortality ratio Modeled estimate per 100,000 live births	Contraceptive prevalence rate % of married women ages 15–49		HIV prevalence % of population ages 15–49	Incidence of tuberculosis per 100,000 people	Carbon dioxide emissions per capita metric tons		Proportion of species threatened with extinction %	Access to improved sanitation facilities % of population		Internet users per 100 people[a]
	2005	**1990**	**2002–07[b]**	**2007**	**2007**	**1990**	**2005**	**2008**	**1990**	**2006**	**2007**
Honduras	280	47	65	0.7	59	0.5	1.1	3.5	45	66	6.0
Hungary	6	..	..	0.1	17	5.8	5.6	1.8	100	100	51.9
India	450	43	56	0.3	168	0.8	1.3	3.3	14	28	7.2
Indonesia	420	50	61	0.2	228	0.8	1.9	3.4	51	52	5.8
Iran, Islamic Rep.	140	49	79	0.2	22	4.0	6.5	1.0	83	..	32.4
Iraq	..	14	..	..	..	2.6	..	11.0	..	..	..
Ireland	1	60	..	0.2	13	8.7	10.2	1.8	..	..	56.1
Israel	4	68	..	0.1	8	7.1	9.2	4.3	..	..	27.9
Italy	3	..	..	0.4	7	7.0	7.7	2.2	..	..	53.9
Jamaica	170	55	69	1.6	7	3.3	3.8	7.7	83	83	56.1
Japan	6	58	..	..	21	8.7	9.6	4.9	100	100	69.0
Jordan	62	40	57	..	7	3.2	3.8	3.4	..	85	19.7
Kazakhstan	140	..	51	0.1	129	17.6	11.9	1.1	97	97	12.3
Kenya	560	27	39	..	353	0.2	0.3	3.9	39	42	8.0
Korea, Dem. Rep.	370	62	..	..	344	12.1	3.5	1.3	..	..	0.0
Korea, Rep.	14	79	..	<0.1	90	5.6	9.4	1.7	..	..	75.9
Kuwait	4	..	..	..	24	20.4	36.9	6.3	..	..	33.8
Kyrgyz Republic	150	..	48	0.1	121	2.8	1.1	0.8	..	93	14.3
Lao PDR	660	..	38	0.2	151	0.1	0.3	1.2	..	48	1.7
Latvia	10	..	..	0.8	53	5.4	2.8	1.4	..	78	55.0
Lebanon	150	..	58	0.1	19	3.1	4.2	1.2	..	..	38.3
Lesotho	960	23	37	23.2	637	..	..	0.6	..	36	3.5
Liberia	1,200	..	11	1.7	277	0.2	0.1	3.8	40	32	0.5
Libya	97	..	..	..	17	8.7	9.5	1.6	97	97	4.3
Lithuania	11	..	..	0.1	68	6.6	4.1	0.9	..	..	49.2
Macedonia, FYR	10	..	14	<0.1	29	8.1	5.1	0.9	..	89	27.3
Madagascar	510	17	27	0.1	251	0.1	0.2	6.4	8	12	0.6
Malawi	1,100	13	42	11.9	346	0.1	0.1	3.3	46	60	1.0
Malaysia	62	50	..	0.5	103	3.1	9.3	6.9	..	94	55.7
Mali	970	..	8	1.5	319	0.1	0.0	1.0	35	45	0.8
Mauritania	820	3	..	0.8	318	1.4	0.6	2.9	20	24	1.0
Mauritius	15	75	76	1.7	22	1.4	2.7	24.3	94	94	27.0
Mexico	60	..	71	0.3	20	4.5	4.1	3.2	56	81	22.7
Moldova	22	..	68	0.4	141	5.4	2.1	1.3	..	79	18.4
Mongolia	46	..	66	0.1	205	4.7	3.4	1.1	..	50	12.3
Morocco	240	42	63	0.1	92	1.0	1.6	1.9	52	72	21.4
Mozambique	520	..	17	12.5	431	0.1	0.1	2.9	20	31	0.9
Myanmar	380	17	34	0.7	171	0.1	0.2	2.7	23	82	0.1
Namibia	210	29	55	15.3	767	0.0	1.3	2.1	26	35	4.9
Nepal	830	23	48	0.5	173	0.0	0.1	1.1	9	27	1.4
Netherlands	6	76	..	0.2	8	9.3	7.7	1.3	100	100	84.2
New Zealand	9	..	..	0.1	7	6.5	7.2	5.1	..	..	69.2
Nicaragua	170	..	72	0.2	49	0.6	0.7	1.3	42	48	2.8
Niger	1,800	4	11	0.8	174	0.1	0.1	1.0	3	7	0.3
Nigeria	1,100	6	13	3.1	311	0.5	0.8	4.3	26	30	6.8
Norway	7	74	..	0.1	6	7.1	11.4	1.5	..	..	84.8
Oman	64	9	..	..	13	5.6	12.5	4.2	85	..	13.1
Pakistan	320	15	30	0.1	181	0.6	0.9	1.7	33	58	10.8
Panama	130	..	..	1.0	47	1.3	1.8	2.9	..	74	22.3
Papua New Guinea	470	..	..	1.5	250	0.6	0.7	3.6	44	45	1.8
Paraguay	150	48	73	0.6	58	0.5	0.7	0.5	60	70	8.7
Peru	240	59	71	0.5	126	1.0	1.4	2.8	55	72	27.4
Philippines	230	36	51	..	290	0.7	0.9	6.6	58	78	6.0
Poland	8	49	..	0.1	25	9.1	7.9	1.2	..	..	44.0
Portugal	11	..	..	0.5	30	4.3	5.9	2.8	92	99	40.1
Puerto Rico	18	..	..	..	4	..	..	3.6	..	..	25.4

1.3 Millennium Development Goals: protecting our common environment

	Improve maternal health			Combat HIV/AIDS and other diseases		Ensure environmental sustainability					Develop a global partnership for development
	Maternal mortality ratio Modeled estimate per 100,000 live births	Contraceptive prevalence rate % of married women ages 15–49		HIV prevalence % of population ages 15–49	Incidence of tuberculosis per 100,000 people	Carbon dioxide emissions per capita metric tons		Proportion of species threatened with extinction %	Access to improved sanitation facilities % of population		Internet users per 100 people[a]
	2005	1990	2002–07[b]	2007	2007	1990	2005	2008	1990	2006	2007
Romania	24	..	70	0.1	115	6.7	4.1	1.6	72	72	23.9
Russian Federation	28	34	..	1.1	110	15.3	10.5	1.3	87	87	21.1
Rwanda	1,300	21	17	2.8	397	0.1	0.1	1.6	29	23	1.1
Saudi Arabia	18	..	..	..	46	12.1	16.5	3.8	91	99	26.4
Senegal	980	..	12	1.0	272	0.4	0.4	2.2	26	28	6.6
Serbia	14[c]	..	41	0.1	32	6.2[d]	6.5[d]	..	..	92	20.3
Sierra Leone	2,100	..	5	1.7	574	0.1	0.2	3.2	..	11	0.2
Singapore	14	65	..	0.2	27	13.8	13.2	9.7	100	100	65.7
Slovak Republic	6	74	..	<0.1	17	9.7	6.8	1.1	100	100	55.9
Slovenia	6	..	..	<0.1	13	9.0	7.4	2.1	..	..	52.6
Somalia	1,400	1	15	0.5	249	0.0	0.1	3.2	..	23	1.1
South Africa	400	57	60	18.1	948	9.4	8.7	1.6	55	59	8.3
Spain	4	..	..	0.5	30	5.5	7.9	3.8	100	100	51.3
Sri Lanka	58	..	68	..	60	0.2	0.6	14.0	71	86	3.9
Sudan	450	9	8	1.4	243	0.2	0.3	2.4	33	35	9.1
Swaziland	390	20	51	26.1	1,198	0.6	0.8	0.8	..	50	3.7
Sweden	3	..	..	0.1	6	5.8	5.4	1.4	100	100	79.7
Switzerland	5	..	..	0.6	6	6.4	5.5	1.4	100	100	76.3
Syrian Arab Republic	130	..	58	..	24	2.8	3.6	2.0	81	92	17.4
Tajikistan	170	..	38	0.3	231	4.4	0.8	0.8	..	92	7.2
Tanzania	950	10	26	6.2	297	0.1	0.1	5.1	35	33	1.0
Thailand	110	..	77	1.4	142	1.8	4.3	3.4	78	96	21.0
Timor-Leste	380	..	20	..	322	..	0.2	..	..	41	0.1
Togo	510	34	17	3.3	429	0.2	0.2	1.2	13	12	5.0
Trinidad and Tobago	45	..	43	1.5	11	13.8	24.7	1.7	93	92	16.0
Tunisia	100	50	..	0.1	26	1.6	2.2	2.1	74	85	16.8
Turkey	44	63	71	..	30	2.5	3.4	1.4	85	88	16.5
Turkmenistan	130	..	48	<0.1	68	8.7	8.6	10.7	..	..	1.4
Uganda	550	5	24	5.4	330	0.0	0.1	2.5	29	33	2.5
Ukraine	18	..	67	1.6	102	13.2	6.9	1.1	96	93	21.5
United Arab Emirates	37	..	..	..	16	29.3	30.1	14.1	97	97	51.8
United Kingdom	8	..	84	0.2	15	9.9	9.1	2.8	..	..	71.7
United States	11	71	..	0.6	4	19.2	19.5	5.7	100	100	73.5
Uruguay	20	..	..	0.6	22	1.3	1.7	2.6	100	100	29.1
Uzbekistan	24	..	65	0.1	113	6.1	4.3	1.0	93	96	4.5
Venezuela, RB	57	..	..	..	34	5.9	5.6	1.1	83	..	20.8
Vietnam	150	53	76	0.5	171	0.3	1.2	3.5	29	65	21.0
West Bank and Gaza	..	..	50	..	20	..	..	..	..	80	9.6
Yemen, Rep.	430	10	28	..	76	0.8	1.0	12.6	28	46	1.4
Zambia	830	15	34	15.2	506	0.3	0.2	0.7	42	52	4.2
Zimbabwe	880	43	60	15.3	782	1.6	0.9	0.9	44	46	10.1
World	**400 w**	**57 w**	**60 w**	**0.8 w**	**139 w**	**4.3[e] w**	**4.5[e] w**		**51 w**	**60 w**	**21.8 w**
Low income	780	22	33	2.1	269	0.7	0.6		26	39	5.2
Middle income	260	61	68	0.6	129	2.8	3.3		48	60	15.2
Lower middle income	300	63	69	0.3	134	1.8	2.8		41	55	12.4
Upper middle income	97	52	..	1.7	108	6.9	5.5		77	83	26.6
Low & middle income	440	54	60	0.9	162	2.4	2.7		44	55	13.1
East Asia & Pacific	150	75	78	0.2	136	1.9	3.6		48	66	14.6
Europe & Central Asia	44	..	..	0.6	84	10.4	7.0		88	89	21.4
Latin America & Carib.	130	56	..	0.5	50	2.3	2.5		68	78	26.9
Middle East & N. Africa	200	42	62	0.1	41	2.5	3.7		67	77	17.1
South Asia	500	40	53	0.3	174	0.7	1.1		18	33	6.6
Sub-Saharan Africa	900	15	23	5.0	369	0.9	0.8		26	31	4.4
High income	10	72	..	0.3	16	11.8	12.6		100	100	65.7
Euro area	5	..	..	0.3	13	8.4	8.1		..	..	59.2

a. Data are from the International Telecommunication Union's (ITU) World Telecommunication Development Report database. Please cite ITU for third-party use of these data. b. Data are for the most recent year available. c. Includes Montenegro. d. Includes Kosovo and Montenegro. e. Includes emissions not allocated to specific countries.

Millennium Development Goals: protecting our common environment

1.3

About the data

The Millennium Development Goals address concerns common to all economies. Diseases and environmental degradation do not respect national boundaries. Epidemic diseases, wherever they occur, pose a threat to people everywhere. And environmental damage in one location may affect the well-being of plants, animals, and humans far away. The indicators in the table relate to goals 5, 6, and 7 and the targets of goal 8 that address access to new technologies. For the other targets of goal 8, see table 1.4.

The target of achieving universal access to reproductive health has been added to goal 5 to address the importance of family planning and health services in improving maternal health and preventing maternal death. Women with multiple pregnancies are more likely to die in childbirth. Access to contraception is an important way to limit and space births.

Measuring disease prevalence or incidence can be difficult. Most developing economies lack reporting systems for monitoring diseases. Estimates are often derived from survey data and report data from sentinel sites, extrapolated to the general population. Tracking diseases such as HIV/AIDS, which has a long latency

between contraction of the virus and the appearance of symptoms, or malaria, which has periods of dormancy, can be particularly difficult. The table shows the estimated prevalence of HIV among adults ages 15–49. Prevalence among older populations can be affected by life-prolonging treatment. The incidence of tuberculosis is based on case notifications and estimates of cases detected in the population.

Carbon dioxide emissions are the primary source of greenhouse gases, which contribute to global warming, threatening human and natural habitats. In recognition of the vulnerability of animal and plant species, a new target of reducing biodiversity loss has been added to goal 7.

Access to reliable supplies of safe drinking water and sanitary disposal of excreta are two of the most important means of improving human health and protecting the environment. Improved sanitation facilities prevent human, animal, and insect contact with excreta.

Internet use includes narrowband and broadband Internet. Narrowband is often limited to basic applications; broadband is essential to promote e-business, e-learning, e-government, and e-health.

Definitions

- **Maternal mortality ratio** is the number of women who die from pregnancy-related causes during pregnancy and childbirth, per 100,000 live births. Data are from various years and adjusted to a common 2005 base year. The values are modeled estimates (see *About the data* for table 2.18). • **Contraceptive prevalence rate** is the percentage of women ages 15–49 married or in-union who are practicing, or whose sexual partners are practicing, any form of contraception. • **HIV prevalence** is the percentage of people ages 15–49 who are infected with HIV.
- **Incidence of tuberculosis** is the estimated number of new tuberculosis cases (pulmonary, smear positive, and extrapulmonary). • **Carbon dioxide emissions** are those stemming from the burning of fossil fuels and the manufacture of cement. They include emissions produced during consumption of solid, liquid, and gas fuels and gas flaring (see table 3.8).
- **Proportion of species threatened with extinction** is the total number of threatened mammal (excluding whales and porpoises), bird, and higher native, vascular plant species as a percentage of the total number of known species of the same categories.
- **Access to improved sanitation facilities** is the percentage of the population with at least adequate access to excreta disposal facilities (private or shared, but not public) that can effectively prevent human, animal, and insect contact with excreta (facilities do not have to include treatment to render sewage outflows innocuous). Improved facilities range from simple but protected pit latrines to flush toilets with a sewerage connection. To be effective, facilities must be correctly constructed and properly maintained. • **Internet users** are people with access to the worldwide network.

Location of indicators for Millennium Development Goals 5–7   1.3a

Goal 5. Improve maternal health	Table
5.1 Maternal mortality ratio	1.3, 2.18
5.2 Proportion of births attended by skilled health personnel	2.18, 2.21
5.3 Contraceptive prevalence rate	1.3, 2.18, 2.21
5.4 Adolescent fertility rate	2.18
5.5 Antenatal care coverage	1.5, 2.18, 2.21
5.6 Unmet need for family planning	2.18
Goal 6. Combat HIV/AIDS, malaria, and other diseases	
6.1 HIV prevalence among population ages 15–24	1.3*, 2.20*
6.2 Condom use at last high-risk sex	2.20*
6.3 Proportion of population ages 15–24 with comprehensive, correct knowledge of HIV/AIDS	—
6.4 Ratio of school attendance of orphans to school attendance of nonorphans ages 10–14	—
6.5 Proportion of population with advanced HIV infection with access to antiretroviral drugs	—
6.6 Incidence and death rates associated with malaria	—
6.7 Proportion of children under age 5 sleeping under insecticide-treated bednets	2.17
6.8 Proportion of children under age 5 with fever who are treated with appropriate antimalarial drugs	2.17
6.9 Incidence, prevalence, and death rates associated with tuberculosis	1.3, 2.20
6.10 Proportion of tuberculosis cases detected and cured under directly observed treatment short course	2.17
Goal 7. Ensure environmental sustainability	
7.1 Proportion of land area covered by forest	3.1
7.2 Carbon dioxide emissions, total, per capita, and per $1 purchasing power parity GDP	3.8
7.3 Consumption of ozone-depleting substances	3.9*
7.4 Proportion of fish stocks within safe biological limits	—
7.5 Proportion of total water resources used	3.5
7.6 Proportion of terrestrial and marine areas protected	—
7.7 Proportion of species threatened with extinction	1.3
7.8 Proportion of population using an improved drinking water source	1.3, 2.17, 3.5
7.9 Proportion of population using an improved sanitation facility	1.3, 2.17, 3.11
7.10 Proportion of urban population living in slums	—

— No data are available in the *World Development Indicators* database. * Table shows information on related indicators.

Data sources

The indicators here and throughout this book have been compiled by World Bank staff from primary and secondary sources. Efforts have been made to harmonize the data series used to compile this table with those published on the United Nations Millennium Development Goals Web site (www. un.org/millenniumgoals), but some differences in timing, sources, and definitions remain. For more information see the data sources for the indicators listed in table 1.3a.

Development Assistance Committee members

	Official development assistance (ODA) by donor		Least developed countries' access to high-income markets								Support to agriculture
	Net % of donor GNI	For basic social services[a] % of total sector-allocable ODA	Goods (excluding arms) admitted free of tariffs % of exports from least developed countries		Average tariff on exports of least developed countries						
					Agricultural products %		Textiles %		Clothing %		% of GDP
	2007	**2007**	**2000**	**2006**	**2000**	**2006**	**2000**	**2006**	**2000**	**2006**	**2007[b]**
Australia	0.32	9.1	95.9	100.0	0.2	0.0	5.7	0.0	22.5	0.0	0.28
Canada	0.29	31.2	39.0	99.7	0.3	0.1	6.0	0.2	19.3	1.7	0.68
European Union			97.8	97.8	3.0	2.4	0.0	0.1	0.0	1.2	0.91
Austria	0.50	9.0									
Belgium	0.43	20.6									
Denmark	0.81	10.1									
Finland	0.39	13.9									
France	0.38	6.0									
Germany	0.37	10.0									
Greece	0.16	15.0									
Ireland	0.55	35.1									
Italy	0.19	9.8									
Luxembourg	0.91	33.9									
Netherlands	0.81	18.1									
Portugal	0.22	3.1									
Spain	0.37	15.6									
Sweden	0.93	13.1									
United Kingdom	0.36	57.6									
Japan	0.17	3.8	49.1	26.7	4.7	4.4	5.0	2.7	0.4	0.1	1.04
New Zealand	0.27	32.0	85.9[c]	99.2[c]	0.0[c]	13.1[c]	9.3[c]	0.0[c]	12.9[c]	0.0[c]	0.22
Norway	0.95	21.2	99.0	99.0	3.6	0.2	4.6	0.0	1.4	1.0	0.79
Switzerland	0.37	6.3	99.4	96.7	6.1	2.6	0.0	0.0	0.0	0.0	1.11
United States	0.16	31.6	50.3	76.6	6.9	6.4	7.0	5.8	14.1	11.3	0.73

Heavily indebted poor countries (HIPCs)

| | HIPC decision point[d] | HIPC completion point[d] | HIPC Initiative assistance[e] | MDRI assistance[f] | | | HIPC decision point[d] | HIPC completion point[d] | HIPC Initiative assistance[e] | MDRI assistance[f] |
			$ millions	$ millions					$ millions	$ millions
Afghanistan	Jul. 2007	Floating	571	..		Honduras	Jul. 2000	Apr. 2005	776	1,543
Benin	Jul. 2000	Mar. 2003	366	604		Liberia	Mar. 2008	Floating	2,845	..
Bolivia[g]	Feb. 2000	Jun. 2001	1,856	1,596		Madagascar	Dec. 2000	Oct. 2004	1,167	1,292
Burkina Faso[g,h]	Jul. 2000	Apr. 2002	772	603		Malawi[h]	Dec. 2000	Aug. 2006	1,310	705
Burundi	Aug. 2005	Jan. 2009	908	53[i]		Mali[g]	Sep. 2000	Mar. 2003	752	1,043
Cameroon	Oct. 2000	Apr. 2006	1,768	747		Mauritania	Feb. 2000	Jun. 2002	868	450
Central African Republic	Sep. 2007	Floating	611	..		Mozambique[g]	Apr. 2000	Sep. 2001	2,992	1,057
Chad	May 2001	Floating	227	..		Nicaragua	Dec. 2000	Jan. 2004	4,618	954
Congo, Dem. Rep.	Jul. 2003	Floating	7,636	..		Niger[h]	Dec. 2000	Apr.2004	899	519
Congo, Rep.	Apr. 2006	Floating	1,847	..		Rwanda[h]	Dec. 2000	Apr. 2005	908	225
Ethiopia[h]	Nov. 2001	Apr. 2004	2,575	1,458		São Tomé & Príncipe[h]	Dec. 2000	Mar. 2007	163	26
Gambia, The	Dec. 2000	Dec. 2007	93	199		Senegal	Jun. 2000	Apr. 2004	682	1,374
Ghana	Feb. 2002	Jul. 2004	2,910	2,095		Sierra Leone	Mar. 2002	Dec. 2006	857	352
Guinea	Dec. 2000	Floating	761	..		Tanzania	Apr. 2000	Nov. 2001	2,828	2,038
Guinea-Bissau	Dec. 2000	Floating	581	..		Togo	Nov. 2008	Floating	270	..
Guyana[g]	Nov. 2000	Dec. 2003	852	402		Uganda[g]	Feb. 2000	May 2000	1,434	1,805
Haiti	Nov. 2006	Floating	147	..		Zambia	Dec. 2000	Apr. 2005	3,489	1,632

a. Includes primary education, basic life skills for youth, adult and early childhood education, basic health care, basic health infrastructure, basic nutrition, infectious disease control, health education, health personnel development, population policy and administrative management, reproductive health care, family planning, sexually transmitted disease control including HIV/AIDS, personnel development for population and reproductive health, basic drinking water supply and basic sanitation, and multisector aid for basic social services. b. Provisional data. c. Calculated by World Bank staff using the World Integrated Trade Solution based on the United Nations Conference on Trade and Development's Trade Analysis and Information Systems database. d. Refers to the Enhanced HIPC Initiative. e. Total HIPC assistance (committed debt relief) assuming of full participation of creditors, in end-2007 net present value terms. Topping-up assistance and assistance provided under the original HIPC Initiative were committed in net present value terms as of the decision point and are converted to end-2007 terms. f. Multilateral Debt Relief Initiative (MDRI) assistance has been delivered in full to all post-completion point countries, shown in end-2007 net present value terms. g. Also reached completion point under the original HIPC Initiative. The assistance includes original debt relief. h. Assistance includes topping up at completion point. i. Excludes $15 million (in nominal terms) of committed debt relief by the International Monetary Fund.

Achieving the Millennium Development Goals requires an open, rule-based global economy in which all countries, rich and poor, participate. Many poor countries, lacking the resources to finance development, burdened by unsustainable debt, and unable to compete globally, need assistance from rich countries. For goal 8—develop a global partnership for development—many indicators therefore monitor the actions of members of the Organisation for Economic Co-operation and Development's (OECD) Development Assistance Committee (DAC).

Official development assistance (ODA) has risen in recent years as a share of donor countries' gross national income (GNI), but the poorest economies need additional assistance to achieve the Millennium Development Goals. After rising to a record $107 billion in 2005, net ODA disbursements from DAC donors fell 3.3 percent in 2007 to $103.5 billion in nominal terms.

One important action that high-income economies can take is to reduce barriers to exports from low- and middle-income economies. The European Union has begun to eliminate tariffs on developing economy exports of "everything but arms," and the United States offers special concessions to Sub-Saharan African exports. However, these programs still have many restrictions.

Average tariffs in the table reflect high-income OECD member tariff schedules for exports of countries designated least developed countries by the United Nations. Although average tariffs have been falling, averages may disguise high tariffs on specific goods (see table 6.8 for each country's share of tariff lines with "international peaks"). The averages in the table include ad valorem duties and equivalents.

Subsidies to agricultural producers and exporters in OECD countries are another barrier to developing economies' exports. Agricultural subsidies in OECD economies are estimated at $365 billion in 2007.

The Debt Initiative for Heavily Indebted Poor Countries (HIPCs), an important step in placing debt relief within the framework of poverty reduction, is the first comprehensive approach to reducing the external debt of the world's poorest, most heavily indebted countries. A 1999 review led to an enhancement of the framework. In 2005, to further reduce the debt of HIPCs and provide resources for meeting the Millennium Development Goals, the Multilateral Debt Relief Initiative (MDRI), proposed by the Group of Eight countries, was launched.

Under the MDRI four multilateral institutions—the International Development Association (IDA), International Monetary Fund (IMF), African Development Fund (AfDF), and Inter-American Development Bank (IDB) —provide 100 percent debt relief on eligible debts due to them from countries having completed the HIPC Initiative process. Data in the table refer to status as of February 2009 and might not show countries that have since reached the decision or completion point. Debt relief under the HIPC Initiative has reduced future debt payments by $51.3 billion for 34 countries that have reached the decision point. And 23 countries that have reached the completion point have received additional assistance of $22.8 billion under the MDRI.

Location of indicators for Millennium Development Goal 8 — 1.4a

Goal 8. Develop a global partnership for development	Table
8.1	Net ODA as a percentage of DAC donors' gross national income	1.4, 6.13
8.2	Proportion of ODA for basic social services	1.4, 6.14b*
8.3	Proportion of ODA that is untied	6.14b
8.4	Proportion of ODA received in landlocked countries as a percentage of GNI	—
8.5	Proportion of ODA received in small island developing states as a percentage of GNI	—
8.6	Proportion of total developed country imports (by value, excluding arms) from least developed countries admitted free of duty	1.4
8.7	Average tariffs imposed by developed countries on agricultural products and textiles and clothing from least developed countries	1.4, 6.8*
8.8	Agricultural support estimate for OECD countries as a percentage of GDP	1.4
8.9	Proportion of ODA provided to help build trade capacity	—
8.10	Number of countries reaching HIPC decision and completion points	1.4
8.11	Debt relief committed under new HIPC initiative	1.4
8.12	Debt services as a percentage of exports of goods and services	6.10*
8.13	Proportion of population with access to affordable, essential drugs on a sustainable basis	—
8.14	Telephone lines per 100 people	1.3*, 5.10
8.15	Cellular subscribers per 100 people	1.3*, 5.10
8.16	Internet users per 100 people	5.11

— No data are available in the *World Development Indicators* database. * Table shows information on related indicators.

• **Net official development assistance (ODA)** is grants and loans (net of repayments of principal) that meet the DAC definition of ODA and are made to countries on the DAC list of recipients. • **ODA for basic social services** is aid reported by DAC donors for basic education, primary health care, nutrition, population policies and programs, reproductive health, and water and sanitation services. • **Goods admitted free of tariffs** are exports of goods (excluding arms) from least developed countries admitted without tariff. • **Average tariff** is the unweighted average of the effectively applied rates for all products subject to tariffs. • **Agricultural products** are plant and animal products, including tree crops but excluding timber and fish products. • **Textiles** and **clothing** are natural and synthetic fibers and fabrics and articles of clothing made from them. • **Support to agriculture** is the value of gross transfers from taxpayers and consumers arising from policy measures, net of associated budgetary receipts, regardless of their objectives and impacts on farm production and income or consumption of farm products. • **HIPC decision point** is the date when a heavily indebted poor country with an established track record of good performance under adjustment programs supported by the IMF and the World Bank commits to additional reforms and a poverty reduction strategy. • **HIPC completion point** is the date when a country successfully completes the key structural reforms agreed on at the decision point, including implementing a poverty reduction strategy. The country then receives the bulk of debt relief under the HIPC Initiative without further policy conditions. • **HIPC Initiative assistance** is the debt relief committed as of the decision point in end-2007 net present value. • **MDRI assistance** is the debt relief from IDA, IMF, AfDF, and IDB, delivered to countries having reached the HIPC completion point in end-2007 net present value.

Data sources

Data on ODA are from the OECD. Data on goods admitted free of tariffs and average tariffs are from the World Trade Organization, in collaboration with the United Nations Conference on Trade and Development and the International Trade Centre. These data are available at www.mdg-trade.org. Data on subsidies to agriculture are from the OECD's *Producer and Consumer Support Estimates, OECD Database 1986–2007*. Data on the HIPC Initiative and MDRI are from the World Bank's Economic Policy and Debt Department.

1.5 | Women in development

	Female population	Life expectancy at birth		Pregnant women receiving prenatal care	Teenage mothers	Women in nonagricultural sector	Unpaid family workers		Women in parliaments	
			years		% of women ages 15–19	% of nonagricultural wage employment	Male % of male employment	Female % of female employment	% of total seats	
	% of total 2007	Male 2007	Female 2007	% 2002–07[a]	2002–07[a]	2006	2002–07[a]	2002–07[a]	1990	2008
Afghanistan	..	..	..	..	..	..	..	..	4	28
Albania	50.3	73	80	97	..	..	..	..	29	7
Algeria	49.5	71	74	89	..	17	7.1	13.6	2	8
Angola	50.7	41	44	80	..	..	..	..	15	37
Argentina	51.1	72	79	99	..	45	0.7[b]	1.6[b]	6	40
Armenia	53.5	68	75	93	5	46	..	..	36	8
Australia	50.2	79	84	..	..	49	0.2	0.4	6	27
Austria	51.0	77	83	..	..	47	2.0	2.9	12	32
Azerbaijan	51.4	64	71	77	6	50	16.8	16.8	..	11
Bangladesh	48.8	63	65	51	33	..	9.7	60.1	10	15
Belarus	53.5	65	76	99	..	..	..	..	..	29
Belgium	51.0	77	83	..	..	46	0.4	2.9	9	35
Benin	49.6	56	58	84	21	..	..	..	3	11
Bolivia	50.2	63	68	79	16	..	12.6	34.8	9	17
Bosnia and Herzegovina	51.4	72	77	99	..	35	3.0	11.0	..	12
Botswana	50.3	50	51	..	..	42	2.2	2.2	5	11
Brazil	50.7	69	76	97	..	..	4.6[b]	8.1[b]	5	9
Bulgaria	51.6	69	76	..	..	53	0.7	1.6	21	22
Burkina Faso	50.0	51	54	85	23	..	..	..	..	15
Burundi	51.1	48	51	92	..	..	..	..	..	31
Cambodia	51.2	57	62	69	8	52	..	..	..	16
Cameroon	50.0	50	51	82	28	..	..	..	14	14
Canada	50.5	78	83	..	..	50	0.1	0.2	13	21
Central African Republic	51.2	43	46	69	..	..	..	..	4	11
Chad	50.3	49	52	39	37	..	..	..	..	5
Chile	50.5	75	82	..	..	39	0.9	2.8	..	15
China	48.4	71	75	90	..	..	..	..	21	21
Hong Kong, China	52.1	79	85	..	..	48	0.1[b]	1.1[b]	..	..
Colombia	50.8	69	77	94	21	49	3.2	6.1	5	8
Congo, Dem. Rep.	50.5	45	48	85	24	..	..	..	5	8
Congo, Rep.	50.4	54	57	86	27	..	..	..	14	7
Costa Rica	49.2	76	81	92	..	41	1.3	2.8	11	37
Côte d'Ivoire	49.3	48	49	85	..	..	..	..	6	9
Croatia	51.9	72	79	100	4	44[c]	1.1	3.7	..	22
Cuba	50.0	76	80	100	..	43	..	..	34	43
Czech Republic	51.2	74	80	..	..	46	0.2	1.1	..	16
Denmark	50.5	76	81	..	..	49	0.3	1.0	31	38
Dominican Republic	49.9	69	75	99	21	39	2.8	4.9	8	20
Ecuador	49.9	72	78	84	..	42	4.4	11.1	5	25
Egypt, Arab Rep.	49.9	69	74	70	9	21	8.6[b]	32.6[b]	4	2
El Salvador	50.9	69	75	86	..	49	8.8	9.9	12	17
Eritrea	50.9	56	60	70	14	..	..	..	..	22
Estonia	53.9	67	79	..	..	53	0.0[d]	0.0[d]	..	21
Ethiopia	50.3	52	54	28	17	47	7.8	12.7	..	22
Finland	51.0	76	83	..	..	51	0.6	0.4	32	42
France	51.3	78	85	..	..	48	0.3	1.0	7	18
Gabon	50.0	56	57	..	..	..	..	..	13	17
Gambia, The	49.9	59	60	98	..	..	..	..	8	9
Georgia	52.8	67	75	94	..	49	19.0	39.0	..	6
Germany	51.1	77	82	..	..	47	0.4	1.8	..	32
Ghana	49.3	60	60	92	14	..	..	..	..	11
Greece	50.5	77	82	..	..	42	3.7	10.7	7	15
Guatemala	51.2	67	74	84	..	38	21.3	24.5	7	12
Guinea	49.5	54	58	82	32	..	..	..	..	19
Guinea-Bissau	50.6	45	48	78	..	..	..	..	20	14
Haiti	50.5	59	63	85	14	..	..	..	..	4

	Female population	Life expectancy at birth		Pregnant women receiving prenatal care	Teenage mothers	Women in nonagricultural sector	Unpaid family workers		Women in parliaments	
			years				Male	Female		
	% of total	Male	Female	%	% of women ages 15–19	% of nonagricultural wage employment	% of male employment	% of female employment	% of total seats	
	2007	2007	2007	2002–07[a]	2002–07[a]	2006	2002–07[a]	2002–07[a]	1990	2008
Honduras	50.3	67	74	92	22	45	12.1	8.3	10	23
Hungary	52.4	69	77	..	..	48	0.3	0.7	21	11
India	48.2	63	66	74	16	18	..	..	5	9
Indonesia	50.1	69	73	93	10	29	7.8	33.6	12	12
Iran, Islamic Rep.	49.3	69	73	..	..	..	5.4	32.7	2	3
Iraq	..	..	..	..	..	..	..	..	11	26
Ireland	50.1	77	82	..	..	48	0.4	0.9	8	13
Israel	50.5	79	83	..	..	49	0.1	0.4	7	14
Italy	51.4	79	84	..	..	43	1.3	2.6	13	21
Jamaica	50.7	70	75	91	..	48	0.5	2.2	5	13
Japan	51.2	79	86	..	..	42	1.1	7.3	1	9
Jordan	48.6	71	74	99	4	26	..	..	0	6
Kazakhstan	52.2	61	72	100	7	49	1.0	1.3	..	16
Kenya	50.2	53	55	88	23	..	..	..	1	9
Korea, Dem. Rep.	50.7	65	69	..	..	..	..	..	21	20
Korea, Rep.	50.0	76	82	..	..	42	1.2	12.7	2	14
Kuwait	40.1	76	80	..	..	..	..	..	..	3
Kyrgyz Republic	50.7	64	72	97	..	52	8.8	19.3	..	26
Lao PDR	50.2	63	66	..	..	50	..	..	6	25
Latvia	53.9	66	77	..	..	53	1.5	1.6	..	20
Lebanon	51.0	70	74	96	..	..	..	..	0	5
Lesotho	52.9	43	42	90	20	..	..	..	..	25
Liberia	50.0	45	47	..	32	..	..	..	..	13
Libya	48.2	72	77	..	..	..	..	..	..	8
Lithuania	53.4	65	77	..	..	54	1.1	2.4	..	23
Macedonia, FYR	50.1	72	77	98	..	40	7.0	14.9	..	32
Madagascar	50.3	58	61	80	34	38	32.1	73.0	7	8
Malawi	50.3	48	48	92	34	..	..	..	10	13
Malaysia	49.2	72	77	79	..	38	2.7	8.8	5	11
Mali	51.3	52	57	70	36	35	18.4	10.2	..	10
Mauritania	49.4	62	66	..	..	..	..	..	..	22
Mauritius	50.4	69	76	..	..	38	0.9	4.7	7	17
Mexico	51.2	73	77	..	..	39	4.9	10.0	12	23
Moldova	52.1	65	72	98	6	54	1.3	3.4	..	22
Mongolia	50.1	64	70	99	..	53	18.4	31.7	25	4
Morocco	50.8	69	73	68	7	28	17.0	55.3	0	11
Mozambique	51.5	42	42	85	41	..	..	..	16	35
Myanmar	50.5	59	65	..	..	..	..	..	..	..
Namibia	50.7	52	53	95	..	47	3.2	5.8	7	27
Nepal	50.4	63	64	44	19	..	..	..	6	33
Netherlands	50.5	78	82	..	..	47	0.2	1.0	21	39
New Zealand	50.7	78	82	..	..	47	0.8	1.5	14	33
Nicaragua	50.2	70	76	90	..	..	12.2	9.1	15	19
Niger	49.3	58	56	46	39	..	..	..	5	12
Nigeria	50.0	46	47	58	25	21	..	..	..	7
Norway	50.3	78	83	..	..	49	0.2	0.3	36	36
Oman	44.1	74	77	..	..	..	..	..	..	0
Pakistan	48.6	65	66	61	9	11	18.6	61.9	10	23
Panama	49.6	73	78	..	..	43	2.3	4.0	8	17
Papua New Guinea	49.3	55	60	..	..	..	..	..	0	1
Paraguay	49.5	70	74	94	..	..	10.8[b]	8.9[b]	6	13
Peru	49.9	69	74	91	26	36	4.7[b]	9.9[b]	6	29
Philippines	49.6	70	74	88	8	42	9.0	18.0	9	21
Poland	51.7	71	80	..	..	47	2.8	6.0	14	20
Portugal	51.6	75	82	..	..	47	0.7	1.5	8	28
Puerto Rico	52.1	74	83	..	..	41	0.0[d]	0.0[d]	..	..

	Female population	Life expectancy at birth		Pregnant women receiving prenatal care	Teenage mothers	Women in nonagricultural sector	Unpaid family workers		Women in parliaments	
		years			% of women ages 15–19	% of nonagricultural wage employment	Male % of male employment	Female % of female employment	% of total seats	
	% of total	Male	Female	%						
	2007	2007	2007	2002–07[a]	2002–07[a]	2006	2002–07[a]	2002–07[a]	1990	2008
Romania	51.3	69	76	94	..	47	6.5	19.9	34	9
Russian Federation	53.7	62	74	..	..	51	0.1	0.1	..	14
Rwanda	51.8	45	48	94	4	..	..	..	17	56
Saudi Arabia	45.0	71	75	..	..	13	..	..	..	0
Senegal	50.2	61	65	87	19	..	..	..	13	22
Serbia	50.5	71	76	98	..	42	3.1	11.9	..	22
Sierra Leone	50.7	41	44	81	..	23	14.8	21.6	..	13
Singapore	49.7	78	83	..	..	50	0.4	1.3	5	25
Slovak Republic	51.5	71	78	..	..	50	0.1[b]	0.1[b]	..	19
Slovenia	51.2	74	82	..	..	48	3.1	7.1	..	13
Somalia	50.4	47	49	26	..	..	..	..	4	8
South Africa	50.8	49	52	92	..	43	0.3	0.6	3	33
Spain	50.7	78	84	..	..	43	0.7	1.6	15	36
Sri Lanka	50.7	69	76	99	..	45	4.4[b]	21.7[b]	5	6
Sudan	49.6	57	60	70	..	..	..	..	..	18
Swaziland	51.6	40	39	85	23	..	..	..	4	11
Sweden	50.4	79	83	..	..	50	0.3	0.3	38	47
Switzerland	51.3	79	84	..	..	47	1.7	3.2	14	29
Syrian Arab Republic	49.5	72	76	84	..	..	..	..	9	12
Tajikistan	50.4	64	69	79	..	..	..	..	..	18
Tanzania	50.3	51	54	78	26	..	9.7	13.0	..	30
Thailand	51.3	66	75	98	..	47	14.0	29.9	3	12
Timor-Leste	49.2	60	62	61	..	..	..	..	..	29
Togo	50.5	57	60	84	..	..	..	..	5	11
Trinidad and Tobago	50.8	68	72	96	..	43	0.3	1.7	17	27
Tunisia	49.7	72	76	..	..	..	..	..	4	23
Turkey	49.6	69	74	81	..	21	5.6	38.2	1	9
Turkmenistan	50.8	59	68	99	..	..	..	..	26	16
Uganda	50.0	51	52	94	25	..	10.3[b]	40.5[b]	12	31
Ukraine	53.9	63	74	99	..	55	0.4	0.3	..	8
United Arab Emirates	32.4	77	81	..	..	..	..	..	0	23
United Kingdom	51.0	77	82	..	..	50	0.2	0.5	6	20
United States	50.8	75	81	..	..	47	0.1	0.1	7	17
Uruguay	51.7	72	80	..	..	45	0.9[b]	3.0[b]	6	12
Uzbekistan	50.3	64	70	99	..	..	..	..	..	18
Venezuela, RB	49.8	71	77	..	..	41	0.6	1.6	10	19
Vietnam	50.0	72	76	91	3	46	18.9	47.2	18	26
West Bank and Gaza	49.1	72	75	99	..	17	6.6	31.5	..	..
Yemen, Rep.	49.4	61	64	41	..	..	..	..	4	0[d]
Zambia	50.2	42	42	93	32	..	..	..	7	15
Zimbabwe	50.3	44	43	94	21	..	10.4	13.6	11	15
World	**49.6 w**	**67 w**	**71 w**	**81 w**		**.. w**	**.. w**	**.. w**	**13 w**	**18 w**
Low income	49.8	56	59	67		..	..	..	..	18
Middle income	49.3	67	72	86		..	..	..	13	17
Lower middle income	48.9	67	71	84		..	..	..	13	15
Upper middle income	51.2	67	75	..		45	3.3	7.3	13	19
Low & middle income	49.4	65	69	81		..	..	..	13	17
East Asia & Pacific	48.9	70	74	90		..	..	..	17	18
Europe & Central Asia	52.1	65	74	..		48	2.4	6.3	..	15
Latin America & Carib.	50.6	70	76	95		..	4.0	7.5	12	22
Middle East & N. Africa	49.7	68	72	76		..	..	..	4	9
South Asia	48.4	63	66	69		18	..	..	6	20
Sub-Saharan Africa	50.2	50	52	72		..	..	..	..	18
High income	50.6	77	82	..		46	0.5	2.4	12	22
Euro area	51.1	77	83	..		45	0.8	2.1	12	25

a. Data are for the most recent year available. b. Limited coverage. c. Data are for 2007. d. Less than 0.5.

Despite much progress in recent decades, gender inequalities remain pervasive in many dimensions of life—worldwide. But while disparities exist throughout the world, they are most prevalent in developing countries. Gender inequalities in the allocation of such resources as education, health care, nutrition, and political voice matter because of the strong association with well-being, productivity, and economic growth. These patterns of inequality begin at an early age, with boys routinely receiving a larger share of education and health spending than do girls, for example.

Because of biological differences girls are expected to experience lower infant and child mortality rates and to have a longer life expectancy than boys. This biological advantage may be overshadowed, however, by gender inequalities in nutrition and medical interventions and by inadequate care during pregnancy and delivery, so that female rates of illness and death sometimes exceed male rates, particularly during early childhood and the reproductive years. In high-income countries women tend to outlive men by four to eight years on average, while in low-income countries the difference is narrower—about two to three years. The difference in child mortality rates (table 2.22) is another good indicator of female social disadvantage because nutrition and medical interventions are particularly important for the 1–4 age group. Female child mortality rates that are as high as or higher than male child mortality rates may indicate discrimination against girls.

Having a child during the teenage years limits girls' opportunities for better education, jobs, and income. Pregnancy is more likely to be unintended during the teenage years, and births are more likely to be premature and are associated with greater risks of complications during delivery and of death. In many countries maternal mortality (tables 1.3 and 2.18) is a leading cause of death among women of reproductive age. Most maternal deaths result from preventable causes—hemorrhage, infection, and complications from unsafe abortions. Prenatal care is essential for recognizing, diagnosing, and promptly treating complications that arise during pregnancy. In high-income countries most women have access to health care during pregnancy, but in developing countries an estimated 200 million women suffer pregnancy-related complications, and over half a million die every year (Glasier and others 2006). This is reflected in the differences in maternal mortality ratios between high- and low-income countries.

Women's wage work is important for economic growth and the well-being of families. But restricted access to education and vocational training, heavy workloads at home and in nonpaid domestic and market activities, and labor market discrimination often limit women's participation in paid economic activities, lower their productivity, and reduce their wages. When women are in salaried employment, they tend to be concentrated in the nonagricultural sector. However, in many developing countries women are a large part of agricultural employment, often as unpaid family workers. Among people who are unsalaried, women are more likely than men to be unpaid family workers, while men are more likely than women to be self-employed or employers. There are several reasons for this.

Few women have access to credit markets, capital, land, training, and education, which may be required to start a business. Cultural norms may prevent women from working on their own or from supervising other workers. Also, women may face time constraints due to their traditional family responsibilities. Because of biases and misclassification substantial numbers of employed women may be underestimated or reported as unpaid family workers even when they work in association or equally with their husbands in the family enterprise.

Women are vastly underrepresented in decision-making positions in government, although there is some evidence of recent improvement. Gender parity in parliamentary representation is still far from being realized. In 2008 women accounted for 18 percent of parliamentarians worldwide, compared with 9 percent in 1987. Without representation at this level, it is difficult for women to influence policy.

For information on other aspects of gender, see tables 1.2 (Millennium Development Goals: eradicating poverty and saving lives), 1.3 (Millennium Development Goals: protecting our common environment), 2.3 (Employment by economic activity), 2.4 (Decent work and productive employment), 2.5 (Unemployment), 2.6 (Children at work), 2.10 (Assessing vulnerability and security), 2.13 (Education efficiency), 2.14 (Education completion and outcomes), 2.15 (Education gaps by income and gender), 2.18 (Reproductive health), 2.20 (Health risk factors and future challenges), 2.21 (Health gaps by income and gender), and 2.22 (Mortality).

• **Female population** is the percentage of the population that is female. • **Life expectancy at birth** is the number of years a newborn infant would live if prevailing patterns of mortality at the time of its birth were to stay the same throughout its life. • **Pregnant women receiving prenatal care** are the percentage of women attended at least once during pregnancy by skilled health personnel for reasons related to pregnancy. • **Teenage mothers** are the percentage of women ages 15–19 who already have children or are currently pregnant. • **Women in nonagricultural sector** are female wage employees in the nonagricultural sector as a percentage of total nonagricultural wage employment. • **Unpaid family workers** are those who work without pay in a market-oriented establishment or activity operated by a related person living in the same household. • **Women in parliaments** are the percentage of parliamentary seats in a single or lower chamber held by women.

Data sources

Data on female population and life expectancy are from the World Bank's population database. Data on pregnant women receiving prenatal care are from household surveys, including Demographic and Health Surveys by Macro International and Multiple Indicator Cluster Surveys by the United Nations Children's Fund (UNICEF), and UNICEF's *State of the World's Children 2009*. Data on teenage mothers are from Demographic and Health Surveys by Macro International. Data on labor force and employment are from the International Labour Organization's *Key Indicators of the Labour Market,* fifth edition. Data on women in parliaments are from the Inter-Parliamentary Union.

	Population	Surface area	Population density	Gross national income				Gross domestic product		Life expectancy at birth	Adult literacy rate	Carbon dioxide emissions
						PPP[a]						
							Per capita		Per capita		% ages 15	thousand
	thousands	thousand sq. km	people per sq. km	$ millions	Per capita $	$ millions	$	% growth	% growth	years	and older	metric tons
	2007	2007	2007	2007[b]	2007[b]	2007	2007	2006–07	2006–07	2007	2007	2005
American Samoa	65	0.2	325	..	..[c]	..	..	..	..	..	..	..
Andorra	82	0.5	175	..	..[d]	..	..	..	..	..	..	..
Antigua and Barbuda	85	0.4	193	980	11,650	1,487[e]	17,680[e]	–1.2	–2.1	..	99	421
Aruba	101	0.2	561	..	..[d]	..	..	..	..	..	98	2,308
Bahamas, The	331	13.9	33	..	..[d]	..	..	2.8	1.6	73	..	2,107
Bahrain	753	0.7	1,060	12,607	17,390	19,720	27,210	7.8	5.6	76	89	19,668
Barbados	294	0.4	684	..	..[d]	4,711[e]	16,140[e]	..	..	77	..	1,315
Belize	304	23.0	13	1,144	3,760	1,847[e]	6,080[e]	1.2	–0.9	76	..	817
Bermuda	64	0.1	1,280	..	..[d]	..	..	4.6	4.3	79	..	572
Bhutan	657	47.0	14	1,166	1,770	3,275	4,980	19.1	17.5	66	53	414
Brunei Darussalam	389	5.8	74	10,211	26,740	19,540	50,200	0.6	–1.3	77	95	5,892
Cape Verde	530	4.0	132	1,287	2,430	1,557	2,940	7.0	4.6	71	84	286
Cayman Islands	54	0.3	206	..	..[d]	..	..	..	..	..	99	315
Channel Islands	149	0.2	785	10,241	68,640	..	..	5.9	5.7	79	..	..
Comoros	628	1.9	338	425	680	721	1,150	–1.0	–3.3	65	75	88
Cyprus	855	9.3	92	19,617[f]	24,940[f]	20,549	24,040	4.4	3.3	79	98	7,017
Djibouti	833	23.2	36	908	1,090	1,885	2,260	4.0	2.2	55	..	374
Dominica	73	0.8	97	292	4,030	501[e]	6,930[e]	3.2	2.6	..	..	114
Equatorial Guinea	508	28.1	18	6,527	12,860	10,770	21,220	12.5	9.9	52	..	4,335
Faeroe Islands	48	1.4	35	..	..[d]	..	..	..	..	79	..	656
Fiji	834	18.3	46	3,125	3,750	3,538	4,240	–6.6	–7.1	69	..	1,641
French Polynesia	263	4.0	72	..	..[d]	..	..	..	..	74	..	685
Greenland	57	410.5	0[g]	..	..[d]	..	..	..	..	..	..	557
Grenada	106	0.3	311	414	3,920	579[e]	5,480[e]	3.0	2.9	69	..	234
Guam	173	0.5	321	..	..[d]	..	..	..	..	76	..	..
Guyana	739	215.0	4	926	1,250	1,907[e]	2,580[e]	9.1	9.2	67	..	1,491
Iceland	311	103.0	3	17,959	57,750	10,596	34,070	3.8	1.4	81	..	2,184
Isle of Man	77	0.6	136	3,517	45,810	..	..	7.7	6.7	..	..	..

About the data

The table shows data for 56 economies with populations between 30,000 and 1 million and for smaller economies if they are members of the World Bank. Where data on gross national income (GNI) per capita are not available, the estimated range is given. For more information on the calculation of GNI (gross national product, or GNP, in the System of National Accounts 1968) and purchasing power parity (PPP) conversion factors, see *About the data* for table 1.1. Additional data for the economies in the table are available on the *World Development Indicators* CD-ROM or at *WDI Online*.

Definitions

• **Population** is based on the de facto definition of population, which counts all residents regardless of legal status or citizenship—except for refugees not permanently settled in the country of asylum, who are generally considered part of the population of their country of origin. The values shown are midyear estimates. See also table 2.1. • **Surface area** is a country's total area, including areas under inland bodies of water and some coastal waterways. • **Population density** is midyear population divided by land area in square kilometers. • **Gross national income (GNI)** is the sum of value added by all resident producers plus any product taxes (less subsidies) not included in the valuation of output plus net receipts of primary income (compensation of employees and property income) from abroad. Data are in current U.S. dollars converted using the *World Bank Atlas* method (see *Statistical methods*). • **GNI per capita** is GNI divided by midyear population. GNI per capita in U.S. dollars is converted using the *World Bank Atlas* method. • **Purchasing power parity (PPP) GNI** is GNI converted to international dollars using PPP rates. An international dollar has the same purchasing power over GNI that a U.S. dollar has in the United States. • **Gross domestic product (GDP)** is the sum of value added by all resident producers plus any product taxes (less subsidies) not included in the valuation of output.

	Population	Surface area	Population density	Gross national income				Gross domestic product		Life expectancy at birth	Adult literacy rate	Carbon dioxide emissions
						PPP[a]						
	thousands	thousand sq. km	people per sq. km	$ millions	Per capita $	$ millions	Per capita $	% growth	Per capita % growth	years	% ages 15 and older	thousand metric tons
	2007	2007	2007	2007[b]	2007[b]	2007	2007	2006–07	2006–07	2007	2007	2005
Kiribati	95	0.8	117	107	1,120	194[e]	2,040[e]	1.7	0.1	61	..	26
Liechtenstein	35	0.2	220	..	..[d]	..	..	..	..	..	..	..
Luxembourg	480	2.6	185	34,234	72,430	29,239	61,860	4.5	2.9	79	..	11,314
Macao, China	480	0.0	17,026	..	..[d]	..	..	27.3	26.6	81	94	2,235
Maldives	305	0.3	1,018	974	3,190	1,500	4,910	6.6	4.9	68	97	714
Malta	409	0.3	1,279	6,825	16,680	9,192	22,460	3.8	3.1	80	92	2,550
Marshall Islands	58	0.2	324	189	3,240	..	..	3.5	1.2	..	..	84
Mayotte	186	0.4	497	..	..[c]	..	..	..	..	..	..	..
Micronesia, Fed. Sts.	111	0.7	159	253	2,280	334[e]	3,010[e]	–3.2	–3.5	69	..	..
Monaco	33	0.0	16,769	..	..[d]	..	..	..	..	..	..	..
Montenegro	599	14.0	43	3,154	5,270	7,056	11,780	10.7	11.1	75	..	..
Netherlands Antilles	191	0.8	239	..	..[d]	..	..	..	..	75	96	3,891
New Caledonia	242	18.6	13	..	..[d]	..	..	..	..	76	96	2,638
Northern Mariana Islands	84	0.5	182	..	..[d]	..	..	..	..	..	..	..
Palau	20	0.5	44	167	8,270	..	..	2.5	1.9	69	..	114
Qatar	836	11.0	76	..	..[d]	..	..	6.1	1.8	76	93	49,816
Samoa	181	2.8	64	489	2,700	789[e]	4,350[e]	6.1	5.6	72	99	150
San Marino	31	0.1	510	1,430	46,770	..	..	4.5	3.1	82	..	..
Sao Tome and Principe	158	1.0	165	138	870	258	1,630	6.0	4.1	65	88	103
Seychelles	85	0.5	185	762	8,960	1,313[e]	15,440[e]	6.3	5.8	73	..	579
Solomon Islands	495	28.9	18	374	750	845[e]	1,710[e]	10.2	7.7	64	..	176
St. Kitts and Nevis	49	0.3	188	488	9,990	668[e]	13,680[e]	3.3	2.5	..	..	136
St. Lucia	168	0.6	275	928	5,520	1,552[e]	9,240[e]	3.2	2.0	74	..	370
St. Vincent & Grenadines	120	0.4	309	507	4,210	863[e]	7,170[e]	6.7	6.2	72	..	191
Suriname	458	163.3	3	2,166	4,730	3,498[e]	7,640[e]	5.3	4.7	70	90	2,374
Tonga	102	0.8	142	254	2,480	397[e]	3,880[e]	–0.3	–0.6	73	99	117
Vanuatu	226	12.2	19	417	1,840	771[e]	3,410[e]	5.0	2.6	70	78	88
Virgin Islands (U.S.)	108	0.4	310	..	..[d]	..	..	..	..	79	..	..

a. PPP is purchasing power parity, see *Definitions*. b. Calculated using the *World Bank Atlas* method. c. Estimated to be upper middle income ($3,706–$11,455). d. Estimated to be high income ($11,456 or more). e. Based on regression; others are extrapolated from the 2005 International Comparison Program benchmark estimates. f. Excludes Turkish Cypriot side. g. Less than 0.5.

Growth is calculated from constant price GDP data in local currency. • **GDP per capita** is GDP divided by midyear population. • **Life expectancy at birth** is the number of years a newborn infant would live if prevailing patterns of mortality at the time of its birth were to stay the same throughout its life. • **Adult literacy rate** is the percentage of adults ages 15 and older who can, with understanding, read and write a short, simple statement about their everyday life. • **Carbon dioxide emissions** are those stemming from the burning of fossil fuels and the manufacture of cement. They include carbon dioxide produced during consumption of solid, liquid, and gas fuels and gas flaring.

Data sources

The indicators here and throughout the book are compiled by World Bank staff from primary and secondary sources. More information about the indicators and their sources can be found in the *About the data*, *Definitions*, and *Data sources* entries that accompany each table in subsequent sections.

PEOPLE

Decent and productive work

Sustainable development is about improving the quality of people's lives and expanding their ability to shape their futures. These generally call for higher per capita incomes, but they also involve equitable education and job opportunities, better health and nutrition, and a more sustainable natural environment.

The Millennium Development Goals are the world's time-bound targets to measure and monitor the progress of countries in improving people's welfare. They address extreme poverty in its many dimensions—income, hunger, and disease—while promoting education, gender equality, health, and sanitation. At the midpoint between their adoption in 2000 and the target date of 2015, the goals related to human development (primary school completion rate, under-five and maternal mortality) have recorded slower progress than those related to economic growth and infrastructure development (income poverty, gender parity, access to clean water and sanitation; figure 2a).

Income from work is the main determinant of living conditions and well-being (World Bank 1995). Therefore, breaking the cycle of poverty involves creating local wealth and new cycles of opportunity through decent and productive employment. Economic growth is a vehicle for poverty reduction, but economic advances in a variety of countries over the past decade have not helped lift a majority of people and their families out of poverty because many poor people were deprived of opportunities to benefit from economic expansion. That is why decent and productive work has been added as a target, with four specific indicators. Target 1b under Goal 1 is to achieve full and productive employment and decent work for all, including women and young people. The indicators cover employment, vulnerable employment, the working poor, and labor productivity.

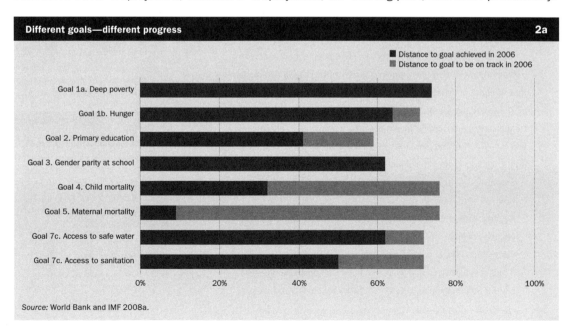

Different goals—different progress   **2a**

Legend: ■ Distance to goal achieved in 2006   ■ Distance to goal to be on track in 2006

Categories: Goal 1a. Deep poverty; Goal 1b. Hunger; Goal 2. Primary education; Goal 3. Gender parity at school; Goal 4. Child mortality; Goal 5. Maternal mortality; Goal 7c. Access to safe water; Goal 7c. Access to sanitation

Source: World Bank and IMF 2008a.

New indicators on decent and productive work

Measuring the achievement of decent and productive work in its many facets (box 2b) is challenging. Nevertheless, it is clear that increased opportunities for decent and productive employment have led to greater earnings for many workers in high-income economies. In contrast, jobs in the formal economy are often beyond the reach of most people in low-income economies, where many workers still continue to toil long hours in poor conditions with low remuneration and low productivity.

A set of indicators has been adopted to assess the achievement of the Millennium Development Goal target for full and productive employment and decent work for all: employment to population ratios, the share of vulnerable employment in total employment, the share of working poor (earning less than $1.25 a day) in total employment, and labor productivity growth rates. The four indicators should:

- Provide relevant measures of progress toward the new target.
- Provide a basis for international comparison.
- Link to country monitoring systems.
- Be based on international standards, recommendations, and best practices.
- Be constructed from well established data sources, quantifiable and consistent, enabling measurement over time.

Employment to population ratios

The employment to population ratio—the number of people employed as a percentage of the population for the corresponding age group (ages 15 and older or ages 15–24) and sex—is a good indicator of the efficiency of an economy in providing jobs. Although there is no optimal employment to population ratio, most economies have ratios in the range of 55–75 percent. Ratios above 80 percent could point to an abundance of low-quality jobs.

The ratios for people ages 15 and older changed little between 1991 and 2007 (figure 2c), but they hide wide variations across regions (figure 2d). Developed economies have lower ratios than developing economies because their higher productivity and incomes require fewer workers to meet the needs of the entire population.

For developing economies there is no correct, or optimal, ratio. During the development process employment to population ratios and poverty indicators can both be high because people must work to survive, which is the case for some countries in South Asia and Sub-Saharan Africa (figure 2e). When unemployment rates are very high, signifying

Employment to population ratios have not changed much over time. . .   2c

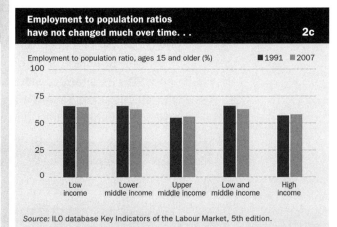

Employment to population ratio, ages 15 and older (%)   ■ 1991 ■ 2007

Source: ILO database Key Indicators of the Labour Market, 5th edition.

. . . But variations are wide across regions   2d

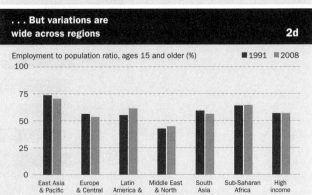

Employment to population ratio, ages 15 and older (%)   ■ 1991 ■ 2008

Source: ILO 2008.

that people are looking for work but not finding it, efforts are needed to increase the employment to population ratio. Efforts to boost ratios are also needed when unemployment rates are low as a result of discouragement, indicating that people may have given up hope of finding a job. On the other hand, increases in employment to population ratios should be moderate, since sharp spikes could be the result of a decline in productivity.

Two regions experienced increases in employment to population ratios over this period: Latin America and the Caribbean and Middle East and North Africa. In both, the increases were fueled by increases in the labor force participation of women. But despite this, the employment to population ratio in the Middle East and North Africa remained the lowest in the world.

Globally, employment to population ratios are lower for women than for men, resulting in a large untapped potential of female labor (figure 2f). The Middle East and North Africa has the largest gender gap, attributable to low participation of women in the workforce. The opposite is true in East Asia

and Pacific, where the high employment to population ratio is in part explained by the high employment to population ratio for women, and the gender gap in employment to population ratios is the lowest of all regions. Gender gaps in these ratios may be the result of women choosing not to work, but especially in developing countries women are likely to face cultural or other constraints to labor market participation. If such constraints become less binding over time, ratios for women will gradually increase.

High ratios among youth, as in some East Asian and Pacific economies, indicate that more young people are working rather than attending school and investing in their future (figure 2g). A reduction in youth employment to population ratios can be a positive trend if related to increased enrollments. Ratios generally are negatively correlated to school enrollment: the higher the enrollment, the lower the employment (figure 2h). But Nigeria and Sudan have low secondary school enrollments and low youth employment, indicating that young people are neither working nor preparing for future work.

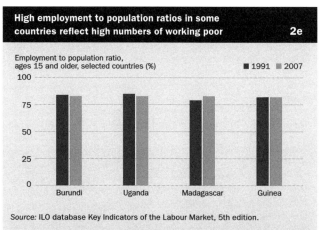

High employment to population ratios in some countries reflect high numbers of working poor — 2e

Employment to population ratio, ages 15 and older, selected countries (%) ■ 1991 ■ 2007

Source: ILO database Key Indicators of the Labour Market, 5th edition.

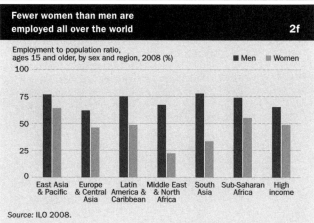

Fewer women than men are employed all over the world — 2f

Employment to population ratio, ages 15 and older, by sex and region, 2008 (%) ■ Men ■ Women

Source: ILO 2008.

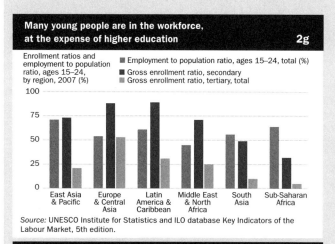

Many young people are in the workforce, at the expense of higher education — 2g

Enrollment ratios and employment to population ratio, ages 15–24, by region, 2007 (%) ■ Employment to population ratio, ages 15–24, total (%) ■ Gross enrollment ratio, secondary ■ Gross enrollment ratio, tertiary, total

Source: UNESCO Institute for Statistics and ILO database Key Indicators of the Labour Market, 5th edition.

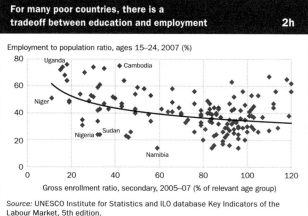

For many poor countries, there is a tradeoff between education and employment — 2h

Employment to population ratio, ages 15–24, 2007 (%)

Gross enrollment ratio, secondary, 2005–07 (% of relevant age group)

Source: UNESCO Institute for Statistics and ILO database Key Indicators of the Labour Market, 5th edition.

Share of vulnerable employment in total employment

The share of vulnerable employment in total employment captures the proportion of workers who are less likely to have access to social security, income protection, and effective coverage under labor legislation—and are thus more likely to lack critical elements of decent work. Such elements include mechanisms for dialogue that could improve their working conditions or ensure rights at work. The fact that the vulnerable are most likely to lack social protection and safety nets in times of low economic demand can increase their poverty, a big concern in the current global economic crisis.

Vulnerable employment accounted for just over half of world employment in 2007 (50.5 percent), down from 52.6 percent in 2000. It is very high in South Asia and Sub-Saharan Africa (figure 2i), accounting for three-quarters of all jobs, and in East Asia and Pacific. The lowest share of vulnerable employment outside high-income economies is in Europe and Central Asia. Women are more likely than men to be vulnerable (figure 2j), and the difference is more than 10 percentage points in Sub-Saharan Africa, South Asia, and the Middle East and North Africa. Shares of women in vulnerable employment are very low in high-income regions.

The share of working poor in total employment

Working poor are employed people living in a household in which each member is estimated to be below the poverty line ($1.25 a day). Measurements of the working poor indicate the lack of decent work: if a person's work does not provide a sufficient income to lift the family out of poverty, this work does not fulfill the income component of decent work. Unemployment is not an option for the poor, who have no savings or other sources of income and cannot rely on safety nets. Measuring decent work remains a challenge.

Harsh labor market conditions in South Asia and Sub-Saharan Africa are reflected in the share of working poor in total employment (figure 2k). Almost 60 percent of workers in Sub-Saharan Africa and 40 percent in South Asia are extremely poor ($1.25 a day). It will take many years in these regions to make decent work for all a realistic objective. East Asia and Pacific advanced most toward improving the incomes of workers, reducing the share of working poor from 36 percent to 13 percent.

The global financial crisis, which has turned into a global jobs crisis, will likely increase the share of working poor and the share of vulnerable employment in developing economies. But with 2008 data not yet available for many countries, it is difficult to estimate the impact (box 2m).

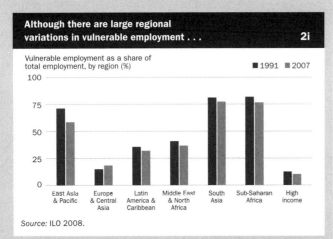

Although there are large regional variations in vulnerable employment . . .   **2i**

Vulnerable employment as a share of total employment, by region (%)   ■ 1991 ■ 2007

Source: ILO 2008.

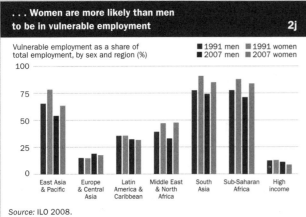

. . . Women are more likely than men to be in vulnerable employment   **2j**

Vulnerable employment as a share of total employment, by sex and region (%)   ■ 1991 men ■ 1991 women ■ 2007 men ■ 2007 women

Source: ILO 2008.

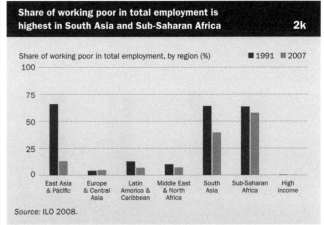

Share of working poor in total employment is highest in South Asia and Sub-Saharan Africa   **2k**

Share of working poor in total employment, by region (%)   ■ 1991 ■ 2007

Source: ILO 2008.

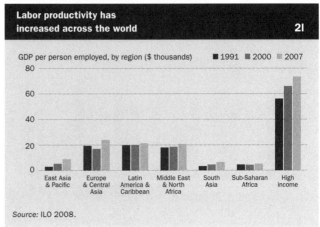

Labor productivity has increased across the world   **2l**

GDP per person employed, by region ($ thousands)   ■ 1991 ■ 2000 ■ 2007

Source: ILO 2008.

Labor productivity growth rates

Labor productivity assesses the likelihood that an economy provides the opportunity to create and sustain decent employment with fair and equitable remuneration and better working conditions. Higher productivity improves the social and economic environment, reducing poverty through investments in human and physical capital, social protection, and technological progress.

Higher productivity comes from enterprises' combining of capital, labor, and technology. There has been an increase in labor productivity since 2000 across the world.

Productivity gains have been greatest in high-income economies and in Europe and Central Asia (figure 2l). Productivity increased slightly in Latin America and the Caribbean, and the share of working poor subsequently fell. The fairly low and often volatile productivity changes in Sub-Saharan Africa may explain the limited decline in workers in vulnerable employment there. The number of working poor is unlikely to decline without increased productivity.

Challenge of measuring decent work

The multifaceted Decent Work Agenda links full and productive employment with rights at work, social protection, and a social dialogue. A major challenge lies in refining indicators of the qualitative elements of decent work and collecting the data. Future action will include:

- Compiling definitions for statistical indicators based on agreed international statistical standards and providing guidance on interpreting indicators, including limitations and possible pitfalls.
- Carrying out developmental work on statistical indicators in areas highlighted by experts, such as maternity protection, paid annual leave, sick leave, and sustainable enterprises.
- Generating reliable and reproducible indicators to comply with fundamental principles and rights at work.

The indicators are a start at measuring progress toward decent work, but challenges remain, particularly for developing economies, at different stages of statistical development and with different statistical capacities.

Scenarios for 2008   2m

In response to the financial crisis and dwindling access to funding, many businesses are reducing operating costs by postponing investments and shedding workers. The economic weight and market size of the high-income economies, and the global linkages of the financial sector, mean that the crisis is hitting funding and export markets in other parts of the world, especially those for commodities.

Since data on working poverty and vulnerable employment are lacking for 2008, global scenarios for 2008 are presented instead (ILO 2009).

Both the share of working poor and workers in vulnerable employment will have increased in 2008, reversing the encouraging trends to 2007. The slight decline in vulnerable employment in recent years raised hopes that in 2008, for the first time, the share of workers in vulnerable employment would fall below 50 percent (figure 1). But a second scenario finds it likely to rise to 52.6 percent. The projections in figure 2 would result in a decrease in the share of extreme working poverty in total employment from 2007 in the first and second scenarios. However, in the third scenario, the share would increase 4 percent over the share from 2007 (figure 2). Given the sharp decline in economic growth for many economies in 2008, the third scenario may be most likely.

The negative impact in these scenarios is realistic, since people who lose their wage and salaried employment will most likely end up out of work altogether or working as own-account workers and unpaid contributing family workers. And new entrants to labor markets will have fewer opportunities in wage and salaried jobs, most likely ending up in vulnerable employment.

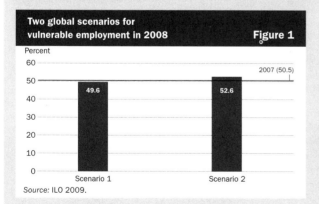

Two global scenarios for vulnerable employment in 2008 — Figure 1

Source: ILO 2009.

Scenario 1. Based on labor market data to date and IMF November 2008 revised estimates for economic growth.
Scenario 2. Based on a simultaneous increase in vulnerable employment in all economies equal to half the largest increase since 1991 and IMF November 2008 revised estimates for economic growth.

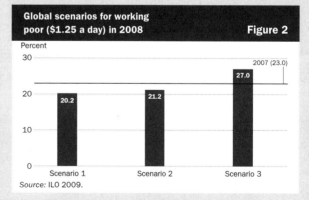

Global scenarios for working poor ($1.25 a day) in 2008 — Figure 2

Source: ILO 2009.

Scenario 1. Based on labor market data to date and IMF November 2008 revised estimates for economic growth.
Scenario 2. Based on a 5 percent higher poverty line.
Scenario 3. Based on a 10 percent higher poverty line.

	Population			Average annual population growth		Population age composition			Dependency ratio		Crude death rate	Crude birth rate
							%		% of working-age population		per 1,000 people	per 1,000 people
		millions			%	Ages 0–14	Ages 15–64	Ages 65+	Young	Old		
	1990	2007	2015	1990–2007	2007–15	2007	2007	2007	2007	2007	2007	2007
Afghanistan	..	..	..	..	..	..	..	..	..	..	..	..
Albania	3.3	3.2	3.3	−0.2	0.4	25	66	9	38	14	6	16
Algeria	25.3	33.9	38.0	1.7	1.5	28	67	5	42	7	5	21
Angola	10.5	16.9	20.7	2.8	2.5	46	51	2	90	5	21	47
Argentina	32.6	39.5	42.5	1.1	0.9	26	64	10	40	16	8	18
Armenia	3.5	3.0	3.0	−1.0	0.1	19	69	12	28	17	10	13
Australia	17.1	21.0	22.5	1.2	0.8	19	67	13	28	20	7	14
Austria	7.7	8.3	8.4	0.4	0.1	15	68	17	23	25	9	9
Azerbaijan	7.2	8.6	9.1	1.0	0.8	23	69	7	34	10	6	18
Bangladesh	113	158.6	180.0	2.0	1.6	34	62	4	55	6	8	25
Belarus	10.2	9.7	9.3	−0.3	−0.6	15	71	14	21	20	14	10
Belgium	10	10.6	10.7	0.4	0.1	17	66	17	25	26	9	11
Benin	5.2	9.0	11.3	3.3	2.8	44	54	3	82	5	11	40
Bolivia	6.7	9.5	10.9	2.1	1.6	37	58	5	64	8	8	27
Bosnia and Herzegovina	4.3	3.8	3.7	−0.8	−0.1	17	69	14	25	21	10	9
Botswana	1.4	1.9	2.1	1.9	1.2	35	62	3	56	6	14	25
Brazil	149.5	191.6	209.4	1.5	1.1	27	66	6	41	10	6	19
Bulgaria	8.7	7.7	7.2	−0.8	−0.8	13	69	17	19	25	15	10
Burkina Faso	8.9	14.8	18.6	3.0	2.9	46	51	3	90	6	14	44
Burundi	5.7	8.5	11.2	2.4	3.5	44	53	3	84	5	16	47
Cambodia	9.7	14.4	16.6	2.3	1.8	36	61	3	59	5	9	26
Cameroon	12.2	18.5	21.5	2.4	1.9	41	55	4	74	6	14	35
Canada	27.8	33.0	35.3	1.0	0.8	17	70	13	24	19	7	11
Central African Republic	3	4.3	5.0	2.2	1.8	42	54	4	78	7	18	36
Chad	6.1	10.8	13.4	3.3	2.7	46	51	3	91	6	15	45
Chile	13.2	16.6	17.8	1.4	0.9	24	68	9	35	13	5	15
China	1,135.2	1,318.3	1,375.7	0.9	0.5	21	71	8	29	11	7	12
Hong Kong, China	5.7	6.9	7.4	1.1	0.9	14	73	12	20	16	6	10
Colombia	33.2	44.0	48.4	1.7	1.2	29	65	5	45	8	6	19
Congo, Dem. Rep.	37.9	62.4	78.5	2.9	2.9	47	50	3	95	5	18	50
Congo, Rep.	2.4	3.8	4.5	2.6	2.1	42	55	3	76	6	11	35
Costa Rica	3.1	4.5	5.0	2.2	1.3	27	67	6	41	9	4	18
Côte d'Ivoire	12.8	19.3	22.3	2.4	1.9	41	56	3	74	6	15	35
Croatia	4.8	4.4	4.4	−0.4	−0.2	15	68	17	22	26	12	9
Cuba	10.6	11.3	11.2	0.4	−0.1	18	70	12	26	17	8	10
Czech Republic	10.4	10.3	10.3	0.0[a]	−0.1	14	71	15	20	20	10	11
Denmark	5.1	5.5	5.5	0.4	0.1	19	66	16	28	24	10	12
Dominican Republic	7.3	9.7	10.6	1.7	1.1	33	61	6	54	9	6	23
Ecuador	10.3	13.3	14.6	1.5	1.1	32	62	6	51	10	5	21
Egypt, Arab Rep.	55.1	75.5	86.2	1.8	1.7	33	62	5	52	8	6	24
El Salvador	5.1	6.9	7.6	1.7	1.3	33	61	6	55	9	6	23
Eritrea	3.2	4.8	6.2	2.5	3.0	43	55	2	78	4	9	39
Estonia	1.6	1.3	1.3	−0.9	−0.3	15	68	17	22	24	13	12
Ethiopia	48.0	79.1	96.0	2.9	2.4	44	53	3	82	6	13	38
Finland	5.0	5.3	5.4	0.3	0.2	17	67	16	26	24	9	11
France	56.7	61.7	63.3	0.5	0.3	18	65	16	28	25	8	13
Gabon	0.9	1.3	1.5	2.2	1.5	35	61	5	58	8	12	26
Gambia, The	1.0	1.7	2.1	3.4	2.5	41	55	4	74	7	10	35
Georgia	5.5	4.4	4.2	−1.3	−0.6	18	68	14	26	21	12	11
Germany	79.4	82.3	81.1	0.2	−0.2	14	66	20	21	30	10	8
Ghana	15.6	23.5	27.3	2.4	1.9	38	58	4	66	6	9	30
Greece	10.2	11.2	11.2	0.6	0.0[b]	14	67	19	21	28	10	10
Guatemala	8.9	13.3	16.2	2.4	2.4	43	53	4	80	8	6	33
Guinea	6.0	9.4	11.4	2.6	2.4	43	54	3	80	6	12	40
Guinea-Bissau	1.0	1.7	2.2	3.0	3.0	48	49	3	97	6	18	50
Haiti	7.1	9.6	11.0	1.8	1.7	37	59	4	63	7	9	28

	Population			Average annual population growth		Population age composition			Dependency ratio		Crude death rate	Crude birth rate
	millions			%		Ages 0–14	% Ages 15–64	Ages 65+	% of working-age population Young	Old	per 1,000 people	per 1,000 people
	1990	**2007**	**2015**	**1990–2007**	**2007–15**	**2007**	**2007**	**2007**	**2007**	**2007**	**2007**	**2007**
Honduras	4.9	7.1	8.3	2.2	1.9	39	57	4	68	7	6	28
Hungary	10.4	10.1	9.8	−0.2	−0.3	15	69	16	22	22	13	10
India	849.5	1,124.8	1,249.6	1.7	1.3	32	63	5	51	8	8	24
Indonesia	178.2	225.6	245.1	1.4	1.0	28	67	6	42	9	6	19
Iran, Islamic Rep.	54.4	71.0	78.9	1.6	1.3	27	69	4	39	6	6	18
Iraq	18.5	..	..	..	..	..	..	..	..	..	..	..
Ireland	3.5	4.4	4.8	1.3	1.2	21	68	11	30	16	6	16
Israel	4.7	7.2	8.1	2.5	1.6	28	62	10	45	16	6	21
Italy	56.7	59.4	58.4	0.3	−0.2	14	66	20	21	30	10	9
Jamaica	2.4	2.7	2.8	0.7	0.5	31	62	7	50	12	6	17
Japan	123.5	127.8	124.5	0.2	−0.3	14	66	21	21	32	9	9
Jordan	3.2	5.7	6.8	3.5	2.1	36	61	3	59	5	4	29
Kazakhstan	16.3	15.5	16.8	−0.3	1.0	24	69	8	35	11	10	20
Kenya	23.4	37.5	46.1	2.8	2.6	43	55	3	78	5	12	39
Korea, Dem. Rep.	20.1	23.8	24.4	1.0	0.3	23	68	9	34	13	10	13
Korea, Rep.	42.9	48.5	49.2	0.7	0.2	18	72	10	24	14	5	10
Kuwait	2.1	2.7	3.2	1.3	2.1	23	75	2	31	3	2	18
Kyrgyz Republic	4.4	5.2	5.8	1.0	1.2	30	65	6	46	9	7	23
Lao PDR	4.1	5.9	6.7	2.1	1.7	38	58	4	65	6	7	27
Latvia	2.7	2.3	2.2	−0.9	−0.5	14	69	17	20	25	15	10
Lebanon	3.0	4.1	4.4	1.9	1.0	28	65	7	43	11	7	18
Lesotho	1.6	2.0	2.1	1.3	0.6	40	55	5	72	9	19	29
Liberia	2.1	3.7	4.7	3.3	2.8	47	51	2	93	4	18	50
Libya	4.4	6.2	7.1	2.0	1.8	30	66	4	46	6	4	23
Lithuania	3.7	3.4	3.3	−0.5	−0.5	16	69	16	23	23	14	10
Macedonia, FYR	1.9	2.0	2.0	0.4	0.0[a]	19	70	11	27	16	9	11
Madagascar	12.0	19.7	24.1	2.9	2.5	43	54	3	81	6	10	36
Malawi	9.4	13.9	17.0	2.3	2.5	47	50	3	94	6	15	41
Malaysia	18.1	26.5	30.0	2.3	1.5	30	65	5	47	7	4	21
Mali	7.7	12.3	15.7	2.8	3.0	48	49	4	97	7	15	48
Mauritania	1.9	3.1	3.8	2.8	2.4	40	57	4	70	6	8	32
Mauritius	1.1	1.3	1.3	1.0	0.6	24	70	7	34	10	7	14
Mexico	83.2	105.3	113.7	1.4	1.0	30	64	6	46	10	5	19
Moldova	4.4	3.8	3.7	−0.8	−0.4	19	70	11	27	16	12	11
Mongolia	2.1	2.6	2.8	1.3	1.0	27	69	4	39	6	6	22
Morocco	24.2	30.9	33.9	1.4	1.2	29	65	5	45	8	6	21
Mozambique	13.5	21.4	24.7	2.7	1.8	44	52	3	85	6	20	39
Myanmar	40.1	48.8	51.9	1.1	0.8	26	68	6	39	8	10	18
Namibia	1.4	2.1	2.3	2.3	1.5	37	59	4	64	6	12	26
Nepal	19.1	28.1	32.2	2.3	1.7	38	58	4	65	6	8	28
Netherlands	15.0	16.4	16.5	0.5	0.1	18	67	15	27	22	8	11
New Zealand	3.4	4.2	4.5	1.2	0.8	21	67	12	31	19	7	15
Nicaragua	4.1	5.6	6.3	1.8	1.4	37	59	4	62	7	5	25
Niger	7.8	14.2	18.5	3.5	3.3	48	49	3	98	7	14	49
Nigeria	94.5	148.0	175.6	2.6	2.1	44	53	3	82	6	17	40
Norway	4.2	4.7	4.9	0.6	0.5	19	66	15	29	22	9	12
Oman	1.8	2.6	3.0	2.0	2.0	32	65	3	50	4	3	22
Pakistan	108.0	162.5	192.3	2.4	2.1	36	60	4	59	7	7	27
Panama	2.4	3.3	3.8	1.9	1.5	30	64	6	47	10	5	21
Papua New Guinea	4.1	6.3	7.3	2.5	1.8	40	58	2	69	4	10	30
Paraguay	4.2	6.1	7.0	2.2	1.6	35	60	5	58	8	6	25
Peru	21.8	27.9	30.7	1.5	1.2	31	64	6	48	9	6	21
Philippines	61.2	87.9	101.0	2.1	1.7	35	61	4	59	7	5	26
Poland	38.1	38.1	37.5	0.0[b]	−0.2	15	71	13	22	19	10	10
Portugal	9.9	10.6	10.7	0.4	0.1	16	67	17	23	25	10	10
Puerto Rico	3.5	3.9	4.1	0.6	0.5	21	66	13	32	20	8	13

	Population (millions)			Average annual population growth (%)		Population age composition (%)			Dependency ratio (% of working-age population)		Crude death rate (per 1,000 people)	Crude birth rate (per 1,000 people)
	1990	2007	2015	1990–2007	2007–15	Ages 0–14 2007	Ages 15–64 2007	Ages 65+ 2007	Young 2007	Old 2007	2007	2007
Romania	23.2	21.5	20.5	−0.4	−0.6	15	70	15	22	21	12	10
Russian Federation	148.3	142.1	135.6	−0.3	−0.6	15	72	13	21	19	15	11
Rwanda	7.3	9.7	12.1	1.7	2.8	43	55	2	78	4	17	44
Saudi Arabia	16.4	24.2	28.3	2.3	2.0	33	65	3	50	4	4	25
Senegal	7.9	12.4	15.4	2.7	2.7	42	54	4	77	8	9	35
Serbia	7.6	7.4	7.3	−0.2	−0.1	18[c]	67[c]	15[c]	27[c]	22[c]	14	9
Sierra Leone	4.1	5.8	6.9	2.1	2.1	43	54	3	80	6	22	46
Singapore	3.0	4.6	4.8	2.4	0.5	18	73	9	25	12	5	10
Slovak Republic	5.3	5.4	5.4	0.1	0.0[a]	16	72	12	22	16	10	10
Slovenia	2.0	2.0	2.0	0.1	−0.2	14	70	16	20	23	9	10
Somalia	6.7	8.7	10.9	1.5	2.8	44	53	3	83	5	17	43
South Africa	35.2	47.9	49.5	1.8	0.4	32	64	4	50	7	17	22
Spain	38.8	44.9	45.7	0.9	0.2	15	69	17	21	25	9	11
Sri Lanka	17.1	20.0	20.5	0.9	0.3	23	70	7	33	10	6	19
Sudan	25.9	38.6	45.6	2.3	2.1	40	56	4	71	6	10	32
Swaziland	0.8	1.1	1.2	2.3	0.7	39	58	3	67	6	21	29
Sweden	8.6	9.1	9.4	0.4	0.3	17	66	18	26	27	10	12
Switzerland	6.7	7.6	7.7	0.7	0.2	16	68	16	24	24	8	10
Syrian Arab Republic	12.7	19.9	23.5	2.6	2.1	36	61	3	58	5	3	27
Tajikistan	5.3	6.7	7.7	1.4	1.6	38	58	4	65	7	6	27
Tanzania	25.5	40.4	48.9	2.7	2.4	44	53	3	84	6	13	39
Thailand	54.3	63.8	66.6	1.0	0.5	21	71	8	30	12	8	15
Timor-Leste	0.7	1.1	1.4	2.1	3.2	45	53	3	85	5	9	42
Togo	4.0	6.6	8.0	3.0	2.5	43	54	3	79	6	10	37
Trinidad and Tobago	1.2	1.3	1.4	0.5	0.4	21	72	7	30	9	8	15
Tunisia	8.2	10.2	11.2	1.3	1.1	25	69	6	36	9	6	17
Turkey	56.2	73.9	81.0	1.6	1.2	27	67	6	41	9	7	19
Turkmenistan	3.7	5.0	5.5	1.8	1.3	30	65	5	46	7	8	22
Uganda	17.8	30.9	40.6	3.2	3.4	49	48	2	101	5	13	47
Ukraine	51.9	46.5	43.6	−0.6	−0.8	14	70	16	20	23	16	10
United Arab Emirates	1.9	4.4	5.3	5.0	2.4	20	79	1	25	1	1	16
United Kingdom	57.2	61.0	62.5	0.4	0.3	18	66	16	27	25	9	13
United States	249.6	301.6	324.1	1.1	0.9	20	67	12	31	18	8	14
Uruguay	3.1	3.3	3.4	0.4	0.2	23	63	14	37	22	9	15
Uzbekistan	20.5	26.9	30.0	1.6	1.4	32	64	5	49	7	5	21
Venezuela, RB	19.8	27.5	31.1	1.9	1.5	31	64	5	47	8	5	22
Vietnam	66.2	85.2	94.1	1.5	1.3	28	66	6	42	8	5	19
West Bank and Gaza	2.0	3.7	4.5	3.7	2.5	45	52	3	88	6	4	36
Yemen, Rep.	12.3	22.4	28.2	3.5	2.9	45	53	2	85	4	7	38
Zambia	8.1	11.9	13.8	2.3	1.9	46	52	3	88	6	19	39
Zimbabwe	10.5	13.4	14.8	1.4	1.3	38	58	4	66	6	18	28
World	**5,259.1 s**	**6,610.3 s**	**7,210.6 s**	**1.3 w**	**1.1 w**	**28 w**	**65 w**	**7 w**	**43 w**	**12 w**	**8 w**	**20 w**
Low income	866.5	1,295.8	1,532.9	2.4	2.1	39	57	4	69	6	11	33
Middle income	3,457.9	4,258.2	4,586.3	1.2	0.9	27	67	7	40	10	7	18
Lower middle income	2,751.9	3,434.5	3,721.4	1.3	1.0	27	67	6	41	10	7	19
Upper middle income	706.0	823.7	865.0	0.9	0.6	24	67	9	36	13	9	17
Low & middle income	4,324.4	5,554.0	6,119.2	1.5	1.2	30	64	6	46	9	8	22
East Asia & Pacific	1,596.0	1,912.4	2,026.0	1.1	0.7	23	70	7	33	10	7	14
Europe & Central Asia	436.2	445.6	447.3	0.1	0.0[b]	19	69	11	28	17	12	14
Latin America & Carib.	435.1	560.6	614.2	1.5	1.1	29	64	6	45	10	6	20
Middle East & N. Africa	223.7	313.2	358.7	2.0	1.7	32	63	4	51	7	6	24
South Asia	1,120.2	1,522.0	1,711.6	1.8	1.5	33	62	5	53	8	8	25
Sub-Saharan Africa	513.2	800.0	961.4	2.6	2.3	43	54	3	80	6	15	39
High income	934.7	1,056.3	1,091.3	0.7	0.4	18	67	15	26	22	8	12
Euro area	301.6	324.2	325.5	0.4	0.1	15	67	18	23	27	9	10

a. More than −0.05. b. Less than 0.05. c. Includes Kosovo.

Population estimates are usually based on national population censuses, but the frequency and quality vary by country. Most countries conduct a complete enumeration no more often than once a decade. Estimates for the years before and after the census are interpolations or extrapolations based on demographic models. Errors and undercounting occur even in high-income countries; in developing countries errors may be substantial because of limits in the transport, communications, and other resources required to conduct and analyze a full census.

The quality and reliability of official demographic data are also affected by public trust in the government, government commitment to full and accurate enumeration, confidentiality and protection against misuse of census data, and census agencies' independence from political influence. Moreover, comparability of population indicators is limited by differences in the concepts, definitions, collection procedures, and estimation methods used by national statistical agencies and other organizations that collect the data.

Of the 153 economies in the table and the 56 economies in table 1.6, 180 (about 86 percent) conducted a census during the 2000 census round (1995–2004). A quarter of countries have completed a census for the 2010 census round (2005–14). All told, 195 countries (93 percent) have conducted a census during 1995–2008. The currentness of a census and the availability of complementary data from surveys or registration systems are objective ways to judge demographic data quality. Some European countries' registration systems offer complete information on population in the absence of a census. See *Primary data documentation* for the most recent census or survey year and for the completeness of registration.

Current population estimates for developing countries that lack recent census data and pre- and post-census estimates for countries with census data are provided by the United Nations Population Division and other agencies. The standard estimation method requires fertility, mortality, and net migration data, often collected from sample surveys, which can be small or limited in coverage. Population estimates are from demographic modeling and so are susceptible to biases and errors from shortcomings in the model and in the data. Population projections use the cohort component method.

The growth rate of the total population conceals age-group differences in growth rates. In many developing countries the once rapidly growing under-15 population is shrinking. Previously high fertility rates and declining mortality rates are now reflected in the larger share of the working-age population.

Dependency ratios account for variations in the proportions of children, elderly people, and working-age people in the population. Calculations of young and old-age dependency suggest the dependency burden that the working-age population bears in relation to children and the elderly. But dependency ratios show only the age composition of a population, not economic dependency. Some children and elderly people are part of the labor force, and many working-age people are not.

Vital rates are based on data from birth and death registration systems, censuses, and sample surveys by national statistical offices and other organizations, or on demographic analysis. The 2007 estimates for many countries are projections based on extrapolations of levels and trends from earlier years or interpolations of population estimates and projections from the United Nations Population Division. Data for most high-income countries are provisional estimates based on vital registers.

Vital registers are the preferred source for these data, but in many developing countries systems for registering births and deaths are absent or incomplete because of deficiencies in the coverage of events or geographic areas. Many developing countries carry out special household surveys that ask respondents about recent births and deaths. Estimates derived in this way are subject to sampling errors and recall errors.

The United Nations Statistics Division monitors the completeness of vital registration systems. The share of countries with at least 90 percent complete vital registration rose from 45 percent in 1988 to 61 percent in 2007. Still, some of the most populous developing countries—China, India, Indonesia, Brazil, Pakistan, Bangladesh, Nigeria—lack complete vital registration systems. From 2000 to 2007, on average 64 percent of births, 62 percent of deaths, and 45 percent of infant deaths were registered and reported to the United Nations Statistics Division.

International migration is the only other factor besides birth and death rates that directly determines a country's population growth. From 1990 to 2005 the number of migrants in high-income countries rose 40 million. About 190 million people (3 percent of the world population) live outside their home country. Estimating migration is difficult. At any time many people are located outside their home country as tourists, workers, or refugees or for other reasons. Standards for the duration and purpose of international moves that qualify as migration vary, and estimates require information on flows into and out of countries that is difficult to collect.

• **Population** is based on the de facto definition of population, which counts all residents regardless of legal status or citizenship—except for refugees not permanently settled in the country of asylum, who are generally considered part of the population of their country of origin. The values shown are mid-year estimates for 1990 and 2007 and projections for 2015. • **Average annual population growth** is the exponential change for the period indicated. See *Statistical methods* for more information. • **Population age composition** is the percentage of the total population that is in specific age groups. • **Dependency ratio** is the ratio of dependents—people younger than 15 or older than 64—to the working-age population—those ages 15–64. • **Crude death rate** and **crude birth rate** are the number of deaths and the number of live births occurring during the year, per 1,000 people, estimated at midyear. Subtracting the crude death rate from the crude birth rate provides the rate of natural increase, which is equal to the population growth rate in the absence of migration.

The World Bank's population estimates are compiled and produced by its Human Development Network and Development Data Group in consultation with its operational staff and country offices. Important inputs to the World Bank's demographic work come from the United Nations Population Division's *World Population Prospects: The 2006 Revision;* census reports and other statistical publications from national statistical offices; household surveys conducted by national agencies, Macro International, and the U.S. Centers for Disease Control and Prevention; Eurostat, *Demographic Statistics* (various years); Secretariat of the Pacific Community, Statistics and Demography Programme; and U.S. Bureau of the Census, International Database.

2.2 Labor force structure

	Labor force participation rate				Labor force				
	% ages 15 and older				Total millions		Ages 15 and older average annual % growth	Female % of labor force	
	Male		Female						
	1990	2007	1990	2007	1990	2007	1990–2007	1990	2007
Afghanistan	..	..	..	..	..	..	..	..	..
Albania	84	71	67	50	1.7	1.4	−0.9	43.4	41.9
Algeria	75	78	23	37	7.0	13.9	4.0	23.6	31.9
Angola	90	89	74	75	4.5	7.5	2.9	46.4	46.6
Argentina	79	76	29	50	12.0	18.3	2.5	28.4	41.1
Armenia	79	68	66	56	1.8	1.5	−1.1	48.0	49.9
Australia	76	72	52	57	8.5	10.9	1.5	41.2	44.8
Austria	70	68	43	52	3.5	4.2	1.0	40.8	44.7
Azerbaijan	78	71	66	60	3.4	4.3	1.4	48.2	48.1
Bangladesh	89	85	62	57	50.9	74.3	2.2	39.5	39.2
Belarus	75	66	60	53	5.3	4.9	−0.5	48.9	48.8
Belgium	61	60	36	46	3.9	4.7	1.0	39.0	44.4
Benin	88	86	51	59	1.9	3.7	3.9	38.2	40.5
Bolivia	85	83	46	66	2.5	4.4	3.3	36.1	45.0
Bosnia and Herzegovina	83	67	69	53	2.5	1.9	−1.7	46.7	46.1
Botswana	78	63	44	48	0.5	0.7	2.4	37.7	43.7
Brazil	85	82	39	60	59.3	97.7	2.9	32.1	43.3
Bulgaria	64	57	57	46	4.2	3.4	−1.3	48.4	46.2
Burkina Faso	90	90	76	77	3.9	6.7	3.2	47.4	46.8
Burundi	90	90	91	90	2.8	4.2	2.4	52.5	51.4
Cambodia	85	87	77	75	4.3	7.5	3.2	52.4	48.7
Cameroon	79	75	53	52	4.4	7.0	2.7	40.8	41.3
Canada	76	73	58	63	14.7	18.5	1.3	44.1	46.6
Central African Republic	88	87	69	67	1.3	1.9	2.2	46.6	45.5
Chad	84	77	57	71	2.3	4.3	3.6	41.4	48.7
Chile	77	72	32	39	5.0	7.0	2.0	30.6	36.0
China	85	80	73	71	650.6	785.7	1.1	44.8	45.7
Hong Kong, China	80	70	47	53	2.9	3.6	1.4	36.3	45.3
Colombia	77	79	44	64	13.4	22.1	2.9	35.9	44.2
Congo, Dem. Rep.	86	90	60	54	14.6	23.5	2.8	42.5	38.6
Congo, Rep.	84	83	57	56	0.9	1.5	2.8	41.4	41.1
Costa Rica	85	79	36	43	1.2	2.0	3.0	29.2	34.5
Côte d'Ivoire	89	85	42	39	4.6	7.1	2.5	29.6	30.6
Croatia	75	60	52	45	2.4	2.0	−1.2	43.2	44.5
Cuba	73	69	36	45	4.5	5.2	0.9	33.2	39.2
Czech Republic	80	68	61	51	5.7	5.2	−0.5	45.5	44.2
Denmark	75	71	62	61	2.9	2.9	0.0[a]	46.1	46.7
Dominican Republic	82	73	26	57	2.5	4.2	3.1	24.0	43.8
Ecuador	78	79	33	52	3.5	5.9	3.2	29.5	40.0
Egypt, Arab Rep.	74	71	24	24	15.9	24.0	2.4	24.4	25.3
El Salvador	80	79	51	47	2.0	2.8	2.2	41.2	38.8
Eritrea	88	86	55	55	1.2	1.9	2.8	40.4	41.0
Estonia	72	65	61	54	0.8	0.7	−1.0	50.3	49.8
Ethiopia	89	91	63	80	19.7	37.9	3.8	42.4	47.3
Finland	71	65	59	58	2.6	2.7	0.2	47.5	48.0
France	65	62	46	50	24.8	28.0	0.7	43.3	46.0
Gabon	83	80	63	62	0.4	0.6	2.6	44.0	43.8
Gambia, The	86	84	70	70	0.4	0.8	3.5	45.4	45.8
Georgia	83	74	67	55	3.1	2.3	−1.6	48.2	46.3
Germany	73	66	46	51	39.3	41.4	0.3	40.9	44.8
Ghana	74	73	73	72	6.4	10.5	3.0	49.4	48.9
Greece	67	65	36	43	4.2	5.2	1.3	36.2	40.4
Guatemala	89	85	28	45	2.8	4.9	3.2	23.7	37.1
Guinea	90	89	80	79	2.8	4.5	2.7	47.2	47.1
Guinea-Bissau	87	90	56	54	0.4	0.6	2.8	40.3	38.4
Haiti	81	83	49	39	2.6	3.6	2.0	39.4	33.4

	Labor force participation rate				Labor force				
	% ages 15 and older				Total millions		Ages 15 and older average annual % growth	Female % of labor force	
	Male		Female						
	1990	**2007**	**1990**	**2007**	**1990**	**2007**	**1990–2007**	**1990**	**2007**
Honduras	87	82	37	37	1.6	2.6	2.6	30.0	31.7
Hungary	66	59	47	44	4.6	4.3	−0.4	44.6	45.2
India	85	82	35	34	321.9	447.7	1.9	27.6	28.2
Indonesia	81	86	50	50	75.3	110.5	2.3	38.4	36.9
Iran, Islamic Rep.	81	75	22	32	15.6	27.8	3.4	20.2	29.2
Iraq	74	..	12	..	4.4	..	..	13.3	..
Ireland	70	73	36	53	1.3	2.2	2.9	34.3	42.5
Israel	62	61	41	50	1.7	2.9	3.2	40.6	46.3
Italy	66	61	36	39	24.0	25.3	0.3	37.0	40.4
Jamaica	80	74	66	55	1.1	1.2	0.3	46.6	44.0
Japan	77	72	50	48	63.9	65.7	0.2	40.6	41.2
Jordan	68	72	11	16	0.7	1.6	5.0	12.6	16.9
Kazakhstan	78	75	62	65	7.8	8.2	0.3	47.0	49.3
Kenya	90	87	75	74	9.9	17.4	3.3	46.0	46.4
Korea, Dem. Rep.	79	78	51	58	9.6	12.4	1.5	40.6	44.0
Korea, Rep.	73	73	47	49	19.1	24.3	1.4	39.3	40.8
Kuwait	81	81	34	43	0.8	1.4	2.9	21.6	24.0
Kyrgyz Republic	74	75	58	53	1.8	2.3	1.5	46.1	42.8
Lao PDR	83	80	80	79	1.8	2.9	2.6	49.6	50.5
Latvia	77	69	63	54	1.4	1.2	−1.2	49.6	48.2
Lebanon	83	77	22	25	1.0	1.5	2.4	22.8	25.6
Lesotho	85	75	68	68	0.7	0.9	1.5	50.9	52.4
Liberia	85	85	54	55	0.8	1.4	3.3	39.3	39.8
Libya	78	78	17	26	1.2	2.3	3.6	15.5	23.5
Lithuania	74	61	59	51	1.9	1.6	−1.1	48.1	49.5
Macedonia, FYR	73	66	54	42	0.9	0.9	−0.1	42.7	39.3
Madagascar	85	88	80	82	5.5	9.5	3.3	48.8	48.8
Malawi	80	80	76	76	3.9	5.7	2.3	50.7	50.1
Malaysia	81	80	43	45	7.0	11.6	2.9	34.4	35.2
Mali	69	65	34	37	2.0	3.2	2.8	34.9	38.3
Mauritania	84	80	58	60	0.8	1.3	3.1	42.0	42.9
Mauritius	82	77	40	42	0.5	0.6	1.4	33.1	36.1
Mexico	84	80	34	41	29.9	44.4	2.3	30.0	35.6
Moldova	74	48	61	45	2.1	1.4	−2.2	48.6	51.3
Mongolia	65	61	55	58	0.7	1.1	2.5	46.2	49.1
Morocco	82	80	24	25	7.7	11.2	2.3	23.5	24.7
Mozambique	84	77	86	88	6.2	9.9	2.8	54.7	56.1
Myanmar	88	86	69	69	20.2	27.9	1.9	44.7	45.3
Namibia	65	59	49	49	0.4	0.7	2.7	45.2	46.3
Nepal	80	76	48	59	7.1	11.7	2.9	37.9	45.2
Netherlands	70	71	43	57	6.9	8.5	1.2	39.1	45.0
New Zealand	74	75	54	61	1.7	2.3	1.7	43.1	45.9
Nicaragua	85	87	39	38	1.4	2.2	2.8	32.1	31.0
Niger	87	88	41	39	2.6	4.7	3.6	32.5	30.7
Nigeria	75	71	37	39	28.4	45.3	2.7	34.0	35.9
Norway	73	71	57	62	2.2	2.5	0.8	44.7	47.1
Oman	81	77	20	26	0.6	1.0	3.0	14.2	19.6
Pakistan	86	85	11	21	30.1	56.2	3.7	10.9	18.7
Panama	81	80	37	48	0.9	1.5	2.9	30.9	37.1
Papua New Guinea	75	73	71	71	1.8	2.7	2.6	46.7	49.2
Paraguay	83	84	52	71	1.7	3.1	3.6	38.0	45.2
Peru	76	82	48	64	8.3	14.1	3.1	39.1	43.9
Philippines	83	80	47	50	23.5	36.9	2.7	36.6	38.3
Poland	72	61	55	47	18.1	17.3	−0.2	45.4	45.4
Portugal	73	70	50	56	4.8	5.6	0.9	42.8	46.3
Puerto Rico	61	58	31	38	1.2	1.5	1.4	35.8	42.3

	Labor force participation rate				Labor force				
	% ages 15 and older				Total millions		Ages 15 and older average annual % growth	Female % of labor force	
	Male		Female						
	1990	2007	1990	2007	1990	2007	1990–2007	1990	2007
Romania	67	60	55	46	10.8	9.7	−0.6	46.7	45.0
Russian Federation	76	69	60	57	77.0	75.8	−0.1	48.5	49.5
Rwanda	88	79	86	81	3.2	4.4	2.0	51.7	52.9
Saudi Arabia	80	80	15	19	5.1	8.7	3.2	11.2	14.9
Senegal	90	86	61	62	3.3	5.3	2.9	40.1	42.2
Serbia	..	60	..	43	..	3.1	..	..	42.5
Sierra Leone	65	67	66	65	1.6	2.2	2.0	51.6	50.3
Singapore	79	76	51	54	1.6	2.4	2.7	39.1	41.1
Slovak Republic	79	69	66	52	2.9	2.7	−0.3	47.2	44.6
Slovenia	76	65	60	52	1.1	1.0	−0.3	46.3	45.9
Somalia	89	89	52	54	2.6	3.4	1.7	37.6	38.9
South Africa	64	60	44	47	11.6	17.4	2.4	41.9	45.2
Spain	69	68	34	47	15.9	22.0	1.9	34.4	41.5
Sri Lanka	79	75	46	43	7.3	9.0	1.2	36.1	37.2
Sudan	78	72	24	31	7.3	11.9	2.9	23.4	30.4
Swaziland	79	69	66	62	0.3	0.5	2.7	51.1	50.1
Sweden	72	69	63	61	4.7	4.9	0.2	47.7	47.0
Switzerland	79	75	49	60	3.6	4.2	1.0	39.4	45.8
Syrian Arab Republic	81	78	18	21	3.3	6.4	4.0	18.3	20.8
Tajikistan	84	67	75	56	2.4	2.6	0.4	48.2	46.6
Tanzania	93	90	89	87	12.5	19.9	2.7	50.1	49.8
Thailand	87	81	76	66	31.6	36.6	0.9	47.3	46.8
Timor-Leste	81	83	52	58	0.3	0.4	2.0	38.1	40.4
Togo	89	87	53	52	1.5	2.6	3.2	38.6	38.3
Trinidad and Tobago	76	77	39	55	0.5	0.7	2.4	34.9	42.6
Tunisia	76	71	21	26	2.4	3.7	2.5	21.6	26.5
Turkey	81	71	34	24	21.0	24.2	0.8	29.4	26.8
Turkmenistan	75	71	63	59	1.5	2.2	2.4	47.3	46.9
Uganda	92	90	80	82	8.0	13.5	3.1	47.4	47.8
Ukraine	72	65	57	53	26.0	23.3	−0.6	49.4	49.3
United Arab Emirates	92	93	25	40	1.0	2.7	6.2	9.8	14.5
United Kingdom	75	70	53	56	29.5	31.4	0.4	43.3	45.5
United States	76	72	57	59	129.3	156.6	1.1	44.3	45.7
Uruguay	72	75	43	53	1.3	1.6	1.2	39.8	43.5
Uzbekistan	85	70	76	58	9.7	11.8	1.1	48.3	46.0
Venezuela, RB	82	81	32	52	7.0	12.7	3.5	27.8	38.9
Vietnam	81	76	74	69	31.4	44.4	2.0	48.4	47.9
West Bank and Gaza	67	67	10	14	0.4	0.8	4.1	11.9	16.9
Yemen, Rep.	70	66	15	22	2.5	5.4	4.6	17.5	24.4
Zambia	81	81	59	60	3.1	4.6	2.3	42.6	43.2
Zimbabwe	80	80	68	60	4.2	5.7	1.9	46.4	43.3
World	**81 w**	**78 w**	**52 w**	**53 w**	**2,352.2 t**	**3,098.8 t**	**1.6 w**	**39.3 w**	**40.3 w**
Low income	84	82	56	56	342.8	542.8	2.7	40.1	40.7
Middle income	83	79	53	52	1,565.5	2,039.7	1.6	38.6	39.5
Lower middle income	84	80	55	53	1,270.7	1,661.6	1.6	38.6	38.9
Upper middle income	78	73	46	50	294.8	378.1	1.5	38.7	42.1
Low & middle income	83	79	53	53	1,908.3	2,582.5	1.8	38.9	39.7
East Asia & Pacific	84	80	69	67	858.7	1,081.5	1.4	44.2	44.5
Europe & Central Asia	76	67	57	50	206.6	207.2	0.0[a]	46.1	45.5
Latin America & Carib.	82	80	38	53	165.1	262.2	2.7	32.1	40.8
Middle East & N. Africa	77	74	21	26	62.4	106.2	3.1	21.3	26.1
South Asia	85	82	36	36	421.5	607.9	2.2	28.2	29.1
Sub-Saharan Africa	82	80	58	60	194.1	317.5	2.9	42.3	43.5
High income	74	70	49	52	443.9	516.3	0.9	41.4	43.4
Euro area	69	65	42	48	135.8	154.3	0.7	39.9	43.8

a. Less than 0.05.

Labor force structure

About the data

The labor force is the supply of labor available for producing goods and services in an economy. It includes people who are currently employed and people who are unemployed but seeking work as well as first-time job-seekers. Not everyone who works is included, however. Unpaid workers, family workers, and students are often omitted, and some countries do not count members of the armed forces. Labor force size tends to vary during the year as seasonal workers enter and leave.

Data on the labor force are compiled by the International Labour Organization (ILO) from labor force surveys, censuses, establishment censuses and surveys, and administrative records such as employment exchange registers and unemployment insurance schemes. For some countries a combination of these sources is used. Labor force surveys are the most comprehensive source for internationally comparable labor force data. They can cover all noninstitutionalized civilians, all branches and sectors of the economy, and all categories of workers, including people holding multiple jobs. By contrast, labor force data from population censuses are often based on a limited number of questions on the economic characteristics of individuals, with little scope to probe. The resulting data often differ from labor force survey data and vary considerably by country, depending on the census scope and coverage. Establishment censuses and surveys provide data only on the employed population, not unemployed workers, workers in small establishments, or workers in the informal sector (ILO, *Key Indicators of the Labour Market 2001–2002*).

The reference period of a census or survey is another important source of differences: in some countries data refer to people's status on the day of the census or survey or during a specific period before the inquiry date, while in others data are recorded without reference to any period. In developing countries, where the household is often the basic unit of production and all members contribute to output, but some at low intensity or irregularly, the estimated labor force may be much smaller than the numbers actually working.

Differing definitions of employment age also affect comparability. For most countries the working age is 15 and older, but in some countries children younger than 15 work full- or part-time and are included in the estimates. Similarly, some countries have an upper age limit. As a result, calculations may systematically over- or underestimate actual rates. For

further information on source, reference period, or definition, consult the original source.

The labor force participation rates in the table are from the ILO database, Key Indicators of the Labour Market, 5th edition. These harmonized estimates use strict data selection criteria and enhanced methods to ensure comparability across countries and over time, including collection and tabulation methodologies and methods applied to such country-specific factors as military service requirements. Estimates are based mainly on labor force surveys, with other sources (population censuses and nationally reported estimates) used only when no survey data are available.

Participation rates indicate the relative size of the labor supply. Beginning in the 2008 edition of *World Development Indicators,* the indicator covers the population ages 15 and older, to include people who continue working past age 65. In previous editions the indicator was for the population ages 15–64, so participation rates are not comparable across editions.

The labor force estimates in the table were calculated by applying labor force participation rates from the ILO database to World Bank population estimates to create a series consistent with these population estimates. This procedure sometimes results in labor force estimates that differ slightly from those in the ILO's *Yearbook of Labour Statistics* and its database Key Indicators of the Labour Market.

Estimates of women in the labor force and employment are generally lower than those of men and are not comparable internationally, reflecting that demographic, social, legal, and cultural trends and norms determine whether women's activities are regarded as economic. In many countries many women work on farms or in other family enterprises without pay, and others work in or near their homes, mixing work and family activities during the day.

• **Labor force participation rate** is the proportion of the population ages 15 and older that is economically active: all people who supply labor for the production of goods and services during a specified period. • **Total labor force** is people ages 15 and older who meet the ILO definition of the economically active population. It includes both the employed and the unemployed. • **Average annual percentage growth of the labor force** is calculated using the exponential endpoint method (see *Statistical methods* for more information). • **Female labor force as as a percentage of the labor force** shows the extent to which women are active in the labor force.

Data on labor force participation rates are from the ILO database Key Indicators of the Labour Market, 5th edition. Labor force numbers were calculated by World Bank staff, applying labor force participation rates from the ILO database to population estimates.

2009 World Development Indicators **47**

	Agriculture				Industry				Services			
	Male % of male employment		Female % of female employment		Male % of male employment		Female % of female employment		Male % of male employment		Female % of female employment	
	1990–92[a]	2003–06[a]	1990–92[a]	2003–06[a]	1990–92[a]	2003–06[a]	1990–92[a]	2003–06[a]	1990–92[a]	2003–06[a]	1990–92[a]	2003–06[a]
Afghanistan	..	..	..	..	..	..	..	..	..	..	..	..
Albania	..	..	..	..	..	..	..	..	..	..	..	..
Algeria	..	23	..	11	..	24	..	25	..	53	..	64
Angola	..	..	..	..	..	..	..	..	..	..	..	..
Argentina	0[b,c]	2[c]	0[b,c]	1[c]	40[c]	33[c]	18[c]	11[c]	59[c]	66[c]	81[c]	88[c]
Armenia	..	..	..	..	..	..	..	..	..	..	..	..
Australia	6	5	4	3	32	31	12	9	61	65	84	88
Austria	6	6[c]	8	6[c]	47	40[c]	20	13[c]	46	55[c]	72	81[c]
Azerbaijan	..	41	..	37	..	15	..	9	..	44	..	54
Bangladesh	54	50	85	59	16	12	9	18	25	38	2	23
Belarus	..	..	..	..	..	..	..	..	..	..	..	..
Belgium	3[c]	2[c]	2[c]	2[c]	41[c]	35[c]	16[c]	11[c]	56[c]	62[c]	81[c]	86[c]
Benin	..	..	..	..	..	..	..	..	..	..	..	..
Bolivia	3[c]	..	1[c]	..	42[c]	..	17[c]	..	55[c]	..	82[c]	..
Bosnia and Herzegovina	..	..	..	..	..	..	..	..	..	..	..	..
Botswana	..	29	..	13	..	28	..	17	..	43	..	71
Brazil	31[c]	25[c]	25[c]	16[c]	27[c]	27[c]	10[c]	13[c]	43[c]	48[c]	65[c]	71[c]
Bulgaria	..	11	..	7	..	39	..	29	..	50	..	64
Burkina Faso	..	..	..	..	..	..	..	..	..	..	..	..
Burundi	..	..	..	..	..	..	..	..	..	..	..	..
Cambodia	..	..	..	..	..	..	..	..	..	..	..	..
Cameroon	53	..	68	..	14	..	4	..	26	..	23	..
Canada	6[c]	4[c]	2[c]	2[c]	31[c]	32[c]	11[c]	11[c]	64[c]	64[c]	87[c]	88[c]
Central African Republic	..	..	..	..	..	..	..	..	..	..	..	..
Chad	..	..	..	..	..	..	..	..	..	..	..	..
Chile	24	17	6	6	32	29	15	12	45	54	79	83
China	..	..	..	..	..	..	..	..	..	..	..	..
Hong Kong, China	1	0[b]	0[b]	0[b]	37	22	27	7	63	77	73	93
Colombia	2[c]	32	1[c]	8	35[c]	21	25[c]	16	63[c]	48	74[c]	76
Congo, Dem. Rep.	..	..	..	..	..	..	..	..	..	..	..	..
Congo, Rep.	..	..	..	..	..	..	..	..	..	..	..	..
Costa Rica	32	21	5	5	27	26	25	13	41	52	69	82
Côte d'Ivoire	..	..	..	..	..	..	..	..	..	..	..	..
Croatia	..	12[d]	..	14[d]	..	40[d]	..	18[d]	..	48[d]	..	67[d]
Cuba	..	28	..	10	..	23	..	14	..	50	..	76
Czech Republic	9	5	7	3	55	49	33	27	36	46	61	71
Denmark	7	4	3	2	37	34	16	12	56	62	81	86
Dominican Republic	26	21	3	3	23	26	21	15	52	53	76	82
Ecuador	10[c]	11[c]	2[c]	4[c]	29[c]	27[c]	17[c]	12[c]	62[c]	62[c]	81[c]	84[c]
Egypt, Arab Rep.	35	28	52	39	25	23	10	6	41	49	37	55
El Salvador	48	30	15	3	23	25	23	22	29	45	63	75
Eritrea	..	..	..	..	..	..	..	..	..	..	..	..
Estonia	23[c]	7[c]	13[c]	4[c]	42[c]	44[c]	30[c]	24[c]	36[c]	49[c]	57[c]	72[c]
Ethiopia	..	84	..	76	..	5	..	8	..	10	..	16
Finland	11	7	6	3	38	38	15	12	51	56	78	84
France	..	5	..	2	..	35	..	12	..	60	..	85
Gabon	..	..	..	..	..	..	..	..	..	..	..	..
Gambia, The	..	..	..	..	..	..	..	..	..	..	..	..
Georgia	..	52	..	57	..	14	..	4	..	34	..	38
Germany	4	3	4	2	50	41	24	16	47	56	72	82
Ghana	66	..	59	..	10	..	10	..	23	..	32	..
Greece	20[c]	12[c]	26[c]	14[c]	32[c]	30[c]	17[c]	10[c]	48[c]	58[c]	56[c]	76[c]
Guatemala	..	..	..	..	..	..	..	..	..	..	..	..
Guinea	..	..	..	..	..	..	..	..	..	..	..	..
Guinea-Bissau	..	..	..	..	..	..	..	..	..	..	..	..
Haiti	..	..	..	..	..	..	..	..	..	..	..	..

Employment by economic activity | **2.3**

	Agriculture				Industry				Services			
	Male % of male employment		Female % of female employment		Male % of male employment		Female % of female employment		Male % of male employment		Female % of female employment	
	1990–92[a]	2003–06[a]	1990–92[a]	2003–06[a]	1990–92[a]	2003–06[a]	1990–92[a]	2003–06[a]	1990–92[a]	2003–06[a]	1990–92[a]	2003–06[a]
Honduras	53[c]	51[c]	6[c]	13[c]	18[c]	20[c]	25[c]	23[c]	29[c]	29[c]	69[c]	63[c]
Hungary	..	7[c]	..	3[c]	..	42[c]	..	21[c]	..	51[c]	..	76[c]
India	..	..	..	..	..	..	..	..	..	..	..	..
Indonesia	54	41[d]	57	41[d]	15	21[d]	13	15[d]	31	38[d]	31	44[d]
Iran, Islamic Rep.	..	23	..	34	..	31	..	28	..	46	..	37
Iraq	..	14	..	33	..	20	..	7	..	66	..	60
Ireland	19	9	3	1	33	39	18	12	48	51	78	86
Israel	5	3	2	1	38	31	15	11	57	65	83	88
Italy	8	5	9	3	37	39	22	18	55	56	70	79
Jamaica	36	25	16	9	25	27	12	5	39	48	72	86
Japan	6	4	7	5	40	35	27	18	54	59	65	77
Jordan	..	4	..	2	..	23	..	12	..	73	..	84
Kazakhstan	..	35	..	32	..	24	..	10	..	41	..	58
Kenya	19[c]	..	20[c]	..	23[c]	..	9[c]	..	58[c]	..	71[c]	..
Korea, Dem. Rep.	..	..	..	..	..	..	..	..	..	..	..	..
Korea, Rep.	14	7	18	9	40	34	28	17	46	59	54	74
Kuwait	..	..	..	..	..	..	..	..	..	..	..	..
Kyrgyz Republic	..	39	..	39	..	23	..	11	..	38	..	50
Lao PDR	..	..	..	..	..	..	..	..	..	..	..	..
Latvia	..	15[c]	..	8[c]	..	35[c]	..	16[c]	..	49[c]	..	75[c]
Lebanon	..	..	..	..	..	..	..	..	..	..	..	..
Lesotho	..	..	..	..	..	..	..	..	..	..	..	..
Liberia	..	..	..	..	..	..	..	..	..	..	..	..
Libya	..	..	..	..	..	..	..	..	..	..	..	..
Lithuania	25	17[c]	15	11[c]	46	37[c]	31	21[c]	29	46[c]	54	68[c]
Macedonia, FYR	..	20	..	19	..	34	..	30	..	46	..	51
Madagascar	..	77	..	79	..	7	..	6	..	16	..	15
Malawi	..	..	..	..	..	..	..	..	..	..	..	..
Malaysia	23	16	20	11	31	35	32	27	46	49	48	62
Mali	..	50	..	30	..	18	..	15	..	32	..	55
Mauritania	..	..	..	..	..	..	..	..	..	..	..	..
Mauritius	15	11	13	9	36	34	48	29	48	55	39	62
Mexico	34	21	11	5	25	30	19	19	41	49	70	76
Moldova	..	41	..	40	..	21	..	12	..	38	..	48
Mongolia	..	43	..	37	..	19	..	15	..	38	..	48
Morocco	..	40	..	61	..	21	..	16	..	39	..	23
Mozambique	..	..	..	..	..	..	..	..	..	..	..	..
Myanmar	..	..	..	..	..	..	..	..	..	..	..	..
Namibia	45	..	52	..	21	..	8	..	34	..	40	..
Nepal	75	..	91	..	4	..	1	..	20	..	8	..
Netherlands	5	4	3	2	33	30	10	8	60	62	82	86
New Zealand	13	9	8	5	31	32	13	11	56	59	80	84
Nicaragua	..	41	..	10	..	19	..	17	..	33	..	52
Niger	..	..	..	..	..	..	..	..	..	..	..	..
Nigeria	..	..	..	..	..	..	..	..	..	..	..	..
Norway	7	5	3	2	34	32	10	8	58	63	86	90
Oman	..	..	..	..	..	..	..	..	..	..	..	..
Pakistan	45	38	69	67	20	21	15	15	35	41	16	18
Panama	35	22	3	4	20	22	11	9	45	56	85	86
Papua New Guinea	..	..	..	..	..	..	..	..	..	..	..	..
Paraguay	3[c]	39[c]	0[b,c]	20[c]	33[c]	19[c]	19[c]	10[c]	64[c]	42[c]	80[c]	70[c]
Peru	1[c]	1[c]	0[b,c]	0[b,c]	30[c]	31[c]	13[c]	13[c]	69[c]	68[c]	87[c]	86[c]
Philippines	53[c]	45	32[c]	25	17[c]	17	14[c]	12	29[c]	39	55[c]	64
Poland	..	18[c]	..	17[c]	..	39[c]	..	17[c]	..	43[c]	..	66[c]
Portugal	10[c]	11[c]	13[c]	13[c]	39[c]	41[c]	24[c]	19[c]	51[c]	48[c]	63[c]	68[c]
Puerto Rico	5	3	0[b]	0[b]	27	25	19	11	67	72	80	89

	Agriculture				Industry				Services			
	Male % of male employment		Female % of female employment		Male % of male employment		Female % of female employment		Male % of male employment		Female % of female employment	
	1990–92[a]	2003–06[a]	1990–92[a]	2003–06[a]	1990–92[a]	2003–06[a]	1990–92[a]	2003–06[a]	1990–92[a]	2003–06[a]	1990–92[a]	2003–06[a]
Romania	29	31	38	33	44	35	30	25	28	34	33	42
Russian Federation	..	12	..	8	..	38	..	21	..	50	..	71
Rwanda	..	..	..	..	..	..	..	..	..	..	..	..
Saudi Arabia	..	5	..	0[b]	..	11	..	1	..	85	..	99
Senegal	..	..	..	..	..	..	..	..	..	..	..	..
Serbia	..	21[e]	..	20[e]	..	37[e]	..	20[e]	..	42[e]	..	60[e]
Sierra Leone	..	..	..	..	..	..	..	..	..	..	..	..
Singapore	1	0	0[b]	0	36	36	32	21	63	63	68	79
Slovak Republic	..	6[c]	..	3[c]	..	50[c]	..	25[c]	..	44[c]	..	72[c]
Slovenia	..	9	..	9	..	47	..	25	..	43	..	65
Somalia	..	..	..	..	..	..	..	..	..	..	..	..
South Africa	..	13	..	7	..	33	..	14	..	54	..	79
Spain	11[c]	6[c]	8[c]	4[c]	41[c]	41[c]	16[c]	12[c]	49[c]	52[c]	76[c]	84[c]
Sri Lanka	..	..	..	..	..	..	..	..	..	..	..	..
Sudan	..	..	..	..	..	..	..	..	..	..	..	..
Swaziland	..	..	..	..	..	..	..	..	..	..	..	..
Sweden	5[c]	3[c]	2[c]	1[c]	40[c]	34[c]	12[c]	9[c]	55[c]	63[c]	86[c]	90[c]
Switzerland	4[c]	5[c]	4[c]	3[c]	37[c]	32[c]	15[c]	11[c]	59[c]	63[c]	81[c]	86[c]
Syrian Arab Republic	23	23	54	49	28	29	8	8	49	48	38	43
Tajikistan	..	..	..	..	..	..	..	..	..	..	..	..
Tanzania	78[c]	..	90[c]	..	7[c]	..	1[c]	..	15[c]	..	8[c]	..
Thailand	60	44	62	41	18	22	13	19	22	34	25	41
Timor-Leste	..	..	..	..	..	..	..	..	..	..	..	..
Togo	..	..	..	..	..	..	..	..	..	..	..	..
Trinidad and Tobago	15	6	6	2	34	41	14	16	51	52	80	82
Tunisia	..	..	..	..	..	..	..	..	..	..	..	..
Turkey	33	22	72	52	26	28	11	15	41	50	17	33
Turkmenistan	..	..	..	..	..	..	..	..	..	..	..	..
Uganda	91	60[c]	91	77[c]	4	11[c]	6	5[c]	5	29[c]	3	18[c]
Ukraine	..	..	..	..	..	..	..	..	..	..	..	..
United Arab Emirates	..	..	..	..	..	..	..	..	..	..	..	..
United Kingdom	3	2	1	1	41	33	16	9	55	65	82	90
United States	4	2	1	1	34	30	14	10	62	68	85	90
Uruguay	7[c]	7[c]	1[c]	2[c]	36[c]	29[c]	21[c]	13[c]	57[c]	64[c]	78[c]	86[c]
Uzbekistan	..	..	..	..	..	..	..	..	..	..	..	..
Venezuela, RB	17	16[c]	2	2[c]	32	25[c]	16	11[c]	52	59[c]	82	86[c]
Vietnam	..	56	..	60	..	21	..	14	..	23	..	26
West Bank and Gaza	..	12	..	34	..	28	..	8	..	59	..	56
Yemen, Rep.	44	..	83	..	14	..	2	..	38	..	13	..
Zambia	..	..	..	..	..	..	..	..	..	..	..	..
Zimbabwe	..	..	..	..	..	..	..	..	..	..	..	..
World	.. w	.. w	.. w	.. w	.. w	.. w	.. w	.. w	.. w	.. w	.. w	.. w
Low income	..	..	..	..	..	..	..	..	..	..	..	..
Middle income	..	..	..	..	..	..	..	..	..	..	..	..
Lower middle income	..	..	..	..	..	..	..	..	..	..	..	..
Upper middle income	..	20	..	14	..	30	..	17	..	49	..	68
Low & middle income	..	..	..	..	..	..	..	..	..	..	..	..
East Asia & Pacific	..	..	..	..	..	..	..	..	..	..	..	..
Europe & Central Asia	..	19	..	19	..	34	..	20	..	47	..	62
Latin America & Carib.	21	21	14	10	30	27	14	15	49	52	71	76
Middle East & N. Africa	..	..	..	..	..	..	..	..	..	..	..	..
South Asia	..	..	..	..	..	..	..	..	..	..	..	..
Sub-Saharan Africa	..	..	..	..	..	..	..	..	..	..	..	..
High income	6	4	5	3	38	34	19	13	56	62	76	84
Euro area	7	5	7	3	42	38	21	14	50	56	72	82

Note: Data across sectors may not sum to 100 percent because of workers not classified by sectors.
a. Data are for the most recent year available. b. Less than 0.5. c. Limited coverage. d. Data are for 2007. e. Data are for 2008.

Employment by economic activity **2.3**

The International Labour Organization (ILO) classifies economic activity using the International Standard Industrial Classification (ISIC) of All Economic Activities, revision 2 (1968) and revision 3 (1990). Because this classification is based on where work is performed (industry) rather than type of work performed (occupation), all of an enterprise's employees are classified under the same industry, regardless of their trade or occupation. The categories should sum to 100 percent. Where they do not, the differences are due to workers who cannot be classified by economic activity.

Data on employment are drawn from labor force surveys, household surveys, official estimates, censuses and administrative records of social insurance schemes, and establishment surveys when no other information is available. The concept of employment generally refers to people above a certain age who worked, or who held a job, during a reference period. Employment data include both full-time and part-time workers.

There are many differences in how countries define and measure employment status, particularly members of the armed forces, self-employed workers, and unpaid family workers. Where members of the armed forces are included, they are allocated to the service sector, causing that sector to be somewhat overstated relative to the service sector in economies where they are excluded. Where data are obtained from establishment surveys, data cover only employees; thus self-employed and unpaid family workers are excluded. In such cases the employment share of the agricultural sector is severely underreported. Caution should be also used where the data refer only to urban areas, which record little or no agricultural work. Moreover, the age group and area covered could differ by country or change over time within a country. For detailed information on breaks in series, consult the original source.

Countries also take different approaches to the treatment of unemployed people. In most countries unemployed people with previous job experience are classified according to their last job. But in some countries the unemployed and people seeking their first job are not classifiable by economic activity. Because of these differences, the size and distribution of employment by economic activity may not be fully comparable across countries.

The ILO's *Yearbook of Labour Statistics* and its database Key Indicators of the Labour Market report data by major divisions of the ISIC revision 2 or revision 3. In the table the reported divisions or categories are aggregated into three broad groups: agriculture, industry, and services. Such broad classification may obscure fundamental shifts within countries' industrial patterns. A slight majority of countries report economic activity according to the ISIC revision 2 instead of revision 3. The use of one classification or the other should not have a significant impact on the information for the three broad sectors presented in the table.

The distribution of economic wealth in the world remains strongly correlated with employment by economic activity. The wealthier economies are those with the largest share of total employment in services, whereas the poorer economies are largely agriculture based.

The distribution of economic activity by gender reveals some clear patterns. Men still make up the majority of people employed in all three sectors, but the gender gap is biggest in industry. Employment in agriculture is also male-dominated, although not as much as industry. Segregating one sex in a narrow range of occupations significantly reduces economic efficiency by reducing labor market flexibility and thus the economy's ability to adapt to change. This segregation is particularly harmful for women, who have a much narrower range of labor market choices and lower levels of pay than men. But it is also detrimental to men when job losses are concentrated in industries dominated by men and job growth is centered in service occupations, where women have better chances, as has been the recent experience in many countries.

There are several explanations for the rising importance of service jobs for women. Many service jobs—such as nursing and social and clerical work—are considered "feminine" because of a perceived similarity to women's traditional roles. Women often do not receive the training needed to take advantage of changing employment opportunities. And the greater availability of part-time work in service industries may lure more women, although it is unclear whether this is a cause or an effect.

• **Agriculture** corresponds to division 1 (ISIC revision 2) or tabulation categories A and B (ISIC revision 3) and includes hunting, forestry, and fishing.
• **Industry** corresponds to divisions 2–5 (ISIC revision 2) or tabulation categories C–F (ISIC revision 3) and includes mining and quarrying (including oil production), manufacturing, construction, and public utilities (electricity, gas, and water). • **Services** correspond to divisions 6–9 (ISIC revision 2) or tabulation categories G–P (ISIC revision 3) and include wholesale and retail trade and restaurants and hotels; transport, storage, and communications; financing, insurance, real estate, and business services; and community, social, and personal services.

Data sources

Data on employment are from the ILO database Key Indicators of the Labour Market, 5th edition.

2.4 Decent work and productive employment

	Employment to population ratio				Gross enrollment ratio, secondary		Vulnerable employment				Labor productivity	
	Total % ages 15 and older		Youth % ages 15–24		% of relevant age group		Unpaid family workers and own-account workers				GDP per person employed % growth	
							Male % of male employment		Female % of female employment			
	1991	2007	1991	2007	1991	2007a	1990	2007	1990	2007	1992	2008
Afghanistan	..	..	..	..	..	..	..	..	..	..	..	..
Albania	53	51	39	36	88	..	..	..	..	..	−3.9	4.9
Algeria	39	51	25	34	60	83	..	..	..	..	−0.1	0.1
Angola	76	76	69	68	11	17	..	..	..	..	−10.3	7.8
Argentina	54	58	43	39	72	84	..	22b	..	17b	9.6	5.0
Armenia	39	40	24	26	..	89	..	..	..	..	−39.5	11.2
Australia	57	62	58	64	83	150	12	11	9	7	0.4	0.6
Austria	54	57	61	53	102	102	..	9	..	9	0.3	0.2
Azerbaijan	57	61	38	39	88	..	..	41	..	66	−23.7	9.3
Bangladesh	75	68	67	56	20	..	..	85	..	87	5.2	2.3
Belarus	59	53	40	34	93	95	..	..	..	..	−8.7	9.6
Belgium	46	49	31	27	101	110	..	11	..	9	0.3	0.3
Benin	71	72	64	59	10	32	..	..	..	..	−2.1	1.6
Bolivia	62	70	48	49	44	82	32b	..	50b	..	0.0	2.7
Bosnia and Herzegovina	52	41	28	16	..	85	..	..	..	..	0.8	4.7
Botswana	49	46	39	26	48	76	..	..	..	..	0.8	−0.7
Brazil	56	65	54	53	58	105	29b	30	30b	24	−8.2	3.8
Bulgaria	46	47	28	26	86	105	..	10	..	7	−11.6	4.6
Burkina Faso	81	81	77	74	7	16	..	..	..	..	−3.0	1.2
Burundi	84	83	73	72	5	15	..	..	..	..	−1.0	0.2
Cambodia	78	79	68	75	25	42	..	..	..	..	4.7	3.8
Cameroon	59	59	39	35	26	25	..	..	..	..	−5.8	1.1
Canada	59	64	57	61	101	..	..	12b	..	9b	2.1	−0.6
Central African Republic	72	71	57	57	11	..	..	..	..	..	−9.0	0.4
Chad	66	69	50	49	7	19	..	..	..	..	3.0	−3.5
Chile	51	51	34	24	73	91	..	25	..	24	6.9	2.8
China	76	73	72	56	40	76	..	..	..	..	11.8	8.6
Hong Kong, China	63	59	54	39	80	86	..	10	..	4	5.7	1.8
Colombia	52	63	37	44	50	85	30b	41	26b	41	−0.1	2.0
Congo, Dem. Rep.	67	66	58	61	21	33	..	..	..	..	−13.6	5.0
Congo, Rep.	65	64	48	45	46	..	..	..	..	..	−0.4	5.9
Costa Rica	57	59	48	44	45	87	26	20	21	20	4.2	1.7
Côte d'Ivoire	62	60	51	45	21	..	..	..	..	..	−3.1	0.6
Croatia	46	47	25	29	..	91	..	18b	..	18b	−11.5	1.6
Cuba	53	56	39	32	94	93	..	..	..	..	..	..
Czech Republic	58	56	45	29	91	96	..	15	..	9	−1.1	3.6
Denmark	62	63	65	62	109	120	..	..	..	..	1.7	0.7
Dominican Republic	44	53	28	33	..	79	42	49	30	30	6.4	4.4
Ecuador	52	60	39	39	55	70	33b	29b	41b	41b	−3.1	2.8
Egypt, Arab Rep.	43	42	22	22	71	..	..	20	..	44	1.8	4.5
El Salvador	59	58	42	41	36	64	..	29	..	44	6.9	1.6
Eritrea	65	65	58	53	..	29	..	..	..	..	15.3	−2.5
Estonia	63	57	44	30	104	100	2	8	3	4	−18.5	2.1
Ethiopia	72	81	65	74	13	30	..	48	..	56	−11.7	7.7
Finland	59	57	45	44	116	112	..	..	..	..	3.8	1.1
France	50	51	28	29	98	114	..	8	..	5	1.7	0.5
Gabon	58	59	37	34	39	..	..	..	..	..	−7.5	−0.7
Gambia, The	72	72	58	54	17	49	..	..	..	..	−0.3	2.3
Georgia	58	56	28	22	95	90	..	64	..	65	−43.3	4.1
Germany	56	54	58	43	98	102	..	..	..	..	3.8	−0.7
Ghana	69	65	40	40	34	49	..	..	..	..	−1.2	3.8
Greece	46	50	31	28	94	103	..	28	..	27	−2.0	1.6
Guatemala	56	63	52	53	23	56	..	..	..	..	3.4	1.0
Guinea	82	82	75	73	10	35	..	..	..	..	−0.9	2.2
Guinea-Bissau	66	66	57	62	6	..	..	..	..	..	−2.2	0.5
Haiti	56	56	37	48	21	..	..	..	..	..	−10.2	0.0

Decent work and productive employment | **2.4**

	Employment to population ratio				Gross enrollment ratio, secondary		Vulnerable employment				Labor productivity	
								Unpaid family workers and own-account workers				GDP per person employed
	Total % ages 15 and older		Youth % ages 15–24		% of relevant age group		Male % of male employment		Female % of female employment		% growth	
	1991	2007	1991	2007	1991	2007[a]	1990	2007	1990	2007	1992	2008
Honduras	59	56	49	43	33	61	48[b]	..	50[b]	..	−0.4	1.9
Hungary	50	47	39	21	86	96	8	8	7	6	−3.0	2.3
India	59	55	47	39	42	55	..	..	..	..	2.4	5.4
Indonesia	63	62	46	41	45	66	..	60	..	68	4.3	4.2
Iran, Islamic Rep.	46	48	33	35	57	73	..	40	..	56	2.6	1.4
Iraq	35	..	23	..	44	..	..	..	..	..	..	..
Ireland	45	60	38	47	100	112	25	16	9	5	2.5	0.0
Israel	46	51	25	27	92	92	..	9	..	5	1.3	2.3
Italy	45	46	30	26	83	100	..	27	..	16	0.9	−0.4
Jamaica	62	58	39	32	65	87	46	38	37	31	0.9	−0.7
Japan	63	57	43	41	97	101	15	10	26	12	−0.3	0.4
Jordan	36	39	24	19	82	89	..	..	..	..	8.2	1.7
Kazakhstan	64	64	46	42	100	92[d]	..	..	..	..	−1.5	2.8
Kenya	72	73	61	59	46	50	..	..	..	..	−5.2	−1.1
Korea, Dem. Rep.	62	65	46	40	..	..	..	..	..	..	..	..
Korea, Rep.	59	59	36	29	90	98	..	23	..	28	3.9	1.9
Kuwait	62	66	30	32	43	91	..	..	..	..	52.3	3.0
Kyrgyz Republic	60	59	41	40	100	86	..	47	..	47	−14.3	5.6
Lao PDR	80	78	74	64	23	44	..	..	..	..	3.8	4.3
Latvia	59	57	42	35	92	99	..	9	..	6	−31.7	1.7
Lebanon	46	46	32	28	62	81	..	..	..	..	1.0	6.2
Lesotho	51	56	43	43	24	37	..	..	..	..	5.6	4.8
Liberia	66	66	57	57	..	..	..	..	..	..	−34.1	4.3
Libya	46	49	28	28	..	94	..	..	..	..	−5.5	4.5
Lithuania	55	53	35	20	92	99	..	..	..	..	−20.0	8.3
Macedonia, FYR	38	35	19	14	..	84	..	24	..	20	−5.7	4.3
Madagascar	79	83	65	70	17	26	..	84	..	89	−2.8	3.1
Malawi	72	72	49	49	8	28	..	..	..	..	−10.6	5.0
Malaysia	60	61	47	44	57	69	31	23	25	21	6.2	3.6
Mali	48	46	39	34	8	32	..	..	..	..	5.2	1.8
Mauritania	54	47	43	31	14	25	..	..	..	..	−0.9	2.7
Mauritius	56	55	46	37	55	88	13	18	7	15	−2.5	2.9
Mexico	57	58	50	43	53	87	29	28	15	32	−0.2	0.6
Moldova	59	44	38	17	78	89	..	35	..	30	−28.6	7.6
Mongolia	51	52	40	35	82	92	..	..	..	..	−12.8	7.9
Morocco	46	46	40	34	36	56	..	47	..	65	−7.1	4.2
Mozambique	79	77	66	64	7	18	..	..	..	..	−13.1	4.3
Myanmar	75	75	62	54	23	..	..	..	..	..	7.1	3.0
Namibia	46	42	24	14	45	59	..	..	..	..	3.6	0.2
Nepal	61	62	54	45	34	48[d]	..	..	..	..	−0.6	1.7
Netherlands	53	61	55	65	120	118	..	..	..	..	−0.3	0.5
New Zealand	57	65	55	56	90	120	15	14	10	10	0.1	−0.4
Nicaragua	53	59	41	48	42	66	..	45	..	46	−5.5	0.4
Niger	60	60	50	51	7	11	..	..	..	..	−10.0	2.4
Nigeria	52	51	28	24	24	32	..	..	..	..	0.2	2.4
Norway	60	65	49	56	103	113	..	8	..	3	4.1	1.0
Oman	53	51	30	29	45	90	..	..	..	..	1.6	2.8
Pakistan	48	51	39	43	25	33	..	58	..	75	4.6	1.8
Panama	50	60	34	40	62	70	44	30	19	24	1.9	7.4
Papua New Guinea	70	70	58	55	12	..	..	..	..	..	11.8	4.2
Paraguay	62	73	51	58	31	66	17[b]	45	31[b]	50	−2.1	2.2
Peru	58	68	45	52	67	94	30[b]	33[b]	46[b]	47[b]	−3.6	6.7
Philippines	59	61	42	40	71	83	..	44	..	47	−3.4	3.1
Poland	54	49	32	26	87	100	..	21	..	18	4.1	1.3
Portugal	59	58	53	36	66	97	18[b]	18	21[b]	19	3.3	−0.2
Puerto Rico	38	42	21	29	..	..	..	..	..	..	..	..

Decent work and productive employment

	Employment to population ratio				Gross enrollment ratio, secondary		Vulnerable employment				Labor productivity	
	Total % ages 15 and older		Youth % ages 15–24		% of relevant age group		Unpaid family workers and own-account workers				GDP per person employed % growth	
							Male % of male employment		Female % of female employment			
	1991	2007	1991	2007	1991	2007[a]	1990	2007	1990	2007	1992	2008
Romania	57	50	42	24	92	86	7[b]	32	11[b]	33	–13.3	9.4
Russian Federation	58	59	34	33	93	84	1	6	1	6	–19.2	6.3
Rwanda	87	80	79	64	9	18	..	..	..	..	13.7	5.2
Saudi Arabia	51	51	27	25	44	94	..	..	..	..	2.0	2.7
Senegal	67	66	59	54	15	24	77	..	91	..	–1.6	0.7
Serbia	50[c]	49[c]	28[c]	30[c]	..	88	..	25	..	20	..	..
Sierra Leone	64	64	39	42	17	32	..	..	..	..	–19.5	3.8
Singapore	64	62	56	37	..	..	10	12	6	7	3.5	–0.9
Slovak Republic	56	53	43	30	..	96	..	13[b]	..	5[b]	–8.0	4.6
Slovenia	56	56	38	33	89	95	..	14	..	13	1.4	3.6
Somalia	65	66	58	57	..	..	..	..	..	..	..	..
South Africa	40	41	20	14	69	96	..	2	..	3	–6.0	2.7
Spain	43	53	36	38	105	119	20	13	24	10	3.7	7.1
Sri Lanka	52	55	32	35	71	..	..	39[b]	..	44[b]	5.1	4.3
Sudan	46	47	29	24	21	35[d]	..	..	..	..	4.3	5.2
Swaziland	54	51	34	26	42	47	..	..	..	..	–0.5	1.3
Sweden	65	61	59	45	90	103	..	..	..	..	3.3	0.6
Switzerland	68	64	69	63	99	93	8	10	11	11	0.3	1.5
Syrian Arab Republic	47	45	38	33	48	72	..	..	..	..	8.1	1.5
Tajikistan	54	55	36	55	102	84	..	..	..	..	–27.4	3.2
Tanzania	88	78	79	70	5	..	..	82[b]	..	93[b]	–2.8	4.2
Thailand	78	72	70	47	33	83	67	51	74	56	6.8	3.3
Timor-Leste	64	67	51	58	..	53	..	..	..	..	..	..
Togo	65	64	57	52	20	39	..	..	..	..	–6.5	–2.4
Trinidad and Tobago	45	62	33	47	82	76	22	17	21	13	–4.8	2.7
Tunisia	41	42	29	23	45	85	..	..	..	..	4.7	2.1
Turkey	53	43	48	31	48	79	..	32	..	50	4.4	0.1
Turkmenistan	56	59	34	34	..	..	..	..	..	..	–8.7	7.2
Uganda	85	83	78	76	11	18	..	..	..	..	0.2	6.1
Ukraine	59	54	37	34	94	94	..	..	..	..	–8.8	3.0
United Arab Emirates	71	75	43	47	68	92	..	..	..	..	–3.3	4.7
United Kingdom	58	59	66	56	87	98	..	..	..	..	2.7	1.0
United States	61	62	56	52	92	94	..	..	..	..	2.7	3.0
Uruguay	54	58	43	38	84	101	..	26	..	24	4.4	9.7
Uzbekistan	55	58	36	38	99	102	..	..	..	..	–11.4	5.7
Venezuela, RB	52	60	36	38	53	79	..	28	..	33	0.7	2.7
Vietnam	76	71	75	52	32	..	..	..	..	..	5.8	4.0
West Bank and Gaza	29	32	19	16	..	92	..	34	..	47	..	..
Yemen, Rep.	38	39	23	22	..	46	..	..	..	..	2.6	–0.2
Zambia	57	61	40	47	23	43	56	..	81	..	–3.9	3.2
Zimbabwe	70	67	48	51	49	40	..	..	..	..	..	..
World	**63 w**	**61 w**	**53 w**	**45 w**	**51 w**	**66 w**	**.. w**	**.. w**	**.. w**	**.. w**	**–0.4 w**	**3.1 w**
Low income	66	65	55	51	25	38	..	..	..	..	–0.5	3.8
Middle income	64	62	54	43	51	70	..	..	..	..	–1.7	6.1
Lower middle income	66	63	56	44	47	65	..	..	..	..	3.1	7.7
Upper middle income	55	56	43	38	68	91	..	23	..	20	–7.2	3.9
Low & middle income	64	62	54	45	45	61	..	..	..	..	–1.6	5.8
East Asia & Pacific	74	71	67	52	47	73	..	..	..	..	8.5	8.6
Europe & Central Asia	56	54	38	32	85	88	..	19	..	18	–11.9	4.6
Latin America & Carib.	55	61	47	46	51	89	30	31	28	31	–1.8	3.4
Middle East & N. Africa	43	45	28	28	57	71	..	34	..	52	1.2	3.2
South Asia	59	56	48	42	38	49	..	..	..	..	3.0	6.5
Sub-Saharan Africa	64	64	50	49	21	32	..	..	..	..	–4.0	3.7
High income	57	58	47	44	92	101	..	..	..	..	2.0	1.9
Euro area	50	52	41	37	..	..	..	14	..	9	2.2	1.4

a. Provisional data. b. Limited coverage. c. Includes Montenegro. d. Data are for 2008.

Decent work and productive employment | 2.4

Four targets were added to the UN Millennium Declaration at the 2005 World Summit High-Level Plenary Meeting of the 60th Session of the UN General Assembly. One was full and productive employment and decent work for all, which is seen as the main route for people to escape poverty. The four indicators for this target have an economic focus, and three of them are presented in the table.

The employment to population ratio indicates how efficiently an economy provides jobs for people who want to work. A high ratio means that a large proportion of the population is employed. But a lower employment to population ratio can be seen as a positive sign, especially for young people, if it is caused by an increase in their education. This indicator has a gender bias because women who do not consider their work employment or who are not perceived as working tend to be undercounted. This bias has different effects across countries.

Comparability of employment ratios across countries is also affected by variations in definitions of employment and population (see *About the data* for table 2.3). The biggest difference results from the age range used to define labor force activity. The population base for employment ratios can also vary (see table 2.1). Most countries use the resident, noninstitutionalized population of working age living in private households, which excludes members of the armed forces and individuals residing in mental, penal, or other types of institutions. But some countries include members of the armed forces in the population base of their employment ratio while excluding them from employment data (International Labour Organization, *Key Indicators of the Labour Market,* 5th edition).

The proportion of unpaid family workers and own-account workers in total employment is derived from information on status in employment. Each status group faces different economic risks, and unpaid family workers and own-account workers are the most vulnerable—and therefore the most likely to fall into poverty. They are the least likely to have formal work arrangements, are the least likely to have social protection and safety nets to guard against economic shocks, and often are incapable of generating sufficient savings to offset these shocks. A high proportion of unpaid family workers in a country indicates weak development, little job growth, and often a large rural economy.

Data on employment by status are drawn from labor force surveys and household surveys, supplemented by official estimates and censuses for a small group of countries. The labor force survey is the most comprehensive source for internationally comparable employment, but there are still some limitations for comparing data across countries and over time even within a country. Information from labor force surveys is not always consistent in what is included in employment. For example, information provided by the Organisation for Economic Cooperation and Development relates only to civilian employment, which can result in an underestimation of "employees" and "workers not classified by status," especially in countries with large armed forces. While the categories of unpaid family workers and self-employed workers, which include own-account workers, would not be affected, their relative shares would be. Geographic coverage is another factor that can limit cross-country comparisons. The employment by status data for most Latin American countries covers urban areas only. Similarly, in some countries in Sub-Saharan Africa, where limited information is available anyway, the members of producer cooperatives are usually excluded from the self-employed category. For detailed information on definitions and coverage, consult the original source.

Labor productivity is used to assess a country's economic ability to create and sustain decent employment opportunities with fair and equitable remuneration. Productivity increases obtained through investment, trade, technological progress, or changes in work organization can increase social protection and reduce poverty, which in turn reduce vulnerable employment and working poverty. Productivity increases do not guarantee these improvements, but without them—and the economic growth they bring—improvements are highly unlikely. For comparability of individual sectors labor productivity is estimated according to national accounts conventions. However, there are still significant limitations on the availability of reliable data. Information on consistent series of output in both national currencies and purchasing power parity dollars is not easily available, especially in developing countries, because the definition, coverage, and methodology are not always consistent across countries. For example, countries employ different methodologies for estimating the missing values for the nonmarket service sectors and use different definitions of the informal sector.

• **Employment to population ratio** is the proportion of a country's population that is employed. People ages 15 and older are generally considered the working-age population. People ages 15–24 are generally considered the youth population. • **Gross enrollment ratio, secondary,** is the ratio of total enrollment in secondary education, regardless of age, to the population of the age group that officially corresponds to secondary education. • **Vulnerable employment** is unpaid family workers and own-account workers as a percentage of total employment. • **Labor productivity** is the growth rate of gross domestic product (GDP) divided by total employment in the economy.

Data on employment to population ratio, vulnerable employment, and labor productivity are from the International Labour Organization database Key Indicators of the Labour Market, 5th edition. Data on gross enrollment ratios are from the UNESCO Institute for Statistics.

	Unemployment						Long-term unemployment			Unemployment by educational attainment		
	Total % of total labor force		Male % of male labor force		Female % of female labor force		% of total unemployment			% of total unemployment		
							Total	Male	Female	Primary	Secondary	Tertiary
	1990–92[a]	2004–07[a]	1990–92[a]	2004–07[a]	1990–92[a]	2004–07[a]	2004–07[a]	2004–07[a]	2004–07[a]	2004–07[a]	2004–07[a]	2004–07[a]
Afghanistan	..	..	..	..	..	..	..	..	..	..	..	..
Albania	..	..	..	..	..	..	..	..	..	98.3	..	1.7
Algeria	23.0	12.3	24.2	..	20.3	..	..	..	..	59.3	23.0	11.4
Angola	..	..	..	..	..	..	..	..	..	..	..	..
Argentina	6.7[b]	9.5[b]	6.4[b]	7.8[b]	7.0[b]	11.6[b]	..	..	..	37.3[b]	41.8[b]	19.7[b]
Armenia	..	9.6	..	5.7	..	13.8	..	..	..	5.2	83.0	11.9
Australia	10.8	4.4	11.4	4.0	10.0	4.8	15.5[b]	16.5[b]	14.4[b]	48.0	34.1	17.9
Austria	3.6	4.4	3.5	3.9	3.8	5.0	26.8	26.6	27.1	37.9[b]	52.1[b]	10.0[b]
Azerbaijan	..	..	..	..	..	..	..	..	..	6.3	78.9	14.9
Bangladesh	..	4.3	..	3.4	..	7.0	..	..	..	33.0	24.4	15.9
Belarus	..	..	..	..	..	..	..	..	..	10.0	39.0	51.0
Belgium	6.7	7.6	4.8	6.7	9.5	8.7	50.0	49.1	51.0	42.1	38.2	19.7
Benin	1.5	..	2.2	..	0.6	..	..	..	..	..	..	..
Bolivia	5.5[b]	..	5.5[b]	..	5.6[b]	..	..	..	..	..	..	..
Bosnia and Herzegovina	17.6	31.1	15.5	28.9	21.6	34.8	..	..	..	..	..	..
Botswana	..	17.6	..	15.3	..	19.9	..	..	..	..	..	..
Brazil	6.4[b]	8.9[b]	5.4[b]	6.8[b]	7.9[b]	11.7[b]	..	..	..	51.6[b]	33.6[b]	3.6[b]
Bulgaria	..	8.9	..	8.6	..	9.3	..	..	..	41.8	49.7	8.6
Burkina Faso	..	..	..	..	..	..	..	..	..	..	..	..
Burundi	0.5	..	0.7	..	0.3	..	..	..	..	..	..	..
Cambodia	..	..	..	..	..	..	..	..	..	..	..	..
Cameroon	..	..	..	..	..	..	..	..	..	..	..	..
Canada	11.2[b]	6.0[b]	12.0[b]	6.4[b]	10.2[b]	5.6[b]	7.5[b]	8.4[b]	6.3[b]	27.7[b]	41.1[b]	31.2[b]
Central African Republic	..	..	..	..	..	..	..	..	..	..	..	..
Chad	..	..	..	..	..	..	..	..	..	..	..	..
Chile	4.4	8.9	3.9	..	5.3	..	..	..	..	17.0	57.9	24.8
China	2.3[b]	4.0[b]	..	..	..	..	..	..	..	..	..	..
Hong Kong, China	2.0	4.0	2.0	4.5	1.9	3.4	..	..	..	40.8	41.4	16.6
Colombia	9.5	10.9	6.8	8.7	13.0	13.8	..	..	..	76.6	..	20.6
Congo, Dem. Rep.	..	..	..	..	..	..	..	..	..	..	..	..
Congo, Rep.	..	..	..	..	..	..	..	..	..	..	..	..
Costa Rica	4.1	4.6	3.5	3.3	5.4	6.8	..	..	..	65.2	27.3	6.4
Côte d'Ivoire	6.7	..	..	..	..	..	..	..	..	..	..	..
Croatia	..	9.6	..	8.3	..	11.2	58.8	54.6	61.8	20.4	67.8	11.8
Cuba	..	1.9	..	1.7	..	2.2	..	..	..	43.0	52.4	4.6
Czech Republic	..	5.3	..	4.2	..	6.7	53.4	51.7	54.7	26.8	68.8	4.3
Denmark	9.0	3.6	8.3	3.2	9.9	4.0	18.2	18.4	17.9	35.9	35.1	23.0
Dominican Republic	20.7	17.9	12.0	11.3	35.2	28.8	..	..	..	..	..	..
Ecuador	8.9	7.9	6.0	5.8	13.2	10.8	..	..	..	74.0	..	23.6
Egypt, Arab Rep.	9.0	9.0	6.4	6.0	17.0	18.6	..	..	..	..	..	..
El Salvador	7.9	6.6	8.4	8.5	7.2	3.9	..	..	..	..	..	..
Eritrea	..	..	..	..	..	..	..	..	..	..	..	..
Estonia	3.7	4.7	3.9	5.4	3.5	3.9	..	..	..	23.1	57.8	16.6
Ethiopia	..	5.4	..	2.7	..	8.2	..	..	..	35.9	13.3	3.2
Finland	11.6	6.8	13.3	6.4	9.6	7.3	23.0	26.5	19.5	35.5	45.9	18.6
France	10.0	8.0	7.9	7.4	12.7	8.5	40.4	40.6	40.1	39.9	39.6	19.9
Gabon	..	..	..	..	..	..	..	..	..	..	..	..
Gambia, The	..	..	..	..	..	..	..	..	..	..	..	..
Georgia	..	13.3	..	13.9	..	12.6	..	..	..	5.1	52.5	42.3
Germany	6.6	8.6	5.3	8.5	8.4	8.8	56.6	57.5	55.6	33.1	56.3	10.6
Ghana	4.7	..	3.7	..	5.5	..	..	..	..	..	..	..
Greece	7.8	8.1	4.9	5.0	12.9	12.6	50.3	42.1	54.9	29.3	48.4	21.8
Guatemala	..	3.1	..	2.8	..	3.7	..	..	..	..	..	..
Guinea	..	..	..	..	..	..	..	..	..	..	..	..
Guinea-Bissau	..	..	..	..	..	..	..	..	..	..	..	..
Haiti	12.7	..	11.9	..	13.8	..	..	..	..	..	..	..

Unemployment | 2.5

	Unemployment						Long-term unemployment			Unemployment by educational attainment		
	Total % of total labor force		Male % of male labor force		Female % of female labor force		% of total unemployment			% of total unemployment		
							Total	Male	Female	Primary	Secondary	Tertiary
	1990–92[a]	2004–07[a]	1990–92[a]	2004–07[a]	1990–92[a]	2004–07[a]	2004–07[a]	2004–07[a]	2004–07[a]	2004–07[a]	2004–07[a]	2004–07[a]
Honduras	3.2	4.2	3.3	3.2	3.0	6.2	..	..	..	..	..	..
Hungary	9.9	7.4	11.0	7.1	8.7	7.7	47.5	47.3	47.9	33.1	58.7	8.1
India	..	5.0[b]	..	4.9[b]	..	5.3[b]	..	..	..	29.0	37.7	33.3
Indonesia	2.8	9.1	2.7	8.1	3.0	10.8	..	..	..	44.4	40.7	9.6
Iran, Islamic Rep.	11.1	10.5	9.5	9.3	24.4	15.7	..	..	..	41.8	34.7	19.6
Iraq	..	..	..	..	..	..	..	..	..	..	..	..
Ireland	15.2	4.6	15.2	4.8	15.2	4.3	30.3	36.0	21.9	39.8	37.2	18.2
Israel	11.2[b]	7.3[b]	9.2[b]	6.7[b]	13.9[b]	7.9[b]	..	..	..	12.2	12.8	72.5
Italy	11.5	6.1	8.1	4.9	17.3	7.9	49.9	47.3	52.3	46.5	40.6	11.3
Jamaica	15.7	9.4	9.5	5.5	22.8	14.3	..	..	..	9.7	4.3	8.4
Japan	2.2	3.9	2.1	4.0	2.2	3.7	32.0	40.3	19.4	67.2	..	32.8
Jordan	..	12.4	..	11.8	..	16.5	..	..	..	..	..	..
Kazakhstan	..	8.4	..	7.0	..	9.8	..	..	..	7.1	49.0	43.9
Kenya	..	..	..	..	..	..	..	..	..	..	..	..
Korea, Dem. Rep.	..	..	..	..	..	..	..	..	..	..	..	..
Korea, Rep.	2.5	3.2	2.8	3.7	2.1	2.6	0.6	0.7	0.3	15.2	49.7	35.2
Kuwait	..	1.7	..	..	..	..	..	..	..	19.4	41.4	9.6
Kyrgyz Republic	..	8.3	..	7.7	..	9.0	..	..	..	13.3	77.1	9.6
Lao PDR	..	1.4	..	1.3	..	1.4	..	..	..	..	..	..
Latvia	..	6.0	..	6.3	..	5.4	..	..	..	24.3	59.9	14.6
Lebanon	..	8.1	..	..	..	..	..	..	..	..	..	..
Lesotho	..	..	..	..	..	..	..	..	..	..	..	..
Liberia	..	5.6	..	6.8	..	4.2	..	..	..	..	..	..
Libya	..	..	..	..	..	..	..	..	..	..	..	..
Lithuania	..	4.3	..	4.3	..	4.4	..	..	..	14.2	70.4	15.4
Macedonia, FYR	..	34.9	..	34.5	..	35.5	..	..	..	..	..	..
Madagascar	..	2.6	..	1.7	..	3.5	..	..	..	67.7	..	9.3
Malawi	..	7.8	..	5.4	..	10.0	..	..	..	..	..	..
Malaysia	3.7	3.1	..	3.2	..	3.4	..	..	..	13.3	61.6	25.1
Mali	..	8.8	..	7.2	..	10.9	..	..	..	..	..	..
Mauritania	..	33.0	..	25.2	..	..	..	..	..	..	..	..
Mauritius	..	8.5	..	5.3	..	14.4	..	..	..	44.2	48.5	6.4
Mexico	3.1	3.4	2.7	3.2	4.0	3.7	2.7[b]	3.0[b]	2.3[b]	50.7	24.5	22.9
Moldova	..	5.1	..	6.2	..	3.9	..	..	..	..	..	..
Mongolia	..	2.8	..	..	..	..	..	..	..	35.1	45.8	18.5
Morocco	16.0[b]	10.0	13.0[b]	10.1	25.3[b]	10.0	..	..	..	51.1[b]	22.4[b]	21.6[b]
Mozambique	..	..	..	..	..	..	..	..	..	..	..	..
Myanmar	6.0	..	4.7	..	8.8	..	..	..	..	..	..	..
Namibia	19.0	21.9	20.0	19.4	19.0	25.0	..	..	..	..	..	..
Nepal	..	..	..	..	..	..	..	..	..	..	..	..
Netherlands	5.5	3.6	4.3	3.2	7.3	4.1	41.7	43.9	39.8	41.3	39.7	17.0
New Zealand	10.4[b]	3.6[b]	11.0[b]	3.3[b]	9.6[b]	3.9[b]	5.7[b]	6.1[b]	5.4[b]	30.6	38.8	26.9
Nicaragua	14.4	5.2	11.3	5.4	19.5	4.9	..	..	..	72.8	2.1	18.0
Niger	..	..	..	..	..	..	..	..	..	..	..	..
Nigeria	..	..	..	..	..	..	..	..	..	..	..	..
Norway	5.9	2.5	6.6	2.5	5.1	2.4	8.8	10.2	7.1	25.4	49.2	20.6
Oman	..	..	..	..	..	..	..	..	..	..	..	..
Pakistan	5.2	5.3	3.8	4.5	14.0	8.4	..	..	..	14.3	11.4	26.0
Panama	14.7	6.8	10.8	5.3	22.3	9.3	..	..	..	36.0	39.6	24.0
Papua New Guinea	7.7	..	9.0	..	5.9	..	..	..	..	..	..	..
Paraguay	5.3[b]	5.6[b]	6.4[b]	4.2[b]	3.8[b]	7.6[b]	..	..	..	49.9	38.0	9.9
Peru	9.4[b]	6.7[b]	7.5[b]	5.6[b]	12.5[b]	8.0[b]	..	..	..	30.0[b]	31.9[b]	37.6[b]
Philippines	8.6	6.3	7.9	6.4	9.9	6.0	..	..	..	13.6	46.2	39.4
Poland	13.3	9.6	12.2	9.0	14.7	10.3	45.9	45.8	46.0	16.4	73.2	10.4
Portugal	4.1[b]	8.0	3.5[b]	6.6	5.0[b]	9.6	47.3	48.2	46.7	68.1	15.4	13.2
Puerto Rico	16.9	10.9	19.1	12.0	13.3	9.5	..	..	..	..	..	..

	Unemployment						Long-term unemployment			Unemployment by educational attainment		
	Total % of total labor force		Male % of male labor force		Female % of female labor force		% of total unemployment			% of total unemployment		
	1990–92[a]	2004–07[a]	1990–92[a]	2004–07[a]	1990–92[a]	2004–07[a]	Total 2004–07[a]	Male 2004–07[a]	Female 2004–07[a]	Primary 2004–07[a]	Secondary 2004–07[a]	Tertiary 2004–07[a]
Romania	..	6.4	..	7.2	..	5.4	..	..	..	25.8	66.3	6.1
Russian Federation	5.3	6.1	5.4	6.4	5.2	5.8	..	..	..	13.7	54.2	32.1
Rwanda	0.3	..	0.6	..	0.2	..	..	..	..	..	..	..
Saudi Arabia	..	5.6	..	4.2	..	13.2	..	..	..	12.3	43.9	40.0
Senegal	..	..	..	..	..	..	..	..	..	40.2	6.9	2.5
Serbia	..	13.3[c]	..	11.7[c]	..	15.2[c]	70.5	79.3	82.2	..	..	..
Sierra Leone	..	3.4	..	4.5	..	2.3	..	..	..	..	..	..
Singapore	2.7	4.0	2.7	3.7	2.6	4.3	..	..	..	31.0	25.6	43.2
Slovak Republic	..	11.0	..	9.8	..	12.5	70.8	72.3	69.4	29.2[b]	65.3[b]	5.3[b]
Slovenia	..	4.6	..	3.9	..	6.1	..	..	..	25.0	60.4	12.5
Somalia	..	..	..	..	..	..	..	..	..	..	..	..
South Africa	..	23.0	..	20.0	..	26.6	..	..	..	36.2	56.3	4.5
Spain	18.1	8.3	13.9	6.4	25.8	10.9	27.6	23.9	30.5	54.8	23.6	20.4
Sri Lanka	13.3[b]	6.0[b]	10.1[b]	4.3[b]	19.9[b]	9.0[b]	..	..	..	45.4[b]	22.0[b]	32.6[b]
Sudan	..	..	..	..	..	..	..	..	..	..	..	..
Swaziland	..	..	..	..	..	..	..	..	..	..	..	..
Sweden	5.7	6.1	6.7	5.8	4.6	6.4	13.0	14.5	11.4	32.2	46.0	17.1
Switzerland	2.8	3.6	2.3	2.9	3.5	4.5	40.8	37.9	43.0	28.8	53.2	17.9
Syrian Arab Republic	6.8	..	5.2	..	14.0	..	..	..	..	..	..	..
Tajikistan	..	..	..	..	..	..	..	..	..	66.5	28.8	4.6
Tanzania	3.6[b]	4.7	2.8[b]	..	4.3[b]	..	..	..	..	..	..	..
Thailand	1.4	1.2	1.3	1.3	1.5	1.1	..	..	..	40.5	45.5	0.1
Timor-Leste	..	..	..	..	..	..	..	..	..	..	..	..
Togo	..	..	..	..	..	..	..	..	..	..	..	..
Trinidad and Tobago	19.6	6.5	17.0	4.4	23.9	9.6	..	..	..	..	..	..
Tunisia	..	14.2	..	13.1	..	17.3	..	..	..	79.1	..	13.6
Turkey	8.5	9.9	8.8	9.8	7.8	10.2	30.4	27.1	39.5	52.3	28.2	12.7
Turkmenistan	..	..	..	..	..	..	..	..	..	..	..	..
Uganda	..	..	..	..	..	..	..	..	..	..	..	..
Ukraine	..	6.8	..	7.0	..	6.6	..	..	..	8.5	52.2	39.3
United Arab Emirates	..	3.1	..	2.5	..	7.1	..	..	..	24.3	36.0	21.6
United Kingdom	9.7	5.2	11.5	5.5	7.3	4.9	24.7	29.7	18.2	37.3	47.7	14.3
United States	7.5[b]	4.6[b]	7.9[b]	4.7[b]	7.0[b]	4.5[b]	10.0[b]	10.7[b]	9.0[b]	18.7[b]	35.5[b]	45.7[b]
Uruguay	9.0[b]	9.2[b]	6.8[b]	6.6[b]	11.8[b]	12.4[b]	..	..	..	59.1	27.0	13.8
Uzbekistan	..	..	..	..	..	..	..	..	..	..	..	..
Venezuela, RB	7.7	7.5	8.2	7.1	6.8	8.1	..	..	..	..	..	..
Vietnam	..	2.1	..	1.9	..	2.4	..	..	..	..	..	..
West Bank and Gaza	..	21.6	..	22.1	..	19.0	..	..	..	54.3	14.2	23.5
Yemen, Rep.	..	..	..	..	..	..	..	..	..	..	..	..
Zambia	18.9	..	16.3	..	22.4	..	..	..	..	..	..	..
Zimbabwe	..	4.2	..	4.2	..	4.1	..	..	..	..	..	..
World	.. w	**6.4 w**	.. w	.. w	.. w	.. w	.. w	.. w	.. w	.. w	.. w	.. w
Low income	..	..	..	..	..	..	..	..	..	..	..	..
Middle income	..	6.4	..	..	..	..	..	..	..	..	..	..
Lower middle income	..	5.7	..	..	..	..	..	..	..	..	..	..
Upper middle income	6.3	8.7	5.9	8.0	7.1	9.6	..	..	..	37.8	43.6	13.7
Low & middle income	..	6.4	..	..	..	..	..	..	..	..	..	..
East Asia & Pacific	2.5	4.5	..	..	..	..	..	..	..	..	..	..
Europe & Central Asia	..	7.8	..	8.1	..	7.4	..	..	..	23.4	53.1	22.3
Latin America & Carib.	6.7	8.8	5.4	6.9	8.4	11.5	..	..	..	53.4	32.2	12.9
Middle East & N. Africa	12.8	12.1	10.8	10.4	21.7	18.4	..	..	..	..	..	..
South Asia	..	5.3	..	5.1	..	6.0	..	..	..	27.8	34.5	32.2
Sub-Saharan Africa	..	..	..	..	..	..	..	..	..	..	..	..
High income	7.4	5.5	7.0	5.2	7.9	5.8	25.6	27.3	23.1	35.3	41.3	26.7
Euro area	9.5	7.5	7.5	6.6	12.5	8.6	45.2	44.4	45.5	41.4	42.9	14.9

a. Data are for the most recent year available. b. Limited coverage. c. Data are for 2008.

Unemployment and total employment are the broadest indicators of economic activity as reflected by the labor market. The International Labour Organization (ILO) defines the unemployed as members of the economically active population who are without work but available for and seeking work, including people who have lost their jobs or who have voluntarily left work. Some unemployment is unavoidable. At any time some workers are temporarily unemployed—between jobs as employers look for the right workers and workers search for better jobs. Such unemployment, often called frictional unemployment, results from the normal operation of labor markets.

Changes in unemployment over time may reflect changes in the demand for and supply of labor; they may also reflect changes in reporting practices. Paradoxically, low unemployment rates can disguise substantial poverty in a country, while high unemployment rates can occur in countries with a high level of economic development and low rates of poverty. In countries without unemployment or welfare benefits people eke out a living in vulnerable employment. In countries with well developed safety nets workers can afford to wait for suitable or desirable jobs. But high and sustained unemployment indicates serious inefficiencies in resource allocation.

The ILO definition of unemployment notwithstanding, reference periods, the criteria for people considered to be seeking work, and the treatment of people temporarily laid off or seeking work for the first time vary across countries. In many developing countries it is especially difficult to measure employment and unemployment in agriculture. The timing of a survey, for example, can maximize the effects of seasonal unemployment in agriculture. And informal sector employment is difficult to quantify where informal activities are not tracked.

Data on unemployment are drawn from labor force sample surveys and general household sample surveys, censuses, and official estimates, which are generally based on information from different sources and can be combined in many ways. Administrative records, such as social insurance statistics and employment office statistics, are not included in the table because of their limitations in coverage. Labor force surveys generally yield the most comprehensive data because they include groups not covered in other unemployment statistics, particularly people seeking work for the first time. These surveys generally use a definition of unemployment that follows the international recommendations more closely than that used by other sources and therefore generate statistics that are more comparable internationally. But the age group, geographic coverage, and collection methods could differ by country or change over time within a country. For detailed information, consult the original source.

Women tend to be excluded from the unemployment count for various reasons. Women suffer more from discrimination and from structural, social, and cultural barriers that impede them from seeking work. Also, women are often responsible for the care of children and the elderly and for household affairs. They may not be available for work during the short reference period, as they need to make arrangements before starting work. Furthermore, women are considered to be employed when they are working part-time or in temporary jobs, despite the instability of these jobs or their active search for more secure employment.

Long-term unemployment is measured by the length of time that an unemployed person has been without work and looking for a job. The data in the table are from labor force surveys. The underlying assumption is that shorter periods of joblessness are of less concern, especially when the unemployed are covered by unemployment benefits or similar forms of support. The length of time that a person has been unemployed is difficult to measure, because the ability to recall that time diminishes as the period of joblessness extends. Women's long-term unemployment is likely to be lower in countries where women constitute a large share of the unpaid family workforce.

Unemployment by level of educational attainment provides insights into the relation between the educational attainment of workers and unemployment and may be used to draw inferences about changes in employment demand. Information on educational attainment is the best available indicator of skill levels of the labor force. Besides the limitations to comparability raised for measuring unemployment, the different ways of classifying the education level may also cause inconsistency. Education level is supposed to be classified according to International Standard Classification of Education 1997 (ISCED97). For more information on ISCED97, see *About the data* for table 2.11.

• **Unemployment** is the share of the labor force without work but available for and seeking employment. Definitions of labor force and unemployment may differ by country (see *About the data*). • **Long-term unemployment** is the number of people with continuous periods of unemployment extending for a year or longer, expressed as a percentage of the total unemployed. • **Unemployment by educational attainment** is the unemployed by level of educational attainment as a percentage of the total unemployed. The levels of educational attainment accord with the ISCED97 of the United Nations Educational, Scientific, and Cultural Organization.

Data on unemployment are from the ILO database Key Indicators of the Labour Market, 5th edition.

2.6 Children at work

	Survey year	Children in employment					Employment by economic activity[a]			Status in employment[a]		
		% of children ages 7–14			% of children ages 7–14 in employment		% of children ages 7–14 in employment			% of children ages 7–14 in employment		
		Total	Male	Female	Work only	Study and work	Agriculture	Manufacturing	Services	Self-employed	Wage	Unpaid family
Afghanistan		..	..	..	..	..	..	..	..	..	..	..
Albania	2000	36.6	41.1	31.8	43.1	56.9	..	..	..	..	1.4	93.1
Algeria		..	..	..	..	..	..	..	..	..	..	..
Angola[b]	2001	30.1	30.0	30.1	26.6	73.4	..	..	..	..	6.2	80.1
Argentina	2004	12.9	15.7	9.8	4.8	95.2	..	..	..	34.2	8.1	56.2
Armenia		..	..	..	..	..	..	..	..	..	..	..
Australia		..	..	..	..	..	..	..	..	..	..	..
Austria		..	..	..	..	..	..	..	..	..	..	..
Azerbaijan	2000	9.7	12.0	7.3	4.2	95.8	..	..	..	..	2.1	88.9
Bangladesh	2006	16.2	25.7	6.4	37.8	62.2	..	..	..	–	17.0	77.8
Belarus	2005	11.7	12.1	11.2	0.0	100.0	..	..	..	..	9.2	78.8
Belgium		..	..	..	..	..	..	..	..	..	..	..
Benin	2006	74.4	72.8	76.1	36.1	63.9	..	..	..	..	..	..
Bolivia	2005	22.0	23.9	20.1	8.1	91.9	84.4	4.3	10.1	1.2	4.4	92.9
Bosnia and Herzegovina	2006	10.6	11.7	9.5	0.1	99.9	..	..	..	..	1.6	92.1
Botswana		..	..	..	..	..	..	..	..	..	..	..
Brazil	2004	7.0	9.4	4.6	7.2	92.8	60.8	6.6	30.9	6.8	21.5	58.0
Bulgaria		..	..	..	..	..	..	..	..	..	..	..
Burkina Faso	2004	50.0	49.0	51.0	98.1	1.9	97.2	0.4	2.2	1.3	0.4	98.3
Burundi	2000	37.0	38.4	35.7	48.3	51.7	..	..	..	3.9	85.3	..
Cambodia	2001	52.3	52.4	52.1	16.5	83.5	76.1	5.0	18.0	1.5	4.7	90.2
Cameroon[c]	2001	15.9	14.5	17.4	52.5	47.5	88.2	2.1	7.1	..	..	..
Canada		..	..	..	..	..	..	..	..	..	..	..
Central African Republic	2000	67.0	66.5	67.6	54.9	45.1	..	..	..	..	2.0	56.4
Chad	2004	60.4	64.4	56.2	49.1	50.9	..	..	..	..	1.8	77.2
Chile	2003	4.1	5.1	3.1	3.2	96.8	24.1	6.9	66.9	..	..	..
China		..	..	..	..	..	..	..	..	..	..	..
Hong Kong, China		..	..	..	..	..	..	..	..	..	..	..
Colombia	2005	4.0	6.2	1.8	32.8	67.2	..	..	..	12.6	39.1	48.3
Congo, Dem. Rep.[c]	2000	39.8	39.9	39.8	35.7	64.3	..	..	..	..	6.6	76.7
Congo, Rep	2005	30.1	29.9	30.2	9.9	90.1	..	..	..	..	4.2	84.5
Costa Rica[c]	2004	5.7	8.1	3.5	44.6	55.4	40.3	9.5	49.0	15.8	57.7	26.6
Côte d'Ivoire	2006	45.7	47.7	43.6	46.8	53.2	..	..	..	..	2.4	88.0
Croatia		..	..	..	..	..	..	..	..	..	..	..
Cuba		..	..	..	..	..	..	..	..	..	..	..
Czech Republic		..	..	..	..	..	..	..	..	..	..	..
Denmark		..	..	..	..	..	..	..	..	..	..	..
Dominican Republic[c]	2005	5.8	9.0	2.7	6.2	93.8	18.5	9.8	57.5	23.8	19.5	56.2[d]
Ecuador	2004	12.0	14.6	9.3	27.0	73.0	70.0	4.7	23.7	6.0	15.8	75.5
Egypt, Arab Rep.	2005	7.9	11.5	4.3	21.0	79.0	..	..	..	..	11.4	87.4
El Salvador	2003	12.7	17.1	8.1	19.5	80.5	51.0	12.5	35.4	1.5	15.3	78.4
Eritrea		..	..	..	..	..	..	..	..	..	..	..
Estonia		..	..	..	..	..	..	..	..	..	..	..
Ethiopia	2005	56.0	64.3	47.1	69.4	30.6	94.6	1.5	3.7	1.7	2.4	95.8
Finland		..	..	..	..	..	..	..	..	..	..	..
France		..	..	..	..	..	..	..	..	..	..	..
Gabon		..	..	..	..	..	..	..	..	..	..	..
Gambia, The	2005	43.5	33.9	52.3	32.1	67.9	..	..	..	..	1.1	87.3
Georgia		..	..	..	..	..	..	..	..	..	..	..
Germany		..	..	..	..	..	..	..	..	..	..	..
Ghana	2003	6.0	6.0	5.9	71.2	28.8	78.8	2.8	15.2	10.8	5.5	78.4
Greece		..	..	..	..	..	..	..	..	..	..	..
Guatemala	2004	16.8	23.1	10.5	31.3	68.7	66.1	9.1	23.5	3.4	17.8	78.9
Guinea	1994	48.3	47.2	49.5	98.6	1.4	..	..	..	..	..	..
Guinea-Bissau	2000	67.5	67.4	67.5	63.7	36.3	..	..	..	..	0.9	81.1
Haiti	2005	33.4	37.3	29.6	17.7	82.3	..	..	..	..	1.8	79.4

Children at work | 2.6

	Survey year	Children in employment					Employment by economic activity[a]			Status in employment[a]		
		% of children ages 7–14			% of children ages 7–14 in employment		% of children ages 7–14 in employment			% of children ages 7–14 in employment		
		Total	Male	Female	Work only	Study and work	Agriculture	Manufacturing	Services	Self-employed	Wage	Unpaid family
Honduras	2004	6.8	10.4	3.2	48.6	51.4	63.4	8.3	24.7	2.7	19.9	73.8
Hungary		..	..	..	..	..	..	..	..	..	..	..
India	2004–05	4.2	4.2	4.2	84.9	15.2	69.4	16.0	12.4	7.1	6.8	59.3
Indonesia	2000	8.9	8.8	9.1	24.9	75.1	..	..	..	..	17.8	75.8[d]
Iran, Islamic Rep.		..	..	..	..	..	..	..	..	..	..	..
Iraq	2006	14.7	17.9	11.3	32.4	67.6	..	..	..	..	7.0	85.3
Ireland		..	..	..	..	..	..	..	..	..	..	..
Israel		..	..	..	..	..	..	..	..	..	..	..
Italy		..	..	..	..	..	..	..	..	..	..	..
Jamaica	2002	1.1	1.5	0.6	17.1	82.9	31.3	7.7	51.4	21.6	35.1	43.3
Japan		..	..	..	..	..	..	..	..	..	..	..
Jordan		..	..	..	..	..	..	..	..	..	..	..
Kazakhstan	2006	3.6	4.4	2.8	1.6	98.4	..	..	..	..	4.0	75.0
Kenya	2000	37.7	40.1	35.2	14.1	85.9	..	..	..	..	..	..
Korea, Dem. Rep.		..	..	..	..	..	..	..	..	..	..	..
Korea, Rep.		..	..	..	..	..	..	..	..	..	..	..
Kuwait		..	..	..	..	..	..	..	..	..	..	..
Kyrgyz Republic	2006	5.2	5.8	4.6	7.9	92.1	..	..	..	..	3.7	81.9
Lao PDR		..	..	..	..	..	..	..	..	..	..	..
Latvia		..	..	..	..	..	..	..	..	..	..	..
Lebanon		..	..	..	..	..	..	..	..	..	..	..
Lesotho	2000	30.8	34.2	27.5	17.6	82.4	..	..	..	..	3.6	83.3
Liberia	2007	37.4	37.8	37.1	45.0	55.0	..	..	..	..	1.7	79.3
Libya		..	..	..	..	..	..	..	..	..	..	..
Lithuania		..	..	..	..	..	..	..	..	..	..	..
Macedonia, FYR	2005	11.8	14.8	8.6	2.8	97.2	..	..	..	..	3.9	89.5
Madagascar	2001	25.6	26.1	25.1	85.1	14.9	94.0	1.0	2.4	6.8	1.5	91.4
Malawi	2006	40.3	41.3	39.4	10.5	89.5	..	..	..	..	6.7	75.5
Malaysia		..	..	..	..	..	..	..	..	..	..	..
Mali	2006	49.5	55.0	44.1	59.5	40.5	..	..	..	..	1.6	80.4
Mauritania		..	..	..	..	..	..	..	..	..	..	..
Mauritius		..	..	..	..	..	..	..	..	..	..	..
Mexico[e]	2004	8.9	12.2	5.6	34.1	65.9	38.1	12.3	48.0	3.7	52.0	44.2
Moldova	2000	33.5	34.1	32.8	3.8	96.2	..	..	..	..	2.9	82.0
Mongolia	2005	12.4	14.1	10.7	8.7	91.3	..	..	..	..	3.9	91.3
Morocco	1998–99	13.2	13.5	12.8	93.2	6.8	60.6	8.3	10.1	2.1	10.0	81.7
Mozambique[c]	1996	1.8	1.9	1.7	100.0	0.0	..	..	..	..	..	..
Myanmar		..	..	..	..	..	..	..	..	..	..	..
Namibia	1999	15.4	16.2	14.7	9.5	90.5	91.5	0.4	8.0	0.1	4.5	95.0
Nepal	1999	47.2	42.2	52.4	35.6	64.4	87.0	1.4	11.1	4.2	3.3	92.4
Netherlands		..	..	..	..	..	..	..	..	..	..	..
New Zealand		..	..	..	..	..	..	..	..	..	..	..
Nicaragua	2005	10.1	16.2	3.9	30.8	69.2	70.5	9.7	19.3	1.2	13.8	85.0[f]
Niger	2006	47.1	49.2	45.0	66.5	33.5	..	..	..	4.8	74.5	..
Nigeria		..	..	..	..	..	..	..	..	..	..	..
Norway		..	..	..	..	..	..	..	..	..	..	..
Oman		..	..	..	..	..	..	..	..	..	..	..
Pakistan		..	..	..	..	..	..	..	..	..	..	..
Panama[c]	2003	5.1	7.7	2.2	38.4	61.6	57.6	3.1	38.1	12.4	24.9	50.3[f]
Papua New Guinea		..	..	..	..	..	..	..	..	..	..	..
Paraguay[c]	2005	15.3	22.6	7.7	24.2	75.7	60.8	6.2	32.1	9.3	24.8	65.8
Peru	2000	24.1	25.7	22.3	4.8	95.2	72.6	2.8	24.5	1.9	6.8	91.4
Philippines	2001	13.3	16.3	10.0	14.8	85.2	64.3	4.1	30.6	4.1	22.8	73.1
Poland		..	..	..	..	..	..	..	..	..	..	..
Portugal	2001	3.6	4.6	2.6	3.6	96.4	48.5	11.2	33.3	..	..	..
Puerto Rico		..	..	..	..	..	..	..	..	..	..	..

	Survey year	Children in employment					Employment by economic activity[a]			Status in employment[a]		
		% of children ages 7–14			% of children ages 7–14 in employment		% of children ages 7–14 in employment			% of children ages 7–14 in employment		
		Total	Male	Female	Work only	Study and work	Agriculture	Manufacturing	Services	Self-employed	Wage	Unpaid family
Romania	2000	1.4	1.7	1.1	20.7	79.3	97.1	0.0	2.3	4.5	..	92.9[d]
Russian Federation		..	..	..	..	..	..	..	..	..	..	..
Rwanda	2000	33.1	36.1	30.3	27.5	72.5	..	..	..	..	2.9	85.7
Saudi Arabia		..	..	..	..	..	..	..	..	..	..	..
Senegal	2005	18.5	24.4	12.6	61.9	38.1	79.1	5.0	14.0	6.3	4.4	84.1
Serbia	2005	6.9	7.2	6.6	2.1	97.9	..	..	..	..	5.2	89.4
Sierra Leone	2005	62.7	63.6	61.8	29.9	70.1	..	..	..	..	1.0	71.1
Singapore		..	..	..	..	..	..	..	..	..	..	..
Slovak Republic		..	..	..	..	..	..	..	..	..	..	..
Slovenia		..	..	..	..	..	..	..	..	..	..	..
Somalia	2006	43.5	45.5	41.5	53.5	46.5	..	..	..	..	1.6	94.8
South Africa	1999	27.7	29.0	26.4	5.1	94.9	..	..	..	7.1	7.1	85.8
Spain		..	..	..	..	..	..	..	..	..	..	..
Sri Lanka	1999	17.0	20.4	13.4	5.4	94.6	71.2	13.1	15.0	2.9	8.3	88.0
Sudan[g]	2000	19.1	21.5	16.8	55.9	44.1	..	..	..	..	7.3	81.3
Swaziland	2000	11.2	11.4	10.9	14.0	86.0	..	..	..	..	10.4	85.9
Sweden		..	..	..	..	..	..	..	..	..	..	..
Switzerland		..	..	..	..	..	..	..	..	..	..	..
Syrian Arab Republic	2006	6.6	8.8	4.3	34.6	65.4	..	..	..	..	21.5	68.8
Tajikistan	2005	8.9	8.7	9.1	9.0	91.0	..	..	..	..	24.2	71.3
Tanzania	2001	40.4	41.5	39.2	40.0	60.0	78.5	0.2	21.3	0.9	1.0	98.2[d]
Thailand	2005	15.1	15.7	14.4	4.2	95.8	..	..	..	..	13.5	80.0
Timor-Leste		..	..	..	..	..	..	..	..	..	..	..
Togo	2006	38.7	39.8	37.4	29.8	70.2	82.9	1.3	15.1	5.0	1.6	93.4
Trinidad and Tobago	2000	3.9	5.2	2.8	12.8	87.2	..	..	..	..	29.8	64.9
Tunisia		..	..	..	..	..	..	..	..	..	..	..
Turkey	1999	4.5	5.2	3.8	66.8	33.2	65.4	15.9	18.7	3.7	34.9	61.4
Turkmenistan		..	..	..	..	..	..	..	..	..	..	..
Uganda	2005–06	38.2	39.8	36.5	7.7	92.3	95.5	1.4	3.0	1.4	1.5	97.1
Ukraine	2005	17.3	18.0	16.6	0.1	99.9	..	..	..	..	3.1	79.3
United Arab Emirates		..	..	..	..	..	..	..	..	..	..	..
United Kingdom		..	..	..	..	..	..	..	..	..	..	..
United States		..	..	..	..	..	..	..	..	..	..	..
Uruguay		..	..	..	..	..	..	..	..	..	..	..
Uzbekistan	2005	5.1	5.3	4.9	1.0	99.0	..	..	..	..	3.8	78.6
Venezuela, RB[c]	2005	5.4	7.1	3.6	24.7	75.3	28.3	8.0	61.1	18.9	25.3	54.0
Vietnam	2006	21.3	21.0	21.6	11.9	88.1	..	..	..	..	5.9	91.2
West Bank and Gaza		..	..	..	..	..	..	..	..	..	..	..
Yemen, Rep.	1999	13.1	12.4	14.0	64.3	35.7	92.0	1.0	6.2	4.1	5.4	86.8
Zambia	2005	47.9	48.9	46.8	25.9	74.1	95.9	0.6	3.5	2.6	0.7	96.5
Zimbabwe	1999	14.3	15.3	13.3	12.0	88.0	..	..	..	3.4	28.4	68.2

a. Shares may not sum to 100 percent because of a residual category not included in the table. b. Covers only Angola-secured territory. c. Covers children ages 10–14. d. Refers to family workers, regardless of whether they are paid. e. Covers children ages 12–14. f. Refers to unpaid workers, regardless of whether they are family workers. g. Covers northern Sudan only.

Children at work | 2.6

The data in the table refer to children's work in the sense of "economic activity"—that is, children in employment, which is a broader concept than child labor (see ILO forthcoming for details on this distinction).

In line with the definition of economic activity adopted by the 13th International Conference of Labour Statisticians, the threshold for classifying a person as employed is to have been engaged at least one hour in any activity during the reference period relating to the production of goods and services set by the 1993 United Nations System of National Accounts. Children seeking work are thus not included in employment. Economic activity covers all market production and certain types of nonmarket production, including production of goods for own use. It excludes unpaid household services (commonly called "household chores")—that is, the production of domestic and personal services by household members for consumption within their own household.

The data are from household surveys conducted by the International Labor Organization (ILO), the United Nations Children's Fund (UNICEF), the World Bank, and national statistical offices. These surveys yield a variety of data on education, employment, health, expenditure, and consumption indicators that relate to children's work.

Household survey data generally include information on work type—for example, whether a child is

working for payment in cash or in kind or is involved in unpaid work, whether a child is working for someone who is not a member of the household, whether a child is involved in any type of family work (on the farm or in a business), and the like. The ages used in country surveys to define child labor range from 5 to 17 years. The data in the table have been recalculated to present statistics for children ages 7–14.

Although efforts are made to harmonize the definition of employment and the questions on employment used in survey questionnaires, significant differences remain in the survey instruments used to collect data on children in employment and in the sampling design underlying these surveys. Differences exist not only across different household surveys in the same country, but also across the same type of survey carried out in different countries.

Because of the differences in the underlying survey instruments and dates, estimates of working children are not fully comparable across countries. Caution should be used in drawing conclusions concerning relative levels of child economic activity across countries or regions based on the data.

The table aggregates the distribution of children in employment by the industrial categories of the International Standard Industrial Classification (ISIC): agriculture, manufacturing, and services. A residual category—which includes mining and quarrying; electricity, gas, and water; construction; extraterritorial organization and other inadequately defined activities—is not presented. Both ISIC revision 2 and revision 3 are used, depending solely on the codification applied by each country in describing the economic activity. The use of two different classifications does not affect the definition of the groups presented in the table.

The table aggregates the distribution of children in employment by status in employment. Status in employment is based on the International Classification of Status in Employment (1993), which shows the distribution of children in employment by three major categories: self-employed workers, wage workers (also known as employees), and unpaid family workers. A residual category—which includes those not classifiable by status—is not presented.

• **Survey year** is the year in which the underlying data were collected. • **Children in employment** are children involved in any economic activity for at least one hour in the reference week of the survey. • **Work only** refers to children who are employed and not attending school. • **Study and work** refer to children attending school in combination with employment. • **Employment by economic activity** is the distribution of children in employment by the major industrial categories (ISIC revision 2 or revision 3). • **Agriculture** corresponds to division 1 (ISIC revision 2) or categories A and B (ISIC revision 3) and includes agriculture and hunting, forestry and logging, and fishing. • **Manufacturing** corresponds to division 3 (ISIC revision 2) or category D (ISIC revision 3). • **Services** correspond to divisions 6–9 (ISIC revision 2) or categories G–P (ISIC revision 3) and include wholesale and retail trade, hotels and restaurants, transport, financial intermediation, real estate, public administration, education, health and social work, other community services, and private household activity. • **Self-employed workers** are people whose remuneration depends directly on the profits derived from the goods and services they produce, with or without other employees, and include employers, own-account workers, and members of producers cooperatives. • **Wage workers** (also known as employees) are people who hold explicit (written or oral) or implicit employment contracts that provide basic remuneration that does not depend directly on the revenue of the unit for which they work. • **Unpaid family workers** are people who work without pay in a market-oriented establishment operated by a related person living in the same household.

Data on children at work are estimates produced by the Understanding Children's Work project based on household survey data sets made available by the ILO's International Programme on the Elimination of Child Labour under its Statistical Monitoring Programme on Child Labour, UNICEF under its Multiple Indicator Cluster Survey program, the World Bank under its Living Standards Measurement Study program, and national statistical offices. Information on how the data were collected and some indication of their reliability can be found at www.ilo.org/public/english/standards/ipec/simpoc/, www.childinfo.org, and www.worldbank.org/lsms. Detailed country statistics can be found at www.ucw-project.org.

Average work time among children ages 7–14 who study and work, 2005 (hours per week)

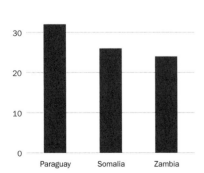

Children in many countries work long hours, often combining studying with working. In Paraguay children work more than 30 hours a week, leaving very little time for studying or any other activities.

Source: Understanding Children's Work Project.

	Population below national poverty line								Poverty gap at national poverty line			
	Survey year	Rural %	Urban %	National %	Survey year	Rural %	Urban %	National %	Survey year	Rural %	Urban %	National %
Afghanistan	2007	45.0	27.0	42.0		..	..	..		..	..	..
Albania	2002	29.6	19.5	25.4	2005	24.2	11.2	18.5	2005	5.3	2.3	4.0
Algeria	1988	16.6	7.3	12.2	1995	30.3	14.7	22.6	1995	4.5	1.8	3.2
Argentina	1998	..	28.8	..	2002	..	53.0	..	2002	..	28.5	..
Armenia	1998–99	50.8	58.3	55.1	2001	48.7	51.9	50.9	2001	..	..	15.1
Azerbaijan	1995	..	..	68.1	2001	42.0	55.0	49.6	2001	..	..	15.5
Bangladesh	2000	52.3	35.1	48.9	2005	43.8	28.4	40.0	2005	9.8	6.5	9.0
Belarus	2002	..	..	30.5	2004	..	..	17.4		..	..	..
Benin	1999	33.0	23.3	29.0	2003	46.0	29.0	39.0	2003	14.0	8.0	12.0
Bolivia	1999	80.1	51.4	62.0	2002	82.2	53.9	64.6	2002	43.4	23.8	31.2
Bosnia and Herzegovina	2001–02	19.9	13.8	19.5		..	..	..	2001–02	4.9	2.8	4.6
Brazil	1998	51.4	14.7	22.0	2002–03	41.0	17.5	21.5	2002–03	28.4	17.8	19.6
Bulgaria	1997	..	..	36.0	2001	..	..	12.8	2001	..	..	4.2
Burkina Faso	1998	61.1	22.4	54.6	2003	52.4	19.2	46.4	2003	17.6	5.1	15.3
Burundi	1998	64.6	66.5	68.0		..	..	..		..	..	..
Cambodia	1994	..	..	47.0	2004	38.0	18.0	35.0	2004	7.8	1.2	6.7
Cameroon	1996	59.6	41.4	53.3	2001	49.9	22.1	40.2				
Chad	1995–96	48.6	..	43.4		..	..	..	1995–96	26.3	..	27.5
Chile	1996	..	..	19.9	1998	..	..	17.0	1998	..	..	5.7
China	1998	4.6	..	4.6	2004	..	..	2.8		..	..	..
Colombia	1995	79.0	48.0	60.0	1999	79.0	55.0	64.0	1999	44.0	26.0	34.0
Congo, Dem. Rep.	2004–05	75.7	61.5	71.3		..	..	..	2004–05	34.9	26.2	32.2
Congo, Rep.	2005	49.2	..	42.3		..	..	..		..	..	..
Costa Rica	1989	35.8	26.2	31.7	2004	28.3	20.8	23.9	2004	10.8	7.0	8.6
Croatia	2002	..	..	11.2	2004	..	..	11.1		..	..	..
Dominican Republic	2000	45.3	18.2	27.7	2004	55.7	34.7	42.2	2004	24.0	12.9	16.8
Ecuador	1998	69.0	30.0	46.0	2001	..	..	45.2	2001	..	..	18.0
Egypt, Arab Rep.	1995–96	23.3	22.5	22.9	1999–2000	..	..	16.7	1999–2000	..	..	3.0
El Salvador	1995	64.8	38.9	50.6	2002	49.8	28.5	37.2	2002	24.2	11.1	16.5
Eritrea	1993–94	..	..	53.0		..	..	..		..	..	..
Estonia	1995	14.7	6.8	8.9		..	..	..	1995	6.6	1.8	3.1
Ethiopia	1995–96	47.0	33.3	45.5	1999–2000	45.0	37.0	44.2	1999–2000	12.0	10.0	12.0
Gambia, The	1998	61.0	48.0	57.6	2003	63.0	57.0	61.3	2003	..	..	25.9
Georgia	2002	55.4	48.5	52.1	2003	52.7	56.2	54.5		..	..	..
Ghana	1998–99	49.6	19.4	39.5	2005–06	39.2	10.8	28.5	2005–06	13.5	3.1	9.6
Guatemala	1989	71.9	33.7	57.9	2000	74.5	27.1	56.2	2000	..	..	22.6
Guinea	1994	..	..	40.0		..	..	..		..	..	..
Guinea-Bissau	2002	..	52.6	65.7		..	..	..	2000	..	17.5	25.7
Haiti	1987	..	..	65.0	1995	66.0	..	..		..	..	..
Honduras	1998–99	71.2	28.6	52.5	2004	70.4	29.5	50.7	2004	34.5	9.1	22.3
Hungary	1993	..	..	14.5	1997	..	..	17.3	1997	4.1	..	..
India	1993–94	37.3	32.4	36.0	1999–2000	30.2	24.7	28.6	1999–2000	5.6	6.9	..
Indonesia	1996	19.8	13.6	17.6	2005	..	..	16.0	2004	..	..	2.9
Jamaica	1995	37.0	18.7	27.5	2000	25.1	12.8	18.7		..	..	..
Jordan	1997	27.0	19.7	21.3	2002	18.7	12.9	14.2	2002	4.7	2.9	3.3
Kazakhstan	2001	..	..	17.6	2002	..	..	15.4	2002	4.5	2.0	3.1
Kenya	1994	47.0	29.0	40.0	1997	53.0	49.0	52.0		..	..	..
Kyrgyz Republic	2003	57.5	35.7	49.9	2005	50.8	29.8	43.1	2005	12.0	7.0	10.0
Lao PDR	1997–98	41.0	26.9	38.6	2002–03	..	..	33.0	2002–03	..	..	8.0
Latvia	2002	11.6	..	7.5	2004	12.7	..	5.9	2004	..	..	1.2
Lesotho	1994/95	68.9	36.7	66.6	2002/03	60.5	41.5	56.3		..	..	..
Macedonia, FYR	2002	25.3	..	21.4	2003	22.3	..	21.7	2003	6.5	..	6.7
Madagascar	1997	76.0	63.2	73.3	1999	76.7	52.1	71.3	1999	36.1	21.4	32.8
Malawi	1990–91	..	..	54.0	1997–98	66.5	54.9	65.3		..	..	..
Malaysia	1989	..	..	15.5		..	..	..		..	..	..
Mali	1998	75.9	30.1	63.8		..	..	..		..	..	..

Poverty rates at national poverty lines **2.7**

	Population below national poverty line							Poverty gap at national poverty line			
	Survey year	Rural %	Urban %	National %	Survey year	Rural %	Urban %	National %	Survey year	Rural %	Urban %	National %
Mauritania	1996	65.5	30.1	50.0	2000	61.2	25.4	46.3		..	..	..
Mauritius	1992	..	..	10.6		..	..	..		..	..	..
Mexico	2002	34.8	11.4	20.3	2004	27.9	11.3	17.6	2002	12.2	2.8	6.3
Moldova	2001	64.1	58.0	62.4	2002	67.2	42.6	48.5	2002	..	..	16.5
Mongolia	1998	32.6	39.4	35.6	2002	43.4	30.3	36.1	2002	13.2	9.2	11.0
Morocco	1990–91	18.0	7.6	13.1	1998–99	27.2	12.0	19.0	1998–99	6.7	2.5	4.4
Mozambique	1996–97	71.3	62.0	69.4	2002–03	55.3	51.5	54.1	2002–03	20.9	19.7	20.5
Nepal	1995–96	43.3	21.6	41.8	2003–04	34.6	9.6	30.9	2003–04	8.5	2.2	7.5
Nicaragua	1998	68.5	30.5	47.9	2001	64.3	28.7	45.8	2001	25.9	8.7	17.0
Niger	1989–93	66.0	52.0	63.0		..	..	..		..	..	..
Nigeria	1985	49.5	31.7	43.0	1992–93	36.4	30.4	34.1		..	..	..
Pakistan	1993	33.4	17.2	28.6	1998–99	35.9	24.2	32.6	1998–99	7.9	5.0	7.0
Panama	1997	64.9	15.3	37.3		..	..	..	1997	32.1	3.9	16.4
Papua New Guinea	1996	41.3	16.1	37.5		..	..	..	1996	13.8	4.3	12.4
Paraguay[a]	1990	28.5	19.7	20.5		..	..	..	1990	10.5	5.6	6.0
Peru	2001	77.1	42.0	54.3	2004	72.1	42.9	53.1	2004	28.3	12.4	18.0
Philippines	1994	45.4	18.6	32.1	1997	36.9	11.9	25.1	1997	10.0	2.6	6.4
Poland	1996	..	..	14.6	2001	..	..	14.8		..	..	..
Romania	1995	..	..	25.4	2002	..	..	28.9	2002	..	..	7.6
Russian Federation	1998	..	..	31.4	2002	..	..	19.6	2002	..	..	5.1
Rwanda	1993	..	..	51.2	1999–2000	65.7	14.3	60.3		..	..	..
Senegal	1992	40.4	23.7	33.4		..	..	..	1992	16.4	3.1	13.9
Sierra Leone	1989	..	..	82.8	2003–04	79.0	56.4	70.2	2003–04	34.0	..	29.0
Slovak Republic	2004	..	..	16.8		..	..	..	2004	..	..	5.5
Sri Lanka	1995–96	27.0	15.0	25.0	2002	7.9	24.7	22.7	2002	5.6	1.7	5.1
Swaziland	2000–01	75.0	49.0	69.2		..	..	..	2000–01	..	..	32.9
Tajikistan	1999	..	..	74.9	2003	..	..	44.4	2003	..	..	12.7
Tanzania	1991	40.8	31.2	38.6	2000–01	38.7	29.5	35.7		..	..	..
Thailand	1994	..	..	9.8	1998	..	..	13.6	1998	..	..	3.0
Timor-Leste	2001	..	..	39.7		..	..	..	2001	..	..	11.9
Togo	1987–89	..	..	32.3		..	..	..	1987–89	..	..	10.0
Trinidad and Tobago	1992	20.0	24.0	21.0		..	..	..	1992	6.2	7.4	7.3
Tunisia	1990	13.1	3.5	7.4	1995	13.9	3.6	7.6	1990	3.3	0.9	1.7
Turkey	1994	..	..	28.3	2002	34.5	22.0	27.0	2002	..	..	0.3
Uganda	1999–2000	37.4	9.6	33.8	2002–03	41.7	12.2	37.7	2002–03	12.6	3.0	11.3
Ukraine	2000	34.9	..	31.5	2003	28.4	..	19.5		..	..	..
Uruguay	1994	..	20.2	..	1998	..	24.7	..	1998	..	8.6	..
Uzbekistan	2000–01	33.6	27.8	31.5	2003	29.8	22.6	27.2		..	..	..
Venezuela, RB	1989	..	..	31.3	1997–99	..	..	52.0	1997–99	..	..	24.0
Vietnam	1998	45.5	9.2	37.4	2002	35.6	6.6	28.9	2002	8.7	1.3	6.9
Yemen, Rep.	1998	45.0	30.8	41.8		..	..	..	1998	14.7	8.2	13.2
Zambia	1998	83.1	56.0	72.9	2004	78.0	53.0	68.0	2004	44.0	22.0	36.0
Zimbabwe	1990–91	35.8	3.4	25.8	1995–96	48.0	7.9	34.9		..	..	..

a. Covers Asunción metropolitan area only.

The World Bank periodically prepares poverty assessments of countries in which it has an active program, in close collaboration with national institutions, other development agencies, and civil society groups, including poor people's organizations. Poverty assessments report the extent and causes of poverty and propose strategies to reduce it. Since 1992 the World Bank has conducted about 200 poverty assessments, which are the main source of the poverty estimates presented in the table. Countries report similar assessments as part of their Poverty Reduction Strategies.

The poverty assessments are the best available source of information on poverty estimates using national poverty lines. They often include separate assessments of urban and rural poverty. Data are derived from nationally representative household surveys conducted by national statistical offices or by private agencies under the supervision of government or international agencies and obtained from government statistical offices and World Bank Group country departments.

Some poverty assessments analyze the current poverty status of a country using the latest available household survey data, while others use survey data for several years to analyze poverty trends. Thus, poverty estimates for more than one year might be derived from a single poverty assessment. A poverty assessment might not use all available household surveys, or survey data might become available at a later date even though data were collected before the poverty assessment date. Thus poverty assessments may not fully represent all household survey data.

Over the last 20 years there has been considerable expansion in the number of countries that field surveys and in the frequency of the surveys. The quality of their data has improved greatly as well.

Data availability

The number of data sets within two years of any given year rose dramatically, from 13 between 1978 and 1982 to 158 between 2001 and 2006. Data coverage is improving in all regions, but the Middle East and North Africa and Sub-Saharan Africa continue to lag. The database, maintained by a team in the World Bank's Development Research Group, is updated annually as new survey data become available, and a major reassessment of progress against poverty is made about every three years. A complete overview of data availability by year and country is available at http://iresearch.worldbank.org/povcalnet/.

Data quality

Poverty assessments are based on surveys fielded to collect, among other things, information on income or consumption from a sample of households. To be useful for poverty estimates, surveys must be nationally representative and include sufficient information to compute a comprehensive estimate of total household consumption or income (including consumption or income from own production), from which it is possible to construct a correctly weighted distribution of consumption or income per person. There remain many potential problems with household survey data, including selective nonresponse and differences in the menu of consumption items presented and the length of the period over which respondents must recall their expenditures. These issues are discussed in *About the data* for table 2.8.

National poverty lines

National poverty lines are used to make estimates of poverty consistent with the country's specific economic and social circumstances and are not intended for international comparisons of poverty rates. The setting of national poverty lines reflects local perceptions of the level of consumption or income needed not to be poor. The perceived boundary between poor and not poor rises with the average income of a country and so does not provide a uniform measure for comparing poverty rates across countries. Nevertheless, national poverty estimates are clearly the appropriate measure for setting national policies for poverty reduction and for monitoring their results.

Almost all the national poverty lines use a food bundle based on prevailing diets that attains predetermined nutritional requirements for good health and normal activity levels, plus an allowance for nonfood spending. The rise in poverty lines with average income is driven more by the gradient in the nonfood component of the poverty lines than in the food component, although there is still an appreciable share attributable to the gradient in food poverty lines. While nutritional requirements tend to be fairly similar even across countries at different levels of economic development, richer countries tend to use a more expensive food bundle—more meat and vegetables, less starchy staples, and more processed foods generally—for attaining the same nutritional needs.

• **Survey year** is the year in which the underlying data were collected. • **Rural population below national poverty line** is the percentage of the rural population living below the national rural poverty line. • **Urban population below national poverty line** is the percentage of the urban population living below the national urban poverty line. • **National population below national poverty line** is the percentage of the country's population living below the national poverty line. National estimates are based on population-weighted subgroup estimates from household surveys. • **Poverty gap at national poverty line** is the mean shortfall from the poverty line (counting the nonpoor as having zero shortfall) as a percentage of the poverty line. This measure reflects the depth of poverty as well as its incidence.

The poverty measures are prepared by the World Bank's Development Research Group, based on data from World Bank's country poverty assessments and country Poverty Reduction Strategies. Summaries of poverty assessments are available at www.worldbank.org/povertynet, by selecting "Poverty assessments" from the left side bar. Poverty assessment documents are available at www-wds.worldbank.org, under "By topic," "Poverty reduction," "Poverty assessment." Further discussion of how national poverty lines vary across countries can be found in Ravallion, Chen, and Sangraula's "Dollar a Day Revisited" (2008).

Poverty rates at international poverty lines

	International poverty line in local currency		International poverty line									
	$1.25 a day 2005	$2 a day 2005	Survey year	Population below $1.25 a day %	Poverty gap at $1.25 a day %	Population below $2 a day %	Poverty gap at $2 a day %	Survey year	Population below $1.25 a day %	Poverty gap at $1.25 a day %	Population below $2 a day %	Poverty gap at $2 a day %
Albania	75.51	120.82	2002[a]	<2	<0.5	8.7	1.4	2005[a]	<2	<0.5	7.8	1.4
Algeria	48.42[b]	77.48[b]	1988[a]	6.6	1.8	23.8	6.6	1995[a]	6.8	1.4	23.6	6.4
Angola	88.13	141.01		..	..	..	..	2000[a]	54.3	29.9	70.2	42.3
Argentina	1.69	2.71	2002[c,d]	9.9	2.9	19.7	7.4	2005[c,d]	4.5	1.0	11.3	3.6
Armenia	245.24	392.38	2002[a]	15.0	3.1	46.7	13.6	2003[a]	10.6	1.9	43.4	11.3
Azerbaijan	2,170.94	3,473.51	2001[a]	6.3	1.1	27.1	6.8	2005[a]	<2	<0.5	<2	<0.5
Bangladesh	31.87	50.99	2000[a]	57.8[e]	17.3[e]	85.4[e]	38.7[e]	2005[a]	49.6[e]	13.1[e]	81.3[e]	33.8[e]
Belarus	949.53	1,519.25	2002[a]	<2	<0.5	<2	<0.5	2005[a]	<2	<0.5	<2	<0.5
Benin	343.99	550.38		..	..	..	..	2003[a]	47.3	15.7	75.3	33.5
Bhutan	23.08	36.93		..	..	..	..	2003[a]	26.2	7.0	49.5	18.8
Bolivia	3.21	5.14	2002[d]	22.8	12.4	34.2	18.5	2005[a]	19.6	9.7	30.3	15.5
Bosnia and Herzegovina	1.09	1.74	2001[a]	<2	<0.5	<2	<0.5	2004[a]	<2	<0.5	<2	<0.5
Botswana	4.23	6.77	1985–86[a]	35.6	13.8	54.7	25.8	1993–94[a]	31.2	11.0	49.4	22.3
Brazil	1.96	3.14	2005[d]	7.8	1.6	18.3	5.9	2007[d]	5.2	1.3	12.7	4.1
Bulgaria	0.92	1.47	2001[a]	2.6	<0.5	7.8	2.2	2003[a]	<2	<0.5	<2	0.9
Burkina Faso	303.02	484.83	1998[a]	70.0	30.2	87.6	49.1	2003[a]	56.5	20.3	81.2	39.2
Burundi	558.79	894.07	1998[a]	86.4	47.3	95.4	64.1	2006[a]	81.3	36.4	93.4	56.0
Cambodia	2,019.12	3,230.60	1993–94[a,f]	48.6	13.8	77.8	33.3	2004[a]	40.2	11.3	68.2	28.0
Cameroon	368.12	588.99	1996[a]	51.5	18.9	74.4	36.0	2001[a]	32.8	10.2	57.7	23.6
Cape Verde	97.72	156.35		..	..	..	..	2001[a]	20.6	5.9	40.2	14.9
Central African Republic	384.33	614.93	1993[a]	82.8	57.0	90.7	68.4	2003[a]	62.4	28.3	81.9	45.3
Chad	409.46	655.14		..	..	..	..	2002–03[a]	61.9	25.6	83.3	43.9
Chile	484.20	774.72	2003[d]	<2	<0.5	5.3	1.3	2006[d]	<2	<0.5	2.4	0.39
China	5.11[g]	8.17[g]	2002[a]	28.4[h]	8.7[h]	51.1[h]	20.6[h]	2005[a]	15.9[h]	4.0[h]	36.3[h]	12.2[h]
Colombia	1,489.68	2,383.48	2003[d]	15.4	6.1	26.3	10.9	2006[d]	16.0	5.7	27.9	11.9
Comoros	368.01	588.82		..	..	..	..	2004[a]	46.1	20.8	65.0	34.2
Congo, Dem. Rep.	395.29	632.46		..	..	..	..	2005–06[a]	59.2	25.3	79.5	42.4
Congo, Rep.	469.46	751.14		..	..	..	..	2005[a]	54.1	22.8	74.4	38.8
Costa Rica	348.70[b]	557.92[b]	2003[d]	5.6	2.4	11.5	4.7	2005[d]	2.4	<0.5	8.6	2.3
Croatia	5.58	8.92	2001[a]	<2	<0.5	<2	<0.5	2005[a]	<2	<0.5	<2	<0.5
Czech Republic	19.00	30.39	1993[d]	<2	<0.5	<2	<0.5	1996[d]	<2	<0.5	<2	<0.5
Côte d'Ivoire	407.26	651.62	1998[a]	24.1	6.7	49.1	18.1	2002[a]	23.3	6.8	46.8	17.6
Djibouti	134.76	215.61	1996[a]	4.8	1.6	15.1	4.5	2002[a]	18.8	5.3	41.2	14.6
Dominican Republic	25.50[b]	40.79[b]	2003[d]	6.1	1.5	16.3	5.1	2005[d]	5.0	0.9	15.1	4.3
Ecuador	0.63	1.00	2005[d]	9.8	3.2	20.4	7.6	2007[d]	4.7	1.2	12.8	4.0
Egypt, Arab Rep.	2.53	4.04	1999–2000[a]	<2	<0.5	19.3	3.5	2004–05[a]	<2	<0.5	18.4	3.5
El Salvador	6.02[b]	9.62[b]	2003[d]	14.3	6.7	25.3	11.6	2005[d]	11.0	4.8	20.5	8.9
Estonia	11.04	17.66	2002[a]	<2	<0.5	2.5	0.6	2004[a]	<2	<0.5	<2	<0.5
Ethiopia	3.44	5.50	1999–2000[a]	55.6	16.2	86.4	37.9	2005[a]	39.0	9.6	77.5	28.8
Gabon	554.69	887.50		..	..	..	..	2005[a]	4.8	0.9	19.6	5.0
Gambia, The	12.93	20.69	1998[a]	66.7	34.7	82.0	50.0	2003–04[a]	34.3	12.1	56.7	24.9
Georgia	0.98	1.57	2002[a]	15.1	4.7	34.2	12.2	2005[a]	13.4	4.4	30.4	10.9
Ghana	5,594.78	8,951.64	1998–99[a]	39.1	14.4	63.3	28.5	2006[a]	30.0	10.5	53.6	22.3
Guatemala	5.68[b]	9.08[b]	2002[d]	16.9	6.5	29.8	12.9	2006[d]	11.7	3.5	24.3	8.9
Guinea-Bissau	355.34	568.55	1993–94[a]	52.1	20.6	75.7	37.4	2002–03[a]	48.8	16.5	77.9	34.8
Guinea	1,849.46	2,959.13	1994[a]	36.8	11.5	63.8	26.4	2002–03[a]	70.1	32.2	87.2	50.2
Guyana	131.47[b]	210.35[b]	1993[d]	5.8	2.6	15.0	5.4	1998[d]	7.7	3.9	16.8	6.9
Haiti	24.21[b]	38.73[b]		..	..	..	..	2001[d]	54.9	28.2	72.1	41.8
Honduras	12.08[b]	19.32[b]	2005[d]	22.2	10.2	34.8	16.7	2006[d]	18.2	8.2	29.7	14.2
Hungary	171.90	275.03	2002[a]	<2	<0.5	<2	<0.5	2004[a]	<2	<0.5	<2	<0.5
India	19.50[i]	31.20[i]	1993–94[a]	49.4[h]	14.4[h]	81.7[h]	35.3[h]	2004–05[a]	41.6[h]	10.8[h]	75.6[h]	30.4[h]
Iran, Islamic Rep.	3,393.53	5,429.65	1998[a]	<2	<0.5	8.3	1.8	2005[a]	<2	<0.5	8.0	1.8
Jamaica	54.20[b]	86.72[b]	2002[a]	<2	<0.5	8.7	1.6	2004[a]	<2	<0.5	5.8	0.9
Jordan	0.62	0.99	2002–03[a]	<2	<0.5	11.0	2.1	2006[a]	<2	<0.5	3.5	0.6
Kazakhstan	81.21	129.93	2002[a]	5.2	0.9	21.5	5.4	2003[a]	3.1	<0.5	17.2	3.9

	International poverty line in local currency			International poverty line								
	$1.25 a day 2005	$2 a day 2005	Survey year	Population below $1.25 a day %	Poverty gap at $1.25 a day %	Population below $2 a day %	Poverty gap at $2 a day %	Survey year	Population below $1.25 a day %	Poverty gap at $1.25 a day %	Population below $2 a day %	Poverty gap at $2 a day %
Kenya	40.85	65.37	1997[a]	19.6	4.6	42.7	14.7	2005–06[a]	19.7	6.1	39.9	15.1
Kyrgyz Republic	16.25	26.00	2002[a]	34.0	8.8	66.6	24.9	2004[a]	21.8	4.4	51.9	16.8
Lao PDR	4,677.02	7,483.24	1997–98	49.3[e]	14.9[e]	79.9[e]	34.4[e]	2002–03[a]	44.0[e]	12.1[e]	76.8[e]	31.0[e]
Latvia	0.43	0.69	2002[a]	<2	<0.5	<2	0.6	2004[a]	<2	<0.5	<2	<0.5
Lesotho	4.28	6.85	1995[a]	47.6	26.7	61.1	37.3	2002–03[a]	43.4	20.8	62.2	33.0
Liberia	0.64	1.02		..	..	..	..	2007[a]	83.7	40.8	94.8	59.5
Lithuania	2.08	3.32	2002[a]	<2	<0.5	<2	<0.5	2004[a]	<2	<0.5	<2	<0.5
Macedonia, FYR	29.47	47.16	2002[a]	<2	<0.5	3.1	0.7	2003[a]	<2	<0.5	3.2	0.7
Madagascar	945.48	1,512.76	2001[a]	76.3	41.4	88.7	57.2	2005[a]	67.8	26.5	89.6	46.9
Malawi	71.15	113.84	1997–98[d]	83.1	46.0	93.5	62.3	2004–05[a,j]	73.9	32.3	90.4	51.8
Malaysia	2.64	4.23	1997[d]	<2	<0.5	6.8	1.3	2004–05[d]	<2	<0.5	7.8	1.4
Mali	362.10	579.36	2001[a]	61.2	25.8	82.0	43.6	2006[a]	51.4	18.8	77.1	36.5
Mauritania	157.08	251.33	1995–96[a]	23.4	7.1	48.3	17.8	2000[a]	21.2	5.7	44.1	15.9
Mexico	9.56	15.30	2004[a]	2.8	1.4	7.0	2.6	2006[a]	<2	<0.5	4.8	1.0
Moldova	6.03	9.65	2002[a]	17.1	4.0	40.3	13.2	2004[a]	8.1	1.7	28.9	7.9
Mongolia	653.12	1,044.99	2002[a]	15.5	3.6	38.8	12.3	2005[a]	22.4	6.2	49.0	17.2
Morocco	6.89	11.02	2000[a]	6.3	0.9	24.3	6.3	2007[a]	2.5	0.5	14.0	3.1
Mozambique	14,532.12	23,251.39	1996–97[a]	81.3	42.0	92.9	59.4	2002–03[a]	74.7	35.4	90.0	53.5
Namibia	6.33	10.13		..	..	..	..	1993[d]	49.1	24.6	62.2	36.5
Nepal	33.08	52.93	1995–96[a]	68.4	26.7	88.1	46.8	2003–04[a]	55.1	19.7	77.6	37.8
Nicaragua	9.12[b]	14.59[b]	2001[d]	19.4	6.7	37.5	14.4	2005[d]	15.8	5.2	31.8	12.3
Niger	334.16	534.66	1994[a]	78.2	38.6	91.5	56.5	2005[a]	65.9	28.1	85.6	46.6
Nigeria	98.23	157.17	1996–97[a]	68.5	32.1	86.4	49.7	2003–04[a]	64.4	29.6	83.9	46.9
Pakistan	25.89	41.42	2001–02[a]	35.9	7.9	73.9	26.4	2004–05[a]	22.6	4.4	60.3	18.7
Panama	0.76[b]	1.22[b]	2004[d]	9.2	2.7	18.0	6.8	2006[d]	9.5	3.1	17.8	7.1
Papua New Guinea	2.11[b]	3.37[b]		..	..	..	..	1996[a]	35.8	12.3	57.4	25.5
Paraguay	2,659.74	4,255.59	2005[d]	9.3	3.4	18.4	7.3	2007[d]	6.5	2.7	14.2	5.5
Peru	2.07	3.31	2005[d]	8.2	2.0	19.4	6.3	2006[d]	7.9	1.9	18.5	6.0
Philippines	30.22	48.36	2003[a]	22.0	5.5	43.8	16.0	2006[a]	22.6	5.5	45.0	16.3
Poland	2.69	4.31	2002[a]	<2	<0.5	<2	<0.5	2005[a]	<2	<0.5	<2	<0.5
Romania	2.15	3.44	2002[a]	2.9	0.8	13.0	3.2	2005[a]	<2	<0.5	3.4	0.9
Russian Federation	16.74	26.78	2002[a]	<2	<0.5	3.7	0.6	2005[a]	<2	<0.5	<2	<0.5
Rwanda	295.93	473.49	1984–85[a]	63.3	19.7	88.4	41.8	2000[a]	76.6	38.2	90.3	55.7
Senegal	372.81	596.49	2001[a]	44.2	14.3	71.3	31.2	2005[a]	33.5	10.8	60.3	24.6
Sierra Leone	1,745.26	2,792.42	1989–90[a]	62.8	44.8	75.0	54.0	2002–03[a]	53.4	20.3	76.1	37.5
Slovak Republic	23.53	37.66	1992[d]	<2	<0.5	<2	<0.5	1996[d]	<2	<0.5	<2	<0.5
Slovenia	198.25	317.20	2002[a]	<2	<0.5	<2	<0.5	2004[a]	<2	<0.5	<2	<0.5
South Africa	5.71	9.14	1995[a]	21.4	5.2	39.9	15.0	2000[a]	26.2	8.2	42.9	18.3
Sri Lanka	50.05	80.08	1995–96[a]	16.3	3.0	46.7	13.7	2002[a]	14.0	2.6	39.7	11.8
St. Lucia	2.37[b]	3.80[b]		..	..	..	..	1995[d]	20.9	7.2	40.6	15.5
Suriname	2.29[b]	3.67[b]		..	..	..	..	1999[d]	15.5	5.9	27.2	11.7
Swaziland	4.66	7.45	1994–95[a]	78.6	47.7	89.3	61.6	2000–01[a]	62.9	29.4	81.0	45.8
Tajikistan	1.16	1.85	2003[a]	36.3	10.3	68.8	26.7	2004[a]	21.5	5.1	50.8	16.8
Tanzania	603.06	964.90	1991–92[a]	72.6	29.7	91.3	50.1	2000–01[a]	88.5	46.8	96.6	64.4
Thailand	21.83	34.93	2002[a]	<2	<0.5	15.1	2.8	2004[a]	<2	<0.5	11.5	2.0
Timor-Leste	0.61[b]	0.98[b]		..	..	..	..	2001[a]	52.9	19.1	77.5	37.0
Togo	352.82	564.51		..	..	..	..	2006[a]	38.7	11.4	69.3	27.9
Trinidad and Tobago	5.77[b]	9.23[b]	1988[d]	<2	<0.5	8.6	1.9	1992[d]	4.2	1.1	13.5	3.9
Tunisia	0.87	1.39	1995[a]	6.5	1.3	20.4	5.8	2000[a]	2.6	<0.5	12.8	3.0
Turkey	1.25	2.00	2002[a]	2.0	<0.5	9.6	2.3	2005[a]	2.7	0.9	9.0	2.6
Turkmenistan	5,961.06[b]	9,537.69[b]	1993[d]	63.5	25.8	85.7	44.8	1998[a]	24.8	7.0	49.6	18.4
Uganda	930.77	1,489.24	2002[a]	57.4	22.7	79.8	40.6	2005[a]	51.5	19.1	75.6	36.4
Ukraine	2.14	3.42	2002[a]	<2	<0.5	3.4	0.7	2005[a]	<2	<0.5	<2	<0.5
Uruguay	19.14	30.62	2005[c,d]	<2	<0.5	4.5	0.7	2006[d]	<2	<0.5	4.2	0.6
Uzbekistan	470.09[b]	752.14[b]	2002[a]	42.3	12.4	75.6	30.6	2003[a]	46.3	15.0	76.7	33.2
Venezuela, RB	1,563.90	2,502.24	2003[d]	18.4	8.8	31.7	14.6	2006[d]	3.5	1.2	10.2	3.2

Poverty rates at international poverty lines | **2.8**

	International poverty line in local currency			International poverty line								
	$1.25 a day **2005**	$2 a day **2005**	Survey year	Population below $1.25 a day %	Poverty gap at $1.25 a day %	Population below $2 a day %	Poverty gap at $2 a day %	Survey year	Population below $1.25 a day %	Poverty gap at $1.25 a day %	Population below $2 a day %	Poverty gap at $2 a day %
Vietnam	7,399.87	11,839.79	2004[a]	24.2	5.1	52.5	17.9	2006[a]	21.5	4.6	48.4	16.2
Yemen, Rep.	113.83	182.12	1998[a]	12.9	3.0	36.3	11.1	2005[a]	17.5	4.2	46.6	14.8
Zambia	3,537.91	5,660.65	2002–03[a]	64.6	27.1	85.1	45.8	2004–05[a]	64.3	32.8	81.5	48.3

a. Expenditure based. b. PPP imputed using regression. c. Covers urban area only. d. Income based. e. Adjusted by spatial consumer price index information. f. Due to security concerns, the survey covered only 56 percent of rural villages and 65 percent of the rural population. g. PPP conversion factor based on urban prices. h. Weighted average of urban and rural estimates. i. Weighted average of urban and rural poverty lines. j. Due to change in survey design, the most recent survey is not strictly comparable with the previous one.

Regional poverty estimates and progress toward the Millennium Development Goals

Global poverty measured at the $1.25 a day poverty line has been decreasing since the 1980s. The share of population living on less than $1.25 a day fell 10 percentage points, to 42 percent, in 1990 and then fell nearly 17 percentage points between 1990 and 2005. The number of people living in extreme poverty fell from 1.9 billion in 1981 to 1.8 billion in 1990 to about 1.4 billion in 2005 (figure 2.8a). This substantial reduction in extreme poverty over the past quarter century, however, disguises large regional differences.

The greatest reduction in poverty occurred in East Asia and Pacific, where the poverty rate declined from 78 percent in 1981 to 17 percent in 2005 and the number of people living on less than $1.25 a day dropped more than 750 million (figure 2.8b). Much of this decline was in China, where poverty fell from 84 percent to 16 percent, leaving 620 million fewer people in poverty.

Over the same period the poverty rate in South Asia fell from 59 percent to 40 percent (table 2.8c). In contrast, the poverty rate fell only slightly in Sub-Saharan Africa—from less than 54 percent in 1981 to more than 58 percent in 1999 then down to 51 percent in 2005. But the number of people living below the poverty line has nearly doubled.

Only East Asia and Pacific is consistently on track to meet the Millennium Development Goal target of reducing 1990 poverty rates by half by 2015. A slight acceleration over historical growth rates could lift Latin America and the Caribbean and South Asia to the target. However, the recent slowdown in the global economy may leave these regions and many countries short of the target. Preliminary estimates for 2009 suggest that lower economic growth rates will likely leave 46 million more people below the $1.25 a day poverty line than had been expected before the crisis.

Most of the people who have escaped extreme poverty remain very poor by the standards of middle-income economies. The median poverty line for developing countries in 2005 was $2.00 a day. The poverty rate for all developing countries measured at this line fell from nearly 70 percent in 1981 to 47 percent in 2005, but the number of people living on less than $2.00 a day has remained nearly constant at 2.5 billion. The largest decrease, both in number and proportion, occurred in East Asia and Pacific, led by China. Elsewhere, the number of people living on less than $2.00 a day increased, and the number of people living between $1.25 and $2.00 a day nearly doubled, to 1.18 billion. In 2009 the global growth deceleration will likely leave 53 million more people below the $2 a day poverty line.

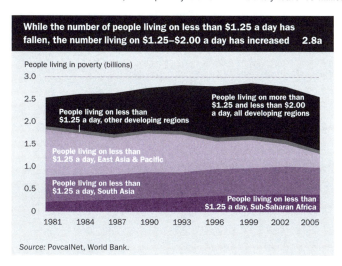

Source: PovcalNet, World Bank.

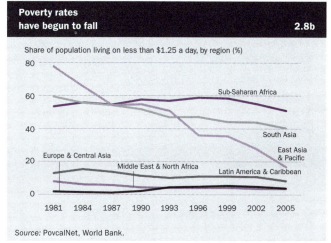

Source: PovcalNet, World Bank.

Regional poverty estimates   2.8c

Region	1981	1984	1987	1990	1993	1996	1999	2002	2005
People living on less than 2005 PPP $1.25 a day (millions)									
East Asia & Pacific	1,072	947	822	873	845	622	635	507	316
China	835	720	586	683	633	443	447	363	208
Europe & Central Asia	7	6	5	9	20	21	24	21	17
Latin America & Caribbean	47	59	56	49	46	53	55	56	45
Middle East & North Africa	14	12	12	10	10	10	11	10	11
South Asia	548	548	569	579	559	594	589	616	596
India	420	416	428	435	444	442	447	460	456
Sub-Saharan Africa	211	241	256	295	317	355	382	390	388
Total	1,898	1,812	1,721	1,816	1,797	1,657	1,696	1,600	1,373
Share of people living on less than 2005 PPP $1.25 a day (%)									
East Asia & Pacific	77.7	65.5	54.2	54.7	50.8	36.0	35.5	27.6	16.8
China	84.0	69.4	54.0	60.2	53.7	36.4	35.6	28.4	15.9
Europe & Central Asia	1.8	1.4	1.1	2.1	4.4	4.8	5.3	4.8	3.8
Latin America & Caribbean	12.9	15.3	13.7	11.3	10.1	10.9	10.9	10.7	8.2
Middle East & North Africa	7.9	6.1	5.7	4.3	4.1	4.1	4.2	3.6	3.6
South Asia	59.4	55.6	54.2	51.7	46.9	47.1	44.1	43.8	40.3
India	59.8	55.5	53.6	51.3	49.4	46.6	44.8	43.9	41.6
Sub-Saharan Africa	53.4	55.8	54.5	57.6	56.9	58.8	58.4	55.0	50.9
Total	52.2	47.0	42.1	42.0	39.5	34.7	33.9	30.7	25.3
People living on less than 2005 PPP $2.00 a day (millions)									
East Asia & Pacific	1,278	1,280	1,238	1,273	1,262	1,108	1,105	954	728
China	972	963	907	961	926	792	770	655	473
Europe & Central Asia	35	28	25	31	47	55	66	55	41
Latin America & Caribbean	89	109	102	95	95	106	110	113	94
Middle East & North Africa	46	43	47	44	48	52	51	50	51
South Asia	799	836	881	926	950	1,008	1,030	1,083	1,091
India	609	635	669	702	735	757	783	813	827
Sub-Saharan Africa	291	325	348	390	423	471	508	535	555
Total	2,538	2,622	2,642	2,760	2,825	2,800	2,870	2,791	2,560
Share of people living on less than 2005 PPP $2.00 a day (%)									
East Asia & Pacific	92.6	88.5	81.5	79.8	75.8	64.1	61.8	51.9	38.6
China	97.8	92.9	83.7	84.6	78.6	65.0	61.4	51.1	36.3
Europe & Central Asia	8.7	6.8	5.9	7.1	10.8	12.4	14.9	12.5	9.2
Latin America & Caribbean	24.6	28.1	24.9	21.9	20.7	22.0	21.8	21.5	17.1
Middle East & North Africa	26.7	23.0	22.7	19.7	19.8	20.2	18.9	17.6	16.9
South Asia	86.5	84.8	83.9	82.7	79.7	79.8	77.2	77.0	73.9
India	86.6	84.8	83.8	82.6	81.7	79.8	78.4	77.5	75.6
Sub-Saharan Africa	73.8	75.5	74.0	76.0	75.9	77.9	77.6	75.6	72.9
Total	69.9	68.1	64.7	63.8	62.0	58.6	57.4	53.6	47.3

Source: World Bank PovcalNet.

Poverty rates at international poverty lines | **2.8**

About the data

The World Bank produced its first global poverty estimates for developing countries for *World Development Report 1990: Poverty* using household survey data for 22 countries (Ravallion, Datt, and van de Walle 1991). Since then there has been considerable expansion in the number of countries that field household income and expenditure surveys. The World Bank's poverty monitoring database now includes more than 600 surveys representing 115 developing countries. More than 1.2 million randomly sampled households were interviewed in these surveys, representing 96 percent of the population of developing countries.

Data availability

The number of data sets within two years of any given year rose dramatically, from 13 between 1978 and 1982 to 158 between 2001 and 2006. Data coverage is improving in all regions, but the Middle East and North Africa and Sub-Saharan Africa continue to lag. The database, maintained by a team in the World Bank's Development Research Group, is updated annually as new survey data become available, and a major reassessment of progress against poverty is made about every three years. A complete overview of data availability by year and country is available at http://iresearch.worldbank.org/povcalnet/.

Data quality

Besides the frequency and timeliness of survey data, other data quality issues arise in measuring household living standards. The surveys ask detailed questions on sources of income and how it was spent, which must be carefully recorded by trained personnel. Income is generally more difficult to measure accurately, and consumption comes closer to the notion of living standards. And income can vary over time even if living standards do not. But consumption data are not always available: the latest estimates reported here use consumption for about two-thirds of countries.

However, even similar surveys may not be strictly comparable because of differences in timing or in the quality and training of enumerators. Comparisons of countries at different levels of development also pose a potential problem because of differences in the relative importance of the consumption of nonmarket goods. The local market value of all consumption in kind (including own production, particularly important in underdeveloped rural economies) should be included in total consumption expenditure, but may not be. Most survey data now include valuations for consumption or income from own production, but valuation methods vary.

The statistics reported here are based on consumption data or, when unavailable, on income surveys. Analysis of some 20 countries for which income and consumption expenditure data were both available from the same surveys found income to yield a higher mean than consumption but also higher inequality. When poverty measures based on consumption and income were compared, the two effects roughly cancelled each other out: there was no significant statistical difference.

International poverty lines

International comparisons of poverty estimates entail both conceptual and practical problems. Countries have different definitions of poverty, and consistent comparisons across countries can be difficult. Local poverty lines tend to have higher purchasing power in rich countries, where more generous standards are used, than in poor countries.

Poverty measures based on an international poverty line attempt to hold the real value of the poverty line constant across countries, as is done when making comparisons over time. Since *World Development Report 1990* the World Bank has aimed to apply a common standard in measuring extreme poverty, anchored to what *poverty* means in the world's poorest countries. The welfare of people living in different countries can be measured on a common scale by adjusting for differences in the purchasing power of currencies. The commonly used $1 a day standard, measured in 1985 international prices and adjusted to local currency using purchasing power parities (PPPs), was chosen for *World Development Report 1990* because it was typical of the poverty lines in low-income countries at the time.

Early editions of *World Development Indicators* used PPPs from the Penn World Tables to convert values in local currency to equivalent purchasing power measured in U.S dollars. Later editions used 1993 consumption PPP estimates produced by the World Bank. International poverty lines were recently revised using the new data on PPPs compiled in the 2005 round of the International Comparison Program, along with data from an expanded set of household income and expenditure surveys. The new extreme poverty line is set at $1.25 a day in 2005 PPP terms, which represents the mean of the poverty lines found in the poorest 15 countries ranked by per capita consumption. The new poverty line maintains the same standard for extreme poverty—the poverty line typical of the poorest countries in the world—but updates it using the latest information on the cost of living in developing countries.

PPP exchange rates are used to estimate global poverty, because they take into account the local prices of goods and services not traded internationally. But PPP rates were designed for comparing aggregates from national accounts, not for making international poverty comparisons. As a result, there is no certainty that an international poverty line measures the same degree of need or deprivation across countries. So called poverty PPPs, designed to compare the consumption of the poorest people in the world, might provide a better basis for comparison of poverty across countries. Work on these measures is ongoing.

Definitions

• **International poverty line in local currency** is the international poverty lines of $1.25 and $2.00 a day in 2005 prices, converted to local currency using the PPP conversion factors estimated by the International Comparison Program. • **Survey year** is the year in which the underlying data were collected. • **Population below $1.25 a day** and **population below $2 a day** are the percentages of the population living on less than $1.25 a day and $2.00 a day at 2005 international prices. As a result of revisions in PPP exchange rates, poverty rates for individual countries cannot be compared with poverty rates reported in earlier editions. • **Poverty gap** is the mean shortfall from the poverty line (counting the nonpoor as having zero shortfall), expressed as a percentage of the poverty line. This measure reflects the depth of poverty as well as its incidence.

Data sources

The poverty measures are prepared by the World Bank's Development Research Group. The international poverty lines are based on nationally representative primary household surveys conducted by national statistical offices or by private agencies under the supervision of government or international agencies and obtained from government statistical offices and World Bank Group country departments. The World Bank Group has prepared an annual review of its poverty work since 1993. For details on data sources and methods used in deriving the World Bank's latest estimates, and further discussion of the results, see Shaohua Chen and Martin Ravallion's "The Developing World Is Poorer Than We Thought, but No Less Successful in the Fight against Poverty?" (2008).

	Survey year	Gini index	Percentage share of income or consumption[a]						
			Lowest 10%	Lowest 20%	Second 20%	Third 20%	Fourth 20%	Highest 20%	Highest 10%
Afghanistan		..	..	..	..	..	..	..	..
Albania	2005[b]	33.0	3.2	7.8	12.2	16.6	22.6	40.9	25.9
Algeria	1995[b]	35.3	2.8	6.9	11.5	16.3	22.8	42.4	26.9
Angola	2000[b]	58.6	0.6	2.0	5.7	10.8	19.7	61.9	44.7
Argentina[c]	2005[d]	50.0	1.2	3.4	7.8	13.3	21.6	53.9	37.3
Armenia	2003[b]	33.8	3.7	8.6	12.3	15.7	20.7	42.8	28.9
Australia	1994[d]	35.2	2.0	5.9	12.0	17.2	23.6	41.3	25.4
Austria	2000[d]	29.1	3.3	8.6	13.3	17.4	22.9	37.8	23.0
Azerbaijan	2005[b]	16.8	6.1	13.3	16.2	18.7	21.7	30.2	17.5
Bangladesh	2005[b]	31.0	4.3	9.4	12.6	16.1	21.1	40.8	26.6
Belarus	2005[b]	27.9	3.6	8.8	13.6	17.8	23.1	36.7	22.0
Belgium	2000[d]	33.0	3.4	8.5	13.0	16.3	20.8	41.4	28.1
Benin	2003[b]	38.6	2.9	6.9	10.9	15.1	21.2	45.9	31.0
Bolivia	2005[b]	58.2	0.5	1.8	5.9	11.4	20.2	60.7	44.1
Bosnia and Herzegovina	2004[b]	35.8	2.8	6.9	11.5	16.2	22.6	42.8	27.4
Botswana	1993–95[b]	61.0	1.3	3.1	5.8	9.6	16.4	65.0	51.2
Brazil	2007[d]	55.0	1.1	3.0	6.9	11.8	19.6	58.7	43.0
Bulgaria	2003[b]	29.2	3.5	8.7	13.5	17.4	22.3	38.1	23.8
Burkina Faso	2003[b]	39.6	3.0	7.0	10.6	14.7	20.6	47.1	32.4
Burundi	2006[b]	33.3	4.1	9.0	11.9	15.4	21.0	42.8	28.0
Cambodia	2007[b]	40.7	3.0	7.1	10.6	14.0	19.6	48.8	34.2
Cameroon	2001[b]	44.6	2.4	5.6	9.3	13.7	20.5	50.9	35.5
Canada	2000[d]	32.6	2.6	7.2	12.7	17.2	23.0	39.9	24.8
Central African Republic	2003[b]	43.6	2.1	5.2	9.4	14.3	21.7	49.4	33.0
Chad	2002–03[b]	39.8	2.6	6.3	10.4	15.0	21.8	46.6	30.8
Chile	2006[d]	52.0	1.6	4.1	7.7	12.2	19.3	56.8	41.7
China	2005[d]	41.5	2.4	5.7	9.8	14.7	22.0	47.8	31.4
Hong Kong, China	1996[d]	43.4	2.0	5.3	9.4	13.9	20.7	50.7	34.9
Colombia	2006[d]	58.5	0.8	2.3	6.0	11.0	19.1	61.6	45.9
Congo, Dem. Rep.	2005–06[b]	44.4	2.3	5.5	9.2	13.8	20.9	50.6	34.7
Congo, Rep.	2005[b]	47.3	2.1	5.0	8.4	13.0	20.5	53.1	37.1
Costa Rica	2005[d]	47.2	1.5	4.2	8.6	13.9	21.7	51.8	35.5
Côte d'Ivoire	2002[b]	48.4	2.0	5.0	8.7	12.9	19.3	54.1	39.6
Croatia	2005[b]	29.0	3.6	8.7	13.3	17.5	22.8	37.7	23.1
Cuba		..	..	..	..	..	..	..	..
Czech Republic	1996[d]	25.8	4.3	10.2	14.3	17.5	21.7	36.2	22.7
Denmark	1997[d]	24.7	2.6	8.3	14.7	18.2	22.9	35.8	21.3
Dominican Republic	2005[d]	50.0	1.5	4.0	8.0	12.9	20.6	54.5	38.7
Ecuador	2007[d]	54.4	1.2	3.4	7.2	11.8	19.2	58.5	43.3
Egypt, Arab Rep.	2004–05[b]	32.1	3.9	9.0	12.6	16.1	20.9	41.5	27.6
El Salvador	2005[d]	49.7	1.0	3.3	8.1	13.6	21.6	53.4	37.0
Eritrea		..	..	..	..	..	..	..	..
Estonia	2004[b]	36.0	2.7	6.8	11.6	16.2	22.5	43.0	27.7
Ethiopia	2005[b]	29.8	4.1	9.3	13.2	16.8	21.4	39.4	25.6
Finland	2000[d]	26.9	4.0	9.6	14.1	17.5	22.1	36.7	22.6
France	1995[d]	32.7	2.8	7.2	12.6	17.2	22.8	40.2	25.1
Gabon	2005[b]	41.5	2.5	6.1	10.1	14.6	21.2	47.9	32.7
Gambia, The	2003[b]	47.3	2.0	4.8	8.6	13.2	20.6	52.8	36.9
Georgia	2005[b]	40.8	1.9	5.4	10.4	15.4	22.4	46.4	30.6
Germany	2000[d]	28.3	3.2	8.5	13.7	17.8	23.1	36.9	22.1
Ghana	2006[b]	42.8	1.9	5.2	9.8	14.8	21.9	48.3	32.5
Greece	2000[d]	34.3	2.5	6.7	11.9	16.8	23.0	41.5	26.0
Guatemala	2006[d]	53.7	1.3	3.4	7.2	12.0	19.5	57.8	42.4
Guinea	2003[b]	43.3	2.4	5.8	9.6	14.1	20.8	49.7	34.4
Guinea-Bissau	2002[b]	35.5	2.9	7.2	11.6	16.0	22.1	43.0	28.0
Haiti	2001[d]	59.5	0.9	2.5	5.9	10.5	18.1	63.0	47.8

Distribution of income or consumption **2.9**

	Survey year	Gini index	Percentage share of income or consumption[a]						
			Lowest 10%	Lowest 20%	Second 20%	Third 20%	Fourth 20%	Highest 20%	Highest 10%
Honduras	2006[d]	55.3	0.7	2.5	6.7	12.1	20.4	58.4	42.2
Hungary	2004[b]	30.0	3.5	8.6	13.1	17.1	22.5	38.7	24.1
India	2004–05[b]	36.8	3.6	8.1	11.3	14.9	20.4	45.3	31.1
Indonesia	2005[b]	39.4	3.0	7.1	10.7	14.4	20.5	47.3	32.3
Iran, Islamic Rep.	2005[b]	38.3	2.6	6.4	10.9	15.6	22.2	45.0	29.6
Iraq		..	..	..	..	..	..	..	..
Ireland	2000[d]	34.3	2.9	7.4	12.3	16.3	21.9	42.0	27.2
Israel	2001[d]	39.2	2.1	5.7	10.5	15.9	23.0	44.9	28.8
Italy	2000[d]	36.0	2.3	6.5	12.0	16.8	22.8	42.0	26.8
Jamaica	2004[b]	45.5	2.1	5.2	9.0	13.8	20.9	51.2	35.6
Japan	1993[d]	24.9	4.8	10.6	14.2	17.6	22.0	35.7	21.7
Jordan	2006[b]	37.7	3.0	7.2	11.1	15.2	21.1	45.4	30.7
Kazakhstan	2003[b]	33.9	3.1	7.4	11.9	16.6	23.0	41.3	25.9
Kenya	2005[b]	47.7	1.8	4.7	8.8	13.3	20.3	53.0	37.8
Korea, Dem. Rep.		..	..	..	..	..	..	..	..
Korea, Rep.	1998[d]	31.6	2.9	7.9	13.6	18.0	23.1	37.5	22.5
Kuwait		..	..	..	..	..	..	..	..
Kyrgyz Republic	2004[b]	32.9	3.6	8.1	12.0	16.2	22.3	41.4	25.9
Lao PDR	2002–03[b]	32.6	3.7	8.5	12.3	16.2	21.6	41.4	27.0
Latvia	2004[b]	35.7	2.7	6.8	11.6	16.3	22.6	42.7	27.4
Lebanon		..	..	..	..	..	..	..	..
Lesotho	2003[b]	52.5	1.0	3.0	7.2	12.5	21.0	56.4	39.4
Liberia	2007[b]	52.6	2.4	6.4	11.4	15.7	21.6	45.0	30.1
Libya		..	..	..	..	..	..	..	..
Lithuania	2004[b]	35.8	2.7	6.8	11.5	16.3	22.7	42.8	27.4
Macedonia, FYR	2003[b]	39.0	2.4	6.1	10.6	15.6	22.5	45.2	29.5
Madagascar	2005[b]	47.2	2.6	6.2	9.6	13.1	17.7	53.5	41.5
Malawi	2004–05[b]	39.0	2.9	7.0	10.8	14.9	20.9	46.4	31.7
Malaysia	2004[d]	37.9	2.6	6.4	10.8	15.8	22.8	44.4	28.5
Mali	2006[b]	39.0	2.7	6.5	10.7	15.2	21.6	46.0	30.5
Mauritania	2000[b]	39.0	2.5	6.2	10.5	15.4	22.3	45.7	29.6
Mauritius		..	..	..	..	..	..	..	..
Mexico	2006[b]	48.1	1.8	4.6	8.6	13.2	20.3	53.3	37.9
Moldova	2004[b]	35.6	3.0	7.3	11.6	16.0	22.0	43.1	28.2
Mongolia	2005[b]	33.0	2.9	7.2	12.2	17.1	23.4	40.2	24.8
Morocco	2007[b]	40.9	2.7	6.5	10.5	14.5	20.6	47.9	33.2
Mozambique	2002–03[b]	47.1	2.1	5.4	9.2	13.1	19.0	53.3	39.2
Myanmar		..	..	..	..	..	..	..	..
Namibia	1993[d]	74.3	0.6	1.5	2.8	5.5	12.0	78.3	65.0
Nepal	2003–04[b]	47.3	2.7	6.1	8.9	12.5	18.4	54.2	40.4
Netherlands	1999[d]	30.9	2.5	7.6	13.2	17.2	23.3	38.7	22.9
New Zealand	1997[d]	36.2	2.2	6.4	11.4	15.8	22.6	43.8	27.8
Nicaragua	2005[d]	52.3	1.4	3.8	7.7	12.3	19.4	56.9	41.8
Niger	2005[b]	43.9	2.3	5.9	9.8	13.9	20.1	50.3	35.7
Nigeria	2003–04[b]	42.9	2.0	5.1	9.7	14.7	21.9	48.6	32.4
Norway	2000[d]	25.8	3.9	9.6	14.0	17.2	22.0	37.2	23.4
Oman		..	..	..	..	..	..	..	..
Pakistan	2004–05[b]	31.2	3.9	9.1	12.8	16.3	21.3	40.5	26.5
Panama	2006[d]	54.9	0.8	2.5	6.6	12.1	20.8	58.0	41.4
Papua New Guinea	1996[b]	50.9	1.9	4.5	7.7	12.1	19.3	56.4	40.9
Paraguay	2007[d]	53.2	1.1	3.4	7.6	12.2	19.4	57.4	42.3
Peru	2006[d]	49.6	1.5	3.9	8.0	13.2	21.0	54.0	37.9
Philippines	2006[b]	44.0	2.4	5.6	9.1	13.7	21.2	50.4	33.9
Poland	2005[b]	34.9	3.0	7.3	11.7	16.2	22.4	42.4	27.2
Portugal	1997[d]	38.5	2.0	5.8	11.0	15.5	21.9	45.9	29.8
Puerto Rico		..	..	..	..	..	..	..	..

	Survey year	Gini index	Percentage share of income or consumption[a]						
			Lowest 10%	Lowest 20%	Second 20%	Third 20%	Fourth 20%	Highest 20%	Highest 10%
Romania	2005[b]	31.5	3.3	8.2	12.8	16.8	22.3	39.9	25.3
Russian Federation	2005[b]	37.5	2.6	6.4	11.0	15.9	22.7	44.1	28.4
Rwanda	2000[b]	46.7	2.3	5.4	9.0	13.2	19.6	52.8	38.2
Saudi Arabia		..	..	..	..	..	..	..	..
Senegal	2005[b]	39.2	2.5	6.2	10.6	15.3	22.0	45.9	30.1
Serbia[e]	2003[b]	30.0	3.4	8.3	13.0	17.3	23.0	38.4	23.4
Sierra Leone	2003[b]	42.5	2.6	6.1	9.7	14.0	20.9	49.3	33.6
Singapore	1998[d]	42.5	1.9	5.0	9.4	14.6	22.0	49.0	32.8
Slovak Republic	1996[d]	25.8	3.1	8.8	14.9	18.6	22.9	34.8	20.8
Slovenia	2004[b]	31.2	3.4	8.2	12.8	17.0	22.6	39.4	24.6
Somalia		..	..	..	..	..	..	..	..
South Africa	2000[b]	57.8	1.3	3.1	5.6	9.9	18.8	62.7	44.9
Spain	2000[d]	34.7	2.6	7.0	12.1	16.4	22.5	42.0	26.6
Sri Lanka	2002[b]	41.1	2.9	6.8	10.4	14.4	20.5	48.0	33.3
Sudan		..	..	..	..	..	..	..	..
Swaziland	2001[b]	50.7	1.8	4.5	8.0	12.3	19.4	55.9	40.8
Sweden	2000[d]	25.0	3.6	9.1	14.0	17.6	22.7	36.6	22.2
Switzerland	2000[d]	33.7	2.9	7.6	12.2	16.3	22.6	41.3	25.9
Syrian Arab Republic		..	..	..	..	..	..	..	..
Tajikistan	2004[b]	33.6	3.2	7.7	12.0	16.4	22.4	41.4	26.4
Tanzania	2000–01[b]	34.6	3.1	7.3	11.8	16.3	22.3	42.3	27.0
Thailand	2004[b]	42.5	2.6	6.1	9.8	14.2	21.0	49.0	33.7
Timor-Leste	2001[b]	39.5	2.9	6.7	10.4	14.8	21.3	46.8	31.3
Togo	2006[b]	34.4	3.3	7.6	11.7	16.1	22.2	42.4	27.1
Trinidad and Tobago	1992[d]	40.3	2.1	5.5	10.3	15.5	22.7	45.9	29.9
Tunisia	2000[b]	40.8	2.4	5.9	10.2	14.9	21.8	47.2	31.6
Turkey	2005[b]	43.2	1.9	5.2	9.8	14.6	21.6	48.8	33.2
Turkmenistan	1998[b]	40.8	2.5	6.0	10.2	14.9	21.7	47.2	31.8
Uganda	2005[b]	42.6	2.6	6.1	9.8	14.1	20.7	49.3	34.1
Ukraine	2005[b]	28.2	3.8	9.0	13.4	17.6	22.9	37.2	22.5
United Arab Emirates		..	..	..	..	..	..	..	..
United Kingdom	1999[d]	36.0	2.1	6.1	11.4	16.0	22.5	44.0	28.5
United States	2000[d]	40.8	1.9	5.4	10.7	15.7	22.4	45.8	29.9
Uruguay	2006[d]	46.2	1.7	4.5	8.7	14.0	21.8	51.1	34.8
Uzbekistan	2003[b]	36.7	2.9	7.1	11.5	15.7	21.5	44.2	29.5
Venezuela, RB	2006[d]	43.4	1.7	4.9	9.6	14.8	22.1	48.6	32.7
Vietnam	2006[b]	37.8	3.1	7.1	10.8	15.2	21.6	45.4	29.8
West Bank and Gaza		..	..	..	..	..	..	..	..
Yemen, Rep.	2005[b]	37.7	2.9	7.2	11.3	15.3	21.0	45.3	30.8
Zambia	2004–05[b]	50.7	1.3	3.6	7.8	12.8	20.6	55.2	38.9
Zimbabwe	1995[b]	50.1	1.8	4.6	8.1	12.2	19.3	55.7	40.3

a. Percentage shares by quintile may not sum to 100 percent because of rounding. b. Refers to expenditure shares by percentiles of population, ranked by per capita expenditure. c. Urban data. d. Refers to income shares by percentiles of population, ranked by per capita income. e. Includes Montenegro.

Distribution of income or consumption | 2.9

Inequality in the distribution of income is reflected in the percentage shares of income or consumption accruing to portions of the population ranked by income or consumption levels. The portions ranked lowest by personal income receive the smallest shares of total income. The Gini index provides a convenient summary measure of the degree of inequality. Data on the distribution of income or consumption come from nationally representative household surveys. Where the original data from the household survey were available, they have been used to directly calculate the income or consumption shares by quintile. Otherwise, shares have been estimated from the best available grouped data.

The distribution data have been adjusted for household size, providing a more consistent measure of per capita income or consumption. No adjustment has been made for spatial differences in cost of living within countries, because the data needed for such calculations are generally unavailable. For further details on the estimation method for low- and middle-income economies, see Ravallion and Chen (1996).

Because the underlying household surveys differ in method and type of data collected, the distribution data are not strictly comparable across countries. These problems are diminishing as survey methods improve and become more standardized,

but achieving strict comparability is still impossible (see *About the data* for tables 2.7 and 2.8).

Two sources of noncomparability should be noted in particular. First, the surveys can differ in many respects, including whether they use income or consumption expenditure as the living standard indicator. The distribution of income is typically more unequal than the distribution of consumption. In addition, the definitions of income used differ more often among surveys. Consumption is usually a much better welfare indicator, particularly in developing countries. Second, households differ in size (number of members) and in the extent of income sharing among members. And individuals differ in age and consumption needs. Differences among countries in these respects may bias comparisons of distribution.

World Bank staff have made an effort to ensure that the data are as comparable as possible. Wherever possible, consumption has been used rather than income. Income distribution and Gini indexes for high-income economies are calculated directly from the Luxembourg Income Study database, using an estimation method consistent with that applied for developing countries.

• **Survey year** is the year in which the underlying data were collected. • **Gini index** measures the extent to which the distribution of income (or consumption expenditure) among individuals or households within an economy deviates from a perfectly equal distribution. A Lorenz curve plots the cumulative percentages of total income received against the cumulative number of recipients, starting with the poorest individual. The Gini index measures the area between the Lorenz curve and a hypothetical line of absolute equality, expressed as a percentage of the maximum area under the line. Thus a Gini index of 0 represents perfect equality, while an index of 100 implies perfect inequality. • **Percentage share of income or consumption** is the share of total income or consumption that accrues to subgroups of population indicated by deciles or quintiles.

The Gini coefficient and ratio of income or consumption of the richest quintile to the poorest quintiles are closely correlated 2.9a

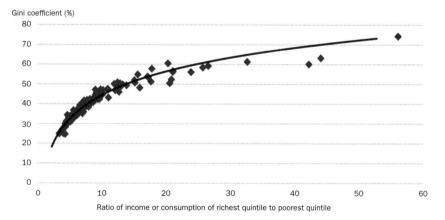

Source: World Development Indicators data files.

There are many ways to measure income or consumption inequality. The Gini coefficient shows inequality over the entire population; the ratio of income or consumption of the richest quintile to the poorest quintiles shows differences only at the tails of the population distribution. Both measures are closely correlated and provide similar information. At low levels of inequality the Gini coefficient is a more sensitive measure, but above a Gini value of 45–55 percent the inequality ratio rises faster.

Data on distribution are compiled by the World Bank's Development Research Group using primary household survey data obtained from government statistical agencies and World Bank country departments. Data for high-income economies are from the Luxembourg Income Study database.

Assessing vulnerability and security

	Youth unemployment		Female-headed households	Pension contributors			Public expenditure on pensions			
	Male % of male labor force ages 15–24 2003–05a	Female % of female labor force ages 15–24 2003–05a	% of total 2004–07a	Year	% of labor force	% of working-age population	Year	% of GDP	Year	Average pension % of average wage
Afghanistan	..	..	..		..	..	2005	0.5		..
Albania	..	..	..	2004	48.9	33.0	2005	5.4		..
Algeria	43	46	..	2002	36.7	22.1	2002	3.2		..
Angola	..	..	..		..	..		..		..
Argentina	22b	28b	..	2004	35.0	25.9	2007	8.0	2000	43.8
Armenia	..	..	36	2002	64.4	48.3	2004	3.4	2007	20.3
Australia	11b	11b	..	2005	92.6	69.6	2004	4.9		..
Austria	11	10	..	2005	96.4	68.7	2005	14.7		..
Azerbaijan	..	..	25	2007	36.8	30.2	2000	3.3	2006	24.3
Bangladesh	7	6	10	2004	2.8	2.1	2001	0.5		..
Belarus	..	..	54	1992	97.0	94.0	2002	12.1	2002	41.6
Belgium	21	19	..	2005	94.2	61.6	2003	11.0		..
Benin	..	..	23	1996	4.8	..	2006	1.5		..
Bolivia	..	..	..	2002	10.1	7.8	2000	4.5		..
Bosnia and Herzegovina	..	..	..	2004	36.0	27.0	2004	8.8		..
Botswana	..	..	..		..	..		..		..
Brazil	14b	23b	..	2004	52.6	39.1	2004	12.6		..
Bulgaria	23	21	..	1994	64.0	63.0	2005	8.9	2004	42.9
Burkina Faso	..	..	..	1993	3.1	3.0	1992	0.3		..
Burundi	..	..	..	1993	3.3	3.0	1991	0.2		..
Cambodia	..	..	24		..	..		..		..
Cameroon	..	..	24	1993	13.7	11.5	2001	0.8		..
Canada	14b	11b	..	2005	90.5	71.4	2004	4.8		..
Central African Republic	..	..	..	2004	1.5	1.3	2004	0.8		..
Chad	..	..	20	1990	1.1	1.0	1997	0.1		..
Chile	15	21	..	2003	58.0	35.2	2001	2.9	2006	53.5
China	..	..	..	2005	20.5	17.2	1996	2.7		..
Hong Kong, China	14	8	..		..	..		..		..
Colombia	12	19	19	2006	24.5	18.8	2006	2.7		..
Congo, Dem. Rep.	..	..	21		..	..		..		..
Congo, Rep.	..	..	23	1992	5.8	5.6	2004	0.9		..
Costa Rica	11	22	..	2004	55.3	37.6	2006	2.4		..
Côte d'Ivoire	..	..	..	1997	9.3	9.1	1997	0.3		..
Croatia	21c	28c	..	2007	75.2	51.0	2007	11.3	2005	32.4
Cuba	..	..	46		..	..	1992	12.6		..
Czech Republic	19	19	..	2007	84.5	67.3	2005	9.4	2005	40.7
Denmark	6	10	..	2007	94.4	86.9	2005	8.5		..
Dominican Republic	..	..	35	2000	31.0	20.7	2000	0.8		..
Ecuador	12b	21b	..	2004	27.0	20.8	2002	2.5		..
Egypt, Arab Rep.	..	..	12	2004	55.5	27.7	2004	4.1		..
El Salvador	13	9	..	2005	29.8	19.7	2006	1.9		..
Eritrea	..	..	..		..	..	2001	0.3		..
Estonia	16	15	..	2004	95.2	68.6	2003	6.0	2007	35.4
Ethiopia	4	11	23		..	..	2007	0.3		..
Finland	21	19	..	2005	88.7	67.2	2005	8.0		..
France	21b	25b	..	2005	89.9	61.4	2005	14.0		..
Gabon	..	..	..	1995	15.0	14.0		..		..
Gambia, The	..	..	..	2003	3.8	2.9		..		..
Georgia	27	31	..	2004	29.9	22.7	2004	3.0	2003	13.0
Germany	16	14	..	2005	88.2	65.5	2005	12.6		..
Ghana	..	..	..	2004	9.1	7.1	2002	1.3		..
Greece	18	35	..	2005	85.2	58.5	2005	12.0		..
Guatemala	..	..	17	2005	24.0	18.0	2005	1.0		..
Guinea	..	..	..	1993	1.5	1.8		..		..
Guinea-Bissau	..	..	..	2004	1.9	1.5	2005	2.1		..
Haiti	..	..	44		..	..		..		..

	Youth unemployment		Female-headed households	Pension contributors			Public expenditure on pensions			
	Male % of male labor force ages 15–24 **2003–05[a]**	Female % of female labor force ages 15–24 **2003–05[a]**	% of total **2004–07[a]**	Year	% of labor force	% of working-age population	Year	% of GDP	Year	Average pension % of average wage
Honduras	5[b]	11[b]	26	2006	16.1	12.4	1994	0.6		..
Hungary	20	19	..	2007	93.0	62.6	2005	11.1	2005	39.8
India	10[b]	11[b]	14	2004	9.0	5.7	2007	2.0		..
Indonesia	25	34	..	2002	15.5	11.3		..		..
Iran, Islamic Rep.	20	32	..	2001	35.1	20.0	2000	1.1		..
Iraq	..	..	..		..	..		..		..
Ireland	9	7	..	2005	88.0	63.9	2003	3.4		..
Israel	17	19	..	1992	82.0	63.0	1996	5.9		..
Italy	22	27	..	2005	92.4	58.4	2005	14.7		..
Jamaica	22	36	41	2004	17.4	12.6	1996	..		..
Japan	10[b]	7[b]	..	2005	95.3	75.0	2005	9.5		..
Jordan	..	..	..	2004	32.2	18.6	2001	2.2		..
Kazakhstan	13	16	..	2004	33.8	26.4	2004	4.9	2003	24.9
Kenya	..	..	..	2005	8.0	6.7	2003	1.1		
Korea, Dem. Rep.	..	..	..		..	..		..		..
Korea, Rep.	12	9	..	2005	78.0	55.0	2005	2.0		..
Kuwait	..	..	..		..	..	1990	3.5		..
Kyrgyz Republic	14	18	25	2006	42.2	28.9	2006	4.8	2003	27.5
Lao PDR	..	..	..		..	..		..		..
Latvia	12	14	..	2003	92.4	66.5	2002	7.5	2005	33.1
Lebanon	..	..	..	2003	33.1	19.9	2003	2.1		..
Lesotho	..	..	37	2005	5.7	3.6		..		..
Liberia	..	..	31		..	..		..		..
Libya	..	..	..	2004	65.5	38.1	2001	2.1		..
Lithuania	16	15	..	2004	79.7	56.0	2003	6.8	2005	30.9
Macedonia, FYR	63	62	8	2000	63.8	38.9	2006	8.5	2006	55.0
Madagascar	7	7	22	1993	5.4	4.8	1990	0.2		..
Malawi	..	..	25		..	..		..		..
Malaysia	..	..	..	2000	65.0	..	1999	6.5		..
Mali	..	..	12	1990	2.5	2.0	1991	0.4		..
Mauritania	..	..	..	1995	5.0	4.0	1992	0.2		..
Mauritius	21	34	..	2000	51.4	33.6	1999	4.4		..
Mexico	6	7	..	2002	34.5	22.7	2005	0.9		..
Moldova	19	18	34	2000	60.6	43.1	2003	8.0	2003	20.9
Mongolia	20	21	17	2002	61.4	49.1	2002	5.8		..
Morocco	16	14	17	2003	22.4	12.8	2003	1.9		..
Mozambique	..	..	..	1995	2.0	2.1	1996	0.0		..
Myanmar	..	..	..		..	..		..		..
Namibia	..	..	..		..	..		..		..
Nepal	..	..	23	2003	2.1	1.4	2003	0.3		..
Netherlands	10	10	..	2005	90.3	70.4	2005	8.4		..
New Zealand	9[b]	10[b]	..		..	..	2005	7.2		..
Nicaragua	11	16	..	2005	17.9	11.5	1996	2.5		..
Niger	..	..	19	2006	1.3	1.2	2006	0.7		..
Nigeria	..	..	..	2005	1.7	1.2	1991	0.1		..
Norway	13	12	..	2005	90.8	75.7	2003	8.4		..
Oman	..	..	..		..	..		..		..
Pakistan	11	15	10	2004	6.4	4.0	1993	0.9		..
Panama	19	30	..	1998	51.6	40.7	1996	4.3		..
Papua New Guinea	..	..	..		..	..		..		..
Paraguay	12[b]	21[b]	..	2004	11.6	9.1	2001	1.2		..
Peru	21[b]	21[b]	22	2003	16.3	12.3	2000	2.6		..
Philippines	15	19	..	2007	20.8	15.5	1993	1.0		..
Poland	37	39	..	2005	84.9	54.5	2005	14.1	2007	47.1
Portugal	14	19	..	2005	91.4	71.9	2004	10.4		..
Puerto Rico	25[b]	21[b]	..		..	..		..		..

	Youth unemployment		Female-headed households	Pension contributors			Public expenditure on pensions			
	Male % of male labor force ages 15–24 2003–05[a]	Female % of female labor force ages 15–24 2003–05[a]	% of total 2004–07[a]	Year	% of labor force	% of working-age population	Year	% of GDP	Year	Average pension % of average wage
Romania	21	18	..	2007	53.4	36.3	2003	6.9	2005	41.5
Russian Federation	..	..	..		..	..	2004	5.8	2003	29.2
Rwanda	..	..	34	2004	4.8	4.1		..		..
Saudi Arabia	..	..	..		..	..	1998	0.2		..
Senegal	..	..	23	2003	5.3	3.9	2003	1.3		..
Serbia	..	..	29	2003	46.0[d]	32.2[d]	2003	12.4[d]		
Sierra Leone	..	..	..	2004	4.6	3.6				
Singapore	4	6	..	2000	70.0	..	1996	1.4		..
Slovak Republic	31	29	..	2003	78.5	55.3	2005	6.5	2005	44.7
Slovenia	11	12	..	1995	86.0	68.7	2003	10.1	2005	44.3
Somalia	..	..	..		..	..		..		..
South Africa	56	65	..		..	..		..		..
Spain	17	24	..	2005	91.0	63.2	2005	10.4	2006	58.6
Sri Lanka	20[b]	37[b]	..	2004	35.6	22.2	2002	2.0		..
Sudan	..	..	19	1995	12.1	12.0		..		..
Swaziland	..	..	48		..	..		..		..
Sweden	23	22	..	2005	91.0	72.3	2005	11.4		..
Switzerland	9	9	..	2005	100.0	79.1	2005	9.2	2000	40.0
Syrian Arab Republic	..	..	..	2004	17.4	11.4	2004	1.3		..
Tajikistan	..	..	..		..	..	1996	3.0	2003	25.7
Tanzania	..	..	25	1996	2.0	2.0		..		..
Thailand	5	5	30	2005	27.2	21.8		..		..
Timor-Leste	..	..	..		..	..		..		..
Togo	..	..	..	1997	15.9	15.0	1997	0.6		..
Trinidad and Tobago	..	..	..	2004	55.6	..	1996	0.6		..
Tunisia	31	29	..	2004	45.3	25.4	2003	4.3		..
Turkey	19	19	..	2007	55.0	30.5	2003	3.2	2007	61.3
Turkmenistan	..	..	..		..	..	1996	2.3		..
Uganda	..	..	30	2004	10.7	9.3	2003	0.3		..
Ukraine	15	14	..	2007	68.2	47.4	2005	15.4	2007	48.3
United Arab Emirates	..	..	..		..	..		..		..
United Kingdom	13	10	..	2005	92.7	71.4	2005	7.6		..
United States	12[b]	10[b]	..	2005	92.5	72.5	2003	7.3	2006	29.2
Uruguay	25	35	..	2004	55.0	44.3	2007	10.0		..
Uzbekistan	..	..	18		..	..	2005	6.5	2005	40.0
Venezuela, RB	24	35	..	2004	31.8	23.8	2001	2.7		..
Vietnam	4	5	..	2005	13.2	10.8	1998	1.6		..
West Bank and Gaza	39	45	..	2000	18.8	7.8	2001	0.8		..
Yemen, Rep.	..	..	..	2005	10.0	5.5	1999	0.9		..
Zambia	..	..	..	2000	5.9	4.9	2006	0.2		..
Zimbabwe	..	..	38	1995	12.0	10.0	2002	2.3		..
World	.. w	.. w								
Low income	..	..								
Middle income	..	..								
Lower middle income	..	..								
Upper middle income	21	26								
Low & middle income	..	..								
East Asia & Pacific	..	..								
Europe & Central Asia	..	..								
Latin America & Carib.	14	21								
Middle East & N. Africa	..	..								
South Asia	11	12								
Sub-Saharan Africa	..	..								
High income	14	13								
Euro area	18	21								

a. Data are for the most recent year available. b. Limited coverage. c. Data are for 2007. d. Includes Montenegro.

About the data

As traditionally measured, poverty is a static concept, and vulnerability a dynamic one. Vulnerability reflects a household's resilience in the face of shocks and the likelihood that a shock will lead to a decline in well-being. Thus, it depends primarily on the household's assets and insurance mechanisms. Because poor people have fewer assets and less diversified sources of income than do the better-off, fluctuations in income affect them more.

Enhancing security for poor people means reducing their vulnerability to such risks as ill health, providing them the means to manage risk themselves, and strengthening market or public institutions for managing risk. Tools include microfinance programs, public provision of education and basic health care, and old age assistance (see tables 2.11 and 2.16).

Poor households face many risks, and vulnerability is thus multidimensional. The indicators in the table focus on individual risks—youth unemployment, female-headed households, income insecurity in old age—and the extent to which publicly provided services may be capable of mitigating some of these risks. Poor people face labor market risks, often having to take up precarious, low-quality jobs and to increase their household's labor market participation by sending their children to work (see tables 2.4 and 2.6). Income security is a prime concern for the elderly.

Youth unemployment is an important policy issue for many economies. Experiencing unemployment may permanently impair a young person's productive potential and future employment opportunities. The table presents unemployment among youth ages 15–24, but the lower age limit for young people in a country could be determined by the minimum age for leaving school, so age groups could differ across countries. Also, since this age group is likely to include school leavers, the level of youth unemployment varies considerably over the year as a result of different school opening and closing dates. The youth unemployment rate shares similar limitations on comparability as the general unemployment rate. For further information, see *About the data* for table 2.5 and the original source.

The definition of female-headed household differs greatly across countries, making cross-country comparison difficult. In some cases it is assumed that a woman cannot be the head of any household with an adult male, because of sex-biased stereotype. Caution should be used in interpreting the data.

Pension scheme coverage may be broad or even universal where eligibility is determined by citizenship, residency, or income status. In contribution-related schemes, however, eligibility is usually restricted to individuals who have contributed for a minimum number of years. Definitional issues—relating to the labor force, for example—may arise in comparing coverage by contribution-related schemes over time and across countries (for country-specific information, see Hinz and Pallares-Miralles forthcoming). The share of the labor force covered by a pension scheme may be overstated in countries that do not try to count informal sector workers as part of the labor force.

Public interventions and institutions can provide services directly to poor people, although whether these interventions and institutions work well for the poor is debated. State action is often ineffective, in part because governments can influence only a few of the many sources of well-being and in part because of difficulties in delivering goods and services. The effectiveness of public provision is further constrained by the fiscal resources at governments' disposal and the fact that state institutions may not be responsive to the needs of poor people.

The data on public pension spending cover the pension programs of the social insurance schemes for which contributions had previously been made. In many cases noncontributory pensions or social assistance targeted to the elderly and disabled are also included. A country's pattern of spending is correlated with its demographic structure—spending increases as the population ages.

Definitions

• **Youth unemployment** is the share of the labor force ages 15–24 without work but available for and seeking employment. • **Female-headed households** are the percentage of households with a female head. • **Pension contributors** are the share of the labor force or working-age population (here defined as ages 15 and older) covered by a pension scheme. • **Public expenditure on pensions** is all government expenditures on cash transfers to the elderly, the disabled, and survivors and the administrative costs of these programs. • **Average pension** is the average pension payment of all pensioners of the main pension schemes divided by the average wage of all formal sector workers.

Data sources

Data on youth unemployment are from the ILO database Key Indicators of the Labour Market, 5th edition. Data on female-headed household are from Demographic and Health Surveys by Macro International. Data on pension contributors and pension spending are from Richard Paul Hinz and Montserrat Pallares-Miralles' *International Patterns of Pension Provision II* (forthcoming).

Education inputs

	Public expenditure per student						Public expenditure on education		Trained teachers in primary education	Primary school pupil-teacher ratio
			% of GDP per capita				% of GDP	% of total government expenditure	% of total	pupils per teacher
	Primary		Secondary		Tertiary					
	1991	2007[a]	1999	2007[a]	1999	2007[a]	2007[a]	2007[a]	2007[a]	2007[a]
Afghanistan	..	..	..	..	..	..	..	..	..	..
Albania	..	..	..	..	..	..	..	..	..	..
Algeria	26.5	..	..	..	..	..	..	..	99.2	24
Angola	..	3.7	..	36.9	..	78.3	2.6	..	..	41
Argentina	..	12.0	..	19.6	17.7	..	..	..	..	17
Armenia	..	..	..	..	..	..	2.7	15.0	77.5	19
Australia	..	17.3	15.4	15.4	27.2	23.1	4.8	..	..	..
Austria	18.2	23.5	29.9	26.3	51.6	50.0	5.4	10.9	..	12
Azerbaijan	..	..	15.4	..	..	..	2.6	12.6	..	13
Bangladesh	..	..	13.4	..	50.1	46.2	2.6	15.8	..	..
Belarus	30.1	14.4	..	27.0	..	18.3	5.2	9.3	99.8	16
Belgium	15.8	20.2	23.7	33.4	38.3	35.1	6.0	12.1	..	11
Benin	..	13.4	26.3	..	170.4	165.4	3.9	18.0	71.8	44
Bolivia	..	..	11.7	..	44.1	..	..	..	..	..
Bosnia and Herzegovina	..	..	..	..	..	..	..	..	..	..
Botswana	..	16.1	..	41.2	..	449.6	8.1	21.0	86.9	24
Brazil	..	15.4	9.5	13.2	57.1	35.1	4.5	14.5	..	21
Bulgaria	..	24.5	18.8	23.4	17.9	24.8	4.5	..	..	16
Burkina Faso	..	36.0	..	23.3	..	236.5	4.5	15.4	87.7	48
Burundi	13.4	19.9	..	77.5	1,078.2	363.1	5.1	17.7	87.4	52
Cambodia	..	..	11.5	..	43.7	8.5	1.6	12.4	98.4	51
Cameroon	..	7.6	16.8	41.6	64.4	126.3	3.9	17.0	36.3	44
Canada	..	..	..	..	47.1	..	4.9	..	..	..
Central African Republic	11.9	7.5	..	..	..	305.2	1.4	..	..	102[b]
Chad	8.0	7.1	28.3	29.2	..	348.2	1.9	10.1	26.8	60
Chile	..	11.1	14.8	12.4	19.4	11.8	3.2	16.0	..	26
China	..	..	11.5	..	90.1	..	..	..	..	18
Hong Kong, China	..	12.5	17.7	16.5	..	47.3	3.5	23.2	94.6	17
Colombia	..	15.6	16.9	12.6	39.6	52.7	4.9	12.6	..	28
Congo, Dem. Rep.	..	..	..	..	..	..	..	..	96.0	38
Congo, Rep.	..	3.0	..	..	379.5	..	1.8	8.1	86.6	58
Costa Rica	7.8	..	23.2	..	55.0	..	4.9	20.6	89.5	19
Côte d'Ivoire	..	..	55.5	..	216.6	..	..	..	100.0	41
Croatia	..	..	..	..	41.5	..	4.6	9.3	..	17
Cuba	21.6	51.1	41.4	60.1	86.6	43.5	13.3	20.6	100.0	10
Czech Republic	..	12.6	21.7	22.9	33.7	27.2	4.3	9.5	..	16
Denmark	..	25.1	38.1	35.0	65.9	55.3	8.3	15.5	..	..
Dominican Republic	..	10.3	..	4.7	..	..	2.4	11.0	88.3	24
Ecuador	..	..	9.7	..	..	..	..	..	71.6	23
Egypt, Arab Rep.	..	..	..	..	..	..	3.8	12.6	..	27
El Salvador	..	9.0	7.9	10.5	9.4	15.5	3.0	13.1	93.3	40
Eritrea	..	9.6	38.5	9.6	444.1	..	2.4	..	87.1	48
Estonia	..	19.4	27.9	23.0	32.6	18.3	4.9	14.6	..	11
Ethiopia	22.1	12.5	..	8.9	..	785.5	5.5	23.3	..	..
Finland	21.7	18.0	25.8	32.3	40.3	34.4	6.3	12.5	..	16
France	11.8	17.4	28.5	27.0	29.7	33.3	5.7	10.6	..	19
Gabon	..	..	..	..	..	..	..	..	..	..
Gambia, The	13.2	..	..	..	..	..	..	..	76.3	41
Georgia	..	..	..	..	..	..	2.7	7.8	..	..
Germany	..	16.3	20.5	21.5	..	..	4.5	9.7	..	14
Ghana	..	18.4	..	29.1	..	213.4	5.4	..	56.3	35
Greece	7.5	14.1	13.5	18.2	22.8	21.5	3.5	9.2	..	11
Guatemala	..	10.5	4.3	6.0	..	19.3	3.1	..	..	30
Guinea	..	..	..	..	..	192.9	1.7	..	98.8	45
Guinea-Bissau	..	..	..	..	..	..	..	..	..	..
Haiti	9.1	..	..	..	..	..	..	..	..	..

	Public expenditure per student						Public expenditure on education		Trained teachers in primary education	Primary school pupil-teacher ratio
	Primary		% of GDP per capita Secondary		Tertiary		% of GDP	% of total government expenditure	% of total	pupils per teacher
	1991	2007[a]	1999	2007[a]	1999	2007[a]	2007[a]	2007[a]	2007[a]	2007[a]
Honduras	..	..	..	..	..	..	..	..	..	28
Hungary	..	25.7	19.1	23.1	34.2	23.8	5.5	10.9	..	10
India	..	8.9	24.7	16.7	90.8	57.8	3.2	..	..	..
Indonesia	..	..	..	..	..	..	3.5	17.5	..	20
Iran, Islamic Rep.	..	15.4	9.9	22.3	34.8	27.7	5.5	19.5	70.8	19
Iraq	..	..	..	..	..	..	..	..	..	..
Ireland	11.5	14.7	16.8	21.8	28.5	24.8	4.8	13.9	..	17
Israel	..	20.7	22.4	20.5	31.7	23.1	6.3	..	..	13
Italy	14.9	23.1	27.7	26.9	27.6	22.3	4.4	9.2	..	11
Jamaica	9.9	14.6	23.6	21.5	79.0	..	5.3	8.8	..	28
Japan	..	22.2	20.9	22.4	15.1	19.2	3.5	9.5	..	19
Jordan	..	15.4	15.8	19.0	..	..	..	..	..	..
Kazakhstan	..	..	..	..	..	8.0	2.9	..	..	17[b]
Kenya	..	22.4	15.2	22.1	209.4	..	7.1	17.9	..	40
Korea, Dem. Rep.	..	..	..	..	..	..	..	..	..	..
Korea, Rep.	11.8	18.8	15.7	23.4	8.4	9.3	4.4	15.3	..	27
Kuwait	35.4	9.2	..	14.1	..	79.8	3.6	12.9	100.0	10
Kyrgyz Republic	..	..	..	..	27.7	22.3	5.6	..	62.4	24
Lao PDR	..	9.1	4.3	4.7	66.5	25.2	3.2	15.8	89.7	30
Latvia	..	..	23.7	..	27.9	..	..	..	..	12
Lebanon	..	8.3	..	8.8	14.2	14.8	2.7	9.6	12.2	14
Lesotho	..	25.0	71.6	49.8	1,295.1	1,141.5	13.3	29.8	66.1	40
Liberia	..	6.0	..	..	..	..	..	..	40.2[b]	24[b]
Libya	..	..	..	..	23.9	..	..	..	..	..
Lithuania	..	15.9	..	20.2	34.2	18.2	5.0	14.7	..	14
Macedonia, FYR	..	..	..	..	..	..	..	..	..	19
Madagascar	..	9.5	..	12.7	182.1	145.2	3.4	16.4	55.2	49
Malawi	7.2	..	..	..	..	..	..	..	..	..
Malaysia	10.1	..	22.6	..	84.3	..	..	..	..	17
Mali	..	21.3	53.0	31.7	227.7	..	4.6	16.8	100.0	52
Mauritania	..	9.6	35.3	24.2	77.8	39.2	2.9	10.1	100.0	43
Mauritius	10.1	10.3	15.3	17.4	40.4	29.8	3.9	12.7	100.0	22
Mexico	4.8	15.1	14.2	15.6	47.8	40.0	5.5	..	..	28
Moldova	..	33.6	..	40.7	..	41.4	8.3	19.8	..	16
Mongolia	..	14.9	..	14.8	..	..	5.1	..	98.7	32
Morocco	15.4	14.6	44.5	39.3	94.8	73.9	5.5	26.1	100.0	27
Mozambique	..	15.1	..	86.9	..	..	5.2	21.0	63.2	65
Myanmar	..	..	6.8	..	27.5	..	..	..	99.0	29
Namibia	..	21.4	36.2	22.0	156.9	141.3	..	..	94.8	30
Nepal	..	15.3[b]	13.1	11.3[b]	141.6	..	3.8[b]	..	61.4[b]	38[b]
Netherlands	12.1	17.7	21.1	24.2	42.8	39.9	5.2	11.5	..	..
New Zealand	17.2	17.8	24.3	20.6	41.6	26.4	6.2	15.5	..	16
Nicaragua	..	9.8	..	4.5	..	..	..	..	73.6	33
Niger	..	28.7	60.9	46.1	..	371.4	3.4	17.6	98.2	40
Nigeria	..	..	..	..	..	..	..	..	51.2	40
Norway	32.7	18.9	26.8	28.8	45.8	49.2	7.0	16.7	..	..
Oman	10.5	15.1	21.9	12.7	..	14.0	4.0	31.1	100.0	14
Pakistan	..	..	..	..	..	..	2.9	11.2	84.6	39
Panama	11.3	12.4	19.1	15.1	33.6	..	..	..	90.8	25
Papua New Guinea	..	..	..	..	..	..	..	..	..	36
Paraguay	..	..	18.4	..	58.9	..	..	..	..	..
Peru	..	7.0	10.7	9.0	20.9	10.5	2.5	15.4	..	22
Philippines	..	8.6	10.8	9.1	15.1	11.5	2.5	15.2	..	35
Poland	..	23.7	16.5	22.2	21.1	21.4	5.5	..	..	11
Portugal	16.3	23.2	27.5	34.7	28.1	27.1	5.4	11.3	..	11
Puerto Rico	..	..	..	..	..	..	..	..	..	..

	Public expenditure per student						Public expenditure on education		Trained teachers in primary education	Primary school pupil-teacher ratio
	Primary		Secondary		Tertiary		% of GDP	% of total government expenditure	% of total	pupils per teacher
			% of GDP per capita							
	1991	2007[a]	1999	2007[a]	1999	2007[a]	2007[a]	2007[a]	2007[a]	2007[a]
Romania	..	10.7	16.0	16.0	32.6	23.7	3.5	..	..	17
Russian Federation	..	..	..	..	..	12.6	3.1	..	..	17
Rwanda	..	10.2	30.2	35.1	699.4	372.8	4.9	19.0	98.1	69
Saudi Arabia	..	18.5	..	18.4	..	..	..	..	91.5	11
Senegal	18.9	17.9	..	32.9	..	225.2	4.8	26.3	100.0	34
Serbia	..	..	..	..	..	..	4.2[b]	9.4[b]	..	13
Sierra Leone	..	..	..	..	..	..	3.8	..	49.4	44
Singapore	..	9.3[b]	..	14.1[b]	..	..	2.9[b]	15.3[b]	96.1	20
Slovak Republic	..	14.8	18.3	15.2	32.6	24.2	3.9	..	..	17
Slovenia	17.4	25.1	26.0	32.0	28.3	22.7	5.8	12.7	..	15
Somalia	..	..	..	..	..	..	..	..	..	..
South Africa	20.2	15.6	20.0	16.7	60.7	44.3	5.4	17.4	..	30
Spain	11.3	19.1	24.4	23.4	19.6	22.8	4.2	11.0	..	14
Sri Lanka	..	..	..	..	..	..	..	..	..	23
Sudan	..	..	..	..	..	..	..	..	58.7	37
Swaziland	6.7	15.4	26.1	43.7	388.4	343.6	7.6	..	90.8	33
Sweden	45.8	25.7	26.6	33.5	52.7	41.5	7.1	..	..	10
Switzerland	36.1	24.5	27.7	28.3	54.5	56.2	5.8	..	..	13
Syrian Arab Republic	..	20.3	21.7	..	..	..	..	..	..	..
Tajikistan	..	9.4[b]	6.5	14.4[b]	27.4	11.8	3.7[b]	19.3[b]	87.4	22
Tanzania	..	..	..	..	..	..	..	..	99.4[b]	53[b]
Thailand	11.6	..	15.5	..	35.1	28.0	4.3	25.0	..	18
Timor-Leste	..	27.6	..	..	..	..	..	..	..	31
Togo	..	9.8	31.1	20.0	..	162.5	3.7	15.8[b]	14.6	39
Trinidad and Tobago	..	..	12.3	..	149.3	..	..	..	..	17
Tunisia	..	20.9	27.1	24.2	89.4	55.9	7.2	20.8	..	19
Turkey	10.7	..	14.3	..	45.5	..	..	..	..	..
Turkmenistan	..	..	..	..	..	..	..	..	..	..
Uganda	..	..	..	..	..	..	..	..	84.8	49
Ukraine	..	15.8	11.2	24.3	36.5	25.5	5.4	20.2	99.8	16
United Arab Emirates	..	4.4	11.5	6.2	41.5	..	1.4	28.3	100.0	17
United Kingdom	15.0	18.9	24.3	20.3	26.2	32.3	5.5	12.5	..	18
United States	..	22.2	22.5	24.6	27.0	25.4	5.7	13.7	..	14
Uruguay	7.8	8.8	11.3	10.8	19.1	18.8	2.9	11.6	..	20
Uzbekistan	..	..	..	..	..	..	..	..	100.0	18
Venezuela, RB	..	9.1	..	8.1	..	24.4	3.7	..	84.0	19
Vietnam	..	..	..	..	..	..	..	..	95.6	21
West Bank and Gaza	..	..	..	..	..	..	..	..	100.0	30
Yemen, Rep.	..	..	..	..	..	..	..	..	..	..
Zambia	..	2.3	19.4	8.1	164.3	..	1.5	..	..	49
Zimbabwe	20.7	..	19.6	..	196.1	..	..	..	..	38
World	.. m	15.3 m	.. m	.. m	.. m	.. m	4.5 m	14.2 m		25 w
Low income	..	..	..	..	..	..	..	..		41
Middle income	..	..	..	..	..	..	4.5	14.2		24
Lower middle income	..	..	..	..	..	..	3.2	..		26
Upper middle income	..	14.5	18.1	19.7	38.6	24.2	4.5	13.0		20
Low & middle income	..	..	..	..	..	..	..	..		28
East Asia & Pacific	..	..	8.1	..	37.8	..	..	..		20
Europe & Central Asia	..	..	..	..	..	..	4.1	13.1		18
Latin America & Carib.	..	12.0	13.1	13.2	37.1	..	3.5	13.1		23
Middle East & N. Africa	..	..	..	..	..	..	..	..		24
South Asia	..	..	13.4	..	90.8	..	..	..		..
Sub-Saharan Africa	..	11.8	..	..	..	..	4.1	..		45
High income	15.8	18.9	22.4	23.1	32.6	25.4	5.1	12.5		15
Euro area	14.9	18.0	24.4	26.3	29.1	26.0	5.2	11.2		14

a. Provisional data. b. Data are for 2008.

Data on education are compiled by the United Nations Educational, Scientific, and Cultural Organization (UNESCO) Institute for Statistics from official responses to surveys and from reports provided by education authorities in each country. The data are used for monitoring, policymaking, and resource allocation. However, coverage and data collection methods vary across countries and over time within countries, so comparisons should be made with caution.

For most countries the data on education spending in the table refer to public spending—government spending on public education plus subsidies for private education—and generally exclude foreign aid for education. They may also exclude spending by religious schools, which play a significant role in many developing countries. Data for some countries and some years refer to ministry of education spending only and exclude education expenditures by other ministries and local authorities.

Many developing countries seek to supplement public funds for education, some with tuition fees to recover part of the cost of providing education services or to encourage development of private schools. Fees raise difficult questions of equity, efficiency, access, and taxation, however, and some governments have used scholarships, vouchers, and other public finance methods to counter criticism. For greater detail, consult the country- and indicator-specific notes in the original source.

The share of public expenditure devoted to education allows an assessment of the priority a government assigns to education relative to other public investments, as well as a government's commitment to investing in human capital development. It also reflects the development status of a country's education system relative to that of others. However, returns on investment to education, especially primary and lower secondary education, cannot be understood simply by comparing current education indicators with national income. It takes a long time before currently enrolled children can productively contribute to the national economy (Hanushek 2002).

Data on education finance are generally of poor quality. This is partly because ministries of education, from which the UNESCO Institute for Statistics collects data, may not be the best source for education finance data. Other agencies, particularly ministries of finance, need to be consulted, but coordination is not easy. It is also difficult to track actual spending from the central government to local institutions. And private spending adds to the complexity of collecting accurate data on public spending.

The share of trained teachers in primary education measures the quality of the teaching staff. It does not take account of competencies acquired by teachers through their professional experience or self-instruction or of such factors as work experience, teaching methods and materials, or classroom conditions, which may affect the quality of teaching. Since the training teachers receive varies greatly (pre-service or in-service), care should be taken in making comparisons across countries.

The primary school pupil-teacher ratio reflects the average number of pupils per teacher. It differs from the average class size because of the different practices countries employ, such as part-time teachers, school shifts, and multigrade classes. The comparability of pupil-teacher ratios across countries is affected by the definition of teachers and by differences in class size by grade and in the number of hours taught, as well as the different practices mentioned above. Moreover, the underlying enrollment levels are subject to a variety of reporting errors (for further discussion of enrollment data, see *About the data* for table 2.12). While the pupil-teacher ratio is often used to compare the quality of schooling across countries, it is often weakly related to the value added of schooling systems.

In 1998 UNESCO introduced the new International Standard Classification of Education 1997 (ISCED 1997). Consistent historical time series with reclassification of the pre–ISCED 1997 series were produced for a selection of indicators in 2008. The full set of the historical series is forthcoming.

In 2006 the UNESCO Institute for Statistics also changed its convention for citing the reference year of education data and indicators to the calendar year in which the academic or financial year ends. Data that used to be listed for 2006, for example, are now listed for 2007. This change was implemented to present the most recent data available and to align the data reporting with that of other international organizations (in particular the Organisation for Economic Co-operation and Development and Eurostat).

• **Public expenditure per student** is public current and capital spending on education divided by the number of students by level as a percentage of gross domestic product (GDP) per capita. • **Public expenditure on education** is current and capital public expenditure on education as a percentage of GDP and as a percentage of total government expenditure. • **Trained teachers in primary education** are the percentage of primary school teachers who have received the minimum organized teacher training (pre-service or in-service) required for teaching in their country. • **Primary school pupil-teacher ratio** is the number of pupils enrolled in primary school divided by the number of primary school teachers (regardless of their teaching assignment).

Data on education inputs are from the UNESCO Institute for Statistics, which compiles international data on education in cooperation with national commissions and national statistical services.

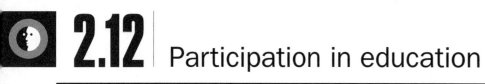

	Gross enrollment ratio				Net enrollment ratio				Adjusted net enrollment ratio, primary		Children out of school	
		% of relevant age group				% of relevant age group			% of primary-school-age children		thousand primary-school-age children	
	Preprimary	Primary	Secondary	Tertiary	Primary		Secondary		Male	Female	Male	Female
	2007[a]	2007[a]	2007[a]	2007[a]	1991	2007[a]	1991	2007[a]	2007[a]	2007[a]	2007[a]	2007[a]
Afghanistan	..	..	..	..	..	..	..	..	..	..	..	..
Albania	..	..	..	..	96	..	..	..	..	..	..	..
Algeria	30	110	83	24	89	95	53	..	97	95	61	88
Angola	61	199	17	3	50	..	..	..	..	..	..	..
Argentina	66	112	84	64	94	99	..	78	100	98	5	31
Armenia	37	110	89	34	..	85	..	86	92	95	5	2
Australia	104	105	150	73	99	96	80	87	96	97	36	27
Austria	90	102	102	50	88	97	..	..	97	98	6	3
Azerbaijan	..	..	..	..	89	..	..	..	..	..	..	..
Bangladesh	..	..	..	7	76	..	..	..	..	..	..	..
Belarus	103	97	95	69	85	91	..	87	91	89	18	21
Belgium	121	102	110	63	96	97	86	87	97	98	9	8
Benin	6	96	32	5	41	80	..	..	90	75	71	173
Bolivia	50	109	82	..	..	95	..	71	96	97	30	22
Bosnia and Herzegovina	10	98	85	..	79	..	..	..	..	..	..	..
Botswana	15	107	76	5	88	84	39	56	83	86	27	22
Brazil	69	137	105	25	84	94	..	79	94	97	383	214
Bulgaria	82	100	105	46	..	92	..	88	94	94	8	9
Burkina Faso	3	65	16	3	27	52	..	12	58	48	514	608
Burundi	2	114	15	2	53	81	..	..	82	80	116	128
Cambodia	13	119	42	5	72	89	..	31	..	..	..	..
Cameroon	21	110	25	7	69	..	..	..	..	..	..	..
Canada	68	98	..	..	98	..	89	..	..	..	..	..
Central African Republic	..	80[b]	..	1	52	61[b]	..	..	71[b]	51[b]	103[b]	174[b]
Chad	1	74	19	1	34	..	..	..	..	..	..	..
Chile	55	104	91	47	89	..	55	..	..	..	..	..
China	39	111	76	22	98	..	..	..	..	..	..	..
Hong Kong, China	66	98	86	34	92	91	..	79	97	93	7	16
Colombia	41	116	85	32	68	87	34	67	91	91	219	194
Congo, Dem. Rep.	3	85	33	4	54	..	..	..	..	..	..	..
Congo, Rep.	10	106	..	..	82	54	..	..	56	52	129	142
Costa Rica	61	110	87	25	87	..	38	64	..	..	..	..
Côte d'Ivoire	3	72	..	8	45	..	..	..	..	..	..	..
Croatia	50	99	91	44	70	90	..	87	98	100	2	0[c]
Cuba	111	102	93	109	94	98	73	86	99	99	4	6
Czech Republic	114	100	96	50	87	93	..	..	91	94	22	15
Denmark	95	99	120	80	98	96	87	89	95	97	10	7
Dominican Republic	32	107	79	..	..	82	..	61	84	86	104	90
Ecuador	100	118	70	..	98	97	..	59	..	..	..	..
Egypt, Arab Rep.	17	105	..	35	86	96	..	..	100	95	10	222
El Salvador	49	118	64	22	..	92	..	54	93	94	32	27
Eritrea	14	55	29	..	15	41	..	25	45	40	167	181
Estonia	93	99	100	65	..	94	..	91	97	97	1	1
Ethiopia	3	91	30	3	22	71	..	24	75	69	1,667	2,054
Finland	62	98	112	93	98	97	93	96	97	97	6	5
France	116	110	114	56	100	99	..	99	99	99	18	9
Gabon	..	..	..	..	94	..	..	..	..	..	..	..
Gambia, The	22	86	49	..	46	76	..	36	74	78	33	27
Georgia	57	99	90	37	97	94	..	82	96	93	7	11
Germany	106	103	102	..	84	98	..	..	98	99	28	19
Ghana	60	98	49	6	54	72	..	45	73	71	477	490
Greece	69	102	103	95	95	99	83	92	100	100	1	1
Guatemala	29	113	56	18	64	95	..	38	98	95	17	53
Guinea	10	91	35	5	27	74	..	28	80	70	146	216
Guinea-Bissau	..	..	..	..	38	..	..	..	..	..	..	..
Haiti	..	..	..	..	21	..	..	..	..	..	..	..

	Gross enrollment ratio				Net enrollment ratio				Adjusted net enrollment ratio, primary		Children out of school	
		% of relevant age group				% of relevant age group			% of primary-school-age children		thousand primary-school-age children	
	Preprimary	Primary	Secondary	Tertiary	Primary		Secondary		Male	Female	Male	Female
	2007[a]	2007[a]	2007[a]	2007[a]	1991	2007[a]	1991	2007[a]	2007[a]	2007[a]	2007[a]	2007[a]
Honduras	36	117	61	..	88	96	21	..	96	98	21	12
Hungary	86	97	96	69	87	88	..	90	94	95	12	11
India	40	112	55	12	..	89	..	..	96	92	2,529	4,613
Indonesia	37	114	66	17	96	95	39	60	99	96	142	544
Iran, Islamic Rep.	54	121	73	31	92	94		77	..	..	..	..
Iraq	..	..	..	..	94	..	..	..	..	..	..	..
Ireland	..	104	112	59	90	95	80	87	94	95	13	10
Israel	91	110	92	58	..	97	..	89	96	98	13	9
Italy	104	103	100	67	100	99	..	94	100	99	5	12
Jamaica	92	95	87	..	96	90	64	78	91	91	16	15
Japan	86	100	101	57	100	100	97	99	..	..	..	..
Jordan	32	97	89	39	95	90	..	82	93	95	31	22
Kazakhstan	39[b]	109[b]	92[b]	47[b]	88	90[b]	..	86[b]	99[b]	100[b]	6[b]	2[b]
Kenya	49	106	50	..	..	75	..	43	76	77	708	662
Korea, Dem. Rep.	..	..	..	..	..	..	..	..	..	..	..	..
Korea, Rep.	101	105	98	93	100	98	86	96	..	..	..	..
Kuwait	77	98	91	18	49	88	..	77	95	93	5	7
Kyrgyz Republic	16	95	86	43	92	84	..	81	93	92	16	16
Lao PDR	13	118	44	9	62	86	..	35	88	84	44	59
Latvia	89	95	99	74	94	90	..	..	90	94	4	3
Lebanon	66	95	81	52	66	83	..	73	84	83	38	38
Lesotho	18	114	37	4	72	72	15	24	71	74	54	47
Liberia	125[b]	83[b]	..	..	..	31[b]	..	..	32[b]	30[b]	221[b]	226[b]
Libya	9	110	94	..	..	..	..	..	..	..	..	..
Lithuania	69	95	99	76	..	89	..	92	92	92	7	6
Macedonia, FYR	33	98	84	30	..	92	..	81	97	97	2	1
Madagascar	8	141	26	3	64	98	..	17	99	100	17	3
Malawi	..	116	28	0[c]	49	87	..	24	84	91	198	117
Malaysia	63	100	69	29	93	100	..	69	..	..	..	..
Mali	3	83	32	4	25	63	6	..	70	56	312	452
Mauritania	2	103	25	4	36	80	..	16	79	83	51	38
Mauritius	99	101	88	14[b]	91	95	..	73	95	96	3	2
Mexico	106	113	87	26	98	98	45	70	100	99	12	61
Moldova	70	94	89	41	86	88	..	81	90	90	8	9
Mongolia	54	100	92	48	90	89	..	81	96	99	5	1
Morocco	60	107	56	11	56	89	..	..	92	87	157	237
Mozambique	..	111	18	1	42	70	..	3	72	67	578	671
Myanmar	..	..	..	..	99	..	..	..	..	..	..	..
Namibia	32	109	59	6	86	87	..	49	84	89	30	21
Nepal	57[b]	124[b]	48[b]	..	63	80[b]	..	..	82[b]	78[b]	338[b]	376[b]
Netherlands	90	107	118	60	95	98	84	88	99	98	7	14
New Zealand	92	102	120	80	98	99	85	..	99	100	1	1
Nicaragua	52	116	66	..	70	90	..	43	91	92	38	34
Niger	2	53	11	1	24	45	6	9	52	39	574	689
Nigeria	15	97	32	10	55	63	..	..	69	60	3,608	4,582
Norway	90	98	113	78	100	98	88	96	98	98	5	4
Oman	31	80	90	25	69	73	..	79	74	76	46	41
Pakistan	52	84	33	5	33	66	..	32	73	57	2,705	4,116
Panama	70	113	70	45	92	98	..	64	99	99	2	3
Papua New Guinea	..	55	..	..	66	..	..	..	..	..	..	..
Paraguay	34	111	66	26	94	94	26	57	95	95	23	19
Peru	68	116	94	35	88	96	..	72	..	..	..	..
Philippines	45	110	83	28	96	91	..	60	91	93	553	400
Poland	57	98	100	66	96	96	..	94	96	97	55	44
Portugal	79	115	97	55	98	98	..	82	99	99	2	3
Puerto Rico	..	..	..	..	..	..	..	..	..	..	..	..

	Gross enrollment ratio				Net enrollment ratio				Adjusted net enrollment ratio, primary		Children out of school	
		% of relevant age group				% of relevant age group			% of primary-school-age children		thousand primary-school-age children	
	Preprimary	Primary	Secondary	Tertiary	Primary		Secondary		Male	Female	Male	Female
	2007[a]	2007[a]	2007[a]	2007[a]	1991	2007[a]	1991	2007[a]	2007[a]	2007[a]	2007[a]	2007[a]
Romania	72	105	86	52	81	93	..	73	95	96	21	19
Russian Federation	83	96	84	70	98	..	..	..	..	..	..	..
Rwanda	..	147	18	3	67	94	8	..	92	95	56	38
Saudi Arabia	11	98	94	30	59	85	31	73	85	84	245	252
Senegal	9	84	24	6	45	72	..	20	73	73	254	253
Serbia	59	97	88	..	..	95	..	..	95	95	8	7
Sierra Leone	5	147	32	..	43	..	..	23	..	..	..	..
Singapore	..	..	..	..	..	..	..	..	..	..	..	..
Slovak Republic	93	100	96	45	..	92	..	..	92	92	10	9
Slovenia	81	100	95	83	96	95	..	90	97	97	2	1
Somalia	..	..	..	..	..	..	..	..	..	..	..	..
South Africa	43	103	96	15	90	86	45	72	91	92	332	274
Spain	121	105	119	67	100	100	..	94	100	99	1	6
Sri Lanka	..	108	..	..	84	..	..	..	..	..	..	..
Sudan	27[b]	72[b]	35[b]	..	..	..	..	..	..	..	..	..
Swaziland	17	106	47	4	75	78	30	32	78	79	23	22
Sweden	95	96	103	79	100	95	85	99	95	95	17	17
Switzerland	99	97	93	46	84	89	80	82	93	94	18	17
Syrian Arab Republic	10	126	72	..	91	..	43	66	..	..	..	..
Tajikistan	9[b]	100[b]	84	20[b]	77	98[b]	..	81	99	96	2	15
Tanzania	35[b]	112[b]	..	1	51	98	..	..	99	97	50	93
Thailand	94	106	83	50	88	94	..	76	..	..	..	..
Timor-Leste	10	91	53	..	..	63	..	..	64	62	35	36
Togo	4	97	39	5	64	77	15	..	84	74	83	139
Trinidad and Tobago	85	95	76	11	89	85	..	65	89	90	8	7
Tunisia	..	108	85	31	93	96	..	..	97	98	18	9
Turkey	13	94	79	35	89	91	42	69	93	89	291	439
Turkmenistan	..	..	..	..	..	..	..	..	..	..	..	..
Uganda	3	117	18	..	51	..	..	16	..	..	..	..
Ukraine	94	100	94	76	81	89	..	84	90	90	85	82
United Arab Emirates	85	107	92	23	99	91	60	79	99	98	2	3
United Kingdom	72	105	98	59	98	98	80	92	99	100	16	0[c]
United States	61	98	94	82	97	92	84	88	92	94	1,004	723
Uruguay	79	115	101	46	91	100	..	..	98	97	4	4
Uzbekistan	27	95	102	10	78	91	..	92	95	92	60	86
Venezuela, RB	62	106	79	52	91	92	..	68	94	94	105	90
Vietnam	..	..	..	..	90	..	..	..	..	..	..	..
West Bank and Gaza	30	80	92	46	..	73	..	89	77	78	56	52
Yemen, Rep.	1	87	46	9	..	75	..	37	85	65	275	632
Zambia	..	119	43	..	78	94	..	41	95	96	60	48
Zimbabwe	..	101	40	..	84	88	..	37	88	89	149	132
World	**41 w**	**105 w**	**66 w**	**25 w**	**81 w**	**86 w**	**.. w**	**58 w**	**90**	**87 w**		
Low income	22	94	38	6	56	73	..	34	77	70		
Middle income	44	111	70	24	87	91	..	62	95	93		
Lower middle income	39	111	65	19	85	90	..	..	94	92		
Upper middle income	68	111	91	42	90	94	..	76	96	96		
Low & middle income	37	106	61	19	79	85	..	54	89	86		
East Asia & Pacific	42	110	73	21	96	93	..	..	94	94		
Europe & Central Asia	52	97	88	53	89	91	..	81	94	92		
Latin America & Carib.	65	118	89	31	86	94	..	70	95	96		
Middle East & N. Africa	33	105	71	25	83	90	..	67	93	90		
South Asia	36	108	49	10	69	85	..	..	92	87		
Sub-Saharan Africa	14	94	32	5	53	70	..	25	73	68		
High income	78	101	101	67	95	95	..	90	96	96		
Euro area	106	..	..	..	..	..	..	..	..	..		

a. Provisional data. b. Data are for 2008. c. Less than 0.5.

About the data

School enrollment data are reported to the United Nations Educational, Scientific, and Cultural Organization (UNESCO) Institute for Statistics by national education authorities and statistical offices. Enrollment ratios help monitor whether a country is on track to achieve the Millennium Development Goal of universal primary education by 2015 (a net primary enrollment ratio of 100 percent), and whether an education system has the capacity to meet the needs of universal primary education, as indicated in part by gross enrollment ratios.

Enrollment ratios, while a useful measure of participation in education, have limitations. They are based on annual school surveys, which are typically conducted at the beginning of the school year and do not reflect actual attendance or dropout rates during the year. And school administrators may exaggerate enrollments, especially if there is a financial incentive to do so.

Also, as international indicators, the gross and net primary enrollment ratios have an inherent weakness: the length of primary education differs across countries, although the International Standard Classification of Education tries to minimize the difference. A relatively short duration for primary education tends to increase the ratio; a relatively long one to decrease it (in part because more older children drop out).

Overage or underage enrollments are frequent, particularly when parents prefer children to start school at other than the official age. Age at enrollment may be inaccurately estimated or misstated, especially in communities where registration of births is not strictly enforced.

Other problems of cross-country comparison stem from errors in school-age population estimates. Age-sex structures drawn from censuses or vital registrations, the primary data sources on school-age population, commonly underenumerate (especially young children) to circumvent laws or regulations. Errors are also introduced when parents round children's ages. While census data are often adjusted for age bias, adjustments are rarely made for inadequate vital registration systems. Compounding these problems, pre- and postcensus estimates of school-age children are model interpolations or projections that may miss important demographic events (see discussion of demographic data in *About the data* for table 2.1).

Gross enrollment ratios indicate the capacity of each level of the education system, but a high ratio may reflect a substantial number of overage children

enrolled in each grade because of repetition rather than a successful education system. The net enrollment ratio excludes overage and underage students to capture more accurately the system's coverage and internal efficiency but does not account for children who fall outside the official school age because of late or early entry rather than grade repetition. Differences between gross and net enrollment ratios show the incidence of overage and underage enrollments.

Adjusted net primary enrollment (called total net primary enrollment in the 2008 edition), recently added as a Millennium Development Goal indicator, captures primary-school-age children who have progressed to secondary education, which the traditional net enrollment ratio excludes.

The data on children out of school (primary-school-age children not enrolled in primary or secondary education) are compiled by the UNESCO Institute for Statistics using administrative data. Children out of school include dropouts, children never enrolled, and children of primary age enrolled in preprimary education. Large numbers of children out of school create pressure to enroll children and provide classrooms, teachers, and educational materials, a task made difficult in many countries by limited education budgets. However, getting children into school is a high priority for countries and crucial for achieving the Millennium Development Goal of universal primary education.

In 2006 the UNESCO Institute for Statistics changed its convention for citing the reference year. For more information, see *About the data* for table 2.11.

Definitions

• **Gross enrollment ratio** is the ratio of total enrollment, regardless of age, to the population of the age group that officially corresponds to the level of education shown. • **Preprimary education** refers to the initial stage of organized instruction, designed primarily to introduce very young children to a school-type environment. • **Primary education** provides children with basic reading, writing, and mathematics skills along with an elementary understanding of such subjects as history, geography, natural science, social science, art, and music. • **Secondary education** completes the provision of basic education that began at the primary level and aims at laying the foundations for lifelong learning and human development by offering more subject- or skill-oriented instruction using more specialized teachers. • **Tertiary education** refers to a wide range of post-secondary education institutions, including technical and vocational education, colleges, and universities, whether or not leading to an advanced research qualification, that normally require as a minimum condition of admission the successful completion of education at the secondary level. • **Net enrollment ratio** is the ratio of total enrollment of children of official school age based on the International Standard Classification of Education 1997 to the population of the age group that officially corresponds to the level of education shown. • **Adjusted net enrollment ratio, primary,** is the ratio of total enrollment of children of official school age for primary education who are enrolled in primary or secondary education to the total primary-school-age population. • **Children out of school** are the number of primary-school-age children not enrolled in primary or secondary school.

Data sources

Data on gross and net enrollment ratios and out of school children are from the UNESCO Institute for Statistics.

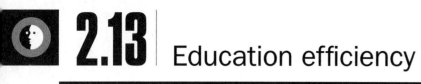

Education efficiency

2.13

	Gross intake rate in grade 1		Cohort survival rate						Repeaters in primary school		Transition to secondary school	
	% of relevant age group		% of grade 1 students						% of enrollment		%	
			Reaching grade 5				Reaching last grade of primary education					
	Male	Female	Male		Female		Male	Female	Male	Female	Male	Female
	2007ª	2007ª	1991	2006ª	1991	2006ª	2006ª	2006ª	2007ª	2007ª	2006ª	2006ª
Afghanistan	..	..	..	..	..	..	..	..	..	..	..	..
Albania	..	..	..	..	..	..	..	..	..	..	..	..
Algeria	102	100	95	95	94	97	89	95	14	8	78	84
Angola	..	..	..	..	..	..	..	..	..	..	..	..
Argentina	109	108	..	88	..	91	85	89	8	5	92	94
Armenia	130	133	..	..	..	..	98	97	0ᵇ	0ᵇ	99	100
Australia	106	105	98	..	99	..	..	..	..	..	..	..
Austria	102	100	..	..	..	..	..	..	..	..	..	..
Azerbaijan	94	92	..	..	..	..	98	100	..	..	99	100
Bangladesh	..	..	..	..	..	..	..	..	..	..	..	..
Belarus	103	101	..	..	..	..	99	100	0ᵇ	0ᵇ	100	100
Belgium	98	99	90	96	92	97	93	94	3	3	..	..
Benin	122	108	54	72	56	71	67	63	8	8	72	70
Bolivia	122	122	..	..	..	..	..	..	1	1	..	..
Bosnia and Herzegovina	..	..	..	..	..	..	..	..	..	..	..	..
Botswana	124	120	81	80	87	85	71	78	..	..	97	98
Brazil	..	..	..	..	..	..	..	..	..	..	..	..
Bulgaria	100	100	..	..	..	..	95	95	3	2	96	96
Burkina Faso	86	76	71	79	68	82	71	74	12	12	47	44
Burundi	144	137	65	65	58	68	56	61	32	32	37	24
Cambodia	141	132	..	61	..	64	53	56	13	10	81	78
Cameroon	118	103	..	..	..	..	..	..	20	20	35	37
Canada	..	..	95	..	98	..	..	..	..	..	..	..
Central African Republic	99ᶜ	73ᶜ	24	53	22	45	43	35	28	28	44	51
Chad	109	79	56	34	41	32	27	23	22	24	56	42
Chile	100	99	94	99	91	99	..	..	3	2	96	98
China	88	87	58	..	78	..	..	..	0ᵇ	0ᵇ	..	..
Hong Kong, China	88	83	..	99	..	100	99	100	1	1	100	100
Colombia	123	121	..	85	..	92	85	92	4	3	99	100
Congo, Dem. Rep.	114	99	58	..	50	..	..	..	16	16	..	..
Congo, Rep.	89	86	56	..	65	..	..	..	21	21	58	58
Costa Rica	101	102	83	86	85	89	82	86	9	6	100	97
Côte d'Ivoire	76	64	75	83	70	73	83	66	22	21	49	48
Croatia	97	97	..	..	..	..	99	100	0ᵇ	0ᵇ	100	100
Cuba	98	98	..	97	..	97	97	97	1	0ᵇ	98	98
Czech Republic	109	108	..	100	..	100	100	100	1	1	99	99
Denmark	97	98	94	100	94	100	92	92	0	0	100	100
Dominican Republic	123	116	..	66	..	71	58	65	7	4	93	98
Ecuador	141	139	..	80	..	83	79	82	2	1	81	77
Egypt, Arab Rep.	105	102	..	96	..	97	94	96	4	2	..	..
El Salvador	111	107	..	72	..	76	67	71	8	5	91	92
Eritrea	44	38	..	59	..	61	59	61	15	14	78	76
Estonia	96	95	..	97	..	97	96	97	3	1	96	99
Ethiopia	144	128	16	64	23	65	57	59	7	5	90	87
Finland	97	96	100	99	100	100	99	100	1	0ᵇ	98	99
France	..	..	69	..	95	..	..	..	..	..	..	..
Gabon	..	..	..	..	..	..	..	..	..	..	..	..
Gambia, The	88	95	..	..	..	..	..	..	6	6	95	93
Georgia	109	103	..	86	..	90	83	89	0ᵇ	0ᵇ	98	100
Germany	104	103	..	..	..	..	98	99	1	1	100	99
Ghana	105	110	81	..	79	..	..	..	6	6	..	..
Greece	100	99	100	97	100	100	97	100	1	1	100	99
Guatemala	124	122	..	69	..	67	63	62	13	11	94	90
Guinea	97	90	64	87	48	79	82	72	9	10	69	59
Guinea-Bissau	..	..	..	..	..	..	..	..	..	..	..	..
Haiti	..	..	..	..	..	..	..	..	..	..	..	..

Education efficiency 2.13

	Gross intake rate in grade 1		Cohort survival rate						Repeaters in primary school		Transition to secondary school	
	% of relevant age group		% of grade 1 students						% of enrollment		%	
			Reaching grade 5				Reaching last grade of primary education					
	Male	Female	Male		Female		Male	Female	Male	Female	Male	Female
	2007a	2007a	1991	2006a	1991	2006a	2006a	2006a	2007a	2007a	2006a	2006a
Honduras	136	131	..	64	..	69	58	64	8	6	68	74
Hungary	97	96	..	..	..	..	97	98	2	2	99	99
India	133	126	..	66	..	65	66	65	3	3	86	82
Indonesia	123	119	34	83	78	86	78	81	4	3	88	89
Iran, Islamic Rep.	109	106	91	..	89	..	..	..	3	1	89	77
Iraq	..	..	..	..	..	..	..	..	..	..	..	..
Ireland	97	99	99	97	100	100	..	..	1	1	..	..
Israel	95	98	..	100	..	99	100	99	2	1	73	72
Italy	105	104	..	99	..	100	99	100	0b	0b	100	99
Jamaica	94	92	..	..	..	..	..	..	3	2	100	97
Japan	99	99	100	..	100	..	..	..	..	..	..	..
Jordan	89	90	..	97	..	96	96	95	1	1	97	96
Kazakhstan	117c	117c	..	..	..	..	99d	100d	0b,c	0b,c	100d	100d
Kenya	112	108	..	81	..	85	..	..	6	6	..	..
Korea, Dem. Rep.	..	..	..	..	..	..	..	..	..	..	..	..
Korea, Rep.	106	109	99	99	100	99	99	99	0b	0b	99	99
Kuwait	97	94	..	100	..	99	100	99	1	1	100	100
Kyrgyz Republic	97	97	..	..	..	..	96	97	0b	0b	99	99
Lao PDR	135	126	..	62	..	61	62	61	18	16	79	76
Latvia	95	95	..	..	..	..	98	98	4	2	97	97
Lebanon	89	87	..	97	..	100	94	99	11	8	85	90
Lesotho	105	99	58	68	73	80	53	71	24	18	68	68
Liberia	100c	100c	..	..	..	..	..	..	7c	6c	..	..
Libya	..	..	..	..	..	..	..	..	..	..	..	..
Lithuania	98	94	..	..	..	..	97	97	1	0b	98	99
Macedonia, FYR	99	99	..	..	..	..	98	99	0b	0b	100	99
Madagascar	171	168	22	42	21	43	42	43	20	18	61	60
Malawi	137	147	71	44	57	43	37	35	21	20	76	71
Malaysia	98	98	97	99	97	100	..	..	..	..	100	99
Mali	92	79	71	83	67	79	75	70	17	17	52	47
Mauritania	115	120	76	63	75	65	54	55	3	3	57	47
Mauritius	100	102	97	99	98	99	98	98	4	3	65	77
Mexico	112	110	35	94	71	95	91	93	5	3	95	93
Moldova	96	96	..	..	..	..	96	96	0b	0b	99	99
Mongolia	124	126	..	86	..	83	86	83	1	0b	95	97
Morocco	116	112	75	85	76	83	79	76	14	10	80	79
Mozambique	166	156	36	68	32	60	48	41	6	6	56	61
Myanmar	136	135	..	68	..	72	68	72	1	0b	75	70
Namibia	102	103	60	84	65	90	73	80	19	14	75	80
Nepal	125c	127c	51	60d	51	64d	60d	64d	17c	17c	81d	81d
Netherlands	103	101	..	99	..	100	..	..	..	..	..	..
New Zealand	105	104	..	..	..	..	..	..	..	..	..	..
Nicaragua	173	163	11	50	37	57	46	55	11	8	..	..
Niger	72	58	61	74	65	69	72	67	5	5	42	37
Nigeria	106	90	..	..	..	..	..	..	3	3	..	..
Norway	100	100	99	100	100	100	99	100	0	0	99	100
Oman	77	78	97	98	96	99	97	98	1	2	97	97
Pakistan	125	100	..	68	..	72	68	72	2	2	69	75
Panama	115	113	..	90	..	90	88	89	7	4	100	98
Papua New Guinea	..	..	70	..	68	..	..	..	..	..	..	..
Paraguay	113	110	73	86	75	90	82	86	6	4	89	89
Peru	109	110	..	90	..	89	86	84	9	8	97	94
Philippines	131	121	..	70	..	78	66	75	3	2	100	98
Poland	97	98	..	..	..	..	..	..	1	0b	..	..
Portugal	108	109	..	..	..	..	..	..	..	..	..	..
Puerto Rico	..	..	..	..	..	..	..	..	..	..	..	..

	Gross intake rate in grade 1		Cohort survival rate						Repeaters in primary school		Transition to secondary school	
	% of relevant age group		% of grade 1 students						% of enrollment		%	
			Reaching grade 5				Reaching last grade of primary education					
			Male		Female							
	Male	Female	1991	2006[a]	1991	2006[a]	Male 2006[a]	Female 2006[a]	Male 2007[a]	Female 2007[a]	Male 2006[a]	Female 2006[a]
	2007[a]	2007[a]										
Romania	97	97	..	..	..	..	93	94	3	2	98	98
Russian Federation	101	100	..	..	..	..	..	..	1	1	..	..
Rwanda	209	205	61	..	59	..	..	..	15	15	..	..
Saudi Arabia	98	99	82	..	84	..	..	..	3	3	..	..
Senegal	98	103	..	65	..	65	54	53	11	10	52	48
Serbia	..	..	..	..	..	..	..	..	..	..	..	..
Sierra Leone	188	172	..	..	..	..	..	..	10	10	..	..
Singapore	..	..	..	..	..	..	..	..	..	..	..	..
Slovak Republic	102	101	..	..	..	..	97	98	3	2	98	98
Slovenia	95	96	..	..	..	..	..	..	1	0[b]	..	..
Somalia	..	..	..	..	..	..	..	..	..	..	..	..
South Africa	117	109	..	..	..	..	..	..	8	8	87	89
Spain	104	104	..	100	..	100	100	100	3	2	..	..
Sri Lanka	112	112	92	93	93	94	93	94	1	1	96	97
Sudan	90[c]	80[c]	90	72	99	69	64	60	3	3	90[d]	98[d]
Swaziland	111	103	74	81	80	87	66	75	19	15	88	89
Sweden	96	95	100	..	100	..	..	..	..	..	..	..
Switzerland	88	92	..	..	..	..	..	..	2	1	99	100
Syrian Arab Republic	123	119	97	..	95	..	95	96	8	6	95	96
Tajikistan	106	102	..	..	..	..	100	97	0[b]	0[b]	100[c]	97[c]
Tanzania	116[c]	114[c]	81	85	82	89	81	85	4	4	64[d]	52[d]
Thailand	71	83	..	..	..	..	..	..	12	6	85	89
Timor-Leste	113	111	..	..	..	..	..	..	15	14	..	..
Togo	97	90	52	58	42	50	49	39	23	24	56	49
Trinidad and Tobago	96	92	..	90	..	92	80	87	6	4	94	92
Tunisia	97	100	94	96	77	97	94	95	7	5	86	90
Turkey	95	92	98	89	97	90	95	93	3	3	93	90
Turkmenistan	..	..	..	..	..	..	..	..	..	..	..	..
Uganda	145	147	..	49	..	49	26	25	13	13	42	43
Ukraine	101	100	..	..	..	..	97	99	0[b]	0[b]	100	100
United Arab Emirates	108	106	80	100	80	100	100	100	2	2	98	99
United Kingdom	..	..	..	..	..	..	..	..	0	0	..	..
United States	105	102	..	96	..	98	..	..	0	0	..	..
Uruguay	100	101	96	92	98	95	91	94	8	6	76	87
Uzbekistan	95	92	..	..	..	..	99	99	0[b]	0[b]	100	100
Venezuela, RB	106	104	..	96	..	100	95	100	6	4	98	98
Vietnam	..	..	..	..	..	..	..	..	..	..	..	..
West Bank and Gaza	80	79	..	..	..	..	99	99	1	1	97	98
Yemen, Rep.	122	102	..	67	..	65	61	57	5	4	83	82
Zambia	126	129	..	94	..	84	83	67	7	6	54	64
Zimbabwe	..	..	72	..	81	..	..	..	..	..	..	..
World	**114 w**	**108 w**	**.. w**	**.. w**	**.. w**	**.. w**	**.. w**	**.. w**	**4 w**	**3 w**	**.. w**	**.. w**
Low income	118	108	..	..	..	..	..	..	8	8	..	..
Middle income	114	110	..	..	..	..	..	..	3	3	..	..
Lower middle income	114	110	..	..	..	..	..	..	3	3	..	..
Upper middle income	111	107	..	..	..	..	..	..	..	..	..	..
Low & middle income	115	109	..	..	..	..	..	..	4	4	..	..
East Asia & Pacific	99	97	55	..	78	..	..	..	2	1	..	..
Europe & Central Asia	99	97	..	..	..	..	..	..	1	1	..	..
Latin America & Carib.	122	117	..	..	..	..	..	..	..	..	..	..
Middle East & N. Africa	108	105	..	..	..	..	..	..	7	4	86	83
South Asia	131	122	..	67	..	66	67	66	4	4	83	81
Sub-Saharan Africa	115	105	..	..	..	..	..	..	9	9	..	..
High income	103	102	..	..	..	..	..	..	..	..	..	..
Euro area	104	103	..	..	..	..	98	99	2	1	..	..

a. Provisional data. b. Less than 0.5. c. Data are for 2008. d. Data are for 2007.

About the data

The United Nations Educational, Scientific, and Cultural Organization (UNESCO) Institute for Statistics estimates indicators of students' progress through school. These indicators measure an education system's success in reaching all students, efficiently moving students from one grade to the next, and imparting a particular level of education.

The gross intake rate indicates the level of access to primary education and the education system's capacity to provide access to primary education. Low gross intake rates in grade 1 reflect the fact that many children do not enter primary school even though school attendance, at least through the primary level, is mandatory in all countries. Because the gross intake rate includes all new entrants regardless of age, it can exceed 100 percent. Once enrolled, students drop out for a variety of reasons, including low quality schooling, lack of relevant curriculum (real or perceived by parents or students), repetition, discouragement over poor performance, and direct and indirect schooling costs. Students' progress to higher grades may also be limited by the availability of teachers, classrooms, and materials.

The cohort survival rate is the estimated proportion of an entering cohort of grade 1 students that eventually reaches grade 5 or the last grade of primary education. It measures an education system's holding power and internal efficiency. Rates approaching 100 percent indicate high retention and low dropout levels. Cohort survival rates are typically estimated from data on enrollment and repetition by grade for two consecutive years. This procedure, called the reconstructed cohort method, makes three simplifying assumptions: dropouts never return to school; promotion, repetition, and dropout rates remain constant over the period in which the cohort is enrolled in school; and the same rates apply to all pupils enrolled in a grade, regardless of whether they previously repeated a grade (Fredricksen 1993). Cross-country comparisons should thus be made with caution, because other flows—caused by new entrants, reentrants, grade skipping, migration, or transfers during the school year—are not considered.

Research suggests that five to six years of schooling, which is how long primary education lasts in most countries, is a critical threshold for achieving sustainable basic literacy and numeracy skills. But the indicator only indirectly reflects the quality of schooling, and a high rate does not guarantee these learning outcomes. Measuring actual learning outcomes requires setting curriculum standards and measuring students' learning progress against those standards through standardized assessments, actions that many countries do not systematically undertake.

Data on repeaters are often used to indicate an education system's internal efficiency. Repeaters not only increase the cost of education for the family and the school system, but also use limited school resources. Country policies on repetition and promotion differ; in some cases the number of repeaters is controlled because of limited capacity. Care should be taken in interpreting this indicator.

The transition rate from primary to secondary school conveys the degree of access or transition between the two levels. As completing primary education is a prerequisite for participating in lower secondary school, growing numbers of primary completers will inevitably create pressure for more available places at the secondary level. A low transition rate can signal such problems as an inadequate examination and promotion system or insufficient secondary school capacity. The quality of data on the transition rate is affected when new entrants and repeaters are not correctly distinguished in the first grade of secondary school. Students who interrupt their studies after completing primary school could also affect data quality.

In 2006 the UNESCO Institute for Statistics changed its convention for citing the reference year. For more information, see *About the data* for table 2.11.

Definitions

• **Gross intake rate in grade 1** is the number of new entrants in the first grade of primary education regardless of age as a percentage of the population of the official primary school entrance age. • **Cohort survival rate** is the percentage of children enrolled in the first grade of primary school who eventually reach grade 5 or the last grade of primary education. The estimate is based on the reconstructed cohort method (see *About the data*). • **Repeaters in primary school** are the number of students enrolled in the same grade as in the previous year as a percentage of all students enrolled in primary school. • **Transition to secondary school** is the number of new entrants to the first grade of secondary school in a given year as a percentage of the number of students enrolled in the final grade of primary school in the previous year.

Data sources

Data on education efficiency are from the UNESCO Institute for Statistics.

	Primary completion rate						Youth literacy rate				Adult literacy rate	
	% of relevant age group						% ages 15–24				% ages 15 and older	
	Total		Male		Female		Male		Female		Male	Female
	1991	2007[a]	1991	2007[a]	1991	2007[a]	1990	2005–07[b]	1990	2005–07[b]	2005–07[b]	2005–07[b]
Afghanistan	..	..	..	..	..	..	..	..	..	..	..	..
Albania	..	96	..	97	..	96	..	99	..	99	99	99
Algeria	80	95	86	94	73	96	86	94	62	91	84	66
Angola	35	..	..	..	..	..	..	..	..	..	..	..
Argentina	..	97	..	95	..	99	98	99	99	99	98	98
Armenia	..	98	..	96	..	100	100	100	100	100	100	99
Australia	..	..	..	..	..	..	..	..	..	..	..	..
Austria	..	103	..	103	..	102	..	..	..	..	..	..
Azerbaijan	..	..	..	..	..	..	..	100	..	100	100	99
Bangladesh	..	72	..	70	..	74	52	71	38	73	59	48
Belarus	94	92	..	93	..	92	100	100	100	100	100	100
Belgium	79	87	76	86	82	88	..	..	..	..	..	..
Benin	21	64	28	76	13	52	55	63	27	41	53	28
Bolivia	71	101	78	102	64	100	96	100	92	99	96	86
Bosnia and Herzegovina	..	..	..	..	..	..	..	..	..	..	..	..
Botswana	89	95	82	91	97	98	86	93	92	95	83	83
Brazil	90	106	..	..	..	..	..	97	..	99	90	90
Bulgaria	90	98	88	98	92	98	..	98	..	97	99	98
Burkina Faso	20	33	24	37	15	29	27	47	14	33	37	22
Burundi	46	39	49	42	43	36	59	..	48	..	..	..
Cambodia	..	85	..	85	..	85	..	90	..	83	86	68
Cameroon	53	55	57	61	49	50	..	..	..	..	..	..
Canada	..	..	..	..	..	..	..	..	..	..	..	..
Central African Republic	27	24	35	30	18	19	63	..	35	..	..	..
Chad	18	31	29	41	7	21	..	53	..	35	43	21
Chile	..	95	..	96	..	95	98	99	99	99	97	96
China	105	..	..	..	..	..	97	99	91	99	96	90
Hong Kong, China	102	102	..	104	..	99	..	..	..	..	..	..
Colombia	70	107	67	105	73	109	89	97	92	98	92	93
Congo, Dem. Rep.	46	51	58	61	34	41	..	..	..	..	..	..
Congo, Rep.	54	72	59	75	49	70	..	..	..	..	..	..
Costa Rica	79	91	77	90	81	93	..	98	..	98	96	96
Côte d'Ivoire	43	45	55	53	32	36	60	..	38	..	..	..
Croatia	..	96	..	97	..	95	100	100	100	100	99	98
Cuba	99	93	..	93	..	93	..	100	..	100	100	100
Czech Republic	..	94	..	95	..	93	..	..	..	..	..	..
Denmark	98	101	98	101	98	102	..	..	..	..	..	..
Dominican Republic	62	89	..	87	..	91	..	95	..	97	89	90
Ecuador	..	106	..	105	..	107	97	95	96	96	87	82
Egypt, Arab Rep.	..	98	..	101	..	96	71	88	54	82	75	58
El Salvador	61	91	60	89	62	93	85	93	85	94	85	80
Eritrea	..	46	..	52	..	41	..	..	..	..	..	..
Estonia	..	100	..	102	..	98	100	100	100	100	100	100
Ethiopia	..	46	..	51	..	41	39	..	28	..	..	..
Finland	97	97	98	97	97	97	..	..	..	..	..	..
France	104	..	..	..	..	..	..	..	..	..	..	..
Gabon	..	..	..	..	..	..	94	98	92	96	90	82
Gambia, The	..	72	..	70	..	73	..	..	..	..	..	..
Georgia	..	92	..	..	..	..	..	..	..	..	..	..
Germany	..	97	..	97	..	98	..	..	..	..	..	..
Ghana	61	71	69	73	54	68	..	80	..	76	72	58
Greece	..	103	..	104	..	103	99	99	99	99	98	96
Guatemala	..	77	..	80	..	74	82	88	71	83	79	68
Guinea	17	64	25	73	9	55	..	..	..	..	..	..
Guinea-Bissau	..	..	..	..	..	..	..	..	..	..	..	..
Haiti	27	..	29	..	26	..	..	..	..	..	..	..

Education completion and outcomes

	Primary completion rate						Youth literacy rate				Adult literacy rate	
	% of relevant age group						% ages 15–24				% ages 15 and older	
	Total		Male		Female		Male		Female		Male	Female
	1991	2007[a]	1991	2007[a]	1991	2007[a]	1990	2005–07[b]	1990	2005–07[b]	2005–07[b]	2005–07[b]
Honduras	64	88	67	85	61	90	..	93	..	95	84	83
Hungary	87	96	93	96	95	96	99	98	99	99	99	99
India	64	86	75	88	52	83	74[c]	87	49[c]	77	77	54
Indonesia	91	99	..	99	..	99	97	97	95	96	95	89
Iran, Islamic Rep.	91	105	97	98	85	113	92	97	81	96	87	77
Iraq	..	..	..	..	..	..	..	..	..	..	..	..
Ireland	..	96	..	91	..	101	..	..	..	..	..	..
Israel	..	101	..	100	..	101	..	..	..	..	..	..
Italy	104	100	104	100	104	99	..	100	..	100	99	99
Jamaica	90	82	86	81	94	84	..	91	..	98	81	91
Japan	101	..	101	..	102	..	..	..	..	..	..	..
Jordan	101	99	101	100	101	98	..	99	..	99	95	87
Kazakhstan	..	104[d]	..	104[d]	..	105[d]	100	100	100	100	100	99
Kenya	..	93	..	94	..	92	..	..	..	..	..	..
Korea, Dem. Rep.	..	..	..	..	..	..	..	..	..	..	..	..
Korea, Rep.	98	101	98	106	98	95	..	..	..	..	..	..
Kuwait	..	98	..	98	..	98	..	98	..	99	95	93
Kyrgyz Republic	..	95	..	95	..	94	..	100	..	100	100	99
Lao PDR	45	77	..	81	..	72	..	89	..	79	82	63
Latvia	..	92	..	93	..	91	100	100	100	100	100	100
Lebanon	..	82	..	80	..	83	..	98	..	99	93	86
Lesotho	59	78	42	65	76	92	..	..	..	..	..	..
Liberia	..	55[d]	..	60[d]	..	50[d]	56	68	47	76	60	51
Libya	..	..	..	..	..	..	99	100	91	98	94	78
Lithuania	89	93	..	92	..	93	100	100	100	100	100	100
Macedonia, FYR	..	97	..	96	..	98	99	99	99	99	99	95
Madagascar	33	62	33	62	34	61	..	..	..	..	..	..
Malawi	29	55	36	55	21	56	70	84	49	82	79	65
Malaysia	91	98	91	98	91	98	96	98	95	98	94	90
Mali	13	49	15	59	10	40	..	47	..	31	35	18
Mauritania	34	59	41	59	27	60	..	70	..	62	63	48
Mauritius	107	94	107	92	107	95	91	95	92	97	90	85
Mexico	88	104	..	104	..	104	96	98	95	98	94	91
Moldova	..	93	..	93	..	93	100	100	100	100	100	99
Mongolia	..	110	..	108	..	113	..	94	..	97	97	98
Morocco	48	83	57	87	39	79	71	84	46	67	69	43
Mozambique	26	46	32	53	21	39	..	58	..	47	57	33
Myanmar	..	..	..	..	..	..	..	..	..	..	..	..
Namibia	..	77	..	73	..	81	86	91	90	94	89	87
Nepal	51	78[d]	..	79[d]	..	78[d]	68	85	33	73	70	44
Netherlands	..	..	..	..	..	..	..	..	..	..	..	..
New Zealand	100	..	101	..	99	..	..	..	..	..	..	..
Nicaragua	42	73	..	70	..	77	..	85	..	89	78	78
Niger	18	40	22	47	13	32	..	52	..	23	43	15
Nigeria	..	72	..	80	..	65	81	89	62	85	80	64
Norway	100	96	100	95	100	97	..	..	..	..	..	..
Oman	74	88	78	88	70	88	..	99	..	98	89	77
Pakistan	..	62	..	70	..	53	..	79	..	58	68	40
Panama	..	99	..	98	..	99	95	97	95	96	94	93
Papua New Guinea	46	..	51	..	42	..	..	63	..	65	62	53
Paraguay	68	95	68	94	69	96	96	99	95	99	96	93
Peru	..	101	..	101	..	101	97	98	94	97	95	85
Philippines	88	94	..	90	..	97	96	94	97	95	93	94
Poland	96	97	..	..	..	..	100	100	100	99	100	99
Portugal	95	104	94	102	95	107	99	100	99	100	97	93
Puerto Rico	..	..	..	..	..	..	92	..	94	..	..	..

2.14 Education completion and outcomes

	Primary completion rate						Youth literacy rate				Adult literacy rate	
	% of relevant age group						% ages 15–24				% ages 15 and older	
	Total		Male		Female		Male		Female		Male	Female
	1991	2007[a]	1991	2007[a]	1991	2007[a]	1990	2005–07[b]	1990	2005–07[b]	2005–07[b]	2005–07[b]
Romania	100	101	100	101	100	101	99	97	99	98	98	97
Russian Federation	..	..	..	..	..	..	100	100	100	100	100	99
Rwanda	35	35	40	36	31	35	..	..	..	..	..	..
Saudi Arabia	55	93	60	96	51	91	94	98	81	96	89	79
Senegal	43	49	52	51	33	47	49	58	28	45	52	33
Serbia	..	..	..	..	..	..	99[e]	..	98[e]	..	..	..
Sierra Leone	..	81	..	92	..	70	..	64	..	44	50	27
Singapore	..	..	..	..	..	..	99	100	99	100	97	92
Slovak Republic	..	93	..	94	..	92	..	..	..	..	..	..
Slovenia	..	..	..	..	..	..	100	100	100	100	100	100
Somalia	..	..	..	..	..	..	..	..	..	..	..	..
South Africa	76	92	71	92	80	92	..	95	..	96	89	87
Spain	103	99	104	99	103	99	100	100	100	100	99	97
Sri Lanka	102	106	103	106	102	107	..	97	..	98	93	89
Sudan	42	50	47	54	37	46	..	..	..	..	..	..
Swaziland	60	67	57	64	63	69	83	..	84	..	..	..
Sweden	96	..	96	..	96	..	..	..	..	..	..	..
Switzerland	53	88	53	88	54	89	..	..	..	..	..	..
Syrian Arab Republic	89	114	94	116	84	113	..	95	..	92	90	76
Tajikistan	..	95	..	..	..	..	100	100	100	100	100	100
Tanzania	62	112[d]	62	115[d]	63	109[d]	86	79	78	76	79	66
Thailand	..	101	..	99	..	104	..	98	..	98	96	93
Timor-Leste	..	69	..	69	..	69	..	..	..	..	..	..
Togo	35	57	48	67	22	48	..	..	..	..	..	..
Trinidad and Tobago	101	88	98	86	104	90	99	100	99	100	99	98
Tunisia	74	120	79	122	70	117	..	97	..	94	86	69
Turkey	90	96	93	101	86	91	97	99	88	94	96	81
Turkmenistan	..	..	..	..	..	..	..	100	..	100	100	99
Uganda	..	54	..	57	..	51	77	88	63	84	82	66
Ukraine	94	101	..	101	..	101	..	100	..	100	100	100
United Arab Emirates	103	105	104	103	103	106	..	94	..	97	89	91
United Kingdom	..	..	..	..	..	..	..	..	..	..	..	..
United States	..	95	..	94	..	96	..	..	..	..	..	..
Uruguay	94	99	91	98	96	100	..	98	..	99	97	98
Uzbekistan	..	97	..	99	..	96	..	..	..	..	..	..
Venezuela, RB	81	98	76	96	86	100	95	98	96	99	95	95
Vietnam	..	..	..	..	..	..	94	..	93	..	..	..
West Bank and Gaza	..	83	..	83	..	83	..	99	..	99	97	90
Yemen, Rep.	..	60	..	74	..	46	83	93	35	67	77	40
Zambia	..	88	..	94	..	83	67	82	66	68	81	61
Zimbabwe	97	..	99	..	96	..	97	94	94	88	94	88
World	**79 w**	*86 w*	**86 w**	*88 w*	**75 w**	*84 w*	**88 w**	*91 w*	**79 w**	*87 w*	**88 w**	**79 w**
Low income	..	65	..	70	..	60	70	79	56	69	72	55
Middle income	84	93	90	94	79	92	90	94	81	91	90	80
Lower middle income	83	91	90	93	76	90	89	93	78	89	88	77
Upper middle income	90	101	90	101	90	101	96	98	96	98	95	93
Low & middle income	78	85	85	87	73	83	97	90	92	85	86	75
East Asia & Pacific	101	98	105	98	97	98	99	98	98	98	96	90
Europe & Central Asia	93	98	93	99	92	96	93	99	94	99	99	90
Latin America & Carib.	84	100	84	100	85	101	86	97	76	97	92	90
Middle East & N. Africa	78	90	84	93	72	88	85	93	69	86	82	65
South Asia	62	80	75	83	52	77	71	84	48	74	74	52
Sub-Saharan Africa	51	60	57	65	47	55	71	77	59	67	71	54
High income	..	97	..	97	..	97	100	100	99	100	99	99
Euro area	101	..	100	..	100	..	..	..	..	..	..	..

a. Provisional data. b. Data are for the most recent year available. c. Includes the Indian-held part of Jammu and Kashmir. d. Data are for 2008. e. Includes Montenegro.

Education completion and outcomes | 2.14

Many governments publish statistics that indicate how their education systems are working and developing—statistics on enrollment and such efficiency indicators as repetition rates, pupil-teacher ratios, and cohort progression. The World Bank and the United Nations Educational, Scientific, and Cultural Organization (UNESCO) Institute for Statistics jointly developed the primary completion rate indicator. Increasingly used as a core indicator of an education system's performance, it reflects an education system's coverage and the educational attainment of students. The indicator is a key measure of education outcome at the primary level and of progress toward the Millennium Development Goals and the Education for All initiative. However, because curricula and standards for school completion vary across countries, a high primary completion rate does not necessarily mean high levels of student learning.

The primary completion rate reflects the primary cycle as defined by the International Standard Classification of Education, ranging from three or four years of primary education (in a very small number of countries) to five or six years (in most countries) and seven (in a small number of countries).

The table shows the proxy primary completion rate, calculated by subtracting the number of repeaters in the last grade of primary school from the total number of students in that grade and dividing by the total number of children of official graduation age. Data limitations preclude adjusting for students who drop out during the final year of primary school. Thus proxy rates should be taken as an upper estimate of the actual primary completion rate.

There are many reasons why the primary completion rate can exceed 100 percent. The numerator may include late entrants and overage children who have repeated one or more grades of primary school as well as children who entered school early, while the denominator is the number of children of official completing age. Other data limitations contribute to completion rates exceeding 100 percent, such as the use of population estimates of varying reliability, the conduct of school and population surveys at different times of year, and other discrepancies in the numbers used in the calculation.

Basic student outcomes include achievements in reading and mathematics judged against established standards. In many countries national assessments are enabling the ministry of education to monitor progress in these outcomes. Internationally comparable assessments are not yet available, except for a few, mostly industrialized, countries. The UNESCO

Institute for Statistics has established literacy as an outcome indicator based on an internationally agreed definition.

The literacy rate is the percentage of people who can, with understanding, both read and write a short, simple statement about their everyday life. In practice, literacy is difficult to measure. To estimate literacy using such a definition requires census or survey measurements under controlled conditions. Many countries estimate the number of literate people from self-reported data. Some use educational attainment data as a proxy but apply different lengths of school attendance or levels of completion. Because definitions and methodologies of data collection differ across countries, data should be used cautiously.

The reported literacy data are compiled by the UNESCO Institute for Statistics based on national censuses and household surveys during 1985–2007. For countries that have not reported national estimates, the UNESCO Institute for Statistics derived the modeled estimates. For detailed information on sources, definitions, and methodology, consult the original source.

Literacy statistics for most countries cover the population ages 15 and older, but some include younger ages or are confined to age ranges that tend to inflate literacy rates. The literacy data in the narrower age range of 15–24 better captures the ability of participants in the formal education system and reflects recent progress in education. The youth literacy rate reported in the table measures the accumulated outcomes of primary education over the previous 10 years or so by indicating the proportion of people who have passed through the primary education system and acquired basic literacy and numeracy skills.

• **Primary completion rate** is the percentage of students completing the last year of primary school. It is calculated by taking the total number of students in the last grade of primary school, minus the number of repeaters in that grade, divided by the total number of children of official completing age. • **Youth literacy rate** is the percentage of people ages 15–24 that can, with understanding, both read and write a short, simple statement about their everyday life. • **Adult literacy rate** is the literacy rate among people ages 15 and older.

Data on primary completion rates and literacy rates are from the UNESCO Institute for Statistics.

Education gaps by income and gender

	Survey year	Gross intake rate in grade 1		Gross primary participation rate		Average years of schooling		Primary completion rate				Children out of school	
		% of relevant age group		% of relevant age group		Ages 15–24		% of relevant age group				% of children ages 6–11	
		Poorest quintile	Richest quintile	Poorest quintile	Richest quintile	Poorest quintile	Richest quintile	Poorest quintile	Richest quintile	Male	Female	Poorest quintile	Richest quintile
Armenia	2000	105	93	177	181	9	11	96	98	96	98	14	13
Bangladesh	2004	193	156	107	120	3	8	26	70	47	58	25	10
Benin	2001	74	112	51	115	1	6	7	45	23	15	66	21
Bolivia	2003	98	95	92	98	6	11	48	90	75	75	24	5
Burkina Faso	2003	24	97	20	98	1	6	8	52	24	20	87	32
Cambodia	2000	146	187	78	134	2	7	4	45	18	17	50	12
Cameroon	2004	115	100	94	122	3	9	12	69	36	37	42	4
Central African Republic	1994–95	103	118	57	130	2	6	0[a]	18	8	6	65	21
Chad	2004	3	14	15	98	0[a]	5	1	36	15	8	91	36
Colombia	2005	157	85	126	99	6	11	50	90	70	77	8	1
Comoros	1996	84	119	56	147	2	6	4	29	12	12	72	26
Côte d'Ivoire	1994	26	39	41	103	2	6	6	41	25	17	70	23
Dominican Republic	2002	170	103	149	156	6	11	38	87	57	69	14	4
Egypt, Arab Rep.	2003	87	120	96	103	6	11	58	87	77	71	24	5
Eritrea	1995	55	117	42	154	1	7	3	65	21	24	84	10
Ethiopia	2000	87	257	61	186	1	5	4	44	15	12	87	42
Gabon	2000	..	..	155	140	5	8	12	60	35	40	8	3
Ghana	2003	90	90	71	108	4	9	15	66	38	41	57	20
Guatemala	1995	114	124	62	122	2	9	9	76	41	40	58	8
Guinea	1999	13	39	10	38	1	5	3	27	18	9	95	77
Haiti	2000	141	200	94	152	3	8	1	40	13	18	64	21
India	1999	99	72	87	122	3	10	31	87	64	55	35	2
Indonesia	2002–03	85	92	103	104	7	11	75	97	86	89	19	6
Jordan	2002	..	..	101	99	10	12	93	98	97	97	11	9
Kazakhstan	1999	..	..	125	130	10	11	98	100	98	99	24	18
Kenya	2003	128	123	104	118	5	9	14	57	30	36	24	4
Kyrgyz Republic	1997	..	..	133	138	10	10	86	88	85	87	21	18
Madagascar	1997	84	87	59	134	2	7	1	47	13	16	60	6
Malawi	2002	180	226	103	126	4	8	10	52	32	14	29	9
Mali	2001	45	89	36	101	1	5	3	37	16	11	75	29
Morocco	2003–04	109	85	98	116	2	9	17	78	47	46	26	2
Mozambique	2003	104	134	79	150	2	5	2	17	8	7	59	13
Namibia	1992	..	..	138	116	5	8	15	65	25	34	22	9
Nepal	2001	240	249	116	160	3	7	18	59	37	28	33	6
Nicaragua	2001	127	108	79	104	3	10	14	88	47	59	46	5
Niger	1998	11	69	15	77	1	4	8	46	22	13	90	44
Nigeria	2003	77	106	67	111	4	10	16	70	39	37	56	5
Pakistan	1990–91	68	173	45	127	2	8	11	55	32	22	72	13
Paraguay	1990	137	106	103	114	5	10	29	77	49	54	21	10
Peru	2000	114	94	112	109	6	11	41	93	72	72	9	1
Philippines	2003	131	102	103	102	6	11	46	88	67	79	17	2
Rwanda	2000	216	197	100	126	3	6	7	28	14	14	43	23
Tanzania	1999	95	231	63	119	4	7	27	55	34	34	74	27
Uganda	2000–01	145	127	106	120	4	8	7	43	19	21	28	6
Uzbekistan	1996	..	..	102	114	10	10	84	87	84	86	29	23
Vietnam	2002	121	105	139	127	5	10	58	97	84	84	8	2
Zambia	2001–02	83	119	74	112	4	9	16	79	38	43	61	18
Zimbabwe	1994	138	114	104	109	7	10	36	80	51	57	22	8

a. Less than 0.5.

Education gaps by income and gender | 2.15

The data in the table describe basic information on school participation and educational attainment by individuals in different socioeconomic groups within countries. The data are from Demographic and Health Surveys conducted by Macro International with the support of the U.S. Agency for International Development. These large-scale household sample surveys, conducted periodically in developing countries, collect information on a large number of health, nutrition, and population measures as well as on respondents' social, demographic, and economic characteristics using a standard set of questionnaires. The data presented here draw on responses to individual and household questionnaires.

Typically, Demographic and Health Surveys collect basic information on educational attainment and enrollment levels from every household member ages 5 or 6 and older as background characteristics. As the surveys are intended for the collection of demographic and health information, the education section of the survey is not as robust and detailed as the health section; however, it still provides useful micro-level information on education that cannot be explained by aggregate national-level data.

Socioeconomic status as displayed in the table is based on a household's assets, including ownership of consumer items, features of the household's dwelling, and other characteristics related to wealth. Each household asset on which information was

collected was assigned a weight generated through principal-component analysis. The resulting scores were standardized to a standard normal distribution with a mean of zero and a standard deviation of one. The standardized scores were then used to create break-points defining wealth quintiles, expressed as quintiles of individuals in the population.

The selection of the asset index for defining socioeconomic status was based on pragmatic rather than conceptual considerations: Demographic and Health Surveys do not collect income or consumption data but do have detailed information on households' ownership of consumer goods and access to a variety of goods and services. Like income or consumption, the asset index defines disparities primarily in economic terms. It therefore excludes other possibilities of disparities among groups, such as those based on gender, education, ethnic background, or other facets of social exclusion. To that extent the index provides only a partial view of the multidimensional concepts of poverty, inequality, and inequity.

Creating one index that includes all asset indicators limits the types of analysis that can be performed. In particular, the use of a unified index does not permit a disaggregated analysis to examine which asset indicators have a more or less important association with education status. In addition, some asset indicators may reflect household wealth better in some countries than in others—or reflect different degrees of wealth in different countries. Taking such information into account and creating country-specific asset indexes with country-specific choices of asset indicators might produce a more effective and accurate index for each country. The asset index used in the table does not have this flexibility.

The analysis was carried out for 48 countries. The table shows the estimates for the poorest and richest quintiles only; the full set of estimates for 32 indicators is available in the country reports (see *Data sources*). The data in the table differ from data for similar indicators in preceding tables either because the indicator refers to a period a few years preceding the survey date or because the indicator definition or methodology is different. Findings should be used with caution because of measurement error inherent in the use of survey data.

• **Survey year** is the year in which the underlying data were collected. • **Gross intake rate in grade 1** is the number of students in the first grade of primary education regardless of age as a percentage of the population of the official primary school entrance age. These data may differ from those in table 2.13. • **Gross primary participation rate** is the ratio of total students attending primary school regardless of age to the population of the age group that officially corresponds to primary education. • **Average years of schooling** are the years of formal schooling received, on average, by youths and adults ages 15–24. • **Primary completion rate** is the percentage of children of the official primary school completing age to the official primary school completing age plus four who have completed the last year of primary school or higher. These data differ from those in table 2.14 because the definition and methodology are different. • **Children out of school** are the percentage of children ages 6–11 who are not in school. These data differ from those in table 2.12 because the definition and methodology are different.

Highest level of education, Liberia, 2007 (%)

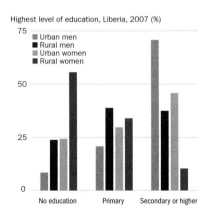

Rural women are the most disadvantaged in Liberia, with more than 55 percent having no education and only 10 percent having secondary or higher education.

Source: Demographic and Health Surveys.

Data on education gaps by income and gender are from an analysis of Demographic and Health Surveys by Macro International and the World Bank. Country reports are available at www.worldbank.org/education/edstats/.

	Health expenditure					Year last national health account completed	Health workers per 1,000 people		Year of last health survey[a]	Hospital beds per 1,000 people	Outpatient visits per capita
	Total % of GDP	Public % of total	Out of pocket % of private	Per capita $	Per capita PPP$		Physicians	Nurses and midwives			
	2006	**2006**	**2006**	**2006**	**2006**		**2002–07[b]**	**2002–07[b]**		**2002–07[b]**	**2000–07[b]**
Afghanistan	9.2	32.4	78.5	..	..		..	..	2003	..	..
Albania	6.5	37.3	94.9	187	1,332	2003	1.2	4.1	2005	3.0	1.5
Algeria	4.2	81.1	94.6	148	..	2001	1.1	2.2	2006	1.7	..
Angola	2.6	86.8	100.0	71	187		0.1	1.4	2001	0.8	..
Argentina	10.1	45.5	43.8	551	2,723	1997	..	..		..	..
Armenia	4.7	41.2	87.6	98	763	2007	3.7	4.9	2005	4.4	2.8
Australia	8.7	67.7	56.4	3,302	4,152	2005	2.5	..		4.0	6.2
Austria	10.2	75.9	65.8	3,974	5,424	2004	3.7	6.6		7.6	6.7
Azerbaijan	4.1	26.1	86.4	102	1,031		3.6	8.4	2006	8.0	4.6
Bangladesh	3.2	31.8	88.3	12	119	2005	0.3	0.3	2006	0.3	..
Belarus	6.4	74.9	68.8	243	1,997		4.8	12.5	2005	11.3	13.2
Belgium	9.9	72.5	79.0	3,726	4,821	2006	4.2	14.2		5.3	7.0
Benin	4.7	50.2	94.9	26	154	2003	0.0[c]	0.8	2006	0.5	..
Bolivia	6.4	62.8	81.0	79	699	2007	..	..	2003	1.1	..
Bosnia and Herzegovina	9.5	55.2	100.0	296	1,102	2006	1.4	4.7	2006	3.0	3.3
Botswana	7.1	76.5	27.5	379	1,054	2003	0.4	2.7	2000	2.4	..
Brazil	7.5	47.9	63.8	427	1,460	2005	..	..	1996	2.4	..
Bulgaria	7.2	56.7	97.1	297	1,709	2006	3.7	4.6		6.4	..
Burkina Faso	6.3	56.9	91.5	27	161	2005	0.1	0.5	2003	0.9	..
Burundi	8.7	8.6	57.4	10	92		0.0[c]	0.2	2000	0.7	..
Cambodia	5.9	26.0	84.7	30	437		..	..	2005	0.1	..
Cameroon	4.6	21.2	94.8	45	202	1995	0.2	1.6	2006	1.5	..
Canada	10.0	70.4	49.0	3,917	4,651	2007	1.9	10.1		3.4	6.3
Central African Republic	4.0	38.3	95.0	14	56		0.1	0.4	2006	1.2	..
Chad	4.9	53.9	96.2	29	379		0.0[c]	0.3	2004	0.4	..
Chile	5.3	52.7	54.8	473	1,290	2006	1.1	0.6		2.3	..
China	4.6	40.7	83.1	94	1,124	2006	1.5	1.0	2006	2.2	..
Hong Kong, China	..	..	..	..	..		..	..		..	..
Colombia	7.3	85.4	43.9	217	989	2003	1.4[d]	0.6	2005	1.0	..
Congo, Dem. Rep.	6.8	18.7	48.9	10	47		0.1	0.5	2007	0.8	..
Congo, Rep.	2.1	71.7	100.0	44	188		0.2	1.0	2005	1.6	..
Costa Rica	7.7	68.4	86.7	402	..	2003	..	..	1993	1.3	..
Côte d'Ivoire	3.8	23.6	87.8	35	..		0.1	0.6	2006	0.4	..
Croatia	8.2	76.8[e]	92.2	996[e]	2,101		2.7	5.5		5.3	6.4
Cuba	7.7	91.6	93.3	362	..		5.9	7.4	2006	4.9	..
Czech Republic	6.9	88.0	95.5	953	3,270	2006	3.6	8.9	1993	8.2	15.0
Denmark	10.8	85.9	90.1	5,447	5,165	2006	3.6	10.1		3.8	4.1
Dominican Republic	5.6	37.0	64.3	206	..	2002	..	..	2007	1.0	..
Ecuador	5.3	43.6	85.6	166	928	2005	..	..	2004	1.7	..
Egypt, Arab Rep.	6.3	41.4	94.9	92	1,174	2002	2.4	3.4	2005	2.1	..
El Salvador	6.6	61.8	88.9	181	..	2007	1.5	0.8	2002/03	0.7	..
Eritrea	3.6	45.9	100.0	8	..		0.1	0.6	2002	1.2	..
Estonia	5.2	73.3	93.3	632	2,043	2006	3.3	7.0		5.7	6.9
Ethiopia	3.9	59.3	80.6	7	77	2005	0.0[c]	0.2	2005	0.2	..
Finland	8.2	76.0	77.6	3,232	3,607	2006	3.3	8.9		6.8	4.3
France	11.0	79.7	33.2	3,937	5,189	2006	3.4	8.0		7.3	6.9
Gabon	4.5	73.0	100.0	351	1,338		0.3	5.0	2000	2.0	..
Gambia, The	5.0	56.8	71.2	15	142	2004	0.1	1.3	2005/06	0.8	..
Georgia	8.4	21.5	91.9	147	1,063	2007	4.7	4.0	2005	3.3	2.2
Germany	10.6	76.9	57.1	3,718	5,210	2006	3.4	8.0		8.3	7.0
Ghana	5.1	34.2	77.8	33	214	2002	0.2	0.9	2006	0.9	..
Greece	9.5	62.0	94.8	2,280	3,745		5.0	3.6		4.8	..
Guatemala	5.8	28.7	92.5	157	..	2007	..	..	2002	0.7	..
Guinea	5.8	14.1	99.5	20	105		0.1	0.5	2005	0.3	..
Guinea-Bissau	5.8	26.3	55.8	12	69		0.1	0.7	2006	0.7	..
Haiti	8.4	67.6	89.6	42	..	2006	..	..	2005	1.3	..

	Health expenditure					Year last national health account completed	Health workers		Year of last health survey[a]	Hospital beds	Outpatient visits
	Total % of GDP	Public % of total	Out of pocket % of private	Per capita $	PPP$		per 1,000 people Physicians	Nurses and midwives		per 1,000 people	per capita
	2006	**2006**	**2006**	**2006**	**2006**		**2002–07[b]**	**2002–07[b]**		**2002–07[b]**	**2000–07[b]**
Honduras	6.4	47.8	87.1	99	..	2005	..	..	2005	1.0	..
Hungary	8.3	70.9	77.6	929	2,761	2006	3.0	9.2		7.1	12.9
India	3.6	25.0	91.4	29	426	2001	0.6	1.3	2005/06	0.9	..
Indonesia	2.5	50.5	70.4	39	213	2004	0.1	0.8	2002/03	0.6	..
Iran, Islamic Rep.	6.8	50.7	94.8	215	3,057	2001	0.9	1.6	2000	1.7	..
Iraq	3.5[f]	78.1[f]	100.0[f]	..	..		..	..	2006	..	..
Ireland	7.5	78.3	57.2	3,871	4,270		2.9	19.5		5.6	..
Israel	8.0	56.0	75.3	1,675	3,028		3.7	6.2		6.0	7.1
Italy	9.0	77.2	88.5	2,813	3,190		3.7	7.2		3.9	6.1
Jamaica	4.7	53.1	63.7	180	..	2006	0.9	1.7	2005	2.0	..
Japan	8.1	81.3	80.8	2,759	4,693	2006	2.1	9.5		14.0	14.4
Jordan	9.7[g]	43.3[g]	75.9	238[g]	988[g]	2001	2.4	3.2	2007	1.9	..
Kazakhstan	3.6	64.3	98.4	190	1,608	2007	3.9	7.6	2006	8.1	6.6
Kenya	4.6	47.8	80.0	29	205	2002	0.1	1.2	2004	1.4	..
Korea, Dem. Rep.	3.5	85.6	100.0	..	..		3.3	4.1	2000	13.2	..
Korea, Rep.	6.4	55.7	81.0	1,168	3,341	2007	1.6	1.9		8.6	..
Kuwait	2.2	78.2	91.6	803	1,614		1.8	3.7	1996	1.9	..
Kyrgyz Republic	6.4	43.0	94.1	35	524	2006	2.4	5.8	2005/06	4.9	3.6
Lao PDR	4.0	18.6	76.1	24	401		0.4	1.0	2006	1.2	..
Latvia	6.6	59.2	97.2	582	2,320	2005	3.1	5.6		7.5	5.5
Lebanon	8.8	44.3	76.1	494	1,694	2005	2.4	1.3	2000	3.4	..
Lesotho	6.8	58.9	68.9	51	403		0.1	0.6	2004	1.3	..
Liberia	4.8	25.8	65.7	7	46		0.0[c]	0.3	2007	..	..
Libya	2.4	66.3	100.0	219	..		1.3	4.8	2000	3.7	..
Lithuania	6.2	70.0	98.3	547	2,046	2006	4.0	7.7		8.1	6.6
Macedonia, FYR	8.0	70.6	100.0	249	1,522		2.6	4.3	2005	4.6	6.0
Madagascar	3.2	62.8	52.5	9	60	2003	0.3	0.3	2003/04	0.3	0.5
Malawi	12.9	69.0	28.4	21	114	2006	0.0[c]	0.6	2006	1.1	..
Malaysia	4.3	44.6	73.2	259	1,518	2006	0.7	1.8		1.8	..
Mali	5.8	49.6	99.5	31	152	2004	0.1	0.6	2006	0.3	..
Mauritania	2.2	69.5	100.0	19	128		0.1	0.6	2000/01	0.4	..
Mauritius	3.9	51.1	80.6	230	998	2004	1.1	3.7		3.0	..
Mexico	6.6	44.2	93.9	527	1,208	2006	1.5	..	1995	1.6	2.5
Moldova	9.4	46.9	97.7	90	862		2.7	6.2	2005	5.2	6.0
Mongolia	5.7	73.7	44.0	70	984	2003	2.6	3.5	2005	6.1	..
Morocco	5.3	26.2	77.3	113	288	2001	0.5	0.8	2003/04	0.9	..
Mozambique	5.0	70.8	40.6	16	75	1997	0.0[c]	0.3	2003	0.8	..
Myanmar	2.2	13.1	99.4	5	..	2001	0.4	1.0	2000	0.6	..
Namibia	8.7	43.5	5.7	281	957	2000	0.3	3.1	2006/07	3.3	..
Nepal	5.1	30.5	85.2	17	215	2003	0.2	0.5	2006	0.2	..
Netherlands	9.4	80.0	29.3	3,872	5,520	2007	3.7	14.6		4.8	5.4
New Zealand	9.3	77.8	74.6	2,421	3,370	2006	2.2	8.9		6.2	4.4
Nicaragua	9.6	48.2	98.1	92	..	2004	0.4	1.1	2001	1.0	..
Niger	5.9	54.7	96.5	16	78	2004	0.0[c]	0.2	2006	0.3	..
Nigeria	3.8	29.7	90.4	33	184	2002	0.3	1.7	2007	0.5	..
Norway	8.7	83.6	95.2	6,267	5,952	2005	3.8	16.2		4.0	..
Oman	2.3	82.3	57.7	332	906	1998	1.7	3.7	1995	2.0	..
Pakistan	2.0	16.4	97.9	16	187		0.8	0.5	2006/07	1.0	..
Panama	7.3	68.8	80.6	380	..	2003	..	..	2003	2.2	..
Papua New Guinea	3.2	82.0	41.5	29	..	2000	..	..	1996	..	..
Paraguay	7.6	38.3	87.7	117	777	2005	1.1	1.8	2004	1.3	..
Peru	4.4	58.3	77.5	149	587	2005	..	..	2004	1.2	..
Philippines	3.8	32.9	83.5	52	314	2007	1.2	6.1	2003	1.1	..
Poland	6.2	70.0	85.4	555	2,031	2006	2.0	5.2		5.2	6.1
Portugal	10.2	70.5	77.3	1,864	3,014	2006	3.4	4.6		3.5	3.9
Puerto Rico	..	..	..	..	..		..	..	1995/96	..	..

	Health expenditure					Year last national health account completed	Health workers per 1,000 people		Year of last health survey[a]	Hospital beds per 1,000 people	Outpatient visits per capita
	Total % of GDP	Public % of total	Out of pocket % of private	Per capita $	Per capita PPP$		Physicians	Nurses and midwives			
	2006	2006	2006	2006	2006		2002–07[b]	2002–07[b]		2002–07[b]	2000–07[b]
Romania	4.5	76.9	96.8	256	1,244	2006	1.9	4.2	1999	6.5	5.6
Russian Federation	5.3	63.2	81.5	367	2,217	2007	4.3	8.5	1996	9.7	9.0
Rwanda	10.9	42.5	38.6	33	270	2006	0.1	0.4	2005	1.6	..
Saudi Arabia	3.3	77.0	13.4	492	1,386		1.4	3.0	2007	2.2	..
Senegal	5.8	56.9	77.0	44	199	2005	0.1	0.3	2005	0.1	..
Serbia	8.2	69.7	87.9	336	1,717	2005	2.0	4.3	2005-06	4.1	..
Sierra Leone	4.0	36.4	56.4	12	88		0.0[c]	0.5	2005	0.4	..
Singapore	3.3	33.1	93.8	1,017	3,037		1.5	4.4	2005	3.2	..
Slovak Republic	7.1	70.6	79.8	735	2,788	2006	3.1	6.6		6.8	12.5
Slovenia	8.4	72.2	42.5	1,607	3,230	2006	2.4	8.0		4.8	6.6
Somalia	..	..	..	..	..		..	..	2006	..	..
South Africa	8.0	37.7	17.5	425	1,100	1998	0.8	4.1	1998	2.8	..
Spain	8.4	71.2	74.7	2,328	3,935	2006	3.3	7.6		3.4	9.5
Sri Lanka	4.2	47.5	86.7	62	677	2006	0.6	1.7	1987	3.1	..
Sudan	3.8	36.8	100.0	37	167		0.3	0.9	2006	0.7	..
Swaziland	6.3	65.8	41.4	155	1,420		0.2	6.3	2000	2.1	..
Sweden	9.2	81.7	87.9	3,973	4,588	2006	3.3	10.9		..	2.8
Switzerland	10.8	59.1	75.3	5,660	5,446	2007	4.0	..		5.5	..
Syrian Arab Republic	3.9	47.8	100.0	66	482		0.5	1.4	2006	1.5	..
Tajikistan	5.0	23.8[e]	96.6	25[e]	455		2.0	5.0	2005	5.4[d]	8.3[d]
Tanzania	6.4	57.8	54.3	23	324	2006	0.0[c]	0.4	2006	1.1	..
Thailand	3.5	64.5	76.6	113	825	2006	..	..	2005/06	2.2	..
Timor-Leste	17.7	86.0	37.2	52	..		0.1	2.2		..	..
Togo	6.0	21.2	84.2	21	67	2002	0.0[c]	0.4	2006	0.9	..
Trinidad and Tobago	4.4	56.5	88.0	600	..	2000	..	1.8	2006	2.7	..
Tunisia	5.1	44.2	81.7	156	624	2005	1.3	2.9	2006	1.8	..
Turkey	4.8	72.5	84.2	352	866	2005	1.6	2.9	2003	2.7	4.6
Turkmenistan	3.8	66.5	100.0	146	..		2.5	4.7	2006	4.3	3.7
Uganda	7.0	25.4	51.0	24	165	2001	0.1	0.7	2006	1.1	..
Ukraine	6.9	55.4	88.8	160	1,327	2004	3.1	8.5	2007	8.7	10.8
United Arab Emirates	2.5	70.4	69.4	1,018	..		1.7	3.5		1.9	..
United Kingdom	8.2	87.3	91.7	3,332	4,259	2000	2.2	..		3.9	4.9
United States	15.3	45.8	23.5	6,719	6,719	2007	2.3	..	monthly	3.1	9.0
Uruguay	8.2	43.5	31.1	476	1,616	2006	3.7	0.9		2.9	..
Uzbekistan	4.7	50.2	97.1	30	..		2.7	10.9	2006	4.7	8.7
Venezuela, R.B.	4.9	49.5	88.6	332	..		..	..	2000	0.9	..
Vietnam	6.6	32.3	90.2	46	658	2006	0.6	0.8	2006	2.7	..
West Bank and Gaza	..	..	..	..	..		..	..	2006	..	..
Yemen, Rep.	4.5	46.0	95.2	40	367	2003	0.3	0.7	2006	0.7	..
Zambia	6.2	60.7	67.2	58	244	2006	0.1	2.0	2005	2.0	..
Zimbabwe	9.3	48.7	50.3	38	..	2001	0.2	0.7	2005/06	3.0	..
World	**9.8 w**	**60.0 w**	**43.5 w**	**722 w**	**1,466 w**		**.. w**	**.. w**		**2.6 w**	**.. w**
Low income	4.3	36.8	84.6	23	205		..	..		..	..
Middle income	5.4	50.1	77.6	140	945		..	..		2.3	..
Lower middle income	4.5	44.1	85.0	75	794		..	..		1.8	..
Upper middle income	6.3	54.7	70.7	412	1,581		..	..		5.0	..
Low & middle income	5.3	49.5	78.0	114	789		..	..		1.7	..
East Asia & Pacific	4.3	42.1	82.1	83	939		1.5	1.0		2.2	..
Europe & Central Asia	5.5	66.2	85.6	304	1,631		3.2	6.7		7.1	7.5
Latin America & Carib.	6.9	50.0	72.2	374	1,355		..	..		..	..
Middle East & N. Africa	5.7	51.3	90.5	133	1,364		..	..		..	..
South Asia	3.5	25.8	91.4	26	368		0.6	1.3		0.9	..
Sub-Saharan Africa	5.7	41.6	46.8	53	224		..	..		..	..
High income	11.2	61.6	36.5	4,033	4,969		2.6	..		6.1	8.6
Euro area	9.9	76.9	60.0	3,268	4,460		3.5	..		5.7	6.8

a. Survey name can be found in *Primary data documentation*. b. Data are for the most recent year available. c. Less than 0.05. d. Data are for 2008. e. Data are for 2007. f. Excludes northern Iraq. g. Includes contributions from the United Nations Relief and Works Agency for Palestine Refugees.

Health systems—the combined arrangements of institutions and actions whose primary purpose is to promote, restore, or maintain health (WHO 2000)— are increasingly being recognized as key to combating disease and improving the health status of populations. The World Bank's 2007 "Healthy Development: Strategy for Health, Nutrition, and Population Results" emphasizes the need to strengthen health systems, which are weak in many countries, in order to increase the effectiveness of programs aimed at reducing specific diseases and further reduce morbidity and mortality (World Bank 2007c). To evaluate health systems, the World Health Organization (WHO) has recommended that key components—such as financing, service delivery, workforce, information, and governance—be monitored using several key indicators (WHO 2008a). The data in the table are a subset of these indicators. Monitoring health systems allows the effectiveness, efficiency, and equity of different health system models to be compared. Health system data also help identify weaknesses and strengths and areas that need investment, such as additional health facilities, better health information systems, or better trained human resources.

Health expenditure data are broken down into public and private expenditures, with private expenditure further broken down into out-of-pocket expenditure (direct payments by households to providers), which make up the largest proportion of private

expenditures. In general, low-income economies have a higher share of private health expenditure than do middle- and high-income countries. High out-of-pocket expenditures may discourage people from accessing preventive or curative care and can impoverish households that cannot afford needed care. Health financing data are collected through national health accounts, which systematically, comprehensively, and consistently monitoring health system resource flows. To establish a national health account, countries must define the boundaries of the health system and classify health expenditure information along several dimensions, including sources of financing, providers of health services, functional use of health expenditures, and beneficiaries of expenditures. The accounting system can then provide an accurate picture of resource envelopes and financial flows and allow analysis of the equity and efficiency of financing to inform policy.

Many low-income countries use Demographic and Health Surveys or Multiple Indicator Cluster Surveys funded by donors to obtain health system data. Data on health worker (physicians, nurses, and midwives) density shows the availability of medical personnel. The WHO estimates that at least 2.5 physicians, nurses, and midwives per 1,000 people are needed to provide adequate coverage with primary care interventions associated with achieving the Millennium Development Goals (WHO 2006). The WHO compiles data from household and labor force surveys, censuses, and administrative records. Data comparability is limited by differences in definitions and training of medical personnel varies. In addition, human resources tend to be concentrated in urban areas, so that average densities do not provide a full picture of health personnel available to the entire population.

Availability and use of health services, shown by hospital beds per 1,000 people and outpatient visits per capita, reflect both demand and supply side factors. In the absence of a consistent definition these are crude indicators of the extent of physical, financial, and other barriers to health care.

• **Total health expenditure** is the sum of public and private health expenditure. It covers the provision of health services (preventive and curative), family planning and nutrition activities, and emergency aid for health but excludes provision of water and sanitation.
• **Public health expenditure** is recurrent and capital spending from central and local governments, external borrowing and grants (including donations from

international agencies and nongovernmental organizations), and social (or compulsory) health insurance funds. • **Out-of-pocket health expenditure,** part of private health expenditure, is direct household outlays, including gratuities and in-kind payments, for health practitioners and pharmaceutical suppliers, therapeutic appliances, and other goods and services whose primary intent is to restore or enhance health. • **Health expenditure per capita** is total health expenditure divided by population in U.S. dollars and in international dollars converted using 2005 purchasing power parity (PPP) rates for health expenditure. • **Year last national health account completed** is the latest year for which the health expenditure data are available using the national health account approach. • **Physicians** include generalist and specialist medical practitioners.• **Nurses and midwives** include professional nurses and midwives, auxiliary nurses and midwives, enrolled nurses and midwives, and other personnel, such as dental nurses and primary care nurses. • **Year of last health survey** is the latest year the national survey that collects health information was conducted. • **Hospital beds** are inpatient beds for both acute and chronic care available in public, private, general, and specialized hospitals and rehabilitation centers. • **Outpatient visits per capita** are the number of visits to health care facilities per capita, including repeat visits.

Data on health expenditures and year last national health account completed are mostly from the WHO's National Health Account database (www.who.int/nha/en), supplemented by country data. Data on health expenditure per capita in current dollars are from WHO's National Health Account database. Data on health expenditure per capita in PPP dollars are World Bank staff estimates based on the WHO's National Health Account database and the 2005 round of the International Comparison Program. Data on physicians, nurses and midwives, hospital beds, and outpatient visits are from the WHO, OECD, and TransMONEE, supplemented by country data. Information on health survey is from various sources including Macro International and the United Nations Children's Fund.

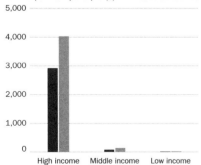

Health expenditure per capita ($)   ■ 2002 ■ 2006

Health expenditure per capita by high-income economies is 300 times more than that by developing economies, and the gap has been increasing.

Source: World Health Organization.

	Access to an improved water source		Access to improved sanitation facilities		Child immunization rate		Children with acute respiratory infection taken to health provider	Children with diarrhea who received oral rehydration and continuous feeding	Children sleeping under treated bednets[a]	Children with fever receiving antimalarial drugs	Tuberculosis treatment success rate	DOTS detection rate
							% of children ages 12–23 months[b]	% of children under age 5 with ARI	% of children under age 5 with diarrhea	% of children under age 5	% of children under age 5 with fever	% of new registered cases	% of new estimated cases
	% of population		% of population		Measles	DTP3							
	1990	2006	1990	2006	2007	2007	2002–07[c]	2002–07[c]	2002–07[c]	2002–07[c]	2006	2007
Afghanistan	..	..	..	..	..	..	..	..	..	..	84	64
Albania	..	97	..	97	97	98	45	50	..	..	93	54
Algeria	94	85	88	94	92	95	53	24	..	..	91	98
Angola	39	51	26	50	88	83	..	..	17.7	29.3	18	102
Argentina	94	96	81	91	99	96	..	..	..	..	63	76
Armenia	..	98	..	91	92	88	36	59	..	..	69	51
Australia	100	100	100	100	94	92	..	..	..	..	85	49
Austria	100	100	100	100	79	85	..	..	..	..	71	41
Azerbaijan	68	78	..	80	97	95	33	45	..	..	60	46
Bangladesh	78	80	26	36	88	90	30	49	..	..	92	66
Belarus	100	100	..	93	99	95	90	54	..	..	70	40
Belgium	..	..	..	..	92	99	..	..	..	..	73	58
Benin	63	65	12	30	61	67	36	42	20.1	54.0	87	86
Bolivia	72	86	33	43	81	81	52	54	..	..	83	71
Bosnia and Herzegovina	97	99	..	95	96	95	91	53	..	..	97	81
Botswana	93	96	38	47	90	97	..	..	..	..	72	57
Brazil	83	91	71	77	99	98	..	..	..	..	72	69
Bulgaria	99	99	99	99	96	95	..	..	..	..	80	81
Burkina Faso	34	72	5	13	94	99	39	42	9.6	48.0	73	18
Burundi	70	71	44	41	75	74	38	23	8.3	30.0	83	27
Cambodia	19	65	8	28	79	82	48	50	4.2	0.2	93	61
Cameroon	49	70	39	51	74	82	35	22	13.1	57.8	74	91
Canada	100	100	100	100	94	94	..	..	..	..	57	62
Central African Republic	58	66	11	31	62	54	32	47	15.1	57.0	65	71
Chad	..	48	5	9	23	20	12	27	0.6	44.0	54	18
Chile	91	95	84	94	91	94	..	..	..	..	85	105
China	67	88	48	65	94	93	..	..	..	..	94	80
Hong Kong, China	..	..	..	..	..	..	..	..	..	..	78	60
Colombia	89	93	68	78	95	93	62	39	..	..	71	81
Congo, Dem. Rep.	43	46	15	31	79	87	42	..	5.8	29.8	86	61
Congo, Rep.	..	71	..	20	67	80	48	39	6.1	48.0	53	56
Costa Rica	..	98	94	96	90	89	..	..	..	..	88	120
Côte d'Ivoire	67	81	20	24	67	76	35	45	3.0	36.0	73	42
Croatia	99	99	99	99	96	96	..	..	..	..	30	46
Cuba	..	91	98	98	99	93	..	..	..	..	90	109
Czech Republic	100	100	100	99	97	99	..	..	..	..	69	67
Denmark	100	100	100	100	89	75	..	..	..	..	77	69
Dominican Republic	84	95	68	79	96	79	67	42	..	..	78	66
Ecuador	73	95	71	84	99	99	..	..	..	..	74	46
Egypt, Arab Rep.	94	98	50	66	97	98	63	27	..	..	87	72
El Salvador	69	84	73	86	98	96	62	..	..	..	91	65
Eritrea	43	60	3	5	95	97	44	54	4.2	3.6	90	35
Estonia	100	100	95	95	96	95	..	..	..	..	68	76
Ethiopia	13	42	4	11	65	73	19	15	33.1	9.5	84	28
Finland	100	100	100	100	98	99	..	..	..	..	..	0
France	..	100	..	..	87	98	..	..	..	..	..	0
Gabon	..	87	..	36	55	38	..	..	..	..	46	66
Gambia, The	..	86	..	52	85	90	69	38	49.0	62.6	58	64
Georgia	76	99	94	93	97	98	74	37	..	..	75	113
Germany	100	100	100	100	94	97	..	..	..	..	71	54
Ghana	56	80	6	10	95	94	34	29	21.8	60.8	76	36
Greece	96	100	97	98	88	88	..	..	..	..	..	0
Guatemala	79	96	70	84	93	82	64	22	..	..	47	40
Guinea	45	70	13	19	71	75	42	38	1.4	43.5	75	53
Guinea-Bissau	..	57	..	33	76	63	57	25	39.0	45.7	69	68
Haiti	52	58	29	19	58	53	31	43	..	5.1	82	49

Disease prevention coverage and quality 2.17

	Access to an improved water source		Access to improved sanitation facilities		Child immunization rate		Children with acute respiratory infection taken to health provider	Children with diarrhea who received oral rehydration and continuous feeding	Children sleeping under treated bednets[a]	Children with fever receiving antimalarial drugs	Tuberculosis treatment success rate	DOTS detection rate
	% of population		% of population		% of children ages 12–23 months[b]		% of children under age 5 with ARI	% of children under age 5 with diarrhea	% of children under age 5	% of children under age 5 with fever	% of new registered cases	% of new estimated cases
	1990	2006	1990	2006	Measles 2007	DTP3 2007	2002–07[c]	2002–07[c]	2002–07[c]	2002–07[c]	2006	2007
Honduras	72	84	45	66	89	86	56	49	..	0.5	86	87
Hungary	96	100	100	100	99	99	..	..	..	..	46	51
India	71	89	14	28	67	62	69	33	..	8.2	86	68
Indonesia	72	80	51	52	80	75	61	56	..	..	91	91
Iran, Islamic Rep.	92	..	83	..	97	99	..	..	..	..	83	68
Iraq	83	..	..	..	..	..	..	..	..	..	84	37
Ireland	..	..	..	..	87	92	..	..	..	..	..	0
Israel	100	100	..	..	97	96	..	..	..	..	74	61
Italy	..	..	..	..	87	96	..	..	..	..	67	0
Jamaica	92	93	83	83	76	85	75	39	..	..	41	83
Japan	100	100	100	100	98	98	..	..	..	..	53	77
Jordan	97	98	..	85	95	98	75	44	..	..	71	81
Kazakhstan	96	96	97	97	99	93	71	48	..	..	72	69
Kenya	41	57	39	42	80	81	49	33	6.0	26.5	85	72
Korea, Dem. Rep.	..	100	..	..	99	92	93	..	..	..	86	64
Korea, Rep.	..	..	..	..	92	91	..	..	..	..	81	14
Kuwait	..	..	..	..	99	99	..	..	..	..	78	90
Kyrgyz Republic	..	89	..	93	99	94	62	22	..	..	82	60
Lao PDR	..	60	..	48	40	50	..	..	..	..	92	78
Latvia	99	99	..	78	97	98	..	..	..	..	73	89
Lebanon	100	100	..	..	53	74	..	..	..	..	90	62
Lesotho	..	78	..	36	85	83	59	53	..	..	66	16
Liberia	57	64	40	32	95	88	70	..	..	58.5	76	69
Libya	71	..	97	97	98	98	..	..	..	..	77	162
Lithuania	..	..	..	..	97	95	..	..	..	..	74	90
Macedonia, FYR	..	100	..	89	96	95	93	45	..	..	87	74
Madagascar	39	47	8	12	81	82	48	47	0.2	34.2	78	69
Malawi	41	76	46	60	83	87	52	27	24.7	24.9	78	41
Malaysia	98	99	..	94	90	96	..	..	..	..	48	80
Mali	33	60	35	45	68	68	38	38	27.1	31.7	76	23
Mauritania	37	60	20	24	67	75	45	..	..	20.7	41	39
Mauritius	100	100	94	94	98	98	..	..	..	..	92	69
Mexico	88	95	56	81	96	98	..	..	..	..	80	99
Moldova	..	90	..	79	96	92	60	48	..	..	62	67
Mongolia	64	72	..	50	98	95	63	47	..	..	88	76
Morocco	75	83	52	72	95	95	38	46	..	..	87	93
Mozambique	36	42	20	31	77	72	55	47	..	14.9	83	49
Myanmar	57	80	23	82	81	86	66	65	..	..	84	116
Namibia	57	93	26	35	69	86	72	..	10.5	9.8	76	84
Nepal	72	89	9	27	81	82	43	37	..	0.1	88	66
Netherlands	100	100	100	100	96	96	..	..	..	..	84	11
New Zealand	97	..	..	..	79	88	..	..	..	..	70	60
Nicaragua	70	79	42	48	99	87	..	..	..	..	89	97
Niger	41	42	3	7	47	39	47	34	7.4	33.0	77	53
Nigeria	50	47	26	30	62	54	33	28	1.2	33.9	76	23
Norway	100	100	..	..	92	93	..	..	..	..	93	33
Oman	81	..	85	..	97	99	..	..	..	..	86	125
Pakistan	86	90	33	58	80	83	69	37	..	3.3	88	67
Panama	..	92	..	74	89	88	..	..	..	..	79	98
Papua New Guinea	39	40	44	45	58	60	..	..	..	..	73	15
Paraguay	52	77	60	70	80	66	..	..	..	..	83	58
Peru	75	84	55	72	99	80	67	71	..	..	78	93
Philippines	83	93	58	78	92	87	55	76	..	0.2	88	75
Poland	..	..	..	..	98	99	..	..	..	..	75	66
Portugal	96	99	92	99	95	97	..	..	..	..	87	87
Puerto Rico	..	..	..	..	..	..	..	..	..	..	80	77

Disease prevention coverage and quality

	Access to an improved water source		Access to improved sanitation facilities		Child immunization rate		Children with acute respiratory infection taken to health provider	Children with diarrhea who received oral rehydration and continuous feeding	Children sleeping under treated bednets[a]	Children with fever receiving antimalarial drugs	Tuberculosis treatment success rate	DOTS detection rate
	% of population		% of population		% of children ages 12–23 months[b]		% of children ages 12–23 months[b]	% of children under age 5 with ARI	% of children under age 5 with diarrhea	% of children under age 5	% of children under age 5 with fever	% of new registered cases	% of new estimated cases
					Measles	DTP3						
	1990	2006	1990	2006	2007	2007	2002–07[c]	2002–07[c]	2002–07[c]	2002–07[c]	2006	2007
Romania	76	88	72	72	97	97	..	..	..	..	83	85
Russian Federation	94	97	87	87	99	98	..	..	..	..	58	49
Rwanda	65	65	29	23	99	97	28[d]	24	13.0	12.3	86	25
Saudi Arabia	94	96	91	99	96	96	..	..	..	..	69	39
Senegal	67	77	26	28	84	94	47	43	16.4	22.0	76	48
Serbia	..	99[e]	..	92[e]	95	94	93	31	..	..	84	80
Sierra Leone	..	53	..	11	67	64	48	31	5.3	51.9	87	37
Singapore	100	100	100	100	95	96	..	..	..	..	84	96
Slovak Republic	100	100	100	100	99	99	..	..	..	..	81	44
Slovenia	..	..	..	..	96	97	..	..	..	..	92	77
Somalia	..	29	..	23	34	39	13	7	11.4	7.9	89	64
South Africa	81	93	55	59	83	97	..	..	..	..	74	78
Spain	100	100	100	100	97	96	..	..	..	..	..	0
Sri Lanka	67	82	71	86	98	98	58	..	2.9	0.3	87	85
Sudan	64	70	33	35	79	84	..	56	27.6	54.2	82	31
Swaziland	..	60	..	50	91	95	73	22	0.6	0.6	43	55
Sweden	100	100	100	100	96	99	..	..	..	..	63	0
Switzerland	100	100	100	100	86	93	..	..	..	..	..	0
Syrian Arab Republic	83	89	81	92	98	99	77	34	..	..	86	80
Tajikistan	..	67	..	92	85	86	64	22	1.3	1.2	84	30
Tanzania	49	55	35	33	90	83	59	53	16.0	58.2	85	51
Thailand	95	98	78	96	96	98	84	46	..	..	77	72
Timor-Leste	..	62	..	41	63	70	24	..	8.3	47.4	79	61
Togo	49	59	13	12	80	88	23	22	38.4	47.7	67	15
Trinidad and Tobago	88	94	93	92	91	88	74	32	..	..	..	..
Tunisia	82	94	74	85	98	98	..	..	..	..	91	78
Turkey	85	97	85	88	96	96	41	..	..	..	91	76
Turkmenistan	..	..	..	..	99	98	83	25	..	..	84	84
Uganda	43	64	29	33	68	64	73	39	9.7	61.3	70	51
Ukraine	..	97	96	93	98	98	..	..	..	..	59	55
United Arab Emirates	100	100	97	97	92	92	..	..	..	..	79	18
United Kingdom	100	100	..	..	86	92	..	..	..	..	..	0
United States	99	99	100	100	93	96	..	..	..	..	64	87
Uruguay	100	100	100	100	96	94	..	..	..	..	87	95
Uzbekistan	90	88	93	96	99	96	68	28	..	..	81	45
Venezuela, RB	89	..	83	..	55	71	..	..	..	..	82	68
Vietnam	52	92	29	65	83	92	83	65	5.1	2.6	92	82
West Bank and Gaza	..	89	..	80	..	..	..	..	..	..	94	5
Yemen, Rep.	..	66	28	46	74	87	47	48	..	..	83	46
Zambia	50	58	42	52	85	80	68	48	22.8	57.9	85	58
Zimbabwe	78	81	44	46	66	62	25	47	2.9	4.7	60	27
World	**76 w**	**86 w** [c]	**51 w**	**60 w**	**82 w**	**82 w**			**.. w**	**.. w**	**85 w**	**63 w**
Low income	58	68	26	39	76	77			..	26.4	84	51
Middle income	75	89	48	60	84	82			..	..	85	72
Lower middle income	72	88	41	55	82	79			..	..	87	72
Upper middle income	88	95	77	83	94	96			..	..	72	72
Low & middle income	72	84	44	55	81	80			..	..	85	64
East Asia & Pacific	68	87	48	66	90	89			..	..	91	77
Europe & Central Asia	90	95	88	89	97	96			..	..	70	56
Latin America & Carib.	84	91	68	78	93	92			..	..	76	72
Middle East & N. Africa	89	89	67	77	90	92			..	..	86	72
South Asia	73	87	18	33	72	69			..	7.3	87	67
Sub-Saharan Africa	49	58	26	31	73	73			12.3	34.9	76	47
High income	99	100	100	100	93	95			..	..	68	37
Euro area	..	100	..	..	91	96			..	..	..	17

a. For malaria prevention only. b. Refers to children who were immunized before age 12 months or in some cases at any time before the survey (12–23 months). c. Data are for the most recent year available. d. Data are for 2008. e. Includes Kosovo.

People's health is influenced by the environment in which they live. Lack of clean water and basic sanitation is the main reason diseases transmitted by feces are so common in developing countries. Access to drinking water from an improved source and access to improved sanitation do not ensure safety or adequacy, as these characteristics are not tested at the time of the surveys. But improved drinking water technologies and improved sanitation facilities are more likely than those characterized as unimproved to provide safe drinking water and to prevent contact with human excreta. The data are derived by the Joint Monitoring Programme (JMP) of the World Health Organization (WHO) and United Nations Children's Fund (UNICEF) based on national censuses and nationally representative household surveys. The coverage rates for water and sanitation are based on information from service users on the facilities their households actually use rather than on information from service providers, which may include nonfunctioning systems. While the estimates are based on use, the JMP reports use as access, because access is the term used in the Millennium Development Goal target for drinking water and sanitation.

Governments in developing countries usually finance immunization against measles and diphtheria, pertussis (whooping cough), and tetanus (DTP) as part of the basic public health package. In many developing countries lack of precise information on the size of the cohort of one-year-old children makes immunization coverage difficult to estimate from program statistics. The data shown here are based on an assessment of national immunization coverage rates by the WHO and UNICEF. The assessment considered both administrative data from service providers and household survey data on children's immunization histories. Based on the data available, consideration of potential biases, and contributions of local experts, the most likely true level of immunization coverage was determined for each year.

Acute respiratory infection continues to be a leading cause of death among young children, killing about 2 million children under age 5 in developing countries each year. Data are drawn mostly from household health surveys in which mothers report on number of episodes and treatment for acute respiratory infection.

Since 1990 diarrhea-related deaths among children have declined tremendously. Most diarrhea-related deaths are due to dehydration, and many of these deaths can be prevented with the use of oral rehydration salts at home. However, recommendations for the use of oral rehydration therapy have changed over time based on scientific progress, so it is difficult to accurately compare use rates across countries. Until the current recommended method for home management of diarrhea is adopted and applied in all countries, the data should be used with caution. Also, the prevalence of diarrhea may vary by season. Since country surveys are administered at different times, data comparability is further affected.

Malaria is endemic to the poorest countries in the world, mainly in tropical and subtropical regions of Africa, Asia, and the Americas. Insecticide-treated bednets, properly used and maintained, are one of the most important malaria-preventive strategies to limit human-mosquito contact. Studies have emphasized that mortality rates could be reduced by about 25–30 percent if every child under age 5 in malaria-risk areas such as Africa slept under a treated bednet every night.

Prompt and effective treatment of malaria is a critical element of malaria control. It is vital that sufferers, especially children under age 5, start treatment within 24 hours of the onset of symptoms, to prevent progression—often rapid—to severe malaria and death.

Data on the success rate of tuberculosis treatment are provided for countries that have implemented DOTS, the internationally recommended tuberculosis control strategy. The treatment success rate for tuberculosis provides a useful indicator of the quality of health services. A low rate or no success suggests that infectious patients may not be receiving adequate treatment. An essential complement to the tuberculosis treatment success rate is the DOTS detection rate, which indicates whether there is adequate coverage by the recommended case detection and treatment strategy. A country with a high treatment success rate may still face big challenges if its DOTS detection rate remains low.

For indicators that are from household surveys, the year in the table refers to the survey year. For more information, consult the original sources.

• **Access to an improved water source** refers to people with reasonable access to water from an improved source, such as piped water into a dwelling, public tap, tubewell, protected dug well, and rainwater collection. Reasonable access is the availability of at least 20 liters a person a day from a source within 1 kilometer of the dwelling. • **Access to improved sanitation facilities** refers to people with at least adequate access to excreta disposal facilities that can effectively prevent human, animal, and insect contact with excreta. Improved facilities range from protected pit latrines to flush toilets. • **Child immunization rate** refers to children ages 12–23 months who, before 12 months or at any time before the survey, had received one dose of measles vaccine and three doses of diphtheria, pertussis (whooping cough), and tetanus (DTP3) vaccine. • **Children with acute respiratory infection taken to health provider** are children under age 5 with acute respiratory infection in the two weeks before the survey who were taken to an appropriate health provider. • **Children with diarrhea who received oral rehydration and continuous feeding** are children under age 5 with diarrhea in the two weeks before the survey who received either oral rehydration therapy or increased fluids, with continuous feeding. • **Children sleeping under treated bednets** are children under age 5 who slept under an insecticide-treated bednet to prevent malaria the night before the survey. • **Children with fever receiving antimalarial drugs** are children under age 5 who were ill with fever in the two weeks before the survey and received any appropriate (locally defined) antimalarial drugs. • **Tuberculosis treatment success rate** refers to new registered infectious tuberculosis cases that were cured or completed a full course of treatment. • **DOTS detection rate** refers to estimated new infectious tuberculosis cases detected by DOTS, the internationally recommended tuberculosis detection and treatment strategy.

Data on access to water and sanitation are from the WHO and UNICEF's *Progress on Drinking Water and Sanitation* (2008). Data on immunization are from WHO and UNICEF estimates (www.who.int/ immunization_monitoring). Data on children with acute respiratory infection, with diarrhea, sleeping under treated bednets, and receiving antimalarial drugs are from UNICEF's *State of the World's Children 2009*, Childinfo, and Demographic and Health Surveys by Macro International. Data on tuberculosis are from the WHO's *Global Tuberculosis Control Report 2009*.

2.18 Reproductive health

	Total fertility rate		Adolescent fertility rate	Unmet need for contraception	Contraceptive prevalence rate	Newborns protected against tetanus	Pregnant women receiving prenatal care	Births attended by skilled health staff		Maternal mortality ratio	
	births per woman		births per 1,000 women ages 15–19	% of married women ages 15–49	% of married women ages 15–49	% of births	%	% of total		per 100,000 live births National estimates	Modeled estimates
	1990	2007	2007	2002–07a	2002–07a	2007	2002–07a	1990	2002–07a	1990–2007a	2005
Afghanistan	..	..	..		..	..	..	..	..		..
Albania	2.9	1.8	16	..	60	87	97	..	100	20	92
Algeria	4.6	2.4	7	..	61	70	89	77	95	117	180
Angola	7.1	5.8	138	..	..	81	80	..	47	..	1,400
Argentina	3.0	2.3	57	..	..	..	99	96	99	48	77
Armenia	2.5	1.7	30	13	53	..	93	..	98	16	76
Australia	1.9	1.9	14	..	..	..	..	100	100	..	4
Austria	1.5	1.4	12	..	..	..	..	..	..	..	4
Azerbaijan	2.7	2.0	29	23	51	..	77	..	89	29	82
Bangladesh	4.3	2.8	124	11	56	91	51	..	18	322	570
Belarus	1.9	1.3	22	..	73	..	99	..	100	12	18
Belgium	1.6	1.8	7	..	..	94	..	..	..	..	8
Benin	6.7	5.4	120	30	17	93	84	..	74	397	840
Bolivia	4.9	3.5	78	23	58	71	79	43	67	229	290
Bosnia and Herzegovina	1.7	1.2	20	23	36	85	99	97	100	9	3
Botswana	4.6	2.9	52	..	..	78	..	77	..	326	380
Brazil	2.8	2.2	89	..	..	93	97	72	97	53	110
Bulgaria	1.8	1.4	40	..	..	65	..	..	99	7	11
Burkina Faso	7.3	6.0	126	29	17	80	85	..	54	484	700
Burundi	6.8	6.8	55	..	9	78	92	..	34	615	1,100
Cambodia	5.7	3.2	42	25	40	87	69	..	44	472	540
Cameroon	5.9	4.3	118	20	29	81	82	58	63	669	1,000
Canada	1.8	1.6	14	..	..	82	..	..	100	..	7
Central African Republic	5.6	4.6	115	..	19	54	69	..	53	543	980
Chad	6.7	6.2	164	21	3	60	39	..	14	1,099	1,500
Chile	2.6	1.9	60	..	58	..	..	..	100	20	16
China	2.1	1.7	8	..	85	..	90	50	98	41	45
Hong Kong, China	1.3	1.0	5	..	..	..	..	..	100	..	..
Colombia	3.0	2.5	76	6	78	78	94	82	96	75	130
Congo, Dem. Rep.	6.7	6.3	222	24	..	81	85	..	74	1,289	1,100
Congo, Rep.	5.3	4.5	115	16	21	90	86	..	83	781	740
Costa Rica	3.1	2.1	71	..	96	..	92	98	99	36	30
Côte d'Ivoire	6.5	4.5	107	29	13	76	85	..	57	543	810
Croatia	1.6	1.4	14	..	..	97	100	100	100	10	7
Cuba	1.7	1.5	47	8	77	..	100	..	100	21	45
Czech Republic	1.9	1.4	11	..	..	..	..	..	100	8	4
Denmark	1.7	1.9	6	..	..	..	..	..	..	10	3
Dominican Republic	3.3	2.4	108	11	73	85	99	93	98	159	150
Ecuador	3.6	2.6	83	..	73	67	84	..	75	107	210
Egypt, Arab Rep.	4.3	2.9	39	10	59	85	70	37	74	84	130
El Salvador	3.7	2.7	81	..	67	87	86	52	92	71	170
Eritrea	6.2	5.0	72	27	8	80	70	..	28	998	450
Estonia	2.0	1.6	21	..	..	..	..	..	100	7	25
Ethiopia	6.8	5.3	94	34	15	85	28	..	6	673	720
Finland	1.8	1.8	9	..	..	..	..	..	100	6	7
France	1.8	2.0	7	..	..	..	..	..	..	10	8
Gabon	4.7	3.1	82	..	..	67	..	..	..	519	520
Gambia, The	6.0	4.7	104	..	..	90	98	44	57	730	690
Georgia	2.1	1.4	30	..	47	87	94	..	98	23	66
Germany	1.5	1.4	9	..	..	..	..	..	100	8	4
Ghana	5.7	3.8	55	34	17	88	92	40	50	..	560
Greece	1.4	1.4	9	..	..	69	..	..	..	1	3
Guatemala	5.6	4.2	107	..	43	80	84	..	41	133	290
Guinea	6.6	5.4	149	21	9	95	82	31	38	980	910
Guinea-Bissau	7.1	7.1	188	..	10	92	78	..	39	405	1,100
Haiti	5.4	3.8	46	38	32	43	85	23	26	630	670

	Total fertility rate		Adolescent fertility rate	Unmet need for contraception	Contraceptive prevalence rate	Newborns protected against tetanus	Pregnant women receiving prenatal care	Births attended by skilled health staff		Maternal mortality ratio	
	births per woman		births per 1,000 women ages 15–19	% of married women ages 15–49	% of married women ages 15–49	% of births	%	% of total		per 100,000 live births National estimates	Modeled estimates
	1990	2007	2007	2002–07[a]	2002–07[a]	2007	2002–07[a]	1990	2002–07[a]	1990–2007[a]	2005
Honduras	5.1	3.3	93	17	65	94	92	45	67	108	280
Hungary	1.8	1.3	19	..	..	..	..	..	100	8	6
India	4.0	2.7	62	13	56	86	74	..	47	301	450
Indonesia	3.1	2.2	40	9	61	83	93	32	72	307	420
Iran, Islamic Rep.	4.8	2.0	20	..	79	83	..	..	97	25	140
Iraq	5.9	..	..	..	..	..	..	54	..	294	..
Ireland	2.1	1.9	16	..	..	..	..	..	100	6	1
Israel	2.8	2.9	14	..	..	..	..	..	..	5	4
Italy	1.3	1.3	6	..	..	52	..	..	99	7	3
Jamaica	2.9	2.4	78	..	69	54	91	79	97	95	170
Japan	1.5	1.3	3	..	..	86	..	100	100	8	6
Jordan	5.4	3.6	25	11	57	87	99	87	99	41	62
Kazakhstan	2.7	2.4	31	..	51	..	100	..	100	70	140
Kenya	5.8	5.0	104	25	39	74	88	50	42	414	560
Korea, Dem. Rep.	2.4	1.9	1	..	..	91	..	..	97	105	370
Korea, Rep.	1.6	1.3	4	..	..	..	..	98	100	20	14
Kuwait	3.5	2.2	13	..	..	83	..	..	100	5	4
Kyrgyz Republic	3.7	2.7	31	1	48	82	97	..	98	104	150
Lao PDR	6.1	3.2	72	..	38	47	..	..	..	405	660
Latvia	2.0	1.4	14	..	..	..	..	..	100	9	10
Lebanon	3.1	2.2	25	..	58	72	96	..	98	..	150
Lesotho	4.9	3.4	73	31	37	76	90	..	55	762	960
Liberia	6.9	5.2	219	36	11	89	..	..	46	..	1,200
Libya	4.7	2.7	3	..	..	..	..	..	..	77	97
Lithuania	2.0	1.4	18	..	..	..	..	..	100	13	11
Macedonia, FYR	2.0	1.4	21	34	14	..	98	..	98	21	10
Madagascar	6.2	4.8	133	24	27	72	80	57	51	469	510
Malawi	6.9	5.6	135	28	42	86	92	55	54	807	1,100
Malaysia	3.7	2.6	13	..	..	89	79	..	98	28	62
Mali	7.4	6.5	179	31	8	89	70	..	45	464	970
Mauritania	5.8	4.4	85	..	..	60	..	40	..	747	820
Mauritius	2.3	1.7	41	..	76	86	..	91	99	22	15
Mexico	3.4	2.1	65	..	71	87	..	..	93	62	60
Moldova	2.3	1.7	32	7	68	..	98	..	100	16	22
Mongolia	4.0	1.9	45	14	66	87	99	..	99	90	46
Morocco	4.0	2.4	19	10	63	85	68	31	63	227	240
Mozambique	6.2	5.1	149	18	17	82	85	..	48	408	520
Myanmar	3.4	2.1	16	..	34	91	..	..	68	316	380
Namibia	5.7	3.6	59	..	55	82	95	68	81	271	210
Nepal	5.1	3.0	115	25	48	83	44	7	19	281	830
Netherlands	1.6	1.7	5	..	..	..	..	..	100	7	6
New Zealand	2.2	2.2	22	..	..	..	..	..	..	15	9
Nicaragua	4.7	2.8	113	..	72	94	90	..	74	87	170
Niger	7.9	7.0	196	16	11	72	46	15	33	648	1,800
Nigeria	6.7	5.3	126	17	13	53	58	33	35	..	1,100
Norway	1.9	1.9	8	..	..	..	..	100	..	6	7
Oman	6.5	3.0	10	..	..	95	..	..	98	13	64
Pakistan	6.1	3.9	36	25	30	81	61	19	39	533	320
Panama	3.0	2.6	83	..	..	..	..	..	91	66	130
Papua New Guinea	4.8	3.8	51	..	..	60	..	..	42	..	470
Paraguay	4.5	3.1	72	..	73	81	94	66	77	121	150
Peru	3.9	2.5	60	8	71	82	91	80	71	185	240
Philippines	4.3	3.2	47	17	51	65	88	..	60	162	230
Poland	2.0	1.3	13	..	..	..	..	..	100	3	8
Portugal	1.4	1.3	13	..	..	..	..	98	..	8	11
Puerto Rico	2.2	1.8	47	..	..	..	..	..	100	..	18

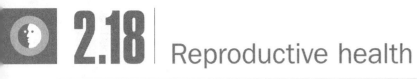

2.18 Reproductive health

	Total fertility rate		Adolescent fertility rate	Unmet need for contraception	Contraceptive prevalence rate	Newborns protected against tetanus	Pregnant women receiving prenatal care	Births attended by skilled health staff		Maternal mortality ratio	
	births per woman		births per 1,000 women ages 15–19	% of married women ages 15–49	% of married women ages 15–49	% of births	%	% of total		per 100,000 live births National estimates	Modeled estimates
	1990	2007	2007	2002–07[a]	2002–07[a]	2007	2002–07[a]	1990	2002–07[a]	1990–2007[a]	2005
Romania	1.8	1.3	32	..	70	..	94	..	98	15	24
Russian Federation	1.9	1.4	28	..	..	..	..	..	100	24	28
Rwanda	7.4	5.9	40	38	17	82	94	26	39	750	1,300
Saudi Arabia	5.9	3.2	28	..	..	56	..	..	96	10	18
Senegal	6.5	5.1	87	32	12	86	87	..	52	401	980
Serbia	1.8	1.4	24	29	41	..	98	..	99	13	14[b]
Sierra Leone	6.5	6.5	160	..	5	94	81	..	43	1,800	2,100
Singapore	1.9	1.3	5	..	..	4	..	..	100	6	14
Slovak Republic	2.1	1.3	20	..	..	73	..	..	100	4	6
Slovenia	1.5	1.4	7	..	..	74	..	100	100	17	6
Somalia	6.8	6.0	66	..	15	68	26	..	33	1,044	1,400
South Africa	3.5	2.7	61	..	60	72	92	..	92	166	400
Spain	1.3	1.4	9	..	..	72	..	..	..	6	4
Sri Lanka	2.5	1.9	25	..	68	91	99	..	99	43	58
Sudan	5.9	4.2	57	6	8	72	70	69	49	..	450
Swaziland	5.6	3.6	33	24	51	86	85	..	69	589	390
Sweden	2.1	1.9	4	..	..	86	..	..	..	5	3
Switzerland	1.6	1.5	4	..	..	93	..	..	100	5	5
Syrian Arab Republic	5.4	3.1	35	..	58	92	84	..	93	65	130
Tajikistan	5.1	3.3	28	..	38	88	80	..	83	97	170
Tanzania	6.1	5.2	121	22	26	88	78	53	43	578	950
Thailand	2.1	1.9	42	..	77	89	98	..	97	12	110
Timor-Leste	5.5	6.5	54	..	20	59	61	..	18	..	380
Togo	6.4	4.8	89	..	17	82	84	31	62	478	510
Trinidad and Tobago	2.4	1.6	35	..	43	..	96	..	98	45	45
Tunisia	3.5	2.0	7	..	..	96	..	69	..	69	100
Turkey	3.0	2.2	37	..	71	69	81	..	83	29	44
Turkmenistan	4.2	2.5	16	..	48	..	99	..	100	14	130
Uganda	7.1	6.7	152	41	24	85	94	38	42	435	550
Ukraine	1.8	1.2	28	..	67	..	99	..	99	17	18
United Arab Emirates	4.3	2.3	18	..	..	..	..	..	100	3	37
United Kingdom	1.8	1.9	24	..	84	..	..	..	..	7	8
United States	2.1	2.1	42	..	..	..	..	99	99	8	11
Uruguay	2.5	2.0	61	..	..	..	..	..	99	35	20
Uzbekistan	4.1	2.4	34	8	65	87	99	..	100	28	24
Venezuela, RB	3.4	2.6	90	..	..	51	..	..	95	61	57
Vietnam	3.6	2.1	17	5	76	86	91	..	88	162	150
West Bank and Gaza	6.3	4.6	79	..	50	..	99	..	99	..	..
Yemen, Rep.	8.0	5.5	71	..	28	52	41	16	36	365	430
Zambia	6.4	5.2	125	27	34	89	93	51	43	729	830
Zimbabwe	5.1	3.7	59	13	60	78	94	70	69	555	880
World	**3.2 w**	**2.5 w**	**52 w**	**.. w**	**60 w**	**.. w**	**81 w**	**50 w**	**65 w**		**400 w**
Low income	5.6	4.2	95	21	33	78	67	..	42		780
Middle income	3.0	2.2	42	..	68	..	86	49	74		260
Lower middle income	3.1	2.3	39	..	69	..	84	45	69		300
Upper middle income	2.7	2.0	56	..	..	..	..	..	95		97
Low & middle income	3.5	2.7	56	..	60	81	81	46	62		440
East Asia & Pacific	2.4	1.9	17	..	78	..	90	48	87		150
Europe & Central Asia	2.3	1.7	29	..	..	..	..	..	95		44
Latin America & Carib.	3.2	2.4	77	..	..	83	95	72	89		130
Middle East & N. Africa	4.8	2.8	30	..	62	78	76	48	80		200
South Asia	4.2	2.9	67	14	53	85	69	32	41		500
Sub-Saharan Africa	6.3	5.1	118	24	23	75	72	..	45		900
High income	1.8	1.8	22	..	..	..	..	..	99		10
Euro area	1.5	1.5	8	..	..	..	..	..	..		5

a. Data are for most recent year available. b. Includes Montenegro.

About the data

Reproductive health is a state of physical and mental well-being in relation to the reproductive system and its functions and processes. Means of achieving reproductive health include education and services during pregnancy and childbirth, safe and effective contraception, and prevention and treatment of sexually transmitted diseases. Complications of pregnancy and childbirth are the leading cause of death and disability among women of reproductive age in developing countries.

Total and adolescent fertility rates are based on data on registered live births from vital registration systems or, in the absence of such systems, from censuses or sample surveys. The estimated rates are generally considered reliable measures of fertility in the recent past. Where no empirical information on age-specific fertility rates is available, a model is used to estimate the share of births to adolescents. For countries without vital registration systems fertility rates are generally based on extrapolations from trends observed in censuses or surveys from earlier years.

More couples in developing countries want to limit or postpone childbearing but are not using effective contraception. These couples have an unmet need for contraception. Common reasons are lack of knowledge about contraceptive methods and concerns about possible side effects. This indicator excludes women not exposed to the risk of unintended pregnancy because of menopause, infertility, or postpartum anovulation.

Contraceptive prevalence reflects all methods—ineffective traditional methods as well as highly effective modern methods. Contraceptive prevalence rates are obtained mainly from household surveys, including Demographic and Health Surveys, Multiple Indicator Cluster Surveys, and contraceptive prevalence surveys (see *Primary data documentation* for the most recent survey year). Unmarried women are often excluded from such surveys, which may bias the estimates.

An important cause of infant mortality in some developing countries, neonatal tetanus can be prevented through immunization of the mother during pregnancy. As in last year's edition, the data on tetanus in the table are estimated by the "protection at birth" model, which tracks the immunization status of women of child-bearing age. The estimates account for the number of vaccine doses received and the time since the mother's last immunization. A currently immune woman's child is considered protected. Because the methodology behind this indicator has changed, these data cannot be compared with those in editions before 2008.

Good prenatal and postnatal care improve maternal health and reduce maternal and infant mortality. But data may not reflect such improvements because health information systems are often weak, maternal deaths are underreported, and rates of maternal mortality are difficult to measure.

The share of births attended by skilled health staff is an indicator of a health system's ability to provide adequate care for pregnant women. Maternal mortality ratios are generally of unknown reliability, as are many other cause-specific mortality indicators. Household surveys such as Demographic and Health Surveys attempt to measure maternal mortality by asking respondents about survivorship of sisters. The main disadvantage of this method is that the estimates of maternal mortality that it produces pertain to 12 years or so before the survey, making them unsuitable for monitoring recent changes or observing the impact of interventions. In addition, measurement of maternal mortality is subject to many types of errors. Even in high-income countries with vital registration systems, misclassification of maternal deaths has been found to lead to serious underestimation.

The national estimates of maternal mortality ratios in the table are based on national surveys, vital registration records, and surveillance data or are derived from community and hospital records. The modeled estimates are based on an exercise by the World Health Organization (WHO), United Nations Children's Fund (UNICEF), United Nations Population Fund (UNFPA), and World Bank. For countries with complete vital registration systems with good attribution of cause of death, the data are used as reported. For countries with national data either from complete vital registration systems with uncertain or poor attribution of cause of death or from household surveys reported maternal mortality was adjusted, usually by a factor of underenumeration and misclassification. For countries with no empirical national data (about 35 percent of countries), maternal mortality was estimated with a regression model using socioeconomic information, including fertility, birth attendants, and GDP. Neither set of ratios can be assumed to provide an exact estimate of maternal mortality for any of the countries in the table.

For the indicators that are from household surveys, the year in the table refers to the survey year. For more information, consult the original sources.

Definitions

• **Total fertility rate** is the number of children that would be born to a woman if she were to live to the end of her childbearing years and bear children in accordance with current age-specific fertility rates. • **Adolescent fertility rate** is the number of births per 1,000 women ages 15–19. • **Unmet need for contraception** is the percentage of fertile, married women of reproductive age who do not want to become pregnant and are not using contraception. • **Contraceptive prevalence rate** is the percentage of women married or in-union ages 15–49 who are practicing, or whose sexual partners are practicing, any form of contraception. • **Newborns protected against tetanus** are the percentage of births by women of child-bearing age who are immunized against tetanus. • **Pregnant women receiving prenatal care** are the percentage of women attended at least once during pregnancy by skilled health personnel for reasons related to pregnancy. • **Births attended by skilled health staff** are the percentage of deliveries attended by personnel trained to give the necessary care to women during pregnancy, labor, and postpartum; to conduct deliveries on their own; and to care for newborns. • **Maternal mortality ratio** is the number of women who die from pregnancy-related causes during pregnancy and childbirth per 100,000 live births.

Data sources

Data on fertility rates are compiled and estimated by the World Bank's Development Data Group. Inputs come from the United Nations Population Division's *World Population Prospects: The 2006 Revision*, census reports and other statistical publications from national statistical offices, and household surveys such as Demographic and Health Surveys. Data on women with unmet need for contraception and contraceptive prevalence rates are from household surveys, including Demographic and Health Surveys by Macro International and Multiple Indicator Cluster Surveys by UNICEF. Data on tetanus vaccinations, pregnant women receiving prenatal care, births attended by skilled health staff, and national estimates of maternal mortality ratios are from UNICEF's *State of the World's Children 2009* and Childinfo and Demographic and Health Surveys by Macro International. Modeled estimates for maternal mortality ratios are from WHO, UNICEF, UNFPA and the World Bank's *Maternal Mortality in 2005* (2007).

Nutrition

	Prevalence of undernourishment		Prevalence of child malnutrition		Prevalence of overweight children	Low-birthweight babies	Exclusive breast-feeding	Consumption of iodized salt	Vitamin A supplementation	Prevalence of anemia	
	% of population		% of children under age 5		% of children under age 5	% of births	% of children under 6 months	% of households	% of children 6–59 months	% Children under age 5	Pregnant women
			Underweight	Stunting							
	1990–92	2003–05	2000–07[a]	2000–07[a]	2000–07[a]	2002–07[a]	2002–07[a]	2002–07[a]	2007	2000–05[a]	2000–05[a]
Afghanistan	..	..	..	..	..	..	..	..	..	..	..
Albania	<5	<5	17.0	39.2	30.0	7	40	60	..	31	34
Algeria	<5	<5	10.2	21.6	15.4	6	7	61	..	43	43
Angola	66	46	27.5	50.8	5.3	..	..	..	36	..	57
Argentina	<5	<5	2.3	8.2	9.9	7	..	..	..	18	25
Armenia	46	21	4.2	18.2	11.7	8	33	97	..	24	12
Australia	<5	<5	..	..	..	..	..	..	..	8	12
Austria	<5	<5	..	..	..	..	..	..	..	11	15
Azerbaijan	27	12	14.0	24.1	6.2	..	12	54	95[b]	32	38
Bangladesh	36	27	39.2	47.8	0.9	22	37	84	95	47	47
Belarus	<5	<5	1.3	4.5	9.7	4	9	55	..	27	26
Belgium	<5	<5	..	..	..	..	..	..	..	9	13
Benin	28	19	21.5	39.1	3.0	15	43	55	73	82	73
Bolivia	24	22	5.9	32.5	9.2	7	54	90	39	52	37
Bosnia and Herzegovina	<5	<5	1.6	11.8	25.6	5	18	62	..	27	35
Botswana	20	26	10.7	29.1	10.4	..	..	..	..	..	21
Brazil	10	6	2.2	7.1	7.3	8	..	..	..	55	29
Bulgaria	<5	<5	1.6	8.8	13.6	..	..	100	..	27	30
Burkina Faso	14	10	35.2	43.1	5.4	16	7	34	95	92	68
Burundi	44	63	38.9	63.1	1.4	11	45	98	83	56	47
Cambodia	38	26	28.4	43.7	1.7	14	60	73	76	63	66
Cameroon	34	23	15.1	35.4	8.7	11	21	49	95	68	51
Canada	<5	<5	..	..	..	..	..	..	..	8	12
Central African Republic	47	43	21.8	44.6	10.8	13	23	62	78	..	..
Chad	59	39	33.9	44.8	4.4	22	2	56	54	71	60
Chile	7	<5	0.6	2.1	9.8	6	85	..	..	24	28
China	15[c]	9[c]	6.8	21.8	9.2	2	51	94	..	20	29
Hong Kong, China	..	..	..	..	..	..	..	..	..	..	..
Colombia	15	10	5.1	16.2	4.2	6	47	..	..	28	31
Congo, Dem. Rep.	29	76	33.6	44.4	6.5	..	36	..	79	71	67
Congo, Rep.	40	22	11.8	31.2	8.5	13	19	82	95	66	55
Costa Rica	<5	<5	..	..	..	7	..	..	..	..	..
Côte d'Ivoire	15	14	16.7	40.1	9.0	17	4	84	63	69	55
Croatia	<5	<5	..	..	..	5	..	..	..	23	28
Cuba	5	<5	..	..	..	5	26	88	..	27	39
Czech Republic	<5	<5	2.1	2.6	4.4	..	..	..	..	18	22
Denmark	<5	<5	..	..	..	..	..	..	..	9	12
Dominican Republic	27	21	4.2	11.7	8.6	11	8	19	..	35	40
Ecuador	24	15	6.2	29.0	5.1	..	40	..	..	38	38
Egypt, Arab Rep.	<5	<5	5.4	23.8	14.1	14	38	78	87[b]	30	45
El Salvador	9	10	6.1	24.6	5.8	7	24	62	20	18	..
Eritrea	67	68	34.5	43.7	1.6	14	52	68	51	70	55
Estonia	<5	<5	..	..	..	..	..	..	..	23	23
Ethiopia	71	46	34.6	50.7	5.1	20	49	20	88	75	63
Finland	<5	<5	..	..	..	..	..	..	..	11	15
France	<5	<5	..	..	..	..	..	..	..	8	11
Gabon	5	<5	8.8	26.3	5.6	..	..	..	90	44	46
Gambia, The	20	30	15.8	27.6	2.7	20	41	7	93	..	..
Georgia	47	13	..	..	..	5	11	87	..	41	42
Germany	<5	<5	..	..	..	..	..	..	..	8	12
Ghana	34	9	18.8	35.6	4.5	9	54	32	95	76	65
Greece	<5	<5	..	..	..	..	..	..	..	12	19
Guatemala	14	16	17.7	54.3	5.6	12	51	40	33	38	22
Guinea	19	17	22.5	39.3	5.1	12	27	51	95	79	63
Guinea-Bissau	20	32	21.9	36.1	5.1	24	16	1	66	75	58
Haiti	63	58	18.9	29.7	3.9	25	41	3	42	65	63

	Prevalence of undernourishment		Prevalence of child malnutrition		Prevalence of overweight children	Low-birthweight babies	Exclusive breast-feeding	Consumption of iodized salt	Vitamin A supplementation	Prevalence of anemia %	
	% of population		% of children under age 5		% of children under age 5	% of births	% of children under 6 months	% of households	% of children 6–59 months	Children under age 5	Pregnant women
	1990–92	2003–05	Underweight 2000–07[a]	Stunting 2000–07[a]	2000–07[a]	2002–07[a]	2002–07[a]	2002–07[a]	2007	2000–05[a]	2000–05[a]
Honduras	19	12	8.6	29.9	5.8	10	30	..	40	30	..
Hungary	<5	<5	..	..	..	..	..	..	..	19	21
India	24	21	43.5	47.9	1.9	28	46	51	33	74	50
Indonesia	19	17	24.4	28.6	5.1	9	40	73	87	44	44
Iran, Islamic Rep.	<5	<5	..	..	..	..	23	99	..	35	..
Iraq	..	..	..	..	..	..	..	..	..	..	..
Ireland	<5	<5	..	..	..	..	..	..	..	10	15
Israel	<5	<5	..	..	..	..	..	..	..	12	17
Italy	<5	<5	..	..	..	..	..	..	..	11	15
Jamaica	11	5	3.1	4.5	7.5	12	15	..	..	..	..
Japan	<5	<5	..	..	..	..	..	..	..	11	15
Jordan	<5	<5	3.6	12.0	4.7	12	22	..	..	28	39
Kazakhstan	<5	<5	4.9	17.5	14.8	6	17	92	..	..	26
Kenya	33	32	16.5	35.8	5.8	10	13	..	22	..	..
Korea, Dem. Rep.	21	32	17.8	44.7	0.9	7	65	40	95	..	..
Korea, Rep.	<5	<5	..	..	..	..	..	..	..	..	23
Kuwait	20	<5	..	..	..	..	..	..	..	32	31
Kyrgyz Republic	17	<5	2.7	18.1	10.7	5	32	76	95	..	34
Lao PDR	27	19	36.4	48.2	2.7	..	..	..	83	48	56
Latvia	<5	<5	..	..	..	..	..	..	..	27	25
Lebanon	<5	<5	..	..	..	..	..	92	..	..	32
Lesotho	15	15	16.6	45.2	6.8	13	36	91	85	49	25
Liberia	30	40	20.4	39.4	4.2	..	29	..	85	..	..
Libya	<5	<5	..	..	..	..	..	..	..	34	34
Lithuania	<5	<5	..	..	..	..	..	..	..	24	24
Macedonia, FYR	<5	<5	1.8	11.5	16.2	6	16	94	..	..	32
Madagascar	32	37	36.8	52.8	6.2	17	67	75	95	68	50
Malawi	45	29	18.4	52.5	10.2	14	57	50	90	73	47
Malaysia	<5	<5	..	..	..	9	..	..	..	32	38
Mali	14	11	27.9	38.5	4.7	19	38	79	95	83	73
Mauritania	10	8	30.4	39.5	3.8	..	..	..	95	68	53
Mauritius	7	6	..	..	..	14	21	..	..	..	..
Mexico	<5	<5	3.4	15.5	7.6	8	..	91	68	..	..
Moldova	<5	<5	3.2	11.3	9.1	6	46	60	..	41	36
Mongolia	30	29	5.3	27.5	14.2	6	57	83	95	21	37
Morocco	5	<5	9.9	23.1	13.3	15	31	21	..	32	37
Mozambique	59	38	21.2	47.0	6.3	15	30	54	48	75	52
Myanmar	44	19	29.6	40.6	2.4	..	15	60	94	63	50
Namibia	29	19	17.5	29.6	4.6	..	24	..	68	41	31
Nepal	21	15	38.8	49.3	0.6	21	53	..	95	..	..
Netherlands	<5	<5	..	..	..	..	..	..	..	9	13
New Zealand	<5	<5	..	..	..	..	..	..	..	11	18
Nicaragua	52	22	7.8	25.2	7.1	..	..	97	95	17	33
Niger	38	29	39.9	54.8	3.5	27	9	46	95	81	66
Nigeria	15	9	27.2	43.0	6.2	14	17	97	74	..	..
Norway	<5	<5	..	..	..	..	..	..	..	6	9
Oman	..	..	..	..	..	9	..	..	..	..	43
Pakistan	22	23	31.3	41.5	4.8	..	37	17	95	51	39
Panama	18	17	..	..	..	10	..	..	4	..	..
Papua New Guinea	..	..	..	..	..	..	..	..	7	60	55
Paraguay	16	11	..	..	..	9	22	94	..	30	39
Peru	28	15	5.2	31.3	11.8	10	63	91	..	50	43
Philippines	21	16	20.7	33.8	2.4	20	34	45	83	36	44
Poland	<5	<5	..	..	..	..	..	..	..	23	25
Portugal	<5	<5	..	..	..	..	..	..	..	13	17
Puerto Rico	..	..	..	..	..	..	..	..	..	..	..

	Prevalence of undernourishment		Prevalence of child malnutrition		Prevalence of overweight children	Low-birthweight babies	Exclusive breast-feeding	Consumption of iodized salt	Vitamin A supplementation	Prevalence of anemia	
	% of population		% of children under age 5		% of children under age 5	% of births	% of children under 6 months	% of households	% of children 6–59 months	Children under age 5	Pregnant women
			Underweight	Stunting						%	
	1990–92	2003–05	2000–07[a]	2000–07[a]	2000–07[a]	2002–07[a]	2002–07[a]	2002–07[a]	2007	2000–05[a]	2000–05[a]
Romania	<5	<5	3.5	12.8	8.3	8	16	74	..	40	30
Russian Federation	<5	<5	..	..	..	6	..	35	..	27	21
Rwanda	45	40	18.0	51.7	6.7	6	88	88	89	..	..
Saudi Arabia	<5	<5	..	..	..	..	..	..	..	33	32
Senegal	28	26	14.5	20.1	2.4	19	34	41	94	70	58
Serbia	<5[d]	<5[d]	1.8	8.1	19.3	5	15	..	..	..	..
Sierra Leone	45	47	28.3	46.9	5.9	24	8	45	95	83	60
Singapore	..	..	3.3	4.4	2.6	..	..	..	..	19	24
Slovak Republic	<5	<5	..	..	..	..	..	..	..	23	25
Slovenia	<5	<5	..	..	..	..	..	..	..	14	19
Somalia	..	..	32.8	42.1	4.7	11	9	1	89	..	..
South Africa	<5	<5	..	..	..	..	7	..	33	..	22
Spain	<5	<5	..	..	..	..	..	..	..	13	18
Sri Lanka	27	21	22.8	18.4	1.0	..	..	94	64	30	29
Sudan	31	21	38.4	47.6	5.2	..	34	11	90	85	58
Swaziland	12	18	9.1	36.6	14.9	9	32	80	59	47	24
Sweden	<5	<5	..	..	..	..	..	..	..	9	13
Switzerland	<5	<5	..	..	..	..	..	..	..	6	..
Syrian Arab Republic	<5	<5	..	..	..	9	29	79	..	41	39
Tajikistan	34	34	14.9	33.1	6.7	10	25	46	92	38	45
Tanzania	28	35	16.7	44.4	4.9	10	41	43	93	72	58
Thailand	29	17	7.0	15.7	8.0	9	5	47	..	..	..
Timor-Leste	18	22	40.6	55.7	5.7	12	31	58	57	32	23
Togo	45	37	..	..	..	12	28	25	95	52	50
Trinidad and Tobago	11	10	4.4	5.3	4.9	19	13	28	..	30	30
Tunisia	<5	<5	..	..	..	..	..	..	..	..	..
Turkey	<5	<5	3.5	15.6	9.1	..	21	64	..	33	40
Turkmenistan	9	6	..	..	..	4	11	87	..	36	30
Uganda	19	15	19.0	44.8	4.9	14	60	96	64	64	41
Ukraine	<5	<5	4.1	22.9	26.5	4	6	18	..	22	27
United Arab Emirates	<5	<5	..	..	..	..	..	..	..	28	28
United Kingdom	<5	<5	..	..	..	..	..	..	..	..	15
United States	<5	<5	1.3	3.9	8.0	8	..	..	..	3	6
Uruguay	5	<5	6.0	13.9	9.4	8	54	..	..	19	27
Uzbekistan	5	14	4.4	19.6	12.8	5	26	53	84	38	..
Venezuela, RB	10	12	..	..	..	9	..	..	..	33	40
Vietnam	28	14	20.2	35.8	2.5	7	17	93	95[b]	34	32
West Bank and Gaza	..	15	..	..	..	7	27	86	..	..	..
Yemen, Rep.	30	32	..	..	..	..	12	30	47[b]	68	58
Zambia	40	45	23.3	52.5	5.9	12	61	77	95	53	..
Zimbabwe	40	40	14.0	35.8	9.1	11	22	91	83	..	..
World	**17 w**	**14 w**	**23.2 w**	**34.7 w**	**5.7 w**	**14 w**	**38 w**	**69 w**	**.. w**	**.. w**	**.. w**
Low income	31	27	28.0	43.8	4.8	15	33	61	82	..	..
Middle income	16	13	22.0	31.8	6.1	15	41	71	..	..	..
Lower middle income	19	14	24.8	34.9	5.8	16	43	71	..	..	..
Upper middle income	6	6	..	..	..	8	..	72	..	38	29
Low & middle income	19	16	24.1	36.0	5.7	15	38	69	..	..	..
East Asia & Pacific	18	11	12.8	25.8	7.1	6	43	86	..	20	29
Europe & Central Asia	7	6	..	..	..	6	..	50	..	29	30
Latin America & Carib.	12	9	4.4	15.8	7.4	9	..	85	..	..	..
Middle East & N. Africa	7	7	..	..	..	12	26	68	..	..	..
South Asia	25	22	41.1	47.3	2.2	27	44	51	50	74	50
Sub-Saharan Africa	31	29	26.6	44.3	5.8	14	31	62	77	..	..
High income	5	5	..	..	..	..	..	..	..	..	13
Euro area	5	5	..	..	..	..	..	..	..	10	14

a. Data are for the most recent year available. b. Country's vitamin A supplementation programs do not target children all the way up to 59 months of age. c. Includes Hong Kong, China; Macao, China; and Taiwan, China. d. Includes Montenegro.

About the data

Data on undernourishment are from the Food and Agriculture Organization (FAO) of the United Nations and measure food deprivation based on average food available for human consumption per person, the level of inequality in access to food, and the minimum calories required for an average person.

From a policy and program standpoint, however, this measure has its limits. First, food insecurity exists even where food availability is not a problem because of inadequate access of poor households to food. Second, food insecurity is an individual or household phenomenon, and the average food available to each person, even corrected for possible effects of low income, is not a good predictor of food insecurity among the population. And third, nutrition security is determined not only by food security but also by the quality of care of mothers and children and the quality of the household's health environment (Smith and Haddad 2000).

Estimates of child malnutrition, based on weight for age (underweight) and height for age (stunting), are from national survey data. The proportion of underweight children is the most common malnutrition indicator. Being even mildly underweight increases the risk of death and inhibits cognitive development in children. And it perpetuates the problem across generations, as malnourished women are more likely to have low-birthweight babies. Height for age reflects linear growth achieved pre- and postnatally; a deficit indicates long-term, cumulative effects of inadequate health, diet, or care. Stunting is often used as a proxy for multifaceted deprivation and as an indicator of long-term changes in malnutrition.

Estimates of overweight children are also from national survey data. Overweight children have become a growing concern in developing countries. Research shows an association between childhood obesity and a high prevalence of diabetes, respiratory disease, high blood pressure, and psychosocial and orthopedic disorders (de Onis and Blössner 2000).

New international growth reference standards for infants and young children were released in 2006 by the World Health Organization (WHO) to monitor children's nutritional status. They are also key in monitoring health targets for the Millennium Development Goals. Differences in growth to age 5 are influenced more by nutrition, feeding practices, environment, and healthcare than by genetics or ethnicity. The previously reported data were based on the U.S. National Center for Health Statistics–WHO growth reference. Because of the change in standards, the data in this edition should not be compared with data in editions prior to 2008.

Low birthweight, which is associated with maternal malnutrition, raises the risk of infant mortality and stunts growth in infancy and childhood. There is also emerging evidence that low-birthweight babies are more prone to noncommunicable diseases such as diabetes and cardiovascular diseases. Estimates of low-birthweight infants are drawn mostly from hospital records and household surveys. Many births in developing countries take place at home and are seldom recorded. A hospital birth may indicate higher income and therefore better nutrition, or it could indicate a higher risk birth, possibly skewing the data on birthweights downward. The data should therefore be used with caution.

Improved breastfeeding can save an estimated 1.3 million children a year. Breast milk alone contains all the nutrients, antibodies, hormones, and antioxidants an infant needs to thrive. It protects babies from diarrhea and acute respiratory infections, stimulates their immune systems and response to vaccination, and may confer cognitive benefits. The data on breastfeeding are derived from national surveys.

Iodine deficiency is the single most important cause of preventable mental retardation, and it contributes significantly to the risk of stillbirth and miscarriage. Widely used and inexpensive, iodized salt is the best source of iodine, and a global campaign to iodize edible salt is significantly reducing the risks (www.childinfo.org). The data on iodized salt are derived from household surveys.

Vitamin A is essential for immune system functioning. Vitamin A deficiency, a leading cause of blindness, also causes a 23 percent greater risk of dying from a range of childhood ailments such as measles, malaria, and diarrhea. Giving vitamin A to new breastfeeding mothers helps protect their children during the first months of life. Food fortification with vitamin A is being introduced in many developing countries.

Data on anemia are compiled by the WHO based mainly on nationally representative surveys between 1993 and 2005, which measured hemoglobin in the blood. WHO's hemoglobin thresholds were then used to determine anemia status based on age, sex, and physiological status. Children under age 5 and pregnant women have the highest risk for anemia. Data should be used with caution because surveys differ in quality, coverage, age group interviewed, and treatment of missing values across countries and over time.

For indicators from household surveys, the year in the table refers to the survey year. For more information, consult the original sources.

Definitions

• **Prevalence of undernourishment** is the percentage of the population whose dietary energy consumption is continuously below a minimum requirement for maintaining a healthy life and carrying out light physical activity with an acceptable minimum weight for height. • **Prevalence of child malnutrition** is the percentage of children under age 5 whose weight for age (underweight) or height for age (stunting) is more than two standard deviations below the median for the international reference population ages 0–59 months. Height is measured by recumbent length for children up to two years old and by stature while standing for older children. Data are for the WHO child growth standards released in 2006. • **Prevalence of overweight children** is the percentage of children under age 5 whose weight for height is more than two standard deviations above the median for the international reference population of the corresponding age as established by the WHO child growth standards released in 2006. • **Low-birthweight babies** are the percentage of newborns weighing less than 2.5 kilograms within the first hours of life, before significant postnatal weight loss has occurred. • **Exclusive breastfeeding** is the percentage of children less than six months old who were fed breast milk alone (no other liquids) in the past 24 hours. • **Consumption of iodized salt** is the percentage of households that use edible salt fortified with iodine. • **Vitamin A supplementation** is the percentage of children ages 6–59 months old who received at least one dose of vitamin A in the previous six months, as reported by mothers. • **Prevalence of anemia, children under age 5,** is the percentage of children under age 5 whose hemoglobin level is less than 110 grams per liter at sea level. • **Prevalence of anemia, pregnant women,** is the percentage of pregnant women whose hemoglobin level is less than 110 grams per liter at sea level.

Data sources

Data on undernourishment are from ww.fao.org/ faostat/foodsecurity/index_en.htm. Data on malnutrition and overweight children are from the WHO's Global Database on Child Growth and Malnutrition (www.who.int/nutgrowthdb). Data on low-birthweight babies, breastfeeding, iodized salt consumption, and vitamin A supplementation are from the United Nations Children's Fund's *State of the World's Children 2009* and Childinfo. Data on anemia are from the WHO's *Worldwide Prevalence of Anemia 1993–2005* (2008).

Health risk factors and future challenges

	Prevalence of smoking		Incidence of tuberculosis	Prevalence of diabetes	Prevalence of HIV							Condom use	
	% of adults		per 100,000 people	% of population ages 20–79	Total % of population ages 15–49		Female % of total population with HIV		Youth % of population ages 15–24		% of population ages 15–24	
	Male	Female							Male	Female	Male	Female
	2008	2008	2007	2007	1990	2007	2001	2007	2007	2007	2000–07[a]	2000–07[a]
Afghanistan	..	..	..	..	..	..	..	..	..	..	..	..
Albania	41	4	17	4.5	..	..	..	..	..	..	..	..
Algeria	27	0[b]	57	8.4	..	0.1	25.0	28.6	0.1	0.1	..	..
Angola	..	..	287	3.3	0.3	2.1	60.9	61.1	0.2	0.3	..	..
Argentina	34	24	31	5.6	0.2	0.5	25.0	26.7	0.6	0.3	..	..
Armenia	55	4	72	7.7	..	0.1	<27.8	<41.7	0.2	0.1	32	7
Australia	28	22	6	5.0	0.1	0.2	<7.1	6.7	0.2	<0.1	..	..
Austria	46	40	12	7.9	<0.1	0.2	27.3	29.6	0.2	0.1	..	..
Azerbaijan	..	1	77	7.3	..	0.2	..	16.7	0.3	0.1	25	1
Bangladesh	43	1	223	5.3	..	..	..	16.7	..	..	..	..
Belarus	64	21	61	7.6	..	0.2	27.5	30.0	0.3	0.1	..	..
Belgium	30	24	12	5.2	0.1	0.2	26.2	27.3	0.2	0.1	..	..
Benin	..	..	91	4.4	0.1	1.2	63.3	62.7	0.3	0.9	39	10
Bolivia	34	26	155	5.8	0.1	0.2	24.6	27.8	0.2	0.1	29	10
Bosnia and Herzegovina	49	35	51	7.0	..	<0.1	..	..	..	..	..	..
Botswana	..	..	731	5.2	4.7	23.9	59.3	60.7	5.1	15.3	..	..
Brazil	20	13	48	6.2	0.4	0.6	34.4	33.8	1.0	0.6	..	..
Bulgaria	48	28	39	7.6	..	..	..	..	..	..	..	..
Burkina Faso	14	1	226	3.7	1.9	1.6	45.4	50.8	0.5	0.9	54	17
Burundi	16	11	367	1.7	1.7	2.0	59.2	58.9	0.4	1.3	..	..
Cambodia	38	6	495	5.0	0.7	0.8	25.8	28.6	0.8	0.3	31	3
Cameroon	10	1	192	3.7	0.8	5.1	61.2	60.0	1.2	4.3	52	24
Canada	19	18	5	7.4	0.2	0.4	26.5	27.4	0.4	0.2	..	..
Central African Republic	..	..	345	4.4	1.8	6.3	66.7	65.0	1.1	5.5	..	..
Chad	13	1	299	3.6	0.7	3.5	60.7	61.1	2.0	2.8	18	7
Chile	42	31	12	5.6	<0.1	0.3	26.0	28.1	0.3	0.2	..	..
China	60	4	98	4.1	..	0.1[c]	25.5[c]	29.0[c]	0.1[c]	0.1[c]	..	..
Hong Kong, China	22	4	62	8.2	..	..	..	..	..	..	..	..
Colombia	27	11	35	5.0	0.1	0.6	26.9	29.4	0.7	0.3	..	23
Congo, Dem. Rep.	11	1	392	3.0	..	..	..	..	..	..	..	..
Congo, Rep.	10	0[b]	403	5.0	5.1	3.5	58.4	58.9	0.8	2.3	36	16
Costa Rica	26	7	11	9.3	0.1	0.4	27.5	28.1	0.4	0.2	..	..
Côte d'Ivoire	12	1	420	4.6	2.2	3.9	58.2	59.5	0.8	2.4	..	..
Croatia	39	29	40	7.1	..	<0.1	..	..	..	..	..	..
Cuba	36	26	6	9.3	..	0.1	<43.5	29.0	0.1	0.1	..	..
Czech Republic	37	25	9	7.6	..	..	<38.5	<33.3	<0.1	..	..	..
Denmark	36	31	8	5.5	0.1	0.2	..	22.9	0.2	0.1	..	..
Dominican Republic	16	11	69	8.7	0.6	1.1	54.0	50.8	0.3	0.6	58	19
Ecuador	24	6	101	5.7	0.1	0.3	25.8	28.4	0.4	0.2	..	..
Egypt, Arab Rep.	25	1	21	11.0	..	..	26.8	28.9	..	..	..	..
El Salvador	22	3	40	9.0	0.1	0.8	25.7	28.5	0.9	0.5	..	..
Eritrea	16	1	95	2.3	0.1	1.3	60.0	60.0	0.3	0.9	..	2
Estonia	50	28	38	7.6	..	1.3	<28.6	24.2	1.6	0.7	..	..
Ethiopia	7	1	378	2.3	0.7	2.1	59.5	59.6	0.5	1.5	18	2
Finland	32	24	6	5.9	..	0.1	<50.0	<41.7	0.1	<0.1	..	..
France	37	27	14	5.9	0.1	0.4	25.0	27.1	0.4	0.2	..	..
Gabon	..	..	406	4.9	0.9	5.9	58.3	58.7	1.3	3.9	..	..
Gambia, The	17	1	258	4.1	..	0.9	59.0	60.0	0.2	0.6	..	..
Georgia	57	6	84	7.4	..	0.1	20.0	37.0	0.1	0.1	..	..
Germany	37	26	6	7.9	<0.1	0.1	27.3	28.8	0.1	0.1	..	..
Ghana	7	1	203	4.2	0.1	1.9	58.3	60.0	0.4	1.3	45	19
Greece	64	40	18	5.9	0.1	0.2	26.5	27.3	0.2	0.1	..	..
Guatemala	25	4	63	8.6	<0.1	0.8	97.9	98.1	..	1.5	..	..
Guinea	..	9	287	4.1	0.2	1.6	59.6	59.3	0.4	1.2	35	10
Guinea-Bissau	..	..	220	3.8	0.2	1.8	59.2	58.0	0.4	1.2	..	..
Haiti	..	4	306	9.0	1.2	2.2	45.7	52.7	0.6	1.4	28	20

Health risk factors and future challenges

	Prevalence of smoking		Incidence of tuberculosis	Prevalence of diabetes	Prevalence of HIV						Condom use	
	% of adults		per 100,000 people	% of population ages 20–79	Total % of population ages 15–49		Female % of total population with HIV		Youth % of population ages 15–24		% of population ages 15–24	
	Male	Female							Male	Female	Male	Female
	2008	2008	2007	2007	1990	2007	2001	2007	2007	2007	2000–07[a]	2000–07[a]
Honduras	..	3	59	9.1	1.3	0.7	25.7	28.5	0.7	0.4	..	7
Hungary	46	34	17	7.6	..	0.1	<35.7	<30.3	0.1	<0.1	..	..
India	28	1	168	6.7	0.1	0.3	38.5	38.3	0.3	0.3	..	..
Indonesia	62	4	228	2.3	..	0.2	10.8	20.0	0.3	0.1	..	1
Iran, Islamic Rep.	24	2	22	7.8	..	0.2	26.7	28.2	0.2	0.1	..	..
Iraq	..	..	..	..	..	..	..	..	..	..	..	..
Ireland	27	26	13	5.1	..	0.2	26.1	27.3	0.2	0.1	..	..
Israel	31	18	8	6.9	<0.1	0.1	60.0	59.2	<0.1	0.1	..	..
Italy	33	19	7	5.8	0.4	0.4	25.7	27.3	0.4	0.2	..	..
Jamaica	19	8	7	10.3	0.3	1.6	26.4	29.2	1.7	0.9	..	..
Japan	44	14	21	4.9	..	..	22.2	24.0	..	..	..	..
Jordan	62	10	7	9.8	..	..	..	..	..	..	..	4
Kazakhstan	43	10	129	5.6	..	0.1	<29.4	27.5	0.2	0.1	..	..
Kenya	24	1	353	3.3	..	..	..	..	..	..	39	9
Korea, Dem. Rep.	59	..	344	5.2	..	..	..	..	..	..	..	..
Korea, Rep.	53	6	90	7.8	..	<0.1	26.5	27.7	<0.1	<0.1	..	..
Kuwait	34	2	24	14.4	..	..	..	..	..	..	..	..
Kyrgyz Republic	47	2	121	5.1	..	0.1	<50	26.2	0.2	0.1	..	..
Lao PDR	61	14	151	3.1	..	0.2	<45.5	24.1	0.2	0.1	..	..
Latvia	54	24	53	7.6	..	0.8	<23.8	27.0	0.9	0.5	..	..
Lebanon	29	7	19	7.7	<0.1	0.1	<45.5	<33.3	0.1	0.1	..	..
Lesotho	48	34	637	3.8	0.8	23.2	58.3	57.7	5.9	14.9	44	26
Liberia	..	..	277	4.6	0.4	1.7	59.1	59.4	0.4	1.3	19	9
Libya	32	2	17	4.4	..	..	..	..	..	..	..	..
Lithuania	45	21	68	7.6	..	0.1	<35.7	<45.5	0.1	0.1	..	..
Macedonia, FYR	40	32	29	7.1	..	<0.1	..	..	..	..	..	..
Madagascar	..	..	251	3.0	..	0.1	23.8	26.2	0.2	0.1	8	2
Malawi	19	2	346	2.1	2.1	11.9	56.4	58.3	2.4	8.4	32	9
Malaysia	51	3	103	10.7	0.1	0.5	23.3	26.6	0.6	0.3	..	..
Mali	14	1	319	4.1	0.2	1.5	60.5	60.2	0.4	1.1	29	4
Mauritania	16	1	318	4.6	<0.1	0.8	25.8	27.9	0.9	0.5	..	..
Mauritius	36	1	22	11.1	<0.1	1.7	<27.8	29.2	1.8	1.0	..	..
Mexico	37	12	20	10.6	0.2	0.3	27.1	28.5	0.3	0.2	..	..
Moldova	46	6	141	7.6	..	0.4	<50.0	29.5	0.4	0.2	55	22
Mongolia	46	7	205	1.9	..	0.1	..	<20.0	0.1	..	..	..
Morocco	26	0[b]	92	8.1	..	0.1	27.5	28.1	0.1	0.1	..	..
Mozambique	20	2	431	3.7	1.4	12.5	59.4	57.9	2.9	8.5	27	12
Myanmar	44	12	171	3.2	0.4	0.7	33.4	41.7	0.7	0.6	..	..
Namibia	36	9	767	4.2	1.2	15.3	60.7	61.1	3.4	10.3	65	42
Nepal	29	26	173	4.2	<0.1	0.5	21.8	25.0	0.5	0.3	24	8
Netherlands	38	30	8	5.2	0.1	0.2	25.6	27.2	0.2	0.1	..	..
New Zealand	30	28	7	6.4	0.1	0.1	<16.7	<35.7	0.1	..	..	..
Nicaragua	..	5	49	10.1	<0.1	0.2	25.6	28.0	0.3	0.1	..	7
Niger	41	11	174	3.7	0.1	0.8	29.3	30.4	0.9	0.5	..	..
Nigeria	9	0[b]	311	4.5	0.7	3.1	60.0	58.3	0.8	2.3	38	8
Norway	34	30	6	3.6	<0.1	0.1	<41.7	<33.3	0.1	0.1	..	..
Oman	24	0[b]	13	13.1	..	..	..	..	..	..	..	..
Pakistan	30	3	181	9.6	..	0.1	26.0	28.7	0.1	0.1	..	..
Panama	52	20	47	9.7	0.4	1.0	26.9	28.9	1.1	0.6	..	..
Papua New Guinea	46	28	250	2.9	..	1.5	34.7	39.6	0.6	0.7	..	..
Paraguay	33	14	58	4.8	<0.1	0.6	26.4	29.0	0.7	0.3	..	..
Peru	43	23	126	6.0	0.1	0.5	26.8	28.4	0.5	0.3	..	9
Philippines	39	9	290	7.6	..	..	<50	26.8	..	..	13	3
Poland	44	27	25	7.6	..	0.1	26.0	28.9	0.1	0.1	..	..
Portugal	41	31	30	5.7	0.2	0.5	26.6	27.6	0.5	0.3	..	..
Puerto Rico	..	..	4	10.7	..	..	..	..	..	..	..	..

2.20 Health risk factors and future challenges

	Prevalence of smoking		Incidence of tuberculosis	Prevalence of diabetes	Prevalence of HIV						Condom use	
	% of adults		per 100,000 people	% of population ages 20–79	Total % of population ages 15–49		Female % of total population with HIV		Youth % of population ages 15–24		% of population ages 15–24	
	Male	Female							Male	Female	Male	Female
	2008	2008	2007	2007	1990	2007	2001	2007	2007	2007	2000–07ᵃ	2000–07ᵃ
Romania	41	25	115	7.6	..	0.1	50.7	50.0	0.2	0.2	..	..
Russian Federation	70	27	110	7.6	..	1.1	22.1	25.5	1.3	0.6	..	..
Rwanda	..	8	397	1.5	9.2	2.8	60.6	60.0	0.5	1.4	19	5
Saudi Arabia	25	3	46	16.7	..	..	..	..	..	..	..	..
Senegal	14	1	272	4.6	0.1	1.0	60.9	59.4	0.3	0.8	48	5
Serbia	44ᵈ	44ᵈ	32	7.1ᵈ	<0.1	0.1	25.5	28.1	0.1	0.1	..	..
Sierra Leone	32	4	574	4.3	0.2	1.7	59.4	58.8	0.4	1.3	..	..
Singapore	26	5	27	10.1	..	0.2	<34.5	29.3	0.2	0.1	..	..
Slovak Republic	42	20	17	7.6	..	<0.1	..	..	..	..	..	..
Slovenia	32	21	13	7.6	..	<0.1	..	..	..	..	..	..
Somalia	..	..	249	2.8	<0.1	0.5	26.5	27.9	0.6	0.3	..	..
South Africa	25	8	948	4.4	0.8	18.1	58.7	59.3	4.0	12.7	57	46
Spain	36	31	30	5.7	0.4	0.5	20.8	20.0	0.6	0.2	..	..
Sri Lanka	25	0ᵇ	60	8.4	..	..	<33.3	37.8	<0.1	..	..	..
Sudan	24	2	243	4.0	0.8	1.4	56.0	58.6	0.3	1.0	..	..
Swaziland	13	3	1,198	4.0	0.9	26.1	60.7	58.8	5.8	22.6	66	44
Sweden	20	25	6	5.2	0.1	0.1	43.4	46.8	0.1	0.1	..	..
Switzerland	31	22	6	7.9	0.4	0.6	33.2	36.8	0.4	0.5	..	..
Syrian Arab Republic	43	..	24	10.6	..	..	..	..	..	..	..	..
Tajikistan	..	..	231	4.9	..	0.3	<20.8	21.0	0.4	0.1	..	..
Tanzania	21	2	297	2.9	4.8	6.2	61.7	58.5	0.5	0.9	36	13
Thailand	37	3	142	6.9	1.0	1.4	36.9	41.7	1.2	1.2	..	..
Timor-Leste	26	1	322	1.7	..	..	..	..	..	..	..	..
Togo	..	..	429	4.1	0.7	3.3	61.0	57.5	0.8	2.4	..	..
Trinidad and Tobago	32	6	11	11.5	0.2	1.5	57.5	59.2	0.3	1.0	..	..
Tunisia	47	1	26	5.2	..	0.1	<45.5	27.8	0.1	<0.1	..	..
Turkey	52	19	30	7.8	..	..	..	..	..	..	..	..
Turkmenistan	27	1	68	5.2	..	<0.1	..	..	..	..	..	1
Uganda	18	2	330	2.0	13.7	5.4	58.9	59.3	1.3	3.9	38	15
Ukraine	64	23	102	7.6	..	1.6	35.7	44.2	1.5	1.5	..	..
United Arab Emirates	26	2	16	19.5	..	..	..	..	..	..	..	..
United Kingdom	37	35	15	2.9	<0.1	0.2	..	..	..	..	..	..
United States	26	22	4	7.8	0.5	0.6	18.0	20.9	0.7	0.3	..	..
Uruguay	37	28	22	5.6	0.1	0.6	25.4	28.0	0.6	0.3	..	..
Uzbekistan	24	1	113	5.1	..	0.1	<35.7	28.8	0.1	0.1	18	2
Venezuela, RB	33	27	34	5.4	..	..	..	..	..	..	..	..
Vietnam	43	2	171	2.9	0.1	0.5	24.7	27.1	0.6	0.3	16	8
West Bank and Gaza	41	3	20	8.4	..	..	..	..	..	..	..	..
Yemen, Rep.	77	29	76	2.9	..	..	..	..	..	..	..	..
Zambia	18	2	506	3.8	8.9	15.2	54.7	57.1	3.6	11.3	36	19
Zimbabwe	21	2	782	4.0	14.2	15.3	58.8	56.7	2.9	7.7	52	9
World	**40 w**	**8 w**	**139 w**	**5.8 w**	**0.3 w**	**0.8 w**	**30.8 w**	**32.9 w**	**0.5 w**	**0.7 w**		
Low income	29	4	269	4.7	1.5	2.1	37.5	40.6	0.7	1.6		
Middle income	44	6	129	5.9	0.1	0.6	30.8	32.6	0.4	0.5		
Lower middle income	44	3	134	5.5	0.1	0.3	30.7	32.7	0.3	0.3		
Upper middle income	41	18	108	7.4	..	1.7	31.1	32.2	1.0	1.4		
Low & middle income	41	6	162	5.6	0.4	0.9	32.1	34.2	0.5	0.8		
East Asia & Pacific	57	4	136	4.2	0.1	0.2	25.4	28.5	0.2	0.2		
Europe & Central Asia	56	21	84	7.3	..	0.6	28.6	30.5	0.8	0.5		
Latin America & Carib.	29	15	50	7.1	0.3	0.5	32.1	32.8	0.7	0.4		
Middle East & N. Africa	31	3	41	8.6	..	0.1	28.0	28.6	..	..		
South Asia	30	2	174	6.9	0.1	0.3	32.9	34.6	0.3	0.3		
Sub-Saharan Africa	15	2	369	3.6	2.1	5.0	57.0	56.9	1.1	3.3		
High income	34	22	16	6.8	0.3	0.3	23.3	24.9	0.5	0.2		
Euro area	37	27	13	6.4	0.2	0.3	25.8	26.9	0.3	0.2		

a. Data are for the most recent year available. b. Less than 0.5. c. Includes Hong Kong, China. d. Includes Montenegro.

About the data

The limited availability of data on health status is a major constraint in assessing the health situation in developing countries. Surveillance data are lacking for many major public health concerns. Estimates of prevalence and incidence are available for some diseases but are often unreliable and incomplete. National health authorities differ widely in capacity and willingness to collect or report information. To compensate for this and improve reliability and international comparability, the World Health Organization (WHO) prepares estimates in accordance with epidemiological models and statistical standards.

Smoking is the most common form of tobacco use and the prevalence of smoking is therefore a good measure of the tobacco epidemic (Corrao and others 2000). Tobacco use causes heart and other vascular diseases and cancers of the lung and other organs. Given the long delay between starting to smoke and the onset of disease, the health impact of smoking in developing countries will increase rapidly only in the next few decades. Because the data present a one-time estimate, with no information on intensity or duration of smoking, and because the definition of adult varies, the data should be used with caution.

Tuberculosis is one of the main causes of adult deaths from a single infectious agent in developing countries. In developed countries tuberculosis has reemerged largely as a result of cases among immigrants. The estimates of tuberculosis incidence in the table are based on an approach in which reported cases are adjusted using the ratio of case notifications to the estimated share of cases detected by panels of 80 epidemiologists convened by the WHO.

Diabetes, an important cause of ill health and a risk factor for other diseases in developed countries, is spreading rapidly in developing countries. Highest among the elderly, prevalence rates are rising among younger and productive populations in developing countries. Economic development has led to the spread of Western lifestyles and diet to developing countries, resulting in a substantial increase in diabetes. Without effective prevention and control programs, diabetes will likely continue to increase. Data are estimated based on sample surveys.

Adult HIV prevalence rates reflect the rate of HIV infection in each country's population. Low national prevalence rates can be misleading, however. They often disguise epidemics that are initially concentrated in certain localities or population groups and threaten to spill over into the wider population. In many developing countries most new infections occur in young adults, with young women especially vulnerable.

The Joint United Nations Programme on HIV/AIDS (UNAIDS) and the WHO estimate HIV prevalence from sentinel surveillance, population-based surveys, and special studies. The estimates in the table are more reliable than previous estimates because of expanded sentinel surveillance and improved data quality. Findings from population-based HIV surveys, which are geographically more representative than sentinel surveillance and include both men and women, influenced a downward adjustment to prevalence rates based on sentinel surveillance. And assumptions about the average time people living with HIV survive without antiretroviral treatment were improved in the most recent model. Thus, estimates in this edition should not be compared with estimates in previous editions.

Estimates from recent Demographic and Health Surveys that have collected data on HIV/AIDS differ somewhat from those of UNAIDS and the WHO, which are based on surveillance systems that focus on pregnant women who attend sentinel antenatal clinics. Caution should be used in comparing the two sets of estimates. Demographic and Health Surveys are household surveys that use a representative sample from the whole population, whereas surveillance data from antenatal clinics are limited to pregnant women. Household surveys also frequently provide better coverage of rural populations. However, respondents who refuse to participate or are absent from the household add considerable uncertainty to survey-based HIV estimates, because the possible association of absence or refusal with higher HIV prevalence is unknown. UNAIDS and the WHO estimate HIV prevalence for the adult population (ages 15–49) by assuming that prevalence among pregnant women is a good approximation of prevalence among men and women. However, this assumption might not apply to all countries or over time. Other potential biases are associated with the use of antenatal clinic data, such as differences among women who attend antenatal clinics and those who do not.

Data on condom use are from household surveys and refer to condom use at last intercourse. However, condoms are not as effective at preventing transmission of HIV unless used consistently. Some surveys have asked directly about consistent use, but the question is subject to recall and other biases. Caution should be used in interpreting the data.

For indicators from household surveys, the year in the table refers to the survey year. For more information, consult the original sources.

Definitions

• **Prevalence of smoking** is the percentage of men and women who smoke cigarettes. The age range varies, but in most countries is 18 and older or 15 and older. • **Incidence of tuberculosis** is the estimated number of new tuberculosis cases (pulmonary, smear positive, extrapulmonary). • **Prevalence of diabetes** refers to the percentage of people ages 20–79 who have type 1 or type 2 diabetes. • **Prevalence of HIV** is the percentage of people who are infected with HIV. Total and youth rates are percentages of the relevant age group. Female rate is as a percentage of the total population with HIV. • **Condom use** is the percentage of the population ages 15–24 who used a condom at last intercourse in the last 12 months.

Data sources

Data on smoking are from Omar Shafey, Michael Eriksen, Hana Ross, and Judith Mackay's *Tobacco Atlas,* 3rd edition (2009). Data on tuberculosis are from the WHO's *Global Tuberculosis Control Report 2009.* Data on diabetes are from the International Diabetes Federation's *Diabetes Atlas,* 3rd edition. Data on prevalence of HIV are from UNAIDS and the WHO's *2008 Report on the Global AIDS Epidemic.* Data on condom use are from Demographic and Health Surveys by Macro International.

	Survey year	Prevalence of child malnutrition				Child immunization rate				Infant mortality rate		Under-five mortality rate	
		Moderate underweight % of children under age 5				% of children ages 12–23 months[a]				per 1,000 live births		per 1,000	
		New reference		Old reference		Measles		DTP3					
		Poorest quintile	Richest quintile	Poorest quintile	Richest quintile	Poorest quintile	Richest quintile	Poorest quintile	Richest quintile	Poorest quintile	Richest quintile	Poorest quintile	Richest quintile
Armenia	2000	3	2	3	1	68	74[b]	89	84[b]	52	27	61	30
Bangladesh	2004	36	19	41	24	60	91	71	91	90	65	121	71
Benin	2001	18	6	21	9	57	83	63	89	112	50	198	93
Bolivia	2003	7	1	10	1	62	74	64	85	87	32	119	37
Brazil	1996	7	2	10	3	78	90	66	82	83	29	99	33
Burkina Faso	2003	19	13	26	16	48	71	45	73	97	78	206	144
Cambodia	2000	27	23	35	28	44	82	39	75	110	50	155	64
Cameroon	2004	..	..	..	..	57	86	55	86	101	52	189	88
Central African Republic	1994–95	20	11	25	15	31	80	27	76	132	54	193	98
Chad	2004	24	16	27	19	8	38	5	42	109	101	176	187
Colombia	2005	7	2	11	3	70	91	73	91	32	14	39	16
Comores	1996	15	12	22	14	51	86	58	92	87	65	129	87[b]
Côte d'Ivoire	1994	17	7	21	10	31	79	26	74	117	63	190	97
Dominican Republic	2002	7	1	9	1	83	94	46	66	50	20	66	22
Egypt, Arab Rep.	2000	4	2	5	2	95	99	94	93	76	30	98	34
Eritrea	1995	..	..	..	..	37	92	30	89	74	68	152	104
Ethiopia	2000	25	22	32	29	18	52	14	43	93	95	159	147
Gabon	2000	10	4	14	7	34	71	18	49	57	36	93	55
Ghana	2003	17	6	22	10	74	88	64	87	61	58	128	88
Guatemala	1998–99	21	9	26	10	80	91	74	76	58	39	78	39
Guinea	1999	17	9	22	13	33	73	30	69	119	70	230	133
Haiti	2000	14	4	18	6	43	63	31	58	100	97	164	109
India	1998–99	28	16	33	21	28	81	36	85	97	38	141	46
Indonesia	2002–03	..	..	..	..	59	85	42	72	61	17	77	22
Jordan	1997	..	..	..	..	90	93	98	93	35	23	42	25
Kazakhstan	1999	3	5	5	6	74	76[b]	90	82[b]	68	42	82	45
Kenya	2003	17	6	22	7	54	88	56	73	96	62	149	91
Kyrgyz Republic	1997	6	5	10	7	82	81	82	87	83	46	96	49
Madagascar	1997	24	18	29	24	32	79	32	81	119	58	195	101
Malawi	2000	18	9	24	12	80	90	79	93	132	86	231	149
Mali	2001	20	10	26	13	40	77	28	71	137	90	248	148
Mauritania	2000–01	18	11	23	15	42	86	18	61	61	62	98	79
Morocco	2003–04	11	2	13	3	83	98	89	98	62	24	78	26
Mozambique	2003	16	5	21	7	61	96	52	96	143	71	196	108
Namibia	2000	17	6	22	9	76	86	76	83	36	23	55	31
Nepal	2001	34	20	40	26	61	83	62	85	86	53	130	68
Nicaragua	2001	9	2	13	2	76	94	77	83	50	16	64	19
Niger	1998	27	18	30	26	23	66	9	68	131	86	282	184
Nigeria	2003	20	9	24	10	16	71	7	61	133	52	257	79
Pakistan	1990–91	28	14	33	19	28	75	24	64	89	63	125	74
Paraguay	1990	3	1	5	1	48	69	40	69	43	16	57	20
Peru	2000	9	1	13	1	81	92	76	93	64	14	93	18
Philippines	2003	..	..	..	..	70	89	64	92	42	19	66	21
Rwanda	2000	15	8	19	12	84	89	80	89	139	88	246	154
Senegal	1997	..	..	..	..	..	..	..	..	85	45	181	70
South Africa	1998	..	..	..	..	74	85	64	85	62	17	87	22
Tanzania	2004	14	8	20	11	65	91	34	36	88	64	137	93
Togo	1998	17	8	23	10	35	63	29	68	84	66	168	97
Turkey	1998	..	..	..	..	64	89	45	81	68	30	85	33
Turkmenistan	2000	..	..	..	..	91	80	97	86	89	58	106	70
Uganda	2000–01	16	7	21	10	49	65	35	55	106	60	192	106
Uzbekistan	1996	11	8	15	10	96	93	89	82	54	46	70	50
Vietnam	2002	..	..	..	..	64	98	53	94	39	14	53	16
Yemen, Rep.	1997	..	..	36	24	16	73	14	71	109	60	163	73
Zambia	2001–02	18	12	24	17	81	88	74	89	115	57	192	92
Zimbabwe	1999	10	5	16	6	80	86	81	86	59	44	100	62

a. Refers to children who were immunized at any time before the survey. b. The data contain large sampling errors because of the small number of cases.

	Survey year	Prevalence of child malnutrition		Child immunization rate				Infant mortality rate		Under-five mortality rate	
		Old reference Moderate underweight % of children under age 5		% of children ages 12–23 months[a]				per 1,000 live births		per 1,000	
				Measles		DTP3					
		Male	Female	Male	Female	Male	Female	Male	Female	Male	Female
Armenia	2000	2	3	71	79	90	89	46	42	51	45
Bangladesh	2004	34	35	76	76	81	81	80	64	102	91
Benin	2001	19	17	69	67	74	71	98	92	162	163
Bolivia	2003	6	6	65	63	70	73	71	64	94	91
Brazil	1996	6	5	87	87	82	80	52	44	60	53
Burkina Faso	2003	25	23	54	58	57	57	95	89	195	192
Cambodia	2000	32	33	57	54	50	47	103	82	133	110
Cameroon	2004	14	15	65	66	65	68	88	74	154	141
Central African Republic	1994–95	21	19	52	53	49	46	109	94	165	152
Chad	2004	23	23	23	23	20	21	122	108	207	198
Colombia	2005	6	6	83	82	84	81	26	18	30	21
Comores	1996	19	17	63	64	68	69	93	75	122	103
Côte d'Ivoire	1994	19	16	54	52	49	45	99	83	163	137
Dominican Republic	2002	5	5	89	88	54	61	38	31	46	40
Egypt, Arab Rep.	2000	4	3	97	97	94	94	55	55	69	70
Eritrea	1995	26	27	52	50	49	49	82	69	163	141
Ethiopia	2000	32	31	28	26	22	19	124	101	197	178
Gabon	2000	10	9	55	55	40	33	74	49	103	80
Ghana	2003	17	17	82	83	81	77	70	59	111	108
Guatemala	1998–99	21	18	82	87	73	74	50	48	64	65
Guinea	1999	17	19	52	52	46	47	112	101	202	188
Haiti	2000	14	13	54	54	43	43	97	83	143	132
India	1998–99	28	30	52	50	56	54	75	71	98	105
Indonesia	2002–03	..	..	73	71	58	59	46	40	58	51
Jordan	1997	4	5	90	90	96	96	34	23	38	30
Kazakhstan	1999	4	4	79	78	89	88	62	47	72	53
Kenya	2003	18	14	73	72	71	74	84	67	122	103
Kyrgyz Republic	1997	11	8	84	85	83	81	72	60	81	70
Madagascar	1997	27	27	47	45	48	49	109	90	176	152
Malawi	2000	20	19	83	83	84	85	117	108	207	199
Mali	2001	24	21	49	48	41	38	136	116	250	226
Mauritania	2000–01	22	22	61	63	39	41	74	59	110	94
Morocco	2003–04	9	8	88	92	95	95	51	37	59	48
Mozambique	2003	18	17	77	76	73	71	127	120	181	176
Namibia	2000	19	18	79	82	78	81	45	34	67	54
Nepal	2001	35	36	73	69	74	70	79	75	105	112
Nicaragua	2001	9	7	87	86	84	81	39	32	48	41
Niger	1998	29	30	36	34	25	25	141	131	299	306
Nigeria	2003	19	20	34	38	19	24	116	102	222	212
Pakistan	1990–91	27	27	55	46	45	40	102	86	122	119
Paraguay	1990	3	4	56	61	50	57	39	33	49	45
Peru	2000	6	6	84	85	85	84	46	40	64	57
Philippines	2003	..	..	78	81	78	80	35	25	48	34
Rwanda	2000	19	19	86	88	85	87	123	112	215	198
Senegal	1997	..	..	..	..	..	..	74	65	144	134
South Africa	1998	..	..	84	81	74	78	49	35	66	48
Tanzania	2004	18	18	80	80	37	33	83	82	135	130
Togo	1998	19	18	45	40	43	41	89	71	156	132
Turkey	1998	7	7	79	78	60	57	51	46	61	58
Turkmenistan	2000	11	10	87	88	93	92	83	60	101	76
Uganda	2000–01	18	17	56	57	45	48	93	85	164	149
Uzbekistan	1996	15	13	91	92	87	90	50	37	65	46
Vietnam	2002	..	..	84	82	72	73	25	25	34	31
Yemen, Rep.	1997	33	30	45	40	41	39	98	80	128	114
Zambia	2001–02	21	21	83	86	78	82	95	93	176	160
Zimbabwe	1999	12	11	77	81	80	82	63	56	95	85

a. Refers to children who were immunized at any time before the survey.

	Survey year	Pregnant women receiving prenatal care		Contraceptive prevalence rate		Births attended by skilled health staff[a]		Total fertility rate		Exclusive breastfeeding	
		%		modern methods % of married women ages 15–49		% of total		births per woman		% of children under 4 months	
		Poorest quintile	Richest quintile	Poorest quintile	Richest quintile	Poorest quintile	Richest quintile	Poorest quintile	Richest quintile	Poorest quintile	Richest quintile
Armenia	2000	85	97	16	29	93	100	2.5	1.6	..	..
Bangladesh	2004	25	81	45	50	3	39	4.1	2.2	62	31
Benin	2001	73	100	4	15	50	99	7.2	3.5	50	42[b]
Bolivia	2003	62	98	23	49	27	98	6.7	2.0	79	31
Brazil	1996	72	98	56	77	72	99	4.8	1.7	33	60[b]
Burkina Faso	2003	56	96	2	27	19	84	6.6	3.6	17	28
Cambodia	2000	22	80	13	25	15	81	4.7	2.2	14	18
Cameroon	2004	65	97	2	27	29	95	6.5	3.2	33	30[b]
Central African Republic	1994–95	39	91	1	9	14	82	5.1	4.9	9	4
Chad	2004	9	77	0	7	1	51	5.1	6.0	1	2
Colombia	2005	84	99	60	72	72	99	4.1	1.4	60	64
Comoros	1996	67	95	7	19	26	85	6.4	3.0	3[b]	..
Côte d'Ivoire	1994	62	98	1	13	17	84	6.4	3.7	0	5
Dominican Republic	2002	97	99	59	70	94	100	4.5	2.1	18	6
Egypt, Arab Rep.	2000	31	84	43	61	31	94	4.0	2.9	72	57
Eritrea	1995	34	90	0[c]	19	5	74	8.0	3.7	64	73
Ethiopia	2000	15	60	3	23	1	25	6.3	3.6	63	46
Gabon	2000	85	98	6	18	67	97	6.3	3.0	6	5[b]
Ghana	2003	83	98	9	26	21	90	6.4	2.8	62[b]	..
Guatemala	1998–99	37	97	5	60	9	92	7.6	2.9	62	..
Guinea	1999	58	97	1	9	12	82	5.8	4.0	9	8
Haiti	2000	65	91	17	24	4	70	6.8	2.7	40	15[b]
India	1998–99	44	93	29	55	16	84	3.4	1.8	64	37
Indonesia	2002–03	78	99	49	58	40	94	3.0	2.2	58	35
Jordan	1997	93	97	28	47	91	99	5.2	3.1	14	14[b]
Kazakhstan	1999	97	91	49	55	99	99	3.4	1.2	..	..
Kenya	2003	75	94	12	44	17	75	7.6	3.1	22	17
Kyrgyz Republic	1997	96	99	44	54	96	100	4.6	2.0	18[b]	..
Madagascar	1997	67	96	2	24	30	89	8.1	3.4	57	65
Malawi	2000	89	98	20	40	43	83	7.1	4.8	53	72
Mali	2001	42	92	4	18	22	89	7.3	5.3	38	18
Mauritania	2000–01	33	89	0[c]	17	15	93	5.4	3.5	28	30
Morocco	2003–04	40	93	51	57	29	95	3.3	1.9	53	36
Mozambique	2003	67	98	14	37	25	89	6.3	3.8	47	27
Namibia	2000	81	96	29	64	55	97	6.0	2.7	100[b]	85[b]
Nepal	2001	30	80	24	55	4	45	5.3	2.3	76	67
Nicaragua	2001	69	97	50	71	78	99	5.6	2.1	53	15[b]
Niger	1998	24	85	1	18	4	63	8.4	5.7	1	3
Nigeria	2003	37	96	4	21	13	85	6.5	4.2	15	34
Pakistan	1990–91	8	72	1	23	5	55	5.1	4.0	36	9
Paraguay	1990	73	98	21	46	41	98	7.9	2.7	7	0
Peru	2000	41	74	37	58	13	88	5.5	1.6	88	59
Philippines	2003	72	97	24	35	25	92	5.9	2.0	60	20
Rwanda	2000	90	95	2	15	17	60	6.0	5.4	89	79
Senegal	1997	67	97	1	24	20	86	7.4	3.6	13	19
South Africa	1998	96	94	34	70	68	98	4.8	1.9	15	11[b]
Tanzania	2004	91	97	11	36	31	87	7.3	3.3	58	55
Togo	1998	69	97	3	13	25	91	7.3	2.9	7	34
Turkey	1998	38	96	24	48	53	98	3.9	1.7	10	4[b]
Turkmenistan	2000	98	97	51	50	97	98	3.4	2.1	11	28[b]
Uganda	2000–01	88	98	11	41	20	77	8.5	4.1	73	59
Uzbekistan	1996	93	96	46	52	92	100	4.4	2.2	..	..
Vietnam	2002	68	100	58	52	58	100	2.2	1.4	18	..
Yemen, Rep.	1997	17	68	1	24	7	50	7.3	4.7	20	13
Zambia	2001–02	89	99	11	53	20	91	7.3	3.6	39	70[b]
Zimbabwe	1999	94	97	41	67	57	94	4.9	2.6	36	46[b]

a. Based on births in the five years before the survey. b. The data contain large sampling errors because of the small number of cases. c. Less than 0.5.

Health gaps by income and gender

About the data

The data in the table describe the health status and use of health services by individuals in different socioeconomic groups and by sex within countries. The data are from Demographic and Health Surveys conducted by Macro International with the support of the U.S. Agency for International Development. These large-scale household sample surveys, conducted periodically in developing countries, collect information on many health, nutrition, and population measures as well as on respondents' social, demographic, and economic characteristics using a standard set of questionnaires. The data presented here draw on responses to individual and household questionnaires.

Socioeconomic status as displayed in the table is based on a household's assets, including ownership of consumer items, features of the household's dwelling, and other characteristics related to wealth. Each household asset on which information was collected was assigned a weight generated through principal-component analysis. The resulting scores were standardized in relation to a standard normal distribution with a mean of zero and a standard deviation of one. The standardized scores were then used to create break-points defining wealth quintiles, expressed as quintiles of individuals in the population rather than quintiles of individuals at risk with respect to any one health indicator.

The choice of the asset index for defining socioeconomic status was based on pragmatic rather than conceptual considerations: Demographic and Health Surveys do not collect income or consumption data but do have detailed information on households' ownership of consumer goods and access to a variety of goods and services. Like income or consumption, the asset index defines disparities primarily in economic terms. It therefore excludes other possibilities of disparities among groups, such as those based on gender, education, ethnic background, or other facets of social exclusion. To that extent the index provides only a partial view of the multidimensional concepts of poverty, inequality, and inequity.

Creating one index that includes all asset indicators limits the types of analysis that can be performed. In particular, the use of a unified index does not permit a disaggregated analysis to examine which asset indicators are more closely associated with health status or use of health services. In addition, some asset indicators may reflect household wealth better in some countries than in others—or reflect different degrees of wealth in different countries. Taking such information into account and creating country-specific asset indexes with country-specific choices of asset indicators might produce a more effective and accurate index for each country. The asset index used in the table does not have this flexibility.

The analysis was carried out for 56 countries, with the results issued in country reports. The table shows the estimates for the poorest and richest quintiles and by sex only; the full set of estimates for up to 117 indicators is available in the country reports (see Data sources).

Demographic and Health Surveys try to collect internationally comparable data, but the age group of the reference population could differ across countries. Caution should be used when comparing the data. The estimates in the table are based on survey data, which refer to a period preceding the survey date, or use a definition or methodology different from the estimates in tables 2.17–2.19 and 2.22. Thus the estimates may differ from those in the other tables, and caution should be used in interpreting the data.

Definitions

• **Survey year** is the year in which the underlying data were collected. • **Prevalence of child malnutrition** is the percentage of children under age 5 whose weight for age is two to three standard deviations below the median reference standard for their age. The table presents malnutrition data using both the old reference standards and the new international child growth standards released in 2006 by the World Health Organization. For more information about the change in standards, see About the data for table 2.19. • **Child immunization rate** is the percentage of children ages 12–23 months at the time of the survey who, at any time before the survey, had received measles vaccine and three doses of diphtheria, tetanus, and pertussis (whooping cough) vaccine (DTP3). • **Infant mortality rate** is the number of infants dying before reaching one year of age, per 1,000 live births. • **Under-five mortality rate** is the probability that a newborn baby will die before reaching age 5, per 1,000, if subject to current age-specific mortality rates. • **Pregnant women receiving prenatal care** are the percentage of women with one or more births during the five years preceding the survey who were attended by skilled health personnel at least once during pregnancy for reasons related to pregnancy. • **Contraceptive prevalence rate** is the percentage of women married or in-union ages 15–49 who are practicing, or whose sexual partners are practicing, any modern method of contraception. • **Births attended by skilled health staff** are the percentage of deliveries attended by personnel trained to give the necessary supervision, care, and advice to women during pregnancy, labor, and the postpartum period; to conduct deliveries on their own; and to care for newborns. Skilled health staff include doctors, nurses, and trained midwives, but exclude trained or untrained traditional birth attendants. • **Total fertility rate** is the number of children that would be born to a woman if she were to live to the end of her childbearing years and bear children in accordance with current age-specific fertility rates. • **Exclusive breastfeeding** refers to the percentage of children ages 0–3 months who received only breast milk in the 24 hours preceding the survey.

Data sources

Data on health gaps by income and gender are from Davidson R. Gwatkin and others' Socio-Economic Differences in Health, Nutrition, and Population (2007). Country reports are available at www.worldbank.org/povertyandhealth/countrydata.

	Life expectancy at birth		Infant mortality rate		Under-five mortality rate		Child mortality rate		Adult mortality rate		Survival to age 65	
	years		per 1,000 live births		per 1,000		per 1,000		per 1,000		% of cohort	
							Male	Female	Male	Female	Male	Female
	1990	2007	1990	2007	1990	2007	2000–07[a,b]	2000–07[a,b]	2005–07[a]	2005–07[a]	2007	2007
Afghanistan	..	..	..	..	..	..	..	..	..	..	..	..
Albania	72	76	37	13	46	15	3	1	106	51	81	90
Algeria	67	72	54	33	69	37	..	..	121	102	78	81
Angola	40	43	150	116	258	158	..	..	479	434	30	36
Argentina	72	75	25	15	29	16	..	..	166	79	74	87
Armenia	68	72	48	22	56	24	8	3	195	87	68	83
Australia	77	81	8	5	10	6	..	..	84	48	88	93
Austria	76	80	8	4	10	4	..	..	111	55	84	93
Azerbaijan	66	67	78	34	98	39	9	5	216	102	62	77
Bangladesh	55	64	105	47	151	61	24	29	231	198	62	67
Belarus	71	70	20	12	24	13	..	..	330	115	52	82
Belgium	76	80	8	4	10	5	..	..	111	61	84	92
Benin	53	57	111	78	184	123	64	65	279	235	53	59
Bolivia	59	66	89	48	125	57	20	26	235	176	63	71
Bosnia and Herzegovina	72	75	18	13	22	14	..	..	145	76	76	86
Botswana	63	51	45	33	57	40	..	..	567	567	32	36
Brazil	67	72	49	20	58	22	..	..	229	120	67	80
Bulgaria	72	73	15	10	19	12	..	..	221	92	70	86
Burkina Faso	50	52	112	104	206	191	110	113	283	183	47	58
Burundi	46	49	113	108	189	180	..	..	404	370	40	45
Cambodia	55	60	87	70	119	91	20	20	346	243	50	61
Cameroon	55	50	85	87	139	148	73	72	414	420	41	43
Canada	77	81	7	5	8	6	..	..	94	57	86	92
Central African Republic	50	45	113	113	171	172	74	82	559	533	28	34
Chad	51	51	120	124	201	209	96	101	355	308	43	49
Chile	74	78	18	8	21	9	..	..	129	64	80	89
China	68	73	36	19	45	22	..	..	151	90	75	83
Hong Kong, China	77	82	..	..	..	..	..	..	77	33	87	94
Colombia	68	73	28	17	35	20	4	3	202	95	71	83
Congo, Dem. Rep.	46	46	127	108	200	161	70	64	435	400	36	40
Congo, Rep.	57	55	67	79	104	125	49	43	391	367	45	50
Costa Rica	76	79	16	10	18	11	..	..	114	61	82	89
Côte d'Ivoire	53	48	104	89	151	127	..	..	420	403	38	43
Croatia	72	76	11	5	13	6	..	..	156	61	76	89
Cuba	75	78	11	5	13	7	..	..	117	72	82	88
Czech Republic	71	77	11	3	13	4	..	..	148	66	78	90
Denmark	75	78	8	4	9	4	..	..	116	69	83	89
Dominican Republic	68	72	53	31	66	38	6	4	219	131	68	79
Ecuador	69	75	43	20	57	22	5	5	169	90	75	85
Egypt, Arab Rep.	62	71	68	30	93	36	10	10	155	91	73	83
El Salvador	66	72	47	21	60	24	..	..	207	125	70	80
Eritrea	49	58	88	46	147	70	55	50	418	319	42	54
Estonia	69	73	12	4	18	6	..	..	283	92	59	85
Ethiopia	48	53	122	75	204	119	56	56	361	325	45	50
Finland	75	79	6	3	7	4	..	..	133	57	83	92
France	77	81	7	4	9	4	..	..	123	57	84	93
Gabon	61	57	60	60	92	91	32	33	379	383	49	51
Gambia, The	51	59	104	82	153	109	46	39	219	181	58	63
Georgia	70	71	41	27	47	30	5	4	213	81	67	84
Germany	75	80	7	4	9	4	..	..	107	56	84	92
Ghana	57	60	76	73	120	115	51	35	285	281	57	59
Greece	77	80	9	4	11	4	..	..	91	41	85	93
Guatemala	63	70	60	29	82	39	..	..	236	130	67	79
Guinea	47	56	137	93	231	150	89	86	272	235	52	59
Guinea-Bissau	42	46	142	118	240	198	110	88	447	401	35	41
Haiti	55	61	105	57	152	76	33	36	306	237	55	63

	Life expectancy at birth		Infant mortality rate		Under-five mortality rate		Child mortality rate		Adult mortality rate		Survival to age 65	
	years		per 1,000 live births		per 1,000		per 1,000		per 1,000		% of cohort	
							Male	Female	Male	Female	Male	Female
	1990	2007	1990	2007	1990	2007	2000–07[a,b]	2000–07[a,b]	2005–07[a]	2005–07[a]	2007	2007
Honduras	66	70	45	20	58	24	8	9	238	139	66	78
Hungary	69	73	15	6	17	7	..	..	256	107	67	86
India	60	65	80	54	117	72	9	12	257	164	60	69
Indonesia	62	71	60	25	91	31	13	11	168	118	72	80
Iran, Islamic Rep.	65	71	54	29	72	33	..	..	152	101	73	81
Iraq	62	..	42	..	53	..	..	..	..	..	..	..
Ireland	75	79	8	4	9	4	..	..	88	56	85	91
Israel	77	81	10	4	12	5	..	..	80	38	87	93
Italy	77	81	8	3	9	4	..	..	84	44	86	93
Jamaica	72	73	28	26	33	31	5	6	220	139	70	79
Japan	79	83	5	3	6	4	..	..	90	44	87	94
Jordan	67	73	33	21	40	24	3	2	164	113	73	81
Kazakhstan	68	66	51	28	60	32	5	4	361	144	50	77
Kenya	59	54	64	80	97	121	42	39	417	396	43	48
Korea, Dem. Rep.	70	67	42	42	55	55	..	..	179	127	66	75
Korea, Rep.	71	79	8	4	9	5	..	..	109	45	82	92
Kuwait	75	78	13	9	15	11	..	..	86	52	85	90
Kyrgyz Republic	68	68	62	34	74	38	8	4	279	131	57	75
Lao PDR	55	64	120	56	163	70	..	..	233	190	62	68
Latvia	69	71	14	7	17	9	..	..	311	114	64	86
Lebanon	69	72	32	26	37	29	..	..	153	101	74	82
Lesotho	59	43	81	68	102	84	22	19	723	720	19	22
Liberia	43	46	138	93	205	133	57	51	460	425	33	38
Libya	68	74	35	17	41	18	..	..	148	92	75	84
Lithuania	71	71	10	7	16	8	..	..	346	116	63	86
Macedonia, FYR	71	74	33	15	38	17	2	1	135	80	77	85
Madagascar	51	59	103	70	168	112	45	45	287	227	55	62
Malawi	49	48	124	71	209	111	52	54	526	519	34	37
Malaysia	70	74	16	10	22	11	..	..	152	87	75	85
Mali	48	54	148	117	250	196	117	114	255	178	49	59
Mauritania	58	64	81	75	130	119	50	48	172	106	64	74
Mauritius	69	72	20	13	24	15	..	..	207	106	68	82
Mexico	71	75	42	29	52	35	..	..	142	79	78	86
Moldova	67	69	30	16	37	18	7	4	294	138	59	77
Mongolia	61	67	71	35	98	43	11	10	262	171	59	71
Morocco	64	71	69	32	89	34	9	11	148	98	74	82
Mozambique	44	42	135	115	201	168	61	64	625	613	24	27
Myanmar	59	62	91	74	130	103	..	..	298	190	54	67
Namibia	62	53	57	47	87	68	24	19	518	512	37	41
Nepal	54	64	99	43	142	55	21	18	230	206	62	66
Netherlands	77	80	7	4	9	5	..	..	81	59	86	91
New Zealand	75	80	8	5	11	6	..	..	92	59	87	91
Nicaragua	64	73	52	28	68	35	10	9	209	120	70	80
Niger	47	57	143	83	304	176	138	135	166	180	60	58
Nigeria	47	47	120	97	230	189	57	57	434	416	37	39
Norway	77	80	7	3	9	4	..	..	86	53	87	92
Oman	70	76	25	11	32	12	..	..	99	73	82	87
Pakistan	60	65	102	73	132	90	14	22	174	142	66	69
Panama	72	76	27	18	34	23	..	..	139	74	78	87
Papua New Guinea	55	57	69	50	94	65	..	..	422	306	41	55
Paraguay	68	72	34	24	41	29	..	..	174	128	72	79
Peru	66	71	58	17	78	20	11	8	200	123	70	80
Philippines	66	72	43	23	62	28	14	9	158	104	73	82
Poland	71	75	19	6	17	7	..	..	209	80	72	89
Portugal	74	78	11	3	15	4	..	..	128	53	83	91
Puerto Rico	75	78	..	..	..	..	..	..	134	53	80	91

	Life expectancy at birth		Infant mortality rate		Under-five mortality rate		Child mortality rate		Adult mortality rate		Survival to age 65	
	years		per 1,000 live births		per 1,000		per 1,000		per 1,000		% of cohort	
							Male	Female	Male	Female	Male	Female
	1990	2007	1990	2007	1990	2007	2000–07[a,b]	2000–07[a,b]	2005–07[a]	2005–07[a]	2007	2007
Romania	70	73	27	13	32	15	..	..	201	85	69	85
Russian Federation	69	68	23	13	27	15	..	..	429	158	43	77
Rwanda	32	46	117	109	195	181	90	87	456	408	34	40
Saudi Arabia	68	73	35	20	44	25	3	4	140	90	76	84
Senegal	57	63	72	59	149	114	69	69	171	102	63	73
Serbia	71	73	..	7	..	8	4	3	157[c]	83[c]	74[c]	85[c]
Sierra Leone	39	43	169	155	290	262	134	124	405	345	33	40
Singapore	74	80	7	2	8	3	..	..	81	46	86	92
Slovak Republic	71	74	12	7	15	8	..	..	196	76	71	88
Slovenia	73	78	8	3	11	4	..	..	149	57	80	91
Somalia	42	48	121	88	203	142	53	54	385	335	39	44
South Africa	62	50	49	46	64	59	13	9	623	598	27	33
Spain	77	81	8	4	9	4	..	..	106	44	85	94
Sri Lanka	70	72	26	17	32	21	..	..	233	99	67	83
Sudan	53	59	79	69	125	109	38	30	305	265	53	59
Swaziland	58	40	70	66	96	91	32	30	772	760	15	18
Sweden	78	81	6	3	7	3	..	..	78	48	88	93
Switzerland	77	82	7	4	9	5	..	..	78	46	87	93
Syrian Arab Republic	68	74	30	15	37	17	5	3	124	84	78	85
Tajikistan	63	67	91	57	117	67	18	13	211	139	63	73
Tanzania	51	52	96	73	157	116	56	52	433	401	41	46
Thailand	67	71	26	6	31	7	..	..	264	159	64	77
Timor-Leste	47	61	138	77	184	97	..	..	266	232	57	62
Togo	58	58	89	65	150	100	55	43	278	236	54	61
Trinidad and Tobago	70	70	30	31	34	35	..	..	240	190	66	73
Tunisia	70	74	41	18	52	21	..	..	124	72	78	86
Turkey	66	72	67	21	82	23	9	9	152	85	73	84
Turkmenistan	63	63	81	45	99	50	19	17	298	142	53	72
Uganda	50	51	106	82	175	130	75	62	429	416	41	44
Ukraine	70	68	22	20	25	24	4	1	385	142	51	80
United Arab Emirates	73	79	13	7	15	8	..	..	74	49	86	91
United Kingdom	76	79	8	5	10	6	..	..	96	60	85	91
United States	75	78	9	7	11	8	..	..	141	82	81	88
Uruguay	73	76	21	12	25	14	..	..	142	67	77	88
Uzbekistan	69	67	61	36	74	41	11	7	240	136	61	74
Venezuela, RB	71	74	27	17	32	19	..	..	179	94	73	84
Vietnam	66	74	40	13	56	15	5	4	137	91	78	84
West Bank and Gaza	69	73	33	24	38	27	3	3	129	92	78	84
Yemen, Rep.	54	63	90	55	127	73	10	11	254	205	59	66
Zambia	48	42	99	103	163	170	89	74	620	619	25	27
Zimbabwe	61	43	62	59	95	90	21	21	687	719	22	22
World	**65 w**	**69 w**	**63 w**	**47 w**	**93 w**	**68 w**			**219 w**	**155 w**	**68 w**	**76 w**
Low income	54	57	103	80	164	126			306	269	53	58
Middle income	65	70	55	35	75	45			201	127	68	78
Lower middle income	64	69	58	38	81	50			197	125	68	77
Upper middle income	69	71	39	21	47	24			225	138	64	80
Low & middle income	63	67	69	51	101	74			224	159	65	74
East Asia & Pacific	67	72	42	22	56	27			163	102	74	81
Europe & Central Asia	69	70	41	21	49	23			303	125	58	81
Latin America & Carib.	68	73	44	22	55	26			196	107	71	82
Middle East & N. Africa	64	70	58	32	77	38			164	112	72	80
South Asia	59	64	87	59	125	78			248	169	60	69
Sub-Saharan Africa	50	51	108	89	183	146			417	390	41	45
High income	76	79	10	6	12	7			117	63	83	91
Euro area	76	80	8	4	10	4			112	54	84	92

a. Data are for the most recent year available. b. Refers to a survey year. Values were estimated directly from surveys and cover the 5 or 10 years preceding the survey. c. Includes Kosovo.

About the data

Mortality rates for different age groups (infants, children, and adults) and overall mortality indicators (life expectancy at birth or survival to a given age) are important indicators of health status in a country. Because data on the incidence and prevalence of diseases are frequently unavailable, mortality rates are often used to identify vulnerable populations. And they are among the indicators most frequently used to compare socioeconomic development across countries.

The main sources of mortality data are vital registration systems and direct or indirect estimates based on sample surveys or censuses. A "complete" vital registration system—covering at least 90 percent of vital events in the population—is the best source of age-specific mortality data. Where reliable age-specific mortality data are available, life expectancy at birth is directly estimated from the life table constructed from age- specific mortality data.

But complete vital registration systems are fairly uncommon in developing countries. Thus estimates must be obtained from sample surveys or derived by applying indirect estimation techniques to registration, census, or survey data (see *Primary data documentation*). Survey data are subject to recall error, and surveys estimating infant deaths require large samples because households in which a birth or an infant death has occurred during a given year cannot ordinarily be pre-selected for sampling. Indirect estimates rely on model life tables that may be inappropriate for the population concerned. Because life expectancy at birth is estimated using infant mortality data and model life tables for many developing countries, similar reliability issues arise for this indicator. Extrapolations based on outdated surveys may not be reliable for monitoring changes in health status or for comparative analytical work.

Estimates of infant and under-five mortality tend to vary by source and method for a given time and place. Years for available estimates also vary by country, making comparison across countries and over time difficult. To make infant and under-five mortality estimates comparable and to ensure consistency across estimates by different agencies, the United Nations Children's Fund (UNICEF) and the World Bank (now working together with other organizations as the Inter-agency Group for Child Mortality Estimation) developed and adopted a statistical method that uses all available information to reconcile differences. The method uses the weighted least squares method to fit a regression line to the relationship between mortality rates and

their reference dates and then extrapolate the trend to the present. (For further discussion of childhood mortality estimates, see UNICEF, WHO, World Bank, and United Nations Population Division 2007; for a graphic presentation and detailed background data, see www.childmortality.org/).

Infant and child mortality rates are higher for boys than for girls in countries in which parental gender preferences are insignificant. Child mortality captures the effect of gender discrimination better than infant mortality does, as malnutrition and medical interventions are more important in this age group. Where female child mortality is higher, as in some countries in South Asia, girls probably have unequal access to resources. Child mortality rates in the table are not compatible with infant mortality and under-five mortality rates because of differences in methodology and reference year. Child mortality data were estimated directly from surveys and cover the 10 years preceding the survey. In addition to estimates from Demographic Health Surveys, new estimates derived from Multiple Indicator Cluster Surveys (MICS) 3 have been added to the table; they cover the 5 years preceding the survey.

Rates for adult mortality and survival to age 65 come from life tables. Adult mortality rates increased notably in a dozen countries in Sub-Saharan Africa between 1995–2000 and 2000–05 and in several countries in Europe and Central Asia during the first half of the 1990s. In Sub-Saharan Africa the increase stems from AIDS-related mortality and affects both sexes, though women are more affected. In Europe and Central Asia the causes are more diverse (high prevalence of smoking, high-fat diet, excessive alcohol use, stressful conditions related to the economic transition) and affect men more.

The percentage of a hypothetical cohort surviving to age 65 reflects both child and adult mortality rates. Like life expectancy, it is a synthetic measure based on current age-specific mortality rates. It shows that even in countries where mortality is high, a certain share of the current birth cohort will live well beyond the life expectancy at birth, while in low-mortality countries close to 90 percent will reach at least age 65.

Definitions

• **Life expectancy at birth** is the number of years a newborn infant would live if prevailing patterns of mortality at the time of its birth were to stay the same throughout its life. • **Infant mortality rate** is the number of infants dying before reaching one year of age, per 1,000 live births in a given year. • **Under-five mortality rate** is the probability per 1,000 that a newborn baby will die before reaching age 5, if subject to current age-specific mortality rates. • **Child mortality rate** is the probability per 1,000 of dying between ages 1 and 5—that is, the probability of a 1-year-old dying before reaching age 5—if subject to current age-specific mortality rates. • **Adult mortality rate** is the probability per 1,000 of dying between the ages of 15 and 60—that is, the probability of a 15-year-old dying before reaching age 60—if subject to current age-specific mortality rates between those ages. • **Survival to age 65** refers to the percentage of a hypothetical cohort of newborn infants that would survive to age 65, if subject to current age-specific mortality rates.

Data sources

Data on infant and under-five mortality rates are the estimates by the Inter-agency Group for Child Mortality Estimation (which comprises the World Health Organization, UNICEF, United Nations Population Division, World Bank, Harvard University, U.S. Census Bureau, Economic Commission for Latin America and the Caribbean, Measure DHS, and other universities and research institutes) and are based mainly on household surveys, censuses, and vital registration data, supplemented by the World Bank's estimates based on household surveys and vital registration and sample registration data. Data on child mortality rates are from Demographic and Health Surveys by Macro International (Measure DHS) and Multiple Indicator Cluster Surveys by UNICEF. Other estimates are compiled and produced by the World Bank's Human Development Network and Development Data Group in consultation with its operational staff and country offices. Important inputs to the World Bank's demographic work come from the United Nations Population Division's *World Population Prospects: The 2006 Revision,* census reports and other statistical publications from national statistical offices and Eurostat, Demographic and Health Surveys by Macro International, and the Human Mortality Database by the University of California, Berkeley, and the Max Planck Institute for Demographic Research (www.mortality.org).

ENVIRONMENT

Energy and a changing climate

The world economy needs ever-increasing amounts of energy to sustain economic growth, raise living standards, and reduce poverty. But today's trends in energy use are not sustainable. As the world's population grows and economies become more industrialized, nonrenewable energy sources will become scarcer and more costly. And carbon dioxide emissions from the use of fossil fuels will continue to build in the atmosphere, accelerating global warming. Energy-related carbon dioxide now accounts for 61–65 percent of global greenhouse gas emissions (IEA 2008a; IPCC 2007a; WRI 2005). Global warming will have particularly pernicious effects for developing economies, with their high exposure and low adaptive capacity. Where energy comes from, how we produce it, and how much we use will profoundly affect development in the 21st century.

This introduction focuses on recent trends in energy use and carbon dioxide emissions—and projections through 2030. There is now a consensus that action is needed to curb the growth in human-made greenhouse-gas emissions (IPCC 2007b; IEA 2008a). A new post-2012 policy regime on global climate change—to be agreed in Copenhagen in late 2009—aims to set a quantified global goal for stabilizing greenhouse gases in the atmosphere and to establish robust policy mechanisms that ensure the goal is achieved.

Without government initiatives on energy or climate change, global temperatures may rise as much as 6°C by the end of the century. This outcome of the Intergovernmental Panel on Climate Change Trend Scenario can be compared with a 3°C rise under a Policy Scenario in which greenhouse gasses are stabilized at 550 parts per million (ppm) of carbon dioxide equivalent and a 2°C rise under a Policy Scenario in which concentrations are stabilized at 450 ppm. The consequences of the Trend Scenario go well beyond what the international community regards as acceptable.

The global financial and economic crisis, while reducing the demand for energy in the short run, may also slow efforts at energy saving by lowering the price of oil and other fossil energy sources. And by discouraging investments in fossil fuel substitutes and more energy-efficient production processes, the crisis may leave the world on a higher carbon dioxide emission path. The world's largest economy and biggest contributor to carbon dioxide emissions has new leadership that could make climate change a top priority and commit resources to finding alternative sources of cleaner energy.

Energy use: unsustainable trend, unacceptable future

In 2006 global energy use from all sources reached 11.5 billion metric tons of oil equivalent—twice as high as its 1971 level (figure 3a). High-income economies, with just 15 percent of world population, use almost half of global energy (figure 3b). Energy use grew by 2.4 percent a year in low-income economies, 2.0 percent in middle-income economies, and 1.6 percent in high-income economies over 1990–2006. It rose 4.4 percent a year in China and 3.5 percent in India. The United States, Russian Federation, Germany, Japan, China, and India are the top energy consumers, accounting for 55 percent of global energy use (figure 3c and table 3.7). On average, high-income economies use more than 11 times the energy per capita of low-income economies, with huge differences across countries and within countries and regions (figure 3d).

The accelerating trend in energy use and the potential consequences have been matters of concern for the international community. The recent global financial crisis, economic downturn, and significant fluctuations in the price of energy, particularly oil, make projections of energy demand difficult. The International Energy Agency forecasts that energy demand in 2030 will be 45 percent higher than energy use in 2006, for an average annual growth of 1.6 percent, or just a little slower than the 1.9 percent from 1980 to 2006 (IEA 2008a, b). More than 80 percent of the energy used in 2006 was from nonrenewable fuels—carbon dioxide–emitting oil, coal, and gas. In the absence of new policies this share is projected to remain above 80 percent in 2030, with demand for coal—cheaper and more abundant—growing faster than that for oil and gas (figure 3e and table 3f).

Growing 2 percent a year on average, world demand for coal is projected to be 60 percent higher in 2030 than in 2006. Most of the increase in demand comes from the power generation sector. China and India together account for 85 percent of this increase. Oil demand grows far more slowly than demand for other fossil fuels, mainly because of high final prices. Yet, oil remains the dominant fuel in the primary mix, even with the drop in its share from 34 percent in 2006 to 30 percent in 2030.

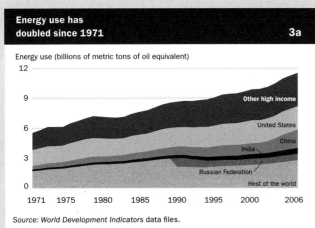

Energy use has doubled since 1971 **3a**

Energy use (billions of metric tons of oil equivalent)

Source: World Development Indicators data files.

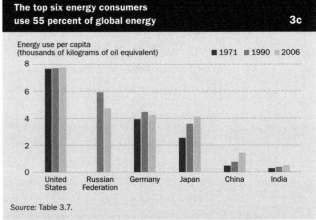

The top six energy consumers use 55 percent of global energy **3c**

Energy use per capita (thousands of kilograms of oil equivalent) ■ 1971 ■ 1990 ■ 2006

Source: Table 3.7.

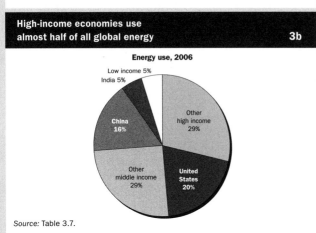

High-income economies use almost half of all global energy **3b**

Energy use, 2006

Low income 5%
India 5%
China 16%
Other high income 29%
Other middle income 29%
United States 20%

Source: Table 3.7.

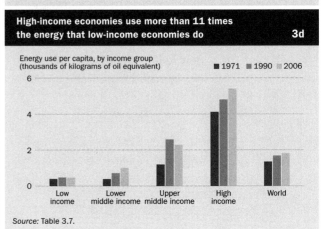

High-income economies use more than 11 times the energy that low-income economies do **3d**

Energy use per capita, by income group (thousands of kilograms of oil equivalent) ■ 1971 ■ 1990 ■ 2006

Source: Table 3.7.

Uncertain supply

It is not going to be easy to meet the expected growth in energy demand, particularly for oil, despite seemingly large available reserves (table 3g). Based on a field by field analysis of production trends, the cost of investment, opportunities for expanding capacity, and possible constraints and risks—both above and below ground—the International Energy Agency has drawn attention to the possibility of an oil-supply crunch by the middle of the 2010s, if upstream investments fall short of requirements. A growing number of oil companies and analysts have suggested that oil production may peak within the next two decades, a result of rising costs, political and geological factors, and limits on the investment that can be mobilized (IEA 2008a). The rate of decline in production from existing fields—especially large, mature fields that have been the mainstay of global output for several decades—has been faster than anticipated (figure 3h). How output from these fields evolves—with or without the deployment of enhanced recovery techniques—will have major implications for the required investment in new fields, which are typically smaller, more complex, and more costly to develop.

Despite the improved environment for emerging, climate-friendly, renewable energy sources and technologies, many barriers remain. The costs of some technologies are high at their early stages, when economies of scale cannot be realized. Research and development were limited until the recent oil price rise. Concerns are growing about the impact on food supplies with more use of crops for energy. And there is skepticism about the net contribution of biofuels to lower greenhouse gas emissions (FAO 2008).

In many countries climate change has risen to the top of the political agenda—the result of a growing body of evidence on global warming and ever more startling predictions of the ecological consequences (IPCC 2007b). The commitment of the new U.S. administration to containing the impact of global climate change and the changing attitudes toward wind and solar energy offer promise of reducing the carbon footprint of energy use.

Nonrenewable fuels are projected to account for 80 percent of energy use in 2030—about the same as in 2006 — 3e

Energy demand, by source
(thousands of megatons of oil equivalent)   ■ 2006 ■ 2030

Source: Table 3.7.

Fossil fuels will remain the main sources of energy through 2030 — 3f

Fuel	1980	2006	2030	Annual growth, 2006–30 (%)
Total (million metric tons oil equivalent)	7,224	11,730	17,014	1.6
Share (% of total)				
Coal	24.8	26.0	28.8	2.0
Oil	43.0	34.3	30.0	1.0
Gas	17.1	20.5	21.6	1.8
Nuclear	2.6	6.2	5.3	0.9
Hydropower	2.0	2.2	2.4	1.9
Biomass and waste	10.4	10.1	9.8	1.4
Other renewables	0.2	0.6	2.1	7.2

Source: IEA 2008a.

Known global oil reserves and countries with highest endowments in 2006 — 3g

Country	Oil reserves (billions of barrels)	Share of world total (%)
Saudi Arabia	264.3	20.4
Canada	178.9	13.8
Iran	132.5	10.3
Iraq	115.0	8.9
Kuwait	101.5	7.9
United Arab Emirates	97.8	7.6
Venezuela, RB	79.7	6.2
Russian Federation	60.0	4.6
Rest of the world	262.8	20.3
Total	1,292.5	

Source: Deutch, Lauvergeon, and Prawiraatmadja 2007.

Production declines from existing oil fields have been rapid — 3h

Production-weighted average post-peak observed decline, by type of producer and year of first production (%)   ■ OPEC ■ Non-OPEC

Source: IEA 2008a.

Energy and climate change

Economic activity, energy use, and carbon dioxide emissions move together (figure 3i). The world is already experiencing the impact of rising average global temperature on physical and biological systems, and the situation is worsening. The 13 warmest years since 1880 have occurred in the last 16 years (IPCC 2007a; Rosenzweig and others 2008). There is a risk of reaching unpredictable tipping points, such as a rise in Arctic temperatures precipitating a massive release of methane from permafrost zones. Thawing permafrost could also threaten oil and gas extraction infrastructure and pipeline stability.

Current carbon dioxide levels

In the 1980s global energy-related carbon dioxide emissions (up 1.7 percent annually) rose more slowly than primary energy demand (up 1.9 percent annually), mainly because the shares of natural gas, nuclear power, and renewables in the power mix expanded. But this decarbonization of energy reversed at the beginning of the 21st century as the share of nuclear energy fell while that of coal rose. In the Trend Scenario recarbonization of the energy sector is projected to continue until after 2020, when changing supply patterns

again cause emissions growth to fall below the rate of growth of primary energy use (figure 3j). But as the world becomes wealthier, energy-related carbon dioxide emissions continue to rise in absolute terms.

World carbon dioxide emissions per capita fell until around 2000, but have since risen rapidly. In the absence of new policies, this upward trend is projected to continue through 2030. Government policies, including those to address climate change, air pollution, and energy security, have slowed the growth in emissions in some countries. But in most, emissions are still rising fast. In 2005 per capita emissions were greatest in the United States, followed by the Russian Federation, Japan, and Germany (table 3.8 and figure 3k). China's per capita emissions were 4.3 tons—close to the global average and about one-third of the level of high-income economies (figure 3l)—while India's were 1.3 tons.

Carbon dioxide emissions are attributed to the country or region consuming the fossil fuel. Yet the consumption benefits from the goods and services produced using the fossil fuel are often realized in a country other than that in which the emissions arise. This concerns some emerging market economies, which tend to be more export-oriented,

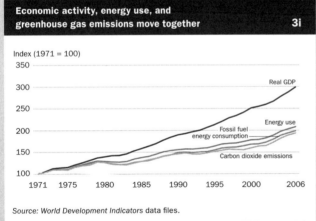

Economic activity, energy use, and greenhouse gas emissions move together 3i

Index (1971 = 100)

Source: World Development Indicators data files.

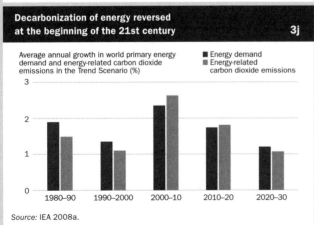

Decarbonization of energy reversed at the beginning of the 21st century 3j

Average annual growth in world primary energy demand and energy-related carbon dioxide emissions in the Trend Scenario (%)

■ Energy demand
■ Energy-related carbon dioxide emissions

Source: IEA 2008a.

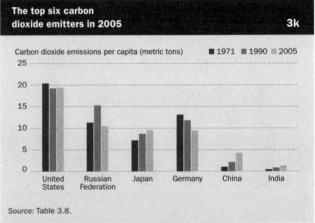

The top six carbon dioxide emitters in 2005 3k

Carbon dioxide emissions per capita (metric tons)   ■ 1971 ■ 1990 ■ 2005

Source: Table 3.8.

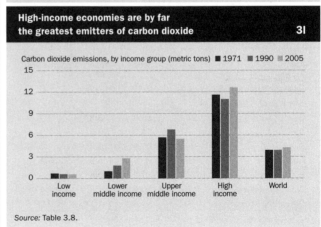

High-income economies are by far the greatest emitters of carbon dioxide 3l

Carbon dioxide emissions, by income group (metric tons)   ■ 1971 ■ 1990 ■ 2005

Source: Table 3.8.

with energy-intensive manufactured exports. A detailed input-output analysis in China tracked the distribution of fuels, raw materials, and intermediate goods to and from industries throughout the economy. Taking carbon intensities and trade data into account, it estimated the energy-related carbon dioxide emissions embedded in domestic production for export at 34 percent of its 2004 emissions (IEA 2007). With China's production facilities expanding rapidly, the figures for later years could be higher (box 3m).

Trend and Policy Scenarios

Annual greenhouse gas emissions are projected to grow from 44 gigatons of carbon dioxide equivalent in 2005 to 60 gigatons in 2030, a 35 percent increase. The share of energy-related carbon dioxide emissions in total emissions is forecast to increase from 61 percent in 2005 to 68 percent in 2030 (IEA 2008a). With emissions of greenhouse gases building in the atmosphere faster than natural processes can remove them, concentrations rise. The Trend Scenario puts us on a path to doubling aggregate concentrations by the end of the century, increasing global average temperatures up to 6°C (IPCC 2007a; IEA 2008a).

In the Trend Scenario rising global use of fossil energy continues to drive up energy-related carbon dioxide emissions over at least the next two decades. Emissions grew by 2.5 gigatons from 1990 to 2000, when their growth accelerated, and increased a further 4.5 gigatons to 28 gigatons by 2006. They are projected to increase a further 45 percent by 2030, approaching 41 gigatons in the Trend Scenario. This acceleration in carbon dioxide emissions calls for urgent stabilization measures.

There is not yet an international consensus on long-term stabilization targets. Most discussions center on stabilization levels between 450 ppm and 550 ppm of carbon dioxide equivalent and their consequences (table 3n and figure 3o; IPCC 2007). The required reduction in energy-related emissions varies with level of international participation by economies sorted by income groups. In both the 450 ppm and 550 ppm Policy Scenarios, even after allowing for international emissions trading and active engagement by non–Organisation for Economic Co-operation and Development (OECD) countries, International Energy Agency projections show that OECD countries would have to substantially reduce emissions domestically (IEA 2008a).

Carbon dioxide emissions embedded in international trade   3m

Energy and energy-related carbon dioxide emissions are embedded in imports as well as exports, and some goods and services are more emissions-intensive than others. There are ways of calculating the emissions embedded in international trade, none of them fully accurate because of the lack of complete, reliable, and up-to-date data. A detailed input-output analysis for China reveals the complexity, involving calculating carbon intensity all along the production chain and across the economy, including outsourcing (IEA 2007; Houser and others 2008).

At the global level the percentage of exports in GDP can be used as a simple proxy for the share of energy-related carbon dioxide emissions embedded in domestic production for export. The countries for which up-to-date trade data are available represent 83 percent of total world energy-related carbon dioxide emissions (IEA 2008a). The International Energy Agency estimate of the share of emissions embedded in exports in 2006 ranges from 15 percent for North America to 48 percent for the Middle East. The difference reflects variations in the amount and type of exports and the carbon intensity of energy use. The shares for China (44 percent) and Asian countries other than China and India (41 percent) are next highest. Of the 23 gigatons of energy-related carbon dioxide emissions in the International Energy Agency sample, one-third were embedded in production for export. China alone accounted for 2.3 gigatons (31 percent) of this, and Europe and the Russian Federation combined for another 1.7 gigatons (23 percent). Africa and Latin America each accounted for just 2 percent of embedded emissions (IEA 2008a).

Impact of Policy Scenarios: carbon dioxide concentration, temperature increase, emissions, and energy demand   3n

| Carbon dioxide concentration (parts per million) | Temperature increase | Global emissions by 2030 (gigatons) | | Global energy demand (metric tons oil equivalent) | |
		Energy-related carbon dioxide	Total greenhouse gases	2020	2030
550	3°C	33	48	14,360	15,480
450	2°C	26[a]	36	14,280	14,360

a. Emissions peak in 2020 at 32.5 gigatons and then decline to 25.7 gigatons in 2030.
Source: IPCC 2007b; IEA 2008a.

Reductions in energy-related carbon dioxide emissions by region in the 550 and 450 parts per million Policy Scenarios relative to the Trend Scenario   3o

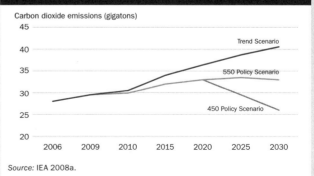

Carbon dioxide emissions (gigatons)

Source: IEA 2008a.

Need for cleaner, more efficient energy

Adequate energy supplies are required for economies to grow and poverty to be reduced, but the current reliance on fossil fuels is not sustainable. Transitioning to new energy sources poses a significant challenge to all economies. Humanity's future on this planet may depend on finding ways to supply the world's growing energy needs without irreparably harming the environment. This could be achieved through new energy technologies, greater energy efficiency, and alternative renewable sources that provide a low-carbon path to growth.

For the low-carbon growth needed to stabilize carbon dioxide emissions, technological innovations are crucial. Because much of today's energy-using capital stock will be replaced only gradually, it will take time before most of the impact of recent and future technological developments that improve energy efficiency are felt. Rates of capital-stock turnover differ greatly by industry and sector. Most of today's cars, trucks, heating and cooling systems, and industrial boilers will be replaced by 2030. But most buildings, roads, railways, and airports and many power stations and refineries will still be in use unless governments encourage or force early retirement. Despite the slow turnover, refurbishment in some cases could significantly improve energy efficiency at an acceptable net economic cost.

On the supply side technological advances can improve the technical and economic efficiency of producing and supplying energy. In some cases they are expected to reduce unit costs and to lead to new and cleaner ways of producing and delivering energy services. Some major new supply-side technologies that are approaching commercialization are expected to become available to some degree before 2030 (IEA 2008a).

- *Carbon capture and storage.* This technology mitigates emissions of carbon dioxide from power plants and other industrial facilities, but it has not yet been deployed on a significant scale (IEA 2008a). The basic technology already exists to capture carbon dioxide gas and transport and store it permanently in geological formations. Four large-scale carbon capture and storage projects are operating around the world, each separating around 1 megaton of carbon dioxide per year from produced natural gas: Sleipner and Snohvit in Norway, Weyburn in Canada (with the carbon dioxide sourced in the United States), and In Salah in Algeria. Yet there are technical, economic, and legal barriers to more widespread deployment, particularly high energy intensity and the cost.

- *Second-generation biofuels.* New biofuel technologies —notably hydrolysis and gasification of woody lignocellulosic feedstock to produce ethanol—are expected to reach commercialization by around 2020. Although the technology already exists, experts believe that more research is needed to improve process efficiencies. There is virtually no commercial production of ethanol yet from cellulosic biomass, but several OECD countries are researching it. A recent Food and Agriculture Organization report is skeptical about the net contribution of biofuels to reduction of greenhouse gasses and blames biofuels production for last year's large food price increases (FAO 2008).

- *Coal-to-liquids.* The conversion of coal to oil products through gasification and synthesis—much like gas to liquid production—has been done commercially for many decades. Yet global production remains limited because it has been uneconomical, mainly because of the large amounts of energy and water used in the process, the high cost of building plants, and the volatility of oil and coal prices.

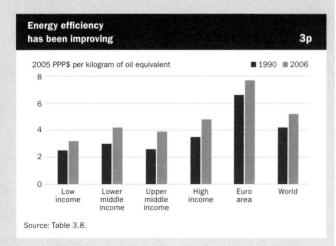

Energy efficiency has been improving   3p

2005 PPP$ per kilogram of oil equivalent ■ 1990 ■ 2006

Source: Table 3.8.

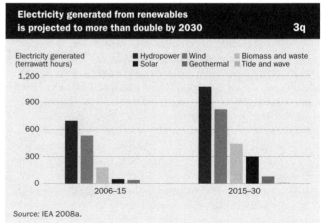

Electricity generated from renewables is projected to more than double by 2030   3q

Electricity generated (terrawatt hours) — ■ Hydropower ■ Wind ■ Solar ■ Geothermal ■ Biomass and waste ■ Tide and wave

Source: IEA 2008a.

Energy efficiency

In recent years there has been an encouraging trend in producing more from each unit of energy (figure 3p), a powerful and cost-effective way to get on the path to a sustainable energy future. Greater energy efficiency can reduce the need for investing in energy infrastructure, cut fuel costs, increase competitiveness, and improve consumer welfare. And by reducing greenhouse gas emissions and air pollution, it can be good for the environment. The International Energy Agency estimates that implementing a host of 25 policy recommendations for promoting energy efficiency could reduce annual carbon dioxide emissions 8.2 gigatons by 2030—equivalent to one-fifth of global energy-related carbon dioxide emissions in the Trend Scenario (IEA 2008b). The recommendations cover policies and technologies for buildings, appliances, transport, and industry as well as end-use applications such as lighting.

Renewable energy

The share of renewables in global primary energy demand, excluding traditional biomass, is projected to climb from 7 percent in 2006 to 10 percent by 2030 in the Trend Scenario (IEA 2008a). This assumes that costs come down as renewable technologies mature, that higher fossil fuel prices make renewables more competitive, and that policy support is strong. The renewables industry could eliminate its reliance on subsidies and bring emerging technologies into the mainstream.

- World renewables-based electricity generation— mostly hydro and wind power—is projected to more than double by 2030 (figure 3q).
- Many countries have already begun exploiting wind to generate electricity (figure 3r). Global wind power is projected to increase 11-fold, becoming the second largest source renewable after hydropower by 2030.

- Biomass, geothermal, and solar thermal met around 6 percent of global heating demand in 2006, a share projected to rise to 7 percent by 2030. Where resources are abundant and conventional energy sources expensive, renewables-based heating can be cost competitive with conventional heating systems.
- The share of biofuels in road transport fuels worldwide is projected to rise from 1.5 percent in 2006 to 5 percent in 2030, spurred by subsidies and high oil prices. Most of the growth comes from the United States, European Union, China, and Brazil.

The cost of power generation from renewables is expected to fall. Greater deployment spurs technological progress and increases economies of scale, lowering investment costs. The costs of the more mature technologies, including geothermal and onshore wind, are assumed to fall least. Renewables account for just under half of the total projected investment in electricity generation. The cost of stabilizing carbon dioxide is significant, but there are also significant savings (box 3s). And the cost of inaction would be far higher.

Cost and savings under the Policy Scenarios   **3s**

The 550 parts per million (ppm) Policy Scenario requires spending $4.1 trillion more on energy efficiency and power plants and reducing consumption of fossil fuels by 22 gigatons of oil equivalent over 2010–30 through more efficient energy use. The International Energy Agency estimates that the net undiscounted savings in the 550 ppm Policy Scenario, compared with the Trend Scenario, amount to more than $4 trillion.

The 450 ppm Policy Scenario requires additional investment of $3.6 trillion in power plants and $5.7 trillion in energy efficiency over 2010–30 relative to the Trend Scenario. This additional investment is much higher in 2021–30 than in 2010–20 (see figure). In the 450 ppm Policy Scenario substantially higher investment is needed in power plants. Also, investment in energy efficiency rises considerably, particularly beyond 2020. During that period improving energy efficiency in buildings will require the highest investment. In the 450 ppm Policy Scenario the additional investment in power plants and demand-side efficiency corresponds to 0.55 percent of cumulative world GDP over 2010–30, compared with 0.24 percent in the 550 ppm Policy Scenario.

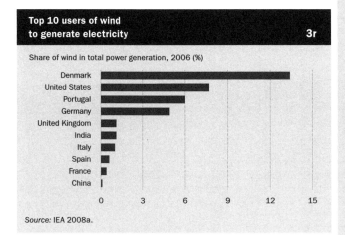

Top 10 users of wind to generate electricity   **3r**

Share of wind in total power generation, 2006 (%)

Source: IEA 2008a.

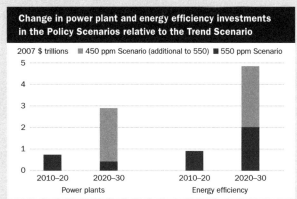

Change in power plant and energy efficiency investments in the Policy Scenarios relative to the Trend Scenario

2007 $ trillions   ■ 450 ppm Scenario (additional to 550)   ■ 550 ppm Scenario

Source: IEA 2008a.

3.1 Rural population and land use

	Rural population			Land area	Land use							
	% of total		average annual % growth	thousand sq. km	Forest area		% of land area Permanent cropland		Arable land		Arable land hectares per 100 people	
	1990	2007	1990–2007	2007	1990	2005	1990	2005	1990	2005	1990–92	2003–05
Afghanistan	..	..	..	652.1	2.0	1.3	0.2	0.2	12.1	12.1	..	..
Albania	64	54	–1.2	27.4	28.8	29.0	4.6	4.5	21.1	21.1	18.7	18.4
Algeria	48	35	–0.1	2,381.7	0.8	1.0	0.2	0.4	3.0	3.1	24.5	23.1
Angola	63	44	0.7	1,246.7	48.9	47.4	0.4	0.2	2.3	2.6	21.2	21.1
Argentina	13	8	–1.6	2,736.7	12.9	12.1	0.4	0.4	9.6	10.4	75.2	74.0
Armenia	33	36	–0.4	28.2	12.0	10.0	2.7	2.1	17.7	17.6	16.1[a]	16.4
Australia	15	11	–0.2	7,682.3	21.9	21.3	0.0	0.0	6.2	6.4	248.9	240.6
Austria	34	33	0.2	82.5	45.8	46.8	1.0	0.8	17.3	16.8	17.3	17.0
Azerbaijan	46	48	1.3	82.7	11.2	11.3	3.7	2.7	20.5	22.3	22.6[a]	22.2
Bangladesh	80	73	1.5	130.2	6.8	6.7	2.3	3.5	70.2	61.1	5.7	5.3
Belarus	34	27	–1.7	207.5	36.0	38.0	0.9	0.6	29.3	26.3	58.4[a]	56.2
Belgium	4	3	–1.4	30.2	23.2[b]	22.1	0.5[b]	0.8	23.9[b]	27.9	8.2	8.1
Benin	66	59	2.7	110.6	30.0	21.3	0.9	2.4	14.6	24.9	33.0	33.0
Bolivia	44	35	0.7	1,084.4	57.9	54.2	0.1	0.2	1.9	2.8	34.9	33.9
Bosnia and Herzegovina	61	53	–1.6	51.2	43.1	42.7	2.9	1.9	16.6	19.5	27.0[a]	26.9
Botswana	58	41	–0.1	566.7	24.2	21.1	0.0	0.0	0.7	0.7	21.5	20.8
Brazil	25	15	–1.6	8,459.4	61.5	56.5	0.8	0.9	6.0	7.0	33.1	32.0
Bulgaria	34	29	–1.6	108.6	30.1	33.4	2.7	1.9	34.9	29.2	43.4	42.0
Burkina Faso	86	81	2.6	273.6	26.1	24.8	0.2	0.2	12.9	17.7	35.9	35.9
Burundi	94	90	2.1	25.7	11.3	5.9	14.0	14.2	36.2	37.8	14.2	13.0
Cambodia	87	79	1.8	176.5	73.3	59.2	0.6	0.9	20.9	21.0	28.4	27.0
Cameroon	59	44	0.7	465.4	52.7	45.6	2.6	2.6	12.8	12.8	36.7	34.2
Canada	23	20	0.0	9,093.5	34.1	34.1	0.7	0.7	5.0	5.0	147.4	142.7
Central African Republic	63	62	2.0	623.0	37.2	36.5	0.1	0.1	3.1	3.1	49.1	46.8
Chad	79	74	2.9	1,259.2	10.4	9.5	0.0	0.0	2.6	3.3	40.7	40.1
Chile	17	12	–0.7	748.8	20.4	21.5	0.3	0.5	3.7	2.6	12.7	12.2
China	73	58	–0.5	9,327.5	16.8	21.2	0.8	1.4	13.3	15.4	11.1	11.0
Hong Kong, China	1	0	..	1.0	..	..	..	..	..	..	..	..
Colombia	32	26	0.5	1,109.5	55.4	54.7	1.5	1.5	3.0	1.8	6.2	5.1
Congo, Dem. Rep.	72	67	2.5	2,267.1	62.0	58.9	0.5	0.5	2.9	3.0	12.9	11.8
Congo, Rep.	46	39	1.7	341.5	66.5	65.8	0.1	0.1	1.4	1.4	15.0	14.0
Costa Rica	49	37	0.5	51.1	50.2	46.8	4.9	6.5	5.1	4.4	5.6	5.3
Côte d'Ivoire	60	52	1.5	318.0	32.1	32.7	11.0	11.3	7.6	11.0	18.2	18.8
Croatia	46	43	–0.8	55.9	37.9	38.2	2.0	2.1	21.7	19.8	32.9[a]	27.6
Cuba	27	24	–0.2	109.8	18.7	24.7	7.4	6.1	27.6	33.4	32.8	32.7
Czech Republic	25	27	0.4	77.3	34.1	34.3	3.1	3.1	41.1	39.4	30.1	29.9
Denmark	15	14	–0.3	42.4	10.5	11.8	0.2	0.2	60.4	52.7	42.6	41.8
Dominican Republic	45	32	–0.3	48.4	28.4	28.4	9.3	10.3	18.6	16.9	9.2	8.8
Ecuador	45	35	0.1	276.8	49.9	39.2	4.8	4.4	5.8	4.9	12.0	10.1
Egypt, Arab Rep.	57	57	1.9	995.5	0.0	0.1	0.4	0.5	2.3	3.0	4.2	4.1
El Salvador	51	40	0.3	20.7	18.1	14.4	12.5	12.1	26.5	31.9	10.4	10.0
Eritrea	84	80	2.2	101.0	15.9	15.4	0.0	0.0	4.9	6.3	14.6	14.0
Estonia	29	31	–0.6	42.4	51.4	53.9	0.3	0.3	26.3	13.9	52.1[a]	40.9
Ethiopia	87	83	2.7	1,000.0	14.7	13.0	0.6	0.8	10.0	13.1	15.1	16.7
Finland	39	37	0.1	304.6	72.9	73.9	0.0	0.0	7.4	7.3	42.2	42.5
France	26	23	–0.2	550.1	26.4	28.3	2.2	2.1	32.7	33.6	31.1	30.5
Gabon	31	15	–1.9	257.7	85.1	84.5	0.6	0.7	1.1	1.3	27.0	25.6
Gambia, The	62	44	1.4	10.0	44.2	47.1	0.5	0.5	18.2	35.0	21.3	21.9
Georgia	45	47	–1.0	69.5	39.7	39.7	4.8	3.8	11.4	11.5	17.1[a]	17.8
Germany	27	26	0.1	348.8	30.8	31.8	1.3	0.6	34.3	34.1	14.3	14.4
Ghana	64	51	1.1	227.5	32.7	24.2	6.6	9.7	11.9	18.4	19.7	19.0
Greece	41	39	0.3	128.9	25.6	29.1	8.3	8.8	22.5	20.4	24.9	24.1
Guatemala	59	52	1.6	108.4	43.8	36.3	4.5	5.6	12.0	13.3	12.2	11.6
Guinea	72	66	2.1	245.7	30.1	27.4	2.0	2.7	3.0	4.9	12.1	13.2
Guinea-Bissau	72	70	2.9	28.1	78.8	73.7	4.2	8.9	10.7	10.7	21.2	19.4
Haiti	72	55	0.2	27.6	4.2	3.8	11.6	11.6	28.3	28.3	8.9	8.5

	Rural population			Land area	Land use							
	% of total		average annual % growth	thousand sq. km	Forest area		Permanent cropland		Arable land		Arable land hectares per 100 people	
	1990	2007	1990–2007	2007	1990	2005	1990	2005	1990	2005	1990–92	2003–05
Honduras	60	53	1.4	111.9	66.0	41.5	3.2	3.2	13.1	9.5	16.9	15.9
Hungary	34	33	−0.4	89.6	20.0	22.1	2.6	2.3	56.2	51.3	45.2	45.5
India	75	71	1.3	2,973.2	21.5	22.8	2.2	3.4	54.8	53.7	15.5	14.8
Indonesia	69	50	−0.6	1,811.6	64.3	48.8	6.5	7.5	11.2	12.7	10.3	10.6
Iran, Islamic Rep.	44	32	−0.3	1,628.6	6.8	6.8	0.8	1.0	9.3	10.2	24.0	24.0
Iraq	30	..	..	437.4	1.8	1.9	0.7	0.6	12.1	13.1	22.0	..
Ireland	43	39	0.7	68.9	6.4	9.7	0.0	0.0	15.1	17.6	29.7	29.5
Israel	10	8	1.7	21.6	7.1	7.9	4.1	3.5	15.9	14.6	5.3	4.8
Italy	33	32	0.0	294.1	28.5	33.9	10.1	8.6	30.6	26.3	14.7	13.6
Jamaica	51	47	0.2	10.8	31.9	31.3	9.2	10.2	11.0	16.1	6.7	6.6
Japan	37	34	−0.3	364.5	68.4	68.2	1.3	0.9	13.1	12.0	3.5	3.4
Jordan	28	22	2.0	88.2	0.9	0.9	0.8	1.0	2.0	2.1	3.9	3.6
Kazakhstan	44	42	−0.5	2,699.7	1.3	1.2	0.1	0.1	13.0	8.3	148.7[a]	149.3
Kenya	82	79	2.5	569.1	6.5	6.2	0.8	0.8	8.8	9.2	15.7	15.1
Korea, Dem. Rep.	42	38	0.4	120.4	68.1	51.4	1.5	1.7	19.0	23.3	11.4	11.7
Korea, Rep.	26	19	−1.2	98.7	64.5	63.5	1.6	2.0	19.8	16.4	3.6	3.4
Kuwait	2	2	0.2	17.8	0.2	0.3	0.1	0.2	0.2	0.8	0.6	0.6
Kyrgyz Republic	62	64	1.1	191.8	4.4	4.5	0.4	0.4	6.9	6.7	27.2[a]	25.9
Lao PDR	85	70	1.0	230.8	75.0	69.9	0.3	0.4	3.5	4.3	17.0	17.8
Latvia	31	32	−0.7	62.3	45.1	47.2	0.4	0.2	27.2	17.5	41.0[a]	44.1
Lebanon	17	13	0.4	10.2	11.8	13.3	11.9	13.9	17.9	18.2	4.7	4.7
Lesotho	86	75	0.5	30.4	0.2	0.3	0.1	0.1	10.4	10.9	17.3	16.8
Liberia	55	41	1.6	96.3	42.1	32.7	2.2	2.3	4.2	4.0	12.0	11.4
Libya	24	23	1.6	1,759.5	0.1	0.1	0.2	0.2	1.0	1.0	33.3	30.6
Lithuania	32	33	−0.4	62.7	31.3	33.5	0.7	0.6	46.0	30.4	58.8[a]	49.0
Macedonia, FYR	42	34	−1.0	25.4	35.6	35.6	2.2	1.8	23.8	22.3	27.9[a]	27.9
Madagascar	76	71	2.4	581.5	23.5	22.1	1.0	1.0	4.7	5.1	17.6	16.3
Malawi	88	82	1.8	94.1	41.4	36.2	1.2	1.5	19.3	27.6	18.4	19.8
Malaysia	50	31	−0.7	328.6	68.1	63.6	16.0	17.6	5.2	5.5	7.6	7.1
Mali	77	68	2.1	1,220.2	11.5	10.3	0.0	0.0	1.7	3.9	45.3	42.6
Mauritania	60	59	2.7	1,030.7	0.4	0.3	0.0	0.0	0.4	0.5	18.5	17.1
Mauritius	56	58	1.2	2.0	19.2	18.2	3.0	3.0	49.3	49.3	8.3	8.1
Mexico	29	23	0.1	1,944.0	35.5	33.0	1.0	1.3	12.5	12.9	25.4	24.6
Moldova	53	58	−0.4	32.9	9.7	10.0	14.2	9.1	52.8	56.2	45.1[a]	47.1
Mongolia	43	43	1.3	1,566.5	7.3	6.5	0.0	0.0	0.9	0.7	49.1	46.7
Morocco	52	44	0.5	446.3	9.6	9.8	1.6	2.1	19.5	19.0	29.7	28.4
Mozambique	79	64	1.4	786.4	25.4	24.5	0.3	0.3	4.4	5.6	21.6	21.8
Myanmar	75	68	0.6	657.6	59.6	49.0	0.8	1.4	14.5	15.3	21.4	21.1
Namibia	72	64	1.5	823.3	10.6	9.3	0.0	0.0	0.8	1.0	42.7	40.9
Nepal	91	83	1.7	143.0	33.7	25.4	0.5	0.9	16.0	16.5	9.4	8.9
Netherlands	31	19	−2.5	33.9	10.2	10.8	0.9	1.0	25.9	26.8	5.7	5.6
New Zealand	15	14	0.5	267.7	28.8	31.0	5.1	7.1	9.9	5.6	38.5	36.7
Nicaragua	48	44	1.2	121.4	53.9	42.7	1.6	1.9	10.7	15.9	37.1	35.7
Niger	85	84	3.4	1,266.7	1.5	1.0	0.0	0.0	8.7	11.4	125.7	113.1
Nigeria	65	52	1.4	910.8	18.9	12.2	2.8	3.3	32.4	35.1	22.6	22.6
Norway	28	23	−0.7	304.3	30.0	30.8	..	..	2.8	2.8	19.6	19.0
Oman	34	28	1.0	309.5	0.0	0.0	0.1	0.1	0.1	0.2	1.6	2.2
Pakistan	69	64	1.9	770.9	3.3	2.5	0.6	1.0	26.6	27.6	15.2	14.1
Panama	46	28	−1.1	74.4	58.8	57.7	2.1	2.0	6.7	7.4	18.1	17.3
Papua New Guinea	85	87	2.7	452.9	69.6	65.0	1.3	1.4	0.4	0.5	3.8	3.9
Paraguay	51	40	0.8	397.3	53.3	46.5	0.2	0.2	5.3	10.6	61.2	70.2
Peru	31	29	1.0	1,280.0	54.8	53.7	0.3	0.5	2.7	2.9	14.2	13.7
Philippines	51	36	0.0	298.2	35.5	24.0	14.8	16.8	18.4	19.1	7.3	6.9
Poland	39	39	0.0	306.3	29.2	30.0	1.1	1.2	47.3	39.6	35.3	32.6
Portugal	52	41	−1.0	91.5	33.9	41.3	8.5	7.1	25.6	13.8	15.4	13.3
Puerto Rico	28	2	−15.1	8.9	45.5	46.0	5.6	4.7	7.3	8.0	1.7	1.8

	Rural population			Land area	Land use							
	% of total		average annual % growth	thousand sq. km	Forest area		Permanent cropland		Arable land		Arable land hectares per 100 people	
					% of land area							
	1990	2007	1990–2007	2007	1990	2005	1990	2005	1990	2005	1990–92	2003–05
Romania	47	46	−0.5	230.0	27.8	27.7	2.6	2.3	41.2	40.4	42.4	43.2
Russian Federation	27	27	−0.1	16,381.4	49.4	49.4	0.1	0.1	8.1	7.4	84.9ᵃ	84.9
Rwanda	95	82	0.9	24.7	12.9	19.5	12.4	11.1	35.7	48.6	11.8	13.2
Saudi Arabia	23	17	0.5	2,000.0ᶜ	1.4	1.4	0.0	0.1	1.6	1.6	17.0	15.7
Senegal	61	58	2.4	192.5	48.6	45.0	0.1	0.2	12.1	13.2	22.9	21.8
Serbia	50	48	−0.3	91.0	..	26.3ᵈ	..	3.2ᵈ	..	33.6ᵈ	..	42.4ᵈ
Sierra Leone	67	63	1.7	71.6	42.5	38.5	0.8	1.1	6.8	8.4	10.8	11.0
Singapore	0	0	..	0.7	3.4	3.3	1.5	0.3	1.5	0.9	0.0	0.0
Slovak Republic	44	44	0.1	48.1	40.0	40.1	1.0	0.5	32.5	28.9	27.1	26.0
Slovenia	50	51	0.2	20.1	59.5	62.8	1.8	1.3	9.9	8.7	8.6ᵃ	8.7
Somalia	70	64	1.0	627.3	13.2	11.4	0.0	0.0	1.6	2.2	15.1	16.5
South Africa	48	40	0.7	1,214.5	7.6	7.6	0.7	0.8	11.1	12.1	33.0	31.8
Spain	25	23	0.5	499.2	27.0	35.9	9.7	9.9	30.7	27.4	32.2	32.0
Sri Lanka	83	85	1.1	64.6	36.4	29.9	15.9	15.5	13.5	14.2	4.8	4.7
Sudan	73	57	0.9	2,376.0	32.1	28.4	0.0	0.1	5.4	8.2	48.1	51.2
Swaziland	77	75	2.2	17.2	27.4	31.5	0.7	0.8	10.5	10.3	16.7	15.9
Sweden	17	16	−0.1	410.3	66.7	67.1	0.0	0.0	6.9	6.6	30.3	29.8
Switzerland	27	27	0.6	40.0	28.9	30.5	0.5	0.6	9.8	10.3	5.7	5.5
Syrian Arab Republic	51	46	2.0	183.8	2.0	2.5	4.0	4.7	26.6	26.5	27.1	25.9
Tajikistan	68	74	1.8	140.0	2.9	2.9	0.9	0.9	6.1	6.6	14.9ᵃ	14.4
Tanzania	81	75	2.2	885.8	46.8	39.8	1.1	1.3	10.2	10.4	25.9	24.5
Thailand	71	67	0.6	510.9	31.2	28.4	6.1	7.0	34.2	27.8	25.9	22.7
Timor-Leste	79	73	1.7	14.9	65.0	53.7	3.9	4.6	7.4	8.2	15.2	13.2
Togo	70	59	2.0	54.4	12.6	7.1	1.7	2.6	38.6	45.8	45.1	41.2
Trinidad and Tobago	92	87	0.2	5.1	45.8	44.1	9.0	9.2	14.4	14.6	5.7	5.7
Tunisia	42	34	0.1	155.4	4.1	6.8	12.5	13.9	18.7	17.6	29.0	27.9
Turkey	41	32	0.1	769.6	12.6	13.2	3.9	3.6	32.0	31.0	34.8	33.2
Turkmenistan	55	52	1.4	469.9	8.8	8.8	0.1	0.1	2.9	4.9	40.5ᵃ	46.9
Uganda	89	87	3.1	197.1	25.0	18.4	9.4	11.2	25.4	27.4	20.0	18.9
Ukraine	33	32	−0.8	579.4	16.1	16.5	1.9	1.6	57.6	56.0	66.9ᵃ	68.4
United Arab Emirates	21	22	5.3	83.6	2.9	3.7	0.2	2.3	0.4	0.8	2.0	1.6
United Kingdom	11	10	−0.3	241.9	10.8	11.8	0.3	0.2	27.4	23.7	9.8	9.6
United States	25	19	−0.6	9,161.9	32.6	33.1	0.2	0.3	20.3	19.0	61.6	59.7
Uruguay	11	8	−1.6	175.0	5.2	8.6	0.3	0.2	7.2	7.8	41.5	41.5
Uzbekistan	60	63	1.9	425.4	7.2	7.7	0.9	0.8	10.5	11.0	18.0ᵃ	18.2
Venezuela, RB	16	7	−2.8	882.1	59.0	54.1	0.9	0.9	3.2	3.0	10.5	10.1
Vietnam	80	73	0.9	310.1	28.8	41.7	3.2	7.6	16.4	21.3	8.2	8.0
West Bank and Gaza	32	28	3.0	6.0	..	1.5	19.1	19.1	18.4	17.8	3.5	3.2
Yemen, Rep.	79	70	2.8	528.0	1.0	1.0	0.2	0.3	2.9	2.9	8.1	7.4
Zambia	61	65	2.6	743.4	66.1	57.1	0.0	0.0	7.1	7.1	49.3	46.7
Zimbabwe	71	63	0.8	386.9	57.5	45.3	0.3	0.3	7.5	8.3	25.2	24.7
World	**57 w**	**51 w**	**0.6 w**	**129,644.6 s**	**31.2 w**	**30.4 w**	**0.9 w**	**1.1 w**	**10.8 w**	**11.0 w**	**23.0 w**	**22.3 w**
Low income	75	68	1.8	21,216.9	26.8	24.7	1.0	1.2	9.0	10.2	18.1	17.6
Middle income	61	52	0.3	74,923.2	33.7	32.7	1.0	1.2	11.1	11.2	20.8	20.2
Lower middle income	68	58	0.4	34,404.7	25.6	25.0	1.5	1.8	13.5	14.3	15.0	14.7
Upper middle income	31	25	−0.4	40,518.4	40.6	39.3	0.6	0.7	9.1	8.6	44.7	43.3
Low & middle income	63	56	0.7	96,140.1	32.2	31.0	1.0	1.2	10.6	11.0	20.2	19.6
East Asia & Pacific	71	57	−0.3	15,870.6	28.8	28.4	2.2	2.9	12.1	13.5	11.6	11.4
Europe & Central Asia	37	36	0.0	23,109.9	38.2	38.3	0.4	0.4	12.4	11.0	58.4	57.7
Latin America & Carib.	29	22	−0.2	20,156.5	48.8	45.4	0.9	1.0	6.5	7.2	27.6	26.8
Middle East & N. Africa	48	43	1.3	8,643.7	2.3	2.4	0.8	0.9	5.8	6.1	18.3	17.6
South Asia	75	71	1.5	4,781.3	16.5	16.8	1.8	2.6	42.6	41.9	14.5	13.8
Sub-Saharan Africa	72	64	1.9	23,578.1	28.5	26.5	0.8	0.9	6.6	8.0	25.5	25.0
High income	27	23	−0.3	33,504.5	28.4	28.8	0.7	0.7	11.4	11.0	37.3	36.4
Euro area	29	27	−0.1	2,513.0	32.5	37.2	4.7	4.3	26.9	25.5	20.6	20.2

a. Data are not available for all three years. b. Includes Luxembourg. c. Provisional estimate. d. Includes Montenegro.

About the data

With 3 billion people, including 70 percent of the world's poor people, living in rural areas, adequate indicators to monitor progress in rural areas are essential. However, few indicators are disaggregated between rural and urban areas (for some that are, see tables 2.7, 3.5, and 3.11). The table shows indicators of rural population and land use. Rural population is approximated as the midyear nonurban population. While a practical means of identifying the rural population, it is not precise (see box 3.1a for further discussion).

The data in the table show that land use patterns are changing. They also indicate major differences in resource endowments and uses among countries. True comparability of the data is limited, however, by variations in definitions, statistical methods, and quality of data. Countries use different definitions of rural and urban population and land use. The Food and Agriculture Organization of the United Nations (FAO), the primary compiler of the data, occasionally adjusts its definitions of land use categories and revises earlier data. Because the data reflect changes in reporting procedures as well as actual changes in land use, apparent trends should be interpreted cautiously.

Satellite images show land use that differs from that of ground-based measures in area under cultivation and type of land use. Moreover, land use data in some countries (India is an example) are based on reporting systems designed for collecting tax revenue. With land taxes no longer a major source of government revenue, the quality and coverage of land use data have declined. Data on forest area may be particularly unreliable because of irregular surveys and differences in definitions (see *About the data* for table 3.4). FAO's *Global Forest Resources Assessment 2005* aims to address this limitation. The FAO has been coordinating global forest resources assessments every 5–10 years since 1946. *Global Forest Resources Assessment 2005,* conducted during 2003–05, covers 229 countries and territories at three points: 1990, 2000, and 2005. The most comprehensive assessment of forests, forestry, and the benefits of forest resources in both scope and number of countries and people involved, it examines status and trends for about 40 variables on the extent, condition, uses, and values of forests and other wooded land.

Definitions

• **Rural population** is calculated as the difference between the total population and the urban population (see *Definitions* for tables 2.1 and 3.11). • **Land area** is a country's total area, excluding area under inland water bodies and national claims to the continental shelf and to exclusive economic zones. In most cases definitions of inland water bodies includes major rivers and lakes. (See table 1.1 for the total surface area of countries.) • **Land use** can be broken into several categories, three of which are presented in the table (not shown are land used as permanent pasture and land under urban developments). • **Forest area** is land under natural or planted stands of trees, whether productive or not. • **Permanent cropland** is land cultivated with crops that occupy the land for long periods and need not be replanted after each harvest, such as cocoa, coffee, and rubber. Land under flowering shrubs, fruit trees, nut trees, and vines is included, but land under trees grown for wood or timber is not. • **Arable land** is land defined by the FAO as under temporary crops (double-cropped areas are counted once), temporary meadows for mowing or for pasture, land under market or kitchen gardens, and land temporarily fallow. Land abandoned as a result of shifting cultivation is excluded.

What is rural? Urban? | 3.1a

The rural population identified in table 3.1 is approximated as the difference between total population and urban population, calculated using the urban share reported by the United Nations Population Division. There is no universal standard for distinguishing rural from urban areas, and any urban-rural dichotomy is an oversimplification (see *About the data* for table 3.11). The two distinct images—isolated farm, thriving metropolis—represent poles on a continuum. Life changes along a variety of dimensions, moving from the most remote forest outpost through fields and pastures, past tiny hamlets, through small towns with weekly farm markets, into intensively cultivated areas near large towns and small cities, eventually reaching the center of a megacity. Along the way access to infrastructure, social services, and nonfarm employment increase, and with them population density and income. Because rurality has many dimensions, for policy purposes the rural-urban dichotomy presented in tables 3.1, 3.5, and 3.11 is inadequate.

A 2005 World Bank Policy Research Paper proposes an operational definition of rurality based on population density and distance to large cities (Chomitz, Buys, and Thomas 2005). The report argues that these criteria are important gradients along which economic behavior and appropriate development interventions vary substantially. Where population densities are low, markets of all kinds are thin, and the unit cost of delivering most social services and many types of infrastructure is high. Where large urban areas are distant, farm-gate or factory-gate prices of outputs will be low and input prices will be high, and it will be difficult to recruit skilled people to public service or private enterprises. Thus, low population density and remoteness together define a set of rural areas that face special development challenges.

Using these criteria and the Gridded Population of the World (CIESIN 2005), the authors' estimates of the rural population for Latin America and the Caribbean differ substantially from those in table 3.1. Their estimates range from 13 percent of the population, based on a population density of less than 20 people per square kilometer, to 64 percent, based on a population density of more than 500 people per square kilometer. Taking remoteness into account, the estimated rural population would be 13–52 percent. The estimate for Latin America and the Caribbean in table 3.1 is 22 percent.

Data sources

Data on urban population shares used to estimate rural population come from the United Nations Population Division's *World Urbanization Prospects: The 2007 Revision.* Data on land area and land use are from the FAO's electronic files. The FAO gathers these data from national agencies through annual questionnaires and country official publications and websites and by analyzing the results of national agricultural censuses.

	Agricultural land[a]		Irrigated land		Land under cereal production		Fertilizer consumption		Agricultural employment		Agricultural machinery	
	% of land area		% of cropland		thousand hectares		hundred grams per hectare of arable land		% of total employment		Tractors per 100 sq. km of arable land	
	1990–92	2003–05	1990–92[b]	2003–05[b]	1990–92	2005–07	1990–92[b]	2003–05[b]	1990–92	2003–05	1990–92	2003–05
Afghanistan	58.3	58.3	33.9	33.8[c]	2,283.3	2,943.7	58.5	47.5	..	..	0	0
Albania	41.1	40.9	55.6	50.5[c]	242.6	141.0	903.3	924.3	..	58.3	177	125
Algeria	16.3	17.1	6.4	6.9[c]	3,104.9	2,664.7	144.5	166.1	..	21.1[c]	128	133
Angola	46.1	46.2	2.3	2.2[c]	892.6	1,476.4	28.8	28.5	..	..	35	31
Argentina	46.6	47.2	5.6	..	8,509.6	9,332.5	72.7	479.7	0.4	1.2	99	86
Armenia	44.7[c]	49.3	49.9[c]	51.5[c]	162.8[c]	180.3	502.0[c]	232.0	..	46.5[c]	293[c]	289
Australia	60.5	57.5	4.2	4.9	12,813.8	18,999.9	274.8	492.8	5.5	3.8	67	65
Austria	42.5	40.0	0.3	2.5[c]	903.2	802.2	1,994.7	3,192.1	7.5	5.4	2,367	2,396
Azerbaijan	53.4[c]	57.5	68.0[c]	69.1	627.0[c]	764.7	440.0[c]	109.9	32.5	39.6	195[c]	126
Bangladesh	73.5	69.2	33.8	56.1[c]	10,985.4	11,547.8	1,135.6	1,723.4	66.4[c]	51.7[c]	2	1
Belarus	45.3[c]	42.7	2.1[c]	2.0[c]	2,578.0[c]	2,261.7	2,292.9[c]	1,455.0	21.7	..	207[c]	101
Belgium	44.0[d]	46.0	2.2[d]	4.7[c]	354.3[d]	319.7	4,545.8[d]	..	2.8	1.9	1,474[d]	1,137
Benin	20.6	31.9	0.6	0.4[c]	659.9	938.1	78.4	2.9	..	..	1	1
Bolivia	32.9	34.6	5.5	4.1[c]	632.9	839.9	41.7	60.8	1.7	..	25	20
Bosnia and Herzegovina	43.0[c]	42.1	0.2[c]	0.3[c]	305.1[c]	313.4	0.0[c]	452.7	..	..	235[c]	287
Botswana	45.9	45.8	0.2	0.3[c]	140.1	84.3	21.6	..	..	21.2[c]	143	159
Brazil	28.9	31.2	4.6	4.4[c]	19,632.5	19,055.2	655.6	1,570.0	25.6[c]	20.9[c]	142	134
Bulgaria	55.7	48.5	29.6	16.6[c]	2,179.3	1,602.5	1,194.1	1,608.2	19.7	9.6	128	100
Burkina Faso	34.9	39.8	0.6	0.5[c]	2,724.5	3,259.9	60.3	75.0	..	..	3	4
Burundi	82.9	90.9	1.2	1.5[c]	218.8	211.8	33.7	16.4	..	..	2	2
Cambodia	25.5	29.6	6.6	7.0[c]	1,800.8	2,586.3	18.7	30.7	..	..	3	9
Cameroon	19.7	19.7	0.3	0.4[c]	816.1	1,138.9	34.1	94.3	60.6[c]	..	1	1
Canada	7.5	7.4	1.4	1.5[c]	20,864.4	16,038.3	476.3	581.5	4.2	2.7	162	161
Central African Republic	8.0	8.4	0.0	0.1[c]	104.0	182.3	5.1	..	..	..	0	0
Chad	38.4	38.9	0.5	0.8[c]	1,241.9	2,510.6	24.6	..	..	..	1	0
Chile	21.0	20.4	57.1	81.0[c]	741.6	619.1	1,214.7	2,910.5	18.8	13.4	144	274
China	57.0	59.5	36.9	35.6[c]	93,430.3	83,522.6	2,321.0	3,148.0	53.5	..	64	71
Hong Kong, China	..	..	..	..	..	..	..	..	0.8	0.3	..	..
Colombia	40.5	38.2	14.3	24.0[c]	1,598.1	1,083.1	1,822.5	3,310.0	1.4	21.3	98	97
Congo, Dem. Rep.	10.1	10.1	0.1	0.1[c]	1,867.6	1,972.9	8.3	..	..	..	4	4
Congo, Rep.	30.8	30.9	0.3	0.4[c]	9.1	17.0	34.6	..	..	..	15	14
Costa Rica	55.7	56.5	15.2	20.2[c]	83.1	57.5	4,521.9	8,528.3	25.2	15.0	259	311
Côte d'Ivoire	59.8	63.4	1.1	1.1[c]	1,434.0	788.5	150.8	203.0	..	..	20	27
Croatia	43.0[c]	50.8	0.2[c]	0.7[c]	592.7[c]	556.2	1,514.2[c]	1,368.6	..	16.8	35[c]	1,574
Cuba	61.5	60.0	22.6	19.5[c]	235.0	287.9	1,288.2	193.0	25.1[c]	21.5[c]	246	205
Czech Republic	..	55.2	..	0.7[c]	..	1,569.5	..	1,404.1	10.1	4.3	..	292
Denmark	65.4	62.0	16.9	9.7	1,581.3	1,485.1	2,249.3	1,159.3	5.4	3.0	625	511
Dominican Republic	71.6	70.7	16.5	20.8[c]	134.2	160.0	1,003.3	..	19.5[c]	14.4	25	23
Ecuador	28.6	26.9	27.9	28.3	861.0	849.7	508.5	1,731.2	7.0	8.9	54	112
Egypt, Arab Rep.	2.7	3.5	100.0	100.0[c]	2,410.2	2,975.4	3,977.2	6,706.7	36.2	29.9[c]	251	324
El Salvador	71.1	82.2	4.9	4.9[c]	452.6	344.6	1,335.5	904.3	17.9	18.7[c]	60	52
Eritrea	..	75.1	..	3.5[c]	..	402.9	..	12.8	..	..	..	8
Estonia	32.4[c]	19.1	0.5[c]	0.7[c]	453.6[c]	282.0	1,010.9[c]	724.0	19.5	5.8	455[c]	646
Ethiopia	..	33.0	..	2.5[c]	4,585.8	8,727.3	..	119.7	..	44.1[c]	..	2
Finland	7.9	7.4	2.8	2.9	1,050.5	1,155.9	1,647.0	1,286.0	8.8	4.9	900	784
France	55.3	53.9	11.0	13.3[c]	9,211.6	9,142.7	2,918.1	2,081.2	..	4.0	784	653
Gabon	20.0	20.0	1.1	1.4[c]	14.4	19.8	25.1	56.9	..	..	28	29
Gambia, The	63.2	80.7	0.9	0.6[c]	89.5	207.7	43.7	81.5	..	..	2	3
Georgia	46.5[c]	43.3	39.9[c]	44.0[c]	248.5[c]	258.8	905.7[c]	195.7	..	54.4	296[c]	222
Germany	49.8	48.8	4.0	4.0[c]	6,673.0	6,710.2	2,615.8	2,145.3	4.0[c]	2.4	1,253	795
Ghana	55.7	64.8	0.7	0.5[c]	1,077.6	1,397.7	37.6	78.0	62.0[c]	..	15	9
Greece	71.3	65.2	31.1	37.9[c]	1,455.2	1,167.5	2,289.4	1,691.3	22.7	13.4	774	970
Guatemala	39.5	42.9	6.8	6.3[c]	768.2	810.4	1,072.1	1,285.4	..	..	33	30
Guinea	48.9	51.0	7.0	5.4[c]	774.2	1,705.7	16.3	26.6	..	..	48	48
Guinea-Bissau	53.2	58.0	4.1	4.5[c]	112.4	138.3	15.2	..	..	..	1	1
Haiti	57.9	57.7	8.0	8.4[c]	406.5	440.2	35.0	..	..	..	2	2

Agricultural inputs | 3.2

	Agricultural land[a]		Irrigated land		Land under cereal production		Fertilizer consumption		Agricultural employment		Agricultural machinery	
	% of land area		% of cropland		thousand hectares		hundred grams per hectare of arable land		% of total employment		Tractors per 100 sq. km of arable land	
	1990–92	2003–05	1990–92[b]	2003–05[b]	1990–92	2005–07	1990–92[b]	2003–05[b]	1990–92	2003–05	1990–92	2003–05
Honduras	29.8	26.2	3.8	5.6[c]	502.3	367.8	203.2	544.8	42.1	37.2	31	50
Hungary	70.7	65.4	4.1	2.5	2,803.5	2,903.3	796.3	1,152.6	11.3[c]	5.3	158	259
India	60.9	60.6	28.3	32.9[c]	100,759.8	99,409.0	757.6	1,140.1	68.1	..	65	165
Indonesia	23.5	26.3	14.5	12.4[c]	13,861.2	15,404.7	1,329.8	1,548.1	54.9	44.5	3	2
Iran, Islamic Rep.	38.5	36.1	39.9	47.2	9,611.9	9,074.1	749.6	928.7	25.6	24.9[c]	136	162
Iraq	21.9	22.9	63.0	58.6[c]	3,506.1	4,110.7	347.0	..	..	17.0[c]	72	127
Ireland	70.2	62.4	..	..	298.0	278.3	6,591.0	4,529.4	14.1	6.3	1,667	1,409
Israel	26.7	24.4	44.4	..	107.8	86.3	2,835.7	20,007.8	3.7	2.0	763	757
Italy	55.4	50.7	22.9	25.8[c]	4,346.9	3,899.0	2,195.5	1,726.2	8.4	4.6[c]	1,619	2,312
Jamaica	44.0	47.4	11.0	0.0[c]	2.6	1.6	1,737.0	611.4	27.3[c]	19.0	242	177
Japan	15.5	12.9	54.3	35.8	2,438.6	2,006.9	3,778.5	4,108.8	6.8	4.5	4,297	4,417
Jordan	12.0	11.5	25.0	27.5	111.9	64.5	969.4	7,294.8	..	3.6[c]	352	328
Kazakhstan	82.0[c]	76.9	9.8[c]	15.7[c]	22,152.4[c]	14,512.3	135.5[c]	68.2	..	34.4[c]	62[c]	21
Kenya	47.3	47.4	1.1	1.8[c]	1,765.9	2,190.8	209.2	375.5	19.0[c]	..	20	25
Korea, Dem. Rep.	21.0	24.9	58.2	50.3[c]	1,569.0	1,293.8	3,522.3	..	..	..	297	234
Korea, Rep.	21.9	19.2	47.1	47.6[c]	1,367.8	1,045.2	4,931.8	5,011.5	16.7	8.3	275	1,344
Kuwait	7.9	8.6	60.0	72.2[c]	0.4	1.4	666.7	10,631.1	..	0.0[c]	215	70
Kyrgyz Republic	52.6[c]	56.2	72.6[c]	73.1	578.0[c]	601.0	242.4[c]	236.7	35.5	43.4	189[c]	159
Lao PDR	7.2	8.5	16.2	16.5[c]	625.3	888.8	31.0	..	..	..	11	11
Latvia	40.8[c]	26.5	1.1[c]	2.1[c]	696.7[c]	..	995.3[c]	435.2	..	13.0	364[c]	548
Lebanon	31.1	38.1	28.1	31.3[c]	41.5	64.9	1,639.3	1,467.0	..	..	188	446
Lesotho	76.7	76.9	0.6	0.9[c]	177.6	160.7	167.3	..	..	..	57	61
Liberia	27.1	27.0	0.5	0.5[c]	135.0	120.0	2.5	..	..	..	8	9
Libya	8.8	8.8	21.8	21.9[c]	355.0	352.8	457.6	506.2	..	..	187	224
Lithuania	54.1[c]	42.5	0.5[c]	0.4[c]	1,134.0[c]	974.1	540.7[c]	1,470.0	18.8	15.9	256[c]	660
Macedonia, FYR	51.4[c]	48.8	12.1[c]	9.0[c]	235.2[c]	180.3	0.0[c]	399.8	..	19.4	730[c]	954
Madagascar	62.5	70.2	30.7	30.6[c]	1,321.0	1,590.9	34.0	32.4	..	78.0[c]	5	2
Malawi	40.2	48.3	1.2	2.2[c]	1,442.6	1,791.8	350.6	235.6	..	..	8	6
Malaysia	22.7	24.0	4.8	0.0[c]	699.3	685.7	..	8,199.7	23.9[c]	14.6[c]	161	241
Mali	26.3	32.4	3.7	4.9[c]	2,392.7	3,184.4	91.0	..	..	41.5[c]	11	5
Mauritania	38.5	38.6	11.8	..	132.9	222.7	132.2	..	..	..	8	8
Mauritius	55.7	55.7	16.0	20.8[c]	0.5	0.1	2,731.5	2,300.9	14.7[c]	10.0	36	52
Mexico	53.8	55.3	22.0	22.8[c]	10,075.0	9,918.6	686.4	714.4	24.7[c]	15.9	128	130
Moldova	77.9[c]	76.7	..	10.7[c]	675.6[c]	915.4	776.5[c]	121.8	..	41.4	310[c]	222
Mongolia	79.9	83.3	5.8	7.0[c]	620.0	135.7	111.5	38.5	..	40.6	73	35
Morocco	68.2	68.1	13.2	15.4[c]	5,373.9	5,308.6	352.9	569.7	..	45.0	46	58
Mozambique	60.7	61.8	2.8	2.6[c]	1,508.6	2,180.5	12.0	51.0	..	..	14	14
Myanmar	15.8	17.1	10.1	17.0[c]	5,282.9	8,454.5	78.8	10.5	69.4[c]	..	12	11
Namibia	47.0	47.2	0.7	1.0[c]	206.4	284.0	0.0	21.6	48.2[c]	..	47	39
Nepal	29.0	29.5	..	47.0	2,957.2	3,339.1	339.6	262.3	81.9	..	23	24
Netherlands	58.9	56.8	61.0	60.2[c]	185.0	215.5	6,297.8	9,126.6	4.3	2.9	2,056	1,647
New Zealand	65.0	64.5	..	..	153.5	123.5	1,911.4	6,740.8	10.7	7.6	323	499
Nicaragua	33.5	43.5	4.0	2.8[c]	299.3	500.7	269.9	317.2	38.7	29.0[c]	20	16
Niger	27.0	30.4	0.5	0.5[c]	7,010.6	8,798.4	1.2	3.7	..	..	0	0
Nigeria	79.4	80.4	0.7	0.8[c]	16,416.7	19,572.3	142.2	63.9	..	..	8	10
Norway	3.3	3.4	..	..	361.4	320.9	2,362.0	2,461.0	5.9	3.5	1,723	1,526
Oman	3.5	5.1	71.6	90.0[c]	2.4	4.5	2,440.6	3,424.2	..	..	42	39
Pakistan	33.7	35.2	..	84.2	11,776.8	12,871.3	962.0	1,594.9	48.9	42.7	133	185
Panama	28.7	30.0	4.8	6.2[c]	182.4	181.9	666.2	426.1	25.8[c]	16.4	103	148
Papua New Guinea	2.0	2.3	..	..	1.9	3.2	621.5	1,805.9	..	..	59	52
Paraguay	56.0	60.7	2.9	1.7[c]	454.7	801.0	91.9	580.9	1.7	31.5[c]	72	43
Peru	17.1	16.6	29.9	27.8[c]	682.5	1,160.7	245.9	853.6	1.0	0.7	36	36
Philippines	37.4	40.9	15.7	14.5[c]	6,957.4	6,737.7	935.5	1,449.1	45.3	37.1	72	111
Poland	61.6	52.8	..	0.6[c]	8,522.7	8,371.6	894.8	1,296.5	25.2	17.9	821	1,119
Portugal	42.8	41.2	..	23.8[c]	780.1	359.5	1,122.9	2,018.6	15.6	12.1	569	1,259
Puerto Rico	47.5	25.1	..	..	0.5	0.3	..	..	3.5	2.1	478	438

	Agricultural land[a] % of land area		Irrigated land % of cropland		Land under cereal production thousand hectares		Fertilizer consumption hundred grams per hectare of arable land		Agricultural employment % of total employment		Agricultural machinery Tractors per 100 sq. km of arable land	
	1990–92	2003–05	1990–92[b]	2003–05[b]	1990–92	2005–07	1990–92[b]	2003–05[b]	1990–92	2003–05	1990–92	2003–05
Romania	64.4	63.8	..	3.2	5,842.3	5,178.7	788.5	428.8	30.6	33.1	146	183
Russian Federation	13.5[c]	13.2	..	3.6	59,541.3[c]	41,831.1	417.4[c]	114.1	..	10.4	98[c]	44
Rwanda	75.6	78.6	0.3	0.6[c]	258.2	333.8	19.9	..	..	..	1	0
Saudi Arabia	57.5	80.8	44.2	42.7[c]	1,061.8	664.1	1,445.8	1,060.3	..	..	20	28
Senegal	41.9	42.6	3.3	4.8[c]	1,153.8	1,130.9	65.1	134.4	..	..	2	3
Serbia[e]	..	54.8	..	0.9	..	1,945.8[c]	..	1,199.5	..	..	..	948
Sierra Leone	38.3	40.0	5.2	4.7[c]	451.7	883.5	22.6	..	..	..	3	1
Singapore	2.2	1.2	..	..	..	..	54,333.3	141,594.4	0.3[c]	0.2	637	1,083
Slovak Republic	..	42.3	..	3.8	..	772.3	..	766.2	..	5.2	..	158
Slovenia	28.0[c]	25.0	..	1.2	112.5[c]	97.3	3,167.8[c]	3,522.5	..	8.9	..	..
Somalia	70.2	70.7	19.2	15.7[c]	531.4	624.6	8.8	..	..	..	16	10
South Africa	80.2	82.0	8.3	9.5[c]	5,735.9	3,570.9	548.6	520.7	..	10.3[c]	101	43
Spain	60.8	58.3	..	20.3[c]	7,588.5	6,357.7	1,185.9	1,601.6	10.7	5.5	494	705
Sri Lanka	36.2	36.5	28.0	38.8[c]	834.3	908.0	2,016.4	2,873.1	44.3	33.9[c]	180	221
Sudan	51.9	57.2	14.1	10.2[c]	6,266.9	9,192.4	51.2	35.6	..	..	8	9
Swaziland	75.8	80.9	24.1	26.0[c]	69.1	59.4	688.5	..	..	..	251	222
Sweden	8.2	7.8	4.1	4.3[c]	1,184.3	989.4	1,112.0	1,050.6	3.3	2.1	604	616
Switzerland	46.9	38.1	6.0	5.8[c]	207.3	163.2	4,031.8	2,147.6	4.2	4.0	2,870	2,632
Syrian Arab Republic	73.7	75.6	14.3	24.3[c]	3,811.9	3,222.8	621.5	856.8	28.2[c]	27.0[c]	137	220
Tajikistan	32.1[c]	30.4	72.9[c]	68.3[c]	266.0[c]	392.8	1,488.4[c]	..	57.9	67.2	415[c]	239
Tanzania	38.4	38.8	1.4	1.8[c]	3,003.3	4,906.7	53.5	69.7	84.2[c]	..	8	23
Thailand	41.9	36.3	21.0	28.2[c]	10,593.6	11,402.1	598.2	1,406.9	61.7	43.3	39	256
Timor-Leste	21.9	22.9	..	..	83.7	107.7	..	..	..	..	8	7
Togo	58.7	66.7	0.3	0.3[c]	610.2	736.6	56.3	61.1	..	..	0	0
Trinidad and Tobago	25.7	25.9	3.3	3.3[c]	6.4	2.0	1,111.4	1,848.1	11.8	4.9	606	683
Tunisia	58.4	63.0	..	7.2	1,524.7	1,484.7	329.9	460.9	..	..	88	140
Turkey	51.8	53.3	..	19.7	13,759.9	13,328.6	756.7	1,095.5	46.5	32.5	287	426
Turkmenistan	68.6[c]	70.2	..	79.5[c]	331.3[c]	1,022.1	1,296.3[c]	..	..	..	465[c]	224
Uganda	61.0	63.9	0.1	0.1[c]	1,097.6	1,669.7	1.5	15.0	91.5[c]	69.1[c]	9	9
Ukraine	72.4[c]	71.4	7.6[c]	6.6[c]	12,542.3[c]	13,875.5	806.9[c]	186.5	20.0	19.8	153[c]	114
United Arab Emirates	3.7	6.7	..	29.9[c]	1.4	0.0	4,810.4	5,531.3	..	..	50	59
United Kingdom	75.0	70.2	2.5	3.0[c]	3,548.5	2,880.3	3,323.1	3,020.0	2.2	1.3	762	872
United States	46.6	45.3	11.3	12.5[c]	64,547.3	57,213.3	1,014.8	1,562.1	2.9	1.6	245	272
Uruguay	84.7	85.4	10.2	14.9[c]	509.4	571.2	610.2	1,387.4	1.5	4.6[c]	259	266
Uzbekistan	65.2[c]	65.6	87.3[c]	84.9[c]	1,225.3[c]	1,601.1	1,631.6[c]	..	..	..	402[c]	362
Venezuela, RB	24.7	24.6	13.9	16.9[c]	798.7	1,092.0	1,388.3	1,747.5	12.6	10.7[c]	176	186
Vietnam	21.0	30.8	44.6	33.7[c]	6,726.1	8,399.2	1,299.3	3,308.9	73.8[c]	58.8[c]	60	247
West Bank and Gaza	62.5	61.8	..	7.0[c]	..	32.7[c]	..	..	..	15.8[c]	441	715
Yemen, Rep.	33.4	33.6	24.3	33.0[c]	738.2	746.2	127.2	50.6	52.6[c]	..	40	43
Zambia	31.4	34.4	0.7	2.9[c]	813.4	837.2	131.1	0.0	..	..	11	11
Zimbabwe	34.1	39.9	3.6	5.2[c]	1,430.8	2,095.0	508.1	328.6	..	..	61	75
World	**37.3 w**	**38.2 w**	**17.0 w**	**18.0 w**	**704,455.8 s**	**689,120.1 s**	**945.2 w**	**1,192.9 w**	**42.6 w**	**.. w**	**186 w**	**208 w**
Low income	36.7	38.7	9.5	18.6	103,608.2	131,441.1	339.8	448.7	..	..	40	47
Middle income	37.1	38.2	22.8	20.8	454,663.6	419,524.9	965.8	1,233.0	51.6	..	115	144
Lower middle income	45.5	47.0	27.5	28.1	287,054.6	283,677.2	1,169.7	1,615.2	54.6	..	102	122
Upper middle income	30.1	30.7	10.1	8.9	167,609.0	135,847.6	603.6	703.9	..	17.5	75	127
Low & middle income	37.0	38.3	20.0	20.4	558,271.9	550,965.9	833.7	1,090.7	52.4	..	166	163
East Asia & Pacific	48.3	50.7	..	..	142,265.1	139,631.3	1,821.0	2,627.6	54.5	..	56	96
Europe & Central Asia	28.1	28.4	16.7	10.9	137,268.0	110,119.5	564.7	359.7	..	20.8	190	186
Latin America & Carib.	34.4	35.7	11.3	12.5	47,712.7	48,655.5	585.7	1,108.1	18.6	16.5	121	118
Middle East & N. Africa	23.5	23.6	31.6	33.7	30,590.3	30,102.1	641.4	1,055.7	..	..	116	151
South Asia	54.7	54.7	28.8	39.2	129,690.1	131,101.8	767.2	1,166.3	65.6	..	67	153
Sub-Saharan Africa	42.1	43.9	3.4	3.5	70,745.7	91,355.7	129.0	119.2	..	..	19	13
High income	37.9	38.0	..	..	146,184.0	138,154.2	1,200.2	1,474.7	5.6	3.4	413	432
Euro area	49.7	47.3	13.9	16.5	32,674.3	31,370.1	2,302.5	2,046.1	7.3	4.5	993	1,002

a. Includes permanent pastures, arable land, and land under permanent crops. b. Data for two periods may not be comparable (see *About the data*). c. Data are not available for all three years. d. Includes Luxembourg. e. Includes Montenegro.

About the data

Agriculture is still a major sector in many economies, and agricultural activities provide developing countries with food and revenue. But agricultural activities also can degrade natural resources. Poor farming practices can cause soil erosion and loss of soil fertility. Efforts to increase productivity by using chemical fertilizers, pesticides, and intensive irrigation have environmental costs and health impacts. Excessive use of chemical fertilizers can alter the chemistry of soil. Pesticide poisoning is common in developing countries. And salinization of irrigated land diminishes soil fertility. Thus, inappropriate use of inputs for agricultural production has far-reaching effects.

The table provides indicators of major inputs to agricultural production: land, fertilizer, labor, and

Nearly 40 percent of land globally is devoted to agriculture   **3.2a**

Total land area in 2005: 130 million sq. km

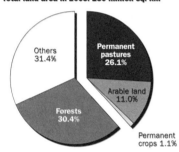

Note: Agricultural land includes permanent pastures, arable land, and land under permanent crops. *Source:* Tables 3.1 and 3.2.

Developing regions lag in agricultural machinery, which reduces their agricultural productivity   **3.2b**

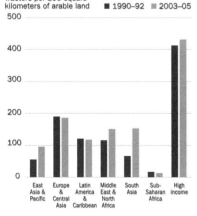

Source: Table 3.2.

machinery. There is no single correct mix of inputs: appropriate levels and application rates vary by country and over time and depend on the type of crops, the climate and soils, and the production process used.

The data shown here and in table 3.3 are collected by the Food and Agriculture Organization of the United Nations (FAO) through annual questionnaires. The FAO tries to impose standard definitions and reporting methods, but complete consistency across countries and over time is not possible. For example, permanent pastures are quite different in nature and intensity in African countries and dry Middle Eastern countries. Thus, despite standard definitions, data on agricultural land in different climates may not be comparable. Data on agricultural employment, in particular, should be used with caution. In many countries much agricultural employment is informal and unrecorded, including substantial work performed by women and children. To address some of these concerns, this indicator is heavily footnoted in the database in sources, definition, and coverage.

Fertilizer consumption measures the quantity of plant nutrients. Consumption is calculated as production plus imports minus exports. Because some chemical compounds used for fertilizers have other industrial applications, the consumption data may overstate the quantity available for crops. The FAO recently revised the time series for fertilizer consumption and irrigation but only for 2002 onward, and data for 2002–05 are not available for all countries. The fertilizer data from the FAO's previous releases are not necessarily comparable with later data. In the previous release data were based on the total consumption of fertilizers, but in the recent release data are based on the nutrients in fertilizers. Caution should thus be used when comparing data over time.

To smooth annual fluctuations in agricultural activity, the indicators in the table have been averaged over three years.

Definitions

• **Agricultural land** is the share of land area that is permanent pastures, arable, or under permanent crops. Permanent pasture is land used for five or more years for forage, including natural and cultivated crops. Arable land includes land defined by the FAO as land under temporary crops (double-cropped areas are counted once), temporary meadows for mowing or for pasture, land under market or kitchen gardens, and land temporarily fallow. Land abandoned as a result of shifting cultivation is excluded. Land under permanent crops is land cultivated with crops that occupy the land for long periods and need not be replanted after each harvest, such as cocoa, coffee, and rubber. Land under flowering shrubs, fruit trees, nut trees, and vines is included, but land under trees grown for wood or timber is not. • **Irrigated land** refers to areas purposely provided with water, including land irrigated by controlled flooding. • **Cropland** is arable land and permanent cropland (see table 3.1). • **Land under cereal production** refers to harvested areas, although some countries report only sown or cultivated area. • **Fertilizer consumption** is the quantity of plant nutrients per unit of arable land. Fertilizer products cover nitrogen, potash, and phosphate (including ground rock phosphate). Traditional nutrients—animal and plant manures—are not included. The time reference for fertilizer consumption is the crop year (July through June). • **Agricultural employment** is employment in agriculture, forestry, hunting, and fishing (see table 2.3). • **Agricultural machinery** refers to wheel and crawler tractors (excluding garden tractors) in use in agriculture at the end of the calendar year specified or during the first quarter of the following year.

Data sources

Data on agricultural inputs are from electronic files that the FAO makes available to the World Bank.

3.3 Agricultural output and productivity

	Crop production index		Food production index		Livestock production index		Cereal yield		Agricultural productivity	
							kilograms per hectare		Agriculture value added per worker 2000 $	
	1999–2001 = 100		1999–2001 = 100		1999–2001 = 100					
	1990–92	2003–05	1990–92	2003–05	1990–92	2003–05	1990–92	2005–07	1990–92	2003–05
Afghanistan	97.4	135.9	78.3	116.5	64.1	99.5	1,153	1,650	..	..
Albania	87.5	102.4	72.0	109.4	63.9	113.0	2,372	3,580	778	1,449
Algeria	86.3	136.6	83.3	123.1	80.7	106.6	915	1,465	1,911	2,225
Angola	60.3	154.3	64.9	136.3	75.6	99.9	378	526	165	174
Argentina	67.3	112.6	73.9	107.0	89.1	97.3	2,652	4,077	6,767	10,072
Armenia	106.4[a]	126.6	104.4[a]	122.6	101.3[a]	115.5	1,843[a]	1,605	1,476[a]	3,692
Australia	60.3	97.9	68.7	98.9	83.3	94.9	1,739	1,411	20,839	29,908
Austria	93.4	98.5	95.8	98.1	97.3	97.8	5,400	5,917	12,048	21,920
Azerbaijan	135.4[a] ·	129.3	103.3[a]	127.9	94.7[a]	122.0	2,113[a]	2,637	1,084[a]	1,143
Bangladesh	75.6	107.7	74.0	107.5	73.8	105.1	2,567	3,769	254	338
Belarus	113.0[a]	126.0	127.2[a]	114.6	141.2[a]	104.2	2,739[a]	2,767	1,977[a]	3,153
Belgium	77.6[b]	107.3	87.8[b]	100.1	93.8[b]	96.9	6,122[b]	8,248	..	39,243
Benin	58.4	118.2	62.6	119.7	87.9	112.4	880	1,173	326	519
Bolivia	63.7	119.6	68.9	115.3	76.9	108.4	1,384	1,939	670	773
Bosnia and Herzegovina	106.5[a]	106.7	115.4[a]	106.9	137.8[a]	107.6	3,548[a]	3,922	..	8,270
Botswana	96.4	112.4	114.4	106.2	118.2	104.7	312	508	536	390
Brazil	77.3	125.2	71.0	122.6	65.3	121.1	1,916	3,206	1,507	3,119
Bulgaria	148.7	102.6	144.9	99.2	143.3	97.6	3,633	3,010	2,500	7,159
Burkina Faso	74.0	124.6	73.3	114.7	68.0	115.6	783	1,132	110	173
Burundi	112.6	105.3	112.3	105.3	134.7	99.9	1,370	1,316	108	70
Cambodia	65.4	109.6	64.6	110.8	65.9	110.3	1,356	2,482	..	314
Cameroon	71.5	108.9	74.2	108.2	85.5	100.6	1,166	1,355	389	648
Canada	..	..	..	..	..	..	2,559	3,083	28,243	44,133
Central African Republic	74.0	96.5	69.8	108.8	68.1	117.6	883	1,100	287	381
Chad	68.4	111.2	72.1	110.7	84.8	107.6	636	907	173	215
Chile	78.5	115.9	73.8	114.2	67.9	111.1	3,949	6,073	3,573	5,309
China	70.0	113.9	61.3	116.7	49.4	122.5	4,307	5,322	258	407
Hong Kong, China	..	..	..	..	..	..	..	..	..	..
Colombia	96.6	112.1	82.5	112.2	80.4	112.6	2,492	3,792	3,080	2,749
Congo, Dem. Rep.	124.5	96.8	121.9	97.1	101.4	96.3	794	772	184	149
Congo, Rep.	80.0	106.4	78.9	108.8	75.8	118.8	688	788	..	..
Costa Rica	71.3	103.8	71.3	104.5	79.7	100.7	3,188	3,110	3,143	4,506
Côte d'Ivoire	73.9	96.5	74.1	101.7	75.6	124.7	863	1,785	598	795
Croatia	80.3[a]	90.6	92.3[a]	93.3	126.4[a]	101.0	3,975[a]	5,215	4,915[a]	9,975
Cuba	112.1	112.3	116.6	107.5	130.4	89.0	2,092	2,742	..	..
Czech Republic	..	95.8	..	94.6	..	93.4	..	4,480	..	5,521
Denmark	103.7	99.8	93.8	102.3	89.0	103.5	5,448	5,863	15,190	38,441
Dominican Republic	118.9	106.4	99.5	108.9	79.1	111.6	4,078	4,426	2,268	4,586
Ecuador	79.5	103.1	72.9	110.1	65.8	117.2	1,724	2,751	1,686	1,676
Egypt, Arab Rep.	69.5	110.7	66.7	113.3	65.4	119.0	5,738	7,624	1,528	2,072
El Salvador	102.2	91.3	85.2	103.5	74.3	108.3	1,871	2,785	1,633	1,638
Eritrea	..	80.4	..	90.9	..	100.3	..	436	..	71
Estonia	123.5[a]	92.0	151.3[a]	99.0	167.5[a]	103.0	1,304[a]	2,644	3,002[a]	3,129
Ethiopia	..	108.6	..	111.0	..	116.6	1,234	1,557	..	158
Finland	97.8	104.0	103.6	105.5	106.6	106.3	3,246	3,471	18,818	31,276
France	94.1	97.4	95.6	97.7	97.5	98.2	6,370	6,731	22,234	44,080
Gabon	87.3	102.3	89.2	101.8	86.8	100.0	1,712	1,648	1,176	1,592
Gambia, The	56.0	97.2	60.1	97.8	98.7	103.4	1,114	1,122	224	235
Georgia	115.6[a]	94.3	97.3[a]	104.3	79.3[a]	113.7	1,998[a]	1,650	2,443[a]	1,791
Germany	84.0	96.5	97.5	98.9	108.4	100.6	5,578	6,538	13,724	25,657
Ghana	59.1	118.4	61.1	118.3	90.7	111.0	1,084	1,365	293	320
Greece	86.0	89.1	91.5	91.7	101.4	98.1	3,589	3,867	7,536	8,818
Guatemala	77.7	103.2	75.8	106.7	76.5	103.9	1,882	1,501	2,120	2,623
Guinea	74.0	110.8	72.9	113.7	60.6	115.6	1,423	1,433	142	190
Guinea-Bissau	71.3	104.6	73.3	105.5	81.1	109.8	1,529	1,544	205	238
Haiti	108.7	98.3	98.5	101.6	69.8	111.8	997	921	..	..

	Crop production index		Food production index		Livestock production index		Cereal yield		Agricultural productivity	
	1999–2001 = 100		1999–2001 = 100		1999–2001 = 100		kilograms per hectare		Agriculture value added per worker 2000 $	
	1990–92	2003–05	1990–92	2003–05	1990–92	2003–05	1990–92	2005–07	1990–92	2003–05
Honduras	92.5	129.4	87.2	158.2	69.1	180.3	1,371	1,519	1,193	1,483
Hungary	115.0	111.2	119.5	105.1	126.7	95.8	4,551	5,135	4,105	6,987
India	80.2	103.2	76.3	105.3	69.3	112.6	1,947	2,464	324	392
Indonesia	82.7	118.8	83.1	120.4	85.5	134.2	3,826	4,374	484	583
Iran, Islamic Rep.	74.8	117.1	72.8	114.1	68.2	105.2	1,523	2,481	1,954	2,561
Iraq	102.0	118.5	99.0	118.8	92.6	117.8	872	794	..	1,756
Ireland	94.1	105.2	94.1	98.2	94.3	97.1	6,653	7,185	..	17,107
Israel	97.6	111.9	83.2	115.2	72.9	117.5	3,132	3,153	..	..
Italy	97.5	97.2	96.2	96.8	95.0	95.8	4,340	5,311	11,528	23,967
Jamaica	85.0	97.2	85.3	98.9	86.8	102.0	1,298	1,211	2,016	1,889
Japan	113.0	93.0	109.4	96.5	106.9	99.7	5,713	6,013	20,445	35,668
Jordan	100.2	134.9	85.9	119.3	70.4	99.6	1,167	1,263	1,892	1,360
Kazakhstan	168.7[a]	110.9	173.9[a]	112.7	178.0[a]	117.2	1,338[a]	1,158	1,795[a]	1,557
Kenya	84.9	103.3	85.3	106.4	85.4	110.4	1,645	1,723	334	333
Korea, Dem. Rep.	125.7	110.1	128.7	112.0	145.2	120.9	5,073	3,638	..	..
Korea, Rep.	88.3	93.1	80.3	96.8	68.1	101.7	5,885	6,291	5,679	11,286
Kuwait	33.9	122.3	30.0	115.0	27.9	110.9	3,112	2,621	..	13,521[a]
Kyrgyz Republic	67.4[a]	103.7	82.8[a]	103.7	109.1[a]	101.8	2,772[a]	2,523	675[a]	979
Lao PDR	62.3	113.8	59.3	115.4	60.2	112.9	2,355	3,517	360	459
Latvia	137.3[a]	120.3	199.4[a]	111.1	253.7[a]	102.9	1,641[a]	2,669	1,790[a]	2,704
Lebanon	109.7	94.1	100.0	103.0	65.6	126.7	2,001	2,666	..	29,950
Lesotho	67.9	105.6	85.7	102.8	108.7	100.0	703	546	428	423
Liberia	62.4	99.2	77.7	97.5	89.9	109.7	951	1,156	..	..
Libya	79.5	98.5	77.8	99.2	75.8	100.5	706	617	..	..
Lithuania	77.5[a]	104.5	133.1[a]	103.7	184.7[a]	103.0	1,938[a]	2,625	..	4,760
Macedonia, FYR	107.1[a]	99.9	106.2[a]	101.1	103.8[a]	104.2	2,652[a]	2,938	2,256[a]	3,487
Madagascar	92.3	105.6	91.6	104.6	93.2	101.0	1,935	2,493	186	174
Malawi	57.3	94.4	48.9	95.7	85.3	102.1	871	1,416	72	116
Malaysia	74.4	121.4	71.0	120.1	81.0	118.2	2,827	3,336	386	525
Mali	73.9	118.2	78.7	113.6	81.7	116.8	840	1,109	208	241
Mauritania	64.5	90.5	85.7	107.1	90.0	110.5	802	763	574	356
Mauritius	110.7	103.3	98.6	106.5	70.7	116.4	4,117	7,666	3,942	5,011
Mexico	83.0	106.8	76.6	108.8	71.2	110.1	2,520	3,145	2,256	2,793
Moldova	134.6[a]	112.5	152.9[a]	113.1	214.5[a]	105.2	2,928[a]	2,113	1,286[a]	816
Mongolia	260.7	114.2	103.3	72.2	93.2	69.6	967	839	870	907
Morocco	100.9	139.3	93.5	126.3	81.0	102.2	1,094	986	1,430	1,746
Mozambique	64.2	108.7	69.4	106.5	94.5	101.3	330	949	107	148
Myanmar	61.7	119.6	61.8	121.3	64.2	128.5	2,739	3,629	..	..
Namibia	72.0	113.2	106.2	130.8	114.1	135.2	388	420	820	1,103
Nepal	73.7	114.2	75.3	112.9	80.1	110.0	1,831	2,271	191	207
Netherlands	93.4	98.0	100.9	93.4	104.4	91.4	7,145	7,753	24,914	42,049
New Zealand	78.7	105.1	78.1	115.5	81.0	115.2	5,257	7,071	19,155	27,189
Nicaragua	76.2	118.6	63.7	123.6	57.1	124.0	1,543	1,880	..	2,071
Niger	73.3	110.7	73.5	105.3	71.7	92.3	323	437	152	157[a]
Nigeria	68.7	105.0	69.2	105.2	76.8	107.0	1,135	1,460	..	..
Norway	121.1	104.5	102.8	100.1	98.1	99.0	3,744	3,924	19,500	37,039
Oman	62.8	87.3	63.0	93.0	65.6	104.1	2,206	3,214	1,005	1,302[a]
Pakistan	80.9	106.6	71.0	109.5	67.4	112.5	1,818	2,639	594	696
Panama	109.9	108.2	87.8	103.1	69.5	98.1	1,862	1,939	2,363	3,904
Papua New Guinea	78.5	102.5	79.9	107.7	80.9	113.1	2,504	3,672	500	595
Paraguay	85.3	124.6	77.2	116.3	86.7	97.8	1,905	2,201	1,596	2,052
Peru	52.4	109.2	56.6	112.1	68.0	116.5	2,463	3,603	930	1,481
Philippines	84.4	113.0	77.5	114.6	61.9	118.2	2,070	3,164	905	1,075
Poland	110.9	91.1	112.5	97.8	115.4	106.7	2,958	3,029	1,502[a]	2,182
Portugal	104.0	97.7	95.6	97.9	85.5	98.2	1,939	2,882	4,642	6,220
Puerto Rico	167.7	117.4	127.5	97.6	118.3	93.5	1,100	1,826	..	..

	Crop production index		Food production index		Livestock production index		Cereal yield kilograms per hectare		Agricultural productivity Agriculture value added per worker 2000 $	
	1999–2001 = 100		1999–2001 = 100		1999–2001 = 100					
	1990–92	2003–05	1990–92	2003–05	1990–92	2003–05	1990–92	2005–07	1990–92	2003–05
Romania	93.0	116.4	103.0	114.3	120.3	110.3	2,777	2,680	2,196	4,646
Russian Federation	125.9[a]	115.9	142.0[a]	110.3	161.8[a]	103.8	1,743[a]	1,865	1,825[a]	2,519
Rwanda	110.2	115.1	106.7	116.4	81.2	123.6	1,088	1,117	167	182
Saudi Arabia	121.4	115.0	93.9	111.6	67.5	108.4	4,212	4,464	7,875	15,780
Senegal	72.5	88.9	74.0	90.1	87.5	104.4	803	968	225	215
Serbia	..	116.3[c]	..	107.0[c]	..	95.1[c]	..	3,839	..	1,679[c]
Sierra Leone	128.9	115.7	121.3	114.5	93.4	106.9	1,223	1,023	..	..
Singapore	157.1	105.3	402.4	114.0	413.8	114.4	..	..	22,695	40,419
Slovak Republic	..	105.6	..	101.4	..	97.2	1,031[a]	4,081	..	5,026
Slovenia	94.0[a]	111.8	82.1[a]	104.8	75.7[a]	101.1	3,279[a]	5,498	12,042[a]	..
Somalia	102.8	106.3	85.6	105.1	83.3	104.9	622	432	..	..
South Africa	79.8	104.9	84.7	107.7	93.9	109.8	1,602	3,081	1,786	2,495
Spain	88.1	103.4	85.3	106.2	80.0	110.5	2,310	3,050	9,511	18,619
Sri Lanka	86.9	101.3	89.1	103.0	93.6	115.5	2,950	3,636	679	702
Sudan	68.8	115.9	66.6	112.0	67.4	109.4	596	681	414	667
Swaziland	105.6	99.9	107.1	104.6	129.6	110.2	1,299	1,196	1,231	1,330
Sweden	102.0	101.5	98.3	99.4	95.9	98.1	4,272	4,791	22,533	35,378
Switzerland	112.2	97.4	107.4	99.6	105.7	100.4	6,102	6,364	19,884	23,588
Syrian Arab Republic	73.9	115.7	75.4	120.6	75.4	121.7	947	1,749	2,344	3,261
Tajikistan	122.8[a]	147.7	132.7[a]	150.1	192.6[a]	152.3	1,037[a]	2,275	346[a]	409
Tanzania	92.8	107.3	89.0	106.9	82.9	109.5	1,276	1,162	238	295
Thailand	81.9	106.3	83.5	104.5	86.2	103.8	2,186	2,907	497	624
Timor-Leste	93.7	106.8	102.0	112.0	101.4	129.0	1,694	1,230	..	..
Togo	73.8	113.4	75.1	108.2	93.4	109.1	791	1,152	312	347
Trinidad and Tobago	116.4	78.5	92.7	112.9	73.4	142.6	3,159	2,647	1,666	1,745
Tunisia	105.6	122.7	90.0	115.0	60.5	99.1	1,401	1,320	2,422	2,700
Turkey	88.3	103.8	89.2	105.3	92.1	108.0	2,192	2,529	1,770	1,846
Turkmenistan	110.9[a]	126.0	63.0[a]	142.2	56.1[a]	139.7	2,210[a]	3,065	1,222[a]	..
Uganda	77.9	107.2	80.0	107.8	82.3	111.4	1,487	1,527	155	175
Ukraine	128.5[a]	117.2	145.5[a]	111.7	171.7[a]	103.5	2,834[a]	2,368	1,195[a]	1,702
United Arab Emirates	23.5	55.7	29.7	64.5	71.5	122.2	2,042	2,000	10,454	25,841
United Kingdom	105.0	98.4	105.4	98.0	105.8	97.6	6,321	7,082	22,664	26,942
United States	88.4	105.8	85.7	104.2	83.4	103.1	4,875	6,512	20,793	42,744
Uruguay	71.3	..	76.7	..	83.5	..	2,445	4,223	5,714	7,973
Uzbekistan	108.0[a]	115.6	97.6[a]	118.1	100.1[a]	115.8	1,777[a]	4,042	1,272[a]	1,800
Venezuela, RB	79.6	98.6	74.6	94.8	73.4	91.7	2,561	3,365	4,483	6,331
Vietnam	60.2	120.4	62.1	122.1	57.9	131.1	3,097	4,726	214	305
West Bank and Gaza	..	104.6	..	109.9	..	117.9	1,105	2,091[a]	..	..
Yemen, Rep.	75.2	100.9	72.3	105.3	66.3	112.0	906	885	271	328[a]
Zambia	80.8	104.3	84.2	105.3	79.9	98.9	1,251	1,697	159	204
Zimbabwe	69.4	65.1	76.2	84.7	90.0	99.8	1,125	674	240	222
World	**82.0 w**	**109.4 w**	**81.1 w**	**109.7 w**	**82.2 w**	**110.1 w**	**2,839 w**	**3,301 w**	**746 w**	**908 w**
Low income	76.1	109.3	75.1	110.4	76.5	112.4	1,596	2,105	270	319
Middle income	80.5	112.0	78.6	112.9	78.3	114.9	2,639	3,093	467	650
Lower middle income	76.7	111.7	71.5	113.5	64.6	117.6	2,789	3,354	371	513
Upper middle income	91.7	113.0	96.0	111.5	103.6	110.0	1,992	2,553	1,987	2,819
Low & middle income	79.8	111.6	78.1	112.6	78.1	114.7	2,421	2,858	433	579
East Asia & Pacific	71.9	114.4	64.8	116.6	53.1	122.0	3,816	4,681	295	438
Europe & Central Asia	113.8	109.8	128.3	108.7	152.2	106.8	1,961	2,211	1,756	2,108
Latin America & Carib.	78.0	116.3	74.2	114.8	72.5	112.9	2,234	3,308	2,125	3,055
Middle East & N. Africa	79.4	117.3	76.5	115.7	71.2	110.3	1,544	2,206	1,583	2,204
South Asia	80.0	104.2	75.6	106.3	69.2	112.1	1,977	2,581	335	406
Sub-Saharan Africa	75.5	106.1	76.9	107.2	83.1	108.8	1,003	1,228	262	278
High income	89.9	101.9	89.6	101.9	90.0	101.8	4,259	5,072	14,543	25,594
Euro area	90.6	98.5	93.6	99.8	97.1	100.8	4,621	5,419	12,587	22,134

a. Data are not available for all three years. b. Includes Luxembourg. c. Includes Montenegro.

Agricultural output and productivity 3.3

About the data

The agricultural production indexes in the table are prepared by the Food and Agriculture Organization of the United Nations (FAO). The FAO obtains data from official and semiofficial reports of crop yields, area under production, and livestock numbers. If data are unavailable, the FAO makes estimates. The indexes are calculated using the Laspeyres formula: production quantities of each commodity are weighted by average international commodity prices in the base period and summed for each year. Because the FAO's indexes are based on the concept of agriculture as a single enterprise, estimates of the amounts retained for seed and feed are subtracted from the production data to avoid double counting. The resulting aggregate represents production available for any use except as seed and feed. The FAO's indexes may differ from those from other sources because of differences in coverage, weights, concepts, time periods, calculation methods, and use of international prices.

To facilitate cross-country comparisons, the FAO uses international commodity prices to value production. These prices, expressed in international dollars (equivalent in purchasing power to the U.S. dollar), are derived using a Geary-Khamis formula applied to agricultural outputs (see System of National Accounts 1993, sections 16.93–96). This method assigns a single price to each commodity so that, for example, one metric ton of wheat has the same price regardless of where it was produced. The use of international prices eliminates fluctuations in the value of output due to transitory movements of nominal exchange rates unrelated to the purchasing power of the domestic currency.

Data on cereal yield may be affected by a variety of reporting and timing differences. Millet and sorghum, which are grown as feed for livestock and poultry in Europe and North America, are used as food in Africa, Asia, and countries of the former Soviet Union. So some cereal crops are excluded from the data for some countries and included elsewhere, depending on their use. To smooth annual fluctuations in agricultural activity, the indicators in the table have been averaged over three years.

Definitions

• **Crop production index** is agricultural production for each period relative to the base period 1999–2001. It includes all crops except fodder crops. The regional and income group aggregates for the FAO's production indexes are calculated from the underlying values in international dollars, normalized to the base period 1999–2001. • **Food production index** covers food crops that are considered edible and that contain nutrients. Coffee and tea are excluded because, although edible, they have no nutritive value. • **Livestock production index** includes meat and milk from all sources, dairy products such as cheese, and eggs, honey, raw silk, wool, and hides and skins. • **Cereal yield,** measured in kilograms per hectare of harvested land, includes wheat, rice, maize, barley, oats, rye, millet, sorghum, buckwheat, and mixed grains. Production data on cereals refer to crops harvested for dry grain only. Cereal crops harvested for hay or harvested green for food, feed, or silage, and those used for grazing, are excluded. The FAO allocates production data to the calendar year in which the bulk of the harvest took place. But most of a crop harvested near the end of a year will be used in the following year. • **Agricultural productivity** is the ratio of agricultural value added, measured in 2000 U.S. dollars, to the number of workers in agriculture. Agricultural productivity is measured by value added per unit of input. (For further discussion of the calculation of value added in national accounts, see *About the data* for tables 4.1 and 4.2.) Agricultural value added includes that from forestry and fishing. Thus interpretations of land productivity should be made with caution.

Cereal yield in low-income economies was less than 40 percent of the yield in high-income countries 3.3a

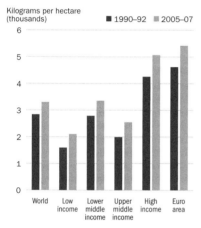

Kilograms per hectare (thousands)   ■ 1990–92   ■ 2005–07

Source: Table 3.3.

Sub-Saharan Africa had the lowest yield, while East Asia and Pacific is closing the gap with high-income economies 3.3b

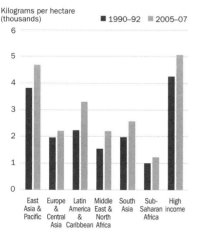

Kilograms per hectare (thousands)   ■ 1990–92   ■ 2005–07

Source: Table 3.3.

Data sources

Data on agricultural production indexes, cereal yield, and agricultural workers are from electronic files that the FAO makes available to the World Bank. The files may contain more recent information than published versions. Data on agricultural value added are from the World Bank's national accounts files.

	Forest area		Average annual deforestation[a]		Animal species		Higher plants[b]		GEF benefits index for biodiversity	Nationally protected areas		Marine protected areas	
	thousand sq. km		%		Total known species	Threatened species	Total known species	Threatened species	0–100 (no biodiversity to maximum biodiversity)	thousand sq. km	% of total land area	thousand sq. km	% of surface area
	1990	2005	1990–2000	2000–05	2004	2008	2004	2008	2008	2006[c]	2006[c]	2004	2004
Afghanistan	13	9	2.5	3.1	578	30	4,000	2	3.4	2.2	0.3	..	..
Albania	8	8	0.3	−0.6	376	45	3,031	0	0.2	0.2	0.7	0.3	1.0
Algeria	18	23	−1.8	−1.2	472	72	3,164	3	2.9	118.8	5.0	0.9	0.0
Angola	610	591	0.2	0.2	1,226	62	5,185	26	8.3	125.5	10.1	29.1	2.3
Argentina	353	330	0.4	0.4	1,413	152	9,372	44	17.7	173.6	6.3	7.8	0.3
Armenia	3	3	1.0	1.5	380	35	3,553	1	0.2	2.4	8.7	..	..
Australia	1,679	1,637	0.2	0.1	1,227	568	15,638	55	87.7	734.1	9.6	680.8	8.8
Austria	38	39	−0.2	−0.1	513	62	3,100	4	0.3	23.5	28.5	..	..
Azerbaijan	9	9	0.0	0.0	446	38	4,300	0	0.8	4.0	4.8	1.2	1.4
Bangladesh	9	9	0.0	0.3	735	89	5,000	12	1.4	0.9	0.7	0.3	0.2
Belarus	75	79	−0.5	−0.1	297	17	2,100	..	0.0	10.8	5.2	..	..
Belgium	8[d]	7	..	..	519	29	1,550	1	0.0	1.0	3.2	0.0	0.0
Benin	33	24	2.1	2.5	644	34	2,500	14	0.2	26.1	23.6	..	..
Bolivia	628	587	0.4	0.5	1,775	80	17,367	71	12.5	218.5	20.2	..	..
Bosnia and Herzegovina	22	22	0.1	0.0	390	55	..	1	0.4	0.2	0.5	..	..
Botswana	137	119	0.9	1.0	739	18	2,151	0	1.4	174.4	30.8	..	..
Brazil	5,200	4,777	0.5	0.6	2,290	343	56,215	382	100.0	1,515.2	17.9	47.4	0.6
Bulgaria	33	36	−0.1	−1.4	485	47	3,572	0	0.8	11.0	10.1	0.0	0.0
Burkina Faso	72	68	0.3	0.3	581	13	1,100	2	0.3	38.2	14.0	..	..
Burundi	3	2	3.7	5.2	713	48	2,500	2	0.3	1.5	6.0	..	..
Cambodia	129	104	1.1	2.0	648	82	..	31	3.5	41.5	23.5	1.9	1.1
Cameroon	245	212	0.9	1.0	1,258	157	8,260	355	12.5	39.9	8.6	3.9	0.8
Canada	3,101	3,101	0.0	0.0	683	77	3,270	2	21.5	473.2	5.2	362.7	3.6
Central African Republic	232	228	0.1	0.1	850	17	3,602	15	1.5	94.7	15.2	..	..
Chad	131	119	0.6	0.7	635	21	1,600	2	2.2	114.9	9.1	..	..
Chile	153	161	−0.4	−0.4	604	95	5,284	40	15.3	27.8	3.7	114.5	15.1
China	1,571	1,973	−1.2	−2.2	1,801	351	32,200	446	66.6	1,437.8	15.4	16.0	0.2
Hong Kong, China	..	..	..	..	363	37	..	6	0.0	0.3	24.7	0.3	26.5
Colombia	614	607	0.1	0.1	2,288	382	51,220	223	51.5	282.7	25.5	8.1	0.7
Congo, Dem. Rep.	1,405	1,336	0.4	0.2	1,578	126	11,007	65	19.9	196.1	8.6	..	..
Congo, Rep.	227	225	0.1	0.1	763	37	6,000	35	3.6	48.7	14.3	..	..
Costa Rica	26	24	0.8	−0.1	1,070	131	12,119	111	9.7	11.2	21.8	4.8	9.4
Côte d'Ivoire	102	104	−0.1	−0.1	931	73	3,660	105	3.4	38.9	12.2	0.3	0.1
Croatia	21	21	0.0	−0.1	461	78	4,288	1	0.6	3.1	5.6	2.5	4.4
Cuba	21	27	−1.7	−2.2	423	115	6,522	163	12.5	1.5	1.4	31.7	28.6
Czech Republic	26	26	0.0	−0.1	474	39	1,900	4	0.1	12.5	16.1	..	..
Denmark	4	5	−0.9	−0.6	508	28	1,450	3	0.2	2.5	5.8	5.1	11.8
Dominican Republic	14	14	0.0	0.0	260	81	5,657	30	6.0	11.8	24.4	8.6	17.6
Ecuador	138	109	1.5	1.7	1,856	340	19,362	1,839	29.3	62.6	22.6	141.0	49.7
Egypt, Arab Rep.	0[e]	1	−3.0	−2.6	599	59	2,076	2	2.9	53.2	5.3	76.7	7.7
El Salvador	4	3	1.5	1.7	571	29	2,911	26	0.9	0.2	1.0	0.1	0.4
Eritrea	16	16	0.2	0.3	607	38	..	3	0.8	5.0	5.0	..	..
Estonia	22	23	−0.3	−0.4	334	14	1,630	0	0.1	20.0	47.1	..	..
Ethiopia	147	130	0.7	1.1	1,127	86	6,603	22	8.4	186.2	18.6	..	..
Finland	222	225	−0.1	0.0	501	19	1,102	1	0.2	29.5	9.7	1.1	0.3
France	145	156	−0.5	−0.3	665	117	4,630	8	5.3	55.6	10.1	0.5	0.1
Gabon	219	218	0.0	0.0	798	43	6,651	108	3.0	34.9	13.5	1.0	0.4
Gambia, The	4	5	−0.4	−0.4	668	31	974	4	0.1	0.3	3.5	0.2	1.9
Georgia	28	28	0.0	0.0	366	46	4,350	0	0.6	2.7	3.9	0.0	0.1
Germany	107	111	−0.3	0.0	613	59	2,682	12	0.6	75.8	21.7	9.1	2.6
Ghana	74	55	2.0	2.0	978	56	3,725	117	1.9	36.3	15.9	..	..
Greece	33	38	−0.9	−0.8	530	95	4,992	11	2.8	4.0	3.1	2.5	1.9
Guatemala	47	39	1.2	1.3	877	133	8,681	83	8.0	35.4	32.6	0.1	0.1
Guinea	74	67	0.7	0.5	855	61	3,000	22	2.3	15.0	6.1	..	..
Guinea-Bissau	22	21	0.4	0.5	560	29	1,000	4	0.6	2.9	10.2	..	..
Haiti	1	1	0.6	0.7	312	91	5,242	29	5.2	0.1	0.3	..	..

	Forest area (thousand sq. km)		Average annual deforestation[a] (%)		Animal species		Higher plants[b]		GEF benefits index for biodiversity 0–100 (no biodiversity to maximum biodiversity)	Nationally protected areas		Marine protected areas	
					Total known species	Threatened species	Total known species	Threatened species		thousand sq. km	% of total land area	thousand sq. km	% of surface area
	1990	2005	1990–2000	2000–05	2004	2008	2004	2008	2008	2006[c]	2006[c]	2004	2004
Honduras	74	46	3.0	3.1	900	102	5,680	110	7.2	21.9	19.6	1.9	1.7
Hungary	18	20	−0.6	−0.7	455	55	2,214	1	0.2	5.2	5.8	..	..
India	639	677	−0.6	0.0	1,602	313	18,664	246	39.9	151.7	5.1	16.1	0.5
Indonesia	1,166	885	1.7	2.0	2,271	464	29,375	386	81.0	203.1	11.2	130.1	6.8
Iran, Islamic Rep.	111	111	0.0	0.0	656	75	8,000	1	7.3	103.9	6.4	6.2	0.4
Iraq	8	8	−0.2	−0.1	498	40	..	0	1.6	0.0	0.0	..	..
Ireland	4	7	−3.3	−1.9	471	15	950	1	0.6	0.8	1.1	0.0	0.0
Israel	2	2	−0.6	−0.8	649	79	2,317	0	0.8	3.4	15.6	0.1	0.6
Italy	84	100	−1.2	−1.1	610	119	5,599	19	3.8	19.4	6.6	1.5	0.5
Jamaica	3	3	0.1	0.1	333	61	3,308	209	4.4	1.6	15.0	8.2	74.5
Japan	250	249	0.0	0.0	763	190	5,565	12	36.0	34.5	9.5	10.6	2.8
Jordan	1	1	0.0	0.0	490	43	2,100	0	0.4	9.3	10.6	0.0	0.0
Kazakhstan	34	33	0.1	0.2	642	55	6,000	16	5.1	77.4	2.9	0.5	0.0
Kenya	37	35	0.3	0.3	1,510	172	6,506	103	8.8	69.1	12.1	3.1	0.5
Korea, Dem. Rep.	82	62	1.8	1.9	474	44	2,898	3	0.7	3.2	2.6	..	..
Korea, Rep.	64	63	0.1	0.1	512	54	2,898	0	1.7	3.5	3.5	3.5	3.5
Kuwait	0[e]	0[e]	−3.4	−2.7	381	23	234	..	0.1	0.0	0.0	0.3	1.5
Kyrgyz Republic	8	9	−0.2	−0.3	265	22	4,500	14	1.1	6.2	3.2	..	..
Lao PDR	173	161	0.5	0.5	919	77	8,286	21	5.0	37.5	16.3	..	..
Latvia	28	29	−0.3	−0.4	393	23	1,153	0	0.0	10.4	16.7	0.2	0.2
Lebanon	1	1	−0.8	−0.8	447	38	3,000	0	0.2	0.0	0.4	0.0	0.0
Lesotho	0	0	−3.4	−2.7	370	11	1,591	1	0.3	0.1	0.2	..	..
Liberia	41	32	1.6	1.8	759	60	2,200	46	2.6	15.2	15.8	0.6	0.5
Libya	2	2	0.0	0.0	413	31	1,825	1	1.6	1.2	0.1	0.5	0.0
Lithuania	20	21	−0.3	−0.8	298	20	1,796	..	0.0	3.6	5.7	0.5	0.8
Macedonia, FYR	9	9	0.0	0.0	380	34	3,500	0	0.2	1.8	7.1	..	..
Madagascar	137	128	0.5	0.3	427	262	9,505	281	29.2	15.2	2.6	0.2	0.0
Malawi	39	34	0.9	0.9	865	141	3,765	14	3.5	18.4	19.5	..	..
Malaysia	224	209	0.4	0.7	1,083	225	15,500	686	13.9	59.7	18.2	5.0	1.5
Mali	141	126	0.7	0.8	758	21	1,741	6	1.5	26.0	2.1	..	..
Mauritania	4	3	2.7	3.4	615	44	1,100	..	1.3	2.5	0.2	15.0	1.5
Mauritius	0[e]	0[e]	0.3	0.5	151	65	750	88	3.3	0.1	3.3	0.1	4.4
Mexico	690	642	0.5	0.4	1,570	579	26,071	261	68.7	102.5	5.3	82.1	4.2
Moldova	3	3	−0.2	−0.2	253	28	1,752	0	0.0	0.5	1.4	..	..
Mongolia	115	103	0.7	0.8	527	38	2,823	0	4.2	217.9	13.9	..	..
Morocco	43	44	−0.1	−0.2	559	76	3,675	2	3.5	4.7	1.1	0.5	0.1
Mozambique	200	193	0.3	0.3	913	93	5,692	46	7.2	45.3	5.8	22.5	2.8
Myanmar	392	322	1.3	1.4	1,335	118	7,000	38	10.0	35.5	5.4	0.2	0.0
Namibia	88	77	0.9	0.9	811	55	3,174	24	5.2	42.8	5.2	74.0	9.0
Nepal	48	36	2.1	1.4	477	72	6,973	7	2.1	22.8	16.0	..	..
Netherlands	3	4	−0.4	−0.3	539	26	1,221	0	0.2	4.3	12.7	0.8	1.9
New Zealand	77	83	−0.6	−0.2	424	124	2,382	21	20.2	64.7	24.2	22.7	8.4
Nicaragua	65	52	1.6	1.3	813	59	7,590	39	3.3	21.3	17.6	1.3	1.0
Niger	19	13	3.7	1.0	616	20	1,460	2	0.9	84.1	6.6	..	..
Nigeria	172	111	2.7	3.3	1,189	79	4,715	171	6.0	56.5	6.2	..	..
Norway	91	94	−0.2	−0.2	525	32	1,715	2	1.3	15.5	5.1	1.3	0.4
Oman	0[e]	0[e]	0.0	0.0	557	50	1,204	6	3.7	0.2	0.1	29.6	9.6
Pakistan	25	19	1.8	2.1	820	78	4,950	2	4.9	65.3	8.5	2.2	0.3
Panama	44	43	0.2	0.1	1,145	121	9,915	194	10.9	7.6	10.2	10.0	13.3
Papua New Guinea	315	294	0.5	0.5	980	158	11,544	142	25.4	36.2	8.0	3.5	0.8
Paraguay	212	185	0.9	0.9	864	39	7,851	10	2.8	23.4	5.9	..	..
Peru	702	687	0.1	0.1	2,222	238	17,144	275	33.4	175.9	13.7	3.4	0.3
Philippines	106	72	2.8	2.1	812	253	8,931	216	32.3	30.0	10.1	16.6	5.5
Poland	89	92	−0.2	−0.3	534	38	2,450	4	0.5	75.4	24.6	0.7	0.2
Portugal	31	38	−1.5	−1.1	606	147	5,050	16	5.5	4.6	5.0	2.0	2.2
Puerto Rico	4	4	−0.1	0.0	348	47	2,493	53	4.0	0.3	3.3	1.7	19.1

	Forest area (thousand sq. km)		Average annual deforestation[a] (%)		Animal species		Higher plants[b]		GEF benefits index for biodiversity 0–100 (no biodiversity to maximum biodiversity)	Nationally protected areas		Marine protected areas	
					Total known species	Threatened species	Total known species	Threatened species		thousand sq. km	% of total land area	thousand sq. km	% of surface area
	1990	2005	1990–2000	2000–05	2004	2008	2004	2008	2008	2006[c]	2006[c]	2004	2004
Romania	64	64	0.0	0.0	466	64	3,400	1	0.7	5.2	2.2	6.1	2.6
Russian Federation	8,090	8,088	0.0	0.0	941	153	11,400	7	34.1	1,113.4	6.8	301.8	1.8
Rwanda	3	5	−0.8	−6.9	871	49	2,288	3	0.9	2.0	8.1	..	..
Saudi Arabia	27	27	0.0	0.0	527	45	2,028	3	3.2	818.3	38.1	5.2	0.3
Senegal	93	87	0.5	0.5	803	55	2,086	7	1.0	21.6	11.2	0.9	0.4
Serbia	26[f]	27[f]	−0.3[f]	−0.3[f]	477[f]	42	4,082[f]	1	0.2[f]	3.3[f]	3.2[f]	0.1[f]	0.1[f]
Singapore	0[e]	0[e]	0.0	0.0	473	44	2,282	54	0.1	0.0	4.2	0.0	0.1
Slovak Republic	19	19	0.0	−0.1	419	44	3,124	2	0.1	9.6	20.0	..	..
Slovenia	12	13	−0.3	−0.4	437	80	3,200	..	0.2	1.3	6.7	0.0	0.0
Somalia	83	71	1.0	1.0	824	55	3,028	17	6.1	1.9	0.3	3.3	0.5
South Africa	92	92	0.0	0.0	1,149	323	23,420	74	20.7	73.7	6.1	3.4	0.3
Spain	135	179	−2.0	−1.7	647	170	5,050	49	6.8	41.4	8.3	1.8	0.4
Sri Lanka	24	19	1.2	1.5	504	177	3,314	280	7.9	11.3	17.5	2.3	3.5
Sudan	764	675	0.8	0.8	1,254	47	3,137	17	5.1	114.1	4.8	0.3	0.0
Swaziland	5	5	−0.9	−0.9	614	16	2,715	11	0.1	0.5	3.1	..	..
Sweden	274	275	0.0	0.0	542	30	1,750	3	0.3	42.4	10.3	4.3	1.0
Switzerland	12	12	−0.4	−0.4	475	44	3,030	3	0.2	11.8	29.5	..	..
Syrian Arab Republic	4	5	−1.5	−1.3	432	59	3,000	0	0.9	1.2	0.7	..	..
Tajikistan	4	4	0.0	0.0	427	27	5,000	14	0.7	19.6	14.0	..	..
Tanzania	414	353	1.0	1.1	1,431	299	10,008	240	14.8	342.7	38.7	2.3	0.2
Thailand	160	145	0.7	0.4	1,271	157	11,625	86	8.0	101.7	19.9	5.8	1.1
Timor-Leste	10	8	1.2	1.3	..	..	..	0	0.6	0.9	6.3	..	..
Togo	7	4	3.4	4.5	740	33	3,085	10	0.3	6.0	11.1	..	..
Trinidad and Tobago	2	2	0.3	0.2	551	38	2,259	1	2.2	0.2	4.7	0.1	1.3
Tunisia	6	11	−4.1	−1.9	438	52	2,196	0	0.5	2.4	1.5	0.2	0.1
Turkey	97	102	−0.4	−0.2	581	121	8,650	3	6.2	12.7	1.6	4.5	0.6
Turkmenistan	41	41	0.0	0.0	421	44	..	3	1.8	12.6	2.7	..	..
Uganda	49	36	1.9	2.2	1,375	131	4,900	38	2.8	62.9	31.9	..	..
Ukraine	93	96	−0.2	−0.1	445	58	5,100	1	0.5	19.4	3.3	3.1	0.5
United Arab Emirates	2	3	−2.4	−0.1	298	27	..	..	0.2	0.2	0.2	..	..
United Kingdom	26	28	−0.7	−0.4	660	38	1,623	14	3.5	47.5	19.6	22.5	9.2
United States	2,986	3,031	−0.1	−0.1	1,356	937	19,473	244	94.2	1,379.2	15.1	909.5	9.4
Uruguay	9	15	−4.5	−1.3	532	66	2,278	1	1.2	0.6	0.3	0.1	0.0
Uzbekistan	31	33	−0.4	−0.5	434	33	4,800	15	1.1	8.7	2.0	..	..
Venezuela, RB	520	477	0.6	0.6	1,745	166	21,073	69	25.3	638.1	72.3	21.3	2.3
Vietnam	94	129	−2.3	−2.0	1,116	152	10,500	147	12.1	16.0	5.2	0.7	0.2
West Bank and Gaza	..	0[e]	..	0.0	..	..	..	0	0.0	..	..	..	..
Yemen, Rep.	5	5	0.0	0.0	459	47	1,650	159	3.2	0.0	0.0	..	..
Zambia	491	425	0.9	1.0	1,025	38	4,747	8	3.8	300.5	40.4	..	..
Zimbabwe	222	175	1.5	1.7	883	35	4,440	17	1.9	57.2	14.8	..	..
World	**40,457 s**	**39,426 s**	**0.2 w**	**0.2 w**						**14,042.4 s**	**11.0 w**	**4,348.8 s**	**3.8 w**
Low income	5,697	5,251	0.5	0.7						2,179.4	10.8	57.5	..
Middle income	25,266	24,520	0.2	0.2						7,908.5	10.6	1,218.4	1.7
Lower middle income	8,822	8,609	0.2	0.0						3,734.7	11.0	559.4	1.8
Upper middle income	16,443	15,911	0.2	0.2						4,173.8	10.3	659.0	1.6
Low & middle income	30,962	29,771	0.3	0.3						10,087.9	10.7	1,275.8	1.6
East Asia & Pacific	4,580	4,507	0.3	−0.2						2,221.7	14.0	192.0	1.3
Europe & Central Asia	8,834	8,857	0.0	0.0						1,401.3	6.1	321.4	1.4
Latin America & Carib.	9,834	9,147	0.5	0.5						3,365.2	16.7	495.6	2.7
Middle East & N. Africa	200	211	−0.4	−0.3						294.8	3.6	85.1	1.1
South Asia	789	801	−0.2	0.1						266.6	5.6	20.9	0.5
Sub-Saharan Africa	6,727	6,247	0.4	0.6						2,538.3	11.3	160.7	..
High income	9,495	9,656	−0.1	−0.1						3,954.5	11.8	3,073.0	8.9
Euro area	817	936	−1.1	−0.6						262.5	10.6	19.6	0.8

a. Negative values indicate an increase in forest area. b. Flowering plants only. c. Data reported by the World Conservation Monitoring Centre in 2006 are the most recent year available. d. Includes Luxembourg. e. Less than 0.5. f. Includes Montenegro.

About the data

Biological diversity is defined in terms of variability in genes, species, and ecosystems. A 2008 comprehensive assessment of world species shows that at least 1,141 of 5,487 known mammals are threatened with extinction. As threats to biodiversity mount, the international community is increasingly focusing on conserving diversity. Deforestation is a major cause of loss of biodiversity, and habitat conservation is vital for stemming this loss. Conservation efforts have focused on protecting areas of high biodiversity.

The Food and Agriculture Organization of the United Nations (FAO) *Global Forest Resources Assessment 2005* provides detailed information on forest cover in 2005 and adjusted estimates of forest cover in 1990 and 2000. The current survey uses a uniform definition of forest. Because of space limitations, the table does not break down forest cover between natural forest and plantation, a breakdown the FAO provides for developing countries. Thus the deforestation data in the table may underestimate the rate at which natural forest is disappearing in some countries.

Measures of species richness are a straightforward way to indicate an area's importance for biodiversity. The number of threatened species is also an important measure of the immediate need for conservation in an area. Global analyses of the status of threatened species have been carried out for few groups of organisms. Only for mammals, birds, and amphibians has the status of virtually all known species been assessed. Threatened species are defined using the World Conservation Union's (IUCN) classification: *endangered* (in danger of extinction and unlikely to survive if causal factors continue operating) and *vulnerable* (likely to move into the endangered category in the near future if causal factors continue operating).

Unlike birds and mammals, it is difficult to accurately count plants. The number of plant species is highly debated. The *2008 IUCN Red List of Threatened Species*, the result of more than 20 years' work by botanists worldwide, is the most comprehensive list of threatened species on a global scale. Only 5 percent of plant species have been evaluated, and 70 percent of these are threatened with extinction. Plant species data may not be comparable across countries because of differences in taxonomic concepts and coverage and so should be used with caution. However, the data identify countries that are major sources of global biodiversity and that show national commitments to habitat protection.

More than information about species richness is needed to set priorities for conserving biodiversity. The

Global Environment Facility's (GEF) benefits index for biodiversity is a comprehensive indicator of national biodiversity status and is used to guide its biodiversity priorities. The indicator incorporates information on individual species range maps available from the IUCN for virtually all mammals (5,487), amphibians (5,915), and endangered birds (1,098); country data from the World Resources Institute for reptiles and vascular plants; country data from FishBase for 31,190 fish species; and the ecological characteristics of 867 world terrestrial ecoregions from WWF International. For each country the biodiversity indicator incorporates the best available and comparable information in four relevant dimensions: represented species, threatened species, represented ecoregions, and threatened ecoregions. To combine these dimensions into one measure, the indicator uses dimensional weights that reflect the consensus of conservation scientists at the GEF, IUCN, WWF International, and other nongovernmental organizations.

The World Conservation Monitoring Centre (WCMC) compiles data on protected areas, numbers of certain species, and numbers of those species under threat from various sources. Because of differences in definitions, reporting practices, and reporting periods, cross-country comparability is limited.

Nationally protected areas are defined using the six IUCN management categories for areas of at least 1,000 hectares: *scientific reserves* and strict nature reserves with limited public access; *national parks* of national or international significance and not materially affected by human activity; *natural monuments* and natural landscapes with unique aspects; *managed nature reserves* and wildlife sanctuaries; *protected landscapes* (which may include cultural landscapes); and *areas managed mainly for the sustainable use* of natural systems to ensure long-term protection and maintenance of biological diversity. The data in the table cover these six categories as well as terrestrial protected areas that were not assigned to a category by the IUCN. Designating land as a protected area does not mean that protection is in force. And for small countries that only have protected areas smaller than 1,000 hectares, the size limit in the definition leads to an underestimate of protected areas.

Due to variations in consistency and methods of collection, data quality is highly variable across countries. Some countries update their information more frequently than others, some have more accurate data on extent of coverage, and many underreport the number or extent of protected areas.

Definitions

• **Forest area** is land under natural or planted stands of trees, whether productive or not. • **Average annual deforestation** is the permanent conversion of natural forest area to other uses, including agriculture, ranching, settlements, and infrastructure. Deforested areas do not include areas logged but intended for regeneration or areas degraded by fuelwood gathering, acid precipitation, or forest fires. • **Animal species** are mammals (excluding whales and porpoises) and birds (included within a country's breeding or wintering ranges). • **Higher plants** are native vascular plant species. • **Threatened species** are the number of species classified by the IUCN as endangered and vulnerable. • **GEF benefits index for biodiversity** is a composite index of relative biodiversity potential based on the species represented in each country and their threat status and diversity of habitat types. The index has been normalized from 0 (no biodiversity potential) to 100 (maximum biodiversity potential). • **Nationally protected areas** are totally or partially protected areas of at least 1,000 hectares that are designated as scientific reserves with limited public access, national parks, natural monuments, nature reserves or wildlife sanctuaries, protected landscapes, and areas managed mainly for sustainable use. Marine areas, unclassified areas, littoral (intertidal) areas, and sites protected under local or provincial law are excluded. Total area protected is a percentage of total land area (see table 3.1). • **Marine protected areas** are areas of intertidal or subtidal terrain—and overlying water and associated flora and fauna and historical and cultural features—that have been reserved to protect part or all of the enclosed environment.

Data sources

Data on forest area and deforestation are from the FAO's *Global Forest Resources Assessment 2005*. Data on species are from the electronic files of the United Nations Environment Programme and WCMC and *2008 IUCN Red List of Threatened Species*. The GEF benefits index for biodiversity is from Kiran Dev Pandey, Piet Buys, Ken Chomitz, and David Wheeler's "Biodiversity Conservation Indicators: New Tools for Priority Setting at the Global Environment Facility" (2006). Data on protected areas are from the United Nations Environment Programme and WCMC, as compiled by the World Resources Institute.

3.5 Freshwater

	Renewable internal freshwater resources[a]		Annual freshwater withdrawals					Water productivity	Access to an improved water source	
	Flows billion cu. m 2007	Per capita cu. m 2007	billion cu. m 2007[b]	% of internal resources 2007[b]	% for agriculture 2007[b]	% for industry 2007[b]	% for domestic 2007[b]	GDP/water use 2000 $ per cu. m 2007[b]	% of urban population 2006	% of rural population 2006
Afghanistan	55	..	23.3	42.3	98	0	2	..	..	..
Albania	27	8,456	1.7	6.4	62	11	27	2.2	97	97
Algeria	11	332	6.1	54.0	65	13	22	9.0	87	81
Angola	148	8,696	0.4	0.2	60	17	23	26.1	62	39
Argentina	276	6,987	29.2	10.6	74	9	17	9.7	98	80
Armenia	9	3,023	3.0	32.5	66	4	30	0.6	99	96
Australia	492	23,412	23.9	4.9	75	10	15	16.9	100	100
Austria	55	6,614	2.1	3.8	1	64	35	91.9	100	100
Azerbaijan	8	947	12.2	150.5	76	19	4	0.8	95	59
Bangladesh	105	662	79.4	75.6	96	1	3	0.6	85	78
Belarus	37	3,834	2.8	7.5	30	47	23	4.6	100	99
Belgium	12	1,129	..	..	..	..	..	..	100	..
Benin	10	1,141	0.1	1.3	45	23	32	18.2	78	57
Bolivia	304	31,892	1.4	0.5	81	7	13	5.8	96	69
Bosnia and Herzegovina	36	9,409	..	..	..	..	..	..	100	98
Botswana	2	1,276	0.2	8.1	41	18	41	31.8	100	90
Brazil	5,418	28,277	59.3	1.1	62	18	20	10.9	97	58
Bulgaria	21	2,742	10.5	50.0	19	78	3	1.2	100	97
Burkina Faso	13	846	0.8	6.4	86	1	13	3.3	97	66
Burundi	10	1,184	0.3	2.9	77	6	17	2.5	84	70
Cambodia	121	8,346	4.1	3.4	98	0	1	0.9	80	61
Cameroon	273	14,731	1.0	0.4	74	8	18	10.2	88	47
Canada	2,850	86,426	46.0	1.6	12	69	20	15.8	100	99
Central African Republic	141	32,463	0.0	0.0	4	16	80	38.4	90	51
Chad	15	1,394	0.2	1.5	83	0	17	6.0	71	40
Chile	884	53,270	12.6	1.4	64	25	11	6.0	98	72
China	2,812	2,132	630.3	22.4	68	26	7	1.9	98	81
Hong Kong, China	..	..	..	..	..	..	..	..	..	..
Colombia	2,112	48,014	10.7	0.5	46	4	50	8.8	99	77
Congo, Dem. Rep.	900	14,423	0.4	0.0	31	17	53	12.0	82	29
Congo, Rep.	222	58,937	0.0	0.0	9	22	70	76.1	95	35
Costa Rica	112	25,189	2.7	2.4	53	17	29	6.0	99	96
Côte d'Ivoire	77	3,988	0.9	1.2	65	12	24	11.2	98	66
Croatia	38	8,499	..	..	..	..	..	..	100	98
Cuba	38	3,386	8.2	21.5	69	12	19	..	95	78
Czech Republic	13	1,272	2.6	19.6	2	57	41	22.0	100	100
Denmark	6	1,099	1.3	21.2	43	25	32	126.0	100	100
Dominican Republic	21	2,153	3.4	16.1	66	2	32	5.8	97	91
Ecuador	432	32,385	17.0	3.9	82	5	12	0.9	98	91
Egypt, Arab Rep.	2	24	68.3	3,794.4	86	6	8	1.5	99	98
El Salvador	18	2,590	1.3	7.2	59	16	25	10.3	94	68
Eritrea	3	578	0.6	20.8	95	0	5	1.2	74	57
Estonia	13	9,475	0.2	1.2	5	38	57	35.6	100	99
Ethiopia	122	1,543	5.6	4.6	94	0	6	1.6	96	31
Finland	107	20,232	2.5	2.3	3	84	14	49.2	100	100
France	179	2,893	40.0	22.4	10	74	16	33.2	100	100
Gabon	164	123,291	0.1	0.1	42	8	50	42.2	95	47
Gambia, The	3	1,758	0.0	1.0	65	12	23	13.8	91	81
Georgia	58	13,224	1.6	2.8	65	13	22	2.7	100	97
Germany	107	1,301	47.1	44.0	20	68	12	40.4	100	100
Ghana	30	1,291	1.0	3.2	66	10	24	5.1	90	71
Greece	58	5,182	7.8	13.4	80	3	16	16.2	100	99
Guatemala	109	8,181	2.0	1.8	80	13	6	9.6	99	94
Guinea	226	24,093	1.5	0.7	90	2	8	2.1	91	59
Guinea-Bissau	16	9,441	0.2	1.1	82	5	13	1.2	82	47
Haiti	13	1,354	1.0	7.6	94	1	5	3.9	70	51

	Renewable internal freshwater resources[a]		Annual freshwater withdrawals					Water productivity	Access to an improved water source	
	Flows billion cu. m 2007	Per capita cu. m 2007	billion cu. m 2007[b]	% of internal resources 2007[b]	% for agriculture 2007[b]	% for industry 2007[b]	% for domestic 2007[b]	GDP/water use 2000 $ per cu. m 2007[b]	% of urban population 2006	% of rural population 2006
Honduras	96	13,527	0.9	0.9	80	12	8	8.3	95	74
Hungary	6	597	7.6	127.3	32	59	9	6.3	100	100
India	1,261	1,122	645.8	51.2	86	5	8	0.7	96	86
Indonesia	2,838	12,578	82.8	2.9	91	1	8	2.0	89	71
Iran, Islamic Rep.	129	1,809	93.3	72.6	92	1	7	1.4	99	84
Iraq	35	..	66.0	187.5	79	15	7	0.4	..	..
Ireland	49	11,223	1.1	2.3	0	77	23	85.3	100	..
Israel	1	104	2.0	260.5	58	6	36	67.0	100	100
Italy	183	3,074	44.4	24.3	45	37	18	24.7	100	..
Jamaica	9	3,514	0.4	4.4	49	17	34	19.6	97	88
Japan	430	3,365	88.4	20.6	62	18	20	52.8	100	100
Jordan	1	119	0.9	138.0	65	4	31	12.1	99	91
Kazakhstan	75	4,871	35.0	46.4	82	17	2	0.5	99	91
Kenya	21	552	2.7	13.2	79	4	17	5.0	85	49
Korea, Dem. Rep.	67	2,817	9.0	13.5	55	25	20	..	100	100
Korea, Rep.	65	1,338	18.6	28.7	48	16	36	27.5	97	71
Kuwait	..	..	0.9	..	54	2	44	42.9	..	..
Kyrgyz Republic	46	8,873	10.1	21.7	94	3	3	0.1	99	83
Lao PDR	190	32,495	3.0	1.6	90	6	4	0.6	86	53
Latvia	17	7,355	0.3	1.8	13	33	53	26.1	100	96
Lebanon	5	1,172	1.3	27.3	60	11	29	15.7	100	100
Lesotho	5	2,607	0.1	1.0	20	40	40	17.1	93	74
Liberia	200	53,290	0.1	0.1	55	18	27	5.1	72	52
Libya	1	97	4.3	721.0	83	3	14	8.0	72	68
Lithuania	16	4,610	0.3	1.7	7	15	78	42.3	..	..
Macedonia, FYR	5	2,651	..	..	..	..	..	..	100	99
Madagascar	337	17,133	15.0	4.4	96	2	3	0.3	76	36
Malawi	16	1,159	1.0	6.3	80	5	15	1.7	96	72
Malaysia	580	21,846	9.0	1.6	62	21	17	10.4	100	96
Mali	60	4,865	6.5	10.9	90	1	9	0.4	86	48
Mauritania	0	128	1.7	425.0	88	3	9	0.6	70	54
Mauritius	3	2,182	0.7	26.4	68	3	30	6.9	100	100
Mexico	409	3,885	78.2	19.1	77	5	17	7.4	98	85
Moldova	1	264	2.3	231.0	33	58	10	0.6	96	85
Mongolia	35	13,322	0.4	1.3	52	27	20	2.5	90	48
Morocco	29	940	12.6	43.4	87	3	10	2.9	100	58
Mozambique	100	4,693	0.6	0.6	87	2	11	6.7	71	26
Myanmar	881	18,051	33.2	3.8	98	1	1	..	80	80
Namibia	6	2,971	0.3	4.9	71	5	24	11.4	99	90
Nepal	198	7,051	10.2	5.1	96	1	3	0.5	94	88
Netherlands	11	672	7.9	72.2	34	60	6	48.5	100	100
New Zealand	327	77,336	2.1	0.6	42	9	48	24.1	100	..
Nicaragua	190	33,854	1.3	0.7	83	2	15	3.0	90	63
Niger	4	247	2.2	62.3	95	0	4	0.8	91	32
Nigeria	221	1,493	8.0	3.6	69	10	21	5.7	65	30
Norway	382	81,119	2.2	0.6	11	67	23	76.8	100	100
Oman	1	539	1.3	94.4	88	1	10	16.9	85	73
Pakistan	55	339	169.4	308.0	96	2	2	0.4	95	87
Panama	147	44,130	0.8	0.6	28	5	67	14.2	96	81
Papua New Guinea	801	126,658	0.1	0.0	1	42	56	49.6	88	32
Paraguay	94	15,358	0.5	0.5	71	8	20	14.4	94	52
Peru	1,616	57,925	20.1	1.2	82	10	8	2.6	92	63
Philippines	479	5,450	28.5	6.0	74	9	17	2.7	96	88
Poland	54	1,406	16.2	30.2	8	79	13	10.6	100	..
Portugal	38	3,582	11.3	29.6	78	12	10	10.0	99	100
Puerto Rico	7	1,801	..	..	..	..	..	..	..	..

	Renewable internal freshwater resources[a]		Annual freshwater withdrawals					Water productivity	Access to an improved water source	
	Flows billion cu. m 2007	Per capita cu. m 2007	billion cu. m 2007[b]	% of internal resources 2007[b]	% for agriculture 2007[b]	% for industry 2007[b]	% for domestic 2007[b]	GDP/water use 2000 $ per cu. m 2007[b]	% of urban population 2006	% of rural population 2006
Romania	42	1,963	23.2	54.8	57	34	9	1.6	99	76
Russian Federation	4,313	30,350	76.7	1.8	18	63	19	3.4	100	88
Rwanda	10	976	0.2	1.6	68	8	24	11.6	82	61
Saudi Arabia	2	99	23.7	986.1	88	3	9	9.9	97	..
Senegal	26	2,079	2.2	8.6	93	3	4	2.2	93	65
Serbia	44[c]	5,419[c]	..	..	..	..	..	..	99[d]	..
Sierra Leone	160	27,358	0.4	0.2	92	3	5	1.7	83	32
Singapore	1	131	..	..	..	..	..	..	100	..
Slovak Republic	13	2,334	..	..	..	..	..	..	100	100
Slovenia	19	9,251	..	..	..	..	..	..	..	..
Somalia	6	690	3.3	55.0	99	0	0	..	63	10
South Africa	45	936	12.5	27.9	63	6	31	10.6	100	82
Spain	111	2,478	35.6	32.0	68	19	13	16.3	100	100
Sri Lanka	50	2,499	12.6	25.2	95	2	2	1.3	98	79
Sudan	30	778	37.3	124.4	97	1	3	0.3	78	64
Swaziland	3	2,306	1.0	39.5	97	1	2	1.4	87	51
Sweden	171	18,692	3.0	1.7	9	54	37	83.0	100	100
Switzerland	40	5,351	2.6	6.4	2	74	24	97.2	100	100
Syrian Arab Republic	7	352	16.7	238.4	88	4	9	1.3	95	83
Tajikistan	66	9,837	12.0	18.0	92	5	4	0.1	93	58
Tanzania	84	2,078	5.2	6.2	89	0	10	2.0	81	46
Thailand	210	3,290	87.1	41.5	95	2	2	1.4	99	97
Togo	12	1,748	0.2	1.5	45	2	53	8.2	86	40
Trinidad and Tobago	4	2,881	0.3	8.1	6	26	68	26.3	97	93
Tunisia	4	410	2.6	62.9	82	4	14	7.4	99	84
Turkey	227	3,072	40.1	17.7	74	11	15	7.0	98	95
Turkmenistan	1	274	24.7	1,812.5	98	1	2	0.1	..	..
Uganda	39	1,261	..	..	..	..	..	..	90	60
Ukraine	53	1,142	37.5	70.7	52	35	12	0.8	97	97
United Arab Emirates	0	34	4.0	2,665.3	83	2	15	24.5	100	100
United Kingdom	145	2,377	9.5	6.6	3	75	22	152.1	100	100
United States	2,800	9,283	479.3	17.1	41	46	13	20.4	100	94
Uruguay	59	17,750	3.2	5.3	96	1	3	6.6	100	100
Uzbekistan	16	608	58.3	357.0	93	2	5	0.2	98	82
Venezuela, RB	722	26,287	8.4	1.2	47	7	46	14.0	..	..
Vietnam	367	4,304	71.4	19.5	68	24	8	0.4	98	90
West Bank and Gaza	..	..	..	..	..	..	..	..	90	88
Yemen, Rep.	2	94	3.4	161.9	90	2	8	2.8	68	65
Zambia	80	6,728	1.7	2.2	76	7	17	1.9	90	41
Zimbabwe	12	915	4.2	34.3	79	7	14	1.6	98	72
World	**43,464 s**	**6,624 w**	**3,850.0 s**	**9.0 w**	**70 w**	**20 w**	**10 w**	**10.3 w**	**96 w**	**77 w**
Low income	5,985	4,619	554.6	9.4	90	5	5	1.0	84	60
Middle income	27,963	6,589	2,374.8	8.5	76	15	9	3.7	97	83
Lower middle income	14,116	4,117	2,929.5	8.7	78	13	8	3.2	96	82
Upper middle income	13,847	16,993	1,937.8	13.8	80	12	8	2.5	98	83
Low & middle income	33,947	6,128	437.0	3.2	57	26	17	8.8	94	76
East Asia & Pacific	9,454	4,945	959.0	10.2	74	20	7	3.4	96	81
Europe & Central Asia	5,167	11,806	368.4	7.2	60	30	10	3.7	99	88
Latin America & Carib.	13,425	23,965	264.9	2.0	71	10	19	9.9	97	73
Middle East & N. Africa	225	728	275.6	122.3	86	6	8	2.7	95	81
South Asia	1,819	1,196	941.1	51.7	89	4	6	1.1	94	84
Sub-Saharan Africa	3,858	4,823	120.5	3.2	87	3	10	4.1	81	46
High income	9,516	9,313	920.5	10.4	43	42	15	31.6	100	98
Euro area	930	2,907	200.0	22.3	38	48	15	33.7	100	100

a. Excludes river flows from other countries because of data unreliability. b. Refers to data reported to the Food and Agriculture Organization as of 2007. See *Primary data documentation* for year of most recent water withdrawals survey. c. Includes Montenegro. d. Includes Kosovo.

The data on freshwater resources are based on estimates of runoff into rivers and recharge of groundwater. These estimates are based on different sources and refer to different years, so cross-country comparisons should be made with caution. Because the data are collected intermittently, they may hide significant variations in total renewable water resources from year to year. The data also fail to distinguish between seasonal and geographic variations in water availability within countries. Data for small countries and countries in arid and semiarid zones are less reliable than those for larger countries and countries with greater rainfall.

Caution should also be used in comparing data on annual freshwater withdrawals, which are subject to variations in collection and estimation methods. In addition, inflows and outflows are estimated at different times and at different levels of quality and precision, requiring caution in interpreting the data, particularly for water-short countries, notably in the Middle East and North Africa.

Water productivity is an indication only of the efficiency by which each country uses its water resources. Given the different economic structure of each country, these indicators should be used carefully, taking into account the countries' sectoral activities and natural resource endowments.

The data on access to an improved water source measure the percentage of the population with ready access to water for domestic purposes. The data are based on surveys and estimates provided by governments to the Joint Monitoring Programme of the World Health Organization (WHO) and the United Nations Children's Fund (UNICEF). The coverage rates are based on information from service users on actual household use rather than on information from service providers, which may include nonfunctioning systems. Access to drinking water from an improved source does not ensure that the water is safe or adequate, as these characteristics are not tested at the time of survey. While information on access to an improved water source is widely used, it is extremely subjective, and such terms as *safe, improved, adequate,* and *reasonable* may have different meaning in different countries despite official WHO definitions (see *Definitions*). Even in high-income countries treated water may not always be safe to drink. Access to an improved water source is equated with connection to a supply system; it does not take into account variations in the quality and cost (broadly defined) of the service.

• **Renewable internal freshwater resources flows** are internal renewable resources (internal river flows and groundwater from rainfall) in the country. • **Renewable internal freshwater resources per capita** are calculated using the World Bank's population estimates (see table 2.1). • **Annual freshwater withdrawals** are total water withdrawals, not counting evaporation losses from storage basins. Withdrawals also include water from desalination plants in countries where they are a significant source. Withdrawals can exceed 100 percent of total renewable resources where extraction from nonrenewable aquifers or desalination plants is considerable or where water reuse is significant. Withdrawals for agriculture and industry are total withdrawals for irrigation and livestock production and for direct industrial use (including for cooling thermoelectric plants). Withdrawals for domestic uses include drinking water, municipal use or supply, and use for public services, commercial establishments, and homes. • **Water productivity** is calculated as GDP in constant prices divided by annual total water withdrawal. • **Access to an improved water source** is the percentage of the population with reasonable access to an adequate amount of water from an improved source, such as piped water into a dwelling, plot, or yard; public tap or standpipe; tubewell or borehole; protected dug well or spring; and rainwater collection. Unimproved sources include unprotected dug wells or springs, carts with small tank or drum, bottled water, and tanker trucks. Reasonable access is defined as the availability of at least 20 liters a person a day from a source within 1 kilometer of the dwelling.

Agriculture is still the largest user of water, accounting for some 70 percent of global withdrawals 3.5a

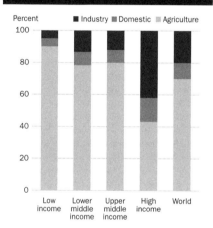

Source: Table 3.5.

The share of withdrawals for agriculture approaches 90 percent in some developing regions 3.5b

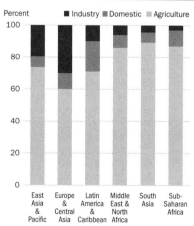

Source: Table 3.5.

Data sources

Data on freshwater resources and withdrawals are from the Food and Agriculture Organization of the United Nations AQUASTAT data. The GDP estimates used to calculate water productivity are from the World Bank national accounts database. Data on access to water are from WHO and UNICEF's *Progress on Drinking Water and Sanitation* (2008).

	Emissions of organic water pollutants				Industry shares of emissions of organic water pollutants							
									% of total			
	thousand kilograms per day		kilograms per day per worker		Primary metals	Paper and pulp	Chemicals	Food and beverages	Stone, ceramics, and glass	Textiles	Wood	Other
	1990	2005a	1990	2005a	2005a	2005a	2005a	2005a	2005a	2005a	2005a	2005a
Afghanistan	5.9	0.2	0.16	0.21	..	19.7	27.9	14.1	11.7	23.3	..	3.1
Albania	2.4	2.5	0.25	0.23	0.0	0.0	0.0	33.4	0.0	66.6	0.0	0.0
Algeria	107.0	..	0.25	..	..	..	..	..	..	..	..	..
Angola	4.5	..	0.19	..	..	..	..	..	..	..	..	..
Argentina	181.4	155.5	0.21	0.23	3.8	8.4	15.8	30.5	3.5	14.3	2.1	21.6
Armenia	37.9	7.1	0.11	0.28	..	..	..	77.6		22.4	..	..
Australia	186.1	111.7	0.18	0.18	12.4	22.8	6.7	43.5	0.2	5.3	2.8	6.3
Austria	90.5	85.2	0.15	0.14	5.5	7.2	9.2	12.4	5.2	4.8	5.9	49.7
Azerbaijan	41.3	18.1	0.15	0.18	9.6	2.4	19.3	18.1	6.5	13.7	1.2	29.3
Bangladesh	250.8	303.0	0.15	0.14	0.7	2.3	3.0	7.6	2.6	79.3	0.5	4.2
Belarus	..	..	..	..	..	..	..	..	..	..	..	..
Belgium	107.8	99.6	0.17	0.17	6.2	7.7	17.5	15.7	5.4	7.4	2.2	37.9
Benin	..	..	..	..	..	..	..	..	..	..	..	..
Bolivia	11.3	11.5	0.24	0.25	0.9	9.8	13.1	35.4	7.7	18.4	5.3	9.5
Bosnia and Herzegovina	50.7	..	0.14	..	..	..	..	..	..	..	..	..
Botswana	2.5	3.4	0.30	0.34	0.0	2.9	0.0	70.5	0.0	5.6	0.0	21.1
Brazil	780.4	..	0.19	..	..	..	..	..	..	..	..	..
Bulgaria	124.3	100.6	0.17	0.17	3.6	4.2	7.1	17.6	4.3	31.4	3.0	28.7
Burkina Faso	..	..	..	..	..	..	..	..	..	..	..	..
Burundi	1.6	..	0.24	..	..	..	..	..	..	..	..	..
Cambodia	3.6	..	0.21	..	..	..	..	..	..	..	..	..
Cameroon	14.0	10.0	0.28	0.19	0.4	5.2	36.1	48.8	0.0	3.8	5.0	0.8
Canada	300.9	310.3	0.17	0.16	4.4	9.1	10.6	13.9	2.8	7.9	6.7	44.6
Central African Republic	1.0	..	0.18	..	..	..	..	..	..	..	..	..
Chad	..	..	..	..	..	..	..	..	..	..	..	..
Chile	..	96.5	..	0.25	7.1	6.4	13.5	35.5	3.6	9.3	6.7	18.0
China	7,038.1	6,088.7	0.14	0.14	20.4	10.9	14.8	28.1	0.5	15.5	0.9	8.8
Hong Kong, China	86.1	34.3	0.12	0.20	1.2	43.5	3.9	30.5	0.1	16.2	0.2	4.6
Colombia	..	87.0	..	0.20	2.3	8.9	17.3	21.3	5.3	24.1	0.9	19.9
Congo, Dem. Rep.	..	..	..	..	..	..	..	..	..	..	..	..
Congo, Rep.	2.5	..	0.32	..	..	..	..	..	..	..	..	..
Costa Rica	27.2	31.2	0.20	0.22	1.6	10.0	8.2	65.7	0.1	10.2	1.3	2.9
Côte d'Ivoire	7.9	..	0.22	..	..	..	..	..	..	..	..	..
Croatia	48.5	41.2	0.17	0.17	3.3	7.2	9.5	17.9	5.9	16.2	4.8	35.1
Cuba	173.0	..	0.25	..	..	..	..	..	..	..	..	..
Czech Republic	176.8	152.4	0.15	0.13	5.4	4.6	9.9	11.4	4.9	8.3	4.0	51.6
Denmark	84.3	62.0	0.18	0.17	1.0	12.3	13.8	17.6	4.2	2.4	4.0	44.8
Dominican Republic	88.6	88.6	0.18	0.18	0.1	1.3	2.3	18.6	1.4	73.1	0.1	3.1
Ecuador	28.6	44.7	0.24	0.28	1.8	7.8	12.8	46.4	4.4	12.3	2.2	12.3
Egypt, Arab Rep.	206.5	206.5	0.19	0.19	5.8	4.0	13.9	20.0	8.2	31.1	0.6	16.4
El Salvador	5.5	..	0.22	..	..	..	..	..	..	..	..	..
Eritrea	2.4	2.9	0.19	0.21	0.3	4.1	8.6	31.8	14.8	24.1	0.0	16.4
Estonia	21.7	16.5	0.15	0.15	0.3	7.3	7.8	15.8	4.7	10.9	16.9	36.4
Ethiopia	18.5	24.1	0.23	0.22	1.6	6.9	10.7	29.7	8.3	28.6	1.4	12.8
Finland	72.0	59.2	0.19	0.15	1.6	17.0	8.5	9.4	4.1	3.1	7.1	49.3
France	326.5	604.7	0.11	0.16	3.2	7.4	16.1	16.1	3.7	5.4	2.3	45.8
Gabon	2.0	..	0.25	..	..	..	..	..	..	..	..	..
Gambia, The	0.8	..	0.34	..	..	..	..	..	..	..	..	..
Georgia	..	..	..	..	..	..	..	..	..	..	..	..
Germany	806.6	960.3	0.13	0.14	3.8	7.1	12.1	11.7	3.4	2.6	2.1	57.2
Ghana	..	15.4	..	0.17	3.1	2.8	15.0	19.2	4.2	10.0	34.3	11.4
Greece	50.9	46.5	0.19	0.20	4.5	7.8	13.2	22.8	6.9	20.0	2.0	22.9
Guatemala	21.6	..	0.23	..	..	..	..	..	..	..	..	..
Guinea	..	..	..	..	..	..	..	..	..	..	..	..
Guinea-Bissau	..	..	..	..	..	..	..	..	..	..	..	..
Haiti	0.1	0.0	0.01	0.01	0.0	2.0	0.0	0.0	0.0	0.0	0.0	98.0

	Emissions of organic water pollutants				Industry shares of emissions of organic water pollutants							
	thousand kilograms per day		kilograms per day per worker						% of total			
					Primary metals	Paper and pulp	Chemicals	Food and beverages	Stone, ceramics, and glass	Textiles	Wood	Other
	1990	2005[a]	1990	2005[a]	2005[a]	2005[a]	2005[a]	2005[a]	2005[a]	2005[a]	2005[a]	2005[a]
Honduras	17.8	..	0.23	..	..	..	..	..	..	..	..	..
Hungary	7.0	123.2	0.36	0.15	2.5	6.5	10.3	16.1	3.7	12.1	3.5	45.3
India	1,410.6	1,519.8	0.20	0.20	12.2	7.6	9.2	53.7	0.3	12.7	0.3	3.9
Indonesia	721.8	731.0	0.18	0.18	1.3	3.8	13.1	21.7	3.5	30.5	8.0	18.1
Iran, Islamic Rep.	131.6	163.2	0.16	0.15	7.0	2.9	12.5	16.1	14.0	11.8	0.7	34.9
Iraq	7.7	7.7	0.27	0.27	13.1	25.6	29.9	16.9	5.4	9.1	..	..
Ireland	36.0	33.6	0.19	0.20	1.2	11.9	12.1	24.5	2.7	2.1	3.7	41.8
Israel	43.9	42.8	0.18	0.18	2.2	8.5	15.0	19.7	0.0	9.1	1.5	43.9
Italy	378.3	481.3	0.13	0.12	3.5	5.3	10.4	8.7	5.4	15.0	2.9	48.9
Jamaica	18.7	..	0.29	..	..	..	..	..	..	..	..	..
Japan	1,451.4	1,133.1	0.14	0.15	3.1	7.2	11.2	15.2	3.7	5.6	2.0	52.0
Jordan	15.0	27.1	0.18	0.18	2.7	6.4	15.0	21.9	11.3	16.1	2.7	23.9
Kazakhstan	1.3	1.7	0.40	0.41	0.0	50.0	0.0	47.6	0.0	0.0	0.0	2.4
Kenya	42.6	56.1	0.23	0.24	..	11.5	5.4	66.8	0.1	12.8	1.7	1.8
Korea, Dem. Rep.	..	..	..	..	..	..	..	..	..	..	..	..
Korea, Rep.	366.9	317.0	0.12	0.12	4.3	5.5	12.3	6.5	3.1	10.2	0.9	57.2
Kuwait	9.1	11.9	0.16	0.17	2.1	16.6	11.1	50.2	0.4	11.6	2.8	5.2
Kyrgyz Republic	28.9	11.5	0.14	0.19	7.1	6.2	8.3	23.6	15.2	12.0	1.8	25.9
Lao PDR	0.5	0.5	0.44	0.44	0.0	26.3	0.0	73.7	0.0	0.0	0.0	0.0
Latvia	39.8	29.9	0.12	0.18	2.4	7.3	5.2	21.7	3.6	13.5	20.2	26.1
Lebanon	14.7	14.7	0.19	0.19	0.5	7.5	6.0	25.5	12.9	16.7	4.5	26.3
Lesotho	..	13.2	..	0.13	1.0	0.5	1.4	3.4	0.5	90.8	..	2.4
Liberia	0.6	..	0.30	..	..	..	..	..	..	..	..	..
Libya	..	..	..	..	..	..	..	..	..	..	..	..
Lithuania	54.0	42.9	0.15	0.17	0.8	4.9	7.1	20.3	4.2	21.3	11.1	30.3
Macedonia, FYR	32.4	..	0.18	..	..	..	..	..	..	..	..	..
Madagascar	11.0	88.9	..	0.14	0.3	1.6	12.4	7.6	2.8	58.9	6.3	10.0
Malawi	37.2	32.7	0.40	0.39	..	1.4	3.7	82.1	0.6	7.5	1.1	3.6
Malaysia	104.7	187.6	..	0.12	2.8	4.7	15.1	9.2	3.7	8.1	7.6	48.9
Mali	..	..	..	..	..	..	..	..	..	..	..	..
Mauritania	..	..	..	..	..	..	..	..	..	..	..	..
Mauritius	0.3	0.4	0.05	0.06	0.0	13.7	0.0	0.0	..	0.0	0.0	86.3
Mexico	370.8	..	0.19	0.20	7.8	12.5	10.4	55.6	0.2	7.5	0.9	5.1
Moldova	29.2	22.4	0.44	0.45	0.0	3.4	0.0	95.6	0.0	0.0	..	1.0
Mongolia	10.2	..	0.18	..	..	..	..	..	..	..	..	..
Morocco	..	72.8	..	0.16	0.9	3.0	9.3	16.0	7.1	45.5	1.9	16.3
Mozambique	20.4	10.2	0.27	0.31	1.1	7.1	2.7	81.2	0.1	5.8	1.4	0.7
Myanmar	7.7	6.2	0.17	0.18	56.5	4.6	13.2	14.9	0.4	2.9	1.7	5.8
Namibia	7.4	..	0.35	..	..	..	..	..	..	..	..	..
Nepal	26.4	26.8	0.14	0.16	1.6	3.9	7.2	19.2	29.9	29.4	2.0	6.8
Netherlands	137.0	119.2	0.20	0.18	1.3	13.1	15.6	18.8	3.7	2.9	2.6	42.1
New Zealand	46.7	55.6	0.24	0.22	2.2	10.4	8.4	28.9	3.0	7.2	8.3	31.7
Nicaragua	10.5	..	0.27	..	..	..	..	..	..	..	..	..
Niger	..	0.4	..	0.32	..	17.0	4.4	76.9	0.3	..	0.8	0.6
Nigeria	70.8	..	0.22	..	..	..	..	..	..	..	..	..
Norway	51.8	49.2	0.20	0.20	3.9	14.6	7.6	21.0	3.8	2.1	5.7	41.2
Oman	3.8	6.5	0.15	0.18	3.9	6.2	16.1	22.1	23.4	6.2	2.2	19.8
Pakistan	104.1	..	0.18	..	..	..	..	..	..	..	..	..
Panama	10.3	12.9	0.30	0.31	1.6	10.2	8.2	53.8	5.6	7.5	1.7	11.4
Papua New Guinea	5.7	..	0.25	..	..	..	..	..	..	..	..	..
Paraguay	15.3	10.8	0.20	0.28	3.1	9.3	16.7	42.6	5.9	11.0	4.5	6.9
Peru	56.1	..	0.20	..	..	..	..	..	..	..	..	..
Philippines	118.4	98.5	0.26	0.24	6.7	6.9	15.2	34.7	7.3	3.4	0.0	25.9
Poland	446.7	364.2	0.16	0.16	3.1	5.1	10.7	19.0	5.6	11.8	5.2	39.6
Portugal	140.6	107.2	0.14	0.15	2.3	7.0	6.2	14.5	8.6	25.3	3.9	32.2
Puerto Rico	19.0	9.2	0.15	0.18	1.9	14.9	21.9	34.4	0.2	15.5	1.4	9.7

| | Emissions of organic water pollutants | | | | Industry shares of emissions of organic water pollutants | | | | | | | |
| | thousand kilograms per day | | kilograms per day per worker | | Primary metals | Paper and pulp | Chemicals | Food and beverages | Stone, ceramics, and glass | Textiles | Wood | Other |
	1990	2005ᵃ	1990	2005ᵃ	2005ᵃ	2005ᵃ	2005ᵃ	2005ᵃ	2005ᵃ	2005ᵃ	2005ᵃ	2005ᵃ
Romania	407.0	235.1	0.12	0.15	4.8	3.2	6.7	12.7	4.0	28.9	5.2	34.4
Russian Federation	1,521.4	1,425.9	0.16	0.17	9.8	4.8	11.7	17.5	7.9	6.8	4.3	37.3
Rwanda	7.1	7.1	0.44	0.44	..	..	0.0	97.0	0.0	0.0	0.0	3.0
Saudi Arabia	18.5	..	0.15	..	..	..	..	..	..	..	..	..
Senegal	6.1	6.6	0.30	0.29	4.9	6.3	23.8	44.6	3.9	10.5	0.8	5.3
Serbia	..	..	..	..	..	..	..	..	..	..	..	..
Sierra Leone	4.2	..	0.32	..	..	..	..	..	..	..	..	..
Singapore	32.4	34.3	0.09	0.10	1.4	24.6	16.0	25.4	0.1	3.9	1.6	26.9
Slovak Republic	72.8	54.6	0.13	0.14	7.3	4.8	8.0	10.5	5.7	14.3	3.2	46.3
Slovenia	55.6	38.4	0.16	0.16	33.7	14.7	8.3	23.7	0.2	10.8	2.0	6.7
Somalia	6.2	..	0.38	..	..	..	..	..	..	..	..	..
South Africa	260.5	183.8	0.17	0.17	6.7	7.3	11.7	16.5	5.0	7.0	4.6	41.3
Spain	348.0	372.5	0.16	0.15	3.1	7.8	10.6	14.9	7.6	9.6	3.8	42.6
Sri Lanka	53.0	78.4	0.19	0.18	0.5	7.2	6.6	51.5	0.2	31.6	1.1	1.2
Sudan	..	38.6	..	0.29	0.6	1.9	7.0	57.5	14.2	8.0	1.7	9.1
Swaziland	146.0	..	0.16	..	..	..	..	..	..	..	..	..
Sweden	116.8	100.1	0.15	0.15	5.3	12.4	9.7	9.0	2.5	1.4	5.4	54.3
Switzerland	..	..	..	..	..	..	..	..	..	..	..	..
Syrian Arab Republic	6.6	4.5	0.45	0.45	0.0	6.2	0.0	93.8	0.0	0.0	0.0	0.0
Tajikistan	29.1	16.1	0.17	0.23	21.9	1.4	5.1	20.2	7.6	37.5	0.4	5.9
Tanzania	31.1	35.2	0.24	0.25	1.5	9.4	2.7	69.3	0.1	14.0	1.5	1.4
Thailand	369.4	333.8	0.15	0.16	1.8	4.1	13.2	16.5	3.4	22.5	2.4	36.1
Timor-Leste	..	..	..	..	..	..	..	..	..	..	..	..
Togo	..	..	..	..	..	..	..	..	..	..	..	..
Trinidad and Tobago	7.0	7.6	0.23	0.29	0.0	18.1	21.4	39.1	0.4	7.6	8.5	4.9
Tunisia	44.6	55.8	0.18	0.14	2.5	6.1	5.5	35.8	0.4	43.3	1.9	4.6
Turkey	174.9	177.7	0.18	0.16	5.2	3.0	9.8	15.2	6.2	35.7	1.0	24.0
Turkmenistan	..	..	..	..	..	..	..	..	..	..	..	..
Uganda	2.7	2.1	0.27	0.23	..	7.8	7.3	34.8	13.3	17.2	0.0	19.6
Ukraine	..	527.2	..	0.19	14.6	4.1	10.3	19.0	6.4	6.6	2.2	36.8
United Arab Emirates	5.6	..	0.14	..	..	..	..	..	..	..	..	..
United Kingdom	599.9	539.7	0.16	0.17	2.5	12.4	13.6	14.4	3.8	4.6	2.4	46.2
United States	2,307.0	1,960.3	0.14	0.14	3.4	9.0	13.0	11.8	3.6	5.0	4.0	50.3
Uruguay	38.7	15.8	0.23	0.28	1.2	3.7	6.6	79.2	0.1	7.4	0.6	1.2
Uzbekistan	..	..	..	..	..	..	..	..	..	..	..	..
Venezuela, RB	96.5	..	0.21	..	..	..	..	..	..	..	..	..
Vietnam	141.0	470.2	0.16	0.15	1.4	3.7	6.6	14.3	7.1	40.3	3.7	22.9
West Bank and Gaza	..	..	..	..	..	..	..	..	..	..	..	..
Yemen, Rep.	1.5	1.0	0.43	0.41	..	79.9	0.0	20.1	0.0	0.0	0.0	0.0
Zambia	15.9	..	0.23	..	..	..	..	..	..	..	..	..
Zimbabwe	29.3	29.3	0.20	0.20	8.0	4.7	11.0	21.5	6.3	25.2	1.7	21.5

a. Data are derived using the United Nations Industrial Development Organization's (UNIDO) industry database four-digit International Standard Industrial Classification (ISIC). Data in italics are for the most recent year available and are derived using UNIDO's industry database at the three-digit ISIC.

About the data

Emissions of organic pollutants from industrial activities are a major cause of degradation of water quality. Water quality and pollution levels are generally measured as concentration or load—the rate of occurrence of a substance in an aqueous solution. Polluting substances include organic matter, metals, minerals, sediment, bacteria, and toxic chemicals. The table focuses on organic water pollution resulting from industrial activities. Because water pollution tends to be sensitive to local conditions, the national-level data in the table may not reflect the quality of water in specific locations.

The data in the table come from an international study of industrial emissions that may have been the first to include data from developing countries (Hettige, Mani, and Wheeler 1998). These data were updated through 2005 by the World Bank's Development Research Group. Unlike estimates from earlier studies based on engineering or economic models, these estimates are based on actual measurements of plant-level water pollution. The focus is on organic water pollution caused by organic waste, measured in terms of biochemical oxygen demand (BOD), because the data for this indicator are the most plentiful and reliable for cross-country comparisons of emissions. BOD measures the strength of an organic waste by the amount of oxygen consumed in breaking it down. A sewage overload in natural waters exhausts the water's dissolved oxygen content. Wastewater treatment, by contrast, reduces BOD.

Data on water pollution are more readily available than are other emissions data because most industrial pollution control programs start by regulating emissions of organic water pollutants. Such data are fairly reliable because sampling techniques for measuring water pollution are more widely understood and much less expensive than those for air pollution.

Hettige, Mani, and Wheeler (1998) used plant- and sector-level information on emissions and employment from 13 national environmental protection agencies and sector-level information on output and employment from the United Nations Industrial Development Organization (UNIDO). Their econometric analysis found that the ratio of BOD to employment in each industrial sector is about the same across countries. This finding allowed the authors to estimate BOD loads across countries and over time. The estimated BOD intensities per unit of employment were multiplied by sectoral employment numbers from UNIDO's industry database for 1980–98. These estimates of sectoral emissions were then used to calculate kilograms of emissions of organic water pollutants per day for each country and year. The data in the table were derived by updating these estimates through 2005.

Definitions

• **Emissions of organic water pollutants** are measured as biochemical oxygen demand, or the amount of oxygen that bacteria in water will consume in breaking down waste, a standard water treatment test for the presence of organic pollutants. Emissions per worker are total emissions divided by the number of industrial workers. • **Industry shares of emissions of organic water pollutants** are emissions from manufacturing activities as defined by two-digit divisions of the International Standard Industrial Classification (ISIC) revision 3.

Emissions of organic water pollutants declined in most economies from 1990 to 2005, even in some of the top emitters

3.6a

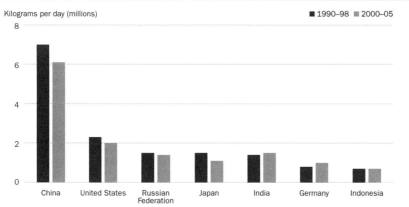

Kilograms per day (millions)

■ 1990–98 ■ 2000–05

Note: Data are for the most recent year available during the period specified.

Source: Table 3.6.

Data sources

Data on water pollutants are from the 1998 study by Hemamala Hettige, Muthukumara Mani, and David Wheeler, "Industrial Pollution in Economic Development: Kuznets Revisited" (available at www.worldbank.org/nipr). The data were updated through 2005 by the World Bank's Development Research Group using the same methodology as the initial study. Data on industrial sectoral employment are from UNIDO's industry database.

3.7 | Energy production and use

	Energy production		Energy use										Clean energy production	
	Total million metric tons of oil equivalent		Total million metric tons of oil equivalent		average annual % growth	Per capita kilograms of oil equivalent		% of total						% of total energy use	
								Fossil fuel		Combustible renewables and waste					
	1990	2006	1990	2006	1990–2006	1990	2006	1990	2006	1990	2006			1990	2006
Afghanistan	..	..	..	..	..	..	..	..	..	..	..			..	..
Albania	2.4	1.2	2.7	2.3	2.2	809	715	76.5	68.5	13.6	10.1			9.2	19.0
Algeria	104.4	173.2	23.9	36.7	2.5	946	1,100	99.9	99.7	0.1	0.2			0.1	0.1
Angola	28.7	79.2	6.3	10.3	3.2	597	620	30.2	33.9	68.8	63.9			1.0	2.2
Argentina	48.4	83.9	46.1	69.1	2.0	1,414	1,766	88.7	88.4	3.7	3.7			7.5	7.6
Armenia	0.1	0.8	7.9	2.6	–4.8	2,228	859	97.3	68.3	0.1	0.0			1.7	32.7
Australia	157.5	267.8	87.7	122.5	2.2	5,138	5,917	94.0	94.7	4.5	4.1			1.5	1.3
Austria	8.1	9.9	25.1	34.2	2.0	3,249	4,132	79.4	75.6	9.9	13.1			10.9	9.6
Azerbaijan	21.3	38.1	26.1	14.1	–3.3	3,643	1,659	..	97.9	0.0	0.0			0.2	1.5
Bangladesh	10.8	20.3	12.8	25.0	4.5	113	161	45.9	65.8	53.5	33.7			0.6	0.5
Belarus	3.3	3.9	42.3	28.6	–2.3	4,153	2,939	95.5	91.9	0.5	5.0			0.0	0.0
Belgium	13.6	15.5	49.7	61.0	1.4	4,988	5,782	75.6	72.5	2.6	5.9			22.4	20.0
Benin	1.8	1.7	1.7	2.8	3.0	324	321	5.8	37.1	93.2	61.1			0.0	0.0
Bolivia	4.9	14.3	2.8	5.8	4.2	416	625	69.1	83.1	27.2	13.8			3.6	3.2
Bosnia and Herzegovina	4.6	4.0	7.0	5.4	1.7	1,633	1,427	93.9	90.6	2.3	3.4			3.7	9.4
Botswana	0.9	1.1	1.3	2.0	2.6	931	1,054	66.3	69.2	33.1	23.2			0.1	0.0
Brazil	103.7	206.7	140.0	224.1	3.0	936	1,184	51.2	53.7	34.0	29.6			13.1	15.0
Bulgaria	9.6	11.1	28.8	20.7	–1.5	3,305	2,688	84.4	72.8	0.6	3.9			13.8	26.5
Burkina Faso	..	..	..	..	..	..	..	..	..	..	..			..	..
Burundi	..	..	..	..	..	..	..	..	..	..	..			..	..
Cambodia	..	3.6	..	5.0	3.6	..	351	..	28.4	..	71.3			..	0.1
Cameroon	11.0	10.3	5.0	7.1	2.3	411	390	19.5	16.3	75.9	79.2			4.5	4.5
Canada	273.7	411.7	209.5	269.7	1.7	7,539	8,262	74.7	75.0	3.9	4.7			21.4	20.9
Central African Republic	..	..	..	..	..	..	..	..	..	..	..			..	..
Chad	..	..	..	..	..	..	..	..	..	..	..			..	..
Chile	7.6	10.0	14.1	29.8	5.0	1,067	1,812	74.8	73.5	19.0	15.9			6.2	9.9
China	886.3	1,749.3	863.2	1,878.7	4.4	760	1,433	75.5	85.1	23.2	12.0			1.3	3.0
Hong Kong, China	0.0	0.0	10.7	18.2	3.1	1,872	2,653	99.5	96.7	0.5	0.3			0.0	0.0
Colombia	48.2	84.6	24.7	30.2	0.5	747	695	68.1	73.4	22.3	14.9			9.6	12.2
Congo, Dem. Rep.	12.0	17.8	11.9	17.5	2.4	314	289	12.0	4.6	84.0	92.4			4.1	3.9
Congo, Rep.	8.7	15.4	0.8	1.2	2.6	329	327	35.0	36.8	59.5	57.6			5.3	2.7
Costa Rica	1.0	2.3	2.0	4.6	5.0	658	1,040	48.3	48.6	36.6	15.5			14.4	35.8
Côte d'Ivoire	3.4	9.3	4.4	7.3	3.4	345	385	24.9	35.7	72.0	63.8			2.6	1.8
Croatia	5.1	4.1	9.1	9.0	1.3	1,905	2,017	86.7	84.7	3.4	4.1			3.6	5.8
Cuba	6.6	5.0	16.8	10.6	–1.6	1,587	944	65.1	88.0	34.9	11.9			0.0	0.1
Czech Republic	40.1	33.4	49.0	46.1	0.1	4,726	4,485	93.2	83.0	0.0	4.0			6.9	15.3
Denmark	10.1	29.6	17.9	20.9	0.4	3,486	3,850	89.9	87.3	6.4	12.9			0.3	2.6
Dominican Republic	1.0	1.5	4.1	7.8	4.4	567	816	75.1	80.4	24.2	18.0			0.7	1.5
Ecuador	16.5	29.8	6.1	11.2	3.8	597	851	79.5	88.2	13.5	5.2			7.0	5.5
Egypt, Arab Rep.	54.9	77.8	32.0	62.5	4.6	580	843	94.0	95.9	3.3	2.3			2.7	1.9
El Salvador	1.7	2.6	2.5	4.7	3.8	496	697	32.0	44.0	48.2	31.6			19.8	24.4
Eritrea	0.7	0.5	0.9	0.7	–2.2	277	150	19.7	27.0	80.3	73.0			0.0	0.0
Estonia	5.1	3.6	9.6	4.9	–2.8	6,122	3,638	..	88.7	2.0	10.7			0.0	0.2
Ethiopia	14.1	20.4	15.0	22.3	2.6	313	289	6.6	8.8	92.8	90.0			0.6	1.3
Finland	12.1	18.0	28.7	37.4	1.8	5,758	7,108	56.0	52.2	15.9	20.4			20.7	18.6
France	112.4	137.0	227.6	272.7	1.2	4,012	4,444	58.6	52.6	5.1	4.4			38.1	44.9
Gabon	14.6	12.1	1.2	1.8	2.2	1,354	1,391	35.4	39.2	59.8	56.3			4.9	4.4
Gambia, The	..	..	..	..	..	..	..	..	..	..	..			..	..
Georgia	1.8	1.2	12.3	3.3	–8.2	2,255	754	88.7	65.1	3.7	19.3			5.3	14.0
Germany	186.2	136.8	355.6	348.6	0.0	4,477	4,231	87.0	81.8	1.3	4.6			11.6	13.9
Ghana	4.4	6.5	5.3	9.5	3.6	343	413	19.0	31.7	73.1	63.3			9.2	5.1
Greece	9.2	10.0	22.2	31.1	2.5	2,188	2,792	94.8	93.1	4.0	3.3			0.9	2.5
Guatemala	3.4	5.4	4.5	8.2	4.1	503	628	28.8	44.5	67.9	51.5			3.4	4.0
Guinea	..	..	..	..	..	..	..	..	..	..	..			..	..
Guinea-Bissau	..	..	..	..	..	..	..	..	..	..	..			..	..
Haiti	1.3	2.0	1.6	2.6	3.3	223	272	20.9	23.3	76.5	75.8			2.5	0.9

Energy production and use | 3.7

	Energy production		Energy use									Clean energy production	
	Total million metric tons of oil equivalent		Total million metric tons of oil equivalent		average annual % growth	Per capita kilograms of oil equivalent		% of total				% of total energy use	
								Fossil fuel		Combustible renewables and waste			
	1990	2006	1990	2006	1990–2006	1990	2006	1990	2006	1990	2006	1990	2006
Honduras	1.7	2.0	2.4	4.3	3.2	494	621	31.1	53.3	62.0	41.5	8.1	5.1
Hungary	14.3	10.3	28.6	27.6	0.1	2,753	2,740	82.4	80.3	1.3	4.3	12.9	13.2
India	291.1	435.6	319.9	565.8	3.5	377	510	55.8	69.0	41.7	28.3	2.4	2.7
Indonesia	170.0	307.7	102.8	179.1	3.4	577	803	54.7	67.1	43.8	29.2	1.5	3.7
Iran, Islamic Rep.	179.8	309.3	68.8	170.9	5.5	1,265	2,438	98.2	98.6	1.0	0.5	0.8	0.9
Iraq	104.9	101.1	19.1	32.0	3.2	1,029	1,123	98.7	99.4	0.1	0.1	1.2	0.1
Ireland	3.5	1.6	10.3	15.5	3.2	2,943	3,628	85.3	91.8	1.0	1.4	0.6	1.3
Israel	0.4	2.7	12.1	21.3	3.6	2,599	3,017	97.3	97.3	0.0	0.0	3.0	3.4
Italy	25.3	27.4	148.1	184.2	1.6	2,611	3,125	93.5	90.7	0.6	2.6	3.8	4.6
Jamaica	0.5	0.5	2.9	4.6	2.5	1,233	1,724	83.5	89.2	16.2	10.5	0.3	0.3
Japan	75.2	101.1	443.9	527.6	1.1	3,593	4,129	84.7	81.6	1.1	1.3	14.2	17.1
Jordan	0.2	0.3	3.5	7.2	4.1	1,103	1,294	98.3	98.0	0.1	0.0	1.7	1.4
Kazakhstan	90.5	131.0	73.6	61.4	−2.3	4,505	4,012	97.0	98.7	0.2	0.1	0.9	1.1
Kenya	9.0	14.3	11.2	17.9	2.9	479	491	19.5	20.6	75.9	73.6	4.4	5.9
Korea, Dem. Rep.	28.9	22.2	33.2	21.7	−2.4	1,649	913	93.1	90.2	2.9	4.8	4.0	5.0
Korea, Rep.	22.6	43.7	93.4	216.5	5.3	2,178	4,483	83.9	80.8	0.8	1.1	15.4	18.1
Kuwait	50.4	150.6	8.0	25.3	8.0	3,762	9,729	99.9	100.0	0.1	0.0	0.0	0.0
Kyrgyz Republic	2.5	1.5	7.6	2.8	−4.9	1,713	542	93.6	62.0	0.1	0.1	11.3	45.5
Lao PDR	..	..	..	..	..	..	..	..	..	..	..	..	..
Latvia	1.1	1.8	7.9	4.6	−3.0	2,941	2,017	81.8	64.2	8.4	25.9	4.9	5.1
Lebanon	0.1	0.2	2.3	4.8	4.6	777	1,173	93.7	94.2	4.5	2.7	1.9	1.4
Lesotho	..	..	..	..	..	..	..	..	..	..	..	..	..
Liberia	..	..	..	..	..	..	..	..	..	..	..	..	..
Libya	73.2	102.0	11.5	17.8	2.3	2,645	2,943	98.9	99.1	1.1	0.9	0.0	0.0
Lithuania	4.9	3.5	16.2	8.5	−2.8	4,394	2,517	76.0	62.1	1.8	8.8	27.9	27.4
Macedonia, FYR	1.5	1.5	2.7	2.8	−0.3	1,423	1,355	98.2	82.9	0.0	6.0	1.5	5.5
Madagascar	..	..	..	..	..	..	..	..	..	..	..	..	..
Malawi	..	..	..	..	..	..	..	..	..	..	..	..	..
Malaysia	50.3	97.9	23.3	68.3	6.1	1,288	2,617	89.4	95.3	9.1	4.1	1.5	0.9
Mali	..	..	..	..	..	..	..	..	..	..	..	..	..
Mauritania	..	..	..	..	..	..	..	..	..	..	..	..	..
Mauritius	..	..	..	..	..	..	..	..	..	..	..	..	..
Mexico	193.4	256.0	123.0	177.4	2.2	1,478	1,702	88.3	89.1	6.0	4.6	5.8	6.4
Moldova	0.1	0.1	9.9	3.4	−6.1	2,265	884	..	88.7	0.4	2.2	0.2	0.2
Mongolia	2.7	3.0	3.4	2.8	−1.9	1,624	1,080	96.9	95.7	2.5	3.8	0.0	0.0
Morocco	0.8	0.7	7.2	14.0	3.9	298	458	94.0	94.5	4.4	3.2	1.5	1.1
Mozambique	5.6	10.7	6.0	8.8	2.7	441	420	6.2	6.9	93.2	81.6	0.4	14.4
Myanmar	10.7	22.1	10.7	14.3	1.9	266	295	14.6	25.9	84.4	72.1	1.0	2.0
Namibia	0.2	0.3	0.7	1.5	5.1	443	721	62.0	67.3	16.0	12.7	17.5	8.8
Nepal	5.5	8.3	5.8	9.4	3.2	304	340	5.3	11.3	93.4	86.2	1.3	2.4
Netherlands	60.5	60.8	67.1	80.1	1.2	4,489	4,901	96.0	92.9	1.4	3.3	1.4	1.5
New Zealand	12.0	13.1	13.8	17.5	1.6	3,991	4,192	65.4	70.0	4.0	6.0	30.7	24.0
Nicaragua	1.5	2.1	2.1	3.5	3.1	512	624	29.2	39.0	53.2	52.2	17.3	8.7
Niger	..	..	..	..	..	..	..	..	..	..	..	..	..
Nigeria	150.5	235.3	70.9	105.1	2.4	751	726	19.7	19.8	79.8	79.6	0.5	0.6
Norway	119.1	222.9	21.4	26.1	1.9	5,050	5,598	52.8	54.9	4.8	5.1	48.6	39.6
Oman	38.3	60.6	4.6	15.4	7.1	2,475	6,057	100.0	100.0	0.0	0.0	0.0	0.0
Pakistan	34.4	61.3	43.4	79.3	3.7	402	499	53.3	60.9	43.2	34.9	3.5	4.2
Panama	0.6	0.8	1.5	2.8	3.6	618	845	58.4	71.7	28.3	17.4	12.8	11.1
Papua New Guinea	..	..	..	..	..	..	..	..	..	..	..	..	..
Paraguay	4.6	6.7	3.1	4.0	1.5	731	660	21.6	30.5	72.3	52.0	75.8	116.5
Peru	10.6	11.5	10.0	13.6	2.1	457	491	64.1	68.5	26.9	17.4	9.0	14.0
Philippines	13.7	24.7	26.2	43.0	3.6	427	498	50.8	51.0	29.2	26.1	20.0	22.9
Poland	99.4	77.9	99.9	97.7	−0.6	2,620	2,562	97.7	95.3	2.2	5.5	0.1	0.2
Portugal	3.4	4.3	17.2	25.4	3.1	1,742	2,402	81.0	81.1	14.4	11.9	4.7	5.2
Puerto Rico	..	..	..	..	..	..	..	..	..	..	..	..	..

	Energy production — Total million metric tons of oil equivalent		Energy use — Total million metric tons of oil equivalent		Energy use — average annual % growth	Energy use — Per capita kilograms of oil equivalent		% of total — Fossil fuel		% of total — Combustible renewables and waste		Clean energy production — % of total energy use	
	1990	**2006**	**1990**	**2006**	**1990–2006**	**1990**	**2006**	**1990**	**2006**	**1990**	**2006**	**1990**	**2006**
Romania	40.8	28.0	62.5	40.1	–2.3	2,693	1,860	96.2	85.1	1.0	8.1	1.6	7.6
Russian Federation	1,280.3	1,220.0	878.9	676.2	–1.5	5,927	4,745	93.4	89.4	1.4	1.1	5.2	8.3
Rwanda	..	..	..	..	..	..	..	..	..	..	..	..	..
Saudi Arabia	370.8	570.7	61.3	146.1	4.7	3,744	6,170	100.0	100.0	0.0	0.0	0.0	0.0
Senegal	1.0	1.2	1.8	3.0	3.8	233	250	48.0	59.5	52.0	39.6	0.0	0.7
Serbia	13.4[a]	10.6	19.5[a]	17.1	..	2,569[a]	2,303	90.7[a]	90.2	6.0[a]	4.7	4.2[a]	5.5
Sierra Leone	..	..	..	..	..	..	..	..	..	..	..	..	..
Singapore	0.0	0.0	13.4	30.7	3.8	4,384	6,968	100.0	100.0	0.0	0.0	0.0	0.0
Slovak Republic	5.3	6.6	21.3	18.7	–0.1	4,035	3,465	81.6	70.9	0.8	2.6	15.5	27.5
Slovenia	2.9	3.3	5.6	7.3	2.2	2,792	3,618	70.6	69.2	4.8	6.5	26.2	24.2
Somalia	..	..	..	..	..	..	..	..	..	..	..	..	..
South Africa	114.5	158.7	91.2	129.8	2.1	2,592	2,739	86.2	87.1	11.4	10.5	2.5	2.7
Spain	34.6	31.4	91.2	144.6	3.3	2,349	3,277	77.7	82.8	4.5	3.6	17.9	13.8
Sri Lanka	4.2	5.5	5.5	9.4	3.7	322	472	24.1	41.4	71.0	54.3	4.9	4.2
Sudan	8.8	30.7	10.7	17.7	3.5	411	470	17.7	21.8	81.5	77.5	0.8	0.7
Swaziland	..	..	..	..	..	..	..	..	..	..	..	..	..
Sweden	29.7	32.8	47.6	51.3	0.5	5,557	5,650	37.8	34.9	11.6	18.4	50.5	44.5
Switzerland	9.7	12.1	24.8	28.2	0.7	3,695	3,770	61.5	56.1	3.7	7.2	35.5	35.9
Syrian Arab Republic	22.3	26.5	11.7	18.9	2.9	918	975	98.0	98.2	0.0	0.0	2.0	1.8
Tajikistan	2.0	1.5	5.6	3.6	–2.7	1,051	548	72.7	59.5	0.0	0.0	25.5	39.1
Tanzania	9.1	19.4	9.8	20.8	4.8	385	527	7.6	8.3	91.0	91.0	1.4	0.6
Thailand	26.5	56.2	43.9	103.4	5.2	809	1,630	65.5	82.3	33.4	16.6	1.0	0.7
Timor-Leste	..	..	..	..	..	..	..	..	..	..	..	..	..
Togo	1.1	2.0	1.3	2.4	4.6	328	375	17.3	13.4	80.6	84.5	0.6	0.3
Trinidad and Tobago	12.6	34.6	6.0	14.3	5.8	4,934	10,768	99.2	99.8	0.8	0.2	0.0	0.0
Tunisia	5.7	6.6	5.1	8.7	3.7	630	863	87.5	86.6	12.4	13.3	0.1	0.1
Turkey	25.8	26.3	52.9	94.0	3.5	943	1,288	81.9	89.1	13.6	5.5	4.6	5.5
Turkmenistan	74.9	61.6	19.6	17.3	1.1	5,352	3,524	..	100.0	0.0	0.0	0.3	0.0
Uganda	..	..	..	..	..	..	..	..	..	..	..	..	..
Ukraine	135.8	82.8	253.8	137.4	–3.5	4,891	2,937	91.9	82.2	0.1	0.4	8.2	17.9
United Arab Emirates	110.2	177.3	23.2	46.9	4.4	12,416	11,036	100.0	100.0	0.0	0.0	0.0	0.0
United Kingdom	208.0	186.6	212.3	231.1	0.5	3,708	3,814	90.9	89.2	0.3	1.7	8.3	8.9
United States	1,649.4	1,654.2	1,926.3	2,320.7	1.3	7,717	7,768	86.5	85.7	3.2	3.4	10.2	10.8
Uruguay	1.1	0.8	2.3	3.2	1.2	725	962	58.7	67.8	24.3	14.9	26.8	9.7
Uzbekistan	38.6	58.2	46.4	48.5	0.6	2,261	1,829	99.2	98.9	0.0	0.0	1.2	1.1
Venezuela, RB	148.9	195.5	43.9	62.2	1.6	2,224	2,302	91.5	88.2	1.2	0.9	7.2	11.0
Vietnam	24.7	71.9	24.3	52.3	5.1	367	621	20.4	49.8	77.7	46.4	1.9	3.9
West Bank and Gaza	..	..	..	..	..	..	..	..	..	..	..	..	..
Yemen, Rep.	9.4	18.7	2.6	7.1	6.4	208	326	97.0	98.9	3.0	1.1	0.0	0.0
Zambia	4.9	6.7	5.5	7.3	1.7	673	625	16.6	11.1	73.4	78.2	12.5	11.0
Zimbabwe	8.6	8.8	9.4	9.6	–0.2	895	724	45.3	29.2	50.4	63.3	4.0	5.0
World	**8,821.7 t**	**11,786.0 t**	**8,637.3 t**	**11,525.2 t**	**1.8 w**	**1,686 w**	**1,820 w**	**81.2 w**	**80.9 w**	**10.0 w**	**9.8 w**	**8.7 w**	**9.2 w**
Low income	451.2	734.4	400.2	575.5	2.4	482	478	44.5	43.1	52.9	53.8	2.8	3.2
Middle income	4,623.1	6,447.4	3,797.2	5,348.7	2.0	1,097	1,267	81.2	82.4	14.6	12.3	4.1	5.2
Lower middle income	2,272.0	3,782.9	1,973.3	3,468.8	3.3	716	1,019	74.4	81.0	22.7	15.2	3.0	3.9
Upper middle income	2,351.1	2,664.4	1,823.9	1,879.8	0.2	2,584	2,300	88.4	84.8	5.9	7.0	5.3	7.6
Low & middle income	5,058.6	7,147.8	4,181.1	5,899.7	2.1	990	1,108	78.1	79.0	17.9	15.9	4.0	5.0
East Asia & Pacific	1,223.4	2,372.6	1,140.5	2,382.5	4.2	718	1,258	71.8	82.1	26.4	14.7	1.8	3.2
Europe & Central Asia	1,862.0	1,772.5	1,695.2	1,302.8	–1.5	3,887	2,930	93.2	89.1	1.6	2.2	5.0	8.1
Latin America & Carib.	608.6	926.1	457.6	685.9	2.4	1,054	1,240	71.4	73.0	19.5	15.9	9.1	11.0
Middle East & N. Africa	563.0	827.2	190.2	385.5	4.3	849	1,254	97.3	97.8	1.6	1.2	1.1	0.9
South Asia	348.8	535.6	390.8	694.8	3.5	350	468	54.0	66.8	43.5	30.4	2.5	2.8
Sub-Saharan Africa	475.6	762.2	313.3	467.6	2.5	685	670	41.8	41.1	56.1	56.3	2.2	2.6
High income	3,780.4	4,663.1	4,479.4	5,659.1	1.6	4,807	5,416	84.1	82.9	2.8	3.4	13.0	13.5
Euro area	477.4	463.1	1,075.7	1,268.9	1.2	3,567	3,936	80.0	76.4	3.2	4.9	16.4	18.3

a. Includes Kosovo and Montenegro.

3.7

About the data

In developing economies growth in energy use is closely related to growth in the modern sectors—industry, motorized transport, and urban areas—but energy use also reflects climatic, geographic, and economic factors (such as the relative price of energy). Energy use has been growing rapidly in low- and middle-income economies, but high-income economies still use almost five times as much energy on a per capita basis.

Energy data are compiled by the International Energy Agency (IEA). IEA data for economies that are not members of the Organisation for Economic Co-operation and Development (OECD) are based on national energy data adjusted to conform to annual questionnaires completed by OECD member governments.

Total energy use refers to the use of primary energy before transformation to other end-use fuels (such as electricity and refined petroleum products). It includes energy from combustible renewables and waste—solid biomass and animal products, gas and liquid from biomass, and industrial and municipal waste. Biomass is any plant matter used directly as fuel or converted into fuel, heat, or electricity. Data for combustible renewables and waste are often based on small surveys or other incomplete information and thus give only a broad impression of developments and are not strictly comparable across countries. The IEA reports include country notes that explain some of these differences (see *Data sources*). All forms of energy—primary energy and primary electricity—are converted into oil equivalents. A notional thermal efficiency of 33 percent is assumed for converting nuclear electricity into oil equivalents and 100 percent efficiency for converting hydroelectric power.

The IEA makes these estimates in consultation with national statistical offices, oil companies, electric utilities, and national energy experts. The IEA occasionally revises its time series to reflect political changes, and energy statistics undergo continual changes in coverage or methodology as more detailed energy accounts become available. Breaks in series are therefore unavoidable.

Definitions

• **Energy production** refers to forms of primary energy—petroleum (crude oil, natural gas liquids, and oil from nonconventional sources), natural gas, solid fuels (coal, lignite, and other derived fuels), and combustible renewables and waste—and primary electricity, all converted into oil equivalents (see *About the data*). • **Energy use** refers to the use of primary energy before transformation to other end-use fuels, which is equal to indigenous production plus imports and stock changes, minus exports and fuels supplied to ships and aircraft engaged in international transport (see *About the data*). • **Fossil fuel** comprises coal, oil, petroleum, and natural gas products. • **Combustible renewables and waste** comprise solid biomass, liquid biomass, biogas, industrial waste, and municipal waste. • **Clean energy production** is noncarbohydrate energy that does not produce carbon dioxide when generated. It includes hydropower and nuclear, geothermal, and solar power, among others.

A person in a high-income economy uses an average of more than 11 times as much energy as a person in a low-income economy

3.7a

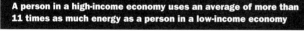

Energy use per capita (thousands of kilograms of oil equivalent) ■ 1990 ■ 2006

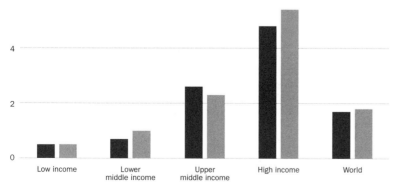

Source: Table 3.7.

Data sources

Data on energy production and use are from IEA electronic files and are published in IEA's annual publications, *Energy Statistics and Balances of Non-OECD Countries, Energy Statistics of OECD Countries,* and *Energy Balances of OECD Countries.*

3.8 Energy dependency and efficiency and carbon dioxide emissions

| | Net energy imports[a] (% of energy use) | | GDP per unit of energy use (2005 PPP $ per kilogram of oil equivalent) | | Carbon dioxide emissions | | | | | | | |
| | | | | | Total (million metric tons) | | Carbon intensity (kilograms per kilogram of oil equivalent energy use) | | Per capita (metric tons) | | kilograms per 2005 PPP $ of GDP | |
	1990	2006	1990	2006	1990	2005	1990	2005	1990	2005	1990	2005
Afghanistan	..	..	..	..	2.6	0.7	..	..	..	..	..	0.0
Albania	8	47	4.8	8.9	7.3	3.5	2.7	1.5	2.2	1.1	0.6	0.2
Algeria	−337	−372	6.6	6.5	77.0	137.5	3.2	4.0	3.0	4.2	0.5	0.6
Angola	−356	−671	5.4	6.9	4.6	9.0	0.7	0.9	0.4	0.6	0.1	0.2
Argentina	−5	−21	5.3	6.6	109.7	152.7	2.4	2.4	3.4	3.9	0.5	0.4
Armenia	98	67	1.3	5.5	4.2	4.3	0.5	1.7	1.2	1.4	0.4	0.3
Australia	−80	−119	4.6	5.4	293.1	368.9	3.3	3.1	17.2	18.1	0.7	0.6
Austria	68	71	8.0	8.4	57.6	73.6	2.3	2.2	7.5	8.9	0.3	0.3
Azerbaijan	18	−171	1.3	3.6	46.1	36.6	1.8	2.6	6.4	4.4	1.4	1.0
Bangladesh	16	19	6.1	7.0	15.4	40.0	1.2	1.7	0.1	0.3	0.2	0.2
Belarus	92	86	1.5	3.2	107.8	63.3	2.5	2.4	10.6	6.5	1.6	0.8
Belgium	73	75	5.0	5.7	99.1	102.6	2.0	1.7	9.9	9.8	0.4	0.3
Benin	−6	39	3.2	3.8	0.7	2.6	0.4	1.0	0.1	0.3	0.1	0.2
Bolivia	−77	−144	7.4	6.2	5.5	9.3	2.0	1.7	0.8	1.0	0.3	0.3
Bosnia and Herzegovina	35	27	..	4.6	6.9	26.3	1.0	5.2	1.6	6.9	..	1.1
Botswana	29	45	7.3	11.7	2.2	4.6	1.7	2.4	1.6	2.5	0.2	0.2
Brazil	26	8	7.7	7.3	202.6	325.5	1.4	1.5	1.4	1.7	0.2	0.2
Bulgaria	67	46	2.3	3.7	75.3	44.4	2.6	2.2	8.6	5.7	1.1	0.6
Burkina Faso	..	..	..	..	0.6	0.7	..	..	0.1	0.1	0.1	0.1
Burundi	..	..	..	..	0.2	0.2	..	..	0.0	0.0	0.1	0.1
Cambodia	..	29	..	4.5	0.5	0.5	..	0.1	0.0	0.0	..	0.0
Cameroon	−118	−46	5.0	5.1	1.6	3.7	0.3	0.5	0.1	0.2	0.1	0.1
Canada	−31	−53	3.6	4.3	428.5	537.5	2.0	2.0	15.4	16.6	0.6	0.5
Central African Republic	..	..	..	..	0.2	0.3	..	..	0.1	0.1	0.1	0.1
Chad	..	..	..	..	0.1	0.1	..	..	0.0	0.0	0.0	0.0
Chile	46	67	6.2	7.0	35.3	66.1	2.5	2.2	2.7	4.1	0.4	0.3
China	−3	7	1.4	3.2	2,399.2	5,547.8	2.8	3.2	2.1	4.3	1.9	1.0
Hong Kong, China	100	100	12.7	14.3	26.2	38.6	2.5	2.1	4.6	5.7	0.2	0.2
Colombia	−95	−180	8.1	11.0	57.4	58.6	2.3	2.0	1.7	1.4	0.3	0.2
Congo, Dem. Rep.	−1	−2	1.9	0.9	4.0	2.1	0.3	0.1	0.1	0.0	0.2	0.1
Congo, Rep.	−997	−1,180	10.5	10.5	1.2	2.0	1.5	1.6	0.5	0.6	0.1	0.2
Costa Rica	49	49	9.5	9.3	2.9	7.3	1.4	1.8	0.9	1.7	0.2	0.2
Cote d'Ivoire	23	−28	5.4	4.1	5.4	8.7	1.2	1.1	0.4	0.5	0.2	0.3
Croatia	43	54	6.0	6.9	24.6	22.9	2.7	2.6	5.1	5.2	0.5	0.4
Cuba	61	53	..	..	32.0	24.3	1.9	2.5	3.0	2.2	..	..
Czech Republic	18	27	3.5	4.8	161.7	119.7	3.3	2.6	15.6	11.7	1.0	0.6
Denmark	44	−41	7.3	8.9	49.8	46.1	2.8	2.3	9.7	8.5	0.4	0.3
Dominican Republic	75	80	5.9	7.2	9.6	18.8	2.3	2.4	1.3	2.0	0.4	0.4
Ecuador	−169	−165	9.2	8.1	16.6	29.3	2.7	2.8	1.6	2.2	0.3	0.3
Egypt, Arab Rep.	−72	−25	5.8	5.7	75.4	173.5	2.4	2.8	1.4	2.4	0.4	0.5
El Salvador	32	44	7.8	7.6	2.6	6.4	1.0	1.4	0.5	1.0	0.1	0.2
Eritrea	20	27	1.9	4.0	..	0.8	..	1.0	..	0.2	..	0.3
Estonia	47	27	1.7	5.0	28.3	18.2	3.0	3.6	18.1	13.5	1.8	0.8
Ethiopia	7	9	1.8	2.3	3.0	7.9	0.2	0.4	0.1	0.1	0.1	0.2
Finland	58	52	4.1	4.5	50.6	53.2	1.8	1.5	10.1	10.1	0.4	0.3
France	51	50	6.2	7.0	363.3	377.7	1.6	1.4	6.4	6.2	0.3	0.2
Gabon	−1,077	−566	11.2	9.9	6.0	1.5	4.8	0.8	6.5	1.2	0.4	0.1
Gambia, The	..	..	..	..	0.2	0.3	..	..	0.2	0.2	0.2	0.2
Georgia	85	64	2.4	5.2	17.3	4.8	1.4	1.5	3.2	1.1	0.6	0.3
Germany	48	61	5.7	7.6	980.6	784.0	2.8	2.3	12.3	9.5	0.5	0.3
Ghana	18	32	2.5	2.9	3.8	7.3	0.7	0.8	0.2	0.3	0.3	0.3
Greece	59	68	8.0	9.3	72.2	95.4	3.2	3.1	7.1	8.6	0.4	0.3
Guatemala	24	34	6.6	6.6	5.1	11.4	1.1	1.4	0.6	0.9	0.2	0.2
Guinea	..	..	..	..	1.0	1.4	..	..	0.2	0.2	0.2	0.1
Guinea-Bissau	..	..	..	..	0.2	0.3	..	..	0.2	0.2	0.3	0.4
Haiti	21	23	7.3	4.0	1.0	1.8	0.6	0.7	0.1	0.2	0.1	0.2

	Net energy importsª		GDP per unit of energy use		Carbon dioxide emissions							
	% of energy use		2005 PPP $ per kilogram of oil equivalent		Total million metric tons		Carbon intensity kilograms per kilogram of oil equivalent energy use		Per capita metric tons		kilograms per 2005 PPP $ of GDP	
	1990	2006	1990	2006	1990	2005	1990	2005	1990	2005	1990	2005
Honduras	30	53	5.4	5.5	2.6	7.4	1.1	1.9	0.5	1.1	0.2	0.3
Hungary	50	63	4.5	6.5	60.1	56.4	2.1	2.0	5.8	5.6	0.5	0.3
India	9	23	3.2	4.7	679.9	1,402.4	2.1	2.6	0.8	1.3	0.7	0.6
Indonesia	−65	−72	3.6	4.2	149.3	419.6	1.5	2.4	0.8	1.9	0.4	0.6
Iran, Islamic Rep.	−161	−81	4.9	4.0	218.3	451.6	3.2	2.9	4.0	6.5	0.6	0.7
Iraq	−451	−216	..	..	48.5	84.5	2.5	2.8	2.6	..	..	..
Ireland	66	90	6.0	10.9	30.6	42.3	3.0	2.8	8.7	10.2	0.5	0.3
Israel	96	88	6.9	7.9	33.1	63.6	2.7	3.0	7.1	9.2	0.4	0.4
Italy	83	85	9.1	9.1	395.7	452.1	2.7	2.4	7.0	7.7	0.3	0.3
Jamaica	84	89	4.2	3.6	8.0	10.2	2.7	2.6	3.3	3.8	0.6	0.6
Japan	83	81	7.2	7.5	1,080.7	1,230.0	2.4	2.3	8.7	9.6	0.3	0.3
Jordan	95	96	3.0	3.5	10.2	20.5	2.9	2.9	3.2	3.8	1.0	0.9
Kazakhstan	−23	−113	1.6	2.4	288.1	180.9	3.9	3.2	17.6	11.9	2.5	1.4
Kenya	20	21	3.0	2.8	5.8	11.1	0.5	0.6	0.2	0.2	0.2	0.2
Korea, Dem. Rep.	13	−3	..	..	244.6	82.6	7.4	3.9	12.1	3.5	..	..
Korea, Rep.	76	80	4.9	5.0	241.6	452.2	2.6	2.1	5.6	9.4	0.5	0.4
Kuwait	−530	−495	2.8	4.6	43.4	93.6	5.4	3.3	20.4	36.9	0.6	0.8
Kyrgyz Republic	67	47	1.5	3.3	12.6	5.6	1.7	2.0	2.8	1.1	1.1	0.6
Lao PDR	..	..	..	..	0.2	1.4	..	..	0.1	0.3	0.1	0.1
Latvia	86	60	3.4	7.3	14.5	6.5	1.8	1.4	5.4	2.8	0.5	0.2
Lebanon	94	96	6.8	8.1	9.1	16.9	3.9	3.0	3.1	4.2	0.6	0.4
Lesotho	..	..	..	..	..	..	..	..	..	..	..	..
Liberia	..	..	..	..	0.5	0.5	..	..	0.2	0.1	0.4	0.4
Libya	−534	−474	..	4.4	37.8	56.1	3.3	3.2	8.7	9.5	..	0.8
Lithuania	70	59	2.9	6.1	24.3	14.0	1.5	1.6	6.6	4.1	0.5	0.3
Macedonia, FYR	47	47	5.9	5.9	15.5	10.3	5.7	3.7	8.1	5.1	1.0	0.7
Madagascar	..	..	..	..	0.9	2.8	..	..	0.1	0.2	0.1	0.2
Malawi	..	..	..	..	0.6	1.0	..	..	0.1	0.1	0.1	0.1
Malaysia	−116	−43	5.2	4.7	55.3	239.8	2.4	3.6	3.1	9.3	0.5	0.8
Mali	..	..	..	..	0.4	0.6	..	..	0.1	0.0	0.0	0.0
Mauritania	..	..	..	..	2.6	1.6	..	..	1.4	0.6	0.9	0.3
Mauritius	..	..	..	..	1.5	3.4	..	..	1.4	2.7	0.2	0.3
Mexico	−57	−44	6.8	7.7	375.2	421.5	3.1	2.4	4.5	4.1	0.4	0.3
Moldova	99	97	1.7	2.6	23.8	8.1	2.4	2.3	5.4	2.1	1.4	0.9
Mongolia	20	−7	1.4	2.6	10.0	8.8	2.9	3.4	4.7	3.4	2.0	1.3
Morocco	89	95	9.3	8.3	23.5	48.0	3.3	3.6	1.0	1.6	0.4	0.4
Mozambique	6	−22	0.9	1.7	1.0	1.9	0.2	0.2	0.1	0.1	0.2	0.1
Myanmar	0	−55	1.3	2.9	4.3	11.3	0.4	0.8	0.1	0.2	0.3	0.3
Namibia	67	79	8.1	6.5	0.0	2.6	0.0	1.8	0.0	1.3	0.0	0.3
Nepal	5	11	2.3	2.9	0.6	3.1	0.1	0.3	0.0	0.1	0.0	0.1
Netherlands	10	24	5.8	7.3	139.7	125.8	2.1	1.5	9.3	7.7	0.4	0.2
New Zealand	13	26	4.6	5.9	22.5	29.9	1.6	1.7	6.5	7.2	0.4	0.3
Nicaragua	29	39	3.7	3.8	2.6	3.9	1.2	1.2	0.6	0.7	0.3	0.3
Niger	..	..	..	..	1.0	1.1	..	..	0.1	0.1	0.2	0.1
Nigeria	−112	−124	2.0	2.5	45.3	114.3	0.6	1.1	0.5	0.8	0.3	0.5
Norway	−456	−755	6.4	8.6	30.3	52.9	1.4	1.6	7.1	11.4	0.2	0.2
Oman	−740	−293	5.7	3.6	10.3	31.4	2.3	2.2	5.6	12.5	0.4	0.6
Pakistan	21	23	4.2	4.6	68.0	134.3	1.6	1.8	0.6	0.9	0.4	0.4
Panama	59	72	9.8	11.6	3.1	5.9	2.1	2.3	1.3	1.8	0.2	0.2
Papua New Guinea	..	..	..	..	2.4	4.4	..	..	0.6	0.7	0.3	0.4
Paraguay	−48	−69	5.5	6.0	2.3	3.9	0.7	1.0	0.5	0.7	0.1	0.2
Peru	−6	15	9.8	14.0	21.0	37.0	2.1	2.7	1.0	1.4	0.2	0.2
Philippines	48	43	5.7	6.1	43.9	75.0	1.7	1.7	0.7	0.9	0.3	0.3
Poland	1	20	3.1	5.7	347.6	302.4	3.5	3.3	9.1	7.9	1.1	0.6
Portugal	80	83	9.1	8.7	42.3	62.4	2.5	2.3	4.3	5.9	0.3	0.3
Puerto Rico	..	..	..	..	..	..	..	..	..	..	..	..

	Net energy imports[a] (% of energy use)		GDP per unit of energy use (2005 PPP $ per kilogram of oil equivalent)		Carbon dioxide emissions							
					Total million metric tons		Carbon intensity kilograms per kilogram of oil equivalent energy use		Per capita metric tons		kilograms per 2005 PPP $ of GDP	
	1990	2006	1990	2006	1990	2005	1990	2005	1990	2005	1990	2005
Romania	35	30	2.9	5.4	155.1	89.1	2.5	2.3	6.7	4.1	0.9	0.4
Russian Federation	−46	−80	2.1	2.7	2,261.7	1,503.3	2.6	2.3	15.3	10.5	1.2	0.9
Rwanda	..	..	..	..	0.5	0.6	..	..	0.1	0.1	0.1	0.1
Saudi Arabia	−505	−291	5.1	3.5	197.4	381.1	3.2	2.7	12.1	16.5	0.6	0.8
Senegal	48	59	5.8	6.2	3.1	5.1	1.7	1.7	0.4	0.4	0.3	0.3
Serbia	31[b]	38	5.1[b]	4.1	65.4[b]	52.5[b]	3.0[b]	..	6.2[b]	6.5[b]	..	..
Sierra Leone	..	..	..	..	0.3	0.9	..	..	0.1	0.2	0.1	0.3
Singapore	100	100	5.4	6.5	41.9	56.3	3.1	1.8	13.8	13.2	0.6	0.3
Slovak Republic	75	65	3.1	5.1	51.4	36.6	2.4	1.9	9.7	6.8	0.8	0.4
Slovenia	48	54	5.9	6.8	18.0	14.8	3.2	2.0	9.0	7.4	0.6	0.3
Somalia	..	..	..	..	0.0	0.6	..	..	0.0	0.1	..	..
South Africa	−26	−22	3.0	3.2	331.9	408.8	3.6	3.2	9.4	8.7	1.2	1.0
Spain	62	78	8.4	8.5	211.8	343.7	2.3	2.4	5.5	7.9	0.3	0.3
Sri Lanka	24	41	6.3	8.0	3.8	11.0	0.7	1.2	0.2	0.6	0.1	0.2
Sudan	18	−73	2.5	3.9	5.4	10.6	0.5	0.6	0.2	0.3	0.2	0.2
Swaziland	..	..	..	..	0.4	1.0	..	..	0.6	0.8	0.1	0.2
Sweden	38	36	4.4	5.9	49.5	48.5	1.0	0.9	5.8	5.4	0.2	0.2
Switzerland	61	57	9.1	9.7	42.7	41.2	1.7	1.5	6.4	5.5	0.2	0.2
Syrian Arab Republic	−91	−40	3.2	4.2	35.8	68.4	3.1	3.7	2.8	3.6	1.0	0.9
Tajikistan	64	59	2.9	2.8	23.4	5.2	4.2	1.5	4.4	0.8	1.4	0.5
Tanzania	8	7	2.2	2.1	2.3	4.7	0.2	0.2	0.1	0.1	0.1	0.1
Thailand	40	46	5.1	4.5	95.7	270.9	2.2	2.7	1.8	4.3	0.4	0.6
Timor-Leste	..	..	..	..	..	0.2	..	..	..	0.2	..	0.2
Togo	19	15	2.6	2.0	0.8	1.3	0.6	0.6	0.2	0.2	0.2	0.3
Trinidad and Tobago	−109	−142	2.1	2.0	16.9	32.7	2.8	2.6	13.8	24.7	1.4	1.3
Tunisia	−11	24	6.4	7.8	13.3	22.0	2.6	2.6	1.6	2.2	0.4	0.3
Turkey	51	72	8.3	8.9	141.5	247.9	2.7	2.9	2.5	3.4	0.3	0.3
Turkmenistan	−281	−257	..	1.4	32.0	41.6	1.6	2.5	8.7	8.6	..	1.8
Uganda	..	..	..	..	0.8	2.3	..	..	0.0	0.1	0.1	0.1
Ukraine	47	40	1.6	2.1	684.0	327.1	2.7	2.3	13.2	6.9	1.6	1.2
United Arab Emirates	−375	−278	4.1	4.7	54.7	123.7	2.4	2.7	29.3	30.1	0.6	0.6
United Kingdom	2	19	6.4	8.6	569.2	546.4	2.7	2.3	9.9	9.1	0.4	0.3
United States	14	29	4.1	5.5	4,797.5	5,776.4	2.5	2.5	19.2	19.5	0.6	0.5
Uruguay	49	75	9.7	10.3	3.9	5.6	1.7	1.9	1.3	1.7	0.2	0.2
Uzbekistan	17	−20	0.9	1.2	125.3	112.4	2.7	2.4	6.1	4.3	3.1	2.1
Venezuela, RB	−239	−214	4.3	4.7	117.4	148.1	2.7	2.5	5.9	5.6	0.6	0.6
Vietnam	−2	−38	2.5	3.7	21.4	101.8	0.9	2.0	0.3	1.2	0.4	0.6
West Bank and Gaza	..	..	..	..	..	..	..	..	..	..	..	..
Yemen, Rep.	−266	−164	8.5	6.7	9.6	20.1	3.7	2.9	0.8	1.0	0.4	0.4
Zambia	10	9	1.8	2.0	2.4	2.4	0.4	0.3	0.3	0.2	0.2	0.2
Zimbabwe	9	9	..	..	16.6	11.5	1.8	1.2	1.6	0.9	..	..
World	**−2[c] w**	**−2[c] w**	**4.2 w**	**5.2 w**	**22,584.9[d] t**	**29,257.0[d] t**	**2.6[d] w**	**2.6[d] w**	**4.3[d] w**	**4.5[d] w**	**0.6[d] w**	**0.5[d] w**
Low income	−13	−28	2.5	3.2	518.7	722.5	1.3	1.3	0.7	0.6	0.3	0.4
Middle income	−22	−21	3.0	4.2	9,675.3	13,842.1	2.5	2.7	2.8	3.3	0.9	0.7
Lower middle income	−15	−9	2.6	3.9	4,882.2	9,447.7	2.5	2.9	1.8	2.8	1.0	0.8
Upper middle income	−29	−42	3.5	4.8	4,793.1	4,393.3	2.6	2.4	6.9	5.5	0.8	0.5
Low & middle income	−21	−21	3.0	4.1	10,193.8	14,564.1	2.4	2.6	2.4	2.7	0.8	0.6
East Asia & Pacific	−7	0	2.0	3.4	3,029.7	6,769.2	2.7	3.1	1.9	3.6	1.3	0.9
Europe & Central Asia	−10	−36	2.3	3.5	4,365.8	3,087.2	2.6	2.4	10.4	7.0	1.1	0.7
Latin America & Carib.	−33	−35	6.8	7.3	1,020.2	1,360.7	2.2	2.1	2.3	2.5	0.3	0.3
Middle East & N. Africa	−196	−115	5.5	5.0	565.4	1,112.6	3.0	3.0	2.5	3.7	0.5	0.6
South Asia	11	23	3.4	4.8	770.5	1,592.6	2.0	2.4	0.7	1.1	0.6	0.5
Sub-Saharan Africa	−52	−63	2.7	3.0	463.4	649.3	1.5	1.4	0.9	0.8	0.6	0.5
High income	16	18	5.2	6.3	11,003.2	13,099.7	2.5	2.3	11.8	12.6	0.5	0.4
Euro area	56	64	6.6	7.7	2,529.7	2,585.0	2.4	2.0	8.4	8.1	0.4	0.3

a. Negative values indicate that a country is a net exporter. b. Includes Kosovo and Montenegro. c. Deviation from zero is due to statistical errors and changes in stock. d. Includes emissions not allocated to specific countries.

About the data

Because commercial energy is widely traded, its production and use need to be distinguished. Net energy imports show the extent to which an economy's use exceeds its production. High-income economies are net energy importers; middle-income economies are their main suppliers.

The ratio of gross domestic product (GDP) to energy use indicates energy efficiency. To produce comparable and consistent estimates of real GDP across economies relative to physical inputs to GDP—that is, units of energy use—GDP is converted to 2005 constant international dollars using purchasing power parity (PPP) rates. Differences in this ratio over time and across economies reflect structural changes in an economy, changes in sectoral energy efficiency, and differences in fuel mixes.

Carbon dioxide emissions, largely by-products of energy production and use (see table 3.7), account for the largest share of greenhouse gases, which are associated with global warming. Anthropogenic carbon dioxide emissions result primarily from fossil fuel combustion and cement manufacturing. In combustion different fossil fuels release different amounts of carbon dioxide for the same level of energy use: oil releases about 50 percent more carbon dioxide than natural gas, and coal releases about twice as much. Cement manufacturing releases about half a metric ton of carbon dioxide for each metric ton of cement produced.

The U.S. Department of Energy's Carbon Dioxide Information Analysis Center (CDIAC) calculates annual anthropogenic emissions from data on fossil fuel consumption (from the United Nations Statistics Division's World Energy Data Set) and world cement manufacturing (from the U.S. Bureau of Mines's Cement Manufacturing Data Set). Carbon dioxide emissions, often calculated and reported as elemental carbon, were converted to actual carbon dioxide mass by multiplying them by 3.664 (the ratio of the mass of carbon to that of carbon dioxide). Although estimates of global carbon dioxide emissions are probably accurate within 10 percent (as calculated from global average fuel chemistry and use), country estimates may have larger error bounds. Trends estimated from a consistent time series tend to be more accurate than individual values. Each year the CDIAC recalculates the entire time series since 1949, incorporating recent findings and corrections. Estimates exclude fuels supplied to ships and aircraft in international transport because of the difficulty of apportioning the fuels among benefiting countries. The ratio of carbon dioxide per unit of energy shows carbon intensity, which is the amount of carbon dioxide emitted as a result of using one unit of energy in the process of production. The proportion of carbon dioxide per unit of GDP indicates how clean production processes are.

Definitions

• **Net energy imports** are estimated as energy use less production, both measured in oil equivalents.
• **GDP per unit of energy use** is the ratio of gross domestic product (GDP) per kilogram of oil equivalent of energy use, with GDP converted to 2005 constant international dollars using purchasing power parity (PPP) rates. An international dollar has the same purchasing power over GDP that a U.S. dollar has in the United States. Energy use refers to the use of primary energy before transformation to other end-use fuel, which is equal to indigenous production plus imports and stock changes minus exports and fuel supplied to ships and aircraft engaged in international transport (see *About the data* for table 3.7). • **Carbon dioxide emissions** are emissions from the burning of fossil fuels and the manufacture of cement and include carbon dioxide produced during consumption of solid, liquid, and gas fuels and gas flaring.

High-income economies depend on imported energy . . .   3.8a

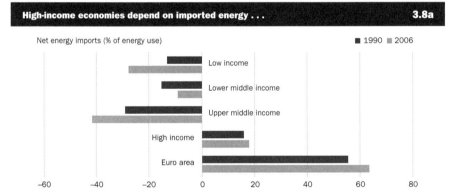

Net energy imports (% of energy use)   ■ 1990 ■ 2006

Note: Negative values indicate that the income group is a net energy exporter.
Source: Table 3.8.

. . . mostly from middle-income economies in the Middle East and North Africa and Latin America and the Caribbean   3.8b

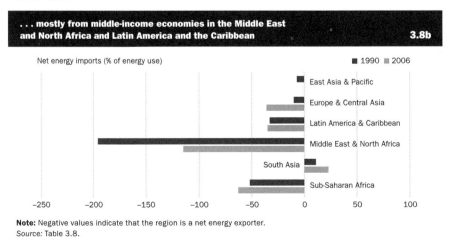

Net energy imports (% of energy use)   ■ 1990 ■ 2006

Note: Negative values indicate that the region is a net energy exporter.
Source: Table 3.8.

Data sources

Data on energy use are from the electronic files of the International Energy Agency. Data on carbon dioxide emissions are from the CDIAC, Environmental Sciences Division, Oak Ridge National Laboratory, Tennessee, United States.

3.9 | Trends in greenhouse gas emissions

	Carbon dioxide emissions		Methane emissions				Nitrous oxide emissions				Other greenhouse gas emissions	
	average annual % growth[a] 1990–2005	% change[b] 1990–2005	Total thousand metric tons of carbon dioxide equivalent 2005	% change[b] 1990–2005	% of total Industrial 2005	% of total Agricultural 2005	Total thousand metric tons of carbon dioxide equivalent 2005	% change[b] 1990–2005	% of total Industrial 2005	% of total Agricultural 2005	Total thousand metric tons of carbon dioxide equivalent 2005	% change[b] 1990–2005
Afghanistan	−9.3	−73.5	..	..	..	..	..	..	..	..	..	..
Albania	−0.9	−51.9	2,170	−2.7	11.5	70.0	1,390	−40.6	0.0	97.1	50	..
Algeria	3.9	78.6	24,310	30.9	66.3	15.3	10,330	17.7	7.2	89.1	110	−52.2
Angola	4.1	93.5	37,020	171.6	11.6	39.1	28,350	454.8	0.0	35.9	0	..
Argentina	2.0	39.2	94,340	14.9	13.0	63.9	83,410	28.2	0.2	97.7	930	−50.5
Armenia	0.3	3.6	2,300	−25.6	25.2	50.9	450	−50.5	0.0	93.3	10	..
Australia	1.3	25.9	116,840	12.3	24.6	61.5	114,500	7.9	1.3	94.9	4,580	74.8
Austria	1.5	27.8	7,210	−12.2	14.6	50.1	4,620	−19.5	9.1	85.3	3,310	173.6
Azerbaijan	−3.2	−31.8	11,550	−20.4	45.2	45.4	4,040	−0.5	0.0	93.6	50	−72.2
Bangladesh	6.8	160.1	92,530	13.4	11.6	69.2	37,100	65.5	0.0	91.9	0	..
Belarus	−3.3	−41.3	16,620	−13.6	43.0	38.8	10,360	−32.2	32.3	65.6	440	..
Belgium	−0.2	3.6	7,610	−25.6	17.0	59.7	9,650	−14.2	12.0	65.4	9,380	7,115.4
Benin	8.0	259.0	4,840	77.3	8.9	47.5	4,660	119.8	0.0	68.0	0	..
Bolivia	3.0	68.2	27,120	74.4	2.8	34.5	28,300	97.8	0.0	43.3	0	..
Bosnia and Herzegovina	16.0	280.4	2,850	42.5	51.9	32.6	1,020	−10.5	0.0	82.4	850	84.8
Botswana	4.2	110.0	4,480	3,346.2	17.9	71.9	2,460	..	0.0	96.3	0	..
Brazil	3.3	60.6	421,820	47.7	3.0	67.1	300,300	31.8	3.2	74.4	7,760	46.7
Bulgaria	−3.1	−41.0	6,140	−35.8	31.9	32.7	5,880	−55.6	29.9	64.5	650	..
Burkina Faso	1.8	33.6	..	..	..	..	..	..	..	..	..	..
Burundi	1.1	15.1	..	..	..	..	..	..	..	..	..	..
Cambodia	1.0	19.5	14,890	..	5.4	71.5	3,820	..	0.0	74.1	0	..
Cameroon	4.5	131.5	15,110	43.9	17.9	56.0	14,540	75.4	0.0	85.0	890	9.9
Canada	1.8	25.4	103,830	25.1	46.6	22.2	51,390	1.4	4.5	86.7	11,010	−14.1
Central African Republic	1.8	27.7	..	..	..	..	..	..	..	..	..	..
Chad	2.9	−2.6	..	..	..	..	..	..	..	..	..	..
Chile	4.7	87.1	19,560	37.8	12.1	29.9	12,590	54.1	6.9	88.7	10	..
China	4.6	131.2	995,760	11.2	34.2	50.0	566,680	24.5	3.0	92.7	119,720	1,285.6
Hong Kong, China	2.4	47.3	1,090	−7.6	40.4	0.9	200	−4.8	0.0	5.0	330	..
Colombia	−0.7	2.1	61,690	25.4	15.7	55.1	24,530	16.0	0.9	78.0	330	73.7
Congo, Dem. Rep.	−5.3	−46.0	5,750	115.4	49.6	11.8	2,250	174.4	0.0	15.6	0	..
Congo, Rep.	1.9	70.6	50,320	81.5	7.7	26.3	38,680	99.5	0.0	23.2	0	..
Costa Rica	5.3	150.4	2,450	−34.1	1.6	58.0	2,850	−17.2	0.0	98.9	0	..
Cote d'Ivoire	2.0	61.5	15,320	183.2	11.2	20.6	12,350	402.0	0.0	25.0	0	..
Croatia	1.8	−6.9	3,690	−6.6	44.2	29.8	3,590	5.9	22.3	63.8	720	7.5
Cuba	−1.8	−24.1	9,490	−4.0	6.4	62.4	8,330	−39.0	8.0	87.4	110	..
Czech Republic	−1.5	−26.0	14,930	−32.9	58.7	17.2	6,570	−38.8	16.4	75.0	3,530	17,550.0
Denmark	−1.3	−7.4	4,920	−12.9	16.3	67.7	7,380	−26.2	7.7	78.6	1,460	461.5
Dominican Republic	5.4	96.3	5,960	12.9	4.0	62.1	2,850	−31.2	0.0	96.1	0	..
Ecuador	3.2	76.8	12,890	5.9	16.3	57.4	8,500	−3.8	0.0	97.6	0	..
Egypt, Arab Rep.	5.9	130.0	32,960	41.8	31.2	44.2	27,810	63.8	11.5	85.6	1,820	−19.1
El Salvador	5.4	144.5	3,200	16.8	12.5	48.1	2,250	9.8	0.0	95.1	0	..
Eritrea	11.2	..	2,410	15.3	7.5	77.6	2,350	75.4	0.0	99.1	0	..
Estonia	−2.8	−35.8	1,230	−52.9	43.1	35.0	610	−62.6	0.0	83.6	60	..
Ethiopia	8.0	165.9	47,740	22.1	10.0	77.2	63,130	24.4	0.0	98.6	0	..
Finland	1.5	5.1	5,470	−26.1	10.2	30.3	5,330	−11.6	27.0	59.5	1,030	368.2
France	0.1	4.0	43,520	−23.3	10.7	71.1	78,090	−11.7	12.1	77.3	27,010	151.5
Gabon	−8.9	−74.9	2,040	−34.6	79.9	4.4	420	−77.3	0.0	57.1	0	..
Gambia, The	3.2	50.0	..	..	..	..	..	..	..	..	..	..
Georgia	−8.8	−72.3	4,330	−25.2	29.6	51.7	3,390	0.0	17.4	49.3	10	..
Germany	1.8	178.1	58,100	−47.1	45.7	39.2	69,470	−10.3	13.3	74.2	41,980	273.8
Ghana	4.7	94.3	8,630	62.5	10.7	49.6	10,520	131.7	0.0	88.6	170	−10.5
Greece	2.3	32.0	7,410	16.0	9.7	39.1	13,090	0.2	3.3	91.3	1,620	105.1
Guatemala	6.2	125.0	8,990	51.9	11.3	42.7	7,980	66.9	0.0	70.8	0	..
Guinea	2.0	34.1	..	..	..	..	..	..	..	..	..	..
Guinea-Bissau	1.9	29.8	..	..	..	..	..	..	..	..	..	..
Haiti	6.9	77.9	3,740	30.3	6.4	61.2	4,290	73.7	0.0	98.4	0	..

	Carbon dioxide emissions		Methane emissions				Nitrous oxide emissions				Other greenhouse gas emissions	
	average annual % growth[a] 1990–2005	% change[b] 1990–2005	Total thousand metric tons of carbon dioxide equivalent 2005	% change[b] 1990–2005	% of total Industrial 2005	% of total Agricultural 2005	Total thousand metric tons of carbon dioxide equivalent 2005	% change[b] 1990–2005	% of total Industrial 2005	% of total Agricultural 2005	Total thousand metric tons of carbon dioxide equivalent 2005	% change[b] 1990–2005
Honduras	7.6	186.9	5,380	7.2	5.8	71.9	3,860	8.7	0.0	97.9	0	..
Hungary	−0.5	−6.2	11,050	−22.3	52.6	18.3	8,760	−26.7	20.7	76.0	1,540	102.6
India	4.8	106.3	712,330	13.9	14.7	64.8	300,680	33.5	0.5	93.0	9,510	18.7
Indonesia	5.7	181.0	224,330	24.5	36.2	41.2	69,910	16.1	0.3	72.6	900	−34.8
Iran, Islamic Rep.	4.9	106.9	95,060	73.7	64.7	21.8	66,140	36.0	0.9	97.6	1,560	−26.8
Iraq	3.6	74.2	10,980	−1.3	48.7	14.7	3,990	−39.3	0.0	93.0	470	20.5
Ireland	2.6	38.3	3,660	−68.3	24.3	32.0	12,320	−4.0	0.2	92.6	2,050	1,763.6
Israel	4.9	92.0	1,170	15.8	9.4	36.8	1,820	−4.2	0.0	83.5	1,140	35.7
Italy	0.9	14.2	36,670	−13.3	19.1	37.7	37,200	4.6	23.7	70.5	27,710	480.9
Jamaica	2.0	27.6	1,160	−4.9	3.4	47.4	1,020	−16.4	0.0	96.1	0	..
Japan	0.9	13.8	53,480	−7.3	30.0	13.4	23,590	−26.2	8.4	49.3	70,570	165.7
Jordan	4.0	101.4	1,610	49.1	13.0	24.2	1,240	6.9	0.0	93.5	10	..
Kazakhstan	−3.6	−37.2	28,270	−48.9	49.1	37.9	5,530	−76.6	0.0	90.2	0	..
Kenya	4.8	90.5	20,310	4.6	18.0	65.0	19,060	−12.7	0.0	96.4	0	..
Korea, Dem. Rep.	−10.4	−66.2	10,650	8.7	29.0	36.4	23,160	152.0	0.0	97.5	860	186.7
Korea, Rep.	4.2	87.2	31,280	14.0	18.5	31.1	22,020	132.3	56.6	36.1	8,700	61.1
Kuwait	2.7	115.6	11,200	64.7	93.9	1.5	540	116.0	0.0	81.5	390	56.0
Kyrgyz Republic	−5.5	−55.8	3,520	−24.8	10.5	72.2	3,260	−23.1	0.0	98.8	60	..
Lao PDR	15.5	520.7	..	..	..	..	..	..	..	..	..	..
Latvia	−5.9	−55.5	2,290	−47.0	40.6	29.3	1,390	−48.3	0.0	88.5	110	..
Lebanon	4.1	85.7	980	34.2	12.2	18.4	1,020	37.8	0.0	93.1	0	..
Lesotho	..	..	..	..	..	..	..	..	..	..	..	..
Liberia	3.1	1.6	..	..	..	..	..	..	..	..	..	..
Libya	2.9	48.5	8,540	−2.4	77.6	8.9	2,050	−28.3	0.0	91.7	290	190.0
Lithuania	−4.2	−42.6	3,650	−52.8	44.1	38.1	2,860	−31.3	0.0	90.2	150	..
Macedonia, FYR	−0.8	−33.9	..	..	..	..	..	..	..	..	..	..
Madagascar	8.4	198.9	..	..	..	..	..	..	..	..	..	..
Malawi	4.1	65.2	..	..	..	..	..	..	..	..	..	..
Malaysia	7.4	333.9	25,510	19.8	57.2	22.3	9,920	−14.5	3.9	64.3	530	−44.8
Mali	2.1	33.9	..	..	..	..	..	..	..	..	..	..
Mauritania	−6.1	−38.1	..	..	..	..	..	..	..	..	..	..
Mauritius	6.2	133.1	..	..	..	..	..	..	..	..	..	..
Mexico	0.5	12.3	120,100	25.3	22.2	39.6	75,500	7.5	1.2	90.1	3,160	63.7
Moldova	−8.1	−66.2	2,590	−45.8	43.6	30.9	970	−70.3	0.0	94.8	360	..
Mongolia	−1.7	−12.0	4,840	−34.4	2.9	83.9	22,850	128.5	0.0	99.6	0	..
Morocco	4.0	104.4	13,240	46.0	2.6	41.6	15,510	7.9	0.0	75.2	0	..
Mozambique	4.1	88.6	11,680	23.9	16.9	64.3	9,930	236.6	0.0	99.7	0	..
Myanmar	6.1	165.3	60,840	51.5	6.8	70.0	25,900	80.0	0.0	66.8	10	..
Namibia	51.7	34,883.6	4,260	−1.4	4.7	89.9	4,620	9.0	0.0	99.1	0	..
Nepal	9.4	395.9	36,040	6.6	10.4	80.5	7,100	24.6	0.0	88.5	0	..
Netherlands	−0.2	−10.0	15,180	−21.4	23.6	49.2	16,800	−13.0	33.8	51.5	5,300	−10.9
New Zealand	2.4	33.4	27,490	0.4	10.4	82.3	27,960	−17.6	0.1	99.4	820	105.0
Nicaragua	4.4	47.9	6,350	35.4	4.7	80.2	3,210	−14.4	0.0	96.9	0	..
Niger	−0.4	1.0	..	..	..	..	..	..	..	..	..	..
Nigeria	6.2	152.1	78,290	31.2	45.5	33.7	39,030	39.1	0.0	87.1	80	−33.3
Norway	3.4	74.7	12,080	58.5	61.8	14.3	4,680	−11.5	37.8	53.0	1,770	−64.5
Oman	8.3	206.3	4,260	110.9	76.1	12.9	1,140	31.0	0.0	96.5	0	..
Pakistan	4.5	97.4	110,300	33.2	14.1	66.3	80,040	44.5	0.8	96.4	620	−11.4
Panama	4.4	88.1	3,040	2.4	4.3	72.4	2,070	−17.9	0.0	95.7	0	..
Papua New Guinea	3.6	82.7	..	..	..	..	..	..	..	..	..	..
Paraguay	3.7	71.5	17,750	51.8	1.7	70.9	12,870	29.0	0.0	81.8	0	..
Peru	3.3	76.0	21,510	24.6	6.4	48.1	18,720	30.9	0.0	89.4	80	..
Philippines	3.9	70.7	44,860	15.5	8.0	66.7	18,940	5.3	0.1	95.6	350	250.0
Poland	−1.2	−13.0	60,060	−33.3	67.0	18.4	26,110	−17.3	22.3	72.5	1,270	176.1
Portugal	2.7	47.3	7,140	−4.2	8.0	52.9	7,000	1.2	9.9	80.7	1,050	707.7
Puerto Rico	−8.9	−82.1	..	..	..	..	..	..	..	..	..	..

Trends in greenhouse gas emissions

	Carbon dioxide emissions		Methane emissions				Nitrous oxide emissions				Other greenhouse gas emissions	
	average annual % growth[a] 1990–2005	% change[b] 1990–2005	Total thousand metric tons of carbon dioxide equivalent 2005	% change[b] 1990–2005	% of total Industrial 2005	% of total Agricultural 2005	Total thousand metric tons of carbon dioxide equivalent 2005	% change[b] 1990–2005	% of total Industrial 2005	% of total Agricultural 2005	Total thousand metric tons of carbon dioxide equivalent 2005	% change[b] 1990–2005
Romania	–3.5	–42.6	23,260	–45.0	52.4	30.1	11,790	–52.3	25.9	69.6	2,220	48.0
Russian Federation	–2.6	–33.5	501,380	–20.6	77.3	7.9	42,650	–67.0	8.0	76.2	56,600	192.1
Rwanda	1.6	14.6	..	..	..	..	..	..	..	..	..	..
Saudi Arabia	2.2	93.0	63,500	59.9	91.8	1.9	7,720	–6.2	0.0	92.1	1,530	–32.3
Senegal	2.9	61.9	6,340	14.2	4.7	75.9	10,250	64.8	0.0	99.0	10	..
Serbia[c]	–2.4	–59.8	6,720	–47.7	16.4	59.2	4,700	–48.2	11.1	81.5	840	147.1
Sierra Leone	5.3	181.3	..	..	..	..	..	..	..	..	..	..
Singapore	0.8	34.2	1,260	70.3	27.0	4.8	7,970	4,327.8	95.7	0.8	1,300	225.0
Slovak Republic	–1.6	–28.8	5,290	–29.0	54.3	19.5	2,760	–40.6	32.2	58.0	710	7,000.0
Slovenia	0.8	–17.6	1,630	–6.3	20.9	47.9	1,100	2.8	0.0	88.2	210	–63.8
Somalia	44.7	3,123.5	..	..	..	..	..	..	..	..	..	..
South Africa	1.2	23.2	59,200	13.3	54.3	23.8	29,250	10.5	7.3	82.7	2,600	79.3
Spain	3.4	62.2	38,010	20.1	11.3	44.1	48,520	37.5	3.5	85.7	15,050	239.0
Sri Lanka	8.0	193.1	10,280	0.0	12.3	61.8	3,130	29.9	0.0	89.1	0	..
Sudan	6.5	97.3	67,310	69.3	21.5	73.3	59,750	51.6	0.0	96.2	0	..
Swaziland	10.8	125.0	..	..	..	..	..	..	..	..	..	..
Sweden	–0.2	–1.9	6,460	–15.8	6.5	41.5	6,070	–4.1	8.4	76.8	1,620	63.6
Switzerland	–0.2	–3.6	4,150	–13.4	8.7	68.0	2,840	–10.4	8.1	78.2	3,310	335.5
Syrian Arab Republic	2.9	90.9	7,960	37.0	33.8	34.7	9,430	20.0	2.8	94.9	0	..
Tajikistan	–10.0	–77.7	3,270	–11.4	10.1	68.5	1,590	–48.9	0.0	99.4	120	50.0
Tanzania	3.9	100.2	39,460	46.9	20.3	63.5	31,690	36.0	0.0	84.3	0	..
Thailand	6.2	182.9	78,840	14.4	9.4	76.1	27,990	31.2	0.7	87.9	940	–40.5
Timor-Leste	..	..	..	..	..	..	..	..	..	..	..	..
Togo	4.7	79.0	2,840	58.7	14.8	48.6	5,470	174.9	0.0	88.8	0	..
Trinidad and Tobago	4.0	93.1	3,820	52.2	78.0	1.0	360	5.9	0.0	91.7	0	..
Tunisia	3.2	65.7	4,390	17.4	32.1	34.2	7,230	69.7	4.1	94.2	30	..
Turkey	3.6	75.2	23,140	–14.5	15.3	59.5	47,950	8.3	9.0	88.0	1,480	–47.9
Turkmenistan	2.5	30.2	23,060	–30.6	81.8	15.2	3,200	–22.9	20.0	78.8	250	..
Uganda	7.4	183.8	..	..	..	..	..	..	..	..	..	..
Ukraine	–5.1	–52.2	75,640	–48.3	68.9	15.7	23,270	–66.5	41.6	54.2	1,390	2,216.7
United Arab Emirates	6.9	126.3	34,250	79.2	96.8	1.7	2,730	193.5	0.0	90.5	480	118.2
United Kingdom	–0.3	–4.0	39,400	–41.8	35.7	50.7	65,480	–4.4	37.1	52.2	14,030	138.6
United States	1.3	20.4	810,280	–5.5	56.4	18.4	456,210	10.5	5.5	74.7	108,420	18.8
Uruguay	1.2	42.2	17,700	25.4	0.6	90.3	15,630	3.0	0.0	99.6	20	..
Uzbekistan	13.1	1,602.7	51,480	23.7	70.1	23.2	14,660	2.3	0.3	98.3	760	..
Venezuela, RB	2.6	26.2	65,730	58.3	42.0	33.6	26,460	21.9	0.1	77.8	2,300	72.9
Vietnam	11.9	376.0	75,080	41.7	17.8	66.8	37,470	169.2	0.0	94.9	10	..
West Bank and Gaza	..	..	..	..	..	..	..	..	..	..	..	..
Yemen, Rep.	4.5	110.2	9,040	95.7	44.5	27.7	7,080	38.6	0.0	98.9	10	..
Zambia	–1.1	–3.2	16,770	70.8	5.7	68.6	11,410	137.7	3.7	65.1	0	..
Zimbabwe	–3.2	–31.2	10,400	–4.1	24.8	60.4	10,160	13.3	0.0	97.1	20	..
World	**1.6 w**	**29.5 w**	**6,607,490 s**	**7.0 w**	**34.8 w**	**43.1 w**	**3,787,800 s**	**14.0 w**	**5.2 w**	**82.6 w**	**601,890 s**	**126.9 w**
Low income	0.9	39.4	742,160	32.7	21.1	59.3	477,730	53.9	0.2	89.6	2,730	96.4
Middle income	2.0	43.1	4,255,740	8.6	32.2	46.4	2,179,990	13.7	3.3	84.8	221,040	244.3
Lower middle income	3.8	93.5	2,731,100	14.2	27.8	51.7	1,448,600	25.7	2.4	86.7	139,690	428.9
Upper middle income	–0.6	–8.3	1,524,640	–0.2	39.9	36.9	731,390	–4.3	5.1	81.0	81,350	115.3
Low & middle income	1.9	42.9	4,997,900	11.6	30.5	48.3	2,657,720	19.3	2.8	85.7	223,770	241.2
East Asia & Pacific	4.2	123.4	..	..	30.5	51.9	..	..	2.2	90.0	..	..
Europe & Central Asia	–2.3	–29.3	851,260	–26.2	69.1	16.2	215,350	–46.5	15.6	77.5	67,550	163.6
Latin America & Carib.	1.9	33.4	929,970	36.0	10.7	57.9	645,520	24.6	1.9	80.8	14,700	38.4
Middle East & N. Africa	4.4	96.8	209,070	47.8	52.0	25.9	151,830	29.4	3.4	92.0	4,300	–15.7
South Asia	4.8	106.7	961,480	15.3	14.1	66.0	428,050	37.6	0.5	93.4	10,130	16.3
Sub-Saharan Africa	2.0	40.3	..	..	24.4	49.4	..	..	0.6	78.5	..	..
High income	1.3	26.9	1,609,590	–5.0	47.9	26.9	1,130,080	3.2	10.7	75.3	378,120	89.4
Euro area	1.2	43.2	232,220	–25.9	22.2	47.6	303,960	–3.1	12.8	76.4	135,750	236.8

a. Calculated using the least squares method, which accounts for ups and downs of all data points in the period (see *Statistical methods*). b. Calculated as the change in emission since 1990, which is the baseline for Kyoto Protocol requirements. c. Includes Kosovo and Montenegro.

3.9

ENVIRONMENT

About the data

Greenhouse gases—which include carbon dioxide, methane, nitrous oxide, hydrofluorocarbons, perfluorocarbons, and sulfur hexafluoride—contribute to climate change.

Carbon dioxide emissions, largely a by-product of energy production and use (see table 3.7), account for the largest share of greenhouse gases. Anthropogenic carbon dioxide emissions result primarily from fossil fuel combustion and cement manufacturing. Burning oil releases more carbon dioxide than burning natural gas, and burning coal releases even more for the same level of energy use. Cement manufacturing releases about half a metric ton of carbon dioxide for each metric ton of cement produced.

Methane emissions result largely from agricultural activities, industrial production landfills and wastewater treatment, and other sources such as tropical forest and other vegetation fires. The emissions are usually expressed in carbon dioxide equivalents using the global warming potential, which allows the effective contributions of different gases to be

compared. A kilogram of methane is 21 times as effective at trapping heat in the earth's atmosphere as a kilogram of carbon dioxide within 100 years.

Nitrous oxide emissions are mainly from fossil fuel combustion, fertilizers, rainforest fires, and animal waste. Nitrous oxide is a powerful greenhouse gas, with an estimated atmospheric lifetime of 114 years, compared with 12 years for methane. The per kilogram global warming potential of nitrous oxide is nearly 310 times that of carbon dioxide within 100 years.

Other greenhouse gases covered under the Kyoto Protocol are hydrofluorocarbons, perfluorocarbons, and sulfur hexafluoride. Although emissions of these artificial gases are small, they are more powerful greenhouse gases than carbon dioxide, with much higher atmospheric lifetimes and high global warming potential.

For a discussion of carbon dioxide sources and the methodology behind emissions calculation, see *About the data* for table 3.8.

Definitions

• **Carbon dioxide emissions** are emissions from the burning of fossil fuels and the manufacture of cement and include carbon dioxide produced during consumption of solid, liquid, and gas fuels and gas flaring. • **Methane emissions** are emissions from human activities such as agriculture and from industrial methane production. • **Industrial methane emissions** are emissions from the handling, transmission, and combustion of fossil fuels and biofuels. • **Agricultural methane emissions** are emissions from animals, animal waste, rice production, agricultural waste burning (nonenergy, on-site), and savannah burning. • **Nitrous oxide emissions** are emissions from agricultural biomass burning, industrial activities, and livestock management. • **Industrial nitrous oxide emissions** are emissions produced during the manufacturing of adipic acid and nitric acid. • **Agricultural nitrous oxide emissions** are emissions produced through fertilizer use (synthetic and animal manure), animal waste management, agricultural waste burning (nonenergy, on-site), and savannah burning. • **Other greenhouse gas emissions** are by-product emissions of hydrofluorocarbons, perfluorocarbons, and sulfur hexafluoride.

The 10 largest contributors to methane emissions account for about 62 percent of emissions

3.9a

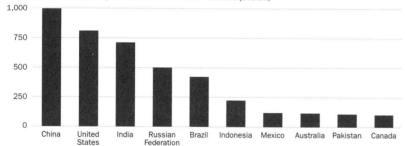

Methane emissions, 2005 (million metric tons of carbon dioxide equivalent)

Source: Table 3.9.

The 10 largest contributors to nitrous oxide emissions account for about 56 percent of emissions

3.9b

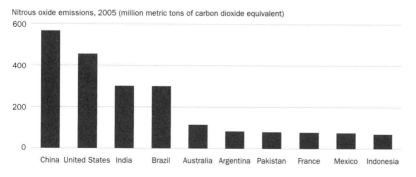

Nitrous oxide emissions, 2005 (million metric tons of carbon dioxide equivalent)

Source: Table 3.9.

Data sources

Data on carbon dioxide emissions are from the Carbon Dioxide Information Analysis Center, Environmental Sciences Division, Oak Ridge National Laboratory, Tennessee, United States. Data on methane, nitrous oxide, and other greenhouse gases emissions are compiled by the International Energy Agency.

	Electricity production		Sources of electricity[a]									
	billion kilowatt hours		Coal		Gas		Oil		Hydropower		Nuclear power	
							% of total					
	1990	2006	1990	2006	1990	2006	1990	2006	1990	2006	1990	2006
Afghanistan	..	..	..	..	..	..	..	..	..	..	..	..
Albania	3.2	5.1	0.0	0.0	0.0	0.0	10.9	1.8	89.1	98.2	0.0	0.0
Algeria	16.1	35.2	0.0	0.0	93.7	97.2	5.4	2.2	0.8	0.6	0.0	0.0
Angola	0.8	3.0	0.0	0.0	0.0	0.0	13.8	9.9	86.2	90.1	0.0	0.0
Argentina	50.7	115.0	1.3	1.8	39.2	50.2	9.8	7.0	35.2	33.0	14.3	6.7
Armenia	10.4	5.9	0.0	0.0	16.4	24.8	68.6	0.0	15.0	30.7	0.0	44.4
Australia	154.3	251.3	77.1	79.2	10.6	12.2	2.7	0.9	9.2	6.2	0.0	0.0
Austria	49.3	60.7	14.2	13.7	15.7	17.6	3.8	2.7	63.9	57.4	0.0	0.0
Azerbaijan	23.2	23.6	0.0	0.0	0.0	63.5	97.0	25.9	3.0	10.7	0.0	0.0
Bangladesh	7.7	24.3	0.0	0.0	84.3	87.6	4.3	6.7	11.4	5.7	0.0	0.0
Belarus	39.5	31.8	0.0	0.0	58.1	95.0	41.8	4.6	0.1	0.1	0.0	0.0
Belgium	70.3	84.3	28.2	10.9	7.7	27.3	1.9	1.6	0.4	0.4	60.8	55.3
Benin	0.0	0.1	0.0	0.0	0.0	0.0	100.0	100.0	0.0	0.0	0.0	0.0
Bolivia	2.1	5.3	0.0	0.0	37.6	39.3	5.3	16.7	55.3	40.8	0.0	0.0
Bosnia and Herzegovina	14.6	13.3	71.8	54.9	0.0	0.0	7.3	1.2	20.9	43.9	0.0	0.0
Botswana	0.9	1.0	88.1	99.4	0.0	0.0	11.9	0.6	0.0	0.0	0.0	0.0
Brazil	222.8	419.3	2.0	2.4	0.0	4.4	2.2	3.0	92.8	83.2	1.0	3.3
Bulgaria	42.1	45.5	50.3	42.2	7.6	4.7	2.9	0.8	4.5	9.3	34.8	42.8
Burkina Faso	..	..	..	..	..	..	..	..	..	..	..	..
Burundi	..	..	..	..	..	..	..	..	..	..	..	..
Cambodia	..	1.2	..	0.0	..	0.0	..	95.7	..	4.1	..	0.0
Cameroon	2.7	4.0	0.0	0.0	0.0	0.0	1.5	5.9	98.5	94.1	0.0	0.0
Canada	481.9	612.5	17.1	17.1	2.0	5.5	3.4	1.5	61.6	58.0	15.1	16.0
Central African Republic	..	..	..	..	..	..	..	..	..	..	..	..
Chad	..	..	..	..	..	..	..	..	..	..	..	..
Chile	18.4	57.6	34.3	17.1	1.3	19.9	7.6	1.6	55.3	59.5	0.0	0.0
China	621.2	2,864.2	71.3	80.4	0.4	0.5	7.9	1.8	20.4	15.2	0.0	1.9
Hong Kong, China	28.9	38.6	98.3	68.9	0.0	30.8	1.7	0.3	0.0	0.0	0.0	0.0
Colombia	36.4	54.3	10.1	7.5	12.4	12.4	1.0	0.2	75.6	78.7	0.0	0.0
Congo, Dem. Rep.	5.7	7.9	0.0	0.0	0.0	0.0	0.4	0.3	99.6	99.7	0.0	0.0
Congo, Rep.	0.5	0.5	0.0	0.0	0.0	17.9	0.6	0.0	99.4	82.1	0.0	0.0
Costa Rica	3.5	8.7	0.0	0.0	0.0	0.0	2.5	6.1	97.5	75.9	0.0	0.0
Côte d'Ivoire	2.0	5.5	0.0	0.0	0.0	72.7	33.3	0.0	66.7	27.3	0.0	0.0
Croatia	9.2	12.3	6.8	18.3	20.2	16.7	31.6	15.9	41.3	48.8	0.0	0.0
Cuba	15.0	16.5	0.0	0.0	0.2	0.0	91.5	96.7	0.6	0.6	0.0	0.0
Czech Republic	62.3	83.7	76.4	60.4	0.6	3.9	0.9	0.3	1.9	3.0	20.2	31.1
Denmark	26.0	45.7	90.7	53.9	2.7	20.6	3.4	3.5	0.1	0.1	0.0	0.0
Dominican Republic	3.7	14.2	1.2	13.4	0.0	9.1	88.6	67.3	9.4	10.0	0.0	0.0
Ecuador	6.3	15.4	0.0	0.0	0.0	9.6	21.5	44.1	78.5	46.3	0.0	0.0
Egypt, Arab Rep.	42.3	115.4	0.0	0.0	39.6	72.1	36.9	16.1	23.5	11.2	0.0	0.0
El Salvador	2.2	5.6	0.0	0.0	0.0	0.0	6.9	44.2	73.5	35.1	0.0	0.0
Eritrea	0.1	0.3	0.0	0.0	0.0	0.0	100.0	99.3	0.0	0.0	0.0	0.0
Estonia	17.4	9.7	85.8	90.2	5.9	8.0	8.3	0.3	0.0	0.1	0.0	0.0
Ethiopia	1.2	3.3	0.0	0.0	0.0	0.0	11.6	0.3	88.4	99.7	0.0	0.0
Finland	54.4	82.3	18.5	20.6	8.6	15.0	3.1	0.6	20.0	14.0	35.3	27.8
France	417.2	569.2	8.5	4.6	0.7	3.9	2.1	1.2	12.9	9.8	75.3	79.1
Gabon	1.0	1.7	0.0	0.0	16.4	15.3	11.2	29.5	72.1	54.8	0.0	0.0
Gambia, The	..	..	..	..	..	..	..	..	..	..	..	..
Georgia	13.7	7.3	0.0	0.0	15.6	26.7	29.2	0.3	55.2	72.9	0.0	0.0
Germany	547.7	629.4	58.7	48.0	7.4	12.1	1.9	1.5	3.2	3.2	27.8	26.6
Ghana	5.7	8.4	0.0	0.0	0.0	0.0	0.0	33.3	100.0	66.7	0.0	0.0
Greece	34.8	60.2	72.4	53.6	0.3	17.6	22.3	16.0	5.1	9.7	0.0	0.0
Guatemala	2.3	7.9	0.0	13.6	0.0	0.0	9.0	25.3	76.0	48.3	0.0	0.0
Guinea	..	..	..	..	..	..	..	..	..	..	..	..
Guinea-Bissau	..	..	..	..	..	..	..	..	..	..	..	..
Haiti	0.6	0.6	0.0	0.0	0.0	0.0	20.6	52.5	76.5	47.5	0.0	0.0

	Electricity production		Sources of electricity[a]									
			% of total									
	billion kilowatt hours		Coal		Gas		Oil		Hydropower		Nuclear power	
	1990	2006	1990	2006	1990	2006	1990	2006	1990	2006	1990	2006
Honduras	2.3	6.0	0.0	0.0	0.0	0.0	1.7	56.1	98.3	43.2	0.0	0.0
Hungary	28.4	35.9	30.5	19.8	15.7	36.7	4.8	1.5	0.6	0.5	48.3	37.5
India	289.4	744.1	66.2	68.3	3.4	8.3	3.5	4.2	24.8	15.3	2.1	2.5
Indonesia	33.3	133.1	31.5	44.1	2.3	14.6	42.7	29.1	20.2	7.2	0.0	0.0
Iran, Islamic Rep.	59.1	201.0	0.0	0.0	52.5	73.7	37.3	17.2	10.3	9.1	0.0	0.0
Iraq	24.0	31.9	0.0	0.0	0.0	0.0	89.2	98.5	10.8	1.5	0.0	0.0
Ireland	14.2	27.7	41.6	21.3	27.7	52.3	10.0	9.8	4.9	2.6	0.0	0.0
Israel	20.9	51.8	50.1	69.3	0.0	17.5	49.9	13.1	0.0	0.1	0.0	0.0
Italy	213.1	307.7	16.8	16.4	18.6	51.4	48.2	14.9	14.8	12.0	0.0	0.0
Jamaica	2.5	7.5	0.0	0.0	0.0	0.0	92.4	96.4	3.6	2.2	0.0	0.0
Japan	835.5	1,090.5	14.0	27.4	20.0	23.3	18.5	8.5	10.7	7.9	24.2	27.8
Jordan	3.6	11.6	0.0	0.0	11.9	70.4	87.8	29.2	0.3	0.4	0.0	0.0
Kazakhstan	87.4	71.7	71.1	70.3	10.5	11.8	10.0	7.0	8.4	10.8	0.0	0.0
Kenya	3.2	6.5	0.0	0.0	0.0	0.0	7.1	30.5	76.6	50.6	0.0	0.0
Korea, Dem. Rep.	27.7	22.4	40.1	40.9	0.0	0.0	3.6	2.8	56.3	56.2	0.0	0.0
Korea, Rep.	105.4	402.3	16.8	38.0	9.1	18.1	17.9	5.6	6.0	0.9	50.2	37.0
Kuwait	18.5	47.6	0.0	0.0	45.7	27.5	54.3	72.5	0.0	0.0	0.0	0.0
Kyrgyz Republic	15.7	17.1	13.1	3.3	23.5	9.6	0.0	0.0	63.5	87.2	0.0	0.0
Lao PDR	..	..	..	..	..	..	..	..	..	..	..	..
Latvia	6.6	4.9	0.0	0.0	26.1	42.9	5.4	0.1	67.6	55.2	0.0	0.0
Lebanon	1.5	9.3	0.0	0.0	0.0	0.0	66.7	92.5	33.3	7.5	0.0	0.0
Lesotho	..	..	..	..	..	..	..	..	..	..	..	..
Liberia	..	..	..	..	..	..	..	..	..	..	..	..
Libya	10.2	24.0	0.0	0.0	0.0	40.9	100.0	59.1	0.0	0.0	0.0	0.0
Lithuania	28.4	12.1	0.0	0.0	23.8	20.4	14.6	1.7	1.5	3.3	60.0	71.6
Macedonia, FYR	5.8	7.0	89.7	72.9	0.0	0.0	1.8	3.5	8.5	23.6	0.0	0.0
Madagascar	..	..	..	..	..	..	..	..	..	..	..	..
Malawi	..	..	..	..	..	..	..	..	..	..	..	..
Malaysia	23.0	91.6	12.3	25.3	22.0	64.0	48.4	3.0	17.3	7.7	0.0	0.0
Mali	..	..	..	..	..	..	..	..	..	..	..	..
Mauritania	..	..	..	..	..	..	..	..	..	..	..	..
Mauritius	..	..	..	..	..	..	..	..	..	..	..	..
Mexico	124.1	249.6	6.3	12.7	11.6	45.5	56.7	21.6	18.9	12.2	2.4	4.4
Moldova	16.2	3.8	30.8	0.0	42.3	97.5	25.4	0.0	1.6	2.0	0.0	0.0
Mongolia	3.5	3.6	92.4	96.9	0.0	0.0	7.6	3.1	0.0	0.0	0.0	0.0
Morocco	9.6	23.2	23.0	58.1	0.0	12.8	64.4	21.4	12.7	6.9	0.0	0.0
Mozambique	0.5	14.7	13.9	0.0	0.0	0.1	23.6	0.1	62.6	99.9	0.0	0.0
Myanmar	2.5	6.2	1.6	0.0	39.3	40.2	10.9	5.8	48.1	53.9	0.0	0.0
Namibia	1.4	1.6	1.5	5.2	0.0	0.0	3.3	0.6	95.2	94.1	0.0	0.0
Nepal	0.9	2.7	0.0	0.0	0.0	0.0	0.1	0.4	99.9	99.6	0.0	0.0
Netherlands	71.9	98.4	38.3	26.9	50.9	57.6	4.3	2.1	0.1	0.1	4.9	3.5
New Zealand	32.3	43.5	1.9	12.5	17.6	22.6	0.0	0.1	72.3	53.9	0.0	0.0
Nicaragua	1.4	3.0	0.0	0.0	0.0	0.0	39.8	72.2	28.8	12.5	0.0	0.0
Niger	..	..	..	..	..	..	..	..	..	..	..	..
Nigeria	13.5	23.1	0.1	0.0	53.7	57.8	13.7	8.8	32.6	33.4	0.0	0.0
Norway	121.6	121.3	0.1	0.1	0.0	0.4	0.0	0.0	99.6	98.5	0.0	0.0
Oman	4.5	13.6	0.0	0.0	81.6	82.0	18.4	18.0	0.0	0.0	0.0	0.0
Pakistan	37.7	98.4	0.1	0.1	33.6	36.4	20.6	28.6	44.9	32.5	0.8	2.3
Panama	2.7	6.0	0.0	0.0	0.0	0.0	14.7	38.9	83.2	59.8	0.0	0.0
Papua New Guinea	..	..	..	..	..	..	..	..	..	..	..	..
Paraguay	27.2	53.8	0.0	0.0	0.0	0.0	0.0	0.0	99.9	100.0	0.0	0.0
Peru	13.8	27.4	0.0	3.0	1.7	9.5	21.5	8.4	75.8	78.5	0.0	0.0
Philippines	25.2	56.7	7.7	27.0	0.0	28.8	46.7	8.2	24.0	17.5	0.0	0.0
Poland	134.4	160.8	97.5	93.6	0.1	1.9	1.2	1.5	1.1	1.3	0.0	0.0
Portugal	28.4	48.6	32.1	30.8	0.0	25.4	33.1	10.8	32.3	22.6	0.0	0.0
Puerto Rico	..	..	..	..	..	..	..	..	..	..	..	..

3.10 Sources of electricity

	Electricity production		Sources of electricity[a]									
							% of total					
	billion kilowatt hours		Coal		Gas		Oil		Hydropower		Nuclear power	
	1990	2006	1990	2006	1990	2006	1990	2006	1990	2006	1990	2006
Romania	64.3	62.7	28.8	40.3	35.1	18.9	18.4	2.6	17.7	29.3	0.0	9.0
Russian Federation	1,082.2	993.9	14.3	17.9	47.3	46.1	11.9	2.5	15.3	17.4	10.9	15.7
Rwanda	..	..	..	..	..	..	..	..	..	..	..	..
Saudi Arabia	69.2	179.8	0.0	0.0	48.1	47.7	51.9	52.3	0.0	0.0	0.0	0.0
Senegal	0.9	2.4	0.0	0.0	2.3	1.9	93.0	85.1	0.0	9.6	0.0	0.0
Serbia	40.9[b]	36.5	69.1[b]	68.7	3.2[b]	0.3	4.6[b]	0.9	23.1[b]	30.1	0.0[b]	0.0
Sierra Leone	..	..	..	..	..	..	..	..	..	..	..	..
Singapore	15.7	39.4	0.0	0.0	0.0	78.0	100.0	22.0	0.0	0.0	0.0	0.0
Slovak Republic	25.5	31.3	31.9	18.3	7.1	6.1	6.4	2.3	7.4	14.1	47.2	57.6
Slovenia	12.0	15.1	31.9	36.0	0.0	2.5	4.8	0.3	24.7	23.8	38.7	36.7
Somalia	..	..	..	..	..	..	..	..	..	..	..	..
South Africa	165.4	251.9	94.3	93.5	0.0	0.0	0.0	0.0	0.6	1.5	5.1	4.7
Spain	151.2	299.1	40.1	22.8	1.0	30.2	5.7	8.0	16.8	8.5	35.9	20.1
Sri Lanka	3.2	9.4	0.0	0.0	0.0	0.0	0.2	50.6	99.8	49.4	0.0	0.0
Sudan	1.5	4.2	0.0	0.0	0.0	0.0	36.8	67.5	63.2	32.5	0.0	0.0
Swaziland	..	..	..	..	..	..	..	..	..	..	..	..
Sweden	146.0	143.3	1.1	1.1	0.3	0.4	0.9	1.2	49.7	43.1	46.7	46.7
Switzerland	55.0	62.1	0.1	0.0	0.6	1.3	0.7	0.3	54.2	49.8	43.0	44.8
Syrian Arab Republic	11.6	37.3	0.0	0.0	20.5	38.0	56.0	51.2	23.5	10.7	0.0	0.0
Tajikistan	18.1	16.9	0.0	0.0	9.1	2.3	0.0	0.0	90.9	97.7	0.0	0.0
Tanzania	1.6	2.8	0.0	3.8	0.0	43.8	4.9	0.6	95.1	51.7	0.0	0.0
Thailand	44.2	138.7	25.0	18.0	40.2	67.8	23.5	6.1	11.3	5.9	0.0	0.0
Timor-Leste	..	..	..	..	..	..	..	..	..	..	..	..
Togo	0.2	0.2	0.0	0.0	0.0	0.0	39.9	57.5	60.1	41.2	0.0	0.0
Trinidad and Tobago	3.6	7.0	0.0	0.0	99.0	99.4	0.1	0.2	0.0	0.0	0.0	0.0
Tunisia	5.8	14.1	0.0	0.0	63.7	84.9	35.5	14.2	0.8	0.7	0.0	0.0
Turkey	57.5	176.3	35.1	26.5	17.7	45.8	6.9	2.5	40.2	25.1	0.0	0.0
Turkmenistan	14.6	13.7	0.0	0.0	95.2	100.0	0.0	0.0	4.8	0.0	0.0	0.0
Uganda	..	..	..	..	..	..	..	..	..	..	..	..
Ukraine	298.6	193.2	38.2	33.6	16.7	12.7	16.1	0.4	3.5	6.7	25.5	46.7
United Arab Emirates	17.1	66.8	0.0	0.0	96.3	98.0	3.7	2.0	0.0	0.0	0.0	0.0
United Kingdom	317.8	394.5	65.0	38.5	1.6	35.8	10.9	1.3	1.6	1.2	20.7	19.1
United States	3,202.8	4,274.3	53.1	49.8	11.9	19.6	4.1	1.9	8.5	6.8	19.1	19.1
Uruguay	7.4	5.6	0.0	0.0	0.0	0.1	5.1	35.1	94.2	64.0	0.0	0.0
Uzbekistan	56.3	49.3	7.4	4.7	76.4	69.6	4.4	12.8	11.8	12.8	0.0	0.0
Venezuela, RB	59.3	110.4	0.0	0.0	26.2	13.4	11.5	14.6	62.3	72.0	0.0	0.0
Vietnam	8.7	56.5	23.1	17.2	0.1	37.0	15.0	4.1	61.8	41.8	0.0	0.0
West Bank and Gaza	..	..	..	..	..	..	..	..	..	..	..	..
Yemen, Rep.	1.7	5.3	0.0	0.0	0.0	0.0	100.0	100.0	0.0	0.0	0.0	0.0
Zambia	8.0	9.4	0.5	0.2	0.0	0.0	0.3	0.4	99.2	99.4	0.0	0.0
Zimbabwe	9.4	9.8	53.3	43.0	0.0	0.0	0.0	0.2	46.7	56.8	0.0	0.0
World	**11,845.0 t**	**18,977.0 t**	**37.3 w**	**40.8 w**	**14.6 w**	**20.1 w**	**10.3 w**	**5.5 w**	**18.0 w**	**15.9 w**	**17.0 w**	**14.7 w**
Low income	261.0	449.1	9.4	5.8	29.0	30.2	7.3	12.4	41.9	38.8	0.1	0.5
Middle income	4,017.2	7,919.8	35.3	48.3	20.6	18.6	14.4	6.1	22.3	20.6	6.3	5.1
Lower middle income	1,705.1	4,921.3	47.0	61.2	10.6	11.9	15.9	6.0	20.7	16.3	4.8	3.4
Upper middle income	2,312.1	2,998.3	26.6	27.0	28.0	29.5	13.4	6.2	23.5	27.6	7.4	7.8
Low & middle income	4,278.5	8,376.6	33.7	45.9	21.1	19.2	14.0	6.4	23.5	21.5	5.9	4.8
East Asia & Pacific	794.1	3,394.2	61.1	72.1	3.4	6.7	12.5	3.3	21.5	15.0	0.0	1.6
Europe & Central Asia	2,085.5	1,966.8	27.7	29.4	34.3	35.5	13.0	2.8	13.9	17.4	10.8	14.4
Latin America & Carib.	606.2	1,192.1	3.8	5.2	9.2	19.3	18.9	12.5	63.7	57.3	2.1	2.7
Middle East & N. Africa	187.9	515.0	1.2	2.6	36.9	60.7	48.3	27.8	12.4	7.4	0.0	0.0
South Asia	341.7	886.2	56.1	57.4	8.5	13.5	5.3	7.5	27.4	17.4	1.9	2.4
Sub-Saharan Africa	260.2	416.8	62.2	57.8	2.8	4.6	1.9	3.2	15.9	18.0	3.2	2.8
High income	7,585.5	10,644.0	39.2	36.6	10.9	20.7	8.2	4.7	14.9	11.4	23.2	22.5
Euro area	1,693.6	2,324.4	33.7	24.6	8.6	21.2	9.5	5.0	11.1	9.1	35.6	33.3

a. Shares may not sum to 100 percent because some sources of generated electricity (such as wind, solar, and geothermal) are not shown. b. Includes Kosovo and Montenegro.

Use of energy is important in improving people's standard of living. But electricity generation also can damage the environment. Whether such damage occurs depends largely on how electricity is generated. For example, burning coal releases twice as much carbon dioxide—a major contributor to global warming—as does burning an equivalent amount of natural gas (see *About the data* for table 3.8). Nuclear energy does not generate carbon dioxide emissions, but it produces other dangerous waste products. The table provides information on electricity production by source.

The International Energy Agency (IEA) compiles data on energy inputs used to generate electricity. IEA data for countries that are not members of the Organisation for Economic Co-operation and Development (OECD) are based on national energy data adjusted to conform to annual questionnaires completed by OECD member governments. In addition, estimates are sometimes made to complete major aggregates from which key data are missing, and adjustments are made to compensate for differences in definitions. The IEA makes these estimates in consultation with national statistical offices, oil companies, electric utilities, and national energy experts. It occasionally revises its time series to reflect political changes. For example, the IEA has constructed historical energy statistics for countries of the former Soviet Union. In addition, energy statistics for other countries have undergone continuous changes in coverage or methodology in recent years as more detailed energy accounts have become available. Breaks in series are therefore unavoidable.

• **Electricity production** is measured at the terminals of all alternator sets in a station. In addition to hydropower, coal, oil, gas, and nuclear power generation, it covers generation by geothermal, solar, wind, and tide and wave energy as well as that from combustible renewables and waste. Production includes the output of electric plants designed to produce electricity only, as well as that of combined heat and power plants. • **Sources of electricity** are the inputs used to generate electricity: coal, gas, oil, hydropower, and nuclear power. • **Coal** is all coal and brown coal, both primary (including hard coal and lignite-brown coal) and derived fuels (including patent fuel, coke oven coke, gas coke, coke oven gas, and blast furnace gas). Peat is also included in this category. • **Gas** is natural gas but not natural gas liquids. • **Oil** is crude oil and petroleum products. • **Hydropower** is electricity produced by hydroelectric power plants. • **Nuclear power** is electricity produced by nuclear power plants.

World

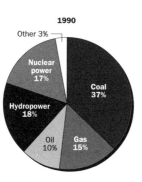
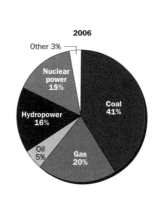

Source: Table 3.10.

Developing economies

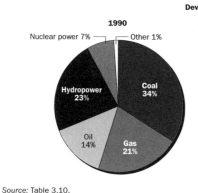
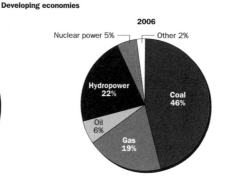

Source: Table 3.10.

Data on electricity production are from the IEA's electronic files and its annual publications *Energy Statistics and Balances of Non-OECD Countries, Energy Statistics of OECD Countries,* and *Energy Balances of OECD Countries.*

	Urban population					Population in urban agglomerations of more than 1 million		Population in largest city		Access to improved sanitation facilities			
	millions		% of total population		average annual % growth	% of total population		% of urban population		% of urban population		% of rural population	
	1990	2007	1990	2007	1990–2007	1990	2007	1990	2007	1990	2006	1990	2006
Afghanistan	2.3	6.4	18	24	6.0	11	12	62	51	..	45	..	25
Albania	1.2	1.5	36	46	1.2	..	..	..	..	97	98	..	97
Algeria	13.2	21.9	52	65	3.0	8	10	14	15	99	98	77	87
Angola	3.9	9.5	37	56	5.2	15	23	40	42	55	79	9	16
Argentina	28.3	36.3	87	92	1.4	39	39	37	35	86	92	45	83
Armenia	2.4	1.9	68	64	−1.3	33	37	49	57	94	96	..	81
Australia	14.6	18.6	85	89	1.4	60	61	25	24	100	100	100	100
Austria	5.1	5.6	66	67	0.5	27	28	41	41	100	100	100	100
Azerbaijan	3.8	4.4	54	52	0.8	24	22	45	43	..	90	..	70
Bangladesh	22.4	42.3	20	27	3.7	8	12	29	32	56	48	18	32
Belarus	6.7	7.1	66	73	0.3	16	19	24	26	..	91	..	97
Belgium	9.6	10.3	96	97	0.4	10	17	10	17	..	..	..	..
Benin	1.8	3.7	35	41	4.3	..	..	..	..	32	59	2	11
Bolivia	3.7	6.2	56	65	3.0	25	32	29	26	47	54	15	22
Bosnia and Herzegovina	1.7	1.8	39	47	0.3	..	..	..	..	99	99	..	92
Botswana	0.6	1.1	42	59	3.9	..	..	..	..	60	60	22	30
Brazil	111.8	163.1	75	85	2.2	34	38	13	12	82	84	37	37
Bulgaria	5.8	5.4	66	71	−0.4	14	16	21	22	100	100	96	96
Burkina Faso	1.2	2.8	14	19	4.9	..	8	49	41	23	41	2	6
Burundi	0.4	0.9	6	10	5.1	..	..	..	..	41	44	44	41
Cambodia	1.2	3.0	13	21	5.3	6	10	49	48	..	62	2	19
Cameroon	5.0	10.4	41	56	4.3	14	19	19	18	47	58	34	42
Canada	21.3	26.5	77	80	1.3	40	44	18	20	100	100	99	99
Central African Republic	1.1	1.7	37	38	2.4	..	..	..	..	21	40	5	25
Chad	1.3	2.8	21	26	4.7	..	..	38	35	19	23	1	4
Chile	11.0	14.6	83	88	1.7	35	34	42	39	91	97	48	74
China	311.0	556.3	27	42	3.4	13	18	3	3	61	74	43	59
Hong Kong, China	5.7	6.9	100	100	1.2	100	100	100	100	..	..	..	..
Colombia	22.6	32.6	68	74	2.2	32	35	22	23	81	85	39	58
Congo, Dem. Rep.	10.5	20.8	28	33	4.0	15	17	35	38	53	42	1	25
Congo, Rep.	1.3	2.3	54	61	3.3	29	36	53	59	..	19	..	21
Costa Rica	1.6	2.8	51	63	3.4	24	29	47	46	96	96	92	95
Côte d'Ivoire	5.1	9.3	40	48	3.5	16	20	41	41	39	38	8	12
Croatia	2.6	2.5	54	57	−0.1	..	..	..	..	99	99	98	98
Cuba	7.8	8.5	73	76	0.5	20	19	27	26	99	99	95	95
Czech Republic	7.8	7.6	75	74	−0.2	12	11	16	16	100	100	98	98
Denmark	4.4	4.7	85	86	0.5	26	20	31	23	100	100	100	100
Dominican Republic	4.0	6.7	55	68	3.0	21	22	38	32	77	81	57	74
Ecuador	5.7	8.7	55	65	2.5	26	32	28	29	88	91	50	72
Egypt, Arab Rep.	24.0	32.2	44	43	1.7	22	21	38	37	68	85	37	52
El Salvador	2.5	4.1	49	60	2.9	19	21	39	35	88	90	59	80
Eritrea	0.5	1.0	16	20	4.0	..	..	..	..	20	14	0	3
Estonia	1.1	0.9	71	69	−1.1	..	..	..	..	96	96	94	94
Ethiopia	6.1	13.2	13	17	4.6	4	4	30	22	19	27	2	8
Finland	3.1	3.3	61	63	0.5	17	21	28	34	100	100	100	100
France	42.0	47.6	74	77	0.7	23	22	22	21	..	..	..	..
Gabon	0.6	1.1	69	85	3.4	..	..	..	..	..	37	..	30
Gambia, The	0.4	0.9	38	56	5.6	..	..	..	..	..	50	..	55
Georgia	3.0	2.3	55	53	−1.5	22	25	41	48	96	94	91	92
Germany	58.1	60.5	73	74	0.2	8	9	6	6	100	100	100	100
Ghana	5.7	11.6	36	49	4.2	12	16	21	18	11	15	3	6
Greece	6.0	6.8	59	61	0.8	30	29	51	48	100	99	93	97
Guatemala	3.7	6.4	41	48	3.3	..	8	22	16	87	90	58	79
Guinea	1.7	3.2	28	34	3.7	15	16	53	47	19	33	10	12
Guinea-Bissau	0.3	0.5	28	30	3.3	..	..	..	..	..	48	..	26
Haiti	2.0	4.4	29	45	4.5	16	21	56	46	49	29	20	12

	Urban population					Population in urban agglomerations of more than 1 million		Population in largest city		Access to improved sanitation facilities			
	millions		% of total population		average annual % growth	% of total population		% of urban population		% of urban population		% of rural population	
	1990	2007	1990	2007	1990–2007	1990	2007	1990	2007	1990	2006	1990	2006
Honduras	2.0	3.4	40	47	3.1	..	..	29	29	68	78	29	55
Hungary	6.8	6.7	66	67	−0.1	19	17	29	25	100	100	100	100
India	216.6	329.1	26	29	2.5	10	12	6	6	44	52	4	18
Indonesia	54.5	113.6	31	50	4.3	9	9	14	8	73	67	42	37
Iran, Islamic Rep.	30.6	48.3	56	68	2.7	23	23	21	16	86	..	78	..
Iraq	12.9	19.4	70	67	2.4	26	22	32	26	75	80	..	69
Ireland	2.0	2.7	57	61	1.7	26	25	46	40	..	..	..	..
Israel	4.2	6.6	90	92	2.6	43	60	48	49	100	100	..	..
Italy	37.8	40.3	67	68	0.4	19	17	9	8	..	..	..	..
Jamaica	1.2	1.4	49	53	1.1	..	..	..	..	82	82	83	84
Japan	78.0	84.7	63	66	0.5	46	48	42	42	100	100	100	100
Jordan	2.3	4.5	72	78	4.0	27	18	37	30	..	88	..	71
Kazakhstan	9.2	8.9	56	58	−0.2	7	8	12	14	97	97	96	98
Kenya	4.3	8.0	18	21	3.7	6	8	32	38	18	19	44	48
Korea, Dem. Rep.	11.8	14.8	58	62	1.4	15	19	21	22	..	..	..	..
Korea, Rep.	31.6	39.4	74	81	1.3	51	48	33	25	..	..	..	..
Kuwait	2.1	2.6	98	98	1.3	65	72	67	74	..	..	..	..
Kyrgyz Republic	1.7	1.9	38	36	0.7	..	..	38	43	..	94	..	93
Lao PDR	0.6	1.7	15	30	6.0	..	..	..	..	..	87	..	38
Latvia	1.9	1.5	69	68	−1.0	..	..	..	..	..	82	..	71
Lebanon	2.5	3.6	83	87	2.1	43	45	52	52	100	100	..	..
Lesotho	0.2	0.5	14	25	4.7	..	..	..	..	..	43	30	34
Liberia	1.0	2.2	45	59	4.9	..	28	55	47	59	49	24	7
Libya	3.3	4.8	76	77	2.2	48	55	45	46	97	97	96	96
Lithuania	2.5	2.3	68	67	−0.6	..	..	..	..	..	..	..	..
Macedonia, FYR	1.1	1.4	58	66	1.2	..	..	..	..	..	92	..	81
Madagascar	2.8	5.7	24	29	4.1	8	9	33	30	15	18	6	10
Malawi	1.1	2.5	12	18	5.0	..	..	..	..	50	51	46	62
Malaysia	9.0	18.4	50	69	4.2	6	5	12	8	95	95	..	93
Mali	1.8	3.9	23	32	4.6	10	12	42	38	53	59	30	39
Mauritania	0.8	1.3	40	41	2.9	..	..	..	..	33	44	11	10
Mauritius	0.5	0.5	44	42	0.8	..	..	..	..	95	95	94	94
Mexico	59.4	81.0	71	77	1.8	32	34	26	23	74	91	8	48
Moldova	2.1	1.6	47	42	−1.5	..	..	..	..	..	85	..	73
Mongolia	1.2	1.5	57	57	1.3	..	..	48	60	..	64	..	31
Morocco	11.7	17.2	48	56	2.3	16	19	23	18	80	85	25	54
Mozambique	2.9	7.7	21	36	5.8	6	7	27	19	..	53	12	19
Myanmar	10.0	15.6	25	32	2.6	7	8	29	26	47	85	15	81
Namibia	0.4	0.8	28	36	3.8	..	..	..	..	73	66	8	18
Nepal	1.7	4.7	9	17	6.0	..	..	23	19	36	45	6	24
Netherlands	10.3	13.3	69	81	1.5	14	12	10	8	100	100	100	100
New Zealand	2.9	3.7	85	86	1.3	25	30	30	34	..	..	88	..
Nicaragua	2.2	3.2	52	56	2.2	18	21	34	38	59	57	23	34
Niger	1.2	2.3	15	16	3.9	..	..	36	39	16	27	1	3
Nigeria	33.3	70.5	35	48	4.4	11	14	14	13	33	35	22	25
Norway	3.1	3.6	72	77	1.0	..	..	22	22	..	..	..	..
Oman	1.2	1.9	66	72	2.5	..	..	..	..	97	97	61	..
Pakistan	33.0	58.0	31	36	3.3	16	18	22	21	76	90	14	40
Panama	1.3	2.4	54	72	3.7	35	38	65	53	..	78	..	63
Papua New Guinea	0.6	0.8	15	13	1.5	..	..	..	..	67	67	41	41
Paraguay	2.1	3.7	49	60	3.4	22	31	45	51	88	89	34	42
Peru	15.0	19.9	69	71	1.7	27	29	39	40	73	85	15	36
Philippines	29.9	56.4	49	64	3.7	14	14	27	20	71	81	46	72
Poland	23.4	23.4	61	61	0.0	4	4	7	7	..	..	..	..
Portugal	4.7	6.2	48	59	1.6	37	39	54	45	97	99	88	98
Puerto Rico	2.6	3.9	72	98	2.4	44	67	60	69	..	..	..	..

	Urban population					Population in urban agglomerations of more than 1 million		Population in largest city		Access to improved sanitation facilities			
	millions		% of total population		average annual % growth	% of total population		% of urban population		% of urban population		% of rural population	
	1990	2007	1990	2007	1990–2007	1990	2007	1990	2007	1990	2006	1990	2006
Romania	12.3	11.6	53	54	−0.3	8	9	14	17	88	88	52	54
Russian Federation	108.8	103.5	73	73	−0.3	18	18	8	10	93	93	70	70
Rwanda	0.4	1.8	5	18	8.8	..	..	56	48	31	34	29	20
Saudi Arabia	12.5	19.9	77	81	2.7	30	40	19	22	100	100	..	..
Senegal	3.1	5.2	39	42	3.1	18	21	45	50	52	54	9	9
Serbia	3.8	3.8	50	52	0.0	..	11	..	21	..	96[a]	..	88[a]
Sierra Leone	1.3	2.2	33	37	2.9	..	..	40	39	..	20	..	5
Singapore	3.0	4.6	100	100	2.4	99	100	99	100	100	100	..	..
Slovak Republic	3.0	3.0	57	56	0.1	..	..	..	..	100	100	99	99
Slovenia	1.0	1.0	50	49	−0.1	..	..	..	..	..	..	..	..
Somalia	2.0	3.1	30	36	2.7	14	13	47	35	..	51	..	7
South Africa	18.3	28.8	52	60	2.7	25	33	10	12	64	66	45	49
Spain	29.3	34.5	75	77	1.0	22	24	15	16	100	100	100	100
Sri Lanka	2.9	3.0	17	15	0.2	..	..	..	..	85	89	68	86
Sudan	6.9	16.4	27	43	5.1	9	12	34	29	53	50	26	24
Swaziland	0.2	0.3	23	25	2.8	..	..	..	..	..	64	..	46
Sweden	7.1	7.7	83	84	0.5	17	14	21	16	100	100	100	100
Switzerland	4.9	5.5	73	73	0.7	14	15	19	20	100	100	100	100
Syrian Arab Republic	6.2	10.7	49	54	3.2	26	31	25	25	94	96	69	88
Tajikistan	1.7	1.8	32	26	0.3	..	..	..	..	..	95	..	91
Tanzania	4.8	10.1	19	25	4.4	5	7	27	29	29	31	36	34
Thailand	16.0	21.1	29	33	1.6	11	10	37	32	92	95	72	96
Timor-Leste	0.2	0.3	21	27	3.7	..	..	..	..	..	64	..	32
Togo	1.2	2.7	30	41	4.8	16	22	52	53	25	24	8	3
Trinidad and Tobago	0.1	0.2	9	13	2.9	..	..	..	..	93	92	93	92
Tunisia	4.7	6.8	58	66	2.1	..	..	..	..	95	96	44	64
Turkey	33.2	50.4	59	68	2.4	22	27	20	20	96	96	69	72
Turkmenistan	1.7	2.4	45	48	2.2	..	..	..	..	..	..	..	..
Uganda	2.0	4.0	11	13	4.1	4	5	38	36	27	29	29	34
Ukraine	34.7	31.6	67	68	−0.5	12	11	7	9	98	97	93	83
United Arab Emirates	1.5	3.4	79	78	4.9	25	31	32	40	98	98	95	95
United Kingdom	50.8	54.8	89	90	0.5	26	26	15	16	..	..	..	..
United States	188.0	245.5	75	81	1.6	41	43	9	8	100	100	99	99
Uruguay	2.8	3.1	89	92	0.6	41	45	46	49	100	100	99	99
Uzbekistan	8.2	9.9	40	37	1.1	10	8	25	22	97	97	91	95
Venezuela, RB	16.6	25.6	84	93	2.5	34	32	17	12	90	..	47	..
Vietnam	13.4	23.3	20	27	3.2	13	13	30	22	62	88	21	56
West Bank and Gaza	1.3	2.7	68	72	4.0	..	..	..	..	..	84	..	69
Yemen, Rep.	2.6	6.7	21	30	5.7	5	9	25	30	79	88	14	30
Zambia	3.2	4.2	39	35	1.6	9	11	24	32	49	55	38	51
Zimbabwe	3.0	4.9	29	37	2.9	10	12	34	32	65	63	35	37
World	**2,252.1 s**	**3,260.9 s**	**43 w**	**50 w**	**2.2 w**	**18 w**	**20 w**	**17 w**	**16 w**	**76 w**	**78 w**	**34 w**	**44 w**
Low income	219.6	410.5	25	32	3.7	11	12	28	26	50	54	19	33
Middle income	1,361.3	2,049.5	39	48	2.4	15	18	14	12	72	76	33	45
Lower middle income	873.3	1,430.3	32	42	2.9	13	16	12	10	64	71	31	43
Upper middle income	488.0	619.3	69	75	1.4	..	28	17	17	86	89	53	64
Low & middle income	1,580.9	2,460.1	37	44	2.6	14	17	16	14	69	73	30	41
East Asia & Pacific	460.0	827.7	29	43	3.5	..	..	9	7	65	75	42	59
Europe & Central Asia	273.7	283.3	63	64	0.2	15	16	13	14	95	94	77	79
Latin America & Carib.	308.0	438.8	71	78	2.1	32	34	24	22	81	86	35	51
Middle East & N. Africa	115.7	179.3	52	57	2.6	20	21	27	24	83	88	51	62
South Asia	279.2	443.9	25	29	2.7	10	12	10	11	49	57	8	23
Sub-Saharan Africa	144.3	287.1	28	36	4.0	..	13	26	25	41	42	20	24
High income	671.1	800.9	73	77	1.0	..	..	20	19	100	100	99	99
Euro area	213.0	236.7	71	73	0.6	18	18	15	15	..	..	..	..

a. Includes Kosovo.

About the data

There is no consistent and universally accepted standard for distinguishing urban from rural areas, in part because of the wide variety of situations across countries. Most countries use an urban classification related to the size or characteristics of settlements. Some define urban areas based on the presence of certain infrastructure and services. And other countries designate urban areas based on administrative arrangements.

The population of a city or metropolitan area depends on the boundaries chosen. For example, in 1990 Beijing, China, contained 2.3 million people in 87 square kilometers of "inner city" and 5.4 million in 158 square kilometers of "core city." The population of "inner city and inner suburban districts" was 6.3 million and that of "inner city, inner and outer suburban districts, and inner and outer counties" was 10.8 million. (Most countries use the last definition.) For further discussion of urban-rural issues see box 3.1a in *About the data* for table 3.1.

Estimates of the world's urban population would change significantly if China, India, and a few other populous nations were to change their definition of urban centers. According to China's State Statistical Bureau, by the end of 1996 urban residents accounted for about 43 percent of China's population, more than double the 20 percent considered urban in 1994. In addition to the continuous migration of people from rural to urban areas, one of the main reasons for this shift was the rapid growth in the hundreds of towns reclassified as cities in recent years.

Because the estimates in the table are based on national definitions of what constitutes a city or metropolitan area, cross-country comparisons should be made with caution. To estimate urban populations, UN ratios of urban to total population were applied to the World Bank's estimates of total population (see table 2.1).

The table shows access to improved sanitation facilities for both urban and rural populations to allow comparison of access. Definitions of access and urban areas vary, however, so comparisons between countries can be misleading.

Definitions

- **Urban population** is the midyear population of areas defined as urban in each country and reported to the United Nations (see *About the data*). • **Population in urban agglomerations of more than 1 million** is the percentage of a country's population living in metropolitan areas that in 2005 had a population of more than 1 million. • **Population in largest city** is the percentage of a country's urban population living in that country's largest metropolitan area. • **Access to improved sanitation facilities** is the percentage of the urban or rural population with access to at least adequate excreta disposal facilities (private or shared but not public) that can effectively prevent human, animal, and insect contact with excreta. Improved facilities range from simple but protected pit latrines to flush toilets with a sewerage connection. To be effective, facilities must be correctly constructed and properly maintained.

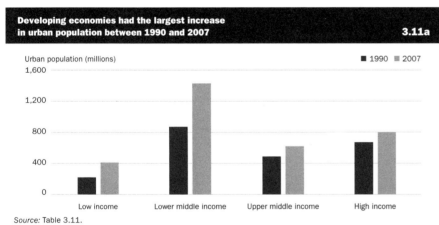

Developing economies had the largest increase in urban population between 1990 and 2007

3.11a

Urban population (millions)   ■ 1990   ■ 2007

Source: Table 3.11.

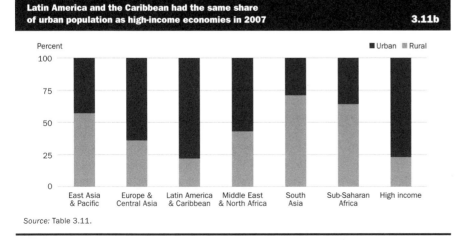

Latin America and the Caribbean had the same share of urban population as high-income economies in 2007

3.11b

Percent   ■ Urban ■ Rural

Source: Table 3.11.

Data sources

Data on urban population and the population in urban agglomerations and in the largest city are from the United Nations Population Division's *World Urbanization Prospects: The 2007 Revision*. Data on total population are World Bank estimates. Data on access to sanitation are from the World Health Organization and United Nations Children's Fund's *Progress on Drinking Water and Sanitation* (2008).

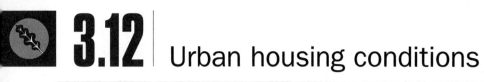

3.12 Urban housing conditions

	Census year	Household size		Overcrowding		Durable dwelling units		Home ownership		Multiunit dwellings		Vacancy rate	
		number of people		Households living in overcrowded dwellings[a] % of total		Buildings with durable structure % of total		Privately owned dwellings % of total		% of total		Unoccupied dwellings % of total	
		National	Urban	National	Urban	National	Urban	National	Urban	National	Urban	National	Urban
Afghanistan		..	..	..	..	..	..	..	..	..	..	..	..
Albania	2001	4.2	3.9	..	..	..	..	65[b]	30[b]	..	..	12	13
Algeria	1998	4.9	..	..	..	..	..	67	..	..	..	19	..
Angola		..	..	..	..	..	..	..	..	..	..	..	..
Argentina	2001	3.6	..	19	..	97	..	..	..	4	..	16[b]	..
Armenia	2001	4.1	4.0	4	6	93	93	95	90	1	1	..	..
Australia	2001	3.8	..	1	..	..	..	..	..	..	..	..	..
Austria	1991	2.6	..	2	..	..	..	..	..	50	..	13	..
Azerbaijan	1999	4.7	4.4	..	..	..	..	74	62	4	5	..	..
Bangladesh	2001	4.8	4.8	..	..	21[b]	42[b]	88[b]	61[b]	..	..	..	..
Belarus	1999	..	..	..	..	..	..	..	..	..	..	..	..
Belgium	2001	2.6	..	0[b]	..	..	..	67	..	32[b]	..	..	..
Benin	1992	5.9	..	..	..	26	..	59	..	..	..	..	..
Bolivia	2001	4.2	4.3	40	..	43	58	70	59	3[b]	5[b]	6	4
Bosnia and Herzegovina		..	..	..	..	..	..	..	..	..	..	..	..
Botswana	2001	4.2	3.9	27	47	88	90[b]	61	47	1	..	..	..
Brazil	2000	3.8	3.7	..	..	..	..	74	75	..	..	..	..
Bulgaria	2001	2.7	2.7	..	..	79	89	98	98	..	..	23	17
Burkina Faso	1996	6.2	5.8	30	53	..	..	..	..	..	..	..	..
Burundi	1990	4.7	..	..	..	..	..	..	..	..	..	..	..
Cambodia	1998	5.2	..	..	..	..	..	..	..	..	..	..	..
Cameroon	1987	5.2	5.1	67	77	77	..	73	48	27	42	..	..
Canada	2001	2.6	..	..	..	..	..	64	..	32	..	8	..
Central African Republic	2003	5.2	5.8	32	36[b]	78	92	85	74	..	..	..	..
Chad	1993	5.1	5.1	..	..	..	..	..	..	..	..	..	..
Chile	2002	3.4	3.5	..	..	91	92	66	65	13	15	11	10
China	2000	3.4	3.2	..	..	82	..	88	74	..	..	1	..
Hong Kong, China		..	..	..	..	..	..	..	..	..	..	..	..
Colombia	1993	4.8	..	27[b]	..	83[b]	..	68[b]	..	13	..	10[b]	..
Congo Dem Rep	1984	5.4	..	55		..	..	..	..	..	..	..	..
Congo Rep	1984	10.5	..	..	..	..	..	76	..	..	..	..	..
Costa Rica	2000	4.0	..	22	..	88	..	72	..	2	3	9	6
Côte d'Ivoire	1998	5.4	..	..	..	..	..	..	..	..	..	..	..
Croatia	2001	3.0	..	..	..	..	..	..	..	..	..	12	..
Cuba	1981	4.2	4.2	..	..	..	..	..	..	15	21	0	0
Czech Republic	2001	2.4	..	..	..	..	..	52	..	49	..	12	..
Denmark	2001	2.2	..	..	..	..	..	..	..	..	..	..	..
Dominican Republic	2002	3.9	..	..	..	97	..	..	..	8	..	11	..
Ecuador	2001	3.5	3.7	30	..	81	88	68[b]	58[b]	9	14	12	7
Egypt	1996	4.7	..	..	..	..	..	..	..	75	..	..	..
El Salvador	1992	..	..	63	..	67	83	70	68	3	6	11	11
Eritrea		..	..	..	..	..	..	..	..	..	..	..	..
Estonia	2000	2.4	2.3	3	..	..	..	..	..	72	..	13	..
Ethiopia	1994	4.8	4.7	..	..	..	23	..	54	..	..	..	..
Finland	2000	2.2	..	..	..	..	..	64	..	44	..	..	..
France	1999	2.5	..	..	..	..	..	55	..	..	..	7	..
Gabon	2003	5.2	..	..	..	..	..	..	..	..	..	..	..
Gambia	1993	8.9	..	..	..	18	..	68	..	..	..	..	..
Georgia	2002	3.5	3.5	..	..	..	..	..	..	..	..	..	..
Germany	2001	2.3	..	..	..	..	..	43	..	..	..	7	..
Ghana	2000	5.1	5.1	..	..	45	..	57	..	53	..	5	..
Greece	2001	3.0	..	1	..	..	..	..	..	..	..	..	..
Guatemala	2002	4.4	4.7	..	..	67	80	81	74	2	4	13	11
Guinea		..	..	..	..	..	..	..	..	..	..	..	..
Guinea-Bissau		..	..	..	..	..	..	..	..	..	..	..	..
Haiti	1982	4.2	..	26	..	..	..	92	68	..	..	9	19

	Census year	Household size		Overcrowding		Durable dwelling units		Home ownership		Multiunit dwellings		Vacancy rate	
		number of people		Households living in overcrowded dwellings[a] % of total		Buildings with durable structure % of total		Privately owned dwellings % of total		% of total		Unoccupied dwellings % of total	
		National	Urban	National	Urban	National	Urban	National	Urban	National	Urban	National	Urban
Honduras	2001	4.4	..	..	..	69	85	..	..	..	..	14	..
Hungary	1990	2.7	..	..	..	..	..	..	..	..	..	4	..
India	2001	5.3	5.3	77	71	83	81	87	67	..	..	6	9
Indonesia	2000	4.0	..	..	..	..	..	..	..	..	..	..	..
Iran, Islamic Rep.	1996	4.8	4.6	33[b]	26[b]	72	76	73	67	..	..	..	..
Iraq	1997	7.7	7.2	..	..	88	96	70	66	4	5	13	15
Ireland	2002	3.0	..	..	..	..	..	..	..	8[b]	..	..	..
Israel	1995	3.5	..	..	..	..	..	..	..	..	..	..	..
Italy	2001	2.8	..	..	..	..	..	..	..	..	..	21	..
Jamaica	2001	3.5	..	..	..	98[b]	..	58[b]	..	2[b]	..	..	..
Japan	2000	2.7	..	..	..	..	..	61	..	37	..	..	..
Jordan	1994	6.2	6.0	1	..	97	97	69	64	57	67	..	..
Kazakhstan		..	..	..	..	..	..	..	..	..	..	..	..
Kenya	1999	4.6	3.4	..	..	35	72	72	25	..	..	39	17
Korea, Dem Rep	2000	3.8	..	23	..	..	..	50	..	15	..	..	..
Korea, Rep.	1993	4.4	..	..	..	..	..	..	..	..	..	..	..
Kuwait	1995	6.4	..	..	..	..	..	..	..	9[b]	..	11	..
Kyrgyz Republic	1999	4.4	3.6	..	..	..	..	..	..	..	..	..	..
Laos	1995	6.1	6.1	..	..	49	77	96	86	..	..	..	..
Latvia	2000	3.0	2.6	4	..	88	..	58	..	74	..	0	..
Lebanon		..	..	..	..	..	..	..	..	..	..	..	..
Lesotho	2001	5.0	..	10[b]	..	..	..	84	..	0	..	..	..
Liberia	1974	4.8	..	31	..	20	..	1	..	..	..	..	..
Libya		6.4	..	..	..	..	..	..	..	..	..	7	..
Lithuania	2001	2.6	..	7	..	..	..	..	..	..	..	..	..
Macedonia, FYR	2002	3.6	3.6[b]	8[b]	..	95[b]	95[b]	48[b]	..	..	..	7[b]	3[b]
Madagascar	1993	4.9	4.8	64	57	..	..	81	59	..	..	..	..
Malawi	1998	4.4	4.4	30	..	48	84	86	47	..	..	..	..
Malaysia	2000	4.5	4.4	..	..	..	..	..	..	10[b]	16[b]	..	..
Mali	1998	5.6	..	..	..	..	..	..	..	..	..	..	..
Mauritania	1988	..	..	..	..	..	..	..	..	..	..	..	..
Mauritius	2000	3.9	3.8	6	7	91	94	87	81	..	..	7	6
Mexico	2000	4.4	..	27[b]	..	87	..	78	..	6	..	..	..
Moldova	2003	..	..	..	..	..	..	..	..	..	..	..	..
Mongolia	2000	4.4	4.5	..	..	..	..	..	..	48	56	..	..
Morocco	1982	5.9	5.3	..	..	..	..	..	..	..	..	..	..
Mozambique	1997	4.4	4.9	37	28	7	20	92	83	1	1	0	..
Myanmar		..	..	..	..	..	..	..	..	..	..	..	..
Namibia	2001	5.3	..	..	..	..	..	..	..	..	..	..	..
Nepal	2001	5.4	4.9	..	..	..	..	88	..	..	..	0	..
Netherlands		..	..	..	..	..	..	..	..	..	..	..	..
New Zealand	2001	2.8	..	1[b]	..	..	..	65	..	17	..	10	..
Nicaragua	1995	5.3	..	..	..	79	87	84	86	0	0	8	..
Niger	2001	6.4	6.0	..	..	..	..	77	40	..	..	..	..
Nigeria	1991	5.0	4.7	..	..	..	..	..	..	..	..	..	..
Norway	1980	2.7	..	1	..	..	..	67	..	38	..	..	..
Oman	2003	7.1	..	..	..	..	..	..	..	..	..	..	..
Pakistan	1998	6.8	6.8	..	..	58	86	81	..	..	..	..	..
Panama	2000	4.1	..	28[b]	..	88	98[b]	80	66[b]	10[b]	10[b]	14	..
Papua New Guinea	1990	4.5[b]	6.5	..	..	..	..	..	44	..	8	..	..
Paraguay	2002	4.6	4.5	38[b]	..[b]	95[b]	98[b]	79	75	1[b]	2[b]	6[b]	6[b]
Peru	1993	..	..	..	..	49	64	..	..	..	..	7	3
Philippines	1990	5.3	5.3	..	..	62	..	83	76	6	11	4	4
Poland	1988	3.2	..	..	..	..	..	..	..	..	..	1	..
Portugal	2001	2.8	..	..	..	..	..	76	..	86	..	..	..
Puerto Rico	1990	3.3	..	..	..	..	..	72	..	..	..	11	..

	Census year	Household size		Overcrowding		Durable dwelling units		Home ownership		Multiunit dwellings		Vacancy rate	
		number of people		Households living in overcrowded dwellings[a] % of total		Buildings with durable structure % of total		Privately owned dwellings % of total		% of total		Unoccupied dwellings % of total	
		National	Urban	National	Urban	National	Urban	National	Urban	National	Urban	National	Urban
Romania	1992	3.1	3.1	..	..	58	..	87	77	39	71	6	4
Russia	2002	2.8	2.7	7	5	..	..	..	..	73	86	..	..
Rwanda	1991	4.7	..	..	..	79	78	92	73	19	25	..	..
Saudi Arabia	2004	5.5	..	..	..	92[b]	..	43	..	..	..	..	..
Senegal		..	..	..	..	..	..	..	..	..	..	..	..
Serbia	2001	2.9	2.2	..	..	..	..	..	..	..	..	..	..
Sierra Leone	1985	6.8	..	..	..	34	..	68	..	..	..	..	..
Singapore	2000	4.4	..	..	..	..	..	..	..	..	..	..	..
Slovak Republic		..	..	..	..	..	..	..	..	..	..	..	..
Slovenia	1991	3.1	..	..	..	..	..	69	..	37	..	9	..
Somalia	1975	..	..	..	..	..	..	..	..	..	..	..	..
South Africa	2001	4.0	..	..	..	..	..	..	..	7	..	..	..
Spain	1991	3.3	..	0	..	..	..	78	..	..	..	..	..
Sri Lanka	2001	3.8	..	..	..	93[b]	92[b]	70[b]	58[b]	1	14[b]	13	1[b]
Sudan	1993	5.8	6.0	..	..	..	..	86[b]	58[b]	0[b]	1[b]	..	..
Swaziland	1997	5.4	3.7	..	..	..	..	..	..	..	..	..	..
Sweden	1990	2.0	..	..	..	..	..	..	..	54	..	1	..
Switzerland	1990	2.4	2.1	..	..	..	..	31	24	28	32	11	7
Syrian Arab Republic	1981	6.3	6.0	..	..	..	..	..	..	..	..	..	..
Tajikistan	2000	..	..	..	..	..	..	..	..	..	..	..	..
Tanzania	2002	4.9	4.5[b]	33[b]	7[b]	..	..	82[b]	43[b]	..	..	..	..
Thailand	2000	3.8	..	..	..	93	93	81	62	3	..	3	..
Timor-Leste		..	..	..	..	..	..	..	..	..	..	..	..
Togo		..	..	..	..	..	..	..	..	..	..	..	..
Trinidad and Tobago	2000	3.7	..	9[b]	..	98[b]	..	74[b]	..	17[b]	..	..	..
Tunisia	1994	8.0	..	..	..	99	..	71	89[b]	6	10[b]	15	12[b]
Turkey	1990	5.0	..	..	..	..	..	70	..	..	..	..	..
Turkmenistan		..	..	..	..	..	..	..	..	..	..	..	..
Uganda	1991	4.9	4.0[b]	..	..	21[b]	..	80[b]	24[b]	0[b]	2[b]	..	..
Ukraine	2003	..	..	..	..	..	..	..	..	..	..	..	..
United Arab Emirates		..	..	..	..	..	..	..	..	..	1	..	..
United Kingdom	2001	..	2.4	..	..	..	..	..	69	..	19	..	..
United States	2000	2.7	..	..	..	..	..	66	..	..	..	9	7
Uruguay	1996	3.3	3.4[b]	22[b]	..	..	..	57[b]	57[b]	..	..	13[b]	13[b]
Uzbekistan		..	..	..	..	..	..	..	..	..	..	..	..
Venezuela. RB	2001	4.4	..	..	..	..	..	78	..	14	..	16	..
Vietnam	1999	4.6	4.5	..	..	77	89	95	86	..	..	..	..
West Bank and Gaza	1997	7.1	..	..	..	..	..	78	..	45	..	..	..
Yemen	1994	6.7	6.8	54[b]	6[b]	..	..	88[b]	68[b]	3[b]	11[b]	..	..
Zambia	2000	5.3	5.9	..	..	..	..	94	30	..	..	..	..
Zimbabwe	1992	4.8	4.2	..	..	..	..	94	30	6	..	..	..

a. More than two people per room. b. Data are from a previous census.

About the data

Urbanization can yield important social benefits, improving access to public services and the job market. It also leads to significant demands for services. Inadequate living quarters and demand for housing and shelter are major concerns for policymakers.

The unmet demand for affordable housing, along with urban poverty, has led to the emergence of slums in many poor countries. Improving the shelter situation requires a better understanding of the mechanisms governing housing markets and the processes governing housing availability. That requires good data and adequate policy-oriented analysis so that housing policy can be formulated in a global comparative perspective and drawn from lessons learned in other countries. Housing policies and outcomes affect such broad socioeconomic conditions as the infant mortality rate, performance in school, household saving, productivity levels, capital formation, and government budget deficits. A good understanding of housing conditions thus requires an extensive set of indicators within a reasonable framework.

There is a strong demand for quantitative indicators that can measure housing conditions on a regular basis to monitor progress. However, data deficiencies and lack of rigorous quantitative analysis hamper informed decisionmaking on desirable policies to improve housing conditions. The data in the table are from housing and population censuses, collected using similar definitions. The table will incorporate household survey data in future editions. The table focuses attention on urban areas, where housing conditions are typically most severe. Not all the compiled indicators are presented in the table because of space limitations.

Definitions

• **Census year** is the year in which the underlying data were collected. • **Household size** is the average number of people within a household, calculated by dividing total population by the number of households in the country and in urban areas. • **Overcrowding** refers to the number of households living in dwellings with two or more people per room as a percentage of total households in the country and in urban areas. • **Durable dwelling units** are the number of housing units in structures made of durable building materials (concrete, stone, cement, brick, asbestos, zinc, and stucco) expected to maintain their stability for 20 years or longer under local conditions with normal maintenance and repair, taking into account location and environmental hazards such as floods, mudslides, and earthquakes, as a percentage of total dwellings. • **Home ownership** refers to the number of privately owned dwellings as a percentage of total dwellings. When the number of private dwellings is not available from the census data, the share of households that own their housing unit is used. Privately owned and owner-occupied units are included, depending on the definition used in the census data. State- and community-owned units and rented, squatted, and rent-free units are excluded. • **Multiunit dwellings** are the number of multiunit dwellings, such as apartments, flats, condominiums, barracks, boardinghouses, orphanages, retirement houses, hostels, hotels, and collective dwellings, as a percentage of total dwellings. • **Vacancy rate** is the percentage of completed dwelling units that are currently unoccupied. It includes all vacant units, whether on the market or not (such as second homes).

Selected housing indicators for smaller economies — 3.12a

	Census year	Household size	Overcrowding	Durable dwelling units	Home ownership	Multiunit dwellings	Vacancy rate
			Households living in overcrowded dwellings[a]	Buildings with durable structure	Privately owned dwellings		Unoccupied dwellings
		number of people	% of total	% of total	% of total	% of total	% of total
Antigua and Barbuda	2001	3.0	..	99[b]	65[b]	3[b]	22
Bahamas	1990	3.8	12	99	55	13	14
Bahrain	2001	5.9	..	94[b]	51	28	6
Barbados	1990	3.5	3	100	76	9	9
Belize	2000	4.6	..	93	63	4	..
Cape Verde	1990	5.1	28	78	72	2	..
Cayman Islands	1999	3.1	..	100	53	38	19
Equatorial Guinea	1993	7.5	14	56[b]	75	14	..
Fiji	1996	5.4	..	60	65	7	..
Guam	2000	4.0	2[b]	93	48	29	19
Isle of Man	2001	2.4	0	..	68	16	..
Maldives	2000	6.6	..	93	..	1	15
Marshall Islands	1999	7.8	..	95	72	12	8
Netherlands Antilles	2001	2.9	24[b]	99	60	16	12
New Caledonia	1989	4.1	..	77	53	9	13
Northern Mariana Islands	1995	4.9	9[b]	99	33	27	17
Palau	2000	5.7	8	76	79	11	3
Seychelles	1997	4.2	15[b]	97	78	..	0
Solomon Islands	1999	6.3	51	23	85	1	..
St. Vincent & Grenadines	1991	3.9	..	98	71	7	..
Turks and Caicos	1990	3.3	4	96	66	11	..
Virgin Islands (UK)	1991	3.0	2	99	40	46	..
Western Samoa	1991	7.3	..	42	90	47	30

a. More than two people per room. b. Data are from a previous census.
Source: National population and housing censuses.

Data sources

Data on urban housing conditions are from national population and housing censuses.

	Motor vehicles		Passenger cars	Road density	Road sector fuel consumption		Transport sector fuel consumption		Fuel price		Particulate matter concentration	
	per 1,000 people	per kilometer of road	per 1,000 people	km. of road per 100 sq. km. of land area	% of total consumption	liters per capita	liters per capita Diesel	Gasoline	$ per liter Super grade gasoline	Diesel	Urban-population-weighted PM10 micrograms per cubic meter	
	2006	2006	2006	2006	2006	2006	2006	2006	2008	2008	1990	2006
Afghanistan	..	9	..	6	..	..	..	..	1.05	0.96	78	41
Albania	97	15	71	63	27	225	156	77	1.36	1.31	92	44
Algeria	91	27	58	5	14	179	98	60	0.34	0.20	115	71
Angola	..	..	8	4	11	82	48	31	0.53	0.39	142	66
Argentina	..	..	146	8	19	396	217	94	0.78	0.58	105	73
Armenia	..	..	..	25	7	71	0	67	1.08	1.11	453	59
Australia	671	17	542	11	19	1,321	418	781	0.74	0.94	23	15
Austria	552	43	507	128	20	964	631	275	1.37	1.43	38	33
Azerbaijan	61	10	57	68	11	211	92	100	0.74	0.56	226	60
Bangladesh	2	1	1	166	4	8	9	2	1.17	0.70	231	135
Belarus	..	..	183	46	5	171	129	62	1.33	1.06	23	6
Belgium	535	36	474	499	13	897	731	163	1.50	1.34	30	22
Benin	..	..	13	17	22	83	29	50	1.03	1.03	75	46
Bolivia	49	7	15	6	20	149	70	56	0.68	0.53	120	94
Bosnia and Herzegovina	..	..	..	43	15	250	159	87	1.13	1.18	36	19
Botswana	113	7	47	4	26	327	114	199	0.88	1.02	95	67
Brazil	170	18	136	20	22	308	166	86	1.26	1.03	40	23
Bulgaria	360	63	314	37	12	383	220	92	1.28	1.37	111	57
Burkina Faso	7	7	5	34	..	..	..	..	1.38	1.33	151	84
Burundi	..	..	1	48	..	..	..	..	1.39	1.23	56	29
Cambodia	36	37	25	22	8	32	19	12	0.94	0.89	86	46
Cameroon	11	3	11	11	10	46	25	19	1.14	1.04	116	62
Canada	582	13	561	14	16	1,537	452	1,084	0.76	0.90	25	17
Central African Republic	..	..	1	4	..	..	..	..	1.44	1.44	62	44
Chad	6	2	..	3	..	..	..	..	1.30	1.32	217	109
Chile	157	26	97	11	18	378	232	149	0.95	0.95	88	48
China	28	11	18	36	5	76	48	45	0.99	1.01	114	73
Hong Kong, China	70	245	52	180	8	250	187	53	1.95	1.16	..	..
Colombia	59	16	37	15	23	186	83	90	1.04	0.73	39	22
Congo, Dem. Rep.	..	..	..	7	1	3	0	3	1.23	1.21	73	47
Congo, Rep.	..	..	8	5	22	85	55	27	0.81	0.57	135	64
Costa Rica	198	24	146	70	29	358	175	164	1.24	1.10	45	36
Côte d'Ivoire	..	..	7	25	5	24	19	9	1.33	1.20	94	36
Croatia	366	56	323	51	21	487	295	184	1.27	1.37	44	30
Cuba	..	..	..	55	7	79	23	47	1.67	1.51	44	17
Czech Republic	394	31	399	163	12	650	399	230	1.37	1.45	67	21
Denmark	437	33	354	168	20	904	520	390	1.54	1.54	30	19
Dominican Republic	115	..	78	26	20	192	62	119	1.04	0.94	44	20
Ecuador	66	20	39	15	31	310	180	148	0.51	0.27	38	25
Egypt, Arab Rep.	..	..	29	9	16	157	93	52	0.49	0.20	223	119
El Salvador	..	..	24	48	20	161	84	69	0.78	0.81	46	33
Eritrea	..	..	..	3	6	11	10	1	2.53	1.07	118	56
Estonia	477	11	367	126	14	619	375	269	1.18	1.30	45	13
Ethiopia	2	4	1	3	5	16	13	2	0.92	0.89	112	68
Finland	542	36	470	23	11	898	499	416	1.57	1.39	23	18
France	598	39	496	141	15	809	590	191	1.52	1.45	18	13
Gabon	..	..	..	3	8	128	91	32	1.14	0.90	10	8
Gambia, The	7	3	5	33	..	..	..	..	0.79	0.75	144	86
Georgia	71	16	56	29	16	139	44	87	1.09	1.16	208	47
Germany	598	213	565	185	15	748	374	312	1.56	1.56	27	19
Ghana	18	9	12	25	12	58	29	29	0.90	0.90	39	34
Greece	522	47	409	89	21	674	269	415	1.23	1.41	67	36
Guatemala	68	53	53	13	20	149	66	76	0.86	0.82	63	62
Guinea	14	4	8	10	..	..	..	..	1.02	1.02	108	70
Guinea-Bissau	1	1	..	12	..	..	..	..	0.00	0.00	119	72
Haiti	..	..	..	15	5	16	19	15	1.16	0.89	70	37

Traffic and congestion

	Motor vehicles		Passenger cars	Road density	Road sector fuel consumption		Transport sector fuel consumption		Fuel price		Particulate matter concentration	
	per 1,000 people	per kilometer of road	per 1,000 people	km. of road per 100 sq. km. of land area	% of total consumption	liters per capita	liters per capita		$ per liter		Urban-population-weighted PM10 micrograms per cubic meter	
							Diesel	Gasoline	Super grade gasoline	Diesel		
	2006	2006	2006	2006	2006	2006	2006	2006	2008	2008	1990	2006
Honduras	67	31	52	12	17	127	64	57	0.80	0.80	45	43
Hungary	374	20	292	172	15	496	307	176	1.27	1.38	36	19
India	12	3	8	100	6	33	23	10	1.09	0.70	112	65
Indonesia	109	62	..	20	12	117	50	69	0.60	0.46	137	83
Iran, Islamic Rep.	..	..	24	10	21	612	239	331	0.53	0.03	86	51
Iraq	..	..	30	10	32	428	161	244	0.03	0.01	146	115
Ireland	447	20	382	132	29	1,222	676	518	1.56	1.64	25	16
Israel	293	115	239	85	16	574	185	357	1.47	1.27	71	31
Italy	667	81	595	162	21	779	480	252	1.57	1.63	42	27
Jamaica	188	24	138	201	12	246	163	230	0.74	0.84	59	43
Japan	586	63	441	316	14	689	252	406	1.74	1.54	43	30
Jordan	127	91	88	9	22	332	167	156	0.61	0.61	110	45
Kazakhstan	139	23	114	3	5	241	46	207	0.83	0.72	43	19
Kenya	18	10	9	11	6	34	21	13	1.20	1.14	67	36
Korea, Dem. Rep.	..	..		21	2	16	9	7	0.76	0.95	165	68
Korea, Rep.	328	156	240	102	12	653	363	171	1.65	1.33	51	35
Kuwait	422	181	349	32	13	1,441	356	1,002	0.24	0.20	75	97
Kyrgyz Republic	..	..	39	9	9	55	0	52	0.80	0.88	75	22
Lao PDR	57	10	..	13	..	..	..	..	0.92	0.76	91	49
Latvia	415	14	357	108	22	528	342	191	1.12	1.23	38	16
Lebanon	..	..	403	67	28	384	3	355	0.76	0.76	43	36
Lesotho	..	..		20	..	..	..	..	0.79	0.93	86	41
Liberia	..	..	6	10	..	..	..	..	0.74	1.03	61	40
Libya	257	..	232	5	18	620	364	227	0.14	0.12	106	88
Lithuania	513	22	468	123	16	475	284	119	1.13	1.22	53	19
Macedonia, FYR	163	25	150	52	12	196	109	62	1.15	1.12	46	21
Madagascar	..	..		8	..	..	..	..	1.55	1.43	78	34
Malawi	..	..	..	16	..	..	..	..	1.78	1.67	75	33
Malaysia	272	72	225	28	19	588	211	355	0.53	0.53	37	23
Mali	..	..	..	1	..	..	..	..	1.30	1.10	274	152
Mauritania	..	..	..	1	..	..	..	..	1.49	1.06	147	86
Mauritius	138	89	104	99	..	..	..	..	0.74	0.56	23	18
Mexico	222	65	147	18	26	514	151	335	0.74	0.54	69	36
Moldova	94	31	84	38	7	75	55	22	1.20	1.04	97	36
Mongolia	43	2	28	3	11	144	39	127	1.38	1.42	198	110
Morocco	59	29	46	13	3	16	8	15	1.29	0.83	34	21
Mozambique	..	..	..	4	4	19	16	4	1.71	1.37	111	28
Myanmar	6	..	4	4	8	29	19	9	0.43	0.52	107	58
Namibia	85	4	42	5	37	316	101	196	0.78	0.88	74	47
Nepal	..	..	3	12	3	12	8	2	1.13	0.82	67	34
Netherlands	486	62	429	372	14	826	492	300	1.68	1.45	46	34
New Zealand	722	32	609	35	25	1,237	536	660	1.09	0.85	16	14
Nicaragua	46	13	18	14	14	101	63	37	0.87	0.82	48	28
Niger	5	4	4	1	..	..	..	..	0.99	0.97	220	132
Nigeria	..	..	17	21	7	64	8	52	0.59	1.13	175	45
Norway	546	27	439	29	13	863	644	378	1.63	1.63	24	15
Oman	..	..	156	11	9	649	61	548	0.31	0.38	148	108
Pakistan	14	8	10	34	10	56	47	8	0.84	0.77	224	120
Panama	103	27	73	15	16	164	140	153	0.67	0.68	58	35
Papua New Guinea	..	..	5	4	..	..	..	..	0.94	0.90	34	21
Paraguay	85	15	50	7	27	206	165	32	1.17	0.96	106	77
Peru	47	16	30	6	25	145	103	32	1.42	0.99	98	54
Philippines	34	14	9	67	14	82	53	36	0.91	0.81	55	23
Poland	416	35	351	135	13	388	198	125	1.43	1.40	59	37
Portugal	507	67	471	90	24	683	473	186	1.61	1.47	51	23
Puerto Rico	..	..	..	289	..	..	..	..	0.65	0.78	27	21

3.13 | Traffic and congestion

	Motor vehicles		Passenger cars	Road density	Road sector fuel consumption		Transport sector fuel consumption		Fuel price		Particulate matter concentration	
	per 1,000 people	per kilometer of road	per 1,000 people	km. of road per 100 sq. km. of land area	% of total consumption	liters per capita	liters per capita		$ per liter		Urban-population-weighted PM10 micrograms per cubic meter	
							Diesel	Gasoline	Super grade gasoline	Diesel		
	2006	2006	2006	2006	2006	2006	2006	2006	2008	2008	1990	2006
Romania	180	20	156	83	10	218	138	78	1.11	1.22	36	14
Russian Federation	228	35	188	5	6	338	119	230	0.89	0.86	41	18
Rwanda	3	..	1	57	..	..	..	..	1.37	1.37	49	26
Saudi Arabia	..	20	415	10	18	1,329	590	672	0.16	0.09	161	113
Senegal	14	9	10	7	16	47	38	9	1.35	1.26	97	95
Serbia	244	46	204	44	14	236	160	68	1.11	1.29	33[a]	15[a]
Sierra Leone	4	2	2	16	..	..	..	..	0.91	0.91	92	50
Singapore	141	194	105	461	7	608	374	206	1.07	0.90	106	41
Slovak Republic	287	35	247	89	9	379	227	132	1.57	1.68	41	15
Slovenia	531	28	493	190	21	879	485	372	1.18	1.26	40	30
Somalia	..	..	..	3	..	..	..	..	1.12	1.15	78	31
South Africa	151	16	103	30	11	345	136	198	0.87	0.95	34	21
Spain	550	35	445	132	22	866	708	185	1.23	1.28	42	32
Sri Lanka	55	11	17	148	16	92	63	27	1.43	0.75	94	82
Sudan	..	..	..	1	12	68	44	21	0.65	0.45	296	165
Swaziland	84	25	40	21	..	..	..	..	0.86	0.93	56	33
Sweden	516	7	462	155	14	948	414	485	1.38	1.52	15	12
Switzerland	564	59	520	173	20	871	291	548	1.30	1.52	37	26
Syrian Arab Republic	48	23	19	21	24	277	148	115	0.85	0.53	159	75
Tajikistan	..	..	19	19	37	238	0	226	1.03	1.00	103	50
Tanzania	..	..	1	8	4	28	20	6	1.11	1.30	57	25
Thailand	..	..	54	35	17	328	217	98	0.87	0.64	88	71
Timor-Leste	..	..	..	..	..	..	..	..	1.22	1.35	..	..
Togo	..	..	10	13	8	35	18	16	0.89	0.88	57	35
Trinidad and Tobago	..	..	..	162	5	640	250	357	0.36	0.24	142	101
Tunisia	95	49	83	12	17	174	118	47	0.96	0.84	74	30
Turkey	124	20	84	55	13	199	133	44	1.87	1.63	68	40
Turkmenistan	..	..	..	5	5	228	0	217	0.22	0.20	177	55
Uganda	5	..	2	17	..	..	..	..	1.30	1.22	28	12
Ukraine	128	36	118	28	5	186	70	119	0.88	0.96	72	21
United Arab Emirates	..	..	228	5	17	2,147	1,108	936	0.37	0.52	266	127
United Kingdom	517	80	457	171	17	775	427	352	1.44	1.65	25	15
United States	814[b]	31	461[b,c]	68	23	2,104	548	1,468	0.56	0.78	30	21
Uruguay	176	..	151	102	24	274	182	76	1.18	1.17	237	175
Uzbekistan	..	..	..	18	3	71	15	53	1.35	0.75	85	55
Venezuela, RB	..	..	94	11	25	678	120	489	0.02	0.01	22	11
Vietnam	8	..	..	68	12	87	47	38	0.80	0.77	123	55
West Bank and Gaza	36	18	29	80	..	..	..	..	1.34	1.25	..	..
Yemen, Rep.	..	..	19	14	31	119	34	73	0.30	0.17	..	..
Zambia	..	..	..	12	4	30	16	16	1.70	1.61	96	40
Zimbabwe	..	..	45	25	4	34	21	13	1.30	1.05	35	27
World	.. w	.. w	118 w	26 w	14 w	301 w	128 w	164 w	1.11 m	1.03 m	80 w	50 w
Low income	..	..	..	..	7	42	21	20	1.12	1.03	143	69
Middle income	46	13	41	23	10	146	72	72	0.91	0.90	91	56
Lower middle income	19	10	14	40	8	95	53	46	0.88	0.83	112	67
Upper middle income	172	..	139		13	360	154	178	1.12	1.03	53	30
Low & middle income	38	..	38	15	10	125	62	61	1.03	0.95	98	58
East Asia & Pacific	27	11	18	35	6	95	55	51	0.92	0.85	112	69
Europe & Central Asia	162	30	184	9	8	263	116	139	1.13	1.13	63	27
Latin America & Carib.	155		115	18	23	329	143	152	0.87	0.83	59	35
Middle East & N. Africa	..	..	33	..	20	297	131	146	0.61	0.53	124	72
South Asia	12	3	8	75	6	33	24	9	1.09	0.76	134	78
Sub-Saharan Africa	..	..	..		8	66	27	37	1.14	1.06	113	53
High income	630	41	455	76	19	1,210	468	691	1.28	1.36	37	26
Euro area	604	66	418[d]	123	17	801	514	257	1.54	1.44	33	23

a. Includes Montenegro. b. Data are from the U.S. Federal Highway Administration. c. Excludes personal passenger vans, passenger minivans, and utility-type vehicles, which are all treated as trucks. d. Data are from the European Commission and the European Road Federation.

About the data

Traffic congestion in urban areas constrains economic productivity, damages people's health, and degrades the quality of life. The particulate air pollution emitted by motor vehicles—the dust and soot in exhaust—is far more damaging to human health than once believed. (For information on particulate matter and other air pollutants, see table 3.14.)

In recent years ownership of passenger cars has increased, and expanded economic activity has led to more goods and services transported by road over greater distances (see table 5.9). These developments have increased demand for roads and vehicles, adding to urban congestion, air pollution, health hazards, and traffic accidents and injuries. Congestion, the most visible cost of expanding vehicle ownership, is reflected in the indicators in the table. Other relevant indicators—such as average vehicle speed in major cities and the cost of congestion, which takes a heavy toll on economic productivity—are not included because data are incomplete or difficult to compare.

The data in the table—except those on fuel prices and particulate matter—are compiled by the International Road Federation (IRF) through questionnaires sent to national organizations. The IRF uses a hierarchy of sources to gather as much information as possible. Primary sources are national road associations. If they lack data or do not respond, other agencies are contacted, including road directorates, ministries of transport or public works, and central statistical offices. As a result, data quality is uneven. Coverage of each indicator may differ across countries because of different definitions. Comparability is also limited when time series data are reported. The IRF took steps to improve the quality of the data in its *World Road Statistics 2008*. Because this effort covers 1999–2006 only, time series data may not

be comparable. Another reason is coverage. For example, for the United States the 2005 estimate for passenger cars from the U.S. Federal Highway Administration excludes personal passenger vans, passenger minivans, and utility-type vehicles, which are all treated as trucks. Moreover, the data do not cover vehicle quality or age. Road density is a rough indicator of accessibility and does not capture road width, type, or condition. Thus comparisons over time and across countries should be made with caution.

Data on fuel prices are compiled by the German Agency for Technical Cooperation (GTZ), from its global network, and other sources, including the Allgemeiner Deutscher Automobile Club (for Europe) and the Latin American Energy Organization (for Latin America). Local prices are converted to U.S. dollars using the exchange rate in the *Financial Times* international monetary table on the survey date. When multiple exchange rates exist, the market, parallel, or black market rate is used. Prices were compiled in mid-November 2008, when crude oil prices had dropped to $48 a barrel Brent (from a high of $148 in July).

Considerable uncertainty surrounds estimates of particulate matter concentrations, and caution should be used in interpreting them. They allow for cross-country comparisons of the relative risk of particulate matter pollution facing urban residents. Major sources of urban outdoor particulate matter pollution are traffic and industrial emissions, but nonanthropogenic sources such as dust storms may also be a substantial contributor for some cities. Country technology and pollution controls are important determinants of particulate matter. Data on particulate matter for selected cities are in table 3.14. Estimates of economic damages from death and illness due to particulate matter pollution are in table 3.16.

Definitions

• **Motor vehicles** include cars, buses, and freight vehicles but not two-wheelers. Population figures refer to the midyear population in the year for which data are available. Roads refer to motorways, highways, main or national roads, and secondary or regional roads. A motorway is a road designed and built for motor traffic that separates the traffic flowing in opposite directions. • **Passenger cars** are road motor vehicles, other than two-wheelers, intended for the carriage of passengers and designed to seat no more than nine people (including the driver). • **Road density** is the ratio of the length of the country's total road network to the country's land area. The road network includes all roads in the country—motorways, highways, main or national roads, secondary or regional roads, and other urban and rural roads. • **Road sector fuel consumption** is the average fuel used per capita in the roads sector. • **Transport sector fuel consumption** is the average volume of fuel consumed per capita in the transport sector. • **Fuel price** is the pump price of super grade gasoline (usually 95 octane) and of diesel fuel. Prices are converted from the local currency to U.S. dollars (see *About the data*). • **Particulate matter concentration** is fine suspended particulates of less than 10 microns in diameter (PM10) that are capable of penetrating deep into the respiratory tract and causing significant health damage. Data are urban-population-weighted PM10 levels in residential areas of cities with more than 100,000 residents. The estimates represent the average annual exposure level of the average urban resident to outdoor particulate matter.

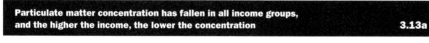

Particulate matter concentration has fallen in all income groups, and the higher the income, the lower the concentration   3.13a

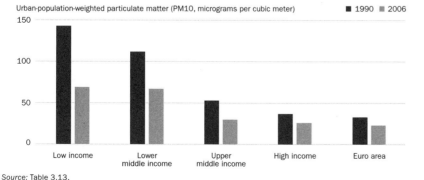

Urban-population-weighted particulate matter (PM10, micrograms per cubic meter)   ■ 1990   ■ 2006

Source: Table 3.13.

Data sources

Data on vehicles, road density, and fuel consumption are from the IRF's electronic files and its annual *World Road Statistics*, except where noted. Data on fuel prices are from the GTZ's electronic files. Data on particulate matter concentrations are from Kiran Dev Pandey, David Wheeler, Bart Ostro, Uwe Deichmann, Kirk Hamilton, and Katie Bolt's "Ambient Particulate Matter Concentrations in Residential and Pollution Hotspot Areas of World Cities: New Estimates Based on the Global Model of Ambient Particulates (GMAPS)" (2006).

3.14 Air pollution

City		City population	Particulate matter concentration	Sulfur dioxide	Nitrogen dioxide
			Urban-population-weighted PM10 micrograms per cubic meter	micrograms per cubic meter	micrograms per cubic meter
		thousands **2007**	**2006**	**2001**[a]	**2001**[a]
Argentina	Córdoba	1,452	55	..	97
Australia	Melbourne	3,728	12	..	30
	Perth	1,532	12	5	19
	Sydney	4,327	19	28	81
Austria	Vienna	2,315	39	14	42
Belgium	Brussels	1,743	25	20	48
Brazil	Rio de Janeiro	11,748	29	129	..
	São Paulo	18,845	34	43	83
Bulgaria	Sofia	1,185	63	39	122
Canada	Montréal	3,678	17	10	42
	Toronto	5,213	20	17	43
	Vancouver	2,146	12	14	37
Chile	Santiago	5,720	54	29	81
China	Anshan	1,639	83	115	88
	Beijing	11,106	90	90	122
	Changchun	3,183	75	21	64
	Chengdu	4,123	87	77	74
	Chongqing	6,461	124	340	70
	Dalian	3,167	50	61	100
	Guangzhou	8,829	64	57	136
	Guiyang	3,662	71	424	53
	Harbin	3,621	77	23	30
	Jinan	2,798	95	132	45
	Kunming	2,931	71	19	33
	Lanzhou	2,561	92	102	104
	Liupanshui	1,221	60	102	..
	Nanchang	2,350	79	69	29
	Pingxiang	905	67	75	..
	Quingdao	2,817	62	190	64
	Shanghai	14,987	74	53	73
	Shenyang	4,787	102	99	73
	Taiyuan	2,794	89	211	55
	Tianjin	7,180	126	82	50
	Wulumqi	2,025	57	60	70
	Wuhan	7,243	80	40	43
	Zhengzhou	2,636	98	63	95
	Zibo	3,061	75	198	43
Colombia	Bogotá	7,772	30	..	..
Croatia	Zagreb	908	32	31	..
Cuba	Havana	2,174	20	1	5
Czech Republic	Prague	1,162	21	14	33
Denmark	Copenhagen	1,085	19	7	54
Ecuador	Guayaquil	2,514	23	15	..
	Quito	1,701	30	22	..
Egypt, Arab Rep.	Cairo	11,893	149	69	..
Finland	Helsinki	1,115	19	4	35
France	Paris	9,904	11	14	57
Germany	Berlin	3,406	21	18	26
	Frankfurt	668	18	11	45
	Munich	1,275	19	8	53
Ghana	Accra	2,121	33	..	..
Greece	Athens	3,242	38	34	64
Hungary	Budapest	1,679	20	39	51
Iceland	Reykjavik	164	18	5	42
India	Ahmadabad	5,375	76	30	21
	Bengaluru	6,787	41	..	..

About the data

Indoor and outdoor air pollution place a major burden on world health. More than half the world's people rely on dung, wood, crop waste, or coal to meet basic energy needs. Cooking and heating with these fuels on open fires or stoves without chimneys lead to indoor air pollution, which is responsible for 1.6 million deaths a year—one every 20 seconds. In many urban areas air pollution exposure is the main environmental threat to health. Long-term exposure to high levels of soot and small particles contributes to a range of health effects, including respiratory diseases, lung cancer, and heart disease. Particulate pollution, alone or with sulfur dioxide, creates an enormous burden of ill health.

Sulfur dioxide and nitrogen dioxide emissions lead to deposition of acid rain and other acidic compounds over long distances, which can lead to the leaching of trace minerals and nutrients critical to trees and plants. Sulfur dioxide emissions can damage human health, particularly that of the young and old. Nitrogen dioxide is emitted by bacteria, motor vehicles, industrial activities, nitrogen fertilizers, fuel and biomass combustion, and aerobic decomposition of organic matter in soils and oceans.

Where coal is the primary fuel for power plants without effective dust controls, steel mills, industrial boilers, and domestic heating, high levels of urban air pollution are common—especially particulates and sulfur dioxide. Elsewhere the worst emissions are from petroleum product combustion.

Sulfur dioxide and nitrogen dioxide concentration data are based on average observed concentrations at urban monitoring sites, which not all cities have.

The data on particulate matter are estimated average annual concentrations in residential areas away from air pollution "hotspots," such as industrial districts and transport corridors. The data are from the World Bank's Development Research Group and Environment Department estimates of annual ambient concentrations of particulate matter in cities with populations exceeding 100,000 (Pandey and others 2006b). A country's technology and pollution controls are important determinants of particulate matter concentrations.

Pollutant concentrations are sensitive to local conditions, and even monitoring sites in the same city may register different levels. Thus these data should be considered only a general indication of air quality, and comparisons should be made with caution. Current World Health Organization (WHO) air quality guidelines are annual mean concentrations of 20 micrograms per cubic meter for particulate matter less than 10 microns in diameter and 40 micrograms for nitrogen dioxide and daily mean concentrations of 20 micrograms per cubic meter for sulfur dioxide.

	City	City population	Particulate matter concentration	Sulfur dioxide	Nitrogen dioxide
			Urban-population-weighted PM10 micrograms per cubic meter	micrograms per cubic meter	micrograms per cubic meter
		thousands 2007	2006	2001[a]	2001[a]
India	Chennai	7,163	34	15	17
	Delhi	15,926	136	24	41
	Hyderabad	6,376	37	12	17
	Kanpur	3,162	99	15	14
	Kolkata	14,787	116	49	34
	Lucknow	2,695	99	26	25
	Mumbai	18,978	57	33	39
	Nagpur	2,454	50	6	13
	Pune	4,672	42	..	..
Indonesia	Jakarta	9,125	84	..	..
Iran, Islamic Rep.	Tehran	7,873	50	209	..
Ireland	Dublin	1,059	16	20	..
Italy	Milan	2,945	30	31	248
	Rome	3,339	29	..	..
	Turin	1,652	43	..	..
Japan	Osaka-Kobe	11,294	33	19	63
	Tokyo	35,676	38	18	68
	Yokohama	3,366	29	100	13
Kenya	Nairobi	3,010	40	..	..
Korea, Rep.	Pusan	3,480	35	60	51
	Seoul	9,796	37	44	60
	Taegu	2,460	40	81	62
Malaysia	Kuala Lumpur	1,448	23	24	..
Mexico	Mexico City	19,028	48	74	130
Netherlands	Amsterdam	1,031	34	10	58
New Zealand	Auckland	1,245	13	3	20
Norway	Oslo	802	18	8	43
Philippines	Manila	11,100	28	33	..
Poland	Katowice	2,914	39	83	79
	Lódz	776	38	21	43
	Warsaw	1,707	42	16	32
Portugal	Lisbon	2,812	21	8	52
Romania	Bucharest	1,942	16	10	71
Russian Federation	Moscow	10,452	19	109	..
	Omsk	1,135	19	20	34
Singapore	Singapore	4,436	41	20	30
Slovak Republic	Bratislava	456	15	21	27
South Africa	Cape Town	3,215	13	21	72
	Durban	2,729	25	31	..
	Johannesburg	3,435	26	19	31
Spain	Barcelona	4,920	33	11	43
	Madrid	5,567	29	24	66
Sweden	Stockholm	1,264	11	3	20
Switzerland	Zurich	1,108	24	11	39
Thailand	Bangkok	6,704	76	11	23
Turkey	Ankara	3,716	39	55	46
	Istanbul	10,061	46	120	..
Ukraine	Kiev	2,709	26	14	51
United Kingdom	Birmingham	2,285	14	9	45
	London	8,567	19	25	77
	Manchester	2,230	15	26	49
United States	Chicago	8,990	23	14	57
	Los Angeles	12,500	32	9	74
	New York-Newark	19,040	20	26	79
Venezuela, RB	Caracas	2,985	16	33	57

a. Data are for the most recent year available.

Definitions

• **City population** is the number of residents of the city or metropolitan area as defined by national authorities and reported to the United Nations. • **Particulate matter concentration** is fine suspended particulates of less than 10 microns in diameter (PM10) that are capable of penetrating deep into the respiratory tract and causing significant health damage. Data are urban-population-weighted PM10 levels in residential areas of cities with more than 100,000 residents. The estimates represent the average annual exposure level of the average urban resident to outdoor particulate matter. • **Sulfur dioxide** is an air pollutant produced when fossil fuels containing sulfur are burned. • **Nitrogen dioxide** is a poisonous, pungent gas formed when nitric oxide combines with hydrocarbons and sunlight, producing a photochemical reaction. These conditions occur in both natural and anthropogenic activities.

Data sources

Data on city population are from the United Nations Population Division. Data on particulate matter concentrations are from Kiran D. Pandey, David Wheeler, Bart Ostro, Uwe Deichman, Kirk Hamilton, and Kathrine Bolt's "Ambient Particulate Matter Concentration in Residential and Pollution Hotspot Areas of World Cities: New Estimates Based on the Global Model of Ambient Particulates (GMAPS)" (2006). Data on sulfur dioxide and nitrogen dioxide concentrations are from the WHO's Healthy Cities Air Management Information System and the World Resources Institute.

	Environmental strategies or action plans	Biodiversity assessments, strategies, or action plans	Participation in treaties[a]								
			Climate change[b]	Ozone layer	CFC control	Law of the Sea[c]	Biological diversity[b]	Kyoto Protocol	CITES	CCD	Stockholm Convention
			1992	1985	1987	1982	1992	1997	1973	1994	2001
Afghanistan	..	..	2002	2004[d]	2004[d]	..	2002		1985[d]	1995[d]	..
Albania	1993	..	1995	1999[d]	1999[d]	2003[d]	1994[d]	2005[d]	2003[d]	2000[d]	2004
Algeria	2001	..	1994	1992[d]	1992[d]	1996	1995	2005[d]	1983[d]	1996	2006
Angola	..	..	2000	2000[d]	2000[d]	1994	1998	2007	..	1997	2006
Argentina	1992	..	1994	1990	1990	1995	1994	2001	1981	1997	2005
Armenia	..	..	1994	1999[d]	1999[d]	2002[d]	1993[e]	2008[e]	..	1997	2003
Australia	1992	1994	1994	1987[d]	1989	1994	1993	..	1976	2000	2004
Austria	..	..	1994	1987	1989	1995	1994	2002	1982[d]	1997[d]	2002
Azerbaijan	1998	..	1995	1996[d]	1996[d]	..	2000[f]	2000[d]	1998[d]	1998[d]	2004[d]
Bangladesh	1991	1990	1994	1990[d]	1990[d]	2001	1994	2001[d]	1981	1996	2007
Belarus	..	..	2000	1986[e]	1988[e]	2006[d]	1993	2007[e]	1995[d]	2001[d]	2004[d]
Belgium	..	..	1996	1988	1988	1998	1996	2002	1983	1997[d]	2006
Benin	1993	..	1994	1993[d]	1993[d]	1997	1994	2002[d]	1984[d]	1996	2004
Bolivia	1994	1988	1995	1994[d]	1994[d]	1995	1994	1999	1979	1996	2003
Bosnia and Herzegovina	..	..	2000	1992[g]	1992[g]	1994[g]	2002[d]	2007	2002	2002[d]	..
Botswana	1990	1991	1994	1991[d]	1991[d]	1994	1995	2003[d]	1977[d]	1996	2002[d]
Brazil	..	1988	1994	1990[d]	1990[d]	1994	1994	2002	1975	1997	2004
Bulgaria	..	1994	1995	1990[d]	1990[d]	1996	1996	2002	1991[d]	2001[d]	2004
Burkina Faso	1993	..	1994	1989	1989	2005	1993	2005[d]	1989[d]	1996	2004
Burundi	1994	1989	1997	1997[d]	1997[d]	..	1997	2001[d]	1988[d]	1997	2005
Cambodia	1999	..	1996	2001[d]	2001[d]	..	1995[d]	2002[d]	1997	1997	2006
Cameroon	..	1989	1995	1989[d]	1989[d]	1994	1994	2002[d]	1981[d]	1997	..
Canada	1990	1994	1994	1986	1988	2003	1992	2002	1975	1995	2001
Central African Republic	..	..	1995	1993[d]	1993[d]	..	1995	2008	1980[d]	1996	..
Chad	1990	..	1994	1989[d]	1994	..	1994	..	1989[d]	1996	2004
Chile	..	1993	1995	1990	1990	1997	1994	2002	1975	1997	2005
China	1994	1994	1994	1989[d]	1991[d]	1996	1993	2002[f]	1981[d]	1997	2004
Hong Kong, China	..	..	..	..	..	..	..	..	..	..	..
Colombia	1998	1988	1995	1990[d]	1993[d]		1994	2001[d]	1981	1999	..
Congo, Dem. Rep.	..	1990	1995	1994[d]	1994[d]	1995	1996	2005[d]	1976[d]	1997	2005[d]
Congo, Rep.	..	1990	1997	1994[d]	1994[d]	2008	1994	2007	1983[d]	1999	2007
Costa Rica	1990	1992	1994	1991[d]	1991[d]	1994	1994	2002	1975	1998	2007
Côte d'Ivoire	1994	1991	1995	1993[d]	1993[d]	1994	1994	2007	1994[d]	1997	2004
Croatia	2001	2000	1996	1991[e]	1991[e]	1994[g]	1996	..	2000[d]	2000[e]	2007
Cuba	..	..	1994	1992[d]	1992[d]	1994	1994	2002	1990[d]	1997	2007
Czech Republic	1994	..	1994	1993[e]	1993[e]	1996	1993[f]	2007[e]	993[g]	2000[d]	2002
Denmark	1994	..	1994	1988	1988	2004	1993	2002	1977	1995[d]	2003
Dominican Republic	..	1995	1999	1993[d]	1993[d]	..	1996	2002[d]	1986[d]	1997[d]	2007
Ecuador	1993	1995	1994	1990[d]	1990[d]	..	1993	2000	1975	1995	2004
Egypt, Arab Rep.	1992	1988	1995	1988	1988	1994	1994	2005[d]	1978	1995	2003
El Salvador	1994	1988	1996	1992	1992	..	1994	1998	1987[d]	1997[d]	..
Eritrea	1995	..	1995	2005[d]	2005[d]	..	1996[d]	2005[d]	1994[d]	1996	2005[d]
Estonia	1998	..	1994	1996[d]	1996[d]	2005[d]	1994	2002	1992[d]	..	..
Ethiopia	1994	1991	1994	1994[d]	1994[d]	..	1994	2005[d]	1989[d]	1997	2003
Finland	1995	..	1994	1986	1988	1996	1994[e]	2002	1976[d]	1995[e]	2002[e]
France	1990	..	1994	1987[f]	1988[f]	1996	1994	2002[f]	1978	1997	2004[f]
Gabon	..	1990	1998	1994[d]	1994[d]	1998	1997	..	1989[d]	1996[d]	2007
Gambia, The	1992	1989	1994	1990[d]	1990[d]	1994	1994	2001[d]	1977[d]	1996	2006
Georgia	1998	..	1994	1996[d]	1996[d]	1996[d]	1994[d]	1999[d]	1996[d]	1999	2006
Germany	..	..	1994	1988	1988	1994[d]	1993	2002	1976	1996	2002
Ghana	1992	1988	1995	1989[d]	1989	1994	1994	2003[d]	1975	1996	2003
Greece	..	..	1994	1988	1988	1995	1994	2002	1992[d]	1997	2006
Guatemala	1994	1988	1996	1987[d]	1989[d]	1997	1995	1999	1979	1998[d]	..
Guinea	1994	1988	1994	1992[d]	1992[d]	1994	1993	2000[d]	1981[d]	1997	..
Guinea-Bissau	1993	1991	1996	2002[d]	2002[d]	1994	1995	..	1990[d]	1995	2008
Haiti	1999	..	1996	2000[d]	2000[d]	1996	1996	2005[d]	..	1996	..

	Environ-mental strategies or action plans	Biodiversity assessments, strategies, or action plans	Participation in treaties[a]								
			Climate change[b] 1992	Ozone layer 1985	CFC control 1987	Law of the Sea[c] 1982	Biological diversity[b] 1992	Kyoto Protocol 1997	CITES 1973	CCD 1994	Stockholm Convention 2001
Honduras	1993	..	1996	1993[d]	1993[d]	1994	1995	2000	1985[d]	1997	2005
Hungary	1995	..	1994	1988[d]	1989[d]	2002	1994	2002[d]	1985[d]	1999[d]	2008
India	1993	1994	1994	1991[d]	1992[d]	1995	1994	2008[e]	1976	1996	2006
Indonesia	1993	1993	1994	1992[d]	1992	1994	1994	2004	1978[d]	1998	..
Iran, Islamic Rep.	..	..	1996	1990[d]	1990[d]	..	1996	2005[d]	1976	1997	2006
Iraq	..	..	..	..	..	1994	..	..	..	..	..
Ireland	..	..	1994	1988[d]	1988	1996	1996	2002	2002	1997	..
Israel	..	..	1996	1992[d]	1992	..	1995	2004	1979	1996	..
Italy	..	..	1994	1988	1988	1995	1994	2002	1979	1997	..
Jamaica	1994	..	1995	1993[d]	1993[d]	1994	1995	1999[d]	1997[d]	1997[d]	2007
Japan	..	..	1994	1988[d]	1988	1996	1993[e]	2002[e]	1980	1998[e]	2002[d]
Jordan	1991	..	1994	1989[d]	1989[d]	1995[d]	1993	2003[d]	1978[d]	1996	2004
Kazakhstan	..	..	1995	1998[d]	1998[d]	..	1994	..	2000[d]	1997	..
Kenya	1994	1992	1994	1988[d]	1988	1994	1994	2005[d]	1978	1997	2004
Korea, Dem. Rep.	..	..	1995	1995[d]	1995[d]	..	1994[f]	2005[d]	..	2003[d]	2002[d]
Korea, Rep.	..	..	1994	1992	1992	1996	1994	2002	1993[d]	1999	2007
Kuwait	..	..	1995	1992[d]	1992[d]	1994	2002	2005[d]	2002	1997	2006
Kyrgyz Republic	1995	..	2000	2000[d]	2000[d]	..	1996[f]	2003[d]	..	1997[d]	2006
Lao PDR	1995	..	1995	1998[d]	1998[d]	1998	1996[f]	2003[d]	2004[d]	1996[e]	2006
Latvia	..	..	1995	1995[d]	1995[d]	2004[d]	1995	2002	1997[d]	2002[d]	2004
Lebanon	..	..	1995	1993[d]	1993[d]	1995	1994	2006	..	1996	2003
Lesotho	1989	..	1995	1994[d]	1994[d]	2007	1995	2000[d]	2003	1995	2002
Liberia		2003	1996[d]	1996[d]	2008	2000	2002[d]	2005[d]	1998[d]	2002[d]
Libya	..	..	1999	1990[d]	1990[d]	..	2001	2006	2003[d]	1996	2005[d]
Lithuania	..	..	1995	1995[d]	1995[d]	2003[d]	1996	2003	2001[d]	2003[d]	2006
Macedonia, FYR	..	..	1998	1994[g]	1994[g]	1994[g]	1997[d]	2004[d]	2000[d]	2002[d]	2004
Madagascar	1988	1991	1999	1996[d]	1996[d]	2001	1996	2003[d]	1975	1997	..
Malawi	1994	..	1994	1991[d]	1991[d]	..	1994	2001[d]	1982[d]	1996	..
Malaysia	1991	1988	1994	1989[d]	1989[d]	1996	1994	2002	1977[d]	1997	..
Mali	..	1989	1995	1994[d]	1994[d]	1994	1995	2002	1994[d]	1995	2003
Mauritania	1988	..	1994	1994[d]	1994[d]	1996	1996	2005[d]	1998[d]	1996	2005
Mauritius	1990	..	1994	1992[d]	1992[d]	1994	1992	2001[d]	1975	1996	2004
Mexico	..	1988	1994	1987	1988	1994	1993	2000	1991[d]	1995	2003
Moldova	2002	..	1995	1996[d]	1996[d]	2007	1995	2008[e]	2001[d]	1999[d]	2004
Mongolia	1995	..	1994	1996[d]	1996[d]	1996	1993	1999[d]	1996[d]	1996	2004
Morocco	..	1988	1996	1995	1995	2007	1995	2002[d]	1975	1996	2004
Mozambique	1994	..	1995	1994[d]	1994[d]	1997	1995	2005[d]	1981[d]	1997	2005
Myanmar	..	1989	1995	1993[d]	1993[d]	1996	1995	2003[d]	1997[d]	1997[d]	2004[d]
Namibia	1992	..	1995	1993[d]	1993[d]	1994	1997	2003[d]	1990[d]	1997	2005[d]
Nepal	1993	..	1994	1994[d]	1994[d]	1998	1993	2005[d]	1975[d]	1996	2007
Netherlands	1994	..	1994	1988[d]	1988[e]	1996	1994[e]	2002[d]	1984	1995[e]	2002[e]
New Zealand	1994	..	1994	1987	1988	1996	1993	2002	1989[d]	2000[d]	2004
Nicaragua	1994	..	1996	1993[d]	1993[d]	2000	1995	1999	1977[d]	1998	..
Niger	..	1991	1995	1992[d]	1992[d]	..	1995	2004	1975	1996	2006
Nigeria	1990	1992	1994	1988[d]	1988[d]	1994	1994	2004[d]	1974	1997	2004
Norway	..	1994	1994	1986	1988	1996	1993	2008[e]	1976	1996	2002
Oman	..	..	1995	1999[d]	1999[d]	1994	1995	2005[d]	..	1996[d]	2005
Pakistan	1994	1991	1994	1992[d]	1992[d]	1997	1994	2005[d]	1976[d]	1997	..
Panama	1990	..	1995	1989[d]	1989	1996	1995	1999	1978	1996	2003
Papua New Guinea	1992	1993	1994	1992[d]	1992[d]	1997	1993	2002	1975[d]	2000[d]	2003
Paraguay	..	..	1994	1992[d]	1992[d]	1994	1994	1999	1976	1997	2004
Peru	..	1988	1994	1989	1993[d]	..	1993	2002	1975	1995	2005
Philippines	1989	1989	1994	1991[d]	1991	1994	1993	2003	1981	2000	2004
Poland	1993	1991	1994	1990[d]	1990[d]	1998	1996	2002	1989	2001[d]	2008
Portugal	1995	..	1994	1988[d]	1988	1997	1993	2002[f]	1980	1996	2004[e]
Puerto Rico	..	..	..	..	..	..	..	..	..	..	..

	Environmental strategies or action plans	Biodiversity assessments, strategies, or action plans	Participation in treaties[a]								
			Climate change[b] 1992	Ozone layer 1985	CFC control 1987	Law of the Sea[c] 1982	Biological diversity[b] 1992	Kyoto Protocol 1997	CITES 1973	CCD 1994	Stockholm Convention 2001
Romania	1995	..	1994	1993[d]	1993[d]	1996	1994	2001	1994[d]	1998[d]	2004
Russian Federation	1999	1994	1995	1986[e]	1988[e]	1997	1995	2008[e]	1992	2003[d]	..
Rwanda	1991	..	1998	2001[d]	2001[d]	..	1996	2004[d]	1980[d]	1998	2002[d]
Saudi Arabia	..	..	1995	1993[d]	1993[d]	1996	2001[f]	2005[d]	1996[d]	1997[d]	..
Senegal	1984	1991	1995	1993[d]	1993	1994	1994	2001[d]	1977[d]	1995	2003
Serbia and Montenegro			2001	2001[g]	2001[g]	2001[g]	2002	2007	2002	..	2002
Sierra Leone	1994	..	1995	2001[d]	2001[d]	1994	1994[f]	2006[d]	1994[d]	1997	2003[d]
Singapore	1993	1995	1997	1989[d]	1989[d]	1994	1995	2006[d]	1986[d]	1999[d]	2005
Slovak Republic	..	..	1994	1993[d]	1993[g]	1996	1994[f]	2002	1993	2002[d]	2002
Slovenia	1994		1996	1992[g]	1992[g]	1995[g]	1996	2002	2000[d]	2001[d]	2004
Somalia			..	2001[d]	2001[d]	1994	..		1985[d]	2002[d]	..
South Africa	1993		1997	1990[d]	1990[d]	1997	1995	2002[d]	1975	1997	2002
Spain	..	..	1994	1988[d]	1988	1997	1995	2002	1986[d]	1996	2004
Sri Lanka	1994	1991	1994	1989[d]	1989[d]	1994	1994	2002[d]	1979[d]	1998[d]	..
Sudan			1994	1993[d]	1993[d]	1994	1995	2004[d]	1982	1995	2006
Swaziland			1997	1992[d]	1992[d]	..	1994	..	1997[d]	1996	2006
Sweden	..	..	1994	1986	1988	1996	1993	2002	1974	1995	2002
Switzerland	..	..	1994	1987	1988	..	1994	2006[d]	1974	1996	2003
Syrian Arab Republic	1999	..	1996	1989[d]	1989[d]	..	1996	2006[d]	2003[d]	1997	2005
Tajikistan	..	..	1998	1996[d]	1998[d]	..	1997[f]	..	..	1997[d]	2007
Tanzania	1994	1988	1996	1993[d]	1993[d]	1994	1996	2002[d]	1979	1997	2004
Thailand	..	..	1995	1989[d]	1989	..	2004	2002	1983	2001[d]	2005
Togo	1991	..	1995	1991[d]	1991	1994	1995[e]	2004[d]	1978	1995[e]	2004
Trinidad and Tobago	..	..	1994	1989[d]	1989[d]	1994	1996	1999	1984[d]	2000[d]	2002[d]
Tunisia	1994	1988	1994	1989[d]	1989[d]	1994	1993	2003[d]	1974	1995	2004
Turkey	1998	..	2004	1991[d]	1991[d]	..	1997	..	1996[d]	1998	..
Turkmenistan	..	..	1995	1993[d]	1993[d]	..	1996[f]	2008[e]	..	1996	..
Uganda	1994	1988	1994	1988[d]	1988	1994	1993	2002[d]	1991[d]	1997	2004[d]
Ukraine	1999	..	1997	1986[e]	1988[e]	1999	1995	2004	1999[d]	2002[d]	..
United Arab Emirates	..	..	1996	1989[d]	1989[d]	2000	2000	2005[d]	1990[d]	1998[d]	2002
United Kingdom	1995	1994	1994	1987	1988	1997[d]	1994	2002	1976	1996	2005
United States	1995	1995	1994	1986	1988		..	..	1974	2000	..
Uruguay	..	..	1994	1989[d]	1991[d]	1994	1993	2001	1975	1999[d]	2004
Uzbekistan	..	..	1994	1993[d]	1993[d]	..	1995[f]	2007[e]	1997[d]	1995	..
Venezuela	..	..	1995	1988[d]	1989	..	1994	..	1977	1998[d]	2005
Vietnam	..	1993	1995	1994[d]	1994[d]	2006[d]	1994	2008[e]	1994[d]	1998[d]	2002
West Bank and Gaza	..	..	..	..	..	..	..	..	..	..	
Yemen, Rep.	1996	1992	1996	1996[d]	1996[d]	1994	1996	2004[d]	1997[d]	1997[d]	2004
Zambia	1994	..	1994	1990[d]	1990[d]	1994	1993	2006[d]	1980[d]	1996	2006
Zimbabwe	1987	..	1994	1992[d]	1992[d]	1994	1994	..	1981[d]	1997	..

a. Ratification of the treaty. b. Year the treaty entered into force in the country. c. Convention became effective November 16, 1994. d. Accession. e. Acceptance. f. Approval. g. Succession.

About the data

National environmental strategies and participation in international treaties on environmental issues provide some evidence of government commitment to sound environmental management. But the signing of these treaties does not always imply ratification, nor does it guarantee that governments will comply with treaty obligations.

In many countries efforts to halt environmental degradation have failed, primarily because governments have neglected to make this issue a priority, a reflection of competing claims on scarce resources. To address this problem, many countries are preparing national environmental strategies—some focusing narrowly on environmental issues, and others integrating environmental, economic, and social concerns. Among such initiatives are conservation strategies and environmental action plans. Some countries have also prepared country environmental profiles and biodiversity strategies and profiles.

National conservation strategies—promoted by the World Conservation Union (IUCN)—provide a comprehensive, cross-sectoral analysis of conservation and resource management issues to help integrate environmental concerns with the development process. Such strategies discuss current and future needs, institutional capabilities, prevailing technical conditions, and the status of natural resources in a country.

National environmental action plans, supported by the World Bank and other development agencies, describe a country's main environmental concerns, identify the principal causes of environmental problems, and formulate policies and actions to deal with them. These plans are a continuing process in which governments develop comprehensive environmental policies, recommend specific actions, and outline the investment strategies, legislation, and institutional arrangements required to implement them.

Biodiversity profiles—prepared by the World Conservation Monitoring Centre and the IUCN—provide basic background on species diversity, protected areas, major ecosystems and habitat types, and legislative and administrative support. In an effort to establish a scientific baseline for measuring progress in biodiversity conservation, the United Nations Environment Programme (UNEP) coordinates global biodiversity assessments.

To address global issues, many governments have also signed international treaties and agreements launched in the wake of the 1972 United Nations Conference on the Human Environment in Stockholm and the 1992 United Nations Conference on Environment and Development (the Earth Summit) in Rio de Janeiro, which produced Agenda 21—an array of actions to address environmental challenges:

- The Framework Convention on Climate Change aims to stabilize atmospheric concentrations of greenhouse gases at levels that will prevent human activities from interfering dangerously with the global climate.
- The Vienna Convention for the Protection of the Ozone Layer aims to protect human health and the environment by promoting research on the effects of changes in the ozone layer and on alternative substances (such as substitutes for chlorofluorocarbon) and technologies, monitoring the ozone layer, and taking measures to control the activities that produce adverse effects.
- The Montreal Protocol for Chlorofluorocarbon Control requires that countries help protect the earth from excessive ultraviolet radiation by cutting chlorofluorocarbon consumption by 20 percent over their 1986 level by 1994 and by 50 percent over their 1986 level by 1999, with allowances for increases in consumption by developing countries.
- The United Nations Convention on the Law of the Sea, which became effective in November 1994, establishes a comprehensive legal regime for seas and oceans, establishes rules for environmental standards and enforcement provisions, and develops international rules and national legislation to prevent and control marine pollution.
- The Convention on Biological Diversity promotes conservation of biodiversity through scientific and technological cooperation among countries, access to financial and genetic resources, and transfer of ecologically sound technologies.

But 10 years after the Earth Summit in Rio de Janeiro the World Summit on Sustainable Development in Johannesburg recognized that many of the proposed actions had yet to materialize. To help developing countries comply with their obligations under these agreements, the Global Environment Facility (GEF) was created to focus on global improvement in biodiversity, climate change, international waters, and ozone layer depletion. The UNEP, United Nations Development Programme, and World Bank manage the GEF according to the policies of its governing body of country representatives. The World Bank is responsible for the GEF Trust Fund and chairs the GEF.

Definitions

- **Environmental strategies or action plans** provide a comprehensive analysis of conservation and resource management issues that integrate environmental concerns with development. They include national conservation strategies, environmental action plans, environmental management strategies, and sustainable development strategies. The date is the year a country adopted a strategy or action plan. • **Biodiversity assessments, strategies, or action plans** include biodiversity profiles (see *About the data*). • **Participation in treaties** covers nine international treaties (see *About the data*). • **Climate change** refers to the Framework Convention on Climate Change (signed in 1992). • **Ozone layer** refers to the Vienna Convention for the Protection of the Ozone Layer (signed in 1985). • **CFC control** refers to the Protocol on Substances That Deplete the Ozone Layer (the Montreal Protocol for Chlorofluorocarbon Control) (signed in 1987). • **Law of the Sea** refers to the United Nations Convention on the Law of the Sea (signed in 1982). • **Biological diversity** refers to the Convention on Biological Diversity (signed at the Earth Summit in 1992). • **Kyoto Protocol** refers to the protocol on climate change adopted at the third conference of the parties to the United Nations Framework Convention on Climate Change in December 1997. • **CITES** is the Convention on International Trade in Endangered Species of Wild Fauna and Flora, an agreement among governments to ensure that the survival of wild animals and plants is not threatened by uncontrolled exploitation. Adopted in 1973, it entered into force in 1975. • **CCD** is the United Nations Convention to Combat Desertification, an international convention addressing the problems of land degradation in the world's drylands. Adopted in 1994, it entered into force in 1996. • **Stockholm Convention** is an international legally binding instrument to protect human health and the environment from persistent organic pollutants. Adopted in 2001, it entered into force in 2004.

Data sources

Data on environmental strategies and participation in international environmental treaties are from the Secretariat of the United Nations Framework Convention on Climate Change, the Ozone Secretariat of the UNEP, the World Resources Institute, the UNEP, the Center for International Earth Science Information Network, and the United Nations Treaty Series.

	Gross savings	Consumption of fixed capital	Net national savings	Education expenditure	Energy depletion	Mineral depletion	Net forest depletion	Carbon dioxide damage	Particulate emission damage	Adjusted net savings
	% of GNI 2007	% of GNI 2007	% of GNI 2007	% of GNI 2007	% of GNI 2007	% of GNI 2007	% of GNI 2007	% of GNI 2007	% of GNI 2007	% of GNI 2007
Afghanistan	..	..	..	..	..	..	..	..	..	..
Albania	19.2	10.9	8.3	2.8	0.0	0.0	0.0	0.2	0.2	10.7
Algeria	57.9	11.6	46.3	4.5	29.7	0.1	0.1	1.2	0.3	19.4
Angola	31.8	14.3	17.5	2.3	55.6	0.0	0.0	0.2	1.3	−37.3[a]
Argentina	27.2	12.4	14.8	4.0	7.7	0.6	0.0	0.5	1.6	8.3
Armenia	29.7	10.7	18.9	2.2	0.0	1.1	0.0	0.4	1.6	18.1
Australia	22.8	15.3	7.5	4.8	2.9	3.8	0.0	0.3	0.1	5.2
Austria	26.2	15.1	11.1	5.3	0.2	0.0	0.0	0.1	0.3	15.7
Azerbaijan	59.9	13.5	46.4	2.8	52.6	0.0	0.0	2.0	1.2	−6.6
Bangladesh	32.2	7.7	24.5	1.8	2.9	0.0	0.7	0.4	0.5	21.8
Belarus	26.9	11.8	15.1	4.9	0.1	0.0	0.0	1.4	..	18.5[a]
Belgium	24.8	14.6	10.2	5.8	0.0	0.0	0.0	0.0	0.2	15.7
Benin	..	8.8	..	3.6	0.0	0.0	0.9	0.3	0.4	..
Bolivia	30.1	10.1	20.0	6.3	21.6	2.4	0.0	0.5	1.4	0.4
Bosnia and Herzegovina	8.9	11.1	−2.2	..	0.2	0.0	..	0.9	0.1	..
Botswana	57.9	12.8	45.0	6.6	0.2	8.2	0.0	0.3	..	42.9[a,b]
Brazil	17.0	12.6	4.4	4.4	2.3	1.6	0.0	0.2	0.2	4.5
Bulgaria	17.8	11.9	5.9	4.1	0.6	1.1	0.0	1.0	1.5	5.7
Burkina Faso	..	8.4	..	4.3	0.0	0.0	1.1	0.1	1.3	..
Burundi	..	6.6	..	5.1	0.0	0.8	11.5	0.2	0.1	..
Cambodia	15.9	9.1	6.8	1.7	0.0	0.0	0.2	0.1	0.3	7.9
Cameroon	19.7	9.7	10.0	2.6	6.4	0.1	0.0	0.2	0.8	5.3
Canada	23.0	14.9	8.1	4.8	4.1	0.9	0.0	0.4	0.1	7.4[c]
Central African Republic	4.5	8.2	−3.7	1.3	0.0	0.0	0.0	0.1	0.4	−2.9
Chad	26.9	10.2	16.6	1.2	40.7	0.0	0.0	0.0	1.1	−24.0
Chile	28.7	14.3	14.4	3.4	0.2	16.7	0.0	0.4	0.6	−0.1
China	54.4	10.7	43.7	1.8	4.5	1.3	0.0	1.4	1.6	36.8
Hong Kong, China	33.8	13.8	20.1	3.0	0.0	0.0	0.0	0.2	..	22.9[a]
Colombia	19.6	12.1	7.5	4.8	6.6	1.7	0.0	0.3	0.1	3.6
Congo, Dem. Rep.	12.1	7.0	5.1	0.9	3.1	2.9	0.0	0.2	0.6	−0.8
Congo, Rep.	45.4	13.4	32.0	2.3	56.5	0.0	0.0	0.4	0.7	−23.4
Costa Rica	19.2	12.4	6.8	4.1	0.0	0.0	0.1	0.2	0.3	10.2
Cote d'Ivoire	9.6	10.0	−0.4	4.7	7.0	0.0	0.0	0.2	0.3	−3.2
Croatia	24.6	13.4	11.3	4.3	0.7	0.0	0.2	0.4	0.5	13.8
Cuba	..	..	..	8.2	..	..	..	..	0.1	..
Czech Republic	27.0	14.4	12.6	4.0	0.4	0.0	0.1	0.6	0.1	15.4
Denmark	24.0	14.9	9.1	7.8	2.3	0.0	0.0	0.1	0.1	14.4
Dominican Republic	21.0	12.0	9.0	3.5	0.0	3.5	0.0	0.6	0.1	8.4
Ecuador	26.9	11.7	15.2	1.4	18.4	0.5	0.0	0.5	0.1	−2.9
Egypt, Arab Rep.	22.4	10.2	12.2	4.4	13.4	0.1	0.2	1.0	1.0	0.9
El Salvador	12.5	11.3	1.2	2.8	0.0	0.0	0.5	0.3	0.2	3.0
Eritrea	..	7.8	..	1.9	0.0	0.0	0.9	0.4	0.4	..
Estonia	21.9	14.5	7.4	4.6	0.8	0.0	0.1	0.9	0.0	10.2
Ethiopia	20.9	7.5	13.4	3.7	0.0	0.4	5.4	0.4	0.3	10.6
Finland	26.5	14.8	11.6	5.9	0.0	0.1	0.0	0.2	0.1	17.1
France	19.2	13.3	5.9	5.1	0.0	0.0	0.0	0.1	0.0	10.9
Gabon	46.3	14.2	32.1	3.1	33.3	0.0	0.0	0.1	..	1.7[a]
Gambia, The	12.6	8.7	3.9	2.0	0.0	0.0	0.6	0.4	0.7	4.2
Georgia	17.0	10.4	6.5	2.8	0.0	0.0	0.0	0.4	1.3	7.7
Germany	24.9	14.6	10.4	4.4	0.2	0.0	0.0	0.2	0.1	14.3
Ghana	23.2	8.9	14.2	4.7	0.0	4.5	2.3	0.4	0.1	11.5
Greece	9.5	14.6	−5.1	2.8	0.2	0.2	0.0	0.3	0.7	−3.7
Guatemala	16.8	10.9	5.9	2.8	0.6	0.0	0.8	0.3	0.5	6.5
Guinea	8.8	8.6	0.2	2.0	0.0	4.9	1.7	0.2	0.3	−4.9
Guinea-Bissau	24.0	7.5	16.5	2.3	0.0	0.0	0.0	0.6	0.9	17.3
Haiti	..	9.8	..	1.5	0.0	0.0	0.6	0.2	0.4	..

Toward a broader measure of savings 3.16

	Gross savings	Consumption of fixed capital	Net national savings	Education expenditure	Energy depletion	Mineral depletion	Net forest depletion	Carbon dioxide damage	Particulate emission damage	Adjusted net savings
	% of GNI	% of GNI	% of GNI	% of GNI	% of GNI	% of GNI	% of GNI	% of GNI	% of GNI	% of GNI
	2007	2007	2007	2007	2007	2007	2007	2007	2007	2007
Honduras	23.8	10.8	13.0	3.5	0.0	2.0	0.0	0.5	0.4	13.6
Hungary	17.7	14.2	3.5	5.4	0.6	0.0	0.0	0.4	0.1	7.9
India	38.8	9.6	29.2	3.2	2.7	0.7	0.9	1.1	0.7	26.4
Indonesia	27.2	10.8	16.3	1.1	6.9	2.0	0.9	0.8	1.1	6.7
Iran, Islamic Rep.	43.4	11.6	31.8	4.9	26.8	0.6	0.0	1.3	0.7	7.3
Iraq	..	..	..	..	..	..	..	..	..	..
Ireland	25.6	18.1	7.6	5.1	0.0	0.2	0.0	0.2	0.0	12.3[c]
Israel	..	13.9	..	6.0	0.2	0.0	0.0	0.4	0.4	..
Italy	19.8	14.6	5.2	4.2	0.2	0.0	0.0	0.2	0.2	8.9
Jamaica	..	13.2	..	5.4	0.0	1.9	0.0	0.7	0.3	..
Japan	31.0	14.0	17.0	3.2	0.0	0.0	0.0	0.2	0.5	19.5[c]
Jordan	8.2	10.4	−2.2	5.6	0.3	0.5	0.0	0.9	0.6	1.1
Kazakhstan	32.5	13.8	18.7	4.4	28.3	2.4	0.0	2.0	0.3	−9.9
Kenya	17.1	8.8	8.3	6.6	0.0	0.1	1.2	0.3	0.1	13.1
Korea, Dem. Rep.	..	..	..	..	..	..	..	..	..	..
Korea, Rep.	29.9	13.7	16.2	3.9	0.0	0.0	0.0	0.4	0.6	19.1
Kuwait	..	13.3	..	3.0	32.5	0.0	0.0	0.5	1.4	..
Kyrgyz Republic	6.7	9.1	−2.4	5.2	0.1	0.0	0.0	1.2	0.2	1.2
Lao PDR	23.5	9.3	14.2	1.3	0.0	0.0	0.0	0.3	1.2	14.0
Latvia	15.4	13.9	1.6	5.6	0.0	0.0	0.6	0.3	0.0	6.2
Lebanon	0.4	12.1	−11.7	2.5	0.0	0.0	0.0	0.5	0.8	−10.6
Lesotho	32.7	7.3	25.4	10.0	0.0	0.0	1.3	..	0.2	..
Liberia	−19.3	9.4	−28.7	..	0.0	0.0	6.6	0.6	0.4	..
Libya	..	12.4	..	..	45.1	0.0	0.0	0.9	..	..
Lithuania	17.0	13.5	3.5	4.8	0.1	0.0	0.1	0.3	0.2	7.6
Macedonia, FYR	21.1	11.4	9.6	4.9	0.0	0.0	0.2	1.2	0.1	13.1
Madagascar	13.4	8.2	5.2	3.1	0.0	0.0	0.2	0.3	0.2	7.7
Malawi	9.6	7.6	2.0	3.5	0.0	0.0	0.8	0.3	0.2	4.3
Malaysia	38.4	12.5	25.9	5.5	10.3	0.1	0.0	0.8	0.1	20.2
Mali	13.6	9.0	4.6	3.6	0.0	0.0	0.0	0.1	1.6	6.5
Mauritania	28.0	8.9	19.1	2.8	0.0	17.0	0.5	0.8	2.3	1.2
Mauritius	19.7	11.8	7.9	3.4	0.0	0.0	0.0	0.4	..	10.9[a]
Mexico	25.7	12.9	12.8	5.5	6.9	0.4	0.0	0.4	0.4	10.3
Moldova	20.4	8.8	11.6	6.6	0.0	0.0	0.1	1.4	0.6	16.0
Mongolia	42.5	10.3	32.3	4.6	2.5	14.0	0.0	2.2	2.0	16.3
Morocco	32.8	10.9	21.9	5.2	0.0	1.0	0.0	0.5	0.1	25.6
Mozambique	3.1	8.9	−5.8	3.8	7.1	0.0	0.6	0.2	0.2	−10.2
Myanmar	..	..	..	0.8	..	..	..	..	0.6	..
Namibia	40.3	11.3	29.0	7.3	0.0	4.2	0.0	0.3	0.1	31.7
Nepal	28.2	8.0	20.2	2.4	0.0	0.0	4.4	0.2	0.1	17.9
Netherlands	27.6	14.6	12.9	4.8	1.4	0.0	0.0	0.1	0.6	15.6
New Zealand	..	15.5	..	6.7	1.3	0.2	0.0	0.2	0.0	..
Nicaragua	14.6	9.7	4.9	3.0	0.0	0.7	0.0	0.6	0.1	6.5
Niger	..	7.7	..	2.6	0.0	0.0	2.4	0.2	0.9	..
Nigeria	..	10.8	..	0.9	25.2	0.0	0.1	0.7	0.5	..
Norway	38.3	15.7	22.6	6.5	13.4	0.0	0.0	0.2	0.0	15.5
Oman	..	..	..	3.9	..	..	0.0	..	1.4	..
Pakistan	24.5	9.1	15.4	2.1	3.3	0.0	0.9	0.7	1.5	11.0
Panama	24.7	12.9	11.8	4.4	0.0	0.0	0.0	0.3	0.2	15.7
Papua New Guinea	39.2	10.6	28.7	..	18.0	30.0	0.0	0.4	0.0	..
Paraguay	19.6	10.3	9.4	3.9	0.0	0.0	0.0	0.3	0.7	12.3
Peru	25.7	12.4	13.3	2.6	1.5	10.5	0.0	0.3	0.6	3.1
Philippines	31.6	9.3	22.3	2.2	0.4	1.6	0.1	0.5	0.2	21.7
Poland	22.0	13.3	8.7	5.3	0.9	0.5	0.1	0.7	0.4	11.5
Portugal	12.6	14.4	−1.8	5.4	0.0	0.1	0.0	0.2	0.3	3.0
Puerto Rico	..	..	..	..	..	..	..	..	..	..

	Gross savings	Consumption of fixed capital	Net national savings	Education expenditure	Energy depletion	Mineral depletion	Net forest depletion	Carbon dioxide damage	Particulate emission damage	Adjusted net savings
	% of GNI 2007	% of GNI 2007	% of GNI 2007	% of GNI 2007	% of GNI 2007	% of GNI 2007	% of GNI 2007	% of GNI 2007	% of GNI 2007	% of GNI 2007
Romania	21.1	12.4	8.7	3.4	2.1	0.1	0.0	0.5	0.0	9.3
Russian Federation	31.3	12.9	18.4	3.5	17.9	1.3	0.0	1.1	0.2	1.4
Rwanda	16.2	8.0	8.2	4.6	0.0	0.0	3.6	0.2	0.1	9.0
Saudi Arabia	..	13.4	..	7.2	42.1	0.0	0.0	0.7	1.4	..
Senegal	21.8	9.4	12.4	4.5	0.0	0.1	0.0	0.3	1.2	15.2
Serbia	..	..	..	..	..	..	..	..	..	..
Sierra Leone	9.8	7.9	2.0	3.9	0.0	0.9	1.6	0.4	0.9	2.1
Singapore	..	15.1	..	2.7	0.0	0.0	0.0	0.3	0.9	..
Slovak Republic	24.0	13.8	10.2	3.8	0.1	0.0	0.4	0.5	0.0	13.1
Slovenia	28.0	14.2	13.7	5.5	0.1	0.0	0.2	0.3	0.2	18.4
Somalia	..	..	..	..	..	..	..	..	..	..
South Africa	14.5	12.4	2.1	5.3	3.1	2.2	0.2	1.3	0.1	0.4
Spain	21.9	14.8	7.1	3.9	0.0	0.0	0.0	0.4	0.4	10.4
Sri Lanka	23.3	10.3	13.0	2.6	0.0	0.0	0.6	0.3	0.3	14.3
Sudan	13.2	10.8	2.4	0.9	15.7	0.1	0.0	0.2	0.4	–13.2
Swaziland	19.8	10.6	9.2	6.4	0.0	0.0	0.0	0.3	0.1	15.2
Sweden	27.5	14.7	12.8	7.2	0.0	0.3	0.0	0.1	..	19.6[a]
Switzerland	..	13.9	..	4.8	0.0	0.0	0.0	0.1	0.2	..
Syrian Arab Republic	19.7	10.6	9.1	2.6	19.2	0.0	0.0	1.3	0.9	–9.7
Tajikistan	13.9	8.9	5.0	3.2	0.3	0.0	0.0	1.3	0.4	6.3
Tanzania	..	8.2	..	2.4	0.5	5.6	0.0	0.2	0.1	..
Thailand	34.0	11.8	22.2	4.8	4.1	0.0	0.2	0.9	0.4	21.4
Timor-Leste	..	1.9	..	..	..	0.0	..	0.1	..	..
Togo	..	8.3	..	2.5	0.0	0.6	2.6	0.6	0.2	..
Trinidad and Tobago	31.0	14.0	16.9	4.0	41.9	0.0	0.0	1.6	0.3	–22.8
Tunisia	23.9	11.8	12.0	6.7	4.6	0.6	0.1	0.6	0.2	12.5
Turkey	16.0	12.7	3.2	3.7	0.2	0.1	0.0	0.3	1.1	5.3
Turkmenistan	..	11.1	..	..	92.6	0.0	..	2.5	1.0	..
Uganda	14.0	8.3	5.7	4.0	0.0	0.0	4.6	0.1	..	4.9[a]
Ukraine	23.1	11.2	11.9	4.4	3.0	0.0	0.0	2.2	0.3	10.7
United Arab Emirates	..	..	..	..	..	..	..	..	..	..
United Kingdom	15.7	14.7	1.0	5.0	1.5	0.0	0.0	0.2	0.0	4.3[c]
United States	14.0	14.8	–0.8	4.8	1.2	0.1	0.0	0.3	0.3	2.0[c]
Uruguay	13.4	12.5	1.0	2.6	0.0	0.0	0.3	0.2	1.9	1.2
Uzbekistan	38.6	9.2	29.4	9.4	38.5	0.0	0.0	5.8	0.7	–6.2
Venezuela, RB	34.8	12.3	22.5	3.4	18.7	0.7	0.0	0.7	0.0	5.9
Vietnam	35.5	9.4	26.1	2.8	11.6	0.1	0.4	1.2	0.5	15.2
West Bank and Gaza	..	..	..	..	..	..	..	..	..	..
Yemen, Rep.	..	10.1	..	..	22.5	0.0	0.0	0.8	..	..
Zambia	26.2	10.7	15.5	2.1	0.1	19.8	0.0	0.2	0.6	–3.0
Zimbabwe	..	..	..	6.9	..	..	..	..	0.1	..
World	**22.7 w**	**13.7 w**	**8.9 w**	**4.3 w**	**3.0 w**	**0.4 w**	**0.0 w**	**0.4 w**	**0.4 w**	**8.8 w**
Low income	25.4	9.3	16.2	2.6	9.8	0.9	0.8	0.7	0.7	5.8
Middle income	32.3	11.7	20.6	3.5	7.1	1.2	0.1	0.9	0.8	14.0
Lower middle income	41.7	10.7	31.0	2.6	6.6	1.2	0.2	1.2	1.1	23.5
Upper middle income	23.2	12.8	10.5	4.4	7.6	1.3	0.0	0.6	0.4	4.9
Low & middle income	32.0	11.6	20.4	3.4	7.2	1.2	0.1	0.9	0.8	13.6
East Asia & Pacific	48.0	10.7	37.3	2.1	4.9	1.3	0.0	1.3	1.3	30.6
Europe & Central Asia	24.0	12.8	11.2	4.0	9.8	0.7	0.0	1.0	0.5	3.2
Latin America & Carib.	22.9	12.6	10.3	4.5	5.4	1.9	0.0	0.3	0.4	6.7
Middle East & N. Africa	33.3	11.3	22.0	4.7	21.3	0.4	0.0	1.0	0.6	3.4
South Asia	36.2	9.5	26.8	3.0	2.7	0.6	0.9	1.0	0.8	23.9
Sub-Saharan Africa	17.4	11.1	6.3	3.6	11.7	1.5	0.5	0.7	0.4	–5.0
High income	20.6	14.5	6.1	4.6	1.5	0.2	0.0	0.3	0.3	8.5
Euro area	22.3	14.4	7.8	4.6	0.2	0.0	0.0	0.2	0.2	11.9

a. Excludes particulate emissions damage. b. Likely to be overestimated because mineral depletion excludes diamonds. c. World Bank staff estimate.

ENVIRONMENT

Adjusted net savings measure the change in value of a specified set of assets, excluding capital gains. If a country's net savings are positive and the accounting includes a sufficiently broad range of assets, economic theory suggests that the present value of social welfare is increasing. Conversely, persistently negative adjusted net savings indicate that an economy is on an unsustainable path.

The table provides a check on the extent to which today's rents from a number of natural resources and changes in human capital are balanced by net savings, or this generation's bequest to future generations.

Adjusted net savings are derived from standard national accounting measures of gross savings by making four adjustments. First, estimates of capital consumption of produced assets are deducted to obtain net savings. Second, current public expenditures on education are added to net savings (in standard national accounting these expenditures are treated as consumption). Third, estimates of the depletion of a variety of natural resources are deducted to reflect the decline in asset values associated with their extraction and harvest. And fourth, deductions are made for damages from carbon dioxide and particulate emissions.

The exercise treats public education expenditures as an addition to savings. However, because of the wide variability in the effectiveness of public education expenditures, these figures cannot be construed as the value of investments in human capital. A current expenditure of $1 on education does not necessarily yield $1 of human capital. The calculation should also consider private education expenditure, but data are not available for a large number of countries.

While extensive, the accounting of natural resource depletion and pollution costs still has some gaps. Key estimates missing on the resource side include the value of fossil water extracted from aquifers, net depletion of fish stocks, and depletion and degradation of soils. Important pollutants affecting human health and economic assets are excluded because no internationally comparable data are widely available on damage from ground-level ozone or sulfur oxides.

Estimates of resource depletion are based on the "change in real wealth" method described in Hamilton and Ruta (2008), which estimates depletion as the ratio between the total value of the resource and the remaining reserve lifetime. The total value of the resource is the present value of current and future rents from resource extractions. An economic rent represents an excess return to a given factor of production. Natural resources give rise to rents because they are not produced; in contrast, for produced goods and services competitive forces will expand supply until economic profits are driven to zero. For each type of resource and each country, unit resource rents are derived by taking the difference between world prices (to reflect the social opportunity cost of resource extraction) and the average unit extraction or harvest costs (including a "normal" return on capital). Unit rents are then multiplied by the physical quantity extracted or harvested to arrive at total rent. To estimate the value of the resource, rents are assumed to be constant over the life of the resource (the El Serafy approach), and the present value of the rent flow is calculated using a 4 percent social discount rate. For details on the estimation of natural wealth see World Bank (2006a).

A positive net depletion figure for forest resources implies that the harvest rate exceeds the rate of natural growth; this is not the same as deforestation, which represents a change in land use (see *Definitions* for table 3.4). In principle, there should be an addition to savings in countries where growth exceeds harvest, but empirical estimates suggest that most of this net growth is in forested areas that cannot currently be exploited economically. Because the depletion estimates reflect only timber values, they ignore all the external and nontimber benefits associated with standing forests.

Pollution damage from emissions of carbon dioxide is calculated as the marginal social cost per unit multiplied by the increase in the stock of carbon dioxide. The unit damage figure represents the present value of global damage to economic assets and to human welfare over the time the unit of pollution remains in the atmosphere.

Pollution damage from particulate emissions is estimated by valuing the human health effects from exposure to particulate matter pollution in urban areas. The estimates are calculated as willingness to pay to avoid illness and death from cardiopulmonary disease and lung cancer in adults and acute respiratory infections in children that is attributable to particulate emissions.

For a detailed note on methodology, see www.worldbank.org/data.

- **Gross savings** are the difference between gross national income and public and private consumption, plus net current transfers. • **Consumption of fixed capital** is the replacement value of capital used up in production. • **Net national savings** are gross savings minus consumption of fixed capital. • **Education expenditure** is public current operating expenditures in education, including wages and salaries and excluding capital investments in buildings and equipment. • **Energy depletion** is the ratio of the value of the stock of energy resources to the remaining reserve lifetime (capped at 25 years). It covers coal, crude oil, and natural gas. • **Mineral depletion** is the ratio of the value of the stock of mineral resources to the remaining reserve lifetime (capped at 25 years). It covers tin, gold, lead, zinc, iron, copper, nickel, silver, bauxite, and phosphate. • **Net forest depletion** is unit resource rents times the excess of roundwood harvest over natural growth. • **Carbon dioxide damage** is estimated at $20 per ton of carbon (the unit damage in 1995 U.S. dollars) times tons of carbon emitted. • **Particulate emission damage** is the willingness to pay to avoid illness and death attributable to particulate emissions.• **Adjusted net savings** are net savings plus education expenditure minus energy depletion, mineral depletion, net forest depletion, and carbon dioxide and particulate emissions damage.

Data on gross savings are from World Bank national accounts data files (see table 4.8). Data on consumption of fixed capital are from the United Nations Statistics Division's *National Accounts Statistics: Main Aggregates and Detailed Tables, 1997*, extrapolated to 2007. Data on education expenditure are from the United Nations Statistics Division's *Statistical Yearbook 1997* and from the United Nations Educational, Scientific, and Cultural Organization Institute for Statistics online database. Missing data are estimated by World Bank staff. Data on energy, mineral, and forest depletion are estimates based on sources and methods in Arundhati Kunte and others' "Estimating National Wealth: Methodology and Results" (1998). Data on carbon dioxide damage are from Samuel Fankhauser's *Valuing Climate Change: The Economics of the Greenhouse* (1995). Data on particulate emission damage are from Kiran D. Pandey and others' "The Human Costs of Air Pollution: New Estimates for Developing Countries" (2006). The conceptual underpinnings of the savings measure appear in Kirk Hamilton and Michael Clemens' "Genuine Savings Rates in Developing Countries" (1999).

ECONOMY

The global economy in 2007

Global output grew 3.8 percent in 2007, receding slightly from 4 percent in 2006. The downturn was greatest in high-income economies, where growth fell from 3 percent to 2.5 percent, affected by the cooling of the housing market, a precursor to the 2008 financial crisis. Low- and middle-income economies, which have grown faster on average, reached a peak of 8.1 percent annual growth in 2007. Their strong performance was led by the economies of East Asia and Pacific and South Asia (figure 4a), dominated by China at 13 percent annual growth and India at 9 percent. After a decade of sustained growth India's gross national income (GNI) per capita (using the *World Bank Atlas* method) now places it with China among the lower middle-income economies. Cambodia, Lao PDR, Malaysia, Mongolia, the Philippines, and Vietnam in East Asia and Pacific all grew faster than 6 percent, as did all South Asian economies except Afghanistan and Nepal (figure 4b).

Sub-Saharan Africa achieved 6.2 percent growth for the second year in a row, thanks to higher prices for its oil and commodity exports. The commodity boom also helped the Middle East and North Africa and Latin America and the Caribbean achieve their highest growth rate since 2004. Egypt, Iran, Jordan, Libya, Syria, and Tunisia grew more than 6 percent. About half the countries in Latin America and the Caribbean grew more than 6 percent, with Argentina at 9 percent and Venezuela at 8 percent. Similarly, 28 of the 47 Sub-Saharan countries grew 5 percent or more. Growth slowed in Europe and Central Asia, but annual rates remained above 5 percent, except for Moldova.

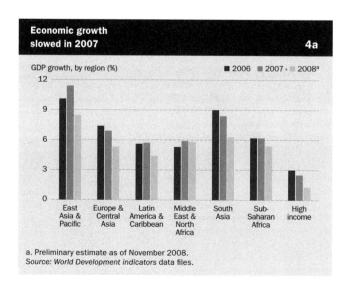

Economic growth slowed in 2007 **4a**

GDP growth, by region (%)

■ 2006 ■ 2007 ▪ 2008ᵃ

a. Preliminary estimate as of November 2008.
Source: World Development indicators data files.

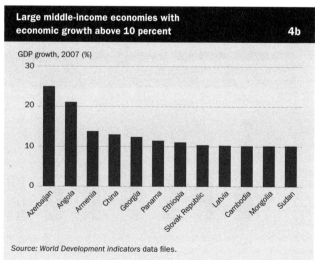

Large middle-income economies with economic growth above 10 percent **4b**

GDP growth, 2007 (%)

Source: World Development indicators data files.

Savings and investment were higher in 2007

The rapid growth of developing economies since 2000 has been marked by large increases in investment (figure 4c). Between 2000 and 2007 investment rates rose from 32 percent of gross domestic product (GDP) to 38 percent in East Asia and Pacific and from 23 percent to 34 percent in South Asia. Investment in China, India, Lao PDR, Mongolia, and Vietnam exceeded 37 percent of GDP during 2005–07. Sub-Saharan Africa saw its investment grow 73 percent, Europe and Central Asia 91 percent, and the Middle East and North Africa 63 percent. At 34 percent, investment growth in Latin America and the Caribbean was not as rapid.

Most of the increase was financed by rising savings. Annual gross savings in developing economies grew from 25 percent of GDP to 31 percent between 2000 and 2007. East Asia and Pacific saw the largest increase, from 36 percent of GDP to 47 percent, followed by South Asia, from 25 percent to 34 percent (figure 4d). Countries enjoying a surge in demand for their exports of fuels, other commodities, or manufactures—such as Algeria, Azerbaijan, Botswana, China, Gabon, Iran, and Mongolia—saved more than 40 percent of their GDP during 2005–07.

High-income economies still dominate manufactured output and exports

During their industrial revolutions today's developed economies transformed themselves from agrarian economies into producers and exporters of manufactured goods. Manufacturing has yet to take off in most developing economies. Value added in manufacturing accounted for as much as 20 percent of GDP in only about a dozen developing countries in 2007, among them China, Indonesia, Lao PDR, Philippines, and Vietnam. China's share was 32 percent. Some developing economies have been investing in and expanding their services, which in 38 countries accounted for more then 50 percent of GDP, among them Bangladesh, India, Pakistan, and Sri Lanka. Resource extraction remains important for many countries: minerals and petroleum were the leading sources of growth in many Sub-Saharan, and Middle Eastern and North African economies.

Services are now the largest sector in high-income economies, accounting for more than 70 percent of GDP. Although their manufacturing share has fallen, they still accounted for 73 percent of global manufactured output in 2006, down from 79 percent in 2000 (figure 4e). They also accounted for the largest share of manufactures exports (figure 4f). East Asia and Pacific made the largest inroads, improving its share of global manufactured output by 4 percentage points, from 9 percent to 13 percent.

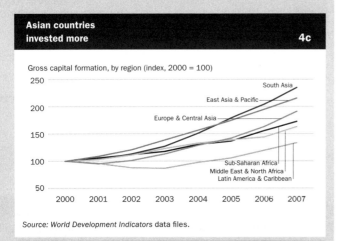

Asian countries invested more   **4c**

Gross capital formation, by region (index, 2000 = 100)

Source: *World Development Indicators* data files.

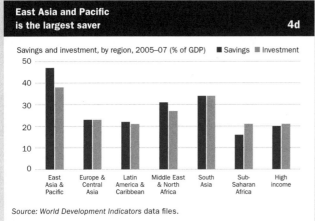

East Asia and Pacific is the largest saver   **4d**

Savings and investment, by region, 2005–07 (% of GDP) ■ Savings ■ Investment

Source: *World Development Indicators* data files.

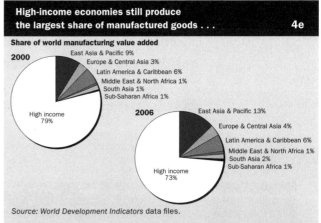

High-income economies still produce the largest share of manufactured goods . . .   **4e**

Share of world manufacturing value added

Source: *World Development Indicators* data files.

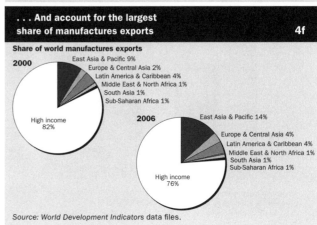

. . . And account for the largest share of manufactures exports   **4f**

Share of world manufactures exports

Source: *World Development Indicators* data files.

Macroeconomic stability and fiscal space

Macroeconomic stability is good for economic growth. Despite concerns that strict fiscal and monetary policies were preventing countries from pursuing aggressive antipoverty programs and progressing toward the Millennium Development Goals, most developing economies have reduced their fiscal deficits, controlled inflation, and kept real interest rates low.

In periods of rapid growth monetary policy is crucial in maintaining macroeconomic stability. But in a deep recession it has limitations because interest rates cannot go below zero.

The current financial crisis has renewed interest in fiscal policy to stimulate economic growth. Discretionary fiscal spending is possible when a country has "fiscal space," the difference between current government spending and the maximum spending a government can undertake without jeopardizing its fiscal solvency—that is, without jeopardizing its current and future ability to service its debt. Indicators that assess fiscal space include the ratios of public debt to GDP, external debt to GDP, and fiscal balance to GDP. The ratio of the current account balance to GDP and of private capital flows excluding foreign direct investment to GDP are also relevant to determining the extent of fiscal space.

Fiscal space can be created without issuing new debt, through improved efficiency and public expenditure, increased revenue mobilization, and additional grant aid. But some countries may also be able to undertake fiscal stimulus programs by taking on additional debt within the available fiscal space. Among large economies with data for 2005–07, 34 had a cash surplus and 16 had a cash deficit greater than 2 percent and 12 developing economies had a deficit greater than 3 percent (figure 4g). In 2007, five developing economies had a public debt to GDP ratio greater than 60 percent (figure 4h).

Maintaining fiscal solvency is one aspect of fiscal policy. A second is macroeconomic stability. The ability to increase public spending while maintaining macroeconomic stability has been referred to as having "macroeconomic space."

High inflation limits the possibility of fiscal expansion. Rapid growth, supply constraints, and rising demand for commodities by developed and developing economies boosted prices globally, and inflation rose modestly in many countries (figure 4i), even as the highest rates were being brought under control.

Some countries responded by raising interest rates between 2005 and 2007, but real interest rates continued to fall in many others (figure 4j). Now, faced with a crisis that began in the United States in 2007 and spread to other economies in 2008, developing economies will face difficult policy choices as they continue to grow while maintaining a stable—and sustainable—fiscal stance.

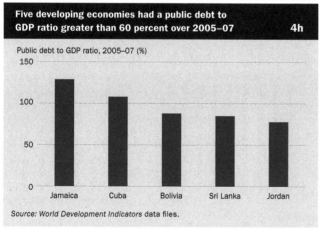

Twelve developing economies had a cash deficit greater than 3 percent of GDP   **4g**

Cash deficit, 2005–07 (% of GDP)

Source: *World Development Indicators* data files.

Five developing economies had a public debt to GDP ratio greater than 60 percent over 2005–07   **4h**

Public debt to GDP ratio, 2005–07 (%)

Source: *World Development Indicators* data files.

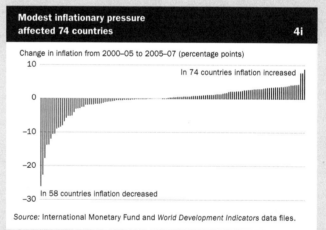

Modest inflationary pressure affected 74 countries   **4i**

Change in inflation from 2000–05 to 2005–07 (percentage points)

In 74 countries inflation increased

In 58 countries inflation decreased

Source: International Monetary Fund and *World Development Indicators* data files.

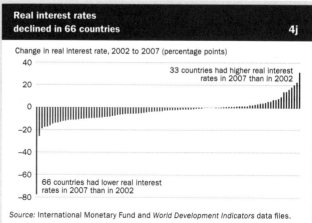

Real interest rates declined in 66 countries   **4j**

Change in real interest rate, 2002 to 2007 (percentage points)

33 countries had higher real interest rates in 2007 than in 2002

66 countries had lower real interest rates in 2007 than in 2002

Source: International Monetary Fund and *World Development Indicators* data files.

Growth in GDP and investment

Quarterly data for selected major economies in each of the six developing regions show that the 2008 global crisis has affected countries differently (figure 4k–4p). In Brazil GDP rose slightly in 2008 over 2007. In China and India GDP growth has declined but remains above 7 percent. The GDP growth rate fell significantly in the Russian Federation in the fourth quarter of 2008, to 1.1 percent. South Africa and Egypt saw their GDP growth rates decline rapidly in the second half of 2008. However, overall GDP growth remained positive in all six countries.

Growth in industrial production

In the current global crisis growth in the industrial sector, particularly the manufacturing sector, has fallen sharply. The large developing economies shown here, with the exception of China, saw their industrial production fall into the negative range by the end of 2008 (figures 4q–4v). Even China saw a large decline in its industrial output due to falling demand.

Lending and inflation rates

Countries need macroeconomic space to pursue monetary policies to stimulate their economies. But many countries are still experiencing double-digit inflation despite cooling economies (figure 4w–4bb). Egypt has a high inflation rate. But China's lending rate and inflation rate are both below 10 percent.

Central government debt

With monetary policy limited in scope during the current crisis, countries are looking to fiscal policy to lift them out of the economic crisis (figures 4cc–4hh). China seems to have the fiscal space to afford a large stimulus package. Brazil and India have a more constrained fiscal environment, limiting the actions they can take without affecting fiscal solvency. For the Russian Federation the falling price of oil and the depreciation of the ruble may also limit the scope for fiscal policy.

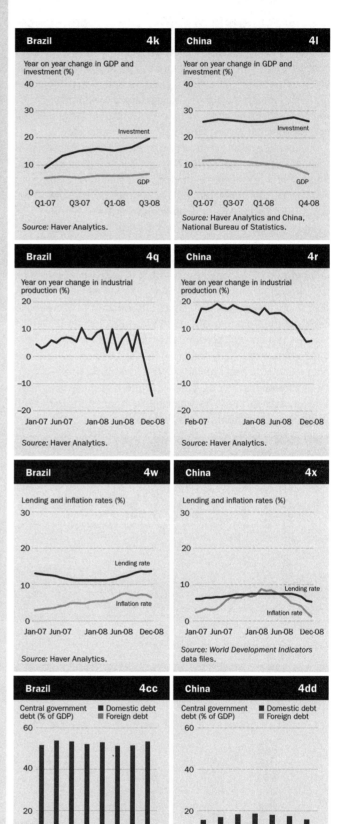

Brazil   4k
Year on year change in GDP and investment (%)
Source: Haver Analytics.

China   4l
Year on year change in GDP and investment (%)
Source: Haver Analytics and China, National Bureau of Statistics.

Brazil   4q
Year on year change in industrial production (%)
Source: Haver Analytics.

China   4r
Year on year change in industrial production (%)
Source: Haver Analytics.

Brazil   4w
Lending and inflation rates (%)
Source: Haver Analytics.

China   4x
Lending and inflation rates (%)
Source: World Development Indicators data files.

Brazil   4cc
Central government debt (% of GDP) ■ Domestic debt ■ Foreign debt
Source: Banco Central do Brasil.

China   4dd
Central government debt (% of GDP) ■ Domestic debt ■ Foreign debt
Source: Haver Analytics.

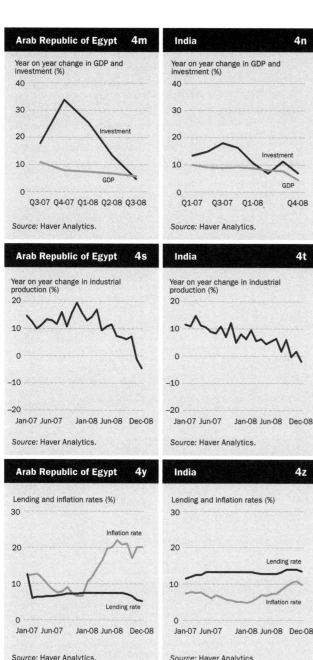

Arab Republic of Egypt   4m

Year on year change in GDP and investment (%)

Investment

GDP

Q3-07 Q4-07 Q1-08 Q2-08 Q3-08

Source: Haver Analytics.

India   4n

Year on year change in GDP and investment (%)

Investment

GDP

Q1-07 Q3-07 Q1-08 Q4-08

Source: Haver Analytics.

Russian Federation   4o

Year on year change in GDP and investment (%)

Investment

GDP

Q1-07 Q3-07 Q1-08 Q4-08

Source: Haver Analytics.

South Africa   4p

Year on year change in GDP and investment (%)

Investment

GDP

Q1-07 Q3-07 Q1-08 Q4-08

Source: Haver Analytics.

Arab Republic of Egypt   4s

Year on year change in industrial production (%)

Jan-07 Jun-07 Jan-08 Jun-08 Dec-08

Source: Haver Analytics.

India   4t

Year on year change in industrial production (%)

Jan-07 Jun-07 Jan-08 Jun-08 Dec-08

Source: Haver Analytics.

Russian Federation   4u

Year on year change in industrial production (%)

Jan-07 Jun-07 Jan-08 Jun-08 Dec-08

Source: Haver Analytics.

South Africa   4v

Year on year change in industrial production (%)

Jan-07 Jun-07 Jan-08 Jun-08 Dec-08

Source: Haver Analytics.

Arab Republic of Egypt   4y

Lending and inflation rates (%)

Inflation rate

Lending rate

Jan-07 Jun-07 Jan-08 Jun-08 Dec-08

Source: Haver Analytics.

India   4z

Lending and inflation rates (%)

Lending rate

Inflation rate

Jan-07 Jun-07 Jan-08 Jun-08 Dec-08

Source: Haver Analytics.

Russian Federation   4aa

Lending and inflation rates (%)

Inflation rate

Lending rate

Jan-07 Jun-07 Jan-08 Jun-08 Dec-08

Source: Haver Analytics.

South Africa   4bb

Lending and inflation rates (%)

Lending rate

Inflation rate

Jan-07 Jun-07 Jan-08 Jun-08 Dec-08

Source: Haver Analytics.

Arab Republic of Egypt   4ee

Central government debt (% of GDP)
■ Domestic debt
■ Foreign debt

Q1-07 Q3-07 Q1-08 Q4-08

Source: Haver Analytics.

India   4ff

Central government debt (% of GDP)
■ Domestic debt
■ Foreign debt

Q1-07 Q3-07 Q1-08 Q3-08

Source: Haver Analytics.

Russian Federation   4gg

Central government debt (% of GDP)
■ Domestic debt
■ Foreign debt

Q1-07 Q3-07 Q1-08 Q4-08

Source: Haver Analytics.

South Africa   4hh

Central government debt (% of GDP)
■ Domestic debt
■ Foreign debt

Q1-07 Q3-07 Q1-08 Q4-08

Source: Haver Analytics.

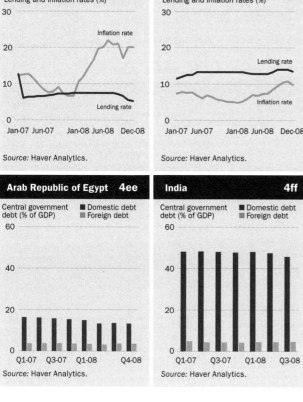
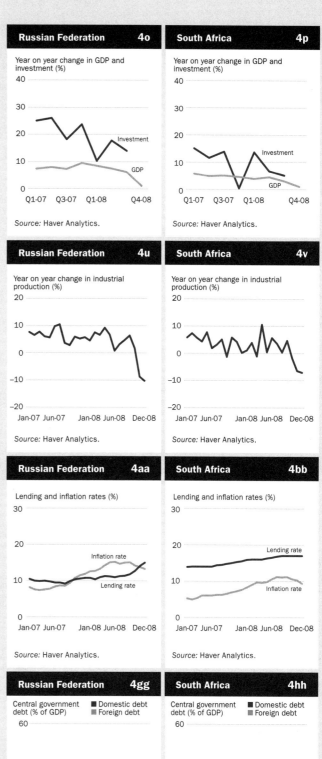
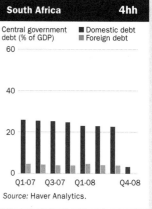

2009 World Development Indicators   **201**

4.a

	Gross domestic product		Exports of goods and services		Imports of goods and services		GDP deflator		Current account balance		Gross international reserves	
	average annual % growth		average annual % growth		average annual % growth		% growth		% of GDP		$ millions	months of import coverage
	2007	2008[a]	2007	2008[a]	2007	2008[a]	2007	2008[a]	2007	2008[a]	2008[a]	2008[a]
Algeria	3.1	3.0	−0.6	4.4	7.6	5.6	7.5	9.0	..	20.2	138,945	31.0
Angola	21.1	14.8	..	..	..	..	7.1	32.5	15.3	19.5	..	..
Argentina	8.7	6.0	9.0	..	20.6	..	14.2	10.0	2.7	0.9	..	..
Armenia	13.8	6.8	−3.5	−13.8	13.0	9.6	4.2	8.5	−6.4	−12.8	1,405	3.0
Azerbaijan	25.0	10.8	43.3	6.0	14.0	20.9	14.4	20.8	28.9	29.5	18,038	28.9
Bangladesh	6.4	6.2	13.0	8.7	16.0	14.5	6.8	8.0	1.3	0.9	5,788	2.8
Belarus	8.2	10.0	7.3	1.2	0.0	16.8	12.1	20.6	−6.8	−7.6	3,061	0.9
Bolivia	4.6	6.1	3.3	9.4	4.8	16.3	7.4	14.9	13.7	11.9	7,722	16.6
Bosnia and Herzegovina	6.8	6.0	12.6	13.1	16.6	17.2	6.0	7.4	−12.7	−15.5	4,497	5.4
Botswana	5.3	2.4	8.8	−20.8	13.6	19.6	11.7	12.2	19.8	−1.9	9,200	21.3
Brazil	5.4	5.5	6.6	2.9	20.7	23.0	4.1	7.5	0.1	−1.8	207,467	10.2
Bulgaria	6.2	6.0	5.2	2.8	9.9	4.8	7.8	10.3	−22.0	−24.3	17,923	5.4
Burundi	3.6	4.5	..	34.0	..	4.3	9.5	24.5	−11.9	−13.0	154	3.9
Cameroon	3.5	3.9	−12.1	4.7	6.2	5.1	2.0	1.7	−2.6	1.3	3,991	6.5
Chile	5.1	3.5	7.8	1.8	14.3	13.4	4.9	8.7	4.4	−2.6	23,162	4.8
China	11.9	9.0	19.9	7.8	13.9	3.7	5.2	7.2	12.0	8.9	1,950,000	19.1
Colombia	8.2	3.5	12.2	7.9	18.4	3.2	2.9	8.7	−2.9	−3.2	23,671	6.9
Congo, Dem. Rep.	6.8	8.2	9.8	−0.2	9.1	12.1	17.0	19.7	0.0	−12.3	83	0.2
Congo, Rep.	−1.6	7.6	..	6.2	..	−0.6	−7.9	33.3	−28.5	6.5	5,507	22.2
Costa Rica	7.3	2.9	8.4	3.2	4.5	7.0	9.6	13.0	−6.0	−8.0	4,216	2.9
Côte d'Ivoire	1.7	2.8	−9.9	7.4	1.3	0.3	2.7	5.0	−0.7	−0.5	..	..
Croatia	5.6	2.2	5.7	12.9	5.8	18.0	4.0	6.6	−8.7	−10.0	14,327	4.9
Dominican Republic	8.5	5.3	7.6	−10.9	6.7	12.7	5.7	10.6	−6.1	−9.6	2,644	1.8
Ecuador	2.6	3.1	−1.7	1.5	6.5	5.4	4.7	11.9	3.6	2.8	4,473	2.4
Egypt, Arab Rep.	7.1	7.2	23.3	28.8	28.8	26.3	12.6	12.3	0.3	0.5	34,603	6.6
El Salvador	4.7	3.8	3.9	4.0	8.1	10.8	4.4	6.3	−5.5	−6.1	2,515	2.7
Ethiopia	11.1	11.6	10.2	0.6	3.8	10.7	16.8	25.9	−4.3	−10.5	906	..
Gabon	5.6	2.1	4.2	−0.9	22.0	10.9	5.2	14.2	..	17.1	1,954	5.1
Ghana	6.3	7.2	2.6	4.7	8.9	8.9	14.8	18.1	−14.2	19.9	1,896	2.1
Guatemala	5.7	4.6	10.8	8.1	7.0	12.5	6.1	8.5	−5.0	−5.5	4,564	3.5
Honduras	6.3	4.0	3.6	11.0	8.0	17.6	7.0	9.8	−10.0	−13.3	2,532	3.8
India	9.0	7.0	7.5	9.7	7.7	4.7	4.3	9.5	..	−2.6	254,613	9.2
Indonesia	6.3	6.1	8.0	9.5	8.9	10.0	11.5	18.3	2.4	..	51,639	4.9
Iran, Islamic Rep.	7.8	5.0	2.8	−40.0	4.9	−13.0	20.5	25.0	..	10.3	63,450	7.4
Jamaica	..	−1.3	..	..	..	..	..	21.1	..	−13.8	1,600	2.7
Jordan	6.0	5.5	0.8	−3.5	6.5	11.1	6.0	14.9	−17.5	−14.0	8,344	4.8
Kazakhstan	8.9	3.2	9.0	8.0	25.5	3.2	15.5	20.0	−7.0	6.7	19,401	4.7
Kenya	7.0	3.6	6.0	−4.2	12.7	8.2	4.7	27.0	−4.6	−7.1	2,928	3.0
Latvia	10.3	−4.6	12.5	−1.8	16.9	−13.7	13.3	15.2	−23.9	−13.2	5,248	7.1
Lebanon	2.0	5.5	6.6	32.6	8.9	7.5	4.9	7.5	−8.4	−17.4	17,062	12.6
Lesotho	4.9	3.9	14.6	−21.8	13.3	7.7	6.2	8.3	13.2	−3.7	982	6.6

	Gross domestic product		Exports of goods and services		Imports of goods and services		GDP deflator		Current account balance		Gross international reserves	
	average annual % growth		average annual % growth		average annual % growth		% growth		% of GDP		$ millions	months of import coverage
	2007	2008[a]	2007	2008[a]	2007	2008[a]	2007	2008[a]	2007	2008[a]	2008[a]	2008[a]
Lithuania	8.8	3.2	4.7	13.1	9.1	11.6	8.6	12.1	−13.7	−12.6	6,441	2.4
Macedonia, FYR	5.0	5.3	11.8	6.4	15.2	20.0	5.1	6.6	..	−13.2	2,115	3.2
Malawi	7.9	8.7	−1.1	−5.4	−4.2	−4.6	7.4	8.6	..	−17.9	209	1.3
Malaysia	6.3	5.1	4.2	9.2	5.4	3.5	5.2	1.3	15.5	12.8	91,400	7.4
Mauritius	4.7	5.3	4.7	5.4	5.9	2.9	7.0	7.6	−6.0	−6.3	2,570	4.9
Mexico	3.2	1.3	6.2	−3.5	7.0	1.3	4.7	7.4	−0.5	−1.7	85,421	2.9
Moldova	3.0	7.2	9.5	−7.8	13.4	−6.1	15.8	9.7	−15.8	−15.4	1,672	4.2
Mongolia	10.2	8.9	..	19.6	..	50.3	12.3	22.4	..	−9.6	637	2.1
Montenegro	10.3	7.5	10.3	6.1	10.3	12.3	7.2	9.0	..	−31.3	468	..
Morocco	2.7	5.8	5.2	−8.0	15.0	5.6	3.8	3.0	−0.2	−4.6	25,350	7.0
Nicaragua	3.9	3.5	9.7	3.9	16.3	11.4	9.2	16.8	−18.3	−24.4	1,206	2.5
Nigeria	5.9	6.2	..	..	..	..	5.1	15.8	13.3	6.2	52,800	12.0
Pakistan	6.0	6.0	2.3	−8.9	−2.8	−2.1	7.9	13.4	−5.8	−8.3	9,385	2.2
Panama	11.5	9.0	15.0	14.4	19.3	16.5	1.9	9.3	−7.3	−9.8	2,602	3.5
Papua New Guinea	6.2	6.9	−13.4	13.6	−1.4	13.9	2.4	11.4	..	2.8	2,090	4.4
Paraguay	6.8	5.8	9.6	32.4	10.8	39.3	10.2	7.1	1.0	−2.0	2,864	3.7
Peru	8.9	9.0	6.2	10.1	21.3	24.1	2.0	5.8	1.4	−1.6	37,297	10.0
Philippines	7.2	4.0	5.6	2.5	−4.5	3.6	2.8	8.5	4.4	1.5	36,659	5.4
Poland	6.6	4.8	8.5	10.8	15.0	11.4	3.3	3.5	−4.4	−5.5	62,180	3.8
Romania	6.0	7.8	12.0	13.8	12.0	9.4	10.8	13.5	−13.9	−12.9	37,972	5.7
Russian Federation	8.1	7.3	6.4	5.7	27.3	19.4	13.5	15.0	5.9	7.6	614,638	16.5
Senegal	4.8	2.7	−1.8	14.1	8.7	13.5	5.2	7.4	..	−12.4	1,610	3.2
Serbia	7.5	6.0	16.3	12.1	23.9	12.0	6.8	11.1	..	−17.4	14,383	5.7
Seychelles	6.3	0.1	30.6	16.2	43.6	19.2	7.3	29.6	−36.2	−32.1	51	0.7
South Africa	5.1	3.1	8.3	3.0	10.4	..	8.9	10.5	−7.3	−8.1	34,089	3.0
Sri Lanka	6.8	6.3	..	5.2	..	4.0	14.0	23.5	−4.2	−7.5	1,753	1.5
Sudan	10.2	8.3	33.6	23.0	−4.4	0.3	7.0	15.8	−7.1	−8.3	..	..
Swaziland	3.5	2.0	−1.9	6.4	3.0	3.5	9.0	9.7	−2.3	−1.3	685	2.9
Syrian Arab Republic	6.6	5.1	2.5	−2.4	8.4	2.5	3.5	12.3	..	0.0	5,516	3.4
Thailand	4.8	2.6	7.1	5.5	3.5	7.5	3.2	4.5	6.4	−0.1	111,008	6.6
Tunisia	6.3	5.0	8.5	1.1	6.1	6.0	2.4	5.0	−2.6	−4.6	8,769	4.2
Togo	1.9	0.8	..	5.6	..	8.9	1.3	4.8	..	−7.0	..	3.7
Turkey	4.6	1.0	7.3	..	10.7	..	7.6	10.1	−5.7	−5.5	72,946	4.3
Uganda	7.9	9.5	12.2	7.3	16.7	28.1	6.9	6.3	−6.3	−9.1	2,673	6.4
Ukraine	7.6	2.1	3.2	−0.4	19.9	6.7	21.8	28.2	−3.7	−6.7	31,543	3.9
Uruguay	7.4	10.6	10.2	12.0	12.5	20.0	8.5	6.5	−0.8	−2.7	6,329	8.6
Uzbekistan	9.5	8.0	32.4	15.8	36.8	20.0	24.0	17.0	..	17.9	2,684	3.6
Venezuela, RB	8.4	4.9	−5.6	0.0	33.6	2.7	14.0	38.0	8.8	12.0	43,127	9.3
Vietnam	8.5	6.2	21.0	5.6	30.8	9.2	8.2	21.7	−10.2	−10.2	22,420	4.0
Zambia	6.0	5.8	21.2	−5.9	16.2	13.1	9.4	11.0	−4.4	−8.9	976	2.3
Zimbabwe	..	..	..	..	29.4	..	..	..	..	..	..	..

a. Data are preliminary estimates.
Source: *World Development Indicators* data files.

4.1 Growth of output

	Gross domestic product		Agriculture		Industry		Manufacturing		Services	
	average annual % growth		average annual % growth		average annual % growth		average annual % growth		average annual % growth	
	1990–2000	2000–07	1990–2000	2000–07	1990–2000	2000–07	1990–2000	2000–07	1990–2000	2000–07
Afghanistan	..	10.7	..	..	..	..	..	..	..	..
Albania	3.5	5.3	4.3	1.4	−0.5	3.6	..	−0.2	6.9	7.2
Algeria	1.9	4.5	3.6	6.3	1.8	3.9	−2.1	2.3	1.8	5.0
Angolaª	1.6	12.9	−1.4	14.3	4.4	14.0	−0.3	20.2	−2.2	9.1
Argentina	4.3	4.7	3.5	3.7	3.8	6.2	2.7	5.8	4.5	3.6
Armenia	−1.9	12.7	0.5	7.8	−7.8	15.9	−4.3	6.5	6.4	13.7
Australia	3.6	3.2	3.1	0.2	2.7	2.5	1.8	1.2	4.2	3.7
Austria	2.4	2.0	1.6	−0.4	2.7	3.0	2.7	2.3	2.3	1.8
Azerbaijan	−6.3	17.6	−2.1	6.1	−2.1	23.0	−15.7	11.0	−2.3	15.1
Bangladesh	4.8	5.7	2.9	3.1	7.3	7.9	7.2	7.7	4.5	5.9
Belarus	−1.7	8.3	−4.0	6.4	−1.8	11.5	−0.7	11.3	−0.4	6.3
Belgium	2.1	2.0	2.7	−1.7	1.8	1.3	3.1	0.7	1.9	2.2
Beninª	4.8	3.8	5.8	4.6	4.1	3.8	5.8	2.7	4.2	3.2
Bolivia	4.0	3.6	2.9	3.4	4.1	4.4	3.8	4.1	4.3	2.6
Bosnia and Herzegovina	..	5.3	..	5.0	..	7.1	..	8.1	..	3.9
Botswana	6.0	5.3	−1.2	−1.5	5.8	4.6	4.4	2.8	7.8	5.9
Brazil	2.7	3.3	3.6	4.0	2.4	3.1	2.0	3.2	3.8	3.4
Bulgaria	−1.8	5.7	3.0	−4.1	−5.0	5.9	..	6.6	−5.2	6.3
Burkina Faso	5.5	5.8	5.9	6.2	5.9	7.3	5.9	6.3	3.9	5.5
Burundi	−2.9	2.7	−1.9	−1.5	−4.3	−6.2	−8.7	..	−2.8	10.4
Cambodia	7.0	9.9	3.7	5.5	14.3	14.2	18.6	13.8	7.1	10.2
Cameroon	1.7	3.5	5.5	3.4	−0.9	−0.4	1.4	5.8	0.2	6.2
Canada	3.1	2.7	1.1	2.3	3.2	1.5	..	0.1	3.0	3.2
Central African Republic	2.0	0.0	3.8	0.7	0.7	0.8	−0.2	1.1	0.2	−1.6
Chad	2.2	12.2	4.9	3.3	0.6	33.2	..	..	0.8	8.4
Chile	6.6	4.5	2.2	5.9	5.6	3.6	4.4	4.0	6.9	4.7
Chinaª	10.6	10.3	4.1	4.2	13.7	11.6	12.9	10.9	10.2	10.6
Hong Kong, China	3.6	5.2	..	−2.2	..	−2.8	..	−3.3	..	4.9
Colombia	2.8	4.9	−2.6	3.0	1.5	5.0	−2.5	5.5	4.1	4.7
Congo, Dem. Rep.	−4.9	5.0	1.4	1.2	−8.0	9.6	−8.7	6.3	−13.0	11.5
Congo, Rep.ª	1.0	4.1	0.7	..	1.7	..	−2.4	..	−0.7	..
Costa Rica	5.3	5.4	4.1	4.1	6.2	5.9	6.8	5.8	4.7	5.6
Côte d'Ivoireª	3.2	0.3	3.5	1.2	6.3	−1.0	5.5	−2.8	2.0	0.4
Croatia	0.6	4.8	−2.1	1.3	−1.1	5.9	−3.5	5.5	1.3	4.7
Cubaª	4.2	3.4	..	..	..	..	..	..	..	..
Czech Republic	1.1	4.6	0.0	0.4	0.2	6.4	4.3	8.2	1.2	4.3
Denmark	2.7	1.8	4.6	0.6	2.5	0.1	2.5	−0.4	2.7	2.0
Dominican Republicª	6.0	4.8	3.9	4.7	7.0	2.2	4.9	2.3	6.0	6.2
Ecuador	1.9	5.0	−1.7	4.8	2.6	5.4	1.5	5.4	2.4	2.7
Egypt, Arab Rep.	4.4	4.3	3.1	3.3	5.1	4.5	6.4	4.0	4.1	4.8
El Salvador	4.8	2.8	1.2	3.2	5.1	2.3	5.2	2.4	4.0	2.9
Eritrea	5.7	1.4	1.5	9.3	15.0	0.8	10.6	−4.9	5.7	0.1
Estonia	0.4	8.1	−6.2	−3.0	−2.4	9.8	7.3	10.5	3.3	7.7
Ethiopia	3.8	7.5	2.6	6.2	4.1	9.0	3.9	6.4	5.2	8.4
Finland	2.6	3.0	−1.1	1.3	4.1	4.5	6.4	4.7	2.5	2.0
France	1.9	1.8	2.0	−0.3	1.0	1.4	..	1.2	2.2	2.0
Gabonª	2.3	2.0	2.0	1.4	1.6	1.2	3.0	3.4	3.1	2.7
Gambia, The	3.0	4.9	3.3	2.6	1.0	7.3	0.9	4.2	3.7	6.0
Georgia	−7.1	8.3	−11.0	1.6	−8.1	12.5	..	10.4	−0.3	9.5
Germany	1.8	1.0	0.1	−0.4	−0.1	1.5	0.2	1.6	2.9	1.1
Ghanaª	4.3	5.5	3.4	2.8	2.7	5.2	−4.5	..	5.6	7.6
Greece	2.2	4.3	0.5	−2.6	1.0	4.8	..	4.0	2.6	4.1
Guatemalaª	4.2	3.6	2.8	3.0	4.3	2.9	2.8	2.8	4.7	4.1
Guinea	4.4	2.8	4.3	4.0	4.9	3.7	4.0	2.6	3.6	1.4
Guinea-Bissau	1.2	0.4	3.9	4.8	−3.1	4.0	−2.0	4.0	−0.6	0.3
Haiti	−1.5	0.2	..	..	..	..	..	..	..	..

Growth of output | **4.1**

	Gross domestic product		Agriculture		Industry		Manufacturing		Services	
	average annual % growth		average annual % growth		average annual % growth		average annual % growth		average annual % growth	
	1990–2000	2000–07	1990–2000	2000–07	1990–2000	2000–07	1990–2000	2000–07	1990–2000	2000–07
Honduras	3.2	5.3	2.2	3.9	3.6	4.3	4.0	5.6	3.8	6.3
Hungary	1.5	4.0	−2.4	4.8	3.6	3.8	7.9	5.6	1.3	4.0
India	5.9	7.8	3.2	3.1	6.1	8.6	6.7	8.0	7.7	9.3
Indonesia[a]	4.2	5.1	2.0	3.2	5.2	4.1	6.7	5.1	4.0	6.8
Iran, Islamic Rep.	3.1	5.9	3.2	5.9	2.6	6.9	5.1	9.9	3.8	5.3
Iraq	..	−11.4	..	..	..	..	..	..	..	..
Ireland	7.4	5.5	0.8	−4.3	12.7	4.9	..	..	7.5	6.1
Israel[a]	5.4	3.2	..	..	..	..	..	..	..	..
Italy	1.5	1.0	2.1	−0.2	1.0	0.3	1.4	−1.2	1.6	1.4
Jamaica	1.8	1.0	−0.3	−1.4	−1.0	1.7	−2.2	−0.2	2.3	0.4
Japan	1.1	1.7	−1.3	−1.7	−0.3	1.7	..	1.9	2.0	1.6
Jordan	5.0	6.3	−3.0	7.5	5.2	8.4	5.6	10.2	5.0	5.8
Kazakhstan	−4.1	10.0	−8.0	5.0	0.6	11.1	2.7	8.6	0.3	10.9
Kenya	2.2	4.4	1.9	3.2	1.2	4.7	1.3	4.2	3.2	4.2
Korea, Dem. Rep.	..	..	..	..	..	..	..	..	..	..
Korea, Rep.	5.8	4.7	1.6	0.3	6.0	6.3	7.3	7.4	5.6	3.7
Kuwait[a]	4.9	9.2	1.0	..	0.3	..	−0.1	..	3.5	..
Kyrgyz Republic	−4.1	4.1	1.5	2.0	−10.3	−0.4	−7.5	−2.4	−4.9	8.3
Lao PDR	6.5	6.7	4.8	3.1	11.1	12.8	11.7	10.1	6.6	7.1
Latvia	−1.5	9.0	−5.2	2.9	−8.3	8.4	−7.3	6.3	2.7	9.5
Lebanon	6.1	3.3	1.9	0.5	−1.8	4.0	−0.8	2.8	3.7	2.6
Lesotho	5.1	3.8	2.4	−5.5	5.3	5.8	6.6	6.7	7.1	3.7
Liberia	4.1	−2.7	..	..	..	..	..	..	..	..
Libya	..	3.7	..	..	..	..	..	..	..	..
Lithuania	−2.7	8.0	−0.8	1.9	3.2	10.3	5.5	9.9	5.5	7.4
Macedonia, FYR	−0.8	2.7	0.2	1.3	−2.3	2.0	−5.3	1.1	0.5	3.2
Madagascar	2.0	3.2	1.9	1.9	2.4	2.7	2.0	3.8	2.3	3.6
Malawi	3.7	3.3	8.6	0.2	2.0	4.6	0.5	2.8	1.6	4.0
Malaysia[a]	7.0	5.4	0.3	3.8	8.6	4.6	9.5	5.8	7.3	6.6
Mali	4.1	5.4	2.6	4.8	6.4	4.5	−1.4	5.1	3.0	6.5
Mauritania	2.9	5.1	−0.2	0.6	3.4	4.2	5.8	−1.4	4.9	6.9
Mauritius	5.2	4.0	−0.5	0.6	5.5	1.4	5.3	0.2	6.4	6.0
Mexico	3.1	2.6	1.5	2.0	3.8	1.7	4.3	1.7	2.9	3.0
Moldova	−9.6	6.5	−11.2	−1.8	−13.6	0.8	−7.1	4.8	0.7	11.5
Mongolia	1.0	7.5	2.5	4.6	−2.5	7.9	−9.7	8.1	0.7	8.4
Morocco	2.4	5.0	−0.4	5.4	3.2	4.4	2.6	3.3	3.1	5.1
Mozambique	6.1	8.1	5.2	7.5	12.3	11.2	10.2	11.0	5.0	6.7
Myanmar[a]	6.9	9.2	5.7	..	10.5	..	7.9	..	7.2	..
Namibia	4.0	4.8	3.8	1.4	2.4	5.9	2.6	3.5	4.5	5.4
Nepal	4.9	3.4	2.5	3.3	7.1	2.7	8.9	0.9	6.2	3.4
Netherlands	3.2	1.6	1.8	1.1	1.7	0.6	2.6	0.7	3.6	2.1
New Zealand	3.2	3.4	2.9	2.5	2.4	2.8	2.2	2.6	3.6	3.9
Nicaragua	3.7	3.4	4.7	3.0	5.5	4.4	5.3	5.5	5.0	3.5
Niger[a]	2.4	3.9	3.0	..	2.0	..	2.6	..	1.9	..
Nigeria	2.5	6.6	..	7.0	..	3.8	..	..	..	14.3
Norway	3.9	2.4	2.6	3.7	3.8	0.6	1.5	3.7	3.9	3.1
Oman[a]	4.5	4.7	5.0	2.2	3.9	−0.5	6.0	9.3	5.0	7.5
Pakistan	3.8	5.6	4.4	3.4	4.1	7.9	3.8	9.9	4.4	6.0
Panama	4.7	6.0	3.1	4.1	6.0	4.0	2.7	0.6	4.5	6.5
Papua New Guinea	3.8	2.3	4.5	1.4	5.4	3.2	4.6	3.2	−0.6	2.7
Paraguay[a]	2.2	3.3	3.3	5.4	0.6	1.7	1.4	1.2	2.5	3.0
Peru	4.7	5.4	5.5	3.6	5.4	6.3	3.8	6.2	4.0	5.3
Philippines[a]	3.3	5.1	1.7	3.8	3.5	4.0	3.0	4.5	4.0	6.5
Poland	4.7	4.1	0.5	3.9	7.1	4.7	9.9	6.9	5.1	3.5
Portugal	2.8	0.9	−0.4	0.5	3.2	−0.4	2.6	−0.1	2.4	1.6
Puerto Rico[a]	4.2	..	..	..	..	..	..	..	..	..

4.1 Growth of output

	Gross domestic product		Agriculture		Industry		Manufacturing		Services	
	average annual % growth		average annual % growth		average annual % growth		average annual % growth		average annual % growth	
	1990–2000	2000–07	1990–2000	2000–07	1990–2000	2000–07	1990–2000	2000–07	1990–2000	2000–07
Romania	−0.6	6.1	−1.9	7.7	−1.2	6.5	..	..	0.9	4.8
Russian Federation	−4.7	6.6	−4.9	3.9	−7.1	5.8	..	..	−1.7	7.2
Rwanda[a]	−0.2	5.8	2.5	4.0	−3.8	8.2	−5.8	6.7	−0.9	6.7
Saudi Arabia[a]	2.1	4.1	1.6	1.4	2.2	4.5	5.6	6.1	2.2	4.1
Senegal	3.0	4.5	2.4	0.7	3.8	4.1	3.1	1.9	3.0	6.1
Serbia	−4.7	5.6	..	..	..	..	..	..	..	..
Sierra Leone	−5.0	11.2	−13.0	..	−4.5	..	6.1	..	−2.9	..
Singapore	7.6	5.8	−2.4	2.9	7.8	5.5	7.0	7.0	7.8	6.0
Slovak Republic	2.2	6.0	0.4	1.4	3.8	7.0	9.3	10.7	5.3	5.4
Slovenia	2.7	4.3	0.4	−1.8	1.6	5.3	1.8	5.3	3.3	4.2
Somalia	..	..	..	..	..	..	..	..	..	..
South Africa	2.1	4.3	1.0	0.4	1.1	3.4	1.6	3.2	2.7	5.0
Spain	2.7	3.4	3.1	−1.6	2.3	2.8	..	1.1	2.7	3.7
Sri Lanka[a]	5.3	5.3	1.8	1.8	6.9	5.0	8.1	4.0	5.7	6.3
Sudan	5.5	7.1	7.4	1.8	8.5	10.2	7.5	3.5	1.9	10.3
Swaziland	3.4	2.6	0.9	1.2	3.2	1.7	2.8	1.6	3.9	4.1
Sweden	2.2	3.0	−0.8	2.6	4.3	4.3	..	..	1.8	2.5
Switzerland	1.0	1.8	−0.9	−1.1	0.3	1.7	..	..	1.2	1.4
Syrian Arab Republic	5.1	4.5	6.0	3.6	9.2	2.8	..	16.2	1.5	7.9
Tajikistan	−10.4	8.8	−6.8	8.8	−11.4	9.8	−12.6	9.5	−10.8	8.3
Tanzania[b]	2.9	6.7	3.2	4.9	3.1	9.6	2.7	8.0	2.7	6.2
Thailand[a]	4.2	5.3	1.0	2.6	5.7	6.6	6.9	6.8	3.7	4.7
Timor-Leste[a]	..	0.9	..	..	..	..	..	..	..	..
Togo[a]	3.5	2.6	4.0	2.8	1.8	8.1	1.8	7.5	3.9	−0.7
Trinidad and Tobago	3.2	8.8	2.7	−10.8	3.2	12.3	4.9	8.7	3.2	5.2
Tunisia[a]	4.7	4.8	2.3	2.9	4.6	3.3	5.5	3.2	5.3	6.0
Turkey	3.9	5.9	1.3	1.5	4.7	6.9	4.7	6.5	4.0	6.1
Turkmenistan	−4.8	..	−5.7	..	−3.4	..	..	..	−5.4	..
Uganda	7.1	7.1	3.7	1.3	12.1	10.3	14.1	6.6	8.2	9.8
Ukraine	−9.3	7.6	−5.6	2.6	−12.6	6.8	−11.2	11.1	−8.1	7.2
United Arab Emirates	4.8	7.7	13.2	3.6	3.0	6.0	11.9	8.1	7.2	9.6
United Kingdom	2.7	2.6	−0.3	1.4	1.5	0.1	1.3	−0.4	3.3	3.4
United States	3.5	2.6	3.7	3.2	3.7	1.3	..	2.1	3.4	2.9
Uruguay	3.4	3.3	2.8	6.1	1.1	3.7	−0.1	5.3	3.7	2.3
Uzbekistan	−0.2	6.2	0.5	6.8	−3.4	4.2	0.7	1.9	0.4	7.0
Venezuela, RB	1.6	4.6	1.2	3.8	1.2	2.4	4.5	2.4	−0.1	6.3
Vietnam[a]	7.9	7.8	4.3	3.8	11.9	10.3	11.2	11.9	7.5	7.4
West Bank and Gaza	7.3	−0.9	..	..	..	..	..	..	..	..
Yemen, Rep.[a]	6.0	4.0	5.6	..	8.2	..	5.7	..	5.0	..
Zambia	0.5	5.1	4.2	2.0	−4.2	9.4	0.8	5.3	2.5	6.5
Zimbabwe	2.1	−5.7	4.3	−8.5	0.4	−10.0	0.4	−12.0	2.9	−10.0
World	**2.9 w**	**3.2 w**	**2.0 w**	**2.5 w**	**2.4 w**	**3.0 w**	**.. w**	**3.3 w**	**3.1 w**	**3.0 w**
Low income	3.4	5.6	3.3	3.5	4.5	7.3	4.7	7.8	3.6	5.8
Middle income	3.9	6.2	2.3	3.6	4.7	7.1	6.3	7.1	4.3	6.2
Lower middle income	6.2	8.0	2.9	3.8	7.9	9.1	8.4	9.1	6.3	8.4
Upper middle income	2.2	4.3	0.8	3.2	1.6	4.3	3.7	4.2	3.0	4.4
Low & middle income	3.9	6.2	2.5	3.6	4.7	7.2	6.2	7.2	4.2	6.2
East Asia & Pacific	8.5	9.0	3.5	4.0	11.0	10.1	10.9	9.7	8.0	9.3
Europe & Central Asia	−0.8	6.1	−1.8	3.3	−2.6	6.5	..	..	0.9	6.1
Latin America & Carib.	3.2	3.6	2.1	3.5	3.1	3.3	2.9	3.3	3.5	3.6
Middle East & N. Africa	3.8	4.5	2.9	4.4	4.1	3.6	4.2	6.0	3.4	5.1
South Asia	5.5	7.3	3.3	3.1	6.0	8.3	6.4	8.1	6.9	8.6
Sub-Saharan Africa	2.5	5.1	3.2	3.0	2.0	5.2	2.1	3.2	2.5	5.1
High income	2.7	2.4	1.3	0.7	1.9	1.7	..	2.1	2.9	2.5
Euro area	2.1	1.7	1.6	−0.6	1.1	1.6	1.2	1.1	2.5	1.9

a. Components are at producer prices. b. Covers mainland Tanzania only.

About the data

An economy's growth is measured by the change in the volume of its output or in the real incomes of its residents. The 1993 United Nations System of National Accounts (1993 SNA) offers three plausible indicators for calculating growth: the volume of gross domestic product (GDP), real gross domestic income, and real gross national income. The volume of GDP is the sum of value added, measured at constant prices, by households, government, and industries operating in the economy.

Each industry's contribution to growth in the economy's output is measured by growth in the industry's value added. In principle, value added in constant prices can be estimated by measuring the quantity of goods and services produced in a period, valuing them at an agreed set of base year prices, and subtracting the cost of intermediate inputs, also in constant prices. This double-deflation method, recommended by the 1993 SNA and its predecessors, requires detailed information on the structure of prices of inputs and outputs.

In many industries, however, value added is extrapolated from the base year using single volume indexes of outputs or, less commonly, inputs. Particularly in the services industries, including most of government, value added in constant prices is often imputed from labor inputs, such as real wages or number of employees. In the absence of well defined measures of output, measuring the growth of services remains difficult.

Moreover, technical progress can lead to improvements in production processes and in the quality of goods and services that, if not properly accounted for, can distort measures of value added and thus of growth. When inputs are used to estimate output, as for nonmarket services, unmeasured technical progress leads to underestimates of the volume of output. Similarly, unmeasured improvements in quality lead to underestimates of the value of output and value added. The result can be underestimates of growth and productivity improvement and overestimates of inflation.

Informal economic activities pose a particular measurement problem, especially in developing countries, where much economic activity is unrecorded. A complete picture of the economy requires estimating household outputs produced for home use, sales in informal markets, barter exchanges, and illicit or deliberately unreported activities. The consistency and completeness of such estimates depend on the skill and methods of the compiling statisticians.

Rebasing national accounts

When countries rebase their national accounts, they update the weights assigned to various components to better reflect current patterns of production or uses of output. The new base year should represent normal operation of the economy—it should be a year without major shocks or distortions. Some developing countries have not rebased their national accounts for many years. Using an old base year can be misleading because implicit price and volume weights become progressively less relevant and useful.

To obtain comparable series of constant price data, the World Bank rescales GDP and value added by industrial origin to a common reference year. This year's *World Development Indicators* continues to use 2000 as the reference year. Because rescaling changes the implicit weights used in forming regional and income group aggregates, aggregate growth rates in this year's edition are not comparable with those from earlier editions with different base years.

Rescaling may result in a discrepancy between the rescaled GDP and the sum of the rescaled components. Because allocating the discrepancy would cause distortions in the growth rates, the discrepancy is left unallocated. As a result, the weighted average of the growth rates of the components generally will not equal the GDP growth rate.

Computing growth rates

Growth rates of GDP and its components are calculated using the least squares method and constant price data in the local currency. Constant price U.S. dollar series are used to calculate regional and income group growth rates. Local currency series are converted to constant U.S. dollars using an exchange rate in the common reference year. The growth rates in the table are average annual compound growth rates. Methods of computing growth rates and the alternative conversion factor are described in *Statistical methods*.

Changes in the System of National Accounts

World Development Indicators adopted the terminology of the 1993 SNA in 2001. Although many countries continue to compile their national accounts according to the SNA version 3 (referred to as the 1968 SNA), more and more are adopting the 1993 SNA. Some low-income countries still use concepts from the even older 1953 SNA guidelines, including valuations such as factor cost, in describing major economic aggregates. Countries that use the 1993 SNA are identified in *Primary data documentation*.

Definitions

• **Gross domestic product (GDP)** at purchaser prices is the sum of gross value added by all resident producers in the economy plus any product taxes (less subsidies) not included in the valuation of output. It is calculated without deducting for depreciation of fabricated capital assets or for depletion and degradation of natural resources. Value added is the net output of an industry after adding up all outputs and subtracting intermediate inputs. The industrial origin of value added is determined by the International Standard Industrial Classification (ISIC) revision 3. • **Agriculture** is the sum of gross output less the value of intermediate input used in production for industries classified in ISIC divisions 1–5 and includes forestry and fishing. • **Industry** is the sum of gross output less the value of intermediate input used in production for industries classified in ISIC divisions 10–45, which cover mining, manufacturing (also reported separately), construction, electricity, water, and gas. • **Manufacturing** is the sum of gross output less the value of intermediate input used in production for industries classified in ISIC divisions 15–37. • **Services** correspond to ISIC divisions 50–99. This sector is derived as a residual (from GDP less agriculture and industry) and may not properly reflect the sum of services output, including banking and financial services. For some countries it includes product taxes (minus subsidies) and may also include statistical discrepancies.

Data sources

Data on national accounts for most developing countries are collected from national statistical organizations and central banks by visiting and resident World Bank missions. Data for high-income economies are from Organisation for Economic Co-operation and Development (OECD) data files. The World Bank rescales constant price data to a common reference year. The complete national accounts time series is available on the *World Development Indicators 2009* CD-ROM. The United Nations Statistics Division publishes detailed national accounts for UN member countries in *National Accounts Statistics: Main Aggregates and Detailed Tables* and publishes updates in the *Monthly Bulletin of Statistics*.

4.2 Structure of output

	Gross domestic product		Agriculture		Industry		Manufacturing		Services	
	$ millions		% of GDP		% of GDP		% of GDP		% of GDP	
	1995	2007	1995	2007	1995	2007	1995	2007	1995	2007
Afghanistan	..	8,399	..	36	..	24	..	15	..	39
Albania	2,424	10,831	56	21	22	20	14	..	22	59
Algeria	41,764	135,285	10	8	50	61	11	5	39	31
Angola[a]	5,040	61,403	7	9	66	70	4	5	26	21
Argentina	258,032	262,451	6	9	28	34	18	21	66	57
Armenia	1,468	9,204	42	20	32	44	25	17	26	36
Australia	361,306	820,974	3	2	29	29	15	11	68	69
Austria	239,561	373,192	3	2	30	31	19	20	67	67
Azerbaijan	3,052	31,248	27	6	34	73	13	6	39	21
Bangladesh	37,940	68,415	26	19	25	28	15	18	49	52
Belarus	13,973	44,773	17	9	37	42	31	32	46	48
Belgium	284,321	452,754	2	1	28	24	20	17	70	75
Benin[a]	2,009	5,428	34	32	15	13	9	8	51	54
Bolivia	6,715	13,120	17	13	33	36	19	15	50	51
Bosnia and Herzegovina	1,867	15,144	21	10	26	22	11	13	54	69
Botswana	4,774	12,311	4	2	51	49	5	3	45	49
Brazil	768,951	1,313,361	6	6	28	29	19	18	67	66
Bulgaria	13,107	39,549	14	6	35	32	24	17	50	61
Burkina Faso	2,380	6,767	35	33	21	22	15	14	43	44
Burundi	1,000	974	48	35	19	20	9	9	33	45
Cambodia	3,239	8,350	50	32	15	27	10	19	36	41
Cameroon	8,733	20,686	24	19	31	31	22	17	45	50
Canada	590,517	1,329,885	3	..	31	..	18	..	66	..
Central African Republic	1,122	1,712	46	54	21	14	10	8	33	32
Chad	1,446	7,085	36	23	14	44	11	6	51	32
Chile	71,349	163,913	9	4	35	47	18	14	55	49
China[a]	728,007	3,205,507	20	11	47	49	34	32	33	40
Hong Kong, China	144,230	207,169	0	0	15	8	8	3	85	92
Colombia	92,503	207,786	15	9	32	35	16	18	53	56
Congo, Dem. Rep.	5,643	8,953	57	42	17	28	9	6	26	29
Congo, Rep.[a]	2,116	7,646	10	5	45	60	8	6	45	35
Costa Rica	11,722	26,267	14	9	30	29	22	21	57	63
Côte d'Ivoire[a]	11,000	19,796	25	24	21	25	15	18	55	51
Croatia	18,808	51,278	11	7	34	32	24	21	55	61
Cuba[a]	..	..	6	..	45	..	38	..	49	..
Czech Republic	55,257	174,998	5	3	38	39	24	27	57	59
Denmark	181,985	311,580	3	1	25	26	17	14	71	73
Dominican Republic[a]	12,585	36,686	13	12	33	28	18	13	55	60
Ecuador	20,206	44,490	..	7	..	37	..	10	..	56
Egypt, Arab Rep.	60,159	130,476	17	14	32	36	17	16	51	50
El Salvador	9,500	20,373	14	12	30	29	23	22	56	59
Eritrea	578	1,375	21	24	17	19	9	5	62	56
Estonia	4,343	20,901	6	3	33	30	21	18	61	67
Ethiopia	7,606	19,395	57	46	10	13	5	5	33	40
Finland	130,605	244,661	4	3	33	32	25	24	63	65
France	1,569,983	2,589,839	3	2	25	21	..	12	72	77
Gabon[a]	4,959	11,568	8	5	52	60	5	4	40	35
Gambia, The	382	644	30	29	13	15	6	5	57	56
Georgia	2,694	10,175	52	11	16	24	17	12	32	65
Germany	2,522,792	3,317,365	1	1	32	30	23	23	67	69
Ghana[a]	6,457	15,147	39	34	24	26	9	8	37	41
Greece	131,718	313,354	9	4	21	23	..	13	70	73
Guatemala[a]	14,657	33,855	24	11	20	28	14	18	56	61
Guinea	3,694	4,564	19	17	29	45	4	4	52	38
Guinea-Bissau	254	357	55	64	12	12	8	8	33	24
Haiti	2,908	6,715	25	..	32	..	20	..	44	..

Structure of output 4.2

	Gross domestic product		Agriculture		Industry		Manufacturing		Services	
	$ millions		% of GDP		% of GDP		% of GDP		% of GDP	
	1995	2007	1995	2007	1995	2007	1995	2007	1995	2007
Honduras	3,911	12,234	22	13	31	28	18	20	48	59
Hungary	44,656	138,429	7	4	32	30	24	22	61	66
India	356,299	1,176,890	26	18	28	30	18	16	46	52
Indonesia[a]	202,132	432,817	17	14	42	47	24	27	41	39
Iran, Islamic Rep.	90,829	286,058	18	10	34	44	12	11	47	45
Iraq	10,114	..	9	..	75	..	1	..	16	..
Ireland	67,090	259,018	7	2	38	35	30	23	55	63
Israel[a]	95,907	163,957	..	..	..	..	..	..	..	..
Italy	1,126,042	2,101,637	3	2	30	27	22	18	66	71
Jamaica	5,813	11,430	9	6	37	35	16	15	54	59
Japan	5,247,609	4,384,255	2	1	34	30	23	21	64	68
Jordan	6,727	15,833	4	3	29	29	15	19	67	67
Kazakhstan	20,374	104,853	13	6	32	41	15	12	55	53
Kenya	9,046	24,190	31	26	16	18	10	11	53	56
Korea, Dem. Rep.	..	..	..	..	..	..	..	..	..	..
Korea, Rep.	517,118	969,795	6	3	42	39	28	28	52	58
Kuwait[a]	27,192	112,116	0	..	55	..	4	..	45	..
Kyrgyz Republic	1,661	3,745	44	34	20	19	9	11	37	47
Lao PDR	1,764	4,108	56	42	19	32	14	21	25	26
Latvia	5,236	27,155	9	3	30	22	21	11	61	75
Lebanon	11,719	24,352	7	6	27	24	15	11	66	70
Lesotho	1,009	1,600	16	12	36	47	15	19	48	41
Liberia	135	735	82	54	5	19	3	13	13	27
Libya	25,541	58,333	..	..	..	..	..	..	..	..
Lithuania	7,507	38,332	12	5	34	33	21	19	55	61
Macedonia, FYR	4,449	7,674	13	12	30	30	23	19	57	59
Madagascar	3,160	7,382	27	26	9	17	8	16	64	56
Malawi	1,397	3,563	30	34	20	20	16	14	50	45
Malaysia[a]	88,832	186,719	13	10	41	48	26	28	46	42
Mali	2,466	6,863	50	37	19	24	8	3	32	39
Mauritania	1,415	2,644	37	13	25	47	8	5	37	41
Mauritius	3,820	6,786	10	5	32	28	23	20	58	67
Mexico	286,698	1,022,815	6	4	28	36	21	19	66	60
Moldova	1,753	4,396	33	12	32	15	26	14	35	73
Mongolia	1,227	3,930	41	23	29	41	12	4	30	36
Morocco	32,986	75,119	15	14	34	27	19	15	51	59
Mozambique	2,247	7,790	35	28	15	26	8	15	51	47
Myanmar[a]	..	..	60	..	10	..	7	..	30	..
Namibia	3,503	7,015	12	11	28	30	13	11	60	59
Nepal	4,401	10,315	42	34	23	17	10	8	35	49
Netherlands	418,969	765,818	3	2	27	24	17	13	69	74
New Zealand	62,049	135,667	7	..	27	..	19	..	66	..
Nicaragua	3,191	5,726	23	19	27	30	19	19	49	51
Niger[a]	1,881	4,170	40	..	17	..	6	..	43	..
Nigeria	28,109	165,469	..	33	..	39	..	3	..	28
Norway	148,920	388,413	3	1	34	43	13	10	63	56
Oman[a]	13,803	35,729	3	..	46	..	5	..	51	..
Pakistan	60,636	142,893	26	21	24	27	16	19	50	53
Panama	7,906	19,485	8	7	18	17	9	7	74	77
Papua New Guinea	4,636	6,259	35	35	34	45	8	6	31	20
Paraguay[a]	8,066	12,222	21	22	23	20	16	13	56	58
Peru	53,674	107,297	9	7	31	37	17	16	60	56
Philippines[a]	74,120	144,062	22	14	32	32	23	22	46	54
Poland	139,062	422,090	8	4	35	31	21	18	57	65
Portugal	112,960	222,758	6	3	28	24	18	15	66	73
Puerto Rico[a]	42,647	..	1	..	44	..	42	..	55	..

4.2 Structure of output

	Gross domestic product ($ millions)		Agriculture (% of GDP)		Industry (% of GDP)		Manufacturing (% of GDP)		Services (% of GDP)	
	1995	2007	1995	2007	1995	2007	1995	2007	1995	2007
Romania	35,477	165,976	21	9	43	36	29	22	36	55
Russian Federation	395,529	1,290,082	7	5	37	38	..	19	56	57
Rwanda[a]	1,293	3,339	44	40	16	14	10	6	40	46
Saudi Arabia[a]	142,458	381,683	6	3	49	65	10	10	45	32
Senegal	4,879	11,165	21	14	24	23	17	14	55	62
Serbia	19,681	40,122	..	13	..	28	..	..	..	59
Sierra Leone	871	1,664	43	45	39	24	9	..	18	31
Singapore	84,291	161,347	0	0	35	31	27	25	65	69
Slovak Republic	19,579	74,972	6	3	38	36	27	22	56	61
Slovenia	20,814	47,182	4	2	35	34	26	23	60	63
Somalia	..	..	..	..	..	..	..	..	..	..
South Africa	151,113	283,007	4	3	35	31	21	18	61	66
Spain	596,751	1,436,891	5	3	29	30	..	16	66	67
Sri Lanka[a]	13,030	32,346	23	12	27	30	16	19	50	58
Sudan	13,830	46,228	39	28	11	31	5	6	51	41
Swaziland	1,699	2,894	12	7	45	49	39	44	43	43
Sweden	253,706	454,310	3	2	31	29	..	..	67	70
Switzerland	315,940	424,367	2	1	30	28	..	..	68	71
Syrian Arab Republic	11,397	37,745	32	18	20	35	15	12	48	47
Tajikistan	1,232	3,712	38	21	39	28	28	20	22	51
Tanzania[b]	5,255	16,181	47	45	14	17	7	7	38	37
Thailand[a]	167,896	245,351	10	11	41	44	30	35	50	45
Timor-Leste[a]	..	395	..	..	..	..	..	..	..	..
Togo[a]	1,309	2,499	38	44	22	24	10	10	40	32
Trinidad and Tobago	5,329	20,886	2	0	47	59	9	6	51	41
Tunisia[a]	18,031	35,020	11	10	29	30	19	17	59	60
Turkey	244,946	655,881	11	9	23	28	..	19	66	63
Turkmenistan	2,482	12,933	17	..	63	..	40	..	20	..
Uganda	5,756	11,771	49	24	14	26	7	8	36	50
Ukraine	48,214	141,177	15	8	43	37	35	23	42	55
United Arab Emirates	42,807	163,296	3	2	52	59	10	12	45	39
United Kingdom	1,141,045	2,772,024	2	1	32	23	22	14	66	76
United States	7,342,300	13,751,400	2	1	26	22	19	14	72	77
Uruguay	18,348	23,136	9	10	29	32	20	23	62	58
Uzbekistan	13,350	22,308	32	23	28	31	12	12	40	46
Venezuela, RB	74,889	228,071	6	4	41	58	15	16	53	38
Vietnam[a]	20,736	68,643	27	20	29	42	15	21	44	38
West Bank and Gaza	3,220	4,016	..	..	..	..	..	..	..	..
Yemen, Rep.[a]	4,236	22,523	20	..	32	..	14	..	48	..
Zambia	3,478	11,363	18	22	36	38	11	11	46	40
Zimbabwe	7,111	3,418	15	19	29	24	22	14	56	57
World	29,669,867 t	54,583,788 t	4 w	3 w	30 w	28 w	20 w	18 w	65 w	69 w
Low income	301,247	801,382	32	25	23	30	13	16	45	46
Middle income	4,878,804	13,490,034	13	9	35	37	23	19	52	53
Lower middle income	2,149,301	6,896,111	20	13	39	41	25	24	41	46
Upper middle income	2,731,355	6,594,607	7	6	31	33	20	19	62	61
Low & middle income	5,181,211	14,296,294	14	10	34	37	22	18	52	53
East Asia & Pacific	1,312,340	4,365,487	19	12	44	47	31	30	36	41
Europe & Central Asia	998,317	3,156,118	11	7	33	34	..	19	56	60
Latin America & Carib.	1,751,109	3,615,910	7	6	29	33	19	18	64	61
Middle East & N. Africa	315,655	850,182	16	11	34	40	15	12	50	49
South Asia	476,196	1,443,539	26	18	27	29	17	17	46	53
Sub-Saharan Africa	327,582	847,438	18	15	29	32	16	14	53	53
High income	24,484,804	40,309,714	2	1	30	26	20	17	68	72
Euro area	7,274,362	12,277,625	3	2	29	27	22	18	68	71

a. Components are at producer prices. b. Covers mainland Tanzania only.

About the data

An economy's gross domestic product (GDP) represents the sum of value added by all producers in the economy. Value added is the value of the gross output of producers less the value of intermediate goods and services consumed in production, before taking account of the consumption of fixed capital in the production process. The United Nations System of National Accounts calls for estimates of value added to be valued at either basic prices (excluding net taxes on products) or producer prices (including net taxes on products paid by producers but excluding sales or value added taxes). Both valuations exclude transport charges that are invoiced separately by producers. Total GDP shown in the table and elsewhere in this volume is measured at purchaser prices. Value added by industry is normally measured at basic prices. When value added is measured at producer prices, this is noted in *Primary data documentation*.

While GDP estimates based on the production approach are generally more reliable than estimates compiled from the income or expenditure side, different countries use different definitions, methods, and reporting standards. World Bank staff review the quality of national accounts data and sometimes make adjustments to improve consistency with international guidelines. Nevertheless, significant discrepancies remain between international standards and actual practice. Many statistical offices, especially those in developing countries, face severe limitations in the resources, time, training, and budgets required to produce reliable and comprehensive series of national accounts statistics.

Data problems in measuring output

Among the difficulties faced by compilers of national accounts is the extent of unreported economic activity in the informal or secondary economy. In developing countries a large share of agricultural output is either not exchanged (because it is consumed within the household) or not exchanged for money.

Agricultural production often must be estimated indirectly, using a combination of methods involving estimates of inputs, yields, and area under cultivation. This approach sometimes leads to crude approximations that can differ from the true values over time and across crops for reasons other than climate conditions or farming techniques. Similarly, agricultural inputs that cannot easily be allocated to specific outputs are frequently "netted out" using equally crude and ad hoc approximations. For further discussion of the measurement of agricultural production, see *About the data* for table 3.3.

Ideally, industrial output should be measured through regular censuses and surveys of firms. But in most developing countries such surveys are infrequent, so earlier survey results must be extrapolated using an appropriate indicator. The choice of sampling unit, which may be the enterprise (where responses may be based on financial records) or the establishment (where production units may be recorded separately), also affects the quality of the data. Moreover, much industrial production is organized in unincorporated or owner-operated ventures that are not captured by surveys aimed at the formal sector. Even in large industries, where regular surveys are more likely, evasion of excise and other taxes and nondisclosure of income lower the estimates of value added. Such problems become more acute as countries move from state control of industry to private enterprise, because new firms enter business and growing numbers of established firms fail to report. In accordance with the System of National Accounts, output should include all such unreported activity as well as the value of illegal activities and other unrecorded, informal, or small-scale operations. Data on these activities need to be collected using techniques other than conventional surveys of firms.

In industries dominated by large organizations and enterprises, such as public utilities, data on output, employment, and wages are usually readily available and reasonably reliable. But in the services industry the many self-employed workers and one-person businesses are sometimes difficult to locate, and they have little incentive to respond to surveys, let alone to report their full earnings. Compounding these problems are the many forms of economic activity that go unrecorded, including the work that women and children do for little or no pay. For further discussion of the problems of using national accounts data, see Srinivasan (1994) and Heston (1994).

Dollar conversion

To produce national accounts aggregates that are measured in the same standard monetary units, the value of output must be converted to a single common currency. The World Bank conventionally uses the U.S. dollar and applies the average official exchange rate reported by the International Monetary Fund for the year shown. An alternative conversion factor is applied if the official exchange rate is judged to diverge by an exceptionally large margin from the rate effectively applied to transactions in foreign currencies and traded products.

Definitions

• **Gross domestic product (GDP)** at purchaser prices is the sum of gross value added by all resident producers in the economy plus any product taxes (less subsidies) not included in the valuation of output. It is calculated without deducting for depreciation of fabricated assets or for depletion and degradation of natural resources. Value added is the net output of an industry after adding up all outputs and subtracting intermediate inputs. The industrial origin of value added is determined by the International Standard Industrial Classification (ISIC) revision 3. • **Agriculture** is the sum of gross output less the value of intermediate input used in production for industries classified in ISIC divisions 1–5 and includes forestry and fishing. • **Industry** is the sum of gross output less the value of intermediate input used in production for industries classified in ISIC divisions 10–45, which cover mining, manufacturing (also reported separately), construction, electricity, water, and gas. • **Manufacturing** is the sum of gross output less the value of intermediate input used in production for industries classified in ISIC divisions 15–37. • **Services** correspond to ISIC divisions 50–99. This sector is derived as a residual (from GDP less agriculture and industry) and may not properly reflect the sum of services output, including banking and financial services. For some countries it includes product taxes (minus subsidies) and may also include statistical discrepancies.

Data sources

Data on national accounts for most developing countries are collected from national statistical organizations and central banks by visiting and resident World Bank missions. Data for high-income economies are from Organisation for Economic Co-operation and Development (OECD) data files. The complete national accounts time series is available on the *World Development Indicators 2009* CD-ROM. The United Nations Statistics Division publishes detailed national accounts for UN member countries in *National Accounts Statistics: Main Aggregates and Detailed Tables* and publishes updates in the *Monthly Bulletin of Statistics*.

4.3 Structure of manufacturing

	Manufacturing value added		Food, beverages, and tobacco		Textiles and clothing		Machinery and transport equipment		Chemicals		Other manufacturing[a]	
	$ millions		% of total		% of total		% of total		% of total		% of total	
	1995	2007	1995	2005	1995	2005	1995	2005	1995	2005	1995	2005
Afghanistan	..	1,053	..	..	..	..	..	..	..	..	..	..
Albania	405	1,830	..	20	..	..	..	..	..	..	..	80
Algeria	4,366	6,393	..	..	..	..	..	..	..	..	..	..
Angola	202	3,074	..	..	..	..	..	..	..	..	..	..
Argentina	44,502	51,305	30	..	6	..	10	..	9	..	54	..
Armenia	356	1,380	..	..	..	..	..	..	..	..	..	..
Australia	50,044	81,096	20	17	6	1	11	5	..	7	63	69
Austria	41,681	58,005	11	10	5	2	27	31	2	6	56	52
Azerbaijan	352	1,604	..	28	..	1	..	11	..	7	..	53
Bangladesh	5,586	11,755	28	..	44	..	4	..	11	..	13	..
Belarus	3,909	12,194	..	..	..	..	..	..	..	..	..	..
Belgium	51,721	59,893	13	13	6	4	22	21	8	20	51	42
Benin	174	322	..	..	..	..	..	..	..	..	..	..
Bolivia	1,123	1,498	36	..	5	..	1	..	3	..	55	..
Bosnia and Herzegovina	213	1,614	..	..	..	..	..	..	..	..	..	..
Botswana	242	381	44	23	1	0	15	..	5	..	55	77
Brazil	124,976	199,714	21	18	6	4	23	22	13	12	38	44
Bulgaria	2,015	5,395	23	17	12	15	20	18	15	7	30	44
Burkina Faso	336	775	..	..	..	..	..	..	..	..	..	..
Burundi	83	64	..	..	..	..	..	..	..	..	..	..
Cambodia	296	1,447	20	..	3	..	..	..	..	..	80	..
Cameroon	1,758	3,328	..	..	..	..	..	..	..	..	..	..
Canada	100,393	..	13	..	4	..	23	..	10	..	50	..
Central African Republic	108	129	..	..	..	..	..	..	..	..	..	..
Chad	159	398	..	..	..	..	..	..	..	..	..	..
Chile	10,594	21,488	..	16	..	2	..	3	..	8	..	72
China	245,002	1,341,337	4	4	2	2	2	3	..	..	93	93
Hong Kong, China	10,524	5,034	..	..	..	..	..	..	..	..	..	..
Colombia	13,506	33,565	..	27	..	9	..	7	..	13	..	44
Congo, Dem. Rep.	510	543	..	..	..	..	..	..	..	..	..	..
Congo, Rep.	172	456	..	..	..	..	..	..	..	..	..	..
Costa Rica	2,339	4,900	..	..	..	..	..	..	..	..	..	..
Côte d'Ivoire	1,655	3,471	..	..	..	..	..	..	..	..	..	..
Croatia	3,666	8,832	..	..	..	..	..	..	..	..	..	..
Cuba	..	..	..	..	..	..	..	..	..	..	..	..
Czech Republic	12,124	42,681	12	10	6	4	24	29	4	3	55	54
Denmark	26,924	31,100	20	14	2	2	25	18	1	2	52	64
Dominican Republic	2,286	4,852	..	..	..	..	..	..	..	..	..	..
Ecuador	2,830	4,063	26	30	7	4	4	3	4	5	59	58
Egypt, Arab Rep.	9,829	19,520	19	..	13	..	12	..	18	..	38	..
El Salvador	2,026	4,209	..	..	..	..	..	..	..	..	..	..
Eritrea	47	72	55	43	12	12	1	2	19	8	13	35
Estonia	804	3,193	..	13	..	6	..	14	..	5	..	63
Ethiopia	344	923	51	48	20	10	2	1	4	5	23	35
Finland	28,814	43,121	10	7	3	2	27	35	4	4	57	52
France	..	283,186	13	14	5	4	28	29	12	12	41	41
Gabon	224	470	..	..	..	..	..	..	..	..	..	..
Gambia, The	20	28	65	..	..	..	..	..	..	..	35	..
Georgia	523	1,080	..	41	..	2	..	5	..	13	..	39
Germany	516,542	595,045	..	9	..	2	..	42	..	10	..	38
Ghana	602	1,199	..	32	..	6	..	0	..	12	..	49
Greece	..	31,426	25	..	15	..	13	..	10	..	38	..
Guatemala	2,069	6,203	..	..	..	..	..	..	..	..	..	..
Guinea	142	178	..	..	..	..	..	..	..	..	..	..
Guinea-Bissau	19	26	..	..	..	..	..	..	..	..	..	..
Haiti	558	..	..	..	..	..	..	..	..	..	..	..

Structure of manufacturing | **4.3**

	Manufacturing value added		Food, beverages, and tobacco		Textiles and clothing		Machinery and transport equipment		Chemicals		Other manufacturing[a]	
	$ millions		% of total		% of total		% of total		% of total		% of total	
	1995	2007	1995	2005	1995	2005	1995	2005	1995	2005	1995	2005
Honduras	607	2,218	..	..	..	..	..	..	..	..	..	..
Hungary	8,839	25,977	19	13	3	4	10	41	13	10	55	33
India	57,917	175,691	..	9	..	9	..	20	..	16	..	46
Indonesia	48,781	116,894	..	23	..	13	..	18	..	9	..	36
Iran, Islamic Rep.	10,918	29,832	15	9	12	4	18	25	15	15	40	47
Iraq	67	..	12	..	7	..	2	..	..	..	80	..
Ireland	18,096	44,801	15	16	0	0	24	7	13	27	49	50
Israel	..	..	13	11	5	2	15	16	6	10	61	61
Italy	225,514	299,459	9	9	14	11	27	26	8	7	41	46
Jamaica	865	1,631	..	..	..	..	..	..	..	..	..	..
Japan	1,077,348	933,818	11	11	4	2	37	41	10	11	39	35
Jordan	866	2,665	30	23	7	11	5	6	15	16	44	43
Kazakhstan	2,976	12,049	..	..	..	..	..	..	..	..	..	..
Kenya	757	2,355	..	29	..	2	..	..	..	5	..	64
Korea, Dem. Rep.	..	..	..	..	..	..	..	..	..	..	..	..
Korea, Rep.	128,839	240,325	8	7	10	5	39	47	8	8	34	33
Kuwait	1,032	..	..	..	..	..	..	..	..	..	..	..
Kyrgyz Republic	142	367	..	14	..	5	..	5	..	1	..	74
Lao PDR	245	867	..	..	..	..	..	..	..	..	..	..
Latvia	965	2,589	39	20	9	8	18	10	4	4	30	58
Lebanon	1,577	2,284	..	..	..	..	..	..	..	..	..	..
Lesotho	129	272	..	..	..	..	..	..	..	..	..	..
Liberia	4	95	..	..	..	..	..	..	..	..	..	..
Libya	..	..	..	..	..	..	..	..	..	..	..	..
Lithuania	1,390	6,548	..	20	..	11	..	11	..	6	..	52
Macedonia, FYR	873	1,244	35	..	..	..	..	..	..	..	65	..
Madagascar	233	1,062	..	40	..	27	..	1	..	2	..	30
Malawi	195	442	..	..	..	..	..	..	..	..	..	..
Malaysia	23,432	52,223	..	8	..	3	..	37	..	12	..	40
Mali	174	195	..	..	..	..	..	..	..	..	..	..
Mauritania	107	84	..	..	..	..	..	..	..	..	..	..
Mauritius	765	1,198	25	30	..	..	..	..	..	..	75	70
Mexico	54,546	182,916	26	..	4	..	22	..	15	..	33	..
Moldova	400	517	..	50	..	..	..	0	..	..	..	50
Mongolia	143	158	23	..	62	..	1	..	1	..	12	..
Morocco	6,056	10,019	..	36	..	14	..	8	..	14	..	27
Mozambique	166	1,080	..	..	..	..	..	..	..	..	..	..
Myanmar	..	..	..	..	..	..	..	..	..	..	..	..
Namibia	403	728	..	..	..	..	..	..	..	..	..	..
Nepal	393	740	35	..	34	..	2	..	..	..	29	..
Netherlands	65,999	79,146	18	15	3	1	15	14	16	10	48	59
New Zealand	10,645	..	29	25	..	..	..	..	..	..	71	75
Nicaragua	533	946	..	..	..	..	..	..	..	..	..	..
Niger	120	..	..	..	..	..	..	..	..	..	..	..
Nigeria	..	3,760	..	..	..	..	..	..	..	..	..	..
Norway	17,018	34,306	17	19	2	1	24	23	9	9	48	47
Oman	643	..	15	7	8	1	3	3	6	13	68	76
Pakistan	8,864	25,654	..	..	..	..	..	..	..	..	..	..
Panama	694	1,290	54	..	7	..	..	..	7	..	32	..
Papua New Guinea	372	361	..	..	..	..	..	..	..	..	..	..
Paraguay	1,280	1,570	..	..	..	..	..	..	..	..	..	..
Peru	8,105	15,600	28	31	9	14	7	2	9	11	48	42
Philippines	17,043	31,718	29	23	1	1	3	6	2	2	66	68
Poland	25,885	64,821	18	22	8	4	0	19	3	7	81	47
Portugal	18,249	23,509	13	14	22	3	18	15	6	2	41	66
Puerto Rico	17,867	..	..	..	..	..	..	..	..	..	..	..

4.3 | Structure of manufacturing

	Manufacturing value added		Food, beverages, and tobacco		Textiles and clothing		Machinery and transport equipment		Chemicals		Other manufacturing[a]	
	$ millions		% of total		% of total		% of total		% of total		% of total	
	1995	2007	1995	2005	1995	2005	1995	2005	1995	2005	1995	2005
Romania	9,387	32,925	28	15	7	16	10	19	7	6	48	44
Russian Federation	..	210,692	..	15	..	2	..	8	..	8	..	67
Rwanda	132	203	..	..	..	..	..	..	..	..	..	..
Saudi Arabia	13,714	36,349	..	..	..	..	..	..	..	..	..	..
Senegal	730	1,424	..	..	..	..	..	..	..	..	..	..
Serbia	..	..	..	..	..	..	..	..	..	..	..	..
Sierra Leone	75	..	..	..	..	..	..	..	..	..	..	..
Singapore	20,799	38,275	4	3	1	1	60	47	9	24	26	50
Slovak Republic	4,704	10,923	11	7	4	5	14	23	9	2	63	63
Slovenia	4,573	9,677	..	..	..	..	..	..	..	..	..	..
Somalia	..	..	..	..	..	..	..	..	..	..	..	..
South Africa	29,274	45,674	15	17	5	1	19	..	10	7	50	76
Spain	..	175,881	16	15	7	5	23	22	10	8	43	49
Sri Lanka	1,836	5,985	..	..	..	..	..	..	..	..	..	..
Sudan	640	2,679	..	..	..	..	..	..	..	..	..	..
Swaziland	557	1,095	..	..	..	..	..	..	..	..	..	..
Sweden	..	..	7	7	1	1	33	30	3	12	56	51
Switzerland	..	..	..	..	..	..	..	..	..	..	..	..
Syrian Arab Republic	1,574	5,145	..	..	..	..	..	..	..	..	..	..
Tajikistan	331	659	..	..	..	..	..	..	..	..	..	..
Tanzania[b]	349	819	..	..	..	..	..	..	..	..	..	..
Thailand	50,194	85,451	21	..	9	..	29	..	6	..	35	..
Timor-Leste	..	..	..	..	..	..	..	..	..	..	..	..
Togo	130	214	..	..	..	..	..	..	..	..	..	..
Trinidad and Tobago	439	1,157	..	13	..	1	..	2	..	35	..	50
Tunisia	3,419	6,009	..	..	..	..	..	..	..	..	..	..
Turkey	..	109,200	15	..	17	..	16	..	10	..	42	..
Turkmenistan	948	..	..	..	..	..	..	..	..	..	..	..
Uganda	359	851	..	..	..	..	..	..	..	..	..	..
Ukraine	14,922	29,003	..	..	..	..	..	..	..	..	..	..
United Arab Emirates	4,452	19,995	..	..	..	..	..	..	..	..	..	..
United Kingdom	219,282	269,610	13	15	5	3	28	27	11	11	42	45
United States	1,289,100	1,700,000	12	14	4	2	34	29	12	14	38	40
Uruguay	3,614	5,269	..	40	..	10	..	1	..	9	..	39
Uzbekistan	1,376	2,541	..	..	..	..	..	..	..	..	..	..
Venezuela, RB	10,668	21,941	..	..	..	..	..	..	..	..	..	..
Vietnam	3,109	14,673	..	..	..	..	..	..	..	..	..	..
West Bank and Gaza	..	..	..	..	..	..	..	..	..	..	..	..
Yemen, Rep.	599	..	..	55	..	..	..	..	..	..	..	45
Zambia	344	1,187	..	..	..	..	..	..	..	..	..	..
Zimbabwe	1,370	324	30	..	7	..	29	..	6	..	29	..
World	**5,486,528 t**	**7,998,553 t**										
Low income	35,085	90,319										
Middle income	1,002,230	2,355,279										
Lower middle income	514,247	1,409,173										
Upper middle income	499,190	1,100,621										
Low & middle income	1,037,197	2,434,141										
East Asia & Pacific	390,709	1,160,250										
Europe & Central Asia	..	..										
Latin America & Carib.	290,974	580,099										
Middle East & N. Africa	39,388	86,834										
South Asia	75,044	221,220										
Sub-Saharan Africa	45,959	82,642										
High income	4,467,711	5,544,426										
Euro Area	1,343,206	1,691,606										

a. Includes unallocated data. b. Covers mainland Tanzania only.

The data on the distribution of manufacturing value added by industry are provided by the United Nations Industrial Development Organization (UNIDO). UNIDO obtains the data from a variety of national and international sources, including the United Nations Statistics Division, the World Bank, the Organisation for Economic Co-operation and Development, and the International Monetary Fund. To improve comparability over time and across countries, UNIDO supplements these data with information from industrial censuses, statistics from national and international organizations, unpublished data that it collects in the field, and estimates by the UNIDO Secretariat. Nevertheless, coverage may be incomplete, particularly for the informal sector. When direct information on inputs and outputs is not available, estimates may be used, which may result in errors in industry totals. Moreover, countries use different reference periods (calendar or fiscal year) and valuation methods (basic or producer prices) to estimate value added. (See also *About the data* for table 4.2.)

The data on manufacturing value added in U.S. dollars are from the World Bank's national accounts files and may differ from those UNIDO uses to calculate shares of value added by industry, in part because of differences in exchange rates. Thus value added in a particular industry estimated by applying the shares to total manufacturing value added will not match those from UNIDO sources. Classification of manufacturing industries in the table accords with the United Nations International Standard Industrial Classification (ISIC) revision 3 for the first time. Previous editions of *World Development Indicators* used revision 2, first published in 1948. Revision 3 was completed in 1989, and many countries now use it. But revision 2 is still widely used for compiling cross-country data. UNIDO has converted these data to

accord with revision 3. Concordances matching ISIC categories to national classification systems and to related systems such as the Standard International Trade Classification are available.

In establishing classifications systems compilers must define both the types of activities to be described and the units whose activities are to be reported. There are many possibilities, and the choices affect how the statistics can be interpreted and how useful they are in analyzing economic behavior. The ISIC emphasizes commonalities in the production process and is explicitly not intended to measure outputs (for which there is a newly developed Central Product Classification). Nevertheless, the ISIC views an activity as defined by "a process resulting in a homogeneous set of products" (UN 1990 [ISIC, series M, no. 4, rev. 3], p. 9).

Firms typically use multiple processes to produce a product. For example, an automobile manufacturer engages in forging, welding, and painting as well as advertising, accounting, and other service activities. Collecting data at such a detailed level is not practical, nor is it useful to record production data at the highest level of a large, multiplant, multiproduct firm. The ISIC has therefore adopted as the definition of an establishment "an enterprise or part of an enterprise which independently engages in one, or predominantly one, kind of economic activity at or from one location . . . for which data are available . . ." (UN 1990, p. 25). By design, this definition matches the reporting unit required for the production accounts of the United Nations System of National Accounts. The ISIC system is described in the United Nations' *International Standard Industrial Classification of All Economic Activities, Third Revision* (1990). The discussion of the ISIC draws on Jacob Ryten's "Fifty Years of ISIC: Historical Origins and Future Perspectives" (1998).

• **Manufacturing value added** is the sum of gross output less the value of intermediate inputs used in production for industries classified in ISIC major division 3. • **Food, beverages, and tobacco** correspond to ISIC divisions 15 and 16. • **Textiles and clothing** correspond to ISIC divisions 17–19. • **Machinery and transport equipment** correspond to ISIC divisions 29, 30, 32, 34, and 35. • **Chemicals** correspond to ISIC division 24. • **Other manufacturing,** a residual, covers wood and related products (ISIC division 20), paper and related products (ISIC divisions 21 and 22), petroleum and related products (ISIC division 23), basic metals and mineral products (ISIC division 27), fabricated metal products and professional goods (ISIC division 28), and other industries (ISIC divisions 25, 26, 31, 33, 36, and 37).

Manufacturing continues to show strong growth in East Asia through 2007   **4.3a**

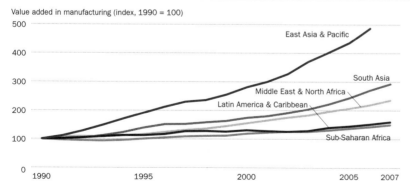

Value added in manufacturing (index, 1990 = 100)

Manufacturing continues to be the dominant sector in East Asia and Pacific, growing an average of about 10 percent a year between 1990 and 2007.

Source: World Development Indicators data files.

Data on manufacturing value added are from the World Bank's national accounts files. Data used to calculate shares of industry value added are provided to the World Bank in electronic files by UNIDO. The most recent published source is UNIDO's *International Yearbook of Industrial Statistics 2008.*

Structure of merchandise exports

	Merchandise exports		Food		Agricultural raw materials		Fuels		Ores and metals		Manufactures	
	$ millions		% of total		% of total		% of total		% of total		% of total	
	1995	2007	1995	2007	1995	2007	1995	2007	1995	2007	1995	2007
Afghanistan	156	480	..	..	..	..	..	..	..	..	..	..
Albania	202	1,072	11	5	9	3	3	7	12	14	65	70
Algeria	10,258	60,163	1	0	0	0	95	98	1	1	3	1
Angola	3,642	39,900	..	..	..	..	..	..	..	..	..	..
Argentina	20,967	55,933	50	50	4	1	10	11	2	4	34	31
Armenia	271	1,157	11	8	5	3	1	1	26	31	54	56
Australia	53,111	141,317	21	13	9	3	18	23	20	29	24	19
Austria	57,738	162,920	4	6	3	2	1	3	3	3	88	82
Azerbaijan	635	10,500	4	8	8	1	66	81	1	3	20	6
Bangladesh	3,501	12,453	10	6	3	2	0	1	0	0	85	91
Belarus	4,803	24,339	..	7	..	2	..	35	..	1	..	53
Belgium	178,265[a]	430,779	10[a]	8	1[a]	1	3[a]	7	4[a]	4	76[a]	78
Benin	420	650	20	26	64	64	7	0	0	1	10	9
Bolivia	1,100	4,490	19	15	9	2	13	48	31	26	17	7
Bosnia and Herzegovina	152	4,166	..	5	..	8	..	8	..	18	..	61
Botswana	2,142	5,117	..	3	..	0	..	0	..	23	..	73
Brazil	46,506	160,649	29	26	5	4	1	8	10	12	53	47
Bulgaria	5,355	18,466	18	9	3	2	7	13	10	18	60	55
Burkina Faso	276	607	23	..	63	..	0	..	0	..	6	..
Burundi	105	62	60	35	3	4	0	4	1	2	2	21
Cambodia	855	4,100	..	..	..	..	..	..	..	..	..	..
Cameroon	1,651	3,604	27	12	28	16	29	62	8	5	8	3
Canada	192,197	418,974	8	8	9	4	9	22	7	9	62	53
Central African Republic	171	195	4	1	20	41	1	0	30	17	45	36
Chad	243	3,450	..	..	..	..	..	..	..	..	..	..
Chile	16,024	68,296	24	15	14	6	0	1	47	65	12	10
China†	148,780	1,217,776	8	3	2	0	4	2	2	2	84	93
Hong Kong, China[b]	173,871	349,386	3	3	0	1	0	2	1	4	94	68
Colombia	10,056	29,991	31	15	5	4	27	36	1	2	34	39
Congo, Dem. Rep.	1,563	2,650	..	..	..	..	..	..	..	..	..	..
Congo, Rep.	1,172	6,100	1	..	8	..	88	..	0	..	3	..
Costa Rica	3,453	9,353	63	30	5	2	1	1	1	1	25	63
Côte d'Ivoire	3,806	8,500	63	39	20	9	10	33	0	0	7	18
Croatia	4,517	12,360	11	10	5	4	8	13	2	5	74	68
Cuba	1,600	3,701	..	11	..	0	..	0	..	2	..	24
Czech Republic	21,335	122,421	6	4	4	1	4	3	3	2	82	90
Denmark	50,906	103,453	24	17	3	3	3	10	1	2	60	66
Dominican Republic	3,780	7,237	11	..	0	..	0	..	0	..	8	..
Ecuador	4,307	13,785	52	27	3	4	35	60	0	1	8	8
Egypt, Arab Rep.	3,450	16,201	10	8	6	2	37	52	6	3	40	19
El Salvador	1,652	3,980	57	35	1	1	0	5	3	4	39	55
Eritrea	86	15	..	..	..	..	..	..	..	..	..	..
Estonia	1,840	10,996	16	8	10	6	7	12	3	3	64	64
Ethiopia	422	1,284	73	61	13	20	3	0	0	3	11	13
Finland	40,490	89,705	2	2	8	5	2	5	3	5	83	81
France	301,162	553,398	14	11	1	1	2	4	3	3	79	79
Gabon	2,713	6,150	0	1	13	7	83	86	2	3	2	4
Gambia, The	16	13	60	82	1	6	0	..	1	0	36	12
Georgia	151	1,240	29	24	3	2	19	4	8	20	41	45
Germany	523,461	1,326,411	5	4	1	1	1	2	3	3	85	83
Ghana	1,724	4,214	41	47	10	5	3	1	6	2	9	11
Greece	11,054	23,809	30	20	4	2	7	12	8	11	50	52
Guatemala	2,155	6,926	65	37	4	4	2	5	0	4	28	50
Guinea	702	1,100	7	..	1	..	0	..	65	..	24	..
Guinea-Bissau	24	95	89	..	11	..	0	..	0	..	0	..
Haiti	110	522	37	..	0	..	0	..	0	..	62	..
†Data for Taiwan, China	113,047	246,377	3	1	2	1	1	6	1	3	93	89

Structure of merchandise exports | 4.4

	Merchandise exports		Food		Agricultural raw materials		Fuels		Ores and metals		Manufactures	
	$ millions		% of total		% of total		% of total		% of total		% of total	
	1995	2007	1995	2007	1995	2007	1995	2007	1995	2007	1995	2007
Honduras	1,769	5,594	87	52	3	2	0	5	0	7	9	29
Hungary	12,865	94,618	21	6	2	1	3	3	5	2	68	81
India	30,630	145,325	19	9	1	2	2	16	4	8	73	64
Indonesia	45,417	118,014	11	15	7	6	25	26	6	11	51	42
Iran, Islamic Rep.	18,360	86,000	4	4	1	0	86	83	1	2	9	10
Iraq	496	41,600	..	0	..	0	..	100	..	0	..	0
Ireland	44,705	121,024	19	10	1	1	0	1	1	1	71	84
Israel	19,046	54,065	5	3	2	1	0	0	1	1	89	76
Italy	233,766	491,507	7	6	1	1	1	4	1	2	89	84
Jamaica	1,427	1,942	22	16	0	0	1	15	51	64	26	5
Japan	443,116	712,769	0	1	1	1	1	1	1	2	95	90
Jordan	1,769	5,700	25	15	2	0	0	1	24	7	49	76
Kazakhstan	5,250	47,755	10	4	3	1	25	66	24	15	38	13
Kenya	1,878	4,080	56	43	7	12	6	4	3	3	28	37
Korea, Dem. Rep.	959	1,690	..	..	..	..	..	..	..	..	..	..
Korea, Rep.	125,058	371,489	2	1	1	1	2	7	1	2	92	89
Kuwait	12,785	62,376	0	..	0	..	95	..	0	..	5	..
Kyrgyz Republic	409	1,135	23	17	13	5	11	12	12	4	41	35
Lao PDR	311	923	..	..	..	..	..	..	..	..	..	..
Latvia	1,305	8,311	14	13	23	16	2	4	1	4	58	60
Lebanon	816	3,574	20	..	1	..	0	..	8	..	69	..
Lesotho	160	805	..	..	..	..	..	..	..	..	..	..
Liberia	820	184	..	..	..	..	..	..	..	..	..	..
Libya	8,975	45,400	0	..	0	..	95	..	0	..	5	..
Lithuania	2,705	17,161	18	17	8	3	11	13	5	2	58	64
Macedonia, FYR	1,204	3,356	18	14	5	1	0	5	18	5	58	76
Madagascar	507	1,190	69	31	6	3	1	5	7	3	14	57
Malawi	405	710	90	86	2	4	0	0	0	0	7	11
Malaysia	73,914	176,211	10	9	6	2	7	14	1	2	75	71
Mali	441	1,480	19	7	61	14	0	0	0	0	2	3
Mauritania	488	1,510	..	25	..	0	..	..	..	69	..	0
Mauritius	1,538	2,231	29	31	1	1	0	0	0	1	70	67
Mexico	79,542	271,990	8	5	1	0	10	16	3	3	77	72
Moldova	745	1,342	72	57	2	1	1	0	3	9	23	32
Mongolia	473	1,889	2	2	28	11	0	9	60	61	10	5
Morocco	6,881	14,656	31	19	3	2	2	4	12	10	51	65
Mozambique	168	2,700	66	11	16	3	2	15	2	64	13	6
Myanmar	860	6,257	..	..	..	..	..	..	..	..	..	..
Namibia	1,409	2,919	..	24	..	1	..	0	..	35	..	39
Nepal	345	888	7	..	1	..	0	..	0	..	91	..
Netherlands	203,171	551,250	20	13	4	3	7	9	3	3	62	60
New Zealand	13,645	26,974	44	52	19	10	2	4	5	5	28	25
Nicaragua	466	1,202	74	81	3	1	1	1	1	2	20	10
Niger	288	733	19	14	1	3	0	2	80	63	1	6
Nigeria	12,342	65,500	2	0	2	0	96	98	0	0	1	1
Norway	41,992	136,377	8	5	2	1	47	64	9	8	27	18
Oman	6,068	24,722	5	2	0	0	79	89	2	1	14	7
Pakistan	8,029	17,838	12	12	4	1	1	6	0	1	83	79
Panama	625	1,164	74	83	0	1	3	1	1	4	20	11
Papua New Guinea	2,654	4,671	13	..	20	..	38	..	25	..	4	..
Paraguay	919	2,785	44	80	36	6	0	0	0	1	19	14
Peru	5,575	27,956	29	14	2	1	5	9	42	49	14	12
Philippines	17,502	50,466	13	6	1	1	2	2	4	5	41	51
Poland	22,895	138,806	10	9	3	1	8	4	7	5	71	80
Portugal	22,783	51,455	7	9	5	2	3	4	2	4	83	74
Puerto Rico	..	..	..	..	..	..	..	..	..	..	..	..

	Merchandise exports		Food		Agricultural raw materials		Fuels		Ores and metals		Manufactures	
	$ millions		% of total		% of total		% of total		% of total		% of total	
	1995	2007	1995	2007	1995	2007	1995	2007	1995	2007	1995	2007
Romania	7,910	40,286	7	4	3	2	8	8	3	5	78	80
Russian Federation	81,095	355,175	2	2	3	3	43	61	10	8	26	17
Rwanda	54	177	57	45	16	5	0	0	12	46	14	5
Saudi Arabia	50,040	233,174	1	1	0	0	88	90	1	0	11	9
Senegal	993	1,698	9	37	7	3	22	19	12	4	48	36
Serbia	..	8,825	28	19	4	2	2	3	15	10	49	66
Sierra Leone	42	244	..	..	..	..	..	..	..	..	..	..
Singapore[b]	118,268	299,272	4	2	1	0	7	14	2	2	84	76
Slovak Republic	8,580	58,171	6	4	4	1	4	5	4	3	82	87
Slovenia	8,316	30,054	4	3	2	2	1	2	3	6	90	88
Somalia	..	..	..	..	..	..	..	..	..	..	..	..
South Africa	27,853[c]	69,788	8[c]	7	4[c]	2	9[c]	11	8[c]	29	43[c]	51
Spain	97,849	241,018	15	13	2	1	2	5	2	3	78	75
Sri Lanka	3,798	7,740	21	22	4	2	0	0	1	4	73	70
Sudan	555	8,879	44	6	46	2	0	90	0	0	6	0
Swaziland	866	2,450	..	21	..	7	..	1	..	1	..	70
Sweden	80,440	169,084	2	4	7	4	2	5	3	4	79	77
Switzerland	81,641	172,060	3	3	1	0	0	2	3	3	93	91
Syrian Arab Republic	3,563	11,700	..	17	..	2	..	40	..	1	..	32
Tajikistan	750	1,468	..	..	..	..	..	..	..	..	..	..
Tanzania	682	2,022	65	35	23	7	0	1	0	13	10	17
Thailand	56,439	153,103	19	12	5	5	1	4	1	2	73	76
Timor-Leste	..	..	..	..	..	..	..	..	..	..	..	..
Togo	378	690	19	16	42	9	0	0	32	13	7	62
Trinidad and Tobago	2,455	15,100	8	3	0	0	48	66	0	3	43	28
Tunisia	5,475	15,029	10	10	1	0	8	16	2	1	79	70
Turkey	21,637	107,215	20	8	1	0	1	5	3	3	74	81
Turkmenistan	1,880	8,920	1	..	13	..	77	..	1	..	8	..
Uganda	460	1,623	86	62	4	8	0	1	1	2	4	21
Ukraine	13,128	49,248	19	13	1	1	4	5	8	6	66	74
United Arab Emirates	28,364	173,000	8	1	0	0	9	62	55	1	28	3
United Kingdom	237,953	437,807	8	5	1	1	6	10	3	4	82	74
United States	584,743	1,162,479	11	8	4	2	2	4	3	4	77	77
Uruguay	2,106	4,485	44	53	15	11	1	4	1	1	39	30
Uzbekistan	3,430	8,029	..	..	..	..	..	..	..	..	..	..
Venezuela, RB	18,457	69,165	3	0	0	0	76	93	7	2	14	5
Vietnam	5,449	48,387	30	19	3	4	18	24	0	1	44	51
West Bank and Gaza	..	..	..	..	..	..	..	..	..	..	..	..
Yemen, Rep.	1,945	7,310	..	5	..	0	..	93	..	0	..	1
Zambia	1,040	4,619	3	7	1	1	3	1	87	78	7	13
Zimbabwe	2,118	2,060	43	16	7	11	1	1	12	19	37	48
World	5,172,481 t	13,952,366 t	9 w	7 w	3 w	2 w	6 w	10 w	3 w	4 w	75 w	72 w
Low income	62,712	230,764	20	14	4	3	36	44	3	2	35	35
Middle income	884,363	3,939,704	14	9	3	2	11	18	5	6	64	61
Lower middle income	413,659	2,196,661	14	8	3	2	11	15	3	4	66	68
Upper middle income	470,822	1,741,884	15	11	4	2	12	21	6	8	62	55
Low & middle income	947,082	4,170,475	14	10	4	2	11	18	5	6	63	60
East Asia & Pacific	354,784	1,784,975	11	7	4	2	6	7	2	3	73	77
Europe & Central Asia	183,585	878,671	9	6	3	2	25	35	8	7	47	45
Latin America & Carib.	223,927	753,753	20	17	3	2	15	14	8	10	54	54
Middle East & N. Africa	62,002	307,393	6	5	1	0	72	75	3	2	18	16
South Asia	46,647	185,551	17	10	2	2	1	14	3	7	76	66
Sub-Saharan Africa	76,554	262,784	17	11	6	3	37	39	8	14	27	30
High income	4,225,020	9,784,163	8	6	2	2	6	8	3	4	78	75
Euro area	1,742,200	4,158,254	10	8	2	1	2	4	3	3	80	78

Note: Components may not sum to 100 percent because of unclassified trade. Exports of gold are excluded.
a. Includes Luxembourg. b. Includes re-exports. c. Refers to the South African Customs Union (Botswana, Lesotho, Namibia, South Africa, and Swaziland).

Structure of merchandise exports | 4.4

About the data

Data on merchandise trade are from customs reports of goods moving into or out of an economy or from reports of financial transactions related to merchandise trade recorded in the balance of payments. Because of differences in timing and definitions, trade flow estimates from customs reports and balance of payments may differ. Several international agencies process trade data, each correcting unreported or misreported data, leading to other differences.

The most detailed source of data on international trade in goods is the United Nations Statistics Division's Commodity Trade (Comtrade) database. The International Monetary Fund (IMF) also collects customs-based data on trade in goods. Exports are recorded as the cost of the goods delivered to the frontier of the exporting country for shipment—the free on board (f.o.b.) value. Many countries report trade data in U.S. dollars. When countries report in local currency, the United Nations Statistics Division applies the average official exchange rate to the U.S. dollar for the period shown.

Countries may report trade according to the general or special system of trade (see *Primary data documentation*). Under the general system exports comprise outward-moving goods that are (a) goods wholly or partly produced in the country; (b) foreign goods, neither transformed nor declared for domestic consumption in the country, that move outward from customs storage; and (c) goods previously included as imports for domestic consumption but subsequently exported without transformation. Under the special system exports comprise categories a and

c. In some compilations categories b and c are classified as re-exports. Because of differences in reporting practices, data on exports may not be fully comparable across economies.

The data on total exports of goods (merchandise) are from the World Trade Organization (WTO), which obtains data from national statistical offices and the IMF's *International Financial Statistics,* supplemented by the Comtrade database and publications or databases of regional organizations, specialized agencies, economic groups, and private sources (such as Eurostat, the Food and Agriculture Organization, and country reports of the Economist Intelligence Unit). Country websites and email contact have improved collection of up-to-date statistics, reducing the proportion of estimates. The WTO database now covers most major traders in Africa, Asia, and Latin America, which together with high-income countries account for nearly 95 percent of world trade. Reliability of data for countries in Europe and Central Asia has also improved.

Export shares by major commodity group are from Comtrade. The values of total exports reported here have not been fully reconciled with the estimates from the national accounts or the balance of payments.

The classification of commodity groups is based on the Standard International Trade Classification (SITC) revision 3. Previous editions contained data based on the SITC revision 1. Data for earlier years in previous editions may differ because of this change in methodology. Concordance tables are available to convert data reported in one system to another.

Definitions

• **Merchandise exports** are the f.o.b. value of goods provided to the rest of the world. • **Food** corresponds to the commodities in SITC sections 0 (food and live animals), 1 (beverages and tobacco), and 4 (animal and vegetable oils and fats) and SITC division 22 (oil seeds, oil nuts, and oil kernels). • **Agricultural raw materials** correspond to SITC section 2 (crude materials except fuels), excluding divisions 22, 27 (crude fertilizers and minerals excluding coal, petroleum, and precious stones), and 28 (metalliferous ores and scrap). • **Fuels** correspond to SITC section 3 (mineral fuels). • **Ores and metals** correspond to the commodities in SITC divisions 27, 28, and 68 (nonferrous metals). • **Manufactures** correspond to the commodities in SITC sections 5 (chemicals), 6 (basic manufactures), 7 (machinery and transport equipment), and 8 (miscellaneous manufactured goods), excluding division 68.

Developing economies' share of world merchandise exports continues to expand   **4.4a**

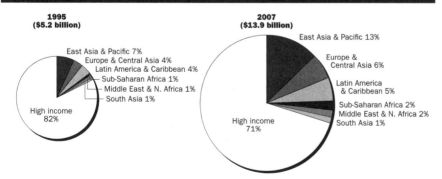

Developing economies' share of world merchandise exports increased 11 percentage points from 1995 to 2007. East Asia and Pacific was the biggest gainer, capturing an additional 5 percentage points. Every region except South Asia increased its share in world trade.

Source: World Development Indicators data files and World Trade Organization.

Data sources

Data on merchandise exports are from the WTO. Data on shares of exports by major commodity group are from Comtrade. The WTO publishes data on world trade in its *Annual Report.* The IMF publishes estimates of total exports of goods in its *International Financial Statistics* and *Direction of Trade Statistics,* as does the United Nations Statistics Division in its *Monthly Bulletin of Statistics.* And the United Nations Conference on Trade and Development publishes data on the structure of exports in its *Handbook of Statistics.* Tariff line records of exports are compiled in the United Nations Statistics Division's Comtrade database.

4.5 Structure of merchandise imports

	Merchandise imports		Food		Agricultural raw materials		Fuels		Ores and metals		Manufactures	
	$ millions		% of total		% of total		% of total		% of total		% of total	
	1995	2007	1995	2007	1995	2007	1995	2007	1995	2007	1995	2007
Afghanistan	387	2,950	..	..	..	..	..	..	..	..	..	..
Albania	714	4,196	34	16	1	1	3	15	1	3	61	65
Algeria	10,100	27,631	29	20	3	2	1	1	2	2	65	75
Angola	1,468	11,400	..	..	..	..	..	..	..	..	..	..
Argentina	20,122	44,780	5	4	2	1	4	6	3	3	86	85
Armenia	674	3,282	31	17	0	1	27	16	0	3	39	59
Australia	61,283	165,334	5	5	2	1	5	13	1	1	86	76
Austria	66,237	162,351	6	6	3	2	4	10	4	5	82	75
Azerbaijan	668	5,712	39	16	1	1	5	3	2	2	53	78
Bangladesh	6,694	18,595	17	17	3	7	8	13	2	3	69	60
Belarus	5,564	28,674	..	7	..	1	..	35	..	4	..	48
Belgium	164,934[a]	413,163	11[a]	8	2[a]	1	6[a]	11	5[a]	5	71[a]	74
Benin	746	1,500	36	30	4	4	0	20	1	1	59	45
Bolivia	1,424	3,444	10	10	2	1	5	8	3	1	81	79
Bosnia and Herzegovina	1,082	9,772	..	16	..	1	..	14	..	4	..	64
Botswana	1,911	4,035	..	13	..	1	..	16	..	2	..	67
Brazil	54,137	126,581	11	5	3	1	12	19	3	5	71	64
Bulgaria	5,660	29,983	8	6	3	1	34	5	4	9	48	62
Burkina Faso	455	1,650	21	..	2	..	14	..	1	..	62	..
Burundi	234	319	21	12	2	1	11	28	1	1	64	58
Cambodia	1,187	5,500	..	..	..	..	..	..	..	..	..	..
Cameroon	1,199	3,760	17	18	3	2	2	31	6	3	72	46
Canada	168,426	389,600	6	6	2	1	4	9	3	3	83	77
Central African Republic	175	230	16	17	10	27	9	17	2	2	64	37
Chad	365	1,500	24	..	1	..	18	..	1	..	57	..
Chile	15,900	47,114	7	7	2	1	9	26	2	4	79	62
China†	132,084	955,950	7	4	5	4	4	12	4	12	79	68
Hong Kong, China	196,072	370,132	5	3	2	1	2	3	2	2	87	90
Colombia	13,853	32,897	9	9	3	1	3	3	2	3	78	83
Congo, Dem. Rep.	871	3,700	..	..	..	..	..	..	..	..	..	..
Congo, Rep.	670	2,900	21	..	1	..	20	..	1	..	58	..
Costa Rica	4,036	12,955	10	8	1	1	9	12	2	2	77	74
Côte d'Ivoire	2,931	6,160	21	17	1	1	19	30	1	1	57	49
Croatia	7,352	25,830	12	8	2	1	12	15	3	3	67	73
Cuba	2,825	10,083	..	12	..	0	..	0	..	1	..	50
Czech Republic	25,085	117,900	7	5	3	1	8	8	4	4	77	81
Denmark	45,939	99,621	12	12	3	2	3	6	2	2	73	77
Dominican Republic	5,170	13,817	..	..	..	..	..	..	..	..	..	..
Ecuador	4,152	13,565	8	8	3	1	6	21	2	1	82	67
Egypt, Arab Rep.	11,760	27,064	28	19	7	4	1	15	3	4	61	42
El Salvador	3,329	8,677	15	17	2	2	9	18	2	1	72	62
Eritrea	454	515	..	..	..	..	..	..	..	..	..	..
Estonia	2,546	15,516	14	8	3	3	11	14	1	1	71	66
Ethiopia	1,145	5,395	14	7	2	1	11	13	1	1	72	77
Finland	29,470	81,491	6	5	4	3	9	14	6	10	74	66
France	289,391	615,229	11	8	3	1	7	14	3	3	76	74
Gabon	882	2,250	19	17	1	0	3	4	1	1	76	78
Gambia, The	182	315	36	31	1	2	14	17	0	1	46	49
Georgia	392	5,217	36	16	0	1	39	18	0	1	24	60
Germany	463,872	1,058,580	10	7	3	1	6	11	4	5	70	67
Ghana	1,906	8,043	8	15	1	..	6	2	3	2	75	81
Greece	25,898	76,149	16	11	2	1	7	15	3	4	71	68
Guatemala	3,292	13,578	12	11	2	1	12	18	1	1	73	68
Guinea	819	1,190	31	..	1	..	19	..	1	..	47	..
Guinea-Bissau	133	140	44	..	0	..	16	..	0	..	40	..
Haiti	653	1,682	..	..	..	..	..	..	..	..	..	..
†Data for Taiwan, China	103,558	219,649	5	3	4	2	7	20	6	9	74	65

Structure of merchandise imports

	Merchandise imports ($ millions)		Food (% of total)		Agricultural raw materials (% of total)		Fuels (% of total)		Ores and metals (% of total)		Manufactures (% of total)	
	1995	2007	1995	2007	1995	2007	1995	2007	1995	2007	1995	2007
Honduras	1,879	8,556	13	15	1	1	12	20	1	1	74	64
Hungary	15,465	95,041	6	4	3	1	12	9	4	3	75	76
India	34,707	216,622	4	3	4	2	24	33	7	6	53	46
Indonesia	40,630	92,381	9	11	6	4	7	30	5	4	73	53
Iran, Islamic Rep.	13,882	46,000	*21*	2	2	1	2	4	3	0	70	*16*
Iraq	665	32,000	..	..	..	..	..	..	..	..	..	..
Ireland	32,340	82,472	8	9	1	1	3	9	2	2	76	73
Israel	29,578	59,039	7	6	2	1	6	16	2	2	82	74
Italy	205,990	504,454	11	8	6	2	7	12	5	6	67	65
Jamaica	2,818	5,899	14	13	2	1	13	34	1	0	68	49
Japan	335,882	621,091	16	9	6	2	16	28	7	9	53	51
Jordan	3,697	13,511	21	15	2	1	13	22	2	3	61	57
Kazakhstan	3,807	32,756	10	7	2	1	25	11	5	2	58	79
Kenya	2,991	8,989	10	11	2	2	15	21	2	2	71	62
Korea, Dem. Rep.	1,380	3,460	..	..	..	..	..	..	..	..	..	..
Korea, Rep.	135,119	356,846	5	4	5	2	14	27	6	8	67	58
Kuwait	7,790	23,642	16	..	1	..	1	..	2	..	81	..
Kyrgyz Republic	522	2,417	18	15	3	2	36	31	3	2	41	50
Lao PDR	589	1,065	..	..	..	..	..	..	..	..	..	..
Latvia	1,815	15,285	10	10	2	3	21	11	1	2	66	70
Lebanon	7,278	12,251	*19*	..	2	..	8	..	2	..	63	..
Lesotho	1,107	1,730	..	..	..	..	..	..	..	..	..	..
Liberia	510	499	..	..	..	..	..	..	..	..	..	..
Libya	5,392	7,750	..	..	..	..	..	..	..	..	..	..
Lithuania	3,650	24,207	13	9	4	2	19	16	4	2	58	70
Macedonia, FYR	1,719	5,228	17	12	3	1	12	19	3	6	54	62
Madagascar	628	2,590	16	15	2	1	14	17	1	0	65	67
Malawi	475	1,450	14	11	1	1	11	14	1	1	73	74
Malaysia	77,691	146,982	5	6	1	1	2	9	3	5	84	75
Mali	772	2,255	*20*	15	*1*	1	*16*	22	*1*	1	63	62
Mauritania	431	1,510	..	25	..	1	..	27	..	0	..	47
Mauritius	1,976	3,895	17	19	3	2	7	18	1	1	72	58
Mexico	75,858	296,275	6	6	2	1	2	7	2	3	80	76
Moldova	840	3,690	8	12	3	2	46	21	2	1	42	64
Mongolia	415	2,117	*14*	12	*1*	0	*19*	27	*1*	1	65	60
Morocco	10,023	31,695	20	12	6	3	14	20	4	4	56	61
Mozambique	704	3,300	22	18	3	1	10	16	1	0	62	47
Myanmar	1,348	3,250	..	..	..	..	..	..	..	..	..	..
Namibia	1,616	3,420	..	15	..	1	..	10	..	1	..	73
Nepal	1,333	2,904	*12*	..	6	..	*13*	..	5	..	63	..
Netherlands	185,232	491,583	14	9	2	1	8	14	4	4	72	61
New Zealand	13,957	30,890	7	8	1	1	5	14	3	3	82	73
Nicaragua	975	3,579	18	16	1	0	18	23	1	0	63	60
Niger	374	970	32	24	1	5	13	17	3	1	51	53
Nigeria	8,222	29,500	*18*	18	*1*	1	*1*	3	2	3	77	76
Norway	32,968	80,281	7	7	3	2	3	4	7	10	80	77
Oman	4,379	16,100	20	10	1	1	2	3	2	5	68	81
Pakistan	11,515	32,590	18	9	5	5	16	26	3	4	57	55
Panama	2,510	6,872	11	10	1	0	14	18	1	1	73	68
Papua New Guinea	1,452	2,909	..	..	..	..	..	..	..	..	..	..
Paraguay	3,144	7,280	19	7	0	0	7	13	1	1	74	78
Peru	7,584	20,180	14	10	2	2	9	19	1	1	75	65
Philippines	28,341	57,985	8	7	2	1	9	17	3	2	58	48
Poland	29,050	162,674	10	6	3	2	9	10	3	4	74	75
Portugal	32,610	78,138	14	12	4	2	8	14	2	3	72	65
Puerto Rico	..	..	..	..	..	..	..	..	..	..	..	..

	Merchandise imports		Food		Agricultural raw materials		Fuels		Ores and metals		Manufactures	
	$ millions		% of total		% of total		% of total		% of total		% of total	
	1995	2007	1995	2007	1995	2007	1995	2007	1995	2007	1995	2007
Romania	10,278	69,863	8	6	2	1	21	11	4	3	63	77
Russian Federation	60,945	223,421	18	13	1	1	3	1	3	2	44	77
Rwanda	236	737	19	14	3	2	12	9	3	3	64	73
Saudi Arabia	28,091	90,157	16	13	1	1	0	0	3	5	75	81
Senegal	1,412	4,452	25	25	2	1	30	27	1	1	42	45
Serbia	..	18,350	14	6	4	2	14	17	7	6	60	69
Sierra Leone	133	445	..	..	..	..	..	..	..	..	..	..
Singapore	124,507	263,155	5	3	1	0	8	20	2	2	83	71
Slovak Republic	8,770	60,218	9	5	3	1	13	11	6	3	70	79
Slovenia	9,492	31,534	8	6	5	3	7	9	4	7	74	74
Somalia	..	..	..	..	..	..	..	..	..	..	..	..
South Africa	30,546[b]	90,990	7[b]	5	2[b]	1	8[b]	19	2[b]	3	78[b]	65
Spain	113,537	372,569	14	9	3	1	8	15	4	4	71	70
Sri Lanka	5,306	11,300	16	12	2	1	6	13	1	3	75	69
Sudan	1,218	8,775	24	5	2	0	14	0	0	0	59	93
Swaziland	1,008	2,650	..	21	..	1	..	16	..	1	..	61
Sweden	65,036	151,269	7	7	2	2	6	11	4	5	80	72
Switzerland	80,152	161,232	6	5	2	1	3	7	3	4	85	82
Syrian Arab Republic	4,709	14,500	..	13	..	3	..	27	..	3	..	52
Tajikistan	810	2,455	..	..	..	..	..	..	..	..	..	..
Tanzania	1,675	5,337	10	12	1	1	1	30	4	1	84	55
Thailand	70,786	140,795	4	4	4	2	7	18	3	5	80	69
Timor-Leste	..	..	..	..	..	..	..	..	..	..	..	..
Togo	594	1,440	18	15	2	1	30	27	1	2	49	55
Trinidad and Tobago	1,714	7,450	16	8	1	1	1	33	6	7	77	50
Tunisia	7,902	18,980	13	10	4	2	7	13	3	3	73	71
Turkey	35,709	170,057	7	3	6	3	13	14	6	8	69	63
Turkmenistan	1,365	4,460	24	..	0	..	3	..	2	..	71	..
Uganda	1,056	3,466	16	12	3	1	2	19	2	1	78	63
Ukraine	15,484	60,670	8	7	2	1	48	26	3	4	38	62
United Arab Emirates	23,778	132,000	15	6	0	1	4	1	6	4	75	62
United Kingdom	267,250	619,575	10	9	2	1	4	10	3	4	80	72
United States	770,852	2,020,403	5	4	2	1	8	18	3	3	79	70
Uruguay	2,867	5,726	10	9	4	3	10	22	1	1	74	65
Uzbekistan	2,750	4,848	..	..	..	..	..	..	..	..	..	..
Venezuela, RB	12,649	46,097	14	7	4	1	1	0	4	1	76	64
Vietnam	8,155	60,830	5	6	2	4	10	15	2	4	76	66
West Bank and Gaza	..	..	..	..	..	..	..	..	..	..	..	..
Yemen, Rep.	1,582	6,500	..	25	..	1	..	22	..	1	..	51
Zambia	700	3,971	10	5	2	0	13	12	2	5	72	76
Zimbabwe	2,660	2,420	6	11	2	4	9	18	2	6	78	54
World	**5,228,953 t**	**14,144,532 t**	**9 w**	**6 w**	**3 w**	**1 w**	**7 w**	**15 w**	**4 w**	**5 w**	**75 w**	**69 w**
Low income	74,778	257,014	14	13	3	3	12	17	2	3	66	62
Middle income	948,310	3,651,462	8	6	3	2	7	14	4	5	75	68
Lower middle income	452,835	1,955,705	9	6	4	3	8	17	4	7	72	63
Upper middle income	495,317	1,691,013	8	6	3	1	7	11	3	4	77	72
Low & middle income	1,023,140	3,908,450	8	7	3	2	7	14	3	5	74	68
East Asia & Pacific	366,057	1,476,968	6	5	4	3	5	14	4	8	78	67
Europe & Central Asia	200,774	939,184	11	7	3	2	14	12	4	4	61	70
Latin America & Carib.	241,363	734,326	8	7	2	1	5	11	2	3	78	72
Middle East & N. Africa	77,167	238,291	22	12	4	2	6	14	3	2	64	50
South Asia	60,322	286,538	8	4	4	2	21	32	6	6	55	48
Sub-Saharan Africa	78,377	242,243	11	10	2	1	10	18	2	2	73	64
High income	4,205,548	10,242,758	9	6	3	1	7	15	4	4	75	70
Euro area	1,644,739	4,068,352	11	8	3	2	7	12	4	5	72	69

Note: Components may not sum to 100 percent because of unclassified trade.
a. Includes Luxembourg. b. Refers to the South African Customs Union (Botswana, Lesotho, Namibia, South Africa, and Swaziland).

Structure of merchandise imports | 4.5

Data on imports of goods are derived from the same sources as data on exports. In principle, world exports and imports should be identical. Similarly, exports from an economy should equal the sum of imports by the rest of the world from that economy. But differences in timing and definitions result in discrepancies in reported values at all levels. For further discussion of indicators of merchandise trade, see *About the data* for tables 4.4 and 6.2.

The value of imports is generally recorded as the cost of the goods when purchased by the importer plus the cost of transport and insurance to the frontier of the importing country—the cost, insurance, and freight (c.i.f.) value, corresponding to the landed cost at the point of entry of foreign goods into the country. A few countries, including Australia, Canada, and the United States, collect import data on a free on board (f.o.b.) basis and adjust them for freight and insurance costs. Many countries report trade data in U.S. dollars. When countries report in local currency, the United Nations Statistics Division applies the average official exchange rate to the U.S. dollar for the period shown.

Countries may report trade according to the general or special system of trade (see *Primary data documentation*). Under the general system imports include goods imported for domestic consumption and imports into bonded warehouses and free trade zones. Under the special system imports comprise goods imported for domestic consumption (including transformation and repair) and withdrawals for

domestic consumption from bonded warehouses and free trade zones. Goods transported through a country en route to another are excluded.

The data on total imports of goods (merchandise) in the table come from the World Trade Organization (WTO). For further discussion of the WTO's sources and methodology, see *About the data* for table 4.4. The import shares by major commodity group are from the United Nations Statistics Division's Commodity Trade (Comtrade) database. The values of total imports reported here have not been fully reconciled with the estimates of imports of goods and services from the national accounts (shown in table 4.8) or those from the balance of payments (table 4.15).

The classification of commodity groups is based on the Standard International Trade Classification (SITC) revision 3. Previous editions contained data based on the SITC revision 1. Data for earlier years in previous editions may differ because of this change in methodology. Concordance tables are available to convert data reported in one system to another.

• **Merchandise imports** are the c.i.f. value of goods purchased from the rest of the world valued in U.S. dollars. • **Food** corresponds to the commodities in SITC sections 0 (food and live animals), 1 (beverages and tobacco), and 4 (animal and vegetable oils and fats) and SITC division 22 (oil seeds, oil nuts, and oil kernels). • **Agricultural raw materials** correspond to SITC section 2 (crude materials except fuels), excluding divisions 22, 27 (crude fertilizers and minerals excluding coal, petroleum, and precious stones), and 28 (metalliferous ores and scrap). • **Fuels** correspond to SITC section 3 (mineral fuels). • **Ores and metals** correspond to the commodities in SITC divisions 27, 28, and 68 (nonferrous metals). • **Manufactures** correspond to the commodities in SITC sections 5 (chemicals), 6 (basic manufactures), 7 (machinery and transport equipment), and 8 (miscellaneous manufactured goods), excluding division 68.

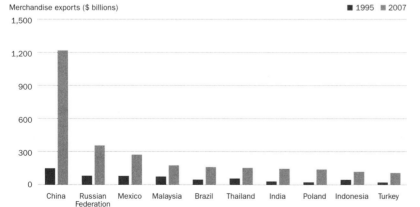

China continues to dominate merchandise exports among developing economies. Even when developed economies are included, China ranks as the third leading merchandise exporter.

Source: World Development Indicators data files and World Trade Organization.

Data on merchandise imports are from the WTO. Data on shares of imports by major commodity group are from Comtrade. The WTO publishes data on world trade in its *Annual Report.* The International Monetary Fund publishes estimates of total imports of goods in its *International Financial Statistics* and *Direction of Trade Statistics,* as does the United Nations Statistics Division in its *Monthly Bulletin of Statistics.* And the United Nations Conference on Trade and Development publishes data on the structure of imports in its *Handbook of Statistics.* Tariff line records of imports are compiled in the United Nations Statistics Division's Comtrade database.

4.6 Structure of service exports

	Commercial service exports		Transport		Travel		Insurance and financial services		Computer, information, communications, and other commercial services	
	$ millions		% of total		% of total		% of total		% of total	
	1995	2007	1995	2007	1995	2007	1995	2007	1995	2007
Afghanistan	..	..	..	..	..	..	..	..	..	..
Albania	94	1,399	19.1	8.2	69.3	71.6	1.4	2.5	10.2	17.6
Algeria	..	..	..	..	..	..	..	..	..	..
Angola	113	311	31.8	5.4	0.7	72.4	9.2	..	59.0	22.2
Argentina	3,676	10,175	27.4	16.5	60.5	42.4	0.2	0.1	11.9	41.0
Armenia	27	571	53.4	23.3	5.2	53.4	6.7	3.3	41.3	20.0
Australia	16,076	39,727	29.3	18.2	50.6	56.4	5.4	3.7	14.8	21.7
Austria	31,692	55,210	11.8	21.7	42.4	34.0	3.9	5.1	41.9	39.2
Azerbaijan	166	1,172	45.9	51.6	42.3	15.2	0.1	0.7	11.7	32.6
Bangladesh	469	685	15.0	11.7	5.3	11.1	0.1	4.6	79.6	72.6
Belarus	466	3,235	64.8	72.5	5.0	10.0	0.5	0.4	29.7	17.1
Belgium	33,619[a]	76,875	29.4[a]	32.3	17.4[a]	14.2	14.8[a]	6.1	38.4[a]	47.4
Benin	159	196	25.8	14.9	53.2	59.2	6.9	2.5	14.1	23.5
Bolivia	174	453	44.8	13.3	31.5	57.2	9.8	12.9	13.9	16.6
Bosnia and Herzegovina	457	1,361	3.8	12.2	54.1	53.6	2.6	3.4	39.5	30.8
Botswana	236	922	16.2	9.0	68.5	59.2	7.8	3.7	7.5	28.1
Brazil	6,005	22,555	43.3	18.0	16.2	22.0	16.9	7.2	23.6	52.8
Bulgaria	1,431	6,333	34.5	30.0	33.0	49.4	7.6	1.3	32.5	19.3
Burkina Faso	38	..	17.3	..	47.8	..	..	..	34.8	..
Burundi	4	7	46.2	21.2	32.4	20.2	0.5	0.0	21.0	58.6
Cambodia	103	1,510	30.5	13.9	51.7	75.1	..	0.9	17.7	10.1
Cameroon	242	476	48.3	38.7	14.8	37.2	7.2	5.1	29.7	19.0
Canada	25,425	61,386	20.7	18.5	31.1	25.4	11.4	9.1	36.8	46.9
Central African Republic	0	..	34.1	..	33.9	..	19.6	..	12.5	..
Chad	23	..	4.5	..	49.8	..	1.7	..	43.9	..
Chile	3,249	8,677	36.8	59.1	28.0	16.4	7.4	3.0	27.8	21.5
China	18,430	121,654	18.2	25.7	47.4	30.6	10.1	0.9	24.4	42.7
Hong Kong, China	33,790	83,563	32.5	30.9	16.8	16.0	9.2	13.3	41.5	39.8
Colombia	1,641	3,559	34.4	31.0	40.0	46.9	6.5	1.9	19.1	20.2
Congo, Dem. Rep.	..	..	..	..	..	..	..	..	..	..
Congo, Rep.	61	303	52.2	4.0	22.4	18.0	0.0	31.4	25.4	46.6
Costa Rica	957	3,598	14.0	9.5	71.2	56.4	-0.2	0.3	14.9	33.8
Côte d'Ivoire	426	787	28.9	28.7	20.9	13.2	12.3	12.8	37.9	58.1
Croatia	2,223	12,524	31.8	12.3	60.7	73.7	1.3	0.7	6.2	13.3
Cuba	..	..	..	..	..	..	..	..	..	..
Czech Republic	6,638	17,144	22.0	29.4	43.4	38.7	1.1	1.8	33.5	30.1
Denmark	15,171	61,608	44.6	47.1	24.3	15.6	..	..	31.0	37.4
Dominican Republic	1,894	4,740	2.2	7.4	82.9	86.1	0.1	0.9	14.9	5.5
Ecuador	687	1,087	46.8	31.9	37.1	57.4	0.0	..	16.0	10.7
Egypt, Arab Rep.	8,262	19,660	38.8	35.3	32.5	47.3	1.0	0.9	27.8	16.5
El Salvador	342	1,454	28.3	25.2	25.0	58.2	7.8	2.7	39.0	13.8
Eritrea	49	..	70.4	..	3.1	..	1.0	..	26.5	..
Estonia	868	4,336	43.0	41.4	41.1	23.9	0.4	3.3	15.5	31.4
Ethiopia	310	1,185	76.9	61.9	5.3	14.9	1.5	4.9	16.4	18.3
Finland	7,334	20,154	28.1	13.8	22.4	14.0	2.0	1.6	47.5	70.7
France	83,108	144,680	24.6	23.1	33.2	37.4	5.3	2.1	36.9	37.3
Gabon	191	120	46.4	22.0	9.0	7.7	3.3	24.1	41.3	46.2
Gambia, The	38	114	21.7	17.4	73.4	65.3	0.3	0.3	4.7	17.0
Georgia	188	976	48.2	52.4	25.0	39.3	..	2.3	26.9	6.0
Germany	73,576	210,820	27.0	24.4	24.5	17.1	5.0	8.3	43.5	50.1
Ghana	139	1,614	58.7	19.4	7.9	56.3	3.0	0.8	30.3	23.6
Greece	9,528	42,984	3.9	54.2	43.4	36.2	0.3	1.3	52.4	8.3
Guatemala	628	1,599	8.6	11.6	33.9	65.9	4.0	1.9	53.6	20.6
Guinea	17	44	75.3	13.6	5.1	0.4	1.4	0.6	18.2	85.4
Guinea-Bissau	2	6	18.2	22.9	14.0	16.6	..	19.5	81.8	41.0
Haiti	98	152	5.1	..	91.9	91.8	0.6	..	2.4	8.2

	Commercial service exports		Transport		Travel		Insurance and financial services		Computer, information, communications, and other commercial services	
	$ millions		% of total		% of total		% of total		% of total	
	1995	2007	1995	2007	1995	2007	1995	2007	1995	2007
Honduras	221	732	25.6	5.6	36.3	76.0	2.0	3.1	36.1	15.2
Hungary	5,086	16,642	8.0	19.4	57.6	28.5	3.2	1.7	31.3	50.4
India	6,763	89,746	28.0	10.2	38.2	11.9	2.5	4.2	31.4	73.7
Indonesia	5,342	12,065	1.1	18.3	97.9	44.3	..	2.5	2.1	34.9
Iran, Islamic Rep.	533	..	25.9	..	12.6	..	8.8	..	52.7	..
Iraq	..	353	..	57.8	..	40.8	..	0.4	..	1.0
Ireland	4,799	88,994	22.2	3.9	46.1	6.9	17.9	24.9	31.7	64.2
Israel	7,906	21,091	25.5	21.3	37.9	14.5	0.2	0.1	36.5	64.1
Italy	61,173	110,468	17.7	16.1	47.0	38.6	6.6	4.9	28.8	40.3
Jamaica	1,568	2,665	16.0	16.8	68.2	71.5	1.1	3.0	14.7	8.7
Japan	63,966	127,060	35.2	33.1	5.0	7.4	0.9	5.9	58.8	53.6
Jordan	1,689	3,298	24.8	19.3	39.1	70.1	0.2	..	36.1	10.6
Kazakhstan	535	3,242	65.7	53.5	22.7	31.3	0.0	3.4	11.6	11.8
Kenya	1,183	2,177	59.4	51.7	35.7	41.8	1.4	0.3	3.4	6.2
Korea, Dem. Rep.	..	..	..	..	..	..	..	..	..	..
Korea, Rep.	22,133	61,536	41.9	54.9	23.3	9.4	0.4	7.3	34.5	28.5
Kuwait	1,124	8,572	83.6	34.1	10.7	2.6	5.7	1.4	..	61.9
Kyrgyz Republic	39	654	39.6	21.3	11.9	52.9	0.6	1.3	48.4	24.5
Lao PDR	68	278	22.8	..	76.0	..	0.6	..	0.6	..
Latvia	718	3,633	91.9	50.8	2.8	18.5	2.4	7.7	3.0	23.0
Lebanon	..	12,516	..	4.6	..	39.9	..	3.1	..	52.4
Lesotho	30	68	7.0	1.0	90.9	63.0	1.4	-0.1	0.7	36.2
Liberia	..	156	..	13.0	..	84.3	..	..	..	2.8
Libya	20	99	62.7	25.4	12.0	74.6	..	..	25.3	..
Lithuania	482	3,980	59.6	59.0	16.0	29.0	0.9	0.6	23.5	11.4
Macedonia, FYR	151	581	32.0	32.0	13.6	22.2	3.6	1.9	50.7	43.9
Madagascar	219	420	29.8	28.2	26.3	43.7	2.2	0.1	41.6	28.1
Malawi	24	..	27.6	..	72.4	..	0.3	..	..	..
Malaysia	11,438	28,184	21.6	25.0	34.7	45.8	0.1	1.6	43.7	27.6
Mali	68	291	32.5	13.4	37.3	60.1	5.1	2.4	25.2	24.1
Mauritania	19	..	9.1	..	57.9	..	..	..	33.0	..
Mauritius	773	2,194	25.8	19.6	55.6	59.4	0.0	1.9	18.5	19.0
Mexico	9,585	17,726	12.1	11.3	64.5	72.8	6.7	11.3	16.7	4.6
Moldova	143	631	29.5	46.3	39.8	26.0	11.6	1.0	19.1	26.7
Mongolia	47	483	31.7	44.4	43.6	46.6	5.3	2.0	19.5	7.0
Morocco	2,020	11,490	20.3	15.8	64.2	62.5	1.4	0.6	14.2	21.1
Mozambique	242	404	24.8	31.8	..	40.4	..	1.6	75.2	26.2
Myanmar	353	321	6.5	35.1	42.7	26.8	0.0	..	50.9	38.1
Namibia	301	580	..	20.7	92.4	74.9	1.5	0.9	6.2	3.5
Nepal	592	340	9.3	10.9	30.0	58.9	..	0.9	60.7	29.3
Netherlands	44,646	94,212	40.4	29.2	14.7	14.2	1.2	2.1	43.7	54.5
New Zealand	4,401	9,178	34.7	21.7	52.7	58.9	0.1	1.2	12.6	18.2
Nicaragua	94	332	17.7	12.8	52.5	76.8	2.5	1.2	27.4	9.2
Niger	12	84	3.3	10.5	57.8	43.1	0.0	4.4	38.9	42.0
Nigeria	608	1,333	16.4	82.8	2.8	16.1	0.6	0.3	80.2	0.8
Norway	13,458	40,357	63.3	47.3	16.6	10.5	3.7	3.2	16.4	39.0
Oman	13	1,163	..	33.1	..	55.5	..	0.7	..	10.7
Pakistan	1,432	2,221	58.0	48.2	7.7	12.4	1.0	4.6	33.4	34.7
Panama	1,298	4,854	60.4	53.7	23.8	24.4	6.1	8.1	9.6	13.8
Papua New Guinea	321	285	10.8	10.9	7.8	1.3	1.2	5.4	80.2	82.4
Paraguay	566	774	13.3	16.6	24.3	13.1	5.0	4.3	57.4	65.9
Peru	1,042	3,209	32.5	19.7	41.1	60.4	7.2	10.0	19.3	9.8
Philippines	9,323	8,448	2.9	15.6	12.2	58.4	0.7	1.2	84.2	24.8
Poland	10,637	28,694	28.6	32.2	21.7	36.9	8.3	1.2	41.4	29.6
Portugal	8,161	22,906	18.6	25.7	59.2	44.4	4.5	2.1	17.7	27.9
Puerto Rico	..	..	..	..	..	..	..	..	..	..

	Commercial service exports		Transport		Travel		Insurance and financial services		Computer, information, communications, and other commercial services	
	$ millions		% of total		% of total		% of total		% of total	
	1995	2007	1995	2007	1995	2007	1995	2007	1995	2007
Romania	1,476	10,398	31.9	24.4	40.0	14.1	5.4	16.6	22.7	44.9
Russian Federation	10,567	39,119	35.8	30.2	40.8	24.6	0.6	4.0	22.8	41.2
Rwanda	11	126	60.6	28.5	21.9	51.8	1.1	0.7	17.6	19.0
Saudi Arabia	3,475	7,901	..	..	..	..	..	..	..	..
Senegal	364	712	15.4	15.9	46.1	35.1	0.6	2.6	37.9	46.4
Serbia	..	3,140	..	23.1	..	27.6	..	1.8	..	47.6
Sierra Leone	71	42	13.7	36.7	80.5	52.0	0.3	2.0	5.6	9.3
Singapore	25,404	69,712	32.7	33.3	30.0	12.5	8.5	11.6	28.9	42.7
Slovak Republic	2,378	7,022	25.9	32.1	26.2	28.9	4.9	4.8	43.0	34.3
Slovenia	2,016	5,643	25.1	30.6	53.8	39.3	0.6	1.4	20.6	28.7
Somalia	..	..	..	..	..	..	..	..	..	..
South Africa	4,414	13,242	24.2	13.6	48.2	63.8	9.9	8.2	17.7	14.4
Spain	40,019	128,340	15.8	16.8	63.4	45.1	3.9	5.9	16.9	32.2
Sri Lanka	800	1,691	41.9	49.6	28.2	22.8	3.4	3.3	26.5	24.3
Sudan	82	342	0.9	3.1	9.7	76.6	3.7	7.9	85.8	12.4
Swaziland	150	447	18.2	2.0	32.2	7.1	0.0	6.9	49.6	84.0
Sweden	15,336	63,054	32.2	17.6	22.6	19.0	2.4	4.4	42.7	58.9
Switzerland	25,179	64,947	15.1	8.4	37.6	18.8	27.8	39.1	19.5	33.8
Syrian Arab Republic	1,632	2,649	14.5	8.2	77.1	76.4	..	2.4	8.4	12.9
Tajikistan	..	116	..	53.9	..	2.8	..	10.7	..	32.6
Tanzania	566	1,675	0.3	19.8	88.6	61.9	0.0	1.6	11.1	16.6
Thailand	14,652	30,124	16.8	21.1	54.8	55.3	0.7	1.0	27.7	22.5
Timor-Leste	..	..	..	..	..	..	..	..	..	..
Togo	64	175	33.9	38.6	19.9	11.8	1.8	3.8	44.3	45.8
Trinidad and Tobago	331	883	58.6	24.4	23.4	51.3	9.2	15.3	8.8	9.0
Tunisia	2,401	4,757	24.9	30.2	63.7	54.1	1.5	2.5	9.8	13.1
Turkey	14,475	28,253	11.8	21.9	34.2	65.4	1.5	3.7	52.4	9.0
Turkmenistan	79	..	79.9	..	9.3	..	0.9	..	10.0	..
Uganda	104	483	17.9	3.1	75.1	73.6	..	7.5	7.0	15.8
Ukraine	2,846	13,651	75.6	44.8	6.7	33.7	2.7	3.0	15.0	18.5
United Arab Emirates	..	..	..	..	..	..	..	..	..	..
United Kingdom	77,549	277,647	20.7	11.8	26.4	13.6	17.5	29.9	35.4	44.7
United States	198,501	472,679	22.7	16.3	37.7	25.2	4.2	14.5	35.5	43.9
Uruguay	1,309	1,735	30.5	35.1	46.7	46.6	1.5	4.6	21.3	13.7
Uzbekistan	..	..	..	..	..	..	..	..	..	..
Venezuela, RB	1,529	1,552	38.2	26.0	55.5	52.6	0.1	0.1	6.1	21.2
Vietnam	2,243	6,030	..	..	..	..	..	..	..	..
West Bank and Gaza	..	..	..	..	..	..	..	..	..	..
Yemen, Rep.	141	562	21.9	5.5	35.3	75.6	..	..	42.8	18.9
Zambia	112	279	64.3	34.5	25.9	49.5	..	6.5	9.8	9.5
Zimbabwe	353	..	26.4	..	50.6	..	0.3	..	22.7	..
World	**1,211,160 t**	**3,355,922 t**	**26.9 w**	**23.7 w**	**32.5 w**	**26.6 w**	**5.9 w**	**8.4 w**	**36.2 w**	**42.1 w**
Low income	11,661	33,841	27.3	26.4	15.9	19.8	..	2.6	55.4	51.3
Middle income	182,607	640,179	24.8	23.3	45.2	45.0	5.9	3.8	26.6	28.0
Lower middle income	90,944	380,479	21.4	23.5	47.6	41.7	6.3	1.7	28.3	33.1
Upper middle income	91,769	265,566	27.5	23.1	43.0	47.5	5.5	5.5	25.0	24.0
Low & middle income	194,194	675,065	24.9	24.4	43.8	44.1	5.7	3.7	27.9	27.9
East Asia & Pacific	62,745	211,292	17.4	23.3	49.2	40.6	7.1	1.3	30.6	34.8
Europe & Central Asia	48,999	168,014	37.2	32.9	32.6	32.9	2.3	3.8	28.1	30.5
Latin America & Carib.	37,663	93,750	24.0	18.2	51.3	55.4	6.9	7.1	17.9	19.3
Middle East & N. Africa	..	..	..	..	..	..	..	..	..	..
South Asia	10,333	95,745	31.8	19.3	29.7	13.7	2.1	4.2	36.4	62.8
Sub-Saharan Africa	12,142	38,309	26.2	32.5	31.3	46.3	5.8	5.5	40.1	16.6
High income	1,014,833	2,679,427	27.5	23.5	29.3	21.7	6.0	9.6	38.5	46.0
Euro Area	422,602	1,083,420	25.6	23.2	31.5	25.1	5.6	5.9	37.6	45.8

a. Includes Luxembourg.

Structure of service exports | 4.6

About the data

Balance of payments statistics, the main source of information on international trade in services, have many weaknesses. Some large economies—such as the former Soviet Union—did not report data on trade in services until recently. Disaggregation of important components may be limited and varies considerably across countries. There are inconsistencies in the methods used to report items. And the recording of major flows as net items is common (for example, insurance transactions are often recorded as premiums less claims). These factors contribute to a downward bias in the value of the service trade reported in the balance of payments.

Efforts are being made to improve the coverage, quality, and consistency of these data. Eurostat and the Organisation for Economic Co-operation and Development, for example, are working together to improve the collection of statistics on trade in services in member countries. In addition, the International Monetary Fund (IMF) has implemented the new classification of trade in services introduced in the fifth edition of its *Balance of Payments Manual* (1993).

Still, difficulties in capturing all the dimensions of international trade in services mean that the record is likely to remain incomplete. Cross-border intrafirm service transactions, which are usually not captured in the balance of payments, have increased in recent years. An example is transnational corporations' use of mainframe computers around the clock for data processing, exploiting time zone differences between their home country and the host countries of their affiliates. Another important dimension of service trade not captured by conventional balance of payments statistics is establishment trade—sales in the host country by foreign affiliates. By contrast, cross-border intrafirm transactions in merchandise may be reported as exports or imports in the balance of payments.

The data on exports of services in the table and on imports of services in table 4.7, unlike those in editions before 2000, include only commercial services and exclude the category "government services not included elsewhere." The data are compiled by the IMF based on returns from national sources. Data on total trade in goods and services from the IMF's Balance of Payments database are shown in table 4.15.

International transactions in services are defined by the IMF's *Balance of Payments Manual* (1993) as the economic output of intangible commodities that may be produced, transferred, and consumed at the same time. Definitions may vary among reporting economies. Travel services include the goods and services consumed by travelers, such as meals, lodging, and transport (within the economy visited), including car rental.

Definitions

• **Commercial service exports** are total service exports minus exports of government services not included elsewhere. • **Transport** covers all transport services (sea, air, land, internal waterway, space, and pipeline) performed by residents of one economy for those of another and involving the carriage of passengers, movement of goods (freight), rental of carriers with crew, and related support and auxiliary services. Excluded are freight insurance, which is included in insurance services; goods procured in ports by nonresident carriers and repairs of transport equipment, which are included in goods; repairs of harbors, railway facilities, and airfield facilities, which are included in construction services; and rental of carriers without crew, which is included in other services. • **Travel** covers goods and services acquired from an economy by travelers in that economy for their own use during visits of less than one year for business or personal purposes. • **Insurance and financial services** cover freight insurance on goods exported and other direct insurance such as life insurance; financial intermediation services such as commissions, foreign exchange transactions, and brokerage services; and auxiliary services such as financial market operational and regulatory services. • **Computer, information, communications, and other commercial services** cover such activities as international telecommunications and postal and courier services; computer data; news-related service transactions between residents and nonresidents; construction services; royalties and license fees; miscellaneous business, professional, and technical services; and personal, cultural, and recreational services.

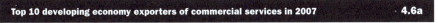

Top 10 developing economy exporters of commercial services in 2007 · 4.6a

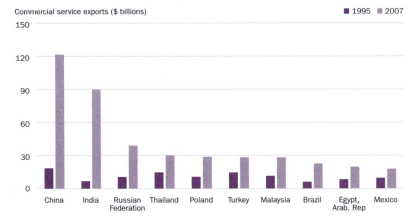

The top 10 developing economy exporters of commercial services accounted for almost 63 percent of developing economy commercial service exports and 13 percent of world commercial service exports.

Source: International Monetary Fund balance of payments data files.

Data sources

Data on exports of commercial services are from the IMF, which publishes balance of payments data in its *International Financial Statistics* and *Balance of Payments Statistics Yearbook.*

4.7 | Structure of service imports

	Commercial service imports		Transport		Travel		Insurance and financial services		Computer, information, communications, and other commercial services	
	$ millions		% of total		% of total		% of total		% of total	
	1995	2007	1995	2007	1995	2007	1995	2007	1995	2007
Afghanistan	..	..	..	..	..	..	..	..	..	..
Albania	98	1,391	61.4	12.8	6.7	66.3	22.1	4.7	9.8	16.1
Algeria	..	..	..	..	..	..	..	..	..	..
Angola	1,665	11,610	18.2	21.6	4.5	1.8	2.7	4.9	74.6	71.7
Argentina	6,992	10,522	30.1	28.6	46.9	37.3	7.1	4.4	15.9	29.7
Armenia	52	772	82.6	46.8	6.2	38.1	10.3	7.0	0.9	8.1
Australia	16,979	38,540	36.9	33.9	30.4	37.0	7.2	3.3	25.6	25.8
Austria	27,552	38,909	11.9	30.7	39.5	27.2	5.6	6.6	43.0	35.6
Azerbaijan	297	3,324	31.1	16.5	49.1	7.9	0.8	5.7	19.0	69.9
Bangladesh	1,192	2,673	65.0	78.6	19.6	5.8	5.6	8.4	9.7	7.2
Belarus	276	1,999	35.9	44.9	31.5	30.3	3.6	2.9	29.0	21.9
Belgium	32,511[a]	72,383	24.1[a]	28.2	27.7[a]	23.9	10.2[a]	4.8	38.0[a]	43.2
Benin	235	342	59.2	63.4	14.7	10.0	10.4	9.9	15.7	16.7
Bolivia	321	810	65.9	35.6	15.0	30.8	9.3	13.8	9.9	19.9
Bosnia and Herzegovina	262	550	51.5	44.1	30.9	35.4	9.5	8.0	8.1	12.6
Botswana	440	970	42.6	41.1	33.0	28.7	8.1	4.3	16.3	25.8
Brazil	13,161	34,776	44.1	24.7	25.8	23.6	9.6	6.1	20.6	45.6
Bulgaria	1,278	4,812	41.5	33.9	15.3	38.0	9.1	4.9	43.2	23.2
Burkina Faso	116	..	56.0	..	19.6	..	4.8	..	19.6	..
Burundi	62	168	49.4	32.0	41.0	61.7	5.9	1.9	3.8	4.3
Cambodia	181	859	46.4	59.4	4.6	14.3	4.3	5.5	44.7	20.8
Cameroon	485	1,413	35.4	49.7	21.7	22.5	7.2	6.7	35.7	21.0
Canada	32,985	79,824	24.1	23.5	31.1	31.2	11.3	11.3	33.5	34.1
Central African Republic	114	..	43.7	..	38.0	..	7.9	..	10.4	..
Chad	174	..	55.0	..	14.9	..	1.5	..	28.6	..
Chile	3,524	9,718	54.0	54.3	19.9	18.1	4.1	8.7	21.9	18.9
China	24,635	129,255	38.7	33.5	15.0	23.0	17.3	8.7	29.0	34.8
Hong Kong, China	24,962	41,234	22.2	31.5	54.0	38.1	6.2	7.1	17.6	23.3
Colombia	2,813	6,170	42.4	42.5	31.2	24.9	11.9	8.1	14.5	24.5
Congo, Dem. Rep.	..	..	..	..	..	..	..	..	..	..
Congo, Rep.	690	3,523	18.6	15.0	7.5	4.8	7.3	5.2	66.6	75.0
Costa Rica	895	1,799	41.4	34.8	36.1	34.9	4.6	7.3	17.9	23.0
Côte d'Ivoire	1,235	2,223	50.5	57.3	15.4	17.8	11.0	9.3	23.2	24.9
Croatia	1,327	3,858	29.5	22.6	31.8	25.5	3.4	4.0	35.3	47.9
Cuba	..	..	..	..	..	..	..	..	..	..
Czech Republic	4,860	14,308	16.5	25.3	33.7	25.5	5.2	6.9	44.7	42.3
Denmark	13,945	53,889	45.1	43.4	30.8	21.8	..	..	24.1	34.8
Dominican Republic	957	1,692	61.1	65.5	18.1	19.3	10.2	7.9	10.6	7.3
Ecuador	1,141	2,481	42.4	53.5	20.6	20.3	5.9	5.8	31.1	20.4
Egypt, Arab Rep.	4,511	13,088	35.1	46.0	28.3	18.7	4.6	10.4	32.0	24.9
El Salvador	488	1,706	55.1	42.6	14.9	35.5	11.0	8.7	19.0	13.2
Eritrea	45	..	1.6	..	6.9	..	0.3	..	93.1	..
Estonia	420	3,022	52.9	42.0	21.5	22.2	4.7	2.9	20.9	33.0
Ethiopia	337	1,740	63.4	64.7	7.5	6.2	7.4	4.1	21.7	25.1
Finland	9,418	21,745	22.8	24.2	24.2	18.3	5.0	2.2	48.0	55.3
France	64,523	129,464	32.9	29.1	25.4	28.4	6.1	4.6	35.6	37.9
Gabon	832	1,020	17.7	31.4	16.5	26.9	8.6	6.5	57.2	35.2
Gambia, The	47	77	59.6	47.2	30.4	9.6	5.8	8.1	4.2	35.1
Georgia	249	872	27.0	58.2	62.8	20.2	8.4	14.1	1.8	7.6
Germany	128,865	257,096	18.4	23.6	46.8	32.3	1.6	4.2	33.2	39.8
Ghana	331	1,808	61.3	47.3	6.2	30.9	6.5	4.6	26.0	17.3
Greece	4,003	19,783	29.9	54.0	33.1	17.3	4.5	8.5	32.5	20.2
Guatemala	672	2,005	41.4	52.2	21.0	29.8	8.7	10.6	28.9	7.5
Guinea	252	248	58.4	38.9	8.4	11.7	7.2	6.2	26.0	43.2
Guinea-Bissau	27	42	53.1	53.5	14.1	30.9	4.7	0.4	28.1	15.1
Haiti	236	476	77.6	83.9	14.7	11.7	1.7	1.5	5.9	3.0

Structure of service imports | **4.7**

	Commercial service imports		Transport		Travel		Insurance and financial services		Computer, information, communications, and other commercial services	
	$ millions		% of total		% of total		% of total		% of total	
	1995	2007	1995	2007	1995	2007	1995	2007	1995	2007
Honduras	326	1,027	60.4	60.9	17.5	29.8	2.5	1.5	19.7	7.8
Hungary	3,765	15,034	12.8	20.3	39.8	19.6	4.9	3.6	42.5	56.5
India	10,062	77,200	56.7	40.0	9.9	11.7	5.6	6.3	27.9	42.1
Indonesia	13,230	24,022	36.7	39.6	16.4	20.4	3.4	4.3	43.4	35.7
Iran, Islamic Rep.	2,192	..	43.0	..	11.0	..	9.9	..	36.1	..
Iraq	..	5,030	..	51.3	..	7.8	..	19.4	..	21.4
Ireland	11,252	94,472	15.9	3.0	18.1	9.2	1.4	17.2	64.6	70.6
Israel	8,131	17,587	44.9	33.1	26.1	18.5	3.0	2.2	26.0	46.2
Italy	54,613	118,261	24.5	23.2	27.2	23.1	9.7	4.0	38.6	49.7
Jamaica	1,073	2,205	..	..	13.8	13.5	9.2	10.5	77.1	76.0
Japan	121,547	148,685	29.6	33.0	30.2	17.8	2.4	5.2	37.8	44.0
Jordan	1,385	3,317	52.3	54.1	30.7	26.6	6.1	8.1	10.9	11.1
Kazakhstan	776	11,370	38.4	18.6	36.4	9.2	1.8	3.9	25.2	68.3
Kenya	900	1,268	46.4	63.8	21.4	20.7	10.4	-6.6	21.8	22.1
Korea, Dem. Rep.	..	..	..	..	..	..	..	..	..	..
Korea, Rep.	25,394	82,523	38.0	36.2	25.0	25.3	1.5	2.2	35.5	36.3
Kuwait	3,826	10,431	39.4	38.1	58.8	58.7	1.7	1.9	0.1	1.3
Kyrgyz Republic	193	577	27.1	58.4	3.4	15.6	4.3	3.2	65.3	22.8
Lao PDR	119	76	43.3	..	25.0	..	4.0	..	27.7	..
Latvia	225	2,678	68.2	29.3	10.8	34.6	7.0	4.0	14.0	32.0
Lebanon	..	9,970	..	17.2	..	31.2	..	3.0	..	48.6
Lesotho	58	88	74.9	78.5	22.6	18.5	0.2	..	2.4	3.1
Liberia	..	214	..	57.3	..	9.8	..	2.3	..	30.6
Libya	510	2,438	60.4	51.8	15.0	36.4	..	7.8	24.7	3.9
Lithuania	457	3,282	63.9	47.7	23.3	34.8	1.1	3.2	11.7	14.3
Macedonia, FYR	300	548	49.6	42.3	8.8	12.9	20.7	4.4	20.9	40.4
Madagascar	277	462	55.6	48.5	21.1	15.9	3.7	1.0	19.6	34.7
Malawi	151	..	66.8	..	26.0	..	0.1	..	7.2	..
Malaysia	14,821	27,784	37.8	39.5	15.6	18.9	..	3.2	46.5	38.3
Mali	412	672	59.6	60.3	11.9	17.9	1.4	5.0	27.1	16.7
Mauritania	197	..	61.5	..	11.6	..	1.4	..	25.4	..
Mauritius	630	1,538	39.9	37.4	25.2	23.5	4.6	5.5	30.3	33.6
Mexico	9,021	22,990	38.0	12.0	35.1	36.4	12.5	48.7	14.4	2.9
Moldova	193	593	51.6	41.3	29.2	35.9	9.3	2.1	9.9	20.7
Mongolia	87	514	69.6	49.5	22.3	36.5	1.8	3.9	8.1	10.1
Morocco	1,350	4,527	48.1	48.8	22.4	19.4	3.5	2.5	25.9	29.2
Mozambique	350	819	32.7	36.0	..	22.0	2.2	2.9	65.1	39.2
Myanmar	233	635	11.0	48.6	7.7	5.8	0.5	..	80.8	45.6
Namibia	538	505	36.5	47.7	16.7	26.2	9.5	6.3	37.3	19.8
Nepal	305	716	36.3	40.1	44.7	38.2	3.0	4.3	15.9	17.4
Netherlands	43,618	83,769	28.9	24.9	26.8	22.8	3.0	3.2	41.3	49.2
New Zealand	4,571	8,940	41.2	33.1	27.5	34.3	5.2	4.1	26.1	28.6
Nicaragua	207	525	39.1	54.3	19.3	23.0	3.3	10.8	38.3	11.9
Niger	120	327	74.4	69.4	11.1	8.5	2.6	3.1	12.0	19.0
Nigeria	4,398	11,837	22.4	28.5	20.6	20.6	2.5	0.0	54.4	50.8
Norway	13,052	38,941	38.2	33.8	32.4	36.1	5.6	3.5	23.7	26.7
Oman	985	4,996	41.8	34.5	4.8	14.9	4.6	7.7	48.8	42.9
Pakistan	2,431	8,409	67.0	38.7	18.4	18.9	4.3	3.2	10.3	39.2
Panama	1,049	2,050	71.0	59.1	11.5	15.0	8.8	14.3	8.7	11.7
Papua New Guinea	642	1,151	25.2	24.2	9.1	4.8	2.8	10.3	63.0	60.7
Paraguay	676	442	66.4	59.1	19.7	24.6	12.4	12.0	1.4	4.3
Peru	1,781	4,133	50.8	45.7	16.7	24.4	10.2	8.1	22.3	21.8
Philippines	6,906	7,245	29.7	52.7	6.1	22.3	1.6	6.7	62.6	18.3
Poland	7,008	23,696	25.2	23.9	5.9	32.7	13.6	3.9	55.3	39.5
Portugal	6,339	13,686	26.8	32.3	33.1	28.7	8.9	4.1	31.1	35.0
Puerto Rico	..	..	..	..	..	..	..	..	..	..

	Commercial service imports		Transport		Travel		Insurance and financial services		Computer, information, communications, and other commercial services	
	$ millions		% of total		% of total		% of total		% of total	
	1995	2007	1995	2007	1995	2007	1995	2007	1995	2007
Romania	1,801	10,047	33.5	32.6	38.7	15.3	5.3	17.8	22.4	34.3
Russian Federation	20,205	57,810	16.4	16.2	57.4	38.5	0.4	4.0	25.9	41.3
Rwanda	58	259	72.8	33.2	17.1	26.7	0.8	0.7	10.1	39.4
Saudi Arabia	8,670	30,798	25.3	28.9	..	..	2.8	3.2	71.9	67.8
Senegal	405	805	57.1	58.5	17.7	6.7	7.0	9.8	18.2	25.0
Serbia	..	3,456	..	28.7	..	30.2	..	2.5	..	38.6
Sierra Leone	79	86	17.4	56.3	62.5	16.5	3.8	9.9	16.3	17.3
Singapore	20,728	72,214	44.8	34.5	22.5	16.4	10.1	6.7	22.6	42.4
Slovak Republic	1,800	6,449	17.0	28.5	17.8	23.8	4.9	9.6	60.2	38.1
Slovenia	1,429	4,186	30.6	24.0	40.2	26.3	1.8	2.6	27.4	47.1
Somalia	..	..	..	..	..	..	..	..	..	..
South Africa	5,756	16,258	39.9	46.9	32.1	24.2	14.1	5.1	13.8	23.9
Spain	22,354	98,431	31.1	25.1	20.3	20.0	7.4	8.1	41.2	46.8
Sri Lanka	1,169	2,569	58.1	62.8	15.9	15.3	5.4	6.0	20.5	15.9
Sudan	150	2,873	27.3	45.6	28.7	51.4	0.3	0.3	43.7	2.7
Swaziland	206	494	15.7	11.7	20.7	10.4	4.3	12.2	59.2	65.7
Sweden	17,112	47,813	28.4	15.9	31.8	29.2	1.4	2.8	38.4	52.1
Switzerland	14,899	33,209	35.2	21.3	49.8	30.9	1.1	8.1	13.9	39.7
Syrian Arab Republic	1,358	2,437	57.2	51.5	36.7	22.2	5.6	15.2	6.1	11.2
Tajikistan	..	590	..	24.1	..	1.1	..	4.7	..	70.1
Tanzania	729	1,424	29.8	34.1	49.4	45.3	2.7	5.4	18.0	15.2
Thailand	18,629	38,173	41.8	47.6	22.9	13.5	5.2	5.0	30.2	33.9
Timor-Leste	..	..	..	..	..	..	..	..	..	..
Togo	148	295	70.8	78.6	12.5	1.8	4.4	11.4	12.3	8.2
Trinidad and Tobago	223	471	..	..	31.0	38.2	7.9	6.5	61.0	55.3
Tunisia	1,245	2,662	45.3	54.8	20.1	16.4	6.5	8.3	28.1	20.5
Turkey	4,654	14,160	30.3	46.0	19.6	23.0	8.4	15.3	41.7	15.6
Turkmenistan	403	..	40.4	..	18.2	..	6.9	..	34.6	..
Uganda	563	1,159	38.2	53.8	14.3	9.7	4.2	6.9	43.3	29.6
Ukraine	1,334	11,055	34.0	35.3	15.7	32.3	7.3	9.5	42.9	22.9
United Arab Emirates	..	..	..	..	..	..	..	..	..	..
United Kingdom	62,524	197,188	27.1	19.1	39.9	36.3	4.4	8.1	28.7	36.5
United States	129,227	341,673	32.3	28.0	35.8	23.7	5.9	18.1	26.0	30.3
Uruguay	814	1,208	46.2	51.4	29.0	19.8	4.5	5.3	20.2	23.5
Uzbekistan	..	..	..	..	..	..	..	..	..	..
Venezuela, RB	4,654	7,243	30.7	51.3	36.8	19.2	2.6	9.8	29.9	19.6
Vietnam	2,304	6,924	..	..	..	..	..	..	..	..
West Bank and Gaza	..	..	..	..	..	..	..	..	..	..
Yemen, Rep.	604	2,069	35.6	42.7	12.5	8.9	7.1	7.9	44.8	40.5
Zambia	282	886	78.9	46.5	9.2	6.3	0.0	8.7	11.9	38.6
Zimbabwe	645	..	56.0	..	18.7	..	2.9	..	22.5	..
World	**1,218,748 t**	**3,075,521 t**	**31.2 w**	**28.4 w**	**30.9 w**	**25.7 w**	**6.2 w**	**9.7 w**	**32.1 w**	**36.3 w**
Low income	22,663	59,403	49.0	47.4	18.0	15.7	4.8	..	29.0	31.4
Middle income	214,348	676,675	38.7	33.7	23.0	25.8	9.9	13.8	29.4	26.8
Lower middle income	107,442	386,677	41.8	40.9	16.3	21.8	10.4	7.5	31.5	29.8
Upper middle income	106,960	291,319	36.0	28.2	28.7	28.9	9.3	18.5	27.6	24.6
Low & middle income	236,387	735,826	39.2	34.4	22.7	25.4	9.6	13.4	29.4	27.0
East Asia & Pacific	82,593	239,360	38.0	38.8	15.5	20.6	12.1	6.7	36.7	34.0
Europe & Central Asia	43,870	165,739	29.3	31.2	26.4	29.7	7.1	8.0	37.7	31.1
Latin America & Carib.	52,171	116,734	41.3	25.9	31.2	30.5	10.1	27.7	17.8	16.1
Middle East & N. Africa	19,235	52,758	44.9	46.4	21.4	18.8	..	9.9	28.2	24.9
South Asia	15,377	92,697	58.6	45.4	13.4	13.1	5.3	6.1	22.6	35.3
Sub-Saharan Africa	24,584	73,653	39.6	43.8	24.1	22.2	8.8	4.0	28.1	30.2
High income	981,892	2,345,145	29.1	27.0	33.1	25.8	5.4	8.9	32.7	38.5
Euro area	421,783	1,001,166	24.9	25.8	31.8	26.0	5.4	5.0	37.9	43.2

a. Includes Luxembourg.

Structure of service imports | 4.7

Trade in services differs from trade in goods because services are produced and consumed at the same time. Thus services to a traveler may be consumed in the producing country (for example, use of a hotel room) but are classified as imports of the traveler's country. In other cases services may be supplied from a remote location; for example, insurance services may be supplied from one location and consumed in another. For further discussion of the problems of measuring trade in services, see *About the data* for table 4.6.

The data on imports of services in the table and on exports of services in table 4.6, unlike those in editions before 2000, include only commercial services and exclude the category "government services not included elsewhere." The data are compiled by the International Monetary Fund (IMF) based on returns from national sources.

International transactions in services are defined by the IMF's *Balance of Payments Manual* (1993) as the economic output of intangible commodities that may be produced, transferred, and consumed at the same time. Definitions may vary among reporting economies.

Travel services include the goods and services consumed by travelers, such as meals, lodging, and transport (within the economy visited), including car rental.

• **Commercial service imports** are total service imports minus imports of government services not included elsewhere. • **Transport** covers all transport services (sea, air, land, internal waterway, space, and pipeline) performed by residents of one economy for those of another and involving the carriage of passengers, movement of goods (freight), rental of carriers with crew, and related support and auxiliary services. Excluded are freight insurance, which is included in insurance services; goods procured in ports by nonresident carriers and repairs of transport equipment, which are included in goods; repairs of harbors, railway facilities, and airfield facilities, which are included in construction services; and rental of carriers without crew, which is included in other services. • **Travel** covers goods and services acquired from an economy by travelers in that economy for their own use during visits of less than one year for business or personal purposes. • **Insurance and financial services** cover freight insurance on goods imported and other direct insurance such as life insurance; financial intermediation services such as commissions, foreign exchange transactions, and brokerage services; and auxiliary services such as financial market operational and regulatory services. • **Computer, information, communications, and other commercial services** cover such activities as international telecommunications, and postal and courier services; computer data; news-related service transactions between residents and nonresidents; construction services; royalties and license fees; miscellaneous business, professional, and technical services; and personal, cultural, and recreational services.

The mix of commercial service imports by developing economies is changing   4.7a

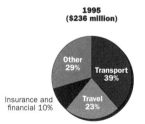

1995
($236 million)

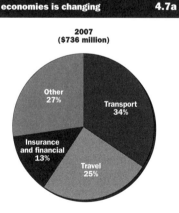

2007
($736 million)

Between 1995 and 2007 developing economies' commercial service imports more than doubled. Insurance and financial services and travel services are displacing transport and other services as the most important services imported.

Source: International Monetary Fund balance of payments data files.

Data sources

Data on imports of commercial services are from the IMF, which publishes balance of payments data in its *International Financial Statistics* and *Balance of Payments Statistics Yearbook*.

4.8 Structure of demand

	Household final consumption expenditure		General government final consumption expenditure		Gross capital formation		Exports of goods and services		Imports of goods and services		Gross savings	
	% of GDP		% of GDP		% of GDP		% of GDP		% of GDP		% of GDP	
	1995	2007	1995	2007	1995	2007	1995	2007	1995	2007	1995	2007
Afghanistan	..	110	..	9	..	25	..	12	..	56	..	24
Albania	87	88	14	9	21	30	12	28	35	54	21	20
Algeria	55	31	17	12	31	33	26	47	29	23	26	57
Angola	51	54	40	..ᵃ	35	14	82	71	68	39	30	25
Argentina	69	59	13	13	18	24	10	25	10	20	16	27
Armenia	109	72	11	11	18	37	24	19	62	39	−7	31
Australia	59	56	18	18	24	27	18	21	20	22	18	22
Austria	57	54	20	18	23	21	35	59	35	52	21	26
Azerbaijan	77	26	13	11	24	21	28	72	42	30	14	50
Bangladesh	83	77	5	6	19	24	11	20	17	27	21	35
Belarus	59	54	21	19	25	33	50	62	54	68	21	27
Belgium	54	52	22	22	20	22	68	89	63	87	25	25
Benin	82	78	11	15	20	20	20	13	33	26	8	11
Bolivia	76	63	14	14	15	15	23	42	27	34	11	30
Bosnia and Herzegovina	..	90	..	22	20	23	20	39	71	74	10	9
Botswana	34	29	29	20	25	41	51	47	38	37	36	55
Brazil	62	61	21	20	18	18	7	14	9	12	16	17
Bulgaria	71	69	15	16	16	37	45	63	46	85	12	18
Burkina Faso	63	75	25	22	24	18	14	12	27	27	18	6
Burundi	89	91	19	29	6	17	13	11	27	48	4	1
Cambodia	95	83	6	3	15	21	31	65	47	73	5	15
Cameroon	72	73	9	9	13	17	24	22	18	21	14	20
Canada	57	56	21	19	19	23	37	36	34	34	18	24
Central African Republic	79	96	15	3	14	9	20	15	28	22	6	4
Chad	91	60	7	6	13	19	22	49	34	34	5	23
Chile	61	55	10	10	26	21	29	47	27	33	25	25
China	42	33	14	14	42	43	23	42	21	32	43	55
Hong Kong, China	62	60	8	8	34	21	143	207	148	196	30	35
Colombia	65	63	15	17	26	24	15	17	21	21	18	19
Congo, Dem. Rep.	81	80	5	11	9	20	28	28	24	39	1	12
Congo, Rep.	49	29	13	14	37	27	65	73	64	43	−3	36
Costa Rica	71	67	14	13	18	25	38	49	40	54	15	19
Côte d'Ivoire	66	77	11	8	16	9	42	47	34	41	12	9
Croatia	64	56	29	20	18	33	39	48	49	56	11	24
Cuba	71	..	24	..	7	..	13	..	16	..	..	..
Czech Republic	51	48	21	20	33	27	51	80	55	75	29	25
Denmark	51	50	25	26	20	23	38	52	34	51	22	24
Dominican Republic	79	79	5	7	19	22	31	35	34	41	18	20
Ecuador	68	66	13	11	22	24	26	34	28	34	17	26
Egypt, Arab Rep.	74	72	11	11	20	21	23	30	28	35	22	23
El Salvador	87	96	9	7	20	20	22	26	38	50	15	12
Eritrea	94	86	44	31	23	11	22	6	83	34	4	10
Estonia	54	56	26	17	28	38	68	74	76	85	24	20
Ethiopia	80	84	8	11	18	25	10	13	16	32	21	21
Finland	52	52	23	21	18	22	36	45	29	40	22	27
France	57	57	24	23	19	22	23	27	22	28	19	19
Gabon	41	36	12	9	23	26	59	65	36	36	33	41
Gambia, The	90	77	14	16	20	23	49	33	73	50	6	12
Georgia	102	70	11	22	4	35	26	32	42	58	−7	17
Germany	58	57	20	18	22	18	24	47	23	40	20	25
Ghana	76	79	12	14	20	34	24	33	33	60	18	23
Greece	75	71	15	17	19	26	17	22	27	35	18	9
Guatemala	86	88	6	8	15	21	19	26	25	42	11	17
Guinea	74	84	8	6	21	13	21	37	25	39	14	9
Guinea-Bissau	95	70	6	16	22	17	12	43	35	46	5	23
Haiti	87	91	7	9	24	29	9	14	27	43	10	..

Structure of demand | 4.8

	Household final consumption expenditure		General government final consumption expenditure		Gross capital formation		Exports of goods and services		Imports of goods and services		Gross savings	
	% of GDP		% of GDP		% of GDP		% of GDP		% of GDP		% of GDP	
	1995	2007	1995	2007	1995	2007	1995	2007	1995	2007	1995	2007
Honduras	64	77	9	16	32	33	44	51	48	78	27	23
Hungary	66	66	11	10	23	22	45	80	45	79	19	16
India	64	54	11	10	27	39	11	21	12	24	27	39
Indonesia	62	63	8	8	32	25	26	29	28	25	28	26
Iran, Islamic Rep.	46	45	16	11	29	33	22	32	13	22	37	43
Iraq	..	..	..	..	..	..	..	..	..	..	..	..
Ireland	54	46	16	16	18	27	76	80	64	69	23	23
Israel	56	56	28	25	25	20	29	43	37	45	13	..
Italy	58	59	18	20	20	21	26	29	22	30	22	20
Jamaica	70	72	11	16	29	30	51	45	61	63	24	15
Japan	55	57	15	18	28	24	9	16	8	15	30	28
Jordan	65	91	24	23	33	27	52	58	73	99	29	9
Kazakhstan	68	47	14	10	23	36	39	49	44	43	18	29
Kenya	70	74	15	17	22	20	33	26	39	37	16	17
Korea, Dem. Rep.	..	..	..	..	..	..	..	..	..	..	..	..
Korea, Rep.	52	55	11	15	38	29	29	46	30	45	36	30
Kuwait	43	30	32	15	15	20	52	65	42	30	..	..
Kyrgyz Republic	75	101	20	18	18	26	29	45	42	90	9	7
Lao PDR	..	68	..	8	..	40	23	37	37	53	15	23
Latvia	63	65	24	18	14	37	43	44	45	65	14	15
Lebanon	101	92	15	15	36	18	11	25	62	50	–3	0
Lesotho	104	98	24	26	56	28	19	55	103	107	27	41
Liberia	..	116	..	15	..	20	9	33	72	84	..	40
Libya	59	..	22	..	12	..	29	..	22	..	..	..
Lithuania	67	66	22	17	22	30	50	55	61	67	13	16
Macedonia, FYR	70	78	19	18	21	23	33	55	43	75	14	21
Madagascar	90	84	7	5	11	27	24	30	32	47	1	13
Malawi	79	84	21	12	17	26	30	24	48	45	–4	10
Malaysia	48	46	12	12	44	22	94	110	98	90	34	38
Mali	83	76	10	11	23	23	21	27	36	37	14	13
Mauritania	77	61	11	20	20	26	37	58	45	65	17	29
Mauritius	63	69	13	14	29	27	58	62	64	71	26	20
Mexico	67	65	10	10	20	26	30	28	28	30	19	25
Moldova	57	95	27	19	25	38	49	46	58	98	19	22
Mongolia	56	48	13	13	32	40	48	64	49	66	35	42
Morocco	68	58	17	18	21	33	27	36	34	45	17	32
Mozambique	90	76	8	12	27	19	16	39	41	46	–6	3
Myanmar	87	..	..[a]	..	14	..	1	..	2	..	14	..
Namibia	54	50	30	25	22	30	49	50	56	54	32	40
Nepal	75	81	9	9	25	28	25	13	35	31	23	29
Netherlands	49	47	24	25	21	20	59	75	54	67	27	28
New Zealand	58	60	17	19	23	23	29	29	28	31	18	15
Nicaragua	83	90	11	12	22	32	19	33	35	67	–1	14
Niger	86	75	14	12	7	23	17	15	24	25	–4	..
Nigeria	..	..	..	..	..	..	44	40	42	30	..	..
Norway	50	42	22	20	22	23	38	46	32	30	26	38
Oman	51	39	25	18	15	19	44	63	36	38	..	..
Pakistan	72	75	12	9	19	23	17	14	19	21	21	25
Panama	52	60	15	11	30	23	101	80	98	75	30	23
Papua New Guinea	44	47	17	11	22	20	61	90	44	68	36	35
Paraguay	76	74	10	11	26	18	59	51	71	54	18	20
Peru	71	61	10	9	25	23	13	29	18	22	25	24
Philippines	74	75	11	10	22	15	36	43	44	42	19	34
Poland	60	60	20	19	19	24	23	41	21	44	20	21
Portugal	65	65	18	20	23	22	29	33	35	40	23	12
Puerto Rico	..	..	..	..	..	..	72	..	97	..	..	..

	Household final consumption expenditure		General government final consumption expenditure		Gross capital formation		Exports of goods and services		Imports of goods and services		Gross savings	
	% of GDP		% of GDP		% of GDP		% of GDP		% of GDP		% of GDP	
	1995	2007	1995	2007	1995	2007	1995	2007	1995	2007	1995	2007
Romania	68	69	14	13	24	30	28	31	33	44	19	21
Russian Federation	52	49	19	18	25	25	29	30	26	22	28	31
Rwanda	97	86	10	11	13	21	5	10	26	28	12	16
Saudi Arabia	47	28	24	23	20	22	38	65	28	38	20	..
Senegal	80	78	13	10	14	33	31	24	37	44	8	22
Serbia	73	81	23	18	12	23	17	29	24	51	6	8
Sierra Leone	88	83	14	10	6	13	19	21	26	28	–3	10
Singapore	41	38	8	10	34	23	..	231	..	202	52	..
Slovak Republic	52	56	22	17	24	28	58	86	56	87	27	23
Slovenia	60	52	19	18	24	31	50	70	52	71	23	27
Somalia	..	..	..	..	..	..	..	..	..	..	..	..
South Africa	63	62	18	20	18	21	23	32	22	35	17	14
Spain	60	57	18	18	22	31	22	26	22	33	22	21
Sri Lanka	73	68	11	15	26	27	36	29	46	40	20	23
Sudan	85	65	5	15	14	24	5	20	10	24	4	12
Swaziland	82	73	15	15	16	13	60	80	74	81	7	20
Sweden	50	47	27	26	17	20	40	52	33	45	20	28
Switzerland	60	59	12	11	23	22	36	52	31	45	30	35
Syrian Arab Republic	66	68	13	12	27	20	31	41	38	41	23	19
Tajikistan	62	114	16	9	29	22	66	21	72	66	23	14
Tanzania[b]	86	73	12	16	20	17	24	22	42	28	0	11
Thailand	55	53	10	13	42	27	42	73	49	66	34	33
Timor-Leste	..	..	..	..	..	..	..	..	..	..	..	..
Togo	77	81	12	19	16	18	32	40	37	57	11	7
Trinidad and Tobago	53	55	12	12	21	13	54	58	39	37	26	30
Tunisia	63	63	16	14	25	25	45	54	49	57	20	23
Turkey	78	71	7	13	18	22	14	22	17	27	15	16
Turkmenistan	44	46	8	13	49	23	75	65	75	48	50	34
Uganda	85	79	11	13	12	22	12	17	21	31	8	14
Ukraine	55	60	21	19	27	27	47	45	50	51	23	23
United Arab Emirates	48	45	16	10	30	21	69	91	63	68	..	..
United Kingdom	63	63	20	22	17	19	28	26	29	29	16	15
United States	68	70	15	16	18	20	11	11	12	17	16	14
Uruguay	73	74	12	11	15	15	19	29	19	30	14	13
Uzbekistan	51	54	22	17	27	19	28	40	28	30	27	39
Venezuela, RB	69	54	7	12	18	28	27	31	22	25	21	35
Vietnam	74	66	8	6	27	42	33	77	42	90	19	35
West Bank and Gaza	98	96	18	33	35	26	16	14	68	68	11	13
Yemen, Rep.	71	..	14	..	22	..	51	..	58	..	20	..
Zambia	72	59	15	10	16	24	36	42	40	36	5	23
Zimbabwe	65	72	18	27	20	17	38	57	41	73	17	0
World	**61 w**	**61 w**	**17 w**	**17 w**	**22 w**	**22 w**	**21 w**	**28 w**	**21 w**	**29 w**	**21 w**	**22 w**
Low income	75	74	11	9	20	25	24	32	29	38	17	26
Middle income	60	55	14	14	27	29	23	33	24	31	26	32
Lower middle income	55	48	13	12	33	35	23	37	24	33	32	42
Upper middle income	64	61	15	15	20	23	23	30	23	28	19	23
Low & middle income	61	55	14	14	26	29	23	33	24	31	25	32
East Asia & Pacific	47	41	13	13	40	38	29	48	29	39	38	48
Europe & Central Asia	63	60	16	16	21	25	26	34	27	36	21	23
Latin America & Carib.	66	62	15	14	20	22	18	24	19	23	18	22
Middle East & N. Africa	63	58	15	13	25	28	26	36	29	34	25	33
South Asia	67	59	10	10	25	35	12	21	15	25	25	36
Sub-Saharan Africa	69	66	15	16	18	22	28	34	30	37	14	17
High income	61	62	17	18	21	21	21	27	20	28	21	20
Euro area	57	57	20	20	21	22	29	41	28	39	21	22

a. Data for general government final consumption expenditure are not available separately; they are included in household final consumption expenditure. b. Covers mainland Tanzania only.

Gross domestic product (GDP) from the expenditure side is made up of household final consumption expenditure, general government final consumption expenditure, gross capital formation (private and public investment in fixed assets, changes in inventories, and net acquisitions of valuables), and net exports (exports minus imports) of goods and services. Such expenditures are recorded in purchaser prices and include net taxes on products.

Because policymakers have tended to focus on fostering the growth of output, and because data on production are easier to collect than data on spending, many countries generate their primary estimate of GDP using the production approach. Moreover, many countries do not estimate all the components of national expenditures but instead derive some of the main aggregates indirectly using GDP (based on the production approach) as the control total. Household final consumption expenditure (private consumption in the 1968 System of National Accounts, or SNA) is often estimated as a residual, by subtracting all other known expenditures from GDP. The resulting aggregate may incorporate fairly large discrepancies. When household consumption is calculated separately, many of the estimates are based on household surveys, which tend to be one-year studies with limited coverage. Thus the estimates quickly become outdated and must be supplemented by estimates using price- and quantity-based statistical procedures. Complicating the issue, in many developing countries the distinction between cash outlays for personal business and those for household use may be blurred. *World Development Indicators* includes in household consumption the expenditures of nonprofit institutions serving households.

General government final consumption expenditure (general government consumption in the 1968 SNA) includes expenditures on goods and services for individual consumption as well as those on services for collective consumption. Defense expenditures, including those on capital outlays (with certain exceptions), are treated as current spending.

Gross capital formation (gross domestic investment in the 1968 SNA) consists of outlays on additions to the economy's fixed assets plus net changes in the level of inventories. It is generally obtained from industry reports of acquisitions and distinguishes only the broad categories of capital formation. The 1993 SNA recognizes a third category of capital formation: net acquisitions of valuables. Included in gross capital formation under the 1993 SNA guidelines are

capital outlays on defense establishments that may be used by the general public, such as schools, airfields, and hospitals, and intangibles such as computer software and mineral exploration outlays. Data on capital formation may be estimated from direct surveys of enterprises and administrative records or based on the commodity flow method using data from production, trade, and construction activities. The quality of data on government fixed capital formation depends on the quality of government accounting systems (which tend to be weak in developing countries). Measures of fixed capital formation by households and corporations—particularly capital outlays by small, unincorporated enterprises—are usually unreliable.

Estimates of changes in inventories are rarely complete but usually include the most important activities or commodities. In some countries these estimates are derived as a composite residual along with household final consumption expenditure. According to national accounts conventions, adjustments should be made for appreciation of the value of inventory holdings due to price changes, but this is not always done. In highly inflationary economies this element can be substantial.

Data on exports and imports are compiled from customs reports and balance of payments data. Although the data from the payments side provide reasonably reliable records of cross-border transactions, they may not adhere strictly to the appropriate definitions of valuation and timing used in the balance of payments or correspond to the change-of-ownership criterion. This issue has assumed greater significance with the increasing globalization of international business. Neither customs nor balance of payments data usually capture the illegal transactions that occur in many countries. Goods carried by travelers across borders in legal but unreported shuttle trade may further distort trade statistics.

Gross savings represent the difference between disposable income and consumption and replace gross domestic savings, a concept used by the World Bank and included in *World Development Indicators* editions before 2006. The change was made to conform to SNA concepts and definitions. For further discussion of the problems in compiling national accounts, see Srinivasan (1994), Heston (1994), and Ruggles (1994). For an analysis of the reliability of foreign trade and national income statistics, see Morgenstern (1963).

• **Household final consumption expenditure** is the market value of all goods and services, including durable products (such as cars and computers), purchased by households. It excludes purchases of dwellings but includes imputed rent for owner-occupied dwellings. It also includes government fees for permits and licenses. Expenditures of nonprofit institutions serving households are included, even when reported separately. Household consumption expenditure may include any statistical discrepancy in the use of resources relative to the supply of resources. • **General government final consumption expenditure** is all government current expenditures for purchases of goods and services (including compensation of employees). It also includes most expenditures on national defense and security but excludes military expenditures with potentially wider public use that are part of government capital formation. • **Gross capital formation** is outlays on additions to fixed assets of the economy, net changes in inventories, and net acquisitions of valuables. Fixed assets include land improvements (fences, ditches, drains); plant, machinery, and equipment purchases; and construction (roads, railways, schools, buildings, and so on). Inventories are goods held to meet temporary or unexpected fluctuations in production or sales, and "work in progress." • **Exports** and **imports of goods and services** are the value of all goods and other market services provided to or received from the rest of the world. They include the value of merchandise, freight, insurance, transport, travel, royalties, license fees, and other services (communication, construction, financial, information, business, personal, government services, and so on). They exclude compensation of employees and investment income (factor services in the 1968 SNA) and transfer payments. • **Gross savings** are gross national income less total consumption, plus net transfers.

Data on national accounts indicators for most developing countries are collected from national statistical organizations and central banks by visiting and resident World Bank missions. Data for high-income economies are from Organisation for Economic Co-operation and Development (OECD) data files.

Growth of consumption and investment

	Household final consumption expenditure				General government final consumption expenditure		Gross capital formation		Goods and services			
	average annual % growth				average annual % growth		average annual % growth		average annual % growth			
	Total		Per capita						Exports		Imports	
	1990–2000	2000–07	1990–2000	2000–07	1990–2000	2000–07	1990–2000	2000–07	1990–2000	2000–07	1990–2000	2000–07
Afghanistan	..	..	..	..	..	..	..	..	..	..	..	..
Albania	4.3	4.3	5.2	3.8	2.4	2.2	25.8	5.5	18.9	11.0	15.7	14.2
Algeria	–0.1	5.5	–1.9	3.9	3.6	4.3	–0.6	9.4	3.2	3.3	–1.0	7.9
Angola	..	..	..	..	..	..	..	..	..	..	..	..
Argentina	2.8	3.8	1.5	2.8	2.2	2.3	7.4	11.2	8.7	7.5	15.6	8.1
Armenia	–0.5	8.6	1.1	9.0	–1.5	11.8	–1.9	24.5	–18.4	13.2	–12.7	11.3
Australia	3.2	3.9	2.0	2.5	2.9	3.2	5.1	7.4	7.7	2.0	7.6	8.8
Austria	1.9	1.4	1.5	0.9	2.5	1.5	2.4	0.8	5.5	6.1	5.0	4.9
Azerbaijan	–1.7	12.4	–2.7	11.4	–1.7	14.2	41.7	26.6	5.7	22.9	14.1	24.0
Bangladesh	2.6	4.1	0.5	2.2	4.7	10.2	9.2	8.6	13.1	11.8	9.7	9.5
Belarus	–0.5	11.2	–0.3	11.7	–1.9	2.2	–7.5	15.2	–4.8	7.8	–8.7	9.6
Belgium	1.8	1.4	1.5	0.8	1.4	1.5	2.7	3.6	4.7	3.3	4.5	3.3
Benin	2.6	2.3	–0.8	–0.9	4.4	8.3	12.2	7.7	1.8	2.7	2.1	1.8
Bolivia	3.6	2.8	1.3	0.8	3.6	3.4	8.5	0.2	4.5	10.2	6.0	6.2
Bosnia and Herzegovina	..	1.7	..	..	..	4.5	..	6.4	..	9.8	..	2.4
Botswana	2.5	4.2	0.1	2.9	6.5	3.9	6.7	–0.3	4.7	4.5	3.8	1.8
Brazil[a]	3.7	2.6	2.2	1.2	1.0	3.0	4.2	2.5	5.9	9.5	11.6	6.0
Bulgaria	–3.7	6.1	–3.0	6.8	–8.4	3.6	–5.0	16.5	3.9	9.5	2.7	12.7
Burkina Faso	5.7	4.5	2.7	1.2	2.9	8.7	3.1	9.0	4.4	10.9	1.9	7.2
Burundi	–4.9	..	..	..	–2.6	..	–0.5	..	–1.2	..	–1.6	..
Cambodia[a]	6.0	8.9	3.4	7.0	7.2	1.9	10.3	13.5	21.7	16.9	14.8	15.4
Cameroon	3.1	4.5	0.5	2.2	0.7	2.8	0.4	3.9	3.2	0.7	5.1	4.0
Canada	2.6	3.4	1.6	2.4	0.3	2.8	4.6	6.5	8.7	0.9	7.1	4.2
Central African Republic[a]	..	–0.9	..	–2.5	..	–1.3	..	1.2	..	–1.5	..	–1.8
Chad[a]	1.5	2.2	–1.8	–1.3	–8.3	5.7	4.0	1.5	2.3	41.9	–1.8	6.2
Chile	7.3	5.6	5.6	4.5	3.7	4.6	9.3	8.8	9.4	6.7	11.7	11.5
China	8.9	7.8	7.8	7.2	9.7	9.1	11.5	13.4	12.9	24.4	14.3	18.6
Hong Kong, China	3.8	3.1	2.0	2.6	3.7	0.9	4.8	2.1	7.8	10.2	8.4	9.0
Colombia	2.2	4.4	0.4	2.9	10.5	4.5	2.0	13.3	5.3	5.2	9.0	10.8
Congo, Dem. Rep.[a]	–4.5	..	–7.2	..	–17.4	..	–0.7	..	–0.5	7.7	–2.4	20.3
Congo, Rep.[a]	–1.8	..	..	..	–4.4	..	10.4	..	3.0	..	2.0	..
Costa Rica[a]	5.1	3.9	2.5	2.0	2.0	1.4	5.1	8.8	10.9	7.8	9.2	6.6
Côte d'Ivoire	4.1	–1.2	1.2	–2.9	0.8	2.7	8.1	–0.8	1.9	4.5	8.2	4.3
Croatia	2.7	4.8	3.4	4.8	1.3	1.1	5.4	12.2	5.9	6.2	4.6	7.9
Cuba	..	..	..	..	..	..	..	..	..	..	..	..
Czech Republic	3.0	3.8	3.0	3.7	–0.9	2.2	4.6	4.7	8.7	11.9	12.0	10.6
Denmark	2.2	3.0	1.8	2.6	2.4	1.5	5.7	3.9	5.1	4.2	6.1	6.8
Dominican Republic[a]	5.3	3.8	3.4	2.2	5.2	5.1	10.4	1.2	9.1	4.2	9.4	1.2
Ecuador[a]	2.1	5.9	0.3	4.7	–1.5	2.9	–0.6	8.1	5.3	7.1	2.8	9.9
Egypt, Arab Rep.	3.7	3.8	1.8	2.0	4.4	2.8	5.8	5.7	3.5	16.7	3.0	13.5
El Salvador	5.3	3.5	3.3	2.0	2.8	1.3	7.1	2.5	13.4	4.9	11.6	5.0
Eritrea	–5.0	1.6	–6.7	–2.3	22.6	1.2	19.1	–1.0	–2.5	–6.3	7.5	–3.7
Estonia	0.6	10.0	2.1	10.3	5.7	1.8	0.5	14.0	11.0	9.0	12.0	12.2
Ethiopia	3.6	9.5	0.4	6.7	9.0	0.4	6.5	9.3	7.1	12.8	5.8	12.9
Finland	1.7	3.5	1.4	3.1	0.6	1.6	2.2	4.2	10.3	5.1	6.5	6.1
France	1.6	2.4	1.2	1.7	1.4	1.7	1.8	2.7	6.9	2.5	5.7	4.4
Gabon[a]	–0.3	4.3	–2.8	2.6	3.7	0.4	3.0	7.3	2.1	–1.6	0.1	4.5
Gambia, The	3.6	1.8	–0.1	–1.4	–2.2	4.2	1.9	10.7	0.1	–0.4	0.1	0.9
Georgia	6.1	9.2	7.5	10.3	12.0	7.3	–12.5	18.4	12.2	6.4	11.2	8.4
Germany	1.9	0.2	1.6	0.2	1.9	0.4	1.1	–0.2	6.0	7.2	5.8	5.4
Ghana	4.1	5.8	1.4	3.5	4.8	–1.0	4.3	14.4	10.1	3.9	10.4	7.2
Greece	2.1	4.4	1.4	4.0	2.1	2.3	4.1	7.6	7.6	3.0	7.4	4.8
Guatemala[a]	4.2	4.0	1.8	1.5	5.1	0.4	6.1	4.1	6.1	2.3	9.2	3.4
Guinea	5.2	3.7	2.0	1.8	–0.5	–0.9	0.1	–5.6	0.3	1.3	–1.1	–1.6
Guinea-Bissau	2.6	6.9	–0.4	3.7	1.9	–0.8	–6.5	–0.4	15.4	4.5	–0.4	0.7
Haiti	..	..	..	..	..	..	..	..	..	..	..	..

Growth of consumption and investment

	Household final consumption expenditure				General government final consumption expenditure		Gross capital formation		Goods and services			
	average annual % growth				average annual % growth		average annual % growth		average annual % growth			
	Total		Per capita						Exports		Imports	
	1990–2000	2000–07	1990–2000	2000–07	1990–2000	2000–07	1990–2000	2000–07	1990–2000	2000–07	1990–2000	2000–07
Honduras[a]	3.0	5.4	0.6	3.4	2.0	5.8	6.9	6.6	1.6	6.9	3.8	7.4
Hungary	−0.1	4.5	0.1	4.7	0.9	2.3	9.6	0.8	9.9	11.2	11.4	10.0
India	4.8	6.0	2.9	4.5	6.6	3.4	6.9	15.1	12.3	15.7	14.4	19.4
Indonesia	6.6	4.1	5.0	2.7	0.1	7.9	−0.6	5.7	5.9	8.3	5.7	9.8
Iran, Islamic Rep.	3.2	7.4	1.6	5.8	1.6	3.6	−0.1	8.3	1.2	5.0	−6.8	13.2
Iraq	..	..	..	..	..	..	..	..	..	..	..	..
Ireland	4.6	4.7	3.7	2.7	6.1	6.0	10.2	5.6	15.7	4.9	14.5	4.4
Israel	4.8	3.2	2.2	1.3	2.7	1.0	1.8	1.7	10.9	5.6	7.5	3.4
Italy	1.5	0.9	1.5	0.2	−0.2	2.0	1.6	1.6	5.9	1.8	4.4	2.8
Jamaica	..	..	..	..	..	..	..	..	..	..	..	..
Japan	1.5	1.3	1.3	1.1	2.9	1.9	−0.8	0.1	4.1	7.7	4.2	4.3
Jordan	4.9	6.7	1.1	4.1	4.7	2.9	0.3	8.7	2.6	8.9	1.5	8.4
Kazakhstan[a]	−8.1	10.3	−7.0	9.7	−7.1	8.1	−18.3	21.3	−2.6	7.4	−11.2	7.4
Kenya	3.6	4.1	0.6	1.4	6.9	2.3	6.1	7.7	1.0	7.7	9.4	8.2
Korea, Dem. Rep.	..	..	..	..	..	..	..	..	..	..	..	..
Korea, Rep.	4.9	2.9	3.9	2.4	4.7	4.9	3.4	3.3	16.0	12.3	10.0	10.0
Kuwait	4.5	5.9	0.6	2.9	−2.4	6.6	1.0	13.7	−1.6	5.4	0.8	9.4
Kyrgyz Republic	−6.5	12.6	−7.4	11.6	−8.8	−0.1	−3.9	−2.4	−1.6	4.6	−8.2	16.0
Lao PDR	..	3.2	..	1.5	..	3.9	..	15.2	..	−11.5	..	−11.5
Latvia	−3.9	11.0	−2.7	11.7	1.8	2.8	−3.7	16.5	4.3	9.4	7.6	13.8
Lebanon	1.8	3.5	0.0	2.3	10.2	1.1	−7.1	0.1	15.5	9.9	−1.0	4.2
Lesotho	1.5	12.0	−0.2	11.1	9.0	2.0	2.8	−4.4	9.7	21.1	2.1	15.0
Liberia	..	..	..	..	..	..	..	..	..	..	..	..
Libya	..	..	..	..	..	..	..	..	..	..	..	..
Lithuania[a]	5.2	10.1	6.0	10.6	1.6	4.3	11.1	13.1	4.9	11.7	7.5	14.5
Macedonia, FYR	2.2	4.4	1.7	4.1	−0.4	−0.3	3.6	3.4	4.2	3.6	7.5	4.2
Madagascar	2.2	3.6	−0.8	0.8	0.0	7.6	3.3	17.0	3.8	3.9	4.1	7.3
Malawi	5.4	4.2	3.4	1.6	−4.4	5.2	−8.4	26.2	4.0	−10.2	−1.1	2.7
Malaysia	5.3	7.5	2.6	5.5	4.8	8.4	5.3	2.7	12.0	6.8	10.3	7.8
Mali	3.0	0.9	0.3	−2.1	3.2	22.2	0.4	6.2	9.9	6.3	3.5	3.9
Mauritania	..	7.4	..	4.4	..	3.1	..	23.8	−1.3	11.5	0.6	14.1
Mauritius	5.1	5.3	3.9	4.4	4.8	4.5	4.7	5.1	5.4	2.7	5.2	2.9
Mexico	3.9	3.8	2.2	2.7	1.8	0.1	4.7	0.6	14.6	5.7	12.3	6.0
Moldova[a]	9.9	10.1	10.7	11.5	−12.4	7.0	−15.5	11.9	0.7	13.0	5.6	15.4
Mongolia[a]	..	..	..	..	..	..	..	..	..	..	..	..
Morocco	1.8	4.6	0.1	3.5	3.9	3.1	2.5	8.7	5.9	7.6	5.1	8.3
Mozambique[a]	5.7	7.2	2.6	4.8	3.2	−9.3	8.6	3.1	13.1	15.9	7.6	4.4
Myanmar	3.9	..	..	..	..	..	15.3	..	10.0	..	5.8	..
Namibia	4.8	2.1	1.9	0.7	3.3	2.0	6.9	8.9	3.8	6.4	5.4	4.7
Nepal	..	..	..	..	..	..	..	..	..	..	..	..
Netherlands	3.1	0.6	2.4	0.2	2.0	2.9	4.4	0.5	7.3	4.6	7.6	4.2
New Zealand	3.2	4.8	2.0	3.3	2.5	3.8	5.9	6.4	5.2	3.2	6.2	7.5
Nicaragua[a]	6.1	3.2	3.9	1.9	−1.5	2.7	11.3	2.2	9.3	8.8	12.2	5.5
Niger	1.8	..	..	..	0.8	..	4.0	..	3.1	..	−2.1	..
Nigeria	..	..	..	..	..	..	..	..	..	..	..	..
Norway	3.5	4.1	2.9	3.4	2.7	2.2	6.0	6.5	5.5	1.0	5.8	5.6
Oman	5.4	1.3	2.6	0.6	2.4	6.1	4.0	17.0	6.2	7.0	5.9	12.8
Pakistan	4.9	5.0	2.3	2.5	0.7	8.5	1.8	6.3	1.7	10.1	2.5	9.5
Panama[a]	6.4	6.7	4.2	4.8	1.7	4.0	10.4	6.7	−0.4	5.8	1.2	6.2
Papua New Guinea	2.5	10.1	−0.2	7.6	2.5	−0.3	1.9	0.7	5.1	−0.4	3.4	4.5
Paraguay	2.6	2.4	0.2	0.5	2.5	2.5	0.7	1.8	3.1	7.4	2.9	5.0
Peru[a]	4.0	4.6	2.3	3.3	5.2	4.5	7.4	8.6	8.5	8.8	9.0	8.6
Philippines	3.7	5.1	1.5	3.0	3.8	2.2	4.1	0.5	7.8	7.1	7.8	4.4
Poland[a]	5.2	3.4	5.1	3.5	3.7	3.3	10.6	4.8	11.3	10.3	16.7	8.6
Portugal	3.0	1.4	2.7	0.8	2.9	1.6	5.8	−1.7	5.3	4.1	7.3	2.8
Puerto Rico	..	..	..	..	..	..	..	..	1.6	..	4.5	..

	Household final consumption expenditure				General government final consumption expenditure		Gross capital formation		Goods and services			
	average annual % growth				average annual % growth		average annual % growth		average annual % growth			
	Total		Per capita						Exports		Imports	
	1990–2000	2000–07	1990–2000	2000–07	1990–2000	2000–07	1990–2000	2000–07	1990–2000	2000–07	1990–2000	2000–07
Romania[a]	1.3	8.0	1.7	8.5	0.8	6.8	−5.1	9.1	8.1	10.8	6.0	11.9
Russian Federation	−0.9	10.1	−0.7	10.6	−2.2	2.1	−19.1	11.7	0.8	9.0	−6.1	19.6
Rwanda[a]	0.4	..	..	..	−2.6	..	0.4	..	−6.4	..	6.1	..
Saudi Arabia	..	..	..	..	..	..	..	..	..	..	..	..
Senegal	2.6	4.2	−0.2	1.5	0.9	0.2	3.5	11.8	4.1	3.0	2.0	6.4
Serbia	..	6.2	..	6.4	..	0.1	..	17.4	..	12.1	..	13.2
Sierra Leone	−4.4	..	..	..	10.4	..	−5.6	..	−11.2	..	−0.2	..
Singapore	..	..	..	..	..	..	..	..	..	..	..	..
Slovak Republic	5.6	5.0	5.4	4.9	1.3	3.2	8.1	7.1	8.8	11.4	12.1	10.1
Slovenia	3.9	3.0	4.0	2.8	2.2	3.2	10.4	7.2	1.7	9.2	5.2	8.8
Somalia	..	..	..	..	..	..	..	..	..	..	..	..
South Africa	2.9	5.6	0.6	4.4	0.3	5.2	5.0	9.1	5.6	3.8	7.1	10.3
Spain	2.4	3.6	2.0	1.9	2.7	5.1	3.2	5.4	10.5	3.7	9.4	6.9
Sri Lanka[a]	5.3	..	4.4	..	10.5	..	6.9	..	7.5	..	8.6	..
Sudan	3.7	6.4	1.1	4.2	5.5	8.1	22.0	13.1	11.6	13.0	8.4	13.6
Swaziland[a]	7.3	5.7	4.0	4.3	7.1	0.2	−4.7	−3.0	6.4	2.8	6.2	4.0
Sweden	1.4	2.3	1.0	1.9	0.6	0.8	1.8	4.3	8.5	5.9	6.3	4.8
Switzerland	1.1	1.3	0.5	0.6	0.5	1.2	0.7	1.1	4.1	3.9	4.3	3.8
Syrian Arab Republic	3.0	7.6	0.3	4.7	2.0	6.9	3.3	3.0	12.0	6.6	4.4	13.1
Tajikistan	−11.8	12.0	−13.1	10.7	−12.6	0.8	−17.6	9.3	−5.3	10.0	−6.0	11.2
Tanzania[b]	4.9	2.8	2.0	0.2	−7.0	16.9	−1.6	7.3	9.3	12.0	3.9	5.7
Thailand	3.7	4.8	2.5	4.1	5.1	4.9	−4.0	7.6	9.5	6.9	4.5	7.6
Timor-Leste	..	..	..	..	..	..	..	..	..	..	..	..
Togo	5.0	0.5	1.7	−2.4	0.0	1.3	−0.1	5.9	1.2	6.0	1.1	3.1
Trinidad and Tobago	0.7	13.3	0.1	12.9	0.3	4.3	12.5	4.2	6.9	5.8	9.9	9.5
Tunisia	4.3	5.1	2.6	4.1	4.1	4.3	3.6	1.3	5.1	4.1	3.8	2.4
Turkey	3.8	6.3	1.9	5.0	4.6	3.6	4.7	11.2	11.1	7.6	10.8	12.3
Turkmenistan	..	..	..	..	..	..	1.9	..	−6.1	13.9	0.6	12.3
Uganda	6.7	7.2	3.3	3.8	7.1	4.1	8.9	11.3	14.7	12.9	10.0	9.6
Ukraine	−6.9	13.7	−6.4	14.6	−4.1	2.5	−18.5	8.8	−3.6	3.8	−6.6	7.1
United Arab Emirates	7.1	12.9	1.1	7.5	6.8	0.8	5.5	5.5	5.5	12.2	6.4	13.6
United Kingdom	2.9	2.7	2.6	2.2	1.0	2.8	4.7	3.8	6.6	4.1	6.8	5.1
United States	3.6	3.0	2.4	2.1	0.7	2.5	7.5	2.5	7.3	3.4	9.8	5.2
Uruguay[a]	5.0	2.2	4.3	2.1	2.3	−1.3	6.3	5.6	6.0	8.3	9.9	5.2
Uzbekistan	..	..	..	..	..	..	−2.5	7.0	2.5	6.7	−0.4	8.3
Venezuela, RB	0.6	8.1	−1.5	6.2	3.7	7.1	11.0	10.8	1.0	−0.9	8.2	14.0
Vietnam	5.4	7.5	3.9	6.1	3.2	7.5	19.8	12.5	19.2	19.5	19.5	20.2
West Bank and Gaza	5.3	−1.5	1.2	−4.8	12.7	1.3	9.2	−3.0	8.7	−3.1	7.5	−2.3
Yemen, Rep.	3.2	..	−0.7	..	1.7	..	11.4	..	16.6	..	8.3	..
Zambia	2.4	0.1	−0.2	−1.7	−8.1	24.9	13.3	6.6	6.7	21.9	15.5	15.6
Zimbabwe	0.0	−3.8	−1.9	−4.5	−2.2	−3.0	−2.5	−10.6	10.5	−7.5	9.4	−3.3
World	**3.0 w**	**2.9 w**	**1.5 w**	**1.7 w**	**1.7 w**	**2.6 w**	**3.3 w**	**3.7 w**	**6.9 w**	**7.1 w**	**7.0 w**	**6.6 w**
Low income	3.5	4.9	1.0	2.6	0.1	6.6	5.2	8.7	7.1	11.8	6.9	11.9
Middle income	4.1	5.6	2.7	4.5	3.5	4.9	2.8	9.8	7.4	12.0	6.6	11.8
Lower middle income	5.3	6.3	3.8	5.2	6.6	6.7	5.9	12.0	8.0	16.3	6.9	13.9
Upper middle income	3.1	4.9	2.0	4.1	1.3	3.0	−0.3	6.3	6.9	7.2	6.3	9.6
Low & middle income	4.0	5.5	2.4	4.2	3.4	4.9	2.9	9.8	7.4	12.0	6.6	11.8
East Asia & Pacific	7.4	7.0	6.1	6.1	8.1	8.5	8.1	12.0	10.9	17.3	10.2	14.1
Europe & Central Asia	1.3	7.4	1.1	7.4	0.2	3.1	−8.4	10.5	2.6	8.8	0.0	12.9
Latin America & Carib.	3.6	3.8	1.9	2.4	2.1	2.7	5.4	4.7	8.5	6.2	10.8	7.1
Middle East & N. Africa	2.9	5.2	0.7	3.3	3.5	3.5	1.2	7.2	4.0	7.6	0.0	10.0
South Asia	4.6	5.7	2.6	4.0	5.9	4.2	6.5	13.9	10.0	14.5	11.2	17.4
Sub-Saharan Africa	3.2	4.9	0.4	2.4	0.4	4.9	4.6	8.0	..	..	6.0	8.4
High income	2.8	2.4	2.0	1.7	1.5	2.2	3.4	2.1	6.8	5.1	7.1	5.3
Euro area	1.9	1.5	1.6	0.9	1.5	1.8	2.2	2.0	6.8	4.7	6.2	4.7

a. Household final consumption expenditure includes statistical discrepancy. b. Covers mainland Tanzania only.

Growth of consumption and investment

4.9

About the data

Measures of growth in consumption and capital formation are subject to two kinds of inaccuracy. The first stems from the difficulty of measuring expenditures at current price levels, as described in *About the data* for table 4.8. The second arises in deflating current price data to measure volume growth, where results depend on the relevance and reliability of the price indexes and weights used. Measuring price changes is more difficult for investment goods than for consumption goods because of the one-time nature of many investments and because the rate of technological progress in capital goods makes capturing change in quality difficult. (An example is computers—prices have fallen as quality has improved.) Several countries estimate capital formation from the supply side, identifying capital goods entering an economy directly from detailed production and international trade statistics. This means that the price indexes used in deflating production and international trade, reflecting delivered or offered prices, will determine the deflator for capital formation expenditures on the demand side.

Growth rates of household final consumption expenditure, household final consumption expenditure per capita, general government final consumption expenditure, gross capital formation, and exports and imports of goods and services are estimated using constant price data. (Consumption, capital formation, and exports and imports of goods and services as shares of GDP are shown in table 4.8.)

To obtain government consumption in constant prices, countries may deflate current values by applying a wage (price) index or extrapolate from the change in government employment. Neither technique captures improvements in productivity or changes in the quality of government services. Deflators for household consumption are usually calculated on the basis of the consumer price index. Many countries estimate household consumption as a residual that includes statistical discrepancies associated with the estimation of other expenditure items, including changes in inventories; thus these estimates lack detailed breakdowns of household consumption expenditures.

Definitions

• **Household final consumption expenditure** is the market value of all goods and services, including durable products (such as cars and computers), purchased by households. It excludes purchases of dwellings but includes imputed rent for owner-occupied dwellings. It also includes government fees for permits and licenses. Expenditures of nonprofit institutions serving households are included, even when reported separately. Household consumption expenditure may include any statistical discrepancy in the use of resources relative to the supply of resources. • **Household final consumption expenditure per capita** is household final consumption expenditure divided by midyear population. • **General government final consumption expenditure** is all government current expenditures for goods and services (including compensation of employees). It also includes most expenditures on national defense and security but excludes military expenditures with potentially wider public use that are part of government capital formation. • **Gross capital formation** is outlays on additions to fixed assets of the economy, net changes in inventories, and net acquisitions of valuables. Fixed assets include land improvements (fences, ditches, drains); plant, machinery, and equipment purchases; and construction (roads, railways, schools, buildings, and so on). Inventories are goods held to meet temporary or unexpected fluctuations in production or sales, and "work in progress." • **Exports** and **imports of goods and services** are the value of all goods and other market services provided to or received from the rest of the world. They include the value of merchandise, freight, insurance, transport, travel, royalties, license fees, and other services (communication, construction, financial, information, business, personal, government services, and so on). They exclude compensation of employees and investment income (factor services in the 1968 System of National Accounts) and transfer payments.

GDP per capita is still lagging in some regions | 4.9a

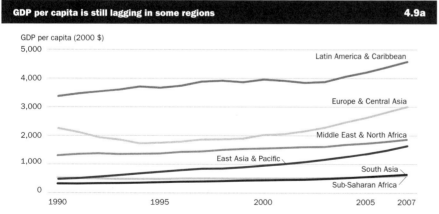

Although GDP per capita more than tripled in East Asia and Pacific between 1990 and 2007, it is still less than GDP per capita in Latin America and Caribbean, Europe and Central Asia, and Middle East and North Africa.

Source: World Development Indicators data files.

Data sources

Data on national accounts indicators for most developing countries are collected from national statistical organizations and central banks by visiting and resident World Bank missions. Data for high-income economies are from Organisation for Economic Co-operation and Development (OECD) data files.

Central government finances

	Revenue[a]		Expense		Cash surplus or deficit		Net incurrence of liabilities				Debt and interest payments	
	% of GDP		% of GDP		% of GDP		% of GDP Domestic		Foreign		Total debt % of GDP	Interest % of revenue
	1995	2007	1995	2007	1995	2007	1995	2007	1995	2007	2007	2007
Afghanistan[b]	..	7.4	..	17.1	..	–1.7	..	0.3	..	2.1	9.3	0.1
Albania[b]	21.2	23.6	25.6	21.9	–8.9	–3.0	7.4	1.9	2.1	1.0	..	15.5
Algeria[b]	30.2	40.1	24.2	18.6	–1.3	6.1	–7.4	–3.6	8.6	–1.2	..	2.1
Angola	..	..	..	..	..	..	..	..	..	..	..	..
Argentina	..	18.1	..	18.3	..	–0.5	..	0.5	..	1.5	..	26.5
Armenia[b]	..	21.0	..	16.6	..	–0.6	..	0.3	..	1.8	..	1.5
Australia	..	27.5	..	25.6	..	1.7	..	..	..	..	21.0	3.5
Austria	37.1	37.1	41.7	38.4	–4.2	–0.9	..	..	..	..	59.2	7.3
Azerbaijan[b]	18.0	..	19.8	..	–3.1	..	..	..	..	..	..	..
Bangladesh[b]	..	10.3	..	10.1	..	–1.3	..	2.4	..	0.5	..	20.7
Belarus[b]	30.0	38.7	28.7	35.0	–2.7	0.4	2.2	0.3	0.4	3.2	9.0	0.9
Belgium	41.5	40.8	45.6	41.1	–3.8	0.3	..	..	..	..	84.1	9.2
Benin[b]	..	17.2	..	13.9	..	0.3	..	–2.7	..	2.5	..	1.3
Bolivia	..	23.3	..	21.8	..	1.2	..	–0.2	..	–0.1	..	8.0
Bosnia and Herzegovina	..	40.3	..	37.5	..	1.0	..	0.3	..	0.3	..	1.2
Botswana[b]	40.5	..	30.4	..	4.9	..	0.2	..	–0.4	..	..	..
Brazil[b]	26.9	..	32.9	..	–2.7	..	..	..	..	..	..	..
Bulgaria[b]	35.5	37.2	39.4	32.0	–5.1	3.5	7.4	–0.6	–0.8	–0.8	..	2.8
Burkina Faso	..	13.0	..	12.8	..	–6.1	..	0.1	..	4.3	..	3.1
Burundi[b]	19.3	..	23.6	..	–4.7	..	3.1	..	4.0	..	..	..
Cambodia	..	9.8	..	8.6	..	–1.7	..	–0.3	..	2.1	..	1.5
Cameroon[b]	11.8	..	10.6	..	0.2	..	–0.3	..	0.3	..	..	..
Canada[b]	20.3	21.0	24.2	19.1	–4.3	1.8	4.9	–0.9	0.0	0.2	45.1	6.1
Central African Republic[b]	..	8.3	..	9.7	..	–0.5	..	1.3	..	0.2	..	8.0
Chad	..	..	..	..	..	..	..	..	..	..	..	..
Chile	..	27.5	..	17.3	..	8.8	..	–1.1	..	–0.3	..	2.2
China[b]	5.4	10.3	..	11.4	..	–1.4	1.6	1.2	..	–0.1	..	4.3
Hong Kong, China	..	..	..	..	..	..	..	..	..	..	..	..
Colombia	..	24.0	..	25.5	..	–1.8	..	1.5	..	–1.0	49.1	26.5
Congo, Dem. Rep.[b]	5.3	..	8.2	..	0.0	..	0.0	..	0.2	..	..	..
Congo, Rep.	..	39.9	..	24.8	..	9.6	..	..	..	..	..	6.5
Costa Rica[b]	20.3	24.7	21.3	21.7	–2.1	1.7	..	..	..	–0.8	..	12.6
Cote d'Ivoire[b]	20.1	19.2	..	20.5	..	–0.8	–1.2	–0.1	3.8	1.2	107.7	8.9
Croatia[b]	43.1	41.0	42.5	39.7	–1.3	–1.3	–2.7	0.7	0.8	–0.5	..	4.8
Cuba	..	..	..	..	..	..	..	..	..	..	..	..
Czech Republic[b]	33.2	31.0	32.6	33.6	–0.9	–1.7	–0.5	1.8	–0.4	0.8	25.0	3.0
Denmark	39.1	40.4	38.2	36.3	1.5	4.8	..	..	..	..	23.9	4.5
Dominican Republic[b]	..	18.1	..	17.2	..	–1.8	..	0.1	..	2.5	..	8.4
Ecuador[b]	30.9	..	26.3	..	0.1	..	..	..	..	..	..	..
Egypt, Arab Rep.[b]	34.8	27.1	28.1	29.3	3.4	–4.6	..	7.3	..	0.5	..	18.7
El Salvador	..	19.2	..	17.2	..	0.8	..	0.4	..	–1.0	40.5	10.8
Eritrea	..	..	..	..	..	..	..	..	..	..	..	..
Estonia	..	32.7	..	27.5	..	3.2	..	..	..	..	4.2	0.2
Ethiopia[b]	..	..	..	..	..	..	..	..	..	..	..	..
Finland	40.6	38.9	49.9	34.0	–7.5	5.5	8.9	–0.4	0.2	–0.8	37.5	3.2
France	43.3	41.8	47.6	44.5	–4.1	–2.3	..	..	..	..	66.7	5.9
Gabon	..	..	..	..	..	..	..	..	..	..	..	..
Gambia, The[b]	23.7	..	..	..	..	..	..	..	..	..	..	..
Georgia[b]	12.2	24.0	15.4	22.9	–4.3	0.8	2.2	–0.1	2.4	0.2	22.7	2.3
Germany	29.9	28.5	38.6	29.0	–8.3	–0.4	..	0.2	..	0.1	40.8	6.0
Ghana[b]	17.0	25.5	..	29.1	..	–7.6	..	5.0	..	2.3	..	9.6
Greece	35.1	38.9	42.6	41.7	–9.1	–3.7	..	..	..	..	113.7	11.1
Guatemala[b]	8.4	12.5	7.6	13.5	–0.5	–2.0	..	1.9	0.4	1.2	22.2	10.7
Guinea[b]	11.2	..	12.1	..	–4.3	..	–0.1	..	4.5	..	..	..
Guinea-Bissau	..	..	..	..	..	..	..	..	..	..	..	..
Haiti	..	..	..	..	..	..	..	..	..	..	..	..

Central government finances | 4.10

	Revenue[a] (% of GDP)		Expense (% of GDP)		Cash surplus or deficit (% of GDP)		Net incurrence of liabilities (% of GDP)				Debt and interest payments	
							Domestic		Foreign		Total debt % of GDP	Interest % of revenue
	1995	2007	1995	2007	1995	2007	1995	2007	1995	2007	2007	2007
Honduras	..	22.1	..	22.5	..	−1.1	..	1.3	..	1.1	..	2.6
Hungary	42.7	38.1	49.6	42.9	−4.7	−4.9	3.9	−0.8	−0.7	4.5	69.4	10.2
India[b]	12.3	13.6	14.4	15.3	−2.2	−1.4	5.1	2.8	0.0	0.2	53.7	23.9
Indonesia[b]	17.7	18.4	9.7	16.9	3.0	−1.1	−0.6	0.0	−0.4	−0.4	28.8	14.8
Iran, Islamic Rep.[b]	24.2	37.2	15.8	20.5	1.1	10.6	..	−0.6	0.1	0.0	..	0.8
Iraq	..	..	..	..	..	..	..	..	..	..	..	..
Ireland	33.6	33.3	37.5	32.2	−2.2	0.4	..	..	..	..	27.4	2.8
Israel	..	40.2	..	42.1	..	0.3	..	..	..	..	..	10.4
Italy	40.4	37.9	48.0	39.8	−7.5	−1.8	..	..	..	..	104.8	12.4
Jamaica[b]	..	64.4	33.3	63.1	..	−28.9	..	..	..	..	128.7	20.1
Japan	20.7	..	..	..	..	..	1.5	..	..	..	..	..
Jordan[b]	28.2	32.3	26.1	36.6	0.9	−5.1	−2.5	3.1	6.1	−3.0	77.5	8.1
Kazakhstan[b]	14.0	15.9	18.7	14.1	−1.8	1.2	0.8	1.0	2.8	−0.4	5.3	1.5
Kenya[b]	21.6	18.9	25.9	19.7	−5.1	−3.0	3.9	2.1	−1.3	0.1	..	10.9
Korea, Dem. Rep.	..	..	..	..	..	..	..	..	..	..	..	..
Korea, Rep.[b]	17.8	26.6	14.3	20.1	2.4	4.6	−0.3	−2.6	−0.1	−0.1	..	5.6
Kuwait	36.8	48.3	46.4	32.0	−13.6	16.3	..	..	..	..	..	0.1
Kyrgyz Republic[b]	16.7	21.0	25.6	18.4	−10.8	−1.5	..	0.1	..	1.3	..	2.6
Lao PDR	..	13.6	..	10.8	..	−3.0	..	0.1	..	3.8	..	3.1
Latvia[b]	25.8	28.1	28.3	27.8	−2.7	0.9	2.4	−0.2	1.5	0.4	..	1.1
Lebanon	..	21.5	..	32.2	..	−11.5	..	3.9	..	2.7	..	56.0
Lesotho[b]	46.1	63.0	31.8	47.4	4.7	9.2	0.0	..	5.8	..	..	4.0
Liberia	..	..	..	..	..	..	..	..	..	..	..	..
Libya	..	..	..	..	..	..	..	..	..	..	..	..
Lithuania	..	29.3	..	29.7	..	−0.9	..	−0.7	..	1.8	19.3	2.2
Macedonia, FYR	..	..	..	..	..	..	..	..	..	..	..	..
Madagascar	..	11.8	..	11.2	..	−2.7	..	0.7	..	2.2	..	7.0
Malawi	..	..	..	..	..	..	..	..	..	..	..	..
Malaysia[b]	24.4	..	17.2	..	2.4	..	..	..	..	−0.8	..	..
Mali	..	16.2	..	15.2	..	−5.6	..	−1.0	..	3.5	..	1.7
Mauritania	..	..	..	..	..	..	..	..	..	..	..	..
Mauritius[b]	21.6	20.9	19.9	21.3	−1.3	−2.3	3.1	−0.6	−0.6	2.1	40.4	14.8
Mexico[b]	15.3	..	15.0	..	−0.6	..	..	..	5.5	..	..	..
Moldova[b]	28.4	34.3	38.4	32.5	−6.3	−0.3	3.0	0.1	2.7	0.2	23.3	3.2
Mongolia	..	40.5	..	25.0	..	7.7	..	2.6	..	2.8	46.9	1.0
Morocco[b]	..	34.8	..	29.2	..	2.5	..	−2.9	..	0.1	..	5.6
Mozambique	..	..	..	..	..	..	..	..	..	..	..	..
Myanmar	6.4	8.0	..	3.4	..	−1.8	..	1.8	..	0.0	..	..
Namibia[b]	31.7	..	35.7	..	−5.0	..	..	..	..	..	..	..
Nepal[b]	10.5	11.9	..	15.1	..	−1.0	0.6	1.2	2.5	0.3	43.0	6.0
Netherlands	41.5	41.3	50.8	40.8	−9.2	0.3	..	..	..	..	44.0	4.4
New Zealand	..	36.8	..	32.7	..	3.1	..	−1.7	..	2.8	38.6	3.4
Nicaragua[b]	12.8	19.5	14.2	19.0	0.6	0.4	..	..	3.4	..	..	6.5
Niger	..	13.9	..	12.0	..	−1.0	..	−2.0	..	2.5	..	1.8
Nigeria	..	..	..	..	..	..	..	..	..	..	..	..
Norway	..	50.3	..	31.7	..	18.0	..	−1.3	..	1.6	46.1	1.6
Oman[b]	27.8	..	32.4	..	−8.9	..	−0.1	..	0.0	..	..	..
Pakistan[b]	17.2	14.4	19.1	16.2	−5.3	−4.1	..	..	..	..	..	29.2
Panama[b]	26.1	..	22.0	..	1.5	..	..	..	..	..	..	..
Papua New Guinea[b]	22.7	..	24.5	..	−0.5	..	1.5	..	−0.7	..	..	..
Paraguay[b]	..	20.3	..	16.8	..	1.8	..	0.9	..	−0.3	..	4.0
Peru[b]	17.4	20.0	17.4	17.0	−1.3	2.0	..	2.1	3.9	−2.0	27.2	8.7
Philippines[b]	17.7	15.8	15.9	17.2	−0.8	−1.5	−0.5	1.2	−0.7	0.9	77.7	26.5
Poland	..	32.7	..	34.5	..	−2.0	..	1.9	..	1.7	47.4	5.9
Portugal	35.3	39.4	37.8	41.9	−3.0	−2.6	−3.5	−0.2	4.1	2.5	70.9	7.0
Puerto Rico	..	..	..	..	..	..	..	..	..	..	..	..

	Revenue[a]		Expense		Cash surplus or deficit		Net incurrence of liabilities				Debt and interest payments	
	% of GDP		% of GDP		% of GDP		Domestic		Foreign		Total debt % of GDP	Interest % of revenue
	1995	2007	1995	2007	1995	2007	1995	2007	1995	2007	2007	2007
Romania	..	25.8	..	26.8	..	−2.4	..	2.0	..	1.2	..	2.6
Russian Federation	..	31.6	..	23.2	..	6.2	..	0.5	..	−0.8	7.2	1.4
Rwanda[b]	10.6	..	15.0	..	−5.6	..	2.9	..	..	..	..	..
Saudi Arabia	..	..	..	..	..	..	..	..	..	..	..	..
Senegal[b]	15.2	..	..	..	..	..	..	..	..	..	..	..
Serbia[b]	..	..	..	..	..	..	..	..	..	..	..	..
Sierra Leone[b]	9.4	12.3	..	23.7	..	−2.5	0.3	..	..	..	..	21.0
Singapore[b]	26.7	21.6	12.4	13.6	19.8	12.5	10.3	13.6	0.0	..	86.7	0.1
Slovak Republic	..	29.1	..	30.6	..	−1.8	..	−1.2	..	1.7	31.3	5.2
Slovenia[b]	35.8	38.6	34.3	38.6	−0.1	−0.7	−0.4	1.5	0.3	−0.4	..	3.7
Somalia	..	..	..	..	..	..	..	..	..	..	..	..
South Africa	..	32.0	..	30.1	..	1.7	..	0.3	..	−0.2	..	8.3
Spain	32.0	27.8	37.1	25.1	−5.8	2.6	..	..	..	..	35.4	4.4
Sri Lanka[b]	20.4	15.8	26.0	20.1	−7.6	−6.5	5.2	4.2	3.2	2.8	85.0	30.7
Sudan[b]	7.2	..	6.8	..	−0.4	..	0.3	..	..	..	..	..
Swaziland[b]	..	..	..	..	..	..	..	..	..	..	..	..
Sweden	35.0	..	44.1	..	−9.3	..	..	..	..	−1.2	47.4	..
Switzerland[b]	22.6	18.6	25.7	18.4	−0.6	0.6	−0.5	−1.1	..	..	25.4	4.6
Syrian Arab Republic[b]	22.9	..	..	..	..	..	..	..	..	..	..	..
Tajikistan[b]	9.3	13.5	11.4	13.7	−3.3	−6.6	0.1	..	2.3	..	..	5.1
Tanzania	..	..	..	..	..	..	..	..	..	..	..	..
Thailand	..	19.6	..	17.7	..	0.1	..	2.7	..	−1.0	26.2	5.6
Timor-Leste	..	..	..	..	..	..	..	..	..	..	..	..
Togo[b]	..	17.0	..	17.5	..	−0.8	..	−0.5	..	0.7	..	5.6
Trinidad and Tobago[b]	27.2	33.4	25.3	28.4	−0.1	1.8	2.8	−0.9	2.6	−0.3	..	6.1
Tunisia[b]	30.0	30.0	28.4	29.0	−2.5	−2.2	0.9	0.3	2.9	−1.0	50.9	8.8
Turkey[b]	..	25.5	..	24.2	..	1.4	..	1.3	..	−0.3	43.8	22.8
Turkmenistan	..	..	..	..	..	..	..	..	..	..	..	..
Uganda[b]	10.6	12.7	..	16.5	..	−1.9	..	1.6	..	1.5	..	7.8
Ukraine[b]	..	34.7	..	35.0	..	−0.6	..	0.5	..	0.4	12.4	1.5
United Arab Emirates[b]	10.1	..	9.3	..	0.5	..	..	..	..	..	..	..
United Kingdom	37.0	38.1	36.9	40.8	0.3	−2.7	−0.3	3.5	0.0	0.0	48.4	5.7
United States	..	19.6	..	21.6	..	−2.1	..	0.7	..	1.7	47.3	11.6
Uruguay[b]	27.6	26.9	27.1	26.9	−1.2	−1.6	7.9	−0.4	1.1	4.4	59.3	14.2
Uzbekistan	..	..	..	..	..	..	..	..	..	..	..	..
Venezuela, RB[b]	16.9	28.3	18.5	25.1	−2.3	2.2	1.1	1.2	0.1	3.3	..	10.4
Vietnam	..	..	..	..	..	..	..	..	..	..	..	..
West Bank and Gaza	..	..	..	..	..	..	..	..	..	..	..	..
Yemen, Rep.[b]	17.3	..	19.1	..	−3.9	..	..	..	..	..	..	..
Zambia[b]	20.0	17.7	21.4	23.0	−3.1	−0.8	28.0	..	16.2	..	..	7.2
Zimbabwe[b]	26.7	..	32.1	..	−5.4	..	−1.4	..	1.6	..	..	..
World	.. w	**26.8 w**	.. w	**27.4 w**	.. w	**−0.8 w**	.. m	.. m	.. m	.. m	.. m	**5.6 m**
Low income	..	..	..	..	..	..	..	..	..	..	..	..
Middle income	16.4	18.2	..	18.6	..	−1.5	..	1.0	..	0.0	..	5.6
Lower middle income	11.9	16.2	..	16.1	..	−1.1	..	1.1	..	0.1	..	5.6
Upper middle income	..	..	..	..	..	..	..	0.3	..	0.4	..	4.8
Low & middle income	..	17.9	..	18.4	..	−1.5	..	..	..	..	..	7.1
East Asia & Pacific	8.4	11.6	..	12.2	..	−1.1	..	2.1	..	..	..	..
Europe & Central Asia	..	30.1	..	27.4	..	1.8	..	0.3	..	0.4	..	2.2
Latin America & Carib.	21.2	..	23.4	..	−1.5	..	..	1.7	..	1.2	..	8.7
Middle East & N. Africa	28.8	33.0	..	25.2	..	2.4	..	−0.2	..	0.1	..	8.1
South Asia	13.1	13.5	15.3	15.1	−2.7	−1.8	3.8	2.6	1.1	0.4	53.7	22.3
Sub-Saharan Africa	..	..	..	..	..	..	..	..	..	..	..	..
High income	..	27.0	..	28.0	..	−1.0	..	..	..	..	44.0	5.2
Euro area	34.8	35.0	42.4	35.9	−7.5	−0.7	..	..	..	..	44.0	5.9

a. Excludes grants. b. Data were reported on a cash basis and have been adjusted to the accrual framework.

Central government finances

4.10 ECONOMY

About the data

Tables 4.10–4.12 present an overview of the size and role of central governments relative to national economies. The tables are based on the concepts and recommendations of the second edition of the International Monetary Fund's (IMF) *Government Finance Statistics Manual 2001*. Before 2005 *World Development Indicators* reported data derived on the basis of the 1986 manual's cash-based method. The 2001 manual, harmonized with the 1993 System of National Accounts, recommends an accrual accounting method, focusing on all economic events affecting assets, liabilities, revenues, and expenses, not only those represented by cash transactions. It takes all stocks into account, so that stock data at the end of an accounting period equal stock data at the beginning of the period plus flows over the period. The 1986 manual considered only the debt stock data. Further, the new manual no longer distinguishes between current and capital revenue or expenditures, and it introduces the concepts of nonfinancial and financial assets. Most countries still follow the 1986 manual, however. The IMF has reclassified historical *Government Finance Statistics Yearbook* data to conform to the 2001 manual's format. Because of reporting differences, the reclassified data understate both revenue and expense.

The 2001 manual describes government's economic functions as the provision of goods and services on a nonmarket basis for collective or individual consumption, and the redistribution of income and wealth through transfer payments. Government activities are financed mainly by taxation and other income transfers, though other financing such as

borrowing for temporary periods can also be used. *Government* excludes public corporations and quasi corporations (such as the central bank).

Units of government at many levels meet this definition, from local administrative units to the national government, but inadequate statistical coverage precludes presenting subnational data. Although data for general government under the 2001 manual are available for a few countries, only data for the central government are shown to minimize disparities. Still, different accounting concepts of central government make cross-country comparisons potentially misleading.

Central government can refer to consolidated or budgetary accounting. For most countries central government finance data have been consolidated into one account, but for others only budgetary central government accounts are available. Countries reporting budgetary data are noted in *Primary data documentation*. Because budgetary accounts may not include all central government units (such as social security funds), they usually provide an incomplete picture.

Data on government revenue and expense are collected by the IMF through questionnaires to member countries and by the Organisation for Economic Co-operation and Development. Despite IMF efforts to standardize data collection, statistics are often incomplete, untimely, and not comparable across countries.

Government finance statistics are reported in local currency. The indicators here are shown as percentages of GDP. Many countries report government finance data by fiscal year; see *Primary data documentation* for information on fiscal year end by country.

Definitions

• **Revenue** is cash receipts from taxes, social contributions, and other revenues such as fines, fees, rent, and income from property or sales. Grants, usually considered revenue, are excluded. • **Expense** is cash payments for government operating activities in providing goods and services. It includes compensation of employees, interest and subsidies, grants, social benefits, and other expenses such as rent and dividends. • **Cash surplus or deficit** is revenue (including grants) minus expense, minus net acquisition of nonfinancial assets. In editions before 2005 nonfinancial assets were included under revenue and expenditure in gross terms. This cash surplus or deficit is close to the earlier overall budget balance (still missing is lending minus repayments, which are included as a financing item under net acquisition of financial assets). • **Net incurrence of liabilities** is domestic financing (obtained from residents) and foreign financing (obtained from nonresidents), or the means by which a government provides financial resources to cover a budget deficit or allocates financial resources arising from a budget surplus. The net incurrence of liabilities should be offset by the net acquisition of financial assets (a third financing item). The difference between the cash surplus or deficit and the three financing items is the net change in the stock of cash. • **Total debt** is the entire stock of direct government fixed-term contractual obligations to others outstanding on a particular date. It includes domestic and foreign liabilities such as currency and money deposits, securities other than shares, and loans. It is the gross amount of government liabilities reduced by the amount of equity and financial derivatives held by the government. Because debt is a stock rather than a flow, it is measured as of a given date, usually the last day of the fiscal year. • **Interest payments** are interest payments on government debt—including long-term bonds, long-term loans, and other debt instruments —to domestic and foreign residents.

Data sources

Data on central government finances are from the IMF's *Government Finance Statistics Yearbook 2008* and data files. Each country's accounts are reported using the system of common definitions and classifications in the IMF's *Government Finance Statistics Manual 2001*. See these sources for complete and authoritative explanations of concepts, definitions, and data sources.

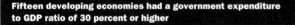

Fifteen developing economies had a government expenditure to GDP ratio of 30 percent or higher   **4.10a**

Central government expense, 2007 (% of GDP)

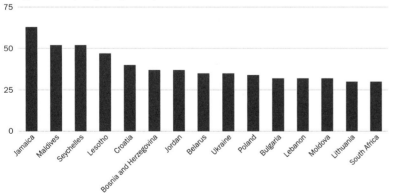

Source: International Monetary Fund, *Government Finance Statistics* data files, and *World Development Indicators* data files.

4.11 Central government expenses

	Goods and services		Compensation of employees		Interest payments		Subsidies and other transfers		Other expense	
	% of expense		% of expense		% of expense		% of expense		% of expense	
	1995	2007	1995	2007	1995	2007	1995	2007	1995	2007
Afghanistan[a]	..	67	..	28	..	0	..	5	..	0
Albania[a]	18	12	14	30	9	17	59	42	0	0
Algeria[a]	6	5	39	28	13	5	34	32	8	29
Angola	..	..	..	..	..	..	..	..	..	..
Argentina	..	5	..	12	..	26	..	50	..	7
Armenia[a]	..	37	..	22	..	2	..	34	..	5
Australia	..	11	..	10	..	4	..	70	..	6
Austria	5	6	8	13	9	7	77	70	3	5
Azerbaijan[a]	49	..	10	..	0	..	41	..	0	..
Bangladesh[a]	..	13	..	25	..	22	..	29	..	11
Belarus[a]	39	14	5	11	1	1	55	68	0	5
Belgium	3	2	7	7	18	9	71	79	3	3
Benin[a]	..	31	..	40	..	2	..	8	..	20
Bolivia	..	14	..	22	..	10	..	47	..	7
Bosnia and Herzegovina	..	24	..	28	..	1	..	43	..	4
Botswana[a]	32	..	30	..	2	..	36	..	2	..
Brazil[a]	5	..	8	..	45	..	45	..	1	..
Bulgaria[a]	18	14	7	18	37	3	38	58	2	6
Burkina Faso	..	21	..	39	..	4	..	35	..	0
Burundi[a]	20	..	30	..	6	..	14	..	10	..
Cambodia	..	41	..	33	..	2	..	19	..	5
Cameroon[a]	17	..	40	..	26	..	14	..	..	..
Canada[a]	8	8	10	12	18	7	64	67	..	6
Central African Republic[a]	..	27	..	53	..	9	..	..	..	11
Chad	..	..	..	..	..	..	..	..	..	..
Chile	..	11	..	21	..	4	..	57	..	11
China[a]	..	27	..	5	..	4	..	60	..	4
Hong Kong, China	..	..	..	..	..	..	..	..	..	..
Colombia	..	5	..	19	..	25	..	45	..	7
Congo, Dem. Rep.[a]	37	..	58	..	1	..	2	..	..	..
Congo, Rep.	..	18	..	18	..	11	..	53	..	0
Costa Rica[a]	12	12	38	42	20	14	26	18	4	15
Côte d'Ivoire[a]	..	34	..	33	..	9	..	18	..	7
Croatia[a]	35	10	27	26	3	5	32	53	3	6
Cuba	..	..	..	..	..	..	..	..	..	..
Czech Republic[a]	7	6	9	9	3	3	75	71	5	12
Denmark	8	9	13	13	13	5	64	70	4	4
Dominican Republic[a]	..	17	..	31	..	9	..	30	..	13
Ecuador[a]	6	..	49	..	26	..	..	..	..	..
Egypt, Arab Rep.[a]	18	8	22	24	26	18	6	39	..	11
El Salvador	..	16	..	40	..	12	..	22	..	11
Eritrea	..	..	..	..	..	..	..	..	..	..
Estonia	..	14	..	22	..	0	..	43	..	4
Ethiopia[a]	..	..	..	..	..	..	..	..	..	..
Finland	8	10	9	10	7	4	68	71	11	7
France	8	6	23	22	6	6	59	62	6	6
Gabon	..	..	..	..	..	..	..	..	..	..
Gambia, The[a]	..	..	..	..	..	..	..	..	..	..
Georgia[a]	52	38	11	16	10	3	26	35	..	9
Germany	4	5	5	5	6	6	67	82	20	3
Ghana[a]	..	15	..	38	..	11	..	37	..	0
Greece	10	11	22	24	27	10	36	45	5	4
Guatemala[a]	15	13	50	24	12	10	18	25	6	27
Guinea[a]	17	..	34	..	28	..	9	..	1	..
Guinea-Bissau	..	..	..	..	..	..	..	..	..	..
Haiti	..	..	..	..	..	..	..	..	..	..

Central government expenses | 4.11

	Goods and services		Compensation of employees		Interest payments		Subsidies and other transfers		Other expense	
	% of expense		% of expense		% of expense		% of expense		% of expense	
	1995	**2007**	**1995**	**2007**	**1995**	**2007**	**1995**	**2007**	**1995**	**2007**
Honduras	..	17	..	49	..	3	..	16	..	16
Hungary	8	9	10	13	20	9	57	61	13	10
India[a]	14	12	10	7	27	21	33	36	0	1
Indonesia[a]	21	8	20	13	16	16	41	63	2	0
Iran, Islamic Rep.[a]	21	10	56	37	0	1	..	32	..	18
Iraq	..	..	..	..	..	..	..	..	..	..
Ireland	5	12	15	24	14	3	33	37	1	1
Israel	..	27	..	25	..	11	..	30	..	9
Italy	4	4	14	16	24	12	54	64	6	6
Jamaica[a]	22	47	24	20	32	21	1	1	21	11
Japan	..	..	..	..	..	..	..	..	..	..
Jordan[a]	7	5	67	26	11	8	12	26	4	35
Kazakhstan[a]	..	23	..	8	3	2	58	64	..	3
Kenya[a]	15	15	28	44	46	11	..	9	2	2
Korea, Dem. Rep.	..	..	..	..	..	..	..	..	..	..
Korea, Rep.[a]	16	7	15	12	3	7	63	58	3	15
Kuwait	33	15	31	24	5	0	24	40	7	20
Kyrgyz Republic[a]	32	25	36	27	5	3	27	34	..	11
Lao PDR	..	37	..	38	..	5	..	18	..	3
Latvia[a]	20	12	20	20	3	1	56	66	0	0
Lebanon	..	3	..	27	..	40	..	22	..	8
Lesotho[a]	32	37	45	33	5	5	8	11	3	6
Liberia	..	..	..	..	..	..	..	..	..	..
Libya	..	..	..	..	..	..	..	..	..	..
Lithuania	..	13	..	18	..	2	..	62	..	9
Macedonia, FYR	..	..	..	..	..	..	..	..	..	..
Madagascar	..	14	..	46	..	10	..	14	..	16
Malawi	..	..	..	..	..	..	..	..	..	..
Malaysia[a]	23	..	34	..	17	..	27	..	1	..
Mali	..	38	..	33	..	2	..	16	..	11
Mauritania	..	..	..	..	..	..	..	..	..	..
Mauritius[a]	12	12	45	35	12	15	28	33	2	5
Mexico[a]	9	..	19	..	19	..	..	..	..	..
Moldova[a]	10	18	8	15	11	4	71	56	1	7
Mongolia	..	37	..	24	..	2	..	36	..	1
Morocco[a]	..	9	..	46	..	7	..	29	..	10
Mozambique	..	..	..	..	..	..	..	..	..	..
Myanmar	..	..	..	..	..	..	..	..	..	..
Namibia[a]	28	..	53	..	1	..	..	..	4	..
Nepal[a]	..	..	..	..	..	7	..	..	..	..
Netherlands	5	8	8	8	9	4	77	79	3	3
New Zealand	..	30	..	25	..	4	..	38	..	7
Nicaragua[a]	14	13	25	36	17	8	29	38	14	6
Niger	..	30	..	30	..	3	..	9	..	28
Nigeria	..	..	..	..	..	..	..	..	..	..
Norway	..	11	..	17	..	2	..	67	..	6
Oman[a]	55	..	30	..	7	..	8	..	0	..
Pakistan[a]	..	31	..	4	28	26	2	31	..	8
Panama[a]	16	..	45	..	8	..	30	..	1	..
Papua New Guinea[a]	19	..	36	..	20	..	26	..	1	..
Paraguay[a]	..	11	..	52	..	5	..	25	..	8
Peru[a]	20	19	19	18	19	10	33	50	8	3
Philippines[a]	15	18	34	31	33	24	15	19	..	8
Poland	..	8	..	12	..	6	..	69	..	7
Portugal	7	7	30	27	10	7	43	49	11	2
Puerto Rico	..	..	..	..	..	..	..	..	..	..

	Goods and services		Compensation of employees		Interest payments		Subsidies and other transfers		Other expense	
	% of expense		% of expense		% of expense		% of expense		% of expense	
	1995	2007	1995	2007	1995	2007	1995	2007	1995	2007
Romania	..	15	..	23	..	3	..	50	..	13
Russian Federation	..	14	..	17	..	2	..	61	..	15
Rwanda[a]	52	..	36	..	12	..	5	..	..	..
Saudi Arabia	..	..	..	..	..	..	..	..	..	..
Senegal[a]	..	..	..	..	..	..	..	..	..	..
Serbia	..	..	..	..	..	..	..	..	..	..
Sierra Leone[a]	..	28	..	26	..	19	..	9	..	18
Singapore[a]	38	44	39	32	8	0	15	24	..	..
Slovak Republic	..	9	..	13	..	5	..	68	..	5
Slovenia[a]	19	12	21	19	3	4	55	62	3	3
Somalia	..	..	..	..	..	..	..	..	..	..
South Africa	..	10	..	14	..	9	..	59	..	8
Spain	5	4	14	9	11	5	42	78	2	5
Sri Lanka[a]	23	11	20	30	22	25	24	23	10	10
Sudan[a]	44	..	38	..	8	..	10	..	..	..
Swaziland[a]	..	..	..	..	..	..	..	..	..	..
Sweden	10	..	5	..	13	..	71	..	1	..
Switzerland[a]	24	8	6	7	4	5	66	75	0	5
Syrian Arab Republic[a]	..	..	..	..	..	..	..	..	..	..
Tajikistan[a]	47	29	8	9	12	5	33	27	..	30
Tanzania	..	..	..	..	..	..	..	..	..	..
Thailand	..	27	..	37	..	6	..	30	..	3
Timor-Leste	..	..	..	..	..	..	..	..	..	..
Togo[a]	..	25	..	31	..	6	..	27	..	12
Trinidad and Tobago[a]	20	16	36	22	20	7	24	36	1	19
Tunisia[a]	7	6	37	38	13	9	36	37	7	10
Turkey[a]	..	7	..	24	..	24	..	37	..	1
Turkmenistan	..	..	..	..	..	..	..	..	..	..
Uganda[a]	..	30	..	12	..	8	..	49	..	0
Ukraine[a]	..	12	..	14	..	1	..	67	..	6
United Arab Emirates[a]	50	..	37	..	..	..	..	..	..	..
United Kingdom	22	19	7	15	9	5	54	53	9	10
United States	..	15	..	13	..	10	..	60	..	2
Uruguay[a]	13	16	17	23	6	14	64	48	0	..
Uzbekistan	..	..	..	..	..	..	..	..	..	..
Venezuela, RB[a]	6	6	22	16	27	12	61	64	2	3
Vietnam	..	..	..	..	..	..	..	..	..	..
West Bank and Gaza	..	..	..	..	..	..	..	..	..	..
Yemen, Rep.[a]	8	..	67	..	16	..	8	..	0	..
Zambia[a]	32	32	35	30	16	7	19	24	0	7
Zimbabwe[a]	16	..	34	..	31	..	19	..	..	..
World	.. m	**13 m**	.. m	**24 m**	.. m	**6 m**	.. m	**40 m**	.. m	**6 m**
Low income	..	..	..	..	..	..	..	..	..	..
Middle income	..	13	..	24	..	6	..	37	..	7
Lower middle income	..	13	..	28	..	6	..	34	..	7
Upper middle income	17	12	25	20	14	5	..	57	..	8
Low & middle income	..	16	..	28	..	7	..	35	..	6
East Asia & Pacific	..	..	..	..	..	..	..	..	..	..
Europe & Central Asia	..	14	..	18	..	2	..	57	..	6
Latin America & Carib.	13	14	26	23	20	10	..	38	..	9
Middle East & N. Africa	8	6	47	28	13	8	..	32	..	10
South Asia	..	13	..	25	27	22	24	29	..	8
Sub-Saharan Africa	..	..	..	..	..	..	..	..	..	..
High income	8	9	14	13	9	5	63	62	3	6
Euro area	5	7	11	13	10	6	61	68	3	5

Note: Components may not sum to 100 percent because of rounding or missing data.
a. Data were reported on a cash basis and have been adjusted to the accrual framework.

Central government expenses | 4.11

The term *expense* has replaced *expenditure* in the table since the 2005 edition of *World Development Indicators* in accordance with use in the International Monetary Fund's (IMF) *Government Finance Statistics Manual 2001*. Government expenses include all nonrepayable payments, whether current or capital, requited or unrequited. The concept of total central government expense as presented in the IMF's *Government Finance Statistics Yearbook* is comparable to the concept used in the 1993 System of National Accounts.

Expenses can be measured either by function (health, defense, education) or by economic type (interest payments, wages and salaries, purchases of goods and services). Functional data are often incomplete, and coverage varies by country because functional responsibilities stretch across levels of government for which no data are available. Defense expenses, usually the central government's responsibility, are shown in table 5.7. For more information on education expenses, see table 2.10; for more on health expenses, see table 2.15.

The classification of expenses by economic type in the table shows whether the government produces goods and services and distributes them, purchases the goods and services from a third party and distributes them, or transfers cash to households to make the purchases directly. When the government produces and provides goods and services, the cost is reflected in compensation of employees, use of goods and services, and consumption of fixed capital. Purchases from a third party and cash transfers to households are shown as subsidies and other transfers, and other expenses. The economic classification can be problematic. For example, the distinction between current and capital expense may be arbitrary, and subsidies to public corporations or banks may be disguised as capital financing. Subsidies may also be hidden in special contractual pricing for goods and services. For further discussion of government finance statistics, see *About the data* for tables 4.10 and 4.12.

• **Goods and services** are all government payments in exchange for goods and services used for the production of market and nonmarket goods and services. Own-account capital formation is excluded. • **Compensation of employees** is all payments in cash, as well as in kind (such as food and housing), to employees in return for services rendered, and government contributions to social insurance schemes such as social security and pensions that provide benefits to employees. • **Interest payments** are payments made to nonresidents, to residents, and to other general government units for the use of borrowed money. (Repayment of principal is shown as a financing item, and commission charges are shown as purchases of services.) • **Subsidies and other transfers** include all unrequited, nonrepayable transfers on current account to private and public enterprises; grants to foreign governments, international organizations, and other government units; and social security, social assistance benefits, and employer social benefits in cash and in kind. • **Other expense** is spending on dividends, rent, and other miscellaneous expenses, including provision for consumption of fixed capital.

4.11a

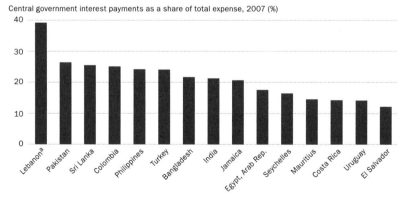

Central government interest payments as a share of total expense, 2007 (%)

Interest payments accounted for more than 12 percent of total expenses in 2007 for 15 countries.

a. Data are for 2005.
Source: International Monetary Fund, *Government Finance Statistics* data files, and *World Development Indicators* data files.

Data on central government expenses are from the IMF's *Government Finance Statistics Yearbook 2008* and data files. Each country's accounts are reported using the system of common definitions and classifications in the IMF's *Government Finance Statistics Manual 2001*. See these sources for complete and authoritative explanations of concepts, definitions, and data sources.

4.12 Central government revenues

	Taxes on income, profits, and capital gains		Taxes on goods and services		Taxes on international trade		Other taxes		Social contributions		Grants and other revenue	
	% of revenue		% of revenue		% of revenue		% of revenue		% of revenue		% of revenue	
	1995	2007	1995	2007	1995	2007	1995	2007	1995	2007	1995	2007
Afghanistan[a]	..	4	..	4	..	8	..	0	..	0	..	83
Albania[a]	8	15	39	49	14	8	1	1	15	18	22	10
Algeria[a]	65	7	10	63	18	4	1	1	..	..	5	26
Angola	..	..	..	..	..	..	..	..	..	..	..	..
Argentina	..	19	..	29	..	16	..	14	..	17	..	5
Armenia[a]	..	18	..	42	..	4	..	10	..	13	..	14
Australia	..	66	..	23	..	2	..	0	..	..	..	9
Austria	26	26	24	24	0	0	2	4	40	40	8	7
Azerbaijan[a]	31	..	34	..	33	..	2	..	23	..	0	..
Bangladesh[a]	..	17	..	28	..	27	..	4	..	..	..	24
Belarus[a]	16	6	33	34	6	17	11	5	31	30	3	8
Belgium	36	37	23	25	..	..	2	1	36	35	3	2
Benin[a]	..	19	..	36	..	24	..	6	..	..	..	15
Bolivia	..	10	..	43	..	3	..	9	..	7	..	28
Bosnia and Herzegovina	..	3	..	49	..	0	..	2	..	33	..	12
Botswana[a]	21	..	4	..	15	..	0	..	..	..	59	..
Brazil[a]	14	..	24	..	2	..	4	..	31	..	26	..
Bulgaria[a]	17	16	28	46	8	1	3	0	21	22	23	15
Burkina Faso	..	15	..	35	..	13	..	2	..	..	..	35
Burundi[a]	14	..	30	..	20	..	1	..	5	..	30	..
Cambodia	..	10	..	40	..	22	..	0	..	..	..	28
Cameroon[a]	17	..	25	..	28	..	3	..	2	..	25	..
Canada[a]	50	55	17	16	2	1	..	..	22	21	10	7
Central African Republic[a]	..	14	..	23	..	19	..	4	..	6	..	34
Chad	..	..	..	..	..	..	..	..	..	..	..	..
Chile	..	40	..	34	..	1	..	2	..	5	..	17
China[a]	9	25	61	57	7	5	0	1	..	..	22	12
Hong Kong, China	..	..	..	..	..	..	..	..	..	..	..	..
Colombia	..	17	..	26	..	6	..	8	..	4	..	39
Congo, Dem. Rep.[a]	21	..	12	..	21	..	5	..	1	..	41	..
Congo, Rep.	..	5	..	6	..	3	..	1	..	1	..	84
Costa Rica[a]	11	16	32	38	15	5	1	2	28	30	12	9
Côte d'Ivoire[a]	15	12	14	15	58	41	3	10	5	7	5	15
Croatia[a]	11	9	42	45	9	1	1	1	33	33	4	11
Cuba	..	..	..	..	..	..	..	..	..	..	..	..
Czech Republic[a]	15	19	32	27	4	0	1	1	40	45	8	8
Denmark	34	44	40	40	..	..	7	2	5	3	14	10
Dominican Republic[a]	..	20	..	53	..	14	..	4	..	1	..	9
Ecuador[a]	50	..	26	..	11	..	1	..	..	..	12	..
Egypt, Arab Rep.[a]	17	28	13	19	10	5	10	3	10	..	41	44
El Salvador	..	24	..	42	..	5	..	1	..	10	..	18
Eritrea	..	..	..	..	..	..	..	..	..	..	..	..
Estonia	..	11	..	41	..	0	..	0	..	34	..	..
Ethiopia[a]	..	..	..	..	..	..	..	..	..	..	..	..
Finland	16	21	31	32	0	0	1	2	34	31	17	14
France	17	25	25	23	0	0	3	4	47	43	8	6
Gabon	..	..	..	..	..	..	..	..	..	..	..	..
Gambia, The[a]	14	..	32	..	42	..	0	..	0	..	7	..
Georgia[a]	7	12	48	56	10	1	..	1	13	17	22	13
Germany	16	18	20	23	..	..	0	..	58	55	6	4
Ghana[a]	15	19	31	34	24	18	..	..	..	..	9	30
Greece	17	19	32	29	0	0	3	3	31	36	16	14
Guatemala[a]	19	28	46	55	23	9	3	1	2	2	6	4
Guinea[a]	8	..	4	..	62	..	2	..	1	..	23	..
Guinea-Bissau	..	..	..	..	..	..	..	..	..	..	..	..
Haiti	..	..	..	..	..	..	..	..	..	..	..	..

Central government revenues

	Taxes on income, profits, and capital gains		Taxes on goods and services		Taxes on international trade		Other taxes		Social contributions		Grants and other revenue	
	% of revenue		% of revenue		% of revenue		% of revenue		% of revenue		% of revenue	
	1995	2007	1995	2007	1995	2007	1995	2007	1995	2007	1995	2007
Honduras	..	21	..	42	..	5	..	1	..	11	..	20
Hungary	18	21	28	33	8	0	1	2	33	35	12	9
India[a]	23	41	28	29	24	15	0	0	0	0	25	15
Indonesia[a]	46	28	33	32	4	3	1	4	6	3	9	30
Iran, Islamic Rep.[a]	12	12	5	2	9	5	1	1	6	12	66	69
Iraq	..	..	..	..	..	..	..	..	..	..	..	..
Ireland	37	37	35	34	0	0	2	6	17	18	9	4
Israel	..	32	..	29	..	1	..	5	..	16	..	17
Italy	32	35	21	21	..	..	5	5	35	35	6	4
Jamaica[a]	..	9	..	18	..	5	..	13	..	5	..	51
Japan	35	..	14	..	1	..	5	..	26	..	18	..
Jordan[a]	10	12	23	40	22	9	9	14	..	0	36	24
Kazakhstan[a]	11	35	28	30	3	7	5	0	48	..	6	29
Kenya[a]	35	37	40	43	14	11	1	1	0	0	10	9
Korea, Dem. Rep.	..	..	..	..	..	..	..	..	..	..	..	..
Korea, Rep.[a]	31	31	32	25	7	3	10	8	8	15	12	18
Kuwait	1	1	0	..	2	1	0	0	..	..	97	98
Kyrgyz Republic[a]	26	9	56	50	5	12	1	..	..	..	11	29
Lao PDR	..	18	..	36	..	9	..	1	..	..	..	36
Latvia[a]	7	13	41	39	3	1	0	0	35	29	13	18
Lebanon	..	13	..	35	..	7	..	12	..	1	..	32
Lesotho[a]	15	17	12	14	49	57	1	0	..	..	24	12
Liberia	..	..	..	..	..	..	..	..	..	..	..	..
Libya	..	..	..	..	..	..	..	..	..	..	..	..
Lithuania	..	21	..	37	..	0	..	0	..	30	..	11
Macedonia, FYR	..	..	..	..	..	..	..	..	..	..	..	..
Madagascar	..	9	..	18	..	35	..	9	..	..	..	29
Malawi	..	..	..	..	..	..	..	..	..	..	..	..
Malaysia[a]	37	..	26	..	12	..	5	..	1	..	19	..
Mali	..	18	..	38	..	9	..	8	..	..	..	27
Mauritania	..	..	..	..	..	..	..	..	..	..	..	..
Mauritius[a]	12	16	25	47	34	14	6	7	6	5	16	12
Mexico[a]	27	..	54	..	4	..	2	..	14	..	16	..
Moldova[a]	6	3	38	49	5	5	1	0	38	27	2	16
Mongolia	..	15	..	20	..	5	..	20	..	9	..	31
Morocco[a]	..	27	..	31	..	7	..	6	..	13	..	15
Mozambique	..	..	..	..	..	..	..	..	..	..	..	..
Myanmar	20	25	26	31	12	2	..	..	..	..	42	42
Namibia[a]	27	..	32	..	28	..	2	..	..	..	11	..
Nepal[a]	10	13	33	36	26	16	4	4	..	..	27	30
Netherlands	26	27	24	28	..	1	2	3	40	34	8	8
New Zealand	..	57	..	26	..	3	..	0	..	0	..	15
Nicaragua[a]	9	23	52	50	7	4	0	0	11	19	31	22
Niger	..	12	..	18	..	26	..	3	..	..	..	41
Nigeria	..	..	..	..	..	..	..	..	..	..	..	..
Norway	..	32	..	24	..	0	..	1	..	18	..	25
Oman[a]	21	..	1	..	3	..	2	..	..	..	74	..
Pakistan[a]	18	25	27	30	24	10	7	1	..	..	24	33
Panama[a]	20	..	17	..	11	..	3	..	16	..	34	..
Papua New Guinea[a]	40	..	8	..	27	..	2	..	0	..	23	..
Paraguay[a]	..	10	..	38	..	7	..	1	..	16	..	28
Peru[a]	15	34	46	36	10	2	8	6	10	8	11	14
Philippines[a]	33	41	26	28	29	20	4	6	..	..	8	11
Poland	..	16	..	39	..	0	..	1	..	36	..	8
Portugal	23	23	32	32	0	0	2	2	29	32	14	
Puerto Rico	..	..	..	..	..	..	..	..	..	..	..	..

	Taxes on income, profits, and capital gains		Taxes on goods and services		Taxes on international trade		Other taxes		Social contributions		Grants and other revenue	
	% of revenue		% of revenue		% of revenue		% of revenue		% of revenue		% of revenue	
	1995	2007	1995	2007	1995	2007	1995	2007	1995	2007	1995	2007
Romania	..	14	..	30	..	1	..	0	..	40	..	14
Russian Federation	..	6	..	24	..	23	..	0	..	19	..	28
Rwanda[a]	11	..	25	..	23	..	3	..	2	..	36	..
Saudi Arabia	..	..	..	..	..	..	..	..	..	..	..	..
Senegal[a]	17	..	19	..	36	..	2	..	..	..	26	..
Serbia[a]	..	..	..	..	..	..	..	..	..	..	..	..
Sierra Leone[a]	15	16	34	9	39	27	0	..	..	..	12	48
Singapore[a]	26	28	20	23	1	0	15	15	..	..	38	33
Slovak Republic	..	12	..	36	..	0	..	0	..	40	..	12
Slovenia[a]	13	18	33	32	9	0	0	3	42	38	3	9
Somalia	..	..	..	..	..	..	..	..	..	..	..	..
South Africa	..	52	..	32	..	4	..	3	..	2	..	7
Spain	28	33	21	16	0	0	0	0	40	46	..	5
Sri Lanka[a]	12	18	49	48	17	14	4	5	1	1	18	13
Sudan[a]	17	..	41	..	27	..	1	..	..	..	14	..
Swaziland[a]	..	..	..	..	..	..	..	..	..	..	..	..
Sweden	12	..	31	..	1	..	7	..	37	..	13	..
Switzerland[a]	11	19	21	32	1	1	2	2	49	36	17	9
Syrian Arab Republic[a]	23	..	37	..	13	..	8	..	0	..	19	..
Tajikistan[a]	6	3	63	54	12	11	0	1	13	12	5	18
Tanzania	..	..	..	..	..	..	..	..	..	..	..	..
Thailand	..	37	..	40	..	6	..	0	..	5	..	12
Timor-Leste	..	..	..	..	..	..	..	..	..	..	..	..
Togo[a]	..	19	..	46	..	20	..	3	..	..	..	12
Trinidad and Tobago[a]	50	60	26	13	6	5	1	9	2	4	15	9
Tunisia[a]	16	27	20	32	28	6	4	5	15	18	17	11
Turkey[a]	..	23	..	42	..	1	..	6	..	..	..	28
Turkmenistan	..	..	..	..	..	..	..	..	..	..	..	..
Uganda[a]	10	19	45	30	7	21	2	0	..	..	37	30
Ukraine[a]	..	13	..	29	..	4	..	0	..	37	..	16
United Arab Emirates[a]	..	..	..	15	..	..	..	..	..	1	..	84
United Kingdom	39	37	31	28	..	..	6	7	19	21	5	6
United States	..	57	..	3	..	1	..	1	..	35	..	3
Uruguay[a]	10	13	32	50	4	5	10	1	31	21	8	10
Uzbekistan	..	..	..	..	..	..	..	..	..	..	..	..
Venezuela, RB[a]	38	21	33	25	9	5	0	4	4	2	19	43
Vietnam	..	..	..	..	..	..	..	..	..	..	..	..
West Bank and Gaza	..	..	..	..	..	..	..	..	..	..	..	..
Yemen, Rep.[a]	17	..	10	..	18	..	3	..	..	..	51	..
Zambia[a]	27	33	22	36	36	8	0	0	0	..	15	23
Zimbabwe[a]	36	..	22	..	17	..	3	..	2	..	19	..
World	.. m	19 m	.. m	32 m	.. m	5 m	.. m	2 m	.. m	.. m	.. m	14 m
Low income	..	..	..	..	..	..	..	..	..	..	..	..
Middle income	..	16	..	38	..	5	..	1	..	13	..	15
Lower middle income	19	17	34	39	14	5	..	1	..	10	16	16
Upper middle income	..	16	..	37	..	4	..	1	..	22	..	14
Low & middle income	..	15	..	35	..	7	..	2	..	..	..	16
East Asia & Pacific	35	26	26	35	12	6	..	..	..	..	20	22
Europe & Central Asia	..	13	..	40	..	1	..	0	..	30	..	15
Latin America & Carib.	..	17	..	38	..	5	..	2	..	8	..	20
Middle East & N. Africa	17	13	13	32	18	6	4	5	..	..	36	26
South Asia	15	18	31	29	24	15	4	..	..	0	25	27
Sub-Saharan Africa	..	..	..	..	..	..	..	..	..	..	..	..
High income	26	28	24	26	..	0	3	2	35	34	9	9
Euro area	26	25	24	28	0	0	2	3	38	36	8	6

Note: Components may not sum to 100 percent because of missing data or adjustment to tax revenue.

a. Data were reported on a cash basis and have been adjusted to the accrual framework.

Central government revenues | 4.12

About the data

The International Monetary Fund (IMF) classifies government revenues as taxes, grants, and property income. Taxes are classified by the base on which the tax is levied, grants by the source, and property income by type (for example, interest, dividends, or rent). The most important source of revenue is taxes. Grants are unrequited, nonrepayable, noncompulsory receipts from other government units and foreign governments or from international organizations. Transactions are generally recorded on an accrual basis.

The IMF's *Government Finance Statistics Manual 2001* describes taxes as compulsory, unrequited payments made to governments by individuals, businesses, or institutions. Taxes are classified in six major groups by the base on which the tax is levied: income, profits, and capital gains; payroll and workforce; property; goods and services; international trade and transactions; and other. However, the distinctions are not always clear. Taxes levied on the income and profits of individuals and corporations are classified as direct taxes, and taxes and duties levied on goods and services are classified as indirect taxes. This distinction may be a useful simplification, but it has no particular analytical significance except with respect to the capacity to fix tax rates.

Direct taxes tend to be progressive, whereas indirect taxes are proportional.

Social security taxes do not reflect compulsory payments made by employers to provident funds or other agencies with a like purpose. Similarly, expenditures from such funds are not reflected in government expenses (see table 4.11). For further discussion of taxes and tax policies, see *About the data* for table 5.6. For further discussion of government revenues and expenditures, see *About the data* for tables 4.10 and 4.11.

Definitions

• **Taxes on income, profits, and capital gains** are levied on the actual or presumptive net income of individuals, on the profits of corporations and enterprises, and on capital gains, whether realized or not, on land, securities, and other assets. Intragovernmental payments are eliminated in consolidation. • **Taxes on goods and services** include general sales and turnover or value added taxes, selective excises on goods, selective taxes on services, taxes on the use of goods or property, taxes on extraction and production of minerals, and profits of fiscal monopolies. • **Taxes on international trade** include import duties, export duties, profits of export or import monopolies, exchange profits, and exchange taxes. • **Other taxes** include employer payroll or labor taxes, taxes on property, and taxes not allocable to other categories, such as penalties for late payment or nonpayment of taxes. • **Social contributions** include social security contributions by employees, employers, and self-employed individuals, and other contributions whose source cannot be determined. They also include actual or imputed contributions to social insurance schemes operated by governments. • **Grants and other revenue** include grants from other foreign governments, international organizations, and other government units; interest; dividends; rent; requited, nonrepayable receipts for public purposes (such as fines, administrative fees, and entrepreneurial income from government ownership of property); and voluntary, unrequited, nonrepayable receipts other than grants.

Rich economies rely more on direct taxes | 4.12a

Taxes on income and capital gains as a share of central government revenue, 2007 (%)

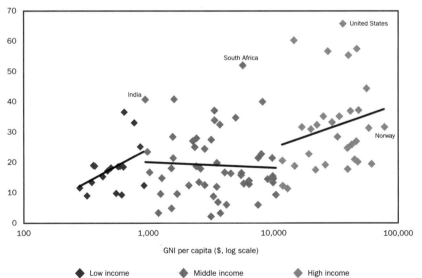

High-income economies tend to tax income and property, whereas low-income economies tend to rely on indirect taxes on international trade and goods and services. But there are exceptions in all groups.

Note: Data are for the most recent year for 2005–07.
Source: International Monetary Fund, *Government Finance Statistics* data files, and *World Development Indicators* data files.

Data sources

Data on central government revenues are from the IMF's *Government Finance Statistics Yearbook 2008* and data files. Each country's accounts are reported using the system of common definitions and classifications in the IMF's *Government Finance Statistics Manual 2001*. The IMF receives additional information from the Organisation for Economic Co-operation and Development on the tax revenues of some of its members. See the IMF sources for complete and authoritative explanations of concepts, definitions, and data sources.

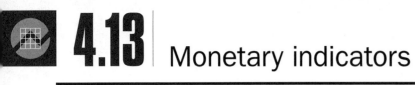
	Money and quasi money		Claims on private sector		Claims on governments and other public entities		Interest rate					
	annual % growth		Annual growth % of M2		Annual growth % of M2		Deposit		% Lending		Real	
	1995	2007	1995	2007	1995	2007	1995	2007	1995	2007	1995	2007
Afghanistan	..	46.0	..	20.1	..	−7.8	..	..	..	18.1	..	7.5
Albania	51.8	13.7	1.8	14.2	−8.3	3.3	15.3	5.7	19.7	14.1	8.9	10.6
Algeria	9.6	22.8	1.0	3.9	−10.0	−19.9	16.6	1.8	18.4	8.0	−7.9	0.5
Angola	4,105.6	38.6	471.4	33.7	119.5	0.7	125.9	6.8	206.3	17.7	−84.7	9.9
Argentina	−2.8	24.5	−1.1	15.2	7.8	−1.1	11.9	8.0	17.9	11.1	14.2	−2.7
Armenia	64.3	42.3	70.3	39.7	7.2	−4.7	63.2	6.3	111.9	17.5	−18.9	12.8
Australia	8.5	29.9	12.5	23.6	0.4	5.9	6.1	4.7	10.7	10.0	9.1	5.1
Austria[a]	..	..	..	..	..	..	2.2	..	6.4	..	6.1	..
Azerbaijan	25.4	73.2	6.1	56.4	−32.7	2.8	..	11.6	..	19.1	..	4.1
Bangladesh	12.1	13.6	25.0	10.5	4.8	4.3	6.0	9.2	14.0	16.0	6.2	8.6
Belarus	158.4	34.7	61.4	46.6	44.7	−31.8	100.8	8.3	175.0	8.6	−63.9	−3.1
Belgium[a]	..	..	..	..	..	..	4.0	..	8.4	8.6	7.1	6.8
Benin	−1.8	19.6	2.2	14.3	6.0	−17.6	3.5	3.5	16.8	..	13.0	..
Bolivia	7.7	26.2	13.7	6.6	1.1	−4.5	18.9	3.5	51.0	12.9	35.5	5.1
Bosnia and Herzegovina	22.0	32.6	23.9	24.1	−0.4	0.8	51.9	3.6	73.5	7.2	76.3	1.1
Botswana	12.3	31.2	−1.7	12.7	10.0	−26.9	9.8	8.6	14.4	16.2	5.2	4.0
Brazil	44.3	18.6	40.5	21.8	14.6	4.6	52.2	10.6	78.2	43.7	65.5	38.1
Bulgaria	40.5	31.3	22.1	44.0	−7.2	−6.5	35.9	3.7	79.4	10.0	10.1	2.0
Burkina Faso	22.3	23.8	2.9	0.9	−7.3	−11.1	3.5	3.5	16.8	..	16.5	..
Burundi	−8.0	13.8	−7.1	4.5	0.2	−1.4	..	..	15.3	16.8	−0.7	6.7
Cambodia	43.6	61.8	12.5	40.2	1.2	−13.1	8.7	1.9	18.7	16.4	6.4	11.2
Cameroon	−6.2	14.9	0.3	3.0	−2.2	−17.1	5.5	4.3	16.0	15.0	6.0	12.7
Canada	4.8	−25.3	3.8	−2.5	0.2	−0.4	5.3	2.1	8.7	6.1	6.2	10.3
Central African Republic	4.3	−3.6	3.9	3.0	−7.9	3.5	5.5	4.3	16.0	15.0	5.2	12.8
Chad	48.8	9.8	6.4	3.5	−18.6	−28.6	5.5	4.3	16.0	15.0	6.6	12.3
Chile	24.3	18.2	34.9	27.1	−2.0	1.6	13.7	5.6	18.2	8.7	7.0	3.6
China	29.5	16.7	22.5	13.4	0.8	3.7	11.0	4.1	12.1	7.5	−1.5	0.0
Hong Kong, China	10.6	18.8	9.8	4.8	−2.4	−3.8	5.6	2.4	8.8	6.8	4.4	3.7
Colombia	28.2	11.9	34.3	30.8	2.9	−6.9	32.3	8.0	42.7	15.4	20.1	10.1
Congo, Dem. Rep.	357.6	50.7	59.6	17.6	−7.9	5.1	60.0	..	293.9	..	−30.5	..
Congo, Rep.	−0.1	7.1	6.3	1.0	2.0	−4.2	5.5	4.3	16.0	15.0	12.2	24.9
Costa Rica	4.7	18.5	−1.4	53.7	5.6	−7.0	23.9	6.4	36.7	12.8	11.9	3.2
Cote d'Ivoire	18.1	23.6	13.3	10.5	0.3	3.7	3.5	3.5	16.8	..	16.8	..
Croatia	40.4	18.2	30.5	14.2	−2.4	−0.8	5.5	2.3	20.2	9.3	14.1	5.1
Cuba	..	..	..	..	..	..	..	..	..	..	..	..
Czech Republic	29.3	12.8	15.8	16.3	2.1	−2.6	7.0	1.3	12.8	5.8	−3.6	2.1
Denmark	6.2	12.1	2.6	38.4	−1.5	−2.2	3.9	..	10.3	..	9.0	..
Dominican Republic	16.6	22.1	14.4	21.8	1.7	9.4	14.9	7.0	30.7	15.8	16.0	9.6
Ecuador	6.8	18.4	15.1	13.1	−74.8	−3.3	43.3	5.0	55.7	12.1	45.7	7.1
Egypt, Arab Rep.	9.9	19.1	12.1	5.7	0.6	2.2	10.9	6.1	16.5	12.5	4.6	−0.1
El Salvador	13.5	17.8	22.6	9.5	−0.9	3.1	14.4	..	19.1	..	7.8	..
Eritrea	21.0	12.1	27.8	2.4	20.5	11.3	..	..	..	..	..	..
Estonia	27.5	13.6	28.9	52.5	−9.3	0.9	8.7	4.4	19.0	6.5	−9.3	−2.9
Ethiopia	9.0	−46.8	13.4	14.7	−3.5	5.4	11.5	3.6	15.1	7.0	2.1	−4.1
Finland[a]	..	..	..	..	..	..	3.2	1.0	7.8	3.7	2.9	3.0
France[a]	..	..	..	..	..	..	4.5	2.9	8.1	6.6	6.7	4.9
Gabon	10.1	6.9	11.9	20.7	5.8	−47.2	5.5	4.3	16.0	15.0	14.5	9.3
Gambia, The	14.2	6.7	−5.0	4.8	15.2	−5.4	12.5	12.9	25.0	27.9	20.3	21.0
Georgia	40.2	49.7	−11.1	79.0	73.8	−1.4	31.0	9.5	58.2	20.4	10.6	9.8
Germany[a]	..	..	..	..	..	..	3.9	..	10.9	..	8.9	..
Ghana	43.2	42.8	10.2	20.1	28.1	10.9	28.7	8.9	..	..	..	..
Greece[a]	..	..	..	..	..	..	15.8	2.2	23.1	..	12.1	..
Guatemala	15.6	11.3	36.1	18.2	−7.1	−1.4	7.9	4.8	21.2	12.8	11.5	6.3
Guinea	11.3	33.4	12.1	19.8	8.4	18.1	17.5	14.4	21.5	..	14.7	..
Guinea-Bissau	43.0	24.9	−6.7	7.5	−20.4	−0.3	3.5	3.5	32.9	..	−8.2	..
Haiti	27.1	11.1	15.7	2.7	0.1	−3.6	4.2	1.5	24.8	47.0	−2.4	22.9

	Money and quasi money		Claims on private sector		Claims on governments and other public entities		Interest rate					
			Annual growth % of M2		Annual growth % of M2				%			
	annual % growth						Deposit		Lending		Real	
	1995	2007	1995	2007	1995	2007	1995	2007	1995	2007	1995	2007
Honduras	28.9	19.3	18.0	27.5	−7.5	0.4	12.0	7.8	27.0	16.6	1.7	9.0
Hungary	20.9	9.5	4.9	19.6	20.2	1.9	24.4	6.8	32.6	9.1	4.6	3.2
India	11.0	22.3	6.0	13.1	3.4	1.5	..	..	15.5	13.0	5.9	7.8
Indonesia	27.5	19.3	25.9	13.3	−2.3	0.5	16.7	8.0	18.9	13.9	8.3	2.2
Iran, Islamic Rep.	30.1	30.6	9.8	37.1	17.3	−0.5	..	11.6	..	12.0	..	−7.0
Iraq	..	37.1	..	3.0	..	−44.3	..	11.4	..	19.7	..	..
Ireland[a]	..	..	..	..	..	..	0.4	0.0	6.6	2.7	3.4	0.1
Israel	21.7	−4.4	18.3	7.5	−0.5	−1.8	14.1	3.5	20.2	6.3	−0.2	6.5
Italy[a]	..	..	..	..	..	..	6.4	..	13.2	6.3	7.9	4.0
Jamaica	28.0	12.6	18.0	15.7	6.1	−1.6	23.2	7.1	43.6	17.2	17.5	−7.9
Japan	4.1	0.8	1.3	−0.1	2.5	−0.4	0.9	0.8	3.5	1.9	4.0	2.5
Jordan	5.7	12.4	9.6	9.4	−3.8	5.3	7.7	5.4	10.7	8.7	8.6	2.6
Kazakhstan	108.2	25.9	−72.5	73.2	24.7	−20.0	..	..	..	..	..	..
Kenya	29.0	20.4	26.7	10.8	6.6	0.8	13.6	5.2	28.8	13.3	15.8	8.3
Korea, Dem. Rep.	..	..	..	..	..	..	..	..	..	..	..	..
Korea, Rep.	15.6	0.3	21.6	18.1	−1.2	−3.7	8.8	5.2	9.0	6.6	1.5	5.3
Kuwait	9.4	19.3	10.9	31.2	−2.0	5.4	6.5	5.4	8.4	8.5	3.4	−7.7
Kyrgyz Republic	14.8	33.2	0.1	29.2	62.6	−8.8	36.7	5.4	65.0	25.3	21.9	10.4
Lao PDR	16.4	38.7	18.1	8.4	−9.7	−1.8	14.0	5.0	25.7	28.5	5.0	24.2
Latvia	−21.4	13.5	−23.8	59.2	6.5	−2.1	14.8	6.1	34.6	10.9	5.5	−2.1
Lebanon	16.4	12.4	13.1	4.9	5.1	0.4	16.3	8.0	24.7	10.3	12.8	5.1
Lesotho	9.8	16.4	−2.3	8.2	−18.7	−52.0	13.3	6.5	16.4	14.1	15.3	7.5
Liberia	29.5	42.4	−6.0	16.6	37.2	67.9	6.4	3.8	15.6	15.1	8.5	−0.8
Libya	9.6	38.0	3.1	2.9	3.6	−38.9	5.5	2.5	7.0	6.0	..	0.6
Lithuania	28.9	21.7	12.7	48.8	−2.4	2.3	20.1	5.4	27.1	6.9	−13.2	−1.6
Macedonia, FYR	1.8	30.7	−138.9	26.7	−229.7	9.0	24.1	4.9	46.0	10.2	24.6	4.9
Madagascar	16.2	20.9	9.4	8.0	−10.3	1.0	18.5	16.5	37.5	45.0	−5.3	31.5
Malawi	56.2	36.6	2.8	9.9	−10.4	1.7	37.3	6.0	47.3	27.7	−16.9	18.9
Malaysia	18.5	10.5	29.2	8.1	−0.7	−1.4	5.9	3.2	8.7	6.4	4.9	1.2
Mali	7.3	13.7	18.9	10.2	−11.6	−2.2	3.5	3.5	16.8	..	14.5	..
Mauritania	−5.1	..	−42.5	..	−28.9	..	9.0	8.0	20.3	23.5	17.0	26.7
Mauritius	18.6	15.4	8.7	14.6	3.0	−0.4	12.2	11.8	20.8	21.9	16.1	13.9
Mexico	31.9	13.8	−2.9	12.0	27.6	1.8	39.8	3.2	59.4	7.6	15.6	2.7
Moldova	65.3	39.8	34.6	37.8	19.1	−5.6	25.4	15.0	36.7	18.8	7.7	2.7
Mongolia	32.6	56.7	14.4	57.5	−31.8	−17.0	74.6	13.5	134.4	17.5	46.9	4.6
Morocco	7.0	16.1	6.9	17.3	5.1	0.2	7.3	3.7	11.3	11.5	3.1	10.4
Mozambique	47.7	26.2	21.8	8.1	−12.5	3.8	38.8	11.9	24.4	19.5	18.0	12.6
Myanmar	36.5	30.0	13.4	4.2	19.7	28.9	9.8	12.0	16.5	17.0	−2.4	−2.2
Namibia	22.6	10.2	30.5	15.7	1.7	−10.0	10.8	7.5	18.5	12.9	12.1	12.0
Nepal	15.4	18.6	18.1	14.6	3.3	4.8	9.6	2.3	12.9	8.0	4.7	0.3
Netherlands[a]	..	..	..	..	..	..	4.4	3.9	7.2	4.6	5.0	3.4
New Zealand	9.3	9.8	15.8	18.7	−3.9	−2.7	8.5	7.8	12.1	12.8	9.9	7.5
Nicaragua	35.1	18.5	30.3	27.4	−21.5	−4.8	11.1	6.1	19.9	13.0	5.7	3.5
Niger	3.8	24.7	−22.8	11.5	10.2	−14.7	3.5	3.5	16.8	..	15.5	..
Nigeria	19.4	64.2	22.3	79.2	−9.1	4.7	13.5	10.3	20.2	16.9	−22.9	11.3
Norway	3.8	..	9.5	..	−1.9	..	5.0	4.9	7.6	6.7	4.4	5.0
Oman	7.7	34.7	9.3	29.9	−2.3	−11.2	6.5	4.1	9.4	7.3	7.5	−0.3
Pakistan	13.8	19.5	10.8	10.0	8.7	7.1	..	5.3	..	11.8	..	3.5
Panama	8.4	17.4	14.5	18.9	−4.3	−6.6	7.2	4.8	11.1	8.3	10.6	6.2
Papua New Guinea	13.7	27.8	0.2	14.4	5.0	−11.3	7.3	1.1	13.1	9.8	−2.3	7.2
Paraguay	0.5	29.5	4.9	28.0	0.1	−7.7	21.2	5.0	33.9	25.0	17.9	13.4
Peru	29.3	23.0	31.1	19.7	−8.1	−9.0	9.6	3.2	36.2	22.9	20.5	20.4
Philippines	23.9	5.4	27.9	2.1	3.0	0.1	8.4	3.7	14.7	8.7	6.6	5.7
Poland	35.6	13.0	19.1	22.3	3.1	−2.5	26.8	2.2	33.5	5.5	−5.2	3.9
Portugal[a]	..	..	..	..	..	..	8.4	..	13.8	..	10.0	..
Puerto Rico	..	..	..	..	..	..	..	..	..	..	..	..

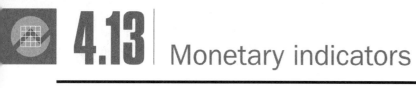

	Money and quasi money		Claims on private sector		Claims on governments and other public entities		Interest rate					
			Annual growth % of M2		Annual growth % of M2		Deposit		Lending		% Real	
	annual % growth											
	1995	**2007**	**1995**	**2007**	**1995**	**2007**	**1995**	**2007**	**1995**	**2007**	**1995**	**2007**
Romania	69.6	33.9	*23.1*	50.3	11.6	5.0	44.7	6.7	50.7	13.4	11.4	2.3
Russian Federation	112.6	44.2	46.2	41.7	73.6	−17.7	102.0	5.1	320.3	10.0	72.3	−3.1
Rwanda	69.5	*18.0*	32.7	*14.5*	−41.0	−13.8	*11.1*	6.8	*18.5*	15.8	6.9	6.4
Saudi Arabia	3.4	20.1	3.4	15.4	1.4	−23.3	6.2	4.8	..	..	..	..
Senegal	7.4	13.1	1.2	6.9	1.0	5.0	3.5	3.5	*16.8*	..	*17.8*	..
Serbia	*33.0*	42.5	*88.5*	36.2	*34.1*	−1.0	*19.1*	4.1	78.0	11.1	23.0	4.1
Sierra Leone	19.6	22.6	1.6	8.5	−101.6	−4.5	7.0	10.0	28.8	25.0	−3.6	13.3
Singapore	8.5	13.4	19.7	12.8	−8.1	3.0	3.5	0.5	6.4	5.3	4.0	1.2
Slovak Republic[a]	18.4	11.1	3.4	14.8	−4.8	−1.4	9.0	3.7	16.8	8.0	7.1	6.8
Slovenia[a]	30.4	*8.4*	31.6	40.5	5.0	−2.3	15.4	3.6	23.4	5.9	−4.0	1.7
Somalia	..	..	..	..	..	..	..	..	..	..	..	..
South Africa	16.0	20.2	18.9	26.2	−4.1	−0.9	13.5	9.2	17.9	13.2	6.9	3.9
Spain[a]	..	..	..	..	..	..	7.7	..	10.1	..	4.9	..
Sri Lanka	35.8	16.5	75.4	15.9	5.4	1.4	12.1	9.1	18.0	17.1	8.0	2.7
Sudan	72.7	10.3	10.6	8.0	389.1	4.2	..	..	..	..	..	..
Swaziland	3.9	21.5	1.3	21.5	−14.8	−50.9	9.4	7.1	17.1	13.2	−1.5	3.9
Sweden	3.1	11.4	−1.1	31.1	−4.0	0.3	6.2	0.8	11.1	3.3	7.2	2.4
Switzerland	4.6	3.3	4.0	10.1	0.2	−0.1	1.3	2.1	5.5	3.2	4.7	1.7
Syrian Arab Republic	9.2	12.4	3.9	4.4	6.1	−18.8	4.0	8.3	9.0	10.2	2.2	6.5
Tajikistan	..	169.9	..	253.7	..	−13.8	23.9	8.4	75.5	22.9	6.2	−3.9
Tanzania	33.0	20.5	−3.9	16.1	16.3	−0.7	24.6	8.7	42.8	16.0	12.6	9.5
Thailand	17.7	2.5	40.3	4.3	−4.2	0.4	11.6	2.9	13.3	7.1	7.3	3.7
Timor-Leste	..	43.9	..	−11.0	..	−135.6	..	0.8	..	15.1	..	2.5
Togo	22.3	16.8	17.6	15.5	14.9	0.8	3.5	3.5	*17.5*	..	*13.8*	..
Trinidad and Tobago	4.0	10.8	9.0	12.0	0.6	8.8	6.9	5.9	15.2	11.8	10.7	7.6
Tunisia	6.6	12.4	10.4	9.8	−1.2	1.2	..	..	..	..	..	..
Turkey	104.2	15.2	66.9	16.2	30.1	3.9	76.0	22.6	..	..	..	..
Turkmenistan	449.5	..	76.3	..	−573.1	..	..	..	..	..	..	..
Uganda	13.9	22.0	9.6	10.7	−41.2	−13.4	7.6	9.3	20.2	19.1	9.9	11.4
Ukraine	115.5	50.8	7.7	68.6	95.4	1.3	70.3	8.1	122.7	13.9	−56.8	−6.5
United Arab Emirates	10.2	41.7	10.7	36.3	−4.3	0.7	..	..	..	..	..	..
United Kingdom	20.3	15.9	19.6	19.9	1.0	−0.3	4.1	..	6.7	5.5	3.9	2.4
United States	6.9	12.1	6.0	7.1	0.2	1.4	..	..	8.8	8.1	6.7	5.3
Uruguay	36.9	5.0	35.2	7.6	1.0	−10.6	57.7	2.4	93.1	8.9	36.9	0.4
Uzbekistan	..	..	..	..	..	..	..	..	..	..	..	..
Venezuela, RB	36.6	28.7	15.3	39.6	32.8	−10.7	24.7	10.7	39.7	17.1	−7.9	2.7
Vietnam	25.8	49.1	18.9	44.5	0.7	−1.0	8.5	7.5	20.1	11.2	*10.5*	2.7
West Bank and Gaza	..	5.6	..	2.9	..	2.4	..	3.0	..	7.7	..	2.3
Yemen, Rep.	50.7	17.0	6.0	7.1	13.3	12.6	23.8	13.0	*31.5*	18.0	−3.2	2.6
Zambia	55.5	25.3	34.2	20.5	185.8	−8.7	30.2	9.2	45.5	18.9	5.4	8.7
Zimbabwe	25.5	64,472.5	25.5	67,582.1	−0.3	11,566.1	25.9	121.5	34.7	579.0	23.0	−0.7

a. As members of the European Monetary Union, these countries share a single currency, the euro.

Money and the financial accounts that record the supply of money lie at the heart of a country's financial system. There are several commonly used definitions of the money supply. The narrowest, M1, encompasses currency held by the public and demand deposits with banks. M2 includes M1 plus time and savings deposits with banks that require prior notice for withdrawal. M3 includes M2 as well as various money market instruments, such as certificates of deposit issued by banks, bank deposits denominated in foreign currency, and deposits with financial institutions other than banks. However defined, money is a liability of the banking system, distinguished from other bank liabilities by the special role it plays as a medium of exchange, a unit of account, and a store of value.

The banking system's assets include its net foreign assets and net domestic credit. Net domestic credit includes credit extended to the private sector and general government and credit extended to the nonfinancial public sector in the form of investments in short- and long-term government securities and loans to state enterprises; liabilities to the public and private sectors in the form of deposits with the banking system are netted out. Net domestic credit also includes credit to banking and nonbank financial institutions.

Domestic credit is the main vehicle through which changes in the money supply are regulated, with central bank lending to the government often playing the most important role. The central bank can regulate lending to the private sector in several ways—for example, by adjusting the cost of the refinancing facilities it provides to banks, by changing market interest rates through open market operations, or by controlling the availability of credit through changes in the reserve requirements imposed on banks and ceilings on the credit provided by banks to the private sector.

Monetary accounts are derived from the balance sheets of financial institutions—the central bank, commercial banks, and nonbank financial intermediaries. Although these balance sheets are usually reliable, they are subject to errors of classification, valuation, and timing and to differences in accounting practices. For example, whether interest income is recorded on an accrual or a cash basis can make a substantial difference, as can the treatment of nonperforming assets. Valuation errors typically arise for foreign exchange transactions, particularly in countries with flexible exchange rates or in countries that have undergone currency devaluation during the

reporting period. The valuation of financial derivatives and the net liabilities of the banking system can also be difficult. The quality of commercial bank reporting also may be adversely affected by delays in reports from bank branches, especially in countries where branch accounts are not computerized. Thus the data in the balance sheets of commercial banks may be based on preliminary estimates subject to constant revision. This problem is likely to be even more serious for nonbank financial intermediaries.

Many interest rates coexist in an economy, reflecting competitive conditions, the terms governing loans and deposits, and differences in the position and status of creditors and debtors. In some economies interest rates are set by regulation or administrative fiat. In economies with imperfect markets, or where reported nominal rates are not indicative of effective rates, it may be difficult to obtain data on interest rates that reflect actual market transactions. Deposit and lending rates are collected by the International Monetary Fund (IMF) as representative interest rates offered by banks to resident customers. The terms and conditions attached to these rates differ by country, however, limiting their comparability. Real interest rates are calculated by adjusting nominal rates by an estimate of the inflation rate in the economy. A negative real interest rate indicates a loss in the purchasing power of the principal. The real interest rates in the table are calculated as $(i - P) / (1 + P)$, where i is the nominal lending interest rate and P is the inflation rate (as measured by the GDP deflator).

• **Money and quasi money** are the sum of currency outside banks, demand deposits other than those of the central government, and the time, savings, and foreign currency deposits of resident sectors other than the central government. This definition of the money supply, often called M2, corresponds to lines 34 and 35 in the IMF's *International Financial Statistics* (IFS). The change in money supply is measured as the difference in end-of-year totals relative to M2 in the preceding year. • **Claims on private sector** (IFS line 32 d) include gross credit from the financial system to individuals, enterprises, nonfinancial public entities not included under net domestic credit, and financial institutions not included elsewhere. • **Claims on governments and other public entities** (IFS line 32 an + 32 b + 32 bx + 32 c) usually comprise direct credit for specific purposes, such as financing the government budget deficit; loans to state enterprises; advances against future credit authorizations; and purchases of treasury bills and bonds, net of deposits by the public sector. Public sector deposits with the banking system also include sinking funds for the service of debt and temporary deposits of government revenues. • **Deposit interest rate** is the rate paid by commercial or similar banks for demand, time, or savings deposits. • **Lending interest rate** is the rate charged by banks on loans to prime customers. • **Real interest rate** is the lending interest rate adjusted for inflation as measured by the GDP deflator.

Data on monetary and financial statistics are published by the IMF in its monthly *International Financial Statistics* and annual *International Financial Statistics Yearbook*. The IMF collects data on the financial systems of its member countries. The World Bank receives data from the IMF in electronic files that may contain more recent revisions than the published sources. The discussion of monetary indicators draws from an IMF publication by Marcello Caiola, *A Manual for Country Economists* (1995). Also see the IMF's *Monetary and Financial Statistics Manual* (2000) for guidelines for the presentation of monetary and financial statistics. Data on real interest rates are derived from World Bank data on the GDP deflator.

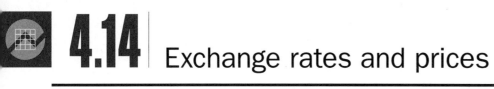

4.14 | Exchange rates and prices

	Official exchange rate		Purchasing power parity (PPP) conversion factor		Ratio of PPP conversion factor to market exchange rate	Real effective exchange rate	GDP implicit deflator		Consumer price index		Wholesale price index	
	local currency units to $		local currency units to international $			Index 2000 = 100	average annual % growth		average annual % growth		average annual % growth	
	2007	2008[a]	1995	2007	2007	2007	1990–2000	2000–07	1990–2000	2000–07	1990–2000	2000–07
Afghanistan	49.96	50.52	..	16.1	0.3	..	..	11.8	..	..	..	..
Albania	90.43	96.84	24.4	43.7	0.5	..	38.0	3.7	27.8	2.9	..	4.8
Algeria	69.29	70.91	15.3	35.8	0.5	82.3	18.5	8.8	17.3	2.6	..	3.5
Angola	76.71	75.13	0.0	51.6	0.7	..	739.4	56.1	711.0	54.4	..	..
Argentina	3.10	3.41	0.9	1.6	0.5	..	5.2	12.3	8.9	10.6	0.1	18.0
Armenia	342.08	307.83	116.6	183.8	0.5	122.6	212.5	4.3	72.8	3.5	..	0.9
Australia	1.20	1.49	1.3	1.4	1.1	133.3	1.5	3.7	2.1	2.9	1.1	3.5
Austria[b]	0.73	0.73	0.9	0.9	1.2	106.7	1.7	1.7	2.2	1.9	0.3	2.4
Azerbaijan	0.86	0.81	0.2	0.4	0.5	..	203.0	8.9	170.9	6.8	..	..
Bangladesh	68.88	68.89	19.2	24.0	0.3	..	4.0	4.4	5.5	6.4	..	..
Belarus	2,146.08	2,189.82	3.5	913.5	0.4	..	355.1	27.6	271.3	22.2	267.8	26.6
Belgium[b]	0.73	0.73	0.9	0.9	1.2	110.8	1.8	2.0	1.9	2.0	1.2	2.3
Benin	479.27	481.53	187.5	219.7	0.5	..	8.7	2.9	8.7	2.7	..	..
Bolivia	7.85	7.02	1.6	2.6	0.3	81.8	8.6	6.8	8.7	4.0	..	..
Bosnia and Herzegovina	1.43	1.44	0.6	0.7	0.5	..	3.7	3.7	..	..	..	..
Botswana	6.14	7.84	1.4	3.0	0.5	..	9.7	7.4	10.4	8.4	..	..
Brazil	1.95	2.39	0.7	1.4	0.7	..	211.8	8.5	199.5	7.7	204.9	11.6
Bulgaria	1.43	1.46	0.0	0.7	0.5	133.9	103.3	5.0	117.5	5.7	85.7	5.5
Burkina Faso	479.27	481.53	189.6	195.3	0.4	..	3.7	2.2	5.5	2.4	..	..
Burundi	1,081.87	1,234.53	126.6	363.9	0.3	68.7	13.4	8.4	16.1	7.4	..	..
Cambodia	4,056.17	4,091.00	1,142.8	1,345.7	0.3	95.3	4.4	3.8	6.3	3.5	..	..
Cameroon	479.27	481.53	241.2	251.4	0.5	114.6	6.3	2.2	6.5	2.1	..	..
Canada	1.07	1.24	1.2	1.2	1.1	132.3	1.5	2.0	1.7	2.2	2.7	1.2
Central African Republic	479.27	481.53	272.0	264.8	0.6	115.1	4.5	2.0	5.3	2.4	6.0	4.4
Chad	479.27	481.53	135.5	213.6	0.4	126.7	7.1	8.2	6.9	2.0	..	..
Chile	522.46	649.32	263.8	371.8	0.7	95.2	7.9	7.0	8.9	2.7	7.0	5.8
China	7.61	6.84	3.4	3.6	0.5	99.1	7.9	3.8	8.6	1.8	..	..
Hong Kong, China	7.80	7.75	7.9	5.5	0.7	..	4.5	–2.3	5.9	–0.5	0.6	0.5
Colombia	2,078.29	2,273.16	423.8	1,143.3	0.6	115.8	22.3	7.0	20.3	5.9	16.4	5.4
Congo, Dem. Rep.	516.75	560.84	0.0	267.8	0.5	31.8	964.9	31.0	932.8	29.5	..	..
Congo, Rep.	479.27	481.53	150.9	277.1	0.6	..	9.0	5.7	9.3	2.8	..	..
Costa Rica	516.62	549.80	103.1	280.5	0.5	95.3	15.9	10.0	15.6	11.1	14.1	12.2
Côte d'Ivoire	479.27	481.53	261.9	291.4	0.6	117.9	9.2	3.0	7.2	2.9	..	..
Croatia	5.37	5.38	3.1	3.9	0.7	112.9	86.0	3.7	86.2	2.5	74.2	2.5
Cuba	..	..	..	..	..	..	3.0	2.6	..	..	..	..
Czech Republic	20.29	19.48	11.1	14.2	0.7	136.8	12.8	2.2	7.8	2.1	8.2	2.3
Denmark	5.44	5.58	8.5	8.6	1.6	109.7	1.6	2.2	2.1	1.9	1.1	2.3
Dominican Republic	33.26	35.44	6.7	18.7	0.6	100.9	9.4	17.4	8.7	17.3	..	..
Ecuador	1.00	1.00	0.4	0.4	0.4	138.5	4.3	9.6	37.1	7.5	..	8.7
Egypt, Arab Rep.	5.73	5.30	1.2	1.8	0.3	..	8.7	7.2	8.8	6.2	6.1	9.5
El Salvador	1.00	1.00	0.4	0.5	0.5	..	6.2	3.5	8.5	3.6	..	4.2
Eritrea	15.38	15.38	1.9	7.0	0.5	..	7.9	18.6	..	..	..	..
Estonia	11.43	11.66	4.8	8.7	0.8	..	53.6	5.2	21.6	3.7	8.1	2.7
Ethiopia	8.95	9.32	2.1	2.8	0.3	99.6	6.4	6.6	5.5	8.3	..	..
Finland[b]	0.73	0.73	1.0	1.0	1.3	106.2	2.0	0.9	1.5	1.2	1.0	1.9
France[b]	0.73	0.73	1.0	0.9	1.2	109.0	1.3	2.1	1.6	1.9	..	1.9
Gabon	479.27	481.53	188.0	274.8	0.6	105.6	7.0	5.0	4.6	1.1	..	..
Gambia, The	24.88	21.64	3.9	7.7	0.3	59.6	4.2	11.9	4.1	9.7	..	..
Georgia	1.67	1.66	0.4	0.8	0.5	109.7	356.7	6.9	24.7	6.7	..	6.6
Germany[b]	0.73	0.73	1.0	0.9	1.2	108.9	1.7	1.1	2.0	1.6	0.4	2.6
Ghana	0.94	1.07	0.1	0.5	0.5	115.5	26.7	19.5	28.4	17.0	..	..
Greece[b]	0.73	0.73	0.6	0.7	1.0	116.8	9.2	3.3	9.0	3.3	3.6	4.0
Guatemala	7.67	7.71	2.9	4.2	0.6	..	10.4	4.7	10.1	7.1	..	..
Guinea	3,644.33	4,478.00	666.8	1,857.1	0.4	..	5.5	18.1	..	..	..	..
Guinea-Bissau	479.27	481.53	114.9	211.4	0.4	..	32.5	1.6	34.0	1.5	..	..
Haiti	36.86	39.82	6.0	22.3	0.6	..	22.8	17.4	21.9	18.9	..	..

Exchange rates and prices 4.14

	Official exchange rate		Purchasing power parity (PPP) conversion factor		Ratio of PPP conversion factor to market exchange rate	Real effective exchange rate	GDP implicit deflator		Consumer price index		Wholesale price index	
	local currency units to $		local currency units to international $			Index 2000 = 100	average annual % growth		average annual % growth		average annual % growth	
	2007	2008ᵃ	1995	2007	2007	2007	1990–2000	2000–07	1990–2000	2000–07	1990–2000	2000–07
Honduras	18.90	18.90	3.0	8.6	0.5	..	19.8	6.2	22.8	7.8	..	..
Hungary	183.63	196.78	61.6	134.8	0.7	142.5	19.6	5.1	20.3	5.5	16.8	3.2
India	41.35	48.64	11.1	15.3	0.4	..	8.1	4.3	9.1	4.4	7.4	4.9
Indonesia	9,141.00	11,836.00	1,031.8	4,724.6	0.5	..	15.8	10.1	13.7	9.3	15.4	9.4
Iran, Islamic Rep.	9,281.15	9,896.38	567.5	3,412.4	0.4	143.1	27.7	17.4	26.0	14.3	28.4	10.7
Iraq	1,254.57	1,203.00	..	558.7	..	..	..	..	..	..	..	..
Irelandᵇ	0.73	0.73	0.8	1.0	1.3	133.1	3.7	2.9	2.3	3.5	1.6	0.3
Israel	4.11	3.87	3.1	3.6	0.9	79.4	11.0	1.1	9.7	1.5	8.1	4.6
Italyᵇ	0.73	0.73	0.8	0.9	1.2	112.3	3.8	2.6	3.7	2.3	2.9	2.7
Jamaica	68.95	73.88	16.8	47.8	0.7	..	23.0	11.2	23.5	10.7	..	..
Japan	117.75	91.32	174.3	120.1	1.0	66.6	0.1	–1.2	0.8	–0.2	–0.9	0.3
Jordan	0.71	0.71	0.4	0.4	0.6	..	3.2	3.0	3.5	3.3	..	9.0
Kazakhstan	122.55	120.58	17.5	76.4	0.6	..	204.7	14.3	67.8	7.5	16.3	11.5
Kenya	67.32	78.04	15.8	31.3	0.4	..	16.6	5.1	15.6	9.4	..	..
Korea, Dem. Rep.	..	..	..	..	..	..	..	..	..	..	..	..
Korea, Rep.	929.26	1,373.84	690.0	749.9	0.8	..	5.7	1.7	5.1	3.1	3.7	2.1
Kuwait	0.28	0.28	0.1	0.2	0.8	..	1.5	8.7	2.0	2.3	1.4	2.5
Kyrgyz Republic	37.32	39.38	3.5	13.3	0.4	..	110.6	6.3	23.3	4.6	35.6	7.9
Lao PDR	9,603.16	8,640.71	309.7	3,096.8	0.3	..	27.0	9.6	28.2	9.5	..	..
Latvia	0.51	0.52	0.2	0.4	0.7	..	48.0	6.9	29.2	5.1	12.0	6.6
Lebanon	1,507.50	1,507.50	837.2	886.4	0.6	..	17.9	2.1	..	..	..	..
Lesotho	7.05	9.97	2.3	3.6	0.5	128.8	7.7	5.4	9.8	7.8	..	..
Liberia	61.27	62.57	0.6	33.5	0.5	..	51.8	10.1	..	..	..	..
Libya	1.26	1.30	..	0.8	0.7	..	..	21.0	5.6	–3.0	..	..
Lithuania	2.52	2.57	1.2	1.6	0.6	..	75.0	2.9	32.6	1.6	24.7	4.3
Macedonia, FYR	44.73	45.73	17.9	18.5	0.4	100.4	79.3	2.8	10.6	1.9	8.4	0.7
Madagascar	1,873.88	1,841.20	287.6	754.2	0.4	..	19.1	11.6	18.7	10.8	..	..
Malawi	139.96	140.60	3.9	47.1	0.3	65.0	33.6	21.2	33.8	13.2	..	..
Malaysia	3.44	3.55	1.4	1.8	0.5	102.1	4.0	3.8	3.6	2.1	3.4	4.6
Mali	479.27	481.53	226.8	246.2	0.5	..	7.0	3.6	5.2	1.7	..	..
Mauritania	258.59	235.99	62.4	118.0	0.4	..	8.7	11.3	6.1	7.5	..	..
Mauritius	31.31	32.10	10.5	15.4	0.5	..	6.4	5.4	6.9	5.9	..	..
Mexico	10.93	13.37	2.9	7.5	0.7	..	19.0	8.6	19.4	4.5	18.4	6.2
Moldova	12.14	10.40	1.2	5.5	0.5	101.9	119.6	11.5	19.2	11.0	..	..
Mongolia	1,170.97	1,228.87	158.7	544.9	0.5	..	57.8	14.1	35.7	6.8	..	..
Morocco	8.19	8.10	4.9	4.9	0.6	92.6	4.0	1.3	3.8	1.8	2.9	..
Mozambique	25.84	24.13	3.9	11.7	0.5	..	34.1	7.9	31.8	11.8	..	..
Myanmar	5.56	5.65	40.2	249.7	..	..	25.5	21.1	25.9	23.6	..	..
Namibia	7.05	9.97	2.5	4.4	0.7	..	10.4	4.8	..	4.7	..	..
Nepal	66.42	78.07	15.4	24.7	0.4	..	8.0	5.6	8.7	5.0	..	..
Netherlandsᵇ	0.73	0.73	0.9	0.9	1.2	113.5	2.1	2.2	2.4	2.0	1.3	2.5
New Zealand	1.36	1.80	1.5	1.5	1.2	137.8	1.7	2.7	1.7	2.6	1.4	2.8
Nicaragua	18.45	19.81	3.5	7.3	0.4	88.6	42.4	7.7	..	7.5	..	..
Niger	479.27	481.53	209.8	224.4	0.5	..	6.0	2.0	6.1	1.8	..	..
Nigeria	125.81	117.73	15.5	71.4	0.6	130.6	29.5	17.9	32.5	13.5	..	..
Norway	5.86	7.01	9.2	9.0	1.5	112.2	2.7	4.2	2.2	1.6	1.6	6.2
Oman	0.39	0.39	0.2	0.2	0.6	..	0.1	5.7	..	1.3	..	..
Pakistan	60.74	79.09	10.1	21.5	0.4	95.6	11.1	6.7	9.7	6.0	10.4	7.0
Panama	1.00	1.00	0.5	0.5	0.5	..	3.6	1.7	1.1	1.5	1.0	2.7
Papua New Guinea	2.97	2.66	0.7	1.4	0.5	96.5	7.6	7.2	9.3	6.1	..	..
Paraguay	5,032.72	4,837.00	949.3	2,267.1	0.5	97.6	11.5	10.8	13.1	8.7	..	11.8
Peru	3.13	3.11	1.2	1.5	0.5	..	26.7	3.6	27.3	2.0	23.7	2.3
Philippines	46.15	48.09	14.1	22.2	0.5	112.3	8.3	5.1	7.7	5.2	5.6	8.2
Poland	2.77	2.97	1.2	1.9	0.7	114.1	24.7	2.4	25.3	2.3	19.8	2.7
Portugalᵇ	0.73	0.73	0.6	0.7	0.9	113.5	5.2	3.0	4.5	2.9	..	2.6
Puerto Rico	1.00	1.00	..	..	..	..	3.0	..	..	..	..	..

4.14 | Exchange rates and prices

	Official exchange rate		Purchasing power parity (PPP) conversion factor		Ratio of PPP conversion factor to market exchange rate	Real effective exchange rate	GDP implicit deflator		Consumer price index		Wholesale price index	
	local currency units to $		local currency units to international $			Index 2000 = 100	average annual % growth		average annual % growth		average annual % growth	
	2007	2008a	1995	2007	2007	2007	1990–2000	2000–07	1990–2000	2000–07	1990–2000	2000–07
Romania	2.44	2.90	0.1	1.5	0.6	140.5	98.0	18.0	100.5	13.8	93.8	17.5
Russian Federation	25.58	28.13	1.5	15.8	0.6	172.7	161.5	16.7	99.1	12.9	99.8	16.9
Rwanda	546.96	551.35	129.3	216.5	0.4	..	14.3	9.7	16.2	7.8	..	..
Saudi Arabia	3.75	3.75	1.8	2.6	0.7	78.5	1.6	8.1	1.0	0.9	1.3	1.9
Senegal	479.27	481.53	252.0	258.5	0.5	..	6.0	2.2	5.4	1.7	..	..
Serbia	58.45	64.71	2.6	31.0	0.5	..	..	18.8	50.2	18.0	..	..
Sierra Leone	2,985.19	2,990.63	387.6	1,251.2	0.4	73.8	31.9	8.8	29.3	8.1	..	..
Singapore	1.51	1.48	1.3	1.1	0.7	95.8	1.3	0.9	1.7	0.8	–1.0	3.4
Slovak Republicb	24.69c	22.65c	13.0	17.1	0.7	158.1	11.1	4.0	8.4	5.4	9.5	5.2
Sloveniab	0.73	0.73	0.4	0.6	0.9	..	29.3	4.4	12.0	4.5	9.1	4.0
Somalia	..	..	..	..	..	..	..	..	..	..	..	..
South Africa	7.05	9.97	2.3	4.3	0.6	94.9	9.9	6.7	8.7	4.9	7.7	6.0
Spainb	0.73	0.73	0.7	0.7	1.0	117.3	3.9	4.1	3.8	3.2	2.4	3.0
Sri Lanka	110.62	111.37	18.3	42.1	0.4	..	9.1	10.0	9.9	9.9	8.1	11.1
Sudan	2.02	2.03	0.3	1.2	0.6	..	65.5	9.6	71.9	7.8	..	..
Swaziland	7.05	9.97	2.2	3.7	0.5	..	10.5	7.3	9.4	6.5	..	..
Sweden	6.76	8.02	9.4	9.1	1.4	98.9	2.2	1.5	1.9	1.4	2.4	2.6
Switzerland	1.20	1.15	2.0	1.7	1.4	98.0	1.1	0.8	1.6	0.9	–0.4	0.8
Syrian Arab Republic	11.23	11.23	12.8	21.0	0.4	..	7.9	6.2	6.4	5.1	4.7	2.2
Tajikistan	3.44	3.42	0.0	1.1	0.3	..	235.0	20.4	..	12.7	..	..
Tanzania	1,245.04	1,273.83	154.8	412.4	0.3	..	21.6	9.0	20.9	4.9	..	..
Thailand	34.52	35.08	15.1	16.3	0.5	..	4.2	2.9	4.9	2.7	3.8	5.3
Timor-Leste	1.00	1.00	..	0.5	0.5	..	..	2.6	..	4.4	..	..
Togo	479.27	481.53	238.6	230.9	0.5	113.5	7.0	0.8	8.5	2.2	..	..
Trinidad and Tobago	6.33	6.26	2.9	4.2	0.7	115.5	5.4	6.4	5.7	5.5	2.8	2.0
Tunisia	1.28	1.34	0.5	0.6	0.5	82.2	4.4	2.7	4.4	3.0	3.6	3.7
Turkey	1.30	1.54	0.0	0.9	0.7	..	74.7	18.7	79.9	20.6	..	8.7
Turkmenistan	..	..	..	3,950.3	0.4	..	408.0	..	..	..	..	..
Uganda	1,723.49	1,959.26	472.8	640.1	0.4	90.0	12.0	4.8	10.5	5.0	..	..
Ukraine	5.05	7.58	0.3	2.2	0.4	112.6	271.0	14.0	155.7	8.5	161.6	12.2
United Arab Emirates	3.67	3.67	1.7	2.7	0.7	..	2.2	7.7	..	..	..	..
United Kingdom	0.50	0.64	0.6	0.6	1.3	107.9	2.9	2.7	2.9	2.8	2.4	1.3
United States	1.00	1.00	1.0	1.0	1.0	88.8	2.0	2.6	2.7	2.7	1.2	4.2
Uruguay	23.47	24.35	5.7	14.5	0.6	79.6	31.1	9.4	33.9	9.9	27.2	15.3
Uzbekistan	..	..	11.2	432.7	0.3	..	245.8	26.5	..	..	..	..
Venezuela, RB	2.15	2.15	0.1	1.5	0.7	81.2	45.3	26.8	49.0	20.2	44.1	27.6
Vietnam	16,105.13	16,600.00	3,170.2	5,167.5	0.3	..	15.2	6.6	4.1	5.8	..	..
West Bank and Gaza	..	..	..	..	..	..	5.7	3.4	..	3.8	..	..
Yemen, Rep.	198.95	200.03	22.0	85.7	0.4	..	22.4	13.5	26.3	12.9	..	..
Zambia	4,002.52	4,882.97	393.5	2,808.8	0.7	151.5	52.1	18.3	57.0	17.6	101.4	..
Zimbabwe	9,675.78	30,000.00	..	..	..	..	26.7	232.0	29.0	497.7	25.9	..

Note: The differences in the growth rates of the GDP deflator and consumer and wholesale price indexes are due mainly to differences in data availability for each of the indexes during the period.

a. Average for December or latest monthly data available. b. As members of the euro area, these countries share a single currency, the euro. c. Koruny. •

About the data

In a market-based economy, household, producer, and government choices about resource allocation are influenced by relative prices, including the real exchange rate, real wages, real interest rates, and other prices in the economy. Relative prices also largely reflect these agents' choices. Thus relative prices convey vital information about the interaction of economic agents in an economy and with the rest of the world.

The exchange rate is the price of one currency in terms of another. Official exchange rates and exchange rate arrangements are established by governments. Other exchange rates recognized by governments include market rates, which are determined largely by legal market forces, and for countries with multiple exchange arrangements, principal rates, secondary rates, and tertiary rates. (Also see *Statistical methods* for alternative conversion factors in the *World Bank Atlas* method of calculating gross national income [GNI] per capita in U.S. dollars.)

Official or market exchange rates are often used to convert economic statistics in local currencies to a common currency in order to make comparisons across countries. Since market rates reflect at best the relative prices of tradable goods, the volume of goods and services that a U.S. dollar buys in the United States may not correspond to what a U.S. dollar converted to another country's currency at the official exchange rate would buy in that country, particularly when nontradable goods and services account for a significant share of a country's output. An alternative exchange rate—the purchasing power parity (PPP) conversion factor—is preferred because it reflects differences in price levels for both tradable and nontradable goods and services and therefore provides a more meaningful comparison of real output. See table 1.1 for further discussion.

The ratio of the PPP conversion factor to the official exchange rate—the national price level or comparative price level—measures differences in the price level at the gross domestic product (GDP) level. The price level index tends to be lower in poorer countries and to rise with income. The market exchange rate (or alternative conversion factor) is the official exchange rate adjusted for some countries by World Bank staff to reflect actual price changes. National price levels vary systematically, rising with GNI per capita. The real effective exchange rate is a nominal effective exchange rate index adjusted for relative movements in national price or cost indicators of the home country, selected countries, and the euro area. A nominal effective exchange rate index is the ratio (expressed on the base 2000 = 100) of an index of a currency's period-average exchange rate to a weighted geometric average of exchange rates

for currencies of selected countries and the euro area. For most high-income countries weights are derived from industrial country trade in manufactured goods. Data are compiled from the nominal effective exchange rate index and a cost indicator of relative normalized unit labor costs in manufacturing. For selected other countries the nominal effective exchange rate index is based on manufactured goods and primary products trade with partner or competitor countries. For these countries the real effective exchange rate index is the nominal index adjusted for relative changes in consumer prices; an increase represents an appreciation of the local currency. Because of conceptual and data limitations, changes in real effective exchange rates should be interpreted with caution.

Inflation is measured by the rate of increase in a price index, but actual price change can be negative. The index used depends on the prices being examined. The GDP deflator reflects price changes for total GDP. The most general measure of the overall price level, it accounts for changes in government consumption, capital formation (including inventory appreciation), international trade, and the main component, household final consumption expenditure. The GDP deflator is usually derived implicitly as the ratio of current to constant price GDP—or a Paasche index. It is defective as a general measure of inflation for policy use because of long lags in deriving estimates and because it is often an annual measure.

Consumer price indexes are produced more frequently and so are more current. They are also constructed explicitly, based on surveys of the cost of a defined basket of consumer goods and services. Nevertheless, consumer price indexes should be interpreted with caution. The definition of a household, the basket of goods, and the geographic (urban or rural) and income group coverage of consumer price surveys can vary widely by country. In addition, weights are derived from household expenditure surveys, which, for budgetary reasons, tend to be conducted infrequently in developing countries, impairing comparability over time. Although useful for measuring consumer price inflation within a country, consumer price indexes are of less value in comparing countries.

Wholesale price indexes are based on the prices at the first commercial transaction of commodities that are important in a country's output or consumption. Prices are farm-gate for agricultural commodities and ex-factory for industrial goods. Preference is given to indexes with the broadest coverage of the economy.

The least-squares method is used to calculate growth rates of the GDP implicit deflator, consumer price index, and wholesale price index.

Definitions

• **Official exchange rate** is the exchange rate determined by national authorities or the rate determined in the legally sanctioned exchange market. It is calculated as an annual average based on monthly averages (local currency units relative to the U.S. dollar). • **Purchasing power parity (PPP) conversion factor** is the number of units of a country's currency required to buy the same amount of goods and services in the domestic market that a U.S. dollar would buy in the United States. • **Ratio of PPP conversion factor to market exchange rate** is the result obtained by dividing the PPP conversion factor by the market exchange rate. • **Real effective exchange rate** is the nominal effective exchange rate (a measure of the value of a currency against a weighted average of several foreign currencies) divided by a price deflator or index of costs. • **GDP implicit deflator** measures the average annual rate of price change in the economy as a whole for the periods shown. • **Consumer price index** reflects changes in the cost to the average consumer of acquiring a basket of goods and services that may be fixed or may change at specified intervals, such as yearly. The Laspeyres formula is generally used. • **Wholesale price index** refers to a mix of agricultural and industrial goods at various stages of production and distribution, including import duties. The Laspeyres formula is generally used.

Data sources

Data on official and real effective exchange rates and consumer and wholesale price indexes are from the International Monetary Fund's *International Financial Statistics*. PPP conversion factors and GDP deflators are from the World Bank's data files.

4.15 | Balance of payments current account

	Goods and services				Net income		Net current transfers		Current account balance		Total reserves[a]	
	Exports		Imports		$ millions		$ millions		$ millions		$ millions	
	$ millions											
	1995	2007	1995	2007	1995	2007	1995	2007	1995	2007	1995	2007
Afghanistan	..	..	..	..	..	..	..	..	..	..	..	..
Albania	304	2,201	836	4,292	44	217	477	1,043	−12	−831	265	2,162
Algeria	..	..	..	..	..	..	..	..	..	..	4,164	114,972
Angola	3,836	44,707	3,519	26,305	−767	−8,778	156	−222	−295	9,402	213	11,197
Argentina	24,987	66,085	26,066	53,353	−4,636	−5,929	597	318	−5,118	7,122	15,979	46,149
Armenia	300	1,777	726	3,589	40	278	168	945	−218	−590	111	1,659
Australia	69,710	182,872	74,841	199,457	−14,036	−40,817	−109	−280	−19,277	−57,682	14,952	26,908
Austria	89,906	217,883	92,055	199,334	−1,597	−5,166	−1,702	−1,352	−5,448	12,031	23,369	18,194
Azerbaijan	785	22,517	1,290	9,424	−6	−5,079	111	1,005	−401	9,019	121	4,273
Bangladesh	4,431	14,091	7,589	19,553	68	−968	2,265	7,287	−824	857	2,376	5,277
Belarus	5,269	27,583	5,752	30,421	−51	−411	76	189	−458	−3,060	377	4,179
Belgium	190,686[b]	402,821	178,798[b]	394,601	6,808[b]	5,816	−4,463[b]	−6,819	14,232[b]	7,216	24,120	16,485
Benin	614	953	895	1,398	−8	−30	121	259	−167	−217	198	1,209
Bolivia	1,234	4,959	1,574	4,078	−207	−173	244	1,091	−303	1,800	1,005	5,314
Bosnia and Herzegovina	..	5,608	..	10,514	..	400	..	2,576	..	−1,930	80	4,525
Botswana	2,421	6,092	2,050	4,417	−32	−346	−39	1,105	300	2,434	4,695	9,790
Brazil	52,641	184,544	63,293	157,871	−11,105	−29,242	3,621	4,029	−18,136	1,460	51,477	180,334
Bulgaria	6,776	24,911	6,502	33,467	−432	−624	132	464	−26	−8,716	1,635	17,545
Burkina Faso	272	..	483	..	−29	..	255	..	15	..	347	1,029
Burundi	129	84	259	435	−13	−6	153	241	10	−116	216	177
Cambodia	969	5,637	1,375	6,327	−57	−360	277	544	−186	−506	192	2,140
Cameroon	2,040	4,952	1,608	5,531	−412	−385	69	416	90	−547	15	2,932
Canada	219,501	495,016	200,991	468,502	−22,721	−12,988	−117	−888	−4,328	12,639	16,369	41,082
Central African Republic	179	..	244	..	−23	..	63	..	−25	..	238	92
Chad	190	..	411	..	−7	..	191	..	−38	..	147	964
Chile	19,358	76,429	18,301	53,938	−2,714	−18,265	307	2,974	−1,350	7,200	14,860	16,843
China†	147,240	1,342,206	135,282	1,034,729	−11,774	25,688	1,435	38,668	1,618	371,833	80,288	1,546,365
Hong Kong, China	..	429,542	..	406,913	..	5,693	..	−2,576	..	25,746	55,424	152,693
Colombia	12,294	34,213	16,012	37,416	−1,596	−7,894	799	5,231	−4,516	−5,866	8,452	20,951
Congo, Dem. Rep.	..	..	..	..	..	..	..	..	..	..	157	181
Congo, Rep.	1,374	6,127	1,346	6,386	−695	−1,885	42	−38	−625	−2,181	64	2,184
Costa Rica	4,451	12,895	4,717	14,092	−226	−850	134	470	−358	−1,578	1,060	4,115
Cote d'Ivoire	4,337	9,419	3,806	8,376	−787	−810	−237	−379	−492	−146	529	2,519
Croatia	6,972	25,148	9,106	29,481	−53	−1,545	802	1,431	−1,385	−4,447	1,896	13,675
Cuba	..	..	..	..	..	..	..	..	..	..	..	..
Czech Republic	28,202	139,971	30,044	131,275	−104	−11,041	572	−887	−1,374	−3,232	14,613	34,907
Denmark	65,655	162,058	57,860	154,725	−4,549	176	−1,391	−5,130	1,855	2,379	11,652	34,318
Dominican Republic	5,731	11,972	6,137	15,370	−769	−2,079	992	3,409	−183	−2,068	373	2,562
Ecuador	5,196	16,038	5,708	15,638	−930	−2,048	442	3,246	−1,000	1,598	1,788	3,521
Egypt, Arab Rep.	13,260	44,398	17,140	53,697	−405	1,388	4,031	8,322	−254	412	17,122	32,214
El Salvador	2,040	5,527	3,623	9,842	−67	−579	1,389	3,776	−262	−1,119	940	2,304
Eritrea	135	..	498	..	8	..	324	..	−32	..	40	25
Estonia	2,573	15,471	2,860	17,828	3	−1,574	126	159	−158	−3,772	583	3,269
Ethiopia	768	2,658	1,446	6,920	−19	40	736	3,395	39	−827	815	833
Finland	47,973	110,338	37,705	99,954	−4,440	1,560	−597	−1,897	5,231	10,048	10,657	8,380
France	362,717	691,775	333,746	731,671	−8,964	39,305	−9,167	−30,658	10,840	−31,249	58,510	115,487
Gabon	2,945	5,610	1,723	2,400	−665	−958	−42	−269	515	1,983	153	1,238
Gambia, The	177	233	232	322	−5	−40	52	76	−8	−53	106	143
Georgia	575	3,182	1,413	5,917	127	39	197	689	−514	−2,006	199	1,361
Germany	600,347	1,571,251	586,662	1,334,445	−2,814	57,894	−38,768	−41,771	−27,897	252,929	121,816	135,932
Ghana	1,582	6,004	2,120	10,060	−129	−139	523	2,043	−144	−2,151	804	2,269
Greece	15,523	67,071	24,711	101,311	−1,684	−12,469	8,008	2,122	−2,864	−44,587	16,119	3,648
Guatemala	2,823	8,721	3,728	14,511	−159	−770	491	4,863	−572	−1,697	783	4,315
Guinea	700	1,252	1,011	1,514	−85	−63	179	−131	−216	−456	87	97
Guinea-Bissau	30	..	89	..	−21	..	46	..	−35	..	20	113
Haiti	192	729	802	2,321	−31	7	553	1,505	−87	−80	199	453
†Data for Taiwan, China	128,369	277,811	124,171	251,157	4,188	10,132	−2,912	−3,807	5,474	32,979	95,559	281,658

	Goods and services				Net income		Net current transfers		Current account balance		Total reservesᵃ	
	$ millions											
	Exports		Imports		$ millions		$ millions		$ millions		$ millions	
	1995	2007	1995	2007	1995	2007	1995	2007	1995	2007	1995	2007
Honduras	1,635	6,344	1,852	9,594	−226	−598	243	2,622	−201	−1,225	270	2,546
Hungary	19,765	111,005	19,916	107,499	−1,701	−10,702	203	452	−1,650	−6,743	12,017	24,052
India	38,013	*198,971*	48,225	*230,232*	−3,734	*−4,264*	8,382	*26,109*	−5,563	−9,415	22,865	276,578
Indonesia	52,923	130,492	54,461	109,571	−5,874	−15,524	981	4,968	−6,431	10,365	14,908	56,936
Iran, Islamic Rep.	18,953	..	15,113	..	−478	..	−4	..	3,358	..	..	..
Iraq	..	*30,887*	..	*24,198*	..	*−3,546*	..	*−462*	..	*2,681*	8,347	*19,655*
Ireland	49,439	204,512	42,169	178,698	−7,325	−36,851	1,776	−1,658	1,721	−12,695	8,770	925
Israel	27,478	70,901	35,287	73,631	−2,654	−25	5,673	7,278	−4,790	4,523	8,123	28,519
Italy	295,618	614,384	250,319	619,592	−15,644	−26,918	−4,579	−18,905	25,076	−51,032	60,690	94,109
Jamaica	3,394	4,928	3,729	8,050	−371	−662	607	2,040	−99	−1,744	681	1,879
Japan	493,991	807,207	419,556	723,705	44,285	138,502	−7,676	−11,514	111,044	210,490	192,620	973,297
Jordan	3,479	9,110	4,903	15,500	−279	835	1,444	2,779	−259	−2,776	2,279	7,925
Kazakhstan	5,975	51,906	6,102	44,887	−146	−12,193	59	−2,160	−213	−7,333	1,660	17,641
Kenya	3,526	6,822	5,922	9,840	−219	−192	1,037	2,108	−1,578	−1,102	384	3,355
Korea, Dem. Rep.	..	..	..	..	..	..	..	..	..	..	..	..
Korea, Rep.	147,761	442,016	155,104	433,181	−1,303	769	−19	−3,649	−8,665	5,954	32,804	262,533
Kuwait	14,215	73,317	12,615	33,707	4,881	12,937	−1,465	−5,076	5,016	47,471	4,543	18,776
Kyrgyz Republic	448	2,021	726	3,218	−35	−52	79	1,020	−235	−228	134	1,177
Lao PDR	408	1,201	748	1,141	−6	−50	110	98	−237	107	99	708
Latvia	2,088	11,898	2,193	17,828	19	−937	71	382	−16	−6,485	602	5,761
Lebanon	..	16,603	..	21,912	..	377	..	2,886	..	−2,046	8,100	20,599
Lesotho	199	881	1,046	1,715	314	420	210	625	−323	212	457	658
Liberia	..	542	..	1,742	..	−150	..	1,139	..	−211	28	119
Libya	7,513	47,069	5,755	20,368	133	1,971	−220	−219	1,672	28,454	7,415	83,260
Lithuania	3,191	21,187	3,902	26,429	−13	−1,614	109	1,163	−614	−5,692	829	7,721
Macedonia, FYR	*1,302*	*2,998*	*1,773*	*4,258*	−30	−3	*213*	*1,239*	−288	−24	275	2,264
Madagascar	749	*1,332*	987	*2,042*	−167	−80	129	*236*	−276	−554	109	847
Malawi	470	..	660	..	−44	..	157	..	−78	..	115	227
Malaysia	83,369	204,674	86,851	167,061	−4,144	−3,995	−1,017	−4,687	−8,644	28,931	24,699	101,995
Mali	529	*1,864*	991	*2,150*	−41	−269	219	*325*	−284	*−231*	323	1,087
Mauritania	504	..	510	..	−48	..	76	..	22	..	90	207
Mauritius	2,349	4,436	2,454	5,202	−19	239	101	119	−22	−408	887	1,832
Mexico	89,321	289,612	82,168	305,775	−12,689	−13,684	3,960	24,323	−1,576	−5,525	17,046	87,208
Moldova	884	2,018	1,006	4,306	−18	414	56	1,179	−85	−695	257	1,334
Mongolia	508	*2,031*	521	*1,880*	−25	*−145*	77	*215*	39	*222*	158	1,396
Morocco	9,044	27,311	11,243	34,732	−1,318	−405	2,330	7,703	−1,186	−122	3,874	24,714
Mozambique	411	2,871	1,055	3,667	−140	−592	339	592	−445	−795	195	1,524
Myanmar	1,307	*4,870*	2,020	*2,890*	−110	*−1,290*	562	*123*	−261	*813*	651	*1,383*
Namibia	1,734	3,521	2,100	3,615	139	−158	403	1,000	176	747	221	896
Nepal	1,029	1,436	1,624	3,655	9	137	230	2,088	−356	6	646	*1,565*
Netherlands	241,517	558,952	216,558	491,853	7,247	4,813	−6,434	−12,326	25,773	59,586	47,162	26,928
New Zealand	17,882	36,591	17,248	38,111	−3,957	−9,164	255	449	−3,068	−10,235	4,410	17,247
Nicaragua	662	2,685	1,150	4,673	−372	−135	138	1,075	−722	−1,048	142	1,103
Niger	321	599	457	*1,077*	−47	*1*	31	*163*	−152	−314	95	593
Nigeria	12,342	66,768	12,841	46,066	−2,878	−16,746	799	18,016	−2,578	21,972	1,709	51,907
Norway	56,058	177,889	46,848	116,784	−1,919	2,001	−2,059	−2,647	5,233	60,459	22,976	60,840
Oman	6,078	25,886	5,035	19,339	−374	−959	−1,469	−3,670	−801	1,918	1,943	9,524
Pakistan	10,214	21,879	14,185	37,525	−1,939	−3,735	2,562	11,086	−3,349	−8,295	2,528	15,798
Panama	7,610	14,263	7,768	14,627	−466	−1,311	153	253	−471	−1,422	781	1,935
Papua New Guinea	2,992	*3,580*	1,905	*2,692*	−488	−538	75	*291*	674	640	267	2,106
Paraguay	4,802	6,317	5,200	6,471	110	−93	195	373	−92	126	1,106	2,462
Peru	6,622	31,298	9,597	23,870	−2,482	−8,418	832	2,495	−4,625	1,505	8,653	27,786
Philippines	26,795	57,960	33,317	65,094	3,662	−542	880	13,977	−1,980	6,301	7,781	33,740
Poland	35,716	173,399	33,825	184,234	−1,995	−16,253	958	8,493	854	−18,595	14,957	65,725
Portugal	32,260	74,902	39,545	89,803	21	−10,135	7,132	3,618	−132	−21,418	22,063	11,512
Puerto Rico	..	..	..	..	..	..	..	..	..	..	..	..

4.15 Balance of payments current account

	Goods and services				Net income		Net current transfers		Current account balance		Total reserves[a]	
	$ millions				$ millions		$ millions		$ millions		$ millions	
	Exports		Imports									
	1995	2007	1995	2007	1995	2007	1995	2007	1995	2007	1995	2007
Romania	9,404	50,794	11,306	74,858	–241	–5,788	369	6,716	–1,774	–23,136	2,624	39,974
Russian Federation	92,987	393,817	82,809	282,673	–3,372	–31,396	157	–3,506	6,963	76,241	18,024	477,950
Rwanda	75	363	374	909	7	–15	350	413	57	–147	99	553
Saudi Arabia	53,450	242,046	34,286	113,396	2,800	238	–27,282	–33,808	–5,318	95,080	10,399	37,592
Senegal	1,506	2,398	1,821	4,032	–124	–63	195	837	–244	–861	272	1,660
Serbia	..	11,945	..	21,432	..	–829	..	3,970	..	–6,346	..	14,214
Sierra Leone	128	335	260	490	–30	–104	43	78	–118	–181	35	217
Singapore	157,658	372,964	144,520	326,455	2,130	–5,752	–894	–1,696	14,373	39,062	68,816	162,957
Slovak Republic	10,969	64,869	10,658	65,245	–14	–3,288	93	–438	390	–4,103	3,863	18,973
Slovenia	10,377	32,772	10,749	33,663	201	–1,000	95	–402	–75	–2,293	1,821	1,066
Somalia	..	..	..	..	..	..	..	..	..	..	..	..
South Africa	34,402	89,746	33,375	98,502	–2,875	–8,923	–645	–2,953	–2,493	–20,631	4,464	32,919
Spain	133,910	385,984	135,000	479,096	–5,402	–43,243	4,525	–9,000	–1,967	–145,355	40,531	19,029
Sri Lanka	4,617	9,452	5,982	12,773	–137	–358	732	2,311	–770	–1,368	2,112	3,654
Sudan	681	9,264	1,238	10,661	–3	–2,253	60	382	–500	–3,268	163	1,378
Swaziland	1,020	2,199	1,274	2,523	81	64	144	194	–30	–66	298	774
Sweden	95,525	234,049	81,142	200,184	–6,473	9,534	–2,970	–4,983	4,940	38,416	25,870	31,033
Switzerland	123,320	266,864	108,916	221,114	10,708	7,600	–4,409	–9,405	20,703	43,946	68,620	75,172
Syrian Arab Republic	5,757	13,169	5,541	11,879	–560	–935	607	565	263	920	..	..
Tajikistan	..	1,706	..	3,707	..	–51	..	1,557	..	–495	39	204
Tanzania	1,265	3,941	2,139	6,334	–110	–79	395	617	–590	–1,856	270	2,886
Thailand	70,292	180,382	82,246	162,904	–2,114	–5,661	487	3,938	–13,582	15,755	36,939	87,472
Timor-Leste	..	..	..	..	..	..	..	..	..	..	..	230
Togo	465	970	671	1,517	–34	–38	118	244	–122	–340	130	438
Trinidad and Tobago	2,799	10,569	2,110	6,265	–390	–760	–4	50	294	3,594	379	6,745
Tunisia	7,979	20,057	8,811	20,826	–716	–1,754	774	1,619	–774	–904	1,689	8,032
Turkey	36,581	144,209	40,113	176,999	–3,204	–7,143	4,398	2,236	–2,338	–37,697	13,891	76,496
Turkmenistan	1,774	..	1,796	..	17	..	5	..	0	..	1,168	..
Uganda	664	2,185	1,490	4,161	–96	–279	639	1,509	–281	–745	459	2,560
Ukraine	17,090	64,001	18,280	72,153	–434	–659	472	3,539	–1,152	–5,272	1,069	32,484
United Arab Emirates	..	..	..	..	..	..	..	..	..	..	7,778	77,239
United Kingdom	322,114	723,781	327,000	824,103	3,393	48,667	–11,943	–27,111	–13,436	–78,765	49,144	57,275
United States	794,397	1,645,726	890,784	2,345,982	20,899	81,751	–38,073	–112,705	–113,561	–731,209	175,996	277,549
Uruguay	3,507	6,825	3,568	6,803	–227	–342	76	134	–213	–186	1,813	4,121
Uzbekistan	..	..	..	..	..	..	..	..	..	..	..	..
Venezuela, RB	20,753	70,838	16,905	52,987	–1,943	2,565	109	–415	2,014	20,001	10,715	33,759
Vietnam	9,498	54,591	12,334	65,845	–384	–2,168	1,200	6,430	–2,020	–6,992	1,324	23,479
West Bank and Gaza	..	..	..	..	..	..	..	..	..	..	..	..
Yemen, Rep.	2,160	7,774	2,471	9,337	–561	–1,152	1,056	1,387	184	–1,328	638	7,757
Zambia	1,222	4,872	1,338	4,524	–249	–1,383	182	530	–182	–505	223	1,090
Zimbabwe	2,344	..	2,515	..	–294	..	40	..	–425	..	888	..
World	6,392,988 t	17,070,490 t	6,233,515 t	16,620,157 t								
Low income	72,352	270,815	99,243	308,995								
Middle income	1,087,015	4,680,736	1,127,240	4,202,021								
Lower middle income	512,935	2,687,262	543,345	2,265,062								
Upper middle income	572,897	2,040,686	584,277	1,943,357								
Low & middle income	1,159,335	4,959,944	1,223,867	4,509,716								
East Asia & Pacific	397,583	1,997,264	413,802	1,634,141								
Europe & Central Asia	238,763	1,079,371	248,679	1,099,718								
Latin America & Carib.	272,861	863,832	288,143	827,588								
Middle East & N. Africa	..	..	103,655	303,535								
South Asia	58,893	244,054	78,652	300,537								
Sub-Saharan Africa	89,262	322,767	99,763	301,623								
High income	5,228,660	12,191,150	5,008,580	12,186,397								
Euro area	2,097,739	5,031,654	1,974,212	4,839,351								

a. International reserves including gold valued at London gold price. b. Includes Luxembourg.

Balance of payments current account | 4.15

The balance of payments records an economy's transactions with the rest of the world. Balance of payments accounts are divided into two groups: the current account, which records transactions in goods, services, income, and current transfers, and the capital and financial account, which records capital transfers, acquisition or disposal of nonproduced, nonfinancial assets, and transactions in financial assets and liabilities. The table presents data from the current account plus gross international reserves.

The balance of payments is a double-entry accounting system that shows all flows of goods and services into and out of an economy; all transfers that are the counterpart of real resources or financial claims provided to or by the rest of the world without a quid pro quo, such as donations and grants; and all changes in residents' claims on and liabilities to nonresidents that arise from economic transactions. All transactions are recorded twice—once as a credit and once as a debit. In principle the net balance should be zero, but in practice the accounts often do not balance, requiring inclusion of a balancing item, net errors and omissions.

Discrepancies may arise in the balance of payments because there is no single source for balance of payments data and therefore no way to ensure that the data are fully consistent. Sources include customs data, monetary accounts of the banking system, external debt records, information provided by enterprises, surveys to estimate service transactions, and foreign exchange records. Differences in collection methods—such as in timing, definitions of residence and ownership, and the exchange rate used to value transactions—contribute to net errors and omissions. In addition, smuggling and other illegal or quasi-legal transactions may be unrecorded or misrecorded. For further discussion of issues relating to the recording of data on trade in goods and services, see *About the data* for tables 4.4–4.7.

The concepts and definitions underlying the data in the table are based on the fifth edition of the International Monetary Fund's (IMF) *Balance of Payments Manual* (1993). That edition redefined as capital transfers some transactions previously included in the current account, such as debt forgiveness, migrants' capital transfers, and foreign aid to acquire capital goods. Thus the current account balance now reflects more accurately net current transfer receipts in addition to transactions in goods, services (previously nonfactor services), and income (previously factor income). Many countries maintain their data collection systems according to the fourth edition of the *Balance of Payments Manual* (1977). Where necessary, the IMF converts such reported data to conform to the fifth edition (see *Primary data documentation*). Values are in U.S. dollars converted at market exchange rates.

• **Exports** and **imports of goods and services** are all transactions between residents of an economy and the rest of the world involving a change in ownership of general merchandise, goods sent for processing and repairs, nonmonetary gold, and services. • **Net income** is receipts and payments of employee compensation for nonresident workers, and investment income (receipts and payments on direct investment, portfolio investment, and other investments and receipts on reserve assets). Income derived from the use of intangible assets is recorded under business services. • **Net current transfers** are recorded in the balance of payments whenever an economy provides or receives goods, services, income, or financial items without a quid pro quo. All transfers not considered to be capital are current. • **Current account balance** is the sum of net exports of goods and services, net income, and net current transfers. • **Total reserves** are holdings of monetary gold, special drawing rights, reserves of IMF members held by the IMF, and holdings of foreign exchange under the control of monetary authorities. The gold component of these reserves is valued at year-end (December 31) London prices ($386.75 an ounce in 1995 and $696.70 an ounce in 2007).

	Total reserves ($ billions)		Share of world total (%)	Annual change (%)	Months of imports
	2006	**2007**	**2007**	**2006–07**	**2007**
China	1,081	1,546	21.8	43.1	17.0
Japan	895	973	13.7	8.7	14.9
Russian Federation	304	478	6.8	57.3	15.9
Taiwan, China	275	282	4.0	2.5	12.8
United States	221	278	3.9	25.5	1.1
India	178	277	3.9	55.3	8.8[a]
Korea, Rep.	239	263	3.7	9.8	7.0
Brazil	86	180	2.5	110.1	10.9
Singapore	136	163	2.3	19.6	5.2
Hong Kong, China	133	153	2.2	14.6	3.6
Germany	112	136	1.9	21.8	1.0
France	98	115	1.6	17.6	1.5
Algeria	81	115	1.6	41.1	..
Malaysia	83	102	1.4	23.1	6.7
Italy	76	94	1.3	24.2	1.5

a. Data are for 2006.
Source: International Monetary Fund, *International Financial Statistics* data files.

Data on the balance of payments are published in the IMF's *Balance of Payments Statistics Yearbook* and *International Financial Statistics*. The World Bank exchanges data with the IMF through electronic files that in most cases are more timely and cover a longer period than the published sources. More information about the design and compilation of the balance of payments can be found in the IMF's *Balance of Payments Manual,* fifth edition (1993), *Balance of Payments Textbook* (1996), and *Balance of Payments Compilation Guide* (1995). The IMF's International Financial Statistics and Balance of Payments databases are available on CD-ROM.

STATES
AND
MARKETS

STATES AND

Information and communication technology for development

Rapid advances in information and communication technology (ICT) have connected people, businesses, and governments around the world, enabling knowledge sharing across cultures and countries. ICTs used in e-government projects can reduce corruption, and some ICTs, such as broadband, can contribute to economic growth (box 5a).

Good government policies and regulations are creating competitive ICT markets, increasing access to ICT services for people everywhere. Recognizing the need to analyze ICT's impact on development, many statistical offices in developing countries are beginning to conduct household and business surveys to improve their ICT policy and analysis. Information on ICT infrastructure, access, use, quality, affordability, applications, and trade are included in tables 5.10 and 5.11.

The well known success of mobile telephony worldwide has been achieved through high demand, low-cost technologies, and market liberalization. Research on the diffusion of advanced telecommunications services in developing economies finds that the rate of adoption depends on an appropriate business environment—which depends in turn on the regulatory and policy environment.

Many countries that have created a competitive market environment for ICTs have more people using ICT services. Competition lowers prices for ICT services and expands markets. Prices for ICT services, such as mobile cellular phone tariffs, have been falling rapidly. But the services are still unaffordable for many people in low-income economies, leaving them yet to realize the potential of ICT for economic and social development.

ICT services range from telecommunication infrastructure (voice, data, and media services) to information applications tailored to specific sectors and functions (such as services in banking and finance, land management, education, and health), to electronic government (e-government), and to the production of equipment.

In developing economies innovative use of ICT services is changing people's lives and providing new opportunities. For example, banking services and job search text messaging services can be delivered through mobile phones and portable devices. Farmers and fishers also use these technologies to track prices and market demand.

Improving governance and contributing to growth	5a

E-government projects increase revenues and improve governance
Successful e-government projects have reduced transaction costs and processing time and increased government revenue. The e-Customs System in Ghana (GCNet) increased revenues 49 percent in the first 18 months of operation and reduced clearance times to two days from three weeks. And a land registration system has cut bribes $18.3 million a year in the Indian state of Karnataka, where an overwhelming proportion of supervisors now sense that the abuse of discretionary power in providing services to citizens has narrowed.

Broadband increases productivity and contributes to growth
Although the benefits of broadband are not yet available to most people in developing economies, access to information and communication technology, especially broadband, supports the growth of firms by lowering costs and raising productivity. Analysis of broadband access in developed economies suggests a robust and noticeable growth dividend. For developing economies the growth benefit of broadband is about the same as that for developed economies—about a 1.4 percentage point increase in per capita GDP for each 10 percent increase in broadband coverage.

Source: World Bank forthcoming.

Mobile phones have captured the market in developing economies

At the end of 2007 there were about 1.1 billion fixed telephone lines and 3.3 billion mobile phone subscribers worldwide. Developing economies increased their share of mobile phone subscribers from about 30 percent of the world total in 2000 to more than 50 percent in 2004 and to about 70 percent in 2007 (figure 5b). But access to mobile phones is still low in many countries, including Burundi, Central African Republic, Eritrea, Ethiopia, and Papua New Guinea, with fewer than 5 mobile phone subscribers per 100 people.

Mobile phone service in developing economies has overtaken fixed-line service. Wireless technology can be deployed more quickly than fixed-line telephone systems and requires less upfront investment in infrastructure. This translates to lower prices and stronger customer demand. Liberalization started later for fixed-line markets (previously dominated by state-owned monopolies), while mobile phone markets were generally opened to one or more new entrants from the start. And even where the opening of mobile phone markets was delayed, once they were opened competition often led to an immediate growth in mobile subscribers (figure 5c). Countries that have taken decisive steps to establish independent regulators and foster competition have seen greater improvements in sector performance. In some cases the announcement of

a plan to issue a new license has been enough to trigger growth, encouraging the existing mobile phone operator to improve service, reduce prices, and increase market penetration before the new entrant starts operations.

The demand for always-on, high-capacity Internet services is increasing. Advanced Internet service—beyond what can be achieved through dial-up connections—has become more important as the demand for data and value-added services grows. Broadband allows for large volumes of data to be transmitted and for cheaper voice communications (say, by routing calls over the Internet). Broadband also enables voice, data, and media services to be transmitted over the same network. This convergence of services can be very good for economic and social development—increasing productivity, lowering transaction costs, facilitating trade, and boosting retail sales and tax revenues. Where broadband has been introduced in rural areas of developing economies, villagers and farmers have gained better access to training, job opportunities, and market prices of crops. But in 2007 broadband reached just 2 percent of the population on average in developing economies, concentrated in urban areas. Why? Because of the relatively high cost of computers and, in rural areas, the limited access to electricity. Internet use (narrowband and broadband) in developing economies is only about one-fifth that in developed economies (figure 5d).

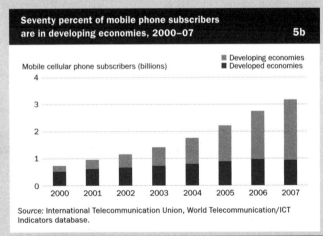

Seventy percent of mobile phone subscribers are in developing economies, 2000–07 — 5b

Mobile cellular phone subscribers (billions)

■ Developing economies
■ Developed economies

Source: International Telecommunication Union, World Telecommunication/ICT Indicators database.

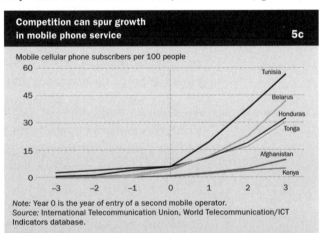

Competition can spur growth in mobile phone service — 5c

Mobile cellular phone subscribers per 100 people

Tunisia
Belarus
Honduras
Tonga
Afghanistan
Kenya

Note: Year 0 is the year of entry of a second mobile operator.
Source: International Telecommunication Union, World Telecommunication/ICT Indicators database.

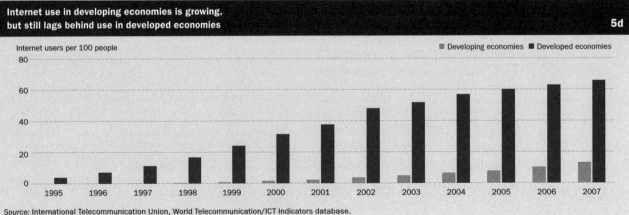

Internet use in developing economies is growing, but still lags behind use in developed economies — 5d

Internet users per 100 people

■ Developing economies ■ Developed economies

Source: International Telecommunication Union, World Telecommunication/ICT Indicators database.

Broadband access is also limited in rural areas of some developed economies, such as the United States, where there is a renewed commitment to improve access to rural areas as part of an economic stimulus package. The goal is to create jobs, bring broadband to every community, and improve the U.S. ranking for per capita broadband access (with about 24 broadband subscribers per 100 people in 2007, the U.S. is below the top tier of developed economies; figure 5e).

Although the capacity of broadband service is measured by the advertised speed available to consumers, speed may be constrained by bandwidth availability (effective rate of data transfer), which is increasing faster in developed economies, with their robust infrastructure, than in developing economies. In high-income economies, average per capita international bandwidth increased from 586 bits per second (bps) in 2000 to 18,240 bps in 2007. Among developing regions Europe and Central Asia and Latin America and the Caribbean have the greatest capacity. Over 2000–07 bandwidth per capita increased from 12 bps to 1,114 bps in Europe and Central Asia and from 8 bps to 1,126 bps in Latin America and the Caribbean. With improved fiber-optic connectivity some countries in South Asia are seeing a rise in international bandwidth, yet South Asia and Sub-Saharan Africa are still well behind other regions in international bandwidth per capita (figure 5f).

To unleash ICT's potential impact on growth, services must be affordable to more people

The price of ICT access continues to fall with technological advances, market growth, and greater competition, a trend that is especially important in allowing people in developing economies to take full advantage of ICT services. In recent years steep price reductions have contributed to the rapid expansion of mobile phone use in many economies (figures 5b and 5g). Prepaid services allow mobile customers to pay in small amounts instead of committing to fixed monthly subscriptions. Prepaid cards give even low-income consumers access to mobile communications, increasing penetration in poor and rural areas.

Pricing for Internet access has also been falling in many countries, including many Sub-Saharan countries (figure 5h). Still, the average price in Sub-Saharan Africa as a whole continues to be well above the world average and, as measured against income, is not affordable for most people. In 2006 the Internet access tariff for Sub-Saharan Africa was about 62 percent of average monthly per capita income, far more than the roughly 12 percent in South Asia, and less than the 9 percent average for all other developing regions. In high-income economies Internet service costs less than 1 percent of the average monthly income.

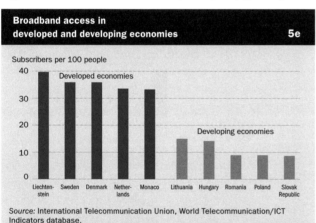

Broadband access in developed and developing economies   **5e**

Subscribers per 100 people

Source: International Telecommunication Union, World Telecommunication/ICT Indicators database.

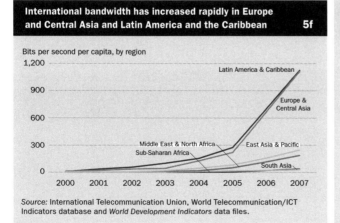

International bandwidth has increased rapidly in Europe and Central Asia and Latin America and the Caribbean   **5f**

Bits per second per capita, by region

Source: International Telecommunication Union, World Telecommunication/ICT Indicators database and World Development Indicators data files.

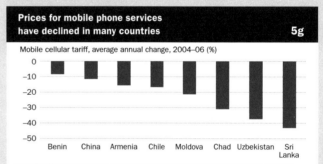

Prices for mobile phone services have declined in many countries   **5g**

Mobile cellular tariff, average annual change, 2004–06 (%)

Note: Tariff is based on the prepaid price for 25 calls per month spread over the same mobile network, other mobile networks, and mobile to fixed calls and during peak, off-peak, and weekend times (Organisation for Economic Co-operation and Development low user definition). It also includes 30 text messages per month. Countries that have experienced significant reductions in mobile phone service prices do not necessarily have the lowest prices.
Source: International Telecommunication Union, World Telecommunication/ICT Indicators database.

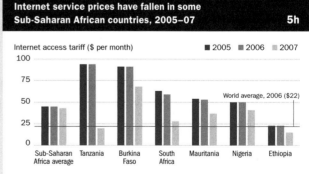

Internet service prices have fallen in some Sub-Saharan African countries, 2005–07   **5h**

Internet access tariff ($ per month) ■ 2005 ■ 2006 ■ 2007

Note: Tariff is based on the cheapest available tariff for accessing the Internet for 20 hours a month (10 hours peak and 10 hours off-peak). The basket does not include the telephone line rental but does include any usage charges.
Source: International Telecommunication Union, World Telecommunication/ICT Indicators database.

Developing economies benefit from ICT exports

Although ICT exports do not necessarily reflect high rates of ICT use, they indicate the importance of a country's ICT sector and its international competitiveness. As barriers to ICT trade are removed, opportunities for developing economies to benefit from such exports will likely grow.

Some developing economies have already become key exporters of ICT goods. China leads in dollar values of ICT export goods in 2006, with $299 billion. For many countries in East Asia and Pacific ICT export goods make up a large share of total goods exports (figure 5i). The share is 56 percent for the Philippines, 46 percent for Singapore, 45 percent for Malaysia, 42 percent for Hong Kong, China, and 31 percent for China.

Trade in ICT services includes communications services (telecommunications, business network services, teleconferencing, support services, and postal services) and computer and information services (databases, data processing, software design and development, maintenance and repair, and news agency services). India's software exports jumped from about $1 billion in 1995 to $22 billion in 2006, generating employment for about 1.6 million people. India leads all other developing economies in exports of communication, computer, and information services as a share of total service exports, at 42 percent in 2006 (table 5j).

ICT applications are transforming how information is shared and transactions are made

Governments are becoming increasingly important users of ICT, particularly for e-government—using Internet technology as a platform for exchanging information, providing services, and transacting with citizens, businesses, and other arms of government. That makes them major actors in fostering ICT uptake and setting information technology standards. E-government initiatives can make public administration more efficient, improve delivery of public services, and increase government accountability and transparency. They can also reduce transaction costs and processing times and increase government revenues. Some e-government projects have also improved governance, so vital for development.

A secure, reliable business-enabling environment is a key element of e-commerce. Privacy and security concerns about the transmission of personal or financial information over the Internet are major issues for both consumers and firms, perhaps explaining why they can be reluctant to use the Internet to make transactions. The number of secure servers indicates how many companies are conducting encrypted transactions over the Internet. Developing economies have only a fraction of the world's secure servers—about 4 percent (figure 5k).

East Asia & Pacific leads in share of information and communication technology goods exports   **5i**

Information and communication technology goods exports as a share of total goods exports, by region (%)

East Asia & Pacific

High income

Latin America & Caribbean

Sub-Saharan Africa   South Asia   Europe & Central Asia

2000 2001 2002 2003 2004 2005 2006

Source: United Nations Statistics Division Commodity Trade (Comtrade) database.

Developing economies have only about 4 percent of the world's secure servers, 2008   **5k**

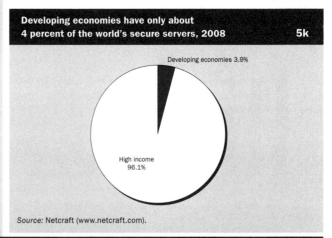

Developing economies 3.9%

High income 96.1%

Source: Netcraft (www.netcraft.com).

India leads developing economies in information and communications technology service export shares, 2007   **5j**

ICT service exports as a share of total service exports (%)

Top five developing economies		Top five developed economies	
Country	**Share (percent)**	**Country**	**Share (percent)**
India	41.6[a]	Kuwait	48.8
Niger	38.8[a]	Ireland	30.1
Guyana	21.5	Israel	28.5
Yemen, Rep.	18.9[a]	Canada	11.1
Romania	16.3	Finland	8.4

a. Data are for 2006.
Source: International Monetary Fund, Balance of Payments Statistics Yearbook database.

Progress in measuring ICT

Improving ICT indicators to analyze the impact of ICT on development was highlighted at the World Summits on the Information Society, held in Geneva in 2003 and Tunis in 2005. Attending were 50 heads of state, prime ministers, and vice presidents—and 80 ministers and vice ministers from 180 countries. The challenge has been taken up by the Partnership on Measuring ICT for Development, with country statistical offices and ICT agencies (box 5I).

The partnership was launched in 2004 with the following objectives to improve ICT measures:

- Continue to raise awareness among policymakers about the importance of statistical indicators for monitoring ICT policies and carrying out impact analysis.
- Expand the core list of indicators to other areas of interest such as ICT in education, government, and health, building on the original core ICT list of access and use by individuals, households and businesses, and production and trade in ICT goods and services.
- Conduct regional workshops to exchange national experiences and discuss methodologies, definitions, survey vehicles, and data collection efforts.
- Assist statistical agencies in developing economies in ICT data collection and dissemination, including national databases to store and analyze survey results.
- Develop a global database of ICT indicators and make it available on the World Wide Web.

In May 2008 the partnership published the *Global Information Society: A Statistical View,* with information on more than 40 core ICT indicators covering ICT infrastructure; access and use of ICT by households, individuals, and businesses; ICT in education; and ICT sector activity and trade in ICT goods (see http://measuring-ict.unctad.org for a complete list).

Partnership on Measuring ICT for Development	5I

Members of the Partnership on Measuring ICT for Development include a wide range of organizations:

- Eurostat.
- International Telecommunication Union.
- Organisation for Economic Co-operation and Development.
- United Nations Conference on Trade and Development.
- United Nations Economic Commission for Africa.
- United Nations Economic Commission for Asia and the Pacific.
- United Nations Economic Commission for Latin America and the Caribbean.
- United Nations Economic Commission for Western Asia.
- United Nations Educational, Scientific, and Cultural Organization's Institute for Statistics.
- World Bank.

	Investment commitments in infrastructure projects with private participation[a]								Domestic credit to private sector	Businesses registered	
					$ millions						
	Telecommunications		Energy		Transport		Water and sanitation		% of GDP	New	Total
	2000–05	2006–07	2000–05	2006–07	2000–05	2006–07	2000–05	2006–07	2007	2007	2007
Afghanistan	466.1	795.4	1.6	..	..	..	..	..	4.0	..	..
Albania	569.2	267.0	790.6	..	308.0	..	8.0	0.0	29.6	2,176	16,110
Algeria	3,422.5	1,263.0	962.0	2,320.0	120.9	161.0	510.0	230.0	13.3	10,662	105,128
Angola	278.7	448.0	45.0	9.4	..	53.0	..	..	10.2	..	..
Argentina	5,836.8	2,134.2	3,826.9	2,320.7	203.6	1,065.7	791.6	..	14.5	16,400	218,700
Armenia	317.1	77.0	74.0	57.0	63.0	10.0	0.0	..	13.6	3,822	56,461
Australia	..	..	..	..	..	..	..	..	127.5	89,960	641,538
Austria	..	..	..	..	..	..	..	..	114.2	3,484	76,374
Azerbaijan	355.6	601.6	375.2	..	..	..	0.0	..	15.3	4,945	69,309
Bangladesh	1,294.3	2,461.8	501.5	..	0.0	0.0	..	..	37.3	5,328	67,459
Belarus	735.4	881.3	..	..	..	..	..	..	25.1	..	..
Belgium	..	..	..	..	..	..	..	..	92.3	28,016	354,489
Benin	116.9	222.0	590.0	..	..	..	..	..	20.0	..	..
Bolivia	520.5	181.0	884.4	117.3	16.6	..	..	..	37.0	1,625	24,649
Bosnia and Herzegovina	0.0	901.5	277.9	800.0	..	..	..	..	54.7	314	23,634
Botswana	104.0	46.0	..	..	..	..	..	..	20.1	7,301	..
Brazil	41,053.8	12,667.3	25,489.2	11,470.5	4,206.4	1,966.2	1,215.3	639.6	49.8	490,542	5,668,003
Bulgaria	2,179.1	1,116.0	3,094.1	909.3	2.1	531.6	152.0	..	66.8	49,328	315,037
Burkina Faso	41.9	378.8	..	..	..	..	..	..	16.8	639	..
Burundi	53.6	0.0	..	..	..	..	..	..	23.6	..	..
Cambodia	148.1	217.0	108.1	648.7	125.3	200.0	..	..	18.2	..	..
Cameroon	394.4	212.4	91.8	440.0	0.0	..	..	0.0	9.2	..	..
Canada	..	..	..	..	..	..	..	..	136.4	207,000	2,500,000
Central African Republic	0.0	12.0	..	..	..	..	..	..	6.7	..	..
Chad	11.0	79.9	0.0	..	..	..	..	..	2.9	..	..
Chile	3,561.6	1,930.7	1,393.2	458.8	4,821.2	538.0	1,495.2	3.1	88.5	25,124	223,345
China	8,548.0	0.0	10,493.2	2,765.2	13,796.8	11,455.2	3,477.0	2,616.6	111.0	..	..
Hong Kong, China	..	..	..	..	..	..	..	..	139.6	80,935	524,445
Colombia	1,570.9	2,704.0	351.6	639.0	1,005.4	2,142.4	314.3	305.0	32.7	28,801	497,778
Congo, Dem. Rep.	473.4	394.0	..	..	..	..	..	..	3.9	..	..
Congo, Rep.	61.8	100.0	..	..	..	..	0.0	..	2.5	237	..
Costa Rica	..	..	80.0	80.0	465.2	373.0	..	..	44.3	10,567	102,311
Cote d'Ivoire	134.9	266.7	0.0	..	176.4	..	..	..	16.1	..	..
Croatia	1,205.7	2,401.0	7.1	..	451.0	492.0	298.7	..	72.1	11,055	200,955
Cuba	100.8	0.0	..	..	0.0	..	600.0	..	..	..	..
Czech Republic	8,508.0	488.0	3,865.3	..	106.7	..	263.7	0.0	47.7	16,395	244,417
Denmark	..	..	..	..	..	..	..	..	202.4	28,811	200,060
Dominican Republic	393.0	77.1	1,306.6	0.0	898.9	250.0	..	..	33.4	..	20,808
Ecuador	357.8	439.7	302.0	129.0	685.0	1,166.0	500.0	..	25.5	3,196	37,434
Egypt, Arab Rep.	3,471.9	6,509.0	678.0	469.0	821.5	730.0	..	..	50.6	9,595	367,559
El Salvador	1,110.6	583.0	85.0	0.0	..	..	..	..	42.8	1,802	..
Eritrea	40.0	0.0	..	..	..	..	..	..	25.6	..	..
Estonia	334.7	132.4	..	..	298.4	..	115.0	..	96.1	..	..
Ethiopia	..	..	..	..	..	..	..	..	23.8	..	..
Finland	..	..	..	..	..	..	..	..	82.0	10,424	120,294
France	..	..	..	..	..	..	..	..	105.2	137,481	1,267,419
Gabon	26.6	131.4	0.0	0.0	177.4	..	..	..	12.0	..	..
Gambia, The	6.6	0.0	..	0.0	..	..	..	..	16.2	..	..
Georgia	173.8	484.2	40.0	557.3	..	228.0	..	435.0	28.3	5,260	59,641
Germany	..	..	..	..	..	..	..	..	105.5	66,747	573,985
Ghana	156.5	635.0	590.0	100.0	10.0	..	0.0	..	17.8	..	..
Greece	..	..	..	..	..	..	..	..	91.5	..	..
Guatemala	560.1	780.1	110.0	226.8	..	..	..	..	35.2	4,251	..
Guinea	50.6	66.0	..	..	..	..	..	..	5.1	..	..
Guinea-Bissau	21.9	39.5	..	..	..	..	..	..	6.1	..	..
Haiti	18.0	306.0	5.5	..	..	..	..	..	11.3	9	300

Private sector in the economy

	Investment commitments in infrastructure projects with private participation[a]								Domestic credit to private sector	Businesses registered	
	$ millions										
	Telecommunications		Energy		Transport		Water and sanitation		% of GDP	New	Total
	2000–05	2006–07	2000–05	2006–07	2000–05	2006–07	2000–05	2006–07	2007	2007	2007
Honduras	135.0	319.9	358.8	..	120.0	..	207.9	..	53.1	..	..
Hungary	5,172.8	1,523.3	851.6	1,707.0	3,297.5	1,588.0	0.0	0.0	61.5	28,153	273,549
India	20,642.0	14,849.4	8,285.8	16,537.1	4,281.3	13,164.7	112.9	142.3	47.3	20,000	732,000
Indonesia	6,557.2	5,192.7	1,763.5	1,116.1	159.2	3,495.9	44.8	20.2	25.4	18,960	271,255
Iran, Islamic Rep.	695.0	221.0	650.0	..	..	..	..	..	49.2	..	..
Iraq	984.0	3,790.0	..	590.0	..	..	..	..	..	..	..
Ireland	..	..	..	..	..	..	..	..	199.6	18,704	180,891
Israel	..	..	..	..	..	..	..	..	90.1	18,814	162,910
Italy	..	..	..	..	..	..	..	..	101.8	77,587	638,987
Jamaica	700.3	166.7	201.0	78.0	565.0	..	..	..	31.1	2,023	54,116
Japan	..	..	..	..	..	..	..	..	171.6	145,151	2,572,088
Jordan	1,589.0	394.3	..	420.0	0.0	675.0	169.0	..	99.0	2,361	..
Kazakhstan	1,153.7	1,473.2	300.0	..	231.0	0.0	100.0	..	58.9	..	..
Kenya	1,434.0	1,496.0	..	116.7	..	404.0	..	..	27.2	7,371	125,102
Korea, Dem. Rep.	..	..	..	..	..	..	..	..	..	..	..
Korea, Rep.	..	..	..	..	..	..	..	..	107.8	..	..
Kuwait	..	..	..	..	..	..	..	..	69.6	..	..
Kyrgyz Republic	11.5	40.9	..	..	..	..	0.0	..	15.3	3,987	..
Lao PDR	87.7	10.0	1,250.0	800.0	0.0	..	..	..	6.8	..	..
Latvia	700.0	283.1	71.1	..	..	135.0	..	..	93.9	12,017	..
Lebanon	138.1	0.0	..	..	153.0	..	0.0	..	75.6	1,030	..
Lesotho	88.4	10.3	0.0	..	..	..	..	..	10.5	..	..
Liberia	70.3	27.5	..	..	..	..	..	..	10.0	..	..
Libya	..	..	..	..	..	..	..	..	7.2	..	..
Lithuania	993.0	326.2	446.3	96.0	..	..	..	..	61.2	6,578	67,095
Macedonia, FYR	706.6	371.0	..	391.0	..	..	..	..	38.0	..	..
Madagascar	12.6	119.6	0.0	..	48.5	0.0	..	..	10.1	1,234	19,305
Malawi	36.3	67.5	0.0	..	..	..	..	..	10.6	420	5,595
Malaysia	3,756.9	1,130.0	6,637.6	203.0	4,461.4	954.0	6,502.2	0.0	105.3	43,279	..
Mali	82.6	87.0	365.9	..	55.4	..	..	..	18.8	..	..
Mauritania	92.1	50.1	..	..	..	..	..	..	..	..	..
Mauritius	413.0	26.1	0.0	..	..	..	..	..	83.5	..	..
Mexico	18,191.4	5,642.2	6,749.3	1,081.0	2,970.4	8,808.4	523.7	303.8	22.0	306,400	4,290,000
Moldova	46.1	197.3	127.2	434.0	0.0	..	..	..	36.9	6,806	73,532
Mongolia	22.1	0.0	..	..	..	..	..	..	45.5	..	..
Morocco	6,139.5	1,466.6	1,049.0	..	200.0	140.0	..	..	69.9	24,811	..
Mozambique	123.0	81.2	1,205.8	..	334.6	..	..	..	13.9	..	..
Myanmar	..	..	..	556.1	..	..	..	..	5.6	..	..
Namibia	35.0	8.5	1.0	..	..	..	0.0	..	65.3	..	..
Nepal	109.3	26.0	39.0	..	..	..	..	..	36.3	..	..
Netherlands	..	..	..	..	..	..	..	..	195.0	116,000	1,030,000
New Zealand	..	..	..	..	..	..	..	..	148.1	74,247	474,212
Nicaragua	218.5	171.2	126.3	95.0	104.0	..	..	..	39.1	2,070	..
Niger	85.5	110.0	..	..	..	..	3.4	..	9.6	..	..
Nigeria	6,950.7	5,296.1	1,920.0	280.0	2,355.4	262.1	..	..	25.4	..	..
Norway	..	..	..	..	..	..	..	..	..	18,082	132,788
Oman	1,005.0	306.0	1,364.3	600.0	473.8	..	..	173.0	32.0	6,362	38,864
Pakistan	6,595.1	5,213.4	524.6	1,494.3	71.0	801.0	..	..	29.4	4,840	..
Panama	211.4	182.5	429.8	495.7	51.4	..	..	..	92.0	..	..
Papua New Guinea	..	150.0	..	..	..	..	..	..	21.4	..	..
Paraguay	199.0	319.7	..	..	..	..	..	..	20.0	..	..
Peru	2,233.4	1,117.0	2,498.9	399.7	522.5	2,290.8	152.0	..	21.0	..	..
Philippines	4,616.4	1,929.4	3,428.4	3,370.8	1,060.5	550.0	0.0	503.9	28.8	18,189	..
Poland	16,800.1	4,970.7	2,341.5	11.2	1,672.0	..	64.3	0.8	39.7	26,388	523,584
Portugal	..	..	..	..	..	..	..	..	169.0	30,934	423,719
Puerto Rico	..	..	..	..	..	..	..	..	..	..	..

	Telecommunications		Energy		Transport		Water and sanitation		Domestic credit to private sector % of GDP	Businesses registered New	Businesses registered Total
	2000–05	**2006–07**	**2000–05**	**2006–07**	**2000–05**	**2006–07**	**2000–05**	**2006–07**	**2007**	**2007**	**2007**
Romania	3,693.9	2,230.7	1,240.8	2,645.0	..	116.8	1,116.0	0.0	35.8	103,733	870,195
Russian Federation	22,049.4	11,757.4	1,726.0	14,011.2	109.4	144.0	935.4	396.2	39.0	489,955	3,267,325
Rwanda	72.3	124.4	1.6	..	..	..	..	..	12.2	..	455
Saudi Arabia	..	..	..	..	..	..	..	..	40.4	..	..
Senegal	593.1	779.0	93.3	..	55.4	..	0.0	0.0	23.0	23	1,000
Serbia	563.5	2,864.1	..	..	..	..	0.0	..	34.2	10,876	83,499
Sierra Leone	48.8	66.3	..	1.2	..	..	..	..	5.3	..	..
Singapore	..	..	..	..	..	..	..	..	99.9	25,904	133,235
Slovak Republic	2,709.9	581.7	3,384.6	1,272.0	..	42.0	..	13.6	42.4	16,025	135,330
Slovenia	..	..	..	..	..	..	..	..	79.0	4,957	47,312
Somalia	13.4	0.0	..	..	..	..	..	..	..	..	..
South Africa	10,519.5	2,574.0	1,251.3	9.9	504.7	3,483.0	31.3	0.0	164.3	41,356	553,425
Spain	..	..	..	..	..	..	..	..	182.7	145,593	2,435,689
Sri Lanka	766.1	723.1	270.8	..	..	..	..	..	33.3	4,529	..
Sudan	747.7	1,184.3	..	..	..	30.0	..	120.7	12.6	..	..
Swaziland	27.7	3.8	..	..	..	..	..	..	25.4	..	..
Sweden	..	..	..	..	..	..	..	..	123.7	27,994	326,052
Switzerland	..	..	..	..	..	..	..	..	177.6	18,284	162,326
Syrian Arab Republic	583.0	104.3	..	..	..	37.0	..	..	16.2	216	2,268
Tajikistan	8.5	11.0	16.0	..	..	..	..	..	28.9	794	..
Tanzania	515.3	485.5	348.0	28.4	27.7	134.0	8.5	..	15.5	3,933	59,163
Thailand	5,602.7	2,180.0	4,693.3	..	939.0	..	287.7	18.8	92.4	25,184	297,084
Timor-Leste	0.0	0.0	..	..	..	..	..	..	25.4	..	..
Togo	0.0	0.0	657.7	..	..	..	..	..	21.3	..	..
Trinidad and Tobago	..	190.0	..	39.0	..	..	120.0	..	33.8	..	..
Tunisia	751.0	2,419.0	30.0	..	..	840.0	..	..	64.3	6,675	63,584
Turkey	12,788.6	4,206.7	5,854.8	328.7	3,118.6	2,598.0	..	..	29.1	93,634	764,240
Turkmenistan	20.0	48.1	..	..	..	..	..	..	..	..	..
Uganda	387.6	500.6	113.9	822.6	..	404.0	0.0	..	10.6	8,906	89,503
Ukraine	3,162.9	2,211.0	160.0	..	..	..	100.0	..	58.8	41,809	528,864
United Arab Emirates	..	..	..	..	..	..	..	..	64.3	..	..
United Kingdom	..	..	..	..	..	..	..	..	190.0	449,700	2,546,200
United States	..	..	..	..	..	..	..	..	210.1	676,830	5,156,000
Uruguay	114.2	60.9	330.0	..	251.1	..	368.0	..	23.7	..	..
Uzbekistan	285.6	362.1	..	..	..	..	0.0	..	..	10,264	56,465
Venezuela, RB	3,337.0	1,683.0	39.5	..	34.0	..	15.0	..	23.6	..	..
Vietnam	430.0	1,326.7	2,360.6	287.0	20.0	400.0	174.0	..	93.3	..	52,506
West Bank and Gaza	279.8	0.0	150.0	..	..	..	..	..	7.5	..	..
Yemen, Rep.	376.8	292.1	..	15.8	..	..	..	..	7.9	50	..
Zambia	208.3	379.0	3.0	..	15.6	..	0.0	..	12.0	5,300	..
Zimbabwe	72.0	20.0	..	..	..	..	..	..	26.6	..	..
World	.. s	.. s	.. s	.. s	.. s	.. s	.. s	.. s	**135.6 w**		
Low income	21,743.0	23,001.5	10,746.1	5,150.7	3,295.8	2,605.1	185.9	0.0	31.2		
Middle income	230,758.0	116,028.5	102,036.5	66,150.7	49,769.0	58,924.6	20,141.7	5,735.9	60.4		
Lower middle income	79,126.8	54,904.0	40,467.3	31,883.7	25,282.6	37,718.9	5,883.5	4,392.4	74.7		
Upper middle income	151,631.2	61,124.5	61,569.2	34,267.0	24,486.5	21,205.7	14,258.2	1,343.5	45.5		
Low & middle income	252,501.0	139,029.9	112,782.6	71,301.4	53,064.8	61,529.7	20,327.6	5,735.9	59.0		
East Asia & Pacific	29,854.1	12,191.0	30,741.7	9,746.8	20,562.2	17,055.1	10,485.7	3,159.5	97.5		
Europe & Central Asia	68,767.4	38,203.5	16,942.6	20,240.6	5,955.1	4,255.4	2,774.4	832.0	39.5		
Latin America & Carib.	80,867.3	31,561.1	44,627.8	17,659.6	16,958.3	18,600.4	6,232.5	1,251.5	36.6		
Middle East & N. Africa	18,430.6	16,459.3	3,519.0	3,814.8	1,475.4	2,883.0	679.0	230.0	42.1		
South Asia	29,926.2	24,086.6	9,623.3	18,031.4	4,352.3	13,965.7	112.9	142.3	44.7		
Sub-Saharan Africa	24,655.4	16,528.5	7,328.3	1,808.2	3,761.6	4,770.1	43.2	120.7	70.4		
High income	..	..	..	..	..	..	..	..	163.2		
Euro area	..	..	..	..	..	..	..	..	121.6		

a. Data refer to total for the period shown. Includes infrastructure projects with private sector participation that reached financial closure in 1990–2007.

About the data

Private sector development and investment—tapping private sector initiative and investment for socially useful purposes—are critical for poverty reduction. In parallel with public sector efforts, private investment, especially in competitive markets, has tremendous potential to contribute to growth. Private markets are the engine of productivity growth, creating productive jobs and higher incomes. And with government playing a complementary role of regulation, funding, and service provision, private initiative and investment can help provide the basic services and conditions that empower poor people—by improving health, education, and infrastructure.

Investment in infrastructure projects with private participation has made important contributions to easing fiscal constraints, improving the efficiency of infrastructure services, and extending delivery to poor people. Developing countries have been in the forefront, pioneering better approaches to infrastructure services and reaping the benefits of greater competition and customer focus.

The data on investment in infrastructure projects with private participation refer to all investment (public and private) in projects in which a private company assumes operating risk during the operating period or development and operating risk during the contract period. Investment refers to commitments not disbursements. Foreign state-owned companies are considered private entities for the purposes of this measure.

Investments are classified into two types: investments in physical assets—the resources a company commits to invest in expanding and modernizing facilities—and payments to the government to acquire state-owned enterprises or rights to provide services in a specific area or to use part of the radio spectrum.

The data are from the World Bank's Private Participation in Infrastructure (PPI) Project database, which tracks infrastructure projects with private participation in developing countries. It provides information on more than 4,100 infrastructure projects in 141 developing economies from 1984 to 2007. The database contains more than 30 fields per project record, including country, financial closure year, infrastructure services provided, type of private participation, investment, technology, capacity, project location, contract duration, private sponsors, bidding process, and development bank support. Data on the projects are compiled from publicly available information. The database aims to be as comprehensive as possible, but some projects—particularly those involving local

and small-scale operators—may be omitted because they are not publicly reported. The database is a joint product of the World Bank's Finance, Economics, and Urban Development Department and the Public-Private Infrastructure Advisory Facility. Geographic and income aggregates are calculated by the World Bank's Development Data Group. For more information, see http://ppi.worldbank.org/.

Credit is an important link in money transmission; it finances production, consumption, and capital formation, which in turn affect economic activity. The data on domestic credit to the private sector are taken from the banking survey of the International Monetary Fund's (IMF) *International Financial Statistics* or, when unavailable, from its monetary survey. The monetary survey includes monetary authorities (the central bank), deposit money banks, and other banking institutions, such as finance companies, development banks, and savings and loan institutions. Credit to the private sector may sometimes include credit to state-owned or partially state-owned enterprises.

Entrepreneurship is essential to the dynamism of the modern market economy, and a greater entry rate of new businesses can foster competition and economic growth. The table includes data on business registrations from the 2008 World Bank Group Entrepreneurship Survey, which includes entrepreneurial activity in more than 100 countries for 2000–08. Survey data are used to analyze firm creation, its relationship to economic growth and poverty reduction, and the impact of regulatory and institutional reforms. The 2008 survey improves on earlier surveys' methodology and country coverage for better cross-country comparability. Data on total and newly registered businesses were collected directly from national registrars of companies. For cross-country comparability, only limited liability corporations that operate in the formal sector are included. For additional information on sources, methodology, calculation of entrepreneurship rates, and data limitations see http://econ.worldbank.org/research/entrepreneurship.

Definitions

• **Investment commitments in infrastructure projects with private participation** refers to infrastructure projects in telecommunications, energy (electricity and natural gas transmission and distribution), transport, and water and sanitation that have reached financial closure and directly or indirectly serve the public. Incinerators, movable assets, standalone solid waste projects, and small projects such as windmills are excluded. Included are operation and management contracts, operation and management contracts with major capital expenditure, greenfield projects (new facilities built and operated by a private entity or a public-private joint venture), and divestitures. Investment commitments are the sum of investments in facilities and investments in government assets. Investments in facilities are resources the project company commits to invest during the contract period in new facilities or in expansion and modernization of existing facilities. Investments in government assets are the resources the project company spends on acquiring government assets such as state-owned enterprises, rights to provide services in a specific area, or use of specific radio spectrums. • **Domestic credit to private sector** is financial resources provided to the private sector—such as through loans, purchases of nonequity securities, and trade credits and other accounts receivable—that establish a claim for repayment. For some countries these claims include credit to public enterprises. • **New businesses registered** are the number of limited liability firms registered in the calendar year. • **Total businesses registered** are the year-end stock of total registered limited liability firms.

Data sources

Data on investment commitments in infrastructure projects with private participation are from the World Bank's PPI Project database (http://ppi.worldbank.org). Data on domestic credit are from the IMF's *International Financial Statistics*. Data on business registration and are from the World Bank's Entrepreneurship Survey and database (http://econ.worldbank.org/research/entrepreneurship).

5.2 Business environment: enterprise surveys

	Survey year	Regulations and tax		Permits and licenses	Corruption	Crime	Informality	Gender	Finance	Infrastructure	Innovation	Trade	Workforce
		Time dealing with officials % of management time	Average number of times meeting with tax officials	Time required to obtain operating license days	Informal payments to public officials % of firms	Losses due to theft, robbery, vandalism, and arson % of sales	Firms that do not report all sales for tax purposes % of firms	Firms with female participation in ownership % of firms	Firms using banks to finance investment % of firms	Value lost due to electrical outages % of sales	Internationally recognized quality certification ownership % of firms	Average time to clear direct exports through customs days	Firms offering formal training % of firms
Afghanistan		..	..	..	..	..	..	..	..	..	..	..	..
Albania	2007	18.7	5.5	21.2	57.7	3.3	..	10.8	12.4	13.7	24.6	1.9	19.9
Algeria[a]	2007	25.1	3.4	19.3	64.7	6.3	..	15.0	8.9	4.0	5.0	14.1	17.3
Angola	2006	7.1	5.2	24.1	46.8	2.4	67.8	23.4	2.1	3.7	5.1	16.5	19.4
Argentina	2006	14.1	4.6	175.8	18.7	3.7	49.1	30.3	6.9	1.4	26.9	5.5	52.2
Armenia	2005	3.0	2.9	..	24.6	0.0	26.2	12.5	35.0	2.5	5.7	5.0	35.9
Australia		..	..	..	..	..	..	..	..	..	..	..	..
Austria		..	..	..	..	..	..	..	..	..	..	..	..
Azerbaijan	2005	5.2	1.3	..	37.8	0.2	38.7	14.4	0.6	5.9	10.3	1.6	16.3
Bangladesh	2007	3.2	1.4	6.1	85.1	1.2	..	16.1	24.7	10.6	7.8	8.4	16.2
Belarus[a]	2008	13.6	2.1	38.2	13.5	1.8	20.0	52.9	35.8	0.8	13.9	2.6	44.4
Belgium		..	..	..	..	..	..	..	..	..	..	..	..
Benin	2004	6.5	6.3	39.9	57.7	0.3	39.6	..	20.8	6.5	2.7	6.3	35.3
Bolivia	2006	13.5	3.5	30.0	32.4	3.3	51.4	41.1	22.2	4.4	13.8	15.3	53.9
Bosnia and Herzegovina	2005	4.3	1.9	..	24.1	0.4	29.2	25.2	17.5	2.4	14.5	2.0	47.2
Botswana	2006	5.0	2.4	13.7	27.6	3.2	65.3	40.9	11.3	1.4	12.7	1.4	37.7
Brazil	2003	7.2	..	..	..	0.4	82.8	..	22.9	1.6	19.1	8.2	67.1
Bulgaria	2007	17.4	4.1	48.2	16.1	1.3	39.7	39.2	40.5	1.2	22.3	2.7	36.5
Burkina Faso	2006	9.5	2.5	5.8	87.0	1.8	58.8	23.3	23.1	3.9	7.4	2.8	43.1
Burundi	2006	5.7	2.1	27.3	56.5	4.9	42.7	34.8	12.3	10.7	7.1	0.0	22.1
Cambodia	2007	5.6	2.3	..	61.2	0.4	..	..	11.3	2.4	..	1.7	48.4
Cameroon	2006	12.8	6.4	15.6	77.6	3.8	38.7	35.3	19.5	3.9	16.4	4.3	42.4
Canada		..	..	..	..	..	..	..	..	..	..	..	..
Central African Republic		..	..	..	..	..	..	..	..	..	..	..	..
Chad		..	..	..	..	..	..	..	..	..	..	..	..
Chile	2006	9.0	5.4	67.7	8.2	1.3	27.9	27.8	29.1	1.8	22.0	5.8	46.9
China	2003	18.3	14.4	11.8	72.6	0.1	49.5	..	9.8	1.3	35.9	6.7	84.8
Hong Kong, China		..	..	..	..	..	..	..	..	..	..	..	..
Colombia	2006	14.3	2.5	28.2	8.2	2.9	38.7	43.0	30.6	2.3	5.9	7.1	39.5
Congo, Dem. Rep.	2006	6.3	10.0	17.8	83.8	6.5	65.4	21.2	3.3	5.6	4.3	3.6	11.4
Congo, Rep.	2009	5.9	2.9	..	48.3	17.3	86.8	27.5	6.3	15.7	23.8	..	38.5
Costa Rica	2005	9.6	0.7	..	33.8	0.4	68.3	34.7	9.3	1.9	10.5	3.5	46.4
Côte d'Ivoire		..	..	..	..	..	..	..	..	..	..	..	..
Croatia	2007	10.9	1.7	26.5	14.5	0.9	33.3	33.5	60.0	0.8	16.5	1.3	28.0
Cuba		..	..	..	..	..	..	..	..	..	..	..	..
Czech Republic	2005	2.1	1.7	..	25.5	0.4	51.1	21.8	11.4	1.6	12.5	3.6	60.3
Denmark		..	..	..	..	..	..	..	..	..	..	..	..
Dominican Republic	2005	8.8	2.7	..	26.3	0.7	73.6	..	3.6	15.2	9.6	11.4	53.3
Ecuador	2006	17.3	2.6	19.9	21.5	3.0	37.6	32.7	24.0	2.7	18.2	7.0	61.6
Egypt, Arab Rep.[a]	2007	..	3.8	81.5	7.3	..	34.8	20.9	9.5	4.7	20.0	6.4	21.2
El Salvador	2006	9.2	4.1	35.4	34.3	5.6	42.3	39.6	17.3	2.9	11.0	2.6	49.6
Eritrea	2002	..	..	..	..	..	..	..	..	..	..	..	..
Estonia	2005	2.3	2.2	..	16.2	0.4	24.7	34.1	17.8	1.1	13.2	1.8	64.9
Ethiopia	2006	3.8	1.8	11.4	12.4	1.4	51.6	30.9	11.0	0.9	4.2	4.3	38.2
Finland		..	..	..	..	..	..	..	..	..	..	..	..
France		..	..	..	..	..	..	..	..	..	..	..	..
Gabon	2009	3.0	22.6	12.7	24.1	3.7	62.7	26.9	5.9	1.8	22.3	3.9	33.7
Gambia, The	2006	7.3	3.2	9.1	52.4	8.7	88.1	21.3	7.6	11.8	22.2	5.0	25.6
Georgia[a]	2008	2.1	1.7	11.8	4.1	7.6	36.0	40.8	38.2	1.4	16.0	3.8	14.5
Germany	2005	4.5	1.3	..	..	0.5	..	20.3	44.3	..	..	4.7	35.4
Ghana	2007	4.0	4.6	6.4	38.8	3.7	59.2	44.0	16.0	6.0	6.8	7.8	33.0
Greece	2005	3.7	1.7	..	21.6	0.0	53.2	24.4	16.1	..	11.7	5.5	20.0
Guatemala	2006	9.2	3.9	75.4	15.7	5.2	44.2	28.4	12.8	4.5	8.0	4.5	28.1
Guinea	2006	2.7	3.6	13.0	84.8	8.3	95.4	25.4	0.9	14.0	5.2	4.3	21.1
Guinea-Bissau	2006	2.9	4.4	30.4	62.7	3.3	68.2	19.9	0.7	5.3	8.4	5.6	12.4
Haiti		..	..	..	..	..	..	..	..	..	..	..	..

Business environment: enterprise surveys

	Survey year	Regulations and tax		Permits and licenses	Corruption	Crime	Informality	Gender	Finance	Infrastructure	Innovation	Trade	Workforce
		Time dealing with officials % of management time	Average number of times meeting with tax officials	Time required to obtain operating license days	Informal payments to public officials % of firms	Losses due to theft, robbery, vandalism, and arson % of sales	Firms that do not report all sales for tax purposes % of firms	Firms with female participation in ownership % of firms	Firms using banks to finance investment % of firms	Value lost due to electrical outages % of sales	Internationally recognized quality certification ownership % of firms	Average time to clear direct exports through customs days	Firms offering formal training % of firms
Honduras	2006	4.6	2.4	31.6	16.7	6.1	36.0	39.9	8.5	3.8	16.5	6.0	33.3
Hungary	2005	4.0	2.5	..	32.1	0.1	40.0	40.1	22.3	1.4	23.1	4.5	39.9
India	2006	6.7	3.1	..	47.5	0.1	59.2	9.1	19.4	6.6	22.5	15.6	15.9
Indonesia	2003	4.0	2.0	18.6	44.2	0.2	44.0	..	13.9	3.3	22.1	4.1	23.8
Iran, Islamic Rep.		..	..	..	..	..	..	..	..	..	..	..	..
Iraq		..	..	..	..	..	..	..	..	..	..	..	..
Ireland	2005	2.3	1.3	..	8.3	0.3	28.8	41.6	20.8	1.5	17.2	2.6	73.2
Israel		..	..	..	..	..	..	..	..	..	..	..	..
Italy		..	..	..	..	..	..	..	..	..	..	..	..
Jamaica	2005	6.3	2.2	..	17.7	1.1	28.8	32.2	10.6	11.8	16.4	4.3	53.5
Japan		..	..	..	..	..	..	..	..	..	..	..	..
Jordan	2006	6.7	2.2	6.4	18.1	1.3	13.0	13.1	8.6	1.7	15.5	3.8	23.9
Kazakhstan	2005	3.1	4.0	..	45.1	0.3	23.2	36.1	15.4	2.2	9.9	6.8	30.7
Kenya[a]	2007	5.1	9.0	23.4	79.2	3.9	45.9	37.1	22.9	6.4	9.8	5.6	40.7
Korea, Dem. Rep.		..	..	..	..	..	..	..	..	..	..	..	..
Korea, Rep.	2005	3.2	2.4	..	14.1	0.0	43.7	19.1	11.5	..	17.6	7.2	39.5
Kuwait		..	..	..	..	..	..	..	..	..	..	..	..
Kyrgyz Republic	2005	6.1	3.5	43.9	66.3	0.7	43.2	27.3	7.9	4.1	11.9	4.1	47.0
Lao PDR	2005	4.5	3.8	..	31.2	1.5	14.9	..	13.8	4.3	3.3	2.0	28.2
Latvia	2005	2.9	2.2	..	31.3	0.5	26.3	42.3	15.1	1.4	9.3	2.0	51.7
Lebanon	2006	12.0	4.7	..	51.2	0.5	67.5	27.9	26.8	6.0	20.9	7.4	67.8
Lesotho	2009	5.7	3.1	10.9	12.9	6.7	..	22.5	26.7	6.0	31.9	8.0	52.7
Liberia	2009	8.5	7.1	16.9	52.9	7.9	90.0	27.6	11.5	3.7	4.7	..	29.4
Libya		..	..	..	..	..	..	..	..	..	..	..	..
Lithuania	2005	5.1	4.2	55.5	44.6	0.4	39.0	25.5	15.6	1.2	15.1	1.8	52.6
Macedonia, FYR	2005	8.2	2.7	..	26.0	0.3	52.2	17.5	9.0	1.8	11.0	2.4	37.4
Madagascar	2005	20.8	2.7	..	24.5	1.9	21.0	..	13.0	6.6	6.6	3.5	48.5
Malawi	2006	5.8	8.9	17.4	35.7	2.3	55.3	15.8	20.6	22.6	17.2	3.5	51.6
Malaysia	2002	7.3	5.2	..	..	0.3	..	..	23.8	1.8	31.4	2.5	42.0
Mali[a]	2007	2.4	2.3	41.0	28.9	3.7	39.7	18.4	7.0	1.8	8.6	4.8	22.5
Mauritania	2006	5.8	1.9	10.7	82.1	5.6	82.5	17.3	3.2	1.6	5.9	3.9	25.5
Mauritius	2005	9.6	2.1	..	17.5	0.1	26.3	..	36.3	2.9	28.4	4.4	62.1
Mexico	2006	20.5	2.3	11.9	22.6	3.4	57.7	24.8	2.6	2.4	20.3	5.4	24.6
Moldova	2005	3.6	2.7	..	36.0	0.1	40.2	27.5	17.7	2.7	6.9	2.6	32.5
Mongolia	2004	6.0	7.3	..	..	0.6	80.4	..	32.8	1.5	20.5	3.5	46.2
Morocco[a]	2007	11.4	5.1	3.4	13.4	0.4	..	13.1	12.3	1.3	17.3	1.8	24.7
Mozambique[a]	2007	3.3	2.7	34.3	14.7	5.1	73.5	24.4	11.3	2.5	18.7	10.0	22.5
Myanmar		..	..	..	..	..	..	..	..	..	..	..	..
Namibia	2006	2.9	1.6	9.6	11.4	3.0	45.5	33.4	8.1	0.7	17.6	1.5	44.5
Nepal		..	..	..	..	..	..	..	..	..	..	..	..
Netherlands		..	..	..	..	..	..	..	..	..	..	..	..
New Zealand		..	..	..	..	..	..	..	..	..	..	..	..
Nicaragua	2006	9.3	2.5	19.7	17.2	3.8	60.4	41.4	13.0	8.7	18.7	5.0	28.9
Niger	2006	11.5	4.3	10.9	69.7	6.1	29.7	10.0	14.6	2.5	4.8	7.4	34.4
Nigeria[a]	2007	6.1	3.7	12.8	40.9	4.1	68.0	20.0	2.7	8.9	8.5	7.5	25.7
Norway		..	..	..	..	..	..	..	..	..	..	..	..
Oman		..	5.2	11.8	33.2	..	42.5	..	6.5	4.2	10.8	4.2	20.9
Pakistan	2002	8.7	4.2	35.2	57.0	0.1	..	..	3.6	4.9	17.0	9.7	11.1
Panama	2006	10.3	2.7	41.2	25.4	2.7	54.2	37.1	19.2	2.4	14.7	5.7	43.9
Papua New Guinea		..	..	..	..	..	..	..	..	..	..	..	..
Paraguay	2006	7.9	2.2	37.8	84.8	3.1	42.8	44.8	8.2	2.5	7.1	5.5	46.9
Peru	2006	13.5	2.5	81.1	11.3	2.4	27.2	32.8	30.9	3.2	14.6	5.6	57.7
Philippines	2003	6.9	3.9	25.0	44.7	0.9	57.9	..	5.5	5.9	15.8	6.6	21.7
Poland	2005	3.0	2.7	..	23.7	0.4	43.9	33.6	20.7	1.6	13.9	3.3	48.4
Portugal	2005	3.3	1.7	..	14.5	0.2	37.3	50.8	9.5	..	12.7	7.2	31.9
Puerto Rico		..	..	..	..	..	..	..	..	..	..	..	..

	Survey year	Regulations and tax		Permits and licenses	Corruption	Crime	Informality	Gender	Finance	Infrastructure	Innovation	Trade	Workforce
		Time dealing with officials % of management time	Average number of times meeting with tax officials	Time required to obtain operating license days	Informal payments to public officials % of firms	Losses due to theft, robbery, vandalism, and arson % of sales	Firms that do not report all sales for tax purposes % of firms	Firms with female participation in ownership % of firms	Firms using banks to finance investment % of firms	Value lost due to electrical outages % of sales	Internationally recognized quality certification ownership % of firms	Average time to clear direct exports through customs days	Firms offering formal training % of firms
Romania	2005	1.1	1.8	..	33.1	0.2	26.9	27.7	23.2	2.1	16.8	2.4	32.7
Russian Federation	2005	6.3	2.5	..	59.9	0.5	40.3	28.6	10.2	2.0	9.3	8.2	37.3
Rwanda	2006	5.9	4.0	6.5	20.0	7.1	28.9	41.0	15.9	8.7	10.8	6.7	27.6
Saudi Arabia		..	..	..	..	..	..	..	..	..	..	..	..
Senegal[a]	2007	2.9	1.8	21.4	18.1	4.1	21.6	26.3	19.8	5.0	6.1	8.9	16.3
Serbia	2005	8.1	4.1	..	31.8	0.6	33.3	25.0	16.7	2.4	11.7	3.2	47.5
Sierra Leone	2009	7.9	2.6	12.0	18.7	4.2	77.3	10.0	12.5	7.8	17.3	..	25.0
Singapore		..	..	..	..	..	..	..	..	..	..	..	..
Slovak Republic	2005	3.0	1.8	..	34.3	0.4	22.0	18.2	13.2	1.2	10.0	5.8	79.4
Slovenia	2005	3.7	1.4	..	11.2	0.2	35.6	34.5	29.6	1.1	20.2	2.9	69.9
Somalia		..	..	..	..	..	..	..	..	..	..	..	..
South Africa	2003	9.2	3.3	6.4	2.1	0.5	15.9	..	24.2	0.4	42.4	4.5	64.0
Spain	2005	0.8	1.5	..	4.4	0.2	18.3	34.1	32.2	3.0	21.3	4.9	51.3
Sri Lanka	2004	3.5	5.1	49.5	16.3	0.5	42.0	..	16.2	..	..	7.6	32.6
Sudan		..	..	..	..	..	..	..	..	..	..	..	..
Swaziland	2006	4.4	1.9	24.0	40.6	3.4	74.6	28.6	7.7	2.5	22.1	4.0	51.0
Sweden		..	..	..	..	..	..	..	..	..	..	..	..
Switzerland		..	..	..	..	..	..	..	..	..	..	..	..
Syrian Arab Republic	2003	10.3	6.0	..	..	..	79.9	..	2.9	8.6	7.4	6.3	21.0
Tajikistan[a]	2008	11.7	2.7	22.6	40.5	4.5	..	34.4	21.4	15.1	16.7	20.4	21.1
Tanzania	2006	4.0	3.3	15.9	49.5	3.9	71.0	30.9	6.8	9.6	14.7	5.7	36.5
Thailand	2006	0.4	1.1	32.1	..	0.1	..	..	74.4	1.5	39.0	1.5	75.3
Timor-Leste		..	..	..	..	..	..	..	..	..	..	..	..
Togo		..	..	..	..	..	..	..	..	..	..	..	..
Trinidad and Tobago		..	..	..	..	..	..	..	..	..	..	..	..
Tunisia		..	..	..	..	..	..	..	..	..	..	..	..
Turkey	2005	10.8	2.2	..	45.7	0.2	63.1	8.9	7.5	2.2	12.6	4.5	25.5
Turkmenistan		..	..	..	..	..	..	..	..	..	..	..	..
Uganda	2006	5.2	2.9	9.3	51.7	4.1	74.5	34.7	7.7	10.2	15.5	4.7	35.0
Ukraine[a]	2008	11.3	3.8	31.0	22.9	3.6	..	47.1	32.1	4.4	13.0	3.5	25.1
United Arab Emirates		..	..	..	..	..	..	..	..	..	..	..	..
United Kingdom		..	..	..	..	..	..	..	..	..	..	..	..
United States		..	..	..	..	..	..	..	..	..	..	..	..
Uruguay	2006	7.0	2.2	133.8	7.3	2.1	45.5	41.6	6.9	0.9	6.8	2.8	24.6
Uzbekistan[a]	2008	11.1	1.7	9.1	56.2	18.3	..	39.8	8.2	5.4	1.3	5.1	9.6
Venezuela, RB	2006	33.6	3.4	41.6	..	6.8	..	..	35.7	4.4	12.5	14.1	42.3
Vietnam	2005	3.1	2.2	..	67.2	0.1	70.3	27.4	29.2	..	11.4	4.9	44.0
West Bank and Gaza	2006	5.7	5.2	21.3	13.3	7.5	25.7	18.0	4.2	4.6	18.2	6.0	26.5
Yemen, Rep.		..	..	..	..	..	..	..	..	..	..	..	..
Zambia[a]	2007	4.6	2.9	47.3	14.8	3.3	..	37.4	10.1	3.6	17.2	3.1	25.4
Zimbabwe		..	..	..	..	..	..	..	..	..	..	..	..

a. Representative sample of the nonagricultural economy, excluding financial and public services.

STATES AND MARKETS

The World Bank Group's Enterprise Survey gathers firm-level data on the business environment to assess constraints to private sector growth and enterprise performance. Standardized surveys are conducted all over the world, and data are available on almost 85,000 firms in 106 countries. The survey covers 11 dimensions of the business environment, including corruption, crime, informality, regulation, and finance. For some countries, firm-level panel data are available, making it possible to track changes in the business environment over time.

Firms evaluating investment options, governments interested in improving business conditions, and economists seeking to explain economic performance have all grappled with defining and measuring the business environment. The firm-level data from Enterprise Surveys provide a useful tool for benchmarking performance and monitoring progress.

Most countries can improve regulation and taxation without compromising broader social interests. Excessive regulation may harm business performance and growth. For example, time spent with tax officials is a burden firms may face in paying taxes. The business environment suffers when governments increase uncertainty and risks or impose unnecessary costs and unsound regulation and taxation. Time to obtain licenses and permits and the associated red tape constrain firm operations.

In some countries doing business requires informal payments to "get things done" in customs, taxes, licenses, regulations, services, and the like. Such corruption harms the business environment by distorting policymaking, undermining government credibility, and diverting public resources. Crime, theft, and disorder also impose costs on businesses and society.

In many developing countries informal businesses operate without licenses. These firms have less access to financial and public services and can engage in fewer types of contracts and investments, constraining growth.

Equal opportunities for men and women contribute to development. Female participation in firm ownership is a measure of women's integration as decisionmakers.

Financial markets connect firms to lenders and investors, allowing firms to grow their businesses: creditworthy firms can obtain credit from financial intermediaries at competitive prices. But too often market imperfections and government-induced distortions limit access to credit and thus restrain growth.

The reliability and availability of infrastructure benefit households and support development. Firms with access to modern and efficient infrastructure—telecommunications, electricity, and transport—can be more productive. Firm-level innovation and use of modern technology may help firms compete.

Delays in clearing customs can be costly, deterring firms from engaging in trade or making them uncompetitive globally. Ill-considered labor regulations discourage firms from creating jobs, and while employed workers may benefit, unemployed, low-skilled, and informally employed workers will not. A trained labor force enables firms to thrive, compete, innovate, and adopt new technology.

Most of the data in the table are from the World Bank Financial and Private Sector Development Group's Enterprise Surveys. Data for 27 countries in Europe and Central Asia and 2 comparator countries in Asia (Republic of Korea and Vietnam) are based on the joint European Bank for Reconstruction and Development (EBRD)–World Bank Business Environment and Enterprise Performance Surveys (BEEPS).

All BEEPS economies plus the Latin American and Caribbean countries, the North African countries for 2007, the Sub-Saharan African countries for 2006 and 2007 (except Burkina Faso, Cameroon, and Cape Verde), Jordan, and Bangladesh for 2007 draw a sample from the universe of registered nonagricultural businesses excluding the financial and public sectors. Economies with samples that are representative of the economy are footnoted. Samples for most of the remaining economies were drawn from the manufacturing sector. Typical Enterprise Survey sample sizes range from 100 to 1,800, depending on the size of the economy. Samples are selected by simple random sampling or stratified random sampling. BEEPS 2005 use a simple random sample method based on GDP contributions, so samples are self-weighted. BEEPS 2008 economies, Latin American and Caribbean, North African, and Sub-Saharan African countries (except Burkina Faso, Cameroon, and Cape Verde), Bangladesh, and Jordan use stratified random sampling. Stratified random sampling allows indicators to be computed by sector, firm size, and geographic region.

At the sector level the strata are composed of selected manufacturing industries and one service sector (retail), plus the rest of the economy, a residual stratum. Firm size is stratified into small (5–19 employees), medium (20–100 employees), and large (more than 100 employees). Geographic stratification is defined by country. Economywide indicators can be computed with more precision under stratified random sampling than under simple random sampling when individual observations are properly weighted.

• **Survey year** is the year in which the underlying data were collected. • **Time dealing with officials** is the time senior management spends dealing with the requirements of government regulation. • **Average number of times meeting with tax officials** is the average number of visits with tax officials. • **Time required to obtain operating license** is the average wait to obtain an operating license from the day applied for to the day granted. • **Informal payments to public officials** are the percentage of firms expected to make informal payments to public officials to "get things done" for customs, taxes, licenses, regulations, services, and the like. • **Losses due to theft, robbery, vandalism, and arson** are the estimated losses from those causes that occurred on establishments' premises as a percentage of annual sales. • **Firms that do not report all sales for tax purposes** are the percentage of firms that expressed that a typical firm reports less than 100 percent of sales for tax purposes; such firms are termed "informal firms." • **Firms with female participation in ownership** are the percentage of firms with a woman among the principal owners. • **Firms using banks to finance investment** are the percentage of firms using banks to finance investments. • **Value lost due to electrical outages** is the percentage of sales lost due to power outages. • **Internationally recognized quality certification ownership** is the percentage of firms that have earned a quality certification recognized by the International Organization for Standardization (ISO). • **Average time to clear direct exports through customs** is the average number of days to clear direct exports through customs. • **Firms offering formal training** are the percentage of firms offering formal training programs for their permanent, full-time employees.

Data on the business environment are from the World Bank Group's Enterprise Surveys website (www.enterprisesurveys.org).

	Starting a business			Registering property		Dealing with construction permits		Employing workers	Enforcing contracts		Protecting investors	Closing a business
	Number of procedures	Time required days	Cost % of per capita income	Number of procedures	Time required days	Number of procedures to build a warehouse	Time required to build a warehouse days	Rigidity of employment index 0–100 (least to most rigid)	Number of procedures	Time required days	Disclosure index 0–10 (least to most disclosure)	Time to resolve insolvency years
	June 2008	June 2008	June 2008	June 2008	June 2008	June 2008	June 2008	June 2008	June 2008	June 2008	June 2008	June 2008
Afghanistan	4	9	59.5	9	250	13	340	27	47	1,642	0	..
Albania	6	8	25.8	6	42	24	331	35	39	390	8	..
Algeria	14	24	10.8	14	51	22	240	48	47	630	6	2.5
Angola	8	68	196.8	7	334	12	328	66	46	1,011	5	6.2
Argentina	15	32	9.0	5	51	28	338	35	36	590	6	2.8
Armenia	9	18	3.6	3	4	19	116	31	49	285	5	1.9
Australia	2	2	0.8	5	5	16	221	3	28	395	8	1.0
Austria	8	28	5.1	3	32	13	194	33	25	397	3	1.1
Azerbaijan	6	16	3.2	4	11	31	207	3	39	237	7	2.7
Bangladesh	7	73	25.7	8	245	14	231	35	41	1,442	6	4.0
Belarus	8	31	7.8	4	21	17	210	27	28	225	5	5.8
Belgium	3	4	5.2	7	132	14	169	20	25	505	8	0.9
Benin	7	31	196.0	4	120	15	410	40	42	825	6	4.0
Bolivia	15	50	112.4	7	92	17	249	79	40	591	1	1.8
Bosnia and Herzegovina	12	60	30.8	7	128	16	296	46	38	595	3	3.3
Botswana	10	78	2.3	4	11	24	167	20	29	987	7	1.7
Brazil	18	152	8.2	14	42	18	411	46	45	616	6	4.0
Bulgaria	4	49	2.0	8	19	24	139	29	39	564	10	3.3
Burkina Faso	5	16	62.3	6	136	15	214	21	37	446	6	4.0
Burundi	11	43	215.0	5	94	20	384	30	44	832	4	..
Cambodia	9	85	151.7	7	56	23	709	45	44	401	5	..
Cameroon	13	37	137.1	5	93	15	426	46	43	800	6	3.2
Canada	1	5	0.5	6	17	14	75	4	36	570	8	0.8
Central African Republic	10	14	232.3	5	75	21	239	61	43	660	6	4.8
Chad	19	75	175.0	6	44	9	181	46	41	743	6	..
Chile	9	27	7.5	6	31	18	155	24	36	480	7	4.5
China	14	40	8.4	4	29	37	336	27	34	406	10	1.7
Hong Kong, China	5	11	2.0	5	54	15	119	0	24	211	10	1.1
Colombia	9	36	14.1	9	23	13	114	24	34	1,346	8	3.0
Congo, Dem. Rep.	13	155	435.4	8	57	14	322	74	43	645	3	5.2
Congo, Rep.	10	37	106.4	7	116	14	169	69	44	560	6	3.0
Costa Rica	12	60	20.5	6	21	23	191	28	40	877	2	3.5
Côte d'Ivoire	10	40	135.1	6	62	21	628	38	33	770	6	2.2
Croatia	8	40	11.5	5	174	19	410	50	38	561	1	3.1
Cuba	..	..	..	..	..	..	..	..	..	..	..	..
Czech Republic	8	15	9.6	4	123	36	180	28	27	820	2	6.5
Denmark	4	6	0.0	6	42	6	69	10	34	380	7	1.1
Dominican Republic	8	19	19.4	7	60	17	214	28	34	460	5	3.5
Ecuador	14	65	38.5	9	16	19	155	51	39	588	1	5.3
Egypt, Arab Rep.	6	7	18.3	7	72	28	249	27	42	1,010	8	4.2
El Salvador	8	17	49.6	5	31	34	155	24	30	786	5	4.0
Eritrea	13	84	102.2	12	101	..	..	20	39	405	4	..
Estonia	5	7	1.7	3	51	14	118	58	36	425	8	3.0
Ethiopia	7	16	29.8	13	43	12	128	34	39	690	4	3.0
Finland	3	14	1.0	3	14	18	38	48	32	235	6	0.9
France	5	7	1.0	9	113	13	137	56	30	331	10	1.9
Gabon	9	58	20.3	8	60	16	210	52	38	1,070	6	5.0
Gambia, The	8	27	254.9	5	371	17	146	27	32	434	2	3.0
Georgia	3	3	4.0	2	3	12	113	7	36	285	8	3.3
Germany	9	18	5.6	4	40	12	100	44	30	394	5	1.2
Ghana	9	34	32.7	5	34	18	220	37	36	487	7	1.9
Greece	15	19	10.2	11	22	15	169	51	39	819	1	2.0
Guatemala	11	26	50.6	5	30	22	215	28	31	1,459	3	3.0
Guinea	13	41	135.7	6	104	32	255	44	50	276	6	3.8
Guinea-Bissau	17	233	257.7	9	211	15	167	66	41	1,140	6	..
Haiti	13	195	159.6	5	405	11	1,179	21	35	508	2	5.7

	Starting a business			Registering property		Dealing with construction permits		Employing workers	Enforcing contracts		Protecting investors	Closing a business
	Number of procedures	Time required days	Cost % of per capita income	Number of procedures	Time required days	Number of procedures to build a warehouse	Time required to build a warehouse days	Rigidity of employment index 0–100 (least to most rigid)	Number of procedures	Time required days	Disclosure index 0–10 (least to most disclosure)	Time to resolve insolvency years
	June 2008	June 2008	June 2008	June 2008	June 2008	June 2008	June 2008	June 2008	June 2008	June 2008	June 2008	June 2008
Honduras	13	20	52.6	7	23	17	125	53	45	900	1	3.8
Hungary	4	5	8.4	4	17	31	204	30	33	335	2	2.0
India	13	30	70.1	6	45	20	224	30	46	1,420	7	10.0
Indonesia	11	76	77.9	6	39	18	176	40	39	570	9	5.5
Iran, Islamic Rep.	8	47	4.6	9	36	19	670	40	39	520	5	4.5
Iraq	11	77	150.7	5	8	14	215	38	51	520	4	..
Ireland	4	13	0.3	5	38	11	185	17	20	515	10	0.4
Israel	5	34	4.4	7	144	20	235	24	35	890	7	4.0
Italy	6	10	18.5	8	27	14	257	38	41	1,210	7	1.8
Jamaica	6	8	7.9	5	54	10	156	4	35	655	4	1.1
Japan	8	23	7.5	6	14	15	187	17	30	316	7	0.6
Jordan	10	14	60.4	8	22	18	122	30	39	689	5	4.3
Kazakhstan	8	21	5.2	5	40	38	231	23	38	230	7	3.3
Kenya	12	30	39.7	8	64	10	100	17	44	465	3	4.5
Korea, Dem. Rep.	..	..	..	..	..	..	..	..	..	..	..	..
Korea, Rep.	10	17	16.9	7	11	13	34	45	35	230	7	1.5
Kuwait	13	35	1.3	8	55	25	104	13	50	566	7	4.2
Kyrgyz Republic	4	15	7.4	7	8	13	159	38	39	177	9	4.0
Lao PDR	8	103	14.1	9	135	24	172	34	42	443	0	..
Latvia	5	16	2.3	7	50	25	187	43	27	279	5	3.0
Lebanon	5	11	87.5	8	25	20	211	25	37	721	9	4.0
Lesotho	7	40	37.8	6	101	15	601	21	41	695	2	2.6
Liberia	8	27	100.2	13	50	25	321	31	41	1,280	4	3.0
Libya	..	..	..	..	..	..	..	..	..	..	..	..
Lithuania	7	26	2.7	2	3	17	162	48	30	210	5	1.7
Macedonia, FYR	7	9	3.8	6	66	21	198	47	38	385	5	3.7
Madagascar	5	7	11.0	7	74	16	178	63	38	871	5	..
Malawi	10	39	125.9	6	88	21	213	25	42	432	4	2.6
Malaysia	9	13	14.7	5	144	25	261	10	30	600	10	2.3
Mali	11	26	121.5	5	29	14	208	38	39	860	6	3.6
Mauritania	9	19	33.9	4	49	25	201	45	46	370	5	8.0
Mauritius	5	6	5.0	4	210	18	107	23	37	750	6	1.7
Mexico	9	28	12.5	5	74	12	138	48	38	415	8	1.8
Moldova	9	15	8.9	6	48	30	292	41	31	365	7	2.8
Mongolia	7	13	4.0	5	11	21	215	34	32	314	5	4.0
Morocco	6	12	10.2	8	47	19	163	63	40	615	6	1.8
Mozambique	10	26	22.9	8	42	17	381	49	30	730	5	5.0
Myanmar	..	..	..	..	..	..	..	..	..	..	..	..
Namibia	10	66	22.1	9	23	12	139	20	33	270	5	1.5
Nepal	7	31	60.2	3	5	15	424	42	39	735	6	5.0
Netherlands	6	10	5.9	2	5	18	230	42	25	514	4	1.1
New Zealand	1	1	0.4	2	2	7	65	7	30	216	10	1.3
Nicaragua	6	39	121.0	8	124	17	219	27	35	540	4	2.2
Niger	11	19	170.1	4	35	17	265	70	39	545	6	5.0
Nigeria	8	31	90.1	14	82	18	350	7	39	457	5	2.0
Norway	6	10	2.1	1	3	14	252	47	33	310	7	0.9
Oman	7	14	3.6	2	16	16	242	24	51	598	8	4.0
Pakistan	11	24	12.6	6	50	12	223	43	47	976	6	2.8
Panama	7	13	19.6	7	44	21	131	66	31	686	1	2.5
Papua New Guinea	8	56	23.6	4	72	24	217	10	43	591	5	3.0
Paraguay	7	35	67.9	6	46	13	291	59	38	591	6	3.9
Peru	10	65	25.7	5	33	21	210	48	41	468	8	3.1
Philippines	15	52	29.8	8	33	24	203	35	37	842	2	5.7
Poland	10	31	18.8	6	197	30	308	37	38	830	7	3.0
Portugal	6	6	2.9	5	42	21	328	48	34	577	6	2.0
Puerto Rico	7	7	0.8	8	194	22	209	25	39	620	7	3.8

	Starting a business			Registering property		Dealing with construction permits		Employing workers	Enforcing contracts		Protecting investors	Closing a business
	Number of procedures	Time required days	Cost % of per capita income	Number of procedures	Time required days	Number of procedures to build a warehouse	Time required to build a warehouse days	Rigidity of employment index 0–100 (least to most rigid)	Number of procedures	Time required days	Disclosure index 0–10 (least to most disclosure)	Time to resolve insolvency years
	June 2008	June 2008	June 2008	June 2008	June 2008	June 2008	June 2008	June 2008	June 2008	June 2008	June 2008	June 2008
Romania	6	10	3.6	8	83	17	243	62	31	512	9	3.3
Russian Federation	8	29	2.6	6	52	54	704	44	37	281	6	3.8
Rwanda	8	14	108.9	4	315	14	210	38	24	310	2	..
Saudi Arabia	7	12	14.9	2	2	18	125	13	44	635	8	1.5
Senegal	4	8	72.7	6	124	16	220	61	44	780	6	3.0
Serbia	11	23	7.6	6	111	20	279	39	36	635	7	2.7
Sierra Leone	7	17	56.2	7	86	25	283	51	40	515	3	2.6
Singapore	4	4	0.7	3	9	11	38	0	21	150	10	0.8
Slovak Republic	6	16	3.3	3	17	13	287	36	30	565	3	4.0
Slovenia	5	19	0.1	6	391	15	208	59	32	1,350	3	2.0
Somalia	..	..	..	..	..	..	..	..	..	..	..	..
South Africa	6	22	6.0	6	24	17	174	42	30	600	8	2.0
Spain	10	47	14.9	4	18	11	233	56	39	515	5	1.0
Sri Lanka	4	38	7.1	8	83	21	214	27	40	1,318	4	1.7
Sudan	10	39	50.8	6	9	19	271	36	53	810	0	..
Swaziland	13	61	35.1	11	46	13	93	13	40	972	0	2.0
Sweden	3	15	0.6	1	2	8	116	44	30	508	6	2.0
Switzerland	6	20	2.1	4	16	14	154	17	32	417	0	3.0
Syrian Arab Republic	8	17	18.2	4	19	26	128	34	55	872	6	4.1
Tajikistan	13	49	27.6	6	37	32	351	51	34	295	4	3.0
Tanzania	12	29	41.5	9	73	21	308	63	38	462	3	3.0
Thailand	8	33	4.9	2	2	11	156	18	35	479	10	2.7
Timor-Leste	10	83	6.6	..	..	22	208	34	51	1,800	3	..
Togo	13	53	251.3	5	295	15	277	57	41	588	6	3.0
Trinidad and Tobago	9	43	0.9	8	162	20	261	7	42	1,340	4	..
Tunisia	10	11	7.9	4	39	20	84	49	39	565	0	1.3
Turkey	6	6	14.9	6	6	25	188	38	35	420	9	3.3
Turkmenistan	..	..	..	..	..	..	..	..	..	..	..	..
Uganda	18	25	100.7	13	227	16	143	3	38	535	2	2.2
Ukraine	10	27	5.5	10	93	30	471	45	30	354	1	2.9
United Arab Emirates	8	17	13.4	3	6	21	125	13	50	607	4	5.1
United Kingdom	6	13	0.8	2	21	19	144	14	30	404	10	1.0
United States	6	6	0.7	4	12	19	40	0	32	300	7	1.5
Uruguay	11	44	43.5	8	66	30	234	31	40	720	3	2.1
Uzbekistan	7	15	10.3	12	78	26	260	34	42	195	4	4.0
Venezuela, RB	16	141	26.8	8	47	11	395	79	29	510	3	4.0
Vietnam	11	50	16.8	4	57	13	194	24	34	295	6	5.0
West Bank and Gaza	11	49	69.1	7	63	21	199	31	44	700	6	..
Yemen, Rep.	7	13	93.0	6	19	13	107	33	37	520	6	3.0
Zambia	6	18	28.6	6	39	17	254	34	35	471	3	2.7
Zimbabwe	10	96	432.7	4	30	19	1,426	33	38	410	8	3.3
World	**9 u**	**38 u**	**47.1 u**	**6 u**	**72 u**	**18 u**	**222 u**	**33 u**	**38 u**	**613 u**	**5 u**	**3.0 u**
Low income	10	49	110.1	7	108	18	304	39	40	626	5	3.6
Middle income	9	42	34.9	6	67	19	213	33	39	652	5	3.2
Lower middle income	9	35	45.9	6	69	19	209	33	39	669	5	3.5
Upper middle income	9	53	19.1	6	64	20	219	32	38	627	5	2.9
Low & middle income	9	44	60.3	6	81	19	243	35	39	643	5	3.3
East Asia & Pacific	9	44	38.0	5	113	19	183	20	37	591	5	3.1
Europe & Central Asia	8	23	9.3	6	59	24	265	37	37	385	6	3.2
Latin America & Carib.	10	70	43.9	7	66	17	233	33	39	714	4	3.2
Middle East & N. Africa	9	27	60.9	7	37	20	215	39	43	716	6	3.5
South Asia	7	33	31.9	6	106	16	245	26	44	1,053	4	5.0
Sub-Saharan Africa	10	46	111.4	7	97	17	273	41	39	662	5	3.4
High income	7	21	7.2	5	47	17	160	29	35	522	6	2.1
Euro area	7	17	5.9	6	69	14	190	44	31	591	6	1.4

The economic health of a country is measured not only in macroeconomic terms but also by other factors that shape daily economic activity such as laws, regulations, and institutional arrangements. The Doing Business indicators measure business regulation, gauge regulatory outcomes, and measure the extent of legal protection of property, the flexibility of employment regulation, and the tax burden on businesses.

The table presents a subset of Doing Business indicators covering 7 of the 10 sets of indicators: starting a business, registering property, dealing with construction permits, employing workers, enforcing contracts, protecting investors, and closing a business. Table 5.5 includes Doing Business measures of getting credit, and table 5.6 presents data on paying taxes.

The fundamental premise of the Doing Business project is that economic activity requires good rules and regulations that are efficient, accessible to all who need to use them, and simple to implement. Thus some Doing Business indicators give a higher score for more regulation, such as stricter disclosure requirements in related-party transactions, and others give a higher score for simplified regulations, such as a one-stop shop for completing business startup formalities.

In constructing the indicators, it is assumed that entrepreneurs know about all regulations and comply with them; in practice, entrepreneurs may not be aware of all required procedures or may avoid legally required procedures altogether. But where regulation is particularly onerous, levels of informality are higher, which comes at a cost: firms in the informal sector usually grow more slowly, have less access to credit, and employ fewer workers—and those workers remain outside the protections of labor law. The indicators in the table can help policymakers understand the business environment in a country and—along with information from other sources such as the World Bank's Enterprise Surveys—provide insights into potential areas of reform.

Doing Business data are collected with a standardized survey that uses a simple business case to ensure comparability across economies and over time—with assumptions about the legal form of the business, its size, its location, and nature of its operation. Surveys in 181 countries are administered through more than 6,700 local experts, including lawyers, business consultants, accountants, freight forwarders, government officials, and other professionals who routinely administer or advise on legal and regulatory requirements.

The Doing Business project encompasses two types of data: data from readings of laws and regulations and data on time and motion indicators that measure efficiency in achieving a regulatory goal. Within the time and motion indicators cost estimates are recorded from official fee schedules where applicable. The data from surveys are subjected to numerous tests for robustness, which lead to revision or expansion of the information collected.

The Doing Business methodology has limitations that should be considered when interpreting the data. First, the data collected refer to businesses in the economy's largest city and may not represent regulations in other locations of the economy. To address this limitation, subnational indicators are being collected for six economies, and data collection is under way in six more. These subnational studies point to significant differences in the speed of reform and the ease of doing business across cities in the same economy. Second, the data often focus on a specific business form—generally a limited liability company of a specified size—and may not represent regulation for other types of businesses such as sole proprietorships. Third, transactions described in a standardized business case refer to a specific set of issues and may not represent the full set of issues a business encounters. Fourth, the time measures involve an element of judgment by the expert respondents. When sources indicate different estimates, the Doing Business time indicators represent the median values of several responses given under the assumptions of the standardized case. Fifth, the methodology assumes that a business has full information on what is required and does not waste time when completing procedures.

• **Number of procedures for starting a business** is the number of procedures required to start a business, including interactions to obtain necessary permits and licenses and to complete all inscriptions, verifications, and notifications to start operations for businesses with specific characteristics of ownership, size, and type of production. • **Time required for starting a business** is the number of calendar days to complete the procedures for legally operating a business using the fastest procedure, independent of cost. • **Cost for starting a business** is normalized as a percentage of gross national income (GNI) per capita. • **Number of procedures for registering property** is the number of procedures required for a business to legally transfer property. • **Time required for registering property** is the number of calendar days for a business to legally transfer property. • **Number of procedures for dealing with licenses to build a warehouse** is the number of interactions of a company's employees or managers with external parties, including government staff, public inspectors, notaries, land registry and cadastre staff, and technical experts apart from architects and engineers. • **Time required for dealing with construction permits to build a warehouse** is the number of calendar days to complete the required procedures for building a warehouse using the fastest procedure, independent of cost. • **Rigidity of employment index,** a measure of employment regulation, is the average of three subindexes: a difficulty of hiring index, a rigidity of hours index, and a difficulty of firing index. Higher values indicate more rigid regulations. • **Number of procedures for enforcing contracts** is the number of independent actions, mandated by law or court regulation, that demand interaction between the parties to a contract or between them and the judge or court officer. • **Time required for enforcing contracts** is the number of calendar days from the time of the filing of a lawsuit in court to the final determination and payment. • **Extent of disclosure index** measures the degree to which investors are protected through disclosure of ownership and financial information. Higher values indicate more disclosure. • **Time to resolve insolvency** is the number of years from time of filing for insolvency in court until resolution of distressed assets and payment of creditors.

Data on the business environment are from the World Bank's Doing Business project (www.doingbusiness.org).

	Market capitalization				Market liquidity		Turnover ratio		Listed domestic companies		S&P/Global Equity Indices	
	$ millions		% of GDP		Value of shares traded % of GDP		Value of shares traded % of market capitalization		number		% change	
	2000	2008	2000	2007	2000	2007	2000	2008	2000	2008	2007	2008
Afghanistan	..	..	..	..	..	..	..	..	..	..	..	..
Albania	..	..	..	..	..	..	..	..	..	..	..	..
Algeria	..	..	..	..	..	..	..	..	..	..	..	..
Angola	..	..	..	..	..	..	..	..	..	..	..	..
Argentina	166,068	52,309	58.4	33.0	2.1	3.1	4.8	19.3	127	107	0.7	−56.2
Armenia	2	105	0.1	1.1	0.0	0.1	4.6	6.1	105	29	..	..
Australia	372,794	1,298,429	92.0	158.2	55.9	161.1	56.5	110.5	1,330	1,913	..	..
Austria	29,935	228,707	15.4	61.3	4.8	32.5	29.8	57.8	97	96	..	..
Azerbaijan	4	..	0.1	..	..	..	..	..	2	..	..	..
Bangladesh	1,186	6,671	2.5	9.9	1.6	7.0	74.4	137.3	221	290	126.4[a]	4.3[a]
Belarus	..	..	..	..	..	..	..	..	..	..	..	..
Belgium	182,481	386,362	78.7	85.3	16.4	56.5	20.7	65.3	174	153	..	..
Benin	..	..	..	..	..	..	..	..	..	..	..	..
Bolivia	1,742	2,263	20.7	17.2	0.8	0.0	0.1	0.0	26	37	..	..
Bosnia and Herzegovina	..	..	..	..	..	..	..	..	..	..	..	..
Botswana	978	3,556	15.8	47.8	0.8	0.9	4.8	3.1	16	19	37.2[a]	−38.4[a]
Brazil	226,152	589,384	35.1	104.3	15.7	44.5	43.5	74.3	459	432	74.7	−57.2
Bulgaria	617	8,858	4.9	55.1	0.5	13.9	9.2	10.8	503	334	39.0[a]	−70.2[a]
Burkina Faso	..	..	..	..	..	..	..	..	..	..	..	..
Burundi	..	..	..	..	..	..	..	..	..	..	..	..
Cambodia	..	..	..	..	..	..	..	..	..	..	..	..
Cameroon	..	..	..	..	..	..	..	..	..	..	..	..
Canada	841,385	2,186,550	116.1	164.4	87.6	123.7	77.3	84.7	1,418	3,881	..	..
Central African Republic	..	..	..	..	..	..	..	..	..	..	..	..
Chad	..	..	..	..	..	..	..	..	..	..	..	..
Chile	60,401	132,428	80.3	129.9	8.1	27.1	9.4	21.2	258	235	22.6	−41.2
China	580,991	2,793,613	48.5	194.2	60.2	243.1	158.3	121.3	1,086	1,604	66.6	−52.7
Hong Kong, China	623,398	1,162,566	368.6	561.2	223.4	442.6	61.3	89.1	779	1,029	..	..
Colombia	9,560	87,032	10.2	49.1	0.4	5.0	3.8	13.2	126	96	12.7[a]	..
Congo, Dem. Rep.	..	..	..	..	..	..	..	..	..	..	..	..
Congo, Rep.	..	..	..	..	..	..	..	..	..	..	..	..
Costa Rica	2,924	2,035	18.3	7.7	0.7	0.2	12.0	3.1	21	12	..	..
Cote d'Ivoire	1,185	7,071	11.4	42.2	0.3	0.8	2.6	4.1	41	38	115.6[a]	−16.9[a]
Croatia	2,742	26,790	14.9	128.7	1.0	8.0	7.4	7.4	64	376	68.1[a]	−59.3[a]
Cuba	..	..	..	..	..	..	..	..	..	..	..	..
Czech Republic	11,002	48,850	19.4	42.0	11.6	24.0	60.3	70.4	131	28	49.7	−45.9
Denmark	107,666	277,746	67.3	89.1	57.2	77.7	86.0	99.1	225	201	..	..
Dominican Republic	141	..	0.8	..	..	..	..	..	6	..	..	..
Ecuador	704	4,562	4.4	9.6	0.1	0.7	5.5	3.6	30	38	3.8[a]	−8.8[a]
Egypt, Arab Rep.	28,741	85,885	28.8	106.8	11.1	40.7	34.7	58.6	1,076	373	52.2	−55.8
El Salvador	2,041	6,743	15.5	33.1	0.2	0.9	1.3	3.7	40	51	..	..
Eritrea	..	..	..	..	..	..	..	..	..	..	..	..
Estonia	1,846	1,951	32.8	28.9	5.8	10.0	18.9	23.2	23	18	−15.5[a]	−65.5[a]
Ethiopia	..	..	..	..	..	..	..	..	..	..	..	..
Finland	293,635	369,168	241.0	150.9	169.6	222.1	64.3	182.0	154	134	..	..
France	1,446,634	2,771,217	108.9	107.0	81.6	132.0	74.1	131.5	808	707	..	..
Gabon	..	..	..	..	..	..	..	..	..	..	..	..
Gambia, The	..	..	..	..	..	..	..	..	..	..	..	..
Georgia	24	1,389	0.8	13.7	0.1	0.4	..	4.4	269	161	..	..
Germany	1,270,243	2,105,506	66.8	63.5	56.3	101.4	79.1	179.7	1,022	658	..	..
Ghana	502	3,394	10.1	15.7	0.2	0.7	1.5	5.2	22	35	21.6[a]	−10.4[a]
Greece	110,839	264,942	88.3	84.6	75.7	48.4	63.7	64.0	329	292	..	..
Guatemala	240	..	1.2	..	0.0	..	0.0	..	44	..	..	..
Guinea	..	..	..	..	..	..	..	..	..	..	..	..
Guinea-Bissau	..	..	..	..	..	..	..	..	..	..	..	..
Haiti	..	..	..	..	..	..	..	..	..	..	..	..

	Market capitalization				Market liquidity		Turnover ratio		Listed domestic companies		S&P/Global Equity Indices	
	$ millions		% of GDP		Value of shares traded % of GDP		Value of shares traded % of market capitalization		number		% change	
	2000	2008	2000	2007	2000	2007	2000	2008	2000	2008	2007	2008
Honduras	458	..	8.8	..	..	..	..	..	46	..	..	..
Hungary	12,021	18,579	25.1	34.4	25.3	34.3	90.7	93.0	60	41	13.1	−62.5
India	148,064	645,478	32.2	154.6	110.8	94.1	133.6	85.2	5,937	4,921	78.6	−64.1
Indonesia	26,834	98,761	16.3	48.9	8.7	26.1	32.9	71.3	290	396	49.3	−61.1
Iran, Islamic Rep.	7,350	45,574	7.3	15.9	1.1	2.9	12.7	19.7	304	329	..	..
Iraq	..	..	..	..	..	..	..	..	..	..	..	..
Ireland	81,882	144,026	85.0	55.6	15.0	52.7	19.2	88.9	76	57	..	..
Israel	64,081	134,463	51.8	144.2	18.9	69.2	36.3	60.2	654	630	34.3	−33.1
Italy	768,364	1,072,692	70.0	51.0	70.9	110.1	104.0	220.4	291	301	..	..
Jamaica	3,582	7,513	44.6	107.9	0.9	3.1	2.5	3.6	46	39	0.3[a]	−38.2[a]
Japan	3,157,222	4,453,475	67.6	101.6	57.7	148.2	69.9	141.6	2,561	3,844	−5.2[b]	−39.7[b]
Jordan	4,943	35,847	58.4	260.3	4.9	110.1	7.7	72.7	163	262	32.6[a]	..
Kazakhstan	1,342	31,075	7.3	39.5	0.5	8.5	25.1	22.2	23	74	−47.0[a]	−47.0[a]
Kenya	1,283	10,917	10.1	55.3	0.4	5.4	3.6	11.8	57	53	11.8[a]	−40.3[a]
Korea, Dem. Rep.	..	..	..	..	..	..	..	..	..	..	..	..
Korea, Rep.	171,587	494,631	33.5	115.9	208.7	203.5	233.2	181.2	1,308	1,798	27.7	−55.6
Kuwait	20,772	107,168	55.1	167.7	11.2	107.7	21.3	83.2	77	202	39.9[a]	..
Kyrgyz Republic	4	121	0.3	3.2	1.7	3.7	..	131.2	80	10	..	..
Lao PDR	..	..	..	..	..	..	..	..	..	..	..	..
Latvia	563	1,609	7.2	11.5	2.9	0.5	48.6	1.8	64	35	1.9[a]	−58.7[a]
Lebanon	1,583	9,641	9.4	44.6	0.7	4.1	6.7	6.9	12	11	40.5[a]	−25.3[a]
Lesotho	..	..	..	..	..	..	..	..	..	..	..	..
Liberia	..	..	..	..	..	..	..	..	..	..	..	..
Libya	..	..	..	..	..	..	..	..	..	..	..	..
Lithuania	1,588	3,625	13.9	26.4	1.8	2.7	14.8	59.9	54	41	14.3[a]	−73.0[a]
Macedonia, FYR	7	2,715	0.2	35.4	3.3	6.6	6.6	26.5	1	38	..	..
Madagascar	..	..	..	..	..	..	..	..	..	..	..	..
Malawi	..	587	..	18.6	..	0.5	13.8	3.5	..	9	..	..
Malaysia	116,935	187,066	124.7	174.4	62.4	80.3	44.6	31.4	795	977	44.6	−43.7
Mali	..	..	..	..	..	..	..	..	..	..	..	..
Mauritania	1,090	..	97.2	..	..	..	..	..	40	..	..	..
Mauritius	1,331	3,443	29.8	83.5	1.7	5.4	5.0	8.9	40	41	94.0[a]	−49.2[a]
Mexico	125,204	232,581	21.5	38.9	7.8	11.3	32.3	34.3	179	125	12.8	−45.1
Moldova	392	..	30.4	..	1.9	2.3	5.8	..	36	..	..	..
Mongolia	37	612	3.4	15.6	0.7	1.4	7.3	14.7	410	384	..	..
Morocco	10,899	65,748	29.4	100.5	3.0	35.0	9.2	31.4	53	77	45.3	−17.0
Mozambique	..	..	..	..	..	..	..	..	..	..	..	..
Myanmar	..	..	..	..	..	..	..	..	..	..	..	..
Namibia	311	619	9.1	10.0	0.6	0.3	4.5	2.8	13	7	39.4[a]	−9.9[a]
Nepal	790	4,909	14.4	47.6	0.6	2.2	6.9	6.9	110	144	..	..
Netherlands	640,456	956,469	166.3	124.9	175.9	235.5	101.4	207.8	234	226	..	..
New Zealand	18,866	47,454	37.1	35.0	21.2	16.0	45.9	46.9	142	154	..	..
Nicaragua	..	..	..	..	..	..	..	..	..	..	..	..
Niger	..	..	..	..	..	..	..	..	..	..	..	..
Nigeria	4,237	49,803	9.2	52.2	0.6	10.1	7.3	29.3	195	213	108.3[a]	..
Norway	65,034	357,420	38.6	92.0	35.7	121.5	93.4	147.8	191	195	..	..
Oman	3,463	14,914	17.4	45.2	2.8	9.3	14.2	44.2	131	127	67.0[a]	..
Pakistan	6,581	23,491	8.9	49.2	44.6	70.3	475.5	116.0	762	653	41.7[a]	..
Panama	2,794	6,568	24.0	31.9	1.3	0.6	1.7	4.0	29	31	−15.7[a]	..
Papua New Guinea	1,520	6,632	49.3	118.9	0.0	0.4	..	0.5	7	15	..	..
Paraguay	224	409	3.5	4.4	0.1	0.0	3.5	0.5	56	55	..	..
Peru	10,562	55,625	19.8	98.8	2.9	6.8	12.6	6.3	230	199	66.4	−41.1
Philippines	25,957	52,101	34.2	71.7	10.8	20.3	15.8	22.2	228	244	36.0	−53.7
Poland	31,279	90,233	18.3	49.1	8.5	20.0	49.9	45.7	225	349	23.2	−57.8
Portugal	60,681	132,258	53.9	59.4	48.3	64.9	85.5	122.2	109	47	..	..
Puerto Rico	..	..	..	..	..	..	..	..	..	..	..	..

	Market capitalization				Market liquidity		Turnover ratio		Listed domestic companies		S&P/Global Equity Indices	
	$ millions		% of GDP		Value of shares traded % of GDP		Value of shares traded % of market capitalization		number		% change	
	2000	2008	2000	2007	2000	2007	2000	2008	2000	2008	2007	2008
Romania	1,069	19,923	2.9	27.1	0.6	4.9	23.1	11.3	5,555	1,824	32.8[a]	−72.2[a]
Russian Federation	38,922	397,183	15.0	116.5	7.8	58.5	36.9	75.0	249	314	21.9	−73.4
Rwanda	..	..	..	..	..	..	..	..	..	..	..	..
Saudi Arabia	67,171	246,337	35.6	135.0	9.2	178.1	27.1	137.8	75	127	35.6	..
Senegal	..	..	..	..	..	..	..	..	..	..	..	..
Serbia	734	23,934	4.6	59.7	0.1	6.4	0.0	14.6	6	1,771	..	..
Sierra Leone	..	..	..	..	..	..	..	..	..	..	..	..
Singapore	152,827	353,489	164.8	219.1	98.7	238.1	52.1	122.0	418	472	..	..
Slovak Republic	1,217	5,079	6.0	9.3	4.4	0.0	129.8	0.4	493	120	57.4[a]	−36.0[a]
Slovenia	2,547	11,772	12.8	61.4	2.3	5.8	20.7	6.9	38	84	95.0[a]	−66.9[a]
Somalia	..	..	..	..	..	..	..	..	..	..	..	..
South Africa	204,952	491,282	154.2	294.5	58.3	150.4	33.9	60.6	616	425	15.5	−41.7
Spain	504,219	1,800,097	86.8	125.3	169.8	206.1	210.7	189.7	1,019	3,498	..	..
Sri Lanka	1,074	4,326	6.6	23.4	0.9	2.9	11.0	17.2	239	234	−10.6[a]	..
Sudan	..	..	..	..	..	..	..	..	..	..	..	..
Swaziland	73	203	4.9	7.0	0.0	0.0	9.8	0.0	6	6	..	..
Sweden	328,339	612,497	133.7	134.8	158.8	213.3	111.2	147.4	292	272	..	..
Switzerland	792,316	1,274,516	317.0	300.3	243.7	418.9	82.0	143.0	252	257	..	..
Syrian Arab Republic	..	..	..	..	..	..	..	..	..	..	..	..
Tajikistan	..	..	..	..	..	..	..	..	..	..	..	..
Tanzania	233	541	2.6	3.8	0.4	0.1	2.4	2.1	4	7	..	..
Thailand	29,489	102,594	24.0	79.9	19.0	44.1	53.2	78.2	381	476	39.4	−50.5
Timor-Leste	..	..	..	..	..	..	..	..	..	..	..	..
Togo	..	..	..	..	..	..	..	..	..	..	..	..
Trinidad and Tobago	4,330	12,157	53.1	74.7	1.7	1.7	3.1	2.6	27	37	−2.8	−9.9
Tunisia	2,828	6,374	14.5	15.3	3.2	1.9	23.3	25.5	44	49	15.6[a]	−3.1[a]
Turkey	69,659	117,930	26.1	43.7	67.1	46.1	206.2	118.5	315	284	74.8[a]	−62.4[a]
Turkmenistan	..	..	..	..	..	..	..	..	..	..	..	..
Uganda	35	116	0.6	1.2	0.0	0.1	..	5.2	2	5	..	..
Ukraine	1,881	24,358	6.0	79.2	0.9	1.4	19.6	3.7	139	251	112.2[a]	−82.2[a]
United Arab Emirates	5,727	97,852	8.1	84.8	0.2	69.2	3.9	89.8	54	96	52.1[a]	..
United Kingdom	2,576,992	3,858,505	177.6	139.2	126.5	372.5	66.6	270.1	1,904	2,588	5.6[c]	−31.3[c]
United States	15,104,037	19,947,284	154.7	145.1	326.3	309.9	200.8	216.5	7,524	5,130	3.5[d]	−38.5[d]
Uruguay	161	159	0.8	0.7	0.0	0.1	0.5	12.0	16	8	..	..
Uzbekistan	32	715	0.2	4.2	0.1	0.4	..	5.9	5	114	..	..
Venezuela, RB	8,128	8,251	6.9	4.5	0.6	0.4	8.9	1.3	85	60	79.0	..
Vietnam	..	9,589	..	28.5	..	18.3	..	28.8	..	171	10.7[a]	−68.2[a]
West Bank and Gaza	765	2,475	18.6	111.1	4.6	52.2	10.0	31.3	24	35	..	..
Yemen, Rep.	..	..	..	..	..	..	..	..	..	..	..	..
Zambia	236	2,346	7.3	20.6	0.2	0.6	20.8	4.1	9	15	..	..
Zimbabwe	2,432	5,333	32.9	70.3	3.8	9.7	10.8	5.1	69	81	−83.8[a]	..
World	**32,187,756 s**	..[e] s	**102.4 w**	**121.3 w**	**152.4 w**	**186.6**	**122.3 w**	..[e] w	**47,877 s**	..[e] s		
Low income	18,702	110,935	7.9	40.5	14.7	24.8	..	69.3	1,575	1,534		
Middle income	1,964,730	6,475,916	36.5	117.0	33.8	94.3	78.5	78.2	20,998	15,300		
Lower middle income	895,510	4,062,921	35.0	144.9	50.6	146.7	112.7	96.2	11,241	9,227		
Upper middle income	1,069,220	2,412,995	37.9	88.5	18.3	40.6	48.6	61.0	9,757	6,073		
Low & middle income	1,983,431	6,586,851	35.3	113.9	33.0	91.3	82.8	77.8	22,573	16,834		
East Asia & Pacific	780,487	3,243,723	47.1	165.1	49.8	191.2	125.0	112.0	3,190	3,868		
Europe & Central Asia	150,122	721,582	17.5	77.3	24.9	38.7	92.4	68.8	7,588	3,882		
Latin America & Carib.	620,263	1,168,004	31.6	71.4	8.4	24.3	27.2	47.0	1,762	1,302		
Middle East & N. Africa	57,110	203,494	19.9	56.1	5.1	18.8	12.4	28.7	1,676	772		
South Asia	157,695	679,965	26.1	133.4	90.2	84.8	167.9	89.3	7,269	6,098		
Sub-Saharan Africa	217,754	570,083	89.9	149.0	32.3	60.9	22.2	29.1	1,088	912		
High income	30,204,325	49,648,498	116.9	123.8	178.2	217.8	130.5	180.5	25,304	29,505		
Euro area	5,433,547	10,468,592	87.0	85.3	80.4	124.0	90.6	162.8	5,028	5,711		

a. Refers to the S&P Frontier BMI index. b. Refers to the Nikkei 225 index. c. Refers to the FT 100 index. d. Refers to the S&P 500 index. e. Aggregates not presented because data for high-income economies are not available for 2008.

The development of an economy's financial markets is closely related to its overall development. Well functioning financial systems provide good and easily accessible information. That lowers transaction costs, which in turn improves resource allocation and boosts economic growth. Both banking systems and stock markets enhance growth, the main factor in poverty reduction. At low levels of economic development commercial banks tend to dominate the financial system, while at higher levels domestic stock markets tend to become more active and efficient relative to domestic banks.

Open economies with sound macroeconomic policies, good legal systems, and shareholder protection attract capital and therefore have larger financial markets. Recent research on stock market development shows that modern communications technology and increased financial integration have resulted in more cross-border capital flows, a stronger presence of financial firms around the world, and the migration of stock exchange activities to international exchanges. Many firms in emerging markets now cross-list on international exchanges, which provides them with lower cost capital and more liquidity-traded shares. However, this also means that exchanges in emerging markets may not have enough financial activity to sustain them, putting pressure on them to rethink their operations.

The stock market indicators in the table are from Standard & Poor's Emerging Markets Data Base. The indicators include measures of size (market capitalization, number of listed domestic companies) and liquidity (value of shares traded as a percentage of gross domestic product, value of shares traded as a percentage of market capitalization). The comparability of such indicators across countries may be limited by conceptual and statistical weaknesses, such as inaccurate reporting and differences in accounting standards. The percentage change in stock market prices in U.S. dollars are from Standard & Poor's Global Equity Indices (S&P IFCI) and Standard & Poor's Frontier Broad Market Index (BMI) and is an important measure of overall performance. Regulatory and institutional factors that can affect investor confidence, such as entry and exit restrictions, the existence of a securities and exchange commission, and the quality of laws to protect investors, may influence the functioning of stock markets but are not included in the table.

Stock market size can be measured in various ways, and each may produce a different ranking of countries. Market capitalization shows the overall size of the stock market in U.S. dollars and as a percentage of GDP. The number of listed domestic companies is another measure of market size. Market size is positively correlated with the ability to mobilize capital and diversify risk.

Market liquidity, the ability to easily buy and sell securities, is measured by dividing the total value of shares traded by GDP. The turnover ratio—the value of shares traded as a percentage of market capitalization—is also a measure of liquidity as well as of transaction costs. (High turnover indicates low transaction costs.) The turnover ratio complements the ratio of value traded to GDP, because the turnover ratio is related to the size of the market and the value traded ratio to the size of the economy. A small, liquid market will have a high turnover ratio but a low value of shares traded ratio. Liquidity is an important attribute of stock markets because, in theory, liquid markets improve the allocation of capital and enhance prospects for long-term economic growth. A more comprehensive measure of liquidity would include trading costs and the time and uncertainty in finding a counterpart in settling trades.

The S&P/EMDB, the source for all the data in the table, provides regular updates on 58 emerging stock markets and 35 frontier markets. Standard & Poor's maintains a series of indexes for investors interested in investing in stock markets in developing countries. The S&P/IFCI index, Standard & Poor's leading emerging markets index, is designed to be sufficiently investable to support index tracking portfolios in emerging market stocks that are legally and practically open to foreign portfolio investment. The S&P/Frontier BMI measures the performance of 35 small and illiquid markets. The individual country indices include all publicly listed equities representing an aggregate of at least 80 percent or more of market capitalization in each market. These indexes are widely used benchmarks for international portfolio management. See www.standardandpoors.com for further information on the indexes.

Because markets included in Standard & Poor's emerging markets category vary widely in level of development, it is best to look at the entire category to identify the most significant market trends. And it is useful to remember that stock market trends may be distorted by currency conversions, especially when a currency has registered a significant devaluation.

About the data is based on Demirgüç-Kunt and Levine (1996), Beck and Levine (2001), and Claessens, Klingebiel, and Schmukler (2002).

• **Market capitalization** (also known as market value) is the share price times the number of shares outstanding. • **Market liquidity** is the total value of shares traded during the period divided by gross domestic product (GDP). This indicator complements the market capitalization ratio by showing whether market size is matched by trading. • **Turnover ratio** is the total value of shares traded during the period divided by the average market capitalization for the period. Average market capitalization is calculated as the average of the end-of-period values for the current period and the previous period. • **Listed domestic companies** are the domestically incorporated companies listed on the country's stock exchanges at the end of the year. This indicator does not include investment companies, mutual funds, or other collective investment vehicles. • **S&P/Global Equity Indices** measure the U.S. dollar price change in the stock markets.

Data on stock markets are from Standard & Poor's *Global Stock Markets Factbook 2008*, which draws on the Emerging Markets Data Base, supplemented by other data from Standard & Poor's. The firm collects data through an annual survey of the world's stock exchanges, supplemented by information provided by its network of correspondents and by Reuters. Data on GDP are from the World Bank's national accounts data files.

	Getting credit				Bank capital to asset ratio	Ratio of bank nonperforming loans to total gross loans	Domestic credit provided by banking sector	Interest rate spread	Risk premium on lending
	Strength of legal rights index 0–10 (weak to strong)	Depth of credit information index 0–6 (low to high)	% of adult population Public credit registry coverage	Private credit bureau coverage	%	%	% of GDP	Lending rate minus deposit rate percentage points	Prime lending rate minus treasury bill rate percentage points
	June 2008	June 2008	June 2008	June 2008	2007	2007	2007	2007	2007
Afghanistan	1	0	0.0	0.0	..	..	−1.6	..	..
Albania	9	4	8.3	0.0	5.8	3.4	62.1	8.4	8.2
Algeria	3	2	0.2	0.0	..	..	−3.5	6.3	7.0
Angola	4	4	2.7	0.0	..	..	1.9	10.9	..
Argentina	4	6	31.2	100.0	13.1	2.7	28.5	3.1	..
Armenia	7	5	2.6	24.4	22.5	2.4	12.1	11.3	11.4
Australia	9	5	0.0	100.0	4.6	0.2	141.8	5.4	..
Austria	7	6	1.3	40.9	6.5	2.1	125.8	..	..
Azerbaijan	8	5	3.1	0.0	14.2	7.2	18.2	7.6	8.5
Bangladesh	8	2	0.9	0.0	6.5	14.0	58.2	6.8	..
Belarus	2	5	2.4	0.0	15.9	0.7	27.2	0.3	..
Belgium	7	4	57.7	0.0	4.3	1.2	113.4	..	4.8
Benin	3	1	10.5	0.0	..	..	8.9	..	..
Bolivia	1	6	11.9	29.7	9.6	5.6	53.5	9.3	6.8
Bosnia and Herzegovina	5	5	0.0	69.2	13.1	3.0	54.7	3.6	..
Botswana	7	4	0.0	52.9	..	..	−16.4	7.6	..
Brazil	3	5	20.2	62.2	9.9	3.0	95.9	33.1	32.2
Bulgaria	8	6	30.7	5.0	7.7	2.1	59.2	6.3	6.2
Burkina Faso	3	1	1.9	0.0	..	..	12.4	..	..
Burundi	2	1	0.3	0.0	..	..	38.5	..	8.2
Cambodia	9	0	0.0	0.0	..	..	12.9	14.6	..
Cameroon	3	2	4.9	0.0	..	..	5.8	10.8	..
Canada	6	6	0.0	100.0	5.5	0.7	165.1	4.0	2.0
Central African Republic	3	2	1.2	0.0	..	..	17.4	10.8	..
Chad	3	1	0.6	0.0	..	..	1.1	10.8	..
Chile	4	5	28.1	34.5	6.7	0.8	90.0	3.1	..
China	6	4	58.8	0.0	5.5	6.7	132.0	3.3	..
Hong Kong, China	10	5	0.0	69.9	12.0	0.9	125.3	4.3	4.8
Colombia	5	5	0.0	42.5	11.4	3.2	41.6	7.4	..
Congo, Dem. Rep.	3	0	0.0	0.0	..	..	5.6	..	..
Congo, Rep.	3	2	6.9	0.0	..	..	−10.1	10.8	..
Costa Rica	5	5	5.9	51.6	10.7	1.2	47.4	6.4	..
Côte d'Ivoire	3	1	2.9	0.0	..	..	20.7	..	..
Croatia	6	3	0.0	71.8	12.5	4.8	82.9	7.0	..
Cuba	..	..	..	..	..	..	..	..	..
Czech Republic	6	5	4.6	65.2	6.0	2.6	52.9	4.5	2.2
Denmark	9	4	0.0	5.0	6.1	0.6	205.1	..	..
Dominican Republic	3	6	33.9	35.0	9.5	4.0	54.0	8.9	..
Ecuador	3	5	37.7	46.8	8.5	2.9	18.7	7.1	..
Egypt, Arab Rep.	3	5	2.2	4.7	5.1	24.7	89.5	6.4	5.7
El Salvador	5	6	18.4	83.0	11.8	2.1	46.3	..	..
Eritrea	2	0	0.0	0.0	..	..	124.5	..	..
Estonia	6	5	0.0	20.6	8.6	0.5	95.1	2.1	..
Ethiopia	4	2	0.1	0.0	..	..	47.2	3.4	6.9
Finland	7	5	0.0	14.8	9.2	0.3	85.6	..	..
France	7	4	28.3	0.0	5.5	2.7	122.0	..	..
Gabon	3	2	20.7	0.0	7.0	7.6	2.9	10.8	..
Gambia, The	5	0	0.0	0.0	..	..	23.9	15.0	..
Georgia	6	6	0.0	4.5	20.4	2.6	31.6	10.9	..
Germany	7	6	0.7	98.4	4.3	3.4	124.9	..	..
Ghana	7	0	0.0	0.0	11.8	6.4	32.9	..	..
Greece	3	4	0.0	39.0	6.6	4.5	108.6	..	..
Guatemala	7	5	16.1	19.7	9.2	5.8	41.4	8.1	..
Guinea	3	0	0.0	0.0	..	..	16.0	..	..
Guinea-Bissau	3	1	1.0	0.0	..	..	12.1	..	..
Haiti	2	2	0.7	0.0	..	..	22.8	45.5	32.7

	Getting credit				Bank capital to asset ratio	Ratio of bank nonperforming loans to total gross loans	Domestic credit provided by banking sector	Interest rate spread	Risk premium on lending
	Strength of legal rights index 0–10 (weak to strong)	Depth of credit information index 0–6 (low to high)	% of adult population Public credit registry coverage	Private credit bureau coverage	%	%	% of GDP	Lending rate minus deposit rate percentage points	Prime lending rate minus treasury bill rate percentage points
	June 2008	June 2008	June 2008	June 2008	2007	2007	2007	2007	2007
Honduras	6	6	11.3	60.5	8.4	6.6	51.0	8.8	..
Hungary	7	5	0.0	10.0	8.3	2.4	74.4	2.3	1.4
India	8	4	0.0	10.5	6.4	2.5	64.2	..	..
Indonesia	3	4	26.1	0.0	10.0	9.3	40.5	5.9	..
Iran, Islamic Rep.	5	3	21.7	0.0	..	..	50.5	0.4	..
Iraq	3	0	0.0	0.0	..	..	..	8.4	–1.3
Ireland	8	5	0.0	100.0	4.5	0.7	195.7	2.6	..
Israel	9	5	0.0	91.0	6.2	1.7	74.8	2.8	1.9
Italy	3	5	11.8	74.9	7.7	4.8	129.7	..	2.3
Jamaica	8	0	0.0	0.0	8.7	2.6	63.9	10.1	4.6
Japan	7	6	0.0	76.2	5.0	1.5	294.1	1.1	1.3
Jordan	4	2	1.0	0.0	6.7	4.1	123.5	3.2	..
Kazakhstan	5	6	0.0	25.6	15.2	2.7	41.0	..	..
Kenya	10	4	0.0	2.1	12.4	22.7	37.6	8.2	6.8
Korea, Dem. Rep.	..	..	..	..	..	..	..	..	..
Korea, Rep.	7	6	0.0	90.4	9.0	0.7	110.2	1.4	..
Kuwait	4	4	0.0	31.2	12.0	3.2	72.5	3.1	5.5
Kyrgyz Republic	7	5	0.0	3.7	..	..	14.2	19.9	20.4
Lao PDR	4	0	0.0	0.0	..	..	6.8	23.5	9.7
Latvia	9	4	3.7	0.0	7.9	0.4	94.8	4.8	6.7
Lebanon	3	5	6.8	0.0	8.1	10.1	186.9	2.3	5.0
Lesotho	8	0	0.0	0.0	14.6	3.0	–18.4	7.7	6.3
Liberia	4	1	0.3	0.0	..	..	160.6	11.3	..
Libya	..	..	..	..	..	..	–66.3	3.5	..
Lithuania	5	6	8.9	7.2	7.4	1.0	61.1	1.5	2.6
Macedonia, FYR	7	4	6.5	0.0	..	9.1	35.5	5.4	..
Madagascar	2	0	0.1	0.0	..	10.1	9.9	28.5	33.2
Malawi	8	0	0.0	0.0	..	..	16.1	21.7	13.8
Malaysia	10	6	52.9	..	7.5	6.6	113.4	3.2	3.0
Mali	3	1	4.1	0.0	..	..	14.9	..	..
Mauritania	3	1	0.2	0.0	..	..	..	15.5	13.1
Mauritius	5	3	20.6	0.0	..	..	110.5	10.1	..
Mexico	4	6	0.0	70.8	14.4	2.5	37.7	4.4	0.4
Moldova	8	0	0.0	0.0	17.3	3.7	40.2	3.8	5.7
Mongolia	6	3	22.7	0.0	..	..	30.1	4.1	..
Morocco	3	2	2.4	0.0	6.9	7.9	90.1	..	..
Mozambique	2	4	1.9	0.0	6.4	2.6	10.4	7.7	4.4
Myanmar	..	..	..	..	..	..	28.1	5.0	..
Namibia	8	5	0.0	59.6	7.9	2.8	63.7	5.3	4.3
Nepal	5	2	0.0	0.2	..	..	49.3	5.8	4.4
Netherlands	6	5	0.0	81.0	3.3	0.8	204.4	0.7	..
New Zealand	9	5	0.0	100.0	..	..	144.4	5.0	5.3
Nicaragua	3	5	13.4	100.0	8.8	8.0	73.5	7.0	..
Niger	3	1	0.9	0.0	..	..	7.1	..	..
Nigeria	8	0	0.1	0.0	16.3	8.4	20.2	6.7	10.1
Norway	7	4	0.0	100.0	5.0	0.6	..	1.8	..
Oman	4	2	23.4	0.0	13.2	3.2	28.7	3.1	..
Pakistan	6	4	4.9	1.5	10.2	8.4	45.7	6.5	2.8
Panama	6	6	0.0	43.7	13.7	1.3	89.3	3.5	..
Papua New Guinea	5	0	0.0	0.0	..	..	22.8	8.7	5.1
Paraguay	3	6	9.7	48.6	11.6	1.3	19.5	20.0	..
Peru	7	6	23.7	33.2	8.8	1.3	16.2	19.6	..
Philippines	3	3	0.0	5.4	11.7	5.8	46.0	5.0	5.3
Poland	8	4	0.0	50.0	7.4	3.1	46.6	3.3	1.3
Portugal	3	4	76.4	11.3	6.2	0.8	172.3	..	..
Puerto Rico	8	5	0.0	61.4	..	..	..	..	..

	Getting credit			Bank capital to asset ratio	Ratio of bank nonperforming loans to total gross loans	Domestic credit provided by banking sector	Interest rate spread	Risk premium on lending
	Strength of legal rights index 0–10 (weak to strong)	Depth of credit information index 0–6 (low to high)	% of adult population				Lending rate minus deposit rate percentage points	Prime lending rate minus treasury bill rate percentage points
			Public credit registry coverage	Private credit bureau coverage	%	%	% of GDP		
	June 2008	**June 2008**	**June 2008**	**June 2008**	**2007**	**2007**	**2007**	**2007**	**2007**
Romania	8	5	4.5	24.7	7.3	9.7	35.7	6.6	6.2
Russian Federation	3	4	0.0	10.0	13.3	2.5	25.7	4.9	..
Rwanda	2	2	0.3	0.0	9.2	27.2	8.7	9.1	8.6
Saudi Arabia	4	6	0.0	14.1	9.9	2.1	17.5	..	..
Senegal	3	1	4.4	0.0	10.4	18.6	24.8	..	..
Serbia	7	5	0.0	91.9	17.1	3.8	30.8	7.1	6.7
Sierra Leone	4	0	0.0	0.0	17.7	31.7	9.8	15.0	6.6
Singapore	10	4	0.0	48.3	9.3	1.8	80.7	4.8	3.0
Slovak Republic	9	4	1.4	39.9	10.6	2.5	51.5	4.3	..
Slovenia	6	2	2.7	0.0	8.4	2.5	82.0	2.3	2.0
Somalia	..	..	..	..	..	..	..	..	..
South Africa	9	6	0.0	64.8	7.9	1.4	198.1	4.0	4.1
Spain	6	5	45.8	8.1	7.0	0.7	192.5	..	..
Sri Lanka	4	5	0.0	8.7	..	9.6	45.0	8.0	0.5
Sudan	5	0	0.0	0.0	..	..	0.2	..	..
Swaziland	6	5	0.0	43.5	22.9	4.0	6.8	6.1	4.1
Sweden	5	4	0.0	100.0	4.0	0.5	131.7	2.5	1.6
Switzerland	8	5	0.0	22.5	4.9	0.3	189.7	1.0	1.0
Syrian Arab Republic	1	0	0.0	0.0	..	..	38.8	1.8	..
Tajikistan	2	0	0.0	0.0	..	..	15.4	14.4	..
Tanzania	8	0	0.0	0.0	..	..	14.1	7.3	2.6
Thailand	4	5	0.0	31.8	9.5	7.9	104.9	4.2	3.6
Timor-Leste	1	0	0.0	0.0	..	..	−29.9	14.3	..
Togo	3	1	2.6	0.0	..	..	22.0	..	..
Trinidad and Tobago	8	4	0.0	37.6	..	..	26.2	5.9	4.8
Tunisia	3	5	14.9	0.0	7.7	17.3	71.5	..	..
Turkey	4	5	12.7	26.3	13.0	3.6	48.7	..	..
Turkmenistan	..	..	..	..	..	..	..	..	..
Uganda	7	0	0.0	0.0	10.3	4.1	5.2	9.8	10.1
Ukraine	9	3	0.0	3.0	12.5	13.2	61.7	5.8	..
United Arab Emirates	4	5	6.5	7.7	12.6	6.3	66.6	..	..
United Kingdom	9	6	0.0	100.0	8.9	0.9	190.5	..	0.0
United States	8	6	0.0	100.0	10.3	1.4	240.6	..	3.6
Uruguay	5	6	15.4	98.0	10.5	1.1	24.8	6.6	1.8
Uzbekistan	3	3	2.3	2.2	..	..	..	..	..
Venezuela, RB	3	0	0.0	0.0	8.3	1.2	22.7	6.4	..
Vietnam	7	4	13.4	0.0	..	..	96.2	3.7	7.0
West Bank and Gaza	0	3	7.8	0.0	..	..	8.3	4.8	..
Yemen, Rep.	2	0	0.1	0.0	..	..	9.9	5.0	2.1
Zambia	9	0	0.0	0.1	..	10.8	16.6	9.7	6.9
Zimbabwe	8	0	0.0	0.0	..	..	93.1	457.5	330.2
World	**5.3 u**	**2.9 u**	**5.6 u**	**20.9 u**	**8.9 m**	**2.7 m**	**162.5 w**	**6.5 m**	
Low income	4.4	1.0	1.2	0.2	..	..	36.9	10.3	
Middle income	5.2	3.2	7.6	19.1	9.6	3.0	75.0	6.6	
Lower middle income	4.7	3.0	7.4	14.4	9.5	3.9	90.5	7.3	
Upper middle income	5.9	3.4	7.9	25.9	9.9	2.5	58.7	6.4	
Low & middle income	4.9	2.4	5.4	12.6	9.7	3.5	73.2	7.1	
East Asia & Pacific	5.4	1.7	8.7	4.2	..	..	116.3	5.9	
Europe & Central Asia	6.3	4.1	4.9	18.2	13.0	3.1	38.8	6.3	
Latin America & Carib.	5.2	3.5	9.9	34.3	10.2	2.3	59.9	7.0	
Middle East & N. Africa	2.6	2.3	4.8	0.4	..	..	47.8	4.3	
South Asia	4.8	2.1	0.7	2.6	6.5	8.4	61.5	6.7	
Sub-Saharan Africa	4.5	1.4	2.5	5.0	..	..	80.6	10.0	
High income	6.5	4.2	6.0	45.7	6.5	1.4	194.8	4.0	
Euro area	5.9	4.2	17.3	36.0	6.4	1.9	138.7	..	

About the data

Financial sector development has positive impacts on economic growth and poverty. The size of the sector determines the resources mobilized for investment. Access to finance can expand opportunities for all with higher levels of access and use of banking services associated with lower financing obstacles for people and businesses. A stable financial system that promotes efficient savings and investment is also crucial for a thriving democracy and market economy. The banking system is the largest sector in the financial system in most countries, so most indicators in the table cover the banking system.

There are several aspects of access to financial services: availability, cost, and quality of services. The development and growth of credit markets depend on access to timely, reliable, and accurate data on borrowers' credit experiences. For secured transactions, such as mortgages or vehicle loans, rapid access to information in property registries is also vital, and for small business loans corporate registry data are needed. Access to credit can be improved by increasing information about potential borrowers' creditworthiness and making it easy to create and enforce collateral agreements. Lenders look at a borrower's credit history and collateral. Where credit registries and effective collateral laws are absent—as in many developing countries— banks make fewer loans. Indicators that cover financial access, or getting credit, include the strength of legal rights index (ranges from 0, weak, to 10, strong), depth of credit information index (ranges from 0, low, to 6, high), public registry coverage, and private bureau coverage.

The strength of legal rights index is based on eight aspects related to legal rights in collateral law and two aspects in bankruptcy law. The methodology for the index in this edition includes three improvements. First, a standardized case scenario with assumptions was introduced to bring the indicator in line with other Doing Business indicators. Second, the indicator focuses on revolving movable collateral, such as accounts receivable and inventory, rather than tangible movable collateral, such as equipment. Third, the indicator no longer considers whether management remains in place during reorganization, thus better accommodating economies that adopt reorganization procedures similar to U.S. Chapter 11 reorganization or *redressement* procedures in civil law systems. The depth of credit information index assesses six features of the public registry or the private credit bureau (or both). For more information on these indexes, see www.doingbusiness.org/MethodologySurveys/.

The size and mobility of international capital flows make it increasingly important to monitor the strength of financial systems. Robust financial systems can increase economic activity and welfare, but instability in the financial system can disrupt financial activity and impose widespread costs on the economy. The ratio of bank capital to assets, a measure of bank solvency and resiliency, shows the extent to which banks can deal with unexpected losses. Capital includes tier 1 capital (paid-up shares and common stock), a common feature in all countries' banking systems, and total regulatory capital, which includes several types of subordinated debt instruments that need not be repaid if the funds are required to maintain minimum capital levels (tier 2 and tier 3 capital). Total assets include all nonfinancial and financial assets. Data are from internally consistent financial statements.

The ratio of bank nonperforming loans to total gross loans, a measure of bank health and efficiency, helps to identify problems with asset quality in the loan portfolio. A high ratio may signal deterioration of the credit portfolio. International guidelines recommend that loans be classified as nonperforming when payments of principal and interest are 90 days or more past due or when future payments are not expected to be received in full. See the International Monetary Fund's (IMF) *Global Financial Stability Report* for details.

Domestic credit by the banking sector as a share of GDP is a measure of banking sector depth and financial sector development in terms of size. In a few countries governments may hold international reserves as deposits in the banking system rather than in the central bank. Since the claims on the central government are a net item (claims on the central government minus central government deposits), this net figure may be negative, resulting in a negative figure of domestic credit provided by the banking sector.

The interest rate spread—the margin between the cost of mobilizing liabilities and the earnings on assets—is a measure of financial sector efficiency in intermediation. A narrow interest rate spread means low transaction costs, which lowers the cost of funds for investment, crucial to economic growth.

The risk premium on lending is the spread between the lending rate to the private sector and the "risk-free" government rate. Spreads are expressed as annual averages. A small spread indicates that the market considers its best corporate customers to be low risk. A negative rate indicates that the market considers its best corporate clients to be lower risk than the government.

Definitions

• **Strength of legal rights index** measures the degree to which collateral and bankruptcy laws protect the rights of borrowers and lenders and thus facilitate lending. Higher values indicate that the laws are better designed to expand access to credit. • **Depth of credit information index** measures rules affecting the scope, accessibility, and quality of information available through public or private credit registries. Higher values indicate the availability of more credit information. • **Public credit registry coverage** is the number of individuals and firms listed in a public credit registry with current information on repayment history, unpaid debts, or credit outstanding as a percentage of the adult population. • **Private credit bureau coverage** is the number of individuals or firms listed by a private credit bureau with current information on repayment history, unpaid debts, or credit outstanding as a percentage of the adult population. • **Bank capital to asset ratio** is the ratio of bank capital and reserves to total assets. Capital and reserves include funds contributed by owners, retained earnings, general and special reserves, provisions, and valuation adjustments. • **Ratio of bank nonperforming loans to total gross loans** is the value of nonperforming loans divided by the total value of the loan portfolio (including nonperforming loans before the deduction of loan loss provisions). The amount recorded as nonperforming should be the gross value of the loan as recorded on the balance sheet, not just the amount overdue. • **Domestic credit provided by banking sector** is all credit to various sectors on a gross basis, except to the central government, which is net. The banking sector includes monetary authorities, deposit money banks, and other banking institutions for which data are available. • **Interest rate spread** is the interest rate charged by banks on loans to prime customers minus the interest rate paid by commercial or similar banks for demand, time, or savings deposits. • **Risk premium on lending** is the interest rate charged by banks on loans to prime private sector customers minus the "risk-free" treasury bill interest rate at which short-term government securities are issued or traded in the market.

Data sources

Data on getting credit are from the World Bank's Doing Business project (www.doingbusiness.org). Data on bank capital and nonperforming loans are from the IMF's *Global Financial Stability Report*. Data on credit and interest rates are from the IMF's *International Financial Statistics*.

5.6 | Tax policies

	Tax revenue collected by central government		Taxes payable by businesses			Highest marginal tax rate[a]		
	% of GDP		Number of payments	Time to prepare, file, and pay taxes hours	Total tax rate % of profit	Individual		Corporate %
						%	On income over $	
	2000	2007	June 2008	June 2008	June 2008	2006–08[b]	2006–08[b]	2006–08[b]
Afghanistan[c]	..	5.8	8	275	36.4	..	..	..
Albania[c]	16.1	..	44	244	50.5	20	2,413	10
Algeria[c]	36.9	29.6	34	451	74.2	..	..	..
Angola	..	..	31	272	53.2	..	..	..
Argentina	9.8	..	9	453	108.1	35	38,339	35
Armenia[c]	..	16	50	958	36.6	..	..	..
Australia	23.7	25.1	12	107	50.3	45	104,167	30
Austria	19.6	20.1	22	170	54.5	50	69,473	25
Azerbaijan[c]	12.7		23	376	41.1	35	13,793	22
Bangladesh[c]	7.6	8	21	302	39.5	..	..	..
Belarus[c]	16.6	24	112	1,188	117.5	..	..	..
Belgium	27.4	25.8	11	156	58.1	50	47,048	33
Benin[c]	15.5	16.3	55	270	73.2	35	..	38
Bolivia	13.2	17	41	1,080	78.1	13	..	25
Bosnia and Herzegovina	..	22.3	51	428	44.1	15	..	30
Botswana[c]	..		19	140	17.1	25	19,967	15
Brazil[c]	11.3	..	11	2,600	69.4	28	13,462	15
Bulgaria[c]	18.3	24.6	17	616	34.9	24	5,414	10
Burkina Faso	..	12	45	270	44.6	..	..	..
Burundi[c]	13.6	..	32	140	278.7	..	..	..
Cambodia	8.2	8.2	27	137	22.6	20	36,973	20
Cameroon[c]	11.2	..	41	1,400	51.4	..	..	..
Canada[c]	15	15.2	9	119	45.4	29	100,970	38
Central African Republic[c]	..	..	54	504	203.8	..	..	..
Chad	..	..	54	122	60.5	..	..	..
Chile	16.7	21.5	10	316	25.9	40	9,722	35
China[c]	6.8	9.4	9	504	79.9	45	175,695	25
Hong Kong, China	..	..	4	80	24.2	17	15,484	18
Colombia	11.7	13.6	31	256	78.4	22	45,564	33
Congo, Dem. Rep.[c]	3.5	..	32	308	229.8	50	4,631	40
Congo, Rep.	9.2	6.2	61	606	65.5	..	4,681	..
Costa Rica[c]	12.1	15.2	43	282	55.7	15	14,575	30
Côte d'Ivoire[c]	14.6	15.5	66	270	45.4	10	5,386	35
Croatia[c]	26.2	23.4	17	196	32.5	45	4,014	..
Cuba	..	..	..	..	..	..	..	..
Czech Republic[c]	15.4	15.1	12	930	48.6	15	53,482	21
Denmark	31	35.5	9	135	29.9	59	63,598	25
Dominican Republic[c]	..	16.6	9	480	35.7	30	26,209	30
Ecuador[c]	..	..	8	600	34.9	25	62,800	25
Egypt, Arab Rep.[c]	13.4	15.4	29	711	46.1	20	..	20
El Salvador	10.7	14	53	320	34.9	..	13,600	25
Eritrea	..	..	18	216	84.5	..	..	..
Estonia	15.9	17.2	10	81	48.6	21	..	21
Ethiopia[c]	10.2	..	20	198	31.1	35	..	30
Finland	24.6	21.8	20	269	47.8	32	84,457	26
France	23.2	21.8	11	132	65.4	..	..	33
Gabon	..	..	26	272	44.7	..	..	..
Gambia, The[c]	..	..	50	376	292.4	..	..	..
Georgia[c]	7.7	17.7	30	387	38.6	12	..	20
Germany	11.9	11.8	16	196	50.5	45	340,553	15
Ghana[c]	17.2	22.6	33	224	32.7	25	10,435	22
Greece	23.3	19.9	10	224	47.4	40	102,650	25
Guatemala[c]	10.1	11.9	39	344	36.5	31	38,714	31
Guinea[c]	11.1	..	56	416	49.9	..	..	..
Guinea-Bissau	..	..	46	208	45.9	..	..	..
Haiti	..	..	42	160	40.1	..	..	..

| | Tax revenue collected by central government | | Taxes payable by businesses | | | Highest marginal tax rate[a] | | |
| | % of GDP | | Number of payments | Time to prepare, file, and pay taxes hours | Total tax rate % of profit | Individual % | On income over $ | Corporate % |
	2000	2007	June 2008	June 2008	June 2008	2006–08[b]	2006–08[b]	2006–08[b]
Honduras	..	16.4	47	224	49.3	25	26,455	25
Hungary	21.9	21.5	14	330	57.5	36	..	16
India[c]	9	11.6	60	271	71.5	30	6,344	30
Indonesia[c]	11.6	..	51	266	37.3	35	22,173	30
Iran, Islamic Rep.[c]	6.3	7.3	22	344	44.2	35	9,183	25
Iraq	..	..	13	312	24.7	..	..	..
Ireland	26.1	25.6	9	76	28.8	42	43,591	13
Israel	29	28.4	33	230	33.9	49	111,695	27
Italy	23.2	23.3	15	334	73.3	43	102,166	28
Jamaica[c]	24.7	28.9	72	414	51.3	..	..	..
Japan	..	..	13	355	55.4	40	157,895	30
Jordan[c]	19	26.7	26	101	31.1	..	..	..
Kazakhstan[c]	10.2	12.3	9	271	36.4	20	..	30
Kenya[c]	16.8	18	41	417	50.9	..	..	..
Korea, Dem. Rep.	..	..	..	..	..	..	..	..
Korea, Rep.[c]	16.1	17.9	14	250	33.7	35	69,980	25
Kuwait	1.3	0.9	14	118	14.4	0	..	..
Kyrgyz Republic[c]	11.7	16.6	75	202	61.4	..	..	..
Lao PDR	..	10.5	34	560	33.7	..	..	..
Latvia[c]	14.2	16.6	7	279	33.0	25	..	15
Lebanon	12.2	15.2	19	180	36.0	..	..	..
Lesotho[c]	32.7	56.8	21	324	18.0	..	..	..
Liberia	..	..	32	158	35.8	..	..	..
Libya	..	..	..	..	..	..	..	..
Lithuania	14.6	18.1	15	166	46.4	27	..	15
Macedonia, FYR[c]	..	..	40	75	18.4	24	17,283	15
Madagascar	11.3	11.4	25	238	42.8	..	..	..
Malawi	..	..	19	292	31.4	..	..	..
Malaysia[c]	13.8	..	12	145	34.5	28	72,254	26
Mali	13.2	15.5	58	270	51.4	..	..	..
Mauritania	..	..	38	696	98.7	..	..	..
Mauritius[c]	18.2	17.6	7	161	22.2	15	..	15
Mexico[c]	11.7	..	27	549	51.5	28	9,496	28
Moldova[c]	14.7	20.6	53	234	42.1	18	2,423	0
Mongolia	..	25.3	42	204	30.3	..	..	..
Morocco[c]	19.9	25.2	28	358	44.6	..	..	..
Mozambique	..	..	37	230	34.3	32	38,814	32
Myanmar	3	4.7	..	..	..	..	..	..
Namibia[c]	30	..	37	375	25.3	35	28,694	35
Nepal[c]	8.7	9.8	34	408	34.1	..	..	..
Netherlands	22.3	23.9	9	180	39.1	52	72,631	26
New Zealand	29.5	31.4	8	70	35.6	39	40,463	30
Nicaragua[c]	13.8	18	64	240	63.2	30	26,455	30
Niger	..	11.7	42	270	42.3	..	..	..
Nigeria	..	..	35	938	32.2	..	..	..
Norway	27.4	28.9	4	87	41.6	..	120,148	28
Oman[c]	7.2	..	14	62	21.6	0	..	..
Pakistan[c]	10.1	9.8	47	560	28.9	35	11,490	37
Panama[c]	10.2	..	59	482	50.6	27	30,000	30
Papua New Guinea[c]	19	..	33	194	41.7	..	..	..
Paraguay[c]	..	11.5	35	328	35.0	8	..	10
Peru[c]	12.2	15.6	9	424	41.2	30	62,100	30
Philippines[c]	13.7	14	47	195	50.8	32	12,077	35
Poland	16	18.4	40	418	40.2	40	35,052	19
Portugal	21.5	22.6	8	328	43.6	42	85,202	25
Puerto Rico	..	..	16	218	64.7	33	50,000	19

	Tax revenue collected by central government		Taxes payable by businesses			Highest marginal tax rate[a]		
	% of GDP		Number of payments	Time to prepare, file, and pay taxes hours	Total tax rate % of profit	Individual		Corporate %
						%	On income over $	
	2000	**2007**	**June 2008**	**June 2008**	**June 2008**	**2006–08[b]**	**2006–08[b]**	**2006–08[b]**
Romania	11.7	12	113	202	48.0	16	..	16
Russian Federation	13.6	16.7	22	448	48.7	13	..	24
Rwanda[c]	..	..	34	160	33.7	..	..	..
Saudi Arabia	..	..	14	79	14.5	0	..	..
Senegal[c]	16.1	..	59	666	46.0	..	..	..
Serbia[c]	..	..	66	279	34.0	15	..	10
Sierra Leone[c]	10.2	..	28	399	233.5	..	..	..
Singapore[c]	15.4	14.4	5	84	27.9	20	222,222	18
Slovak Republic	..	14.1	31	325	47.4	19	..	19
Slovenia[c]	20.6	21	22	260	36.7	41	19,582	22
Somalia	..	..	..	..	..	..	..	..
South Africa	24	29.1	9	200	34.2	40	52,688	28
Spain	16.2	13.9	8	234	60.2	27	72,752	30
Sri Lanka[c]	14.5	14.2	62	256	63.7	35	4,419	35
Sudan[c]	6.4	..	42	180	31.6	..	..	..
Swaziland[c]	..	..	33	104	36.6	33	10,760	30
Sweden	20.6	..	2	122	54.5	32	77,239	28
Switzerland[c]	11.1	10.5	24	63	28.9	..	..	..
Syrian Arab Republic[c]	17.4	..	20	336	43.5	..	..	..
Tajikistan[c]	7.7	..	54	224	85.5	..	..	..
Tanzania	..	..	48	172	45.1	30	..	30
Thailand	..	16.2	23	264	37.8	37	118,624	30
Timor-Leste	..	..	15	640	28.3	..	..	..
Togo[c]	..	16.4	53	270	48.2	..	..	..
Trinidad and Tobago[c]	22.1	29.1	40	114	33.1	25	..	25
Tunisia[c]	21.3	21.2	22	228	59.1	..	..	..
Turkey[c]	..	18.5	15	223	45.5	35	36,752	20
Turkmenistan	..	..	..	..	..	..	..	..
Uganda[c]	10.4	12.3	32	222	34.5	30	2,899	30
Ukraine[c]	14.1	16.7	99	848	58.4	15	..	25
United Arab Emirates[c]	1.7	..	14	12	14.4	0	..	..
United Kingdom	28.9	28	8	105	35.3	40	50,435	28
United States	12.7	12.2	10	187	42.3	35	326,450	35
Uruguay[c]	16.7	18.7	53	336	58.5	25	3,970	25
Uzbekistan	..	..	106	196	90.6	25	..	10
Venezuela, RB[c]	13.3	15.5	70	864	56.6	34	93,767	34
Vietnam	..	..	32	1,050	40.1	40	..	28
West Bank and Gaza	..	..	27	154	16.8	..	..	..
Yemen, Rep.[c]	9.4	..	44	248	47.8	..	..	..
Zambia[c]	18.6	17.2	37	132	16.1	..	..	..
Zimbabwe[c]	..	..	52	256	63.7	..	..	..
World	**15.7 w**	**16.8 w**	**31 u**	**300 u**	**49.3 u**	**..**	**..**	**..**
Low income	..	..	41	314	68.4	..	..	..
Middle income	11.7	14.1	34	352	44.1	..	..	..
Lower middle income	8.9	11.6	34	346	42.9	..	..	..
Upper middle income	..	..	34	361	45.8	..	..	..
Low & middle income	11.6	14.0	36	339	52.3	..	..	..
East Asia & Pacific	7.7	10.1	28	270	39.9	..	..	..
Europe & Central Asia	14.8	17.3	50	384	48.5	..	..	..
Latin America & Carib.	11.4	..	35	428	48.6	..	..	..
Middle East & N. Africa	15.1	16.4	27	295	42.2	..	..	..
South Asia	9.3	11.3	32	293	40.4	..	..	..
Sub-Saharan Africa	..	..	38	312	66.9	..	..	..
High income	16.5	17.0	16	181	40.3	..	..	..
Euro area	19.1	18.5	14	201	48.2	..	..	..

a. Data are from PriceWaterhouseCooper's *Worldwide Tax Summaries* online. b. Data are for the most recent year available. c. Data on central government taxes were reported on a cash basis and have been adjusted to the accrual framework of the International Monetary Fund's *Government Finance Statistics Manual 2001*.

About the data

Taxes are the main source of revenue for most governments. The sources of tax revenue and their relative contributions are determined by government policy choices about where and how to impose taxes and by changes in the structure of the economy. Tax policy may reflect concerns about distributional effects, economic efficiency (including corrections for externalities), and the practical problems of administering a tax system. There is no ideal level of taxation. But taxes influence incentives and thus the behavior of economic actors and the economy's competitiveness.

The level of taxation is typically measured by tax revenue as a share of gross domestic product (GDP). Comparing levels of taxation across countries provides a quick overview of the fiscal obligations and incentives facing the private sector. The table shows only central government data, which may significantly understate the total tax burden, particularly in countries where provincial and municipal governments are large or have considerable tax authority.

Low ratios of tax revenue to GDP may reflect weak administration and large-scale tax avoidance or evasion. Low ratios may also reflect a sizable parallel economy with unrecorded and undisclosed incomes. Tax revenue ratios tend to rise with income, with higher income countries relying on taxes to finance a much broader range of social services and social security than lower income countries are able to.

The indicators covering taxes payable by businesses measure all taxes and contributions that are government mandated (at any level—federal, state, or local), apply to standardized businesses, and have an impact in their income statements. The taxes covered go beyond the definition of a tax for government national accounts (compulsory, unrequited payments to general government) and also measure any imposts that affect business accounts. The main differences are in labor contributions and value-added taxes. The indicators account for government-mandated contributions paid by the employer to a requited private pension fund or workers insurance fund but exclude value-added taxes because they do not affect the accounting profits of the business—that is, they are not reflected in the income statement.

To make the data comparable across countries, several assumptions are made about businesses. The main assumptions are that they are limited liability companies, they operate in the country's most populous city, they are domestically owned, they perform general industrial or commercial activities, and

they have certain levels of start-up capital, employees, and turnover. For details about the assumptions, see the World Bank's *Doing Business 2009.*

A potentially important influence on both domestic and international investors is a tax system's progressivity, as reflected in the highest marginal tax rate levied at the national level on individual and corporate income. Data for individual marginal tax rates generally refer to employment income. In some countries the highest marginal tax rate is also the basic or flat rate, and other surtaxes, deductions, and the like may apply. And in many countries several different corporate tax rates may be levied, depending on the type of business (mining, banking, insurance, agriculture, manufacturing), ownership (domestic or foreign), volume of sales, and whether surtaxes or exemptions are included. The corporate tax rates in the table are mainly general rates applied to domestic companies. For more detailed information, see the country's laws, regulations, and tax treaties and PricewaterhouseCoopers's *Worldwide Tax Summaries Online* (www.pwc.com).

Definitions

• **Tax revenue collected by central government** is compulsory transfers to the central government for public purposes. Certain compulsory transfers such as fines, penalties, and most social security contributions are excluded. Refunds and corrections of erroneously collected tax revenue are treated as negative revenue. The analytic framework of the International Monetary Fund's (IMF) *Government Finance Statistics Manual 2001* (GFSM 2001) is based on accrual accounting and balance sheets. For countries still reporting government finance data on a cash basis, the IMF adjusts reported data to the GFSM 2001 accrual framework. These countries are footnoted in the table. • **Number of tax payments by businesses** is the total number of taxes paid by businesses during one year. When electronic filing is available, the tax is counted as paid once a year even if payments are more frequent. • **Time to prepare, file, and pay taxes** is the time, in hours per year, it takes to prepare, file, and pay (or withhold) three major types of taxes: the corporate income tax, the value-added or sales tax, and labor taxes, including payroll taxes and social security contributions. • **Total tax rate** is the total amount of taxes payable by businesses (except for consumption taxes) after accounting for deductions and exemptions as a percentage of profit. For further details on the method used for assessing the total tax payable, see the World Bank's *Doing Business 2009.* • **Highest marginal tax rate** is the highest rate shown on the national schedule of tax rates applied to the annual taxable income of individuals and corporations. Also presented are the income levels for individuals above which the highest marginal tax rates levied at the national level apply.

Data sources

Data on central government tax revenue are from print and electronic editions of the IMF's *Government Finance Statistics Yearbook.* Data on taxes payable by businesses are from *Doing Business 2009* (www.doingbusiness.org). Data on individual and corporate tax rates are from PricewaterhouseCoopers's *Worldwide Tax Summaries Online* (www.pwc.com).

	Military expenditures				Armed forces personnel				Arms transfers			
	% of GDP		% of central government expenditure		thousands		% of labor force		1990 $ millions			
									Exports		Imports	
	2000	2007	2000	2007	2000	2007	2000	2007	2000	2007	2000	2007
Afghanistan	..	1.5	..	8.7	400	51	6.3	0.6	..	..	33	37
Albania	1.2	1.8	5.4	..	68	15	5.2	1.0	..	..	3	5
Algeria	3.4	2.9	16.5	15.7	305	334	2.8	2.4	..	..	428	700
Angola	2.4	3.7	..	..	118	117	1.9	1.6	1	..	157	4
Argentina	1.3	0.7	6.2	..	102	107	0.6	0.6	2	..	224	41
Armenia	3.6	3.0	..	18.1	42	42	3.1	2.8	..	..	2	..
Australia	1.9	2.0	7.5	7.8	52	55	0.5	0.5	43	1	366	685
Austria	1.0	1.0	2.5	2.5	41	35	1.0	0.8	21	86	25	335
Azerbaijan	2.3	3.0	13.8	..	87	82	2.4	1.9	..	..	3	27
Bangladesh	1.4	1.1	14.9	11.7	137	221	0.2	0.3	..	..	205	17
Belarus	1.3	1.6	5.3	4.7	91	183	1.9	3.8	293	35	41	254
Belgium	1.4	1.1	3.2	2.6	39	39	0.9	0.8	22	10	39	171
Benin	0.6	1.1	4.7	7.6	7	8	0.3	0.2	..	..	6	3
Bolivia	1.7	1.2	6.5	5.7	70	83	2.0	1.9	..	..	19	5
Bosnia and Herzegovina	3.6	1.3	..	3.5	76	9	4.1	0.5	4	..	25	..
Botswana	3.0	2.6	..	..	10	11	1.6	1.6	..	..	50	..
Brazil	1.6	1.6	7.1	..	673	721	0.8	0.7	26	24	126	175
Bulgaria	2.5	2.0	7.8	6.3	114	75	3.5	2.2	2	7	7	38
Burkina Faso	1.2	1.4	..	9.6	11	11	0.2	0.2	..	..	..	4
Burundi	6.0	4.8	30.3	..	46	51	1.4	1.2	..	..	1	..
Cambodia	2.2	0.9	16.8	12.8	360	191	6.1	2.6	..	..	..	36
Cameroon	1.3	1.4	12.0	..	22	23	0.4	0.3	..	..	1	0
Canada	1.1	1.3	6.0	7.0	69	64	0.4	0.3	109	343	560	623
Central African Republic	1.0	1.1	..	..	5	3	0.3	0.2	..	..	..	9
Chad	1.9	1.0	..	..	35	35	1.0	0.8	..	..	15	3
Chile	3.7	3.4	17.7	19.5	117	103	1.9	1.5	1	..	177	615
China	1.8a	2.0a	19.6a	17.9a	3,910	2,885	0.5	0.4	228	355	1,874	1,424
Hong Kong, China	..	..	..	..	..	..	..	..	..	..	..	..
Colombia	3.6	3.1	19.0	12.3	247	411	1.3	1.8	..	..	62	38
Congo, Dem. Rep.	1.0	1.7	11.4	..	93	143	0.5	0.6	..	..	41	17
Congo, Rep.	1.4	1.1	5.9	5.2	15	12	1.2	0.8	..	..	0	1
Costa Rica	..	..	..	..	15	10	0.9	0.5	..	..	..	..
Côte d'Ivoire	..	1.5	..	7.1	15	19	0.2	0.3	..	..	32	..
Croatia	3.6	2.0	7.8	5.0	101	21	5.0	1.1	2	..	70	14
Cuba	..	..	..	..	85	76	1.6	1.5	..	..	..	..
Czech Republic	2.0	1.5	6.1	4.5	63	27	1.2	0.5	78	13	16	15
Denmark	1.5	1.3	4.2	3.7	22	30	0.8	1.0	20	5	64	201
Dominican Republic	0.9	0.5	..	3.5	40	65	1.1	1.5	..	..	13	2
Ecuador	1.7	2.8	..	..	58	58	1.2	1.0	..	..	12	45
Egypt, Arab Rep.	3.2	2.5	12.3	8.4	679	866	3.4	3.6	38	..	826	418
El Salvador	0.9	0.6	4.3	3.3	29	33	1.2	1.2	..	..	16	..
Eritrea	36.4	..	..	..	200	202	14.1	10.4	0	..	4	271
Estonia	1.4	1.9	4.7	7.0	8	7	1.1	1.0	..	..	27	30
Ethiopia	7.6	1.9	18.0	..	353	138	1.2	0.4	..	..	125	..
Finland	1.3	1.3	3.7	3.7	35	32	1.4	1.2	9	24	518	110
France	2.5	2.3	5.7	5.3	389	353	1.5	1.3	1,033	2,690	58	63
Gabon	1.8	1.1	..	..	7	7	1.3	1.1	..	..	..	21
Gambia, The	0.8	0.6	..	..	1	1	0.1	0.1	..	..	..	..
Georgia	0.6	7.5	5.3	32.7	33	33	1.4	1.4	22	..	6	4
Germany	1.5	1.3	4.7	4.4	221	244	0.5	0.6	1,622	3,395	135	85
Ghana	1.0	0.7	3.3	2.6	8	14	0.1	0.1	..	..	1	13
Greece	4.3	3.5	9.8	8.3	163	161	3.4	3.1	2	23	651	2,089
Guatemala	0.8	0.5	7.5	3.6	53	35	1.7	0.7	..	..	1	..
Guinea	1.5	..	11.8	..	19	19	0.5	0.4	..	..	19	..
Guinea-Bissau	4.4	4.0	..	..	9	9	1.8	1.4	..	..	..	..
Haiti	..	..	..	..	5	0	0.2	0.0	..	..	..	..

	Military expenditures				Armed forces personnel				Arms transfers			
	% of GDP		% of central government expenditure		thousands		% of labor force		1990 $ millions			
									Exports		Imports	
	2000	2007	2000	2007	2000	2007	2000	2007	2000	2007	2000	2007
Honduras	0.5	0.6	..	2.8	14	20	0.6	0.8	..	..	..	..
Hungary	1.7	1.1	4.1	2.6	58	37	1.4	0.9	..	6	14	192
India	3.1	2.5	19.5	16.5	2,372	2,576	0.6	0.6	16	14	826	1,318
Indonesia	1.0	1.2	5.7	..	492	582	0.5	0.5	16	8	170	475
Iran, Islamic Rep.	3.8	3.0	22.5	14.7	753	563	3.6	2.0	0	10	413	297
Iraq	..	..	..	..	479	362	7.8	5.0	..	..	..	244
Ireland	0.7	0.5	2.6	1.6	12	10	0.7	0.5	..	..	0	13
Israel	7.9	8.3	17.6	19.8	181	185	7.3	6.5	316	238	364	891
Italy	2.0	1.8	5.2	4.5	503	436	2.1	1.7	192	562	241	176
Jamaica	0.5	0.7	1.5	1.1	3	3	0.3	0.3	..	..	5	1
Japan	1.0	0.9	..	..	249	242	0.4	0.4	..	..	431	519
Jordan	6.2	6.9	23.1	19.0	149	111	11.6	6.8	..	13	130	83
Kazakhstan	0.8	1.2	5.7	8.5	99	81	1.3	1.0	16	12	144	21
Kenya	1.3	1.8	7.8	9.3	27	29	0.2	0.2	..	..	..	25
Korea, Dem. Rep.	..	..	..	..	1,244	1,295	11.2	10.4	13	..	19	9
Korea, Rep.	2.5	2.7	14.4	13.3	688	692	3.0	2.8	8	214	1,266	1,807
Kuwait	7.1	4.3	18.9	13.5	20	23	1.8	1.7	99	..	245	117
Kyrgyz Republic	2.9	3.3	18.0	18.1	14	21	0.7	0.9	..	..	..	1
Lao PDR	2.0	..	..	..	129	129	5.4	4.5	..	..	7	4
Latvia	0.9	1.8	3.2	6.6	9	17	0.8	1.4	..	..	3	51
Lebanon	5.5	5.8	17.7	17.9	77	76	5.8	5.1	45	..	4	3
Lesotho	3.6	2.5	7.8	5.3	2	2	0.3	0.2	..	..	6	1
Liberia	..	0.8	..	..	15	2	1.3	0.1	..	..	8	..
Libya	3.1	1.1	..	..	77	76	4.1	3.4	11	9	145	3
Lithuania	1.4	1.2	5.2	3.9	17	24	1.0	1.5	3	..	5	4
Macedonia, FYR	1.9	2.1	..	..	24	19	2.8	2.1	0	..	11	0
Madagascar	1.2	1.1	11.5	10.0	29	22	0.4	0.2	..	..	..	..
Malawi	0.7	1.2	..	..	6	7	0.1	0.1	1	..	..	..
Malaysia	1.6	2.1	10.5	..	116	134	1.2	1.2	8	..	40	550
Mali	2.4	2.3	20.7	15.3	15	12	0.6	0.4	..	..	7	7
Mauritania	3.5	3.1	..	..	21	21	2.0	1.6	..	..	31	..
Mauritius	0.2	0.2	1.0	0.8	2	2	0.3	0.3	..	..	..	4
Mexico	0.5	0.4	3.4	..	208	286	0.5	0.6	..	..	227	11
Moldova	0.4	0.4	1.4	1.3	13	9	0.7	0.6	3	4	..	..
Mongolia	2.2	1.2	..	5.0	16	16	1.7	1.4	..	..	..	..
Morocco	2.3	3.2	12.0	11.0	241	246	2.4	2.2	..	..	123	44
Mozambique	1.3	0.9	..	..	6	11	0.1	0.1	..	..	0	..
Myanmar	2.3	..	..	..	429	513	1.7	1.8	..	..	3	20
Namibia	2.7	3.4	8.6	..	9	15	1.5	2.2	..	..	18	72
Nepal	1.0	1.5	..	12.6	90	131	1.0	1.1	..	..	11	5
Netherlands	1.6	1.5	4.0	3.6	57	41	0.7	0.5	259	1,355	142	210
New Zealand	1.2	1.1	3.5	3.2	9	9	0.5	0.4	1	..	45	70
Nicaragua	0.8	0.7	4.7	3.5	16	14	0.9	0.6	..	..	..	..
Niger	1.1	1.0	..	10.6	11	10	0.3	0.2	..	..	..	0
Nigeria	0.8	0.6	..	..	107	162	0.3	0.4	..	..	42	15
Norway	1.7	1.4	5.3	4.5	27	19	1.1	0.8	3	14	263	483
Oman	10.6	11.3	40.4	..	48	47	5.4	4.9	..	1	120	4
Pakistan	4.0	3.5	23.4	21.7	900	921	2.2	1.6	3	9	..	..
Panama	1.0	..	4.6	..	12	12	0.9	0.8	..	..	0	..
Papua New Guinea	0.9	0.5	2.9	..	4	3	0.2	0.1	..	..	..	..
Paraguay	1.1	0.8	..	4.5	35	26	1.4	0.8	..	..	6	1
Peru	1.7	1.1	9.7	6.7	193	198	1.7	1.4	4	..	24	172
Philippines	1.1	0.8	6.2	4.7	149	147	0.5	0.4	..	4	9	28
Poland	1.9	2.0	5.7	5.8	239	142	1.4	0.8	43	135	159	985
Portugal	2.0	1.7	5.1	4.2	91	91	1.7	1.6	..	30	2	2
Puerto Rico	..	..	..	..	..	..	..	..	..	..	..	..

	Military expenditures				Armed forces personnel				Arms transfers			
	% of GDP		% of central government expenditure		thousands		% of labor force		1990 $ millions Exports		Imports	
	2000	2007	2000	2007	2000	2007	2000	2007	2000	2007	2000	2007
Romania	2.5	1.8	8.9	6.8	283	153	2.4	1.6	3	16	23	70
Russian Federation	3.7	3.6	19.3	15.4	1,427	1,476	2.0	1.9	4,190	4,588	..	4
Rwanda	3.5	1.7	..	..	76	35	2.1	0.8	..	..	14	3
Saudi Arabia	10.6	9.3	..	..	217	238	3.2	2.7	..	36	81	72
Senegal	1.3	1.7	10.4	..	15	19	0.4	0.4	..	..	..	15
Serbia	5.4	2.4	..	..	136	24	..	0.8	7	5	1	..
Sierra Leone	3.7	1.8	12.8	..	4	11	0.2	0.5	..	..	13	..
Singapore	4.7	4.3	28.7	31.5	169	167	8.2	6.8	10	3	612	707
Slovak Republic	1.7	1.7	..	5.4	41	17	1.6	0.6	92	7	2	4
Slovenia	1.1	1.5	2.9	4.0	14	12	1.4	1.2	..	..	1	2
Somalia	..	..	..	..	50	..	..	1.8	..	..	1	..
South Africa	1.6	1.4	5.6	4.7	72	62	0.5	0.4	18	80	16	855
Spain	1.2	1.2	3.9	4.7	242	222	1.3	1.0	46	529	332	385
Sri Lanka	4.5	2.9	19.7	14.6	204	213	2.6	2.4	..	..	226	1
Sudan	4.7	4.3	53.0	..	120	127	1.2	1.1	..	..	146	49
Swaziland	1.8	..	..	..	3	..	0.8	..	..	..	1	..
Sweden	2.0	1.3	5.5	..	88	18	1.9	0.4	308	413	210	85
Switzerland	1.1	0.8	4.2	4.4	28	23	0.7	0.5	104	211	14	126
Syrian Arab Republic	5.4	3.9	..	..	425	401	8.8	6.3	..	3	439	30
Tajikistan	1.2	..	13.4	..	7	17	0.4	0.7	..	..	..	13
Tanzania	1.5	1.0	..	..	35	28	0.2	0.1	..	..	..	9
Thailand	1.4	1.4	..	7.8	417	420	1.2	1.1	..	..	93	9
Timor-Leste	..	..	..	..	..	1	..	0.2	..	..	..	..
Togo	..	1.6	..	9.8	8	10	0.4	0.4	..	..	..	..
Trinidad and Tobago	..	..	..	..	8	4	1.3	0.6	..	..	10	..
Tunisia	1.7	1.4	6.2	4.9	47	48	1.5	1.3	..	..	11	18
Turkey	3.7	2.1	..	8.6	828	612	3.5	2.5	15	33	1,042	944
Turkmenistan	2.9	..	..	..	15	22	0.8	1.0	..	..	..	..
Uganda	2.5	1.7	16.0	12.4	51	47	0.5	0.3	..	..	6	5
Ukraine	3.6	2.9	13.5	8.3	420	215	1.8	0.9	280	109	0	..
United Arab Emirates	3.4	1.9	45.7	..	66	51	3.5	1.9	..	3	309	1,040
United Kingdom	2.4	2.5	6.7	6.2	213	160	0.7	0.5	1,356	1,151	808	698
United States	3.1	4.2	15.6	19.4	1,455	1,555	1.0	1.0	7,505	7,454	268	587
Uruguay	1.5	1.3	5.0	4.8	25	26	1.6	1.6	1	..	4	33
Uzbekistan	0.8	..	..	..	79	87	0.8	0.7	73	4	6	..
Venezuela, RB	1.2	1.1	5.4	5.2	79	115	0.8	0.9	..	1	89	887
Vietnam	..	..	..	..	524	495	1.4	1.1	..	..	5	1
West Bank and Gaza	..	..	..	..	..	56	..	6.8	..	..	..	2
Yemen, Rep.	5.0	4.7	23.9	..	136	138	3.4	2.6	..	..	158	57
Zambia	1.8	1.8	10.3	7.6	23	16	0.6	0.4	..	..	27	3
Zimbabwe	0.0	0.0	..	..	62	51	1.2	0.9	3	..	2	20
World	**2.3 w**	**2.5 w**	**10.2 w**	**11.2 w**	**29,353 s**	**27,254 s**	**1.0 w**	**0.9 w**	**18,266 s**	**24,192 s**	**18,066 s**	**23,493 s**
Low income	2.4	1.8	..	..	5,806	5,359	1.3	1.0	17	9	724	148
Middle income	2.0	2.0	15.3	14.2	17,507	16,185	0.9	0.8	5,135	5,459	8,181	10,718
Lower middle income	2.2	2.1	17.3	15.6	12,481	11,528	0.8	0.7	549	481	5,846	5,396
Upper middle income	1.9	1.9	..	..	5,026	4,657	1.4	1.2	4,586	4,978	2,335	5,322
Low & middle income	2.1	2.0	15.3	14.2	23,313	21,544	1.0	0.8	5,152	5,459	8,905	10,866
East Asia & Pacific	1.7	1.8	18.4	16.8	7,794	6,815	0.8	0.6	241	359	2,211	2,532
Europe & Central Asia	3.1	2.7	12.6	11.0	4,220	3,394	2.1	1.6	4,869	4,973	1,397	2,163
Latin America & Carib.	1.4	1.3	6.5	..	2,084	2,408	0.9	0.9	4	25	966	1,978
Middle East & N. Africa	3.5	3.0	13.1	13.5	3,379	3,289	4.0	3.1	0	22	2,522	1,824
South Asia	3.1	2.6	19.9	16.9	4,114	4,113	0.8	0.7	19	23	1,257	1,373
Sub-Saharan Africa	1.8	1.5	..	..	1,724	1,525	0.7	0.5	19	80	552	996
High income	2.3	2.6	10.0	10.6	6,040	5,710	1.2	1.1	13,114	18,733	9,161	12,627
Euro area	1.8	1.6	4.8	4.6	1,820	1,690	1.3	1.1	3,204	8,681	2,146	3,641

Note: For some countries data are partial or uncertain or based on rough estimates; see SIPRI (2008).

a. Estimates differ from official statistics of the government of China, which has published the following estimates: military expenditure as 1.2 percent of GDP in 2000 and 1.4 percent in 2006 and 7.6 percent of central government expenditure in 2000 and 7.4 percent in 2006 (see National Bureau of Statistics of China, www.stats.gov.cn).

Although national defense is an important function of government and security from external threats that contributes to economic development, high levels of military expenditures for defense or civil conflicts burden the economy and may impede growth. Data on military expenditures as a share of gross domestic product (GDP) are a rough indicator of the portion of national resources used for military activities and of the burden on the national economy. As an "input" measure military expenditures are not directly related to the "output" of military activities, capabilities, or security. Comparisons of military spending between countries should take into account the many factors that influence perceptions of vulnerability and risk, including historical and cultural traditions, the length of borders that need defending, the quality of relations with neighbors, and the role of the armed forces in the body politic.

Data on military spending reported by governments are not compiled using standard definitions. They are often incomplete and unreliable. Even in countries where the parliament vigilantly reviews budgets and spending, military expenditures and arms transfers rarely receive close scrutiny or full, public disclosure (see Ball 1984 and Happe and Wakeman-Linn 1994). Therefore, SIPRI has adopted a definition of military expenditure derived from the North Atlantic Treaty Organization (NATO) definition (see *Definitions*). The data on military expenditures as a share of GDP and as a share of central government expenditure are estimated by the Stockholm International Peace Research Institute (SIPRI). Central government expenditures are from the International Monetary Fund (IMF). Therefore the data in the table may differ from comparable data published by national governments.

SIPRI's primary source of military expenditure data is official data provided by national governments. These data are derived from national budget documents, defense white papers, and other public documents from official government agencies, including governments' responses to questionnaires sent by SIPRI, the United Nations, or the Organization for Security and Co-operation in Europe. Secondary sources include international statistics, such as those of NATO and the IMF's *Government Finance Statistics Yearbook*. Other secondary sources include country reports of the Economist Intelligence Unit, country reports by IMF staff, and specialist journals and newspapers.

In the many cases where SIPRI cannot make independent estimates, it uses the national data provided. Because of the differences in definitions and the difficulty in verifying the accuracy and completeness of data, data on military expenditures are not strictly comparable across countries. More information on SIPRI's military expenditure project can be found at www.sipri.org/contents/milap/.

Data on armed forces refer to military personnel on active duty, including paramilitary forces. Because data exclude personnel not on active duty, they underestimate the share of the labor force working for the defense establishment. Governments rarely report the size of their armed forces, so such data typically come from intelligence sources.

SIPRI's Arms Transfers Project collects data on arms transfers from open sources. Since publicly available information is inadequate for tracking all weapons and other military equipment, SIPRI covers only what it terms *major conventional weapons*. Data cover the supply of weapons through sales, aid, gifts, and manufacturing licenses; therefore the term *arms transfers* rather than *arms trade* is used. SIPRI data also cover weapons supplied to or from rebel forces in an armed conflict as well as arms deliveries for which neither the supplier nor the recipient can be identified with acceptable certainty; these data are available in SIPRI's database.

SIPRI's estimates of arms transfers are designed as a trend-measuring device in which similar weapons have similar values, reflecting both the value and quality of weapons transferred. SIPRI cautions that the estimated values do not reflect financial value (payments for weapons transferred) because reliable data on the value of the transfer are not available, and even when values are known, the transfer usually includes more than the actual conventional weapons, such as spares, support systems, and training, and details of the financial arrangements (such as credit and loan conditions and discounts) are usually not known.

Given these measurement issues, SIPRI's method of estimating the transfer of military resources includes an evaluation of the technical parameters of the weapons. Weapons for which a price is not known are compared with the same weapons for which actual acquisition prices are available (core weapons) or for the closest match. These weapons are assigned a value in an index that reflects their military resource value in relation to the core weapons. These matches are based on such characteristics as size, performance, and type of electronics, and adjustments are made for secondhand weapons. More information on SIPRI's Arms Transfers Project is available at www.sipri.org/contents/armstrad/.

• **Military expenditures** are SIPRI data derived from the NATO definition, which includes all current and capital expenditures on the armed forces, including peacekeeping forces; defense ministries and other government agencies engaged in defense projects; paramilitary forces, if judged to be trained and equipped for military operations; and military space activities. Such expenditures include military and civil personnel, including retirement pensions and social services for military personnel; operation and maintenance; procurement; military research and development; and military aid (in the military expenditures of the donor country). Excluded are civil defense and current expenditures for previous military activities, such as for veterans benefits, demobilization, and weapons conversion and destruction. This definition cannot be applied for all countries, however, since that would require more detailed information than is available about military budgets and off-budget military expenditures (for example, whether military budgets cover civil defense, reserves and auxiliary forces, police and paramilitary forces, and military pensions).
• **Armed forces personnel** are active duty military personnel, including paramilitary forces if the training, organization, equipment, and control suggest they may be used to support or replace regular military forces. Reserve forces, which are not fully staffed or operational in peace time, are not included. The data also exclude civilians in the defense establishment and so are not consistent with the data on military expenditures on personnel. • **Arms transfers** cover the supply of military weapons through sales, aid, gifts, and manufacturing licenses. Weapons must be transferred voluntarily by the supplier, have a military purpose, and be destined for the armed forces, paramilitary forces, or intelligence agencies of another country. The trends shown in the table are based on actual deliveries only. Data cover major conventional weapons such as aircraft, armored vehicles, artillery, radar systems, missiles, and ships designed for military use. Excluded are transfers of other military equipment such as small arms and light weapons, trucks, small artillery, ammunition, support equipment, technology transfers, and other services.

Data on military expenditures are from SIPRI's *Yearbook 2008: Armaments, Disarmament, and International Security.* Data on armed forces personnel are from the International Institute for Strategic Studies' *The Military Balance 2009.* Data on arms transfers are from SIPRI's Arms Transfer Project (www.sipri.org/contents/armstrad/).

5.8 Public policies and institutions

	IDA Resource Allocation Index 1–6 (low to high)	Economic management 1–6 (low to high)				Structural policies 1–6 (low to high)			
		Macroeconomic management	Fiscal policy	Debt policy	Average	Trade	Financial sector	Business regulatory environment	Average
	2007	**2007**	**2007**	**2007**	**2007**	**2007**	**2007**	**2007**	**2007**
Afghanistan	2.5	3.5	3.0	3.0	3.2	2.5	2.0	2.5	2.3
Angola	2.7	3.0	3.0	3.0	3.0	4.0	2.5	2.0	2.8
Armenia	4.4	5.5	5.0	6.0	5.5	4.5	3.5	4.0	4.0
Azerbaijan	3.8	4.5	4.5	5.0	4.7	4.0	3.0	3.5	3.5
Bangladesh	3.5	4.0	3.5	4.5	4.0	3.5	3.0	3.5	3.3
Benin	3.6	4.5	4.0	3.5	4.0	4.0	3.5	3.5	3.7
Bhutan	3.9	4.5	4.5	4.5	4.5	3.0	3.0	3.5	3.2
Bolivia	3.7	4.0	4.0	4.5	4.2	5.0	3.5	2.5	3.7
Bosnia and Herzegovina	3.7	4.5	3.5	4.0	4.0	3.5	4.0	4.0	3.8
Burkina Faso	3.7	4.5	4.5	4.0	4.3	4.0	3.0	3.0	3.3
Burundi	3.0	3.5	3.5	2.5	3.2	3.5	3.0	2.5	3.0
Cambodia	3.2	4.5	3.0	3.5	3.7	3.5	2.5	3.5	3.2
Cameroon	3.2	4.0	4.0	3.0	3.7	3.5	3.0	3.0	3.2
Cape Verde	4.2	4.5	4.5	4.5	4.5	4.0	4.0	3.5	3.8
Central African Republic	2.5	3.5	3.0	2.0	2.8	3.5	2.5	2.0	2.7
Chad	2.6	3.0	2.5	2.5	2.7	3.0	3.0	2.5	2.8
Comoros	2.4	2.5	1.5	2.0	2.0	3.0	2.5	2.5	2.7
Congo, Dem. Rep.	2.8	3.5	3.5	2.5	3.2	4.0	2.0	3.0	3.0
Congo, Rep.	2.7	3.0	2.0	2.5	2.5	3.5	2.5	2.5	2.8
Côte d'Ivoire	2.6	3.0	2.5	1.5	2.3	3.5	3.0	3.0	3.2
Djibouti	3.1	3.5	2.5	2.5	2.8	4.0	3.5	3.5	3.7
Dominica	3.9	4.0	4.5	3.0	3.8	4.0	4.0	4.5	4.2
Eritrea	2.4	2.0	2.0	2.5	2.2	1.5	2.0	2.0	1.8
Ethiopia	3.4	3.0	4.0	3.5	3.5	3.0	3.0	3.5	3.2
Gambia, The	3.2	4.0	3.5	2.5	3.3	4.0	3.0	3.5	3.5
Georgia	4.3	4.5	4.5	5.0	4.7	5.5	3.5	5.0	4.7
Ghana	4.0	4.0	4.0	4.0	4.0	4.0	4.0	4.0	4.0
Grenada	3.7	3.5	2.5	3.0	3.0	4.0	3.5	4.5	4.0
Guinea	3.0	3.0	3.5	2.5	3.0	4.0	3.0	3.0	3.3
Guinea-Bissau	2.6	2.0	2.5	1.5	2.0	4.0	3.0	2.5	3.2
Guyana	3.4	3.5	3.5	4.0	3.7	4.0	3.5	3.0	3.5
Haiti	2.9	3.5	3.5	2.5	3.2	4.0	3.0	2.5	3.2
Honduras	3.8	4.0	3.5	4.0	3.8	5.0	3.5	4.5	4.3
India	3.9	4.5	3.5	4.5	4.2	4.0	4.0	3.5	3.8
Kenya	3.6	4.5	4.0	4.0	4.2	4.0	3.5	4.0	3.8
Kiribati	3.1	2.5	2.0	5.0	3.2	3.0	3.0	3.0	3.0
Kyrgyz Republic	3.7	4.5	4.0	4.0	4.2	5.0	3.5	3.5	4.0
Lao PDR	3.1	4.5	3.5	3.5	3.8	3.5	2.0	3.0	2.8

About the data

The International Development Association (IDA) is the part of the World Bank Group that helps the poorest countries reduce poverty by providing concessional loans and grants for programs aimed at boosting economic growth and improving living conditions. IDA funding helps these countries deal with the complex challenges they face in meeting the Millennium Development Goals.

The World Bank's IDA Resource Allocation Index (IRAI), presented in the table, is based on the results of the annual Country Policy and Institutional Assessment (CPIA) exercise, which covers the IDA-eligible countries. The table does not include Liberia, Myanmar, and Somalia because they were not rated in the 2007

exercise even though they are IDA eligible. Albania and Indonesia are no longer included in the table because they have graduated from IDA. Country assessments have been carried out annually since the mid-1970s by World Bank staff. Over time the criteria have been revised from a largely macroeconomic focus to include governance aspects and a broader coverage of social and structural dimensions. Country performance is assessed against a set of 16 criteria grouped into four clusters: economic management, structural policies, policies for social inclusion and equity, and public sector management and institutions. IDA resources are allocated to a country on per capita terms based on its IDA country performance rating and, to a limited

extent, based on its per capita gross national income. This ensures that good performers receive a higher IDA allocation in per capita terms. The IRAI is a key element in the country performance rating.

The CPIA exercise is intended to capture the quality of a country's policies and institutional arrangements, focusing on key elements that are within the country's control, rather than on outcomes (such as economic growth rates) that are influenced by events beyond the country's control. More specifically, the CPIA measures the extent to which a country's policy and institutional framework supports sustainable growth and poverty reduction and, consequently, the effective use of development assistance.

Public policies and institutions **5.8**

	IDA Resource Allocation Index 1–6 (low to high)	Economic management 1–6 (low to high)					Structural policies 1–6 (low to high)			
		Macroeconomic management	Fiscal policy	Debt policy	Average		Trade	Financial sector	Business regulatory environment	Average
	2007	**2007**	**2007**	**2007**	**2007**		**2007**	**2007**	**2007**	**2007**
Lesotho	3.5	4.0	4.0	4.0	4.0		3.5	3.5	3.0	3.3
Madagascar	3.7	4.0	3.0	4.0	3.7		4.0	3.5	4.0	3.8
Malawi	3.4	3.5	3.5	3.0	3.3		4.0	3.0	3.5	3.5
Maldives	3.6	3.0	2.5	3.0	2.8		4.0	4.0	4.0	4.0
Mali	3.7	4.5	4.0	4.5	4.3		4.0	3.0	3.5	3.5
Mauritania	3.4	3.5	3.0	4.0	3.5		4.5	2.5	3.5	3.5
Moldova	3.8	4.0	4.0	4.0	4.0		4.5	3.5	3.5	3.8
Mongolia	3.4	3.5	3.0	3.0	3.2		4.5	3.0	3.5	3.7
Mozambique	3.6	4.0	4.0	4.5	4.2		4.0	3.5	3.0	3.7
Nepal	3.4	4.5	3.5	3.5	3.8		4.0	3.0	3.0	3.3
Nicaragua	3.8	4.0	4.0	4.5	4.2		4.5	3.5	3.5	3.8
Niger	3.3	4.0	3.5	3.5	3.7		4.0	3.0	3.0	3.3
Nigeria	3.4	4.0	4.5	4.5	4.3		3.0	3.5	3.0	3.2
Pakistan	3.6	3.5	3.5	4.5	3.8		4.0	4.5	4.0	4.2
Papua New Guinea	3.3	4.5	3.5	4.5	4.2		4.5	3.0	3.0	3.5
Rwanda	3.7	4.0	4.0	3.5	3.8		3.5	3.5	3.5	3.5
Samoa	3.9	4.0	3.5	4.0	3.8		4.5	4.0	3.5	4.0
São Tome and Principe	3.0	3.0	3.0	2.5	2.8		4.0	2.5	3.0	3.2
Senegal	3.7	4.5	4.0	4.0	4.2		4.0	3.5	4.0	3.8
Sierra Leone	3.1	4.0	3.5	3.5	3.7		3.5	3.0	2.5	3.0
Solomon Islands	2.7	3.5	3.0	2.5	3.0		3.0	3.0	2.5	2.8
Sri Lanka	3.5	2.5	3.0	3.5	3.0		3.5	4.0	4.0	3.8
St. Lucia	4.0	4.5	3.5	4.0	4.0		4.0	4.0	4.5	4.2
St. Vincent & Grenadines	3.8	4.0	3.5	3.5	3.7		4.0	4.0	4.5	4.2
Sudan	2.5	3.5	3.0	1.5	2.7		2.5	2.5	3.0	2.7
Tajikistan	3.2	4.0	4.0	3.0	3.7		4.0	3.0	3.5	3.5
Tanzania	3.9	4.5	4.5	4.0	4.3		4.0	3.5	3.5	3.7
Timor-Leste	2.7	2.5	3.0	3.5	3.0		3.5	2.5	1.5	2.5
Togo	2.5	2.5	2.5	1.5	2.2		4.0	2.5	3.0	3.2
Tonga	3.0	3.0	2.5	3.0	2.8		3.5	3.0	3.0	3.2
Uganda	3.9	4.5	4.5	4.5	4.5		4.0	3.5	4.0	3.8
Uzbekistan	3.1	3.5	3.5	4.0	3.7		2.5	2.5	3.0	2.7
Vanuatu	3.3	4.0	3.0	4.0	3.7		3.5	3.0	3.5	3.3
Vietnam	3.8	4.5	4.5	4.0	4.3		3.5	3.0	3.5	3.3
Yemen, Rep.	3.2	3.5	3.0	4.0	3.5		4.5	2.5	3.5	3.5
Zambia	3.5	4.0	3.5	3.5	3.7		4.0	3.5	3.5	3.7
Zimbabwe	1.7	1.0	1.0	1.0	1.0		2.0	2.5	1.5	2.0

All criteria within each cluster receive equal weight, and each cluster has a 25 percent weight in the overall score, which is obtained by averaging the average scores of the four clusters. For each of the 16 criteria countries are rated on a scale of 1 (low) to 6 (high). The scores depend on the level of performance in a given year assessed against the criteria, rather than on changes in performance compared with the previous year. All 16 CPIA criteria contain a detailed description of each rating level. In assessing country performance, World Bank staff evaluate the country's performance on each of the criteria and assign a rating. The ratings reflect a variety of indicators, observations, and judgments based on country knowledge and on relevant publicly available indicators. In interpreting the assessment scores, it should be noted that the criteria are designed in a developmentally neutral manner. Accordingly, higher scores can be attained by a country that, given its stage of development, has a policy and institutional framework that more strongly fosters growth and poverty reduction.

The country teams that prepare the ratings are very familiar with the country, and their assessments are based on country diagnostic studies prepared by the World Bank or other development organizations and on their own professional judgment. An early consultation is conducted with country authorities to make sure that the assessments are informed by up-to-date information. To ensure that scores are consistent across countries, the process involves two key phases. In the benchmarking phase a small representative sample of countries drawn from all regions is rated. Country teams prepare proposals that are reviewed first at the regional level and then in a Bankwide review process. A similar process is followed to assess the performance of the remaining countries, using the benchmark countries' scores as guideposts. The final ratings are determined following a Bankwide review. The overall numerical IRAI score and the separate criteria scores were first publicly disclosed in June 2006.

See IDA's website at www.worldbank.org/ida for more information.

| | Policies for social inclusion and equity 1–6 (low to high) | | | | | | Public sector management and institutions 1–6 (low to high) | | | | | |
| | Gender equality | Equity of public resource use | Building human resources | Social protection and labor | Policies and institutions for environmental sustainability | Average | Property rights and rule-based governance | Quality of budgetary and financial manage-ment | Efficiency of revenue mobilization | Quality of public administration | Transparency, accountability, and corruption in the public sector | Average |
	2007	2007	2007	2007	2007	2007	2007	2007	2007	2007	2007	2007
Afghanistan	2.0	2.5	3.0	2.0	2.0	2.3	1.5	3.0	2.5	2.0	2.0	2.2
Angola	3.0	2.5	2.5	2.5	3.0	2.7	2.0	2.5	2.5	2.5	2.5	2.4
Armenia	4.5	4.5	4.0	4.5	3.5	4.2	3.5	4.0	3.5	4.0	3.5	3.7
Azerbaijan	4.0	4.0	3.5	4.0	3.0	3.7	3.0	4.0	3.5	3.0	2.5	3.2
Bangladesh	4.0	3.5	4.0	3.5	3.0	3.6	3.0	3.0	3.0	3.0	3.0	3.0
Benin	3.5	3.0	3.5	3.0	3.5	3.3	3.0	3.5	3.5	3.0	3.5	3.3
Bhutan	4.0	4.0	4.5	3.5	4.5	4.1	3.5	3.5	4.0	4.0	4.0	3.8
Bolivia	4.0	4.0	4.0	3.5	3.5	3.8	2.5	3.5	4.0	3.0	3.5	3.3
Bosnia and Herzegovina	4.5	3.0	3.5	3.5	3.5	3.6	3.0	3.5	4.0	3.0	3.0	3.3
Burkina Faso	3.5	4.0	3.5	3.5	3.5	3.6	3.5	4.0	3.5	3.5	3.0	3.5
Burundi	4.0	3.5	3.0	3.0	3.0	3.3	2.5	3.0	3.0	2.5	2.0	2.6
Cambodia	4.0	3.0	3.5	3.0	3.0	3.3	2.5	3.0	3.0	2.5	2.5	2.7
Cameroon	3.0	3.0	3.5	3.0	3.0	3.1	2.5	3.5	3.5	3.0	2.5	3.0
Cape Verde	4.5	4.5	4.5	4.5	3.5	4.3	4.0	4.0	3.5	4.0	4.5	4.0
Central African Republic	2.5	2.0	2.0	2.0	2.5	2.2	2.0	2.0	2.5	2.5	2.5	2.3
Chad	2.5	3.0	2.5	2.5	2.5	2.6	2.0	2.0	2.5	2.5	2.0	2.2
Comoros	3.0	3.0	3.0	2.5	2.0	2.7	2.5	1.5	2.5	2.0	2.5	2.2
Congo, Dem. Rep.	3.0	3.0	3.0	3.0	2.5	2.9	2.0	2.5	2.5	2.5	2.0	2.3
Congo, Rep.	3.0	2.5	3.0	2.5	2.5	2.7	2.5	2.5	3.0	2.5	2.5	2.6
Côte d'Ivoire	2.5	1.5	2.5	2.5	2.5	2.3	2.0	2.0	4.0	2.0	2.0	2.4
Djibouti	2.5	3.0	3.5	3.0	3.0	3.0	2.5	3.0	3.5	2.5	2.5	2.8
Dominica	3.5	3.5	4.0	3.5	3.5	3.6	4.0	3.5	4.0	3.5	4.0	3.8
Eritrea	3.5	3.0	3.5	3.0	2.0	3.0	2.5	2.5	3.5	3.0	2.0	2.7
Ethiopia	3.0	4.5	4.0	3.5	3.5	3.7	3.0	4.0	4.0	3.0	2.5	3.3
Gambia, The	3.5	3.0	3.5	2.5	3.0	3.1	3.5	3.0	3.5	3.0	2.0	3.0
Georgia	4.5	4.5	4.0	4.0	3.0	4.0	3.5	4.0	4.5	3.5	3.0	3.7
Ghana	4.0	4.0	4.5	3.5	3.5	3.9	3.5	4.0	4.5	3.5	4.0	3.9
Grenada	5.0	3.5	4.0	3.5	4.0	4.0	3.5	4.0	3.5	3.5	4.0	3.7
Guinea	3.5	3.0	3.0	3.0	2.5	3.0	2.0	3.0	3.0	3.0	2.5	2.7
Guinea-Bissau	2.5	3.0	2.5	2.5	2.5	2.6	2.5	2.5	3.0	2.5	2.5	2.6
Guyana	4.0	3.5	3.5	3.0	3.0	3.4	3.0	3.5	3.5	2.5	3.0	3.1
Haiti	3.0	3.0	2.5	2.5	2.5	2.7	2.0	3.0	2.5	2.5	2.0	2.4
Honduras	4.0	4.0	4.0	3.5	3.0	3.7	3.5	4.0	4.0	3.0	3.0	3.5
India	3.5	4.0	4.0	3.5	3.5	3.7	3.5	4.0	4.0	3.5	3.5	3.7
Kenya	3.0	3.0	3.5	3.0	3.5	3.2	2.5	3.5	4.0	3.5	3.0	3.3
Kiribati	3.0	3.0	2.5	3.0	3.0	2.9	3.5	3.0	3.0	3.0	3.5	3.2
Kyrgyz Republic	4.5	3.5	3.5	3.5	3.0	3.6	2.5	3.0	3.5	3.0	2.5	2.9
Lao PDR	3.5	3.5	3.0	2.5	3.5	3.2	3.0	3.0	2.5	3.0	2.0	2.7

Definitions

• **IDA Resource Allocation Index** is obtained by calculating the average score for each cluster and then by averaging those scores. For each of 16 criteria countries are rated on a scale of 1 (low) to 6 (high) • **Economic management** cluster: **Macroeconomic management** assesses the monetary, exchange rate, and aggregate demand policy framework. • **Fiscal policy** assesses the short- and medium-term sustainability of fiscal policy (taking into account monetary and exchange rate policy and the sustainability of the public debt) and its impact on growth. • **Debt policy** assesses whether the debt management strategy is conducive to minimizing budgetary risks and ensuring long-term debt

sustainability. • **Structural policies** cluster: **Trade** assesses how the policy framework fosters trade in goods. • **Financial sector** assesses the structure of the financial sector and the policies and regulations that affect it. • **Business regulatory environment** assesses the extent to which the legal, regulatory, and policy environments help or hinder private businesses in investing, creating jobs, and becoming more productive. • **Policies for social inclusion and equity** cluster: **Gender equality** assesses the extent to which the country has installed institutions and programs to enforce laws and policies that promote equal access for men and women in education, health, the economy, and protection under law.

• **Equity of public resource use** assesses the extent to which the pattern of public expenditures and revenue collection affects the poor and is consistent with national poverty reduction priorities. • **Building human resources** assesses the national policies and public and private sector service delivery that affect the access to and quality of health and education services, including prevention and treatment of HIV/AIDS, tuberculosis, and malaria. • **Social protection and labor** assess government policies in social protection and labor market regulations that reduce the risk of becoming poor, assist those who are poor to better manage further risks, and ensure a minimal level of welfare to all people. • **Policies**

Public policies and institutions | 5.8

	Policies for social inclusion and equity 1–6 (low to high)						Public sector management and institutions 1–6 (low to high)					
	Gender equality 2007	Equity of public resource use 2007	Building human resources 2007	Social protection and labor 2007	Policies and institutions for environmental sustainability 2007	Average 2007	Property rights and rule-based governance 2007	Quality of budgetary and financial management 2007	Efficiency of revenue mobilization 2007	Quality of public administration 2007	Transparency, accountability, and corruption in the public sector 2007	Average 2007
Lesotho	4.0	3.0	3.5	3.0	3.5	3.4	3.5	3.0	4.0	3.0	3.5	3.4
Madagascar	3.5	4.0	3.5	3.5	4.0	3.7	3.5	3.5	3.5	3.5	3.5	3.5
Malawi	3.5	3.5	3.0	3.5	3.5	3.4	3.5	3.0	4.0	3.5	3.0	3.4
Maldives	4.0	4.0	4.0	3.5	4.0	3.9	4.0	3.0	4.0	4.0	2.5	3.5
Mali	3.5	3.5	3.5	3.5	3.5	3.5	3.5	3.5	4.0	3.0	3.5	3.5
Mauritania	4.0	3.5	3.5	3.0	3.5	3.5	3.0	2.5	3.5	3.0	3.0	3.0
Moldova	5.0	3.5	4.0	3.5	3.5	3.9	3.5	4.0	3.5	3.0	3.0	3.4
Mongolia	3.5	3.5	3.5	3.5	3.0	3.4	3.0	4.0	3.5	3.5	3.0	3.4
Mozambique	3.5	3.5	3.5	3.0	3.0	3.3	3.0	3.5	4.0	3.0	3.0	3.3
Nepal	3.5	3.5	4.0	3.0	3.0	3.4	3.0	3.5	3.5	3.0	3.0	3.2
Nicaragua	3.5	4.0	3.5	3.5	3.5	3.6	3.0	4.0	4.0	3.0	3.0	3.4
Niger	2.5	3.5	3.0	3.0	3.0	3.0	3.0	3.5	3.5	3.0	3.0	3.2
Nigeria	3.0	3.5	3.0	3.5	3.0	3.2	2.5	3.0	3.0	3.0	3.0	2.9
Pakistan	2.0	3.5	3.5	3.0	3.5	3.1	3.0	3.5	3.5	3.5	2.5	3.2
Papua New Guinea	2.5	3.5	2.5	3.0	2.0	2.7	2.0	3.5	3.5	2.5	3.0	2.9
Rwanda	3.5	4.5	4.5	3.5	3.0	3.8	3.0	4.0	3.5	3.5	3.5	3.5
Samoa	3.5	4.0	4.0	3.5	4.0	3.8	4.0	3.5	4.0	4.0	4.0	3.9
São Tome and Principe	3.0	3.0	3.0	2.5	2.5	2.8	2.5	3.0	3.5	3.0	3.5	3.1
Senegal	3.5	3.5	3.5	3.0	3.5	3.4	3.5	3.5	4.0	3.5	3.0	3.5
Sierra Leone	3.0	3.0	3.5	3.0	2.0	2.9	2.5	3.5	2.5	3.0	2.5	2.8
Solomon Islands	3.0	2.5	3.0	2.5	2.0	2.6	2.5	2.5	2.5	2.0	3.0	2.5
Sri Lanka	4.0	3.5	4.0	3.5	3.5	3.7	3.0	4.0	3.5	3.0	3.0	3.3
St. Lucia	3.5	4.0	4.0	4.0	3.5	3.8	4.0	3.5	4.0	3.5	4.5	3.9
St. Vincent & Grenadines	4.0	3.5	4.0	3.5	3.5	3.7	4.0	3.5	4.0	3.5	4.0	3.8
Sudan	2.0	2.5	2.5	2.5	2.5	2.4	2.0	2.0	3.0	2.5	2.0	2.3
Tajikistan	3.5	3.5	3.0	3.5	2.5	3.2	2.5	3.0	3.0	2.5	2.0	2.6
Tanzania	4.0	4.0	4.0	3.5	3.5	3.8	3.5	4.0	4.0	3.5	3.5	3.7
Timor-Leste	3.5	3.0	2.5	2.0	2.5	2.7	1.5	3.0	3.0	2.5	3.0	2.6
Togo	3.0	2.0	3.0	2.5	2.5	2.6	2.5	2.0	2.5	2.0	2.0	2.2
Tonga	2.5	3.5	4.0	3.0	3.0	3.2	3.5	2.5	3.0	3.0	2.5	2.9
Uganda	3.5	4.5	4.0	3.5	4.0	3.9	3.5	4.0	3.0	3.0	3.0	3.3
Uzbekistan	4.0	3.5	4.0	3.5	3.5	3.7	2.5	3.0	3.0	2.5	1.5	2.5
Vanuatu	3.5	3.5	2.5	2.0	3.0	2.9	3.0	3.5	3.5	2.5	3.0	3.1
Vietnam	4.5	4.5	4.0	3.5	3.5	4.0	3.5	4.0	3.5	3.5	3.0	3.5
Yemen, Rep.	2.0	3.5	3.0	3.5	3.0	3.0	2.5	3.0	3.0	3.0	3.0	2.9
Zambia	3.5	3.5	3.5	3.0	3.5	3.4	3.0	3.5	3.5	3.0	3.0	3.2
Zimbabwe	2.5	1.5	1.5	1.0	2.5	1.8	1.0	2.0	3.5	1.5	1.0	1.8

and institutions for environmental sustainability assess the extent to which environmental policies foster the protection and sustainable use of natural resources and the management of pollution. • **Public sector management and institutions** cluster: **Property rights and rule-based governance** assess the extent to which private economic activity is facilitated by an effective legal system and rule-based governance structure in which property and contract rights are reliably respected and enforced. • **Quality of budgetary and financial management** assesses the extent to which there is a comprehensive and credible budget linked to policy priorities, effective financial management systems, and timely and

accurate accounting and fiscal reporting, including timely and audited public accounts. • **Efficiency of revenue mobilization** assesses the overall pattern of revenue mobilization—not only the de facto tax structure, but also revenue from all sources as actually collected. • **Quality of public administration** assesses the extent to which civilian central government staff is structured to design and implement government policy and deliver services effectively. • **Transparency, accountability, and corruption in the public sector** assess the extent to which the executive can be held accountable for its use of funds and for the results of its actions by the electorate, the legislature, and the judiciary and the extent

to which public employees within the executive are required to account for administrative decisions, use of resources, and results obtained. The three main dimensions assessed are the accountability of the executive to oversight institutions and of public employees for their performance, access of civil society to information on public affairs, and state capture by narrow vested interests.

Data sources

Data on public policies and institutions are from the World Bank Group's CPIA database available at www.worldbank.org/ida.

	Roads				Railways			Ports	Air		
	Total road network km	Paved roads %	Passengers carried million passenger-km	Goods hauled million ton-km	Rail lines total route-km	Passengers carried million passenger-km	Goods hauled million ton-km	Port container traffic thousand TEU	Registered carrier departures worldwide thousands	Passengers carried thousands	Air freight million ton-km
	2000–06[a]	2000–06[a]	2000–06[a]	2000–06[a]	2000–07[a]	2000–07[a]	2000–07[a]	2007	2007	2007	2007
Afghanistan	42,150	29.3	..	..	..	..	..	..	..	..	..
Albania	18,000	39.0	197	2,200	423	51	53	..	4	213	0
Algeria	108,302	70.2	..	..	3,572	821	1,429	..	44	2,813	17
Angola	51,429	10.4	166,045	4,709	..	..	..	..	5	277	73
Argentina	231,374	30.0	..	..	35,753	..	12,871	1,874	79	7,037	133
Armenia	7,504	89.0	2,344	432	711	27	678	..	6	606	7
Australia	812,972	..	290,280	168,630	9,639	1,309	46,036	6,229	354	48,729	2,348
Austria	107,262	100.0	69,000	26,411	5,818	9,051	18,996	..	151	9,141	454
Azerbaijan	59,141	49.4	10,892	7,536	2,122	1,109	10,374	..	13	1,441	12
Bangladesh	239,226	9.5	..	..	2,855	4,164	817	978	11	1,243	89
Belarus	94,797	88.6	9,343	15,779	5,494	9,366	47,933	..	6	344	1
Belgium	152,256	78.2	130,868	51,572	3,374	9,932	8,149	10,258	158	3,641	740
Benin	19,000	9.5	..	..	..	..	..	..	..	..	..
Bolivia	62,479	7.0	..	..	..	..	..	..	24	1,745	9
Bosnia and Herzegovina	21,846	52.3	..	300	1,103	88	1,138	..	..	..	..
Botswana	25,798	32.6	..	..	..	..	..	..	7	228	0
Brazil	1,751,868	5.5	..	..	29,487	..	232,297	6,454	650	45,287	1,478
Bulgaria	40,231	98.4	13,688	11,843	4,027	2,424	5,242	..	12	855	3
Burkina Faso	92,495	4.2	..	..	..	..	..	..	2	78	0
Burundi	12,322	10.4	..	..	..	..	..	..	..	..	..
Cambodia	38,257	6.3	201	3	650	45	92	..	4	308	2
Cameroon	51,346	8.4	..	..	974	370	1,055	..	12	453	26
Canada	1,408,900	39.9	493,814	184,774	57,042	2,858	353,227	4,605	1,189	52,104	1,430
Central African Republic	24,307	..	..	..	..	..	..	..	..	..	..
Chad	40,000	0.8	..	..	..	..	..	..	..	..	..
Chile	79,604	20.2	..	..	6,008	732	3,957	2,681	101	7,191	1,295
China	3,456,999	70.7	1,013,085	975,420	63,637	689,616	2,211,246	104,559	1,754	183,613	11,190
Hong Kong, China	1,983	100.0	..	..	..	..	..	23,998	130	21,796	8,326
Colombia	164,278	..	157	39,726	2,137	..	7,751	1,897	186	11,631	1,070
Congo, Dem. Rep.	153,497	1.8	..	..	3,641	79	331	..	..	..	..
Congo, Rep.	17,289	5.0	..	..	795	211	234	..	..	..	..
Costa Rica	35,983	25.2	..	..	..	..	..	977	37	1,017	10
Côte d'Ivoire	80,000	8.1	..	..	639	10	675	710	..	..	..
Croatia	28,788	89.0	3,537	10,502	2,722	1,611	3,574	175	22	2,288	3
Cuba	60,856	49.0	5,121	2,133	..	..	..	..	12	857	31
Czech Republic	128,512	100.0	90,055	46,600	9,491	6,855	16,972	..	76	4,870	33
Denmark	72,361	100.0	70,635	11,058	2,133	5,724	2,030	775	14	582	1
Dominican Republic	12,600	49.4	..	..	..	..	..	884	..	..	..
Ecuador	43,670	14.8	11,410	5,453	..	..	..	671	45	2,631	6
Egypt, Arab Rep.	92,370	81.0	..	..	5,195	40,837	3,917	5,311	51	5,829	207
El Salvador	10,029	19.8	..	..	..	..	..	..	22	2,537	22
Eritrea	4,010	21.8	..	..	..	..	..	..	..	..	..
Estonia	57,016	22.7	3,190	7,641	962	273	8,153	..	9	651	1
Ethiopia	39,477	12.7	219,113	2,456	..	..	..	..	38	2,290	160
Finland	78,941	65.3	70,900	26,400	5,899	3,778	10,434	1,564	119	8,289	490
France	951,500	100.0	724,000	197,000	29,488	83,299	40,635	4,928	825	61,551	6,425
Gabon	9,170	10.2	..	..	810	76	2,202	..	9	535	70
Gambia, The	3,742	19.3	16	..	..	..	..	..	..	..	..
Georgia	20,329	38.6	5,200	570	1,513	809	7,379	..	5	272	3
Germany	644,480	100.0	1,062,700	251,372	33,897	74,740	91,013	16,713	1,127	106,102	8,529
Ghana	57,614	14.9	..	..	977	85	242	..	..	..	..
Greece	117,533	91.8	..	18,360	2,551	1,954	835	1,820	138	10,206	72
Guatemala	14,095	34.5	..	..	..	..	..	853	..	..	..
Guinea	44,348	9.8	..	..	..	..	..	..	..	..	..
Guinea-Bissau	3,455	27.9	..	..	..	..	..	..	..	..	..
Haiti	4,160	24.3	..	..	..	..	..	..	..	..	..

	Roads				Railways			Ports	Air		
	Total road network km 2000–06[a]	Paved roads % 2000–06[a]	Passengers carried million passenger-km 2000–06[a]	Goods hauled million ton-km 2000–06[a]	Rail lines total route-km 2000–07[a]	Passengers carried million passenger-km 2000–07[a]	Goods hauled million ton-km 2000–07[a]	Port container traffic thousand TEU 2007	Registered carrier departures worldwide thousands 2007	Passengers carried thousands 2007	Air freight million ton-km 2007
Honduras	13,600	20.4	..	..	..	..	..	553	..	..	..
Hungary	159,600	43.9	13,300	9,090	7,730	6,953	8,537	..	46	2,592	20
India	3,316,452	47.4	..	..	63,327	694,764	480,993	7,372	569	51,897	968
Indonesia	391,009	55.4	..	..	..	25,535	4,698	4,481	358	30,406	485
Iran, Islamic Rep.	172,927	72.8	..	..	7,265	12,549	20,542	1,723	138	13,916	95
Iraq	45,550	84.3	..	..	..	..	..	..	..	..	..
Ireland	96,602	100.0	..	15,900	1,919	2,007	129	1,175	350	50,738	131
Israel	17,719	100.0	..	..	958	1,831	1,175	1,957	47	4,663	1,133
Italy	487,700	100.0	97,560	192,700	16,668	47,113	22,340	10,435	432	37,831	1,550
Jamaica	22,056	73.3	..	..	..	..	..	2,017	21	1,527	15
Japan	1,196,999	79.3	947,562	327,632	20,050	252,579	23,145	19,008	657	99,842	8,435
Jordan	7,694	100.0	..	..	293	..	517	..	29	2,246	277
Kazakhstan	91,563	91.4	100,865	53,816	14,205	13,613	191,189	..	19	1,295	17
Kenya	63,265	14.1	..	22	1,917	226	1,399	..	32	2,857	298
Korea, Dem. Rep.	25,554	2.8	..	..	..	..	..	..	2	105	2
Korea, Rep.	102,062	88.6	97,854	12,545	3,399	31,596	10,927	16,640	243	36,655	9,040
Kuwait	5,749	85.0	..	..	..	..	..	750	21	2,628	239
Kyrgyz Republic	18,500	91.1	5,874	1,336	..	..	..	..	5	275	1
Lao PDR	29,811	13.4	..	..	..	..	..	..	10	328	3
Latvia	69,675	100.0	2,780	2,729	2,269	983	16,735	..	29	1,410	13
Lebanon	6,970	..	..	..	..	..	..	948	11	969	74
Lesotho	5,940	18.3	..	..	..	..	..	..	..	..	..
Liberia	10,600	6.2	..	..	..	..	..	..	..	..	..
Libya	83,200	57.2	..	..	..	..	..	..	13	1,204	0
Lithuania	79,987	28.3	43,167	18,134	1,766	409	14,373	..	11	424	1
Macedonia, FYR	13,182	..	842	4,100	947	109	961	..	2	209	0
Madagascar	49,827	11.6	..	..	..	..	..	..	37	616	24
Malawi	15,451	45.0	..	..	710	26	38	..	6	155	1
Malaysia	93,109	79.8	..	..	1,667	2,193	1,355	14,873	185	21,326	2,662
Mali	18,709	18.0	..	..	733	196	189	..	..	..	..
Mauritania	11,066	26.8	..	..	..	..	..	..	2	155	0
Mauritius	2,021	100.0	..	..	..	..	..	..	12	1,278	203
Mexico	356,945	50.0	436,999	209,392	26,662	84	75,600	3,071	310	20,953	482
Moldova	12,838	85.5	1,640	1,577	..	..	..	..	4	274	1
Mongolia	49,250	3.5	557	242	1,810	1,289	9,219	..	6	381	5
Morocco	57,625	61.9	..	1,256	1,907	3,659	5,837	..	69	4,624	45
Mozambique	30,400	18.7	..	..	..	..	..	..	11	443	6
Myanmar	27,000	11.9	..	..	..	..	..	..	29	1,663	3
Namibia	42,237	12.8	47	591	..	..	..	..	7	431	0
Nepal	17,280	56.9	..	..	..	..	..	..	7	528	8
Netherlands	126,100	90.0	..	77,100	2,776	15,546	4,331	11,287	260	28,857	5,006
New Zealand	93,576	65.6	..	..	..	..	4,078	2,029	219	12,546	868
Nicaragua	18,669	11.4	..	..	..	..	..	..	..	..	..
Niger	18,550	20.5	..	..	..	..	..	..	..	..	..
Nigeria	193,200	15.0	..	..	3,528	174	77	..	17	1,363	10
Norway	92,864	77.5	58,247	14,966	..	..	..	..	..	..	..
Oman	34,965	27.7	..	..	..	..	..	2,877	..	..	..
Pakistan	260,420	65.4	263,788	129,249	7,791	25,621	5,907	1,936	51	5,439	314
Panama	11,643	34.6	..	..	..	..	..	4,070	33	2,029	36
Papua New Guinea	19,600	3.5	..	..	..	..	..	..	22	919	23
Paraguay	29,500	50.8	..	..	..	..	..	..	10	459	0
Peru	78,986	13.9	..	..	..	119	1,159	1,178	62	5,273	162
Philippines	200,037	9.9	..	..	491	144	1	3,835	65	8,818	286
Poland	423,997	69.7	247,388	136,490	19,419	17,081	43,548	..	89	4,270	83
Portugal	82,900	86.0	..	23,187	2,838	3,610	2,585	1,138	138	10,320	323
Puerto Rico	25,645	95.0	..	10	..	..	..	1,695	..	..	..

	Roads				Railways			Ports	Air		
	Total road network km 2000–06[a]	Paved roads % 2000–06[a]	Passengers carried million passenger-km 2000–06[a]	Goods hauled million ton-km 2000–06[a]	Rail lines total route-km 2000–07[a]	Passengers carried million passenger-km 2000–07[a]	Goods hauled million ton-km 2000–07[a]	Port container traffic thousand TEU 2007	Registered carrier departures worldwide thousands 2007	Passengers carried thousands 2007	Air freight million ton-km 2007
Romania	198,817	30.2	7,985	51,531	10,646	7,417	13,471	1,411	51	3,004	6
Russian Federation	933,000	80.9	..	25,200	84,158	173,411	2,090,337	2,657	468	33,188	1,224
Rwanda	14,008	19.0	..	..	..	..	..	..	..	..	..
Saudi Arabia	221,372	21.5	..	..	1,412	345	1,630	4,209	151	17,141	1,230
Senegal	13,576	29.3	..	..	906	88	384	..	0	539	0
Serbia	38,799	62.7	3,865	452	3,819	762	4,234	..	20	1,042	4
Sierra Leone	11,300	8.0	..	..	..	..	..	..	0	19	10
Singapore	3,262	100.0	..	..	..	..	..	27,932	85	19,566	7,981
Slovak Republic	43,761	87.0	32,214	22,114	3,629	2,148	9,331	..	24	2,679	45
Slovenia	38,562	100.0	850	12,112	1,228	812	3,603	..	20	861	2
Somalia	22,100	11.8	..	..	..	..	..	..	..	..	..
South Africa	364,131	17.3	..	434	24,487	14,856	108,513	3,734	153	12,870	939
Spain	666,292	99.0	397,117	132,868	14,832	21,225	11,064	11,148	658	60,665	1,204
Sri Lanka	97,286	81.0	21,067	..	1,200	4,682	135	3,382	21	3,101	325
Sudan	11,900	36.3	..	..	5,478	40	766	..	9	598	46
Swaziland	3,594	30.0	..	..	..	..	..	..	..	..	..
Sweden	697,794	58.2	106,583	40,123	9,821	6,467	11,500	1,439	..	..	..
Switzerland	71,298	100.0	93,480	16,337	3,619	15,771	16,736	..	139	12,298	1,105
Syrian Arab Republic	38,923	100.0	589	..	2,043	744	2,552	..	19	1,371	18
Tajikistan	27,767	..	414	25,604	..	..	14,529	..	8	581	2
Tanzania	78,891	8.6	..	..	4,460[b]	433[b]	728[b]	..	5	251	1
Thailand	180,053	98.5	..	..	4,044	9,195	4,037	6,200	130	21,192	2,455
Timor-Leste	..	..	..	..	..	..	..	..	..	..	..
Togo	7,520	31.6	..	..	..	..	..	..	..	..	..
Trinidad and Tobago	8,320	51.1	..	..	..	..	..	..	15	1,086	47
Tunisia	19,232	65.8	..	16,611	2,218	1,407	2,197	..	22	2,055	19
Turkey	426,951	..	187,592	177,399	8,697	5,553	9,680	4,488	197	22,895	466
Turkmenistan	24,000	81.2	..	..	..	..	..	..	16	1,851	11
Uganda	70,746	23.0	..	..	259	..	218	..	0	55	34
Ukraine	169,323	97.4	51,820	23,895	21,891	53,230	240,810	979	30	1,736	18
United Arab Emirates	4,030	100.0	..	..	..	..	..	13,160	..	..	..
United Kingdom	398,351	100.0	736,000	163,000	16,208	48,511	22,110	9,383	1,045	101,623	6,154
United States	6,544,257	65.3	7,814,575	2,116,532	191,771	..	2,820,061[c]	41,625	9,816[d]	744,302[d]	40,618[d]
Uruguay	77,732	10.0	..	..	3,003	12	331	..	9	569	4
Uzbekistan	81,600	87.3	..	1,200	4,005	2,339	19,281	..	22	1,940	66
Venezuela, RB	96,155	33.6	..	..	336	..	81	1,332	141	5,495	2
Vietnam	222,179	..	..	..	3,147	4,659	3,881	3,937	60	7,194	258
West Bank and Gaza	5,147	100.0	..	..	..	..	..	..	..	..	..
Yemen, Rep.	71,300	8.7	..	..	..	..	..	..	14	1,073	41
Zambia	91,440	22.0	..	..	1,273	183	..	..	6	62	0
Zimbabwe	97,267	19.0	..	..	..	..	..	..	7	255	8
World	**35.9 m**	**.. m**	**.. m**	**.. s**	**.. m**	**.. m**	**465,594 s**	**24,654 s**	**2,058,936 s**	**124,628 s**
Low income	12.1	..	..	..	..	..	..	422	30,709	1,320
Middle income	47.7	..	..	..	1,295	6,608	193,415	6,368	554,986	26,769
Lower middle income	39.0	..	..	..	1,025	3,046	142,654	3,711	359,286	17,503
Upper middle income	41.8	..	..	..	2,309	13,471	50,761	2,658	195,701	9,266
Low & middle income	23.1	..	..	..	..	..	200,266	6,791	585,695	28,088
East Asia & Pacific	11.4	..	..	..	2,893	1,902	137,886	2,699	277,535	17,475
Europe & Central Asia	..	10,062	15,477	187,104	1,975	13,471	..	970	76,387	1,916
Latin America & Carib.	22.0	..	..	..	..	..	27,286	1,684	112,436	4,726
Middle East & N. Africa	81.0	..	..	..	2,533	2,552	..	378	33,077	699
South Asia	56.9	..	..	..	25,621	5,907	13,668	638	59,108	1,378
Sub-Saharan Africa	11.9	..	..	..	..	..	..	421	27,153	1,895
High income	87.0	..	46,600	..	6,467	11,064	265,328	17,864	1,473,241	96,540
Euro area	100.0	97,840	39,474	124,917	9,051	9,883	72,409	3,871	335,641	24,098

a. Data are for the latest year available in the period shown. b. Includes Tazara railway. c. Refers to class 1 railways only. d. Covers only carriers designated by the U.S. Department of Transportation as major and national air carriers.

Transport infrastructure—highways, railways, ports and waterways, and airports and air traffic control systems—and the services that flow from it are crucial to the activities of households, producers, and governments. Because performance indicators vary widely by transport mode and focus (whether physical infrastructure or the services flowing from that infrastructure), highly specialized and carefully specified indicators are required. The table provides selected indicators of the size, extent, and productivity of roads, railways, and air transport systems and of the volume of traffic in these modes as well as in ports.

Data for transport sectors are not always internationally comparable. Unlike for demographic statistics, national income accounts, and international trade data, the collection of infrastructure data has not been "internationalized." But data on roads are collected by the International Road Federation (IRF), and data on air transport by the International Civil Aviation Organization (ICAO).

National road associations are the primary source of IRF data. In countries where a national road association is lacking or does not respond, other agencies are contacted, such as road directorates, ministries of transport or public works, or central statistical offices. As a result, definitions and data collection methods and quality differ, and the compiled data are of uneven quality. Moreover, the quality of transport service (reliability, transit time, and condition of goods delivered) is rarely measured, though it may be as important as quantity in assessing an economy's transport system.

Unlike the road sector, where numerous qualified motor vehicle operators can operate anywhere on the road network, railways are a restricted transport system with vehicles confined to a fixed guideway. Considering the cost and service characteristics, railways generally are best suited to carry—and can effectively compete for—bulk commodities and containerized freight for distances of 500–5,000 kilometers, and passengers for distances of 50–1,000 kilometers. Below these limits road transport tends to be more competitive, while above these limits air transport for passengers and freight and sea transport for freight tend to be more competitive. The railways indicators in the table focus on scale and output measures: total route-kilometers, passenger-kilometers, and goods (freight) hauled in ton-kilometers.

Measures of port container traffic, much of it commodities of medium to high value added, give some indication of economic growth in a country. But when traffic is merely transshipment, much of the economic benefit goes to the terminal operator and ancillary services for ships and containers rather than to the country more broadly. In transshipment centers empty containers may account for as much as 40 percent of traffic.

The air transport data represent the total (international and domestic) scheduled traffic carried by the air carriers registered in a country. Countries submit air transport data to ICAO on the basis of standard instructions and definitions issued by ICAO. In many cases, however, the data include estimates by ICAO for nonreporting carriers. Where possible, these estimates are based on previous submissions supplemented by information published by the air carriers, such as flight schedules.

The data cover the air traffic carried on scheduled services, but changes in air transport regulations in Europe have made it more difficult to classify traffic as scheduled or nonscheduled. Thus recent increases shown for some European countries may be due to changes in the classification of air traffic rather than actual growth. For countries with few air carriers or only one, the addition or discontinuation of a home-based air carrier may cause significant changes in air traffic.

• **Total road network** covers motorways, highways, main or national roads, secondary or regional roads, and all other roads in a country. • **Paved roads** are roads surfaced with crushed stone (macadam) and hydrocarbon binder or bituminized agents, with concrete, or with cobblestones. • **Passengers carried by road** are the number of passengers transported by road times kilometers traveled. • **Goods hauled by road** are the volume of goods transported by road vehicles, measured in millions of metric tons times kilometers traveled. • **Rail lines** are the length of railway route available for train service, irrespective of the number of parallel tracks. • **Passengers carried by railway** are the number of passengers transported by rail times kilometers traveled. • **Goods hauled by railway** are the volume of goods transported by railway, measured in metric tons times kilometers traveled. • **Port container traffic** measures the flow of containers from land to sea transport modes and vice versa in twenty-foot-equivalent units (TEUs), a standard-size container. Data cover coastal shipping as well as international journeys. Transshipment traffic is counted as two lifts at the intermediate port (once to off-load and again as an outbound lift) and includes empty units. • **Registered carrier departures worldwide** are domestic takeoffs and takeoffs abroad of air carriers registered in the country. • **Passengers carried by air** include both domestic and international passengers of air carriers registered in the country. • **Air freight** is the volume of freight, express, and diplomatic bags carried on each flight stage (operation of an aircraft from takeoff to its next landing), measured in metric tons times kilometers traveled.

Data on roads are from the IRF's *World Road Statistics,* supplemented by World Bank staff estimates. Data on railways are from a database maintained by the World Bank's Transport and Urban Development Department, Transport Division, based on data from the International Union of Railways. Data on port container traffic are from Containerisation International's *Containerisation International Yearbook.* Data on air transport are from the ICAO's *Civil Aviation Statistics of the World* and ICAO staff estimates.

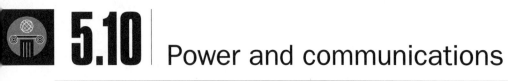
	Electric power		Telephones							
			Access and use			Quality	Affordability and efficiency			
								$ per month			
	Consumption per capita kWh	Transmission and distribution losses % of output	Fixed lines[a]	per 100 people Mobile cellular subscriptions[a]	International voice traffic[a] minutes per person	Population covered by mobile cellular network[a] %	Residential fixed-line tariff[a]	Mobile cellular prepaid tariff[a]	Telecom-munications revenue[a] % of GDP	Mobile cellular and fixed-line subscribers per employee[a]
	2006	2006	2007	2007	2007	2007	2008	2008	2007	2007
Afghanistan	..	..	..	..	..	..	..	..	5.1	861
Albania	961	52	9	72	125	97	4.3	22.7	6.0	710
Algeria	870	18	9	81	18	82	4.6	8.2	2.7	285
Angola	153	14	1	29	..	40	20.2	11.8	2.0	586
Argentina	2,620	13	24	102	3	94	4.8	12.5	3.1	1,929
Armenia	1,612	13	20	62	128	88	5.1	8.4	3.0	173
Australia	11,332	7	46	101	..	99	27.5	26.5	3.6	310
Austria	8,090	6	41	119	..	99	28.7	24.3	2.1	747
Azerbaijan	2,514	13	15	53	..	99	2.4	15.2	2.6	413
Bangladesh	146	6	1	22	6	90	1.3	1.3	..	..
Belarus	3,322	12	38	72	..	93	..	11.8	2.1	280
Belgium	8,684	5	44	101	..	100	36.4	21.9	3.0	690
Benin	69	..	1	21	11	80	7.5	15.5	1.1	1,539
Bolivia	485	14	7	34	80	46	22.7	5.9	6.8	376
Bosnia and Herzegovina	2,385	17	28	65	241	99	9.5	9.9	5.7	657
Botswana	1,419	15	7	61	93	99	16.9	8.3	3.0	1,074
Brazil	2,060	17	21	63	..	91	29.1	37.0	4.7	358
Bulgaria	4,311	11	30	129	31	100	9.2	18.6	5.9	522
Burkina Faso	..	..	1	11	11	61	10.3	16.9	4.0	440
Burundi	..	..	0	3	..	82	..	12.2	..	..
Cambodia	88	8	0	18	10	87	8.0	5.0	..	..
Cameroon	186	15	1	24	4	58	14.8	17.8	3.1	1,050
Canada	16,753	8	55	61	..	98	32.8	19.2	2.7	424
Central African Republic	..	..	0	3	..	19	10.6	12.6	1.1	293
Chad	..	..	0	9	..	24	..	13.2	..	..
Chile	3,207	12	21	84	40	100	27.0	13.7	..	1,311
China	2,041	6	28	42	9	97	3.7	3.6	2.9	1,310
Hong Kong, China	5,883	12	60	155	1,387	100	11.3	2.6	3.5	813
Colombia	968	19	18	77	106	83	7.6	9.6	3.9	..
Congo, Dem. Rep.	96	4	0	11	4	50	..	11.0	7.6	3,628
Congo, Rep.	155	64	0	34	..	53	..	..	..	..
Costa Rica	1,801	10	32	34	119	87	4.6	4.5	2.2	470
Côte d'Ivoire	182	19	1	37	..	59	22.8	14.8	5.5	1,442
Croatia	3,636	16	42	113	208	100	16.4	18.7	5.3	778
Cuba	1,231	16	9	2	31	77	13.2	22.7	..	58
Czech Republic	6,509	6	23	123	74	100	30.9	18.6	3.7	796
Denmark	6,864	3	52	114	307	114	28.5	5.8	2.6	512
Dominican Republic	1,309	11	9	57	..	90	14.4	9.1	0.5	..
Ecuador	759	45	14	76	90	84	1.1	9.0	4.1	512
Egypt, Arab Rep.	1,382	11	15	40	42	94	3.0	4.7	3.8	538
El Salvador	721	13	16	90	515	95	10.4	10.5	5.7	1,657
Eritrea	49	..	1	2	7	2	..	..	2.0	105
Estonia	5,883	11	37	148	..	100	13.7	13.6	4.8	707
Ethiopia	38	10	1	2	3	10	1.5	3.1	2.2	142
Finland	17,177	4	33	115	..	99	19.3	14.1	2.5	584
France	7,813	6	56	90	243	99	30.9	35.7	2.2	695
Gabon	1,083	18	2	88	74	79	..	14.9	2.0	..
Gambia, The	..	..	4	47	..	85	4.0	6.0	..	481
Georgia	1,549	14	13	59	..	96	7.3	8.5	6.5	355
Germany	7,174	5	65	118	..	100	28.8	10.1	2.6	703
Ghana	304	16	2	32	1	68	4.7	5.9	..	1,261
Greece	5,372	8	54	110	182	100	26.7	25.1	3.7	802
Guatemala	529	12	10	76	..	76	8.7	4.5	..	..
Guinea	..	..	1	21	..	80	3.4	3.5	..	..
Guinea-Bissau	..	..	0	17	..	65	..	21.9	..	..
Haiti	37	38	1	26	..	32	..	4.5	..	..

	Electric power		Telephones								
			Access and use			Quality	Affordability and efficiency				
								$ per month			
	Consumption per capita kWh	Transmission and distribution losses % of output	per 100 people		International voice traffic[a] minutes per person	Population covered by mobile cellular network[a] %	Residential fixed-line tariff[a]	Mobile cellular prepaid tariff[a]	Telecom-munications revenue[a] % of GDP	Mobile cellular and fixed-line subscribers per employee[a]
			Fixed lines[a]	Mobile cellular subscriptions[a]						
	2006	2006	2007	2007	2007	2007	2008	2008	2007	2007
Honduras	642	26	12	59	33	90	..	10.8	6.6	391
Hungary	3,882	11	32	110	120	99	30.2	16.1	4.2	1,009
India	503	25	4	21	..	61	3.5	1.6	2.0	..
Indonesia	530	11	8	36	..	90	4.5	5.3	..	..
Iran, Islamic Rep.	2,290	20	34	42	9	95	0.2	3.8	1.4	913
Iraq	..	6	..	..	..	..	..	..	..	941
Ireland	6,488	8	48	114	..	99	42.2	18.7	2.4	..
Israel	6,889	3	43	124	364	100	..	9.3	4.1	..
Italy	5,755	6	46	152	..	100	27.4	17.1	3.2	1,228
Jamaica	2,453	13	14	100	..	95	10.8	7.0	..	..
Japan	8,220	5	40	84	46	100	18.3	32.2	3.1	1,334
Jordan	1,904	13	10	83	32	99	8.3	4.5	8.3	1,026
Kazakhstan	4,293	9	21	80	47	81	..	11.4	2.9	308
Kenya	145	17	1	30	3	77	11.6	13.4	6.1	1,782
Korea, Dem. Rep.	797	16	5	0	..	0	..	..	..	..
Korea, Rep.	8,063	4	46	90	29	90	6.4	14.6	5.0	637
Kuwait	16,311	11	20	104	..	100	9.3	7.9	..	372
Kyrgyz Republic	2,015	24	9	41	30	24	..	6.4	4.8	311
Lao PDR	..	..	2	25	7	55	3.9	3.0	1.7	748
Latvia	2,876	17	28	97	67	99	11.9	7.3	4.0	697
Lebanon	2,141	16	17	31	279	100	10.9	22.2	8.0	..
Lesotho	..	..	3	23	18	55	12.5	12.6	0.6	1,111
Liberia	..	..	0	15	..	..	..	..	8.2	..
Libya	3,688	7	14	73	66	71	..	6.1	..	..
Lithuania	3,233	9	24	146	54	100	15.0	8.7	3.1	..
Macedonia, FYR	3,495	24	23	96	125	100	8.7	13.2	6.8	1,065
Madagascar	..	..	1	11	1	23	18.3	12.4	3.9	394
Malawi	..	..	1	8	..	93	3.3	12.0	3.3	..
Malaysia	3,388	1	16	88	..	93	5.1	5.9	..	571
Mali	..	..	1	21	2	22	9.9	10.0	6.0	1,490
Mauritania	..	..	1	42	5	51	12.9	9.9	7.5	1,272
Mauritius	..	..	29	74	125	99	5.5	4.4	3.6	492
Mexico	2,003	16	19	63	185	100	22.3	15.0	2.8	789
Moldova	1,516	40	28	49	149	98	3.1	8.9	10.1	294
Mongolia	1,298	12	6	30	5	41	..	5.4	3.9	190
Morocco	685	19	8	65	22	98	27.4	22.2	4.8	..
Mozambique	461	14	0	15	13	44	17.7	10.1	1.2	980
Myanmar	93	27	1	0	..	10	..	..	0.6	81
Namibia	1,546	22	7	38	..	95	14.5	11.5	..	435
Nepal	80	21	2	12	6	10	3.4	2.9	1.0	565
Netherlands	7,055	5	45	118	..	100	31.2	17.7	..	..
New Zealand	9,646	7	41	101	310	98	34.4	23.1	3.0	598
Nicaragua	426	22	4	38	65	70	5.1	13.8	..	..
Niger	..	..	0	6	..	45	13.6	13.8	2.2	328
Nigeria	116	27	1	27	..	60	10.3	12.1	3.1	..
Norway	24,296	8	42	110	193	..	37.6	9.7	1.4	..
Oman	4,456	16	10	96	37	96	32.6	5.5	2.7	858
Pakistan	480	22	3	39	10	90	3.6	1.9	2.7	50
Panama	1,506	17	15	90	66	81	9.1	5.1	3.5	229
Papua New Guinea	..	..	1	5	..	..	4.0	12.8	..	..
Paraguay	900	5	6	77	35	..	7.2	5.7	4.8	799
Peru	899	9	10	55	99	92	15.4	8.0	2.9	624
Philippines	578	12	4	59	..	99	14.2	5.7	4.4	..
Poland	3,585	9	27	109	..	99	28.0	12.5	3.7	566
Portugal	4,799	8	40	127	178	99	25.7	26.4	4.5	1,365
Puerto Rico	..	..	27	86	..	100	..	..	..	..

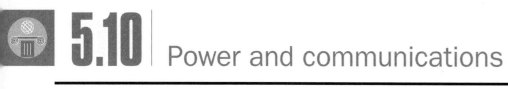

	Electric power		Telephones								
			Access and use			Quality	Affordability and efficiency				
	Consumption per capita kWh	Transmission and distribution losses % of output	per 100 people		International voice traffic[a] minutes per person	Population covered by mobile cellular network[a] %	$ per month		Telecom-munications revenue[a] % of GDP	Mobile cellular and fixed-line subscribers per employee[a]
			Fixed lines[a]	Mobile cellular subscriptions[a]			Residential fixed-line tariff[a]	Mobile cellular prepaid tariff[a]		
	2006	2006	2007	2007	2007	2007	2008	2008	2007	2007
Romania	2,402	10	20	106	41	98	12.2	11.9	3.5	617
Russian Federation	6,122	11	31	115	..	95	11.7	8.6	2.6	439
Rwanda	..	..	0	7	11	90	7.3	10.0	3.2	1,040
Saudi Arabia	7,080	7	17	117	216	98	9.2	8.8	3.0	933
Senegal	150	26	2	29	26	85	17.4	8.4	9.9	1,859
Serbia	4,040	16	41	115	144	92	4.9	4.9	5.0	787
Sierra Leone	..	..	..	13	..	70	..	70.9	..	..
Singapore	8,520	5	41	129	1,531	100	7.1	4.0	2.9	..
Slovak Republic	5,136	4	21	112	97	100	24.5	16.1	3.4	748
Slovenia	7,124	6	42	96	92	100	20.5	12.4	3.2	587
Somalia	..	..	1	7	..	..	..	..	..	..
South Africa	4,810	9	10	88	..	100	22.4	12.3	7.5	1,145
Spain	6,206	9	45	108	..	99	30.8	33.3	4.2	809
Sri Lanka	400	15	14	40	34	90	4.8	2.4	2.5	755
Sudan	95	15	1	21	7	60	4.4	4.8	3.7	1,557
Swaziland	..	..	4	33	..	90	4.8	12.1	12.7	..
Sweden	15,231	8	60	113	..	98	22.8	7.5	2.7	905
Switzerland	8,360	7	65	109	..	100	29.0	35.5	3.2	549
Syrian Arab Republic	1,466	24	17	31	79	96	1.2	9.1	3.0	409
Tajikistan	2,241	16	5	35	..	..	..	23.3	2.9	114
Tanzania	59	21	0	21	0	65	10.9	11.1	..	..
Thailand	2,080	8	11	124	14	38	5.8	3.9	4.0	2,808
Timor-Leste	..	..	0	7	18	69	..	..	8.0	645
Togo	97	46	2	18	5	85	13.1	18.0	7.4	1,059
Trinidad and Tobago	5,006	6	23	113	..	100	19.7	7.9	2.6	..
Tunisia	1,221	13	12	77	73	100	3.0	7.2	4.3	915
Turkey	2,053	14	25	84	30	98	..	12.7	2.5	1,782
Turkmenistan	2,123	14	9	7	..	14	..	17.2	0.7	72
Uganda	..	..	1	14	7	80	12.6	10.4	3.2	255
Ukraine	3,400	12	28	119	57	100	4.2	8.2	5.7	..
United Arab Emirates	14,567	7	32	177	..	100	5.0	4.1	2.7	852
United Kingdom	6,185	8	55	118	..	100	27.3	20.5	3.7	..
United States	13,564	6	54	85	..	100	17.2	15.3	3.1	389
Uruguay	2,042	30	29	90	127	100	13.0	13.8	3.7	661
Uzbekistan	1,694	9	7	22	12	75	..	1.8	2.5	117
Venezuela, RB	3,174	22	18	87	..	90	7.0	24.7	3.8	..
Vietnam	598	11	34	28	..	70	2.3	4.2	4.7	..
West Bank and Gaza	..	..	9	28	..	95	..	9.6	0.8	880
Yemen, Rep.	190	23	4	14	..	68	0.8	4.9	..	..
Zambia	730	6	1	22	..	50	27.7	12.3	2.5	..
Zimbabwe	900	7	3	9	21	75	..	3.4	..	381
World	**2,751 w**	**9 w**	**20 w**	**51 w**	**.. w**	**80 w**	**10.9 m**	**10.1 m**	**3.2 w**	**664 m**
Low income	309	16	4	22	..	54	9.0	10.1	3.3	301
Middle income	1,651	12	17	48	..	83	8.7	8.9	3.2	595
Lower middle income	1,269	11	15	39	..	80	5.4	8.4	3.1	624
Upper middle income	3,242	12	23	84	..	95	11.9	12.3	3.3	566
Low & middle income	1,380	12	14	42	..	76	8.7	9.1	3.3	624
East Asia & Pacific	1,669	7	23	44	9	93	4.5	5.0	3.0	546
Europe & Central Asia	3,835	12	26	95	..	92	9.0	9.4	2.9	532
Latin America & Carib.	1,808	16	18	67	..	91	10.4	9.6	3.8	530
Middle East & N. Africa	1,418	16	17	51	32	93	3.0	7.2	3.1	691
South Asia	453	24	3	23	..	61	3.5	1.9	2.1	660
Sub-Saharan Africa	531	11	2	23	..	56	11.6	11.8	4.7	499
High income	9,675	6	50	100	..	99	27.3	16.1	3.1	747
Euro area	6,956	6	53	117	..	99	28.7	18.7	2.8	725

a. Data are from the International Telecommunication Union's (ITU) World Telecommunication Development Report database. Please cite the ITU for third-party use of these data.

About the data

The quality of an economy's infrastructure, including power and communications, is an important element in investment decisions for both domestic and foreign investors. Government effort alone is not enough to meet the need for investments in modern infrastructure; public-private partnerships, especially those involving local providers and financiers, are critical for lowering costs and delivering value for money. In telecommunications, competition in the marketplace, along with sound regulation, is lowering costs, improving quality, and easing access to services around the globe.

An economy's production and consumption of electricity are basic indicators of its size and level of development. Although a few countries export electric power, most production is for domestic consumption. Expanding the supply of electricity to meet the growing demand of increasingly urbanized and industrialized economies without incurring unacceptable social, economic, and environmental costs is one of the great challenges facing developing countries.

Data on electric power production and consumption are collected from national energy agencies by the International Energy Agency (IEA) and adjusted by the IEA to meet international definitions (for data on electricity production, see table 3.10). Electricity consumption is equivalent to production less power plants' own use and transmission, distribution, and transformation losses less exports plus imports. It includes consumption by auxiliary stations, losses in transformers that are considered integral parts of those stations, and electricity produced by pumping installations. Where data are available, it covers electricity generated by primary sources of energy—coal, oil, gas, nuclear, hydro, geothermal, wind, tide and wave, and combustible renewables. Neither production nor consumption data capture the reliability of supplies, including breakdowns, load factors, and frequency of outages.

Over the past decade new financing and technology, along with privatization and liberalization, have spurred dramatic growth in telecommunications in many countries. With the rapid development of mobile telephony and the global expansion of the Internet, information and communication technologies are increasingly recognized as essential tools of development, contributing to global integration and enhancing public sector effectiveness, efficiency, and transparency. The table presents telecommunications indicators covering access and use, quality, and affordability and efficiency.

Operators have traditionally been the main source of telecommunications data, so information on subscribers has been widely available for most countries. This gives a general idea of access, but a more precise measure is the penetration rate—the share of households with access to telecommunications. During the past few years more information on information and communication technology use has become available from household and business surveys. Also important are data on actual use of telecommunications equipment. Ideally, statistics on telecommunications (and other information and communications technologies) should be compiled for all three measures: subscription and possession, access, and use. The quality of data varies among reporting countries as a result of differences in regulations covering data provision and availability.

Globally, there have been huge improvements in access to telecommunications, driven mainly by mobile telephony. By 2007 worldwide mobile cellular phone subscribers numbered 3.3 billion, far outpacing the 1.1 billion fixed-line subscribers. By 2006 approximately 99 percent of the population in high-income countries and about 77 percent of the population in developing countries were covered by a mobile cellular network (within areas served by a mobile cellular signal). Indeed, in many developing countries, especially in Sub-Saharan Africa, the number of mobile phones has overtaken the number of fixed-line phones.

Although access is the key to delivering telecommunications services to people, if the service is not affordable to most people, then goals of universal usage will not be met. Two indicators of telecommunications affordability are presented in the table: fixed-line telephone service tariff and prepaid mobile cellular service tariff. Telecommunications efficiency is measured by total telecommunications revenue divided by GDP and by mobile cellular and fixed-line telephone subscribers per employee.

Definitions

• **Electric power consumption per capita** measures the production of power plants and combined heat and power plants less transmission, distribution, and transformation losses and own use by heat and power plants divided by midyear population. • **Electric power transmission and distribution losses** are losses in transmission between sources of supply and points of distribution and in distribution to consumers, including pilferage. • **Fixed telephone lines** are telephone lines connecting a subscriber to the telephone exchange equipment. • **Mobile cellular telephone subscriptions** are subscriptions to a public mobile telephone service using cellular technology, which provide access to the public switched telephone network. Post-paid and prepaid subscriptions are included. • **International voice traffic** is the sum of international incoming and outgoing telephone traffic (in minutes) divided by total population. • **Population covered by mobile cellular network** is the percentage of people that live in areas served by a mobile cellular signal regardless of whether they use it. • **Residential fixed-line tariff** is the monthly subscription charge plus the cost of 30 three-minute local calls (15 peak and 15 off-peak). • **Mobile cellular prepaid tariff** is based on the Organisation for Economic Co-operation and Development's low-user definition, which includes the cost of monthly mobile use for 25 outgoing calls per month spread over the same mobile network, other mobile networks, and mobile to fixed-line calls and during peak, off-peak, and weekend times as well as 30 text messages per month. • **Telecommunications revenue** is the revenue from the provision of telecommunications services such as fixed-line, mobile, and data divided by GDP. • **Mobile cellular and fixed-line subscribers per employee** are telephone subscribers (fixed-line plus mobile) divided by the total number of telecommunications employees.

Data sources

Data on electricity consumption and losses are from the IEA's *Energy Statistics and Balances of Non-OECD Countries 2008*, the IEA's *Energy Statistics of OECD Countries 2008*, and the United Nations Statistics Division's *Energy Statistics Yearbook*. Data on telecommunications are from the International Telecommunication Union's World Telecommunication Development Report database and World Bank estimates.

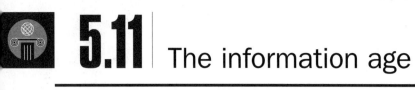

	Daily newspapers	Households with television[b]	Personal computers and the Internet							Information and communications technology trade		
			Access and use		Quality		Affordability	Application		Goods		Services
					Fixed broadband Internet subscribers[b] per 100 people	International Internet bandwidth[b] bits per second per capita	Fixed broadband Internet access tariff[b] $ per month	Secure Internet servers per million people	Information and communications technology expenditures % of GDP	Exports % of total goods exports	Imports % of total goods imports	Exports % of total service exports
	per 1,000 people	%	Personal computers[b]	Internet users[b]								
	2000–07[a]	2006	2007	2007	2007	2007	2008	December 2008	2007	2007	2007	2007
Afghanistan	..	62	..	..	..	..	..	..	..	..	..	..
Albania	24	90	3.8	14.9	0.31	216	31	5	..	1.0	3.5	3.6
Algeria	..	91	1.1	10.3	0.85	89	17	1	2.5	0.0	6.9	..
Angola	2	9	0.7	2.9	0.07	17	164	1	..	..	..	..
Argentina	36	95	9.0	25.9	6.58	2,320	38	18	6.0	0.6	13.1	7.9
Armenia	8	91	31.9	5.7	0.07	..	39	5	..	0.6	5.8	14.6
Australia	155	99[c]	..	68.1	22.98	5,472	28	993	6.6	1.8	12.8	4.6
Austria	311	98	60.7	67.4	19.51	20,288	61	481	5.6	6.3	8.2	6.3
Azerbaijan	16	99	2.4	10.8	0.07	701	85	2	..	0.1	6.1	3.1
Bangladesh	..	48	2.2	0.3	0.00	4	54	0	8.0	..	..	5.7
Belarus	81	97	0.8	29.0	0.12	264	..	2	..	0.8	3.0	6.8
Belgium	165	99	41.7	65.9	25.55	24,945	31	251	5.8	3.7	4.8	8.7
Benin	0	13	0.7	1.7	0.02	17	105	0	..	0.0	3.3	5.4
Bolivia	..	63	2.4	10.5	0.36	42	34	4	5.8	0.1	4.9	12.5
Bosnia and Herzegovina	..	96	6.4	28.0	2.24	530	15	7	..	0.5	3.8	..
Botswana	41	9	4.8	5.3	0.19	43	30	2	..	0.2	5.5	6.8
Brazil	36	91	16.1	35.2	3.54	1,041	47	24	5.8	3.2	14.5	1.8
Bulgaria	79	92	8.9	30.9	8.21	4,909	16	26	7.7	1.8	6.0	4.4
Burkina Faso	..	12	0.6	0.6	0.01	15	1,861	0	..	..	..	..
Burundi	..	15	0.8	0.7	0.00	1	..	0	..	0.5	2.5	0.0
Cambodia	..	43	0.4	0.5	0.06	17	91	1	..	..	..	3.1
Cameroon	..	25	1.1	2.0	0.00	11	184	0	5.0	0.0	3.2	13.0
Canada	175	99	94.3	72.8	27.52	16,193	20	907	6.4	4.7	10.1	11.1
Central African Republic	..	5	0.3	0.3	0.00	0	1,396	0	..	..	..	..
Chad	..	4	0.2	0.6	0.00	1	..	..	..	..	..	..
Chile	51	97	14.1	31.1	7.90	4,086	53	35	4.2	0.1	9.0	2.7
China	74	89	5.7	16.1	5.04	280	19	1	7.9	30.9	28.6	4.5
Hong Kong, China	222	100	68.6	57.2	27.42	15,892	25	287	4.7	42.1	41.8	1.6
Colombia	23	84	8.0	27.5	2.74	971	36	11	4.4	0.3	13.3	7.9
Congo, Dem. Rep.	..	4	0.0	0.4	0.00	0	..	0	..	..	..	..
Congo, Rep.	..	27	0.5	1.9	0.00	0	..	0	..	..	..	..
Costa Rica	65	94	23.1	33.6	2.83	820	17	99	3.9	29.4	25.3	16.4
Côte d'Ivoire	..	35	1.7	1.6	0.05	16	47	1	..	0.4	4.2	11.0
Croatia	..	94	..	44.7	8.73	3,380	21	92	..	5.3	7.5	4.2
Cuba	65	70	3.6	11.6	0.02	19	1,630	0	..	1.9	2.9	..
Czech Republic	183	83	27.4	48.3	12.72	7,075	29	151	7.1	14.2	15.0	8.0
Denmark	353	96	54.9	80.7	35.87	34,506	30	1,041	5.8	7.1	11.9	..
Dominican Republic	39	78	3.5	17.2	1.58	154	28	13	..	..	..	3.7
Ecuador	99	87	13.0	13.2	2.39	324	40	10	6.1	0.3	7.7	6.2
Egypt, Arab Rep.	..	96[c]	4.9	14.0	0.63	143	8	1	5.8	..	..	4.2
El Salvador	38	83	5.2	11.1	1.31	18	18	10	..	0.6	8.4	9.6
Eritrea	..	18	0.8	2.5	0.00	2	..	..	..	..	..	..
Estonia	191	..	52.2	63.7	20.70	11,925	39	280	..	14.2	11.1	6.1
Ethiopia	5	5	0.7	0.4	0.00	3	644	0	..	0.3	7.1	6.3
Finland	431	87	50.0	78.8	30.57	17,221	38	686	5.2	18.9	14.4	8.4
France	164	97	65.2	51.2	25.20	29,466	38	172	5.7	8.0	9.8	4.1
Gabon	..	58	3.6	6.2	0.15	150	..	4	..	0.1	6.6	..
Gambia, The	..	12	3.3	5.9	0.02	36	384	2	..	0.2	4.6	..
Georgia	4	89	5.4	8.2	1.06	745	48	6	..	0.4	7.1	1.5
Germany	267	94	65.6	72.3	23.82	25,654	38	549	6.2	9.6	12.3	7.8
Ghana	..	26[c]	0.6	3.8	0.07	21	64	1	..	0.0	6.3	0.0
Greece	..	100	9.4	32.9	9.09	4,537	25	61	5.4	3.3	6.0	1.6
Guatemala	..	50	2.1	10.1	0.21	187	34	8	..	0.5	9.1	14.8
Guinea	..	10	0.5	0.5	0.00	0	800	0	..	..	..	..
Guinea-Bissau	..	31	0.2	2.2	0.00	1	..	..	..	..	..	..
Haiti	..	27	5.2	10.4	0.00	17	..	1	..	..	..	4.9

	Daily newspapers	Households with television[b]	Personal computers and the Internet							Information and communications technology trade		
			Access and use		Quality		Affordability	Application		Goods		Services
					Fixed broadband Internet subscribers[b] per 100 people	International Internet bandwidth[b] bits per second per capita	Fixed broadband Internet access tariff[b] $ per month	Secure Internet servers per million people	Information and communications technology expenditures % of GDP	Exports % of total goods exports	Imports % of total goods imports	Exports % of total service exports
	per 1,000 people	%	per 100 people									
			Personal computers[b]	Internet users[b]								
	2000–07[a]	2006	2007	2007	2007	2007	2008	December 2008	2007	2007	2007	2007
Honduras	..	61	2.0	6.0	0.00	244	..	6	11.2	0.3	6.9	11.5
Hungary	217	101	25.6	51.9	14.21	4,773	25	83	5.9	26.1	19.9	6.8
India	71	53	3.3	7.2	0.28	32	6	1	5.6	1.3	8.3	41.6
Indonesia	..	65	2.0	5.8	0.11	53	22	1	3.9	5.3	5.4	11.9
Iran, Islamic Rep.	..	..	10.6	32.4	..	153	43	0	3.5	0.1	1.9	..
Iraq	..	..	..	..	..	..	..	..	..	..	..	1.9
Ireland	182	119	58.2	56.1	18.46	15,229	38	679	5.9	22.4	24.1	30.1
Israel	..	92	..	27.9	21.29	2,003	..	273	6.5	10.9	11.4	28.5
Italy	137	98	36.7	53.9	18.29	10,302	26	93	5.8	3.7	7.0	3.5
Jamaica	..	70	6.8	56.1	3.47	19,151	30	32	6.6	0.2	3.6	6.8
Japan	551	99[c]	..	69.0	22.14	3,734	32	472	7.2	19.3	13.7	1.2
Jordan	..	96	6.7	19.7	1.50	164	31	9	9.3	4.8	7.0	0.0
Kazakhstan	..	..	..	12.3	1.75	129	..	2	..	0.1	5.2	2.5
Kenya	..	32[c]	1.4	8.0	0.05	9	168	1	8.2	1.0	5.6	4.1
Korea, Dem. Rep.	..	..	..	0.0	0.00	..	..	..	..	..	..	..
Korea, Rep.	..	100	57.6	75.9	30.36	1,027	20	696	7.1	27.2	16.5	1.4
Kuwait	..	95	23.7	33.8	0.99	871	46	65	4.5	..	..	48.4
Kyrgyz Republic	1	..	1.9	14.3	0.06	114	..	1	..	0.8	5.1	1.9
Lao PDR	3	30	1.8	1.7	0.06	32	268	0	..	..	..	..
Latvia	154	..	32.7	55.0	6.42	3,537	26	98	..	3.4	6.9	4.9
Lebanon	54	95	10.4	38.3	4.88	227	23	13	..	..	..	2.2
Lesotho	..	13	0.3	3.5	0.00	2	49	0	..	..	..	..
Liberia	..	..	..	0.5	..	..	..	..	..	..	..	..
Libya	..	50	2.2	4.3	0.16	50	..	0	..	..	..	2.5
Lithuania	108	98	18.3	49.2	15.04	4,656	16	83	..	4.8	6.4	3.1
Macedonia, FYR	89	98	36.8	27.3	4.93	17	15	12	..	0.4	4.4	14.1
Madagascar	..	18	0.5	0.6	0.01	8	120	0	..	0.5	4.7	0.5
Malawi	..	5	0.2	1.0	0.01	5	900	0	..	0.4	3.8	..
Malaysia	109	95	23.1	55.7	3.81	998	20	27	6.8	41.5	36.0	4.9
Mali	..	15	0.8	0.8	0.03	17	58	1	..	0.2	4.2	..
Mauritania	..	25	4.6	1.0	0.13	70	62	2	..	..	2.1	..
Mauritius	77	96[c]	17.6	27.0	4.88	226	51	60	..	4.7	6.1	2.8
Mexico	93	98	14.4	22.7	4.32	178	37	16	4.0	19.6	14.9	2.3
Moldova	..	74	11.1	18.4	1.24	931	23	7	..	2.6	4.3	15.4
Mongolia	20	33	13.9	12.3	0.28	116	..	9	..	0.1	5.9	3.7
Morocco	12	78	3.6	21.4	1.55	814	20	1	8.3	5.7	6.7	3.3
Mozambique	3	9	1.4	0.9	0.00	3	100	0	..	0.1	5.1	5.0
Myanmar	..	3	0.9	0.1	0.00	2	..	0	..	..	..	..
Namibia	28	41	24.0	4.9	0.01	27	46	9	..	0.5	7.3	2.7
Nepal	..	13	0.5	1.4	0.04	5	23	1	..	..	..	..
Netherlands	307	99	91.2	84.2	33.62	78,159	38	1,108	6.6	18.9	19.8	11.0
New Zealand	182	99	52.6	69.2	20.17	4,544	31	980	5.7	2.3	9.7	5.4
Nicaragua	..	60	4.0	2.8	0.34	144	30	7	..	0.2	7.3	8.2
Niger	0	7	0.1	0.3	0.00	2	58	0	..	0.4	4.4	32.8
Nigeria	..	26	0.8	6.8	0.00	5	690	1	3.4	0.0	6.9	..
Norway	516	97	62.9	84.8	30.57	26,904	57	851	4.4	1.8	9.7	4.2
Oman	..	79	7.1	13.1	0.78	142	31	12	..	0.8	3.8	..
Pakistan	50	..	..	10.8	0.03	44	18	1	5.6	0.5	7.2	6.8
Panama	65	87	4.6	22.3	4.31	15,977	15	87	5.9	0.0	6.7	4.6
Papua New Guinea	9	10	6.4	1.8	0.00	1	144	1	..	..	..	2.2
Paraguay	..	79	7.8	8.7	0.84	163	35	6	..	0.4	28.6	2.2
Peru	..	73	10.3	27.4	2.04	2,704	36	10	3.9	0.1	8.0	2.6
Philippines	79	63	7.3	6.0	0.56	114	23	5	5.7	29.1	20.6	7.0
Poland	114	89	16.9	44.0	8.99	2,748	27	85	6.0	5.6	9.6	4.0
Portugal	..	99	17.2	40.1	14.37	4,790	30	115	5.7	9.0	9.3	4.8
Puerto Rico	..	97	0.8	25.4	3.02	511	..	54	..	..	..	..

5.11 The information age

	Daily newspapers	Households with television[b]	Personal computers and the Internet								Information and communications technology trade		
			Access and use		Quality		Affordability	Application			Goods		Services
					Fixed broadband Internet subscribers[b] per 100 people	International Internet bandwidth[b] bits per second per capita	Fixed broadband Internet access tariff[b] $ per month	Secure Internet servers per million people	Information and communications technology expenditures % of GDP		Exports % of total goods exports	Imports % of total goods imports	Exports % of total service exports
	per 1,000 people	%	per 100 people										
			Personal computers[b]	Internet users[b]									
	2000–07[a]	2006	2007	2007	2007	2007	2008	December 2008	2007		2007	2007	2007
Romania	70	90	19.2	23.9	9.05	2,945	23	16	5.3		3.1	7.6	16.3
Russian Federation	92	98	13.3	21.1	2.81	573	14	7	4.1		0.5	10.1	6.0
Rwanda	..	2	0.3	1.1	0.03	16	92	0	..		0.8	8.0	1.9
Saudi Arabia	..	99	14.8	26.4	2.58	510	40	8	4.7		0.3	7.8	..
Senegal	9	41	2.1	6.6	0.31	137	29	1	10.9		0.5	4.0	18.0
Serbia	..	80	24.4	20.3	4.41	2,861	9	2	..		..	..	..
Sierra Leone	..	..	..	0.2	..	..	..	1	..		..	..	0.2
Singapore	361	98	74.3	65.7	19.51	22,783	22	390	6.5		45.6	38.3	3.1
Slovak Republic	126	78	51.4	55.9	8.75	5,555	28	58	6.0		13.2	10.3	6.6
Slovenia	173	97	42.5	52.6	17.09	6,720	27	171	4.7		3.0	5.3	5.2
Somalia	..	8	0.9	1.1	0.00	0	..	0	..		..	..	..
South Africa	30	59	8.5	8.3	0.79	71	26	37	9.7		1.8	11.3	3.9
Spain	144	96	39.3	51.3	17.98	11,008	29	171	5.5		4.0	7.9	5.4
Sri Lanka	26	32	3.7	3.9	0.32	118	21	3	6.0		1.7	4.9	10.6
Sudan	..	16	11.2	9.1	0.11	345	29	0	..		0.0	7.5	5.4
Swaziland	24	18	3.7	3.7	0.00	1	1,877	5	..		0.0	3.8	1.4
Sweden	481	94	88.1	79.7	35.85	49,828	32	775	6.4		11.2	12.2	13.1
Switzerland	420	86	91.8	76.3	31.52	29,417	32	982	8.0		3.7	7.4	..
Syrian Arab Republic	..	105	9.0	17.4	0.03	53	51	0	..		0.1	2.5	5.8
Tajikistan	..	79	1.3	7.2	0.00	0	..	..	..		..	..	12.6
Tanzania	2	7[c]	0.9	1.0	0.00	3	68	0	..		0.4	6.2	2.5
Thailand	..	92	7.0	21.0	1.43	346	18	10	6.1		24.2	20.0	..
Timor-Leste	..	..	..	0.1	0.00	9	..	..	..		..	..	..
Togo	2	14	3.0	5.0	0.00	4	106	1	..		0.1	4.2	6.9
Trinidad and Tobago	149	88	13.2	16.0	2.66	675	13	46	..		0.2	5.9	..
Tunisia	23	93	7.5	16.8	1.12	303	13	11	6.0		4.2	5.9	1.2
Turkey	..	112	6.0	16.5	6.16	1,381	..	57	5.5		2.0	4.0	1.8
Turkmenistan	9	..	7.2	1.4	..	16	..	..	..		..	..	..
Uganda	..	10	1.7	2.5	0.01	11	170	0	..		6.9	10.0	7.6
Ukraine	131	97	4.5	21.5	1.72	206	21	4	7.1		1.5	3.3	3.6
United Arab Emirates	..	86	33.0	51.8	8.70	2,785	22	126	5.1		4.3	8.6	..
United Kingdom	290	98	80.2	71.7	25.58	39,650	29	908	6.7		20.5	13.6	7.8
United States	193	95	80.5	73.5	24.27	11,277	15	1,174	7.5		16.3	14.6	4.3
Uruguay	..	92	13.6	29.1	4.96	903	24	43	6.0		0.1	6.5	8.8
Uzbekistan	..	99	3.1	4.5	0.03	9	..	0	..		..	..	..
Venezuela, RB	93	90	9.3	20.8	3.12	628	31	7	3.9		0.0	12.1	11.1
Vietnam	..	89	9.6	21.0	1.52	148	17	1	6.1		5.1	7.6	..
West Bank and Gaza	10	93	5.6	9.6	1.50	324	..	1	..		..	..	..
Yemen, Rep.	4	43	2.8	1.4	..	28	226	0	..		0.1	3.7	18.9
Zambia	5	..	1.1	4.2	0.02	3	91	0	..		0.1	5.1	8.5
Zimbabwe	..	32	6.5	10.1	0.11	4	..	1	3.5		0.3	2.0	..
World	**105 w**	**89 m**	**15.3 w**	**21.8 w**	**6.03 w**	**3,297 w**	**31.4 m**	**112 w**	**6.5 w**		**15.4 w**	**15.2 w**	**6.7 w**
Low income	..	16	1.5	5.2	0.02	26	102.4	0	..		1.4	6.7	..
Middle income	71	89	5.6	15.2	2.72	389	28.0	7	5.9		16.9	18.0	4.9
Lower middle income	72	79	4.6	12.4	2.33	199	30.5	2	6.5		20.6	20.2	5.0
Upper middle income	65	92	12.4	26.6	4.28	1,185	26.0	26	5.2		13.5	16.2	4.8
Low & middle income	66	63	5.3	13.1	2.35	318	36.3	5	5.9		16.1	17.5	4.9
East Asia & Pacific	74	53	5.6	14.6	3.70	247	21.7	2	7.3		30.9	28.1	5.2
Europe & Central Asia	109	96	10.8	21.4	4.39	1,114	21.8	24	5.0		1.8	7.0	5.0
Latin America & Carib.	64	84	11.3	26.9	3.64	1,126	34.0	18	4.9		11.4	15.9	4.7
Middle East & N. Africa	..	94	6.3	17.1	..	186	23.0	1	4.5		..	..	..
South Asia	68	42	3.3	6.6	0.24	31	21.0	1	5.7		1.2	8.1	39.0
Sub-Saharan Africa	..	18	1.8	4.4	0.03	36	100.1	3	..		1.1	8.2	..
High income	261	98	67.4	65.7	22.84	18,242	30.2	663	6.7		15.2	14.6	7.0
Euro area	201	97	55.5	59.2	21.60	32,560	30.5	321	5.9		9.4	10.9	8.2

a. Data are for the most recent year available. b. Data are from the International Telecommunication Union's (ITU) World Telecommunication Development Report database. Please cite the ITU for third-party use of these data. c. Data are for 2007.

The digital and information revolution has changed the way the world learns, communicates, does business, and treats illnesses. New information and communications technologies (ICT) offer vast opportunities for progress in all walks of life in all countries—opportunities for economic growth, improved health, better service delivery, learning through distance education, and social and cultural advances.

The table presents indicators of the penetration of the information economy, quality, and secure Internet servers), and some of the economics of the information age.

Comparable statistics on access, use, quality, and affordability of ICT are needed to formulate growth-enabling policies for the sector and to monitor and evaluate the sector's impact on development. Although basic access data are available for many countries, in most developing countries little is known about who uses ICT; what they are used for (school, work, business, research, government); and how they affect people and businesses. The global Partnership on Measuring ICT for Development is helping to set standards, harmonize information and communications technology statistics, and build statistical capacity in developing countries. For more information see www.itu.int/ITU-D/ict/partnership/.

Data on daily newspapers in circulation are from United Nations Educational, Scientific, and Cultural Organization (UNESCO) Institute for Statistics surveys on circulation, online newspapers, journalists, community newspapers, and news agencies.

Estimates of households with television are derived from household surveys. Some countries report only the number of households with a color television set, and so the true number may be higher than reported.

Estimates of personal computers are from an annual International Telecommunication Union (ITU) questionnaire sent to member states, supplemented by other sources. Many governments lack the capacity to survey all places where personal computers are used (homes, schools, businesses, government offices, libraries, Internet cafes) so most estimates are derived from the number of personal computers sold each year. Annual shipment data can also be multiplied by an estimated average useful lifespan before replacement to approximate the number of personal computers. There is no precise method for determining replacement rates, but in general personal computers are replaced every three to five years.

Data on Internet users and related indicators are based on nationally reported data. Some countries derive these data from surveys, but since survey questions and definitions differ, the estimates may not be strictly comparable. Countries without surveys generally derive their estimates by multiplying subscriber counts reported by Internet service providers by a multiplier. This method may undercount actual users, particularly in developing countries, where many commercial subscribers rent out computers connected to the Internet or prepaid cards are used to access the Internet.

Broadband refers to technologies that provide Internet speeds of at least 256 kilobits a second of upstream and downstream capacity and includes digital subscriber lines, cable modems, satellite broadband Internet, fiber-to-home Internet access, ethernet local access networks, and wireless area networks. Bandwidth refers to the range of frequencies available for signals. The higher the bandwidth, the more information that can be transmitted at one time. Reporting countries may have different definitions of broadband, so data are not strictly comparable.

The number of secure Internet servers, from the Netcraft Secure Server Survey, indicates how many companies conduct encrypted transactions over the Internet. The survey examines the use of encrypted transactions through extensive automated exploration, tallying the number of Web sites using a secure socket layer (SSL). Some countries, such as the Republic of Korea, use application layers to establish the encryption channel, which is SSL equivalent.

According to the World Information Technology and Services Alliance's (WITSA) *Digital Planet 2008*, the global marketplace for information and communications technologies was expected to be about $3.4 trillion in 2007 and to rise to almost $3.8 trillion in 2008. The data on information and communications technology expenditures cover the world's 75 largest buyers among countries and regions.

Information and communication technology goods exports and imports are defined by the Working Party on Indicators for the Information Society and are reported in the Organisation for Economic Co-operation and Development's *Guide to Measuring the Information Society*. Information and communication technology service exports data are based on the International Monetary Fund's (IMF) *Balance of Payments Statistics Yearbook* classification.

• **Daily newspapers** are newspapers issued at least four times a week that report mainly on events in the 24-hour period before going to press. The indicator is average circulation (or copies printed) per 1,000 people. • **Households with television** are the percentage of households with a television set. • **Personal computers** are self-contained computers designed for use by a single individual, including laptops and notebooks and excluding terminals connected to mainframe and minicomputers intended primarily for shared use and devices such as smart phones and personal digital assistants. • **Internet users** are people with access to the worldwide network. • **Fixed broadband Internet subscribers** are the number of broadband subscribers with a digital subscriber line, cable modem, or other high-speed technology. • **International Internet bandwidth** is the contracted capacity of international connections between countries for transmitting Internet traffic. • **Fixed broadband Internet access tariff** is the lowest sampled cost per 100 kilobits a second per month and are calculated from low- and high-speed monthly service charges. Monthly charges do not include installation fees or modem rentals. • **Secure Internet servers** are servers using encryption technology in Internet transactions. • **Information and communications technology expenditures** include computer hardware (computers, storage devices, printers, and other peripherals); computer software (operating systems, programming tools, utilities, applications, and internal software development); computer services (information technology consulting, computer and network systems integration, Web hosting, data processing services, and other services); and communications services (voice and data communications services) and wired and wireless communications equipment. • **Information and communication technology goods exports** and **imports** include telecommunications, audio and video, computer and related equipment; electronic components; and other information and communication technology goods. Software is excluded. • **Information and communication technology service exports** include computer and communications services (telecommunications and postal and courier services) and information services (computer data and news-related service transactions).

Data on newspapers are compiled by the UNESCO Institute for Statistics. Data on personal computers and the Internet are from the ITU's World Telecommunication Development Report database. Data on secure Internet servers are from Netcraft (www.netcraft.com/) and official government sources. Data on information and communication technology goods trade are from the United Nations Statistics Division's Commodity Trade (Comtrade) database. Data on information and communication technology expenditures are from WITSA's *Digital Planet 2008* and Global Insight, Inc. Data on information and communication technology service exports are from IMF's Balance of Payments Statistics database.

5.12 Science and technology

	Researchers in R&D	Technicians in R&D	Scientific and technical journal articles	Expenditures for R&D	High-technology exports		Royalty and license fees		Patent applications filed[a,b]		Trademark applications filed[a]	
	per million people 2000–06[c]	per million people 2000–06[c]	2005	% of GDP 2000–06[c]	$ millions 2007	% of manu-factured exports 2007	Receipts 2007	$ millions Payments 2007	Residents 2007	Non-residents 2007	Residents 2007	Non-residents 2007
Afghanistan	..	..	..	..	..	..	..	..	..	..	..	..
Albania	..	..	..	..	8	12	5	8	..	..	186	809
Algeria	170	35	350	0.07	11	2	..	..	84	765	2,235	1,415
Angola	..	..	..	..	..	..	12	1	..	..	..	..
Argentina	895	366	3,058	0.49	1,144	7	85	1,036	0	0	55,252	18,465
Armenia	..	..	180	0.21	9	2	..	..	192	1	883	594
Australia	4,053	904	15,957	1.78	3,541	14	686	2,821	2,717	24,626	40,001	11,176
Austria	3,657	1,462	4,566	2.46	14,566	11	757	1,471	2,271	378	7,844	820
Azerbaijan	..	..	116	0.22	15	4	0	5	281	6	751	1,025
Bangladesh	..	..	193	..	..	..	0	8	22	288	..	..
Belarus	..	..	490	0.68	346	3	7	69	1,188	337	3,666	1,409
Belgium	3,252	1,447	6,841	1.85	25,178	7	1,640	1,867	454	163	22,964[d]	1,695[d]
Benin	..	..	..	..	0	0	0	2	..	..	..	..
Bolivia	120	6	..	0.28	15	5	2	16	..	..	1,873	4,208
Bosnia and Herzegovina	..	..	..	..	76	3	..	..	55	162	320	870
Botswana	..	..	..	0.39	16	0	0	11	..	..	..	..
Brazil	461	394	9,889	0.82	9,295	12	319	2,259	3,810	20,264	76,827	17,842
Bulgaria	1,344	488	764	0.48	618	6	10	73	211	28	6,868	674
Burkina Faso	22	16	..	0.17	..	..	..	..	..	..	..	..
Burundi	..	..	..	..	1	4	0	..	..	..	..	..
Cambodia	17	13	..	0.05	..	..	0	10	..	..	467	1,847
Cameroon	26	..	131	..	3	3	0	6	..	..	..	..
Canada	3,922	1,467	25,836	1.97	29,593	14	3,635	7,552	4,998	35,133	21,101	26,657
Central African Republic	..	..	..	..	0	0	..	..	..	..	..	..
Chad	..	..	..	..	..	..	..	..	..	..	..	..
Chile	833	302	1,559	0.67	401	7	61	434	291	2,924	30,847	13,473
China	926	..	41,596	1.42	336,988	30	343	8,192	153,060	92,101	669,276	56,840
Hong Kong, China	2,090	416	..	0.74	2,370	19	259	1,357	160	13,606	7,902	15,627
Colombia	127	97	400	0.17	338	3	17	188	121	1,860	14,118	9,876
Congo, Dem. Rep.	..	..	..	0.48	..	..	..	..	..	..	..	..
Congo, Rep.	32	35	..	..	..	..	..	..	..	..	..	..
Costa Rica	122	..	105	0.37	2,088	45	0	53	..	..	5,872	5,882
Côte d'Ivoire	68	..	..	..	460	32	0	10	..	..	..	..
Croatia	1,148	538	953	0.87	769	9	40	214	344	93	1,486	946
Cuba	..	..	261	0.51	248	35	..	..	74	210	454	602
Czech Republic	2,578	1,555	3,169	1.54	15,410	14	35	653	716	192	9,156	1,006
Denmark	5,277	1,990	5,040	2.44	11,247	17	..	..	1,660	197	4,444	662
Dominican Republic	..	..	..	..	..	..	0	32	0	0	..	..
Ecuador	51	..	..	0.06	73	7	0	45	0	794	6,078	6,527
Egypt, Arab Rep.	..	..	1,658	0.19	5	0	122	241	516	1,589	..	..
El Salvador	47	..	..	..	42	4	1	24	..	..	..	..
Eritrea	..	..	..	..	..	..	..	..	..	..	..	..
Estonia	2,622	579	439	1.15	840	12	10	40	44	19	1,537	443
Ethiopia	20	10	88	0.20	4	3	0	2	..	..	..	..
Finland	7,681	..	4,811	3.43	15,565	21	1,216	1,326	1,804	211	3,504	629
France	3,353	1,746	30,309	2.12	80,465	19	8,827	4,603	14,722	2,387	70,432	3,151
Gabon	..	..	..	..	71	32	..	..	..	..	..	..
Gambia, The	28	17	..	..	0	2	..	..	..	..	..	..
Georgia	..	..	145	0.18	39	7	11	5	83	79	554	605
Germany	3,386	1,144	44,145	2.52	155,922	14	7,249	9,698	47,853	13,139	72,788	3,377
Ghana	..	..	81	..	5	1	0	..	..	..	..	..
Greece	1,790	795	4,291	0.50	1,005	8	52	600	772	3,889	6,416	889
Guatemala	31	11	..	0.03	119	3	9	79	9	99	5,955	5,048
Guinea	..	..	..	..	..	..	0	0	..	..	..	..
Guinea-Bissau	..	..	..	..	..	..	..	..	..	..	..	..
Haiti	..	..	..	..	..	..	3	0	..	..	..	..

Science and technology

	Researchers in R&D per million people 2000–06c	Technicians in R&D per million people 2000–06c	Scientific and technical journal articles 2005	Expenditures for R&D % of GDP 2000–06c	High-technology exports $ millions 2007	High-technology exports % of manu-factured exports 2007	Royalty and license fees $ millions Receipts 2007	Royalty and license fees $ millions Payments 2007	Patent applications filed[a,b] Residents 2007	Patent applications filed[a,b] Non-residents 2007	Trademark applications filed[a] Residents 2007	Trademark applications filed[a] Non-residents 2007
Honduras	..	..	..	0.05	8	1	..	25	..	..	2,369	5,034
Hungary	1,745	491	2,614	1.00	19,349	25	841	1,596	689	102	3,615	631
India	111	86	14,608	0.69	4,944	5	112	949	4,521	19,984	73,308	12,361
Indonesia	199	..	205	0.05	5,225	11	31	1,052	282	4,324	36,644	16,005
Iran, Islamic Rep.	..	..	2,635	0.59	375	6	..	..	..	..	..	..
Iraq	..	..	..	..	0	0	0	29	..	..	..	..
Ireland	2,882	740	2,120	1.31	28,720	28	1,110	24,669	847	78	1,905	1,116
Israel	..	..	6,309	4.53	3,088	8	784	946	257	7,239	3,293	7,285
Italy	1,407	..	24,645	1.10	27,817	7	1,050	1,680	9,255	870	50,604	4,490
Jamaica	..	..	..	0.07	2	2	15	60	21	132	594	1,114
Japan	5,546	561	55,471	3.40	121,425	19	23,229	16,678	333,498	62,793	118,130	12,796
Jordan	..	..	275	0.34	38	1	0	0	..	..	..	..
Kazakhstan	783	83	96	0.28	1,470	23	0	68	1,433	124	..	..
Kenya	..	..	226	..	81	5	23	24	38	33	1,451	1,187
Korea, Dem. Rep.	..	..	..	..	..	..	..	..	..	..	..	..
Korea, Rep.	4,162	583	16,396	3.23	110,633	33	1,920	5,075	128,701	43,768	112,157	20,131
Kuwait	74	94	233	0.18	..	..	0	0	..	..	..	..
Kyrgyz Republic	..	..	..	0.20	8	2	2	12	155	3	191	424
Lao PDR	..	..	..	..	..	..	..	..	..	..	..	..
Latvia	1,758	648	134	0.69	353	7	13	40	114	37	1,398	479
Lebanon	..	..	234	..	..	..	..	..	..	..	..	..
Lesotho	10	11	..	0.06	..	..	20	..	..	..	..	..
Liberia	..	..	..	..	..	..	..	..	..	..	..	..
Libya	361	493	..	..	..	..	..	0	..	..	..	..
Lithuania	2,358	411	406	0.80	1,214	11	0	22	62	20	2,218	431
Macedonia, FYR	547	83	..	24.77	21	1	3	9	..	..	..	..
Madagascar	43	6	..	0.16	7	1	2	9	4	40	445	432
Malawi	..	..	..	..	2	2	..	..	..	..	222	582
Malaysia	503	63	615	0.60	64,584	52	36	1,195	531	4,269	12,289	13,605
Mali	..	..	..	..	3	7	0	1	..	..	..	..
Mauritania	..	..	..	..	..	..	..	..	..	..	..	..
Mauritius	..	..	..	0.38	112	8	0	6	..	..	..	..
Mexico	464	260	3,902	0.50	33,314	17	120	503	629	15,970	54,610	28,606
Moldova	..	..	89	..	14	5	6	7	333	14	1,262	717
Mongolia	..	..	..	0.26	7	8	..	..	103	110	339	277
Morocco	..	..	443	0.66	858	9	4	36	178	732	5,637	1,365
Mozambique	..	..	..	0.50	3	2	0	2	..	..	553	943
Myanmar	18	139	..	0.16	..	..	..	..	..	..	..	..
Namibia	..	..	..	..	83	5	..	2	..	..	..	..
Nepal	59	137	..	..	..	..	..	..	..	..	..	..
Netherlands	2,524	1,863	13,885	1.69	74,369	26	4,322	3,662	2,079	367	..	..
New Zealand	4,207	768	2,983	1.17	628	10	141	553	1,892	5,952	9,665	9,945
Nicaragua	..	..	..	0.05	5	4	0	..	..	..	1,195	4,780
Niger	8	10	..	..	4	14	0	0	..	..	..	..
Nigeria	..	..	362	..	62	8	..	174	..	..	..	..
Norway	4,668	..	3,644	1.49	4,391	18	700	622	1,223	5,431	3,326	3,286
Oman	..	..	111	..	8	0	..	..	..	..	..	..
Pakistan	80	41	492	0.44	188	1	37	107	0	0	9,033	4,952
Panama	87	206	..	0.25	0	0	0	47	..	..	3,530	6,079
Papua New Guinea	..	..	..	..	..	..	..	..	..	..	76	536
Paraguay	71	122	..	0.09	24	6	206	6	..	..	..	..
Peru	..	..	133	0.15	69	2	2	90	28	1,331	12,778	8,867
Philippines	..	..	178	0.14	13,792	54	5	364	231	3,034	8,398	6,335
Poland	1,562	227	6,844	0.56	4,177	4	108	1,575	2,392	361	13,951	1,100
Portugal	2,007	277	2,910	0.83	3,285	9	105	451	250	31	15,288	959
Puerto Rico	..	..	..	..	..	..	..	..	..	..	..	..

5.12 | Science and technology

	Researchers in R&D	Technicians in R&D	Scientific and technical journal articles	Expenditures for R&D	High-technology exports		Royalty and license fees		Patent applications filed[a,b]		Trademark applications filed[a]	
	per million people 2000–06[c]	per million people 2000–06[c]	2005	% of GDP 2000–06[c]	$ millions 2007	% of manu-factured exports 2007	Receipts $ millions 2007	Payments 2007	Residents 2007	Non-residents 2007	Residents 2007	Non-residents 2007
Romania	952	209	887	0.46	1,178	4	41	242	827	59	10,988	883
Russian Federation	3,255	574	14,412	1.08	4,144	7	396	2,806	27,505	11,934	31,502	10,372
Rwanda	..	..	..	..	1	16	0	1	..	..	..	..
Saudi Arabia	..	..	575	..	121	1	0	0	128	642	..	..
Senegal	..	..	83	0.09	22	4	0	5	..	..	..	..
Serbia	..	..	849	1.65	176	4	..	..	395	121	2,102	2,030
Sierra Leone	..	..	..	..	..	..	..	2	..	..	..	..
Singapore	5,713	549	3,609	2.39	105,549	46	716	9,905	696	9,255	5,383	11,170
Slovak Republic	2,186	424	919	0.49	2,517	5	149	124	239	106	2,889	1,031
Slovenia	2,924	1,476	1,035	1.63	1,246	5	18	169	331	15	1,493	428
Somalia	..	..	..	..	..	..	..	..	..	..	..	..
South Africa	361	109	2,392	0.92	1,859	6	53	1,596	0	5,781	17,106	12,811
Spain	2,639	919	18,336	1.21	9,916	5	536	3,402	3,267	265	55,909	1,924
Sri Lanka	141	77	136	0.19	99	2	0	0	151	279	3,382	2,835
Sudan	..	..	..	0.28	0	1	..	..	..	..	..	..
Swaziland	..	..	..	..	0	0	0	121	..	..	..	..
Sweden	6,139	..	10,012	3.82	20,369	16	4,753	1,810	2,527	398	10,510	800
Switzerland	3,436	2,317	8,749	2.93	33,655	22	..	..	1,692	342	11,723	4,670
Syrian Arab Republic	..	..	77	..	29	1	0	20	124	133	..	..
Tajikistan	..	..	..	0.10	..	..	1	1	26	0	170	612
Tanzania	..	..	107	..	5	1	0	5	..	..	..	..
Thailand	292	211	1,249	0.26	30,925	27	54	2,287	877	511	20,140	13,415
Timor-Leste	..	..	..	..	..	..	..	..	..	..	..	..
Togo	..	..	..	..	0	0	0	7	..	..	..	..
Trinidad and Tobago	..	..	..	0.12	60	2	..	..	0	551	..	..
Tunisia	1,450	41	571	1.03	565	5	15	10	56	282	..	..
Turkey	577	65	7,815	0.76	328	0	..	647	1,810	211	59,028	4,020
Turkmenistan	..	..	..	..	..	..	..	..	..	..	146	380
Uganda	..	..	93	0.19	24	11	1	5	6	1	..	..
Ukraine	..	..	2,105	1.03	1,314	4	53	577	3,474	2,416	19,888	3,858
United Arab Emirates	..	..	229	..	23	1	..	..	..	..	..	..
United Kingdom	3,033	..	45,572	1.80	63,066	19	15,108	10,121	17,375	7,624	28,976	4,999
United States	4,651	..	205,320	2.61	228,655	28	82,614	25,047	241,347	214,807	256,429	33,065
Uruguay	373	51	204	0.26	41	3	0	7	..	..	3,804	8,991
Uzbekistan	..	..	157	..	..	..	..	..	324	198	1,382	680
Venezuela, RB	86	2	534	0.23	80	3	0	276	..	..	..	..
Vietnam	115	..	221	0.19	1,273	6	..	..	180	1,767	12,884	5,134
West Bank and Gaza	..	..	..	..	..	..	..	..	..	..	..	..
Yemen, Rep.	..	..	..	..	1	1	149	9	..	..	..	..
Zambia	..	..	..	0.03	9	2	0	1	..	..	..	..
Zimbabwe	..	..	..	..	48	3	..	..	..	..	..	..
World	**1,173 w**	**.. w**	**708,086 s**	**2.30 w**	**1,807,189 s**	**18 w**	**165,115 s**	**164,279 s**	**1,012,033 s**	**575,469 s**	**1,381,943 s**	**405,931 s**
Low income	..	..	2,103	..	..	7	68	362	485	202	10,852	7,204
Middle income	510	..	123,683	0.94	466,128	19	2,270	26,188	189,511	128,440	408,371	199,853
Lower middle income	336	..	67,280	1.00	339,542	23	964	13,441	155,262	99,433	90,521	66,626
Upper middle income	1,107	304	56,403	0.73	126,586	14	1,306	12,747	34,249	29,007	317,850	133,227
Low & middle income	..	..	125,786	0.92	391,161	19	2,337	26,550	189,996	128,642	419,223	207,057
East Asia & Pacific	926	..	44,064	1.42	..	31	469	13,100	153,937	92,623	32,534	27,686
Europe & Central Asia	2,014	330	36,442	0.86	16,092	6	693	6,369	34,441	13,121	157,537	29,834
Latin America & Carib.	429	283	20,045	0.61	48,714	12	880	4,710	861	20,264	199,614	128,807
Middle East & N. Africa	..	..	6,243	..	..	4	141	296	600	2,354	7,872	2,780
South Asia	111	86	15,429	0.68	..	5	44	115	151	279	12,432	7,919
Sub-Saharan Africa	..	..	3,563	..	2,717	8	110	1,960	6	1	17,106	12,811
High income	3,890	..	582,300	2.48	1,312,001	18	162,778	137,730	822,037	446,827	962,720	198,874
Euro area	2,767	1,237	158,066	2.01	440,779	14	27,601	54,216	81,901	21,591	312,991	21,892

a. Original information was provided by the World Intellectual Property Organization (WIPO). The International Bureau of WIPO assumes no responsibility with respect to the transformation of these data. b. Excludes applications filed under the auspices of the European Patent Office (140,763 by nonresidents) and the Eurasian Patent Organization (2,293 by nonresidents). c. Data are for the most recent year available. d. Includes Luxembourg and the Netherlands.

Technological innovation, often fueled by government-led research and development (R&D), has been the driving force for industrial growth. The best opportunities to improve living standards, including new ways of reducing poverty, will come from science and technology. Countries able to access, generate, and apply scientific knowledge will have a competitive edge. And there is greater appreciation of the need for high-quality scientific input into public policy issues such as regional and global environmental concerns.

Science and technology cover a range of issues too broad and complex to be quantified by a single set of indicators, but those in the table shed light on countries' technology base.

The United Nations Educational, Scientific, and Cultural Organization (UNESCO) Institute for Statistics collects data on researchers, technicians, and expenditure on R&D from around the world, through questionnaires and surveys and from other international sources. R&D covers basic research, applied research, and experimental development. Data on researchers and technicians are normally calculated as full-time equivalents.

Scientific and technical article counts are from a set of journals classified and covered by the Institute for Scientific Information's Science Citation Index (SCI) and Social Sciences Citation Index (SSCI). Counts are based on fractional assignments; for example, an article with two authors from different countries is counted as one-half of an article for each country (see *Definitions* for fields covered). The SCI and SSCI databases cover the core set of scientific journals but may exclude some of regional or local importance. They may also reflect some bias toward English-language journals.

R&D expenditures include all expenditures for R&D performed within a country, including capital expenditures and current costs (annual wages and salaries and all associated costs of researchers, technicians, and supporting staff and other current costs, including noncapital purchases of materials, supplies, and R&D equipment such as utilities, books, journals, reference materials, subscriptions to libraries and scientific societies, and materials for laboratories).

The method for determining a country's high-technology exports was developed by the Organisation for Economic Co-operation and Development in collaboration with Eurostat. Termed the "product approach" to distinguish it from a "sectoral approach," the method is based on R&D intensity (R&D expenditure divided by total sales) for groups of products from Germany, Italy, Japan, the Netherlands, Sweden, and the United States. Because industrial sectors specializing in a few high-technology products may also produce many low-technology products, the product approach is more appropriate than the sectoral approach for analyzing international trade. This method takes only R&D intensity into account, but other characteristics of high technology are also important, such as know-how, scientific and technical personnel, and technology embodied in patents. Considering these characteristics would yield a different list (see Hatzichronoglou 1997). Moreover, the R&D for high-technology exports may not have occurred in the reporting country.

A patent is an exclusive right granted for an invention (a product or process that provides a new way of doing something or a new technical solution to a problem). The invention must be of practical use and display a characteristic unknown in the body of existing knowledge in its technical field. A patent grants protection for a specified period, generally 20 years.

Most countries have systems to protect patentable inventions. The Patent Cooperation Treaty provides a system for filing patent applications. It consists of an international phase followed by a national or regional phase. An applicant files an international application and designates the countries in which patent protection is sought (since 2004 all eligible countries are automatically designated in every application under the treaty). The application is searched and published, and, optionally, an international preliminary examination is conducted. In the national (or regional) phase the applicant requests national processing of the application, pays additional fees, and initiates the national search and granting procedure. International applications under the treaty provide for a national patent grant only—there is no international patent. The national phase filing represents the applicant's seeking of patent protection for a given territory, whereas international filings, while they represent a legal right, do not accurately reflect where patent protection is eventually sought. Resident filings are those from residents of the country or region concerned. Nonresident filings are from applicants outside the country or region. For regional offices such as the European Patent Office, applications from residents of any member state of the regional patent convention are considered a resident filing. Some offices (notably the U.S. Patent and Trademark Office) use the residence of the inventor rather than the applicant to classify resident and nonresident filings. A trademark protects its owner by ensuring exclusive right to use it to identify goods or services or to authorize another to use it in return for payment. The period of protection varies, but a trademark can be renewed indefinitely. Trademarks help consumers identify a product or service whose nature and quality meet their needs.

• **Researchers in R&D** are professionals engaged in conceiving of or creating new knowledge, products, processes, methods, and systems and in managing the projects concerned. Postgraduate doctoral students (ISCED97 level 6) engaged in R&D are considered researchers. • **Technicians in R&D** and equivalent staff are people whose main tasks require technical knowledge and experience in engineering, physical and life sciences (technicians), and social sciences and humanities (equivalent staff). They engage in R&D by performing scientific and technical tasks involving the application of concepts and operational methods, normally under researcher supervision. • **Scientific and technical journal articles** are published articles in physics, biology, chemistry, mathematics, clinical medicine, biomedical research, engineering and technology, and earth and space sciences. • **Expenditures for R&D** are current and capital expenditures on creative work undertaken to increase the stock of knowledge, including on humanity, culture, and society, and the use of knowledge to devise new applications. • **High-technology exports** are products with high R&D intensity, such as in aerospace, computers, pharmaceuticals, scientific instruments, and electrical machinery. • **Royalty and license fees** are payments and receipts between residents and nonresidents for authorized use of intangible, nonproduced, nonfinancial assets and proprietary rights (such as patents, copyrights, trademarks, and industrial processes) and for the use, through licensing, of produced originals of prototypes (such as films and manuscripts). • **Patent applications filed** are worldwide patent applications filed through the Patent Cooperation Treaty procedure or with a national patent office. • **Trademark applications filed** are applications to register a trademark with a national or regional trademark office.

Data on R&D are provided by the UNESCO Institute for Statistics. Data on scientific and technical journal articles are from the U.S. National Science Board's *Science and Engineering Indicators 2008*. Data on high-technology exports are from the United Nations Statistics Division's Commodity Trade (Comtrade) database. Data on royalty and license fees are from the International Monetary Fund's *Balance of Payments Statistics Yearbook*. Data on patents and trademarks are from the World Intellectual Property Organization's *WIPO Patent Report: Statistics on Worldwide Patent Activity* (2008) and www.wipo.int.

GLOBAL LINKS

In a more integrated world the financial crisis reaches more economies faster

Although high-income economies remain the principal source and destination of international trade and investment, globalization has allowed more developing countries to participate in the growth of the global economy. They now account for almost 30 percent of world trade, and their share has been increasing. Developing economies attracted 20 times more foreign direct investment in nominal terms in 2007 than in 1990 and raised 40 times more net portfolio equity. The 12 largest developing economies, which produce 70 percent of developing country output, accounted for 67 percent of developing country exports in 2007. They also received 69 percent of the net private financial inflows to developing economies.

The financial crisis that originated in high-income economies has spread rapidly to developing economies through the same channels that connect them to the global economy: trade, investment, aid, and the movement of people. Although developing economies have previously encountered financial and economic crises, the current one is larger and may last longer. And because the world is more integrated, the crisis will affect more economies and more people.

Even before the current crisis many developing economies' finances suffered from hikes in commodity prices in the first half of 2008, while net exporters of commodities gained. Since then, the prices of primary commodities have declined rapidly. While the net effect is difficult to measure, some developing economies have benefited from improved terms of trade, but price volatility undermines investment in the commodity-producing and exporting sectors— and reduces government revenue.

Export revenues constitute about a third of developing country GDP. But global demand is declining, as economies in recession import less and less. Economies that benefited from growing exports in the past decade will be hurt as export revenues decline.

Weak prospects for international capital markets, foreign investments, and aid flows pose an immediate danger for developing economies. Equity prices plunged during the financial crisis, and developing country asset values declined. Credit conditions have tightened, and cross-border lending has become more expensive. Foreign direct investment is likely to decline as businesses around the world suffer from shrinking profits and growing pressure to raise cash. Lower financial flows affect countries differently, depending on their integration with capital markets and their dependence on foreign capital. In the past, as donor economies entered recession, their aid to developing economies fell. Countries dependent on official flows are likely to face fiscal difficulties if donors fail to keep their aid commitments.

High-income economies are the primary destination for migrant workers. The financial crisis has distressed labor markets in many high-income economies, and millions of workers— including many migrants—are losing their jobs. This may diminish workers' remittances, an important source of foreign capital in many developing economies.

Data in this section provide snapshots of the world's integration and a framework for measuring it, to show how developing economies are likely to be affected by the recent financial crisis. Figures 6y–6vv illustrate just how quickly the financial crisis has spread.

Global trade slows

The importance of trade to low- and middle-income economies can be seen in the ratio of trade (imports plus exports) to GDP, which has risen rapidly, from 47 percent in 1990 to 70 percent in 2007 for low-income economies and 39 percent to 64 percent for middle-income economies, surpassing the share of high-income economies (figure 6a). Increased exports drove many developing economies' GDP growth in the past few years.

Developing economies' share of world trade increased from 18 percent in 1990 to 28 percent in 2007. The 12 largest developing economies— China, India, Russian Federation, Brazil, Mexico, Turkey, Indonesia, Islamic Republic of Iran, Poland, Argentina, Thailand, and South Africa—accounted for 67 percent of developing economies' exports in 2007, a share that has increased over time (figure 6b). China alone accounted for 27 percent. Low-income economies' share of global exports in 2007 was a mere 1.8 percent, but export revenues constituted 33 percent of their GDP.

Although trade between developing economies increased in the last decade, trade with high-income economies still accounts for the largest portion of developing economies' total merchandise exports. In 2007 about 70 percent of middle-income economies' merchandise exports went to high-income economies (figure 6c). Low-income economies exported 67 percent of their goods to high-income markets. And some of the exports to other developing economies are primary goods, which are in turn used for manufactured goods destined for high-income markets.

Since the onset of the financial crisis, the output of high-income economies has fallen and with it global trade. In the third quarter of 2008 the volume of imports by Group of Seven industrial economies declined 1.4 percent over the same quarter in 2007. The sharpest reductions were in Italy (7.1 percent), the United Kingdom (5.2 percent), the United States (3.6 percent), and Japan (1.3 percent) (figure 6d).

Developing economies' exports fell sharply starting in the last quarter of 2008. Merchandise exports in January 2009 fell 17 percent over exports in January 2008 for China, 31 percent for Mexico, and 43 percent for the Russian Federation. Imports by large developing economies from other developing economies have also declined, and the ripple effect is likely to hurt the low-income economies whose main exports are primary commodities such as fuels, metals, minerals, and agricultural raw materials.

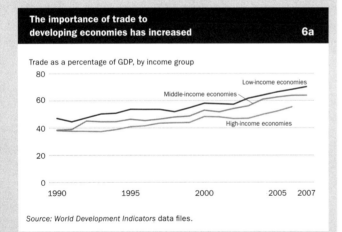

The importance of trade to developing economies has increased   **6a**

Trade as a percentage of GDP, by income group

Source: World Development Indicators data files.

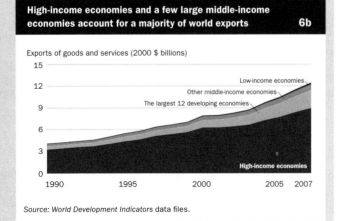

High-income economies and a few large middle-income economies account for a majority of world exports   **6b**

Exports of goods and services (2000 $ billions)

Source: World Development Indicators data files.

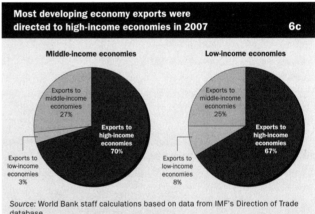

Most developing economy exports were directed to high-income economies in 2007   **6c**

Middle-income economies | Low-income economies

Source: World Bank staff calculations based on data from IMF's Direction of Trade database.

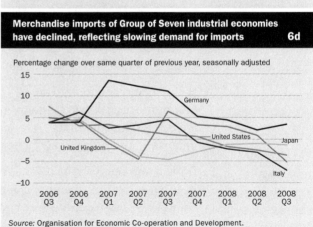

Merchandise imports of Group of Seven industrial economies have declined, reflecting slowing demand for imports   **6d**

Percentage change over same quarter of previous year, seasonally adjusted

Source: Organisation for Economic Co-operation and Development.

Primary commodity prices have been volatile

Commodity prices rose rapidly in early 2008 before collapsing in the second half of the year (figure 6e). Oil prices rose 48 percent between December 2007 and July 2008 and then plunged 69 percent by December 2008. Prices of nonenergy commodities increased an average of 32 percent then dropped 39 percent over the same period. Food, fertilizers, and metals and minerals have been among the most volatile.

The price hikes in early 2008 threatened to impoverish around 200 million people. They also weakened the fiscal positions of developing economies that import large quantities of food and fuel (table 6f), as governments spent more on subsidies and safety nets to offset higher costs. The sharp price decline in the second half of 2008 eased the pressure on net importers of fuel and other commodities, but hurt the export revenues of economies that export mostly oil. Net importers of food and fuel may temporarily benefit from lower prices, but producers of export commodities are likely to suffer. Low prices and uncertain long-term prospects may diminish further investment in primary commodities.

Private financial flows— greater access for some

Developing economies now have greater access to international capital markets and attract more foreign direct investment (FDI). In nominal terms private capital flows to developing economies increased from $208 billion in 2003 to $961 billion in 2007, but 70 percent of that went to the 12 largest economies.

FDI was the source of 55 percent of private financial flows to developing economies in 2007. The 12 largest economies, with greater access to international capital markets, also received large amounts of portfolio equity investment, at 18 percent of total private flows in 2007 (figure 6g). For developing economies with limited or no access to international capital markets, borrowing from private creditors was the second largest source of private flows, at 25 percent in 2007 (figure 6h).

Larger middle-income economies were directly hit by falling equity prices. Sovereign and corporate bond spreads widened, indicating more costly borrowing terms. Cross-border lending by private creditors also slowed, restricting credit to developing economies, especially to the least creditworthy borrowers.

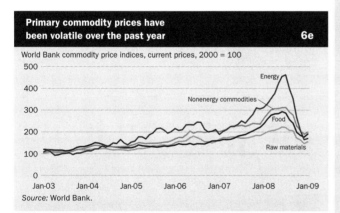

Primary commodity prices have been volatile over the past year — 6e

World Bank commodity price indices, current prices, 2000 = 100

Source: World Bank.

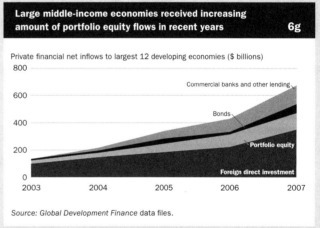

Large middle-income economies received increasing amount of portfolio equity flows in recent years — 6g

Private financial net inflows to largest 12 developing economies ($ billions)

Source: Global Development Finance data files.

For some economies food imports were equivalent to more than 7 percent of household consumption, 2005–07 average — 6f

| Economy | Merchandise imports | | Food imports | Fuel imports |
	Value ($ millions)	Share of PPP GDP (percent)	Share of PPP household consumption (percent)	Share of PPP GDP (percent)
Namibia	3,003	30.1	11.3	1.9
Botswana	3,419	14.3	9.4	2.2
Gambia, The	270	14.1	9.4	2.4
Jordan	11,852	45.9	9.1	10.5
Mauritius	3,560	26.7	8.5	4.6
Senegal	3,694	19.0	8.0	5.2
Swaziland	2,461	47.5	7.6	3.5
Jamaica	5,430	32.8	7.3	9.9
Gabon	1,815	9.6	7.0	0.3

PPP is purchasing power parity.
Source: World Development Indicators data files.

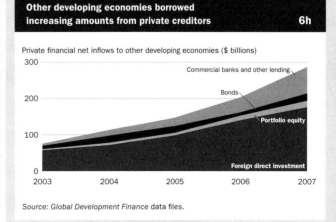

Other developing economies borrowed increasing amounts from private creditors — 6h

Private financial net inflows to other developing economies ($ billions)

Source: Global Development Finance data files.

Foreign direct investment— largest source of private financing

In 2007 high-income economies received about 75 percent of global FDI inflows. The 12 largest developing economies received more than 66 percent of the remainder (figure 6i), with China alone receiving nearly 26 percent. Low-income economies received a mere 1.5 percent of global FDI.

Despite accounting for a small part of global flows, FDI is the largest source of private financing for many developing economies, especially important for low-income economies with limited or no access to international capital markets. Between 2000 and 2007 FDI net inflows to low-income economies more than doubled, from 1.7 percent of GDP to 4.2 percent of GDP (figure 6j). The increase was due partly to increased investments in oil, mineral, and other primary commodity production sectors driven by high commodity prices and partly to an increase in infrastructure projects (many through public-private partnerships). In 2007 FDI net inflows were more than 20 percent of GDP for nine small economies— Republic of Congo, Seychelles, St. Kitts and Nevis, St. Lucia, Montenegro, São Tomé and Principe, Djibouti, Grenada, and Bulgaria.

Foreign direct investment— stable source of financing?

FDI is considered a fairly stable source of external financing, but in past financial crises it declined, sometimes sharply. During the East Asian financial crisis net inflows of FDI fell 105 percent between 1997 and 1998 to Indonesia and 58 percent to Malaysia in parallel with falling output (figure 6k). For Thailand and the Republic of Korea FDI net inflows remained resilient for two to three years (figure 6l).

The current financial crisis originated in high-income economies, so the effect on FDI flows to developing economies may be more drastic than in past crises originating in developing economies. Businesses around the world are lowering their capital spending in response to tighter credit and weaker global demand. And reinvested earnings, which have accounted for a rising share of FDI net inflows, have started to plunge as profits weakened. Likewise, weak commodity prices are likely to undermine new investments in commodity-producing industries, and low real estate prices will weaken FDI in the construction sector. For countries already running current account deficits, a shortfall in FDI may further undermine their ability to manage their balance of payments.

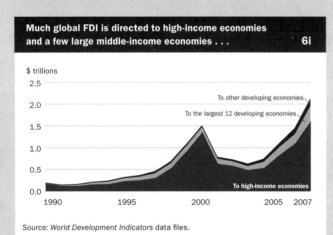

Much global FDI is directed to high-income economies and a few large middle-income economies . . . 6i

Source: World Development Indicators data files.

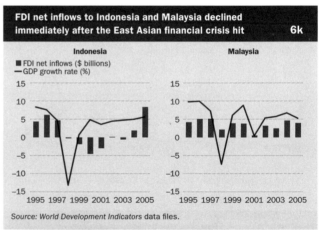

FDI net inflows to Indonesia and Malaysia declined immediately after the East Asian financial crisis hit 6k

Source: World Development Indicators data files.

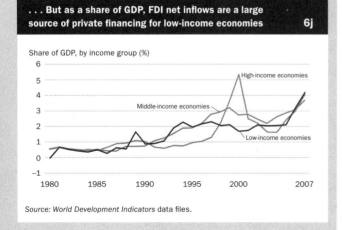

. . . But as a share of GDP, FDI net inflows are a large source of private financing for low-income economies 6j

Source: World Development Indicators data files.

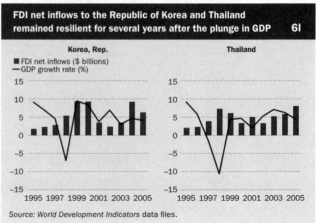

FDI net inflows to the Republic of Korea and Thailand remained resilient for several years after the plunge in GDP 6l

Source: World Development Indicators data files.

Declining portfolio equity flows

In 2007 high-income economies received $577 billion—more than 80 percent of global portfolio equity flows. Developing economies received nearly $140 billion, more than 87 percent of it going to the 12 largest developing economies (figure 6m). And low-income economies received only 1.7 percent of global equity flows.

For larger middle-income economies with developed capital markets, portfolio equity flows are the second largest source of private financial flows. Equities from these economies (emerging market equities) became an attractive investment for high-income investors with appetites for risk, and their prices soared after 2005. Equity markets, declining since October 2007, fell sharply in the last quarter of 2008; investors became more risk averse and were pressed to liquidate their holdings.

Developing economies now play a bigger role in international capital markets. Stock market capitalization of listed companies from developing economies accounted for 23 percent of global market capitalization in end-2007, up from 6 percent in end-2000. In more mature developing markets the stock market capitalization to GDP ratio, at its peak, approached that of high-income economies, around 120 percent. But the ratio has been volatile over the past few years and may be unsustainable for some countries (figure 6n). By December 2008 the stock market capitalization in 42 developing economies where data are available had fallen to 52 percent of GDP, down more than 59 percentage points from its October 2007 peak.

Private debt flows have become more costly

Developing economies raised net capital of $85.4 billion through bond issuance in 2007, up from $20.4 billion in 2003. The five largest bond issuers (Russian Federation, Kazakhstan, India, Turkey, and Ukraine) accounted for 74 percent. Nearly 90 percent of the bond issuance by low-income economies in 2007 was public and publicly guaranteed, while almost 70 percent by middle-income economies was private nonguaranteed. Following the financial crisis, sovereign bond spreads (the spread over 10-year U.S. Treasury notes) widened for most developing economies, raising the cost of borrowing. Corporate bond spreads jumped even more (figure 6o). By January 2009 sovereign bond spreads in 15 developing economies exceeded the "distressed debt" threshold of 1,000 basis points.

Borrowing from private creditors is (after FDI) the second-largest source of private financial flows to developing economies. It is especially important for low-income economies with limited or no access to global equity markets. The financial crisis has made cross-border borrowing more costly. And trade finance tightened in the last quarter of 2008.

Most affected by the slump in debt flows is Europe and Central Asia, where net borrowing from foreign private creditors rapidly increased during the last few years, from $14.5 billion (1 percent of GDP) in 2003 to $131.2 billion (4 percent of GDP) in 2007 (figure 6p).

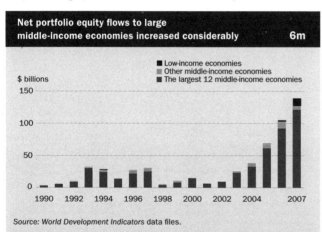

Net portfolio equity flows to large middle-income economies increased considerably · **6m**

Source: World Development Indicators data files.

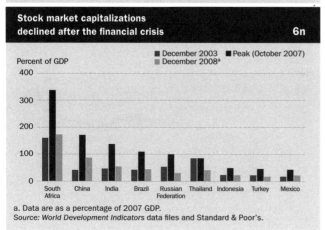

Stock market capitalizations declined after the financial crisis · **6n**

a. Data are as a percentage of 2007 GDP.
Source: World Development Indicators data files and Standard & Poor's.

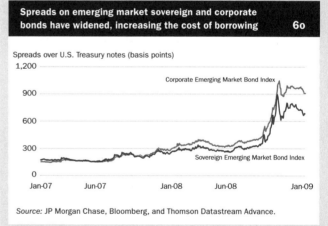

Spreads on emerging market sovereign and corporate bonds have widened, increasing the cost of borrowing · **6o**

Source: JP Morgan Chase, Bloomberg, and Thomson Datastream Advance.

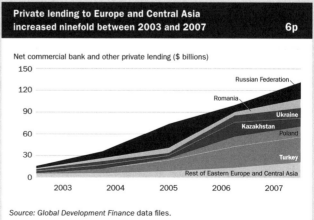

Private lending to Europe and Central Asia increased ninefold between 2003 and 2007 · **6p**

Source: Global Development Finance data files.

External debt declined but the share of private debt has increased

External debt of low-income economies declined from 65 percent of GNI in 2000 to 29 percent in 2007, partly due to debt relief (figure 6q). Public debt from official creditors accounted for nearly 90 percent of the long-term external debt of low-income countries in 2007, and public debt from private creditors for 7 percent. Private nonguaranteed debt was less than 1 percent of GNI.

External debt of middle-income economies declined from 36 percent of GNI in 2000 to less than 25 percent in 2007. More than half their long-term external debt was private nonguaranteed debt, which amounted to 10 percent of GNI in 2007. Public debt from private creditors was 6 percent of GNI and short-term debt 5 percent of GNI, putting some middle-income economies at greater risk from tightening global credit markets.

Net lending of international financial institutions to middle-income economies had been declining since 2002 (figure 6r). But with private capital flows drying up, middle-income economies are again turning to the major international financial institutions. The International Monetary Fund made new commitments to several countries totaling $45 billion as of February 2009. The World Bank created a $2 billion fast-track fund to assist the poorest countries affected by the crisis and plans to increase commitments to all eligible countries in the next few years.

Official development assistance— a lifeline to poor countries

Official development assistance is the main source of external financing for low-income economies (figure 6s). For some countries (Liberia, Burundi, Micronesia, Solomon Islands, Afghanistan, Guinea-Bissau, and Sierra Leone) it is equivalent to more than 30 percent of GNI.

Official development assistance has risen 38 percent in constant prices since 2000, but most of the increase was for debt relief, technical assistance, and emergency relief, which do not provide long-term investment to raise productive capacity. Official development assistance to finance long-term development projects has not increased much since the 1970s (figure 6t). After reaching a record $107 billion in 2005—mainly driven by one-time debt relief—aid declined by 13 percent in 2007.

Official development assistance is a small part of the budgets of the Development Assistance Committee members of the Organisation for Economic Co-operation and Development, averaging only 0.28 percent of their GNI, a small fraction of what they will spend on bailouts and fiscal stimulus in their domestic economies. But for low-income economies that depend on aid for their development, even a small decline can be devastating. To counter the financial crisis and progress toward their development goals, the poorest countries will need more assistance from external donors.

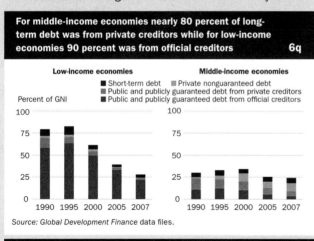

For middle-income economies nearly 80 percent of long-term debt was from private creditors while for low-income economies 90 percent was from official creditors   **6q**

Source: Global Development Finance data files.

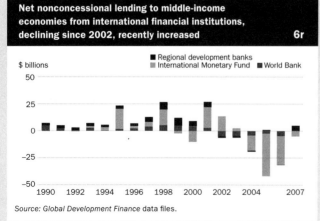

Net nonconcessional lending to middle-income economies from international financial institutions, declining since 2002, recently increased   **6r**

Source: Global Development Finance data files.

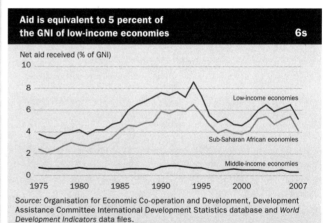

Aid is equivalent to 5 percent of the GNI of low-income economies   **6s**

Source: Organisation for Economic Co-operation and Development, Development Assistance Committee International Development Statistics database and World Development Indicators data files.

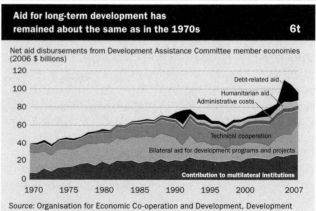

Aid for long-term development has remained about the same as in the 1970s   **6t**

Source: Organisation for Economic Co-operation and Development, Development Assistance Committee International Development Statistics database.

Official development assistance—in historical perspective

Aid flows usually decline after an economic crisis in the donor economy. After Japan's bubble economy burst in 1990 aid flows declined continually through 1996 by 24 percent. After the U.S. savings and loan crisis in the 1980s aid flows dropped 46 percent over the next 10 years. After the Nordic banking crisis in 1991 net aid flows fell 61 percent from Finland, 14 percent from Sweden, and 7 percent from Norway (figure 6u). In Norway aid flows recovered immediately, while Sweden's aid flows continued to decline through 1998.

But donor economies can increase aid flows to developing economies even with difficult conditions at home. After the dot-com bubble burst in 2000, the United States—despite significant economic difficulties—increased its aid flows continually through 2005 (figure 6v). The increase was partly a response to international pressure to increase aid following the 2000 UN Millennium Summit and the 2002 Financing for Development Conference and partly a response to the humanitarian needs of countries at war, such as Afghanistan and Iraq.

Migration and remittances—of increased importance for developing economies

Net migration to high-income economies totaled 18.5 million people during 2000–05, almost twice the number for 1985–90 (figure 6w). Global flows of workers' remittances and compensation of employees also increased, from $68.6 billion in 1990 to $371.3 billion in 2007, more than 75 percent of it received by developing economies, up from 45 percent in 1990 (figure 6x).

Remittances have become an important source of foreign exchange earnings for developing economies, at 2 percent of their GDP in 2007. For low-income economies remittances equaled 7 percent of GDP in 2007, up from 3 percent in 2000. And for Guyana, Lesotho, Liberia, Moldova, Seychelles, Tajikistan, and Tonga remittances accounted for more than 25 percent of GDP in 2007.

The deepening global recession has reduced demand for migrant workers. As labor markets tighten, thousands of workers are losing their jobs, and some migrants are returning home. After a final surge associated with the repatriation of savings and capital assets, remittances are expected to decline, leaving many families with fewer means of support.

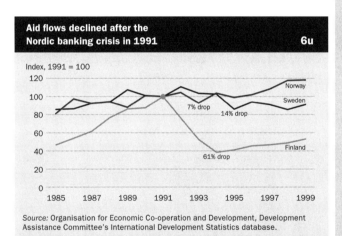

Aid flows declined after the Nordic banking crisis in 1991 — **6u**

Source: Organisation for Economic Co-operation and Development, Development Assistance Committee's International Development Statistics database.

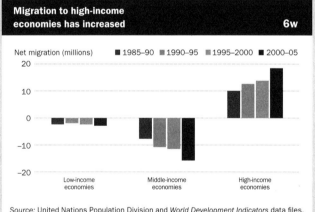

Migration to high-income economies has increased — **6w**

Source: United Nations Population Division and *World Development Indicators* data files.

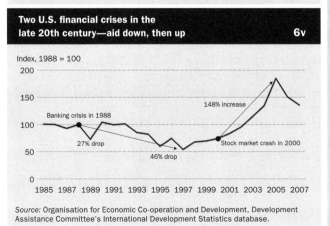

Two U.S. financial crises in the late 20th century—aid down, then up — **6v**

Source: Organisation for Economic Co-operation and Development, Development Assistance Committee's International Development Statistics database.

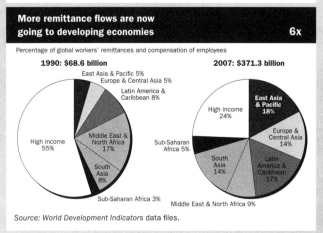

More remittance flows are now going to developing economies — **6x**

Source: *World Development Indicators* data files.

Merchandise trade

Goods make up 70–90 percent of most countries' total exports and imports. Since 2006 Brazil, China, and the Russian Federation have been running current account surpluses, while Egypt, India, and South Africa have had deficits. In the last quarter of 2008 merchandise exports and imports in absolute values and as a share of GDP declined for China, India, the Russian Federation, and South Africa (figures 6y–6dd). Merchandise exports and imports also declined for Brazil, but its GDP declined more.

Equity price indices

Equities of large developing economies had become attractive investments, and their prices soared through October 2007. But equity prices fell back in late 2007 and plunged in the last quarter of 2008 (figures 6ee–6jj). Declines in equity prices undermine the values of developing country assets.

Bond spreads

Following the financial crisis, sovereign bond spreads have widened. Corporate spreads have jumped even more. Bond spreads, measured by J.P. Morgan's Emerging Markets Bond Index Global (EMBI Global) and Corporate Emerging Markets Bond Index (CEMBI) and benchmarked against the yield of 10-year U.S. Treasury notes, indicate that the cost of external borrowing for developing countries is rising (figures 6kk–6pp).

Financing through international capital markets

In 2007 developing economies received increasing amounts of gross private debt and equity flows. But in 2008, even before the intensification of the financial crisis, credit conditions tightened, and transactions slowed. Since October 2008 there has been virtually no new equity issuance, and only a limited amount of new bond issuance and syndicated bank loan commitments (figures 6qq–6vv).

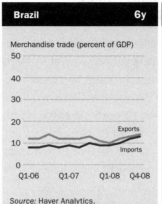

Brazil   **6y**

Merchandise trade (percent of GDP)

Source: Haver Analytics.

China   **6z**

Merchandise trade (percent of GDP)

Source: Haver Analytics.

Brazil   **6ee**

MSCI equity price index
(January 2007 = 100)

Source: MSCI Barra and Thomson
Datastream Advance.

China   **6ff**

MSCI equity price index
(January 2007 = 100)

Source: MSCI Barra and Thomson
Datastream Advance.

Brazil   **6kk**

Spreads over U.S. Treasury notes
(basis points)

Source: JP Morgan Chase, Bloomberg,
and Thomson Datastream Advance.

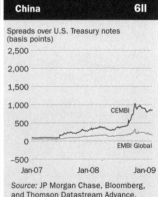

China   **6ll**

Spreads over U.S. Treasury notes
(basis points)

Source: JP Morgan Chase, Bloomberg,
and Thomson Datastream Advance.

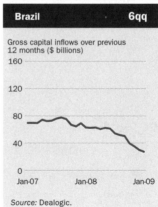

Brazil   **6qq**

Gross capital inflows over previous
12 months ($ billions)

Source: Dealogic.

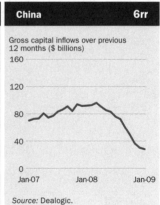

China   **6rr**

Gross capital inflows over previous
12 months ($ billions)

Source: Dealogic.

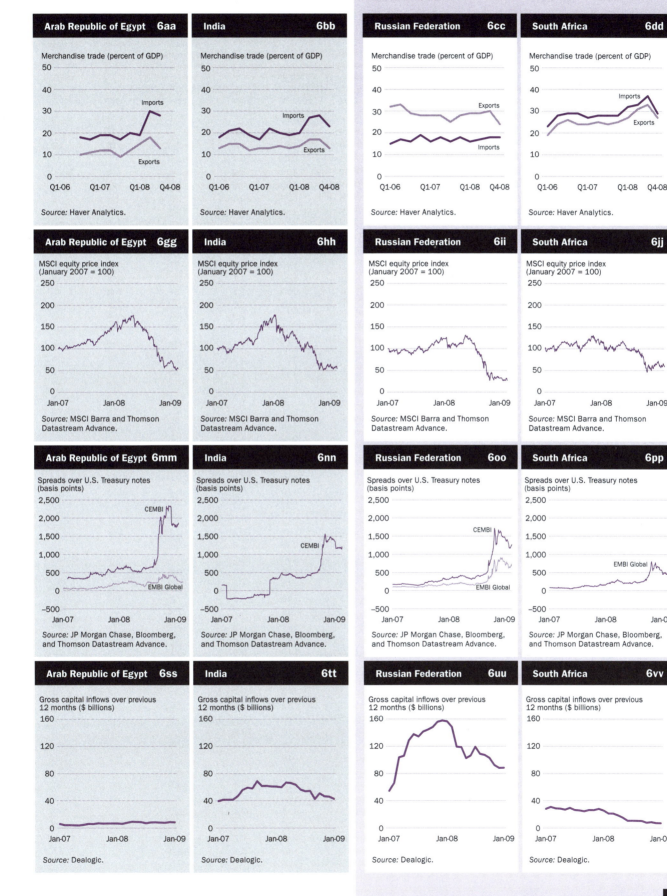

Arab Republic of Egypt 6aa

Merchandise trade (percent of GDP)

Imports

Exports

Source: Haver Analytics.

India 6bb

Merchandise trade (percent of GDP)

Imports

Exports

Source: Haver Analytics.

Russian Federation 6cc

Merchandise trade (percent of GDP)

Exports

Imports

Source: Haver Analytics.

South Africa 6dd

Merchandise trade (percent of GDP)

Imports

Exports

Source: Haver Analytics.

Arab Republic of Egypt 6gg

MSCI equity price index
(January 2007 = 100)

Source: MSCI Barra and Thomson
Datastream Advance.

India 6hh

MSCI equity price index
(January 2007 = 100)

Source: MSCI Barra and Thomson
Datastream Advance.

Russian Federation 6ii

MSCI equity price index
(January 2007 = 100)

Source: MSCI Barra and Thomson
Datastream Advance.

South Africa 6jj

MSCI equity price index
(January 2007 = 100)

Source: MSCI Barra and Thomson
Datastream Advance.

Arab Republic of Egypt 6mm

Spreads over U.S. Treasury notes
(basis points)

CEMBI

EMBI Global

Source: JP Morgan Chase, Bloomberg,
and Thomson Datastream Advance.

India 6nn

Spreads over U.S. Treasury notes
(basis points)

CEMBI

Source: JP Morgan Chase, Bloomberg,
and Thomson Datastream Advance.

Russian Federation 6oo

Spreads over U.S. Treasury notes
(basis points)

CEMBI

EMBI Global

Source: JP Morgan Chase, Bloomberg,
and Thomson Datastream Advance.

South Africa 6pp

Spreads over U.S. Treasury notes
(basis points)

EMBI Global

Source: JP Morgan Chase, Bloomberg,
and Thomson Datastream Advance.

Arab Republic of Egypt 6ss

Gross capital inflows over previous
12 months ($ billions)

Source: Dealogic.

India 6tt

Gross capital inflows over previous
12 months ($ billions)

Source: Dealogic.

Russian Federation 6uu

Gross capital inflows over previous
12 months ($ billions)

Source: Dealogic.

South Africa 6vv

Gross capital inflows over previous
12 months ($ billions)

Source: Dealogic.

6.1 Integration with the global economy

	Trade % of GDP		International finance % of GDP				Movement of people			Communication	
			Financing through international capital markets Gross inflows	Foreign direct investment Net inflows	Net outflows	Workers' remittances and compensation of employees received	Net migration thousands	International migrant stock % of total population	Emigration of people with tertiary education to OECD countries % of population age 25 and older with tertiary education	International voice traffic[a] minutes per person	International Internet bandwidth[a] bits per second per capita
	Merchandise	Services									
	2007	2007	2007	2007	2007	2007	2000–05	2005	2000	2007	2007
Afghanistan	35.6	..	0.0	2.9	..	..	1,112	..	22.6	1	0
Albania	48.6	26.0	0.0	4.4	0.1	9.9	−110	2.6	17.4	125	216
Algeria	64.9	..	0.3	1.2	..	1.6[b]	−140	0.7	9.4	18	89
Angola	83.5	21.1	5.8	−1.5	1.5	..	175	0.4	3.6	..	17
Argentina	38.4	8.1	4.4	2.5	0.6	0.2	−100	3.9	2.8	3	2,320
Armenia	48.2	14.9	0.2	7.6	0.0	9.2	−100	7.8	8.9	128	..
Australia	37.4	9.7	..	4.8	3.0	0.5	593	20.1	2.7	..	5,472
Austria	87.2	25.4	..	8.2	8.4	0.8	180	15.0	13.5	..	20,288
Azerbaijan	51.9	14.8	2.9	−15.2	0.9	4.1	−100	2.2	1.8	..	701
Bangladesh	45.4	6.6	1.0	1.0	0.0	9.6	−500	0.7	4.4	6	4
Belarus	118.4	11.8	0.8	4.0	0.0	0.8	0	12.2	3.2	..	264
Belgium	186.4	33.5	..	15.9	12.2	1.9	180	6.9	5.5	..	24,945
Benin	39.6	12.3	0.0	0.9	0.0	4.1[b]	99	2.1	8.6	11	17
Bolivia	60.5	9.9	0.0	1.6	0.0	7.1	−100	1.3	5.8	80	42
Bosnia and Herzegovina	92.0	12.8	0.9	13.9	0.2	16.6	115	1.1	20.3	241	530
Botswana	74.3	15.5	0.0	−0.2	0.0	1.1	20	4.4	5.1	93	43
Brazil	21.9	4.7	5.3	2.6	0.5	0.3	−229	0.3	2.0	..	1,041
Bulgaria	122.5	28.2	11.9	22.7	0.7	5.3	−43	1.3	9.6	31	4,909
Burkina Faso	33.4	..	0.2	8.9	..	0.7[b]	100	5.5	2.5	11	15
Burundi	39.2	21.4	0.0	0.1	0.0	0.0	192	1.3	7.3	..	1
Cambodia	115.0	29.4	3.2	10.4	0.0	4.2	10	2.2	21.4	10	17
Cameroon	35.6	10.1	0.0	2.1	−0.8	0.8	6	0.8	17.1	4	11
Canada	60.8	10.8	..	8.4	4.1	..	1,041	18.9	4.7	..	16,193
Central African Republic	24.8	..	17.8	1.6	..	..	−45	1.8	7.2	..	0
Chad	69.9	..	0.0	8.5	..	..	219	4.3	9.0	..	1
Chile	70.4	11.4	3.4	8.8	2.3	0.0[b]	30	1.4	6.0	40	4,086
China	67.8	7.9	2.9	4.3	0.5	1.0[b]	−1,900	0.0	3.8	9	280
Hong Kong, China	347.3	60.2	..	26.2	29.5	0.2	300	44.0	29.6	1,387	15,892
Colombia	30.3	4.8	3.1	4.4	0.4	2.2	−120	0.3	10.4	106	971
Congo, Dem. Rep.	70.9	..	0.0	8.0	..	..	−237	0.9	9.0	4	0
Congo, Rep.	117.7	50.3	0.0	56.1	..	0.2	−10	8.0	22.9	..	0
Costa Rica	84.9	20.7	0.1	7.2	1.0	2.4	84	10.2	7.1	119	820
Côte d'Ivoire	74.1	17.1	0.4	2.2	..	0.9	−339	12.8	6.1	..	16
Croatia	74.5	32.1	9.9	9.6	0.5	2.7	100	14.9	24.6	208	3,380
Cuba	..	..	..	..	..	..	−129	0.7	28.8	31	19
Czech Republic	137.3	18.0	..	5.3	0.8	0.8	67	4.4	8.5	74	7,075
Denmark	65.2	37.1	..	3.8	6.4	0.3	46	7.2	7.8	307	34,506
Dominican Republic	57.4	18.0	2.9	4.6	0.0	9.3	−148	1.7	22.4	..	154
Ecuador	61.5	8.4	0.2	0.4	0.0	7.0	−400	0.9	9.5	90	324
Egypt, Arab Rep.	33.2	26.3	5.2	8.9	0.5	5.9	−525	0.2	4.7	42	143
El Salvador	62.1	15.8	0.0	7.5	0.5	18.2	−143	0.4	31.7	515	18
Eritrea	38.6	..	0.0	−0.2	..	..	229	0.3	35.2	7	2
Estonia	126.8	35.7	2.9	12.9	7.5	2.0	1	15.0	9.9	..	11,925
Ethiopia	34.4	16.1	0.0	1.1	0.0	1.8	−140	0.7	9.8	3	3
Finland	70.0	17.2	..	4.7	3.5	0.3	33	3.0	7.2	..	17,221
France	45.1	10.7	..	6.2	8.8	0.5	722	10.6	3.4	243	29,466
Gabon	72.6	13.7	9.6	2.3	0.9	0.1[b]	10	18.9	14.4	74	150
Gambia, The	51.0	29.7	0.0	10.6	..	7.4	31	14.3	67.8	..	36
Georgia	63.5	19.9	7.8	17.0	0.7	6.8	−248	4.3	2.8	..	745
Germany	71.9	14.4	..	1.6	5.2	0.3	1,000	12.3	5.7	..	25,654
Ghana	80.9	25.3	15.2	6.4	0.0	0.8	12	7.4	44.6	1	21
Greece	31.9	20.2	..	0.6	1.7	0.3	154	8.8	12.1	182	4,537
Guatemala	60.6	11.0	0.0	2.1	0.2	12.6	−300	0.4	23.9	..	187
Guinea	50.2	7.5	0.0	2.4	..	3.3	−425	4.5	4.6	..	0
Guinea-Bissau	65.8	..	0.0	2.0	..	8.1[b]	1	1.2	27.7	..	1
Haiti	32.8	13.5	0.0	1.1	..	18.2	−140	0.3	83.4	..	17

	Trade % of GDP		International finance % of GDP				Movement of people			Communication	
	Merchandise	Services	Financing through international capital markets Gross inflows	Foreign direct investment Net inflows	Net outflows	Workers' remittances and compensation of employees received	Net migration thousands	International migrant stock % of total population	Emigration of people with tertiary education to OECD countries % of population age 25 and older with tertiary education	International voice traffic minutes per person	International Internet bandwidth bits per second per capita
	2007	2007	2007	2007	2007	2007	2000–05	2005	2000	2007	2007
Honduras	115.7	14.6	0.0	6.7	0.0	21.5	−150	0.4	24.8	33	244
Hungary	137.0	23.1	8.2	26.9	25.8	0.3	65	3.1	12.8	120	4,773
India	30.8	15.2	5.2	2.0	1.1	3.0[b]	−1,350	0.5	4.3	..	32
Indonesia	48.6	8.5	2.9	1.6	1.1	1.4	−1,000	0.1	2.9	..	53
Iran, Islamic Rep.	46.1	..	0.1	0.3	..	0.4[b]	−1,250	2.8	14.3	9	153
Iraq	..	..	..	..	..	..	−375	..	10.9	..	4
Ireland	78.6	70.8	..	10.1	8.5	0.2	188	14.1	33.7	..	15,229
Israel	69.0	23.8	..	5.9	4.3	0.6	115	38.4	7.8	364	2,003
Italy	47.4	11.1	..	1.9	4.4	0.2	1,125	4.3	9.6	..	10,302
Jamaica	68.6	43.4	33.4	7.6	1.0	18.8	−100	0.7	84.7	..	19,151
Japan	30.4	6.4	..	0.5	1.7	0.0	270	1.6	1.2	46	3,734
Jordan	121.3	43.5	8.9	11.6	0.3	21.7	130	41.1	7.4	32	164
Kazakhstan	76.8	14.5	26.2	9.7	3.1	0.2	−200	16.5	1.2	47	129
Kenya	54.0	17.2	0.0	3.0	0.1	6.6[b]	25	1.0	38.5	3	9
Korea, Dem. Rep.	..	..	..	..	..	..	0	0.2	..	..	..
Korea, Rep.	75.1	15.1	..	0.2	1.6	0.1	−80	1.1	7.5	29	1,027
Kuwait	76.7	20.3	..	0.1	12.2	..	264	65.8	7.1	..	871
Kyrgyz Republic	94.9	33.8	0.0	5.6	0.0	19.1	−75	5.6	0.9	30	114
Lao PDR	48.4	8.6	5.3	7.9	..	0.0[b]	−115	0.4	37.2	7	32
Latvia	86.9	23.5	7.8	8.3	1.2	2.0	−20	19.5	8.5	67	3,537
Lebanon	65.0	92.4	11.8	11.7	−1.0	23.7	0	16.4	43.8	279	227
Lesotho	158.4	11.7	1.2	8.1	..	27.7	−36	0.3	4.1	18	2
Liberia	92.9	216.4	158.1	17.9	0.0	8.8	−119	1.5	44.3	..	..
Libya	91.1	4.7	0.2	8.0	1.3	0.0[b]	10	10.4	4.3	66	50
Lithuania	107.9	19.4	5.3	5.3	1.6	3.7	−30	4.8	8.3	54	4,656
Macedonia, FYR	111.9	18.5	0.5	4.2	0.0	3.5[b]	−10	6.0	29.4	125	17
Madagascar	51.2	22.1	5.7	13.5	..	0.1[b]	−5	0.3	7.7	1	8
Malawi	60.6	..	0.2	1.5	..	0.0[b]	−30	2.1	20.9	..	5
Malaysia	173.1	30.1	7.9	4.5	5.9	1.0[b]	150	6.4	10.5	..	998
Mali	54.4	16.8	2.6	5.2	0.0	3.1[b]	−134	0.4	14.7	2	17
Mauritania	114.2	..	0.0	5.8	..	0.1[b]	30	2.2	8.5	5	70
Mauritius	90.3	55.3	16.2	5.0	0.9	3.2[b]	0	1.7	55.8	125	226
Mexico	55.6	4.1	4.3	2.4	0.8	2.7[b]	−3,983	0.6	15.5	185	178
Moldova	114.5	29.1	0.0	11.2	0.3	34.1	−250	11.4	4.1	149	931
Mongolia	101.9	32.2	1.9	8.3	..	4.9[b]	−50	0.4	7.4	5	116
Morocco	61.7	23.4	4.1	3.7	0.8	9.0	−550	0.4	18.0	22	814
Mozambique	77.0	16.9	11.0	5.5	0.0	1.3	−20	2.0	22.5	13	3
Myanmar	..	..	..	..	..	..[b]	−99	0.2	3.9	..	2
Namibia	90.4	15.9	0.0	2.4	0.0	0.2	−1	7.1	3.4	..	27
Nepal	36.8	12.0	0.0	0.1	..	16.8	−100	3.0	4.0	6	5
Netherlands	136.2	23.7	..	16.1	3.5	0.3	110	10.0	9.5	..	78,159
New Zealand	42.7	13.5	..	2.0	2.1	0.5	102	15.5	21.8	310	4,544
Nicaragua	83.5	16.2	0.0	6.7	0.0	12.9	−210	0.5	30.2	65	144
Niger	40.8	11.7	0.0	0.6	0.0	1.9	−28	0.9	5.4	..	2
Nigeria	57.4	9.5	4.3	3.7	0.3	5.6[b]	−170	0.7	10.5	..	5
Norway	55.8	20.7	..	1.0	3.2	0.2	84	7.4	6.2	193	26,904
Oman	91.3	13.4	6.6	4.5	0.9	0.1	−150	25.0	0.4	37	142
Pakistan	35.3	8.8	1.7	3.7	0.1	4.2	−1,239	2.1	12.7	10	44
Panama	41.2	36.1	15.3	9.8	0.0	0.9	8	3.2	16.7	66	15,977
Papua New Guinea	121.1	29.9	13.2	1.5	0.1	0.2[b]	0	0.4	27.8	..	1
Paraguay	82.3	10.8	0.0	1.6	0.1	3.8	−45	2.9	3.8	35	163
Peru	44.9	7.1	3.1	5.0	..	2.0	−510	0.2	5.8	99	2,704
Philippines	75.3	11.0	6.3	2.0	2.4	11.3	−900	0.4	13.5	..	114
Poland	71.4	12.5	2.1	5.4	1.2	2.5	−200	1.8	14.2	..	2,748
Portugal	58.2	16.7	..	2.5	2.8	1.8	276	7.2	18.9	178	4,790
Puerto Rico	..	..	..	..	..	..	−10	10.7	..	..	511

	Trade % of GDP		International finance % of GDP				Movement of people			Communication	
	Merchandise	Services	Financing through international capital markets Gross inflows	Foreign direct investment Net inflows	Net outflows	Workers' remittances and compensation of employees received	International migrant stock % of total population	Emigration of people with tertiary education to OECD countries % of population age 25 and older with tertiary education	Net migration thousands	International voice traffic[a] minutes per person	International Internet bandwidth[a] bits per second per capita
	2007	2007	2007	2007	2007	2007	2000–05	2005	2000	2007	2007
Romania	66.4	12.4	1.0	5.7	0.0	5.1	−270	0.6	11.2	41	2,945
Russian Federation	44.8	7.6	12.2	4.3	3.6	0.3	917	8.4	1.4	..	573
Rwanda	27.4	13.5	0.4	2.0	−0.4	1.5	43	1.3	26.3	11	16
Saudi Arabia	85.0	10.1	..	−2.1	0.0	..	285	27.5	0.9	216	510
Senegal	55.1	17.7	0.6	0.7	0.1	8.3[b]	−100	2.8	17.1	26	137
Serbia	67.7	..	0.0	7.8	..	12.2[b,c]	−339	6.4[c]	14.6[c]	144	2,861
Sierra Leone	41.4	8.2	0.0	5.7	−0.6	8.9	472	2.1	49.2	..	..
Singapore	348.6	88.2	..	15.0	7.6	..	200	43.2	14.5	1,531	22,783
Slovak Republic	157.9	18.1	3.8	4.5	0.5	2.0	3	2.3	14.3	97	5,555
Slovenia	130.5	20.9	..	3.1	3.3	0.6	22	8.4	10.9	92	6,720
Somalia	..	..	..	..	..	..	100	3.4	34.5	..	0
South Africa	56.8	10.7	9.9	2.0	1.3	0.3	75	2.4	7.4	..	71
Spain	42.7	15.9	..	4.2	8.9	0.7	2,846	11.0	4.2	..	11,008
Sri Lanka	58.9	13.3	3.4	1.9	0.2	7.8	−442	1.9	28.2	34	118
Sudan	38.2	7.2	0.3	5.2	0.0	3.8	−532	1.7	6.8	7	345
Swaziland	176.3	33.2	0.0	1.3	0.8	3.5	−6	4.0	5.3	..	1
Sweden	70.5	24.6	..	2.7	6.3	0.2	152	12.4	4.5	..	49,828
Switzerland	78.5	23.5	..	11.7	11.9	0.5	100	22.3	9.5	..	29,417
Syrian Arab Republic	69.4	16.3	0.0	1.8	0.0	2.2[b]	200	5.2	6.1	79	53
Tajikistan	105.7	20.0	0.0	9.7	0.0	45.5	−345	4.7	0.6	..	0
Tanzania	45.5	19.7	0.5	4.0	0.0	0.1	−345	2.1	12.1	0	3
Thailand	119.8	28.0	1.1	3.9	0.9	0.7	231	1.7	2.2	14	346
Timor-Leste	..	..	0.0	..	..	..	100	0.6	16.5	18	9
Togo	85.2	23.2	..	2.8	−0.6	9.2[b]	−4	2.9	16.3	5	4
Trinidad and Tobago	108.0	9.5	6.1	..	−2.3	0.4[b]	−20	2.8	78.9	..	675
Tunisia	97.1	22.0	1.6	4.6	0.3	4.9	−29	0.4	12.4	73	303
Turkey	42.3	6.7	5.5	3.4	0.3	0.2	−30	1.8	5.8	30	1,381
Turkmenistan	103.5	..	0.0	6.2	..	..	−10	4.6	0.4	..	16
Uganda	43.2	14.2	10.1	4.1	0.0	7.2	−5	1.8	36.0	7	11
Ukraine	77.9	18.3	9.6	7.0	0.5	3.2	−173	14.5	4.3	57	206
United Arab Emirates	150.4	..	..	..	..	..	577	78.3	0.7	..	2,785
United Kingdom	38.1	17.5	..	7.1	9.9	0.3	948	9.0	17.1	..	39,650
United States	23.1	6.3	..	1.7	2.4	0.0	6,493	13.0	0.5	..	11,277
Uruguay	44.1	13.0	5.9	3.8	0.0	0.4	−104	2.5	9.0	127	903
Uzbekistan	57.7	..	0.0	1.2	..	..	−300	4.8	0.8	12	9
Venezuela, RB	50.5	4.0	5.2	0.3	1.0	0.1	40	3.8	3.8	..	628
Vietnam	159.1	18.9	8.5	9.8	0.2	8.0[b]	−200	0.0	26.9	..	148
West Bank and Gaza	..	..	0.0	..	..	14.9[b]	11	48.5	12.0	..	324
Yemen, Rep.	61.3	12.3	0.4	4.1	0.0	5.7[b]	−100	1.3	6.0	..	28
Zambia	75.6	10.5	2.7	8.7	0.0	0.5	−82	2.4	16.4	..	3
Zimbabwe	122.0	..	0.0	3.0	..	..	−75	3.9	13.1	21	4
World	**51.0 w**	**12.0 w**	**.. w**	**4.0 w**	**4.3 w**	**0.7 w**	**..[d] s**	**3.0 w**	**5.4 w**	**.. w**	**3,297 w**
Low income	62.6	12.5	3.3	4.2	0.1	5.7	−2,858	1.7	12.8	..	26
Middle income	55.9	9.6	5.0	3.7	1.1	1.8	−15,770	1.3	6.7	..	389
Lower middle income	59.6	10.6	3.2	3.5	0.6	2.4	−11,295	0.8	6.6	..	199
Upper middle income	52.0	8.8	6.8	3.9	1.5	1.2	−4,475	3.6	6.8	..	1,185
Low & middle income	56.2	9.8	4.9	3.7	1.1	2.0	−18,629	1.4	7.2	..	318
East Asia & Pacific	75.3	10.4	3.2	4.1	0.9	1.5	−3,847	0.2	7.0	9	247
Europe & Central Asia	56.6	10.4	8.3	5.0	1.9	1.6	−1,798	6.8	4.4	..	1,114
Latin America & Carib.	41.2	6.0	4.5	3.0	0.7	1.8	−6,811	1.0	10.6	..	1,126
Middle East & N. Africa	57.5	..	1.9	3.7	..	3.7	−2,618	3.0	10.4	32	186
South Asia	32.7	14.0	4.6	2.1	0.9	3.6	−2,484	0.8	5.3	..	31
Sub-Saharan Africa	59.7	13.6	5.7	3.4	0.7	2.5	−1,070	2.1	12.3	..	36
High income	49.1	12.7	..	4.1	5.2	0.2	18,522	11.2	3.9	..	18,242
Euro area	67.0	17.2	..	6.3	8.4	0.5	6,887	9.5	6.9	..	32,560

a. Data are from the International Telecommunication Union's (ITU) World Telecommunication Development Report database. Please cite the ITU for third-party use of these data. b. World Bank estimates. c. Includes Montenegro. d. World totals computed by the United Nations sum to zero, but because the aggregates shown here refer to World Bank definitions, regional and income group totals do not equal zero.

Globalization—the integration of the world economy—has been a persistent theme of the past quarter century. Growth of cross-border economic activity has changed the structure of economies and the political and social organization of countries. Not all effects of globalization can be measured directly. But the scope and pace of change can be monitored along four key dimensions: trade in goods and services, financial flows, movement of people, and communication.

Trade data are based on gross flows that capture the two-way flow of goods and services. In conventional balance of payments accounting, exports are recorded as a credit and imports as a debit. See tables 4.4 and 4.5 for data on the main trade components of merchandise trade and tables 4.6 and 4.7 for the same data on services trade.

Financing through international capital markets includes gross bond issuance, bank lending, and new equity placement as reported by Dealogic, a company specializing in the investment banking industry. In financial accounting inward investment is a credit and outward investment a debit. Gross flow is a better measure of integration than net flow because gross flow shows the total value of financial transactions over a period, while net flow is the sum of credits and debits and represents a balance in which many transactions are canceled out. Components of financing through international capital markets are reported in U.S. dollars by market sources.

Foreign direct investment (FDI) includes equity investment, reinvested earnings, and short- and long-term loans between parent firms and foreign affiliates. Distinguished from other kinds of international investment, FDI establishes a lasting interest in or effective management control over an enterprise in another country. FDI may be understated in many developing countries because some countries fail to report reinvested earnings and because the definition of long-term loans differs across countries. However, the quality and coverage of the data are improving as a result of continuous efforts by international and national statistics agencies. See *About the data* for table 6.11 for more information.

Workers' remittances are current private transfers from migrant workers resident in the host country for more than a year, irrespective of their immigration status, to recipients in their country of origin. Compensation of employees is the income of migrants who have lived in the host country for less than a year. Migration has increased in importance, now accounting for a substantial part of global integration. The estimates of the international migrant stock are derived from data on foreign-born population—people who reside in one country but were born in another—mainly from population censuses. See *About the data* and *Definitions* for table 6.17 for more information. One negative effect of migration is "brain drain"—emigration of highly educated people. The table shows data on emigration of people with tertiary education, drawn from Docquier, Marfouk, and Lowell (2007). The study analyzes skilled migration using data from censuses and registers of Organisation for Economic Development and Cooperation (OECD) countries and provides data disaggregated by gender for 1990 and 2000.

Well developed communications infrastructure attracts investments and allows investors to capitalize on benefits offered by the digital age. See *About the data* for tables 5.10 and 5.11 for more information.

• **Trade in merchandise** is the sum of merchandise exports and imports. • **Trade in services** is the sum of services exports and imports. • **Financing through international capital markets** is the sum of the absolute values of new bond issuance, syndicated bank lending, and new equity placements. • **Foreign direct investment net inflows** are net inflows of FDI in the reporting economy. FDI is the sum of equity capital, reinvestment of earnings, and other short- and long-term capital. • **Foreign direct investment net outflows** are net outflows of investment from the reporting economy to the rest of the world. • **Workers' remittances and compensation of employees received** are current transfers by migrant workers and wages and salaries of nonresident workers. • **Net migration** is the total number of immigrants minus the total number of emigrants, including citizens and noncitizens, for the five-year period. • **International migrant stock** is the number of people born in a country other than that in which they live, including refugees. • **Emigration of people with tertiary education to OECD countries** is the stock of emigrants ages 25 and older, residing in an OECD country other than that in which they were born, with at least one year of tertiary education. • **International voice traffic** is the sum of international incoming and outgoing telephone traffic (in minutes) divided by total population. • **International Internet bandwidth** is the contracted capacity of international connections between countries for transmitting Internet traffic.

Data on merchandise trade are from the World Trade Organization's *Annual Report*. Data on trade in services are from the International Monetary Fund's (IMF) Balance of Payments database. Data on international capital market financing are based on data reported by Dealogic. Data on FDI are based on balance of payments data reported by the IMF, supplemented by staff estimates using data reported by the United Nations Conference on Trade and Development and official national sources. Data on workers' remittances are World Bank staff estimates based on IMF balance of payments data. Data on net migration are from the United Nations Population Division's *World Population Prospects: The 2006 Revision*. Data on international migrant stock are from the United Nations Population Division's *Trends in Total Migrant Stock: The 2005 Revision*. Data on emigration of people with tertiary education are from Frédéric Docquier, Abdeslam Marfouk, and B. Lindsay Lowell's, "A Gendered Assessment of the Brain Drain" (2007). Data on international voice traffic and international Internet bandwidth are from the International Telecommunication Union's International Development Report database.

Estimating the global emigrant stock	6.1a

Internationally comparable estimates of migrant stock by country of origin are vital for making policies on international migration. The World Bank's Development Research Group and the United Nations Population Division's Department of Economic and Social Affairs are developing estimates of international migrants by country of origin. They have created the Global Migration database, which contains all publicly available data on international migrants, classified by age, sex, place of birth, and country of citizenship enumerated by censuses, population registers, and surveys. Available at www.unmigration.org, the database uses many sources of data, including the United Nations Statistics Division, the United Nations Population Division, and the World Bank's Development Research Group, in collaboration with the University of Nottingham and the University of Sussex. The next step is to develop an appropriate methodology for estimating the emigrant stock for each country at specific points in time.

	Export volume		Import volume		Export value		Import value		Net barter terms of trade index	
	average annual % growth		average annual % growth		average annual % growth		average annual % growth		2000 = 100	
	1990–2000	2000–07[a]	1990–2000	2000–07[a]	1990–2000	2000–07[a]	1990–2000	2000–07[a]	1995	2007[a]
Afghanistan	..	..	..	..	..	..	..	..	..	..
Albania	..	..	..	..	..	..	..	..	..	..
Algeria	2.8	0.7	−0.8	10.8	2.1	18.6	−1.3	16.3	57.9	183.8
Angola	6.2	11.9	7.1	16.3	6.1	31.5	7.8	20.0	80.8	204.1
Argentina	8.4	7.2	17.7	11.0	10.1	12.1	17.0	13.4	91.6	116.2
Armenia	..	..	..	..	..	..	..	..	..	..
Australia[b]	7.3	5.6	9.2	7.1	5.7	17.5	8.7	11.8	99.4	152.4
Austria[b]	4.1	8.2	1.9	8.0	..	..	..	..	..	..
Azerbaijan	..	..	..	..	..	..	..	..	..	..
Bangladesh	12.9	11.1	5.9	5.0	15.7	11.7	10.4	12.2	111.8	69.1
Belarus	..	..	..	..	..	..	..	..	..	..
Belgium[b]	6.0	4.7	5.7	5.0	8.7	6.4	9.1	6.8	104.3	101.2
Benin	1.0	3.6	8.2	0.9	3.3	7.7	9.7	8.5	106.6	80.3
Bolivia	2.8	11.2	9.1	5.0	4.3	22.7	9.7	9.9	89.4	137.2
Bosnia and Herzegovina	..	..	..	..	..	..	..	..	..	..
Botswana	4.8	4.9	4.0	0.8	4.7	9.1	2.7	6.5	89.3	89.6
Brazil	5.1	11.1	16.7	6.0	5.9	18.3	12.5	11.8	110.4	107.8
Bulgaria	..	..	..	..	..	..	..	..	..	..
Burkina Faso	13.2	15.1	3.6	9.6	12.9	20.3	3.6	16.6	131.0	89.6
Burundi	8.6	−3.9	4.0	12.0	−4.3	6.7	−6.9	17.8	163.6	128.6
Cambodia	..	16.0	..	12.0	26.8	17.4	25.2	16.8	..	84.8
Cameroon	0.3	−1.6	5.0	2.0	−3.6	12.1	2.1	10.4	90.4	132.1
Canada[b]	9.1	1.1	9.0	4.6	12.4	2.1	11.9	3.2	103.2	117.6
Central African Republic	20.0	−1.2	4.3	5.0	3.5	1.7	0.2	11.5	193.0	81.3
Chad	..	..	..	..	..	..	..	..	..	..
Chile	11.1	6.7	10.7	12.5	9.4	23.2	10.3	16.3	135.6	194.4
China[†]	13.8	26.2	12.8	18.8	14.5	27.5	13.0	25.0	101.9	98.9
Hong Kong, China	8.4	9.6	8.9	8.8	8.3	9.5	8.8	9.5	99.1	96.8
Colombia	4.5	6.5	8.5	12.3	7.3	14.2	9.7	16.2	86.8	121.4
Congo, Dem. Rep.	−1.8	9.4	4.6	17.8	−7.2	19.4	−0.5	24.8	79.8	119.2
Congo, Rep.	6.6	3.0	4.9	17.5	7.5	20.5	8.7	22.6	52.0	187.1
Costa Rica	14.0	8.3	14.9	8.1	17.0	8.2	13.9	10.8	104.6	84.9
Côte d'Ivoire	5.0	2.0	−0.3	7.9	6.0	13.2	2.4	16.1	122.0	134.5
Croatia	..	..	..	..	..	..	..	..	..	..
Cuba	..	−0.6	..	4.1	−1.7	12.5	2.5	12.7	..	143.5
Czech Republic	..	..	..	..	..	..	..	..	..	..
Denmark[b]	5.4	3.4	5.8	5.1	5.9	4.7	6.8	6.2	102.1	98.9
Dominican Republic	3.9	1.3	11.6	1.4	4.2	3.9	12.0	5.1	98.1	94.7
Ecuador	6.3	10.1	5.9	14.0	6.8	18.8	7.9	19.0	80.6	114.2
Egypt, Arab Rep.	−0.2	8.3	1.8	3.0	0.7	22.8	4.7	10.6	116.3	130.6
El Salvador	2.9	2.4	7.6	5.5	8.9	4.2	10.9	8.5	121.1	95.5
Eritrea	−28.3	−14.5	−3.2	−2.4	−31.1	−13.7	−0.2	2.6	101.7	70.6
Estonia	..	..	..	..	..	..	..	..	..	..
Ethiopia	10.5	7.8	7.3	16.5	10.7	17.0	7.3	23.8	151.0	110.2
Finland	..	..	..	..	..	..	..	..	..	..
France[b]	8.4	4.8	6.6	6.3	6.8	3.7	5.6	5.1	106.3	101.4
Gabon	5.2	1.7	2.5	6.2	0.8	18.3	2.2	10.6	125.4	182.8
Gambia, The	−11.6	−7.8	0.1	2.5	−12.3	−4.0	0.2	9.9	100.0	82.5
Georgia	..	..	..	..	..	..	..	..	..	..
Germany[b]	..	..	..	..	..	..	..	..	107.5	97.2
Ghana	7.7	5.3	8.6	11.6	9.0	14.7	8.3	17.2	106.7	143.3
Greece[b]	8.9	..	9.3	..	8.2	..	8.2	..	89.6	93.3
Guatemala	8.5	4.8	10.0	7.1	10.1	8.3	10.4	12.5	117.9	88.7
Guinea	5.0	−10.4	−1.4	1.0	0.6	5.5	−2.6	7.9	89.6	173.1
Guinea-Bissau	..	..	..	..	..	..	..	..	..	..
Haiti	12.6	8.0	13.3	3.6	12.2	10.4	14.4	8.5	113.2	83.9
[†]Data for Taiwan, China	3.1	7.9	4.8	4.2	7.2	10.0	8.5	10.1	89.9	80.0

Growth of merchandise trade

	Export volume		Import volume		Export value		Import value		Net barter terms of trade index	
	average annual % growth		average annual % growth		average annual % growth		average annual % growth		2000 = 100	
	1990–2000	2000–07[a]	1990–2000	2000–07[a]	1990–2000	2000–07[a]	1990–2000	2000–07[a]	1995	2007[a]
Honduras	2.5	5.8	12.7	8.8	7.2	7.2	13.8	13.4	96.3	80.8
Hungary[b]	10.1	12.5	11.6	9.9	10.1	19.3	11.8	17.4	104.3	95.5
India	6.9	12.4	9	17.6	5.3	21.1	7.9	25.9	108.0	99.3
Indonesia	9.1	1.9	2.9	5.7	7.9	10.1	1.0	15.4	90.4	104.9
Iran, Islamic Rep.	..	1.9	..	10.5	1.2	18.9	−4.8	17.9	..	160.2
Iraq	..	..	..	..	..	..	..	..	..	..
Ireland[b]	15.2	2.6	11.4	3.1	17.3	−0.4	13.8	1.2	98.9	91.3
Israel[b]	9.7	5.1	8.9	2.5	17.9	9.5	16.0	7.9	92.1	91.7
Italy[b]	4.8	1.6	4.2	2.1	10.0	4.4	8.4	5.5	96.8	98.0
Jamaica	2.2	1.4	..	1.3	2.2	8.5	6.9	9.4	..	101.6
Japan[b]	2.6	4.8	5.3	3.5	2.4	7.8	2.9	9.1	105.5	86.0
Jordan	4.7	8.7	3.8	8.2	6.6	17.2	5.1	18.6	115.6	92.4
Kazakhstan	..	..	..	..	..	..	..	..	..	..
Kenya	3.9	6.2	7.4	8.6	6.3	13.1	6.0	17.9	103.9	83.8
Korea, Dem. Rep.	..	..	..	..	..	..	..	..	..	..
Korea, Rep.	15.8	13.6	10.0	8.3	10.1	14.2	7.1	14.5	138.5	72.0
Kuwait	..	5.8	..	12.3	16.5	23.9	5.5	16.3	..	194.3
Kyrgyz Republic	..	..	..	..	..	..	..	..	..	..
Lao PDR	..	11.4	..	6.7	15.4	20.5	12.7	13.4	..	114.0
Latvia[b]	7.2	..	..	..	11.6	..	..	..	..	..
Lebanon	..	14.4	..	2.0	4.1	21.6	8.7	9.0	..	98.8
Lesotho	13.3	20.3	3.1	9.0	12.8	21.2	1.9	14.1	100.0	78.9
Liberia	..	..	..	..	..	..	..	..	..	..
Libya	..	5.9	0.0	11.4	−2.6	24.4	−1.4	22.4	..	172.0
Lithuania	..	..	..	..	..	..	..	..	..	..
Macedonia, FYR	..	..	..	..	..	..	..	..	..	..
Madagascar	4.1	1.2	4.5	8.3	9.0	3.3	6.3	15.1	79.6	74.8
Malawi	2.7	6.4	−2.4	8.0	0.9	9.3	−0.6	14.3	105.7	84.6
Malaysia	13.6	7.4	10.6	7.2	12.2	10.7	9.5	10.4	108.5	100.1
Mali	10.3	2.8	6.4	6.2	6.3	14.6	4.7	14.0	109.6	132.3
Mauritania	1.9	9.1	4.2	14.2	−1.9	24.3	−1.6	20.3	102.2	153.6
Mauritius	2.7	4.7	3.4	9.0	2.2	3.9	3.3	10.4	88.5	86.4
Mexico	15.5	4.1	13.2	4.8	16.1	8.3	14.2	8.0	92.5	104.6
Moldova	..	..	..	..	..	..	..	..	..	..
Mongolia	..	5.4	..	10.3	0.7	21.8	0.5	18.6	..	160.3
Morocco	7.5	2.6	7.2	8.1	7.2	9.5	5.5	15.4	89.1	98.4
Mozambique	15.2	17.4	1.0	10.7	10.2	30.1	1.1	16.7	151.1	127.6
Myanmar	15.5	6.4	13.8	−6.3	14.4	17.3	22.6	−0.5	214.3	122.8
Namibia	2.4	7.8	7.7	8.6	0.9	16.9	3.9	12.6	82.6	139.3
Nepal	..	−1.5	..	0.1	10.7	2.8	9.3	8.9	..	80.0
Netherlands[b]	6.8	4.4	7.0	4.9	7.2	5.9	7.3	5.2	103.2	111.7
New Zealand[b]	4.6	3.3	5.9	8.1	3.9	10.9	5.7	13.9	101.8	118.1
Nicaragua	10.4	8.6	9.3	5.6	10.3	10.9	11.6	11.0	128.9	78.3
Niger	3.1	−8.7	−2.1	11.8	0.0	13.9	0.8	20.0	121.4	313.9
Nigeria	3.3	1.8	2.5	11.6	1.1	19.6	3.1	18.8	55.6	168.4
Norway[b]	6.6	0.6	7.8	6.9	8.6	7.4	7.2	7.6	60.3	134.0
Oman	4.0	−4.5	..	9.6	5.7	12.3	6.1	15.4	..	180.8
Pakistan	2.5	9.3	2.4	10.4	4.3	11.6	3.1	20.3	119.2	65.5
Panama	6.0	−0.5	7.8	5.1	9.4	4.4	8.7	10.8	100.0	94.0
Papua New Guinea	−7.7	−2.7	..	4.9	3.7	15.1	−0.8	12.2	..	177.2
Paraguay	−0.2	15.9	5.4	17.9	1.7	19.2	7.0	21.7	118.3	99.2
Peru	9.4	9.7	10.6	8.2	9.0	24.5	10.8	13.9	123.4	161.9
Philippines	16.0	4.6	11.3	4.3	18.8	4.8	12.5	7.3	80.2	81.7
Poland[b]	9.8	13.9	19.0	10.6	9.4	24.7	16.9	19.6	101.7	109.4
Portugal[b]	0.3	..	0.5	..	−3.0	..	−2.6	..	104.7	..
Puerto Rico	..	..	..	..	..	..	..	..	..	..

	Export volume		Import volume		Export value		Import value		Net barter terms of trade index	
	average annual % growth		average annual % growth		average annual % growth		average annual % growth		2000 = 100	
	1990–2000	2000–07[a]	1990–2000	2000–07[a]	1990–2000	2000–07[a]	1990–2000	2000–07[a]	1995	2007[a]
Romania	..	..	..	..	..	..	..	..	..	..
Russian Federation	..	..	..	..	..	..	..	..	..	..
Rwanda	–8.0	5.7	0.8	8.1	–4.0	17.6	–1.7	14.7	110.1	127.2
Saudi Arabia	2.9	2.2	..	12.7	3.1	21.6	0.8	17.6	..	236.5
Senegal	10.6	2.2	4.9	7.1	4.0	10.2	3.6	15.8	156.3	97.4
Serbia	..	..	..	..	..	..	..	..	..	..
Sierra Leone	..	..	..	..	..	..	..	..	..	..
Singapore	11.7	13.4	8.3	8.9	9.9	14.8	7.8	12.9	104.3	84.5
Slovak Republic	..	..	..	..	..	..	..	..	..	..
Slovenia	..	..	..	..	..	..	..	..	..	..
Somalia	..	..	..	..	..	..	..	..	..	..
South Africa	4.5	2.9	7.6	10.5	2.5	14.3	5.8	19.1	106.0	126.7
Spain[b]	11.4	4.2	9.3	7.2	14.5	5.8	12.0	8.3	104.3	104.7
Sri Lanka	7.4	4.1	8.0	2.3	11.3	6.4	8.9	9.9	99.0	75.8
Sudan	12.6	8.4	8.4	23.9	14.0	26.4	9.8	29.5	100.0	180.7
Swaziland	4.0	10.8	3.1	8.5	5.9	14.9	5.0	14.7	100.0	86.6
Sweden[b]	8.9	3.9	6.4	2.1	7.4	10.2	5.4	10.3	109.5	89.3
Switzerland[b]	3.7	4.9	4.2	3.0	4.4	6.3	3.6	5.1	96.4	96.4
Syrian Arab Republic	2.2	–0.4	..	12.3	0.9	12.8	3.6	19.8	..	134.4
Tajikistan	..	..	..	..	..	..	..	..	..	..
Tanzania	6.0	5.8	–2.0	11.8	6.4	15.9	0.1	20.6	98.0	109.4
Thailand	9.6	9.1	2.6	10.1	10.5	13.6	5.0	14.6	116.0	96.1
Timor-Leste	..	..	..	..	..	..	..	..	..	..
Togo	9.1	8.0	6.0	4.3	6.6	13.7	5.5	16.5	99.1	85.5
Trinidad and Tobago	..	5.3	..	3.3	6.8	21.1	12.1	12.6	..	132.2
Tunisia	5.7	9.3	4.3	5.1	6.0	13.7	5.2	11.2	95.8	91.5
Turkey	10.7	13.6	11.1	12.1	9.2	22.0	10.3	21.3	105.7	94.7
Turkmenistan	..	..	..	..	..	..	..	..	..	..
Uganda	17.8	10.8	22.4	5.5	15.4	19.5	21.0	12.6	197.2	104.2
Ukraine	..	..	..	..	..	..	..	..	..	..
United Arab Emirates	..	7.8	..	16.9	6.5	21.8	10.7	21.7	..	154.0
United Kingdom[b]	6.2	2.5	6.5	5.2	6.2	9.0	6.5	11.0	100.1	104.5
United States[b]	6.6	4.4	9.1	5.2	7.2	6.7	9.5	8.7	103.3	96.6
Uruguay	6.1	9.3	10.5	4.1	5.2	12.6	10.1	9.9	116.2	88.8
Uzbekistan	..	..	..	..	..	..	..	..	..	..
Venezuela, RB	5.2	–1.2	4.8	10.1	5.4	15.5	5.3	16.6	63.4	161.6
Vietnam	..	13.2	..	14.0	22.7	20.4	22.7	22.2	..	92.0
West Bank and Gaza	..	..	..	..	..	..	..	..	..	..
Yemen, Rep.	..	–3.5	4.4	9.1	20.6	13.4	0.6	17.5	..	154.8
Zambia	6.1	8.0	2.9	17.6	–4.6	28.3	1.3	24.8	189.7	193.2
Zimbabwe	8.8	–6.6	8.0	–7.5	3.4	2.4	1.9	2.7	96.8	94.0

a. Data for 2007 are provisional and may differ from data published elsewhere. b. Data are from the International Monetary Fund's International Financial Statistics database.

About the data

Data on international trade in goods are available from each country's balance of payments and customs records. While the balance of payments focuses on the financial transactions that accompany trade, customs data record the direction of trade and the physical quantities and value of goods entering or leaving the customs area. Customs data may differ from data recorded in the balance of payments because of differences in valuation and time of recording. The 1993 United Nations System of National Accounts and the fifth edition of the International Monetary Fund's (IMF) *Balance of Payments Manual* (1993) attempted to reconcile definitions and reporting standards for international trade statistics, but differences in sources, timing, and national practices limit comparability. Real growth rates derived from trade volume indexes and terms of trade based on unit price indexes may therefore differ from those derived from national accounts aggregates.

Trade in goods, or merchandise trade, includes all goods that add to or subtract from an economy's material resources. Trade data are collected on the basis of a country's customs area, which in most cases is the same as its geographic area. Goods provided as part of foreign aid are included, but goods destined for extraterritorial agencies (such as embassies) are not.

Collecting and tabulating trade statistics are difficult. Some developing countries lack the capacity to report timely data, especially landlocked countries and countries whose territorial boundaries are porous. Their trade has to be estimated from the data reported by their partners. (For further discussion of the use of partner country reports, see *About the data* for table 6.3.) Countries that belong to common customs unions may need to collect data through direct inquiry of companies. Economic or political concerns may lead some national authorities to suppress or misrepresent data on certain trade flows, such as oil, military equipment, or the exports of a dominant producer. In other cases reported trade data may be distorted by deliberate under- or over-invoicing to affect capital transfers or avoid taxes. And in some regions smuggling and black market trading result in unreported trade flows.

By international agreement customs data are reported to the United Nations Statistics Division, which maintains the Commodity Trade (Comtrade) and Monthly Bulletin of Statistics databases. The United Nations Conference on Trade and Development (UNCTAD) compiles international trade statistics, including price, value, and volume indexes, from national and international sources such as the IMF's International Financial Statistics database, the United Nations Economic Commission for Latin America and the Caribbean, the United Nations Statistics Division's Monthly Bulletin of Statistics database, the World Bank Africa Database, the U.S. Bureau of Labor Statistics, Japan Customs, and UNCTAD's Commodity Price Statistics. The IMF also compiles data on trade prices and volumes in its International Financial Statistics (IFS) database.

Unless otherwise noted, the growth rates and terms of trade in the table were calculated from index numbers compiled by UNCTAD. The growth rates and terms of trade for selected economies were calculated from index numbers compiled in the IMF's *International Financial Statistics*. In some cases price and volume indexes from different sources vary significantly as a result of differences in estimation procedures. Because the IMF does not publish trade value indexes, for selected economies the trade value indexes were derived from the volume and price indexes. All indexes are rescaled to a 2000 base year.

The terms of trade measures the relative prices of a country's exports and imports. There are several ways to calculate it. The most common is the net barter (or commodity) terms of trade index, or the ratio of the export price index to the import price index. When a country's net barter terms of trade index increases, its exports become more valuable or its imports cheaper.

Definitions

• **Export** and **import volumes** are indexes of the quantity of goods traded. They are derived from UNCTAD's quantum index series and are the ratio of the export or import value indexes to the corresponding unit value indexes. Unit value indexes are based on data reported by countries that demonstrate consistency under UNCTAD quality controls, supplemented by UNCTAD's estimates using the previous year's trade values at the Standard International Trade Classification three-digit level as weights. For economies for which UNCTAD does not publish data, the export and import volume indexes (lines 72 and 73) in the IMF's *International Financial Statistics* are used to calculate the average annual growth rates. • **Export** and **import values** are the current value of exports (f.o.b.) or imports (c.i.f.), converted to U.S. dollars and expressed as a percentage of the average for the base period (2000). UNCTAD's export or import value indexes are reported for most economies. For selected economies for which UNCTAD does not publish data, the value indexes are derived from export or import volume indexes (lines 72 and 73) and corresponding unit value indexes of exports or imports (lines 74 and 75) in the IMF's *International Financial Statistics*. • **Net barter terms of trade index** is calculated as the percentage ratio of the export unit value indexes to the import unit value indexes, measured relative to the base year 2000.

Data sources

Data on trade indexes are from UNCTAD's annual *Handbook of Statistics* for most economies and from the IMF's *International Financial Statistics* for selected economies.

6.3 Direction and growth of merchandise trade

High-income importers

% of world trade, 2007

Source of exports	European Union	Japan	United States	Other high-income	Total
High-income economies	29.0	2.4	7.9	12.1	51.5
European Union	22.7	0.4	2.6	3.8	29.5
Japan	0.7	..	1.1	1.6	3.4
United States	1.7	0.5	..	3.3	5.5
Other high-income economies	3.8	1.5	4.3	3.5	13.1
Low- and middle-income economies	7.6	1.7	5.8	5.5	20.6
East Asia & Pacific	2.2	1.3	2.3	3.8	9.6
China	1.7	0.7	1.7	2.7	6.8
Europe & Central Asia	3.0	0.1	0.1	0.5	3.7
Russian Federation	1.2	0.1	0.1	0.2	1.5
Latin America & Caribbean	0.8	0.1	2.5	0.4	3.8
Brazil	0.3	0.0	0.2	0.1	0.6
Middle East & N. Africa	0.9	0.1	0.3	0.3	1.5
Algeria	0.2	0.0	0.1	0.0	0.4
South Asia	0.3	0.0	0.2	0.3	0.9
India	0.2	0.0	0.2	0.3	0.7
Sub-Saharan Africa	0.4	0.1	0.4	0.2	1.1
South Africa	0.1	0.1	0.1	0.1	0.3
World	36.7	4.1	13.7	17.6	72.1

Low- and middle-income importers

% of world trade, 2007

Source of exports	East Asia & Pacific	Europe & Central Asia	Latin America & Caribbean	Middle East & N. Africa	South Asia	Sub-Saharan Africa	Total
High-income economies	7.5	3.9	3.1	1.1	1.1	1.0	17.7
European Union	1.0	3.1	0.7	0.7	0.4	0.5	6.4
Japan	1.3	0.1	0.2	0.0	0.1	0.1	1.8
United States	0.7	0.2	1.7	0.1	0.2	0.1	2.9
Other high-income economies	4.5	0.4	0.5	0.3	0.5	0.3	6.6
Low- and middle-income economies	2.5	2.5	1.6	0.7	0.7	0.7	8.7
East Asia & Pacific	1.4	0.6	0.4	0.2	0.4	0.2	3.2
China	0.5	0.5	0.4	0.2	0.3	0.2	2.0
Europe & Central Asia	0.2	1.7	0.1	0.2	0.1	0.0	2.3
Russian Federation	0.1	0.7	0.0	0.1	0.0	0.0	1.0
Latin America & Caribbean	0.3	0.1	1.0	0.1	0.0	0.1	1.6
Brazil	0.1	0.0	0.3	0.0	0.0	0.0	0.5
Middle East & N. Africa	0.2	0.1	0.0	0.2	0.0	0.0	0.5
Algeria	0.0	0.0	0.0	0.0	0.0	0.0	0.1
South Asia	0.2	0.0	0.0	0.0	0.1	0.1	0.5
India	0.1	0.0	0.0	0.0	0.1	0.1	0.4
Sub-Saharan Africa	0.2	0.0	0.1	0.0	0.0	0.2	0.6
South Africa	0.0	0.0	0.0	0.0	0.0	0.1	0.1
World	10.0	6.5	4.8	1.8	1.8	1.6	26.4

Nominal growth of trade

High-income importers

annual % growth, 1997–2007

Source of exports	European Union	Japan	United States	Other high-income	Total
High-income economies	9.2	4.6	6.0	6.8	7.8
European Union	9.7	3.7	8.2	7.6	9.2
Japan	4.4	..	2.1	5.3	4.0
United States	5.4	−0.5	..	5.0	4.5
Other high-income economies	9.4	7.2	6.0	8.6	7.7
Low- and middle-income economies	15.0	9.5	12.2	14.0	13.4
East Asia & Pacific	17.7	9.6	15.3	14.1	14.3
China	25.2	12.4	21.7	18.4	19.5
Europe & Central Asia	17.4	10.1	8.5	15.0	16.4
Russian Federation	17.4	9.9	5.3	14.3	15.7
Latin America & Caribbean	11.2	6.9	9.4	12.9	10.0
Brazil	11.5	3.5	10.4	14.2	11.0
Middle East & N. Africa	12.4	15.4	27.4	16.7	14.8
Algeria	11.7	16.5	22.5	23.5	15.4
South Asia	11.6	4.7	10.6	16.0	12.4
India	13.3	7.0	13.0	17.9	14.5
Sub-Saharan Africa	7.6	9.6	14.4	6.3	9.7
South Africa[a]	7.2	9.6	11.2	3.6	7.2
World	10.2	6.4	8.2	8.5	9.1

Low- and middle-income importers

annual % growth, 1997–2007

Source of exports	East Asia & Pacific	Europe & Central Asia	Latin America & Caribbean	Middle East & N. Africa	South Asia	Sub-Saharan Africa	Total
High-income economies	11.5	13.4	6.5	9.5	11.9	9.7	10.6
European Union	10.0	13.6	6.6	8.5	11.8	9.5	11.0
Japan	9.3	17.7	5.1	6.2	8.8	8.7	8.9
United States	8.6	8.2	6.1	7.6	14.7	8.8	7.2
Other high-income economies	13.3	12.9	8.6	13.9	11.8	11.0	12.6
Low- and middle-income economies	19.3	16.2	12.8	18.4	19.0	17.1	16.6
East Asia & Pacific	18.3	30.3	22.7	22.3	22.9	24.0	21.6
China	22.2	33.4	27.2	28.5	29.4	27.5	27.3
Europe & Central Asia	13.9	14.2	13.7	18.2	17.5	17.2	14.6
Russian Federation	13.8	14.7	14.0	22.9	16.9	18.3	15.0
Latin America & Caribbean	22.1	14.0	9.9	10.2	20.8	18.4	12.3
Brazil	18.8	15.1	10.4	13.2	15.7	20.2	12.8
Middle East & N. Africa	24.0	12.6	10.1	21.3	12.0	20.7	17.7
Algeria	59.3	8.6	10.4	23.5	14.4	3.3	14.4
South Asia	22.1	13.0	20.8	18.4	18.4	17.3	18.8
India	23.6	14.1	23.8	21.7	16.9	18.7	20.1
Sub-Saharan Africa	25.0	13.0	19.1	8.8	4.1	11.6	15.6
South Africa[a]	14.2	8.1	5.2	10.9	11.4	7.9	9.5
World	13.0	14.5	8.2	12.2	14.1	12.2	12.2

a. Data for 1997 are based on imports from South Africa reported by other economies because data on exports for South Africa were not available.

About the data

The table provides estimates of the flow of trade in goods between groups of economies. The data are from the International Monetary Fund's (IMF) Direction of Trade database. All high-income economies and major developing economies report trade on a timely basis, covering about 85 percent of trade for recent years. Trade by less timely reporters and by countries that do not report is estimated using reports of trading partner countries. Because the largest exporting and importing countries are reliable reporters, a large portion of the missing trade flows can be estimated from partner reports. Partner country data may introduce discrepancies due to smuggling, confidentiality, different exchange rates, overreporting of transit trade, inclusion or exclusion of freight rates, and different points of valuation and times of recording.

In addition, estimates of trade within the European Union (EU) have been significantly affected by changes in reporting methods following the creation of a customs union. The current system for collecting data on trade between EU members—Intrastat, introduced in 1993—has less exhaustive coverage than the previous customs-based system and has resulted in some problems of asymmetry (estimated imports are about 5 percent less than exports). Despite these issues, only a small portion of world trade is estimated to be omitted from the IMF's *Direction of Trade Statistics Yearbook* and Direction of Trade database.

Most countries report their trade data in national currencies, which are converted into U.S. dollars using the IMF's published period average exchange rate (series rf or rh, monthly averages of the market or official rates) for the reporting country or, if unavailable, monthly average rates in New York. Because imports are reported at cost, insurance, and freight (c.i.f.) valuations, and exports at free on board (f.o.b.) valuations, the IMF adjusts country reports of import values by dividing them by 1.10 to estimate equivalent export values. The accuracy of this approximation depends on the set of partners and the items traded. Other factors affecting the accuracy of trade data include lags in reporting, recording differences across countries, and whether the country reports trade according to the general or special system of trade. (For further discussion of the measurement of exports and imports, see *About the data* for tables 4.4 and 4.5.)

The regional trade flows in the table are calculated from current price values. The growth rates are in nominal terms; that is, they include the effects of changes in both volumes and prices.

Definitions

• **Merchandise trade** includes all trade in goods; trade in services is excluded. • **High-income economies** are those classified as such by the World Bank (see inside front cover). • **European Union** is defined as all high-income EU members: Austria, Belgium, Cyprus, Czech Republic, Denmark, Estonia, Finland, France, Germany, Greece, Hungary, Ireland, Italy, Luxembourg, Malta, the Netherlands, Portugal, Slovenia, Spain, Sweden, and the United Kingdom. • **Other high-income economies** include all high-income economies (both Organisation for Economic Co-operation and Development members and others) except the high-income European Union, Japan, and the United States. • **Low- and middle-income regional groupings** are based on World Bank classifications (see inside back cover for regional groupings) and may differ from those used by other organizations.

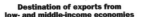

In 2007 around 70 percent of exports from low- and middle-income economies and from high-income economies were directed to high-income economies　　6.3a

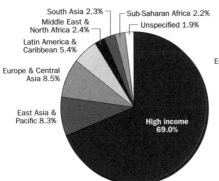

Destination of exports from low- and middle-income economies

South Asia 2.3%
Middle East & North Africa 2.4%
Latin America & Caribbean 5.4%
Europe & Central Asia 8.5%
East Asia & Pacific 8.3%
Sub-Saharan Africa 2.2%
Unspecified 1.9%
High income 69.0%

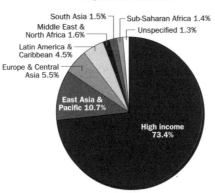

Destination of exports from high-income economies

South Asia 1.5%
Middle East & North Africa 1.6%
Latin America & Caribbean 4.5%
Europe & Central Asia 5.5%
East Asia & Pacific 10.7%
Sub-Saharan Africa 1.4%
Unspecified 1.3%
High income 73.4%

East Asia and Pacific and Europe and Central Asia were the two largest developing region importers from both low- and middle-income economies and high-income economies.

Source: World Bank staff calculations based on data from the International Monetary Fund's Direction of Trade database.

Data sources

Data on the direction and growth of merchandise trade were calculated using the IMF's Direction of Trade database.

Exports to low-income economies

	High-income economies		European Union		Japan		United States	
	1997	2007	1997	2007	1997	2007	1997	2007
Total ($ billions)	**47.8**	**121.4**	**21.1**	**47.2**	**4.9**	**12.2**	**5.2**	**12.6**
% of total exports								
Food	11.7	8.7	13.8	9.4	0.9	0.7	23.8	20.5
Cereals	4.2	2.6	3.7	1.7	0.4	0.1	17.7	13.6
Agricultural raw materials	2.1	2.1	1.5	1.4	1.2	1.6	5.1	6.6
Ores and nonferrous metals	1.2	2.3	0.9	1.2	0.5	1.8	0.7	1.9
Fuels	4.4	13.0	2.7	11.8	1.1	1.1	1.4	3.4
Crude petroleum	0.0	0.7	0.0	0.0	0.0	0.0	0.0	0.0
Petroleum products	3.6	11.9	2.4	11.4	1.0	1.0	1.1	3.0
Manufactured goods	78.4	69.1	78.5	72.5	94.0	92.3	65.6	63.3
Chemical products	12.0	11.7	14.6	12.0	5.3	5.8	9.2	7.2
Iron and steel	3.6	3.5	3.5	2.7	7.8	9.6	1.5	1.3
Machinery and transport equipment	43.5	40.0	43.0	44.5	64.9	64.0	44.2	46.0
Furniture	0.3	0.2	0.5	0.4	0.1	0.2	0.2	0.2
Textiles	6.5	4.1	2.3	1.7	6.1	3.7	3.1	1.0
Footwear	0.5	0.2	0.4	0.2	0.0	0.0	0.4	0.4
Other	12.1	9.4	14.2	11.0	9.9	9.0	7.0	7.3
Miscellaneous goods	1.7	4.2	1.5	3.1	2.3	2.6	3.5	4.2

Imports from low-income economies

	High-income economies		European Union		Japan		United States	
Total ($ billions)	**55.5**	**154.4**	**26.3**	**58.2**	**5.2**	**10.2**	**12.8**	**61.3**
% of total imports								
Food	20.6	12.2	28.0	19.5	26.5	15.4	8.8	4.2
Cereals	0.3	0.4	0.1	0.2	0.0	0.4	0.2	0.1
Agricultural raw materials	7.2	2.5	8.7	4.4	10.9	3.1	0.9	0.5
Ores and nonferrous metals	4.5	5.4	5.1	8.1	9.0	10.9	1.9	0.4
Fuels	29.8	40.1	17.6	22.9	20.6	25.6	54.3	60.8
Crude petroleum	28.4	35.2	17.3	16.6	17.8	17.0	51.3	57.3
Petroleum products	1.1	1.5	0.2	0.6	1.1	3.0	2.9	1.9
Manufactured goods	36.4	37.9	39.5	44.4	32.3	42.7	33.7	33.6
Chemical products	0.6	1.0	0.5	1.4	0.3	1.2	0.7	0.4
Iron and steel	0.5	0.2	0.5	0.3	1.2	0.4	0.3	0.1
Machinery and transport equipment	2.5	3.3	1.8	2.3	2.2	16.9	0.2	1.2
Furniture	0.5	2.2	0.4	1.9	1.6	2.8	0.1	2.6
Textiles	22.1	22.5	21.2	25.7	21.1	10.8	27.6	24.9
Footwear	2.8	3.9	4.5	6.7	1.8	3.7	0.8	1.8
Other	7.3	4.8	10.5	6.1	4.2	6.8	4.1	2.6
Miscellaneous goods	1.5	1.7	1.0	0.6	0.7	2.4	0.4	0.4

Simple applied tariff rates on imports from low-income economies (%)[a]

	High-income economies		European Union		Japan		United States	
Food	7.6	6.9	6.9	4.4	10.2	4.0	3.2	2.9
Cereals	12.9	11	41.5	20.7	4.2	7.9	1.5	2.2
Agricultural raw materials	2.5	3.7	0.2	0.1	1.8	0.2	0.4	0.5
Ores and nonferrous metals	1.5	0.9	0.3	0.4	0.7	0.1	0.2	0.6
Fuels	3.1	0.8	0.0	0.0	1.6	0.2	0.5	0.8
Crude petroleum	1.7	0.5	0.0	0.0	0.9	0.0	0.3	0.0
Petroleum products	5.0	1.1	0.0	0.1	5.6	0.6	1.1	1.4
Manufactured goods	4.9	3.6	1.2	1.0	2.4	1.8	5.9	4.0
Chemical products	3.6	2.6	1.3	1.0	3.0	0.3	1.0	0.8
Iron and steel	5.1	1.8	0.6	0.1	0.1	0.1	1.7	0.5
Machinery and transport equipment	2.3	1.5	0.3	0.2	0.1	0.0	0.5	0.4
Furniture	4.0	3.2	0.1	0.0	0.0	0.0	1.2	1.1
Textiles	8.1	5.9	3.1	2.9	4.5	3.4	11.4	7.5
Footwear	7.9	6.4	3.0	2.5	8.4	9.1	14.2	8.3
Other	3.0	2.14	0.6	0.2	1.4	0.7	3.2	1.1
Miscellaneous goods	0.8	0.3	0.0	0.0	0.0	0.0	0.3	0.1
Average	5.1	4.0	1.9	1.4	3.6	3.2	5.1	3.7

6.4 High-income economy trade with low- and middle-income economies

Exports to middle-income economies

	High-income economies		European Union		Japan		United States	
	1997	2007	1997	2007	1997	2007	1997	2007
Total ($ billions)	**737.3**	**2,001.2**	**287.0**	**837.3**	**100.4**	**235.5**	**189.2**	**357.5**
% of total exports								
Food	7.4	5.1	8.7	5.0	0.4	0.3	9.1	10.1
Cereals	1.6	1.0	1.3	0.6	0.0	0.0	2.5	3.3
Agricultural raw materials	2.0	1.9	1.3	1.4	1.1	0.9	2.7	3.7
Ores and nonferrous metals	1.9	4.0	1.6	2.6	1.3	3.6	1.6	4.3
Fuels	3.1	5.6	1.6	2.6	0.9	1.2	2.6	5.3
Crude petroleum	0.6	0.8	0.1	0.1	0.0	0.0	0.1	0.0
Petroleum products	1.8	3.7	1.3	2.1	0.7	1.0	1.6	4.0
Manufactured goods	83.2	79.2	84.2	84.2	94.6	89.1	80.7	72.7
Chemical products	11.1	13.2	12.7	13.4	6.9	9.8	10.8	13.1
Iron and steel	2.8	3.5	2.7	3.6	6.3	6.6	1.0	1.3
Machinery and transport equipment	49.1	45.8	45.9	47.0	68.1	60.9	49.7	43.3
Furniture	0.6	0.4	0.9	0.7	0.1	0.2	0.6	0.3
Textiles	5.7	2.9	5.4	3.7	2.9	1.6	4.9	2.4
Footwear	0.4	0.2	0.7	0.5	0.0	0.0	0.2	0.1
Other	13.7	13.2	16.1	15.2	10.2	10.1	13.5	12.2
Miscellaneous goods	2.1	3.4	1.9	2.9	1.7	4.8	3.4	3.9

Imports from middle-income economies

	High-income economies		European Union		Japan		United States	
Total ($ billions)	**916.3**	**3,053.0**	**273.8**	**1,123.6**	**109.0**	**264.9**	**291.3**	**895.4**
% of total imports								
Food	10.6	6.3	14.1	7.9	15.5	7.8	7.7	4.8
Cereals	0.4	0.4	0.3	0.5	0.3	0.3	0.2	0.2
Agricultural raw materials	2.9	1.4	3.8	1.9	5.5	2.4	1.5	0.9
Ores and nonferrous metals	5.6	5.6	7.3	6.1	10.0	12.3	2.7	2.8
Fuels	13.7	18.5	18.7	22.5	15.8	17.8	12.4	18.4
Crude petroleum	8.6	12.2	11.9	15.1	7.4	8.8	9.6	14.6
Petroleum products	2.2	3.5	2.9	3.9	1.2	2.2	2.5	3.2
Manufactured goods	65.2	65.7	53.7	58.6	51.8	58.1	73.4	70.9
Chemical products	3.2	3.5	4.3	3.6	2.7	4.2	2.2	2.7
Iron and steel	2.5	3.2	2.2	4.0	1.7	1.6	2.1	2.0
Machinery and transport equipment	25.9	32.3	15.8	25.4	18.0	26.9	34.2	36.5
Furniture	1.4	2.0	1.5	2.0	1.4	1.5	1.8	3.0
Textiles	13.8	8.6	14.9	9.3	13.5	9.6	13.0	8.5
Footwear	3.1	1.5	2.1	1.5	1.9	1.2	4.0	1.9
Other	15.2	14.5	12.9	12.9	12.6	13.2	16.2	16.3
Miscellaneous goods	1.9	1.7	2.2	1.3	1.4	1.6	2.3	2.2

Simple applied tariff rates on imports from middle-income economies (%)[a]

	High-income economies		European Union		Japan		United States	
Food	9.9	9.1	16.4	8.9	12.4	7.7	3.7	3.8
Cereals	13.8	13.9	47.6	25.2	16.8	12.0	1.5	1.4
Agricultural raw materials	2.6	2.6	1.0	0.3	1.3	0.6	0.5	0.6
Ores and nonferrous metals	1.8	1.3	0.9	0.5	0.1	0.1	0.4	0.4
Fuels	3.3	1.4	0.0	0.0	1.3	0.3	0.4	1.3
Crude petroleum	7.1	0.6	0.0	0.0	0.9	0.0	0.4	0.0
Petroleum products	6.2	2.1	0.1	0.1	5.6	1.2	1.3	3.4
Manufactured goods	4.9	3.6	2.0	0.9	1.5	2.4	3.8	2.6
Chemical products	3.4	2.4	1.4	1.0	0.6	0.4	1.4	0.8
Iron and steel	3.5	1.8	1.1	0.1	0.1	0.2	2.9	0.2
Machinery and transport equipment	3.3	2.3	0.7	0.2	0.0	0.0	0.5	0.2
Furniture	5.4	4.3	0.3	0.0	0.0	0.1	0.4	0.3
Textiles	8.7	6.7	5.6	2.9	4.4	6.6	11.0	7.4
Footwear	9.1	8.1	4.6	2.7	13.2	19.3	12.9	7.8
Other	3.2	2.8	1.1	0.3	0.5	0.7	1.0	0.7
Miscellaneous goods	0.7	1.5	0.0	0.0	0.0	0.0	0.4	0.0
Average	**5.3**	**4.1**	**3.3**	**1.7**	**2.7**	**2.8**	**3.6**	**2.6**

a. Includes ad valorem equivalents of specific rates.

About the data

Developing economies are becoming increasingly important in the global trading system. Since the early 1990s trade between high-income economies and low- and middle-income economies has grown faster than trade among high-income economies. The increased trade benefits consumers and producers. But as was apparent at the World Trade Organization's (WTO) Ministerial Conferences in Doha, Qatar, in October 2001; Cancun, Mexico, in September 2003; and Hong Kong, China, in December 2005, achieving a more pro-development outcome from trade remains a challenge. Doing so will require strengthening international consultation. After the Doha meetings negotiations were launched on services, agriculture, manufactures, WTO rules, the environment, dispute settlement, intellectual property rights protection, and disciplines on regional integration. At the most recent negotiations in Hong Kong, China, trade ministers agreed to eliminate subsidies of agricultural exports by 2013; to abolish cotton export subsidies and grant unlimited export access to selected cotton-growing countries in Sub-Saharan Africa; to cut more domestic farm supports in the European Union, Japan, and the United States; and to offer more aid to developing countries to help them compete in global trade.

Trade flows between high-income and low- and middle-income economies reflect the changing mix of exports to and imports from developing economies. While food and primary commodities have continued to fall as a share of high-income economies' imports, manufactures as a share of goods imports from both low- and middle-income economies have grown. And trade between developing economies has grown substantially over the past decade, a result of their increasing share of world output and liberalization of trade, among other influences.

Yet trade barriers remain high. The table includes information about tariff rates by selected product groups. Applied tariff rates are the tariffs in effect for partners in preferential trade agreements such as the North American Free Trade Agreement. When these rates are unavailable, most favored nation rates are used. The difference between most favored nation and applied rates can be substantial. Simple averages of applied rates are shown because they are generally a better indicator of tariff protection than weighted average rates are.

The data are from the United Nations Conference on Trade and Development (UNCTAD). Partner country reports by high-income economies were used for both exports and imports. Because of differences in sources of data, timing, and treatment of missing data, the numbers in the table may not be fully comparable with those used to calculate the direction of trade statistics in table 6.3 or the aggregate flows in tables 4.4, 4.5, and 6.2. Tariff line data were matched to Standard International Trade Classification (SITC) revision 3 codes to define commodity groups. For further discussion of merchandise trade statistics, see *About the data* for tables 4.4, 4.5, 6.2, 6.3, and 6.5, and for information about tariff barriers, see table 6.8.

Definitions

The product groups in the table are defined in accordance with SITC revision 3: **food** (0, 1, 22, and 4) and **cereals** (04); **agricultural raw materials** (2 excluding 22, 27, and 28); **ores and nonferrous metals** (27, 28, and 68); **fuels** (3), **crude petroleum** (crude petroleum oils and oils obtained from bituminous minerals; 333), and **petroleum products** (noncrude petroleum and preparations; 334); **manufactured goods** (5–8 excluding 68), **chemical products** (5), **iron and steel** (67), **machinery and transport equipment** (7), **furniture** (82), **textiles** (65 and 84), **footwear** (85), and **other manufactured goods** (6 and 8 excluding 65, 67, 68, 82, 84, and 85); and **miscellaneous goods** (9). • **Exports** are all merchandise exports by high-income economies to low-income and middle-income economies as recorded in the United Nations Statistics Division's Comtrade database. Exports are recorded free on board (f.o.b.). • **Imports** are all merchandise imports by high-income economies from low-income and middle-income economies as recorded in the United Nations Statistics Division's Commodity Trade (Comtrade) database. Imports include insurance and freight charges (c.i.f.). • **High-, middle-, and low-income economies** are those classified as such by the World Bank (see inside front cover). • **European Union** is defined as all high-income EU members: Austria, Belgium, Cyprus, Czech Republic, Denmark, Estonia, Finland, France, Germany, Greece, Hungary, Ireland, Italy, Luxembourg, Malta, the Netherlands, Portugal, Slovenia, Spain, Sweden, and the United Kingdom.

High-income economies' tariffs on imports from low- and middle-income economies fell between 1997 and 2007 but remain high for some products
6.4a

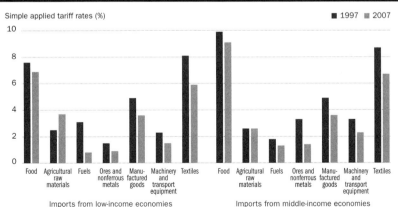

Food and textile products are subject to higher tariff rates than other products are. And tariff rates on agricultural raw material imports from low-income countries have increased significantly.

Source: United Nations Statistics Division's Comtrade database and the United Nations Conference on Trade and Development's Trade Analysis and Information System database.

Data sources

Data on trade values are from United Nations Statistics Division's Comtrade database. Data on tariffs are from UNCTAD's Trade Analysis and Information System database and are calculated by World Bank staff using the World Integrated Trade Solution system.

6.5 Direction of trade of developing economies

	Exports						Imports					
	% of total merchandise exports						% of total merchandise imports					
	To developing economies				To high-income economies		From developing economies				From high-income economies	
	Within region		Outside region				Within region		Outside region			
	1997	2007	1997	2007	1997	2007	1997	2007	1997	2007	1997	2007
East Asia & Pacific	**8.5**	**10.6**	**6.9**	**14.6**	**84.6**	**74.8**	**9.4**	**16.9**	**7.5**	**13.2**	**84.6**	**69.9**
Cambodia	55.5	7.3	1.0	1.9	43.5	90.8	34.3	59.7	0.8	1.4	43.5	38.9
China	4.9	5.5	8.4	17.0	86.6	77.5	6.0	10.7	10.1	17.0	86.6	72.3
Indonesia	11.2	18.9	6.7	12.7	82.1	68.4	8.6	27.8	8.3	10.3	82.1	61.9
Korea, Dem. Rep.	16.8	40.7	33.5	49.6	49.7	9.6	43.0	51.9	18.7	38.6	49.7	9.5
Lao PDR	26.2	71.0	0.0	1.2	73.8	27.8	91.7	85.5	0.1	0.7	73.8	13.8
Malaysia	10.1	19.7	6.5	9.8	83.5	70.5	10.2	26.1	4.4	5.4	83.5	68.5
Mongolia	22.5	72.0	10.8	3.9	66.6	24.1	14.5	34.5	38.9	34.7	66.6	30.8
Myanmar	15.4	61.3	20.2	19.1	64.4	19.6	42.6	63.9	3.0	4.7	64.4	31.4
Papua New Guinea	11.2	15.3	0.7	2.4	88.2	82.2	7.2	18.0	1.0	1.3	88.2	80.7
Philippines	8.4	21.1	1.2	2.2	90.4	76.6	10.4	19.5	5.1	3.4	90.4	77.2
Thailand	13.6	25.1	5.4	11.0	81.0	64.0	11.6	25.6	7.3	7.3	81.0	67.0
Vietnam	14.4	19.8	5.4	3.4	80.2	76.8	13.4	33.9	3.6	4.6	80.2	61.4
Europe & Central Asia	**32.1**	**28.3**	**10.0**	**10.2**	**57.8**	**61.5**	**27.7**	**27.5**	**7.9**	**14.0**	**57.8**	**58.4**
Albania	8.1	8.6	0.1	3.9	91.8	87.6	10.5	23.4	0.5	10.7	91.8	65.9
Armenia	44.1	36.0	21.8	4.9	34.2	59.2	41.4	42.6	12.1	15.1	34.2	42.3
Azerbaijan	55.0	38.2	25.0	21.3	20.0	40.5	69.0	45.3	7.7	11.6	20.0	43.1
Belarus	80.7	58.9	7.3	6.7	12.0	34.4	73.5	72.6	3.3	5.1	12.0	22.3
Bosnia and Herzegovina	39.3	26.9	4.9	2.3	55.9	70.8	33.7	37.2	0.1	1.1	55.9	61.7
Bulgaria	36.3	29.5	9.1	5.9	54.6	64.6	38.2	35.7	9.3	7.7	54.6	56.6
Croatia	23.6	22.9	4.8	2.8	71.6	74.4	9.0	20.3	7.4	9.7	71.6	70.0
Georgia	77.3	46.8	5.6	5.6	17.1	47.6	55.8	56.8	2.5	8.1	17.1	35.2
Kazakhstan	49.2	26.2	11.7	22.3	39.1	51.5	61.1	48.4	3.0	23.5	39.1	28.0
Kyrgyz Republic	54.7	56.6	7.5	17.2	37.8	26.1	68.7	66.5	7.0	16.4	37.8	17.1
Latvia	38.4	37.0	2.3	2.3	59.3	60.7	30.1	35.4	1.6	3.2	59.3	61.4
Lithuania	58.6	45.2	1.0	2.0	40.4	52.9	38.4	39.1	2.9	4.3	40.4	56.6
Macedonia, FYR	20.4	42.4	1.2	0.5	78.4	57.1	28.5	37.5	6.2	4.7	78.4	57.8
Moldova	80.5	65.0	0.5	2.0	19.0	32.9	69.1	67.0	1.6	2.9	19.0	30.2
Poland	27.8	34.4	6.1	10.6	66.1	55.0	21.4	36.5	7.6	23.0	66.1	40.5
Romania	13.6	19.5	14.4	5.8	72.0	74.7	19.0	20.9	7.7	7.1	72.0	72.1
Russian Federation	30.4	28.7	9.9	10.5	59.7	60.8	33.3	20.8	9.2	19.9	59.7	59.3
Tajikistan	43.3	50.9	2.7	6.7	53.9	42.4	66.6	70.3	2.3	17.5	53.9	12.1
Turkey	18.4	19.1	11.7	14.8	69.9	66.1	9.7	22.8	12.6	22.8	69.9	54.5
Turkmenistan	48.2	64.6	31.7	22.9	20.2	12.4	71.5	41.4	4.7	17.7	20.2	40.9
Ukraine	51.2	51.1	22.5	20.1	26.3	28.7	65.4	45.4	3.2	12.1	26.3	42.5
Uzbekistan	62.8	62.8	10.1	14.1	27.1	23.1	46.5	52.4	6.1	14.9	27.1	32.7
Latin America & Carib.	**19.5**	**18.2**	**5.8**	**11.1**	**74.7**	**70.7**	**17.7**	**20.4**	**5.4**	**16.9**	**74.7**	**62.6**
Argentina	50.8	41.1	17.6	27.2	31.6	31.7	31.6	44.5	7.5	18.3	31.6	37.2
Bolivia	43.5	65.2	0.3	2.5	56.2	32.3	43.8	71.3	1.0	4.8	56.2	23.8
Brazil	28.7	25.3	13.0	20.5	58.2	54.2	22.1	17.3	10.2	27.9	58.2	54.8
Chile	21.5	16.9	7.6	23.2	70.9	59.9	29.4	35.8	8.4	21.1	70.9	43.0
Colombia	27.7	35.4	1.9	4.6	70.4	60.0	25.8	31.5	3.7	15.3	70.4	53.2
Costa Rica	26.1	19.5	2.1	18.2	71.8	62.3	32.4	27.6	4.1	7.6	71.8	64.8
Cuba	6.1	13.0	42.7	36.8	51.2	50.2	10.9	39.9	24.7	18.6	51.2	41.5
Dominican Republic	2.9	6.4	0.4	2.8	96.7	90.8	21.2	28.2	1.4	6.2	96.7	65.7
Ecuador	25.9	28.3	7.3	9.4	66.8	62.3	34.2	36.1	4.5	13.4	66.8	50.6
El Salvador	48.0	40.3	0.8	1.4	51.2	58.3	38.9	42.1	1.8	7.1	51.2	50.8
Guatemala	30.1	39.6	3.5	3.0	66.4	57.4	31.2	33.1	2.4	9.5	66.4	57.4
Haiti	0.4	11.9	0.0	3.7	99.6	84.3	14.9	16.8	4.5	10.4	99.6	72.8
Honduras	17.8	17.5	0.0	0.8	82.2	81.7	30.5	27.1	0.0	5.9	82.2	66.9
Jamaica	4.3	2.0	8.1	9.1	87.6	88.9	10.5	29.1	2.3	5.4	87.6	65.5
Mexico	5.1	6.0	0.3	1.6	94.6	92.4	2.3	5.1	3.2	15.4	94.6	79.5
Nicaragua	28.6	44.6	0.1	0.8	71.3	54.6	46.9	58.8	0.5	0.8	71.3	40.4
Panama	23.6	16.9	0.2	8.1	76.2	75.1	30.0	24.2	1.6	7.3	76.2	68.6
Paraguay	61.0	70.0	0.4	8.1	38.6	21.9	53.9	53.6	2.9	10.6	38.6	35.8
Peru	17.9	20.5	13.5	15.9	68.6	63.6	30.4	38.4	2.6	18.3	68.6	43.3
Uruguay	56.6	41.9	9.6	18.6	33.9	39.5	50.7	48.2	7.6	21.3	33.9	30.5
Venezuela, RB	21.9	13.3	0.6	4.8	77.4	81.9	22.2	43.4	1.4	10.2	77.4	46.5

Direction of trade of developing economies

	Exports — % of total merchandise exports						Imports — % of total merchandise imports					
	To developing economies				To high-income economies		From developing economies				From high-income economies	
	Within region		Outside region				Within region		Outside region			
	1997	2007	1997	2007	1997	2007	1997	2007	1997	2007	1997	2007
Middle East & N. Africa	**4.6**	**7.5**	**16.9**	**18.5**	**78.5**	**74.0**	**4.8**	**8.3**	**20.7**	**31.5**	**78.5**	**60.2**
Algeria	1.2	2.5	13.5	11.2	85.3	86.4	3.6	3.3	15.6	31.6	85.3	65.1
Egypt, Arab Rep.	7.0	14.7	12.9	15.3	80.1	70.1	1.3	4.1	24.3	33.6	80.1	62.3
Iran, Islamic Rep.	0.3	2.7	19.6	38.0	80.1	59.3	0.8	0.8	29.4	46.0	80.1	53.2
Iraq	20.2	3.0	17.2	7.0	62.6	90.0	25.8	39.2	28.7	31.9	62.6	28.9
Jordan	28.4	27.5	25.4	17.1	46.3	55.4	17.7	8.6	19.5	25.9	46.3	65.4
Lebanon	16.9	39.6	14.7	11.9	68.4	48.5	7.0	16.5	16.7	22.2	68.4	61.3
Libya	3.5	3.1	10.9	7.1	85.7	89.8	9.2	11.4	10.7	25.5	85.7	63.1
Morocco	6.2	2.7	19.4	21.1	74.4	76.2	4.6	6.3	21.3	20.0	74.4	73.8
Syrian Arab Republic	13.5	53.4	15.6	4.3	70.9	42.3	4.4	21.2	26.9	30.4	70.9	48.5
Tunisia	7.3	9.5	8.3	6.5	84.4	84.0	4.8	7.0	11.8	15.3	84.4	77.7
Yemen, Rep.	0.3	2.1	56.5	66.8	43.2	31.1	3.6	3.3	25.5	34.7	43.2	62.0
South Asia	**4.4**	**6.4**	**17.5**	**26.5**	**78.1**	**67.1**	**3.9**	**4.9**	**21.7**	**32.3**	**78.1**	**62.8**
Afghanistan	24.0	45.9	20.6	21.1	55.4	33.0	9.7	41.8	33.3	28.1	55.4	30.0
Bangladesh	2.5	2.8	9.9	7.1	87.6	90.1	15.0	16.9	23.2	31.3	87.6	51.9
India	4.8	5.2	19.6	29.2	75.5	65.6	0.6	1.1	22.1	33.0	75.5	65.9
Nepal	25.9	72.8	0.4	2.8	73.8	24.4	28.2	66.2	8.2	18.6	73.8	15.2
Pakistan	2.9	13.0	14.1	21.3	83.0	65.7	2.3	3.0	21.3	33.9	83.0	63.1
Sri Lanka	2.8	9.3	15.1	14.3	82.0	76.4	12.1	25.6	21.2	24.9	82.0	49.5
Sub-Saharan Africa	**12.3**	**12.3**	**12.4**	**23.3**	**75.4**	**64.4**	**13.3**	**12.2**	**13.5**	**28.9**	**75.4**	**59.0**
Angola	1.3	4.6	16.4	38.4	82.3	57.0	9.6	7.4	7.7	27.6	82.3	65.0
Benin	7.8	31.5	61.1	44.6	31.1	23.9	15.4	9.0	15.8	59.8	31.1	31.2
Burkina Faso	19.9	16.3	11.0	50.1	69.1	33.6	26.2	41.7	12.0	15.6	69.1	42.7
Burundi	2.5	18.4	0.0	16.6	97.5	65.0	27.0	27.2	6.6	16.5	97.5	56.3
Cameroon	6.6	9.6	9.3	9.5	84.1	80.9	19.2	19.8	10.0	25.1	84.1	55.1
Central African Republic	17.0	8.7	0.1	33.3	82.9	58.0	23.1	24.9	6.8	10.9	82.9	64.2
Chad	6.5	0.5	27.9	4.6	65.7	95.0	22.8	22.0	7.5	14.3	65.7	63.7
Congo, Dem. Rep.	8.6	10.5	4.6	34.1	86.9	55.3	40.6	53.9	9.4	6.7	86.9	39.4
Congo, Rep.	1.1	1.4	11.6	43.1	87.3	55.5	12.2	4.8	6.5	27.8	87.3	67.4
Ethiopia	3.0	2.4	15.3	30.1	81.7	67.4	2.3	2.4	18.7	42.4	81.7	55.2
Gabon	1.0	3.1	11.2	31.1	87.8	65.8	16.0	9.3	5.1	13.0	87.8	77.7
Gambia, The	8.5	8.4	15.3	57.4	76.2	34.2	10.5	21.8	19.7	51.9	76.2	26.3
Ghana	8.2	11.6	13.0	20.3	78.8	68.1	22.9	24.8	13.1	33.2	78.8	42.1
Guinea	5.7	1.9	0.5	35.3	93.8	62.8	12.5	12.2	16.4	33.1	93.8	54.6
Guinea-Bissau	1.6	8.9	55.0	90.2	43.4	0.9	13.3	25.8	20.7	19.7	43.4	54.5
Kenya	41.5	42.8	13.5	16.1	45.0	41.1	13.5	9.1	14.7	29.2	45.0	61.7
Liberia	1.4	2.3	14.0	57.6	84.5	40.0	1.1	2.4	9.1	17.7	84.5	79.9
Madagascar	7.5	2.7	6.3	5.8	86.2	91.6	11.8	14.4	25.0	37.8	86.2	47.8
Malawi	21.6	26.1	13.1	29.1	65.3	44.8	68.0	55.1	5.2	18.0	65.3	27.0
Mali	4.0	6.6	42.7	62.4	53.3	31.0	36.1	43.2	6.5	14.3	53.3	42.5
Mauritania	9.6	13.0	4.6	37.2	85.8	49.8	4.1	6.0	26.2	35.3	85.8	58.7
Mauritius	5.8	12.1	1.2	3.1	93.0	84.9	15.2	10.5	22.1	44.2	93.0	45.3
Mozambique	31.0	21.0	8.0	9.8	61.0	69.2	64.1	47.1	7.2	19.3	61.0	33.5
Niger	28.5	32.8	0.3	2.8	71.2	64.3	27.2	23.3	16.9	17.0	71.2	59.6
Nigeria	8.1	10.2	13.7	14.0	78.2	75.8	3.3	6.0	20.9	28.6	78.2	65.4
Rwanda	5.8	5.5	14.2	40.0	80.0	54.4	30.9	46.6	7.7	11.4	80.0	42.0
Senegal	29.6	49.6	19.5	12.2	51.0	38.2	11.8	9.3	20.8	27.7	51.0	63.0
Sierra Leone	0.0	2.9	0.0	6.2	100.0	90.9	21.2	19.5	9.3	33.6	100.0	46.9
Somalia	0.3	4.0	13.1	29.3	86.6	66.7	13.6	10.9	66.7	66.7	86.6	22.4
South Africa	14.2	14.2	11.7	16.0	74.0	69.8	3.7	6.2	11.6	27.9	74.0	65.9
Sudan	1.3	0.3	30.5	84.2	68.2	15.5	3.2	2.4	41.6	52.8	68.2	44.8
Tanzania	14.6	18.7	25.8	32.4	59.5	48.9	16.5	20.1	23.3	30.5	59.5	49.3
Togo	17.4	55.7	37.5	17.3	45.1	27.0	23.9	6.1	8.9	47.7	45.1	46.2
Uganda	2.4	23.4	7.0	11.1	90.6	65.5	44.2	40.2	9.4	17.4	90.6	42.4
Zambia	13.7	24.1	25.8	18.5	60.5	57.5	55.6	59.1	5.8	11.6	60.5	29.2
Zimbabwe	35.1	55.7	9.6	11.6	55.4	32.7	50.6	67.8	5.6	11.6	55.4	20.7

Note: Bilateral trade data are not available for Timor-Leste, Serbia, West Bank and Gaza, Botswana, Côte d'Ivoire, Eritrea, Lesotho, Namibia, and Swaziland.

6.5 | Direction of trade of developing economies

Developing economies are an increasingly important part of the global trading system. Their share of world trade rose from 18 percent in 1990 to 28 percent in 2007. And trade between high-income economies and low- and middle-income economies has grown faster than trade between high-income economies. This increased trade benefits both producers and consumers in developing and high-income economies.

The table shows trade in goods between developing economies in the same region and other regions and between developing economies and high-income economies. Data on exports and imports are from the International Monetary Fund's (IMF) Direction of Trade database and should be broadly consistent with data from other sources, such as the United Nations Statistics Division's Commodity Trade (Comtrade) database. Generally, data on trade between developing and high-income economies are complete. But trade flows between many developing economies—particularly those in Sub-Saharan Africa—are not well recorded, and the value of trade among developing economies may be understated. The table does not include some developing economies because data on their bilateral trade flows are not available. Data on the direction of trade between selected high-income economies are presented and discussed in tables 6.3 and 6.4.

At the regional level most exports from developing economies are to high-income economies, but the share of intraregional trade is increasing. Geographic patterns of trade vary widely by country and commodity. Larger shares of exports from oil- and resource-rich economies are to high-income economies.

The relative importance of intraregional trade is higher for both landlocked countries and small countries with close trade links to the largest regional economy. For most developing economies—especially smaller ones—there is a "geographic bias" favoring intraregional trade. Despite the broad trend toward globalization and the reduction of trade barriers, the relative share of intraregional trade increased for most economies between 1997 and 2007. This is due partly to trade-related advantages, such as proximity, lower transport costs, increased knowledge from repeated interaction, and cultural and historical affinity. The direction of trade is also influenced by preferential trade agreements that a country has made with other economies. Though formal agreements on trade liberalization do not automatically increase trade, they nevertheless affect the direction of trade between the participating economies. Table 6.7 illustrates the size of existing regional trade blocs that have formal preferential trade agreements.

Although global integration has increased, developing economies still face trade barriers when accessing other markets (see table 6.8).

• **Exports to developing economies within region** are the sum of merchandise exports from the reporting economy to other developing economies in the same World Bank region as a percentage of total merchandise exports by the economy. • **Exports to developing economies outside region** are the sum of merchandise exports from the reporting economy to other developing economies in other World Bank regions as a percentage of total merchandise exports by the economy. • **Exports to high-income economies** are the sum of merchandise exports from the reporting economy to high-income economies as a percentage of total merchandise exports by the economy. • **Imports from developing economies within region** are the sum of merchandise imports by the reporting economy from other developing economies in the same World Bank region as a percentage of total merchandise imports by the economy. • **Imports from developing economies outside region** are the sum of merchandise imports by the reporting economy from other developing economies in other World Bank regions as a percentage of total merchandise imports by the economy. • **Imports from high-income economies** are the sum of merchandise imports by the reporting economy from high-income economies as a percentage of total merchandise imports by the economy.

6.5a

Merchandise exports, 2007 (%)
- ■ To developing economies within region
- ■ To developing economies outside region
- ■ To the United States
- ■ To other high-income economies

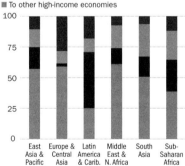

Merchandise imports, 2007 (%)
- ■ From developing economies within region
- ■ From developing economies outside region
- ■ From the United States
- ■ From other high-income economies

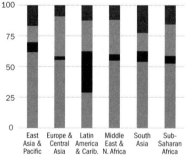

In 2007 most developing economy merchandise trade was with high-income partners, but the degree of dependence varied by region. Latin America and Caribbean is highly integrated with the United States and most likely to be affected by the U.S. recession. Most merchandise exports of Latin America and Caribbean and Europe and Central Asia to developing economies stayed within the same region. Most merchandise imports of East Asia and Pacific and South Asia from developing economies were from within the same region, reflecting strong presence of large regional economies such as China and India.

Source: World Bank staff calculations based on data from International Monetary Fund's Direction of Trade database.

Data on merchandise trade flows are published in the IMF's *Direction of Trade Statistics Yearbook* and *Direction of Trade Statistics Quarterly;* the data in the table were calculated using the IMF's Direction of Trade database. Regional and income group classifications are according to the World Bank classification of economies as of July 1, 2008 and are as shown on the inside covers of this report.

	1970	1980	1990	1995	2000	2002	2003	2004	2005	2006	2007	2008
World Bank commodity price index (2000 = 100)												
Energy	19	153	79	53	100	92	101	123	171	197	207	269
Nonenergy commodities	183	177	115	117	100	105	108	121	135	172	190	215
Agriculture	188	195	113	122	100	112	114	118	121	134	153	181
Beverages	230	273	117	136	100	124	117	109	125	130	144	165
Food	201	199	116	117	100	115	117	123	121	131	156	195
Fats and oils	237	196	105	126	100	115	129	134	120	123	177	219
Grains	204	199	121	124	100	117	112	115	115	134	160	222
Other food	151	205	124	101	100	114	105	117	129	140	126	140
Raw materials	136	143	105	125	100	97	107	109	119	144	149	155
Timber	97	92	88	105	100	92	91	90	100	113	116	119
Other raw materials	179	198	124	146	100	104	124	130	141	179	185	195
Fertilizers	82	177	98	110	100	98	110	125	148	151	203	452
Metals and minerals	185	141	122	106	100	92	96	126	162	251	266	257
Steel products[a]	0	134	131	118	100	92	100	153	170	162	154	228
Commodity prices (2000 prices)												
Energy												
Coal, Australian ($/mt)	..	49	39	33	26	26	25	48	43	44	56	100
Natural gas, Europe ($/mmBtu)	..	5	2	2	4	3	4	4	6	8	7	11
Natural gas, U.S. ($/mmBtu)	1	2	2	1	4	4	5	5	8	6	6	7
Natural gas, liquefied, Japan ($/mmBtu)	..	7	4	3	5	4	5	5	5	6	7	10
Petroleum, avg, spot ($/bbl)	4	45	22	14	28	26	28	34	48	57	60	76
Beverages (cents/kg)												
Cocoa	233	321	123	119	91	185	170	141	140	142	165	203
Coffee, Arabica	397	427	192	277	192	142	137	161	230	225	231	243
Coffee, robusta	321	400	115	230	91	69	79	72	101	133	162	183
Tea, avg., 3 auctions	289	205	200	124	188	157	147	153	150	168	172	191
Tea, Colombo auctions	217	137	182	118	179	163	150	162	167	171	214	220
Tea, Kolkata auctions	343	253	273	145	181	153	142	156	147	157	163	178
Tea, Mombasa auctions	307	224	144	108	203	156	150	141	134	175	141	175
Food												
Fats and oils ($/mt)												
Coconut oil	1,376	831	327	556	450	439	454	600	560	542	778	964
Copra[a]	779	558	224	364	305	278	291	409	376	360	514	643
Groundnut oil	1,312	1,059	937	823	714	717	1,207	1,054	963	867	1,145	1,679
Palm oil	901	719	282	521	310	407	430	428	383	427	661	747
Palm kernel oil[a]	..	..	..	..	444	434	445	588	569	519	753	890
Soybeans	405	365	240	215	212	222	256	278	249	240	325	412
Soybean meal	357	323	195	164	189	183	205	219	195	187	260	339
Soybean oil	992	737	435	519	338	474	538	559	495	535	747	991
Grains ($/mt)												
Barley	..	96	78	86	77	114	102	90	86	104	146	158
Maize	202	154	106	103	89	104	102	102	90	109	139	176
Rice, Thailand, 5%	438	506	263	266	202	200	192	216	260	272	277	512
Sorghum[a]	179	159	101	99	88	106	103	100	87	110	138	164
Wheat, Canada[a]	218	235	152	172	147	183	172	169	179	194	254	358
Wheat, U.S., hard red winter	190	213	132	147	114	155	142	142	138	172	216	257
Wheat, U.S., soft red winter[a]	197	208	125	139	99	136	134	131	123	142	202	214

6.6 Primary commodity prices

	1970	1980	1990	1995	2000	2002	2003	2004	2005	2006	2007	2008
Commodity prices (continued)												
(2000 prices)												
Food (continued)												
Other food												
Bananas, U.S. ($/mt)	573	467	526	369	424	552	364	476	547	605	572	665
Beef (cents/kg)	452	340	249	158	193	220	192	228	238	228	220	247
Chicken meat (cents/kg)	..	85	96	92	119	132	129	138	135	124	133	134
Fishmeal ($/mt)[a]	682	621	401	411	413	632	593	589	664	1,040	997	..
Oranges ($/mt)	582	482	516	441	363	589	661	780	794	741	810	872
Shrimp, Mexico (cents/kg)	..	1,420	1,039	1,253	1,515	1,097	1,110	928	939	915	855	840
Sugar, EU domestic (cents/kg)	39	60	57	57	56	57	58	61	60	58	58	55
Sugar, U.S. domestic (cents/kg)	57	82	50	42	43	48	46	41	43	44	39	37
Sugar, world (cents/kg)	29	78	27	24	18	16	15	14	20	29	19	22
Agricultural raw materials												
Cotton A index (cents/kg)	219	252	177	177	130	106	136	124	110	113	118	124
Logs, Cameroon ($/cu. m)[a]	149	310	334	282	275	246	271	301	304	285	323	415
Logs, Malaysian ($/cu. m)	149	241	172	212	190	170	182	179	184	214	227	230
Rubber, Singapore (cents/kg)	141	176	84	131	67	80	105	118	136	188	194	206
Plywood (cents/sheet)[a]	357	338	345	485	448	410	419	422	462	532	543	511
Sawnwood, Malaysian ($/cu. m)	608	489	518	614	595	549	535	528	599	670	683	701
Tobacco ($/mt)[a]	3,727	2,806	3,297	2,194	2,976	2,864	2,568	2,488	2,533	2,653	2,808	2,801
Woodpulp ($/mt)[a]	615	661	792	708	664	472	510	582	577	624	650	652
Fertilizers ($/mt)												
Diammonium phosphate	187	274	167	180	154	164	174	201	224	233	366	762
Phosphate rock	38	58	39	29	44	42	37	37	38	40	60	272
Potassium chloride	109	143	95	98	123	118	110	113	144	156	170	449
Triple superphosphate	147	222	128	124	138	139	145	169	183	180	287	749
Urea	..	..	116	155	101	98	135	159	199	199	262	388
Metals and minerals												
Aluminum ($/mt)	1,926	1,795	1,593	1,499	1,549	1,408	1,389	1,558	1,724	2,297	2,235	2,027
Copper ($/mt)	4,895	2,690	2,586	2,437	1,813	1,627	1,727	2,602	3,340	6,007	6,030	5,481
Gold ($/toz)[a]	125	750	373	319	279	323	353	372	404	540	590	687
Iron ore (cents/dmtu)	34	35	32	24	29	31	31	34	59	69	72	111
Lead (cents/kg)	105	112	79	52	45	47	50	80	89	115	219	165
Nickel ($/mt)	9,860	8,037	8,614	6,830	8,638	7,066	9,346	12,551	13,387	21,675	31,532	16,635
Silver (cents/toz)[a]	614	2,544	475	431	500	483	477	607	666	1,034	1,136	1,182
Tin (cents/kg)	1,273	2,068	591	516	544	424	475	773	670	785	1,231	1,459
Zinc (cents/kg)	102	94	147	86	113	81	80	95	125	293	275	148
MUV G-5 index (2000 = 100)	29	81	103	120	100	96	103	110	110	112	118	127

Note: bbl = barrel, cu. m = cubic meter, dmtu = dry metric ton unit, kg = kilogram, mmBtu = million British thermal units, mt = metric ton, toz = troy ounce.
a. Series not included in the nonenergy index.

Primary commodities—raw or partially processed materials that will be transformed into finished goods—are often developing countries' most significant exports, and the revenues obtained from them have an important effect on living standards. Price data for primary commodities are collected from a variety of sources, including international commodity study groups, government agencies, industry trade journals, and Bloomberg and Datastream data feed systems. Prices are either compiled in U.S. dollars or converted to U.S. dollars when quoted in local currencies.

The table is based on frequently updated price reports. When available, the prices received by exporters are used; otherwise, the prices paid by importers or trade unit values are used. Annual price series are generally simple averages based on higher frequency data. The constant price series in the table are deflated using the manufactures unit value (MUV) index for the Group of Five (G-5) countries (see below).

The commodity price indices are calculated as Laspeyres index numbers, in which the fixed weights are the 2002–04 average export values for low- and middle-income economies (based on 2001 gross national income) rebased to 2000. As of April 2008 the weights were changed from 1987–89 average export values to 2002–04 averages in order to include the most recent available complete data. Data for exports are collected from various sources, including the United Nations Statistics Division's Commodity Trade Statistics (Comtrade) database Standard International Trade Classification (SITC) revision 3, the Food Agriculture Organization's FAOSTAT database, the International Energy Agency database, BP's *Statistical Review of World Energy,* the World Bureau of Metal Statistics, and World Bank staff estimates.

Each index in the table represents a fixed basket of primary commodity exports over time. The non-energy commodity price index contains 41 price series for 34 nonenergy commodities. The index in previous editions contained only 31 nonenergy commodities. In response to changes in commodity trade shares, minor adjustments have been made to the commodities basket, with barley, poultry meat, and potassium and nitrogen fertilizers added and sorghum dropped.

Separate indices are compiled for energy and steel products, which are not included in the nonenergy commodity price index. The previous petroleum index has been replaced with a new energy index that includes coal, petroleum, and natural gas. The new and old energy indices are similar because petroleum exports account for almost 85 percent of total energy commodity exports from developing countries.

The MUV index is a composite index of prices for manufactured exports from the five major (G-5) industrial economies (France, Germany, Japan, the United Kingdom, and the United States) to low- and middle-income economies, valued in U.S. dollars. The index covers products in groups 5–8 of SITC revision 1. To construct the MUV G-5 index, unit value indexes for each country are combined using weights determined by each country's export share in a base year.

• **Energy price index** is the composite price index for coal, petroleum, and natural gas, weighted by exports of each commodity from low- and middle-income countries. • **Nonenergy commodity price index** covers the 34 nonenergy primary commodities that make up the agriculture, fertilizer, and metals and minerals indexes. • **Agriculture** includes beverages, food, and agricultural raw materials. • **Beverages** include cocoa, coffee, and tea. • **Food** includes fats and oils, grains, and other food items. Fats and oils include coconut oil, groundnut oil, palm oil, soybeans, soybean oil, and soybean meal. Grains include barley, maize, rice, and wheat. Other food items include bananas, beef, chicken, oranges, shrimp, and sugar. • **Agricultural raw materials** include timber and other raw materials. Timber includes tropical hard logs and sawnwood. Other raw materials include cotton, natural rubber, and tobacco. • **Fertilizers** include phosphate, phosphate rock, potassium, and nitrogenous products. • **Metals and minerals** include aluminum, copper, iron ore, lead, nickel, tin, and zinc. • **Steel products price index** is the composite price index for eight steel products based on quotations free on board (f.o.b.) Japan excluding shipments to the United States for all years and to China prior to 2001, weighted by product shares of apparent combined consumption (volume of deliveries) for Germany, Japan, and the United States. • **Commodity prices**—for definitions and sources, see "Commodity price data" (also known as the "Pink Sheet") at the World Bank Prospects for Development website (www.worldbank.org/prospects, click on Products). • **MUV G-5 index** is the manufactures unit value index for G-5 country exports to low- and middle-income economies.

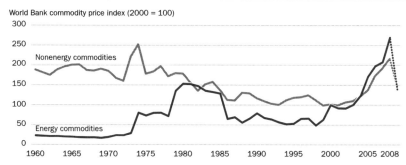

World Bank commodity price index (2000 = 100)

The recent commodity price boom threatened to impoverish millions of people around the world. Although there have been other commodity price booms, the recent boom lasted the longest. The average price of nonenergy commodities increased 115 percent over 2000–08. The increase in energy prices was even more remarkable—169 percent. In the last quarter of 2008, commodity prices declined significantly.

Note: Dotted lines are projections for 2009.
Source: World Bank commodity price data.

Data on commodity prices and the MUV G-5 index are compiled by the World Bank's Development Prospects Group. Monthly updates of commodity prices are available at www.worldbank.org/prospects.

6.7 | Regional trade blocs

Merchandise exports within bloc

	Year of creation	Year of entry into force of the most recent agreement	Type of most recent agreement[a]	$ millions						
				1990	1995	2000	2004	2005	2006	2007
High-income and low- and middle-income economies										
APEC[b]	1989		None	1,000,616	1,688,708	2,261,791	2,924,272	3,310,461	3,775,728	4,191,536
EEA	1994	1994	EIA	998,015	1,330,493	1,702,877	2,643,117	2,846,278	3,218,165	3,774,508
EFTA	1960	2002	EIA	717	925	831	1,128	1,252	1,524	2,196
European Union	1957	1958	EIA, CU	951,373	1,272,211	1,630,509	2,535,600	2,714,582	3,069,912	3,596,135
NAFTA	1994	1994	FTA, EIA	249,474	394,472	676,141	737,591	824,710	902,298	951,587
SPARTECA	1981	1981	PS	5,637	9,101	8,554	13,585	15,181	15,536	18,582
Trans-Pacific SEP	2006	2006	EIA, FTA	1,195	2,614	1,438	2,096	2,345	2,927	3,290
East Asia and Pacific and South Asia										
APTA	1975	1976	PS	5,475	21,728	37,895	99,369	127,277	156,957	198,000
ASEAN	1967	1992	FTA	32,785	79,544	98,060	141,931	165,458	191,392	216,424
PICTA	2001	2003	FTA	5	42	65	130	122	151	187
SAARC	1985	2006	FTA	1,013	2,024	2,680	5,830	7,266	8,310	10,222
Europe, Central Asia,and Middle East										
CEFTA	1992	1994	FTA	..	534	1,038	2,009	2,434	2,819	3,641
CIS	1991	1994	FTA	..	31,529	28,753	43,425	59,423	66,689	97,545
COZ	2003	2004	FTA	..	24,398	22,985	32,629	45,973	49,695	75,700
EAEC	1997	1997	CU	..	13,556	15,467	17,292	27,297	27,930	50,079
ECO	1985	2003	PS	1,232	4,746	4,518	9,982	13,936	19,053	24,584
GCC	1981	2003[c]	CU	4,760	6,832	7,954	12,532	16,635	20,693	24,728
PAFTA (GAFTA)	1997	1998	FTA	10,028	12,948	16,088	35,328	44,511	54,827	65,818
UMA	1989	1994[c]	NNA	1,071	1,109	1,041	1,448	1,934	2,478	3,076
Latin America and the Caribbean										
Andean Community	1969	1988	CU	788	1,788	2,046	3,435	4,572	5,011	5,509
CACM	1961	1961	CU	779	1,594	2,586	3,574	4,342	4,697	5,562
CARICOM	1973	1997	EIA	445	877	1,078	1,746	2,090	2,429	3,759
LAIA (ALADI)	1980	1981	PS	15,769	35,986	44,253	57,741	71,720	90,357	109,130
MERCOSUR	1991	2005	EIA	6,166	16,811	20,082	19,675	24,211	31,197	39,486
OECS	1981	1981[c]	NNA	29	39	38	60	68	84	104
Sub-Saharan Africa										
CEMAC	1994	1999	CU	114	120	96	174	198	245	304
COMESA	1994	1994	FTA	830	1,367	1,443	2,420	2,866	3,468	4,582
EAC	1996	2000	CU	132	628	689	930	1,043	1,279	1,587
ECCAS	1983	2004[c]	NNA	133	157	181	221	251	310	385
ECOWAS	1975	1993	PS	1,384	1,875	2,715	4,366	5,497	5,957	7,341
Indian Ocean Commission	1984	2005[c]	NNA	75	113	106	155	159	172	204
SADC	1992	2000	FTA	1,720	3,615	4,427	6,655	7,798	8,694	11,952
UEMOA	1994	2000	CU	499	560	741	1,233	1,390	1,545	1,917

Note: Regional bloc memberships are as follows: **Andean Community**, Bolivia, Colombia, Ecuador, and Peru; **Arab Maghreb Union (UMA)**, Algeria, Libyan Arab Republic, Mauritania, Morocco, and Tunisia; **Asia Pacific Economic Cooperation (APEC)**, Australia, Brunei Darussalam, Canada, Chile, China, Hong Kong (China), Indonesia, Japan, the Republic of Korea, Malaysia, Mexico, New Zealand, Papua New Guinea, Peru, the Philippines, the Russian Federation, Singapore, Taiwan (China), Thailand, the United States, and Vietnam; **Asia-Pacific Trade Agreement (APTA; formerly Bangkok Agreement),** Bangladesh, China, India, the Republic of Korea, the Lao People's Democratic Republic, and Sri Lanka; **Association of South East Asian Nations (ASEAN)**, Brunei Darussalam, Cambodia, Indonesia, the Lao People's Democratic Republic, Malaysia, Myanmar, the Philippines, Singapore, Thailand, and Vietnam; **Caribbean Community and Common Market (CARICOM)**, Antigua and Barbuda, the Bahamas, Barbados, Belize, Dominica, Grenada, Guyana, Haiti, Jamaica, Montserrat, St. Kitts and Nevis, St. Lucia, St. Vincent and the Grenadines, Suriname, and Trinidad and Tobago; **Central American Common Market (CACM)**, Costa Rica, El Salvador, Guatemala, Honduras, and Nicaragua; **Central European Free Trade Area (CEFTA)**, Albania, Bosnia and Herzegovina, Croatia, Kosovo, Macedonia, Moldova, Montenegro, and Serbia; **Common Economic Zone (COZ),** Belarus, Kazakhstan, the Russian Federation, and Ukraine; **Common Market for Eastern and Southern Africa (COMESA)**, Burundi, Comoros, the Democratic Republic of Congo, Djibouti, the Arab Republic of Egypt, Eritrea, Ethiopia, Kenya, Libyan Arab Republic, Madagascar, Malawi, Mauritius, Rwanda, Seychelles, Sudan, Swaziland, Uganda, Zambia, and Zimbabwe; **Commonwealth of Independent States (CIS)**, Armenia, Azerbaijan, Belarus, Georgia, Kazakhstan, Kyrgyz Republic, Moldova, the Russian Federation, Tajikistan, Turkmenistan, Ukraine, and Uzbekistan; **East African Community (EAC)**, Burundi, Kenya, Rwanda, Tanzania, and Uganda; **Economic and Monetary Community of Central Africa (CEMAC; formerly Central African Customs and Economic Union [UDEAC])**, Cameroon, the Central African Republic, Chad, the Republic of Congo, Equatorial Guinea, and Gabon; **Economic Community of Central African States (ECCAS)**, Angola, Burundi, Cameroon, the Central African Republic, Chad, the Democratic Republic of Congo, the Republic of Congo, Equatorial Guinea, Gabon, and São Tomé and Principe; **Economic Community of West African States (ECOWAS)**, Benin, Burkina Faso, Cape Verde, Côte d'Ivoire, the Gambia, Ghana, Guinea, Guinea-Bissau, Liberia, Mali, Niger, Nigeria, Senegal, Sierra Leone, and Togo; **Economic Cooperation Organization (ECO)**, Afghanistan, Azerbaijan, the Islamic Republic of Iran, Kazakhstan, the Kyrgyz Republic,

Merchandise exports within bloc

	Year of creation	Year of entry into force of the most recent agreement	Type of most recent agreement[a]	% of total bloc exports						
				1990	1995	2000	2004	2005	2006	2007
High-income and low- and middle-income economies										
APEC[b]	1989		None	68.7	71.7	73.1	72.2	70.8	69.5	67.4
EEA	1994	1994	EIA	69.4	67.3	68.6	68.9	68.4	68.6	69.0
EFTA	1960	2002	EIA	0.7	0.7	0.6	0.5	0.5	0.6	0.7
European Union	1957	1958	EIA, CU	67.8	65.8	67.3	67.6	67.0	67.2	67.5
NAFTA	1994	1994	FTA, EIA	42.2	46.2	55.7	55.9	55.8	53.9	51.3
SPARTECA	1981	1981	PS	10.5	12.9	10.7	12.1	11.4	10.2	10.5
Trans-Pacific SEP	2006	2006	EIA, FTA	1.5	1.7	0.8	0.8	0.8	0.8	0.8
East Asia and Pacific and South Asia										
APTA	1975	1976	PS	3.3	6.8	8.0	10.6	11.0	10.9	11.2
ASEAN	1967	1992	FTA	19.8	24.5	23.0	24.9	25.3	25.0	25.2
PICTA	2001	2003	FTA	0.2	1.0	1.7	2.3	1.8	1.9	2.0
SAARC	1985	2006	FTA	3.6	4.4	4.2	5.7	5.6	5.2	5.3
Europe, Central Asia, and Middle East										
CEFTA	1992	1994	FTA	..	7.8	15.3	15.9	16.6	16.1	16.8
CIS	1991	1994	FTA	..	28.6	20.0	17.6	18.0	16.5	19.8
COZ	2003	2004	FTA	..	23.8	17.1	14.0	14.7	13.0	16.2
EAEC	1997	1997	CU	..	14.8	12.5	8.5	9.6	8.0	11.8
ECO	1985	2003	PS	3.2	7.9	5.6	6.7	7.6	8.5	9.2
GCC	1981	2003[c]	CU	5.8	6.8	4.8	5.0	4.9	5.0	5.4
PAFTA (GAFTA)	1997	1998	FTA	8.9	9.8	7.2	10.0	9.9	9.9	10.6
UMA	1989	1994[c]	NNA	3.3	3.8	2.2	2.0	2.0	2.1	2.3
Latin America and the Caribbean										
Andean Community	1969	1988	CU	5.6	8.6	7.7	8.7	9.0	7.8	7.4
CACM	1961	1961	CU	17.6	21.8	19.1	20.9	20.1	15.8	17.0
CARICOM	1973	1997	EIA	8.2	12.1	14.4	12.2	11.6	11.3	15.7
LAIA (ALADI)	1980	1981	PS	12.2	17.3	13.2	13.2	13.6	14.3	15.1
MERCOSUR	1991	2005	EIA	9.9	18.9	16.4	11.1	11.0	12.2	12.8
OECS	1981	1981[c]	NNA	9.0	12.6	10.0	11.7	11.4	8.2	8.1
Sub-Saharan Africa										
CEMAC	1994	1999	CU	2.0	2.1	1.0	1.2	0.9	0.9	1.1
COMESA	1994	1994	FTA	3.6	6.1	4.6	5.0	4.5	4.2	4.7
EAC	1996	2000	CU	7.4	19.5	22.6	18.9	17.6	19.3	20.4
ECCAS	1983	2004[c]	NNA	1.3	1.5	1.0	0.8	0.6	0.5	0.6
ECOWAS	1975	1993	PS	9.7	9.0	7.6	9.3	9.3	8.4	9.4
Indian Ocean Commission	1984	2005[c]	NNA	4.8	5.9	4.4	4.3	4.6	4.8	5.7
SADC	1992	2000	FTA	17.9	32.8	9.5	9.7	9.3	9.1	10.1
UEMOA	1994	2000	CU	11.3	10.3	13.1	12.9	13.4	13.1	15.2

Pakistan, Tajikistan, Turkey, Turkmenistan, and Uzbekistan; **Eurasian Economic Community (EAEC)**, Belarus, Kazakhstan, Kyrgyz Republic, the Russian Federation, Tajikistan, and Uzbekistan; **European Economic Area (EEA)**, European Union plus Iceland, Liechtenstein, and Norway; **European Free Trade Association (EFTA)**, Iceland, Liechtenstein, Norway, and Switzerland; **European Union (EU; formerly European Economic Community and European Community)**, Austria, Belgium, Bulgaria, Cyprus, Czech Republic, Denmark, Estonia, Finland, France, Germany, Greece, Hungary, Ireland, Italy, Latvia, Lithuania, Luxembourg, Malta, the Netherlands, Poland, Portugal, Romania, Slovak Republic, Slovenia, Spain, Sweden, and the United Kingdom; **Gulf Cooperation Council (GCC)**, Bahrain, Kuwait, Oman, Qatar, Saudi Arabia, and the United Arab Emirates; **Indian Ocean Commission**, Comoros, Madagascar, Mauritius, Réunion, and Seychelles; **Latin American Integration Association (LAIA; formerly Latin American Free Trade Area)**, Argentina, Bolivia, Brazil, Chile, Colombia, Cuba, Ecuador, Mexico, Paraguay, Peru, Uruguay, and Bolivarian Republic of Venezuela; **North American Free Trade Agreement (NAFTA)**, Canada, Mexico, and the United States; **Organization of Eastern Caribbean States (OECS)**, Anguilla, Antigua and Barbuda, British Virgin Islands, Dominica, Grenada, Montserrat, St. Kitts and Nevis, St. Lucia, and St. Vincent and the Grenadines; **Pacific Island Countries Trade Agreement (PICTA)**, Cook Islands, Fiji, Federated States of Micronesia, Nauru, Niue, Papua New Guinea, Samoa, Solomon Islands, Tonga, Tuvalu, and Vanuatu; **Pan-Arab Free Trade Area (PAFTA; also known as Greater Arab Trade Area [GAFTA])**, Bahrain, Egypt, Iraq, Jordan, Kuwait, Lebanon, Libya, Morocco, Oman, Qatar, Saudi Arabia, Sudan, Syrian Arab Republic, Tunisia, the United Arab Emirates, and Yemen; **South Asian Association for Regional Cooperation (SAARC)**, Bangladesh, Bhutan, India, Maldives, Nepal, Pakistan, and Sri Lanka; **South Pacific Regional Trade and Economic Cooperation Agreement (SPARTECA)**, Australia, Cook Islands, Fiji, Kiribati, Marshall Islands, Federated States of Micronesia, Nauru, New Zealand, Niue, Papua New Guinea, Solomon Islands, Tonga, Tuvalu, Vanuatu, and Western Samoa; **Southern African Development Community (SADC)**, Angola, Botswana, the Democratic Republic of Congo, Lesotho, Madagascar, Malawi, Mauritius, Mozambique, Namibia, Seychelles, South Africa, Swaziland, Tanzania, Zambia, and Zimbabwe; **Southern Common Market (MERCOSUR)**, Argentina, Brazil, Paraguay, Uruguay, and Bolivarian Republic of Venezuela; **Trans-Pacific Strategic Economic Partnership (Trans-Pacific SEP)**, Brunei Darussalam, Chile, New Zealand, and Singapore; **West African Economic and Monetary Union (UEMOA)**, Benin, Burkina Faso, Côte d'Ivoire, Guinea-Bissau, Mali, Niger, Senegal, and Togo.

6.7 Regional trade blocs

Merchandise exports by bloc

	Year of creation	Year of entry into force of the most recent agreement	Type of most recent agreement[a]	% of world exports						
				1990	1995	2000	2004	2005	2006	2007
High-income and low- and middle-income economies										
APEC[b]	1989		None	41.7	46.3	48.5	44.4	45.1	45.5	45.0
EEA	1994	1994	EIA	41.1	38.9	38.9	42.0	40.2	39.2	39.6
EFTA	1960	2002	EIA	2.8	2.4	2.2	2.3	2.3	2.3	2.3
European Union	1957	1958	EIA, CU	40.1	38.1	38.0	41.0	39.1	38.2	38.6
NAFTA	1994	1994	FTA, EIA	16.9	16.8	19.0	14.5	14.3	14.0	13.4
SPARTECA	1981	1981	PS	1.5	1.4	1.3	1.2	1.3	1.3	1.3
Trans-Pacific SEP	2006	2006	EIA, FTA	2.3	3.0	2.7	2.8	2.9	3.0	2.9
East Asia and Pacific and South Asia										
APTA	1975	1976	PS	4.8	6.3	7.4	10.3	11.2	12.0	12.8
ASEAN	1967	1992	FTA	4.7	6.4	6.7	6.2	6.3	6.4	6.2
PICTA	2001	2003	FTA	0.1	0.1	0.1	0.1	0.1	0.1	0.1
SAARC	1985	2006	FTA	0.8	0.9	1.0	1.1	1.3	1.3	1.4
Europe, Central Asia, and Middle East										
CEFTA	1992	1994	FTA	..	0.1	0.1	0.1	0.1	0.1	0.2
CIS	1991	1994	FTA	..	2.2	2.2	2.7	3.2	3.4	3.6
COZ	2003	2004	FTA	..	2.0	2.1	2.5	3.0	3.2	3.4
EAEC	1997	1997	CU	..	1.8	1.9	2.2	2.7	2.9	3.1
ECO	1985	2003	PS	1.1	1.2	1.3	1.6	1.8	1.9	1.9
GCC	1981	2003[c]	CU	2.4	2.0	2.6	2.7	3.3	3.5	3.3
PAFTA (GAFTA)	1997	1998	FTA	3.2	2.6	3.5	3.9	4.3	4.7	4.5
UMA	1989	1994[c]	NNA	0.9	0.6	0.8	0.8	0.9	1.0	1.0
Latin America and the Caribbean										
Andean Community	1969	1988	CU	0.4	0.4	0.4	0.4	0.5	0.5	0.5
CACM	1961	1961	CU	0.1	0.1	0.2	0.2	0.2	0.2	0.2
CARICOM	1973	1997	EIA	0.2	0.1	0.1	0.2	0.2	0.2	0.2
LAIA (ALADI)	1980	1981	PS	3.7	4.1	5.3	4.8	5.1	5.3	5.2
MERCOSUR	1991	2005	EIA	1.8	1.8	1.9	1.9	2.1	2.1	2.2
OECS	1981	1981[c]	NNA	0.0	0.0	0.0	0.0	0.0	0.0	0.0
Sub-Saharan Africa										
CEMAC	1994	1999	CU	0.2	0.1	0.1	0.1	0.2	0.2	0.2
COMESA	1994	1994	FTA	0.7	0.4	0.5	0.5	0.6	0.7	0.7
EAC	1996	2000	CU	0.1	0.1	0.0	0.1	0.1	0.1	0.1
ECCAS	1983	2004[c]	NNA	0.3	0.2	0.3	0.3	0.4	0.5	0.5
ECOWAS	1975	1993	PS	0.4	0.4	0.6	0.5	0.6	0.6	0.6
Indian Ocean Commission	1984	2005[c]	NNA	0.0	0.0	0.0	0.0	0.0	0.0	0.0
SADC	1992	2000	FTA	0.3	0.2	0.7	0.7	0.8	0.8	0.9
UEMOA	1994	2000	CU	0.1	0.1	0.1	0.1	0.1	0.1	0.1

a. CU is customs union; EIA is economic integration agreement; FTA is free trade agreement; NNA is not notified agreement, which refers to preferential trade arrangements established among member countries that are not notified to the World Trade Organization (these agreements may be functionally equivalent to any of the other agreements); and PS is partial scope agreement. b. No preferential trade agreement c. Years of the most recent agreement are collected from the official website of the trade bloc.

About the data

Trade blocs are groups of countries that have established preferential arrangements governing trade between members. Although in some cases the preferences—such as lower tariff duties or exemptions from quantitative restrictions—may be no greater than those available to other trading partners, such arrangements are intended to encourage exports by bloc members to one another—sometimes called intratrade.

Most countries are members of a regional trade bloc, and more than a third of the world's trade takes place within such arrangements. While trade blocs vary in structure, they all have the same objective: to reduce trade barriers between member countries. But effective integration requires more than reducing tariffs and quotas. Economic gains from competition and scale may not be achieved unless other barriers that divide markets and impede the free flow of goods, services, and investments are lifted. For example, many regional trade blocs retain contingent protections on intrabloc trade, including antidumping, countervailing duties, and "emergency protection" to address balance of payments problems or protect an industry from import surges. Other barriers include differing product standards, discrimination in public procurement, and cumbersome border formalities.

Membership in a regional trade bloc may reduce the frictional costs of trade, increase the credibility of reform initiatives, and strengthen security among partners. But making it work effectively is challenging. All economic sectors may be affected, and some may expand while others contract, so it is important to weigh the potential costs and benefits of membership.

The table shows the value of merchandise intratrade (service exports are excluded) for important regional trade blocs and the size of intratrade relative to each bloc's exports of goods and the share of the bloc's exports in world exports. Although the Asia Pacific Economic Cooperation (APEC) has no preferential arrangements, it is included because of the volume of trade between its members.

The data on country exports are from the International Monetary Fund's (IMF) Direction of Trade database and should be broadly consistent with those from sources such as the United Nations Statistics Division's Commodity Trade (Comtrade) database. However, trade flows between many developing countries, particularly in Sub-Saharan Africa, are not well recorded, so the value of intratrade for certain groups may be understated. Data on trade between developing and high-income countries are generally complete.

Membership in the trade blocs shown is based on the most recent information available (see *Data sources*). Other types of preferential trade agreements may have entered into force earlier than those shown in the table and may still be effective. Unless otherwise indicated in the footnotes, information on the type of agreement and date of enforcement are based on the World Trade Organization's (WTO) list of regional trade agreements.

Although bloc exports have been calculated back to 1990 on the basis of current membership, several blocs came into existence after that and membership may have changed over time. For this reason, and because systems of preferences also change over time, intratrade in earlier years may not have been affected by the same preferences as in recent years. In addition, some countries belong to more than one trade bloc, so shares of world exports exceed 100 percent. Exports of blocs include all commodity trade, which may include items not specified in trade bloc agreements. Differences from previously published estimates may be due to changes in membership or revisions in underlying data.

Definitions

• **Merchandise exports within bloc** are the sum of merchandise exports by members of a trade bloc to other members of the bloc. They are shown both in U.S. dollars and as a percentage of total merchandise exports by the bloc. • **Merchandise exports by bloc** as a share of world exports are the bloc's total merchandise exports (within the bloc and to the rest of the world) as a share of total merchandise exports by all economies in the world. • **Type of most recent agreement** includes customs union, under which members substantially eliminate all tariff and nontariff barriers among themselves and establish a common external tariff for nonmembers; economic integration agreement, which liberalizes trade in services among members and covers a substantial number of sectors, affects a sufficient volume of trade, includes substantial modes of supply, and is nondiscriminatory (in the sense that similarly situated service suppliers are treated the same); free trade agreement, under which members substantially eliminate all tariff and nontariff barriers but set tariffs on imports from nonmembers; partial scope agreement, which is a preferential trade agreement notified to the WTO that is not a free trade agreement, a customs union, or an economic integration agreement; and not notified agreement, which is a preferential trade arrangement established among member countries that is not notified to the World Trade Organization (the agreement may be functionally equivalent to any of the other agreements).

Data sources

Data on merchandise trade flows are published in the IMF's *Direction of Trade Statistics Yearbook* and *Direction of Trade Statistics Quarterly;* the data in the table were calculated using the IMF's Direction of Trade database. Data on trade bloc membership are from the World Bank Policy Research Report *Trade Blocs* (2000a), UNCTAD's *Trade and Development Report 2007,* WTO's Regional Trade Agreements Information System, and the World Bank's International Trade Unit.

The number of trade agreements has increased rapidly since 1990, especially bilateral agreements   **6.7a**

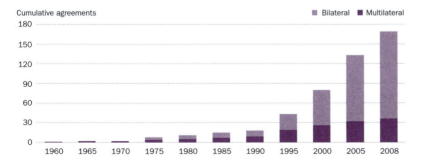

Cumulative agreements

■ Bilateral ■ Multilateral

Note: Data are cumulative number of bilateral and multilateral trade agreements notified to the General Agreement on Tariffs and Trade/World Trade Organization (GATT/WTO) at the time they entered into force. Only agreements that are that are currently in force are included. Agreements on accessions of new members to an existing agreement are not included. Agreements that are in force but have not been notified to GATT/WTO may be excluded. *Source:* World Bank staff calculations based on the World Trade Organization's Regional Trade Agreements Information System.

6.8 Tariff barriers

	Most recent year	Binding coverage	Simple mean bound rate	All products %				Primary products %		Manufactured products %	
				Simple mean tariff	Weighted mean tariff	Share of tariff lines with international peaks	Share of tariff lines with specific rates	Simple mean tariff	Weighted mean tariff	Simple mean tariff	Weighted mean tariff
Afghanistan		..	..	..	..	..	..	..	..	..	..
Albania	2007	100.0	7.0	5.7	5.7	0.0	0.0	7.0	5.2	5.5	6.0
Algeria	2007	..	..	16.2	9.9	40.0	0.0	16.2	9.2	16.2	10.1
Angola	2006	100.0	59.2	7.6	6.5	10.4	0.0	11.5	13.1	6.9	5.0
Antigua and Barbuda	2007	97.9	58.7	11.6	12.6	47.9	0.0	13.7	12.3	11.2	12.7
Argentina	2007	100.0	31.9	10.8	5.7	24.8	0.0	7.8	1.3	11.1	6.4
Armenia	2006	100.0	8.5	3.6	1.8	0.1	0.3	5.5	1.5	3.4	2.0
Australia	2007	97.1	9.9	2.8	1.8	2.6	0.1	0.9	0.3	3.1	2.3
Azerbaijan	2007	..	..	8.6	4.0	47.9	0.5	10.1	3.7	8.4	4.1
Bahamas, The	2006	..	..	28.5	23.9	77.4	0.0	24.4	15.1	29.4	29.7
Bahrain	2007	73.4	34.4	4.2	4.8	0.2	0.0	5.8	5.6	3.9	3.4
Bangladesh	2007	15.9	163.1	14.5	11.0	41.1	0.0	15.2	7.3	14.4	13.0
Barbados	2007	97.9	78.1	15.1	14.8	44.9	0.6	26.4	21.9	13.5	12.3
Belarus	2002	..	..	11.3	8.9	16.4	0.0	11.1	7.1	11.3	10.3
Belize	2007	97.9	58.2	11.6	9.3	43.3	0.0	15.6	6.5	11.1	11.0
Benin	2007	39.0	28.6	13.4	11.8	53.8	0.0	13.4	11.9	13.4	11.7
Bermuda	2007	..	..	18.5	30.2	66.5	0.8	14.0	18.6	19.4	30.9
Bhutan	2007	..	..	18.2	17.8	50.7	0.0	43.7	44.9	15.5	16.0
Bolivia	2007	100.0	40.0	6.2	4.3	0.0	0.0	6.1	4.4	6.2	4.3
Bosnia and Herzegovina	2007	..	..	6.8	4.9	11.4	0.0	3.3	2.0	7.2	6.3
Botswana	2007	96.3	18.9	8.3	8.9	19.0	0.2	4.3	0.9	8.6	9.5
Brazil	2007	100.0	31.4	12.3	6.8	26.4	0.0	7.9	1.2	12.7	9.4
Brunei	2007	95.3	24.3	3.1	6.1	21.6	0.1	0.9	13.2	3.4	4.5
Bulgaria	2006	100.0	24.6	4.1	2.1	13.3	2.0	9.5	4.8	3.5	1.3
Burkina Faso	2007	39.2	41.9	12.1	10.3	44.4	0.0	11.3	7.6	12.2	11.0
Burundi	2007	21.8	68.3	13.5	12.3	27.4	0.0	12.8	13.4	13.7	11.5
Cambodia	2007	..	..	12.5	10.0	49.2	0.0	14.8	10.5	12.1	10.0
Cameroon	2007	13.3	79.9	18.6	12.5	52.6	0.0	21.9	10.8	18.2	14.6
Canada	2007	99.7	5.1	4.2	1.6	7.9	3.6	5.1	3.2	4.0	1.2
Central African Republic	2007	..	..	17.5	13.6	47.4	0.0	19.0	13.8	17.3	13.5
Chad	2007	..	..	17.0	13.6	44.8	0.0	20.8	18.3	16.5	12.7
Chile	2007	100.0	25.1	2.0	1.8	0.0	0.0	2.4	2.2	1.9	1.5
China[†]	2007	100.0	10.0	8.9	5.1	14.9	0.0	9.0	3.0	8.9	6.3
Hong Kong, China	2007	45.6	0.0	0.0	0.0	0.0	0.0	0.0	0.0	0.0	0.0
Colombia	2007	100.0	42.8	10.8	8.8	41.0	0.0	9.7	8.2	10.9	9.0
Congo, Dem. Rep.	2007	..	..	13.0	11.2	43.4	0.0	14.2	10.9	12.8	11.3
Congo, Rep.	2007	16.1	27.3	18.6	14.7	52.6	0.0	22.1	18.6	18.1	14.1
Costa Rica	2007	100.0	42.9	6.1	4.1	0.4	0.0	8.5	5.1	5.8	3.8
Côte d'Ivoire	2007	33.1	11.2	13.4	7.2	50.2	0.0	15.5	4.1	13.0	10.7
Croatia	2007	100.0	6.0	2.5	1.2	4.1	0.0	4.4	1.9	2.3	0.9
Cuba	2007	30.9	21.3	11.3	7.4	34.4	0.0	10.9	5.0	11.3	9.5
Djibouti	2006	100.0	41.0	30.2	29.1	87.9	0.0	23.0	23.1	31.3	31.0
Dominica	2007	94.8	58.7	11.9	7.9	43.3	0.0	19.3	5.7	10.6	9.3
Dominican Republic	2006	100.0	34.9	9.3	8.5	28.6	0.0	12.7	7.3	8.9	9.0
Ecuador	2007	100.0	21.8	10.0	5.9	34.1	0.0	8.7	3.3	10.1	7.1
Egypt, Arab Rep.	2005	99.3	36.8	19.1	13.3	23.0	0.0	86.2	17.7	12.0	11.7
El Salvador	2007	100.0	36.6	5.1	4.6	1.9	0.0	6.9	3.5	4.9	5.3
Equatorial Guinea	2007	..	..	18.3	15.6	52.3	0.0	21.7	21.5	17.8	14.3
Ethiopia	2006	..	..	18.6	12.0	57.4	0.0	18.1	7.8	18.6	13.9
European Union	2007	100.0	4.2	2.4	1.8	5.5	6.4	6.1	1.8	1.6	1.8
Fiji		51.3	40.1	..	..	..	..	..	..	..	..
Gabon	2007	100.0	21.4	18.0	14.5	52.0	0.0	20.0	14.2	17.7	14.6
Gambia, The	2007	13.7	101.8	18.7	15.1	90.7	0.0	17.1	13.3	19.1	17.0
Georgia	2007	100.0	7.2	0.6	0.5	0.0	0.0	4.4	1.3	0.1	0.1
Ghana	2007	14.3	92.5	13.0	9.9	40.8	0.0	16.8	14.4	12.5	8.8
Grenada	2007	100.0	56.8	10.5	8.6	43.0	0.0	13.7	8.4	10.0	8.7
Guatemala	2007	100.0	42.2	5.3	4.6	1.1	0.0	6.7	4.2	5.2	4.9
[†]Data for Taiwan, China	2007	100.0	5.9	5.7	2.0	8.9	0.6	11.1	2.4	4.9	1.9

	Most recent year	Binding coverage	Simple mean bound rate	All products % Simple mean tariff	All products % Weighted mean tariff	Share of tariff lines with international peaks	Share of tariff lines with specific rates	Primary products % Simple mean tariff	Primary products % Weighted mean tariff	Manufactured products % Simple mean tariff	Manufactured products % Weighted mean tariff
Guinea	2005	38.6	20.3	14.2	12.7	58.6	0.0	16.4	14.3	13.9	11.2
Guinea-Bissau	2007	..	..	14.0	14.5	55.3	0.0	16.6	17.6	13.5	12.4
Guyana	2006	100.0	56.7	11.4	6.2	34.5	0.0	17.9	4.1	10.6	7.9
Haiti	2007	100.0	32.4	2.9	3.0	4.7	0.0	5.6	4.4	2.4	2.0
Honduras	2007	..	..	5.4	4.5	0.3	0.0	7.1	5.4	5.2	4.0
Hungary	2002	96.2	9.7	8.9	7.9	10.9	0.0	18.1	6.7	7.8	8.1
Iceland	2007	95.0	13.5	4.1	2.1	10.2	3.4	16.4	5.4	2.4	1.0
India	2005[a]	73.8	49.6	17.0	13.4	15.4	3.9	25.2	14.3	15.9	12.3
Indonesia	2007	96.6	37.1	5.9	3.9	12.7	0.0	6.6	2.5	5.8	4.4
Iran, Islamic Rep.	2007	..	..	21.3	17.6	54.8	0.0	16.9	15.3	21.7	18.5
Israel	2007	75.0	21.5	2.3	1.1	1.0	0.7	4.8	1.3	2.1	1.1
Jamaica	2006	100.0	49.6	9.2	8.9	35.8	0.0	16.0	9.5	8.3	8.5
Japan	2007	99.7	2.9	4.2	3.1	10.1	3.6	11.4	3.8	2.9	2.2
Jordan	2007	100.0	16.3	10.7	5.9	32.7	0.0	14.4	3.8	10.1	7.3
Kazakhstan	2004	..	..	2.4	1.9	0.0	0.0	3.5	3.4	2.3	1.5
Kenya	2007	14.8	95.4	12.3	7.0	37.4	0.0	16.1	7.0	11.9	7.0
Korea, Rep.	2007	94.6	15.8	8.5	8.0	5.1	0.1	20.8	11.5	6.6	4.8
Kuwait	2007	99.9	100.0	4.3	3.9	0.0	0.0	3.4	2.9	4.4	4.0
Kyrgyz Republic	2007	99.9	7.4	2.9	1.1	1.5	1.7	4.7	0.7	2.6	1.4
Lao PDR	2007	..	..	5.8	8.3	15.1	0.0	9.9	8.3	5.3	8.3
Latvia	2001	100.0	12.8	3.3	2.6	3.0	0.0	8.1	5.4	2.6	1.6
Lebanon	2007	..	..	5.6	4.8	11.6	0.0	8.2	5.0	5.2	5.1
Lesotho	2007	..	..	9.0	13.9	21.3	0.5	7.8	5.0	9.0	14.3
Libya	2006	..	..	0.0	0.0	0.0	0.0	0.0	0.0	0.0	0.0
Lithuania	2003	100.0	9.2	1.3	0.6	3.1	0.0	3.3	1.3	1.0	0.4
Macao	2007	28.7	0.0	0.0	0.0	0.0	0.0	0.0	0.0	0.0	0.0
Macedonia, FYR	2007	100.0	6.9	8.6	5.7	31.7	0.0	9.3	5.4	8.6	5.9
Madagascar	2007	30.0	27.3	12.1	8.4	40.4	0.0	14.1	4.4	11.8	10.4
Malawi	2006	31.6	75.4	12.9	8.1	40.4	0.0	12.8	6.1	12.9	8.9
Malaysia	2007	83.7	14.5	5.9	3.1	24.8	0.0	2.8	2.3	6.5	3.4
Maldives	2006	97.1	36.9	21.4	21.1	72.3	0.0	18.1	19.5	22.2	22.0
Mali	2007	40.2	28.5	12.5	8.7	47.2	0.0	11.6	9.8	12.6	8.4
Mauritania	2007	39.3	19.6	12.6	10.1	49.0	0.0	11.2	9.2	12.9	11.0
Mauritius	2007	17.9	94.0	4.3	2.5	9.2	0.0	6.3	2.8	4.0	2.4
Mexico	2006	100.0	35.0	8.0	2.4	10.9	0.3	7.3	1.8	8.1	2.5
Moldova	2006	..	..	4.4	1.7	16.0	1.3	7.2	1.4	4.0	1.9
Mongolia	2007	100.0	17.5	4.9	5.1	0.4	0.0	5.2	5.4	4.9	4.9
Montserrat	1999	..	..	18.2	13.3	41.2	0.0	22.4	15.6	16.4	12.2
Morocco	2007	100.0	41.3	13.3	10.0	45.1	0.0	20.0	11.6	12.6	9.1
Mozambique	2007	..	..	11.0	7.7	36.7	0.0	13.9	8.0	10.5	7.5
Myanmar	2007	17.4	83.6	4.1	3.9	8.1	0.0	5.8	4.5	3.9	3.7
Namibia	2007	96.3	19.2	6.6	1.5	18.0	0.5	4.2	0.7	7.0	1.9
Nepal	2007	..	..	12.6	13.7	42.1	0.0	12.4	9.7	12.7	15.8
New Zealand	2007	99.9	10.0	3.8	2.7	7.5	0.0	2.1	0.4	4.0	3.6
Nicaragua	2007	100.0	41.7	5.4	3.6	0.4	0.0	7.8	3.9	5.1	3.4
Niger	2007	96.7	44.7	12.9	10.1	51.0	0.0	13.2	10.6	12.9	9.6
Nigeria	2006	19.3	118.4	10.6	9.4	33.9	0.0	12.8	13.1	10.3	8.2
Norway	2007	100.0	3.0	4.1	2.6	5.0	5.4	29.8	10.2	0.5	0.2
Oman	2007	100.0	13.8	3.8	3.4	0.2	0.0	4.5	3.0	3.7	3.4
Pakistan	2007	98.7	59.9	14.9	11.4	52.7	0.0	14.2	8.7	15.0	13.3
Panama	2007	99.9	23.4	7.3	7.0	33.6	0.0	11.3	7.8	6.9	6.6
Papua New Guinea	2007	100.0	31.7	5.2	1.6	25.6	0.8	16.2	2.4	3.7	1.1
Paraguay	2007	100.0	33.5	8.0	3.3	17.3	0.0	5.7	0.8	8.2	4.0
Peru	2007	100.0	30.1	8.5	5.2	10.5	0.0	9.3	2.7	8.5	6.4
Philippines	2007	67.0	25.7	5.0	3.6	15.8	0.0	6.0	5.2	4.8	2.7
Poland	2003	96.3	11.9	4.3	2.3	8.8	0.1	18.2	6.7	2.5	1.2
Qatar	2007	100.0	15.9	3.9	4.0	0.1	0.0	3.5	3.8	3.9	4.0

	Most recent year	All products (%)						Primary products (%)		Manufactured products (%)	
		Binding coverage	Simple mean bound rate	Simple mean tariff	Weighted mean tariff	Share of tariff lines with international peaks	Share of tariff lines with specific rates	Simple mean tariff	Weighted mean tariff	Simple mean tariff	Weighted mean tariff
Romania	2005	..	..	6.5	3.1	20.6	0.0	13.4	7.2	5.6	1.8
Russian Federation	2007	..	..	9.9	7.2	34.4	15.2	8.8	9.1	10.1	6.8
Rwanda	2008	100.0	89.5	19.3	11.6	55.2	0.0	17.0	8.8	19.5	12.6
Saudi Arabia	2007	..	..	4.0	3.9	0.1	0.0	3.4	2.8	4.1	4.2
Serbia[b]	2005	..	..	8.1	6.0	17.8	0.0	11.0	4.5	7.8	6.8
Senegal	2007	100.0	30.0	13.5	9.3	51.4	0.0	14.5	7.8	13.3	10.6
Seychelles	2007	..	..	6.5	28.3	12.8	0.0	14.1	50.5	4.8	6.4
Sierra Leone	2004	100.0	47.4	..	..	..	..	..	..	..	..
Singapore	2007	69.7	7.0	0.0	0.0	0.1	0.1	0.2	0.0	0.0	0.0
Slovak Republic	2002	100.0	5.0	5.0	4.6	4.3	0.0	5.6	3.7	4.9	4.9
Solomon Islands	2007	100.0	78.7	10.3	13.3	2.5	1.2	16.2	19.9	9.4	7.8
South Africa	2007	96.3	19.2	8.1	5.0	19.1	0.6	5.9	1.9	8.4	6.5
Sri Lanka	2006[a]	38.1	29.8	11.3	7.1	23.5	0.8	17.8	9.0	10.6	6.4
St. Kitts and Nevis	2007	97.9	75.9	12.1	12.1	43.9	0.2	13.0	11.1	11.9	12.5
St. Lucia	2007	99.6	61.9	9.6	9.0	39.9	0.0	12.8	4.9	9.1	12.3
St. Vincent & Grenadines	2007	..	..	11.3	8.4	44.4	0.2	15.1	7.8	10.6	8.6
Sudan	2006	..	..	17.1	15.3	38.1	0.0	23.0	19.7	16.6	14.7
Suriname	2007	..	..	11.5	11.8	39.4	0.0	17.8	16.0	10.6	10.9
Swaziland	2007	96.3	19.2	9.9	7.9	24.0	0.8	10.3	3.1	9.8	8.7
Switzerland	2007	99.8	0.0	3.9	1.9	10.6	30.9	20.0	9.6	1.1	0.2
Syrian Arab Republic	2002	..	..	14.7	15.5	23.3	0.0	14.4	11.7	14.7	17.1
Tajikistan	2006	..	..	4.9	3.8	0.1	0.7	5.4	2.1	4.8	5.2
Tanzania	2007	13.4	120.0	12.5	7.2	38.0	0.0	16.8	7.5	12.1	7.0
Thailand	2006	75.0	25.7	10.8	4.6	22.9	0.9	13.6	2.1	10.4	5.8
Togo	2007	14.0	80.0	13.9	10.4	55.1	0.0	14.2	9.6	13.8	10.8
Trinidad and Tobago	2007	100.0	55.8	8.8	10.6	43.6	0.4	17.0	3.2	7.6	18.4
Tunisia	2006	57.9	57.9	23.0	18.3	55.5	0.0	32.4	13.9	22.2	20.0
Turkey	2007	50.4	28.6	2.5	2.0	4.7	0.3	14.0	3.8	1.4	1.3
Turkmenistan	2002	..	..	5.4	2.9	14.8	2.8	14.9	12.6	3.8	1.1
Uganda	2007	15.7	73.4	12.1	8.4	37.4	0.0	15.9	9.6	11.6	7.8
Ukraine	2006	..	..	4.9	3.1	4.8	3.7	5.2	0.9	4.8	4.5
United Arab Emirates	2007	100.0	14.7	4.2	3.8	0.2	0.0	4.3	2.9	4.2	4.4
United States	2007	100.0	3.6	2.9	1.6	5.5	4.8	3.0	1.3	2.9	1.7
Uruguay	2007	100.0	31.6	9.5	3.6	25.9	0.0	5.8	1.3	9.8	4.9
Uzbekistan	2007	..	..	10.8	6.6	18.8	0.0	10.2	2.6	10.9	7.4
Vanuatu	2007	..	..	16.9	11.0	64.8	0.0	19.4	18.7	16.4	9.9
Venezuela	2007	99.9	36.5	12.3	10.7	45.6	0.0	11.1	8.5	12.4	11.0
Vietnam	2007	..	..	11.7	10.6	32.2	0.0	14.5	10.2	11.3	11.0
Yemen	2006	..	..	6.7	6.9	1.8	0.0	9.6	8.6	6.3	5.6
Zambia	2005	16.8	106.5	14.6	9.4	34.5	0.0	15.0	9.3	14.6	9.4
Zimbabwe	2007[a]	22.4	89.8	16.6	..	34.3	5.6	17.4	..	16.4	..
World		**79.6**	**32.0**	**7.0**	**3.0**	**15.7**	**0.5**	**8.9**	**2.5**	**6.7**	**3.2**
Low income		**45.9**	**52.4**	**3.9**	**1.9**	**5.6**	**0.0**	**13.8**	**9.2**	**11.6**	**10.3**
Middle income		**89.0**	**32.1**	**4.6**	**1.7**	**7.1**	**0.1**	**10.8**	**4.0**	**7.5**	**5.4**
Lower middle income		88.7	31.0	2.9	1.8	3.4	0.0	12.9	4.0	8.9	6.5
Upper middle income		89.0	33.9	8.2	4.9	21.5	0.1	8.7	3.9	6.2	4.1
Low & middle income		**75.3**	**36.2**	**5.3**	**4.2**	**13.0**	**2.4**	**11.2**	**4.3**	**8.2**	**5.6**
East Asia & Pacific		79.1	32.5	7.9	4.6	21.7	0.0	9.2	3.2	8.0	5.7
Europe & Central Asia		93.8	11.0	14.0	11.0	40.2	0.0	8.1	4.8	4.9	4.0
Latin America & Carib.		97.0	41.6	13.7	8.0	35.8	0.0	9.1	2.9	7.8	5.1
Middle East & N. Africa		91.4	36.9	9.3	5.7	22.9	0.4	24.1	10.7	12.8	11.2
South Asia		64.7	52.3	8.6	5.2	21.8	0.7	16.6	8.2	13.3	7.8
Sub-Saharan Africa		48.0	43.2	11.8	9.9	34.3	0.1	13.6	7.0	11.7	8.3
High income		**92.1**	**21.7**	**7.9**	**5.0**	**20.0**	**0.9**	**5.1**	**1.7**	**3.7**	**1.9**
OECD		98.7	7.2	11.9	7.9	36.4	0.0	3.7	1.7	2.8	1.9
Non-OECD		86.3	33.4	6.5	4.0	17.0	1.3	5.5	1.6	4.4	1.8

Note: Tariff rates include ad valorem equivalents of specific rates whenever available.
a. Rates are most favored nation rates. b. Includes Montenegro.

Poor people in developing countries work primarily in agriculture and labor-intensive manufactures, sectors that confront the greatest trade barriers. Removing barriers to merchandise trade could increase growth in these countries—even more if trade in services (retailing, business, financial, and telecommunications services) were also liberalized.

In general, tariffs in high-income countries on imports from developing countries, though low, are twice those collected from other high-income countries. But protection is also an issue for developing countries, which maintain high tariffs on agricultural commodities, labor-intensive manufactures, and other products and services. In some developing regions new trade policies could make the difference between achieving important Millennium Development Goals—reducing poverty, lowering maternal and child mortality rates, improving educational attainment—and falling far short.

Countries use a combination of tariff and nontariff measures to regulate imports. The most common form of tariff is an ad valorem duty, based on the value of the import, but tariffs may also be levied on a specific, or per unit, basis or may combine ad valorem and specific rates. Tariffs may be used to raise fiscal revenues or to protect domestic industries from foreign competition—or both. Nontariff barriers, which limit the quantity of imports of a particular good, include quotas, prohibitions, licensing schemes, export restraint arrangements, and health and quarantine measures. Because of the difficulty of combining nontariff barriers into an aggregate indicator, they are not included in the table.

Unless specified as most favored nation rates, the tariff rates used in calculating the indicators in the table are effectively applied rates. Effectively applied rates are those in effect for partners in preferential trade arrangements such as the North American Free Trade Agreement. The difference between most favored nation and applied rates can be substantial. As more countries report their free trade agreements, suspensions of tariffs, or other special preferences, *World Development Indicators* will include their effectively applied rates. All estimates are calculated using the most recent information, which is not necessarily revised every year. As a result, data for the same year may differ from data in last year's edition.

Three measures of average tariffs are shown: simple bound rates and the simple and the weighted tariffs. Bound rates are based on all products in a country's tariff schedule, while the most favored nation or applied rates are calculated using all traded items. Weighted mean tariffs are weighted by the value of the country's trade with each trading partner. Simple averages are often a better indicator of tariff protection than weighted averages, which are biased downward because higher tariffs discourage trade and reduce the weights applied to these tariffs. Bound rates result from trade negotiations incorporated into a country's schedule of concessions and are thus enforceable.

Some countries set fairly uniform tariff rates across all imports. Others are selective, setting high tariffs to protect favored domestic industries. The share of tariff lines with international peaks provides an indication of how selectively tariffs are applied. The effective rate of protection—the degree to which the value added in an industry is protected—may exceed the nominal rate if the tariff system systematically differentiates among imports of raw materials, intermediate products, and finished goods.

The share of tariff lines with specific rates shows the extent to which countries use tariffs based on physical quantities or other, non–ad valorem measures. Some countries such as Switzerland apply mainly specific duties. To the extent possible, these specific rates have been converted to their ad valorem equivalent rates and have been included in the calculation of simple and weighted tariffs.

Data are classified using the Harmonized System of trade at the six- or eight-digit level. Tariff line data were matched to Standard International Trade Classification (SITC) revision 3 codes to define commodity groups and import weights. Import weights were calculated using the United Nations Statistics Division's Commodity Trade (Comtrade) database. Data are shown only for the last year for which complete data are available.

• **Binding coverage** is the percentage of product lines with an agreed bound rate. • **Simple mean bound rate** is the unweighted average of all the lines in the tariff schedule in which bound rates have been set. • **Simple mean tariff** is the unweighted average of effectively applied rates or most favored nation rates for all products subject to tariffs calculated for all traded goods. • **Weighted mean tariff** is the average of effectively applied rates or most favored nation rates weighted by the product import shares corresponding to each partner country. • **Share of tariff lines with international peaks** is the share of lines in the tariff schedule with tariff rates that exceed 15 percent. • **Share of tariff lines with specific rates** is the share of lines in the tariff schedule that are set on a per unit basis or that combine ad valorem and per unit rates. • **Primary products** are commodities classified in SITC revision 3 sections 0–4 plus division 68 (nonferrous metals). • **Manufactured products** are commodities classified in SITC revision 3 sections 5–8 excluding division 68.

All indicators in the table were calculated by World Bank staff using the World Integrated Trade Solution system. Data on tariffs were provided by the United Nations Conference on Trade and Development and the World Trade Organization. Data on global imports are from the United Nations Statistics Division's Comtrade database.

6.9 External debt

	Total external debt ($ millions)		Long-term debt						Short-term debt ($ millions)		Use of IMF credit ($ millions)	
					$ millions Public and publicly guaranteed							
			Total		IBRD loans and IDA credits		Private nonguaranteed					
	1995	2007	1995	2007	1995	2007	1995	2007	1995	2007	1995	2007
Afghanistan	..	2,041	..	1,961	..	411	..	0	..	21	..	59
Albania	456	2,697	330	1,787	109	809	0	72	62	748	65	90
Algeria	33,042	5,541	31,303	3,756	2,049	113	0	1,068	261	717	1,478	0
Angola	11,500	12,730	9,543	10,474	81	365	0	0	1,958	2,256	0	0
Argentina	98,465	127,758	54,913	66,110	4,913	5,674	16,066	23,581	21,355	38,067	6,131	0
Armenia	371	2,888	298	1,272	96	970	0	999	2	459	70	158
Australia	..	..	..	..	..	..	..	..	..	..	..	..
Austria	..	..	..	..	..	..	..	..	..	..	..	..
Azerbaijan	321	3,068	206	1,748	30	682	0	143	14	1,074	101	103
Bangladesh	15,927	21,998	15,106	20,151	5,692	10,077	0	0	199	1,347	622	501
Belarus	1,694	9,470	1,301	2,338	116	42	0	1,125	110	6,007	283	0
Belgium	..	..	..	..	..	.	..	..	..	..	..	..
Benin	1,614	857	1,483	852	498	176	0	0	47	1	84	4
Bolivia	5,272	4,947	4,459	2,150	865	259	239	2,621	307	176	268	0
Bosnia and Herzegovina	..	6,378	..	3,014	472	1,521	..	1,774	..	1,587	48	2
Botswana	717	396	707	380	108	6	0	0	10	16	0	0
Brazil	160,469	237,472	98,260	79,957	6,038	9,676	30,830	118,267	31,238	39,248	142	0
Bulgaria	10,379	32,968	8,808	5,243	444	1,604	342	13,689	512	14,036	717	0
Burkina Faso	1,271	1,472	1,140	1,268	608	468	0	0	56	166	75	37
Burundi	1,162	1,456	1,099	1,344	591	830	0	0	15	14	48	98
Cambodia	2,284	3,755	2,110	3,537	65	535	0	0	102	218	72	0
Cameroon	10,807	3,091	9,477	2,204	1,067	239	288	636	991	234	51	17
Canada	..	..	..	..	..	..	..	..	..	..	..	..
Central African Republic	942	972	850	836	414	403	0	0	57	87	35	49
Chad	843	1,793	777	1,712	379	994	0	0	17	25	49	56
Chile	22,038	58,649	7,178	9,378	1,383	357	11,429	35,969	3,431	13,302	0	0
China	118,090	373,635	94,674	87,653	14,248	21,912	1,090	82,284	22,325	203,698	0	0
Hong Kong, China												
Colombia	25,044	44,976	13,946	27,689	2,559	4,758	5,553	11,938	5,545	5,349	0	0
Congo, Dem. Rep.	13,239	12,287	9,636	10,853	1,413	2,402	0	0	3,118	625	485	808
Congo, Rep.	5,896	5,156	4,874	4,807	279	303	0	0	1,004	312	19	37
Costa Rica	3,802	7,846	3,133	3,750	303	46	214	1,134	430	2,962	24	0
Côte d'Ivoire	18,899	13,938	11,902	11,651	2,386	2,388	2,660	591	3,910	1,523	427	173
Croatia	3,830	48,584	1,860	14,212	117	1,101	1,257	29,273	492	5,099	221	0
Cuba	..	..	..	..	..	..	..	..	..	..	..	..
Czech Republic	..	..	..	..	..	..	..	..	..	..	..	..
Denmark	..	..	..	..	..	..	..	..	..	..	..	..
Dominican Republic	4,447	10,312	3,653	6,546	300	482	19	845	616	2,374	160	548
Ecuador	13,903	17,525	11,977	10,447	1,108	697	440	5,184	1,312	1,894	173	0
Egypt, Arab Rep.	33,475	30,444	30,687	26,940	2,356	2,671	313	2,053	2,372	1,451	103	0
El Salvador	2,509	8,790	1,979	5,444	327	411	5	2,376	525	970	0	0
Eritrea	37	875	37	856	24	457	0	0	0	19	0	0
Estonia	..	..	..	..	..	..	..	..	..	..	..	..
Ethiopia	10,308	2,634	9,774	2,544	1,470	711	0	0	460	90	73	0
Finland	..	..	..	..	..	..	..	..	..	..	..	..
France	..	..	..	..	..	..	..	..	..	..	..	..
Gabon	4,360	5,746	3,976	5,177	110	12	0	0	287	545	97	25
Gambia, The	426	732	385	704	162	219	0	0	15	21	26	6
Georgia	1,240	2,257	1,039	1,543	84	885	0	241	85	222	116	252
Germany	..	..	..	..	..	..	..	..	..	..	..	..
Ghana	5,495	4,486	4,200	3,047	2,434	1,104	27	0	620	1,272	648	167
Greece	..	..	..	..	..	..	..	..	..	..	..	..
Guatemala	3,282	6,271	2,328	4,214	158	740	142	78	812	1,979	0	0
Guinea	3,242	3,261	2,987	3,048	847	1,305	0	0	161	148	94	65
Guinea-Bissau	898	744	798	730	210	315	0	0	95	8	6	5
Haiti	821	1,598	766	1,500	389	518	0	0	27	42	29	56

External debt | 6.9

	Total external debt		Long-term debt						Short-term debt		Use of IMF credit	
			$ millions Public and publicly guaranteed									
			Total		IBRD loans and IDA credits		Private nonguaranteed					
	$ millions								$ millions		$ millions	
	1995	2007	1995	2007	1995	2007	1995	2007	1995	2007	1995	2007
Honduras	4,797	3,232	4,193	1,942	828	401	123	624	382	634	99	32
Hungary	..	..	..	..	..	..	..	..	..	..	..	..
India	94,464	220,956	80,422	74,419	27,348	33,432	6,618	102,876	5,049	43,662	2,374	0
Indonesia	124,398	140,783	65,309	68,708	13,259	8,371	33,123	37,132	25,966	34,943	0	0
Iran, Islamic Rep.	21,879	20,058	15,116	11,146	316	699	314	91	6,449	8,821	0	0
Iraq	..	..	..	..	..	..	..	..	..	..	..	..
Ireland	..	..	..	..	..	..	..	..	..	..	..	..
Israel	..	..	..	..	..	..	..	..	..	..	..	..
Italy	..	..	..	..	..	..	..	..	..	..	..	..
Jamaica	4,577	10,063	3,716	6,372	595	360	128	2,189	492	1,502	240	0
Japan	..	..	..	..	..	..	..	..	..	..	..	..
Jordan	7,661	8,397	6,624	7,318	806	908	0	0	785	991	251	88
Kazakhstan	3,750	96,133	2,834	1,698	295	427	103	82,690	381	11,745	432	0
Kenya	7,309	7,327	5,857	6,122	2,412	2,968	445	0	634	936	374	269
Korea, Dem. Rep.	..	..	..	..	..	..	..	..	..	..	..	..
Korea, Rep.	..	..	..	..	..	..	..	..	..	..	..	..
Kuwait	..	..	..	..	..	..	..	..	..	..	..	..
Kyrgyz Republic	609	2,401	472	1,895	141	651	0	280	13	76	124	150
Lao PDR	2,165	3,337	2,091	2,446	285	686	0	860	10	5	64	26
Latvia	463	39,342	271	1,809	55	85	0	20,858	31	16,676	160	0
Lebanon	2,966	24,634	1,550	19,789	113	437	50	530	1,365	4,235	0	80
Lesotho	684	680	642	645	207	297	0	0	4	0	38	35
Liberia	2,154	2,475	1,161	910	269	77	0	0	657	1,214	336	352
Libya	..	..	..	..	..	..	..	..	..	..	..	..
Lithuania	..	..	..	..	..	..	..	..	..	..	..	..
Macedonia, FYR	1,277	3,760	788	1,520	181	587	289	1,044	143	1,196	57	0
Madagascar	4,302	1,661	3,687	1,425	1,121	865	0	0	542	194	73	43
Malawi	2,238	870	2,078	807	1,306	178	0	0	44	32	116	31
Malaysia	34,343	53,717	16,023	18,441	1,059	135	11,046	20,026	7,274	15,250	0	0
Mali	2,958	2,018	2,739	1,989	863	452	0	0	72	17	147	13
Mauritania	2,396	1,704	2,127	1,437	347	203	0	0	169	254	100	13
Mauritius	1,757	4,253	1,148	572	157	90	267	62	342	3,618	0	0
Mexico	165,379	178,108	93,902	105,379	13,823	4,540	18,348	63,723	37,300	9,006	15,828	0
Moldova	695	3,203	450	779	152	432	9	1,169	6	1,095	230	160
Mongolia	520	1,596	472	1,566	59	331	0	5	0	0	47	26
Morocco	23,771	20,293	23,190	15,670	3,999	2,595	331	2,673	198	1,949	52	0
Mozambique	7,458	3,123	5,209	2,533	890	902	1,769	0	279	575	202	15
Myanmar	5,771	7,372	5,378	5,516	777	793	0	0	393	1,856	0	0
Namibia	..	..	..	..	..	..	..	..	..	..	..	..
Nepal	2,410	3,645	2,339	3,485	1,023	1,524	0	0	23	81	48	79
Netherlands	..	..	..	..	..	..	..	..	..	..	..	..
New Zealand	..	..	..	..	..	..	..	..	..	..	..	..
Nicaragua	10,390	3,399	8,566	2,144	341	321	0	361	1,785	809	39	85
Niger	1,576	972	1,319	863	598	235	133	20	72	49	52	40
Nigeria	34,092	9,008	28,140	3,815	3,489	2,309	301	175	5,651	5,018	0	0
Norway	..	..	..	..	..	..	..	..	..	..	..	..
Oman	..	..	..	..	..	..	..	..	..	..	..	..
Pakistan	30,229	40,685	23,788	35,917	6,403	11,161	1,593	1,153	3,235	2,233	1,613	1,381
Panama	6,099	9,862	3,782	8,267	175	216	0	1,061	2,207	529	111	5
Papua New Guinea	2,506	2,254	1,668	1,156	407	256	711	998	78	100	50	0
Paraguay	2,574	3,561	1,453	2,195	189	244	338	572	784	794	0	0
Peru	30,833	32,154	18,931	19,669	1,729	2,649	1,288	6,679	9,659	5,806	955	0
Philippines	39,379	65,845	28,525	37,895	5,185	2,921	4,847	20,867	5,279	7,084	728	0
Poland	44,080	195,374	40,890	43,598	2,067	1,870	1,012	91,412	2,178	60,365	0	0
Portugal	..	..	..	..	..	..	..	..	..	..	..	..
Puerto Rico	..	..	..	..	..	..	..	..	..	..	..	..

	Total external debt		Long-term debt						Short-term debt		Use of IMF credit	
					$ millions Public and publicly guaranteed							
			Total		IBRD loans and IDA credits		Private nonguaranteed					
	$ millions								$ millions		$ millions	
	1995	2007	1995	2007	1995	2007	1995	2007	1995	2007	1995	2007
Romania	6,832	85,380	3,957	15,238	844	2,604	534	39,636	1,303	30,505	1,038	0
Russian Federation	121,401	370,172	101,582	70,396	1,524	4,292	0	220,673	10,201	79,103	9,617	0
Rwanda	1,029	495	971	456	512	204	0	0	32	31	26	8
Saudi Arabia	..	..	..	..	..	..	..	..	..	..	..	..
Senegal	3,916	2,579	3,266	2,029	1,160	663	44	200	260	323	347	27
Serbia	10,785[a]	26,280	6,788[a]	8,224	1,252[a]	2,951	1,773[a]	15,404	2,139[a]	2,652	84[a]	0
Sierra Leone	1,220	348	1,028	308	234	84	0	0	27	3	165	37
Singapore	..	..	..	..	..	..	..	..	..	..	..	..
Slovak Republic	..	..	..	..	..	..	..	..	..	..	..	..
Slovenia	..	..	..	..	..	..	..	..	..	..	..	..
Somalia	2,678	2,944	1,961	1,979	432	448	0	0	551	788	166	177
South Africa	25,358	43,380	9,837	13,868	0	27	4,935	12,954	9,673	16,558	913	0
Spain	..	..	..	..	..	..	..	..	..	..	..	..
Sri Lanka	8,395	14,037	7,175	11,879	1,512	2,357	90	259	535	1,649	595	251
Sudan	17,603	19,224	9,779	12,337	1,279	1,307	496	0	6,368	6,405	960	482
Swaziland	249	393	238	357	25	23	0	0	11	36	0	0
Sweden	..	..	..	..	..	..	..	..	..	..	..	..
Switzerland	..	..	..	..	..	..	..	..	..	..	..	..
Syrian Arab Republic	..	..	..	..	471	19	..	..	..	..	..	..
Tajikistan	634	1,228	590	1,065	0	360	0	40	43	76	0	46
Tanzania	7,421	5,024	6,217	3,684	2,269	1,585	44	4	963	1,319	197	18
Thailand	100,039	63,067	16,826	9,841	1,906	129	39,117	31,585	44,095	21,640	0	0
Timor-Leste	..	..	..	..	..	..	..	..	..	..	..	..
Togo	1,476	1,967	1,286	1,655	541	723	0	0	85	310	105	2
Trinidad and Tobago	..	..	..	..	..	..	..	..	..	..	..	..
Tunisia	10,818	20,231	9,215	16,579	1,766	1,595	0	0	1,310	3,652	293	0
Turkey	73,781	251,477	50,317	75,171	5,069	7,601	7,079	127,344	15,701	41,803	685	7,158
Turkmenistan	402	739	385	648	1	15	0	2	17	89	0	0
Uganda	3,609	1,611	3,089	1,575	1,792	840	0	0	103	26	417	9
Ukraine	8,429	73,600	6,581	10,568	491	2,309	84	39,687	223	22,914	1,542	431
United Arab Emirates	..	..	..	..	..	..	..	..	..	..	..	..
United Kingdom	..	..	..	..	..	..	..	..	..	..	..	..
United States	..	..	..	..	..	..	..	..	..	..	..	..
Uruguay	5,318	12,346	3,833	9,616	513	666	127	357	1,336	2,373	21	0
Uzbekistan	1,799	3,871	1,415	3,086	157	359	15	594	212	191	157	0
Venezuela, RB	35,538	43,148	28,223	27,494	1,639	0	2,013	3,954	3,063	11,700	2,239	0
Vietnam	25,428	24,207	21,778	19,372	231	4,549	0	0	3,272	4,672	377	164
West Bank and Gaza	..	..	..	..	..	..	..	..	..	..	..	..
Yemen, Rep.	6,217	5,930	5,528	5,343	827	2,058	0	0	689	417	0	169
Zambia	6,958	2,783	5,291	1,136	1,434	323	13	990	415	569	1,239	87
Zimbabwe	4,989	5,290	3,462	3,735	896	977	381	16	685	1,421	461	118
World	.. s	.. s	.. s	.. s	.. s	.. s	.. s	.. s	.. s	.. s	.. s	.. s
Low income	253,626	222,664	207,566	182,906	48,542	59,927	8,185	5,945	28,143	28,452	9,732	5,361
Middle income	1,632,033	3,242,545	1,078,726	1,129,584	131,030	145,775	202,778	1,283,874	300,461	818,908	50,068	10,179
Lower middle income	782,620	1,264,349	528,904	512,685	88,208	100,440	95,156	357,936	147,477	390,837	11,084	2,891
Upper middle income	849,412	1,978,196	549,822	616,899	42,822	45,335	107,622	925,938	152,984	428,071	38,984	7,288
Low & middle income	1,885,659	3,465,210	1,286,291	1,312,490	179,572	205,702	210,963	1,289,819	328,604	847,360	59,800	15,540
East Asia & Pacific	455,608	741,426	255,393	256,942	37,604	40,778	90,050	193,785	108,828	290,485	1,337	215
Europe & Central Asia	293,781	1,262,445	231,636	268,016	13,699	32,471	12,497	688,158	33,902	297,721	15,747	8,550
Latin America & Carib.	608,461	825,567	371,667	403,303	38,485	33,226	87,303	281,527	122,859	139,932	26,632	804
Middle East & N. Africa	140,110	136,000	123,482	106,981	12,279	11,222	1,008	6,415	13,443	22,250	2,177	353
South Asia	151,740	304,698	129,135	149,012	42,036	59,126	8,301	104,287	9,051	49,121	5,252	2,277
Sub-Saharan Africa	235,959	195,074	174,978	128,235	35,468	28,878	11,804	15,647	40,522	47,850	8,654	3,341
High income												
Euro area												

a. Includes Montenegro.

About the data

A country's external indebtedness affects its creditworthiness and investor perceptions. Data on the external debt of developing countries are gathered by the World Bank through its Debtor Reporting System. Indebtedness is calculated using loan-by-loan reports submitted by countries on long-term public and publicly guaranteed borrowing and information on short-term debt collected by the countries or from creditors through the reporting systems of the Bank for International Settlements and the Organisation for Economic Co-operation and Development. These data are supplemented by information from major multilateral banks and official lending agencies in major creditor countries and by estimates by World Bank and International Monetary Fund (IMF) staff. The table includes data on long-term private nonguaranteed debt reported to the World Bank or estimated by its staff.

The coverage, quality, and timeliness of data vary across countries. Coverage varies for both debt instruments and borrowers. The widening spectrum of debt instruments and investors alongside the expansion of private nonguaranteed borrowing makes comprehensive coverage of external debt more complex. Reporting countries differ in their capacity to monitor debt, especially private nonguaranteed debt. Even data on public and publicly guaranteed debt are affected by coverage and reporting accuracy—again because of monitoring capacity and sometimes because of an unwillingness to provide information. A key part often underreported is military debt. Currently, 128 developing countries report to the Debtor Reporting System. Nonreporting countries might have outstanding debt with the World Bank, other international financial institutions, and private creditors.

Because debt data are normally reported in the currency of repayment, they have to be converted into a single currency (U.S. dollars) to produce summary tables. Stock figures (amount of debt outstanding) are converted using end-of-period exchange rates, as published in the IMF's *International Financial Statistics* (line ae). Flow figures are converted at annual average exchange rates (line rf). Projected debt service is converted using end-of-period exchange rates. Debt repayable in multiple currencies, goods, or services and debt with a provision for maintenance of the value of the currency of repayment are shown at book value.

Because flow data are converted at annual average exchange rates and stock data at end-of-period exchange rates, year-to-year changes in debt outstanding and disbursed are sometimes not equal to net flows (disbursements less principal repayments); similarly, changes in debt outstanding, including undisbursed debt, differ from commitments less repayments. Discrepancies are particularly notable when exchange rates have moved sharply during the year. Cancellations and reschedulings of other liabilities into long-term public debt also contribute to the differences.

Variations in reporting rescheduled debt also affect cross-country comparability. For example, rescheduling of official Paris Club creditors may be subject to lags between completion of the general rescheduling agreement and completion of the specific bilateral agreements that define the terms of the rescheduled debt. Other areas of inconsistency include country treatment of arrears and of nonresident national deposits denominated in foreign currency.

Definitions

• **Total external debt** is debt owed to nonresidents repayable in foreign currency, goods, or services. It is the sum of public, publicly guaranteed, and private nonguaranteed long-term debt, short-term debt, and use of IMF credit. • **Long-term debt** is debt that has an original or extended maturity of more than one year. It has three components: public, publicly guaranteed, and private nonguaranteed debt. • **Public and publicly guaranteed debt** comprises the long-term external obligations of public debtors, including the national government and political subdivisions (or an agency of either) and autonomous public bodies, and the external obligations of private debtors that are guaranteed for repayment by a public entity. • **IBRD loans and IDA credits** are extended by the World Bank. The International Bank for Reconstruction and Development (IBRD) lends at market rates. The International Development Association (IDA) provides credits at concessional rates. • **Private nonguaranteed debt** consists of the long-term external obligations of private debtors that are not guaranteed for repayment by a public entity. • **Short-term debt** is debt owed to nonresidents having an original maturity of one year or less and interest in arrears on long-term debt. • **Use of IMF credit** denotes members' drawings on the IMF other than those drawn against the country's reserve tranche position and includes purchases and drawings under Stand-By, Extended, Structural Adjustment, Enhanced Structural Adjustment, and Systemic Transformation Facility Arrangements, together with Trust Fund loans.

The levels and the composition of external debt vary by regions 6.9a

$ billions ■ Public and publicly-guaranteed long-term debt ■ Private nonguaranteed long-term debt ■ Short-term debt

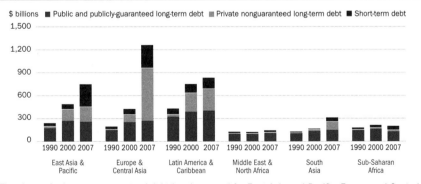

The share of private nonguaranteed debt has increased for East Asia and Pacific, Europe and Central Asia, Latin America and Caribbean, and South Asia. Public and publicly guaranteed debt remain the main source of external borrowing for the Middle East and North Africa and Sub-Saharan Africa.

Source: Global Development Finance data files.

Data sources

Data on external debt are mainly from reports to the World Bank through its Debtor Reporting System from member countries that have received IBRD loans or IDA credits, with additional information from the files of the World Bank, the IMF, the African Development Bank and African Development Fund, the Asian Development Bank and Asian Development Fund, and the Inter-American Development Bank. Summary tables of the external debt of developing countries are published annually in the World Bank's *Global Development Finance* and on its *Global Development Finance* CD-ROM.

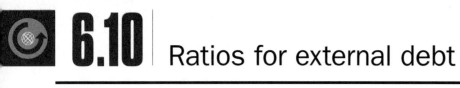

	Total external debt		Total debt service		Multilateral debt service		Short-term debt				Present value of debt	
	% of GNI		% of exports of goods and services and income[a]		% of public and publicly guaranteed debt service		% of total debt		% of total reserves		% of GNI	% of exports of goods, services, and income[a]
	1995	2007	1995	2007	1995	2007	1995	2007	1995	2007	2007[b]	2007[b]
Afghanistan	..	..	..	..	..	52.2	..	1.0	..	..	18[c]	80[c]
Albania	18.4	24.2	1.4	4.1	11.4	51.2	13.7	27.7	23.5	34.6	22	61
Algeria	83.5	4.1	..	..	17.7	3.0	0.8	12.9	6.3	0.6	4	9
Angola	311.9	26.2	12.0	10.2	0.6	0.2	17.0	17.7	919.7	20.2	32	35
Argentina	38.9	49.7	30.1	13.0	21.6	72.2	21.7	29.8	133.6	82.5	63	219
Armenia	25.3	30.5	3.1	7.0	69.8	86.8	0.6	15.9	1.9	27.7	38	117
Australia	..	..	..	..	..	..	..	..	..	..	..	..
Austria	..	..	..	..	..	..	..	..	..	..	..	..
Azerbaijan	10.6	11.7	1.3	0.7	21.8	49.2	4.4	35.0	11.6	25.1	14	16
Bangladesh	40.7	29.9	13.2	3.9	27.1	70.0	1.3	6.1	8.4	25.5	22	84
Belarus	12.2	21.3	3.4	3.9	55.4	8.3	6.5	63.4	29.2	143.8	25	40
Belgium	..	..	..	..	..	..	..	..	..	..	..	..
Benin	82.1	15.8	6.8	..	54.8	35.9	2.9	0.1	23.7	0.0	12[c]	58[c]
Bolivia	81.2	38.2	29.4	11.9	75.5	88.2	5.8	3.6	30.5	3.3	24[c]	52[c]
Bosnia and Herzegovina	..	40.8	..	8.0	..	54.0	..	24.9	..	35.1	42	80
Botswana	15.1	3.4	3.1	0.9	76.0	70.8	1.4	4.0	0.2	0.2	3	5
Brazil	21.2	18.7	36.6	27.8	18.5	13.5	19.5	16.5	60.7	21.8	25	155
Bulgaria	81.8	84.3	16.5	15.5	10.5	49.7	4.9	42.6	31.3	80.0	100	144
Burkina Faso	53.6	21.9	..	..	76.7	53.2	4.4	11.3	16.1	16.1	14[c]	108[c]
Burundi	117.6	154.6	27.6	42.6	70.6	94.1	1.3	0.9	6.9	7.8	97[c]	882[c]
Cambodia	71.8	47.0	0.7	0.5	11.9	80.0	4.5	5.8	53.1	10.2	46	63
Cameroon	131.7	15.0	20.8	9.9	60.8	19.6	9.2	7.6	6,444.5	8.0	5[c]	19[c]
Canada	..	..	..	..	..	..	..	..	..	..	..	..
Central African Republic	85.5	57.1	..	..	100.0	100.0	6.0	9.0	23.8	95.0	48[c]	325[c]
Chad	58.5	29.1	..	..	86.1	83.2	2.0	1.4	11.6	2.6	19[c]	28[c]
Chile	32.1	40.3	24.5	14.2	76.2	7.3	15.6	22.7	23.1	79.0	45	85
China	16.5	11.6	9.9	2.2	7.6	28.1	18.9	54.5	27.8	13.2	13	32
Hong Kong, China	..	..	..	..	..	..	..	..	..	..	..	..
Colombia	27.5	22.5	31.5	22.0	32.7	39.0	22.1	11.9	65.6	25.5	28	133
Congo, Dem. Rep.	271.4	142.9	..	..	..	37.6	23.6	5.1	1,980.9	346.1	111[c]	326[c]
Congo, Rep.	480.0	86.1	13.1	1.2	21.2	44.5	17.0	6.0	1,578.0	14.3	93[c]	88[c]
Costa Rica	33.1	30.8	13.8	4.4	50.7	60.8	11.3	37.8	40.6	72.0	35	62
Côte d'Ivoire	188.7	73.6	23.1	4.5	59.3	95.8	20.7	10.9	739.1	60.4	67[c]	123[c]
Croatia	20.4	97.7	4.8	33.0	73.1	14.6	12.8	10.5	25.9	37.3	109	197
Cuba	..	..	..	..	..	..	..	..	..	..	..	..
Czech Republic	..	..	..	..	..	..	..	..	..	..	..	..
Denmark	..	..	..	..	..	..	..	..	..	..	..	..
Dominican Republic	37.8	29.7	6.1	8.6	39.8	29.1	13.8	23.0	165.3	92.7	33	70
Ecuador	72.1	41.3	24.8	18.7	32.0	53.7	9.4	10.8	73.4	53.8	50	115
Egypt, Arab Rep.	55.8	23.2	13.2	4.4	26.3	22.2	7.1	4.8	13.9	4.5	25	60
El Salvador	26.7	44.4	8.9	11.0	55.1	52.9	20.9	11.0	55.9	42.1	50	104
Eritrea	6.3	64.1	0.1	..	100.0	94.4	0.0	2.2	0.0	..	41[c]	660[c]
Estonia	..	..	..	..	..	..	..	..	..	..	..	..
Ethiopia	136.6	13.6	18.4	4.1	41.7	38.6	4.5	3.4	56.5	..	8[c]	47[c]
Finland	..	..	..	..	..	..	..	..	..	..	..	..
France	..	..	..	..	..	..	..	..	..	..	..	..
Gabon	101.6	56.2	15.3	..	17.9	93.6	6.6	9.5	187.8	44.0	73	99
Gambia, The	113.0	122.7	15.5	12.4	49.1	70.1	3.5	2.9	14.0	15.1	34[c]	63[c]
Georgia	48.2	21.7	..	4.6	0.4	22.3	6.9	9.8	43.0	16.3	20	52
Germany	..	..	..	..	..	..	..	..	..	..	..	..
Ghana	86.9	29.9	24.0	3.1	48.4	32.4	11.3	28.4	77.1	..	22[c]	55[c]
Greece	..	..	..	..	..	..	..	..	..	..	..	..
Guatemala	22.6	18.7	11.1	5.2	47.7	49.4	24.7	31.6	103.7	45.9	21	54
Guinea	89.8	72.5	25.0	13.1	30.4	50.6	5.0	4.5	185.6	..	64[c]	210[c]
Guinea-Bissau	380.7	213.6	51.9	..	88.3	49.8	10.5	1.1	467.0	7.5	263[c]	529[c]
Haiti	28.1	26.1	51.0	4.7	92.2	81.1	3.2	2.6	13.4	9.3	20[c]	57[c]

	Total external debt		Total debt service		Multilateral debt service		Short-term debt				Present value of debt	
	% of GNI		% of exports of goods and services and income[a]		% of public and publicly guaranteed debt service		% of total debt		% of total reserves		% of GNI	% of exports of goods, services, and income[a]
	1995	2007	1995	2007	1995	2007	1995	2007	1995	2007	2007[b]	2007[b]
Honduras	131.5	27.8	34.0	3.7	52.6	45.4	8.0	19.6	141.7	24.9	21[c]	26[c]
Hungary	..	..	..	..	..	..	..	..	..	..	..	..
India	26.8	18.9	29.7	..	24.3	20.8	5.3	19.8	22.1	15.8	20	82
Indonesia	63.4	33.9	29.9	10.5	28.4	33.7	20.9	24.8	174.2	61.4	43	120
Iran, Islamic Rep.	24.3	7.1	30.2	..	1.3	3.7	29.5	44.0	..	..	8	22
Iraq	..	..	..	..	..	..	..	..	..	..	..	..
Ireland	..	..	..	..	..	..	..	..	..	..	..	..
Israel	..	..	..	..	..	..	..	..	..	..	..	..
Italy	..	..	..	..	..	..	..	..	..	..	..	..
Jamaica	82.2	101.0	16.2	17.3	40.6	21.7	10.7	14.9	72.2	80.0	131	183
Japan	..	..	..	..	..	..	..	..	..	..	..	..
Jordan	118.8	50.5	12.4	5.7	33.5	42.5	10.2	11.8	34.4	12.5	54	69
Kazakhstan	18.6	103.7	3.9	49.6	7.8	36.9	10.2	12.2	23.0	66.6	131	218
Kenya	83.8	30.2	24.7	6.0	32.5	60.7	8.7	12.8	164.9	27.9	26	85
Korea, Dem. Rep.	..	..	..	..	..	..	..	..	..	..	..	..
Korea, Rep.	..	..	..	..	..	..	..	..	..	..	..	..
Kuwait	..	..	..	..	..	..	..	..	..	..	..	..
Kyrgyz Republic	37.5	65.0	13.2	6.7	59.0	83.9	2.1	3.2	9.7	6.5	43[c]	65[c]
Lao PDR	123.2	84.4	6.3	18.9	37.4	91.6	0.5	0.2	10.2	0.7	84	267
Latvia	8.8	150.3	1.6	73.3	60.3	49.7	6.7	42.4	5.2	289.5	192	373
Lebanon	24.3	101.8	..	18.7	13.2	4.1	46.0	17.2	16.9	20.6	111	115
Lesotho	50.9	33.7	6.1	7.0	60.3	29.0	0.6	0.0	0.9	..	23	35
Liberia	..	442.1	..	111.6	..	100.0	30.5	49.0	2,340.6	1,016.9	978[c]	976[c]
Libya	..	..	..	..	..	..	..	..	..	..	..	..
Lithuania	..	..	..	..	..	..	..	..	..	..	..	..
Macedonia, FYR	29.0	49.2	..	..	99.9	58.1	11.2	31.8	51.9	52.8	54	100
Madagascar	143.3	22.7	7.6	..	74.3	84.7	12.6	11.7	497.1	22.9	21[c]	70[c]
Malawi	165.8	24.6	24.9	..	51.4	35.8	1.9	3.7	37.8	14.1	9[c]	37[c]
Malaysia	40.6	29.4	7.0	4.6	15.5	8.0	21.2	28.4	29.5	15.0	34	28
Mali	122.3	30.6	13.4	..	45.5	51.5	2.4	0.8	22.2	1.6	16[c]	51[c]
Mauritania	175.3	62.0	22.9	..	49.6	89.5	7.1	14.9	187.9	122.5	85[c]	150[c]
Mauritius	46.2	62.1	9.4	4.9	34.5	25.1	19.5	85.1	38.5	197.5	65	94
Mexico	60.5	17.7	27.0	12.5	19.5	6.7	22.6	5.1	218.8	10.3	20	62
Moldova	40.3	66.5	7.9	9.5	79.1	56.2	0.9	34.2	2.3	82.1	72	98
Mongolia	43.3	41.5	10.1	..	2.8	38.1	0.1	0.0	0.3	0.0	37	52
Morocco	75.1	27.4	33.4	11.4	30.3	34.2	0.8	9.6	5.1	7.9	29	66
Mozambique	360.6	44.3	34.5	1.3	17.4	62.2	3.7	18.4	142.8	37.7	15[c]	34[c]
Myanmar	..	..	17.8	..	15.0	0.5	6.8	25.2	60.4	..	46	119
Namibia	..	..	..	..	..	..	..	..	..	..	..	..
Nepal	54.7	35.0	7.5	4.5	54.2	73.6	0.9	2.2	3.5	..	22[c]	70[c]
Netherlands	..	..	..	..	..	..	..	..	..	..	..	..
New Zealand	..	..	..	..	..	..	..	..	..	..	..	..
Nicaragua	368.3	60.7	38.7	11.7	30.3	76.3	17.2	23.8	1,256.8	73.3	31[c]	52[c]
Niger	86.1	23.0	16.7	..	95.5	94.8	4.5	5.1	75.6	8.3	12[c]	70[c]
Nigeria	131.7	6.1	13.8	1.4	45.4	43.7	16.6	55.7	330.7	9.7	6	12
Norway	..	..	..	..	..	..	..	..	..	..	..	..
Oman	..	..	..	..	..	..	..	..	..	..	..	..
Pakistan	49.5	28.0	26.5	8.9	43.2	53.7	10.7	5.5	128.0	14.1	25	123
Panama	80.9	54.3	3.4	5.3	52.7	26.6	36.2	5.4	282.4	27.4	70	81
Papua New Guinea	57.3	40.2	20.8	..	31.7	78.2	3.1	4.4	29.1	4.7	42	47
Paraguay	31.5	28.6	5.6	6.2	48.0	59.2	30.4	22.3	70.8	32.3	35	60
Peru	60.3	32.6	15.9	25.0	49.9	19.4	31.3	18.1	111.6	20.9	42	125
Philippines	51.7	41.9	16.1	13.7	29.2	17.7	13.4	10.8	67.8	21.0	51	97
Poland	32.2	47.7	11.0	25.6	13.5	8.1	4.9	30.9	14.6	91.8	53	121
Portugal	..	..	..	..	..	..	..	..	..	..	..	..
Puerto Rico	..	..	..	..	..	..	..	..	..	..	..	..

	Total external debt		Total debt service		Multilateral debt service		Short-term debt				Present value of debt	
	% of GNI		% of exports of goods and services and income[a]		% of public and publicly guaranteed debt service		% of total debt		% of total reserves		% of GNI	% of exports of goods, services, and income[a]
	1995	2007	1995	2007	1995	2007	1995	2007	1995	2007	2007[b]	2007[b]
Romania	19.4	51.5	10.5	19.1	21.3	35.3	19.1	35.7	49.7	76.3	67	175
Russian Federation	31.0	29.4	6.3	9.1	9.7	11.1	8.4	21.4	56.6	16.6	39	105
Rwanda	79.2	14.9	20.5	3.2	99.0	72.9	3.1	6.3	32.3	5.6	8[c]	69[c]
Saudi Arabia	..	..	..	..	..	..	..	..	..	..	..	..
Senegal	82.9	23.3	16.8	..	62.2	61.2	6.6	12.5	95.6	19.5	21[c]	59[c]
Serbia	..	68.3	..	..	100.0[d]	44.9	19.8[d]	10.1	..	18.7	86	198
Sierra Leone	149.0	21.4	53.7	2.5	8.4	40.7	2.2	1.0	77.8	1.6	10[c]	37[c]
Singapore	..	..	..	..	..	..	..	..	..	..	..	..
Slovak Republic	..	..	..	..	..	..	..	..	..	..	..	..
Slovenia	..	..	..	..	..	..	..	..	..	..	..	..
Somalia	..	..	..	..	..	..	20.6	26.8	..	..	..	..
South Africa	17.1	15.8	9.5	5.9	0.0	1.5	38.1	38.2	216.7	50.3	19	58
Spain	..	..	..	..	..	..	..	..	..	..	..	..
Sri Lanka	65.3	43.9	8.0	6.7	14.0	25.1	6.4	11.7	25.3	45.1	42	105
Sudan	136.3	46.1	6.7	3.2	100.0	25.3	36.2	33.3	3,898.2	464.8	93[c]	382[c]
Swaziland	14.0	13.3	1.5	1.9	64.0	58.2	4.5	9.3	3.7	4.7	14	17
Sweden	..	..	..	..	..	..	..	..	..	..	..	..
Switzerland	..	..	..	..	..	..	..	..	..	..	..	..
Syrian Arab Republic	..	..	..	..	..	..	..	..	..	..	..	..
Tajikistan	53.6	34.0	..	2.3	..	59.2	6.8	6.2	..	..	30	33
Tanzania	144.6	31.1	17.9	2.5	66.7	37.4	13.0	26.2	356.6	45.7	15[c]	62[c]
Thailand	60.6	26.5	11.6	8.1	20.9	16.2	44.1	34.3	119.4	24.7	29	37
Timor-Leste	..	..	..	..	..	..	..	..	..	..	..	..
Togo	116.7	80.1	6.0	..	75.5	60.9	5.8	15.8	65.1	70.8	80[c]	148[c]
Trinidad and Tobago	..	..	..	..	..	..	..	..	..	..	..	..
Tunisia	63.0	60.8	16.9	11.3	43.8	45.7	12.1	18.1	77.6	45.5	65	106
Turkey	30.5	38.8	27.7	32.1	20.7	11.8	21.3	16.6	113.0	54.6	47	200
Turkmenistan	16.1	5.9	..	..	1.9	4.7	4.3	12.1	1.5	..	7	10
Uganda	63.3	14.0	19.8	2.1	69.7	58.4	2.8	1.6	22.4	1.0	9[c]	37[c]
Ukraine	17.8	52.9	6.6	16.9	13.6	25.3	2.6	31.1	20.9	70.5	66	131
United Arab Emirates	..	..	..	..	..	..	..	..	..	..	..	..
United Kingdom	..	..	..	..	..	..	..	..	..	..	..	..
United States	..	..	..	..	..	..	..	..	..	..	..	..
Uruguay	29.4	54.3	22.1	19.1	27.3	28.3	25.1	19.2	73.7	57.6	69	196
Uzbekistan	13.5	17.3	..	..	1.9	17.0	11.8	4.9	..	..	20	51
Venezuela, RB	48.7	18.7	22.9	7.4	11.5	23.9	8.6	27.1	28.6	34.7	26	66
Vietnam	124.0	36.3	..	2.3	2.9	12.0	12.9	19.3	247.2	19.9	35	45
West Bank and Gaza	..	..	..	..	..	..	..	..	..	..	..	..
Yemen, Rep.	169.0	27.9	3.1	2.7	78.3	59.8	11.1	7.0	107.9	5.4	23	46
Zambia	215.1	27.9	..	2.5	50.6	91.0	6.0	20.5	186.2	52.2	7[c]	16[c]
Zimbabwe	73.5	..	..	..	33.6	5.6	13.7	26.9	77.2	..	121	326
World	.. w	.. w	.. w	.. w	.. w	.. w	.. w	.. w	.. w	.. w		
Low income	87.1	28.9	19.2	4.0	41.7	50.2	11.1	12.8	149.8	16.7		
Middle income	34.7	24.8	17.1	10.6	21.4	19.8	18.4	25.3	66.8	22.4		
Lower middle income	37.6	18.7	16.8	6.2	22.0	25.9	18.8	30.9	63.2	16.3		
Upper middle income	32.3	31.5	17.4	16.4	20.8	15.4	18.0	21.6	70.6	33.5		
Low & middle income	37.7	25.1	17.2	10.2	22.9	21.4	17.4	24.5	70.2	22.2		
East Asia & Pacific	35.5	17.0	12.7	4.0	18.2	23.6	23.9	39.2	64.9	15.5		
Europe & Central Asia	30.0	41.5	10.5	18.7	16.5	16.7	11.5	23.6	53.1	37.9		
Latin America & Carib.	35.9	23.7	26.2	16.0	26.2	21.6	20.2	16.9	88.6	31.1		
Middle East & N. Africa	53.6	18.9	19.8	5.8	19.3	19.7	9.6	16.4	18.4	6.2		
South Asia	32.0	21.1	25.5	12.9	27.4	28.8	6.0	16.1	29.5	16.2		
Sub-Saharan Africa	76.1	24.9	15.9	5.0	35.0	22.4	17.2	24.5	193.5	31.4		
High income												
Euro area												

a. Includes workers' remittances. b. The numerator refers to 2007, whereas the denominator is a three year average of 2005–07 data. c. Data are from debt sustainability analyses for low-income countries. Present value estimates for these countries are for public and publicly guaranteed debt only. d. Includes Montenegro.

6.10 GLOBAL LINKS

A country's external debt burden, both debt outstanding and debt service, affects its creditworthiness and vulnerability. The table shows total external debt relative to a country's size—gross national income (GNI). Total debt service is contrasted with countries' ability to obtain foreign exchange through exports of goods, services, income, and workers' remittances.

Multilateral debt service (shown as a share of the country's total public and publicly guaranteed debt service) are obligations to international financial institutions, such as the World Bank, the International Monetary Fund (IMF), and regional development banks. Multilateral debt service takes priority over private and bilateral debt service, and borrowers must stay current with multilateral debts to remain creditworthy. While bilateral and private creditors often write off debts, international financial institution bylaws prohibit granting debt relief or canceling debts directly. However, the recent decrease in multilateral debt service ratios for some countries reflects debt relief from special programs, such as the Heavily Indebted Poor Countries (HIPC) Debt Initiative and the Multilateral Debt Relief Initiative (MDRI) (see table 1.4.) Other countries have accelerated repayment of debt outstanding. Indebted countries may also apply to the Paris and London Clubs to renegotiate obligations to public and private creditors.

Because short-term debt poses an immediate burden and is particularly important for monitoring vulnerability, it is compared with the total debt and foreign exchange reserves that are instrumental in providing coverage for such obligations. The present value of external debt provides a measure of future debt service obligations.

The present value of external debt is calculated by discounting the debt service (interest plus amortization) due on long-term external debt over the life of existing loans. Short-term debt is included at face value. The data on debt are in U.S. dollars converted at official exchange rates (see *About the data* for table 6.9). The discount rate on long-term debt depends on the currency of repayment and is based on commercial interest reference rates established by the Organisation for Economic Co-operation and Development. Loans from the International Bank for Reconstruction and Development (IBRD), credits from the International Development Association (IDA), and obligations to the IMF are discounted using a special drawing rights reference rate. When the discount rate is greater than the loan interest rate, the present value is less than the nominal sum of future debt service obligations.

Debt ratios are used to assess the sustainability of a country's debt service obligations, but no absolute rules determine what values are too high. Empirical analysis of developing countries' experience and debt service performance shows that debt service difficulties become increasingly likely when the present value of debt reaches 200 percent of exports. Still, what constitutes a sustainable debt burden varies by country. Countries with fast-growing economies and exports are likely to be able to sustain higher debt levels.

• **Total external debt** is debt owed to nonresidents and comprises public, publicly guaranteed, and private nonguaranteed long-term debt, short-term debt, and use of IMF credit. It is presented as a share of GNI. • **Total debt service** is the sum of principal repayments and interest actually paid on total long-term debt (public and publicly guaranteed and private nonguaranteed), use of IMF credit, and interest on short-term debt. • **Exports of goods, services, and income** refer to international transactions involving a change in ownership of general merchandise, goods sent for processing and repairs, nonmonetary gold, services, receipts of employee compensation for nonresident workers, investment income, and workers' remittances. • **Multilateral debt service** is the repayment of principal and interest to the World Bank, regional development banks, and other multilateral and intergovernmental agencies. • **Short-term debt** includes all debt having an original maturity of one year or less and interest in arrears on long-term debt. • **Total reserves** comprise holdings of monetary gold, special drawing rights, reserves of IMF members held by the IMF, and holdings of foreign exchange under the control of monetary authorities. • **Present value of debt** is the sum of short-term external debt plus the discounted sum of total debt service payments due on public, publicly guaranteed, and private nonguaranteed long-term external debt over the life of existing loans.

Data on external debt are mainly from reports to the World Bank through its Debtor Reporting System from member countries that have received IBRD loans or IDA credits, with additional information from the files of the World Bank, the IMF, the African Development Bank and African Development Fund, the Asian Development Bank and Asian Development Fund, and the Inter-American Development Bank. Data on GNI, exports of goods and services, and total reserves are from the World Bank's national accounts files and the IMF's Balance of Payments and International Financial Statistics databases. Summary tables of the external debt of developing countries are published annually in the World Bank's *Global Development Finance* and on its *Global Development Finance* CD-ROM.

The burden of external debt service declined for most regions over 1995–2007 **6.10a**

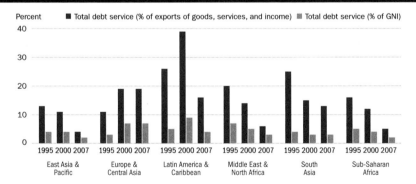

Declines in external debt service ratios for the Middle East and North Africa and Sub-Saharan Africa were due partly to debt relief. Ratios for Europe and Central Asia in 2007 are nearly the same as in 2000 because debt service, GNI, and export revenue increased at a similar rate.

Source: Global Development Finance data files.

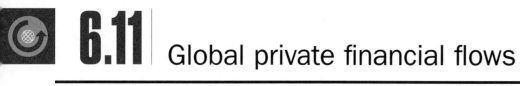

6.11 Global private financial flows

	Equity flows				Debt flows			
	$ millions				$ millions			
	Foreign direct investment		Portfolio equity		Bonds		Commercial bank and other lending	
	1995	**2007**	**1995**	**2007**	**1995**	**2007**	**1995**	**2007**
Afghanistan	..	288	..	0	..	0	..	0
Albania	70	477	0	0	0	0	0	−7
Algeria	0	1,665	0	0	−278	0	788	−642
Angola	472	−893	0	0	0	0	123	1,536
Argentina	5,609	6,462	1,552	1,785	3,705	4,227	754	−135
Armenia	25	699	0	0	0	0	0	502
Australia	12,026	39,596	2,585	17,104	..	..	..	..
Austria	1,901	30,717	1,262	3,684	..	..	..	..
Azerbaijan	330	−4,749	0	2	0	0	0	94
Bangladesh	2	653	−15	153	0	0	−21	−21
Belarus	15	1,785	0	5	0	19	103	257
Belgium	10,689[a]	72,195	..	3,360	..	..	..	..
Benin	13	48	0	0	0	0	0	0
Bolivia	393	204	0	0	0	0	41	230
Bosnia and Herzegovina	0	2,111	0	0	..	0	..	−242
Botswana	70	−29	6	9	0	0	−6	−2
Brazil	4,859	34,585	2,775	26,217	2,636	570	8,283	18,629
Bulgaria	90	8,974	0	101	−6	−87	−93	5,079
Burkina Faso	10	600	0	0	0	0	0	11
Burundi	2	1	0	0	0	0	−1	0
Cambodia	151	867	0	0	0	0	13	0
Cameroon	7	433	0	−13	0	0	−65	−120
Canada	9,319	111,772	−3,077	−42,041	..	..	..	..
Central African Republic	6	27	0	0	0	0	0	0
Chad	33	603	0	0	0	0	0	−1
Chile	2,957	14,457	−249	404	489	−862	1,773	4,664
China	35,849	138,413	0	18,510	317	1,718	4,696	13,898
Hong Kong, China	..	54,365	..	43,625	..	..	..	..
Colombia	968	9,040	165	790	1,008	210	1,250	3,068
Congo, Dem. Rep.	122	720	0	0	0	0	0	−9
Congo, Rep.	125	4,289	0	0	0	0	−50	0
Costa Rica	337	1,896	0	0	−4	−25	−20	272
Côte d'Ivoire	211	427	1	148	0	0	14	−167
Croatia	114	4,916	4	435	0	92	265	5,270
Cuba	..	..	..	..	..	..	..	..
Czech Republic	2,568	9,294	1,236	−268	..	..	..	..
Denmark	4,139	11,858	..	3,017	..	..	..	..
Dominican Republic	414	1,698	0	0	0	411	−31	−15
Ecuador	452	183	13	1	0	0	59	338
Egypt, Arab Rep.	598	11,578	0	−3,199	0	0	−311	−103
El Salvador	38	1,526	0	0	0	−30	−31	−80
Eritrea	..	−3	0	0	0	0	0	0
Estonia	201	2,687	10	260	..	..	..	..
Ethiopia	14	223	0	0	0	0	−48	−44
Finland	1,044	11,568	2,027	5,279	..	..	..	..
France	23,736	159,463	6,823	−68,583	..	..	..	..
Gabon	−315	269	0	0	0	1,000	−75	55
Gambia, The	8	68	0	0	0	0	0	0
Georgia	6	1,728	0	34	0	0	0	75
Germany	11,985	51,543	−1,513	14,314	..	..	..	..
Ghana	107	970	0	0	0	750	38	47
Greece	1,053	1,959	0	10,865	..	..	..	..
Guatemala	75	724	0	0	44	−150	−32	−13
Guinea	1	111	0	0	0	0	−15	0
Guinea-Bissau	0	7	0	0	0	0	0	0
Haiti	7	75	0	0	0	0	0	0

Global private financial flows

	Equity flows				Debt flows			
	$ millions				$ millions			
	Foreign direct investment		Portfolio equity		Bonds		Commercial bank and other lending	
	1995	2007	1995	2007	1995	2007	1995	2007
Honduras	50	816	0	0	−13	0	38	25
Hungary	4,804	37,231	−62	−5,014	..	..	..	..
India	2,144	22,950	1,591	34,986[b]	286	8,227	967	17,704
Indonesia	4,346	6,928	1,493	3,559	2,248	2,843	58	2,317
Iran, Islamic Rep.	17	754	0	0	0	0	−115	−1,284
Iraq	..	..	..	..	..	..	..	..
Ireland	1,447	26,085	0	137,155	..	..	..	..
Israel	1,350	9,664	991	4,306	..	..	..	..
Italy	4,842	40,040	5,358	−14,874	..	..	..	..
Jamaica	147	866	0	0	13	1,796	15	−65
Japan	39	22,180	50,597	45,455	..	..	..	..
Jordan	13	1,835	0	346	0	−2	−201	−16
Kazakhstan	964	10,189	0	841	0	10,243	240	11,029
Kenya	32	728	6	1	0	0	−163	−14
Korea, Dem. Rep.	..	..	..	..	..	..	..	..
Korea, Rep.	1,776	1,579	4,219	−28,726	..	..	..	..
Kuwait	7	119	0	0	..	..	..	..
Kyrgyz Republic	96	208	0	2	0	0	0	−19
Lao PDR	95	324	0	0	0	0	0	305
Latvia	180	2,247	0	−13	43	0	3	6,174
Lebanon	35	2,845	0	791	350	94	333	270
Lesotho	275	130	0	0	0	0	12	−5
Liberia	5	132	0	0	0	0	0	0
Libya	−88	4,689	..	0	..	..	..	..
Lithuania	73	2,017	6	−166	..	..	..	..
Macedonia, FYR	9	320	0	0	0	0	0	200
Madagascar	10	997	0	0	0	0	−4	−1
Malawi	6	55	0	0	0	0	−23	−1
Malaysia	4,178	8,456	0	−669	2,440	−2,170	1,231	873
Mali	111	360	0	0	0	0	0	−1
Mauritania	7	153	0	0	0	0	0	−1
Mauritius	19	339	22	50	150	0	126	−37
Mexico	9,526	24,686	519	−482	3,758	−514	1,401	8,678
Moldova	26	493	−1	2	0	−6	24	364
Mongolia	10	328	0	0	0	75	−14	5
Morocco	92	2,807	20	−64	0	0	158	−170
Mozambique	45	427	0	0	0	0	24	6
Myanmar	280	428	0	0	0	0	36	−137
Namibia	153	170	46	5	..	..	..	..
Nepal	..	6	0	0	0	0	−5	0
Netherlands	12,206	123,609	−743	−98,086	..	..	..	..
New Zealand	3,316	2,753	..	192	..	..	..	..
Nicaragua	89	382	0	0	0	0	−81	77
Niger	7	27	0	0	0	0	−24	−7
Nigeria	1,079	6,087	0	4,648	0	175	−448	−487
Norway	2,393	3,788	636	6,444	..	..	..	..
Oman	46	2,376	0	2,056	..	..	..	..
Pakistan	723	5,333	10	1,276	0	750	317	−247
Panama	223	1,907	0	0	0	930	−12	−17
Papua New Guinea	455	96	0	0	−32	0	−311	103
Paraguay	103	196	0	0	0	0	−16	14
Peru	2,557	5,343	171	814	0	1,003	43	2,086
Philippines	1,478	2,928	0	3,285	1,110	28	−215	2,523
Poland	3,659	22,959	219	−453	250	2,821	228	15,036
Portugal	685	5,534	−179	−664	..	..	..	..
Puerto Rico	..	..	..	..	..	..	..	..

6.11 | Global private financial flows

	Equity flows				Debt flows			
	$ millions				$ millions			
	Foreign direct investment		Portfolio equity		Bonds		Commercial bank and other lending	
	1995	2007	1995	2007	1995	2007	1995	2007
Romania	419	9,492	0	746	0	0	413	12,534
Russian Federation	2,065	55,073	47	18,844	–810	36,505	444	22,824
Rwanda	2	67	0	0	0	0	0	0
Saudi Arabia	–1,875	–8,069	0	0	..	..	..	..
Senegal	32	78	4	0	0	0	–25	–32
Serbia	45c	3,110	0c	0	0c	165	0c	4,072
Sierra Leone	7	94	0	0	0	0	–28	0
Singapore	11,535	24,137	–159	6,743	..	..	..	..
Slovak Republic	236	3,363	–16	232	..	..	..	..
Slovenia	150	1,483	..	275	..	..	..	..
Somalia	1	141	0	0	0	0	0	0
South Africa	1,248	5,746	2,914	8,670	731	4,645	748	305
Spain	8,086	60,122	4,216	15,393	..	..	..	..
Sri Lanka	56	603	0	–322	0	500	103	283
Sudan	12	2,426	0	–17	0	0	0	0
Swaziland	52	37	1	1	0	0	0	–3
Sweden	14,939	12,286	1,853	4,371	..	..	..	..
Switzerland	4,158	49,730	5,851	689	..	..	..	..
Syrian Arab Republic	100	..	..	..	..	..	..	..
Tajikistan	10	360	0	0	0	0	0	3
Tanzania	120	647	0	3	0	0	15	8
Thailand	2,068	9,498	2,253	4,241	2,123	–183	3,702	5,840
Timor-Leste	..	..	..	..	..	..	..	..
Togo	26	69	0	0	0	0	0	0
Trinidad and Tobago	299	..	17	..	..	..	..	..
Tunisia	264	1,620	12	30	588	5	–96	29
Turkey	885	22,195	195	5,138	627	4,415	174	34,243
Turkmenistan	233	804	0	0	0	0	20	–42
Uganda	121	484	0	–48	0	0	–9	–1
Ukraine	267	9,891	0	715	–200	4,068	–19	13,975
United Arab Emirates	..	..	..	..	..	..	..	..
United Kingdom	21,731	197,766	8,070	31,483	..	..	..	..
United States	57,800	237,541	16,523	197,517	..	..	..	..
Uruguay	157	879	0	–27	144	814	39	–58
Uzbekistan	–24	262	0	0	0	0	201	–222
Venezuela, RB	985	646	270	66	–468	760	–247	–1,232
Vietnam	1,780	6,700	0	6,243	0	–26	356	–60
West Bank and Gaza	..	..	..	..	..	..	..	..
Yemen, Rep.	–218	917	0	0	0	0	–2	0
Zambia	97	984	0	4	0	0	–37	198
Zimbabwe	118	69	0	0	–30	0	140	–3
World	**328,380 s**	**2,139,338 s**	**120,570 s**	**715,869 s**	**.. s**	**.. s**	**.. s**	**.. s**
Low income	5,713	31,995	6	12,429	..	1,649	–10	–776
Middle income	93,118	494,617	14,043	126,002	21,280	83,745	26,886	211,782
Lower middle income	54,387	241,019	5,763	63,710	7,233	18,717	10,799	62,434
Upper middle income	38,731	253,598	8,281	62,292	14,047	65,028	16,087	149,348
Low & middle income	98,831	526,612	14,049	138,431	21,218	85,395	26,876	211,006
East Asia & Pacific	50,798	175,340	3,746	35,168	8,206	2,286	9,532	25,832
Europe & Central Asia	9,558	156,437	471	26,232	..	58,236	2,003	131,197
Latin America & Carib.	30,181	107,270	5,216	29,569	11,311	8,699	13,211	36,949
Middle East & N. Africa	817	28,905	32	–2,096	660	97	555	–1,916
South Asia	2,931	29,926	1,585	36,093	286	9,477	1,362	17,719
Sub-Saharan Africa	4,546	28,734	2,999	13,465	851	6,600	213	1,225
High income	229,549	1,612,726	106,520	577,438	..	..	..	..
Euro area	78,432	778,971	17,232	289,878	..	..	..	..

a. Includes Luxembourg. b. Based on data from the Reserve Bank of India. c. Includes Montenegro.

Global private financial flows

About the data

Private financial flows account for the bulk of development finance and are split into two broad categories—equity and debt. Equity flows comprise foreign direct investment (FDI) and portfolio equity. Debt flows are financing raised through bond issuance, bank lending, and supplier credits.

The data on FDI and portfolio equity are based on balance of payments data reported by the International Monetary Fund (IMF). These data are supplemented by staff estimates using data from the United Nations Conference on Trade and Development and official national sources for FDI data and from market sources for portfolio equity data.

Under the internationally accepted definition of FDI, provided in the fifth edition of the IMF's *Balance of Payments Manual* (1993), FDI has three components: equity investment, reinvested earnings, and short- and long-term loans between parent firms and foreign affiliates. Distinguished from other kinds of international investment, FDI is made to establish a lasting interest in or effective management control over an enterprise in another country. The IMF suggests as a guideline that investments should account for at least 10 percent of voting stock to be counted as FDI. In practice many countries set a higher threshold. Also, many countries fail to report reinvested earnings, and the definition of long-term loans differs among countries.

FDI data do not give a complete picture of international investment in an economy. Balance of payments data on FDI do not include capital raised locally, which has become an important source of investment financing in some developing countries. In addition, FDI data capture only cross-border investment flows involving equity participation and thus omit nonequity crossborder transactions such as intrafirm flows of goods and services. For a detailed discussion of the data issues, see the World Bank's *World Debt Tables 1993–94* (vol. 1, chap. 3).

Statistics on bonds, bank lending, and supplier credits are produced by aggregating individual transactions of public and publicly guaranteed debt and private nonguaranteed debt. Data on public and publicly guaranteed debt are reported through the Debtor Reporting System by World Bank member economies that have received either loans from the International Bank for Reconstruction and Development or credits from the International Development Association. These reports are cross-checked with data reported from market sources that also provide transactions data. Information on private nonguaranteed bonds and bank lending is collected from market sources, because official national sources reporting to the Debtor Reporting System are not asked to report the breakdown between private nonguaranteed bonds and private nonguaranteed loans.

Previous editions of the table included portfolio equity flows data only for countries that report to the Debtor Reporting System. The table in this year's edition includes portfolio equity flows data for nonreporting countries based on data from the IMF's International Financial Statistics database. Bonds, bank lending, and supplier credits are shown for only 128 developing countries that report to the Debtor Reporting System; nonreporting countries may also receive debt flows.

The volume of global private financial flows reported by the World Bank generally differs from that reported by other sources because of differences in sources, classification of economies, and method used to adjust and disaggregate reported information. In addition, particularly for debt financing, differences may also result based on whether particular installments of the transactions are included and how certain offshore issuances are treated.

Definitions

• **Foreign direct investment** is net inflows of investment to acquire a lasting interest in or management control over an enterprise operating in an economy other than that of the investor. It is the sum of equity capital, reinvested earnings, other long-term capital, and short-term capital, as shown in the balance of payments. • **Portfolio equity** includes net inflows from equity securities other than those recorded as direct investment and including shares, stocks, depository receipts, and direct purchases of shares in local stock markets by foreign investors • **Bonds** are securities issued with a fixed rate of interest for a period of more than one year. They include net flows through cross-border public and publicly guaranteed and private nonguaranteed bond issues. • **Commercial bank and other lending** includes net commercial bank lending (public and publicly guaranteed and private nonguaranteed) and other private credits.

In 2007 middle-income economies received nearly 20 times more private capital flows than low-income economies did

6.11a

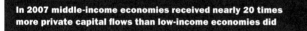

Middle-income economies

Net inflows
($ billions)

- Commercial bank and other lending
- Bonds
- Portfolio equity
- Foreign direct investment
- Official development assistance

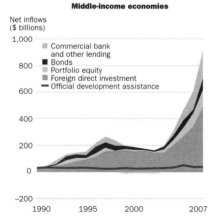

Low-income economies

Net inflows
($ billions)

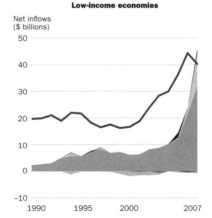

Net private flows to middle-income economies have increased since 2003, reaching $916 billion in 2007—or 24 times the value of aid received. But aid remains the main source of external financing for low-income economies.

Source: Global Development Finance data files and Organisation for Economic Cooperation and Development, Development Assistance Committee's International Development Statistics.

Data sources

Data on equity and debt flows are compiled from a variety of public and private sources, including the World Bank's Debtor Reporting System, the IMF's International Financial Statistics and Balance of Payments databases, and Dealogic. These data are also published in the World Bank's *Global Development Finance 2009*.

	Total ($ millions)		International financial institutions ($ millions)							United Nations[b,c] ($ millions)			
	From bilateral sources 2007	From multilateral sources[a,b] 2007	World Bank[a] IDA 2007	World Bank[a] IBRD 2007	IMF Concessional 2007	IMF Non-concessional 2007	Regional development banks[b] Concessional 2007	Regional development banks[b] Non-concessional 2007	Other institutions 2007	UNICEF 2007	UNRWA 2007	UNTA 2007	Others 2007
Afghanistan	6.9	238.9	41.8	0.0	54.8	0.0	94.3	0.0	0.3	26.4	0.0	3.1	18.2
Albania	6.7	102.8	42.9	5.4	−10.7	3.7	0.0	8.3	48.3	0.7	0.0	0.9	3.3
Algeria	−134.1	−4.3	0.0	−5.9	0.0	0.0	0.0	0.0	−4.3	1.1	0.0	2.3	2.5
Angola	665.0	31.8	3.0	0.0	0.0	0.0	1.0	−0.5	0.0	12.1	0.0	2.6	13.6
Argentina	0.2	−215.2	0.0	−531.6	0.0	0.0	0.0	−5.2	316.3	0.6	0.0	2.0	2.7
Armenia	94.8	83.3	85.8	−0.7	−13.6	0.0	0.0	−6.9	7.2	0.7	0.0	1.2	9.6
Australia													.
Austria													
Azerbaijan	3.1	157.3	52.0	16.0	−25.6	−11.2	13.1	76.0	24.9	1.4	0.0	0.7	10.0
Bangladesh	−69.3	677.4	408.3	0.0	0.0	0.0	127.2	55.4	21.2	16.0	0.0	7.7	41.6
Belarus	1,512.3	−10.4	0.0	−8.7	0.0	0.0	0.0	−5.3	0.0	0.7	0.0	0.8	2.1
Belgium													
Benin	−35.8	121.1	42.5	0.0	1.3	0.0	45.3	0.0	16.4	5.4	0.0	1.9	8.3
Bolivia	36.5	71.2	15.7	0.0	0.0	−14.8	43.8	−45.8	62.1	1.7	0.0	1.4	7.1
Bosnia and Herzegovina	−52.4	42.4	48.0	−23.8	0.0	−18.4	0.0	18.3	7.8	0.8	0.0	0.9	8.8
Botswana	5.1	−20.6	−0.5	−1.1	0.0	0.0	−2.3	−15.2	−8.2	1.2	0.0	1.7	3.8
Brazil	−518.3	811.9	0.0	−198.6	0.0	0.0	0.0	1,031.1	−30.0	2.1	0.0	3.8	3.5
Bulgaria	8.5	−292.7	0.0	136.6	0.0	−347.0	0.0	−14.8	−67.5	..	..	..	..
Burkina Faso	35.9	191.2	80.0	0.0	0.8	0.0	55.4	0.0	24.4	11.4	0.0	2.1	17.1
Burundi	1.0	52.9	1.7	0.0	10.9	0.0	−0.1	0.0	3.4	9.6	0.0	2.2	25.2
Cambodia	74.5	105.2	13.6	0.0	0.0	0.0	52.2	0.0	1.1	6.7	0.0	1.8	29.8
Cameroon	−31.9	109.9	19.9	−5.4	8.1	0.0	17.7	12.6	35.3	6.1	0.0	2.1	13.5
Canada													
Central African Republic	0.0	−6.1	−7.9	0.0	24.2	−19.2	−16.9	−3.6	0.0	6.1	0.0	2.1	9.1
Chad	6.1	25.0	4.9	−4.7	−14.8	0.0	8.2	0.0	1.4	11.8	0.0	2.1	16.1
Chile	−5.0	35.2	−0.7	8.3	0.0	0.0	−0.2	25.1	0.0	0.4	0.0	1.5	0.8
China	−1,038.4	1,094.3	−261.3	285.3	0.0	0.0	0.0	983.3	20.8	13.3	0.0	7.8	45.1
Hong Kong, China	..	..	..	..	..	..	..	..	..	..	..	..	..
Colombia	−112.6	334.5	−0.7	132.4	0.0	0.0	−10.0	476.9	−272.2	1.6	0.0	1.8	4.7
Congo, Dem. Rep.	−138.2	44.3	61.3	0.0	−64.3	0.0	4.5	−24.7	−3.6	43.3	0.0	4.4	23.4
Congo, Rep.	−19.0	0.9	−3.1	0.0	0.0	0.0	0.4	−13.0	3.5	1.8	0.0	4.0	7.3
Costa Rica	2.2	−135.6	−0.2	−8.0	0.0	0.0	−12.3	−56.2	−61.5	0.6	0.0	0.8	1.2
Côte d'Ivoire	16.4	−23.6	−15.9	−29.7	−46.9	62.2	−1.1	−37.6	20.6	9.7	0.0	2.7	12.4
Croatia	−159.6	201.4	0.0	2.3	0.0	0.0	0.0	25.5	169.1	0.3	0.0	1.1	3.1
Cuba	..	..	..	..	..	..	..	..	..	0.8	0.0	1.4	3.5
Czech Republic	..	..	0.0	−9.9	..	..	..	..	..	..	..	..	..
Denmark													
Dominican Republic	125.7	30.8	−0.7	34.4	0.0	63.0	−21.1	−46.4	−2.0	1.1	0.0	1.0	1.5
Ecuador	−222.8	558.3	−1.1	−62.2	0.0	−23.1	−26.5	116.8	550.6	0.8	0.0	1.9	1.1
Egypt, Arab Rep.	−1,140.8	1,212.1	−33.3	626.0	0.0	0.0	0.2	572.2	28.9	3.2	0.0	2.9	12.0
El Salvador	−15.6	−7.8	−0.8	−16.3	0.0	0.0	−22.5	30.6	−5.1	0.7	0.0	1.0	4.6
Eritrea	13.4	44.7	19.6	0.0	0.0	0.0	4.0	0.0	3.5	2.7	0.0	2.0	12.9
Estonia	..	..	0.0	−6.6	..	..	..	..	..	..	..	..	..
Ethiopia	102.5	425.6	132.3	0.0	0.0	0.0	137.2	−18.2	59.0	51.4	0.0	3.8	60.1
Finland													
France													
Gabon	20.8	−37.4	0.0	−7.8	0.0	−34.0	−0.2	−26.4	27.3	0.7	0.0	1.1	1.9
Gambia, The	9.1	38.7	−3.9	0.0	2.4	0.0	10.1	0.0	21.2	1.5	0.0	1.5	5.9
Georgia	−55.3	79.8	65.4	0.0	3.2	0.0	0.0	1.2	0.3	0.8	0.0	1.1	7.8
Germany													
Ghana	−3.2	292.3	247.5	0.0	0.0	0.0	17.9	−14.4	14.3	7.7	0.0	2.1	17.2
Greece			0.0	0.0						..	..	..	..
Guatemala	−40.1	464.1	0.0	98.2	0.0	0.0	−17.6	199.0	176.0	1.1	0.0	1.3	6.1
Guinea	−36.9	4.7	−5.2	0.0	−10.7	0.0	13.9	−7.4	−15.5	5.8	0.0	2.1	21.7
Guinea-Bissau	−8.7	20.4	5.2	0.0	−3.3	0.0	1.8	0.0	0.6	2.5	0.0	1.7	11.9
Haiti	−5.3	117.4	−14.6	0.0	51.6	−30.9	92.0	0.0	1.8	5.0	0.0	1.4	11.1

	Total		International financial institutions							United Nations[b,c]			
	$ millions									$ millions			
			World Bank[a]		IMF		Regional development banks[b]						
	From bilateral sources	From multilateral sources[a,b]	IDA	IBRD	Conces-sional	Non-concessional	Conces-sional	Non-concessional	Other institutions	UNICEF	UNRWA	UNTA	Others
	2007	2007	2007	2007	2007	2007	2007	2007	2007	2007	2007	2007	2007
Honduras	10.6	127.7	45.6	0.0	0.0	0.0	65.4	−18.8	20.6	1.1	0.0	1.5	12.3
Hungary	..	..	0.0	−36.6	..	..	..	..	..	..	..	..	..
India	525.1	1,385.3	44.6	651.8	0.0	0.0	0.0	606.1	−10.8	37.0	0.0	9.6	47.0
Indonesia	−2,013.5	192.3	192.1	−601.5	0.0	0.0	100.9	471.9	0.0	5.5	0.0	6.8	16.6
Iran, Islamic Rep.	−152.3	147.7	0.0	139.5	0.0	0.0	0.0	0.0	0.0	2.2	0.0	2.6	3.4
Iraq	..	..	..	..	..	..	..	..	..	9.4	0.0	1.9	2.9
Ireland													
Israel	..	..	..	..	..	..	..	..	..	..	..	..	..
Italy													
Jamaica	−52.2	−58.1	0.0	−28.9	0.0	0.0	−5.2	−32.1	4.9	0.6	0.0	0.7	1.9
Japan	..	..	..	..	..	..	..	..	..	..	..	..	..
Jordan	−165.0	−0.9	−2.6	−38.4	0.0	−76.2	0.0	0.0	−0.2	2.3	110.9	1.6	1.7
Kazakhstan	−4.5	−109.8	0.0	−76.3	0.0	0.0	−49.0	−10.4	21.6	1.1	0.0	1.0	2.2
Kenya	48.6	151.2	92.8	0.0	104.5	0.0	27.6	−11.0	−111.5	11.0	0.0	2.8	35.0
Korea, Dem. Rep.	..	..	..	..	..	..	..	..	..	5.1	0.0	3.4	2.1
Korea, Rep.	..	..	0.0	−469.8	..	..	..	..	..	..	..	..	..
Kuwait	..	..	..	..	..	..	..	..	..	..	..	..	..
Kyrgyz Republic	5.5	21.3	13.1	0.0	−20.8	0.0	26.5	−6.9	2.3	1.1	0.0	1.0	5.0
Lao PDR	34.3	95.2	16.4	0.0	−3.0	0.0	57.1	0.9	3.8	2.6	0.0	2.1	15.3
Latvia	−0.5	71.6	0.0	−22.2	0.0	0.0	0.0	−1.8	95.6	..	..	..	..
Lebanon	−106.9	236.9	0.0	114.6	0.0	77.7	0.0	0.0	−45.2	2.2	84.0	1.3	2.3
Lesotho	−3.1	28.5	8.0	−3.6	−2.7	0.0	3.3	−1.0	8.5	2.0	0.0	1.4	12.6
Liberia	0.0	−232.9	−35.3	−162.5	0.0	−0.7	−5.9	−52.3	0.0	6.1	0.0	2.1	15.6
Libya	..	..	..	..	..	..	..	..	..	0.0	0.0	0.9	0.3
Lithuania	..	..	0.0	−58.5	..	..	..	..	..	..	..	..	..
Macedonia, FYR	−84.1	−114.5	−4.6	−79.6	−10.5	−46.2	0.0	23.4	−2.5	0.8	0.0	0.7	4.0
Madagascar	7.2	290.2	198.1	0.0	12.0	0.0	36.7	4.2	8.1	12.5	0.0	2.6	16.0
Malawi	6.7	99.7	13.7	0.0	10.2	0.0	26.7	−2.0	7.6	11.9	0.0	2.4	29.2
Malaysia	−1,150.4	−326.9	0.0	−301.8	0.0	0.0	0.0	−36.5	5.7	0.5	0.0	1.5	3.7
Mali	45.5	205.9	138.9	0.0	4.1	0.0	28.4	0.0	2.3	14.5	0.0	2.6	15.1
Mauritania	40.4	81.5	66.1	0.0	12.8	0.0	9.9	−9.1	−20.8	2.4	0.0	1.7	18.5
Mauritius	4.0	24.8	−0.6	19.8	0.0	0.0	−0.1	11.8	−9.0	0.0	0.0	1.6	1.3
Mexico	−213.2	844.9	0.0	329.0	0.0	0.0	0.0	511.2	0.0	1.8	0.0	2.6	0.3
Moldova	−11.9	48.8	38.2	−15.0	27.6	−16.6	0.0	−4.6	7.6	0.7	0.0	1.1	9.8
Mongolia	10.7	44.6	16.4	0.0	−6.6	0.0	17.5	0.0	5.7	1.2	0.0	3.2	7.2
Morocco	240.2	604.2	−1.4	124.1	0.0	0.0	−0.9	113.2	365.1	1.4	0.0	2.8	−0.1
Mozambique	−1.9	372.4	211.9	0.0	5.0	0.0	73.2	7.6	29.9	14.3	0.0	2.4	28.1
Myanmar	−142.2	38.2	0.0	0.0	0.0	0.0	0.0	0.0	−1.3	14.3	0.0	4.7	20.5
Namibia	..	..	0.0	0.0	..	..	..	..	..	0.8	0.0	1.6	4.8
Nepal	−26.6	132.4	0.3	0.0	33.2	0.0	57.1	0.0	−3.0	7.7	0.0	5.5	31.6
Netherlands													
New Zealand													
Nicaragua	1.8	200.7	53.2	0.0	18.2	0.0	112.1	−5.7	8.0	1.7	0.0	1.7	11.5
Niger	−0.2	121.1	36.6	0.0	11.9	0.0	27.9	−2.5	12.7	19.9	0.0	2.6	12.0
Nigeria	68.2	223.5	315.4	−175.9	0.0	0.0	48.0	−33.2	0.0	33.8	0.0	4.8	30.6
Norway	..	..	..	..	..	..	..	..	..	..	..	..	..
Oman	..	..	0.0	0.0	..	..	..	..	..	0.0	0.0	0.7	0.5
Pakistan	−149.9	1,374.6	867.3	−109.0	−122.6	−29.5	279.4	422.5	8.8	17.0	0.0	5.6	35.1
Panama	−3.1	45.3	0.0	30.4	0.0	−10.2	−7.6	1.7	24.5	0.4	0.0	1.0	5.1
Papua New Guinea	−18.5	−88.6	−3.7	−66.1	0.0	0.0	−2.9	−21.2	−3.1	2.2	0.0	2.3	3.9
Paraguay	−40.2	−26.0	−1.5	−14.4	0.0	0.0	−15.1	1.2	1.1	0.9	0.0	0.6	1.2
Peru	−2,404.6	−34.8	0.0	15.3	0.0	−20.5	−7.5	173.2	−204.5	1.4	0.0	2.1	5.7
Philippines	86.9	202.2	−7.0	−30.9	0.0	0.0	−27.4	241.5	3.1	2.6	0.0	3.5	16.8
Poland	−2,275.1	−258.3	0.0	−258.3	0.0	0.0	0.0	0.0	0.0	..	..	..	..
Portugal													
Puerto Rico													

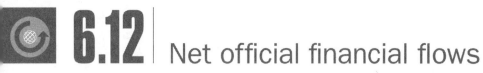

	Total		International financial institutions							United Nations[b,c]			
	$ millions		$ millions							$ millions			
	From bilateral sources[a,b]	From multilateral sources[a,b]	World Bank[a]		IMF		Regional development banks[b]		Other institutions	UNICEF	UNRWA	UNTA	Others
			IDA	IBRD	Concessional	Non-concessional	Concessional	Non-concessional					
	2007	2007	2007	2007	2007	2007	2007	2007	2007	2007	2007	2007	2007
Romania	−10.8	50.3	0.0	21.4	0.0	−105.5	14.0	26.4	94.0	..	..	..	..
Russian Federation	−850.0	−450.0	0.0	−510.1	0.0	0.0	0.0	3.9	56.2	..	..	..	..
Rwanda	−3.4	123.9	27.6	0.0	3.5	0.0	61.2	0.0	−4.7	9.1	0.0	1.8	25.4
Saudi Arabia	..	..	..	..	..	..	..	..	..	0.1	0.0	0.7	0.8
Senegal	51.7	395.0	132.9	0.0	0.0	0.0	50.3	−5.3	188.7	4.8	0.0	2.5	21.1
Serbia	−36.0	213.0	47.4	−17.5	0.0	0.0	0.0	71.2	95.6	0.6	0.0	1.3	14.4
Sierra Leone	−3.0	57.5	14.2	0.0	0.0	0.0	0.9	0.0	6.9	10.7	0.0	2.1	22.7
Singapore	..	..	..	..	..	..	..	..	..	..	..	..	..
Slovak Republic	..	..	0.0	−10.8	..	..	..	..	..	..	..	..	..
Slovenia	..	..	0.0	−13.0	..	..	..	..	..	..	..	..	..
Somalia	0.0	30.2	0.0	0.0	0.0	0.0	0.0	0.0	0.0	12.0	0.0	3.0	15.2
South Africa	0.0	−16.5	0.0	−2.5	0.0	0.0	0.0	−26.3	0.0	1.7	0.0	2.9	7.7
Spain	..	..	..	..	..	..	..	..	..	..	..	..	..
Sri Lanka	124.7	161.4	24.9	0.0	0.0	−5.3	81.3	−2.7	49.7	0.8	0.0	3.7	9.0
Sudan	266.0	157.3	0.0	0.0	0.0	−60.0	0.0	0.0	174.3	18.4	0.0	4.3	20.3
Swaziland	−5.2	3.5	−0.3	−2.3	0.0	0.0	−1.0	0.6	0.2	2.4	0.0	1.3	2.6
Sweden													
Switzerland													
Syrian Arab Republic	..	..	−1.5	0.0	..	..	..	..	..	3.8	42.1	2.5	7.6
Tajikistan	180.6	50.9	7.0	0.0	0.0	0.0	38.3	−0.4	−4.6	3.0	0.0	1.6	6.0
Tanzania	9.4	671.8	474.4	0.0	4.3	0.0	119.4	−0.9	20.0	15.0	0.0	3.0	36.6
Thailand	−826.1	−332.4	−3.4	−272.4	0.0	0.0	−3.8	−42.3	−26.7	1.1	0.0	4.5	10.6
Timor-Leste	..	..	..	..	..	..	..	..	..	2.2	0.0	1.4	4.5
Togo	−2.0	5.7	0.0	0.0	−6.7	0.0	1.0	−1.4	0.3	4.0	0.0	1.5	7.0
Trinidad and Tobago	..	..	..	..	..	..	..	..	..	0.0	0.0	0.3	2.5
Tunisia	−90.3	68.7	−2.1	−8.0	0.0	0.0	0.0	−131.9	204.6	0.7	0.0	1.6	3.8
Turkey	−367.5	−2,421.0	−5.9	557.1	0.0	−4,016.7	0.0	0.0	1,035.0	1.2	0.0	0.9	7.4
Turkmenistan	−78.3	−3.6	0.0	−5.6	0.0	0.0	0.0	0.0	−1.9	1.6	0.0	0.2	2.1
Uganda	−0.6	498.6	373.6	0.0	0.0	0.0	81.2	−2.5	−2.9	18.5	0.0	2.4	28.3
Ukraine	−246.3	−492.8	0.0	−74.4	0.0	−427.1	0.0	−33.9	32.4	1.2	0.0	1.7	7.3
United Arab Emirates	..	..	..	..	..	..	..	..	..	..	..	..	..
United Kingdom													
United States													
Uruguay	−13.2	−2.7	0.0	13.2	0.0	0.0	−2.4	−17.5	0.8	0.5	0.0	0.9	1.8
Uzbekistan	−75.3	48.1	15.8	−7.4	0.0	0.0	0.2	18.3	11.9	2.8	0.0	1.2	5.3
Venezuela, RB	141.3	−589.2	0.0	−50.4	0.0	0.0	0.0	−430.1	−116.2	1.1	0.0	1.2	5.2
Vietnam	335.3	940.7	718.1	0.0	−25.4	0.0	159.2	47.5	10.6	4.3	0.0	5.3	21.1
West Bank and Gaza	..	..	..	..	..	..	..	..	..	6.4	463.3	0.0	3.6
Yemen, Rep.	−23.3	162.3	87.9	0.0	−73.0	−13.5	0.0	0.0	136.6	5.7	0.0	3.5	15.1
Zambia	36.2	140.9	51.2	0.0	42.1	0.0	19.0	5.2	−7.1	10.0	0.0	2.6	17.9
Zimbabwe	126.4	12.7	0.0	0.0	−0.1	0.0	0.0	0.0	−2.4	4.7	0.0	2.0	8.5
World	.. s	.. s	.. s	.. s	.. s	.. s	.. s	.. s	.. s	984.1 s	700.3 s	461.7 s	1,699.4 s
Low income	510.8	8,409.6	4,849.5	−555.3	−1.2	−31.6	1,866.4	297.3	456.8	505.5	0.0	129.0	893.2
Middle income	−10,875.0	5,108.9	539.7	−17.5	−15.5	−5,092.9	298.0	4,820.3	3,015.4	196.0	700.3	167.0	498.1
Lower middle income	−6,793.6	7,488.6	481.3	867.9	−15.5	−652.6	364.1	3,770.0	1,371.1	164.5	616.3	109.5	412.0
Upper middle income	−4,081.4	−2,406.5	58.4	−885.4	0.0	−4,440.3	−66.1	1,050.3	1,644.3	26.9	84.0	36.6	84.8
Low & middle income	−10,364.3	14,260.7	5,389.2	−572.8	−16.8	−5,124.4	2,164.4	5,117.6	3,472.2	979.7	700.3	458.4	1,692.9
East Asia & Pacific	−4,660.1	2,024.0	689.9	−989.1	−34.9	0.0	351.5	1,651.0	27.5	68.8	0.0	55.5	203.8
Europe & Central Asia	−2,427.9	−3,049.3	411.5	−458.6	−50.4	−4,984.7	43.1	187.5	1,651.3	23.5	0.0	17.2	110.3
Latin America & Carib.	−3,362.9	2,731.2	106.9	−244.2	69.8	−41.2	212.7	1,922.2	506.1	28.6	0.0	64.9	105.4
Middle East & N. Africa	−1,595.8	3,030.8	55.1	952.0	−75.8	−12.1	0.3	553.6	693.9	42.0	700.3	58.4	63.1
South Asia	398.8	4,032.8	1,399.2	542.8	−34.6	−34.7	651.0	1,081.3	91.7	107.1	0.0	38.6	190.4
Sub-Saharan Africa	1,283.6	4,840.8	2,726.5	−375.7	109.2	−51.7	905.8	−277.9	501.7	439.6	0.0	128.7	734.6
High income	..	..	..	..	..	..	..	..	..	4.4	0.0	3.3	6.5
Euro area	..	..	..	..	..	..	..	..	..	..	..	..	..

a. Aggregates include amounts for economies that do not report to the World Bank's Debtor Reporting System and may differ from aggregates published in *Global Development Finance 2009*.
b. Aggregates include amounts for economies not specified elsewhere. c. World and income group aggregates include flows not allocated by country or region.

Net official financial flows

About the data

The table shows concessional and nonconcessional financial flows from official bilateral sources and from the major international financial institutions and UN agencies. The international financial institutions fund nonconcessional lending operations primarily by selling low-interest, highly rated bonds backed by prudent lending and financial policies and the strong financial support of their members. Funds are then on-lent to developing countries at slightly higher interest rates with 15- to 20-year maturities. Lending terms vary with market conditions and institutional policies.

Concessional flows from international financial institutions are credits provided through concessional lending facilities. Subsidies from donors or other resources reduce the cost of these loans. Grants are not included in net flows. The Organisation for Economic Co-operation and Development's (OECD) Development Assistance Committee (DAC) defines concessional flows from bilateral donors as flows with a grant element of at least 25 percent, evaluated assuming a 10 percent nominal discount rate.

World Bank concessional lending is done by the International Development Association (IDA) based on gross national income (GNI) per capita and performance standards assessed by World Bank staff. The cutoff for IDA eligibility, set at the beginning of the World Bank's fiscal year, has been $1,095 since July 1, 2008, measured in 2007 U.S. dollars using the *World Bank Atlas* method (see *Users guide*). In exceptional circumstances IDA extends temporary eligibility to countries above the cutoff that are undertaking major adjustments but are not creditworthy for International

Bank for Reconstruction and Development (IBRD) lending. Exceptions are also made for small island economies. The IBRD lends to creditworthy countries at a variable base rate of six-month LIBOR plus a spread, either variable or fixed, for the life of the loan. The lending rate is reset every six months and applies to the interest period beginning on that date. Although some outstanding IBRD loans have a low enough interest rate to be classified as concessional under the DAC definition, all IBRD loans in the table are classified as nonconcessional. Lending by the International Finance Corporation is not included.

The International Monetary Fund makes concessional funds available through its Poverty Reduction and Growth Facility and the IMF Trust Fund. Eligibility is based principally on a country's per capita income and eligibility under IDA.

Regional development banks also maintain concessional windows. Loans from the major regional development banks are recorded in the table according to each institution's classification and not according to the DAC definition.

Data for flows from international financial institutions are available for 128 countries that report to the World Bank's Debtor Reporting System. World Bank flows for nonreporting countries were collected from its operational records. Nonreporting countries may have net flows from other international financial institutions.

Official flows from the United Nations are mainly concessional flows classified as official development assistance but may include nonconcessional flows classified as other official flows in OECD-DAC databases.

• **Total net official financial flows** are disbursements of public or publicly guaranteed loans and credits, less repayments of principal. • **IDA** is the International Development Association, the concessional loan window of the World Bank Group. • **IBRD** is the International Bank for Reconstruction and Development, the founding and largest member of the World Bank Group. • **IMF** is the International Monetary Fund, which provides concessional lending through the Poverty Reduction and Growth Facility and the IMF Trust Fund and nonconcessional lending through credit to its members, mainly for balance of payments needs. • **Regional development banks** are the African Development Bank, which serves all of Africa, including North Africa; the Asian Development Bank, which serves South and Central Asia and East Asia and Pacific; the European Bank for Reconstruction and Development, which serves Europe and Central Asia; and the Inter-American Development Bank, which serves the Americas. • **Concessional** financial flows are disbursements made through concessional lending facilities. • **Nonconcessional** financial flows are all disbursements that are not concessional. • **Other institutions,** a residual category in the World Bank's Debtor Reporting System, includes other multilateral institutions such as the Caribbean Development Fund, Council of Europe, European Development Fund, Islamic Development Bank, and Nordic Development Fund. • **United Nations** includes the United Nations Children's Fund (UNICEF), United Nations Relief and Works Agency for Palestine Refugees in the Near East (UNRWA), United Nations Regular Programme for Technical Assistance (UNTA), and other UN agencies, such as the International Fund for Agricultural Development, Joint United Nations Programme on HIV/AIDS, United Nations Development Programme, United Nations Population Fund, United Nations Refugee Agency, and World Food Programme.

Data on net financial flows from international financial institutions are from the World Bank's Debtor Reporting System and published in the World Bank's *Global Development Finance 2009* and electronically as *GDF Online*. Data on official flows from UN agencies are from the OECD-DAC annual *Development Cooperation Report* and are available electronically on the OECD-DAC's *International Development Statistics* CD-ROM and at www.oecd.org/dac/stats/idsonline.

Net nonconcessional lending from international financial institutions has declined in recent years as countries have paid off previous loans 6.12a

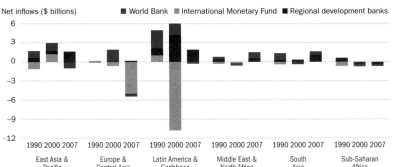

Latin America and the Caribbean paid off International Monetary Fund (IMF) loans in the early 2000s but still receives positive net disbursements from regional development banks, as do East Asia and Pacific, Middle East and North Africa, and South Asia. Europe and Central Asia paid off loans from the IMF and World Bank in 2007. Nonconcessional lending to Sub-Saharan Africa is small because most borrowing is concessional.

Source: Global Development Finance data files.

2009 World Development Indicators **371**

6.13 Financial flows from Development Assistance Committee members

Net disbursements

$ millions	Total net flows[a]	Official development assistance[a]				Other official flows[a]	Private flows[a]					Net grants by NGOs[a]
	2007	Total 2007	Bilateral grants 2007	Bilateral loans 2007	Contributions to multilateral institutions 2007	2007	Total 2007	Foreign direct investment 2007	Bilateral portfolio investment 2007	Multilateral portfolio investment 2007	Private export credits 2007	2007
Australia	10,307	2,669	2,265	3	400	36	6,948	2,367	4,379	..	202	655
Austria	20,553	1,808	1,351	−26	484	−624	19,247	15,802	..	..	3,445	123
Belgium	3,820	1,953	1,268	−29	713	−161	1,686	1,488	..	..	198	342
Canada	17,161	4,080	3,192	−40	928	−4	11,731	7,932	2,386	..	1,413	1,355
Denmark	4,807	2,562	1,722	−72	912	−91	2,242	2,242	..	..	..	94
Finland	2,149	981	575	9	397	96	1,051	11	1,040	..	..	20
France	43,126	9,884	6,690	−431	3,625	−1,179	34,422	14,337	21,925	..	−1,840	..
Germany	39,339	12,291	8,091	−141	4,341	−2,525	28,302	13,521	11,101	−56	3,736	1,271
Greece	3,391	501	249	..	252	4	2,880	2,880	..	..	..	7
Ireland	5,840	1,192	824	..	368	..	4,329	..	4,329	..	..	318
Italy	4,422	3,971	1,252	19	2,700	−261	649	1,353	−3,547	..	2,843	63
Japan	30,315	7,679	5,983	−205	1,901	211	21,979	18,037	3,251	−1,896	2,586	446
Luxembourg	384	376	253	..	122	..	..	..	..	..	..	8
Netherlands	18,142	6,224	4,813	−169	1,580	..	11,575	−1,028	11,951	795	−143	343
New Zealand	404	320	247	..	73	8	26	26	..	..	..	50
Norway	5,221	3,728	2,624	258	845	5	1,488	1,488	..	..	0	..
Portugal	2,215	471	252	18	200	−237	1,980	1,550	..	..	430	2
Spain	21,662	5,140	3,257	82	1,801	6	16,516	16,626	2	..	−111	..
Sweden	6,911	4,339	2,862	71	1,407	−46	2,541	2,232	0	..	309	78
Switzerland	12,561	1,689	1,256	18	416	..	10,368	11,199	..	−833	3	504
United Kingdom	58,319	9,849	6,572	−971	4,247	−43	47,846	31,043	16,587	..	217	667
United States	129,862	21,787	19,729	−827	2,886	−1,632	97,545	45,591	59,796	−7,737	−105	12,161
Total	**440,912**	**103,491**	**75,326**	**−2,433**	**30,598**	**−6,438**	**325,350**	**188,696**	**133,199**	**−9,727**	**13,182**	**18,508**

Official development assistance

	Commitments[b]		Gross disbursements[b]		Net disbursements							
	$ millions		$ millions		$ millions[b]		Per capita[b] $		% of GNI[a]		% of general government disbursements[a]	
	2000	2007	2000	2007	2000	2007	2000	2007	2000	2007	2000	2007
Australia	1,863	1,886	1,605	2,317	1,605	2,317	83	110	0.27	0.32	0.73	0.89
Austria	863	1,695	666	1,648	662	1,622	82	195	0.23	0.50	0.46	1.05
Belgium	1,297	1,968	1,297	1,828	1,262	1,756	123	166	0.36	0.43	0.74	0.90
Canada	3,013	4,244	2,669	3,766	2,632	3,729	86	113	0.25	0.29	0.60	0.75
Denmark	2,461	2,116	2,625	2,394	2,597	2,301	486	420	1.06	0.81	1.96	1.64
Finland	512	948	547	887	537	887	104	167	0.31	0.39	0.64	0.85
France	7,181	10,651	7,657	10,315	6,287	8,867	107	144	0.30	0.38	0.62	0.75
Germany	8,287	12,854	8,412	12,326	7,288	11,069	89	135	0.27	0.37	0.57	0.87
Greece	370	446	370	446	370	446	34	40	0.20	0.16	0.42	0.38
Ireland	388	1,070	388	1,070	388	1,070	102	247	0.29	0.55	0.87	1.47
Italy	2,586	3,787	2,558	3,832	2,202	3,547	39	60	0.13	0.19	0.28	0.41
Japan	14,679	14,424	13,982	13,801	11,587	7,812	91	61	0.28	0.17	0.86	0.50
Luxembourg	202	334	202	334	202	334	459	727	0.72	0.91	1.76	2.19
Netherlands	5,475	6,686	5,135	5,986	4,989	5,629	313	343	0.84	0.81	1.86	1.81
New Zealand	199	308	187	272	187	272	49	64	0.25	0.27	0.57	0.64
Norway	1,954	3,339	2,206	3,350	2,195	3,350	489	707	0.76	0.95	1.83	2.41
Portugal	681	425	681	425	443	420	43	41	0.26	0.22	0.60	0.48
Spain	2,412	4,834	2,412	4,834	2,077	4,566	52	101	0.22	0.37	0.57	1.01
Sweden	1,949	3,333	2,438	3,857	2,438	3,857	275	420	0.80	0.93	1.35	1.90
Switzerland	1,279	1,654	1,260	1,611	1,257	1,605	175	211	0.34	0.37	1.11	1.24
United Kingdom	6,470	10,358	6,470	10,358	6,398	8,774	109	145	0.32	0.36	0.80	0.83
United States	14,698	26,933	12,662	22,111	11,604	21,231	42	70	0.10	0.16	0.31	0.44
Total	**78,821**	**114,295**	**76,430**	**107,770**	**69,210**	**95,462**	**82**	**107**	**0.22**	**0.28**	**0.60**	**0.71**

Note: Components may not sum to totals because of gaps in reporting.
a. At current prices and exchange rates. b. At 2006 prices and exchange rates.

Financial flows from Development Assistance Committee members

6.13 GLOBAL LINKS

About the data

The flows of official and private financial resources from the members of the Development Assistance Committee (DAC) of the Organisation for Economic Co-operation and Development (OECD) to developing economies are compiled by DAC, based principally on reporting by DAC members using standard questionnaires issued by the DAC Secretariat.

The table shows data reported by DAC member economies and does not include aid provided by the Commission of the European Communities—a multilateral member of DAC.

DAC exists to help its members coordinate their development assistance and to encourage the expansion and improve the effectiveness of the aggregate resources flowing to recipient economies. In this capacity DAC monitors the flow of all financial resources, but its main concern is official development assistance (ODA). Grants or loans to countries and territories on the DAC list of aid recipients have to meet three criteria to be counted as ODA. They are undertaken by the official sector. They promote economic development and welfare as the main objective. And they are provided on concessional financial terms (loans must have a grant element of at least 25 percent, calculated at a discount rate of 10 percent). The DAC Statistical Reporting Directives provide the most detailed explanation of this definition and all ODA-related rules.

This definition excludes nonconcessional flows from official creditors, which are classified as "other official flows," and aid for military purposes. Transfer payments to private individuals, such as pensions, reparations, and insurance payouts, are in general not counted. In addition to financial flows, ODA includes technical cooperation, most expenditures for peacekeeping under UN mandates and assistance to refugees, contributions to multilateral institutions such as the United Nations and its specialized agencies, and concessional funding to multilateral development banks.

A DAC revision of the list of countries and territories counted as aid recipients has governed aid reporting for the three years starting in 2005. In the past DAC distinguished aid going to Part I and Part II countries. Part I countries, the recipients of ODA, comprised many of the countries classified by the World Bank as low- and middle-income economies. Part II countries, whose assistance was designated official aid, included the more advanced countries of Central and Eastern Europe, countries of the former Soviet Union, and certain advanced developing countries and territories. This distinction has been

dropped. ODA recipients now comprise all low- and middle-income countries except those that are members of the Group of Eight or the European Union (including countries with a firm date for EU accession). The content and structure of tables 6.13–6.16 were revised to reflect this change. Because official aid flows are quite small relative to ODA, the net effect of these changes is believed to be minor.

Flows are transfers of resources, either in cash or in the form of commodities or services measured on a cash basis. Short-term capital transactions (with one year or less maturity) are not counted. Repayments of the principal (but not interest) of ODA loans are recorded as negative flows. Proceeds from official equity investments in a developing country are reported as ODA, while proceeds from their later sale are recorded as negative flows.

The table is based on donor country reports and does not provide a complete picture of the resources received by developing economies for two reasons. First, flows from DAC members are only part of the aggregate resource flows to these economies. Second, the data that record contributions to multilateral institutions measure the flow of resources made available to those institutions by DAC members, not the flow of resources from those institutions to developing and transition economies.

Aid as a share of gross national income (GNI), aid per capita, and ODA as a share of the general government disbursements of the donor are calculated by the OECD. The denominators used in calculating these ratios may differ from corresponding values elsewhere in this book because of differences in timing or definitions.

Definitions

• **Net disbursements** are gross disbursements of grants and loans minus repayments of principal on earlier loans. • **Total net flows** are ODA or official aid flows, other official flows, private flows, and net grants by nongovernmental organizations. • **Official development assistance** refers to flows that meet the DAC definition of ODA and are made to countries and territories on the DAC list of aid recipients. • **Bilateral grants** are transfers of money or in kind for which no repayment is required. • **Bilateral loans** are loans extended by governments or official agencies that have a grant element of at least 25 percent (calculated at a 10 percent discount rate). • **Contributions to multilateral institutions** are concessional funding received by multilateral institutions from DAC members as grants or capital subscriptions. • **Other**

official flows are transactions by the official sector whose main objective is other than development or whose grant element is less than 25 percent. • **Private flows** are flows at market terms financed from private sector resources in donor countries. They include changes in holdings of private long-term assets by reporting country residents. • **Foreign direct investment** is investment by residents of DAC member countries to acquire a lasting management interest (at least 10 percent of voting stock) in an enterprise operating in the recipient country. The data reflect changes in the net worth of subsidiaries in recipient countries whose parent company is in the DAC source country. • **Bilateral portfolio investment** is bank lending and the purchase of bonds, shares, and real estate by residents of DAC member countries in recipient countries. • **Multilateral portfolio investment** is transactions of private banks and nonbanks in DAC member countries in the securities issued by multilateral institutions. • **Private export credits** are loans extended to recipient countries by the private sector in DAC member countries to promote trade; they may be supported by an official guarantee. • **Net grants by nongovernmental organizations (NGOs)** are private grants by NGOs, net of subsidies from the official sector. • **Commitments** are obligations, expressed in writing and backed by funds, undertaken by an official donor to provide specified assistance to a recipient country or multilateral organization. • **Gross disbursements** are the international transfer of financial resources and goods and services, valued at the cost to the donor.

Data sources

Data on financial flows are compiled by OECD-DAC and published in its annual statistical report, *Geographical Distribution of Financial Flows to Aid Recipients*, and its annual *Development Cooperation Report*. Data are available electronically on the OECD-DAC's *International Development Statistics* CD-ROM and at www.oecd.org/dac/stats/idsonline.

6.14 Allocation of bilateral aid from Development Assistance Committee members

	Net disbursements				Share of bilateral ODA net disbursements								
								%					
			Development projects, programs, and other resource provisions		Technical cooperation[b]		Debt-related aid		Humanitarian assistance		Administrative costs	
	$ millions[a]											
	2000	2007	2000	2007	2000	2007	2000	2007	2000	2007	2000	2007
Australia	758	2,268	28.0	27.3	55.1	51.2	0.8	10.9	9.7	6.6	6.2	4.0
Austria	273	1,324	36.4	26.1	41.8	18.9	12.7	51.1	2.7	1.1	6.4	2.7
Belgium	477	1,240	36.4	28.9	46.9	49.5	3.9	9.5	5.4	7.4	7.5	4.7
Canada	1,160	3,152	39.9	58.8	43.0	24.6	0.7	0.4	5.0	8.7	11.4	7.5
Denmark	1,024	1,651	66.1	70.3	25.3	8.7	0.6	4.8	0.0	8.5	8.0	7.7
Finland	217	584	40.8	28.5	41.4	45.6	0.0	0.0	10.5	18.0	7.2	7.8
France	2,829	6,258	30.7	26.3	50.6	52.3	11.7	15.2	0.4	0.6	6.7	5.7
Germany	2,687	7,950	19.8	25.4	63.8	44.8	3.5	23.0	4.1	3.5	8.7	3.3
Greece	99	249	69.6	28.2	23.8	57.1	0.0	0.0	6.4	5.1	0.2	9.6
Ireland	154	824	79.1	67.3	0.4	4.7	0.0	0.0	15.5	23.1	5.1	5.0
Italy	377	1,270	52.0	61.4	8.1	13.8	15.7	14.3	18.3	6.5	5.9	3.9
Japan	9,768	5,778	61.6	34.8	24.9	31.4	3.1	20.6	0.9	1.6	9.5	11.6
Luxembourg	99	253	84.6	77.5	3.2	3.9	0.6	0.0	10.4	12.0	1.2	6.6
Netherlands	2,243	4,644	43.0	67.1	33.7	13.6	4.9	6.3	9.1	7.3	9.4	5.7
New Zealand	85	247	39.7	51.2	48.1	28.9	0.0	0.0	3.4	11.7	8.8	8.2
Norway	934	2,883	58.1	60.8	23.0	18.8	0.7	1.6	11.3	12.3	6.9	6.5
Portugal	179	270	35.4	37.0	50.4	57.5	9.6	0.1	1.9	0.3	2.7	5.2
Spain	720	3,339	70.2	70.2	17.9	14.5	1.4	4.7	3.7	6.8	6.8	3.8
Sweden	1,242	2,932	61.9	65.4	13.6	15.1	2.1	1.7	14.6	10.5	7.7	7.3
Switzerland	627	1,274	58.8	48.5	19.4	25.6	0.7	3.8	20.2	13.5	0.9	8.5
United Kingdom	2,710	5,602	49.9	67.3	25.5	16.0	3.4	0.7	12.7	6.3	8.4	9.7
United States	7,405	18,901	15.1	71.5	64.4	6.3	1.3	0.5	9.6	15.8	9.7	5.9
Total	**36,064**	**72,894**	**42.3**	**53.1**	**39.4**	**23.3**	**3.6**	**8.7**	**6.1**	**8.6**	**8.6**	**6.3**

a. At current exchange rates and prices. b. Includes aid for promoting development awareness and aid provided to refugees in donor economies.

About the data

Aid can be used in many ways. The sector to which aid goes, the form it takes, and the procurement restrictions attached to it are important influences on aid effectiveness. The data on allocation of official development assistance (ODA) in the table are based principally on reporting by members of the Organisation for Economic Co-operation and Development (OECD) Development Assistance Committee (DAC). For more detailed explanation of ODA, see *About the data* for table 6.13.

The form in which an ODA contribution reaches the benefiting sector or the economy is important. A distinction is made between resource provision and technical cooperation. Resource provision involves mainly cash or in-kind transfers and financing of capital projects, with the deliverables being financial support and the provision of commodities and supplies. Technical cooperation includes grants to nationals of aid-recipient countries receiving education or training at home or abroad, and payments to consultants, advisers, and similar personnel and to teachers and administrators serving in recipient countries. Technical cooperation is spent mostly in the donor economy.

Two other types of aid are presented because they serve distinctive purposes. Debt-related aid aims to

provide debt relief on liabilities that recipient countries have difficulty servicing. Thus, this type of aid may not provide a full value of new resource flows for development, in particular for heavily indebted poor countries. Humanitarian assistance provides relief following sudden disasters and supports food programs in emergency situations. This type of aid does not generally contribute to financing long-term development.

Definitions

• **Net disbursements** are gross disbursements of grants and loans minus repayments of principal on earlier loans • **Development projects, programs, and other resource provisions** are aid provided as cash transfers, aid in kind, development food aid, and the financing of capital projects, intended to increase or improve the recipient's stock of physical capital and to support recipient's development plans and other activities with finance and commodity supply. • **Technical cooperation** is the provision of resources whose main aim is to augment the stock of human intellectual capital, such as the level of knowledge, skills, and technical know-how in the recipient country (including the cost of associated equipment). Contributions take the form mainly of the supply of

human resources from donors or action directed to human resources (such as training or advice). Also included are aid for promoting development awareness and aid provided to refugees in the donor economy. Assistance specifically to facilitate a capital project is not included. • **Debt-related aid** groups all actions relating to debt, including forgiveness, swaps, buybacks, rescheduling, and refinancing. • **Humanitarian assistance** is emergency and distress relief (including aid to refugees and assistance for disaster preparedness). • **Administrative costs** are the total current budget outlays of institutions responsible for the formulation and implementation of donor's aid programs and other administrative costs incurred by donors in aid delivery.

Data sources

Data on aid flows are published by OECD-DAC in its annual statistical report, *Geographical Distribution of Financial Flows to Aid Recipients*, and its annual *Development Cooperation Report*. Data are available electronically on the OECD-DAC's *International Development Statistics* CD-ROM and at www.oecd.org/dac/stats/idsonline.

6.14b Aid by sector

| Share of bilateral ODA commitment (%) | Total sector-allocable aid | Social infrastructure and services | | | | | | Economic infrastructure, services, and production sector | | | Multi-sector or cross-cutting | Untied aid[a] |
| | | Total | Education | Health | Population | Water supply and sanitation | Government and civil society | Total | Transport and communication | Agriculture | | |
	2007	2007	2007	2007	2007	2007	2007	2007	2007	2007	2007	2007
Australia	73.8	48.0	8.9	6.3	1.7	0.7	28.7	9.8	3.4	4.4	15.9	98.4
Austria	26.0	20.3	10.6	2.0	0.3	1.7	4.8	4.4	1.8	1.0	1.4	86.6
Belgium	54.3	39.1	13.7	7.6	1.9	3.6	8.7	10.5	2.0	3.3	4.7	92.0
Canada	63.9	47.3	7.1	14.4	2.5	0.7	21.6	9.6	1.5	2.1	7.0	74.6
Denmark	63.9	33.8	3.6	5.2	4.2	2.1	16.5	23.6	8.6	5.7	6.5	95.5
Finland	58.2	31.7	4.4	3.2	1.9	4.7	14.7	17.4	1.0	6.3	9.0	90.7
France	62.0	35.9	22.8	2.1	0.0	4.6	1.2	16.6	6.5	7.9	9.5	92.6
Germany	62.0	37.9	15.2	2.6	1.3	6.2	10.2	17.4	0.5	2.4	6.7	93.4
Greece	82.9	67.6	24.4	11.3	2.3	1.1	24.3	6.1	0.3	2.6	9.2	42.3[b]
Ireland	64.6	55.5	12.1	15.1	6.1	2.8	15.7	6.1	0.8	4.4	3.0	100.0[b]
Italy	43.9	22.2	3.4	6.3	1.0	4.1	5.7	11.2	2.6	3.8	10.5	59.8
Japan	68.6	26.7	5.5	2.3	0.2	14.9	2.3	33.7	11.2	8.2	8.2	95.1
Luxembourg	68.9	47.5	10.8	14.6	6.7	5.1	6.0	14.9	2.2	4.8	6.6	100.0[b]
Netherlands	56.6	33.8	12.4	2.5	1.0	7.5	9.7	14.7	0.8	1.5	8.0	81.1
New Zealand	53.4	39.3	17.3	3.2	2.2	1.4	14.2	9.5	2.4	2.1	4.6	87.8
Norway	69.9	41.3	9.3	5.1	2.3	1.6	20.1	18.8	0.8	3.5	9.8	99.9
Portugal	91.7	73.3	25.8	3.9	0.1	0.6	35.3	12.4	11.0	0.7	5.9	58.0[b]
Spain	71.7	46.2	10.1	5.3	1.6	3.3	13.8	13.1	4.7	3.2	12.4	89.1[b]
Sweden	52.0	31.3	2.8	6.1	3.2	1.6	14.5	12.4	0.8	4.0	8.2	100.0
Switzerland	49.1	23.6	3.5	3.4	0.2	2.8	12.8	14.8	0.9	5.1	10.7	99.7
United Kingdom	67.4	44.7	12.1	8.1	5.7	1.7	14.3	18.9	1.0	1.6	3.8	100.0[b]
United States	75.3	51.4	3.4	4.6	18.1	1.7	18.6	19.2	5.4	4.9	4.7	68.5
Total	**66.3**	**40.5**	**9.1**	**4.7**	**6.1**	**4.7**	**12.5**	**18.8**	**4.4**	**4.6**	**7.1**	**84.6**

a. Excludes technical cooperation and administrative costs. b. Gross disbursements.

About the data

The Development Assistance Committee (DAC) records the sector classification of aid using a three-level hierarchy. The top level is grouped by themes, such as social infrastructure and services; economic infrastructure, services, and production; and multisector or cross-cutting areas. The second level is more specific. Education and health and transport and storage are examples. The third level comprises subsectors such as basic education and basic health. Some contributions are reported as non-sector-allocable aid.

Reporting on the sectoral destination and the form of aid by donors may not be complete. Also, measures of aid allocation may differ from the perspectives of donors and recipients because of difference in classification, available information, and recording time.

The proportion of untied aid is reported because tying arrangements may prevent recipients from obtaining the best value for their money. Tying requires recipients to purchase goods and services from the donor country or from a specified group of countries. Such arrangements prevent a recipient from misappropriating or mismanaging aid receipts, but they may also be motivated by a desire to benefit donor country suppliers.

Definitions

• **Bilateral official development assistance (ODA) commitments** are firm obligations, expressed in writing and backed by the necessary funds, undertaken by official bilateral donors to provide specified assistance to a recipient country or a multilateral organization. Bilateral commitments are recorded in the full amount of expected transfer, irrespective of the time required for completing disbursements. • **Total sector-allocable aid** is the sum of aid that can be assigned to specific sectors or multisector activities. • **Social infrastructure and services** refer to efforts to develop the human resources potential of aid recipients. • **Education** refers to general teaching and instruction at all levels, as well as construction to improve or adapt educational establishments. Training in a particular field is reported for the sector concerned. • **Health** refers to assistance to hospitals, clinics, other medical and dental services, public health administration, and medical insurance programs. • **Population** refers to all activities related to family planning and research into population problems. • **Water supply and sanitation** refer to assistance for water supply and use, sanitation, and water resources development (including rivers). • **Government and civil society** refer to assistance to strengthen government administrative apparatus

and planning and activities promoting good governance and civil society. • **Economic infrastructure, services, and production sector** group assistance for networks, utilities, services that facilitate economic activity, and contributions to all directly productive sectors. • **Transport and communication** refer to road, rail, water, and air transport; post and telecommunications; and television and print media. • **Agriculture** refers to sector policy, development, and inputs; crop and livestock production; and agricultural credit, cooperatives, and research. • **Multisector or cross-cutting** refers to support for projects that straddle several sectors. • **Untied aid** is ODA not subject to restrictions by donors on procurement sources.

Data sources

Data on aid flows are published annually by the Organisation for Economic Co-operation and Development (OECD) DAC in *Geographical Distribution of Financial Flows to Aid Recipients* and *Development Cooperation Report*. Data are available electronically on the OECD-DAC's *International Development Statistics* CD-ROM and at www.oecd.org/dac/stats/idsonline.

Aid dependency

	Net official development assistance[a]		Aid per capita		Aid dependency ratios							
	$ millions		$		Aid as % of GNI		Aid as % of gross capital formation		Aid as % of imports of goods, services, and income		Aid as % of central government expense	
	2000	2007	2000	2007	2000	2007	2000	2007	2000	2007	2000	2007
Afghanistan	136	3,951	..	..	..	..	..	..	..	..	..	167.7
Albania	317	305	103	96	8.4	2.7	34.8	9.4	21.0	7.0	..	..
Algeria	201	390	7	12	0.4	0.3	1.5	0.9	..	..	1.8	1.5
Angola	302	241	22	14	4.1	0.5	22.0	2.8	4.1	0.7	..	..
Argentina	53	82	1	2	0.0	0.0	0.1	0.1	0.1	0.1	..	..
Armenia	216	352	70	117	11.0	3.7	60.6	10.3	21.2	8.5	..	23.0
Australia												
Austria												
Azerbaijan	139	225	17	26	2.8	0.9	12.8	3.4	5.8	1.5	..	..
Bangladesh	1,172	1,502	8	9	2.4	2.0	10.8	9.0	11.7	7.2	..	21.7
Belarus	40	83	4	9	0.3	0.2	1.2	0.6	0.5	0.3	1.5	0.5
Belgium												
Benin	241	470	33	52	10.7	8.7	56.4	..	32.4	..	..	..
Bolivia	482	476	58	50	5.9	3.7	31.6	23.9	19.7	10.3	..	16.7
Bosnia and Herzegovina	737	443	199	117	12.4	2.8	65.1	12.9	17.4	4.0	..	7.8
Botswana	31	104	18	56	0.5	0.9	1.4	2.1	1.0	2.0	..	..
Brazil	232	297	1	2	0.0	0.0	0.2	0.1	0.2	0.1	..	..
Bulgaria[b]	311	..	39	..	2.5	..	13.5	..	3.7	..	7.6	..
Burkina Faso	338	930	28	63	13.0	13.8	77.2	..	48.9	..	..	..
Burundi	93	466	14	55	12.9	49.5	213.8	..	56.5	103.8	..	..
Cambodia	396	672	31	46	10.9	8.4	60.3	38.7	16.1	9.9	..	..
Cameroon	381	1,933	24	104	4.0	9.4	22.6	54.0	12.9	32.4	..	..
Canada												
Central African Republic	75	176	19	41	8.0	10.4	82.4	116.1	..	..	..	..
Chad	130	352	15	33	9.5	5.7	40.4	26.0	..	..	..	..
Chile	49	120	3	7	0.1	0.1	0.3	0.3	0.2	0.2	0.3	0.4
China	1,728	1,439	1	1	0.1	0.0	0.4	0.1	0.6	0.1	..	..
Hong Kong, China[b]	4	..	1	..	0.0	..	0.0	..	0.0	..	..	..
Colombia	187	731	5	17	0.2	0.4	1.3	1.4	1.1	1.5	..	1.4
Congo, Dem. Rep.	177	1,217	3	19	4.5	14.2	119.1	67.3	..	..	15.2	..
Congo, Rep.	33	127	10	34	1.5	2.1	4.6	6.1	1.6	1.5	..	..
Costa Rica	11	53	3	12	0.1	0.2	0.4	0.8	0.1	0.3	0.3	0.9
Côte d'Ivoire	351	165	21	9	3.6	0.9	31.2	9.7	7.9	1.8	..	4.1
Croatia	66	164	15	37	0.4	0.3	1.8	1.0	0.6	0.5	0.8	0.8
Cuba	44	92	4	8	..	..	..	..	..	..	..	..
Czech Republic[b]	438	..	43	..	0.8	..	2.6	..	1.1	..	2.3	..
Denmark												
Dominican Republic	56	128	6	13	0.3	0.4	1.2	1.6	0.5	0.7	..	..
Ecuador	146	215	12	16	1.0	0.5	4.6	2.0	2.3	1.2	..	..
Egypt, Arab Rep.	1,328	1,083	20	14	1.3	0.8	6.8	4.0	5.6	1.9	..	..
El Salvador	180	88	29	13	1.4	0.4	8.1	2.1	3.0	0.8	..	22.1
Eritrea	176	155	48	32	27.7	11.3	116.7	106.7	34.5	..	..	..
Estonia[b]	64	..	47	..	1.2	..	4.0	..	1.2	..	3.8	..
Ethiopia	686	2,422	10	31	8.5	12.5	41.4	50.1	41.0	34.8	..	..
Finland												
France												
Gabon	12	48	10	36	0.3	0.5	1.1	1.6	0.5	..	..	..
Gambia, The	50	72	36	42	12.4	12.1	67.8	48.5	..	19.6	..	..
Georgia	169	382	36	87	5.3	3.7	20.8	10.9	13.6	6.0	47.9	16.4
Germany												
Ghana	600	1,151	30	49	12.4	7.7	50.2	22.5	17.3	11.2	..	26.0
Greece												
Guatemala	263	450	23	34	1.4	1.3	7.7	6.4	4.4	2.8	12.5	..
Guinea	153	224	19	24	5.0	5.0	24.9	39.0	15.7	13.7	..	..
Guinea-Bissau	80	123	59	73	39.5	35.4	329.8	200.7	..	..	..	..
Haiti	208	701	24	73	5.4	11.4	20.8	40.6	15.1	30.0	..	..

6.15

	Net official development assistance[a] ($ millions)		Aid per capita ($)		Aid dependency ratios							
					Aid as % of GNI		Aid as % of gross capital formation		Aid as % of imports of goods, services, and income		Aid as % of central government expense	
	2000	2007	2000	2007	2000	2007	2000	2007	2000	2007	2000	2007
Honduras	449	464	72	65	6.5	4.0	22.3	11.3	8.9	4.5	..	16.7
Hungary[b]	252	..	25	..	0.6	..	2.0	..	0.6	..	1.3	..
India	1,463	1,298	1	1	0.3	0.1	1.3	0.3	1.8	..	2.0	0.7
Indonesia	1,654	796	8	4	1.1	0.2	4.5	0.7	2.5	0.6	..	..
Iran, Islamic Rep.	130	102	2	1	0.1	0.0	0.4	0.1	0.7	..	0.2	0.2
Iraq	100	9,115	..	..	..	..	..	..	..	..	..	..
Ireland												
Israel[b]	800	..	127	..	0.7	..	3.2	..	1.4	..	1.5	..
Italy												
Jamaica	10	26	4	10	0.1	0.3	0.5	..	0.2	0.3	0.4	0.4
Japan												
Jordan	552	504	115	88	6.4	3.0	29.2	11.6	8.7	3.1	24.1	8.7
Kazakhstan	189	202	13	13	1.1	0.2	5.7	0.5	1.8	0.3	7.5	1.4
Kenya	510	1,275	16	34	4.1	5.3	23.1	26.1	12.9	12.6	23.9	24.0
Korea, Dem. Rep.	73	98	3	4	..	..	..	..	..	..	..	..
Korea, Rep.[b]	−198	..	−4	..	0.0	..	−0.1	..	−0.1	..	−0.2	..
Kuwait[b]	3	..	1	..	0.0	..	0.1	..	0.0	..	..	..
Kyrgyz Republic	215	274	44	52	16.7	7.4	78.3	28.1	28.5	8.3	99.2	39.8
Lao PDR	282	396	54	68	16.9	10.0	57.4	24.2	44.1	32.1	..	89.7
Latvia[b]	91	..	38	..	1.2	..	4.9	..	2.3	..	4.1	..
Lebanon	199	939	53	229	1.2	3.9	5.9	21.5	..	3.9	3.8	12.0
Lesotho	37	130	19	65	3.4	6.4	10.1	29.0	4.4	7.1	..	17.1
Liberia	67	696	22	187	17.4	124.3	..	473.6	..	36.4	..	..
Libya	14	19	3	3	..	0.0	0.3	..	0.2	0.1	..	..
Lithuania[b]	99	..	28	..	0.9	..	4.4	..	1.6	..	3.2	..
Macedonia, FYR	251	213	125	105	7.1	2.8	31.5	12.0	10.6	..	..	..
Madagascar	322	892	20	45	8.4	12.2	55.1	44.2	20.3	..	78.1	108.1
Malawi	446	735	38	53	26.1	20.8	188.7	79.3	65.7	..	..	..
Malaysia	45	200	2	8	0.1	0.1	0.2	0.5	0.0	0.1	0.3	..
Mali	360	1,017	36	82	15.0	15.4	60.5	63.7	34.4	..	128.0	97.4
Mauritania	216	364	84	117	19.8	13.2	103.3	53.1	..	..	..	..
Mauritius	20	75	17	59	0.5	1.1	1.8	4.1	0.7	1.3	2.2	5.0
Mexico	−56	121	−1	1	0.0	0.0	0.0	0.0	0.0	0.0	−0.1	..
Moldova	123	269	30	71	9.4	5.6	39.7	16.0	11.3	5.8	32.9	18.9
Mongolia	217	228	91	87	20.1	5.9	68.8	14.4	27.5	..	..	23.2
Morocco	419	1,090	15	35	1.2	1.5	4.4	4.5	3.1	3.0	..	5.0
Mozambique	906	1,777	50	83	22.5	25.2	68.9	118.9	51.4	39.9	..	..
Myanmar	106	190	2	4	..	..	..	..	4.0	..	..	..
Namibia	152	205	81	99	4.4	3.0	22.8	9.7	8.2	5.1	14.1	..
Nepal	387	598	16	21	7.0	5.7	29.0	20.7	21.2	16.0	..	..
Netherlands												
New Zealand												
Nicaragua	561	834	110	149	15.0	14.9	47.2	45.8	23.5	17.2	86.5	76.4
Niger	208	542	19	38	11.7	12.8	101.4	..	43.0	..	..	108.4
Nigeria	174	2,042	1	14	0.4	1.4	..	..	1.1	3.1	..	..
Norway												
Oman	45	−31	19	−12	0.2	..	1.9	..	0.6	−0.1	0.9	..
Pakistan	700	2,212	5	14	1.0	1.5	5.5	6.8	4.8	5.2	5.7	9.5
Panama	16	−135	5	−40	0.1	−0.7	0.6	−2.9	0.2	−0.8	0.6	..
Papua New Guinea	275	317	51	50	8.3	5.7	35.7	25.7	13.7	..	26.2	..
Paraguay	82	108	15	18	1.1	0.9	6.1	4.9	2.3	1.6	..	5.3
Peru	398	263	15	9	0.8	0.3	3.7	1.1	3.4	0.8	4.2	1.4
Philippines	575	634	8	7	0.7	0.4	3.6	2.9	1.1	0.9	4.3	2.6
Poland[b]	1,396	..	36	..	0.8	..	3.3	..	2.3	..	..	..
Portugal												
Puerto Rico												

6.15 Aid dependency

| | Net official development assistance[a] ($ millions) | | Aid per capita ($) | | Aid dependency ratios | | | | | | | |
| | | | | | Aid as % of GNI | | Aid as % of gross capital formation | | Aid as % of imports of goods, services, and income | | Aid as % of central government expense | |
	2000	2007	2000	2007	2000	2007	2000	2007	2000	2007	2000	2007
Romania[b]	432	..	19	..	1.2	..	6.0	..	2.9	..	..	..
Russian Federation[b]	1,561	..	11	..	0.6	..	3.2	..	2.2	..	..	..
Rwanda	321	713	39	73	18.7	21.5	101.2	100.9	71.2	73.4	..	..
Saudi Arabia	22	–131	1	–5	0.0	0.0	0.1	–0.2	0.1	–0.1	..	..
Senegal	425	843	41	68	9.2	7.6	44.3	23.2	22.0	..	71.2	..
Serbia	1,134[c]	834	151[c]	113	12.6[c]	2.2	150.1[c]	9.0	..	..	..	..
Sierra Leone	181	535	40	92	29.3	32.9	413.2	239.5	68.8	84.0	98.8	..
Singapore[b]	1	..	0	..	0.0	..	0.0	..	0.0	..	0.0	..
Slovak Republic[b]	113	..	21	..	0.6	..	2.1	..	0.7	..	..	..
Slovenia[b]	61	..	31	..	0.3	..	1.1	..	0.5	..	0.9	..
Somalia	101	384	14	44	..	..	..	..	..	..	..	..
South Africa	487	794	11	17	0.4	0.3	2.3	1.3	1.3	0.7	1.3	0.9
Spain												
Sri Lanka	276	589	15	29	1.7	1.8	6.0	6.7	3.2	4.3	7.3	9.1
Sudan	220	2,104	7	55	1.9	5.0	9.7	18.8	8.5	16.1	..	..
Swaziland	13	63	13	55	0.9	2.1	5.1	16.7	0.9	2.3	..	..
Sweden												
Switzerland												
Syrian Arab Republic	158	75	10	4	0.9	0.2	4.7	1.0	2.4	..	..	..
Tajikistan	124	221	20	33	15.8	6.1	125.1	27.1	..	5.9	160.3	..
Tanzania	1,035	2,811	31	70	11.6	17.4	64.7	..	46.4	43.3	..	..
Thailand	698	–312	12	–5	0.6	–0.1	2.5	–0.5	0.9	–0.2	..	–0.7
Timor-Leste	231	278	297	262	71.6	16.3	285.9	..	..	..	..	..
Togo	70	121	13	18	5.4	4.9	29.4	..	10.5	..	..	27.6
Trinidad and Tobago	–2	18	–1	14	0.0	0.1	–0.1	0.7	0.0	..	..	..
Tunisia	222	310	23	30	1.2	0.9	4.2	3.6	2.1	1.3	4.1	3.1
Turkey	327	797	5	11	0.1	0.1	0.6	0.6	0.5	0.4	..	0.5
Turkmenistan	31	28	7	6	1.2	0.2	3.1	..	..	..	..	..
Uganda	845	1,728	34	56	13.9	15.0	70.0	65.7	53.7	38.1	95.5	..
Ukraine	541	405	11	9	1.8	0.3	8.8	1.1	2.8	0.5	6.4	0.8
United Arab Emirates[b]	3	..	1	..	0.0	..	0.0	..	..	..	..	..
United Kingdom												
United States												
Uruguay	17	34	5	10	0.1	0.1	0.6	1.0	0.3	0.4	0.3	0.5
Uzbekistan	186	166	8	6	1.4	0.7	8.3	3.8	..	..	..	..
Venezuela, RB	76	71	3	3	0.1	0.0	0.3	0.1	0.3	0.1	0.3	..
Vietnam	1,681	2,497	22	29	5.5	3.7	18.2	8.7	9.3	3.6	..	..
West Bank and Gaza	637	1,868	219	504	13.3	..	47.4	..	..	..	..	..
Yemen, Rep.	263	225	14	10	3.0	1.1	14.3	..	6.2	2.1	..	..
Zambia	795	1,045	76	88	25.8	10.5	140.8	38.1	53.1	17.6	..	39.9
Zimbabwe	176	465	14	35	2.5	..	17.5	..	..	..	..	..
World	**57,878 s**	**105,056 s**	**10 w**	**16 w**	**0.2 w**	**0.2 w**	**0.8 w**	**.. w**	**0.6 w**	**0.5 w**	**.. w**	**.. w**
Low income	16,632	40,259	15	31	4.6	5.2	23.4	23.3	14.0	11.7	..	..
Middle income	25,713	38,538	6	9	0.5	0.3	1.9	0.9	1.5	0.8	..	..
Lower middle income	17,757	31,700	6	9	0.6	0.5	2.3	1.2	2.2	1.3	..	..
Upper middle income	7,241	6,011	9	7	0.3	0.1	1.2	0.4	0.8	0.3	..	..
Low & middle income	55,145	105,130	11	19	0.9	0.7	3.8	2.5	3.0	2.1	..	..
East Asia & Pacific	8,589	8,611	5	5	0.5	0.2	1.6	0.5	1.4	0.5	..	..
Europe & Central Asia	9,962	5,785	22	13	1.1	0.2	5.3	0.7	3.1	0.5	..	..
Latin America & Carib.	4,850	6,826	9	12	0.2	0.2	1.2	0.8	0.9	0.7	..	..
Middle East & N. Africa	4,489	17,578	16	56	1.0	1.8	4.0	6.7	3.4	5.5	..	..
South Asia	4,206	10,379	3	7	0.7	0.7	3.0	2.0	3.6	..	..	..
Sub-Saharan Africa	13,261	35,362	20	44	4.1	4.5	23.1	21.6	11.0	10.0	..	..
High income	2,732	–74	3	0	0.0	0.0	0.0	0.0	0.0	0.0	..	..
Euro area	..	..	..	..	..	..	..	..	..	..	..	..

Note: Regional aggregates include data for economies not listed in the table. World and income group totals include aid not allocated by country or region—including administrative costs, research on development issues, and aid to nongovernmental organizations. Thus regional and income group totals do not sum to the world total.
a. The distinction between official aid, for countries on the Part II list of the Organisation for Economic Co-operation and Development Development Assistance Committee (DAC), and official development assistance was dropped in 2005. b. No longer on the DAC list of eligible official development assistance recipients. Data for 2000 are official aid. c. Includes Montenegro.

About the data

Unless otherwise noted, aid includes official development assistance (ODA; see *About the data* for table 6.13). The data cover loans and grants from Development Assistance Committee (DAC) member countries, multilateral organizations, and non-DAC donors. They do not reflect aid given by recipient countries to other developing countries. As a result, some countries that are net donors (such as Saudi Arabia) are shown in the table as aid recipients (see table 6.15a). Aid given before 2005 to countries that were Part II recipients (see *About the data* for table 6.13 for more information) is defined as official aid.

The table does not distinguish types of aid (program, project, or food aid; emergency assistance; postconflict peacekeeping assistance; or technical cooperation), which may have different effects on the economy. Expenditures on technical cooperation do not always directly benefit the economy to the extent that they defray costs incurred outside the country on salaries and benefits of technical experts and overhead costs of firms supplying technical services.

Ratios of aid to gross national income (GNI), gross capital formation, imports, and government spending provide measures of recipient country dependency on aid. But care must be taken in drawing policy conclusions. For foreign policy reasons some countries have traditionally received large amounts of aid. Thus aid dependency ratios may reveal as much about a donor's interests as about a recipient's needs. Ratios are generally much higher in Sub-Saharan Africa than in other regions, and they increased in the 1980s. High ratios are due only in part to aid flows. Many African countries saw severe erosion in their terms of trade in the 1980s, which, along with weak policies, contributed to falling incomes, imports, and investment. Thus the increase in aid dependency ratios reflects events affecting both the numerator (aid) and the denominator (GNI).

Because the table relies on information from donors, it is not necessarily consistent with information recorded by recipients in the balance of payments, which often excludes all or some technical assistance—particularly payments to expatriates made directly by the donor. Similarly, grant commodity aid may not always be recorded in trade data or in the balance of payments. Moreover, DAC statistics exclude purely military aid.

The nominal values used here may overstate the real value of aid to recipients. Changes in international prices and exchange rates can reduce the purchasing power of aid. Tying aid, still prevalent though declining in importance, also tends to reduce its purchasing power (see *About the data* for table 6.14).

The aggregates refer to World Bank definitions. Therefore the ratios shown may differ from those of the Organisation for Economic Co-operation and Development (OECD).

Definitions

• **Net official development assistance** is flows (net of repayment of principal) that meet the DAC definition of ODA and are made to countries and territories on the DAC list of aid recipients. See *About the data* for table 6.13. • **Aid per capita** is ODA divided by midyear population. • **Aid dependency ratios** are calculated using values in U.S. dollars converted at official exchange rates. Imports of goods, services, and income refer to international transactions involving a change in ownership of general merchandise, goods sent for processing and repairs, nonmonetary gold, services, receipts of employee compensation for nonresident workers, and investment income. For definitions of GNI, gross capital formation, and central government expense, see *Definitions* for tables 1.1, 4.8, and 4.10.

Official development assistance from non-DAC donors, 2003–07 — 6.15a

Net disbursements ($ millions)

	2003	2004	2005	2006	2007
OECD members (non-DAC)					
Czech Republic	91	108	135	161	179
Hungary	21	70	100	149	103
Iceland	18	21	27	41	48
Korea, Rep.	366	423	752	455	699
Poland	27	118	205	297	363
Slovak Republic	15	28	56	55	67
Turkey	67	339	601	714	602
Arab countries					
Kuwait	138	161	218	158	110
Saudi Arabia	2,391	1,734	1,005	2,095	2,079
United Arab Emirates	188	181	141	249	429
Other donors					
Israel[a]	112	84	95	90	111
Taiwan, China	..	421	483	513	514
Others	4	22	86	195	255
Total	3,436	3,712	3,905	5,172	5,560

Note: The table does not reflect aid provided by several major emerging non–Organisation for Economic Co-operation and Development donors because information on their aid has not been disclosed.
a. Includes $68.8 million in 2003, $47.9 million in 2004, $49.2 million in 2005, $45.5 million in 2006, and $42.9 million in 2007 for first-year sustenance expenses for people arriving from developing countries (many of which are experiencing civil war or severe unrest) or people who have left their country for humanitarian or political reasons.
Source: Organisation for Economic Co-operation and Development.

Data sources

Data on financial flows are compiled by DAC and published in its annual statistical report, *Geographical Distribution of Financial Flows to Aid Recipients,* and in its annual *Development Cooperation Report.* Data are available electronically on the OECD-DAC's *International Development Statistics* CD-ROM and at www.oecd.org/dac/stats/idsonline. Data on population, GNI, gross capital formation, imports of goods and services, and central government expense used in computing the ratios are from World Bank and International Monetary Fund databases.

6.16 Distribution of net aid by Development Assistance Committee members

					Ten major DAC donors $ millions							Other DAC donors $ millions
	Total $ millions 2007	United States 2007	European Commission 2007	Germany 2007	France 2007	Japan 2007	United Kingdom 2007	Netherlands 2007	Spain 2007	Canada 2007	Sweden 2007	2007
Afghanistan	3,300.2	1,514.3	307.5	217.2	19.5	101.0	268.7	88.8	43.5	345.4	56.2	338.2
Albania	251.0	32.1	50.3	46.0	5.0	−1.6	6.8	6.8	19.5	0.8	11.9	73.4
Algeria	375.4	1.7	86.2	9.4	185.2	7.3	0.6	0.0	60.5	0.9	0.9	22.9
Angola	150.5	39.6	64.9	12.3	3.2	23.1	10.0	−49.3	17.6	4.5	6.7	17.9
Argentina	69.9	7.8	6.1	11.9	16.8	15.1	1.0	0.0	21.6	3.6	0.9	−14.9
Armenia	251.2	79.9	20.5	22.5	8.5	85.2	7.5	5.8	0.1	1.9	3.6	15.7
Australia												
Austria												
Azerbaijan	118.8	49.0	9.0	24.3	9.5	11.4	0.4	0.1	0.0	1.5	1.4	12.3
Bangladesh	765.3	49.1	101.5	43.1	−0.9	−6.6	245.6	99.5	12.2	60.2	11.8	150.0
Belarus	55.7	8.1	6.9	18.9	1.2	0.4	0.8	0.0	0.2	0.5	10.5	8.3
Belgium												
Benin	319.7	25.3	81.4	29.6	56.4	6.8	0.0	34.7	2.1	7.0	0.3	76.0
Bolivia	396.6	122.4	43.9	39.8	7.2	36.9	−105.2	48.3	74.6	22.8	26.0	79.9
Bosnia and Herzegovina	352.1	31.6	63.7	29.0	5.6	5.4	9.5	21.1	30.2	10.3	37.0	108.6
Botswana	101.0	44.8	37.3	2.5	9.2	−2.2	0.4	0.1	0.0	2.2	3.7	2.9
Brazil	295.5	3.9	25.7	76.8	112.9	−9.9	3.1	0.2	32.8	9.2	4.0	36.9
Bulgaria												
Burkina Faso	611.2	21.8	199.4	39.9	114.8	20.4	0.0	65.7	4.8	22.7	21.1	100.6
Burundi	321.4	25.9	121.7	23.0	18.3	8.5	13.2	23.1	2.3	6.9	6.0	72.4
Cambodia	462.1	87.2	44.8	37.6	35.0	113.6	24.6	0.2	8.5	15.3	17.9	77.4
Cameroon	1,791.7	30.7	94.9	754.5	596.2	18.6	51.7	2.6	15.3	12.4	73.6	141.3
Canada												
Central African Republic	147.8	18.4	30.0	5.3	54.2	2.6	5.1	6.3	1.0	5.7	7.6	11.8
Chad	298.6	59.6	75.2	29.5	47.9	9.9	5.1	6.8	4.1	11.6	5.9	43.0
Chile	110.5	−1.1	12.5	27.5	10.2	8.8	0.5	0.1	6.7	3.5	0.3	41.6
China	1,387.2	40.8	56.0	289.3	132.3	435.7	162.4	24.8	67.5	32.9	10.6	135.0
Hong Kong, China												
Colombia	702.7	403.5	73.8	23.9	34.4	0.4	1.5	28.0	64.3	20.1	18.6	34.3
Congo, Dem. Rep.	946.4	132.4	158.0	63.0	27.6	22.9	121.2	50.7	17.7	33.0	33.4	286.4
Congo, Rep.	97.8	9.6	50.3	5.8	18.5	5.0	0.2	0.0	1.0	2.5	3.2	1.9
Costa Rica	56.3	−2.9	7.9	3.2	23.1	17.3	−12.0	1.8	10.0	3.9	1.1	2.9
Côte d'Ivoire	179.6	37.0	68.1	19.8	50.7	6.5	−37.1	1.5	3.1	3.9	5.7	20.3
Croatia	155.9	21.1	100.9	7.5	3.2	0.2	1.1	0.1	0.0	0.3	6.1	15.5
Cuba	59.1	12.4	2.1	3.0	2.5	1.8	−4.9	0.2	24.0	8.4	0.1	9.6
Czech Republic												
Denmark												
Dominican Republic	132.3	4.5	107.3	8.7	16.5	3.0	−37.4	0.0	27.3	2.9	0.2	−0.7
Ecuador	215.4	42.7	34.9	22.0	4.0	3.0	−1.3	0.5	71.3	3.5	0.5	34.4
Egypt, Arab Rep.	995.2	462.4	208.1	153.9	77.1	−27.0	0.1	14.6	11.4	17.7	2.4	74.5
El Salvador	96.6	39.0	25.2	9.2	5.7	26.8	−96.7	0.4	61.1	4.2	4.2	17.6
Eritrea	81.6	1.6	36.1	3.9	0.9	8.4	5.2	4.4	0.2	1.4	2.6	16.8
Estonia												
Ethiopia	1,606.8	371.7	364.8	96.5	20.1	36.0	291.5	50.8	27.1	90.5	44.7	213.2
Finland												
France												
Gabon	40.3	1.1	6.7	−1.4	32.2	0.3	0.0	0.0	0.2	1.7	0.0	−0.2
Gambia, The	42.3	1.7	9.2	0.9	0.7	6.4	5.0	10.1	4.8	1.5	0.8	1.1
Georgia	272.3	86.8	28.1	38.3	4.5	7.0	8.7	7.9	0.0	4.2	10.8	76.1
Germany												
Ghana	802.3	70.7	93.9	52.7	41.6	46.5	152.3	142.2	5.8	78.6	1.7	116.5
Greece												
Guatemala	443.2	45.7	30.8	17.3	2.9	17.7	−27.6	25.2	252.9	11.2	28.7	38.5
Guinea	153.1	24.7	30.9	15.8	55.1	12.0	1.1	0.0	2.3	7.1	0.4	3.8
Guinea-Bissau	88.5	6.3	44.9	0.4	3.4	1.1	0.1	0.0	12.6	1.0	0.0	18.9
Haiti	531.8	202.2	97.5	2.7	48.2	6.8	0.0	0.0	15.4	119.2	2.3	37.4

	Total $ millions 2007	Ten major DAC donors $ millions										Other DAC donors $ millions 2007
		United States 2007	European Commission 2007	Germany 2007	France 2007	Japan 2007	United Kingdom 2007	Netherlands 2007	Spain 2007	Canada 2007	Sweden 2007	
Honduras	330.9	71.1	41.3	26.2	1.6	20.8	0.0	0.4	110.8	13.1	19.8	25.9
Hungary												
India	992.8	84.9	89.6	128.0	−48.0	99.9	510.5	6.9	12.6	21.4	13.5	73.5
Indonesia	418.0	117.3	55.9	31.4	−84.0	−222.5	69.7	42.4	−16.2	53.4	16.4	354.0
Iran, Islamic Rep.	77.4	2.2	10.0	42.3	18.1	−12.1	0.5	2.2	6.9	0.1	0.0	7.2
Iraq	9,016.1	3,749.3	24.5	2,095.0	759.2	858.8	60.2	5.9	33.2	43.0	17.4	1,369.6
Ireland												
Israel												
Italy												
Jamaica	20.7	−5.5	37.7	−8.1	−1.2	−8.0	2.1	−5.3	0.5	6.8	0.2	1.4
Japan												
Jordan	344.8	259.5	55.4	27.9	−3.8	−28.3	0.5	0.1	10.3	8.8	0.2	14.3
Kazakhstan	190.2	77.7	9.4	49.6	3.5	43.3	0.7	0.4	0.3	0.6	0.7	4.2
Kenya	938.1	325.2	114.0	62.5	47.8	57.1	111.3	11.0	44.9	22.4	45.5	96.3
Korea, Dem. Rep.	88.3	32.5	16.6	3.1	0.3	0.0	1.2	0.7	1.6	2.1	7.8	22.5
Korea, Rep.												
Kuwait												
Kyrgyz Republic	138.5	39.8	19.9	25.0	1.0	15.7	13.0	0.4	0.3	0.7	7.4	15.5
Lao PDR	230.7	1.4	8.9	23.8	35.5	81.5	1.7	0.1	0.0	4.7	19.8	53.4
Latvia												
Lebanon	524.3	127.1	60.5	32.6	102.6	15.8	7.5	0.6	37.3	10.3	9.1	120.8
Lesotho	79.7	19.5	17.4	6.8	−1.0	4.9	8.1	0.0	1.2	1.4	0.2	21.5
Liberia	265.9	102.7	39.5	10.0	1.1	12.5	10.0	2.9	3.6	2.9	19.8	61.1
Libya	16.3	4.0	1.1	3.9	1.1	0.4	0.3	0.0	0.1	0.0	0.0	5.3
Lithuania												
Macedonia, FYR	210.0	31.3	76.0	18.4	3.5	20.2	1.9	9.0	1.4	0.2	14.1	34.1
Madagascar	554.9	66.9	168.4	14.0	142.0	111.2	1.7	11.9	5.4	3.2	0.5	29.8
Malawi	475.5	79.0	75.0	24.4	0.9	40.3	133.7	6.8	−0.3	16.0	20.4	79.3
Malaysia	192.1	2.3	0.4	9.6	−4.8	223.0	−20.2	0.0	0.0	1.0	0.4	−19.6
Mali	736.7	54.0	178.7	40.6	214.0	9.7	0.0	64.9	17.5	55.9	26.5	75.0
Mauritania	235.2	10.2	101.9	12.9	37.9	23.5	0.1	0.1	39.1	1.7	0.8	7.0
Mauritius	77.3	0.3	33.8	−0.1	39.8	2.8	0.1	0.0	0.0	0.6	0.0	0.2
Mexico	89.8	83.6	10.9	28.2	16.0	−45.2	2.3	−0.3	−17.2	6.7	0.2	4.6
Moldova	159.4	18.9	66.3	9.3	7.3	5.7	6.8	8.0	0.7	0.4	17.1	19.1
Mongolia	142.6	12.7	2.2	30.3	0.7	51.6	1.2	11.1	9.0	2.1	2.2	19.4
Morocco	952.6	5.5	324.7	142.8	218.8	64.7	0.3	−0.3	84.8	8.9	1.3	101.1
Mozambique	1,313.0	153.4	239.8	61.8	25.7	27.8	115.7	80.7	53.8	57.3	103.6	393.5
Myanmar	149.0	15.4	19.7	5.8	1.7	30.5	18.0	2.4	0.0	0.4	11.4	43.8
Namibia	159.8	58.8	16.3	21.2	2.8	5.7	0.9	1.0	28.5	1.9	4.1	18.7
Nepal	402.0	54.0	24.7	48.9	−2.4	48.6	88.4	3.3	0.1	14.8	−17.7	139.3
Netherlands												
New Zealand												
Nicaragua	581.8	76.5	87.8	30.8	2.9	30.6	−6.9	37.0	115.1	22.2	41.9	143.7
Niger	350.2	41.3	117.4	21.4	56.7	28.3	2.4	0.1	8.2	14.5	1.2	58.6
Nigeria	1,558.6	240.6	173.4	25.5	11.8	26.8	286.0	344.0	0.5	20.9	1.1	428.1
Norway												
Oman	9.6	7.3	0.0	0.4	0.9	0.9	0.2	0.0	0.0	0.0	0.0	0.0
Pakistan	1,044.3	433.6	67.9	62.4	52.4	53.2	197.8	36.2	5.7	44.7	14.2	76.1
Panama	−136.5	7.3	3.0	1.1	0.2	2.0	−162.3	0.1	10.6	1.2	0.1	0.3
Papua New Guinea	307.9	0.8	20.4	−1.0	0.1	−10.6	1.0	0.0	0.1	1.2	0.2	295.7
Paraguay	105.7	24.9	23.0	4.8	3.5	28.9	−0.2	0.1	13.3	3.3	1.8	2.4
Peru	236.4	94.1	65.2	7.6	6.2	39.8	−251.0	−0.1	109.4	20.1	5.8	139.4
Philippines	581.8	84.8	34.4	28.2	−4.1	222.2	0.6	4.8	29.2	22.5	6.1	153.3
Poland												
Portugal												
Puerto Rico												

6.16 | Distribution of net aid by Development Assistance Committee members

					Ten major DAC donors $ millions							Other DAC donors $ millions
	Total $ millions 2007	United States 2007	European Commission 2007	Germany 2007	France 2007	Japan 2007	United Kingdom 2007	Netherlands 2007	Spain 2007	Canada 2007	Sweden 2007	2007
Romania												
Russian Federation												
Rwanda	453.1	90.8	79.2	23.1	5.4	19.5	95.0	27.8	8.4	9.7	21.8	72.4
Saudi Arabia	−144.1	0.2	0.0	1.5	7.0	−154.0	0.8	0.0	0.0	0.0	0.0	0.4
Senegal	532.2	39.2	81.3	27.1	176.7	32.0	11.7	22.4	41.6	47.9	0.2	52.2
Serbia	747.2	105.1	271.1	78.4	7.3	7.2	15.5	3.1	2.5	8.0	33.5	215.6
Sierra Leone	452.8	20.9	72.0	36.5	41.7	30.1	88.1	47.1	3.2	5.7	1.7	105.6
Singapore												
Slovak Republic												
Slovenia												
Somalia	335.3	58.7	78.6	13.6	6.2	3.9	26.4	12.4	2.3	12.9	25.8	94.7
South Africa	741.8	227.1	144.7	101.5	105.0	4.7	−20.4	44.9	1.1	14.0	19.4	100.0
Spain												
Sri Lanka	351.8	33.5	53.9	21.3	6.5	44.2	11.5	14.6	14.7	30.7	23.1	97.8
Sudan	1,920.8	710.5	254.7	36.9	13.8	51.6	206.2	202.5	28.4	70.8	68.1	277.5
Swaziland	35.9	3.5	23.7	−5.9	0.3	7.3	2.2	0.0	0.0	1.4	0.0	3.4
Sweden												
Switzerland												
Syrian Arab Republic	49.3	2.5	40.2	8.0	31.7	−45.6	0.1	0.1	3.0	0.5	1.1	8.0
Tajikistan	121.9	34.9	16.0	12.6	4.7	9.4	4.5	0.1	3.0	5.8	13.9	17.2
Tanzania	2,017.8	166.9	187.1	65.0	3.0	721.7	231.8	128.2	8.0	56.7	107.8	341.7
Thailand	−366.0	44.5	30.2	−2.0	5.2	−477.4	0.2	0.7	0.7	5.2	9.1	17.7
Timor-Leste	265.8	25.1	39.6	6.2	0.5	13.1	4.0	0.0	11.4	3.2	6.4	156.3
Togo	95.8	7.4	31.1	12.1	33.7	0.5	0.3	0.0	1.6	2.3	0.8	6.1
Trinidad and Tobago	15.4	0.3	8.5	0.4	4.4	0.1	0.1	0.0	0.0	1.5	0.0	0.1
Tunisia	310.7	−10.9	116.8	27.5	127.9	20.6	0.1	−2.0	21.3	−0.8	0.9	9.4
Turkey	783.4	−11.8	545.9	−55.6	134.2	86.6	1.4	−0.8	55.9	−1.7	7.2	22.0
Turkmenistan	3.8	0.1	2.5	0.8	0.4	−0.5	0.2	0.0	0.0	0.3	0.0	0.0
Uganda	1,119.4	301.6	117.0	47.6	9.0	27.5	167.2	70.4	2.7	20.0	56.6	300.1
Ukraine	333.2	91.1	89.0	69.1	6.5	5.7	7.8	0.0	0.1	16.0	22.1	25.8
United Arab Emirates												
United Kingdom												
United States												
Uruguay	29.1	0.5	9.2	−2.9	2.9	2.6	0.1	0.0	12.7	2.0	0.3	1.7
Uzbekistan	112.7	19.1	10.4	16.5	2.8	56.3	0.1	0.1	0.0	0.5	0.8	6.2
Venezuela, RB	63.0	10.1	18.5	5.6	6.8	2.4	0.1	0.0	15.9	1.6	0.0	2.0
Vietnam	1,556.1	40.6	67.7	97.6	154.5	640.0	97.2	47.7	31.5	28.9	47.0	303.3
West Bank and Gaza	1,369.8	212.3	533.3	75.2	55.9	48.7	22.7	30.3	72.7	42.3	54.3	222.1
Yemen, Rep.	185.1	19.9	17.7	60.8	5.8	9.8	25.3	31.7	0.2	1.6	0.8	11.4
Zambia	834.2	165.3	121.3	40.7	1.1	94.6	74.2	71.5	0.9	23.8	53.7	187.0
Zimbabwe	423.5	139.1	52.1	19.5	15.5	11.7	94.1	7.1	0.7	13.0	19.7	51.2
World	**83,989.0 s**	**18,901.2 s**	**11,095.5 s**	**7,949.8 s**	**6,258.4 s**	**5,778.2 s**	**5,601.5 s**	**4,643.9 s**	**3,338.9 s**	**3,152.2 s**	**2,932.2 s**	**14,337.2 s**
Low income	27,993.9	5,405.8	4,201.8	1,600.9	1,702.6	2,634.3	2,999.3	1,616.8	452.9	1,306.1	831.3	5,242.3
Middle income	33,464.3	8,326.2	5,104.0	4,873.1	3,570.5	1,995.6	552.4	717.5	1,772.4	707.9	697.2	5,147.4
Lower middle income	27,519.4	7,536.3	3,284.8	4,394.4	2,441.9	1,596.7	694.3	530.2	1,500.8	562.6	588.4	4,389.1
Upper middle income	5,182.4	743.4	1,466.8	393.7	1,044.0	398.4	−152.6	170.2	215.8	112.6	103.4	686.7
Low & middle income	84,053.1	18,893.2	11,072.0	7,947.5	6,242.3	5,930.9	5,597.3	4,643.9	3,318.7	3,138.9	2,932.2	14,336.3
East Asia & Pacific	6,548.1	734.8	450.2	604.4	431.6	1,184.3	365.8	136.1	144.4	179.9	172.9	2,143.8
Europe & Central Asia	4,608.9	900.3	1,450.3	436.1	216.8	362.0	86.8	65.8	121.7	51.1	207.3	710.9
Latin America & Carib.	5,805.6	1,398.1	1,042.7	474.0	355.1	225.2	−572.6	268.8	1,181.4	450.2	203.1	779.7
Middle East & N. Africa	14,819.7	4,958.1	1,688.3	2,746.1	1,668.1	917.5	118.2	85.0	386.8	136.8	113.2	2,001.5
South Asia	7,029.5	2,237.2	655.9	544.3	30.0	362.7	1,323.5	256.6	89.4	523.7	103.5	902.9
Sub-Saharan Africa	26,801.6	4,557.6	4,409.5	2,059.4	2,869.0	1,696.8	2,415.5	1,663.0	520.9	1,164.9	995.2	4,449.9
High income	−64.1	8.1	23.5	2.3	16.2	−152.7	4.3	0.0	20.2	13.3	0.0	0.9
Euro area												

Note: Regional aggregates include data for economies not specified elsewhere. World and income group totals include aid not allocated by country or region.

About the data

The table shows net bilateral aid to low- and middle-income economies from members of the Development Assistance Committee (DAC) of the Organisation for Economic Co-operation and Development (OECD). The data include aid to some countries and territories not shown in the table and aid to unspecified economies recorded only at the regional or global level. Aid to countries and territories not shown in the table has been assigned to regional totals based on the World Bank's regional classification system. Aid to unspecified economies is included in regional totals and, when possible, income group totals. Aid not allocated by country or region—including administrative costs, research on development, and aid to nongovernmental organizations—is included in the world total. Thus regional and income group totals do not sum to the world total.

The table is based on donor country reports of bilateral programs, which may differ from reports by recipient countries. Recipients may lack access to information on such aid expenditures as development-oriented research, stipends and tuition costs for aid-financed students in donor countries, and payment of experts hired by donor countries. Moreover, a full accounting would include donor country contributions to multilateral institutions, the flow of resources from multilateral institutions to recipient countries, and flows from countries that are not members of DAC. Previous editions of the table included only DAC member economies. The table also includes net aid from the European Commission—a multilateral member of DAC.

The expenditures that countries report as official development assistance (ODA) have changed. For example, some DAC members have reported as ODA the aid provided to refugees during the first 12 months of their stay within the donor's borders.

Some of the aid recipients shown in the table are also aid donors. See table 6.15a for a summary of ODA from non-DAC countries.

Definitions

• **Net aid** refers to net bilateral official development assistance that meets the DAC definition of official development assistance and is made to countries and territories on the DAC list of aid recipients. See *About the data* for table 6.13 • **Other DAC donors** are Australia, Austria, Belgium, Denmark, Finland, Greece, Ireland, Italy, Luxembourg, New Zealand, Norway, Portugal, and Switzerland.

Most donors increased their proportions of untied aid between 2000 and 2007

6.16a

Proportion of bilateral official development assistance commitment that was untied, 2007 (percent)

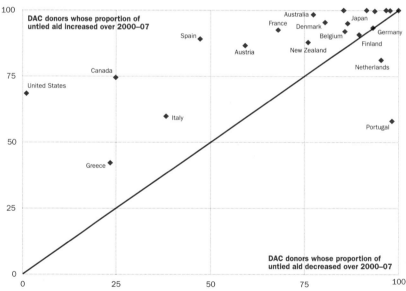

Proportion of bilateral official development assistance commitment that was untied, 2000 (percent)

Six Development Assistance Committee (DAC) donor countries provided nearly 100 percent untied aid in 2007: Sweden, the United Kingdom, Norway, Luxembourg, Ireland, and Switzerland (data points at top right of figure, left to right). Tying aid may prevent recipients from getting the best value for their money. Such arrangements prevent a recipient from misappropriating or mismanaging aid receipts, but they may also be motivated by a desire to benefit donor country suppliers. On average, 85 percent of bilateral commitments by DAC donors in 2007 were untied, up from 81 percent in 2000.

Note: Data for Ireland are for 2001 and 2007 and for New Zealand for 2002 and 2007. The United States did not report amount of untied aid until 2006.
Source: Organisation for Economic Co-operation and Development, Development Assistance Committee.

Data sources

Data on financial flows are compiled by DAC and published in its annual statistical report, *Geographical Distribution of Financial Flows to Aid Recipients,* and its annual *Development Cooperation Report.* Data are available electronically on the OECD-DAC's *International Development Statistics* CD-ROM and at www.oecd.org/dac/stats/idsonline.

	Net migration		International migrant stock		Refugees				Workers' remittances and compensation of employees			
							thousands				$ millions	
	thousands		thousands		By country of origin		By country of asylum		Received		Paid	
	1990–95	2000–05	1995	2005	1995	2007	1995	2007	1995	2007	1995	2007
Afghanistan	3,313	1,112	35	43	2,679.1	3,057.7	19.6	..	..	..	..	..
Albania	−409	−110	71	83	5.8	15.3	4.7	0.1	427	1,071	..	7
Algeria	−50	−140	299	242	1.5	10.6	192.5	94.1	1,120[a]	2,120[a]	..	..
Angola	143	175	38	56	246.7	186.2	10.9	12.1	5	..	210	603
Argentina	50	−100	1,590	1,500	0.3	1.2	10.3	3.3	56	604	190	472
Armenia	−500	−100	455	235	201.4	15.4	219.0	4.6	65	846	17	176
Australia	519	593	4,068	4,097	..	0.1	62.2	22.2	1,651	3,862	700	3,559
Austria	262	180	717	1,234	0.1	0.1	34.4	30.8	1,012	2,945	346	2,985
Azerbaijan	−116	−100	292	182	200.5	15.9	233.7	2.4	3	1,287	9	435
Bangladesh	−260	−500	1,006	1,032	57.0	10.2	51.1	27.6	1,202	6,562	1	3
Belarus	0	0	1,269	1,191	0.1	5.0	29.0	0.6	29	354	12	109
Belgium	85	180	909	719	..	0.1	31.7	17.6	4,937	8,562	3,252	3,192
Benin	105	99	146	175	0.1	0.3	23.8	7.6	100[a]	224[a]	26[a]	67[a]
Bolivia	−100	−100	70	116	0.2	0.4	0.7	0.6	7	927	9	72
Bosnia and Herzegovina	−1,000	115	73	41	769.8	78.3	40.0	7.4	..	2,520	..	65
Botswana	14	20	39	80	..	..	0.3	2.5	59	141	200	120
Brazil	−184	−229	730	641	0.1	1.6	2.1	20.8	3,315	4,382	347	896
Bulgaria	−349	−43	47	104	4.2	3.3	1.3	4.8	42	2,086	34	86
Burkina Faso	−128	100	464	773	0.1	0.6	29.8	0.5	80[a]	50[a]	51[a]	44[a]
Burundi	−250	192	295	100	350.6	375.7	173.0	24.5	..	0	5	0
Cambodia	150	10	116	304	61.2	17.7	..	0.2	12	353	52	157
Cameroon	−5	6	159	137	2.0	11.5	45.8	60.1	11	167	22	103
Canada	643	1,041	5,003	6,106	..	0.5	152.1	175.7	..	..	..	..
Central African Republic	37	−45	67	76	0.2	98.1	33.9	7.5	0	..	27	..
Chad	−10	219	78	437	59.7	55.7	0.1	294.0	1	..	15	..
Chile	90	30	136	231	14.3	1.0	0.3	1.4	..	3[a]	7[a]	6[a]
China	−1,281	−1,900	441	596	104.7	149.1	288.3	301.1	1,053[a]	32,833[a]	19	4,372
Hong Kong, China	300	300	2,432	2,999	0.2	..	1.5	0.1	..	348	..	380
Colombia	−250	−120	108	123	1.9	551.7	0.2	0.2	815	4,523	150	95
Congo, Dem. Rep.	1,208	−237	2,049	539	89.7	370.4	1,433.8	177.4	..	..	..	..
Congo, Rep.	14	−10	169	288	0.2	19.7	19.4	38.5	4	15	27	102
Costa Rica	62	84	228	441	0.2	0.4	24.2	17.2	123	635	36	271
Côte d'Ivoire	214	−339	2,314	2,371	0.2	22.2	297.9	24.6	151	179	457	19
Croatia	153	100	721	661	245.6	100.4	198.7	1.6	544	1,394	17	86
Cuba	−98	−129	90	74	24.9	7.5	1.8	0.6	..	..	..	..
Czech Republic	8	67	454	453	2.0	1.4	2.7	2.0	191	1,332	101	2,625
Denmark	58	46	250	389	..	..	64.8	26.8	523	989	209	2,958
Dominican Republic	−129	−148	118	156	..	0.4	1.0	..	839	3,414	7	28
Ecuador	−50	−400	88	114	0.2	1.3	0.2	264.9	386	3,094	4	83
Egypt, Arab Rep.	−600	−525	172	166	0.9	6.8	5.4	97.6	3,226	7,656	223	180
El Salvador	−90	−143	26	24	23.5	6.0	0.2	..	1,064	3,711	1	29
Eritrea	−359	229	12	15	286.7	208.7	1.1	5.0	..	..	..	..
Estonia	−108	1	309	202	0.4	0.3	..	..	1	426	3	96
Ethiopia	868	−140	795	555	101.0	59.9	393.5	85.2	27	359	1	15
Finland	43	33	103	156	..	..	10.2	6.2	74	772	54	391
France	424	722	6,089	6,471	0.1	0.1	155.3	151.8	4,640	13,746	4,935	4,380
Gabon	20	10	164	245	..	0.1	0.8	8.8	4[a]	11[a]	99[a]	186[a]
Gambia, The	45	31	148	232	0.2	1.3	6.6	14.9	19	47	..	12
Georgia	−560	−248	250	191	0.3	11.8	0.1	1.0	284	696	12	28
Germany	2,688	1,000	9,092	10,144	0.4	0.1	1,267.9	578.9	4,523	8,570	11,270	13,860
Ghana	40	12	1,038	1,669	13.6	5.1	83.2	35.0	17	117	5[a]	6[a]
Greece	470	154	549	974	0.2	0.1	4.4	2.2	3,286	2,484	300	1,460
Guatemala	−360	−300	45	53	42.9	6.2	1.5	0.4	358	4,254	8	18
Guinea	350	−425	870	406	0.4	8.3	672.3	25.2	1	151	10	119
Guinea-Bissau	20	1	32	19	0.8	1.0	15.4	7.9	2[a]	29[a]	3[a]	5[a]
Haiti	−133	−140	22	30	13.9	22.3	..	..	109	1,222	..	96

	Net migration		International migrant stock		Refugees				Workers' remittances and compensation of employees			
							thousands			$ millions		
	thousands		thousands		By country of origin		By country of asylum		Received		Paid	
	1990–95	2000–05	1995	2005	1995	2007	1995	2007	1995	2007	1995	2007
Honduras	–120	–150	31	26	1.2	1.2	0.1	..	124	2,625	8	2
Hungary	101	65	293	316	2.3	3.4	11.4	8.1	152	413	146	235
India	–960	–1,350	6,951	5,700	5.0	20.5	227.5	161.5	6,223[a]	35,262[a]	419[a]	1,580[a]
Indonesia	–725	–1,000	219	160	9.8	20.6	0.1	0.3	651	6,174	..	1,654
Iran, Islamic Rep.	–1,587	–1,250	2,478	1,959	112.4	68.4	2,072.0	963.5	1,600[a]	1,115[a]	..	..
Iraq	170	–375	134	28	718.7	2,309.2	116.7	42.4	..	389	..	781[a]
Ireland	–1	188	264	585	..	..	0.4	9.3	347	580	173	2,554
Israel	484	115	1,919	2,661	0.9	1.5	..	1.2	702	1,041	1,408	2,770
Italy	573	1,125	1,483	2,519	0.1	0.1	74.3	38.1	2,364	3,165	1,824	11,287
Jamaica	–100	–100	20	18	..	0.8	..	..	653	2,144	74	454
Japan	248	270	1,261	2,048	..	0.5	5.4	1.8	1,151	1,577	1,820	4,037
Jordan	509	130	1,618	2,225	0.5	1.8	1,288.9[b]	2,403.8[b]	1,441	3,434	107	479
Kazakhstan	–1,509	–200	3,295	2,502	0.1	5.2	15.6	4.3	116	223	503	4,303
Kenya	222	25	366	345	9.3	7.5	234.7	265.7	298[a]	1,588[a]	4	16
Korea, Dem. Rep.	0	0	35	37	..	0.6	..	..	..	..	..	..
Korea, Rep.	–115	–80	584	551	..	1.2	..	0.1	1,080	1,128	634	4,070
Kuwait	–598	264	996	1,669	0.8	0.7	3.3	38.2	..	..	1,354	3,824
Kyrgyz Republic	–273	–75	482	288	17.1	2.3	13.4	0.7	1	715	41	220
Lao PDR	–30	–115	23	25	58.2	10.0	..	..	22[a]	1[a]	9[a]	1[a]
Latvia	–134	–20	713	449	0.2	0.7	..	..	41	552	1	45
Lebanon	230	0	594	657	13.5	13.1	348.1[b]	464.3[b]	1,225	5,769	..	2,845
Lesotho	–84	–36	5	6	..	..	..	..	411	443	75	21
Liberia	–283	–119	199	50	744.6	91.5	120.1	10.5	..	65	..	0
Libya	10	10	506	618	0.6	2.0	4.0	4.1	..	16[a]	222[a]	945[a]
Lithuania	–99	–30	272	165	0.1	0.5	..	0.7	1	1,427	1	566
Macedonia, FYR	–27	–10	114	121	12.9	8.1	9.1	1.2	68[a]	267[a]	1[a]	18[a]
Madagascar	–7	–5	60	63	0.1	0.3	..	..	14[a]	11[a]	11[a]	21[a]
Malawi	–920	–30	325	279	..	0.1	1.0	2.9	1[a]	1[a]	1[a]	1[a]
Malaysia	287	150	1,135	1,639	0.1	0.6	5.3	32.7	716[a]	1,803[a]	1,329	6,385
Mali	–260	–134	63	46	77.2	4.5	17.9	9.2	112[a]	212[a]	42[a]	57[a]
Mauritania	–15	30	118	66	84.3	33.1	34.4	30.5	5[a]	2[a]	14	..
Mauritius	–7	0	12	21	..	0.1	..	..	132[a]	215[a]	1	12
Mexico	–1,792	–3,983	467	644	0.4	5.6	38.7	1.6	4,368[a]	27,144[a]	..	..
Moldova	–121	–250	473	440	0.5	4.9	..	0.2	1	1,498	1	87
Mongolia	–59	–50	7	9	..	1.1	..	..	..	194[a]	..	77[a]
Morocco	–450	–550	103	132	0.3	4.0	0.1	0.8	1,970	6,730	20	52
Mozambique	650	–20	246	406	125.6	0.2	0.1	2.8	59	99	21	45
Myanmar	–126	–99	112	117	152.3	191.3	..	..	81[a]	125[a]	..	32[a]
Namibia	3	–1	124	143	..	1.1	1.7	6.5	16	16	11	16
Nepal	–101	–100	625	819	0.1	3.4	124.8	130.7	57	1,734	9	4
Netherlands	190	110	1,387	1,638	0.1	0.2	80.0	86.6	1,359	2,548	2,802	7,830
New Zealand	94	102	732	642	..	..	3.8	2.7	1,858	650	584	1,207
Nicaragua	–115	–210	27	28	23.9	1.9	0.6	0.2	75	740	..	..
Niger	–3	–28	139	124	10.3	0.8	27.6	0.3	8	78	29[a]	29[a]
Nigeria	–96	–170	582	971	1.9	13.9	8.1	8.5	804[a]	9,221[a]	5	103
Norway	42	84	231	344	..	..	47.6	34.5	239	613	603	3,642
Oman	23	–150	573	628	..	..	..	..	39	39	1,537	3,670
Pakistan	–2,611	–1,239	4,077	3,254	5.3	31.9	1,202.5	2,035.0	1,712	5,998	4[a]	3[a]
Panama	8	8	73	102	0.2	0.1	0.9	16.9	112	180	20	151
Papua New Guinea	0	0	32	25	2.0	..	9.6	10.0	16[a]	13[a]	16[a]	135[a]
Paraguay	–30	–45	183	168	0.1	0.1	0.1	0.1	287	469	..	..
Peru	–441	–510	51	42	5.9	7.7	0.6	1.0	599	2,131	34	137
Philippines	–900	–900	214	374	0.5	1.6	0.8	0.1	5,360	16,291	151	35
Poland	–77	–200	963	703	19.7	2.9	0.6	9.8	724	10,496	262	1,278
Portugal	–7	276	528	764	0.2	0.1	0.3	0.4	3,953	3,945	527	1,311
Puerto Rico	–4	–10	351	418	..	..	..	..	..	..	..	..

	Net migration thousands		International migrant stock thousands		Refugees thousands By country of origin		By country of asylum		Workers' remittances and compensation of employees $ millions Received		Paid	
	1990–95	2000–05	1995	2005	1995	2007	1995	2007	1995	2007	1995	2007
Romania	−529	−270	135	133	17.0	5.3	0.2	1.8	9	8,533	2	351
Russian Federation	2,263	917	11,707	12,080	207.0	92.9	246.7	1.7	2,503	4,100	3,939	17,716
Rwanda	−1,714	43	60	121	1,819.4	81.0	7.8	53.6	21	51	1	68
Saudi Arabia	−500	285	4,611	6,361	0.3	0.8	13.2	240.7	..	..	16,594	16,068
Senegal	−100	−100	320	326	17.6	15.9	66.8	20.4	146[a]	925[a]	76[a]	96[a]
Serbia	451	−339	760[c]	512[c]	86.1[c]	165.6	650.7[c]	98.0	105[a,c]	4,910[a,c]	..	..
Sierra Leone	−380	472	55	119	379.5	32.1	4.7	8.8	24	148	..	136
Singapore	250	200	992	1,843	..	0.1	0.1	..	..	..	..	..
Slovak Republic	9	3	114	124	0.1	0.3	2.3	0.3	1	1,483	3	73
Slovenia	38	22	200	167	12.9	0.1	22.3	0.3	272	284	31	207
Somalia	−1,193	100	18	282	638.7	457.4	0.6	0.9	..	..	..	..
South Africa	1,125	75	1,098	1,106	0.5	0.5	101.4	36.7	26	834	629	1,186
Spain	292	2,846	1,009	4,790	0.2	2.4	5.9	5.1	3,235	10,687	868	14,728
Sri Lanka	−256	−442	428	368	107.6	135.0	..	0.2	809	2,527	16	314
Sudan	−168	−532	1,111	639	445.3	523.0	674.1	222.7	346	1,769	1	2
Swaziland	−38	−6	38	45	..	..	0.7	0.8	83	100	4	8
Sweden	151	152	906	1,117	..	0.1	199.2	75.1	288	775	336	1,142
Switzerland	200	100	1,471	1,660	0.1	..	82.9	45.7	1,473	2,035	10,114	16,273
Syrian Arab Republic	−70	200	801	985	8.0	13.7	373.5[b]	1,955.3[b]	339[a]	824[a]	15[a]	235[a]
Tajikistan	−313	−345	305	306	59.0	0.9	0.6	1.1	..	1,691	..	184
Tanzania	591	−345	1,130	792	0.1	1.3	829.7	435.6	1	14	1	46
Thailand	172	231	568	1,050	0.2	2.3	106.6	125.6	1,695	1,635	..	..
Timor-Leste	0	100	6	6	..	0.3	..	..	..	..	..	..
Togo	−122	−4	169	183	93.2	22.5	10.9	1.3	15[a]	229[a]	5[a]	35[a]
Trinidad and Tobago	−24	−20	46	38	..	0.2	..	..	32[a]	92[a]	14	..
Tunisia	−22	−29	38	38	0.3	2.5	0.2	0.1	680	1,716	36	15
Turkey	109	−30	1,210	1,328	44.9	221.9	12.8	7.0	3,327	1,209	..	106
Turkmenistan	50	−10	260	224	2.9	0.7	23.3	0.1	4	..	7	..
Uganda	120	−5	610	518	24.2	21.3	229.4	229.0	..	849	..	364
Ukraine	100	−173	7,063	6,833	1.7	26.0	5.2	7.3	6	4,503	1	42
United Arab Emirates	340	577	1,716	3,212	..	0.3	0.4	0.2	..	..	..	..
United Kingdom	167	948	4,198	5,408	0.1	0.2	90.9	299.7	2,469	8,234	2,581	5,048
United States	5,200	6,493	28,522	38,355	0.2	2.2	623.3	281.2	2,179	2,972	22,181	45,643
Uruguay	−20	−104	93	84	0.3	0.2	0.1	0.1	..	97	..	4
Uzbekistan	−340	−300	1,474	1,268	0.1	5.7	2.6	1.1	..	..	..	..
Venezuela, RB	40	40	1,019	1,010	0.5	5.1	1.6	200.9	2	136	203	598
Vietnam	−256	−200	27	21	543.5	327.8	34.4	2.4	..	5,500[a]	..	..
West Bank and Gaza	1	11	1,201	1,680	72.8	341.2	1,201.0[b]	1,793.9[b]	626[a]	598[a]	..	16[a]
Yemen, Rep.	650	−100	228	265	0.4	1.6	53.5	117.4	1,080[a]	1,283[a]	61[a]	120[a]
Zambia	−11	−82	271	275	0.1	0.2	130.0	112.9	..	59	59	124
Zimbabwe	−192	−75	638	511	..	14.4	0.5	4.0	44	..	7	..
World	..[d] s	..[d] s	164,017 s	189,693 s	18,068.7[b,e] s	15,953.5[b,e] s	18,068.7[b,f] s	15,953.5[b,f] s	101,562 s	371,263 s	98,648 s	248,066 s
Low income	−1,910	−2,858	22,337	20,756	8,561.3	5,688.8	6,402.8	4,232.4	6,207	39,940	922	2,388
Middle income	−10,752	−15,770	55,625	54,857	3,935.3	5,342.5	8,611.2	9,530.4	51,121	241,233	9,763	51,507
Lower middle income	−10,710	−11,295	27,196	26,298	3,253.1	4,695.1	7,153.7	8,579.4	32,898	161,264	1,643	12,172
Upper middle income	−42	−4,475	28,429	28,559	682.2	647.4	1,457.6	951.1	18,223	79,970	8,120	39,335
Low & middle income	−12,662	−18,629	77,963	75,613	12,496.6	11,031.3	15,014.0	13,762.8	57,328	281,174	10,685	53,895
East Asia & Pacific	−2,828	−3,847	2,996	4,427	932.7	724.5	447.0	472.4	9,701	65,340	1,618	12,909
Europe & Central Asia	−3,216	−1,798	31,643	29,529	1,877.0	789.6	1,420.6	166.0	7,855	50,377	4,771	25,908
Latin America & Carib.	−3,847	−6,811	5,280	5,713	155.8	624.7	94.0	530.6	13,335	63,107	1,114	3,582
Middle East & N. Africa	−1,224	−2,618	8,207	9,014	948.0	2,775.5	5,683.1	7,943.9	13,319	31,678	702	5,673
South Asia	−976	−2,484	13,133	11,229	2,958.8	3,369.3	1,625.5	2,355.0	10,005	52,086	475	2,007
Sub-Saharan Africa	−572	−1,070	16,704	15,701	5,624.3	2,747.7	5,743.8	2,294.9	3,113	18,586	2,005	3,816
High income	12,645	18,522	86,054	114,080	21.3	14.9	3,055.6	2,190.8	44,234	90,089	87,963	194,171
Euro area	5,099	6,887	22,528	30,461	13.7	0.6	1,688.3	934.2	30,072	61,551	26,446	73,962

a. World Bank estimates. b. Includes Palestinian refugees under the mandate of the United Nations Relief and Works Agency for Palestine Refugees in the Near East, who are not included in data from the UN Refugee Agency (UNHCR). c. Includes Montenegro. d. World totals computed by the United Nations sum to zero, but because the aggregates refer to World Bank definitions, regional and income group totals do not. e. Includes refugees without specified country of origin. f. Regional and income group totals do not sum to the world total because of rounding.

About the data

Movement of people, most often through migration, is a significant part of global integration. Migrants contribute to the economies of both their host country and their country of origin. Yet reliable statistics on migration are difficult to collect and are often incomplete, making international comparisons a challenge.

The United Nations Population Division provides data on net migration and migrant stock. To derive estimates of net migration, the organization takes into account the past migration history of a country or area, the migration policy of a country, and the influx of refugees in recent periods. The data to calculate these official estimates come from a variety of sources, including border statistics, administrative records, surveys, and censuses. When no official estimates can be made because of insufficient data, net migration is derived through the balance equation, which is the difference between overall population growth and the natural increase during the 1990–2000 intercensal period.

The data used to estimate the international migrant stock at a particular time are obtained mainly from population censuses. The estimates are derived from the data on foreign-born population—people who have residence in one country but were born in another country. When data on the foreign-born population are not available, data on foreign population—that is, people who are citizens of a country other than the country in which they reside—are used as estimates.

After the breakup of the Soviet Union in 1991 people living in one of the newly independent countries who were born in another were classified as international migrants. Estimates of migrant stock in the newly independent states from 1990 on are based on the 1989 census of the Soviet Union.

For countries with information on the international migrant stock for at least two points in time, interpolation or extrapolation was used to estimate the international migrant stock on July 1 of the reference years. For countries with only one observation, estimates for the reference years were derived using rates of change in the migrant stock in the years preceding or following the single observation available. A model was used to estimate migrants for countries that had no data.

Registrations, together with other sources—including estimates and surveys—are the main sources of refugee data. But there are difficulties in collecting accurate statistics. Although refugees are often registered individually, the accuracy of registrations varies greatly. Many refugees may not be aware of the need to register or may choose not to do so. And administrative records tend to overestimate the number of refugees because it is easier to register than to de-register. The UN Refugee Agency (UNHCR) collects and maintains data on refugees, except for Palestinian refugees residing in areas under the mandate of the United Nations Relief and Works Agency for Palestine Refugees in the Near East (UNRWA). The UNRWA provides services to Palestinian refugees who live in certain areas and who register with the agency. Registration is voluntary, and estimates by the UNRWA are not an accurate count of the Palestinian refugee population. The table shows estimates of refugees collected by the UNHCR, complemented by estimates of Palestinian refugees under the UNRWA mandate. Thus, the aggregates differ from those published by the UNHCR.

Workers' remittances and compensation of employees are World Bank staff estimates based on data from the International Monetary Fund's (IMF) *Balance of Payments Statistics Yearbook*. The IMF data are supplemented by World Bank staff estimates for missing data for countries where workers' remittances are important. The data reported here are the sum of three items defined in the fifth edition of the IMF's *Balance of Payments Manual*: workers' remittances, compensation of employees, and migrants' transfers.

The distinction among these three items is not always consistent in the data reported by countries to the IMF. In some cases countries compile data on the basis of the citizenship of migrant workers rather than their residency status. Some countries also report remittances entirely as workers' remittances or compensation of employees. Following the fifth edition of the *Balance of Payments Manual* in 1993, migrants' transfers are considered a capital transaction, but previous editions regarded them as current transfers. For these reasons the figures presented in the table take all three items into account.

Definitions

• **Net migration** is the net total of migrants during the period. It is the total number of immigrants less the total number of emigrants, including both citizens and noncitizens. Data are five-year estimates. • **International migrant stock** is the number of people born in a country other than that in which they live. It includes refugees. • **Refugees** are people who are recognized as refugees under the 1951 Convention Relating to the Status of Refugees or its 1967 Protocol, the 1969 Organization of African Unity Convention Governing the Specific Aspects of Refugee Problems in Africa, people recognized as refugees in accordance with the UNHCR statute, people granted refugee-like humanitarian status, and people provided temporary protection. Asylum seekers are people who have applied for asylum or refugee status and who have not yet received a decision or who are registered as asylum seekers. Palestinian refugees are people (and their descendants) whose residence was Palestine between June 1946 and May 1948 and who lost their homes and means of livelihood as a result of the 1948 Arab-Israeli conflict. • **Country of origin** refers to the nationality or country of citizenship of a claimant. • **Country of asylum** is the country where an asylum claim was filed. • **Workers' remittances and compensation of employees** received and paid comprise current transfers by migrant workers and wages and salaries earned by nonresident workers. Remittances are classified as current private transfers from migrant workers resident in the host country for more than a year, irrespective of their immigration status, to recipients in their country of origin. Migrants' transfers are defined as the net worth of migrants who are expected to remain in the host country for more than one year that is transferred to another country at the time of migration. Compensation of employees is the income of migrants who have lived in the host country for less than a year.

Data sources

Data on net migration are from the United Nations Population Division's *World Population Prospects: The 2006 Revision*. Data on migration stock are from the United Nations Population Division's *Trends in Total Migrant Stock: The 2005 Revision*. Data on refugees are from the UNHCR's *Statistical Yearbook 2007*, complemented by statistics on Palestinian refugees under the mandate of the UNRWA as published on its website. Data on remittances are World Bank staff estimates based on IMF balance of payments data.

6.18 Characteristics of immigrants in selected OECD countries

Foreign-born population by country of origin — 6.18a

Country of residence	Country of birth	% of foreign-born population	Country of residence	Country of birth	% of foreign-born population	Country of residence	Country of birth	% of foreign-born population
Australia	United Kingdom	26.1	Germany	Former USSR	17.5	Norway	Sweden	9.6
	New Zealand	8.2		Turkey	15.2		Former Yugoslavia	7.5
	Italy	5.6		Poland	13.1		Denmark	7.1
Austria	Former Yugoslavia	34.5	Greece	Albania	33.7	Portugal	Angola	28.4
	Germany	14.1		Former USSR	18.5		France	14.0
	Turkey	12.2		Germany	9.1		Mozambique	12.9
Belgium	France	13.9	Hungary	Romania	49.5	Slovak Republic	Czech Republic	63.2
	Italy	12.7		Slovak Republic	13.5		Hungary	15.2
	Morocco	11.2		Former Yugoslavia	11.2		Former USSR	8.1
Canada	United Kingdom	11.4	Ireland	United Kingdom	62.3	Spain	Morocco	14.5
	China	5.9		United States	4.4		Ecuador	9.9
	Italy	5.9		Former USSR	2.9		France	7.8
Czech Republic	Slovak Republic	63.8	Italy	Switzerland	8.9	Sweden	Finland	18.4
	Former USSR	11.2		Former Yugoslavia	8.7		Former Yugoslavia	13.1
	Poland	5.6		Germany	8.3		Iraq	5.7
Denmark	Turkey	9.1	Japan[a]	Korea[b]	40.9	Switzerland	Former Yugoslavia	16.1
	Former Yugoslavia	8.5		China	19.9		Italy	15.9
	Germany	7.8		Brazil	13.8		Germany	12.1
Finland	Former USSR	33.6	Netherlands	Indonesia	12.5	United Kingdom	Ireland	11.7
	Sweden	21.9		Turkey	11.2		India	10.1
	Former Yugoslavia	3.5		Morocco	9.3		Pakistan	6.7
France	Algeria	21.6	New Zealand	United Kingdom	33.3	United States	Mexico	26.3
	Morocco	12.3		Samoa	6.9		Philippines	4.3
	Portugal	10.1		Australia	6.7		Puerto Rico	4.1

a. Refers to individuals living in Japan not of Japanese nationality because data based on the country of birth are not available. b. Democratic People's Republic of Korea and Republic of Korea combined.

Foreign-born population by gender, educational attainment, occupation, and sector of employment — 6.18b

	Gender		Educational attainment			Occupation[a]			Sector of employment			
	% of the foreign-born population ages 15 and older		% of the foreign-born population ages 15 and older			% of the employed foreign-born population ages 15 and older			% of the employed foreign-born population ages 15 and older			
	Male	Female	Primary	Secondary	Tertiary	Professionals	Technicians	Operators	Agriculture and industry	Distributive services	Personal and social services	Producer services
Australia	49.4	50.6	41.3	32.8	25.8	31.2	24.2	44.7	26.6	24.6	31.1	17.7
Austria	47.9	52.1	49.4	39.3	11.3	13.3	19.7	67.1	32.9	21.4	31.9	13.8
Belgium	48.1	51.9	53.3	23.8	23.0	31.6	22.0	46.4	28.7	21.2	37.0	13.1
Canada	48.1	51.9	30.1	31.9	38.0	28.8	26.0	45.2	26.9	21.9	32.0	19.3
Czech Republic	45.5	54.5	38.6	48.7	12.8	18.6	21.4	60.0	44.2	20.8	27.4	7.6
Denmark	48.6	51.4	36.9	39.2	23.9	16.9	23.3	59.8	22.9	21.1	38.4	17.6
Finland	49.6	50.4	52.6	28.5	18.9	21.6	20.2	58.1	27.3	19.5	36.3	16.8
France	49.5	50.5	54.8	27.2	18.1	22.1	22.4	55.5	28.3[b]	30.5[b]	36.9[b]	4.3[b]
Germany	50.3	49.7	45.8	39.3	14.9	10.2	20.5	69.3	..	..	..	..
Greece	50.1	49.9	42.7	41.4	15.9	11.2	9.0	79.9	49.7	15.4	28.8	6.1
Hungary	44.1	55.9	41.1	39.1	19.8	31.8	20.1	48.1	33.3	24.5	31.8	10.3
Ireland	49.6	50.4	29.6	29.3	41.1	38.1	19.9	42.0	28.0	17.9	36.0	18.1
Italy	45.6	54.4	54.3	33.5	12.2	17.5	19.9	62.6	45.2	15.5	33.3	6.1
Japan	46.8	53.2	25.9	44.2	30.0	15.6[c]	8.5[c]	75.9[c]	..	..	..	..
Netherlands	48.6	51.4	49.2	31.6	19.2	25.3	27.6	47.1	26.2	19.7	35.6	18.5
New Zealand	48.1	51.9	18.7	50.4	31.0	33.4	25.3	41.3	25.2	23.6	34.2	17.0
Norway	48.9	51.1	18.3	51.2	30.5	20.9	26.0	53.1	18.8	19.2	47.8	14.2
Portugal	49.1	50.9	54.7	25.9	19.3	21.3	24.8	53.9	33.1	19.2	36.4	11.3
Slovak Republic	43.7	56.3	29.3	55.0	15.7	23.8	26.1	50.0	37.4	19.6	34.8	8.2
Spain	50.3	49.7	56.3	22.6	21.1	15.5	14.0	70.5	37.6	17.8	35.9	8.6
Sweden	48.6	51.4	29.5	46.2	24.3	19.0	21.2	59.8	25.0	17.5	43.2	14.3
Switzerland	47.8	52.2	41.6	34.7	23.7	23.1	27.2	49.8	33.0	19.6	32.3	15.1
United Kingdom	46.7	53.3	40.6	24.5	34.8	34.2	26.0	39.8	16.7	22.2	40.2	20.9
United States	49.6	50.4	39.2	34.7	26.1	28.9[c]	11.2[c]	59.9[c]	26.9	18.0	43.8	11.2

a. Excludes armed forces (International Standard Classification of Occupations, ISCO-88, group 0). b. Does not refer to International Standard Industrial Classification revision 3 classifications. c. Does not refer to ISCO-88 classifications.

6.18

GLOBAL LINKS

International migration has become an important element of global integration over the last 20 years. Many countries have adopted policies that encourage the entrance of foreign labor. At the same time remittances—transfers of gifts, wages, and salaries earned by migrants working abroad—have fueled private financing in developing countries. And demographic trends in developing and high-income economies are likely to influence future migration patterns. Despite the importance of international migration, the quality and comparability of data remain limited, in part because of differing national definitions of who is an immigrant. Many countries define immigrants as people with foreign nationality, but others focus on birthplace, considering all those born abroad as immigrants. The lack of comparable data hinders the design and implementation of sound migration policies by both receiving and sending countries. Systematic recording of immigration stock is difficult, especially for poor countries and countries affected by civil disorder and natural disasters.

The table presents the main characteristics of immigrants in selected Organisation for Economic Co-operation and Development (OECD) countries, using data from the Database on Immigrants in OECD Countries, the OECD's effort, in cooperation with national statistical offices, to compile internationally comparable data on foreign-born populations in OECD countries. The database provides comprehensive information on many demographic and labor market characteristics of OECD immigrants. Its main sources of data are population censuses (for 22 countries), population registers (for Denmark, Finland, Norway, and Sweden), and labor force surveys (Germany and the Netherlands). The database includes information on demographic characteristics (age and gender), duration of stay, labor market outcomes (employment status, occupations, sectors of activity), fields of study, educational attainment, and place of birth. The database provides comparable data on foreign-born population for around 2000; time series data are not available. Other national sources that contain time series data use different definitions of immigrant, making comparability across countries difficult.

Although the database includes data on all OECD countries except Iceland and the Republic of Korea, the table presents selected data only for high-income OECD countries with populations of more than 1 million. More data are available from the original source. Though OECD countries are believed to receive the largest number of migrant workers, Gulf countries

and Southern African countries also have a significant share of migrant workers in their labor force.

Census and population register data generally are the most relevant sources for small population groups, but the data are subject to two limitations. First, to ensure international comparability, immigrants are identified as people whose place of birth differs from their current country of residence. Thus, nationals born abroad may be included in the immigrant population. This could be an issue for countries with large repatriated communities (such as France and Portugal) or with large expatriate communities (such as Germany and the United Kingdom). Second, coverage of undocumented migrants, short-term migrants, and asylum seekers may be incomplete.

Table 6.18a presents the top three countries of birth along with their share of the foreign-born population in the reporting country. Because censuses of different countries apply different rules when addressing countries that split, recomposed, or are newly constituted, the coding from the national data collection were maintained. For some countries people born in the Democratic People's Republic of Korea or the Republic of Korea could not be distinguished. In many OECD country censuses countries of the former Union of Soviet Socialist Republics (USSR) are grouped under the name "former USSR." The same applies to the countries of the former Yugoslavia.

Table 6.18b presents the main characteristics of the foreign-born population by gender, educational attainment, occupation, and sector of employment. The database tries to harmonize the classification of variables that are not systematically collected according to international classifications. For example, occupations based on national classifications were mapped to International Standard Classification of Occupations (ISCO-88) classifications, generally with help from national statistical offices. Details of the mapping are in OECD's *A Profile of Immigrant Populations in the 21st Century: Data from OECD Countries* (2008).

Because the database does not provide mapping for Japan and the United States, their data were mapped for the table. For Japan *professionals* refer to managers and officials and professional and technical workers; *technicians* refer to clerical and related workers; *operators* refer to agricultural, forestry, and fisheries workers; production process workers and laborers; protective service workers; sales workers; service workers; and workers in transport and communications. For the United States *professionals* refer to management occupations; business and financial operations occupations; computer and mathematical

science occupations; architecture and engineering occupations; life, physical, and social science occupations; community and social services occupations; legal occupations; education, training, and library occupations; arts, design, entertainment, sports, and media occupations; and healthcare practitioner and technical occupations; *technicians* refer to office and administrative support occupations; *operators* refer to healthcare support occupations; protective service occupations; food preparation and servicing occupations; building and grounds cleaning and maintenance occupations; personal care and service occupations; sales and related occupations; farming, fishing, and forestry occupations; construction and extraction occupations; installation, maintenance, and repair occupations; production occupations; and transportation and material moving occupations.

• **Foreign-born population** is the population ages 15 and older who were born in a country other than the country of residence when the census data were collected. • **Primary education** refers to International Standard Classification of Education 1997 (ISCED) levels 0–2. • **Secondary education** refers to ISCED levels 3–4. • **Tertiary education** refers to ISCED 5–6. • **Professionals** refer to ISCO major groups 1 and 2. • **Technicians** refer to ISCO major groups 3 and 4. • **Operators** refer to ISCO major groups 5–9. • **Agriculture and industry** refer to International Standard Industrial Classification revision 3 (ISIC) major groups A–F. • **Producer services** refer to ISIC major groups J and K. • **Distributive services** refer to ISIC major groups G and I. • **Personal and social services** refer to ISIC major groups H and L–Q.

Data on characteristics of migrants in OECD countries are from OECD's Database on Immigrants in OECD Countries. The methodology of data collection and compilation and the summary report can be found in OECD's *A Profile of Immigrant Populations in the 21st Century: Data from OECD Countries* (2008).

	International tourists				Inbound tourism expenditure				Outbound tourism expenditure			
	thousands				$ millions		% of exports		$ millions		% of imports	
	Inbound		Outbound									
	1995	2007	1995	2007	1995	2007	1995	2007	1995	2007	1995	2007
Afghanistan	..	..	..	..	..	..	..	..	1	..	..	..
Albania	41[a]	57[a]	12	2,979	70	1,055	23.2	47.9	19	940	2.3	21.9
Algeria	520[b,c]	1,743[b,c]	1,090	1,499	32[d]	219[d]	..	..	186[d]	377[d]	..	..
Angola	9	195	3	..	27	236	0.7	0.5	113	473	3.2	1.8
Argentina	2,289	4,562	3,815	4,167	2,550	4,984	10.2	7.5	4,013	5,071	15.4	9.5
Armenia	12	381	..	329	14	343	4.7	19.3	12	345	1.7	9.6
Australia	3,825[e]	5,064[e]	2,519	5,462	11,915	29,065	17.1	15.9	7,260	19,844	9.7	9.9
Austria	17,173[f]	20,766[f]	3,713	9,876	14,529	21,292	16.2	9.8	11,686	12,839	12.7	6.4
Azerbaijan	..	1,010	432	1,631	87	317	11.1	1.4	165	381	12.8	4.0
Bangladesh	156	289	830	2,327	25[g]	76[g]	0.6[g]	0.5[g]	234[g]	514	3.1[g]	2.6
Belarus	161	105	626	517	28	479	0.5	1.7	101	724	1.8	2.4
Belgium	5,560[f]	7,045[f]	5,645	8,371	4,548[g]	12,176	2.4[g]	3.0	8,115[g]	19,095	4.5[g]	4.8
Benin	138	186	..	..	85[g]	124	13.8[g]	12.8	48	75	5.4	5.1
Bolivia	284	556	249	476	92	294	7.5	5.9	72	325	4.6	8.0
Bosnia and Herzegovina	115[f]	306[f]	..	..	257	798	22.9	14.2	97	232	2.4	2.2
Botswana	521	1,675	..	..	176	549	7.3	9.0	153	281	7.5	6.4
Brazil	1,991	5,026	2,600	5,141	1,085	5,284	2.1	2.9	3,982	10,434	6.3	6.6
Bulgaria	3,466	5,151	3,524	4,515	662	3,975	9.8	16.0	312	2,597	4.8	7.8
Burkina Faso	124[h]	289[h]	..	..	..	55	..	..	..	84	..	..
Burundi	34[c]	201[c]	36	..	2	2	1.9	2.7	25[g]	106	9.7[g]	24.4
Cambodia	..	1,873	31	996	71	1,284	7.3	22.8	22	194	1.6	3.1
Cameroon	100[h]	185[h]	..	..	75	221	3.7	4.5	140	476	8.7	8.6
Canada	16,932	17,931	18,206	25,163	9,176	17,985	4.2	3.6	12,658	31,365	6.3	6.7
Central African Republic	26[e]	14[e]	..	11	4[d]	4	..	..	43[d]	32[d]	..	..
Chad	19[h]	25[h]	..	..	43[d]	..	..	..	38[d]	..	..	..
Chile	1,540	2,507	1,070	3,234	1,186	2,172	6.1	2.8	934	2,140	5.1	4.0
China	20,034	54,720	4,520	40,954	8,730[g]	41,126	5.9[g]	3.1	3,688[g]	33,264	2.7[g]	3.2
Hong Kong, China	7,137	17,154	3,023	80,682	9,604[g]	18,015[d]	3.5[g]	4.2[d]	10,497[d,g]	15,086[d,g]	6.5[d,g]	3.7[d,g]
Colombia	1,433[b]	1,195[b]	1,057	1,767	887	2,262	7.2	6.6	1,162	2,093	7.3	5.6
Congo, Dem. Rep.	35	47[e]	50	..	..	..	..	..	..	..	..	..
Congo, Rep.	37[h]	..	..	..	15	54[g]	1.1	0.9[g]	69	168[g]	5.1	2.6[g]
Costa Rica	785	1,980	273	577	763	2,224	17.1	17.2	336	731	7.1	5.2
Côte d'Ivoire	188	..	..	..	103	104[g]	2.4	1.1[g]	312	396[g]	8.2	4.7[g]
Croatia	1,485[f]	9,307[f]	..	..	1,349[g]	9,576	19.3[g]	38.1	422[g]	1,025	4.6[g]	3.5
Cuba	742[e]	2,119[e]	72	194	1,100[d]	2,415[d]	..	..	..	..	..	..
Czech Republic	3,381[f]	6,680[f]	..	..	2,880[g]	7,496	10.2[g]	5.4	1,635[g]	3,771	5.4[g]	2.9
Denmark	2,124[f]	4,716[f]	5,035	6,142	3,691[g]	5,587[g]	5.6[g]	3.9[g]	4,288[g]	7,428[g]	7.4[g]	5.6[g]
Dominican Republic	1,776[c,e]	3,980[c,e]	168	443	1,571[g]	4,026[g]	27.4[g]	33.6[g]	267	517	4.4	3.4
Ecuador	440[b,i]	937[b,i]	271	801	315	626	6.1	3.9	331	733	5.8	4.7
Egypt, Arab Rep.	2,871	10,610	2,683	4,531	2,954	10,327	22.3	23.3	1,371	2,886	8.0	5.4
El Salvador	235	1,339	348	1,012	152	1,158	7.5	21.0	99	690	2.7	7.0
Eritrea	315[b,c]	78[b,c]	..	..	58[d]	60[d]	43.1[d]	..	..	..	..	..
Estonia	530	1,900	1,764	..	452	1,415	17.6	9.1	121	804	4.2	4.5
Ethiopia	103[e]	303[c]	120	..	177	792	23.1	29.8	30	107[g]	2.1	1.5[g]
Finland	2,644	3,519	5,147	5,749	2,383	3,890	5.0	3.5	2,853	4,632	7.6	4.6
France	60,033	81,940	18,686	22,467	31,295	63,609	8.6	9.2	20,699	44,544	6.2	6.1
Gabon	125[e]	..	203	..	94	13	3.2	0.2	182	346	10.6	14.4
Gambia, The	45	143	..	387	28[g]	77	15.8[g]	33.1	16	7[g]	6.9	2.2[g]
Georgia	85[b]	1,052[b]	228	..	75	441	13.1	13.9	171	277	12.1	4.7
Germany	14,847[f]	24,421[f]	55,800	70,400	24,052	46,860	4.0	3.8	66,527	93,515	11.3	7.0
Ghana	286[c]	497[c]	..	..	30	990	1.9	16.5	74	816	3.5	8.1
Greece	10,130	17,518	..	..	4,182	15,687	26.9	23.4	1,495	3,430	6.0	3.4
Guatemala	563[b]	1,628[b]	333	1,168	216	1,055[g]	7.7	12.1[g]	167	736	4.5	5.1
Guinea	12[e]	46[e]	..	..	1	1	0.1	0.1	29	96	2.9	6.3
Guinea-Bissau	..	30[e]	..	..	3	3	5.3	2.6	6	16[g]	6.7	17.3[g]
Haiti	145	112	..	..	90[g]	140[g]	46.8[g]	19.2[g]	35[g]	332	4.4[g]	14.3

	International tourists				Inbound tourism expenditure				Outbound tourism expenditure			
	thousands				$ millions		% of exports		$ millions		% of imports	
	Inbound		Outbound									
	1995	2007	1995	2007	1995	2007	1995	2007	1995	2007	1995	2007
Honduras	271	831	149	315	85	559	5.2	8.8	99	385	5.3	4.0
Hungary	..	8,638	13,083	18,471	2,938	5,693	14.9	5.1	1,501	3,468	7.5	3.2
India	2,124[i]	5,082[i]	3,056	9,780	2,582[g]	10,729[g]	6.8[g]	4.5[g]	996[g]	9,296	2.1[g]	4.0
Indonesia	4,324	5,506	1,782	4,341	5,229[g]	5,833	9.9[g]	4.5	2,172[g]	6,120	4.0[g]	5.6
Iran, Islamic Rep.	489	2,735	1,000	..	205	1,834	1.1	..	247	6,526	1.6	..
Iraq	61[b]	..	..	..	18[d,g]	170	..	0.6	117[d,g]	526	..	2.2
Ireland	4,818	8,332	2,547	6,848	2,698	8,863	5.5	4.3	2,034[g]	8,811	4.8[g]	4.9
Israel	2,215[i]	2,067[i]	2,259	4,147	3,491	3,712	12.7	5.2	2,626	4,250	7.4	5.8
Italy	31,052	43,654	18,173	27,734	30,426	46,144	10.3	7.5	17,219	32,754	6.9	5.3
Jamaica	1,147[c,e]	1,701[c,e]	..	..	1,199	2,137	35.3	43.4	173	340	4.6	4.2
Japan	3,345[b,i]	8,347[b,i]	15,298	17,295	4,894	12,422	1.0	1.5	46,966	37,261	11.2	5.1
Jordan	1,075	3,431[c]	1,128	2,094	973	2,755	28.0	30.2	719	1,024	14.7	6.6
Kazakhstan	..	3,876	523	4,544	155	1,213	2.6	2.3	296	1,355	4.9	3.0
Kenya	896	1,644	..	..	590	1,507	16.7	22.1	183[g]	262[g]	3.1[g]	2.7[g]
Korea, Dem. Rep.	..	..	..	..	..	..	..	..	..	..	..	..
Korea, Rep.	3,753[b,c]	6,448[b,c]	3,819	13,325	6,670	8,947	4.5	2.0	6,947	23,359	4.5	5.4
Kuwait	72[h]	293[h]	878	2,529	307	512	2.2	0.7	2,514	6,678	19.9	19.8
Kyrgyz Republic	36	1,654	42	454	5[g]	392	1.1[g]	19.4	7[g]	193	1.0[g]	6.0
Lao PDR	60	842	..	..	52	189[g]	12.8	15.7[g]	34	..	4.5	..
Latvia	539	1,653	1,812	3,398	37	880	1.8	7.4	62	1,021	2.8	5.7
Lebanon	450	1,017	..	..	710	5,573	..	33.6	..	3,914	..	17.9
Lesotho	87	292	..	..	29	43[g]	14.6	4.9[g]	17	24	1.6	1.4
Liberia	..	..	..	..	..	131[g]	..	24.2[g]	..	48	..	2.8
Libya	56	149	484	..	4	244	0.1	0.6	98	915	1.7	5.8
Lithuania	650	1,486	1,925	3,696	102	1,192	3.2	5.6	107	1,167	2.7	4.4
Macedonia, FYR	147[f]	230[f]	..	..	19[g]	219	2.7	5.2	27[g]	147	1.7	2.6
Madagascar	75[e]	344[e]	39	..	106	506	14.2	21.8	79	94[g]	8.0	3.9[g]
Malawi	192	714	..	..	22	48	4.7	..	53	84	8.0	..
Malaysia	7,469	20,973	20,642	30,761	5,044	16,798	6.1	8.2	2,722	6,245	3.1	3.7
Mali	42[e,h]	164[e,h]	..	..	26	175	4.9	9.4	74	196	7.5	9.1
Mauritania	..	..	..	..	11[g]	..	2.2[g]	..	30	..	5.9	..
Mauritius	422	907	107	213	616	1,663	26.2	37.5	184	388	7.5	7.5
Mexico	20,241[c]	21,424[c]	8,450	15,089	6,847	14,072	7.7	4.9	3,587	9,843	4.4	3.2
Moldova	32	13	71	82	71	221	8.0	11.0	73	270	7.3	6.3
Mongolia	108	452	..	..	33	261	6.5	12.9	22	212	4.2	11.3
Morocco	2,602[c]	7,408[c]	1,317	2,320	1,469	8,307	16.2	30.4	356	1,418	3.2	4.1
Mozambique	..	664	..	..	49[g]	182	10.2[g]	6.3	68	209	6.6	5.7
Myanmar	117	248	..	..	169	59	12.9	1.2	18	40	0.9	1.4
Namibia	272	929	..	..	278[g]	542	16.0[g]	15.4	90[g]	132[g]	4.3[g]	3.7[g]
Nepal	363	527	100	469	232	234	22.5	16.3	167	402	10.3	11.0
Netherlands	6,574[f]	11,008[f]	12,313	17,556	10,611	19,981	4.4	3.6	13,151	19,475	6.1	4.0
New Zealand	1,475[b]	2,434[b]	920	1,978	2,318[g]	5,406[g]	13.0[g]	14.8[g]	1,259[g]	3,066[g]	7.3[g]	8.0[g]
Nicaragua	281	800[c]	255	868	51	255	7.7	9.5	56	195	4.9	4.2
Niger	35	60	10	..	7[g]	39	2.2[g]	6.5	26	42	5.7	3.9
Nigeria	656	1,111	..	..	47	340	0.4	0.5	939	3,494	7.3	7.6
Norway	2,880[a]	4,290	590	3,395	2,730	5,021	4.9	2.8	4,481	14,109	9.6	12.1
Oman	279[h]	1,144[h]	..	..	193[g]	902	2.5[g]	3.5	47[g]	944	0.9[g]	4.9
Pakistan	378	840	..	..	582	900	5.7	4.1	654	2,043	4.6	5.4
Panama	345	1,103	185	314	372	1,796	4.9	12.6	181	457	2.3	3.1
Papua New Guinea	42	104	51	..	25[g]	4	0.8[g]	0.1	58[g]	56	3.0[g]	2.1
Paraguay	438[i]	416[i]	427	242	162	121	3.4	1.9	173	184	3.3	2.8
Peru	479	1,812	508	1,857	521	2,222	7.9	7.1	428	1,274	4.5	5.3
Philippines	1,760[c]	3,092[c]	1,615	2,745	1,141	5,518	4.3	9.5	551	2,007	1.7	3.1
Poland	19,215	14,975	36,387	47,561	6,927	11,686	19.4	6.7	5,865	8,341	17.3	4.5
Portugal	9,511[i]	12,321[c]	..	20,989	5,646	12,917	17.5	17.2	2,540	4,836	6.4	5.4
Puerto Rico	3,131[e]	3,687[e]	1,237	1,441	1,828[d]	3,414[d]	..	..	1,155[d]	1,743[d]	..	..

	International tourists				Inbound tourism expenditure				Outbound tourism expenditure			
	thousands				$ millions		% of exports		$ millions		% of imports	
	Inbound		Outbound									
	1995	2007	1995	2007	1995	2007	1995	2007	1995	2007	1995	2007
Romania	5,445[b]	7,722[b]	5,737	10,980	689	1,922	7.3	3.8	749	1,719	6.6	2.3
Russian Federation	10,290[b]	22,909[b]	21,329	34,285	4,312[g]	12,587	4.6[g]	3.2	11,599[g]	24,289	14.0[g]	8.6
Rwanda	..	..	..	..	4	66	5.4	18.2	13	69	3.5	7.6
Saudi Arabia	3,325	11,531	..	4,817	..	6,020[d]	..	2.5[d]	..	6,279[d]	..	5.5[d]
Senegal		866	..	..	168	329	11.2	13.7	154	139	8.5	3.4
Serbia	..	696[f]				1,011[d]				1,194[d]	..	..
Sierra Leone	38[e]	32[e]	6	71	57[g]	22[g]	44.4[g]	6.6[g]	51	17	19.4	3.5
Singapore	6,070	7,957	2,867	6,024	7,611[g]	8,680[g]	4.8[g]	2.3[g]	4,663[g]	11,844[g]	3.2[g]	3.6[g]
Slovak Republic	903[f]	1,685[f]	218	23,837	630	2,352	5.7	3.6	338	1,825	3.2	2.8
Slovenia	732[f]	1,751[f]	..	2,496	1,128	2,400	10.9	7.3	606	1,219	5.6	3.6
Somalia	..	..	..	..	..	..	..	..	..	..	..	..
South Africa	4,488	9,091	2,520	4,433	2,655	9,890	7.7	11.0	2,414	6,103	7.2	6.2
Spain	34,920	58,973	3,648	11,276	27,369	65,136	20.4	16.9	5,826	24,179	4.3	5.0
Sri Lanka	403[i]	494[i]	504	862	367	750	7.9	7.9	279	709	4.7	5.6
Sudan	29[i]	436[c]	195	..	8[g]	262[g]	1.2[g]	2.8[g]	43[g]	1,477[g]	3.5[g]	13.9[g]
Swaziland	300[a]	870[h]	..	1,130	54	32	5.3	1.5	45	63	3.5	2.5
Sweden	2,310[f]	3,434[f]	10,127	12,681	4,390	13,706	4.6	5.9	6,816	15,696	8.4	7.8
Switzerland	6,946[h]	8,448[h]	11,148	..	11,354	14,777	9.2	5.5	9,478	12,449	8.7	5.6
Syrian Arab Republic	..	4,566	1,746	4,042	1,258[g]	2,113	21.9[g]	16.0	498[g]	585	9.0[g]	4.9
Tajikistan	..	..	..	..	..	16	..	0.9	..	7[g]	..	0.2[g]
Tanzania	285	692	157	..	502[g]	1,053	39.7[g]	26.7	360[g]	666	16.8[g]	10.5
Thailand	6,952[c]	14,464[i]	1,820	4,018	9,257	20,623	13.2	11.4	4,791	6,887	5.8	4.2
Timor-Leste	..	..	..	..	..	..	..	..	..	..	..	..
Togo	53[h]	86[h]	..	..	13[g]	23	2.8[g]	2.4	40	42	6.0	2.8
Trinidad and Tobago	260[e]	449[e]	261	..	232	693	8.3	5.6	91	206	4.3	3.7
Tunisia	4,120[i]	6,758[i]	1,778	2,302	1,838	3,373	23.0	16.8	294	530	3.3	2.5
Turkey	7,083	22,248	3,981	8,938	4,957[g]	20,649	13.6[g]	14.3	911[g]	3,720	2.3[g]	2.1
Turkmenistan	218	8	21	38	13	..	0.7	..	74	..	4.1	..
Uganda	160	642	148	272	78[g]	359	11.7[g]	16.4	80[g]	200	5.4[g]	4.8
Ukraine	3,716	23,122	6,552	16,875	191[g]	5,317	1.1[g]	8.3	210[g]	3,743	1.1[g]	5.2
United Arab Emirates	2,315[a,c]	7,126[a,c]	..	..	632[d]	4,972[d]	..	..	..	8,827[d]	..	..
United Kingdom	21,719	30,870	41,345	69,450	27,577	47,109	8.6	6.5	30,749	88,478	9.4	10.7
United States	43,490	55,986	51,285	64,052	93,700	144,808	11.8	8.8	60,924	109,578	6.8	4.7
Uruguay	2,022	1,752	562	635	725	927	20.7	13.6	332	349	9.3	5.1
Uzbekistan	92	281	246	893	15[d]	43[d]	..	..	..	..	..	..
Venezuela, RB	700	771	534	1,410	995	894	4.8	1.3	1,852	2,101	11.0	4.0
Vietnam	1,351[b]	4,244[b]	..	..	..	3,200[d]	..	7.1[d]	..	..	..	..
West Bank and Gaza	220[h]	264[h]	..	..	255[g]	121[g]	..	..	162[g]	265[g]	..	..
Yemen, Rep.	61[h]	379[h]	..	..	50[g]	425[g]	2.3[g]	5.5[g]	76[g]	247	3.1[g]	2.6
Zambia	163	897	..	..	29[g]	138[g]	2.4[g]	2.8[g]	83	98	6.2	2.2
Zimbabwe	1,416[b]	2,508[b]	256	..	145[d]	365[d]	..	..	106[d]	..	..	..
World	535,972 t	911,470 t	579,267 t	1,100,372 t	486,148 t	1,028,350 t	7.6 w	5.9 w	458,208 t	918,692 t	7.4 w	5.5 w
Low income	9,007	25,153	..	..	4,632	15,333	6.2	5.7	6,137	16,856	5.4	5.5
Middle income	156,729	336,249	164,054	341,298	89,012	279,099	8.3	6.3	63,726	186,323	5.7	4.5
Lower middle income	59,900	165,468	36,644	112,566	42,143	139,002	8.7	5.8	20,688	90,554	3.9	3.9
Upper middle income	97,095	171,571	121,149	203,223	46,881	140,091	7.9	6.8	43,323	95,178	7.4	5.1
Low & middle income	168,466	365,821	195,054	415,707	93,858	295,275	8.2	6.2	69,343	201,988	5.7	4.5
East Asia & Pacific	43,654	108,445	36,055	81,138	31,197	96,536	7.8	4.8	14,769	57,505	3.5	3.5
Europe & Central Asia	55,679	122,293	87,492	151,898	20,529	76,692	8.7	7.1	22,793	57,564	9.3	5.1
Latin America & Carib.	38,965	57,814	21,780	40,970	21,591	50,739	7.5	5.6	18,751	39,665	6.5	4.8
Middle East & N. Africa	13,329	39,685	13,236	25,636	9,771	35,786	12.8	24.6	4,422	15,481	5.2	6.4
South Asia	3,819	8,088	5,151	15,408	4,016	13,343	6.8	5.3	2,393	12,922	3.0	5.1
Sub-Saharan Africa	12,871	29,688	..	..	6,729	22,231	7.6	7.1	6,761	19,233	6.7	6.0
High income	362,515	540,487	336,254	601,882	392,250	733,064	7.5	5.8	388,174	717,338	7.8	5.8
Euro area	202,533	297,435	140,127	225,488	164,023	329,568	7.8	6.5	154,993	276,680	7.8	5.6

Note: Aggregates are based on World Bank country classifications and differ from those of the World Tourism Organization. Regional and income group totals include countries not shown in the table for which data are available.

a. Arrivals in hotels only. b. Arrivals of nonresident visitors at national borders. c. Includes nationals residing abroad. d. Country estimates. e. Arrivals by air only. f. Arrivals in all types of accommodation establishments. g. Expenditure of travel related items only; excludes passenger transport items. h. Arrivals in hotels and similar establishments. i. Excludes nationals residing abroad.

About the data

Tourism is defined as the activities of people traveling to and staying in places outside their usual environment for no more than one year for leisure, business, and other purposes not related to an activity remunerated from within the place visited. The social and economic phenomenon of tourism has grown substantially over the past quarter century.

Statistical information on tourism is based mainly on data on arrivals and overnight stays along with balance of payments information. These data do not completely capture the economic phenomenon of tourism or provide the information needed for effective public policies and efficient business operations. Data are needed on the scale and significance of tourism. Information on the role of tourism in national economies is particularly deficient. Although the World Tourism Organization reports progress in harmonizing definitions and measurement, differences in national practices still prevent full comparability.

The data in the table are from the World Tourism Organization, a United Nations agency. The data on inbound and outbound tourists refer to the number of arrivals and departures, not to the number of people traveling. Thus a person who makes several trips to a country during a given period is counted each time as a new arrival. Unless otherwise indicated in the footnotes, the data on inbound tourism show the arrivals of nonresident tourists (overnight visitors) at national borders. When data on international tourists are unavailable or incomplete, the table shows the arrivals of international visitors, which include tourists, same-day visitors, cruise passengers, and crew members.

Sources and collection methods for arrivals differ across countries. In some cases data are from border statistics (police, immigration, and the like) and supplemented by border surveys. In other cases data are from tourism accommodation establishments. For some countries number of arrivals is limited to arrivals by air and for others to arrivals staying in hotels. Some countries include arrivals of nationals residing abroad while others do not. Caution should thus be used in comparing arrivals across countries.

The World Tourism Organization is improving its coverage of tourism expenditure data, using balance of payments data from the International Monetary Fund (IMF) supplemented by data from individual countries. These data, shown in the table, include travel and passenger transport items as defined in the IMF's (1993) *Balance of Payments Manual.* When the IMF does not report data on passenger transport items, expenditure data for travel items are shown.

The aggregates are calculated using the World Bank's weighted aggregation methodology (see *Statistical methods*) and differ from the World Tourism Organization's aggregates.

Definitions

• **International inbound tourists** (overnight visitors) are the number of tourists who travel to a country other than that in which they usually reside, and outside their usual environment, for a period not exceeding 12 months and whose main purpose in visiting is other than an activity remunerated from within the country visited. When data on number of tourists are not available, the number of visitors, which includes tourists, same-day visitors, cruise passengers, and crew members, is shown instead. • **International outbound tourists** are the number of departures that people make from their country of usual residence to any other country for any purpose other than an activity remunerated in the country visited. • **Inbound tourism expenditure** is expenditures by international inbound visitors, including payments to national carriers for international transport. These receipts include any other prepayment made for goods or services received in the destination country. They may include receipts from same-day visitors, except when these are important enough to justify separate classification. For some countries they do not include receipts for passenger transport items. Their share in exports is calculated as a ratio to exports of goods and services (all transactions between residents of a country and the rest of the world involving a change of ownership from residents to nonresidents of general merchandise, goods sent for processing and repairs, nonmonetary gold, and services). • **Outbound tourism expenditure** is expenditures of international outbound visitors in other countries, including payments to foreign carriers for international transport. These expenditures may include those by residents traveling abroad as same-day visitors, except when these are important enough to justify separate classification. For some countries they do not include expenditures for passenger transport items. Their share in imports is calculated as a ratio to imports of goods and services (all transactions between residents of a country and the rest of the world involving a change of ownership from nonresidents to residents of general merchandise, goods sent for processing and repairs, nonmonetary gold, and services).

Data sources

Data on visitors and tourism expenditure are from the World Tourism Organization's *Yearbook of Tourism Statistics* and *Compendium of Tourism Statistics 2009.* Data in the table are updated from electronic files provided by the World Tourism Organization. Data on exports and imports are from the IMF's *Balance of Payments Statistics Yearbook* and data files.

High-income economies remain the main destination for international travelers, but the share of tourists visiting developing economies is rising   **6.19a**

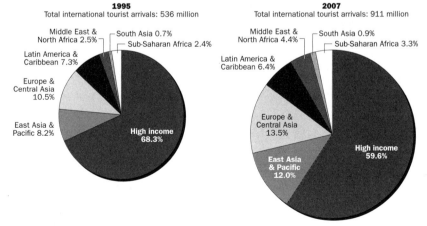

1995
Total international tourist arrivals: 536 million

Middle East & North Africa 2.5%
South Asia 0.7%
Sub-Saharan Africa 2.4%
Latin America & Caribbean 7.3%
Europe & Central Asia 10.5%
East Asia & Pacific 8.2%
High income 68.3%

2007
Total international tourist arrivals: 911 million

Middle East & North Africa 4.4%
South Asia 0.9%
Sub-Saharan Africa 3.3%
Latin America & Caribbean 6.4%
Europe & Central Asia 13.5%
East Asia & Pacific 12.0%
High income 59.6%

Although nearly 60 percent of international tourists traveled to high-income economies in 2007, the share traveling to developing economies has increased since 1995. The share of tourists going to East Asia and Pacific and Europe and Central Asia increased the most—about 3 percentage points.

Source: World Bank staff calculations based on World Tourism Organization data.

PRIMARY DATA DOCUMENTATION

The World Bank is not a primary data collection agency for most areas other than business and enterprise surveys, living standards surveys, and external debt. As a major user of socioeconomic data, however, the World Bank recognizes the importance of data documentation to inform users of differences in the methods and conventions used by primary data collectors—usually national statistical agencies, central banks, and customs services—and by international organizations, which compile the statistics that appear in the World Development Indicators database. These differences may give rise to significant discrepancies over time both within countries and across them. Delays in reporting data and the use of old surveys as the base for current estimates may further compromise the quality of data reported here.

The tables in this section provide information on sources, methods, and reporting standards of the principal demographic, economic, and environmental indicators in *World Development Indicators.* Additional documentation is available from the World Bank's Country Statistical Information Database at www.worldbank.org/data.

The demand for good quality statistical data is increasing. Timely and reliable statistics are key to the broad development strategy often referred to as "managing for results." Monitoring and reporting on publicly agreed indicators are central to implementing poverty reduction strategies and lie at the heart of the Millennium Development Goals and the new Results Measurement System adopted for the 14th replenishment of the International Development Association.

A global action plan to improve national and international statistics was agreed on during the Second Roundtable on Managing for Development Results in February 2004 in Marrakech, Morocco. The plan, now referred to as the Marrakech Action Plan for Statistics, or MAPS, has been widely endorsed and forms the overarching framework for statistical capacity building. The third roundtable conference, held in February 2007 in Hanoi, Vietnam, reaffirmed MAPS as the guiding strategy for improving the capacity of the national and international statistical systems. See www.mfdr.org/RT3 for reports from the conference.

	Currency	National accounts						Balance of payments and trade			Government finance	IMF data dissemination standard
		Base year	Reference year	System of National Accounts	SNA price valuation	Alternative conversion factor	PPP survey year	Balance of Payments Manual in use	External debt	System of trade	Accounting concept	
Afghanistan	Afghan afghani	2002/03			VAB				Preliminary	G	C	G
Albania	Albanian lek	[a]	1996	[b]	VAB		2005	BPM5	Actual	G	C	G
Algeria	Algerian dinar	1980			VAB			BPM5	Actual	S	B	
American Samoa	U.S. dollar											
Andorra	Euro									G		
Angola	Angolan kwanza	1997			VAP	1991–96	2005	BPM5	Actual	S		G
Antigua and Barbuda	Eastern Caribbean dollar	1990			VAB			BPM5		G		G
Argentina	Argentine peso	1993		[b]	VAB	1971–84	2005	BPM5	Actual		C	S
Armenia	Armenian dram	[a]	1996	[b]	VAB	1990–95	2005	BPM5	Actual	G	C	S
Aruba	Aruban florins	1995								S		
Australia	Australian dollar	[a]	2007	[b]	VAB		2005	BPM5		G	C	S
Austria	Euro	2000		[b]	VAB		2005	BPM5		S	C	S
Azerbaijan	New Azeri manat	[a]	2003	[b]	VAB	1992–95	2005	BPM5	Actual	G	C	
Bahamas, The	Bahamian dollar	1991		[b]	VAB			BPM5		G	B	G
Bahrain	Dinar	1985			VAP		2005	BPM5		G	C	G
Bangladesh	Bangladesh taka	1995/96		[b]	VAB		2005	BPM5	Preliminary	G	C	G
Barbados	Barbados dollar	1974			VAB			BPM5		G	C	G
Belarus	Belarusian rubel	[a]	2000	[b]	VAB	1990–95	2005	BPM5	Actual	G	C	G
Belgium	Euro	2000		[b]	VAB		2005	BPM5		S	C	
Belize	Belize dollar	2000		[b]	VAB			BPM5	Actual	G		G
Benin	CFA franc	1985			VAP	1992	2005	BPM5	Preliminary	S	B	G
Bermuda	Bermuda dollar	1996			VAB							
Bhutan	Ngultrum	2000		[b]	VAB		2005		Actual		C	
Bolivia	Boliviano	1990		[b]	VAB	1960–85	2005	BPM5	Actual	S	C	G
Bosnia and Herzegovina	Konvertible mark	[a]	1996	[b]	VAB		2005	BPM5	Actual	G	C	
Botswana	Botswana pula	1993/94		[b]	VAB		2005	BPM5	Preliminary	G	B	G
Brazil	Brazilian real	2000		[b]	VAB		2005	BPM5	Actual	S	C	S
Brunei Darussalam	Brunei dollar	2000			VAP		2005			G		G
Bulgaria	Bulgarian lev	[a]	2002	[b]	VAB	1978–89, 1991–92	2005	BPM5	Actual	G	C	S
Burkina Faso	CFA franc	1999			VAB	1992–93	2005	BPM4	Actual	G	B	G
Burundi	Burundi franc	1980			VAB		2005	BPM5	Actual	S	C	
Cambodia	Cambodian riel	2000			VAB		2005	BPM5	Actual	G	C	G
Cameroon	CFA franc	2000		[b]	VAB		2005	BPM5	Actual	S	B	G
Canada	Canadian dollar	2000		[b]	VAB		2005	BPM5		G	C	S
Cape Verde	Escudos	1980			VAP		2005	BPM5	Actual	S		G
Cayman Islands	Cayman Islands dollar											
Central African Republic	CFA franc	2000			VAB		2005	BPM4	Preliminary	S	B	G
Chad	CFA franc	1995		[b]	VAB		2005	BPM5	Actual		C	G
Channel Islands	Jersey pound & Guernsey pound	2007 & 2003	2007	[b]	VAB							
Chile	Chilean peso	2003		[b]	VAB		2005	BPM5	Actual	S	C	S
China	Chinese yuan	2000		[b]	VAP	1978–93	2005	BPM5	Preliminary	S	B	G
Hong Kong, China	Hong Kong dollar	2006		[b]	VAB		2005	BPM5		G	C	G
Colombia	Colombian peso	2000		[b]	VAB	1992–94	2005	BPM5	Actual	S	B	S
Comoros	CFA franc	1990			VAP		2005		Preliminary			
Congo, Dem. Rep.	Congo franc	1987		[b]	VAB	1999–2001	2005	BPM5	Estimate	S	C	G
Congo, Rep.	CFA franc	1978			VAP	1993	2005	BPM5	Preliminary	S	C	G
Costa Rica	Costa Rican colon	1991		[b]	VAB			BPM5	Actual	S	C	S
Côte d'Ivoire	CFA franc	1996			VAP		2005	BPM5	Actual	S	C	G
Croatia	Croatian kuna	[a]	1997	[b]	VAB		2005	BPM5	Actual	G	C	S
Cuba	Cuban peso	1984			VAP					G		
Cyprus	Euro	[a]	2000		VAB		2005	BPM5		G	C	
Czech Republic	Czech koruna	2000	1995	[b]	VAB		2005	BPM5		G	C	S
Denmark	Danish krone	2000		[b]	VAB		2005	BPM5		G	C	S
Djibouti	CFA franc	1990			VAB		2005		Actual			

PRIMARY DATA DOCUMENTATION

	Latest population census	Latest demographic, education, or health household survey	Source of most recent income and expenditure data	Vital registration complete	Latest agricultural census	Latest industrial data	Latest trade data	Latest water withdrawal data
Afghanistan	1979	MICS, 2003					1977	2000
Albania	2001	MICS, 2005	LSMS, 2005	Yes	1998	2005	2007	2000
Algeria	2008	MICS, 2006	IHS, 1995		2001		2006	2000
American Samoa	2000			Yes				
Andorra	2000			Yes			2006	
Angola	1970	MICS, 2001	IHS, 2000		1964–65		1991	2000
Antigua and Barbuda	2001			Yes			2007	1990
Argentina	2001		IHS, 2005	Yes	2002	2002	2006	2000
Armenia	2001	DHS, 2005	IHS, 2003	Yes			2006	2000
Aruba	2000						2007	
Australia	2006		ES/BS, 1994	Yes	2001	2005	2006	2000
Austria	2001		IS 2000	Yes	1999–2000	2004	2006	2000
Azerbaijan	1999	DHS, 2006	ES/BS, 2005	Yes		2005	2006	2005
Bahamas, The	2000					1998	2007	
Bahrain	2001			Yes			2007	2003
Bangladesh	2001	MICS 2006	IHS, 2005		2005	1998	2006	2000
Barbados	2000			Yes			2007	2000
Belarus	1999	MICS, 2005	ES/BS 2005	Yes	1994		2007	2000
Belgium	2001		IHS, 2000	Yes	1999–2000ᶜ	2004	2006	
Belize	2000	MICS, 2006					2007	2000
Benin	2002	DHS, 2006	CWIQ, 2003		1992		2005	2001
Bermuda	2000			Yes				
Bhutan	2005		IHS, 2003		2000			2000
Bolivia	2001	DHS, 2003	IHS, 2005		1984–88	2001	2006	2000
Bosnia and Herzegovina	1991	MICS, 2006	LSMS, 2004	Yes			2007	
Botswana	2001	MICS, 2000	ES/BS, 1993/94		1993	2005	2007	2000
Brazil	2000	DHS, 1996	IHS, 2007		1996	2004	2006	2000
Brunei Darussalam	2001			Yes			2006	
Bulgaria	2001		ES/BS, 2003	Yes		2005	2006	2000
Burkina Faso	2006	DHS, 2003	CWIQ, 2003		1993		2004	2000
Burundi	1990	MICS, 2000	CWIQ, 2006				2007	2000
Cambodia	2008	DHS, 2005	IHS, 2004			2000	2004	2000
Cameroon	1987	MICS, 2006	PS, 2001		1984		2006	2000
Canada	2006		LFS, 2000	Yes	1996/2001	2002	2006	2000
Cape Verde	2000		ES/BS, 2001	Yes	2004		2007	
Cayman Islands	1999			Yes				
Central African Republic	2003	MICS, 2006	PS, 2003		1985		2005	2000
Chad	1993	DHS, 2004	PS, 2002				1995	2000
Channel Islands	2001			Yes				
Chile	2002		IHS, 2006	Yes	1997	2005	2006	2000
China	2000	NSS, 2006	IHS, 2003		1997	2005	2006	2000
Hong Kong, China	2006			Yes			2006	
Colombia	2005	DHS, 2005	IHS, 2006		2001	2005	2006	2000
Comoros	2003	MICS, 2000	IHS, 2004				2007	
Congo, Dem. Rep.	1984	DHS 2007	1–2–3, 2005		1990		1986	2000
Congo, Rep.	1996	DHS, 2005	CWIQ/ PS, 2005		1985–86		1995	2002
Costa Rica	2000	RHS, 1993	LFS, 2005	Yes	1973		2006	2000
Côte d'Ivoire	1998	MICS, 2006	IHS, 2002		2001		2007	
Croatia	2001		ES/BS, 2005	Yes	2003		2006	
Cuba	2002	MICS, 2006		Yes			2006	2000
Cyprus	2001			Yes		2005	2006	2000
Czech Republic	2001	RHS, 1993	IS 1996/97	Yes	2000	2004	2006	2000
Denmark	2001		ITR 1997	Yes	1999–2000	2004	2006	2000
Djibouti	1983	MICS, 2006	PS, 2002					2000

	Currency	National accounts						Balance of payments and trade			Government finance	IMF data dissemination standard
		Base year	Reference year	System of National Accounts	SNA price valuation	Alternative conversion factor	PPP survey year	Balance of Payments Manual in use	External debt	System of trade	Accounting concept	
Dominica	Eastern Caribbean dollar	1990		b	VAB			BPM5	Actual	G		G
Dominican Republic	Dominican peso	1990			VAP			BPM5	Actual	G	C	G
Ecuador	U.S. dollar	2000		b	VAB		2005	BPM5	Actual	S	B	S
Egypt, Arab Rep.	Egyptian pound	1991/92			VAB		2005	BPM5	Actual	S	B	S
El Salvador	Salvadoran colon	1990			VAB			BPM5	Actual	S	C	S
Equatorial Guinea	CFA franc	2000			VAB	1965–84	2005					
Eritrea	Eritrean nakfa	1992			VAB			BPM4	Actual	G		
Estonia	Estonian kroon	2000		b	VAB	1987–95	2005	BPM5		G	C	S
Ethiopia	Ethiopian birr	1999/2000		b	VAB		2005	BPM5	Actual	G	C	G
Faeroe Islands	Danish krone				VAB			BPM5		G		
Fiji	Fijian dollar	1995			VAB		2005	BPM4	Actual	G	B	G
Finland	Euro	2000		b	VAB		2005	BPM5		G	C	S
France	Euro	a	2000	b	VAB		2005	BPM5		S	C	S
French Polynesia	CFP franc									G		
Gabon	CFA franc	1991			VAP	1993	2005	BPM5	Preliminary	S	B	G
Gambia, The	Gambian dalasi	1987			VAB		2005	BPM5	Estimate	G	B	G
Georgia	Georgian lari	a	1996	b	VAB	1990–95	2005	BPM5	Actual	G	C	G
Germany	Euro	2000		b	VAB		2005	BPM5		S	C	S
Ghana	Ghanaian cedi	1975			VAP	1973–87	2005	BPM5	Preliminary	G	B	S
Greece	Euro	a	2000		VAB		2005	BPM5		S	C	S
Greenland	Danish krone									G		
Grenada	Eastern Caribbean dollar	1990			VAB			BPM5	Actual	G		G
Guam	U.S. dollar											
Guatemala	Guatemalan quetzal	2001		b	VAP			BPM5	Actual	S	B	G
Guinea	Guinean franc	1996			VAB		2005	BPM5	Estimate	S	B	G
Guinea-Bissau	CFA franc	1986			VAB		2005	BPM5	Preliminary	S		G
Guyana	Guyana dollar	1988			VAB			BPM5	Actual	S		
Haiti	Haitian gourde	1975/76			VAB	1991		BPM5	Preliminary	G		
Honduras	Honduran lempira	2000		b	VAB	1988–89		BPM5	Actual	S	B	G
Hungary	Hungarian forint	a	2000	b	VAB		2005	BPM5		S	C	S
Iceland	Iceland kronur	2000			VAB		2005	BPM5		G	C	S
India	Indian rupee	1999/2000		b	VAB		2005	BPM5	Actual	G	C	S
Indonesia	Indonesian rupiah	2000			VAP		2005	BPM5	Actual	G	C	S
Iran, Islamic Rep.	Iranian rial	1997/98			VAB	1980–02	2005	BPM5	Actual	G	C	
Iraq	Iraqi dinar	1997			VAB	1997, 2004	2005	BPM5		S		
Ireland	Euro	2000		b	VAB		2005	BPM5		G	C	S
Isle of Man	Manx pound	2005	2003									
Israel	Israeli new shekel	2005		b	VAP		2005	BPM5		S	C	S
Italy	Euro	2000		b	VAB		2005	BPM5		S	C	S
Jamaica	Jamaica dollar	1996			VAB			BPM5	Actual	G	C	G
Japan	Japanese yen	2000			VAB		2005	BPM5		G	C	S
Jordan	Jordan dinar	1994			VAB		2005	BPM5	Actual	G	B	G
Kazakhstan	Kazakh tenge	a	1995	b	VAB	1987–95	2005	BPM5	Actual	G	C	S
Kenya	Kenya shilling	2001		b	VAB		2005	BPM5	Actual	G	B	G
Kiribati	Australian dollar	1991			VAB					G		G
Korea, Dem. Rep.	Democratic Republic of Korea won							BPM5				
Korea, Rep.	Korean won	2000		b	VAB		2005	BPM5		S	C	S
Kuwait	Kuwaiti dinar	1995			VAP		2005	BPM5		S	C	G
Kyrgyz Republic	Kyrgyz som	a	1995	b	VAB	1990–95	2005	BPM5	Actual	G	C	S
Lao PDR	Lao kip	1990			VAB		2005	BPM5	Preliminary	G		
Latvia	Latvian lat	2000		b	VAB	1987–95	2005	BPM5	Actual	S	C	S
Lebanon	Lebanese pound	2005			VAB		2005	BPM5	Actual	G	B	G
Lesotho	Lesotho loti	1995		b	VAB		2005	BPM5	Actual	G	C	G
Liberia	Liberian dollar	1992			VAB		2005	BPM5	Estimate			G

PRIMARY DATA DOCUMENTATION

	Latest population census	Latest demographic, education, or health household survey	Source of most recent income and expenditure data	Vital registration complete	Latest agricultural census	Latest industrial data	Latest trade data	Latest water withdrawal data
Dominica	2001			Yes			2006	
Dominican Republic	2002	DHS, 2007	IHS, 2005		1971		2001	2000
Ecuador	2001	RHS, 2004	LFS, 2007		1999–2000	2005	2007	2000
Egypt, Arab Rep.	2006	DHS, 2005, SPA 2004	ES/BS, 2005	Yes	1999–2000	2002	2007	2000
El Salvador	2007	RHS, 2002/03	IHS, 2005	Yes	1970–71		2006	2000
Equatorial Guinea	2002							2000
Eritrea	1984	DHS, 2002				2005	2003	2004
Estonia	2000		ES/BS, 2004	Yes	2001	2005	2006	2000
Ethiopia	2007	DHS, 2005	ES/BS, 2004–05		2001–02	2005	2007	2002
Faeroe Islands	2002						2006	
Fiji	2007			Yes			2007	2000
Finland	2000		IS, 2000	Yes	1999–2000	2004	2006	2000
France	2006		ES/BS, 1994/95	Yes	1999–2000	2004	2006	2000
French Polynesia	2007			Yes			2007	
Gabon	2003	DHS, 2000	CWIQ/ IHS, 2005		1974–75		2006	2000
Gambia, The	2003	MICS, 2005/06	IHS, 2003/04		2001–02		2007	2000
Georgia	2002	MICS, 2005	IHS, 2005	Yes	2004	2005	2007	2005
Germany	2004		IHS, 2000	Yes	1999–2000	2004	2006	2000
Ghana	2000	MICS, 2006	LSMS, 2005		1984	2003	2007	2000
Greece	2001		IHS, 2000	Yes	1999–2000	1998	2006	2000
Greenland	2000			Yes			2006	
Grenada	2001			Yes			2006	
Guam	2000			Yes				
Guatemala	2002	RHS, 2002	LSMS, 2006	Yes	2003		2006	2000
Guinea	1996	DHS, 2005	CWIQ/, 2002/03		2000–01		2002	2000
Guinea-Bissau	1991	MICS, 2006	CWIQ, 2002		1988		1995	2000
Guyana	2002	MICS, 2006	IHS, 1998				2006	2000
Haiti	2003	DHS, 2005	IHS, 2001		1971		1997	2000
Honduras	2001	DHS, 2005	IHS, 2006		1993		2006	2000
Hungary	2001		ES/BS, 2004	Yes	2000	2004	2006	2000
Iceland	2000			Yes		2005	2006	2000
India	2001	DHS, 2005/06	IHS, 2004/05		1995–96/ 2000–01	2004	2007	2000
Indonesia	2000	DHS, 2002/03	IHS, 2005		2003	2003	2007	2000
Iran, Islamic Rep.	2006	DHS, 2000	ES/BS, 2005	Yes	2003	2004	2006	2004
Iraq	1997	MICS, 2006			1981	1998	2007	2000
Ireland	2006		IHS, 2000	Yes	2000	2004	2006	2000
Isle of Man	2006			Yes				
Israel	1995		ES/BS, 2001	Yes	1981	2004	2006	2004
Italy	2001		ES/BS, 2000	Yes	2000	2004	2006	2000
Jamaica	2001	MICS 2005	LSMS, 2004		1996		2007	2000
Japan	2005			Yes	2000	2005	2006	2000
Jordan	2004	DHS, 2007	ES/BS, 2004		1997	2005	2006	2005
Kazakhstan	1999	MICS, 2006	ES/BS, 2003	Yes			2007	2000
Kenya	1999	DHS, 2003, SPA, 2004	IHS, 2005		1977–79	2005	2007	2003
Kiribati	2005						2005	
Korea, Dem. Rep.	1993	MICS, 2000						2000
Korea, Rep.	2005		ES/BS, 1998/99	Yes	2000	2005	2006	2000
Kuwait	2005	FHS, 1996		Yes	1970		2007	2002
Kyrgyz Republic	1999	MICS 2005/06	ES/BS, 2004	Yes	2002	2005	2006	2000
Lao PDR	2005	MICS, 2006	ES/BS, 2002		1998–99	1999	1975	2000
Latvia	2000		IHS, 2004	Yes	2001	2005	2006	2000
Lebanon	1970	MICS, 2000			1998–99	1998	2004	2005
Lesotho	2006	DHS, 2004	ES/BS, 2002–03		1999–2000		2004	2000
Liberia	2008	DHS, 2007					1984	2000

	Currency	National accounts						Balance of payments and trade			Government finance	IMF data dissemination standard
		Base year	Reference year	System of National Accounts	SNA price valuation	Alternative conversion factor	PPP survey year	Balance of Payments Manual in use	External debt	System of trade	Accounting concept	
Libya	Libyan dinar	1999			VAB	1986		BPM5		G		
Liechtenstein	Swiss franc				VAB					S		
Lithuania	Lithuanian litas	2000		b	VAB	1990–95	2005	BPM5		G	C	S
Luxembourg	Euro		2000		VAB		2005	BPM5		S	C	S
Macao, China	Pataca	2002			VAB		2005	BPM5		G	C	G
Macedonia, FYR	Macedonian denar	1997	1995	b	VAB		2005	BPM5	Actual	G		G
Madagascar	Malagasy ariary	1984			VAB		2005	BPM5	Actual	S	C	G
Malawi	Malawi kwacha	1994			VAB		2005	BPM5	Actual	G	B	G
Malaysia	Malaysian ringgit	2000			VAP		2005	BPM5	Preliminary	G	C	S
Maldives	Rufiyaa	1995			VAB		2005	BPM5	Actual	G	C	
Mali	CFA franc	1987			VAB		2005	BPM4	Actual	G	B	G
Malta	Euro	1973			VAB		2005	BPM5		G	C	G
Marshall Islands	U.S. dollar	1991			VAB							
Mauritania	Mauritanian ouguiya	1998			VAB		2005	BPM4	Actual	G		G
Mauritius	Mauritian rupee	1997/98			VAB		2005	BPM5	Actual	G	C	G
Mayotte												
Mexico	Mexican new peso	2003		b	VAB		2005	BPM5	Actual	G	C	S
Micronesia, Fed. Sts.	U.S. dollar	1998			VAB							
Moldova	Moldovan leu	a	1996	b	VAB	1990–95	2005	BPM5	Actual	G	C	S
Monaco	Euro											
Mongolia	Mongolian tugrik	2005		b	VAB		2005	BPM5	Estimate	S	C	G
Montenegro	Euro	2000		b	VAB		2005		Actual			
Morocco	Moroccan dirham	1998			VAB		2005	BPM5	Actual	S	C	S
Mozambique	Mozambican metical (New)	2003			VAB	1992–95	2005	BPM5	Preliminary	S		G
Myanmar	Myanmar kyat	1985/86			VAP			BPM5	Estimate	G	C	
Namibia	Namibia dollar	1995/96		b	VAB		2005	BPM5		G	B	G
Nepal	Nepalese rupee	2000/01			VAB		2005	BPM5	Actual	S	C	G
Netherlands Antilles	Netherlands Antilles guilder							BPM5		S		
Netherlands	Euro	a	2000	b	VAB		2005	BPM5		S	C	S
New Caledonia	CFP franc									S		
New Zealand	New Zealand dollar	2000/01			VAB		2005	BPM5		G	C	
Nicaragua	Nicaraguan gold cordoba	1994		b	VAB	1965–95		BPM5	Actual	S	B	G
Niger	CFA franc	1987			VAP	1993	2005	BPM5	Preliminary	S		G
Nigeria	Nigerian naira	2002			VAB	1971–98	2005	BPM5	Preliminary	G		G
Northern Mariana Islands	U.S. dollar											
Norway	Norwegian krone	a	2000	b	VAB		2005	BPM5		G	C	S
Oman	Rial Omani	1988			VAP		2005	BPM5		G	B	G
Pakistan	Pakistan rupee	1999/2000		b	VAB		2005	BPM5	Actual	G	C	G
Palau	U.S. dollar	1995			VAB							
Panama	Panamanian balboa	1996		b	VAB			BPM5	Actual	S	C	G
Papua New Guinea	Papua New Guinea kina	1998			VAB	1989		BPM5	Actual	G	B	
Paraguay	Paraguayan guarani	1994			VAP		2005	BPM5	Actual	S	C	G
Peru	Peruvian new sol	1994			VAB	1985–90	2005	BPM5	Actual	S	C	S
Philippines	Philippine peso	1985			VAP		2005	BPM5	Actual	G	B	S
Poland	Polish zloty	a	2002	b	VAB		2005	BPM5	Actual	S	C	S
Portugal	Euro	2000		b	VAB		2005	BPM5		S	C	S
Puerto Rico	U.S. dollar	1954			VAP					G		
Qatar	Qatar riyals	2001			VAP		2005			G	B	G
Romania	New Romanian leu	a	2005	b	VAB	1987–89, 1992	2005	BPM5	Actual	S	C	S
Russian Federation	Russian ruble	2000		b	VAB	1987–95	2005	BPM5	Preliminary	G	C	S
Rwanda	Rwanda franc	1995			VAP	1994	2005	BPM5	Preliminary	G	C	G

PRIMARY DATA DOCUMENTATION

	Latest population census	Latest demographic, education, or health household survey	Source of most recent income and expenditure data	Vital registration complete	Latest agricultural census	Latest industrial data	Latest trade data	Latest water withdrawal data
Libya	1995	MICS, 2000			2001		2004	2000
Liechtenstein	2000			Yes				
Lithuania	2001		ES/BS, 2004	Yes	2003	2005	2006	2000
Luxembourg	2001			Yes	1999–2000c	2003	2007	
Macao, China	2006			Yes			2007	
Macedonia, FYR	2002	MICS, 2005	ES/BS, 2003	Yes	1994	2001	2007	
Madagascar	1993	DHS, 2003/04	PS 2005		2004	2005	2007	2000
Malawi	2008	MICS 2006	LSMS, 2004		1993	2001	2006	2000
Malaysia	2000		ES/BS, 2004/05	Yes		2004	2006	2000
Maldives	2006	MICS, 2001		Yes			2007	
Mali	1998	DHS, 2006	IHS, 2006		1984		2007	2000
Malta	2005			Yes	2001	2005	2007	2000
Marshall Islands	1999							
Mauritania	2000	DHS, 2000/01	IHS, 2000		1984–85		2006	2000
Mauritius	2000			Yes		2004	2007	2003
Mayotte	2007							
Mexico	2005	ENPF, 1995	LFS, 2006		1991	2000	2007	2000
Micronesia, Fed. Sts.	2000							
Moldova	2004	DHS, 2005	ES/BS, 2004	Yes		2005	2007	2000
Monaco	2000							
Mongolia	2000	MICS, 2005	LSMS, 2005	Yes		2000	2006	2000
Montenegro	2003	MICS, 2005/06		Yes				
Morocco	2004	DHS, 2003/04	ES/BS, 2007		1996	2005	2006	2000
Mozambique	2007	DHS, 2003	ES/BS, 2002/03		1999–2000		2007	2000
Myanmar	1983	MICS, 2000			2003		1992	2000
Namibia	2001	DHS, 2006/07	ES/BS, 1993/94		1996–97		2006	2000
Nepal	2001	DHS, 2006	LSMS, 2003/04		2002	2002	2007	2000
Netherlands Antilles	2001			Yes		2004		2000
Netherlands	2001		IHS, 1999	Yes	1999–2000c	2004	2006	
New Caledonia	2004			Yes			2006	
New Zealand	2006			Yes	2002	2004	2006	2000
Nicaragua	2005	DHS, 2001	LSMS, 2005		2001		2007	2000
Niger	2001	DHS/MICS, 2006			1980		2007	2000
Nigeria	2006	MICS, 2007	IHS, 2003		1960		2006	2000
Northern Mariana Islands	2000							
Norway	2001		IS, 2000	Yes	1999	2004	2006	2000
Oman	2003	FHS, 1995			1978–79	2005	2007	2003
Pakistan	1998	DHS, 2006/07	LSMS, 2004/05		2000		2007	2000
Palau	2005			Yes				
Panama	2000	LSMS, 2003	LFS, 2006		2001	2001	2006	2000
Papua New Guinea	2000	DHS, 1996	IHS, 1996			2001	2004	2000
Paraguay	2002	RHS, 2004	IHS, 2007		1991	2002	2006	2000
Peru	2007	DHS, 2004	LSMS, 2006		1994	2005	2006	2000
Philippines	2007	DHS, 2003	ES/BS, 2006	Yes	2002	2003	2006	2000
Poland	2002		ES/BS, 2005	Yes	1996/2002	2004	2007	2000
Portugal	2001			Yes	1999	2004	2006	2000
Puerto Rico	2000	RHS, 1995/96		Yes	1997/2002			
Qatar	2004			Yes	2000–01	2004	2006	2005
Romania	2002	RHS, 1999	LFS, 2005	Yes	2002	2005	2007	2000
Russian Federation	2002	RHS, 1996	IHS, 2005	Yes	1994–95	2005	2007	2000
Rwanda	2002	DHS, 2005	IHS, 1999		1984	1999	2005	2000

	Currency	Base year	Reference year	System of National Accounts	SNA price valuation	Alternative conversion factor	PPP survey year	Balance of Payments Manual in use	External debt	System of trade	Government finance — Accounting concept	IMF data dissemination standard
Samoa	U.S. dollar	2002			VAB			BPM5	Actual	G		
San Marino	Euro	1995	2000	b	VAB					S	C	G
São Tomé and Principe	Dobras	2001			VAP		2005		Actual	S		G
Saudi Arabia	Saudi Arabian riyal	1999			VAP		2005	BPM4		G		G
Senegal	CFA franc	1999	1987	b	VAB		2005	BPM5	Preliminary	S	B	G
Serbia	Serbian dinar	a	2002	b	VAB		2005		Actual	S	C	
Seychelles	Seychelles rupees	1986			VAP			BPM5	Actual	G	C	G
Sierra Leone	Sierra Leonean leone	1990		b	VAB		2005	BPM5	Preliminary	S	B	G
Singapore	Singapore dollar	2000		b	VAB		2005	BPM5		G	C	S
Slovak Republic	Slovak koruna	2000	1995	b	VAB		2005	BPM5		S	C	S
Slovenia	Euro	a	2000	b	VAB		2005	BPM5		S	C	S
Solomon Islands	Solomon Islands dollar	1990			VAB			BPM5	Actual			
Somalia	Somali shilling	1985			VAB	1977–90			Estimate			
South Africa	South African rand	2000		b	VAB		2005	BPM5	Preliminary	G	C	S
Spain	Euro	2000		b	VAB		2005	BPM5		S	C	S
Sri Lanka	Sri Lankan rupee	2002			VAP		2005	BPM5	Actual	G	B	G
St. Kitts and Nevis	Eastern Caribbean dollar	1990		b	VAB			BPM5	Actual	G	C	G
St. Lucia	Eastern Caribbean dollar	1990			VAB			BPM5	Actual	G		G
St. Vincent & Grenadines	Eastern Caribbean dollar	1990			VAB			BPM5	Actual	G		G
Sudan	Sudanese pound	1981/82d	1996		VAB		2005	BPM5	Actual	G	B	G
Suriname	Suriname guilder	1990		b	VAB			BPM5		G		G
Swaziland	Lilangeni	2000			VAB		2005		Actual	G	C	G
Sweden	Swedish krona	a	2000		VAB		2005	BPM5		G	C	S
Switzerland	Swiss franc	2000			VAB		2005	BPM5		S	C	S
Syrian Arab Republic	Syrian pound	2000			VAB	1970–07	2005	BPM5		S	C	G
Tajikistan	Tajik somoni	a	2000	b	VAB	1990–95	2005	BPM5	Preliminary	G	C	G
Tanzania	Tanzania shilling	1992			VAB		2005	BPM5	Estimate	S		G
Thailand	Thai baht	1988			VAP		2005	BPM5	Preliminary	G	C	S
Timor-Leste	U.S. dollar	2000			VAP							
Togo	CFA franc	1978			VAP		2005	BPM5	Actual	S	B	G
Tonga	Pa'anga	2000/01			VAB			BPM5	Actual			G
Trinidad and Tobago	Trinidad and Tobago dollar	2000		b	VAB			BPM5		S	C	G
Tunisia	Tunisian dinar	1990			VAP		2005	BPM5	Actual	G	C	S
Turkey	Turkish lira	1998			VAB		2005	BPM5	Actual	S	B	S
Turkmenistan	Turkmen manat	a	1987	b	VAB	1987–95, 1997–07		BPM5	Actual	G		
Uganda	Uganda shilling	2001/02			VAB		2005	BPM5	Actual	G	B	G
Ukraine	Ukrainian hryvnia	a	2003	b	VAB	1987–95	2005	BPM5	Preliminary	G	C	S
United Arab Emirates	U.A.E. dirham	1995			VAB			BPM4		G	C	G
United Kingdom	Pound sterling	2000		b	VAB		2005	BPM5		G	C	S
United States	U.S. dollar	a	2000		VAB		2005	BPM5		G	C	S
Uruguay	Uruguayan peso	1983			VAB		2005	BPM5	Actual	S	C	S
Uzbekistan	Uzbek sum	a	1997	b	VAB	1990–95		BPM5	Estimate	G		
Vanuatu	Vatu	1983			VAP			BPM5	Actual			G
Venezuela, RB	Bolivar fuerte	1997			VAB		2005	BPM5	Actual	G	C	G
Vietnam	Vietnamese dong	1994		b	VAP	1991	2005	BPM4	Estimate	G	C	G
Virgin Islands (U.S.)	U.S. dollar	1982			VAB					G		
West Bank and Gaza	Israeli new shekel	1997			VAB						B	G
Yemen, Rep.	Yemen rial	1990			VAP	1990–96	2005	BPM5	Actual	G	B	G
Zambia	Zambian kwacha	1994			VAB	1990–92	2005	BPM5	Preliminary	G	B	G
Zimbabwe	Zimbabwe dollar	1990			VAB	1991, 1998	2005	BPM5	Actual	G	C	G

PRIMARY DATA DOCUMENTATION

	Latest population census	Latest demographic, education, or health household survey	Source of most recent income and expenditure data	Vital registration complete	Latest agricultural census	Latest industrial data	Latest trade data	Latest water withdrawal data
Samoa	2006				1999		2005	
San Marino	2000			Yes				
São Tomé and Principe	2001			Yes			2005	
Saudi Arabia	2004	Demographic survey, 2007			1999		2005	2006
Senegal	2002	DHS, 2005	PS 2005		1998–1999	2002	2006	2002
Serbia	2002	MICS, 2005/06		Yes			2006	
Seychelles	2002			Yes	1998		2006	2003
Sierra Leone	2004	MICS, 2005, DHS 2008	IHS, 2002/03		1984–1985		2007	2000
Singapore	2000	General household, 2005		Yes		2004	2006	
Slovak Republic	2001		IS, 1997	Yes	2001	2004	2006	
Slovenia	2002		ES/BS, 2004	Yes	2000		2006	
Solomon Islands	1999							
Somalia	1987	MICS, 2006					1982	2003
South Africa	2001	DHS, 1998	ES/BS, 2000		2000	2005	2007	2000
Spain	2001		IHS, 2000	Yes	1999	2004	2006	2000
Sri Lanka	2001	DHS, 1987	ES/BS, 2002	Yes	2002		2005	2000
St. Kitts and Nevis	2001			Yes			2006	
St. Lucia	2001		IHS, 1995	Yes			2007	
St. Vincent & Grenadines	2001			Yes				
Sudan	1993	MICS-PAPFAM 2006				2001	2006	2000
Suriname	2004	MICS, 2000	ES/BS, 1999	Yes		2004	2001	2000
Swaziland	2007	DHS, 2006	ES/BS, 2000/01		2003		2007	2000
Sweden	2005		IS, 2000	Yes	1999–2000	2004	2007	2000
Switzerland	2000		ES/BS, 2000	Yes	2000	2003	2006	2000
Syrian Arab Republic	2004	MICS, 2006			1981		2007	2003
Tajikistan	2000	MICS, 2005	LSMS, 2004	Yes	1994		2000	2000
Tanzania	2002	DHS, 2004, SPA, 2006	ES/BS, 2000/01		2002–2003		2007	2002
Thailand	2000	MICS 2005/06	IHS, 2004		2003	2000	2006	2000
Timor-Leste	2004	DGHS, 2003	LSMS, 2001					
Togo	1981	MICS, 2006	CWIQ, 2006		1996		2007	2002
Tonga	2006			Yes	2001		2007	
Trinidad and Tobago	2000	MICS, 2006	IHS, 1992	Yes	2004	2005	2006	2000
Tunisia	2004	MICS, 2006	IHS, 2000		2004		2006	2000
Turkey	2000	DHS, 2003	LFS, 2005		2001	2001	2006	2003
Turkmenistan	1995	DHS,2006	LSMS, 1998	Yes			2000	2000
Uganda	2002	DHS, 2006	PS, 2005		1991	2000	2006	
Ukraine	2001	DHS, 2007	ES/BS, 2005	Yes		2004	2007	2000
United Arab Emirates	2005				1998		2006	2005
United Kingdom	2001		IS, 1999	Yes	1999–2000[c]	2004	2006	2000
United States	2000	CPS(monthly)	LFS 2000	Yes	1997/2002	2004	2007	2000
Uruguay	2004		IHS, 2006	Yes	2000	2004	2006	2000
Uzbekistan	1989	MICS, 2006	ES/BS, 2003	Yes				2000
Vanuatu	1999						2006	
Venezuela, RB	2001	MICS, 2000	IHS, 2006	Yes	1997		2006	
Vietnam	1999	MICS, 2006	IHS, 2006		2001	2000	2006	2000
Virgin Islands (U.S.)	2000			Yes				
West Bank and Gaza	2007	PAPFAM, 2006			1971			
Yemen, Rep.	2004	MICS, 2006	ES/BS, 2005		2002	2004	2006	2000
Zambia	2000	DHS, 2001/02, SPA, 2005	IHS, 2004		1990		2006	2000
Zimbabwe	2002	DHS, 2005/06			1960	1996	2006	2002

Note: For explanation of the abbreviations used in the table see notes following the table.
a. Original chained constant price data are rescaled. b. Country uses the 1993 System of National Accounts methodology. c. Conducted annually. d. Reporting period switch from fiscal year to calendar year from 1996. Pre-1996 data converted to calendar year.

• **Base year** is the base or pricing period used for constant price calculations in the country's national accounts. Price indices derived from national accounts aggregates, such as the implicit deflator for gross domestic product (GDP), express the price level relative to base year prices. • **Reference year** is the year in which the local currency, constant price series of a country is valued. The reference year is usually the same as the base year used to report the constant price series. However, when the constant price data are chain linked, the base year is changed annually, so the data are rescaled to a specific reference year to provide a consistent time series. When the country has not rescaled following a change in base year, World Bank staff rescale the data to maintain a longer historical series. To allow for cross-country comparison and data aggregation, constant price data reported in *World Development Indicators* are rescaled to a common reference year (2000) and currency (U.S. dollars). • **System of National Accounts** identifies countries that use the 1993 System of National Accounts (1993 SNA), the terminology applied in *World Development Indicators* since 2001, to compile national accounts. Although more countries are adopting the 1993 SNA, many still follow the 1968 SNA, and some low-income countries use concepts from the 1953 SNA. • **SNA price valuation** shows whether value added in the national accounts is reported at basic prices (VAB) or producer prices (VAP). Producer prices include taxes paid by producers and thus tend to overstate the actual value added in production. However, VAB can be higher than VAP in countries with high agricultural subsidies. See *About the data* for tables 4.1 and 4.2 for further discussion of national accounts valuation. • **Alternative conversion factor** identifies the countries and years for which a World Bank–estimated conversion factor has been used in place of the official exchange rate (line rf in the International Monetary Fund's [IMF] *International Financial Statistics*). See *Statistical methods* for further discussion of alternative conversion factors. • **Purchasing power parity (PPP) survey year** is the latest available survey year for the International Comparison Program's estimates of PPPs. See *About the data* for table 1.1 for a more detailed description of PPPs. • **Balance of Payments Manual in use** refers to the classification system used to compile and report data on balance of payments items in table 4.15. BPM4 refers to the 4th edition of the IMF's *Balance of Payments Manual* (1977), and BPM5 to the 5th edition (1993). • **External debt** shows debt reporting status for 2007 data. *Actual* indicates that data are as reported, *preliminary* that data are preliminary and include an element of staff estimation, and *estimate* that data are World Bank staff estimates. • **System of trade** refers to the United Nations general trade

system (G) or special trade system (S). Under the general trade system goods entering directly for domestic consumption and goods entered into customs storage are recorded as imports at arrival. Under the special trade system goods are recorded as imports when declared for domestic consumption whether at time of entry or on withdrawal from customs storage. Exports under the general system comprise outward-moving goods: (a) national goods wholly or partly produced in the country; (b) foreign goods, neither transformed nor declared for domestic consumption in the country, that move outward from customs storage; and (c) nationalized goods that have been declared for domestic consumption and move outward without being transformed. Under the special system of trade, exports are categories a and c. In some compilations categories b and c are classified as re-exports. Direct transit trade—goods entering or leaving for transport only—is excluded from both import and export statistics. See *About the data* for tables 4.4, 4.5, and 6.2 for further discussion. • **Government finance accounting concept** is the accounting basis for reporting central government financial data. For most countries government finance data have been consolidated (C) into one set of accounts capturing all central government fiscal activities. Budgetary central government accounts (B) exclude some central government units. See *About the data* for tables 4.10, 4.11, and 4.12 for further details. • **IMF data dissemination standard** shows the countries that subscribe to the IMF's Special Data Dissemination Standard (SDDS) or General Data Dissemination System (GDDS). S refers to countries that subscribe to the SDDS and have posted data on the Dissemination Standards Bulletin Board at http://dsbb.imf.org. G refers to countries that subscribe to the GDDS. The SDDS was established for member countries that have or might seek access to international capital markets to guide them in providing their economic and financial data to the public. The GDDS helps countries disseminate comprehensive, timely, accessible, and reliable economic, financial, and sociodemographic statistics. IMF member countries elect to participate in either the SDDS or the GDDS. Both standards enhance the availability of timely and comprehensive data and therefore contribute to the pursuit of sound macroeconomic policies. The SDDS is also expected to improve the functioning of financial markets. • **Latest population census** shows the most recent year in which a census was conducted and in which at least preliminary results have been released. The preliminary results from the very recent censuses could be reflected in timely revisions if basic data are available, such as population by age and sex, as well as the detailed definition of counting, coverage and completeness. The census includes registration-based censuses for Andorra,

Faeroe Islands, Greenland, Iceland, San Marino, and Sweden. These countries produce similar census tables every 5 or 10 years instead of conducting traditional censuses. A rare case, France has been conducting a rolling census every year since 2004; the 1999 general population census was the last to cover the entire population simultaneously (www.insee.fr/en/recensement/page_accueil_rp.htm). • **Latest demographic, education, or health household survey** indicates the household surveys used to compile the demographic, education, and health data in section 2. CPS is Current Population Survey, DGHS is Demographic and General Health Survey, DHS is Demographic and Health Survey, ENPF is National Family Planning Survey (Encuesta Nacional de Planificacion Familiar), FHS is Family Health Survey, LSMS is Living Standards Measurement Survey, MICS is Multiple Indicator Cluster Survey, NSS is National Sample Survey on Population Change, PAPFAM is Pan Arab Project for Family Health, RHS is Reproductive Health Survey, and SPA is Service Provision Assessments. Detailed information for DHS and SPA are available at www.measuredhs.com/aboutsurveys; for MICS at www.childinfo.org; and for RHS at www.cdc.gov/reproductivehealth/surveys. • **Source of most recent income and expenditure data** shows household surveys that collect income and expenditure data. Names and detailed information on household surveys can be found on the website of the International Household Survey Network (www.surveynetwork.org). Core Welfare Indicator Questionnaire Surveys (CWIQ), developed by the World Bank, measure changes in key social indicators for different population groups—specifically indicators of access, utilization, and satisfaction with core social and economic services. Expenditure survey/budget surveys (ES/BS) collect detailed information on household consumption as well as on general demographic, social, and economic characteristics. Integrated household surveys (IHS) collect detailed information on a wide variety of topics, including health, education, economic activities, housing, and utilities. Income surveys (IS) collect information on the income and wealth of households as well as various social and economic characteristics. Labor force surveys (LFS) collect information on employment, unemployment, hours of work, income, and wages. Living Standards Measurement Studies (LSMS), developed by the World Bank, provide a comprehensive picture of household welfare and the factors that affect it; they typically incorporate data collection at the individual, household, and community levels. Priority surveys (PS) are a light monitoring survey, designed by the World Bank, for collecting data from a large number of households cost-effectively and quickly. Income tax registers (ITR) provide information on a population's income and allowance, such as gross income, taxable income, and taxes by socioeconomic group. 1-2-3 surveys (1-2-3) are implemented in three phases and collect sociodemographic and employment data, data on the informal sector, and information on living conditions and household consumption. • **Vital registration complete** identifies countries judged to have at least 90 percent complete registries of vital (birth and death) statistics by the United Nations Statistics Division and reported in Population and Vital Statistics Reports. Countries with complete vital statistics registries may have more accurate and more timely demographic indicators than other countries. • **Latest agricultural census** shows the most recent year in which an agricultural census was conducted and reported to the Food and Agriculture Organization of the United Nations. • **Latest industrial data** show the most recent year for which manufacturing value added data at the three-digit level of the International Standard Industrial Classification (ISIC, revision 2 or 3) are available in the United Nations Industrial Development Organization database. • **Latest trade data** show the most recent year for which structure of merchandise trade data from the United Nations Statistics Division's Commodity Trade (Comtrade) database are available. • **Latest water withdrawal data** show the most recent year for which data on freshwater withdrawals have been compiled from a variety of sources. See *About the data* for table 3.5 for more information.

Exceptional reporting periods

In most economies the **fiscal year** is concurrent with the calendar year. Exceptions are shown in the table at right. The ending date reported here is for the fiscal year of the central government. Fiscal years for other levels of government and reporting years for statistical surveys may differ. And some countries that follow a fiscal year report their national accounts data on a calendar year basis as shown in the *reporting period* column.

The **reporting period for national accounts data** is designated as either calendar year basis (CY) or fiscal year basis (FY). Most economies report their national accounts and balance of payments data using calendar years, but some use fiscal years. In *World Development Indicators* fiscal year data are assigned to the calendar year that contains the larger share of the fiscal year. If a country's fiscal year ends before June 30, data are shown in the first year of the fiscal period; if the fiscal year ends on or after June 30, data are shown in the second year of the period. Balance of payments data are reported in *World Development Indicators* by calendar year and so are not comparable to the national accounts data of the countries that report their national accounts on a fiscal year basis.

Economies with exceptional reporting periods

Economy	Fiscal year end	Reporting period for national accounts data
Afghanistan	Mar. 20	FY
Australia	Jun. 30	FY
Bangladesh	Jun. 30	FY
Botswana	Jun. 30	FY
Canada	Mar. 31	CY
Egypt, Arab Rep.	Jun. 30	FY
Ethiopia	Jul. 7	FY
Gambia, The	Jun. 30	CY
Haiti	Sep. 30	FY
India	Mar. 31	FY
Indonesia	Mar. 31	CY
Iran, Islamic Rep.	Mar. 20	FY
Japan	Mar. 31	CY
Kenya	Jun. 30	CY
Kuwait	Jun. 30	CY
Lesotho	Mar. 31	CY
Malawi	Mar. 31	CY
Mauritius	Jun. 30	FY
Myanmar	Mar. 31	FY
Namibia	Mar. 31	CY
Nepal	Jul. 14	FY
New Zealand	Mar. 31	FY
Pakistan	Jun. 30	FY
Puerto Rico	Jun. 30	FY
Sierra Leone	Jun. 30	CY
Singapore	Mar. 31	CY
South Africa	Mar. 31	CY
Swaziland	Mar. 31	CY
Sweden	Jun. 30	CY
Thailand	Sep. 30	CY
Uganda	Jun. 30	FY
United States	Sep. 30	CY
Zimbabwe	Jun. 30	CY

Revisions to national accounts data

National accounts data are revised by national statistical offices when methodologies change or data sources improve. National accounts data in *World Development Indicators* are also revised when data sources change. The following notes, while not comprehensive, provide information on revisions from previous data.

• **Bhutan.** Data revisions reflect changes in sources. Current and constant price value added data from 1980 to 2006 are from the government of Bhutan. Current price expenditure data for 1989–2005 and constant price expenditure data for 2000–05 are from the Asian Development Bank's *Key Indicators 2007*. • **Botswana.** Large changes in constant price consumption indicators from 1998–2006 are due to statistical discrepancy. The Central Statistical Office published large-scale revisions of constant price discrepancies in GDP for 1996/97–2004/05 in April 2006 and May 2007. • **Brazil.** The Institute

of Geography and Statistics revised its national accounts data. Among the changes are new sources and a change in base year to 2000. • **Burkina Faso.** National accounts value added and expenditure data have been revised for 1985–2006 according to recently released data from the Ministry of Economy and Finance. Constant price series have been linked back since 1984. Valuation is value added at basic prices, and the new base year is 1999. • **Chile.** Data from 2003 onward reflect the Central Bank's new series using 2003 as the base year. • **China.** The base year for constant price data changed from 1990 to 2000. • **Côte d'Ivoire.** Data for 1999–2006 were revised using data from the IMF, national authorities, and World Bank staff estimates. • **Egypt.** Constant price data are updated from official published national accounts. Constant price import and export data have been revised based on data from the Central Bank website (www.cbe.org.eg), which lists the constant price expenditure components of GDP. • **Fiji.** Data revisions reflect changes in sources. Data for 1996–2005 were revised using data from the Asian Development Bank's *Key Indicators 2007*. • **India.** In May 2007 the Central Statistical Organization published revised national accounts data for 1951–99 consistent with the new series of national accounts statistics released on January 31, 2006. • **Jordan.** Data have been revised by the Central Bank and the Department of Statistics. • **Lebanon.** Data have been revised by the Central Bank. • **Malawi.** The National Statistical Office, with assistance from Norway, revised its national accounts data. The initial outcome is that GDP will increase by approximately 37 percent. • **Morocco.** The government revised national accounts data from 1998 onward. National accounts value added data switched from producer prices to basic prices. The new base year is 1998. • **São Tomé and Principe.** Data have been revised by the National Statistics Institute. Revised GDP estimates are much higher (47.5 percent for the new base year 2001) than those of the previous series and reflect improvements in coverage. • **Senegal.** National accounts data have been revised to conform to 1993 SNA methodology, and the base year has changed to 1999. Value added data are now in basic prices. Agricultural sector data are entered in the year of production (N) in the 1999 base year of the SNA as opposed to the year following the year of production (N+1) in base year 1987. • **Sudan.** Expenditure items in both current and constant prices for 1988–95 were revised using recent United Nations Statistics Division and IMF *World Economic Outlook* estimates. • **Tanzania.** National accounts expenditure data in current and constant prices have been revised from 1995 onward. Data are from IMF and World Bank staff estimates and Tanzanian authorities.

STATISTICAL METHODS

This section describes some of the statistical procedures used in preparing the World Development Indicators. It covers the methods employed for calculating regional and income group aggregates and for calculating growth rates, and it describes the *World Bank Atlas* method for deriving the conversion factor used to estimate gross national income (GNI) and GNI per capita in U.S. dollars. Other statistical procedures and calculations are described in the *About the data* sections following each table.

Aggregation rules

Aggregates based on the World Bank's regional and income classifications of economies appear at the end of most tables. The countries included in these classifications are shown on the flaps on the front and back covers of the book. Most tables also include the aggregate euro area. This aggregate includes the member states of the Economic and Monetary Union (EMU) of the European Union that have adopted the euro as their currency: Austria, Belgium, Cyprus, Finland, France, Germany, Greece, Ireland, Italy, Luxembourg, Malta, Netherlands, Portugal, Slovak Republic, Slovenia, and Spain. Other classifications, such as the European Union and regional trade blocs, are documented in *About the data* for the tables in which they appear.

Because of missing data, aggregates for groups of economies should be treated as approximations of unknown totals or average values. Regional and income group aggregates are based on the largest available set of data, including values for the 153 economies shown in the main tables, other economies shown in table 1.6, and Taiwan, China. The aggregation rules are intended to yield estimates for a consistent set of economies from one period to the next and for all indicators. Small differences between sums of subgroup aggregates and overall totals and averages may occur because of the approximations used. In addition, compilation errors and data reporting practices may cause discrepancies in theoretically identical aggregates such as world exports and world imports.

Five methods of aggregation are used in *World Development Indicators*:

- For group and world totals denoted in the tables by a *t*, missing data are imputed based on the relationship of the sum of available data to the total in the year of the previous estimate. The imputation process works forward and backward from 2000. Missing values in 2000 are imputed using one of several proxy variables for which complete data are available in that year. The imputed value is calculated so that it (or its proxy) bears the same relationship to the total of available data. Imputed values are usually not calculated if missing data account for more than a third of the total in the benchmark year. The variables used as proxies are GNI in U.S. dollars, total population, exports and imports of goods and services in U.S. dollars, and value added in agriculture, industry, manufacturing, and services in U.S. dollars.
- Aggregates marked by an *s* are sums of available data. Missing values are not imputed. Sums are not computed if more than a third of the observations in the series or a proxy for the series are missing in a given year.
- Aggregates of ratios are denoted by a *w* when calculated as weighted averages of the ratios (using the value of the denominator or, in some cases, another

indicator as a weight) and denoted by a *u* when calculated as unweighted averages. The aggregate ratios are based on available data, including data for economies not shown in the main tables. Missing values are assumed to have the same average value as the available data. No aggregate is calculated if missing data account for more than a third of the value of weights in the benchmark year. In a few cases the aggregate ratio may be computed as the ratio of group totals after imputing values for missing data according to the above rules for computing totals.

- Aggregate growth rates are denoted by a *w* when calculated as a weighted average of growth rates. In a few cases growth rates may be computed from time series of group totals. Growth rates are not calculated if more than half the observations in a period are missing. For further discussion of methods of computing growth rates see below.
- Aggregates denoted by an *m* are medians of the values shown in the table. No value is shown if more than half the observations for countries with a population of more than 1 million are missing.

Exceptions to the rules occur throughout the book. Depending on the judgment of World Bank analysts, the aggregates may be based on as little as 50 percent of the available data. In other cases, where missing or excluded values are judged to be small or irrelevant, aggregates are based only on the data shown in the tables.

Growth rates

Growth rates are calculated as annual averages and represented as percentages. Except where noted, growth rates of values are computed from constant price series. Three principal methods are used to calculate growth rates: least squares, exponential endpoint, and geometric endpoint. Rates of change from one period to the next are calculated as proportional changes from the earlier period.

Least-squares growth rate. Least-squares growth rates are used wherever there is a sufficiently long time series to permit a reliable calculation. No growth rate is calculated if more than half the observations in a period are missing. The least-squares growth rate, *r*, is estimated by fitting a linear regression trend line to the logarithmic annual values of the variable in the relevant period. The regression equation takes the form

$$\ln X_t = a + bt$$

which is equivalent to the logarithmic transformation of the compound growth equation,

$$X_t = X_0 (1 + r)^t.$$

In this equation X is the variable, t is time, and $a = \ln X_0$ and $b = \ln (1 + r)$ are parameters to be estimated. If b^* is the least-squares estimate of b, then the average annual growth rate, r, is obtained as $[\exp(b^*) - 1]$ and is multiplied by 100 for expression as a percentage. The calculated growth rate is an average rate that is representative of the available observations over the entire period. It does not necessarily match the actual growth rate between any two periods.

Exponential growth rate. The growth rate between two points in time for certain demographic indicators, notably labor force and population, is calculated from the equation

$$r = \ln(p_n/p_0)/n$$

where p_n and p_0 are the last and first observations in the period, n is the number of years in the period, and ln is the natural logarithm operator. This growth rate is based on a model of continuous, exponential growth between two points in time. It does not take into account the intermediate values of the series. Nor does it correspond to the annual rate of change measured at a one-year interval, which is given by $(p_n - p_{n-1})/p_{n-1}$.

Geometric growth rate. The geometric growth rate is applicable to compound growth over discrete periods, such as the payment and reinvestment of interest or dividends. Although continuous growth, as modeled by the exponential growth rate, may be more realistic, most economic phenomena are measured only at intervals, in which case the compound growth model is appropriate. The average growth rate over n periods is calculated as

$$r = \exp[\ln(p_n/p_0)/n] - 1.$$

Like the exponential growth rate, it does not take into account intermediate values of the series.

World Bank *Atlas* method

In calculating GNI and GNI per capita in U.S. dollars for certain operational purposes, the World Bank uses the *Atlas* conversion factor. The purpose of the *Atlas* conversion factor is to reduce the impact of exchange rate fluctuations in the cross-country comparison of national incomes.

The *Atlas* conversion factor for any year is the average of a country's exchange rate (or alternative conversion factor) for that year and its exchange rates for the two preceding years, adjusted for the difference between the rate of inflation in the country and that in Japan, the United Kingdom, the United States, and the euro area. A country's inflation rate is measured by the change in its GDP deflator.

The inflation rate for Japan, the United Kingdom, the United States, and the euro area, representing international inflation, is measured by the change in the "SDR deflator". (Special drawing rights, or SDRs, are the International Monetary Fund's unit of account.) The SDR deflator is calculated as a weighted average of these countries' GDP deflators in SDR terms, the weights being the amount of each country's currency in one SDR unit. Weights vary over time because both the composition of the SDR and the relative exchange rates for each currency change. The SDR deflator is calculated in SDR terms first and then converted to U.S. dollars using the SDR to dollar *Atlas* conversion factor. The *Atlas* conversion factor is then applied to a country's GNI. The resulting GNI in U.S. dollars is divided by the midyear population to derive GNI per capita.

When official exchange rates are deemed to be unreliable or unrepresentative of the effective exchange rate during a period, an alternative estimate of the exchange rate is used in the *Atlas* formula (see below).

The following formulas describe the calculation of the *Atlas* conversion factor for year t:

$$e_t^* = \frac{1}{3}\left[e_{t-2}\left(\frac{p_t}{p_{t-2}} \Big/ \frac{p_t^{S\$}}{p_{t-2}^{S\$}}\right) + e_{t-1}\left(\frac{p_t}{p_{t-1}} \Big/ \frac{p_t^{S\$}}{p_{t-1}^{S\$}}\right) + e_t\right]$$

and the calculation of GNI per capita in U.S. dollars for year t:

$$Y_t^\$ = (Y_t/N_t)/e_t^*$$

where e_t^* is the *Atlas* conversion factor (national currency to the U.S. dollar) for year t, e_t is the average annual exchange rate (national currency to the U.S. dollar) for year t, p_t is the GDP deflator for year t, $p_t^{S\$}$ is the SDR deflator in U.S. dollar terms for year t, $Y_t^\$$ is the *Atlas* GNI per capita in U.S. dollars in year t, Y_t is current GNI (local currency) for year t, and N_t is the midyear population for year t.

Alternative conversion factors

The World Bank systematically assesses the appropriateness of official exchange rates as conversion factors. An alternative conversion factor is used when the official exchange rate is judged to diverge by an exceptionally large margin from the rate effectively applied to domestic transactions of foreign currencies and traded products. This applies to only a small number of countries, as shown in *Primary data documentation*. Alternative conversion factors are used in the *Atlas* methodology and elsewhere in *World Development Indicators* as single-year conversion factors.

CREDITS

World Development Indicators 2009 draws on a wide range of World Bank reports and numerous external sources, listed in the bibliography following this section. Many people inside and outside the World Bank helped in writing and producing the book. The team would like to particularly acknowledge the help and encouragement of Justin Lin, Senior Vice President and Chief Economist of the World Bank, and Shaida Badiee, Director, Development Data Group. The team is also grateful to the people who provided valuable comments on the entire book. This note identifies many of those who made specific contributions. Many others, too numerous to acknowledge here, helped in many ways for which the team is extremely grateful.

1. World view

The introduction to section 1 was prepared by Sarwar Lateef, Soong Sup Lee, and Eric Swanson. Valuable suggestions were provided by Amar Bhattacharya, Milan Brahmbhatt, Mansoor Dailami, Alan Gelb, and Claudia Paz Sepulveda. Maurizio Bussolo and Rafael de Hoyos of the Development Economics Prospects Group helped in computing the inequality estimates. Changqing Sun prepared the estimates of gross national income in purchasing power parity (PPP) terms. K.M. Vijayalakshmi prepared tables 1.1 and 1.6. Uranbileg Batjargal prepared table 1.4, with valuable assistance from Azita Amjadi. Tables 1.2, 1.3, and 1.5 were prepared by Masako Hiraga. Juan Pedro Schmid and Mona Prasad of the World Bank's Economic Policy and Debt Department provided the estimates of debt relief for the Heavily Indebted Poor Countries Debt Initiative and Multilateral Debt Relief Initiative.

2. People

Section 2 was prepared by Masako Hiraga and Sulekha Patel in partnership with the World Bank's Human Development Network and the Development Research Group in the Development Economics Vice Presidency. Shota Hatakeyama and William Prince provided invaluable assistance in data and table preparation, and Kiyomi Horiuchi prepared the demographic estimates and projections. The introduction was written by the International Labour Organization's (ILO) Employment Trends Team. The poverty estimates were prepared by Shaohua Chen and Prem Sangraula of the World Bank's Poverty Monitoring Group and Changquin Sun. The data on children at work were prepared by Lorenzo Guarcello and Furio Rosati from the Understanding Children's Work project. The data on health gaps by income and gender were based on data prepared by Darcy Gallucio and Davidson Gwatkin of the Human Development Network. Other contributions were provided by Eduard Bos, Charu Garg, Inez Mikkelsen-Lopez, and Emi Suzuki (population, health, and nutrition); Montserrat Pallares-Miralles (pension); Lawrence Jeffrey Johnson of the ILO (labor force); Juan Cruz Perusia and Olivier Labeof the United Nations Educational, Scientific, and Cultural Organization Institute for Statistics (education and literacy); the World Health Organization's Chandika Indikadahena (health expenditure), Monika Bloessner and Mercedes de Onis (malnutrition and overweight), Neeru Gupta (health workers), Mie Inoue and Jessica Ho (hospital beds), Rifat Hossain (water and sanitation),

and Seyed Mehran Hosseini (tuberculosis); Omar Shafey of the American Cancer Society (tobacco); Delice Gan of the International Diabetes Federation (diabetes), and Nyein Nyein Lwin of the United Nations Children's Fund (health). Valuable comments and inputs at all stages of the production process came from Eric Swanson and on the introduction from Sarwar Lateef.

3. Environment

Section 3 was prepared by Mehdi Akhlaghi and M.H. Saeed Ordoubadi in partnership with the World Bank's Sustainable Development Network. Important contributions were made by Carola Fabi and Edward Gillin of the Food and Agriculture Organization of the United Nations; Ricardo Quercioli of the International Energy Agency; Amy Cassara, Christian Layke, Daniel Prager, and Robin White of the World Resources Institute; Laura Battlebury of the World Conservation Monitoring Centre; and Gerhard Metchies of German Technical Cooperation (GTZ). The World Bank's Environment Department devoted substantial staff resources to the book, for which the team is very grateful. M.H. Saeed Ordoubadi wrote the introduction with valuable comments from Sarwar Lateef, Bruce Ross-Larson, and Eric Swanson. Other contributions were made by Susmita Dasgupta, Kirk Hamilton, Craig Meisner, Kiran Pandey, Giovanni Ruta, and Jana Stover.

4. Economy

Section 4 was prepared by K.M. Vijayalakshmi in close collaboration with the Sustainable Development and Economic Data Team of the World Bank's Development Data Group, led by Soong Sup Lee. K.M. Vijayalakshmi wrote the introduction with valuable suggestions from Sarwar Lateef, Soong Sup Lee, and Eric Swanson. Useful comments were provided by Hinh Dinh and Alice Kuegler. Contributions to the section were provided by Azita Amjadi (trade). The national accounts data for low- and middle-income economies were gathered by the World Bank's regional staff through the annual Unified Survey. Maja Bresslauer, Mahyar Eshragh-Tabary, Victor Gabor, Bala Bhaskar Naidu Kalimili, and Soong Sup Lee worked on updating, estimating, and validating the databases for national accounts. The team is grateful to the International Monetary Fund, Organisation for Economic Co-operation and Development, United Nations Industrial Development Organization, and World Trade Organization for access to their databases.

5. States and markets

Section 5 was prepared by David Cieslikowski and Raymond Muhula, in partnership with the World Bank's Financial and Private Sector Development Network, Poverty Reduction and Economic Management Network, Sustainable Development Network, International Finance Corporation, and external partners. David Cieslikowski wrote the introduction with input from Sarwar Lateef and Eric Swanson. Other contributors include Ada Karina Izaguirre (privatization and infrastructure projects); Leora Klapper (business registration); Federica Saliola (Enterprise Surveys); Svetlana Bagaudinova (Doing Business); Alka Banerjee and Isilay Cabuk (Standard & Poor's global stock market indexes); Satish Mannan (public policies and institutions); Nigel Adderley of the International Institute for Strategic Studies (military personnel); Bjorn Hagelin and Petter Stålenheim of the Stockholm International Peace Research Institute (military expenditures and arms transfers); Imed Ben Hamadi of the International Road Federation, Ananthanaryan Sainarayan of the International Civil Aviation Organization, and Helene Stephan (transport); Jane Degerlund of Containerisation International (ports); Vanessa Grey and Esperanza Magpantay of the International Telecommunication Union; Ernesto Fernandez Polcuch of the United Nations Educational, Scientific, and Cultural Organization Institute for Statistics (research and development, researchers, and technicians); and Anders Halvorsen of the World Information Technology and Services Alliance (information and communication technology expenditures).

6. Global links

Section 6 was prepared by Uranbileg Batjargal in partnership with the Financial Data Team of the World Bank's Development Data Group, Development Research Group (trade), Prospects Group (commodity prices), and external partners. Uranbileg Batjargal wrote the introduction, with valuable comments from Sarwar Lateef and Eric Swanson. Olga Akcadag and Nino Kostava provided research assistance. Substantial input for the data and tables came from Azita Amjadi (trade and tariffs) and Nino Kostava (external debt and financial data). Eric Swanson provided guidance on table contents and organization. Other contributors include Frederic Docquier (emigration rates), Flavine Creppy and Yumiko Mochizuki of the United Nations Conference on Trade and Development, and Francis Ng (trade); Betty Dow (commodity prices); Dilek Aykut (foreign direct investment flows); Eung Ju Kim (financing through capital markets); Olga Akcadag (Bloomberg, external debt, and financial data); Yasmin Ahmad and Cecile Sangare of the Organisation for Economic Co-operation and Development (aid); Ibrahim Levent and Alagiriswamy Venkatesan (external debt); Henrik Pilgaard of the United Nations Refugee Agency (refugees); Bela Hovy of the United Nations Population Division (migration); K.M. Vijayalakshmi (remittances); and Teresa Ciller of the World Tourism Organization (tourism). Ramgopal Erabelly, Shelley Lai Fu, and William Prince provided valuable technical assistance.

Other parts of the book

Jeff Lecksell of the World Bank's Map Design Unit coordinated preparation of the maps on the inside covers. David Cieslikowski prepared the *Users guide.* Eric Swanson wrote *Statistical methods.* K.M. Vijayalakshmi coordinated preparation of *Primary data documentation,* and Awatif Abuzeid and Buyant Erdene Khaltarkhuu assisted in updating the *Primary data documentation* table. Richard Fix and Beatriz Prieto-Oramas prepared *Partners* and *Index of indicators.*

Database management

Mehdi Akhlaghi and William Prince coordinated management of the integrated World Development Indicators database. Development and operation of the database management system was made possible by the Data and Information Systems Team, which included Ying Chi, Ramgopal Erabelly, Shelley Fu, Shahin Outadi, and Atsushi Shimo, under the leadership of Reza Farivari.

Design, production, and editing

Richard Fix and Beatriz Prieto-Oramas coordinated all stages of production with Communications Development Incorporated, which provided overall design direction, editing, and layout, led by Meta de Coquereaumont, Bruce Ross-Larson, and Christopher Trott. Elaine Wilson created the graphics and typeset the book. Joseph Caponio and Amye Kenall provided proofreading and production assistance. Communications Development's London partner, Peter Grundy of Peter Grundy Art & Design, provided art direction and design. Staff from External Affairs oversaw printing and dissemination of the book.

Client services

The Development Data Group's Client Services and Communications Team (Azita Amjadi, Richard Fix, Buyant Erdene Khaltarkhuu, Alison Kwong, and Beatriz Prieto-Oramas) contributed to the design and planning of *World Development Indicators 2009* and helped coordinate work with the Office of the Publisher.

Administrative assistance and office technology support

Awatif Abuzeid and Estela Zamora provided administrative assistance. Jean-Pierre Djomalieu, Gytis Kanchas, Nacer Megherbi, and Shahin Outadi provided information technology support.

Publishing and dissemination

The Office of the Publisher, under the direction of Carlos Rossel, provided valuable assistance throughout the production process. Denise Bergeron, Stephen McGroarty, and Nora Ridolfi coordinated printing and supervised marketing and distribution. Merrell Tuck-Primdahl of the Development Economics Vice President's Office managed the communications strategy.

World Development Indicators CD-ROM

Programming and testing were carried out under the coordination of Reza Farivari by Azita Amjadi, Shelley Fu, Buyant Erdene Khaltarkhuu, Vilas K. Mandlekar, Nacer Megherbi, William Prince, and Malarvizhi Veerappan. Masako Hiraga produced the social indicators tables. Kiyomi Horiuchi produced the population projection tables. William Prince coordinated user interface design and overall production and provided quality assurance. Photo credits belong to the World Bank photo library.

WDI Online

Design, programming, and testing were carried out by Reza Farivari and his team: Azita Amjadi, Ramgopal Erabelly, Shelley Fu, Buyant Erdene Khaltarkhuu, and Shahin Outadi. William Prince coordinated production and provided quality assurance. Valentina Kalk and Malika Khek of the Office of the Publisher were responsible for implementation of *WDI Online* and management of the subscription service.

Client feedback

The team is grateful to the many people who have taken the time to provide assistance on its publications. Their feedback and suggestions have helped improve this year's edition.

BIBLIOGRAPHY

Aminian, Nathalie, K.C. Fung, and Francis Ng. 2008. "Integration of Markets vs. Integration by Agreements." Policy Research Working Paper 4546. World Bank, Development Research Group, Washington, D.C.

An, Feng, and Amanda Sauer. 2004. "Comparison of Passenger Vehicle Fuel Economy and Greenhouse Gas Emission Standards around the World." Pew Center on Global Climate Change, Arlington, Va.

Anthoff, David, Robert J. Nichols, Richard S. J. Tol, and Athanasios T. Vafeidis. 2006. "Global and Regional Exposure to Large Rises in Sea-level: A Sensitivity Analysis." Working Paper 96. Tyndall Centre for Climate Change Research, University of East Anglia, Norwich, U.K.

Ashford, Lori S., Davidson R. Gwatkin, and Abdo S. Yazbeck. 2006. *Designing Health and Population Programs to Reach the Poor.* Washington, D.C.: Population Reference Bureau.

Ball, Nicole. 1984. "Measuring Third World Security Expenditure: A Research Note." *World Development* 12 (2): 157–64.

Bank for International Settlements. 2007. *Triennial Central Bank Survey, December 2007. Foreign Exchange and Derivatives Market Activity in 2007.* Basel, Switzerland: Bank for International Settlements.

———. 2008. "OTC Derivatives Market Activity in the First Half of 2008." Bank for International Settlements, Monetary and Economic Department, Basel, Switzerland. [www.bis.org/publ/otc_hy0811.pdf].

———. 2009. *Capital Flows and Emerging Market Economies.* Committee on the Global Financial System Paper 33. Report submitted by a working group chaired by Rakesh Mohan of the Reserve Bank of India. Basel, Switzerland: Bank for International Settlements.

Beck, Thorsten, and Ross Levine. 2001. "Stock Markets, Banks, and Growth: Correlation or Causality?" Policy Research Working Paper 2670. World Bank, Development Research Group, Washington, D.C.

Bhattacharya, Amar. 2008. "Global Financial Governance: From Where….to Where?" Paper prepared for Conference on Governance of a Globalizing World: Whither Asia and the West?, December 4–6, National University of Singapore.

Bhattacharya, Amar, Kemal Derviş, and José Antonio Ocampo. 2008. "Responding to the Financial Crisis, an Agenda for Global Action." Paper for the Global Financial Crisis Meeting, November 13, Columbia University, New York.

Blankfein, Lloyd. 2009. "Do Not Destroy the Essential Catalyst of Risk." *Financial Times.* February 9, p. 7.

Board of Governors of the Federal Reserve System. n.d. "Statistics and Historical Data." [www.federalreserve.gov/econresdata/releases/statisticsdata.htm]

Brahmbhatt, Milan. 2008. "Low Income Countries and the Financial Crisis, Vulnerabilities and Policy Options." World Bank, Poverty Reduction and Economic Management, Washington, D.C.

Brunnermeier, Markus K. 2009. "Deciphering the Liquidity and Credit Crunch 2007–08." *Journal of Economic Perspectives* 23 (1, winter): 77–100.

Burton, Ian, Elliot Diringer, and Joel Smith. 2006. "Climate Change: International Policy Options." Pew Center on Global Climate Change, Arlington, Va.

Caiola, Marcello. 1995. *A Manual for Country Economists.* Training Series 1, Vol. 1. Washington, D.C.: International Monetary Fund.

Caprio, Gerard, Asli Demirgüç-Kunt, and Edward J. Kane. 2008. "The 2007 Meltdown in Structured Securitization, Searching for Lessons, Not Scapegoats." Policy Research Working Paper 4756. World Bank, Washington, D.C.

Caprio, Gerard and Daniel Klingebiel. 1996 "Bank Insolvency: Bad Luck, Bad Policy or Bad Banking?" Paper presented at Annual World Bank Conference on Development Economics 1996, Washington, D.C.

———. 2003. *Episodes of Systemic and Borderline Financial Crisis.* Washington, D.C.: World Bank.

Chen, Shaohua, and Martin Ravallion. 2008. "The Developing World Is Poorer than We Thought, but No Less Successful in the Fight Against Poverty?" Policy Research Working Paper 4703. World Bank, Washington, D.C.

Chomitz, Kenneth M., Piet Buys, and Timothy S. Thomas. 2005. "Quantifying the Rural-Urban Gradient in Latin America and the Caribbean." Policy Research Working Paper 3634. World Bank, Development Research Group, Washington, D.C.

CIESIN (Center for International Earth Science Information Network). 2005. Gridded Population of the World. Columbia University and Centro Internacional de Agricultura Tropical. [http://sedac.ciesin.columbia.edu/gpw/].

Claessens, Stijn, Daniela Klingebiel, and Sergio L. Schmukler. 2002. "Explaining the Migration of Stocks from Exchanges in Emerging Economies to International Centers." Policy Research Working Paper 2816. World Bank, Washington, D.C.

Claessens, Stijn, M. Ayhan Kose, and Marco E. Terrones. 2008. "What Happens During Recessions, Crunches and Busts?" IMF Working Paper 274. International Monetary Fund, Research Department, Washington, D.C.

Commission of the European Communities, IMF (International Monetary Fund), OECD (Organisation for Economic Co-operation and Development), United Nations, and World Bank. 2002. *System of Environmental and Economic Accounts: SEEA 2000.* New York.

Containerisation International. 2008. *Containerisation International Yearbook 2008.* London: Informa Maritime & Transport.

Corrao, Marlo Ann, G. Emmanuel Guindon, Namita Sharma, and Dorna Fakhrabadi Shokoohi. 2000. *Tobacco Control Country Profiles.* Atlanta, Ga.: American Cancer Society.

Dasgupta, Susmita, Denoit Laplante, Craig Meisner, David Wheeler, and Jianping Yan. 2007. "The Impact of Sea Level Rise on Developing Countries: A Comparative Analysis." Policy Research Working Paper 4136. World Bank, Development Research Group, Washington, D.C.

De Grauwe, Paul. 2008. "Lessons from the Banking Crisis: A Return to Narrow Banking." University of Leuven and CESifo.

De Onis, Mercedes, and Monika Blossner. 2000. "The WHO Global Database on Child Growth and Malnutrition: Methodology and Applications." *International Journal of Epidemiology* 32. 518–26.

De Onis, Mercedes, Adelheid W. Onyango, Elaine Borghi, Cutberto Garza, and Hong Yang. 2006. "Comparison of the World Health Organization (WHO) Child Growth

Standards and the National Center for Health Statistics/WHO International Growth Reference: Implications for Child Health Programmes." *Public Health Nutrition* 9 (7): 942–47.

Demirgüç-Kunt, Asli, and Ross Levine. 1996. "Stock Market Development and Financial Intermediaries: Stylized Facts." *World Bank Economic Review* 10 (2): 291–321.

Deutch, John, Anne Lauvergeon, and Widhyawan Prawiraatmadja. 2007. *Energy Security and Climate Change.* Task Force Report 61. Washington, D.C.: The Trilateral Commission.

Docquier, Frédéric, Abdeslam Marfouk, and B. Lindsay Lowell. 2007. "A Gendered Assessment of the Brain Drain." Policy Research Working Paper 4613. World Bank, Washington, D.C.

El-Erian, Mohamed A. 2008. "A Crisis to Remember." *Finance and Development* 45 (4): 15–17.

Eurostat (Statistical Office of the European Communities). Various years. *Demographic Statistics.* Luxembourg.

————. Various years. *Statistical Yearbook.* Luxembourg.

Faiz, Asif, Christopher S. Weaver, and Michael P. Walsh. 1996. *Air Pollution from Motor Vehicles: Standards and Technologies for Controlling Emissions.* Washington, D.C.: World Bank.

Fankhauser, Samuel. 1995. *Valuing Climate Change: The Economics of the Greenhouse.* London: Earthscan.

FAO (Food and Agriculture Organization). 2005. *Global Forest Resources Assessment 2005.* Rome: Food and Agriculture Organization.

————. 2008. *The State of Food and Agriculture 2008.* Rome: Food and Agriculture Organization.

————. n.d. FAOSTAT database. [http://faostat.fao.org/default.aspx].

————. Various years. *Fertilizer Yearbook.* FAO Statistics Series. Rome: Food and Agriculture Organization.

————. Various years. *Production Yearbook.* FAO Statistics Series. Rome: Food and Agriculture Organization.

————. Various years. *State of Food Insecurity in the World.* Rome: Food and Agriculture Organization.

————. Various years. *Trade Yearbook.* FAO Statistics Series. Rome: Food and Agriculture Organization.

Frankhauser, Pierre. 1994. "Fractales, tissus urbains et reseaux de transport." *Revue d'economie politique* 104: 435–55.

Fredricksen, Birger. 1993. *Statistics of Education in Developing Countries: An Introduction to Their Collection and Analysis.* Paris: United Nations Educational, Scientific, and Cultural Organization.

Gardner-Outlaw, Tom, and Robert Engelman. 1997. "Sustaining Water, Easing Scarcity: A Second Update." Population Action International, Washington, D.C.

GEF (Global Environmental Facility). 2007. "Report on Pledging Meeting for Climate Change Funds." GEF Secretariat, Washington, D.C.

Geithner, Timothy F. 2008. "Reducing Systemic Risk in a Dynamic Financial System." Speech given at Federal Reserve Bank of New York, June 9. [www.newyorkfed.org/newsevents/speeches/2008/tfg080609.html].

Glasier A., A. M. Gulmezoglu, G. Schmid, C. Garcia Moreno, and P.F.A. van Look. 2006. "Sexual and Reproductive Health: A Matter of Life and Death." *Lancet* 368(9547): 1595–1607.

Group of Thirty. 2009. *Financial Reform: A Framework for Financial Stability.* Washington, D.C.

Gwatkin, Davidson R., Shea Rutstein, Kiersten Johnson, Eldaw Suliman, Adam Wagstaff, and Agbessi Amouzou. 2007. *Socio Economic Differences in Health, Nutrition, and Population.* Washington, D.C.: World Bank.

Hamilton, Kirk, and Michael Clemens. 1999. "Genuine Savings Rates in Developing Countries." *World Bank Economic Review* 13 (2): 333–56.

Hamilton, Kirk, and Giovanni Ruta. 2008. "Wealth Accounting, Exhaustible Resources and Social Welfare." *Environmental and Resource Economics* 42 (1): 53–64.

Hanushek, Eric. 2002. *The Long-Run Importance of School Quality.* NBER Working Paper 9071. Cambridge, Mass.: National Bureau of Economic Research.

Happe, Nancy, and John Wakeman-Linn. 1994. "Military Expenditures and Arms Trade: Alternative Data Sources." IMF Working Paper 94/69. International Monetary Fund, Policy Development and Review Department, Washington, D.C.

Hatzichronoglou, Thomas. 1997. "Revision of the High-Technology Sector and Product Classification." STI Working Paper 1997/2. Organisation for Economic Co-operation and Development, Directorate for Science, Technology, and Industry, Paris.

Heston, Alan. 1994. "A Brief Review of Some Problems in Using National Accounts Data in Level of Output Comparisons and Growth Studies." *Journal of Development Economics* 44 (1): 29–52.

Hettige, Hemamala, Muthukumara Mani, and David Wheeler. 1998. "Industrial Pollution in Economic Development: Kuznets Revisited." Policy Research Working Paper 1876. World Bank, Development Research Group, Washington, D.C.

Hinz, Richard Paul, and Montserrat Pallares-Miralles. Forthcoming. "International Patterns of Pension Provision II." Social Protection Discussion Paper. World Bank, Washington, D.C.

Houser T., R. Bradley, B. Childs, J. Werksman, and R. Heilmayr. 2008. *Leveling the Carbon Playing Field: International Competition and US Climate Policy Design.* Washington, D.C.: Peterson Institute for International Economics and World Resources Institute.

IEA (International Energy Agency). 2006. *World Energy Outlook.* Paris.

————. 2007. *World Energy Outlook: China and India Insights.* Paris: International Energy Agency.

————. 2008a. *World Energy Outlook.* Paris: International Energy Agency.

————. 2008b. "Energy Technology Perspectives: Scenarios and Strategies to 2050." International Energy Agency, Paris.

BIBLIOGRAPHY

———. 2008c. "Energy Efficiency Indicators for Public Electricity Production From Fossil Fuels." IEA Information Paper. Organisation for Economic Co-operation/ International Energy Agency, Paris.

———. 2008d. *Worldwide Trends in Energy Use and Efficiency: Key Insight from IEA Indicator Analysis*. Paris: International Energy Agency.

———. 2008e. *Towards a Sustainable Energy Future: IEA Programme of Work on Climate Change, Clean Energy and Sustainable Development*. Paris: International Energy Agency.

———. 2008f. *Deploying Renewables: Principles for Effective Policies*. Paris: International Energy Agency.

———. 2008g. *Energy Efficiency Policy Recommendations*. Paris: International Energy Agency.

———. 2008h. *IEA Work for G-8: 2008 Messages*. Paris: International Energy Agency.

———. 2008i. "Sectoral Approach for Greenhouse Gas Mitigation." Organisation for Economic Co-operation and Development / International Energy Agency, Paris.

———. Various years. *Energy Balances of OECD Countries*. Paris: International Energy Agency.

———. Various years. *Energy Statistics and Balances of Non-OECD Countries*. Paris: International Energy Agency.

———. Various years. *Energy Statistics of OECD Countries*. Paris: International Energy Agency.

ILO (International Labour Organization). 1990. "International Standard Classification of Occupations: ISCO-88." International Labour Organization, Geneva. [http://www.ilo.org/public/english/bureau/stat/isco/isco88/index.htm].

———. 2008. *Trends Econometric Models*. Geneva: International Labour Organization.

———. 2009. *Global Employment Trends*. Geneva: International Labour Organization.

———. Forthcoming. *Guide to the New MDG Employment Indicators*. Geneva: International Labour Organization.

———. Various years. *Key Indicators of the Labour Market*. Geneva: International Labour Organization.

———. Various years. *Yearbook of Labour Statistics*. Geneva: International Labour Organization.

IMF (International Monetary Fund). 1977. *Balance of Payments Manual*. Washington, D.C.: International Monetary Fund.

———. 1993. *Balance of Payments Manual*. Washington, D.C.: International Monetary Fund.

———. 1995. *Balance of Payments Compilation Guide*. Washington, D.C.: International Monetary Fund.

———. 1996. *Balance of Payments Textbook*. Washington, D.C.: International Monetary Fund.

———. 2000. *Monetary and Financial Statistics Manual*. Washington, D.C.: International Monetary Fund.

———. 2001. *Government Finance Statistics Manual*. Washington, D.C.: International Monetary Fund.

———. 2004. *Compilation Guide on Financial Soundness Indicators*. Washington, D.C.: International Monetary Fund.

———. 2008a. *Global Financial Stability Report October 2008: Financial Stress and Deleveraging Macrofinancial Implications and Policy*. Washington, D.C.: International Monetary Fund.

———. 2008b. *World Economic Outlook: Financial Stress, Downturns, and Recoveries*. Washington, D.C.: International Monetary Fund.

———. Various issues. *Direction of Trade Statistics Quarterly*. Washington, D.C.: International Monetary Fund.

———. Various issues. *International Financial Statistics*. Washington, D.C.: International Monetary Fund.

———. Various years. *Balance of Payments Statistics Yearbook*. Washington, D.C.: International Monetary Fund.

———. Various years. *Direction of Trade Statistics Yearbook*. Washington, D.C.: International Monetary Fund.

———. Various years. *Government Finance Statistics Yearbook*. Washington, D.C.: International Monetary Fund.

———. Various years. *International Financial Statistics Yearbook*. Washington, D.C.: International Monetary Fund.

International Civil Aviation Organization. 2008. *Civil Aviation Statistics of the World*. Montreal: International Civil Aviation Organization.

International Diabetes Federation. Various years. *Diabetes Atlas*. Brussels: International Diabetes Federation.

International Institute for Strategic Studies. 2009. *The Military Balance 2009*. London: Oxford University Press.

International Road Federation. 2008. *World Road Statistics 2008*. Geneva: International Road Federation.

International Trade Center, UNCTAD (United Nations Conference on Trade and Development), and WTO (World Trade Organization). n.d. The Millennium Development Goals. Online database. [www.mdg-trade.org/].

International Working Group of External Debt Compilers (Bank for International Settlements, International Monetary Fund, Organisation for Economic Co-operation and Development, and World Bank). 1987. *External Debt Definitions*. Washington, D.C.

IPCC (Intergovernmental Panel on Climate Change). 2007a. *Climate Change 2007: The Physical Science Basis. Contribution of Working Group I to the Fourth Assessment Report of the Intergovernmental Panel on Climate Change*. Cambridge, U.K.: Cambridge University Press.

———. 2007b. "Summary for Policymakers." In *Climate Change 2007: The Physical Science Basis. Contribution of Working Group I to the Fourth Assessment Report of the Intergovernmental Panel on Climate Change*. Cambridge, U.K.: Cambridge University Press.

———. 2007c. "Technical Summary." In S. Solomon, D. Qin, M. Manning, Z. Chen, M. Marquis, K.B. Averyt, M. Tignor and H. L. Miller, eds., *Climate Change 2007: Climate Change Impacts, Adaptation and Vulnerability*. WorkingGroup II

Contribution to the Fourth Assessment Report of the Intergovernmental Panel on Climate Change. Cambridge, U.K.: Cambridge University Press.

ITU (International Telecommunication Union). 2008. World Telecommunication Indicators database. Geneva: International Telecommunication Union.

IUCN (World Conservation Union). 2008. *2008 IUCN Red List of Threatened Species.* Gland, Switzerland: World Conservation Union.

Ivanic, Maros, and Will Martin. 2008. "Implications of Higher Global Food Prices for Poverty in Low-Income Countries." Policy Research Working Paper 4594. World Bank, Development Research Group, Washington, D.C.

Kharas, Homi. 2007. "Trends and Issues in Development Aid." Wolfensohn Center for Development Working Paper. The Brookings Institution, Washington, D.C.

Krugman, Paul. 2008. *The Return of Depression Economics and the Crisis of 2008.* New York: W.W. Norton & Company.

Kunte, Arundhati, Kirk Hamilton, John Dixon, and Michael Clemens. 1998. "Estimating National Wealth: Methodology and Results." Environmental Economics Series 57. World Bank, Environment Department, Washington, D.C.

Laeven, Luc, and Fabian Valencia. 2008. "Systemic Banking Crises: A New Database." IMF Working Paper 08/224. International Monetary Fund, Washington, D.C.

Lanjouw, Jean O., and Peter Lanjouw. 2001. "The Rural Non-Farm Sector: Issues and Evidence from Developing Countries." *Agricultural Economics* 26 (1): 1–23.

Lanjouw, Peter, and Gershon Feder. 2001. "Rural Nonfarm Activities and Rural Development: From Experience toward Strategy." Rural Strategy Discussion Paper 4. World Bank, Washington, D.C.

Lin, Justin Yifu. 2009. "How to Solve the Global Economic Crisis: Making Fiscal Stimulus Packages Work across the World." World Bank, Washington, D.C.

Lopez, Alan D., Colin D. Mathers, Majad Ezzati, Dean T. Jamison, and Christopher J.L. Murray, eds. 2006. *Global Burden of Disease and Risk Factors.* Washington, D.C.: World Bank.

Lovei, Magdolna. 1997. "Toward Effective Pollution Management." *Environment Matters* (fall): 52–3.

Macro International. Various years. *Demographic and Health Surveys.* [www.measuredhs.com].

Mani, Muthukumara, and David Wheeler. 1997. "In Search of Pollution Havens? Dirty Industry in the World Economy, 1960–95." World Bank, Policy Research Department, Washington, D.C.

McKinsey Global Institute. 2008. *Mapping Global Capital Markets: Fifth Annual Report.* New York.

Mitchell, Donald. 2008. "A Note on Rising Food Prices." Policy Research Working Paper 4682. World Bank, Washington, D.C.

Morgan Stanley Capital International Barra. 2009. *MSCI Global Investable Market Indices Methodology.* [www.mscibarra.com/products/indices/equity/methodology.jsp].

Morgenstern, Oskar. 1963. *On the Accuracy of Economic Observations.* Princeton, N.J.: Princeton University Press.

National Science Board. 2008. *Science and Engineering Indicators 2008.* Arlington, Va.: National Science Foundation.

Netcraft. 2008. "Netcraft Secure Server Survey." [www.netcraft.com].

NREL (National Renewable Energy Laboratory) Energy Analysis Office. 2005. "Renewable Energy Cost Trends." [www.nrel.gov/analysis/docs/cost_curves_2005.ppt].

OECD (Organisation for Economic Co-operation and Development). 2005. *Guide to Measuring the Information Society.* DSTI/ICCP/ISS (2005)/6. Paris: Organisation for Economic Co-operation and Development.

———. 2006. *OECD Health Data 2006.* Paris: Organisation for Economic Co-operation and Development.

———. 2008a. *A Profile of Immigrant Populations in the 21st Century: Data from OECD Countries.* Paris: Organisation for Economic Co-operation and Development.

———. 2008b. *Agricultural Policies in OECD Countries: Monitoring and Evaluation—At a Glance 2008.* Paris: Organisation for Economic Co-operation and Development.

———. 2008c. *OECD Information Technology Outlook 2008.* Paris: Organisation for Economic Co-operation and Development.

———. 2008d. *Producer and Consumer Support Estimates, 1986–2007.* OECD Online Database. [www.oecd.org/tad/support/psecse].

———. 2009. "Trade Flows Weaken in Third Quarter 2008." OECD International Trade Statistics News Release. January 27. [www.oecd.org/dataoecd/14/55/42058488.pdf].

———. n.d. Database on Immigrants in OECD countries. Online database. [http://stats.oecd.org, select Demography and Population, then select Migration Statistics].

———. Various issues. *Main Economic Indicators.* Paris: Organisation for Economic Co-operation and Development.

———. Various years. *National Accounts.* Vol. 1, Main Aggregates. Paris: Organisation for Economic Co-operation and Development.

———. Various years. *National Accounts.* Vol. 2, Detailed Tables. Paris: Organisation for Economic Co-operation and Development.

OECD (Organisation for Economic Co-operation and Development) DAC (Development Assistance Committee). Various years. International Development Statistics Online. Online database. [www.oecd.org/dac/stats/idsonline].

———. Various years. *Development Cooperation Report.* Paris: Organisation for Economic Co-operation and Development.

———. Various years. *Geographical Distribution of Financial Flows to Aid Recipients.* Paris: Organisation for Economic Co-operation and Development.

Pandey, Kiran D., Piet Buys, Kenneth Chomitz, and David Wheeler. 2006a. "Biodiversity Conservation Indicators: New Tools for Priority Setting at the Global Environmental Facility." World Bank, Development Economics Research Group and Environment Department, Washington, D.C.

Pandey, Kiran D., David Wheeler, Bart Ostro, Uwe Deichmann, Kirk Hamilton, and Katie Bolt. 2006b. "Ambient Particulate Matter Concentrations in Residential

BIBLIOGRAPHY

and Pollution Hotspots of World Cities: New Estimates Based on the Global Model of Ambient Particulates (GMAPS)." World Bank, Development Economics Research Group and Environment Department, Washington, D.C.

Pandey, Kiran D., Katharine Bolt, Uwe Deichmann, Kirk Hamilton, Bart Ostro, and David Wheeler. 2006c. "The Human Cost of Air Pollution: New Estimates for Developing Countries." World Bank, Development Research Group and Environment Department, Washington, D.C.

Partnership on Measuring ICT for Development. 2008. *The Global Information Society: A Statistical View*. Santiago, Chile: United Nations.

Pew Center on Global Climate Change. 2007. "A Look at Emission Targets." Pew Center on Global Climate Change. [www.pewclimate.org/what_s_being_done/targets].

Pricewaterhouse Coopers. 2006. *Worldwide Tax Summaries Online*. New York. [www.pwc.com/extweb/pwcpublications.nsf/docid/9B2B76032544964C8525717E00606CBD].

Ratha, Dilip and William Shaw. 2007. "South-South Migration and Remittances." World Bank, Development Prospects Group, Washington, D.C.

Ravallion, Martin, and Shaohua Chen. 1996. "What Can New Survey Data Tell Us about the Recent Changes in Living Standards in Developing and Transitional Economies?" Policy Research Working Paper 16943. World Bank, Development Research Group, Washington, D.C.

Ravallion, Martin, Shaohua Chen, and Prem Sangraula. 2008. "Dollar a Day Revisited?" Policy Research Working Paper 4620. World Bank, Development Research Group, Washington, D.C.

Ravallion, Martin, Gaurav Datt, and Dominique van de Walle. 1991. "Quantifying Absolute Poverty in the Developing World." *Review of Income and Wealth* 37(4): 345–61.

Reinhart, Carmen M., and Kenneth S. Rogoff. 2008. *Banking Crises: An Equal Opportunity Menace*. NBER Working Paper 14587. Cambridge, Mass.: National Bureau of Economic Research.

———. 2009. *The Aftermath of Financial Crises*. NBER Working Paper 14656. Cambridge, Mass.: National Bureau of Economic Research.

Rosenzweig C., D. Karoly, M. Vicarelli, P. Neofotis, Q. Wu, G. Casassa, A. Menzel, T.L. Root, N. Estrella, B. Seguin, P. Tryjanowski, C. Liu, S. Rawlins, and A. Imeson. 2008. "Attributing Physical and Biological Impacts to Anthropogenic Climate Change." *Nature* 453: 353–57.

Ruggles, Robert. 1994. "Issues Relating to the UN System of National Accounts and Developing Countries." *Journal of Development Economics* 44 (1): 77–85.

Ryten, Jacob. 1998. "Fifty Years of ISIC: Historical Origins and Future Perspectives." ECA/STAT.AC. 63/22. United Nations Statistics Division, New York.

Shafey, O., M. Eriksen, H. Ross, and J. Mackay. 2009. *The Tobacco Atlas*. Third edition. Atlanta, Ga.: American Cancer Society and World Lung Foundation.

SIPRI (Stockholm International Peace Research Institute). 2008. *SIPRI Yearbook 2008: Armaments, Disarmament, and International Security*. Oxford, U.K.: Oxford University Press.

Smith, Lisa, and Laurence Haddad. 2000. "Overcoming Child Malnutrition in Developing Countries: Past Achievements and Future Choices." 2020 Brief 64. International Food Policy Research Institute, Washington D.C.

SPC (Secretariat of the Pacific Community). n.d. Online Statistics and Demography. [www.spc.int].

Srinivasan, T. N. 1994. "Database for Development Analysis: An Overview." *Journal of Development Economics* 44 (1): 3–28.

Standard & Poor's. 2000. *The S&P Emerging Market Indices: Methodology, Definitions, and Practices*. New York.

———. 2008. *Global Stock Markets Factbook 2008*. New York.

Stern, Nicholas. 2006. *The Economics of Climate Change: The Stern Review*. London: Cambridge University Press.

Summers, Lawrence H. 2006. "Reflections on Global Account Imbalances and Emerging Markets Reserve Accumulation." L.K. Jha memorial lecture, Reserve Bank of India, Mumbai, India, March 24. [http://ksghome.harvard.edu/~lsummer/speeches/2006/0324_rbi.html].

UCW (Understanding Children's Work). n.d. Online database. [www.ucw-project.org]

UNAIDS (Joint United Nations Programme on HIV/AIDS) and WHO (World Health Organization). Various years. *Report on the Global AIDS Epidemic*. Geneva.

UNCTAD (United Nations Conference on Trade and Development). 2007. *Trade and Development Report, 2007: Regional Cooperation for Development*. New York and Geneva: United Nations Conference on Trade and Development.

———. 2008a. *Trade and Development Report 2008: Commodity Prices, Capital Flows and the Financing of Investment*. New York and Geneva: United Nations Conference on Trade and Development.

———. 2008b. *World Investment Report 2008: Transnational Corporations and the Infrastructure Challenge*. New York and Geneva: United Nations Conference on Trade and Development.

———. Various years. *Handbook of International Trade and Development Statistics*. Geneva: United Nations Conference on Trade and Development.

———. Various years. *Handbook of Statistics*. Geneva: United Nations Conference on Trade and Development.

UNDP (United Nations Development Programme). 2006. *Human Development Report 2006: Beyond Scarcity: Power, Poverty and Global Water Crisis*. New York: Palgrave Macmillan

———. 2007. *Human Development Report 2007/2008: Fighting Climate Change: Human Solidarity in a Divided World*. New York: United Nations Development Programme.

UNEP (United Nations Environment Programme). 2002. *Global Environment Outlook 3*. London: Earthscan.

UNESCO (United Nations Educational, Scientific, and Cultural Organization). 1997. "International Standard Classification of Education." United Nations Educational, Scientific, and Cultural Organization, Paris.

———. Various years. *EFA Global Monitoring Report*. Paris: United Nations Educational, Scientific, and Cultural Organization.

UNESCO (United Nations Educational, Scientific and Cultural Organization) Institute for Statistics. Various years. *Global Education Digest*. Paris: United Nations Educational, Scientific, and Cultural Organization.

————. Online database. [http://stats.uis.unesco.org/unesco/TableViewer/document.aspx?ReportId=143&IF_Language=eng].

UNHCR (United Nations High Commissioner for Refugees). Various years. *Statistical Yearbook*. Geneva: United Nations High Commissioner for Refugees.

UNICEF (United Nations Children's Fund). n.d. Child Mortality Database. Online database. Childinfo. [www.childmortality.org].

————. Various years. *State of the World's Children*. New York: Oxford University Press.

————. Various years. "Multiple Indicator Cluster Surveys." Childinfo. [http://www.childinfo.org/mics.html].

UNICEF (United Nations Children's Fund), WHO (World Health Organization), World Bank, and United Nations Population Division. 2007. "Levels and Trends of Child Mortality in 2006: Estimates Developed by the Inter-Agency Group for Child Mortality Estimation." Working Paper. United Nations, New York.

UNIDO (United Nations Industrial Development Organization). Various years. *International Yearbook of Industrial Statistics*. Vienna: United Nations Industrial Development Organization.

UNIFEM (United Nations Development Fund for Women). 2005. *Progress of the World's Women*. New York: United Nations Development Fund for Women.

United Nations. 1947. *Measurement of National Income and the Construction of Social Accounts*. Geneva: United Nations.

————. 1968. *A System of National Accounts: Studies and Methods*. Series F, No. 2, Rev. 3. New York: United Nations.

————. 1990. *International Standard Industrial Classification of All Economic Activities, Third Revision*. Statistical Papers Series M, No. 4, Rev. 3. New York: United Nations..

————. 1993. *System of National Accounts*. New York: United Nations.

United Nations Population Division. 2006. *Trends in Total Migrant Stock: 2005 Revision*. New York. [http://esa.un.org/migration/].

————. 2007. *World Population Prospects: The 2006 Revision*. New York: United Nations, Department of Economic and Social Affairs. [http://esa.un.org/unpp/].

————. Various years. *World Urbanization Prospects*. New York: United Nations, Department of Economic and Social Affairs.

United Nations Statistics Division. 1985. *National Accounts Statistics: Compendium of Income Distribution Statistics*. New York: United Nations.

————. n.d. *International Standard Industrial Classification of All Economic Activities, Third Revision (ISIC, Rev. 3)*. Geneva. [http://unstats.un.org/unsd/cr/registry/regcst.asp?Cl=2 /]

————. Various issues. *Monthly Bulletin of Statistics*. New York: United Nations.

————. Various years. *Energy Statistics Yearbook*. New York: United Nations.

————. Various years. *International Trade Statistics Yearbook*. New York: United Nations.

————. Various years. *National Accounts Statistics: Main Aggregates and Detailed Tables*. Parts 1 and 2. New York: United Nations.

————. Various years. *National Income Accounts*. New York: United Nations.

————. Various years. *Population and Vital Statistics Report*. New York: United Nations.

————. Various years. *World Urbanization Prospects*. New York: United Nations.

————. Various years. *Statistical Yearbook*. New York: United Nations.

University of California, Berkeley, and Max Planck Institute for Demographic Research. n.d. Human Mortality Database. [www.mortality.org or www.humanmortality.de].

U.S. Census Bureau. n.d. International Data Base (IDB). [www.census.gov/ipc/www/idb/]

U.S. Census Bureau, Foreign Trade Statistics. 2009. "FT900: U.S. International Trade in Goods and Services. December 2008." *U.S. Census Bureau of Economic Analysis News*. February 11. [http://www.census.gov/foreign-trade/Press-Release/current_press_release/press.html].

U.S. Center for Disease Control and Prevention. Various years. *International Reproductive Health Surveys*. [www.cdc.gov/reproductivehealth/surveys].

U.S. Department of Treasury. 2008. *Report on U.S. Portfolio Holdings of Foreign Securities*. Washington, D.C.: U.S. Department of Treasury. [http://www.ustreas.gov/press/reports.html].

U.S. Environmental Protection Agency. 1995. *National Air Quality and Emissions Trends Report 1995*. Washington, D.C.: U.S. Environmental Protection Agency.

Walsh, Michael P. 1994. "Motor Vehicle Pollution Control: an Increasingly Critical Issue for Developing Countries." World Bank, Washington, D.C.

Watson, Robert, John A. Dixon, Steven P. Hamburg, Anthony C. Janetos, and Richard H. Moss. 1998. *Protecting Our Planet, Securing Our Future: Linkages among Global Environmental Issues and Human Needs*. Nairobi and Washington, D.C.: United Nations Environment Programme, U.S. National Aeronautics and Space Administration, and World Bank.

Watson, Jim, Gordon MacKerron, David Ockwell, and Tao Wang. 2007. "Technology and Carbon Mitigation in Developing Countries: Are Cleaner Coal Technologies a Viable Option?" Background paper for United Nations Development Programme's *Human Development Report 2007*. [http://hdr.undp.org/en/reports/global/hdr2007-2008/papers/watson_mackerron_ockwell_wang.pdf].

WHO (World Health Organization). 2000. *World Health Report 2000: Health Systems: Improving Performance*. Geneva: World Health Organization.

————. 2006. *World Health Report 2006*. Geneva: World Health Organization.

————. 2008a. "Measuring Health System Strengthening and Trends: A Toolkit for Countries." World Health Organization, Geneva. [www.who.int/healthinfo/statistics/toolkit_hss/en/index.html]

————. 2008b. *Worldwide Prevalence of Anemia 1993–2005*. Geneva: World Health Organization.

————. Various years. *Global Tuberculosis Control Report*. Geneva: World Health Organization.

————. Various years. *World Health Statistics*. Geneva: World Health Organization.

BIBLIOGRAPHY

WHO (World Health Organization) and UNICEF (United Nations Children's Fund). 2008. *Progress on Drinking Water and Sanitation.* Geneva.

————. Various years. WHO-UNICEF Estimates of National Immunization Coverage Database. [www.who.int/immunization_monitoring/routine/immunization_coverage/en/index4.html].

WHO (World Health Organization), UNICEF (United Nations Children's Fund), UNFPA (United Nations Population Fund), and World Bank. 2007. *Maternal Mortality in 2005: Estimates Developed by WHO, UNICEF, UNFPA, and the World Bank.* Geneva.

WIPO (World Intellectual Property Organization). 2008. *WIPO Patent Report: Statistics on Worldwide Patent Activity.* Geneva: World Intellectual Property Organization.

WITSA (World Information Technology and Services Alliance). 2008. *Digital Planet 2008: The Global Information Economy.* Vienna, Va.: World Information Technology and Services Alliance.

WMO (World Meteorological Organization). 2006. *Statement on the Status of the Global Climate in 2005.* Geneva: World Meteorological Organization.

————. 2007. "Observing Stations." Publication 9, Volume A, (July 9). [www.wmo.int/pages/prog/www/ois/volumea/vola-home.htm].

Wolf, Holger C. 1997. *Patterns of Intra- and Inter-State Trade.* NBER Working Paper 5939. Cambridge, Mass.: National Bureau of Economic Research.

Wolf, Martin. 2008. "Fixing Global Finance." Baltimore, Md.: John Hopkins University Press.

World Bank. 1990. *World Development Report 1990: Poverty.* New York: Oxford University Press.

————. 1992. *World Development Report 1992: Development and the Environment.* New York: Oxford University Press.

————. 1995. *World Development Report 1995: Workers in an Integrating World.* New York: Oxford University Press.

————. 1996a. *Environment Matters.* Discussion Paper 363. Washington, D.C.: World Bank.

————. 1996b. *Livable Cities for the 21st Century: A Directions in Development Book.* Washington, D.C.: World Bank.

————. 1996c. *National Environmental Strategies: Learning from Experience.* Washington, D.C. :World Bank.

————. 1997a. *Expanding the Measure of Wealth: Indicators of Environmentally Sustainable Development.* Environmentally Sustainable Development Studies and Monographs Series Report 17. Washington, D.C.: World Bank.

————. 1997b. *Rural Development: From Vision to Action.* Environmentally Sustainable Development Studies and Monographs Series Report 12. Washington, D.C.: World Bank.

————. 1999a. *Fuel for Thought: Environmental Strategy for the Energy Sector.* Washington, D.C.: World Bank.

————. 1999b. *Greening Industry: New Roles for Communities, Markets, and Governments.* New York: Oxford University Press.

————. 2000a. *Trade Blocs.* New York: Oxford University Press.

————. 2002. *World Development Report 2003: Sustainable Development in a Dynamic World.* New York: Oxford University Press.

————. 2006a. *Where is the Wealth of Nations? Measuring Capital for the 21st Century.* Washington, D.C.: World Bank.

————. 2006b. "Managing Climate Risk: Integrating Adaptation into World Bank Group Operations." Working Paper 37462. World Bank, Washington, D. C.

————. 2007a. "Clean Energy for Development: The World Bank Group Action." World Bank, Sustainable Development Network, Washington, D.C.

————. 2007b. "An Investment Framework for Clean Energy and Development. A Platform for Convergence of Public and Private Investment." World Bank, Washington D.C.

————. 2007c. "Healthy Development: The World Bank Strategy for Health, Nutrition, and Population Results." World Bank, Washington, D.C.

————. 2008a. "Development and Climate Change: A Strategic Framework for the World Bank Group." Report to Development Committee. World Bank, Washington D.C.

————. 2008b. *Doing Business 2009.* Washington, D.C.: World Bank.

————. 2008c. *East Asia: Navigating the Perfect Storm A World Bank Economic Update for the East Asia and Pacific Region.* Washington, D.C.: World Bank.

————. 2008d. *Global Development Finance.* Washington, D.C.: World Bank.

————. 2008e. "Global Financial Crisis: Responding Today, Securing Tomorrow." Background paper prepared for the G-20 Summit on Financial Markets and the World Economy November 15, Washington, D.C.

————. 2008f. *Global Monitoring Report: MDGs and the Environment.* Washington, D.C.: World Bank.

————. 2008g. Performance Assessments and Allocation of IDA Resources. Online database. [http://web.worldbank.org/WBSITE/EXTERNAL/EXTABOUTUS/IDA/0,,contentMDK:20052347~menuPK:2607525~pagePK:51236175~piPK:437394~theSitePK:73154,00.html].

————. 2008h. Private Participation in Infrastructure Project. Online database. [http://ppi.worldbank.org/].

————. 2008i. "Weathering the Storm: Economic Policy Responses to the Financial Crisis." World Bank, Washington, D.C. [http://siteresources.worldbank.org/NEWS/Resources/weatheringstorm.pdf].

————. 2009a. "Crisis Hitting Poor Hard in Developing World, World Bank Says." Press Release 2009/220/EXC. World Bank, Washington, D.C.

————. 2009b. *Global Economic Prospects 2009: Commodities at the Crossroads.* Washington, D.C.: World Bank.

————. Forthcoming. *Information and Communications for Development 2009: Scaling up the Impact.* Washington, D.C.: World Bank.

————. n.d. Enterprise Surveys Online. [www.enterprisesurveys.org].

————. Various issues. "Commodity Market Review." World Bank, Development Prospects Group, Washington, D.C.

————. Various issues. "Commodity Price Data (Pink sheet)." World Bank, Development Prospects Group, Washington, D.C.

———. Various issues. "Migration and Development Brief." World Bank, Development Prospects Group, Washington, D.C.

———. Various years. *Global Development Finance: Volume I and Volume II.* Washington, D.C.: World Bank.

———. Various years. *World Development Indicators.* Washington, D.C.: World Bank.

———. Various years. *World Debt Tables.* Washington, D.C.: World Bank.

World Bank and IMF (International Monetary Fund). 2006. "Fiscal Policy for Growth and Development: an Interim Report to the Development Committee." Report DC-0003 April 6, 2006. International Monetary Fund, World Bank, Washington D.C.

———. 2008a. *Global Monitoring Report 2008.* Washington, D.C.

———. 2008b. "Heavily Indebted Poor Countries (HIPC) Initiative and Multilateral Debt Relief Initiative (MDRI)—Status of Implementation." International Monetary Fund, World Bank, Washington, D.C.

World Federation of Exchanges. n.d. WFE Online Database. [http://www.world-exchanges.org/statistics]

WRI (World Resources Institute). 2005. "Navigating the Numbers." World Resources Institute, Washington, D.C.

———. 2007. Climate Analysis Indicators Tool (CAIT). Online database. [www.wri.org/climate/project_description2.cfm?pid=93].

———. 2008a. Earth Trends, the Environmental Information Portal. Online database.

———. 2008b. "Energy and Climate Action Plan in China." WRI Fact Sheet. World Resources Institute, Washington D.C.

WRI (World Resources Institute), UNEP (United Nations Environment Programme), UNDP (United Nations Development Programme), and World Bank. Various years. *World Resources: A Guide to the Global Environment.* New York: Oxford University Press.

World Tourism Organization. Various years. *Compendium of Tourism Statistics.* Madrid: World Tourism Organization.

———. Various years. *Yearbook of Tourism Statistics. Vols. 1 and 2.* Madrid: World Tourism Organization.

WTO (World Trade Organization). Various years. *Annual Report.* Geneva: World Trade Organization.

———. n.d. "Regional Trade Agreements Information System." Online database. [http://rtais.wto.org/].

———. n.d. "Regional Trade Agreements Gateway." World Trace Organization, Geneva. [www.wto.org/english/tratop_e/region_e/region_e.htm].

INDEX OF INDICATORS

References are to table numbers.

INDEX OF INDICATORS

INDEX OF INDICATORS

G

INDEX OF INDICATORS

INDEX OF INDICATORS

INDEX OF INDICATORS

INDEX OF INDICATORS

INDEX OF INDICATORS

INDEX OF INDICATORS